BUSINESS
LAW
TODAY

BUSINESS LAW TODAY

ROGER LeROY MILLER
Center for Policy Studies
Clemson University

GAYLORD A. JENTZ
Herbert D. Kelleher
Professor in Business Law
Department of MSIS
University of Texas at Austin

WEST PUBLISHING COMPANY
St. Paul   New York   Los Angeles   San Francisco

COPYRIGHT © 1988 By WEST PUBLISHING COMPANY
50 W. Kellogg Boulevard
P.O. Box 64526
St. Paul, MN 55164-1003

Printed in the United States of America

95 94 93 92 91 90 89   8 7 6 5 4 3

Library of Congress Cataloging-in-Publication Data

Miller, Roger Leroy.
    Business law today.
    Includes index.
    1. Commercial law—United States—Cases.   I. Jentz,
Gaylord A.   II. Title.
KF888.M55   1988   346.73'07   87-37189
ISBN 0-314-62758-8   347.3067

Copy editing: Maggie Jarpey and Debra Annan
Logo: Tom Kovacs
Composition: Parkwood Composition

The Uniform Commercial Code is reproduced with permission of The
American Law Institute and the National Conference of Commissioners
on Uniform State Laws. Copyright © 1987.

Photo Credits

6 Painting by Eben Farrington Commins; 7 The Granger Collection; 13 © 1987 by West Publishing;
15 Steven Falk, Gamma-Liaison; 19 Kagan, Gamma-Liaison; 23 AP/Wide World Photos; 30 Painting
by Charles Sidney Hopkinson; 34 *bottom:* Arthur Grace, Sygma; 38 The Granger Collection; 46 Carl
Bergquist, Gamma-Liaison; 59 Cindy Charles, Gamma-Liaison; 62 Associated Press; 71 Sygma; 79 Wide
World Photos; 86 *left:* Stephen Ferry, Gamma Liaison; *right:* Richard Mims, Sygma; 93 Flip Schulke,
Black Star; 97 J. L. Atlan, Sygma; 100 Sepp Seitz, Woodfin Camp & Associates; 110 Yale University
Art Gallery. Gift of the Class of 1929 Law and friends of the Law School; 126 Jeff Lowenthal, Woodfin
Camp & Associates; 158 *top:* John Bryson, Sygma; *bottom:* Gamma-Liaison; 161 *left:* Gamma-Liaison.
right: Sygma; 179 The Granger Collection; 222 Photo by David Hanover; 241 Columbia University;
263 Gamma-Liaison; 272 Photo by David Hanover; 305 Photo by David Hanover; 315 Photo by David
Farr; 316 Allan Price, Taurus Photos; 393 The Granger Collection; 408 Kirk Land, Sygma; 421 John
Olson, Gamma-Liaison; 490 Wally McNamee, Gamma-Liaison; 537 The Granger Collection; 568 Painting
attributed to George Peter Alexander Healy; 569 Library of Congress; 570 Gamma-Liaison; 594 Bill
Nation Photography; 599 Focus on Sports; 629 *top:* Gamma-Liaison. *bottom:* Randy Taylor, Sygma;
641 Alex Quesaoa, Woodfin Camp & Associates; 646 Alex Quesaoa, Woodfin Camp & Associates;
649 David Burnett, Woodfin Camp & Associates; 666 The Granger Collection; 668 The Granger Col-
lection; 673 Painting by Eben Farrington Commins c 1934; 676 William Strode, Woodfin Camp &
Associates; 694 Photo by David Hanover; 699 James L. Shaffer; 701 Bill Nation, Sygma; 708 John
Chiasson, Gamma-Liaison; 711 Charles Gupton, Stock Boston; 714 James Pozarik, Stock Boston; 715 Tim
Zimberoff, Sygma; 736 Photo by David Hanover; 791 Alain Mingam, Gamma-Liaison; 795 J. Andanson,
Sygma; 809 Wide World Photos, Inc.; 815 Baldev, Sygma; 816 McDonald's Corporations; 817 Photo
by David Hanover.

Contents In Brief

Contents

Chapter 3
Torts   57

Chapter 4
Criminal Law   83

◆ Unit Two
CONTRACTS 105

Why We Study Contract Law 105

Chapter 5
Nature and Classification   107

Chapter 16
Commercial Paper—The Negotiable Instrument, Transferability, and Negotiation 340

Chapter 17
Commercial Paper—Holder in Due Course, Liability, and Defenses 364

Chapter 18
Commercial Paper—Checks and the Banking System 389

Chapter 26
Corporations—Corporate Powers and Management   587

Chapter 27
Corporations—Rights and Duties of Directors, Managers, and
Shareholders   605

Chapter 28
Corporations—Merger, Consolidation, and Termination   625

Preface

We have written *Business Law Today* with one goal in mind—to make business law understandable for the student as he or she prepares to enter the business world. *Business Law Today* offers a clear and comprehensive treatment of all of the important areas of commercial law. The student reader is introduced to courts and procedures, torts, criminal law, contracts, sales, and important topics covered by the Uniform Commercial Code. In addition, we treat partnerships, corporations, and financial regulation, as well as other government regulation with respect to antitrust, the consumer, the environment, and the employee. Finally, we examine property, both real and personal; insurance, wills, and trusts; and international law in a global economy. We conclude our presentation of business law with a special Unit devoted to ethics and social responsibility.

To further enhance our goal of student understanding, we have developed a series of pedagogical features, several of which appear for the first time in a business law text. These features illustrate the relevance of law to students' future business careers, as well as impart a historical sense of the development of our legal system.

❖ Case Selection and Presentation

Generally, in each chapter four to ten cases are presented to illustrate business law. Each case is numbered sequentially for easy reference during class discussions, homework assignments, and exams. We have tried to achieve just the right balance between classic cases and recent cases from the 1980s. Each case is paraphrased in a unique format, which first gives the complete citation. The citation includes the court, the date, the state reporter (if available), and the West Reporter. For each case, there are four clearly labeled sections:

1. **Facts:** The facts of the case are presented in paraphrased form.
2. **Issue:** The issue before the court is described in one or two sentences.
3. **Decision:** The court's decision is presented in one or two sentences.
4. **Reason:** The reason for the decision is paraphrased in a paragraph or two. Where appropriate, direct quotations from the court opinion are included to illustrate the court's reasoning.

A complete explanation of how to read the case and how to find case law is provided in Chapter 1.

❖ Key Highlights in Each Chapter

Virtually all of the chapters have one or more of the following special sections, which are designed to instruct as well as to interest the business law student.

Applications

Nearly all chapters have an *Application* section, in which the student is presented with some practical advice on how to apply the law outlined in the chapter to real-world business problems. Each *Application* ends with a "Checklist" for the future businessperson on how to avoid legal problems. Some of the *Applications* are:

● Law and the Businessperson—To Sue or Not to Sue
● Law and the Entrepreneur—How to Incorporate
● Law and the Businessperson and the Consumer—Stop-Payment Orders
● Law and the Partner—Arranging for a Buyout
● Law and the Employer—Using Independent Contractors

Business Law in Action

Here we show practical and instructive examples of how the law affects people in the business world. Some of topics included in the *Business Law in Action* sections are:

● Business Law As It Applies to the Business of Law
● Hallmark versus "The Little People"
● Combating Computer Crime
● The Athletic Arm of the Sherman Act
● Whistleblowing and Public Policy

Landmarks in the Law

Most of the chapters have a *Landmark in the Law*. The *Landmarks* discuss important cases or statutes affecting business law and the origin of uniform codes. Some of the *Landmarks* are:

● The Interstate Commerce Act
● *The Standard Oil Co. of New Jersey* v. *United States*
● The Statute of Frauds
● Lemon Laws
● The FTC Rule of 1976

Profiles

A number of *Profiles* of important jurists, legal scholars, and other individuals who have had an impact on the law are presented in many of the chapters. For those that are presented, a photograph of the individual under discussion is included. Some of the individuals featured in the *Profiles* are:

- Benjamin Cardozo
- Melvin M. Belli, Sr.
- Karl N. Llewellyn
- John Marshall
- Sandra Day O'Connor

Quotations

Each chapter opens with a brief quotation that is relevant to the material under study. A brief biographical statement is given after the name of the individual quoted. Often, one or two other quotations will be included in the margins of the following pages in the chapter.

Exhibits and Forms

Where appropriate, exhibits illustrating important aspects of the law are given. Additionally, we have included a number of forms for the student's reference. Included are a purchase order form, a bill of lading, a warehouse receipt, a sample promissory note, a stop-payment order, and others.

Full-Color Format

The unique use of a full-color format in key chapters of *Business Law Today* adds a new dimension to business law for students.

Photographs and Cartoons

We believe that appropriate and well-placed photographs and cartoons not only provide visual relief from the printed word but also help the students to relate the material under study to the everyday world around them. We have thus included in this volume approximately sixty photographs and several carefully chosen cartoons.

❖ Other Pedagogical Devices

We have used a number of additional pedagogical devices, including Unit introductions, marginal definitions of important terms, and chapter summaries.

Unit Introductions

Each unit has a concise introduction indicating why the student should study the topics covered within that unit. The unit on contracts, for example, is introduced by a discussion of the function of contracts in the business world and the importance of understanding the nature of contractual relationships.

Marginal Definitions

Legal terminology is a major stumbling block in the study of business law. We have used an important pedagogical device to help the student understand terminology. Whenever an important legal term is introduced, it is done so in boldface type. In the margin of the page, alongside the paragraph in which the term appears, a definition is given of the important term. Additionally, all boldfaced terms are again defined in a *Glossary* at the end of the text.

The authors, as well as a number of student readers, have gone through the text countless times in order to make sure that every important term is defined the first time that it is presented (with a few necessary exceptions). The student reader will not find a confusing mass of undefined terms in this text.

Chapter Summaries

At the end of each chapter, we present in graphic form a thorough *Chapter Summary* designed to aid the student in reviewing the concepts that he or she has just learned. The *Chapter Summaries* can also be used as a reviewing device prior to examinations.

❖ Questions and Case Problems

At the end of every chapter, there are normally eight to ten *Questions and Case Problems*. The questions are hypothetical and number from three to five for each chapter. The case problems are taken directly from actual cases for which full citations are given.

All of the answers to the *Questions and Case Problems* can be found in a separate Solutions Manual.

❖ Appendices

At the end of the text are presented the following appendices:

A. The Constitution of the United States
B. The Uniform Commercial Code
C. The Uniform Partnership Act
D. In recognition of the expanding role of Hispanics in business throughout the United States, *Business Law Today* includes a unique list of the equivalent Spanish terms for important legal terms in English.

❖ Educational Legal Research Software

Business Law Today is the first business law textbook with a direct link to an educational legal research software package. Computer Legal Research Key System (CLERK) permits students with access to IBM-PC and compatible personal computers to retrieve specific cases found in *Business Law Today*. The entire package consists of five disks—

two program disks and three data disks containing the cases. One case from each chapter of *Business Law Today* is included in the CLERK system and is identified by a specific logo ⌨ for easy retrieval. In addition to allowing students to study the facts and issues of the case in greater detail, students who use CLERK will gain valuable experience in conducting legal research.

The educational legal research software package is available free to qualified adopters of *Business Law Today*. An *Instructor's Resource Guide* is available for instructors to facilitate installation and to provide tips for use in class. A *Student User's Guide* is available for purchase by students.

❖ Supplemental Teaching Materials

The text, *Business Law Today*, forms only one part of a fully integrated teaching/learning package. This package consists of the text and the following items:

1. *Student Study Guide*, prepared by Nancy Hart. This workbook contains a general overview of the major points of law discussed within each chapter of the text and a thorough chapter summary. Questions are also included, as are the answers.
2. *Instructor's Resource Guide with Test Bank*, developed by Joseph Zavaglia, Jr. and Nancy Hart.
3. *Transparency Masters*, covering all important exhibits, are available free to adopters.
4. *West's Book of Legal Forms*.

❖ Acknowledgments

A great many people were kind enough to help us on this project. The initial impetus for *Business Law Today* came from our long-time editor, Clyde Perlee, Jr. The design and production coordination were skillfully handled by John Orr. Lavina Miller provided expert research, editing, and proofing services for this project. Additional proofreading was done by Sharon Marsh and Meredith Friedrick. We also thank Edward Garvey for his helpful research assistance, Susanne Walzer for her research and proofing services, and Rosemary Porter for her special assistance.

A number of reviewers were kind enough to give us their ideas and comments on various drafts of the manuscript. They are:

John J. Balek
Morton College, Illinois

Brad Botz
Garden City Community College, Kansas

Lee B. Burgunder
California Polytechnic University—San Luis Obispo

Dale Clark
Corning Community College, New York

Patricia L. DeFrain
Glendale College, California

Joe D. Dillsaver
Northeastern State University, Oklahoma

Larry R. Edwards
Tarrant County Junior College, South Campus, Texas

George E. Eigsti
Kansas City, Kansas, Community College

Jerry Furniss
University of Montana

Nancy L. Hart
Midland College, Texas

Janine S. Hiller
*Virginia Polytechnic Institute & State
    University*

Sarah Weiner Keidan
Oakland Community College, Michigan

Bradley T. Lutz
Hillsborough Community College, Florida

John D. Mallonee
Manatee Community College, Florida

James K. Miersma
*Milwaukee Area Technical Institute,
    Wisconsin*

Jim Lee Morgan
West Los Angeles College

Jack K. Morton
University of Montana

Solange North
Fox Valley Technical Institute, Wisconsin

Robert H. Orr
Florida Community College at Jacksonville

George Otto
Truman College, Illinois

William M. Rutledge
Macomb Community College, Michigan

Anne W. Schacherl
Madison Area Technical, Wisconsin

Edward F. Shafer
Rochester Community College, Minnesota

Lou Ann Simpson
Drake University, Iowa

James E. Walsh, Jr.
Tidewater Community College, Virginia

Edward L. Welsh, Jr.
Phoenix College

Clark W. Wheeler
Santa Fe Community College, Florida

James L. Wittenbach
University of Notre Dame

Joseph Zavaglia, Jr.
Brookdale Community College, New Jersey

We remain solely responsible for all errors and omissions. We welcome comments from all users of this text, both students and instructors.

Roger LeRoy Miller
Gaylord A. Jentz

Unit One

The Legal Environment of Business

❖ Why We Study the Legal Environment of Business

It cannot be doubted that today's business men and women find themselves in an environment that is increasingly legalized. Virtually all activities of businesses are governed by rules enacted by a state legislature or Congress, promulgated by a local, state, or federal agency, or developed through the years in our judicial system. The rules govern all aspects of business: raising capital, hiring and firing personnel, marketing and advertising, repairing or replacing defective products, and so on. In a broad sense, the legal environment of business includes the topic in every chapter of this book. After all, any aspect of business that touches on the law forms the legal environment of business. Thus, the legal environment of business embraces contracts, sales, the formation of partnerships, corporation transactions, government regulations concerning the business environment, insurance policies on business properties, employment, as well as most other transaction relationships. Anyone contemplating a career in the business world cannot escape the legal environment of business, and knowledge of that legal environment can only help the future businessperson become better at whatever job is undertaken.

In this Unit, we discuss law as it reflects social forces. Chapter 1 covers *constitutional law*—law that is directly derived from the Constitution of the United States. In Chapter 2, courts and legal procedures are outlined. No businessperson can realistically assume that he or she will not at some time be exposed to the mechanics of a lawsuit. In Chapter 3, we look at *torts*, or noncontractual wrongs, committed by one party against another. This area is usually called *civil law*, meaning the law governing conduct between private parties. But there is also the *criminal* side of law, including white-collar crimes, and that topic is examined in Chapter 4.

Chapter 1

Law As a Contemporary Social Force

In this introductory chapter, we look at what law is and how it reflects changing social forces. We then examine the history and sources of American law, with emphasis on constitutional law as it relates to business. Because we introduce citations to various cases, we explain how to read case law citations and how to find case law, and discuss the important area of computerized legal research.

❖ What Is Law?

Aristotle saw **law** as a rule of conduct. Plato believed law was a form of social control. Cicero contended the law was the agreement of reason and nature, the distinction between the just and the unjust. The British jurist Sir William Blackstone described law as "a rule of civil conduct prescribed by the supreme power in a state, commanding what is right, and prohibiting what is wrong."

   A typical definition of the term *law* is: Law consists of enforceable rules governing the relationships between individuals and their relationships to society. This definition implies the following:

1.   To have law, there must be established rules, such as constitutions, statutes, administrative agency rules, and judicial decisions (discussed later in this chapter).
2.   These rules must be capable of enforcement; that is, law and order prevails, with resolution in a judicial system (see Chapter 2).
3.   The rules must establish approved conduct by which individuals deal with each other (see Unit Two, dealing with contracts).
4.   The rules must also establish conduct expected of persons dealing with and participating in society—for example, civil rights legislation and criminal law (see Chapter 4).

❖ Law As an Expression of Social Forces

Law both affects, and is affected by, the society in which it functions. Some scholars tend to emphasize the former—that is, law's role as a guiding social force. They

"Logic, and history, and custom, and utility, and the accepted standards of right conduct, are the forces which singly or in combination shape the progress of the law."

Benjamin Cardozo, 1870–1938
(Associate Justice of the U.S. Supreme Court, 1932–1938)

LAW
A body of rules of conduct with legal force and effect, prescribed by the controlling authority.

3

stress the role played by historical legal cases (those prohibiting segregation and discrimination, for example) in spearheading social and political movements (civil rights and equal opportunity legislation, for example). Proponents of this view consider the law itself to be an active social force, helping to bring about changes within a society. Other scholars focus on the law as a conservative element in society. They believe that although the law may change over time in *response* to social changes, it is not a causal force in *bringing about* those changes.

With respect to the law governing commercial transactions, law seems to be less an active social force than a response to social forces at work in our dynamic society. Throughout this text, we present a wide variety of landmark cases that, taken together, show the evolution of business law. For example, the underlying assumption, or watchword, used to be *caveat emptor* (let the buyer beware) but is now *caveat venditor* (let the seller beware). This gradual change in the view of the courts and the legislatures can be seen as a result of changing social forces, the most important being an increasingly better-off (materially) populace that would no longer accept many of the business practices of the past and a populace that was willing to pay, in essence, for changes in the law that provided the consumer with safer products, the worker with better working conditions, and the businessperson with better-defined standards of conduct.

All such legal changes have come about at a cost to our economy, but apparently it is a cost that Americans as a group have been willing to pay. For example, legislation regulating the workplace would have been largely ignored a hundred years ago because the cost of such regulation would not have been acceptable at that time, given average hourly wages and average family income. The concept of environmental law was unheard of a hundred years ago, not only because we produced fewer goods and therefore generated less pollution, but also because we were a poorer nation and would not have been willing to give up very much of our material standard of living at that time in order to preserve the environment.

There are many complaints that today's economy is dominated by large corporations. On the other hand, a person certainly has a better chance at redressing his or her grievance within our judicial system today than was possible a hundred or even fifty years ago. Why? Because the attitude of the courts has changed to reflect concern over the rights of "the little person" in a world increasingly dominated by big business. But one of the reasons the so-called little person has the ability to fight large corporations is that as a nation we have chosen to provide the legal resources to such an individual through public law firms that are in part supported by government funds. Certainly, legislation to provide such funds fifty or a hundred years ago would have never passed because more pressing uses of public monies were at hand.

The law is an ever-changing landscape of rules governing the conduct among individuals and between an individual and his or her government. That landscape will change depending on the social forces that change as America's position with respect to the rest of the world changes, as the economic landscape changes, as social, moral, religious, and ethical values change, and as the form of our government changes.

❖ History and Sources of American Law

Because of our colonial heritage, much of American law is based on the English legal system. A knowledge of this heritage is necessary in order to understand the nature of our legal system today.

Early Courts of Law

In 1066 the Normans conquered England, and William the Conqueror and his successors began the process of unifying the country under their rule. One of the means they used to this end was the establishment of the king's court, or *Curia Regis*. Before the Norman Conquest, disputes had been settled according to local custom. The king's court sought to establish a common or uniform set of customs for the whole country. The body of rules that evolved under the king's court was the beginning of the common law, called "common" because it was meant to be common to the entire English realm. As the number of courts and cases increased, the more important decisions of each year were gathered together and recorded in yearbooks. Judges, settling disputes similar to ones that had been decided before, used the yearbooks as the basis for their decisions. If a case was unique (one of first impression), judges had to create new laws, but they based their decisions whenever possible on the general principles suggested by earlier cases. The body of judge-made law that developed under this system is still used today and is known as the **common law.**

Common Law

Common law began as the ancient unwritten law of England but today includes the statutory and case-law background of England and of the American colonies prior to the American Revolution. The **case law** of the United States since the American Revolution is a predominant part of our common law, consisting of rules of law announced in separate court decisions. The cases may themselves involve a court interpretation of a statute, a regulation, or a provision in a constitution. Such an interpretation becomes part of the authoritative law on the subject and further serves as a **precedent** in the particular jurisdiction. A prior case that is similar in legal principles or in facts to a case under consideration is referred to as a precedent.

Common law must be distinguished from statutory law, such as that enacted by state and federal legislatures. In areas where legislation has not covered the relevant issue, courts still refer to the common law. The history and circumstances of states differ, which has given rise to differences in the common law of each state. Even where legislation has been substituted for common law, courts often rely on common law to interpret the legislation on the theory that the people who drafted the statute intended to codify a previous common-law rule.

Stare Decisis

The practice of deciding new cases with reference to former decisions eventually became a cornerstone of the English and American judicial systems. It forms a doctrine called ***stare decisis*** ("to stand on decided cases"). The doctrine of *stare decisis* suggests that judges attempt to follow precedents. The doctrine helps the courts to be more efficient, because if other courts have carefully reasoned through a similar case, their opinions can serve as guides. *Stare decisis* reflects the experience and wisdom of the past. The doctrine also makes the law more stable and predictable.

The rule of precedent tends to neutralize the prejudices of individual judges, and if the law on a given subject is well settled, someone bringing a case to court can usually rely on the court to make a decision based on what the law has been. Sometimes a court departs from the rule of precedent because it decides that the precedent is incorrect. And sometimes there is no precedent on which to base a decision, or there are conflicting precedents. In these situations, a court is guided in

---

"Reason is the life of the law; nay, the Common Law itself is nothing but reason."

Sir Edward Coke, 1552–1634 *(British jurist and legal scholar)*

COMMON LAW
That body of law developed from custom or judicial decisions in English and American courts, not attributable to a legislature.

CASE LAW
Rules of law announced in court decisions. Case law includes the aggregate of reported cases that interpret judicial precedents, statutes, regulations, and constitutional provisions.

PRECEDENT
A court decision that furnishes an example or authority for deciding subsequent cases in which identical or similar facts are presented.

STARE DECISIS
A flexible doctrine of the courts, recognizing the value of following prior decisions (precedents) in cases similar to the one before the court; the courts' practice of being consistent with prior decisions based on similar facts. See precedent.

Profile

Benjamin Cardozo
(1870–1938)

Benjamin Nathan Cardozo, one of the most notable liberal jurists of the twentieth century and an eminent legal scholar, was born in New York City on May 24, 1870. His productive career began with legal studies at Columbia University Law School, after which he entered private practice in New York. Over the following twenty years, Cardozo's skill as an attorney and his legal knowledge became well known to those within the legal community— eventually leading Chief Justice Charles Evans Hughes to refer to him as "a walking encyclopedia of the law."

In 1913, he accepted a judgeship with the New York Supreme Court (a trial court in New York, the highest court in that state being the Court of Appeals). Within six weeks, however,

he was appointed as a temporary justice to the New York Court of Appeals to help clear the docket of its backlog of cases. He became a permanent justice of that court in 1917 and its chief justice in 1926. In 1932, upon the resignation of Oliver Wendell Holmes, Jr., from the United States Supreme Court, President Hoover nominated Cardozo to the empty "scholar's seat." Cardozo accepted the position and served as an associate justice until his death, six years later, on July 9, 1938.

During his nearly twenty years on the bench of the New York Court of Appeals—the most influential of the state courts—and later as a United States Supreme Court justice, Cardozo's opinions had a profound effect on American jurisprudence. Cardozo served on the United States Supreme Court during the New Deal era of President Franklin D. Roosevelt and, like his fellow justices, was faced with the task of determining the constitutionality of Roosevelt's's legislation. Generally, Cardozo sided with the liberal voices of the court (such as Louis Brandeis and Harlan Stone) in his decisions and felt the Constitution was flexible enough to allow considerable latitude to the government in matters relating to the public welfare. Cardozo made clear on several occasions his conviction that the law should change to meet changing circumstances. "What is critical and urgent changes with the times," he maintained in *Helvering v. Davis*.[1] "Needs that were narrow or parochial

1. 301 U.S. 619, 57 S.Ct. 904, 81 L.Ed. 1307 (1937).

a century ago may be interwoven in our day with the well-being of the nation."

The conviction that legal principles must be flexible and must change over time permeates all of Cardozo's writing. In *The Nature of the Judicial Process* (1921), one of his most influential and widely read works, he wrote of the "uncertainty" that such flexibility must ultimately lend to the law and, consequent upon this uncertainty, the creative nature of the judicial process:

> As the years have gone by, and I have reflected more and more upon the nature of the judicial process, I have become reconciled to the uncertainty, because I have grown to see it as inevitable. I have grown to see that the process in its highest reaches is not discovery, but creation; and that the doubts and misgivings . . . are part of the travail of mind . . . in which principles that have served their day expire, and new principles are born.

Cardozo advised judges and lawmakers to look beyond the specific principles, precedents, and policies of American jurisprudence to the delicate, integrating web of justice that holds them all together. Those who do so, Cardozo suggests, will find, as he did, that ultimately the judicial process involves more creation than discovery.

its decisions by fairness, public policy, and legal reasoning. Cases that overturn precedent often receive a great deal of publicity. In *Brown v. Board of Education*,[1] for example, the U.S. Supreme Court expressly overturned precedent when it concluded that separate educational facilities for whites and blacks, which had been upheld as constitutional in numerous previous cases,[2] were inherently unequal.

Courts have other sources (besides precedent and common law) to consider when making their decisions. These include federal and state constitutions, statutory law, administrative agency regulations, and commercial law codes.

Constitutional Law

The federal government and the states have separate constitutions that set forth the general organization, powers, and limits of their respective governments. The U.S. Constitution[3] is the supreme law of the land. A law in violation of the Constitution, no matter what its source, will be declared unconstitutional and will not be enforced. Similarly, unless they conflict with the U.S. Constitution, state constitutions are supreme within their respective borders. The U.S. Constitution defines the powers and limitations of the federal government. All powers not granted to the federal government are retained by the states or the people.

Statutory Law

Statutes enacted by the U.S. Congress and the various state legislative bodies make up another source of law, which is generally referred to as **statutory law**. The statutory

STATUTORY LAW
Laws enacted by a legislative body (as opposed to constitutional law, administrative law, or case law).

---

1.   347 U.S. 483, 495, 74 S.Ct. 686, 692, 98 L.Ed. 873, 881 (1954).
2.   See *Plessy v. Ferguson*, 163 U.S. 537, 16 S.Ct. 1138, 41 L.Ed. 256 (1896).
3.   See Appendix A for the complete text of the U.S. Constitution.

George Washington presides over the Constitutional Convention in 1787.

law of the United States also includes the ordinances passed by cities and counties, none of which can violate the U.S. Constitution or the relevant state constitution. Today legislative bodies and regulatory agencies assume an ever-increasing share of lawmaking. Much of the work of modern courts consists of interpreting what the rulemakers meant when the law was passed and applying it to a present set of facts.

Administrative Agencies

An administrative agency is created when the executive or legislative branch of the government delegates some of its authority to an appropriate group of persons. At the national level, the executive departments have agencies such as the Food and Drug Administration (FDA), which is under the Department of Health and Human Services (HHS). There are also major independent agencies, such as the Federal Communications Commission (FCC), Securities and Exchange Commission (SEC), and the Federal Trade Commission (FTC). **Administrative law** is the branch of public law concerned with the executive power and actions of administrative agencies, their officials, and their workers. When an individual has a dispute with such an agency, administrative law comes into play. The scope of administrative law has expanded enormously in recent years, and the scope of administrative agencies has increased so much that their activities have come to be called **administrative process,** in contrast to **judicial process.** Administrative process involves the administration of law by nonjudicial agencies, whereas judicial process is the administration of law by judicial bodies (the courts). Disputes involving administrative agencies can, however, be brought before, or appealed to, the federal courts.

❖ Sources of American Commercial Law

The body of law that pertains to commercial dealings is generally referred to as commercial or business law. It includes most of the topics in this text—contracts, partnerships, corporations, and agencies, for example.

Commercial Law Codification

In the interest of uniformity and reform, the legal profession, under the leadership of the American Law Institute, has created several comprehensive codes of laws. The National Conference of Commissioners on Uniform State Laws began meeting in the late 1800s in order to draft uniform statutes. Once these uniform codes were drawn up, the commissioners urged each state legislature to adopt them. Adoption of uniform codes is a state matter, and a state may reject all or part of a code. Hence, the laws throughout the United States are not "uniform." Many uniform codes have been drawn up and adopted in total or in part, by some or all of the states. The most ambitious uniform act was the Uniform Commercial Code.

The Uniform Commercial Code (UCC)

The Uniform Commercial Code (UCC) is designed to assist the legal relationship of parties involved in modern commercial transactions by helping to determine the

ADMINISTRATIVE LAW
A body of law created by administrative agencies—such as the Securities and Exchange Commission (SEC) and the Federal Trade Commission (FTC)—in the form of rules, regulations, orders, and decisions in order to carry out their duties and responsibilities. This law can initially be enforced by these agencies outside the judicial process.

ADMINISTRATIVE PROCESS
The procedure used by administrative agencies in the administration of law.

JUDICIAL PROCESS
The procedures relating to or connected with the administration of justice through the judicial system.

intentions of the parties to a commercial contract and by giving force and effect to their agreement. Moreover, the Code is meant to encourage business transactions by assuring businesspersons that their contracts, if validly entered into, will be enforced. The District of Columbia, the Virgin Islands, and forty-nine states have adopted the entire Uniform Commercial Code.[4] The creation of the Uniform Commercial Code is the subject of "Landmark in the Law" in Chapter 11. The complete text of the Code can be found in Appendix B.

❖ Civil versus Criminal Law

The body of law is huge, but has been broken down into several classifications. **Civil law** spells out the duties that exist between persons or between citizens and their governments, excluding the duty not to commit crimes. Contract law, for example, is part of civil law. The whole body of tort law, which has to do with the infringement by one person of the legally recognized rights of another (discussed in Chapter 3), is also an area of civil law.

Criminal law, in contrast to civil law, has to do with a wrong committed against the public as a whole (see Chapter 4). Criminal acts are proscribed by local, state, or federal government statutes. Criminal law is always public law, whereas civil law is sometimes public and sometimes private. In a criminal case, the government seeks to impose a penalty (monetary and/or imprisonment) upon an allegedly guilty person. In a civil case, one party (sometimes the government) tries to make the other party comply with a duty or pay for the damage caused by failure to so comply.

CIVIL LAW
(*1*) The branch of law dealing with the definition and enforcement of all private or public rights, as opposed to criminal matters. (2) Codified law, such as that compiled by the early Roman jurists.

CRIMINAL LAW
Governs and defines those actions which are crimes and which subject the convicted offender to punishment imposed by the government.

❖ Locating and Analyzing Court Cases

The study of law is enhanced by using the *case method* to present subject matter. When students study law cases, they are learning firsthand how courts interpret the law in specific situations. They learn the major facts of a case, the legal issue or issues presented to the court, and the legal principles and reasoning that guided the court in forming its decision. Before this can be done, however, students must know how to find and how to analyze court cases—subjects to which we now turn.

❖ Finding Case Law

Most trial court decisions are not published. Except for the federal courts and the courts of New York and a few other states that publish selected opinions of their trial proceedings, decisions in trial courts are merely filed in the office of the clerk of the court, where they are available for public inspection. On the other hand, the written decisions of appellate courts are published and distributed (these reported cases are called, somewhat paradoxically, *unwritten law*, in contrast to the *written*, or statutory, law).

---

4. Louisiana has adopted only Articles 1, 3, 4, and 5. There are nine substantive law articles in the Code.

The reported appellate decisions are published in volumes of case reporters called *Reports*, which are numbered consecutively. State court decisions are found in the state reports for most states. Additionally, state reports appear in regional units of the *National Reporter System*, published by West Publishing Company. Most lawyers and libraries have the West reporters because they report cases more quickly and are distributed more widely than the state-published reports. In fact, many states have eliminated their own reports in favor of West's *National Reporter System*.

Geographical Areas

West Publishing Company has divided the states into geographic areas: Atlantic (A. or A.2d), Southeastern (S.E. or S.E.2d), Southwestern (S.W. or S.W.2d), Northwestern (N.W. or N.W.2d), Northeastern (N.E. or N.E.2d), Southern (So. or So.2d), and Pacific (P. or P.2d). After appellate decisions are published, they are usually referred to (cited) by the name of the case; the volume, name, and page of the state report (if any); the volume and page of the *National Reporter*; and the volume, name, and page of any other selected case series. For example, consider the following case citation: *Quality Motors, Inc. v. Hays*, 216 Ark. 264, 225 S.W.2d 326 (1949). We see that the opinion in the case is found in volume 216 of the official *Arkansas Reports* on page 264; and in volume 225 of the *South Western Reporter*, Second Series, on page 326. (When we cite cases in this text, we also give the name of the court and the year of filing for the appellate court decision.) Exhibit 1–1 outlines West's *National Reporter System*.

Federal court decisions are found in the *Federal Reporter* (F. or F.2d) for U.S. Courts of Appeals decisions, *Federal Supplement* (F.Supp.) for U.S. District Court decisions, *Federal Rules Decisions* (F.R.D.), *West's Bankruptcy Reporter* (B.R.), *United States Supreme Court Reports* (U.S.) and *Supreme Court Reporter* (S.Ct.) for Supreme Court of the United States decisions, and the *Lawyer's Edition* (L.Ed.)

Case Titles

In the title of a case such as *Abrams v. Jones*, the *v.* stands for versus, which means against. In the trial court, Abrams was the plaintiff (the person who filed the suit), and Jones was the defendant. If Abrams wins and the case is appealed, however, the appellate court sometimes puts the name of the party appealing the decision first, so that the case may be called *Jones v. Abrams*. Since some appellate courts retain the trial-court order of names, it is often impossible to distinguish the plaintiff from the defendant in the title of a reported appellate court decision. The student must carefully read the facts of each case in order to identify each party.

UNANIMOUS OPINION
A court opinion supported by all the judges or justices involved in deciding the case.

MAJORITY OPINION
A court opinion supported by a majority of the judges or justices involved in deciding the case.

Decisions and Opinions

All decisions reached by the U.S. Supreme Court are written. A decision contains the opinion (the Court's reasons for its decision), the rules of law that apply, and the judgment. There are four types of written opinions for any particular case decided by the U.S. Supreme Court. When all justices unanimously agree on an opinion, the opinion is written for the entire Court (all the justices) and can be deemed a **unanimous opinion**. When there is not a unanimous opinion, a **majority opinion** is written, outlining the views of the majority of the justices involved in the case.

◆ **Exhibit 1–1 National Reporter System—Regional/Federal**

Regional Reporters	Coverage Beginning	Coverage
Atlantic Reporter	1885	Connecticut, Delaware, Maine, Maryland, New Hampshire, New Jersey, Pennsylvania, Rhode Island, Vermont, and District of Columbia Municipal Court of Appeals.
North Eastern Reporter	1885	Illinois, Indiana, Massachusetts, New York, and Ohio.
North Western Reporter	1879	Iowa, Michigan, Minnesota, Nebraska, North Dakota, South Dakota, and Wisconsin.
Pacific Reporter	1883	Alaska, Arizona, California, Colorado, Hawaii, Idaho, Kansas, Montana, Nevada, New Mexico, Oklahoma, Oregon, Utah, Washington, and Wyoming.
South Eastern Reporter	1887	Georgia, North Carolina, South Carolina, Virginia, and West Virginia.
South Western Reporter	1886	Arkansas, Kentucky, Missouri, Tennessee, and Texas.
Southern Reporter	1887	Alabama, Florida, Louisiana, and Mississippi.
Federal Reporters		
Federal Reporter	1880	United States Circuit Court from 1880 to 1912; Commerce Court of the United States from 1911 to 1913; District Courts of the United States from 1880 to 1932; U.S. Court of Claims from 1929 to 1932 and since 1960; the U.S. Court of Appeals from its organization in 1891; the U.S. Court of Customs and Patent Appeals from 1929; and the U.S. Emergency Court of Appeals from 1943.
Federal Supplement	1932	United States Court of Claims from 1932 to 1960; United States District Courts since 1932; United States Customs Court since 1956.
Federal Rules Decisions	1939	United States District Courts involving the Federal Rules of Civil Procedure since 1939 and Federal Rules of Criminal Procedure since 1946.
Supreme Court Reporter	1882	U.S. Supreme Court beginning with the October term of 1882.
Bankruptcy Reporter	1980	Bankruptcy decisions of U.S. Bankruptcy Courts, U.S. District Courts, U.S. Courts of Appeals, and the U.S. Supreme Court.
Military Justice Reporter	1978	United States Court of Military Appeals and Courts of Military Review for the Army, Navy, Air Force, and Coast Guard.

NATIONAL REPORTER SYSTEM MAP

CONCURRING OPINION
An opinion, separate from that which embodies the view and decision of the majority of the court, prepared by a judge or justice who agrees in general but wants to make or clarify a particular point or to voice disapproval of the grounds on which the decision was made, but not the decision itself.

DISSENTING OPINION
A separate opinion in which a judge or justice does not agree with the conclusion reached by the majority of the court and expounds his or her views on the case.

Often one or more justices who feel strongly about making or emphasizing a point that was not made or emphasized in the unanimous or majority opinion will write a **concurring opinion.** That means the justice agrees (concurs) with the judgment given in the unanimous or majority opinion, but for different reasons. In other than unanimous opinions, one or more dissenting opinions are usually written by those justices who did not agree with the majority. The **dissenting opinion** is important because it may form the basis of the arguments used years later in reversing the majority opinion.

Judges and Justices

The terms *judge* and *justice* are usually synonymous and represent two designations given to judges in various courts. All members of the U.S. Supreme Court, for example, are referred to as justices. And "justice" is the formal title usually given to judges of appellate courts, although this is not always the case. In New York, a justice is a trial judge of the trial court (which is called the Supreme Court), and a member of the Court of Appeals (the state's highest court) is called a judge. The term *justice* is commonly abbreviated to J., and *justices* to JJ. A Supreme Court case might refer to Justice White as White, J.; or to Chief Justice Rehnquist as Rehnquist, C. J.

❖ Computerized Legal Research

The days of the hunched-over, bespectacled law clerk searching through copious volumes of dusty tomes filled with ancient cases are not completely over, but, as could be expected, computers have streamlined the legal research techniques used by businesses, lawyers, and members of the judiciary. Today there are a number of data bases—collections of information useful to anyone doing legal research—that can be accessed through several high-speed data-delivery systems. The two most common systems are WESTLAW and LEXIS. WESTLAW is a computer-assisted legal research service of West Publishing Company. LEXIS is a similar service provided by Mead Data Central, Inc. Each system has data-base-access software that makes it possible for the researcher to interact with the delivery system.

In the WESTLAW data-delivery system, data are stored at West's headquarters in St. Paul, Minnesota. User interaction with the data-delivery system can be initiated from a computer terminal or a personal computer running a special WESTLAW access program literally anywhere in the world. The WESTLAW user sends a query, or message, to the computer. The query is then processed and documents are identified that satisfy the search request. The information is transmitted back to the user, where it is seen on a video display terminal (VDT) and can be printed out as "hard copy" on paper. The documents displayed on the VDT can be stored on the user's storage equipment, such as diskettes.

In short, WESTLAW, LEXIS, and similar computerized data-search systems allow for access to virtually all cases, statutes, federal regulations, and the like, with a minimum of time delay and a minimum of physical effort. Often the latest cases can be queried via such a system before they are available to the researcher in his or her geographic location in a local law school or law office library.

WESTLAW is a popular computerized data-search system that allows lawyers immediate access to all cases, statutes, and federal regulations.

❖ Analyzing Case Law

The law consists of case law as well as statutory law. Case law is critical with respect to decision making by businesspeople, since businesses must operate within the boundaries established by law. It is thus essential that businesspeople understand the law as evidenced by adjudicated cases.

The cases in this text have been rewritten and condensed from the full text of a court's opinion. This provides you with concise, real-life illustrations of the applications of certain laws. Those who plan to review court cases for future research projects or need to gain additional legal information will find the following analytical process helpful for understanding a case decision.

The case analyzed here was decided by the Supreme Judicial Court of Maine in 1986. It was brought by a woman against a car dealer because of the automobile's numerous mechanical problems, which were not repaired by the dealer. She sought to revoke her purchase contract.

INNISS v. METHOT BUICK-OPEL, INC.
Supreme Judicial Court of Maine, 1986.
506 A.2d 212.

]— 1
]— 2
]— 3

FACTS   In September of 1982 Kathleen Inniss purchased a 1982 Buick Skylark from Methot Buick-Opel, Inc. The car, which was a demonstrator, had nearly 6,000 miles on it but was accompanied by a new-car, twelve-month or 12,000-mile war-

4 —

ranty. It also had a history of significant mechanical and electrical problems, about which Methot said nothing to Inniss. Shortly after Inniss took possession, she experienced problems with the car. Between September and December of 1982 she took the car back to Methot eight times for repairs. The horn, rear window defogger, throttle, and brakes were repaired, but by the end of the warranty period, several other problems had not been. The temperature gauge continued to malfunction, the car intermittently would not start, it would vibrate in the front end, and the directional indicators would intermittently flash incorrectly when in use. In addition, although the purchase agreement had provided that the car would be rustproofed, much of it had not been.

The state of Maine did not have a "lemon law." Before the twelve-month warranty had lapsed, Inniss sought to revoke her acceptance of the contract and asked for her money back. The trial court held for the dealer and would not allow revocation (voiding) of the contract, although Inniss was awarded some damages for breach of warranty. Inniss appealed.

5 —

ISSUE   Can Inniss revoke her acceptance of the purchase contract and recover the purchase price of the automobile?

6 —

DECISION   Yes. Inniss had sufficient grounds to revoke acceptance in this case.

7 —

REASON   The court held that before revocation could be permitted, Inniss would have to show: (1) that the goods were so nonconforming (did not meet the contract specifications) as to impair substantially their value to her; (2) that it was difficult to discover the nonconformity before acceptance took place; (3) that she revoked within a reasonable period of time; (4) that the revocation took place prior to any substantial change in the condition of the car not caused by its own defects; and (5) that she had given notification of her revocation to Methot. The court reasoned that the history of Inniss's experience with the car was evidence enough that its value to her was substantially impaired. Further, she had met all the other criteria necessary to permit revocation. She was thus entitled to recover the purchase price of the car, plus damages for breach of express warranty and other damages.

Review of Case

1.   The name of the case (the style) is *Inniss v. Methot Buick-Opel, Inc.*, Inniss being the plaintiff, and Methot Buick-Opel, the defendant.
2.   The court deciding this case was the Supreme Judicial Court of the state of Maine. The case was decided in 1986.
3.   The numbers and letters found after the case name constitute the citation. This is what lawyers and legal scholars use to locate the case. This particular case can be found in volume 506 of the *Atlantic Reporter*, Second Series, page 212. Since the state of Maine has no current state reporter, only West's appropriate regional reporter was cited here.
4.   In the facts, we find the background to, and reasons for, the lawsuit which was first heard in a district court (trial court) and then appealed.
5.   The issue is the point or points of law addressed by the case. In this instance, at issue was whether or not Kathleen Inniss could revoke her contract with Methot Buick-Opel, Inc. and recover the money she had paid for her malfunctioning car.

6. The decision consists of the opinion of the majority of the judges or justices hearing the case. In the *Inniss v. Methot Buick-Opel, Inc.* decision, the court held for Inniss and permitted her to revoke her contract and recover the purchase price of the automobile from the car dealer.

7. The reason for the decision indicates what relevant laws and judicial principles were applied in forming the particular conclusion arrived at in the case at bar ("before this court").

❖ The Constitution As It Affects Business

The United States Constitution is the supreme law in this country. Neither Congress nor any state may pass a law that conflicts with the Constitution. In this respect, the U.S. Constitution serves as a limitation on the power of the government.

Conflicts frequently arise regarding the question of which government—federal or state—should be exercising power in a particular area. The United States Supreme Court, as the arbiter of the Constitution, resolves such conflicts by deciding which governmental system is empowered to act under the Constitution. The Constitution expressly grants the federal government the power to regulate commerce among the states.

The Commerce Clause

Article I, Section 8, of the United States Constitution grants Congress the power "[t]o regulate Commerce with foreign Nations, and among the several States, and with the Indian Tribes. . . ." What exactly does "to regulate commerce" mean? What

The U.S. Constitutional Bicentennial Celebration was held in Philadelphia in September of 1987.

does commerce entail? In the following landmark case, Chief Justice John Marshall interpreted the phrase liberally, and today, theoretically, the power over commerce authorizes the federal government to regulate almost every commercial enterprise in the United States. This power was delegated to the federal government to ensure the uniformity of rules governing the movement of goods through the states.

Case 1.1
GIBBONS v. OGDEN
United States Supreme Court, 1824
22 U.S. (9 Wheat.) 1, 6 L.Ed 23

FACTS   Robert Fulton, the inventor of the steamboat, and Robert Livingston, the American minister to France, secured a monopoly over steam navigation in New York state from the New York legislature in 1803. Fulton and Livingston then licensed Aaron Ogden to operate steam-powered ferryboats between New York and New Jersey. Thomas Gibbons decided to compete with Ogden and navigated two steamboats between New York and New Jersey, although he did not have permission from the state of New York to do so. Gibbons's steamboats were licensed under an act of Congress. Ogden sued Gibbons, and the New York state courts granted Ogden an injunction against further operations by Gibbons in New York waters. Gibbons appealed to the U.S. Supreme Court.

ISSUE   This case represented a clash between a federal act licensing vessels to ply the coastal waters of the United States and a state statute. At issue was whether the constitutional power of Congress "to regulate Commerce . . . among the several states" could invalidate the monopoly

granted to Ogden to navigate the waterways within New York state. The Court had to determine (1) whether navigation between New York and New Jersey constituted *commerce* in the sense understood by the framers of the Constitution, and (2) whether the congressional power to regulate commerce *among* the several states could be extended to activities *within* a state when such navigation was related to *interstate* commerce.

DECISION   The Court held that navigation of vessels in and out of ports of the nation did constitute commerce among the several states and that the shipping monopoly granted to Ogden by New York state interfered with the application of the federal act. The decision of the New York courts was therefore reversed.

REASON   Chief Justice Marshall defined commerce as all commercial intercourse—that is, all business dealings. The Court made it clear that the power to regulate commerce also extended to activities within a state, as long as the activities "concerned more states than one." The Court further declared that the power to regulate was "complete in itself, may be exercised to its utmost extent, and acknowledges no limitations, other than are prescribed in the Constitution."

The "Affectation Doctrine"   Traditionally, the commerce clause was interpreted as applying only to interstate, not intrastate, commerce. The Supreme Court, however, now recognizes that Congress has the power to regulate any activity, interstate or intrastate, that "affects" interstate commerce. A farmer's wheat production intended wholly for consumption on his or her own farm, for example, was held to be subject to federal regulation since such home consumption reduces the demand for wheat and thus may have a substantial economic effect on interstate commerce.[5]

   In *McLain v. Real Estate Board of New Orleans, Inc.* the Supreme Court held that local real estate brokers, who were licensed to perform their function only in Louisiana, substantially affected financial transactions and title insurance that were clearly interstate in nature.[6] Thus the brokers' activities affected interstate commerce sufficiently to be regulated by the federal law. The Court acknowledged that the

---

5.   See *Wickard v. Filburn*, 317 U.S. 111, 63 S.Ct. 82, 87 L.Ed. 122 (1942).
6.   444 U.S. 232, 100 S.Ct. 502, 62 L.Ed.2d 441 (1980).

Landmark in the Law

The Interstate Commerce Act

The Interstate Commerce Act of 1887 marks a significant turning point in U.S. history: it represents the first attempt of the federal government to regulate private enterprise and led to the establishment of the first federal regulatory agency—the Interstate Commerce Commission (ICC). The commerce clause of the U.S. Constitution grants the federal government the basic right to regulate interstate trade, and transportation clearly is subject to this clause. For this reason, it is not surprising that the first major form of regulation concerned the transportation industry.

The act was created to regulate the transportation of people and property by carriers within the United States—specifically, railroad carriers. The railroad industry in America was developing at full speed in the 1870s. By the late 1870s and early 1880s, every significant commercial center in the country had far more railroads than necessary to serve its needs. On the route between Atlanta and St. Louis, for example, twenty competing shipping lines operated. Nearly as many serviced the Chicago–New York trade. Owing to the extensive competition and price wars—one railroad at one point reduced its Chicago–New York fare to one dollar—several lines went bankrupt. Those that survived did so by resorting to various tactics to prevail against their competitors. One such tactic was to give rebates to shippers that used the services of one railroad exclusively. Another, for which some of the railway lines became highly unpopular, was the pooling of several competing companies to form a virtual monopoly over a certain route or area.

Such abuses became a major political issue of the day, and several states in the Midwest began to attempt regulation over the railroads in the absence of federal action. By 1887, however, Congress was sufficiently concerned to create regulatory legislation, and President Grover Cleveland signed the Interstate Commerce Act into law that year. The act applied to only those railroads operating within two or more states and required that rates be "reasonable and just." It also prohibited price discrimination, rebates, and pooling efforts. Railway rates were required to be publicly disclosed and could not be changed without ten days' public notice.

Although the ICC was created to enforce the provisions of the new act, it was not very effective during the first decade of its existence. The railroads largely ignored the new rules, and the ICC was powerless to act without the backing of the courts. In fifteen of the first sixteen cases brought against railroads for violating the act, the Supreme Court ruled against the Commission. By 1898, the ICC was virtually powerless. In the following decades, however, Congress succeeded in extending the power and jurisdiction of the ICC to the point where it had regulatory authority over all commercial carriers within the transportation industry.

Legislation during the last decade, such as the Motor Carrier Act of 1980, has significantly curtailed the regulatory power of the ICC in certain areas of transportation. It remains, however, an important independent regulatory agency in the federal government.

commerce clause has "long been interpreted to extend beyond activities actually in interstate commerce to reach other activities, while wholly local in nature, which nevertheless substantially affect interstate commerce."[7]

The Regulatory Power of the States   Another problem that frequently arises regarding the commerce clause is a state's ability to regulate matters within its borders. There is no doubt that states have a strong interest in regulating local activities. As part of their inherent sovereignty, states possess **police powers,** which allow them to regulate private activities to protect or promote the public health, safety, or general welfare of their citizens. States, for example, have a strong interest in keeping their local roads and highways safe for their residents. Most state regulations, however,

POLICE POWERS
Powers possessed by states as part of their inherent sovereignty. These powers may be exercised to protect or promote public health, safety, morals, or the general welfare.

---

7.   444 U.S. 232, 241, 100 S.Ct. 502, 508, 62 L.Ed.2d 441, 449 (1980).

place some burden on interstate commerce, and when state regulations impinge upon interstate commerce, courts must balance the state's interest on the merits and purposes of the regulation against the burden placed on interstate commerce.[8]

Because courts balance the interests involved, it is extremely difficult to predict the outcome in a particular case. State laws enacted pursuant to a state's police powers and affecting the health, safety, and welfare of local citizens do carry a strong presumption of validity. In *Raymond Motor Transportation, Inc. v. Rice*, however, the Supreme Court invalidated Wisconsin administrative regulations limiting the length of trucks travelling on its highways.[9] The court weighed the burden on interstate commerce against the benefits of the regulations and concluded that the challenged regulations "place a substantial burden on interstate commerce and they cannot be said to make more than the most speculative contribution to highway safety."[10]

The following case involves the same type of regulation found in the *Raymond* case.

Case 1.2
KASSEL v. CONSOLIDATED FREIGHTWAYS CORPORATION OF DELAWARE
United States Supreme Court, 1981.
450 U.S. 662, 101 S.Ct. 1309, 67 L.Ed.2d 580.

FACTS Unlike all other states in the West and Midwest, Iowa prohibited by statute the use of sixty-five-foot double-trailer trucks within its borders. Use of fifty-five-foot single-trailer trucks and sixty-foot double-trailer trucks was allowed. The appellee, Consolidated Freightways, owned sixty-five-foot doubles, which it was prohibited from using to carry commodities from other states through Iowa on interstate highways. Consequently, Consolidated filed suit, alleging that Iowa's statutory enactment unconstitutionally burdened interstate commerce. Kassel, an Iowa state official, defended the Iowa statute as a reasonable safety measure. The lower courts held the Iowa law to be unconstitutional because it seriously impeded interstate commerce while providing for slight, if any, safety.

ISSUE Could the Court examine evidence to determine whether a state's interest in safety is substantial enough to justify a statute interfering with interstate commerce?

DECISION Yes. The U.S. Supreme Court held that the Iowa statute was unconstitutional, concluding that the Iowa truck-length limitations burdened interstate commerce.

REASON The Court noted that it has long been recognized that, in the absence of congressional action to set uniform standards, states have the power to make laws governing matters of local concern that nevertheless may affect interstate commerce or even, to some extent, regulate it. But enacting a statute for public health or safety reasons does not insulate a state law from commerce-clause attack. Iowa's statute imposed a disproportionate burden on out-of-state residents and interests. The Court found where, as here, the state's "safety interest is found to be illusory, and its regulations impair significantly the federal interest in efficient and safe interstate transportation, the state law cannot be harmonized with the Commerce Clause."

❖ Business and the Bill of Rights

The importance of a written declaration of the rights of individuals eventually caused the first Congress of the United States to submit ten amendments to the Constitution for the approval by the states. These amendments, commonly known as the **Bill of**

---

8.   See Bibb v. Navajo Freight Lines, Inc., 359 U.S. 520, 79 S.Ct. 962, 3 L.Ed.2d 1003 (1959).
9.   434 U.S. 429, 98 S.Ct. 787, 54 L.Ed.2d 664 (1978).
10.   434 U.S. 429, 447, 98 S.Ct. 787, 797, 54 L.Ed.2d 664, 679 (1978).

Rights, were adopted in 1791 and embody laws that protect the individual against various types of interference by the federal government. Among the guarantees provided for by the Bill of Rights are the First Amendment protections of religion, speech, and assembly; the Fourth Amendment provisions regarding arrest, search, and seizure; and the Sixth Amendment rights to counsel, confrontation, and cross-examination in criminal prosecutions. Furthermore, through the Fourteenth Amendment, passed after the Civil War, most of these guarantees have been held to be so fundamental as to be applicable at the state level as well.

Under the doctrine of *selective incorporation,* those guarantees of individual liberty which are fundamental to the American system of law must be protected by the states. The constitutional rights and liberties of American citizens are referred to in later chapters; the significance of the Fourteenth Amendment in securing these liberties is discussed in the "Landmark" in Chapter 4. Here we discuss two constitutional rights that are being addressed by the courts more and more in relation to business activities—freedom of speech and the freedom of religion.

BILL OF RIGHTS
The first ten amendments to the Constitution.

Freedom of Speech

All of the First Amendment freedoms of religion, speech, press, assembly, and petition have been applied to the states through the due process clause of the Fourteenth Amendment. None of these freedoms, however, confers an absolute right. It is unclear what types of speech the First Amendment was designed to protect, but constitutional protection has never been afforded to certain classes of speech. In 1942, for example, the U.S. Supreme Court concluded:

There are certain well-defined and narrowly limited classes of speech, the prevention and punishment of which have never been thought to raise any Constitutional problem. These include the lewd and obscene, the profane, the libelous, and the insulting or

The First Amendment was designed to protect the right to freedom of expression.

"fighting" words—those which by their very utterance inflict injury or tend to incite an immediate breach of the peace. It has been well observed that such utterances are no essential part of any exposition of ideas, and are of such slight social value as a step to truth that any benefit that may be derived from them is clearly outweighed by the social interest in order and morality.[11]

Although the U.S. Supreme Court initially took the view that language treated as defamatory under state law was not entitled to First Amendment protection, it subsequently concluded that the First Amendment requires that a defense for honest error be allowed where statements are made about *public officials* relating to their *official conduct*. In the well-known case of *New York Times v. Sullivan,* the Court articulated a formal rule in stating that the First Amendment prohibits public officials from recovering damages for defamatory falsehoods relating to their official conduct unless they prove that the statements were made with "actual malice."[12] Actual malice means that a statement must be made *with knowledge that it was false* or *with reckless disregard of whether it was false or not.*

Freedom-of-speech cases generally distinguish between commercial and noncommercial messages. Although commercial advertising is accorded less constitutional protection than political or private speech, it is not completely outside the First Amendment, as the following case indicates.

> "Our nation is founded on the principle that observance of the law is the eternal safeguard of liberty and defiance of the law is the surest road to tyranny."
>
> **John F. Kennedy, 1917–1963 (Thirty-fifth president of the United States, 1961–1963)**

Case 1.3
ZAUDERER v. OFFICE OF DISCIPLINARY COUNSEL
United States Supreme Court, 1985.
471 U.S. 626, 105 S.Ct. 2265, 85 L.Ed.2d 652.

FACTS Philip Zauderer, an attorney practicing in Columbus, Ohio, in 1982 placed a series of newspaper ads directed at women who had used the Dalkon Shield intrauterine device (IUD). In his ads, Zauderer included a drawing of the Dalkon Shield and informed women that they could still sue for any injuries or other harm to their health sustained by its use, even though the IUD was no longer being marketed. As a result of these ads, Zauderer filed lawsuits for 106 of the women who had read the ads. The Ohio Supreme Court deemed such advertisements unethical, and Zauderer was reprimanded by the court for his actions. He was further reprimanded for not having disclosed in his ads that, although his clients would owe no legal fees if they lost, they might still be faced with other costs involved in litigation.

ISSUE The major issue in this case was whether the case-specific type of advertising engaged in by Zauderer

could be protected as "commercial speech" under the First Amendment. A second issue was whether Zauderer's ads were deceptive because they did not disclose the potential costs that clients could incur if they sued.

DECISION The U.S. Supreme Court held that the type of advertising engaged in by Zauderer was commercial speech protected by the First Amendment; the Ohio ruling was thus reversed. On the second issue, the Court upheld the Ohio court's reprimand.

REASON The Court had few precedents upon which to base a determination in this case. In the seminal case of *Bates v. State Bar of Arizona* [433 U.S. 350, 97 S.Ct. 2691, 53 L.Ed.2d 810 (1977)], truthful advertising of the availability and price of routine legal services was accorded protection as commercial speech under the First Amendment. In *Ohralik v. Ohio State Bar Association* [436 U.S. 447, 98 S.Ct. 1912, 56 L.Ed.2d 444 (1976)], however, a lawyer's in-person solicitation for pecuniary gain was not given such protection. In the Zauderer case under consideration, the Court determined that this kind of case-specific solicitation, although forbidden by the Ohio bar's ethical tenets, is "commercial speech" protected by the

---

11. Chaplinsky v. New Hampshire, 315 U.S. 568, 62 S.Ct. 766, 86 L.Ed. 1031 (1942).
12. 376 U.S. 254, 84 S.Ct. 710, 11 L.Ed.2d 686 (1964). Defamation is discussed in Chapter 3.

Case 1.3—Continued

First Amendment. Justice Byron White, writing for the majority, stated that advertisements are not the same as in-person solicitations of clients, which are "rife with possibilities for overreaching . . . and outright fraud."

On the related issue concerning fees, the Court maintained that required disclosures are permissible if they are not unduly burdensome and are reasonably related to the state's interest in preventing deception. Since Zauderer's advertisements did not disclose potential costs to clients, they could be conceived of as misleading. Hence the Ohio court's reprimand was upheld.

Freedom of Religion

The First Amendment requires that the government neither establish any religion nor prohibit the free exercise of religious practices. Government action, both federal and state, must be neutral toward religion. Regulation that does not promote, or place a significant burden on, religion is constitutional, however, even if it has some impact on religion. "Sunday closing laws," for example, make some commercial activities illegal if performed on Sunday. These statutes, also known as "blue laws," have been upheld on the ground that it is a legitimate function of government to provide a day of rest. The U.S. Supreme Court has held that the Sunday closing laws, although originally of a religious character, have taken on the secular purpose of promoting the health and welfare of workers.[13] Even though Sunday closing laws admittedly make it easier for Christians to attend religious services, the Court has

© Sydney Harris.

13. McGowan v. Maryland, 366 U.S. 420, 81 S.Ct. 1101, 6 L.Ed.2d 393 (1961).

viewed this effect as an incidental, not a primary, purpose of Sunday closing laws. Thus, the Constitution does not require a complete separation of church and state, but rather affirmatively mandates accommodation, not merely toleration, of all religions and forbids hostility toward any.[14]

The Supreme Court recently held that the establishment clause of the First Amendment, which prohibits the national government from officially supporting the establishment of a church, does not prohibit a municipality from including a Nativity scene in its annual Christmas display.[15] The Court concluded that whatever benefit the Nativity scene provided to religion was indirect, remote, and incidental.

Another freedom-of-religion issue involves the accommodation that businesses must make for the religious beliefs of their employees. The Equal Employment Opportunity Commission's rule of interpretation of Title VII of the Civil Rights Act of 1964 requires that private employers "reasonably accommodate" the religious practices of their employees, unless to do so would cause undue hardship to the employer's business.

In the following case, an individual felt compelled, on the basis of his religious convictions, to leave his job when he was transferred to an area of his employer's company that was involved in the production of war materials. In such a situation, will that individual be eligible for state unemployment benefits?

Case 1.4
THOMAS v. REVIEW BOARD OF THE INDIANA EMPLOYMENT SECURITY DIVISION

United States Supreme Court, 1981.
450 U.S. 707, 101 S.Ct. 1425, 67 L.Ed.2d 624.

FACTS Thomas worked in the nonmilitary operations of a large firm. When the production of nonmilitary goods was discontinued by the company, Thomas was transferred to a plant producing war materials. Thomas left his job, claiming that it violated his religious principles to participate in the manufacture of materials to be used in destroying life. In effect, he argued, the transfer to the war-materials plant forced him to quit his job. He was denied unemployment compensation by the state, which maintained that Thomas had not been effectively "discharged" by the employer but had voluntarily terminated his employment. The state courts upheld the denial of benefits, and Thomas appealed to the U.S. Supreme Court on the ground that the state's action infringed upon his right to the free expression of religion.

ISSUE May a state deny unemployment benefits to an individual who left his job because he honestly felt it conflicted with his religious convictions?

DECISION No. The judgment of the lower courts was reversed.

REASON The Supreme Court stated that religious beliefs and practices do not have to be acceptable, logical, or comprehensible to others for them to merit the protection of the First Amendment guarantee to the free exercise of religion. Right or wrong, Thomas's religious convictions were honestly and openly held by Thomas, and the Court concluded that his transfer to the war-materials plant, where he was directly involved in the manufacture of weapons, effectively placed Thomas in the position of having to choose between his job and his religious principles. Thomas's departure from the company was thus a result of a decision made by the employer, and Thomas should be entitled to unemployment compensation.

---

14. See Zorach v. Clauson, 343 U.S. 306, 72 S.Ct. 679, 96 L.Ed. 954 (1952).
15. See Lynch v. Donnelly, 465 U.S. 668, 104 S.Ct. 1355, 79 L.Ed.2d 604 (1984).

Business Law in Action

Business Law As It Applies to the Business of Law

The business world also includes those who are in the business of law. Not surprisingly, many aspects of business law apply to the business of law.

The Changing Climate of the Law—Advertising

As we saw in *Zauderer v. Office of Disciplinary Counsel*, which referred to *Bates v. State Bar of Arizona*, the right of commercial free speech by lawyers has been firmly established. The American Bar Association Model Rules of Professional Conduct were modified to allow for advertising so long as it is not false or misleading. The new code has been adopted in various forms by supreme courts in Arizona, Delaware, Minnesota, Missouri, Montana, New Jersey, and Washington, with rulings pending in eleven other states. Not surprisingly, advertising for legal services has become an accepted part of the business of law in many states. One of the biggest beneficiaries of the *Bates* decision is the law clinic.

The Law Clinic—Its Inner Workings

A law clinic is a high-volume, high-efficiency law firm, where case volume is built by advertising and publicity. Much of the routine work is delegated to nonlawyers (sometimes called paralegals). Many clinics allow clients to pay by credit card. Fees are usually standardized, except for cases involving personal injuries. Many

clinics are storefront offices located in shopping malls and even in department stores. Consider an example. Hyatt Legal Services was founded in Cleveland in 1977. It now has more than two hundred offices in twenty-five states. Much of its expansion can be attributed to its special arrangement with H&R Block, the nationwide tax preparers. Block provides administrative services and shares office space with Hyatt. The first law organization to present

Advertising for legal services is only a relatively recent development. This ad for Dan Walker and Associates was among the first ads printed in 1977.

itself as a clinic was Jacoby & Meyers Law Offices, which started in Los Angeles in 1972 and now has eighty outlets on the east and west coasts.

The Sale of Prepaid Legal Plans

Hyatt Legal Services, as well as a number of other services, offer prepaid legal plans. The availability is limited, but where it is available the annual cost is only $96–$120 per family. The services offered are

(continued on next page)

Business Law in Action—Continued

unlimited telephone or in-office consultations with attorneys; simple wills for members and spouses; preparation of powers of attorney, basic deeds, and promissory notes; and review of any documents. Law America, another prepaid legal plan, available to BankAmericard customers only, costs about the same as Hyatt and provides similar services, as well as referrals to local attorneys at reduced hourly rates.

The Law and Mega Law Firms

There are several law firms in the United States with more than 500 lawyers, and the 1,000-lawyer firm may not be far off. Consider the Chicago-based firm of Baker & McKenzie, with almost nine hundred lawyers and forty-five offices worldwide. This firm tops the list of corporate law firms whose sheer size seems to be reshaping the legal profession. These firms, and their

newly powerful managers, are taking over big business law. According to financial writer Mark Stevens, "the genteel corporate firms that dominated the profession for decades are threatened." [1] As a point of comparison, consider that in 1975 the largest law firm, again Baker & McKenzie, had only 326 lawyers.

Law firms are acting in the same way as other big businesses—they are engaged in bidding for the best and the brightest lawyers and luring them away from competing law firms. For example, the eight partners, sixteen associates, and dozens of secretaries who constituted the real estate group at Weil, Gotshal, & Manges, one of the powers in New York real estate law, moved *en masse* to the law firm of Shea & Gould, and brought with them lucrative clients such as Equitable Life Insurance.

1. See Mark Stevens, *Power of Attorney: The Rise of the Giant Law Firms* (New York: McGraw-Hill Book Co., 1986).

Soon Anybody May Be Able to Own a Law Firm

As might be expected, the more the legal profession starts to resemble ordinary business, the more ordinary business practices will come into play. The legal profession now faces a revolutionary change—two bar associations (the District of Columbia and North Dakota) are moving to end rules that prohibit nonlawyers from owning law firms. If these rules are eliminated, such retailers as Sears, Roebuck could add legal counseling to the array of services that they now offer their customers. Mass marketing, power, and price competition would eventually alter the practice of law. "Eventually the distribution of legal services will be no different from any other product," predicts Stephen Gillers, a professor at New York University Law School. [2]

2. Quoted in *Business Week*, January 26, 1987, p. 42.

❖ Chapter Summary: Business Law—Introductory Concepts

The Social Context of Law	Law has evolved slowly over the centuries. It both affects, and is affected by, the customs, habits, and moral and ethical values of the society in which it is operative. The creation of civil rights legislation (such as the Civil Rights Act of 1964) is an example of social and political values altering the law; the enforcement by the courts of civil rights legislation since the 1960s is an example of law strongly affecting its social context. In general, commercial law has evolved in response to social forces and customs of the trade, and has not been itself an active social force.
Sources of American Law	1. *Common law*—Originated in medieval England with the creation of the king's courts; consists of past judicial decisions and reasoning; involves the application of the doctrine of *stare decisis*—the rule of precedent—in applying law.
	2. *Constitutional law*—The law as expressed by federal and state constitutions. The U.S. Constitution is the supreme law of the land. State constitutions are supreme within state borders to the extent that they do not violate a clause of the federal constitution or federal law.
	3. *Statutory law*—Laws or ordinances created by federal, state, and local governing bodies. None of these laws can violate the U.S. Constitution or the relevant state constitution.
	4. *Administrative law*—The branch of law concerned with the power and actions of administrative agencies, boards, and commissions; involves the administration of law by nonjudicial agencies created by the executive or legislative branch of the government.
	5. *Commercial law*—Laws governing trade and commerce. The most important source of commercial law in the United States is the Uniform Commercial Code (UCC), a codification of commercial law that has been adopted by all the states (although only in part by Louisiana).
Civil versus Criminal Law	1. *Civil law*—Law concerned with acts against a person for which the injured party seeks redress in the form of compensation or other relief.
	2. *Criminal law*—Law concerned with acts against society for which society seeks redress in the form of punishment.
The U.S. Constitution and American Business	1. *Commerce Clause*—Gives Congress the right to regulate commerce among the states. On the basis of this constitutional power, as interpreted by the U.S. Supreme Court, the business world in the United States has been subject to the jurisdiction of the federal courts and to regulation by the federal government.
	2. *Bill of Rights*—The first ten amendments to the U.S. Constitution. Particularly important to the business environment are the freedoms of speech and religion guaranteed by the First Amendment and, to some extent, the rights guaranteed by the Fourth and Fifth Amendments.

❖ Questions and Case Problems

1-1. Should judges have the same authority to overrule statutory law as they have to overrule common law? Explain.

1-2. Discuss the difference between common law and *stare decisis?* Should judges have the same power to adopt a rule contrary to common law as they do to depart from *stare decisis?* Explain.

1-3. Joe Caldor entered a hardware store to purchase an item. While he was there, a mounted display shelf holding gallon cans of paint fell on him. He suffered numerous injuries as a result and could not work for three months. He sued the owner of the hardware store for damages. Explain why this is a civil, and not a criminal, proceeding.

1-4. Suppose Georgia enacts a law requiring the use of contoured rear-fender mudguards on trucks and trailers operating within its state lines. The statute further makes it illegal for trucks and trailers to use straight mudguards. In thirty-five other states, straight mudguards are legal. Moreover, in the neighboring state of Florida, straight mudguards are explicitly required by law. There is some evidence suggesting that contoured mudguards might be a little safer than straight mudguards. Discuss whether this Georgia statute would violate the commerce clause of the U.S. Constitution.

1-5. A Los Angeles city ordinance prohibits the posting of signs on public property (such as lamp posts, utility posts, hydrants, traffic signs, and so on). During a campaign in which Roland Vincent was running for City Council, his supporters wanted to post signs on the cross-arms supporting utility poles. The group campaigning for Vincent (called "Taxpayers") challenged the city ordinance prohibiting signs on such property, claiming that the ordinance was unconstitutional because it violated the freedom of speech guaranteed by the First Amendment. Do you agree with Taxpayers? [Los Angeles City Council v. Taxpayers for Vincent, 466 U.S. 789, 104 S.Ct. 2118, 80 L.Ed.2d 772 (1984)]

1-6. New Jersey enacted a law prohibiting the importation of most wastes into the state. Some of the landfill operators in New Jersey, however, had agreements with out-of-state residents, such as those in Philadelphia, to dispose of their solid and liquid waste. Philadelphia brought an action claiming that this statute violated the commerce clause by discriminating against interstate commerce. New Jersey asserted that its statute was justified since its landfills were not big enough for disposing of the state's own waste, and importation had a significant and adverse potential effect on the environment. Explain whether this state regulation of interstate commerce is permissible. [Philadelphia v. New Jersey, 437 U.S. 617, 98 S.Ct. 2531, 57 L.Ed.2d 475 (1978)]

1-7. Under South Carolina law, in order to receive unemployment benefits, a worker must accept employment when it is offered to him or her. Verner, an agent of the state of South Carolina, denied benefits to Sherbert because Sherbert refused to accept a job that required Saturday work. Sherbert was a Seventh Day Adventist, and it was against her religion to work on Saturday, her Sabbath. In all other respects, Sherbert was eligible for unemployment benefits. May the state deny unemployment benefits to Sherbert only on the grounds that she refused to work on Saturday? [Sherbert v. Verner, 374 U.S. 398, 83 S.Ct. 1790, 10 L.Ed.2d 965 (1963)]

Chapter 2

Courts and Procedures

The body of law is vast and complex. As discussed in Chapter 1, American law is based on numerous elements—the case decisions and reasoning that comprise common law; statutes passed by federal and state legislatures; federal and state constitutions; law codifications, such as the Uniform Commercial Code, that have been adopted by the various states; administrative law; and so on. For all that we call this collection of elements "the law," it is, in one sense, not effectively law until it is interpreted and applied by the courts. This is why Justice Holmes, as the opening quote indicates, considered the law *only* to be that which is said and done by the courts.

We may agree or disagree with the eminent jurist on this point, but it cannot be disputed that the courts play a paramount role in fashioning the law and that it is often in the courtrooms that the law touches the lives of Americans. Since at some time or another in their careers, businesspersons will likely face either a potential or an actual lawsuit, it is important to anyone involved in business to have an understanding of American court systems, including the mechanics of lawsuits. Even though there are fifty-two court systems—one for each of the fifty states, one for the District of Columbia, plus a federal system—similarities abound. Keep in mind that the federal courts are not superior to the state courts; they are simply an independently authorized system, whose authority is derived from Article III, Section 2 of the United States Constitution.

Both state and federal court systems are examined in this chapter, and to clarify judicial procedure we follow a typical case through a state court system. We also examine alternative dispute resolution.

"The prophecies of what the courts will do in fact, and nothing more pretentious, are what I mean by the law."

Oliver Wendell Holmes, Jr., 1841–1935
(Associate Justice of the U.S. Supreme Court, 1902–1932)

❖ Jurisdiction

In Latin, *juris* means "law"; *diction* means "to speak." Thus, "the power to speak the law" is the literal meaning of the term **jurisdiction.** Jurisdiction refers either to the geographical area within which a court has the right and power to decide cases or to the right and power of a court to adjudicate matters concerning certain persons, property, or subject matter. Before any court can hear a case, it must have jurisdiction—that is, the power to hear and decide a case. Thus, for a court to exercise

JURISDICTION
The authority of a court to hear and decide a specific action.

valid authority in a case, it must have jurisdiction over the person against whom the suit is brought or over the property involved in the suit, and jurisdiction over the subject matter.

Jurisdiction over Persons and Property

Generally, a court's power is limited to the territorial boundaries of the state in which it is located. Thus, a court has jurisdiction over anyone who can be served with a summons within those boundaries. A court normally will also have jurisdiction over residents of the state and people who do business within the state. In some cases where an individual has committed a wrong, such as causing an automobile injury or selling defective goods within the state, a court can exercise jurisdiction (using the authority of a long-arm statute) even if the individual is outside the state. A **long-arm statute** is a state law permitting courts to obtain jurisdiction over nonresident defendants. A court can further exercise jurisdiction over a corporation in the state where it is incorporated, in the state where the company has its main plant or office, and in any state where it does business.

The deciding issue in the following case concerned whether a court, under a state's long-arm statute, held personal jurisdiction over an out-of-state defendant in a lawsuit.

LONG-ARM STATUTE
Through long-arm statutes, states permit personal jurisdiction to be obtained over nonresident individuals and corporations. Individuals or corporations, however, must have certain "minimum contacts" with that state.

Case 2.1
COTE v. WADEL
United States Court of Appeals, Seventh Circuit, 1986.
796 F.2d 981.

FACTS In January of 1983 Colleen Cote, a Wisconsin resident, hired a Michigan lawyer, Peter Wadel, to represent her in a medical malpractice action in a Michigan state court. Wadel filed an appearance for her on February 10, 1983, and sent her a bill for $118.25 for court costs that he had paid on her behalf. She paid him the following month. In July she learned from the defendant's lawyer that the court had dismissed her case in April for lack of prosecution. On checking with Wadel's office, she was told that settlement negotiations were under way with the defendant's insurer—which Cote knew to be untrue since the defendant was uninsured. She then contacted another lawyer to look into the matter, but the lawyer could obtain no information from Wadel or his law firm concerning the issue. Cote then brought suit, in a Wisconsin federal court (there is at least one federal trial court in each state), against Wadel, alleging malpractice in handling her case.

The federal trial court dismissed her suit for lack of personal jurisdiction over the defendant, whose business

and residence was in Michigan. Cote appealed, claiming that either (1) personal jurisdiction over the Michigan defendant existed or (2) the Wisconsin court should have transferred her case to a court with jurisdiction, instead of dismissing it. Because the statute of limitations (setting a time limit on how long after the event it can be taken to court) had run, the dismissal of the case meant she could not initiate another lawsuit in the appropriate court.

ISSUES (1) Did the Wisconsin federal trial court hearing Cote's case have personal jurisdiction over the Michigan defendant, under Wisconsin's long-arm statute? (2) Did the federal trial court err by dismissing the case instead of transferring it to another district?

DECISION No, to both. The requirements for jurisdiction under Wisconsin's long-arm statute had not been met in this case, and the federal trial court did not err by dismissing the case instead of transferring it.

REASON Under Wisconsin's long-arm statute, jurisdiction is conferred on Wisconsin state and federal courts over nonresident defendants "in any action claiming injury to person or property within or without this state arising out of an act or omission *within this state* by the de-

Case 2.1—Continued

fendant." (Emphasis added.) The court could find no act or omission in Wisconsin by Wadel or any other person in his firm. All of the acts and omissions cited by Cote occurred in Michigan, and "neither Wadel nor anyone else in his firm ever set foot in Wisconsin in connection with this matter." According to the court, "The only significant connection between the suit and Wisconsin is that the plaintiff lives there; and you cannot get jurisdiction over a nonresident just by showing that you are a resident and would prefer to sue in your own state's courts. By that reasoning, there would be no limits to personal jurisdiction over nonresidents."

As to the dismissal of the suit by the federal trial court, the federal appeals court reviewing the case could not find that the federal trial court had been in error. Trial courts have broad discretion in making such determi-nations, and appellate (reviewing) courts can reverse such decisions only when there has been a "clear abuse of discretion." The appellate court could find no such abuse in this case, even though the dismissal meant Cote was "forever barred from bringing a suit that for all we know has great merit." In effect, the dismissal by the federal trial court penalized Cote for filing her suit in the wrong district—an elementary, obvious mistake. "The proper penalty," the federal appellate court stated, "for obvious mistakes that impose costs on opposing parties and on the judicial system is a heavy one." Although the penalty may seem harsh in this case, "litigants [the participants in a lawsuit] and the public will benefit substantially in the long run from better compliance with the rules limiting personal jurisdiction."

Jurisdiction over Subject Matter

Subject matter jurisdiction is a limitation on the types of cases a court can hear. The distinction between courts of general jurisdiction and courts of special, or limited, jurisdiction lies in the subject matter of cases heard. Probate courts—courts that handle only matters relating to wills and estates—are a common example of limited subject matter jurisdiction. A court of general jurisdiction can decide virtually any type of case. The subject matter jurisdiction of a court is usually defined in the statute or constitution creating the court. A court's subject matter jurisdiction can be limited not only by the subject of the lawsuit, but also by the amount of money in controversy, by whether a case is a felony or misdemeanor, or by whether the proceeding is a trial or an appeal.

Original and Appellate Jurisdiction

The distinction between courts of original jurisdiction and courts of appellate juris-diction normally lies in whether the case is being heard for the first time. Courts having **original jurisdiction** are those of the first instance. In other words, these courts are where the trial of a case begins. In contrast, courts having **appellate jurisdiction** act as reviewing courts. In general, cases can be brought to them only on appeal from an order or a judgment of a lower court.

Venue

Jurisdiction has to do with whether a court has authority over a specific subject matter or individual. **Venue,** on the other hand, has to do with the particular geographic area within a judicial district where a suit should be brought. It is a question that arises after a determination of jurisdiction. A particular court may have jurisdiction but not venue.

Basically, the concept of venue reflects the policy that a court trying a suit should be in the geographic neighborhood (usually the county) where the incident leading

ORIGINAL JURISDICTION
The power of a court to take a case, try it, and decide it.

APPELLATE JURISDICTION
The power of a court to hear and decide an appeal; that is to say, the power and authority of a court to review cases that have already been in the lower court for trial, and the power to make decisions about them without actually holding a trial—this process is called appellate review.

VENUE
The geographical district in which the action is tried and from which the jury is selected.

Profile

Oliver Wendell Holmes, Jr. (1841–1935)

The task of a judge or justice can be awesome—especially if you are a justice on the United States Supreme Court. How do you decide what cases are significant enough to warrant the attention of the Court? How do you decide which precedent to apply, when more than one possibility exists? How do you decide at what point justice requires that a well-established precedent be overturned? And finally, how do you know whether you are making a significant decision on the basis of objective reasoning or because of subjective prejudices and biases?

These kinds of questions escape few jurists, and certainly they were among those that preoccupied Oliver Wendell Holmes during his long tenure as a jurist on the Supreme Judicial Court of Massachusetts (twenty years) and then as a Supreme Court Justice (thirty years).

Holmes was a man of ideas. He was an intellectual, a scholar, and a prolific writer. He read avidly, and kept a notebook where he recorded the books he read each year. According to the notebook entries for 1910–1911, Holmes, while serving on the U.S. Supreme Court, also somehow found the time to read forty-nine books, including works by Plato (in Greek), Dante, and Alfred North Whitehead. During his tenure on the bench, Holmes—referred to as the "court scholar"—became celebrated for his pithy philosophical statements concerning law and the human condition in general. He remains probably the most widely quoted of American jurists.

Holmes was greatly influenced by the work of Darwin and by those who transplanted Darwin's "survival of the fittest" principle into a social context. As society is in a constant state of evolution, so, too, must the law remain fluid and open to the moral, political, and economic evolution of the times. In *The Common Law*, written in 1881 and one of his best-known works, Holmes wrote of the practical, experimental nature of the law: "The life of the law has not been logic, it has been experience"; it is affected by the "prejudices which judges share with their fellow men" and corresponds, "as far as it goes, with what is . . . understood to be convenient."

His concern with the role played by personal prejudices and biases in judicial decision making was clearly expressed in his dissenting opinion in *Lochner v. New York* (1905).[1] In *Lochner,* the Supreme Court found unconstitutional a New York state law prohibiting bakery workers from working more than ten hours a day. The Court stated that the New York law violated the due process clause of the Fourteenth Amendment, which provided that no state could "deprive any person of life, liberty, or property without due process of law." The law also violated, according to the Court, the constitutionally guaranteed freedom to contract. Holmes pointed out in his dissent that the majority opinion betrayed the personal biases and prejudices of the justices in favor of freedom of contract and away from an objective consistency in judicial reasoning. After all, Holmes argued, the Supreme Court had, only nine years earlier, upheld a Utah law limiting working hours for miners[2]—a precedent "conveniently" overlooked by the majority on the court.

Probably one of Holmes's greatest insights into the common law was that the same legal rules can be manipulated by judges to serve different policies at different times. The task of judges, in Holmes's opinion, must be to keep their own prejudices and biases out of their decisions, so far as possible, and to be ever vigilant in distinguishing between conclusions based on objective legal reasoning and those stemming from purely subjective biases and attitudes.

1. 198 U.S. 45, 25 S.Ct. 539, 49 L.Ed. 937 (1905).

2. Holden v. Hardy, 169 U.S. 366, 18 S.Ct. 383, 42 L.Ed. 780 (1898).

to the suit occurred or where the parties involved in the suit reside. However, pretrial publicity or other factors may require a change of venue to another community, especially in criminal cases where the defendant's right to a fair and impartial jury is impaired.

The proper venue for a suit is defined by statute. Improper venue does not necessarily deprive the court of power to hear a case, but a party can request a change of venue if venue is not proper.

❖ The State Court System

One can view the typical state system as being made up of trial courts and appellate courts. Trial courts are exactly what their name implies—courts in which trials are held and testimony is taken. Appellate courts are courts of appeal and review.

Consider the typical state court system shown in Exhibit 2-1. It has three main tiers: (1) the state trial court of general, or limited, jurisdiction, (2) the state appellate court, and (3) the state supreme court. Any person who is a party to a lawsuit typically has the opportunity to plead the case before a trial court and then, if he or she loses, before at least one level of appellate court. Finally, if a federal statute or constitutional issue is involved in the decision of the state supreme court, that decision may be further appealed to the United States Supreme Court.

Trial Courts

The state trial courts have either general or limited jurisdiction. Those with limited jurisdiction as to subject matter are often called special inferior trial courts or minor judiciary courts. Some typical courts of limited jurisdiction are domestic relations

◆ **Exhibit 2-1**
   A Typical State Court System

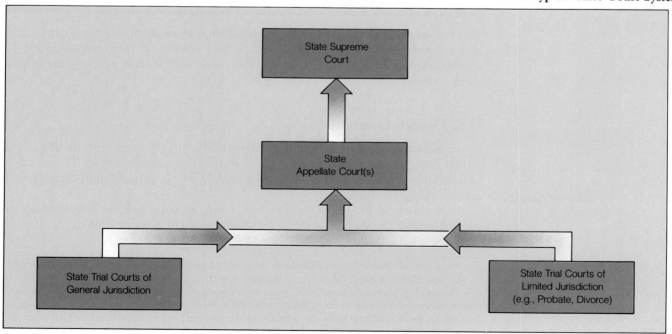

courts, which handle only divorce actions and child custody cases; local municipal courts, which mainly handle traffic cases; probate courts, which handle the administration of wills and estate settlement problems; and small claims and justice of the peace courts.

Trial courts that have general jurisdiction as to subject matter may be called county, district, superior, or circuit courts.[1] The jurisdiction of these courts of general and original jurisdiction is often determined by the size of the county in which the court sits. Many important cases involving businesses originate in these general trial courts.

Courts of Appeal and Review

Although in some states trial courts of general jurisdiction also have limited jurisdiction to hear appeals from the minor judiciary—for example, small claims and traffic cases—when one discusses courts of review, or appellate courts, one usually means courts that are not trial courts.

Every state has at least one court of review, or appellate court. The subject matter jurisdiction of these courts is substantially limited to hearing appeals. These intermediate appellate, or review, courts are often called the courts of appeals. The highest court of the state is usually called the supreme court.[2] Appellate courts try few cases. They examine the record of the case on appeal and determine whether the trial court committed an error. They look at questions of law and procedure, but not usually questions of fact.[3] The decisions of each state's highest court on all questions of state law are final. It is only when issues of federal law are involved that a state's highest court can be overruled by the Supreme Court of the United States.

❖ The Federal Court System

The federal court system is similar in many ways to most state court systems. It is also a three-tiered model consisting of (1) trial courts, (2) intermediate courts of appeals, and (3) the Supreme Court. Exhibit 2-2 shows the organization of the federal court system.

U.S. District Courts

At the federal level, the equivalent of a state trial court of general jurisdiction is the district court. There is at least one federal district court in every state. The number of judicial districts can vary over time, primarily owing to population changes and corresponding caseloads.

In the Federal Judgeship Act of 1984, Congress increased the total number of judicial circuit (reviewing) court and district (trial) court judgeships in the United

---

1. The name in Ohio is Court of Common Pleas; the name in New York is Supreme Court.
2. In New York it is called the Court of Appeals.
3. The appellate court will tamper with a trial court's finding of fact when the finding is clearly erroneous (that is, when it is contrary to the evidence presented at trial) or when there is no evidence to support the finding. Realize, however, that the appeals court has liberal power to reverse on the facts when the case is a nonjury one.

◆ **Exhibit 2-2 The Organization of the Federal Court System**

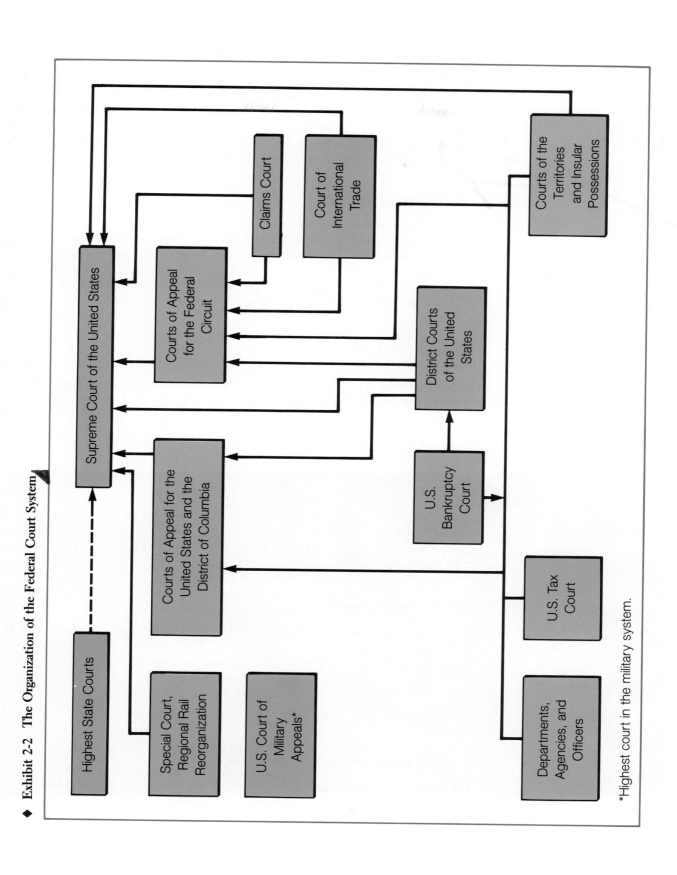

*Highest court in the military system.

States. The law now provides for 168 circuit court judgeships with 13 circuits (including the Federal Circuit) and 563 district court judgeships within the 96 judicial districts.[4]

U.S. district courts have original jurisdiction in federal matters. In other words, district courts are where federal cases originate. There are other trial courts with original, albeit special (or limited) jurisdiction, such as the U.S. Tax Court, the U.S. Bankruptcy Court, and the U.S. Claims Court. Certain administrative agencies and departments with judicial power also have original jurisdiction.

U.S. Courts of Appeals

Congress has established twelve judicial circuits that hear appeals from the district courts located within their respective circuits. The decisions of the courts of appeals are final in most cases, but appeal to the U.S. Supreme Court is possible. Appeals from federal administrative agencies, such as the Federal Trade Commission (FTC), are also made to the U.S. circuit courts of appeals. See Exhibit 2-3 for the geographical boundaries of U.S. district courts and U.S. courts of appeals.

The Supreme Court of the United States

The highest level of the three-tiered model of the federal court system is the Supreme Court of the United States. According to the language of Article III of the U.S.

---

4. See Sections 44(a) and 133 of Title 28, U.S.C.

The Rehnquist Court in 1988.

◆ **Exhibit 2-3 U.S. Courts of Appeals and U.S. District Courts**

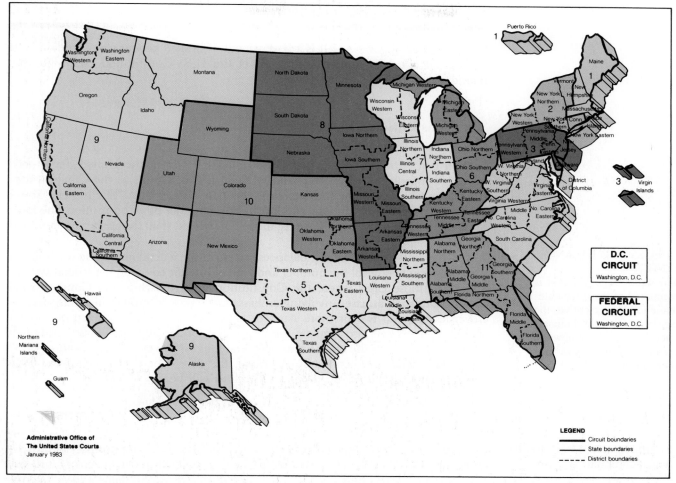

Constitution, there is only one national Supreme Court. All other courts in the federal system are considered "inferior." Congress is empowered to create other inferior courts as it deems necessary. The inferior courts that Congress has created include the second tier in our model—the U.S. courts of appeals—as well as the district courts and any other courts of limited, or specialized, jurisdiction.

The Supreme Court of the United States consists of nine justices; these justices are nominated by the president of the United States and confirmed by the Senate. They (as do all federal district and courts of appeals judges) receive lifetime appointments (since under Article III they "hold their offices during Good Behavior"). Although the U.S. Supreme Court has original, or trial, jurisdiction in rare instances (set forth in Article III, Section 2), most of its work is as an appeals court. The Supreme Court can review any case decided by any of the federal courts of appeals, and it also has the appellate authority over some cases decided in the state courts.

❖ Jurisdiction of the Federal Courts and Judicial Review

Since the federal government is a government of limited powers, the jurisdiction of the federal courts is limited. Article III of the U.S. Constitution established the boundaries of federal judicial power.

The Constitutional Boundaries of Federal Judicial Power

Section I of Article III states that "The judicial Power of the United States shall be vested in one supreme Court and in such inferior Courts as the Congress may from time to time ordain and establish." Section 2 states that "The judicial Power shall extend to all Cases in Law and Equity arising under this Constitution, the Laws of the United States, and Treaties made, or which shall be made, under their Authority. . . ."

In line with the **checks and balances system** of the federal government, Congress has the power to control the number and kind of inferior courts in the federal system. Except in those cases where the Constitution gives the Supreme Court original jurisdiction (such as cases involving ambassadors, consuls, public ministers, or controversies between two or more states or between a state and a citizen of another state), Congress can also regulate the jurisdiction of the Supreme Court. Although the Constitution sets the outer limits of federal judicial power, Congress can set other limits on federal jurisdiction. Furthermore, the courts themselves can promulgate rules that further narrow the types of cases they will hear.

CHECKS AND BALANCES SYSTEM
The national government is composed of three separate branches: the executive, the legislative, and the judicial. Each branch of the government exercises a check upon the actions of the others.

Diversity Jurisdiction

Federal district court jurisdiction also extends to cases involving **diversity of citizenship.** Diversity of citizenship cases are those arising between (1) citizens of different states; (2) a foreign country and citizens of a state or of different states; and (3) citizens of a state and citizens or subjects of a foreign country. The amount in controversy must be more than $50,000 before a federal court can take jurisdiction. For purposes of diversity of citizenship jurisdiction, a corporation is a citizen of the state where it is incorporated and of the state where it has its principal place of business. A case involving diversity of citizenship can commence in the appropriate federal district court or, if the case starts in a state court, it can sometimes be transferred.

Diversity jurisdiction originated in 1789. The authors of the Constitution felt that a state might be biased in favor of its own citizens. Hence, the option of using the federal courts provided by the principle of diversity of citizenship is a means of protecting the out-of-state party. A large percentage of the more than 70,000 cases filed in federal courts each year are based on diversity of citizenship.

DIVERSITY OF CITIZENSHIP
A situation occurring when persons on one side of a case in federal court come from a different state than persons on the other side. This may also involve a foreign country or citizens or subjects of a foreign country and citizens of a state.

Federal Questions

Whenever a plaintiff's cause of action is based, at least in part, on the United States Constitution, a treaty, or a federal law, then a **federal question** arises, and the case comes under the judicial power of federal courts. Any lawsuit involving a federal

FEDERAL QUESTION
A federal question provides jurisdiction for federal courts. This jurisdiction arises from Article III, Section 2, of the Constitution. Federal questions may pertain to the U.S. Constitution, acts of Congress, or treaties.

question can originate in a federal court. People whose claims are based on rights granted by an act of Congress can sue in a federal court. People who claim that their constitutional rights have been violated can begin their suits in a federal court.

When both federal and state courts have the power to hear a case, as is true in suits involving diversity of citizenship, **concurrent jurisdiction** exists. When cases can be tried only in federal courts, **exclusive jurisdiction** exists. Federal courts have exclusive jurisdiction in cases involving federal crimes, bankruptcy, patents, and copyrights; in suits against the United States; and in some areas of admiralty law. (States have exclusive jurisdiction in certain subject matters also—for example, in divorce and adoptions.)

In the following case, a trial court ruled that an employee's federal action was prohibited because it was first brought in a state court. The appellate court makes it clear that federal jurisdiction over federal questions ordinarily cannot be limited by state actions or statutes.

CONCURRENT JURISDICTION
Concurrent jurisdiction exists when two different courts have the power to hear a case. For example, some cases can be heard in a federal or a state court.

EXCLUSIVE JURISDICTION
Jurisdiction is exclusive when a case can only be heard in one particular court.

Case 2.2
LEAMAN v. JOHNSON
United States Court of Appeals, Sixth Circuit, 1986.
794 F.2d 1148.

FACTS A former probationary employee of the Ohio Department of Mental Retardation brought suit in the Ohio Court of Claims against her employer. The employee claimed that her discharge constituted a violation of her right to freedom of speech guaranteed by the First Amendment in that she was fired because she vocally disagreed about the treatment received by a particular mentally retarded person. The state court dismissed her action as a valid personnel decision, without ruling on her constitutional claims. Following the dismissal by the Ohio court, the plaintiff brought suit in federal district court. The federal district court dismissed the constitutional claim against the state officials on the ground that the employee's previous state action constituted "a knowing, intelligent, and voluntary waiver" of her federal action. An Ohio statute provides that "filing a civil action in the Court of Claims results in a complete waiver of any cause of action,

based on the same act or omission . . . against any state officer or employee. . . ." The employee appealed.

ISSUE Can a state statute limit jurisdiction granted by federal law?

DECISION No. The Court of Appeals for the Sixth Circuit concluded that the district court ruling undermined jurisdiction of a federal cause of action against state officials who allegedly injured a citizen in violation of a federal constitutional or statutory right. The state statute in question should be construed, according to the court, only to waive state-created, but not federally-created, claims against state officials.

REASON The court stated, "Statutes enacted by Congress under Article III define the jurisdiction of the federal courts, and ordinarily a state may not withdraw or limit that jurisdiction by the adoption of waiver or election of remedies rules." The court also pointed out that even state courts in Ohio had not previously construed the Ohio statute to limit federal actions.

Judicial Review

The problem often arises as to whether or not a law is contrary to the mandates of the Constitution. **Judicial review** is the process for making such a determination. It is the judicial branch of the national government that has the authority and power to determine whether a particular law violates the Constitution.

The power of judicial review was first established in *Marbury v. Madison* (see the "Landmark" in this chapter). In determining that the Supreme Court had the

JUDICIAL REVIEW
The authority of a court to reexamine a previously considered dispute; the process by which a court decides on the constitutionality of legislative acts.

Landmark in the Law

Marbury v. Madison (1803)

In the edifice of American law, the *Marbury v. Madison* decision in 1803 can be viewed as the keystone of the constitutional arch. The story is often told, and for a reason—it shows how seemingly insignificant cases can have important and enduring results.

Consider the facts behind *Marbury v. Madison*. John Adams had lost his bid for reelection to Thomas Jefferson in 1800. Adams, a Federalist, thought the Jeffersonian Republicans would weaken the power of the national government by asserting states' rights. He also feared the anti-Federalists' antipathy toward business. During the final hours of Adams's presidency, he worked feverishly to "pack" the judiciary with loyal Federalists by appointing what came to be called "midnight judges" just before Jefferson took office.

All of the judicial commissions had to be certified and delivered. The task of delivery fell on Adams's secretary of state, John Marshall. Out of fifty-nine midnight appointments, Marshall delivered only forty-two. He assumed that the remaining seventeen would be sent out by Jefferson's new secretary of state, James Madison. Of course, the new administration would not cooperate in packing the judiciary: Jefferson refused to deliver the remaining commissions. William Marbury, along with three other Federalists to whom the commissions had not been de-

President James Madison

livered, decided to sue. The suit was brought directly to the Supreme Court by a **writ of mandamus,** authorized by Section 13 of the Judiciary Act of 1789.

As fate would have it, the man responsible for the lawsuit, John Marshall, had stepped down as Adams's secretary of state only to become Chief Justice of the Supreme Court. He was now in a position to decide the case for which he was responsible.[1] Marshall was faced with a

1. Today any justice who has been involved in the issue before the Court would probably disqualify himself or herself because of a conflict of interest.

WRIT OF MANDAMUS
A court order telling a public official or governmental department to do something.

power to decide that a law passed by Congress violated the Constitution, the Court stated, "It is emphatically the province and duty of the Judicial Department to say what the law is. . . . If two laws conflict with each other, the courts must decide on the operation of each. . . . So if the law be in opposition to the Constitution. . . . The Court must determine which of these conflicting rules governs the case. This is the very essence of judicial duty."[5]

❖ How Cases Reach the Supreme Court

Many people are surprised to learn that in a typical case there is no absolute right of appeal to the United States Supreme Court. The Supreme Court is given original,

5. 5 U.S. (1 Cranch) 137, 2 L.Ed. 60 (1803).

dilemma: if he ordered the commissions delivered, the new secretary of state could simply refuse. The Court had no way to compel action because it had no police force. Also, Congress was controlled by the Jeffersonian Republicans. It might impeach Marshall for such an action.[2] But if Marshall simply allowed Secretary of State Madison to do as he wished, the Court's power would be severely eroded.

Marshall stated for the unanimous Court that Jefferson and Madison had acted incorrectly in refusing to deliver Marbury's commission. Marshall also stated, however, that the highest court did not have the power to act as a court of original jurisdiction in this particular case, because the section of the law that gave it original jurisdiction was unconstitutional. The Judiciary Act of 1789 specified that the Supreme Court could issue writs of mandamus as part of its original jurisdiction, but Marshall pointed out that Article III of the Constitution, which spelled out the Supreme Court's original jurisdiction, did not mention writs of mandamus. In other words, Congress did not have the right to expand the Court's jurisdiction, so this section of the Judiciary Act of 1789 was unconstitutional and hence null and void.

The decision avoided a showdown between the Federalists and the Jeffersonian Republicans. The power of the Supreme Court was enlarged: "A law repugnant to the Constitution is void."

Was the Marshall Court's assumption of judicial review power justified by the Constitution? Whether or not it was, *Marbury v. Madison* confirmed a doctrine that was part of the legal tradition of the time. Indeed, judicial review was a major (although not articulated) premise upon which the movement to draft constitutions and bills of rights was ultimately based, and was also part of the legal theory underlying the Revolution of 1776. During the decade before the adoption of the federal Constitution, cases in at least eight states involved the power of judicial review. Also, the Supreme Court had considered the constitutionality of an act of Congress in *Hylton v. U.S.*,[3] in which Congress's power to levy certain taxes was challenged. But since that particular act was ruled constitutional rather than unconstitutional, this first federal exercise of true judicial review was not clearly recognized as such.

In any event, since Marshall masterfully fashioned a decision which did not require that anyone do anything, there was no practical legal point to challenge. It still stands today as a judicial and political masterpiece.

---

2. In fact, Congress later did impeach Supreme Court Justice Samuel Chase, although he was not convicted. The charge was abusive behavior under the Sedition Act.

3. 3 Dallas 171 (1796).

---

or trial court, jurisdiction in a small number of situations, as mentioned earlier. In all other cases, its jurisdiction is appellate "with such Exceptions, and under such Regulations as the Congress shall make." Today the exceptions and rules set by Congress, and some of the rules that the Court has set for itself, are quite complex. Thousands of cases are filed with the Supreme Court each year; yet it hears, on average, only about 200. To bring a case before the Supreme Court, a party requests the Court to issue a *writ of certiorari*.[6]

---

6. Between 1790 and 1891, Congress allowed the Supreme Court almost no discretion over which cases to decide. After 1925, the Court could choose in almost ninety-five percent of appealed cases to decide whether to hear arguments and issue an opinion. Beginning with the term in October, 1988, mandatory review was eliminated altogether.

Writ of Certiorari

WRIT OF CERTIORARI
A writ from a higher court asking the lower court for the record of a case. A request for certiorari (or "cert" for short) is similar to an appeal, but one which the higher court is not required to take for decision.

A *writ of certiorari* is an order issued by the Supreme Court to a lower court requiring the latter to send it the record of the case for review. Parties can petition the Supreme Court to issue a *writ of certiorari*, but whether the Court will issue one is entirely within its discretion. In no instance is the Court required to issue a *writ of certiorari*.

Below are some of the situations in which the Supreme Court may issue a *writ of certiorari*:

1. When a state court has decided a substantial federal question that has not been determined by the Supreme Court or when a state court has decided such a question in a way that is probably in disagreement with the trend of the Supreme Court's decisions.
2. When two or more federal courts of appeal are in disagreement with each other.
3. When a federal court of appeals has decided an important state question in conflict with state law, has decided an important federal question not yet addressed by the Court but which should be decided by the Court, has decided a federal question in conflict with applicable decisions of the Court, or has departed from the accepted and usual course of judicial proceedings.
4. When a federal court of appeals holds that a state statute is invalid because it violates federal law.
5. When the highest state court of appeals holds a federal law invalid or upholds a state law that has been challenged as violating federal law.
6. When a federal court holds an act of Congress unconstitutional and the federal government or one of its employees is a party.

Most petitions for *writs of certiorari* are denied. A denial is not a decision on the merits of a case, nor does it indicate agreement with the lower court's opinion. Denial of the writ also has no value as a precedent. The Court will not issue a writ unless at least four justices approve of it. This is called the "rule of four." Typically, only the petitions that raise the possibility of important constitutional questions are granted.

❖ Following a Case through the State Courts

"A judge rarely performs his functions adequately unless the case before him is adequately presented."

**Louis D. Brandeis, 1856–1941
(Associate Justice of the U.S. Supreme Court, 1916–1939)**

American and English courts follow the adversary system of justice. The judge's role is viewed as nonbiased and mostly passive. The lawyer functions as the client's advocate, presenting the client's version of the facts in order to convince the judge or the jury (or both) that they are true. Judges are responsible for the appropriate application of the law. They do not have to accept the legal reasoning of the attorneys, but rather, can base a ruling and a decision on their own study of the law. Judges do not have to be entirely passive; they sometimes ask questions of witnesses and even suggest types of evidence to be presented. For example, if an indigent defendant chooses to act as his or her own counsel, the judge will often play less of a passive role and more of an advocate role, intervening during the trial proceedings to help the defendant.[7]

---

7. See Faretta v. California, 422 U.S. 806, 95 S.Ct. 2525, 45 L.Ed.2d 562 (1975).

Court Procedure

Procedure involves the way in which disputes are handled in the courts. A large body of law—procedural law—establishes the rules and standards for determining disputes in courts. The rules are very complex, and they vary from court to court. There is a set of federal rules of procedure and various sets of rules for state courts. Procedural rules differ in criminal and civil cases.

We will now follow a civil case through the state court system. The case involves an automobile accident in which Kevin Anderson, driving a Mercedes, struck Lisa Marconi, driving a Chevy Sprint. The accident occurred at the intersection of Wilshire Boulevard and Rodeo Drive in Beverly Hills, California. Marconi suffered personal injuries, incurring medical and hospital expenses as well as lost wages for four months. Anderson and Marconi are unable to agree on a settlement, and Marconi sues Anderson. Marconi is the plaintiff and Anderson is the defendant. Both are represented by lawyers.

The Pleadings

Complaint and Summons   Marconi's suit, or action, against Anderson commences when her lawyer files a complaint (sometimes called a petition or declaration) with the clerk of the trial court in the appropriate geographic area. In most states it will be a court having general jurisdiction; in others it may be a court having special jurisdiction with regard to subject matter. The complaint contains: (1) a statement alleging the facts necessary for the court to take jurisdiction, (2) a short statement of the facts necessary to show that the plaintiff is entitled to a remedy, and (3) a statement of the remedy the plaintiff is seeking.

The complaint in this case (as shown in Exhibit 2-4) states that Marconi was driving her car through a green light at the specified intersection, exercising good driving habits and reasonable care, when Anderson carelessly drove his car through a red light and into the intersection from a cross street, striking Marconi and causing serious personal injury and property damage. The complaint goes on to state that she is entitled to $85,000 to cover medical bills, $10,000 to cover lost wages, and $5,000 to cover property damage to her car.

After the complaint has been filed, the sheriff or a deputy of the county serves a summons and a copy of the complaint on defendant Anderson. The summons notifies Anderson that he is required to prepare an answer to the complaint and to file a copy of his answer with both the court and the plaintiff's attorney within a specified time period (usually twenty to thirty days after the summons has been served). The summons also informs Anderson that failure to answer will result in a judgment by default for the plaintiff, meaning the plaintiff will be awarded the damages alleged in her complaint.

Rules vary governing how a summons can be served, but usually the summons is handed to the defendant or is left at the defendant's residence or place of business. In a few states a summons can be served by mail. When the defendant cannot be reached, special rules sometimes permit the summons to be left with a designated person, such as the secretary of state.

Choices Available after Receipt of the Summons and Complaint   Once the defendant is served with a copy of the summons and complaint, he or she must file a responsive pleading (the answer). This filing must be done within the stipulated time

◆ **Exhibit 2-4**
Example of a
Typical Complaint

IN THE LOS ANGELES MUNICIPAL COURT
FOR THE LOS ANGELES JUDICIAL DISTRICT

CIVIL NO. 8-1026

Lisa Marconi
Plaintiff

COMPLAINT

Kevin Anderson
Defendant

Comes now the plaintiff and for her cause of action against the defendant alleges and states as follows:

1. This action is between plaintiff, a California resident living at 1434 Palm Drive, Anaheim, California, and defendant, a California resident living at 6950 Garrison Avenue, Los Angeles, California.

2. On September 10, 1987, plaintiff, Lisa Marconi, was exercising good driving habits and reasonable care in driving her car through the intersection of Rodeo Drive and Wilshire Boulevard when defendant, Kevin Anderson, negligently drove his vehicle through a red light at the intersection and collided with plaintiff's vehicle.

3. As a result of the collision plaintiff suffered severe physical injury, that prevented her from working, and property damage to her car. The cost she incurred included: $85,000 in medical bills, $10,000 in lost wages, and $5,000 automobile repair.

WHEREFORE, plaintiff demands judgment against the defendant for the sum of $100,000 plus interest at the maximum legal rate and the costs of this action.

By _____
Roger Harrington
Attorney for the Plaintiff
800 Orange Avenue
Anaheim CA 91426

1/2/88

period. In the answer, the defendant may file (1) a motion to dismiss, (2) any answer containing an affirmative defense, (3) a counterclaim, or (4) an answer denying the allegations and containing both an affirmative defense and a counterclaim.

MOTION TO DISMISS OR DEMURRER
A pleading in which a defendant admits to the facts as alleged by the plaintiff but asserts that the plaintiff's claim fails to state a cause of action (i.e., has no basis in law).

Motion to Dismiss   If the defendant challenges the sufficiency of the plaintiff's complaint, the defendant can present to the court a **motion to dismiss,** or **demurrer.** (The rules of civil procedure in many states do not use the term *demurrer*; they use only *motion to dismiss*.) The motion to dismiss is an allegation that even if the facts presented in the complaint are true, their legal consequences are such that there is no reason to go further with the suit and no need for the defendant to present an answer. It is a contention that the defendant is not legally liable even if the facts are as the plaintiff alleges. If, for example, Marconi's complaint alleges facts that exclude the possibility of negligence on Anderson's part, Anderson can move to dismiss, and he will not be required to answer because his motion will be granted. The motion to dismiss is often used for the purposes of delay.

If Marconi wishes to discontinue the suit because, for example, an out-of-court settlement has been reached, she can likewise move for dismissal. The court can also dismiss on its own motion. If the court grants the motion to dismiss, the judge is saying that the plaintiff has failed to state a recognized cause of action. The plaintiff generally is given time to file an amended complaint. If the plaintiff does not file this amended complaint, a judgment will be entered against the plaintiff solely on the basis of the pleadings, and the plaintiff will not be allowed to bring suit on the matter again. On the other hand, if the court denies the motion to dismiss, the judge is indicating that the plaintiff has stated a recognized cause of action, and the defendant is given an extension of time to file a further pleading. If the defendant does not do so, a judgment will usually be entered for the plaintiff.

Note that when a judge grants a motion to dismiss, the case being tried is ended, but the losing party does have the right to appeal. Indeed, any direct verdict ends the trial but allows for the right to appeal.

Answer and Counterclaim If the defendant has not chosen to file a motion to dismiss or has filed a motion to dismiss that has been denied, then he or she must file an **answer.** This document either admits the statements or allegations set forth in the complaint or denies them and outlines any defenses that the defendant may have. If Anderson admits to all of Marconi's allegations in his answer, the court will enter a judgment for Marconi. If Anderson denies Marconi's allegations, the matter will proceed to trial.

Anderson can deny Marconi's allegations and set forth his own claim that Marconi was in fact negligent and therefore owes him money for damages to his Mercedes. This is appropriately called a **counterclaim** or a **cross-complaint.** If Anderson files a counterclaim, Marconi will have to answer it with a pleading, normally called a **reply,** which has the same characteristics as an answer.

Answer and Affirmative Defenses Anderson can also admit the truth of Marconi's complaint but raise new facts that may result in dismissal of the action. This is called raising an **affirmative defense.** For example, Anderson could admit that he was negligent but plead that the time period for raising the claim has passed and that Marconi's complaint must therefore be dismissed because it is barred by the statute of limitations (a statutory limit to the time during which one can raise a claim).

The complaint and answer (and the counterclaim and reply) together are called the **pleadings.** The pleadings inform each party of the claims of the other and specify the issues (disputed questions) involved in the case.

Dismissals and Judgments before Trial

Many actions for which pleadings have been filed never come to trial. There are numerous procedural avenues for disposing of a case without a trial. Many of them involve one or the other party's attempts to get the case dismissed through the use of pretrial motions. We have already mentioned the motion to dismiss, or the demurrer. Another equally important motion is the motion for a judgment on the pleadings.

ANSWER
Procedurally, a defendant's response to the complaint.

COUNTERCLAIM, OR CROSS-COMPLAINT
A claim made by a defendant in a civil lawsuit that in effect sues the plaintiff; it can be based on entirely different grounds than those given in the plaintiff's complaint.

REPLY
Procedurally, a plaintiff's response to a defendant's answer.

AFFIRMATIVE DEFENSE
Any response to the plaintiff's claim that does not deny the plaintiff's facts, but asserts a new basis for nonliability. Examples are fraud, duress, and the expiration of the statute of limitations.

PLEADINGS
Statements by the plaintiff and the defendant which detail the facts, charges, and defenses. Modern rules simplify common law pleading, often requiring only the complaint, answer, and sometimes a reply to the answer.

Motion for Judgment on the Pleadings or on the Merits After the pleadings are closed—after the complaint, answer, and any counterclaim and reply have been filed—either of the parties can file a motion for a judgment on the pleadings, or on the merits. This motion is basically the same as a motion to dismiss and may be granted or denied on the same grounds.

Motion for Summary Judgment A lawsuit can be shortened or a trial can be avoided if there are no disagreements about the facts in a case and the only question is which laws apply to those facts. Both sides can agree to the facts and ask the judge to apply the law to them. In this situation, it is appropriate for either party to move for **summary judgment.** Summary judgment will be granted when there are no genuine issues of fact in a case, and the only question is one of law. When the court considers a motion for summary judgment, it can take into account evidence outside the pleadings. This distinguishes the motion for summary judgment from the motion to dismiss. In a pretrial setting, one party can bring in a sworn statement, or affidavit, that refutes the other party's claim. Unless the second party brings in affidavits of conflicting facts, the first party will receive summary judgment.

Discovery

Before a trial begins, the parties can use a number of procedural devices in order to obtain information and gather evidence about the case. Marconi, for example, will want to know how fast Anderson was driving, whether he had been drinking, whether he saw the red light, and so on. The process of obtaining information from the opposing party or from other witnesses is known as **discovery.**

The federal rules of civil procedure and similar rules in the states set forth the guidelines for discovery activity. Discovery includes gaining access to witnesses, documents, records, and other types of evidence. The rules governing discovery are designed to make sure that a witness or party is not unduly harassed, that privileged material is safeguarded, and that only matters relevant to the case at hand are discoverable.

Depositions and Interrogatories Discovery can involve the use of depositions or interrogatories, or both. **Depositions** are sworn testimony by the opposing party or any witness, recorded by an authorized court official. The person deposed gives sworn testimony under oath, and answers questions asked by the attorneys from both sides. The questions and answers are taken down, sworn to, and signed. These answers will, of course, help the attorneys prepare their cases. They can also be used in court to impeach a party or a witness who changes testimony at the trial. In addition, they can be used as testimony if the witness is not available at trial. Lawyers from both sides can prepare for depositions with written questions ahead of time. They then ask the opposing party or witnesses these questions during the deposition.

Interrogatories are a series of written questions for which written answers are prepared and then signed under oath. The main difference between interrogatories and depositions with written questions is that interrogatories are directed to a party to the lawsuit (the plaintiff or the defendant), not to a witness, and the party can prepare answers with the aid of an attorney. The scope of interrogatories is broader because parties are obligated to answer questions, even if it means disclosing information from their records and files. Interrogatories are usually less expensive than depositions.

SUMMARY JUDGMENT
A judgment entered by a trial court prior to trial which is based on the valid assertion by one of the parties that there are no disputed issues of fact which would necessitate a trial.

DISCOVERY
A method by which opposing parties may obtain information from each other to prepare for trial. Generally governed by rules of procedure, but may be controlled by the court.

DEPOSITIONS
A generic term that refers to any evidence verified by oath. As a legal term, it is often limited to the testimony of a witness taken under oath before a trial, with the opportunity of cross-examination.

INTERROGATORIES
A series of written questions for which written answers are prepared and then signed under oath by a party (plaintiff or defendant) to the lawsuit.

Pretrial Hearing

Either party or the court can request a pretrial conference or hearing. Usually the hearing consists of an informal discussion between the judge and the opposing attorneys after discovery has taken place. The purpose of the hearing is to identify the matters that are in dispute and to plan the course of the trial. The pretrial hearing is not intended to compel the parties to settle their case before trial, although judges may encourage them to settle out of court if circumstances suggest that a trial would be a waste of time.

The Right to a Jury Trial

A trial can be held with or without a jury. If there is no jury, the judge determines the truth of the facts alleged in the case. The Seventh Amendment to the U.S. Constitution guarantees the right to a jury trial for cases at law in federal courts when the amount in controversy exceeds $20. Most states have similar guarantees in their own constitutions, although many states put a higher minimum-dollar-amount restriction on the guarantee. For example, Iowa requires the dollar amount of damages to be at least $1,000 before there is a right to a jury trial.

The right to a trial by jury does not have to be exercised, and many cases are tried without a jury. In most states and in federal courts, one of the parties must request a jury or the right is presumed to be waived. In the following case, the right to civil trial by jury—even when no funds exist to pay jurors—is affirmed.

Case 2.3
ARMSTER v. UNITED STATES DISTRICT COURT FOR THE CENTRAL DISTRICT OF CALIFORNIA

United States Court of Appeals, Ninth Circuit, 1986.
792 F.2d 1423.

FACTS On June 16, 1986, the director of the Administrative Office of the U.S. Courts notified the ninety-four federal district courts that no civil jury trials could be initiated until the end of the fiscal year (September 30) due to lack of funds with which to pay the jurors. The petitioners in this case (Armster) claimed that the consequent delay (of three and a half months) in scheduling a jury trial violated the Seventh-Amendment right to a civil jury trial. The Justice Department maintained that unlike the Sixth Amendment, which guarantees a speedy *criminal* jury trial, the Seventh Amendment does not guarantee a speedy *civil* jury trial. The Justice Department further noted that district courts have postponed civil jury trials before, although for other reasons—such as court-calendar congestion, lack of a sufficient number of judges, and

the priority accorded to trying criminal cases before civil actions.

ISSUE Does the suspension of civil jury trials for a period of three and a half months due to lack of funds to pay the jurors violate the Seventh-Amendment right to a trial by jury in civil law cases?

DECISION Yes. The suspension of civil jury trials for a period of three and a half months for budgetary reasons does violate the Seventh Amendment.

REASON The court stated that the Seventh Amendment is violated whenever an individual is not afforded, for a significant period of time, a jury trial that he or she would otherwise receive. Three and a half months were construed to be more than a "significant period of time." The court further concluded that the availability of constitutional rights does not carry a "price tag" and that individual liberties, as mandated by the Constitution, cannot be affected by budget shortages or other variations in the balance of accounts in the national Treasury.

Both attorneys make opening statements concerning the facts they expect to consider during the trial.

Jury Selection

Prior to the commencement of any jury trial, a jury must be selected. The process by which the jury is selected is known as *voir dire* (a French phrase meaning "to speak the truth"). In most jurisdictions, the *voir dire* consists of oral questions that attorneys for the plaintiff and the defendant ask a group of prospective jurors (one at a time) in order to determine whether a potential jury member is biased or has any connection with a party to the action or with a prospective witness. Some trial attorneys go so far as to use psychologists to help them pick juries.

VOIR DIRE
From the French, meaning "to speak the truth." A phrase denoting the preliminary examination used for potential jurors (or witnesses) where competency, interests, etc., may be objected to.

At the Trial

Both attorneys are allowed to make opening statements concerning the facts that they expect to prove during the trial, with the plaintiff's lawyer going first. Since Marconi is the plaintiff and has the burden of proving that her case is correct, Marconi's attorney begins by calling the first witness for the plaintiff and examining (questioning) the witness. (For both attorneys, the type of question and the manner of asking are governed by the rules of evidence.) This questioning is called **direct examination.** After Marconi's attorney is finished, the witness is subject to **cross-examination** by Anderson's attorney. Then Marconi's attorney has another opportunity to question the witness in *redirect examination*, and Anderson's attorney can follow with *recross-examination*. When both attorneys have finished with the first witness, Marconi's attorney calls the succeeding witnesses in the plaintiff's case, each of whom is subject to cross-examination (and redirect and recross, if necessary).

DIRECT EXAMINATION
In a trial, the first questioning of a witness, by the side that called the particular witness.

CROSS-EXAMINATION
The questioning of an opposing witness during the trial.

DIRECTED VERDICT
The verdict in which the judge takes the decision out of the hands of the jury by telling the jury what they must decide, or by actually making the decision.

At the conclusion of the plaintiff's case, the defendant's attorney has the opportunity to ask the judge to direct a verdict for the defendant on the ground that the plaintiff has presented no evidence that would justify the granting of the plaintiff's remedy. This is called a motion for a **directed verdict.** In considering the motion, the judge looks at the evidence in the light most favorable to the plaintiff and grants the motion only if there is insufficient evidence to raise an issue of fact. (Motions for directed verdicts at this stage of trial are seldom granted.)

The defendant's attorney then presents the evidence and witnesses for the defendant's case. Witnesses are called and examined (questioned) by the defendant's attorney. The plaintiff's attorney has the right to cross-examine them, and there is a redirect and recross-examination if necessary. At the end of the defendant's case, either attorney can move for a directed verdict, and the test again is whether the jury can, through any reasonable interpretation of the evidence, find for the party against whom the motion is made.

After the defendant's attorney has finished presenting evidence, the plaintiff's attorney can present a **rebuttal,** which includes additional evidence to refute the defendant's case. The defendant's attorney can meet that evidence in a **rejoinder.** After both sides have rested their cases, the attorneys each present a **closing argument,** with the plaintiff's lawyer going first. In their closing arguments, the two opposing attorneys urge a verdict in favor of their respective clients. The judge instructs the jury (assuming it is a jury trial) in the law that applies to the case. The instructions to the jury are often called charges. Then the jury retires to the jury room to deliberate a verdict. In the Marconi-Anderson case the jury will not only decide for the plaintiff or for the defendant but, if it finds for the plaintiff, it will also decide on the amount of money to be paid to her.

Motion for New Trial   At the end of the trial, a motion can be made to set aside an adverse verdict and any judgment, and to hold a new trial. The motion will be granted if the judge is convinced, after looking at all the evidence, that the jury was in error, but does not feel it is appropriate to grant judgment for the other side. This will usually occur when the jury verdict is the obvious result of a misapplication of the law or misunderstanding of the evidence.

Judgment n.o.v.   If Marconi wins, and if Anderson's attorney had previously moved for a directed verdict, Anderson's attorney can now make a motion for a **judgment n.o.v.** (from the Latin, *non obstante veredicto,* or notwithstanding the verdict). The standards for granting a judgment n.o.v. are the same as those for granting a motion to dismiss. Assume here that this motion is denied and that Anderson appeals the case. (If Marconi wins but receives a smaller money award than she sought, she can appeal also.) These events are illustrated in Exhibit 2-5.

The Appeal

A notice of appeal must be filed with the clerk of the trial court within the prescribed time. Anderson then becomes the appellant or petitioner. His attorney files in the reviewing court (usually an intermediate court of appeals) the record on appeal, which contains the following: (1) the pleadings, (2) a transcript of the trial testimony and copies of the exhibits, (3) the judge's rulings on motions made by the parties, (4) the arguments of counsel, (5) the instructions to the jury, (6) the verdict, (7) the post-trial motions, and (8) the judgment order from which the appeal is taken. Anderson may also be required to post a bond for the appeal.

Anderson's attorney is required to prepare a condensation of the record, known as an abstract. The abstract, the brief, and the arguments are filed with the reviewing court. The brief contains (1) a short statement of the facts, (2) a statement of the

REBUTTAL
Refers to evidence given by the plaintiff's attorney to refute (rebut) evidence introduced by the defendant's attorney.

REJOINDER
The defendant's attorney's answer to the plaintiff's rebuttal.

CLOSING ARGUMENT
Made after the plaintiff and defendant have rested their cases. Closing arguments are made prior to the jury charges.

JUDGMENT n.o.v.
A judgment notwithstanding the verdict; may be entered by the court for the plaintiff (or the defendant) after there has been a jury verdict for the defendant (or the plaintiff).

◆ **Exhibit 2-5   A Typical Lawsuit**

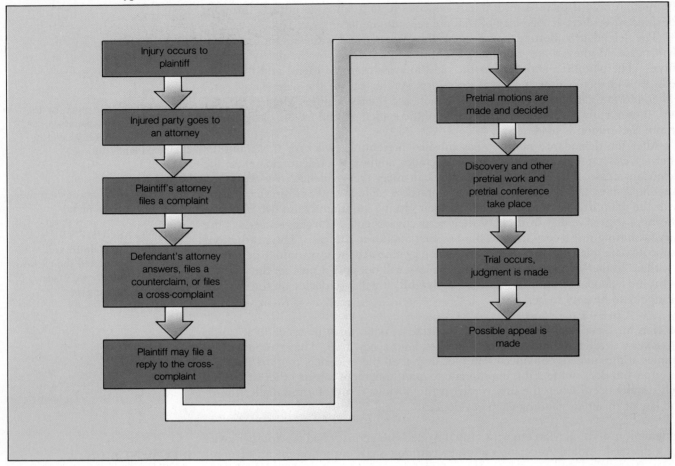

issues, (3) the rulings by the trial court that Anderson contends are erroneous and prejudicial, (5) a statement of the applicable law, and (6) arguments on Anderson's behalf, citing applicable statutes and relevant cases as precedent. The attorney for the appellee, or respondent, Marconi, usually files an answering brief and argument. Anderson's attorney can file a reply, although it is not required. The reviewing court then considers the case.

Appeals courts do not hear any evidence. Their decision concerning a case is based on the abstracts, the record, and the briefs. The attorneys can present oral arguments, after which the case is taken under advisement. In general, the appellate courts do not reverse findings of fact unless the findings are unsupported or contradicted by the evidence. Rather, they review the record for errors of law. If the reviewing court believes that an error was committed during the trial or that the jury was improperly instructed, the judgment will be *reversed*. Sometimes the case will be *remanded* (sent back to the court that originally heard the case) for a new trial. In most cases, the judgment of the lower court is *affirmed*, resulting in the enforcement of the court's judgment or decree.

If the reviewing court is an intermediate appellate court, the losing party normally may appeal to the state supreme court. Such a petition corresponds to a petition for a writ of certiorari in the U.S. Supreme Court. If the petition is granted, new briefs must be filed before the state supreme court and the attorneys may be allowed or requested to present oral arguments. As with the intermediate appellate courts, the supreme court may reverse or affirm the appellate court's decision, or remand the case. At this point, unless a federal question is at issue, the case has reached its end.

It is important to note that most disputes are settled out of court, mainly because of the time and expense of trying a case. Of those cases which go to trial, about 97 percent are resolved at the trial level, as relatively few trial court decisions are changed on appeal.

"Discourage litigation. Persuade your neighbors to compromise whenever you can."

Abraham Lincoln, 1809–1865 (Sixteenth president of the United States, 1861–1865)

❖ Alternative Dispute Resolution

As the number of court cases filling the **dockets** grows every year and as the cost of litigation increases, more and more businesspersons, consumers, and other individuals are turning to alternative dispute resolution (ADR) as an alternative to civil lawsuits. One form of ADR is **mediation,** which involves a mutual third party called the mediator. The mediator's function is to listen to all sides of a dispute, analyze each party's contentions, communicate with each party, and then help them settle the matter. A more formal method of ADR is **arbitration,** where the dispute is formally submitted to a third person (not part of the judiciary), who renders a legally binding decision.

Mediation

In the mediation process, the parties themselves must reach the agreement. The mediator is often a volunteer from the community, and not necessarily a lawyer. The mediator talks face to face with the parties and allows them to discuss their disagreement in an informal atmosphere, such as a community center, church, or neighbor's home. There are few procedural rules, certainly fewer than in a courtroom. In fact, most mediation programs discourage lawyers from participating, and thus legal terminology is frequently avoided. Mediation often results in disputes being settled quickly. Initial meetings between the parties and the mediator often occur within several weeks after a voluntary request to mediate has been made by one or both of the parties.

Mediation is not free. The mediator charges an hourly rate that is similar to what an attorney would charge, but the parties split the cost.

Arbitration

With arbitration, the arbitrator makes a binding decision by which both parties must abide. Often the dispute is formally submitted by the parties because of an arbitration clause in a contract entered into before the dispute arose. Many sales agreements have an arbitration clause requiring that arbitration be entered into if certain clauses in the contract are violated by either party. Virtually any commercial matter can be submitted to arbitration.

DOCKET
The list of cases entered on a court's calendar and thus scheduled to be heard by the court.

MEDIATION
A method of settling disputes outside of court by using the services of a neutral third party, who acts as a communicating agent between the parties; a method of dispute settlement less formal than arbitration.

ARBITRATION
The settling of a dispute by submitting it to a disinterested third party (other than a court), who renders a legally binding decision.

The arbitrator becomes a private judge, but he or she does not have to be a lawyer, even though many are. Arbitrators decide on their own procedural rules as well as their own rules of evidence. The decision of the arbitrator is called the *award*.

When the decision of an arbitrator is contested by a losing party, the courts tend to be reluctant to overturn such a decision, except in the case of evident error. The following case illustrates a court's response to a decision reached through arbitration.

Case 2.4
BEVLES CO., INC. v. TEAMSTERS LOCAL 986

United States Court of Appeals, Ninth Circuit, 1986.
791 F.2d 1391.

FACTS An employer, Bevles Co., Inc., was advised by its attorney that it is unlawful in California to knowingly employ illegal aliens. The employer, following an interrogation of employees suspected of being in this country illegally, summarily dismissed two employees. The Teamsters Union, Local 986, of which the two employees were members, brought a grievance against the employer for their dismissal, claiming the employer lacked "just cause" under a collective bargaining agreement, and the dispute was arbitrated. The arbitrator ruled that the employer violated the collective bargaining agreement because the employer would not have been subject to criminal liability had the employees been retained. The arbitrator ruled that both employees were entitled to reinstatement, and one was entitled to back pay. The district court affirmed the arbitrator's ruling. The employer appealed, contending that the arbitrator's ruling must be vacated because the employees are not legally entitled to work in the United States.

ISSUE Given the fact that neither the employer nor the employees were subject (under federal law) to criminal or civil liability arising from their relationship, did the employer have just cause to dismiss the employees?

DECISION No. The court held that the arbitrator's award of reinstatement and back pay, notwithstanding the immigration status of the employees, neither violates public policy nor is in manifest disregard of the law. The judgment of the trial court was affirmed.

REASON The court stated that, unlike a similar case where illegal aliens had been suspended [*Sure-Tan, Inc.* v. *NLRB,* 467 U.S. 883, 104 S.Ct. 2803, 81 L.Ed.2d 732 (1984)], the discharged employees in this case had not already left the country and no illegal reentry would be involved in reinstating them to their jobs. Thus, no conflict with the Immigration and Naturalization Service (INS) existed. The court also concluded that review of an arbitrator's interpretation of a collective bargaining agreement is much more limited than is a court's review of a decision of the National Labor Relations Board in a labor dispute. In evaluating the California Labor Code, Section 2805, which states that "No employer shall knowingly employ an alien who is not entitled to lawful residence in the United States if such employment would have an adverse effect on lawful resident workers . . .," the court asserted that such provision was not sufficient for the employer to charge the arbitrator with manifest disregard of the law.

AMERICAN ARBITRATION ASSOCIATION (AAA)
The major organization offering arbitration services in the United States.

The Uniform Arbitration Act A number of states have adopted the Uniform Arbitration Act of 1955. Under this act, the parties in a contract agree in advance that all disputes arising thereunder must be submitted to arbitration. The major source of arbitration services is the **American Arbitration Association (AAA)**. The majority of the largest law firms in the nation are members of AAA. Many industries have arbitration programs. The insurance industry, for instance, set up the Insurance Alternative Dispute Resolution Program, which allows insurance companies and policyholders to choose either mediation or binding arbitration of their disputes.

Business Law in Action

The Price of Justice

Former Chief Justice Warren Burger has long favored alternative dispute resolution as a way of reducing the caseloads of the courts and speeding up the settlement of disputes. He maintained that, "If the courts are to retain public confidence, they cannot let disputes wait two, three, and five years or more to be disposed of." Obviously, the former chief justice is not alone in his sentiments. For years, Americans have been seeking—and finding—alternatives to the traditional court system as a means of settling disputes more efficiently and at a lower cost. There are now more than 350 ADR programs in 47 states. Settling claims and disputes by means of arbitration, rent-a-judge courts, and—most recently—for-profit private courts has become a part of the legal environment of our times.

The American Arbitration Association

One of the oldest and most well-known alternative dispute-resolution organizations is the American Arbitration Association (AAA). Founded in 1926, the AAA now settles more than 50,000 disputes a year in its 31 offices throughout the nation. Settlements usually are effected quickly and, at times, in informal settings, such as a hotel room. Cases brought before the AAA are heard by an expert or a panel of experts—about half of whom are usually lawyers—in the area relating to the dispute.

To cover its costs, the nonprofit organization charges a fee, paid by the party filing the claim. In 1987, the AAA typically charged 3 percent for commercial claims up to $20,000 and used a sliding scale for amounts beyond that threshold. In addition, each party to the dispute pays a price ($125 in 1987) for each hearing day, as well as a special additional fee ($100 per party) in cases involving personal injuries or property loss.

Rent-a-Judge Courts

For years, citizens of California have had another alternative for dispute settlement: rent-a-judge courts. Under a California state statute,[1] litigants can bypass the formal court system by having their cases heard before former judges of the California courts. Under the statute, cases can be "tried before a referee selected and paid by the litigants and empowered by the statute to enter decisions having the finality of trial court judgments."

Alternative Private Courts

Given the popularity of alternatives to traditional court proceedings, it was only a matter of time before the profit potential of the business of justice was recognized. In the forefront of this new area of private enterprise is Judicate, a firm based in Philadelphia.

Judicate

Judicate, a for-profit business, was founded in 1983 as a brokerage service bringing together retired judges and citizens seeking efficient, rapid settlement of disputes. According to Alan Epstein, Judicate's founder, "In essence all we are is a scheduling and marketing agency for judges." The goal of Judicate, claims Epstein, "is to become the generic in the alternative resolution system, like McDonald's is for fast food."[2]

Quick and Convenient Justice—For a Price. By using Judicate, you can obtain a decision within six weeks for under $1,000. The process is simple. Your lawyer calls Judicate (800-631-9900), which contacts the other party to the dispute. If both parties are willing to resolve their dispute through Judicate, each party pays a $75 filing fee. Each party also pays $375 per half-day hearing session and $12 for a one-hour settlement conference.[3] The parties decide on the date of the hearing, the presiding judge, whether the judge's decision will be legally binding, and the site of the hearing—which could be in a conference room, a law-school office, or one of a number of other possibilities.

Real Law, Real Procedure. Judicate has contracts with more than 240 former judges, whom it employs in its dispute-resolution services. The judges follow procedures similar to those of the federal courts and use

---

1. Cal. Civ. Proc. Code, Sections 638–645. See also "California Rent-A-Judge Experiment: Constitutional and Policy Considerations of Pay-As-You-Go Courts," 94 *Harv. L. Rev.* 1592 (1981).

2. As quoted in *Forbes*, December 15, 1986, p. 174.
3. As of 1987.

Business Law in Action—Continued

similar rules of law. To those parties who so desire, a courtroom, complete with flag and Bible, is made available. Judicate offers its services in forty-one states and settles disputes concerning contracts, employment, personal injuries, insurance, and so on. It cannot accept criminal cases, and so far it has refused to accept alimony or child-support cases.

Endispute

Another dispenser of lower-cost justice is Endispute (202-429-8782), which opened its doors in 1981 and is headquartered in Washington, D.C. Parties to a dispute can choose between mediation or arbitration services and opt for binding or nonbinding decisions. Each party pays $500 for a half-day session, and

cases are usually heard in an informal setting, such as a conference room. Contract or corporate partnership disputes make up the typical caseload at Endispute.

The Marketing of Justice

Many are concerned, understandably, that the entry of justice into the marketplace may herald abuses. Won't those with the largest pocketbooks end up with the most justice? According to the new entrepreneurs in the field, no. Competition in the marketplace will force them to dispense fair decisions from neutral courts. Judicate's Epstein maintains, for example, that "If you don't get a fair decision, Judicate will be the loser. If it doesn't

deliver its product—justice—it won't remain in business."[4]

In a sense, the rise of for-profit, low-cost alternative private courts parallels the growth of the lower-cost "chain" legal firms discussed in Chapter 1. Both are subjected to the rigors of the marketplace, and both depend for their profits on competitive prices and the quality of their services.

4.   As quoted in *Forbes*, December 15, 1986, p. 174.

Arbitration versus Court Trials   Arbitration is proving to be an increasingly popular alternative to court litigation. Since trials are often characterized by extensive court delays, going to trial is both costly and time consuming. Arbitration offers a less formal way of settling claims. With the assistance of expert arbitrators, disputes can be settled quickly and satisfactorily, without the expense and publicity of court trials. Because of the advantages of arbitration, most states have statutes encouraging arbitration in certain types of disputes; the coverage varies from state to state.

The U.S. District Court for the Southern District of New York has adopted a case-referral project. Under this project, participating judges may order the parties to meet with the director of the AAA's New York regional office within thirty days. During this meeting, available nonjudicial methods for resolving disputes are discussed. Of the cases referred to the AAA, more than half of them have resulted in an agreement to use some method of alternative dispute resolution.

Arbitration is also encouraged on the international level. In a 1985 landmark case, the U.S. Supreme Court held that even antitrust claims—which in a domestic context are not arbitrable—could be subject to arbitration if they were related to transnational contracts.[8]

8.   Mitsubishi Motors Corp. v. Soler Chrysler-Plymouth, Inc., 473 U.S. 614, 105 S.Ct. 3346, 87 L.Ed.2d 444 (1985).

Application

Law and the Businessperson— To Sue or Not to Sue

Wrongs are committed every minute of every day in the United States. These wrongs may be committed inadvertently or on purpose. Sometimes businesspersons believe that wrongs have been committed against them by other businesspersons (employers, employees, or competitors) or by local, state, or federal government. There are many issues to consider when deciding whether or not to sue for a wrong that has been committed against you or your business.

The Question of Cost

Competent legal advice is not inexpensive. Good commercial business law attorneys will charge $75 to $300 an hour, plus expenses. It is almost always worth an initial visit to an attorney who has skills in the area in which you are going to sue, because then you can get an estimate of the expected costs of pursuing a redress for your grievance. You may be charged for the initial visit as well.

Note, also, that less than 10 percent of all corporate lawsuits end up in trial—the rest are settled beforehand. You may end up settling for far less than you thought you were "owed" simply because of the length of time it takes your attorney to bring your case to trial and to finish the trial. And then you might not win, anyway!

Basically, then, you must do a cost-benefit anaysis to determine whether you should sue. Your attorney can give you the costs, and you can guesstimate the benefits. You do this by multiplying the probable size of the award by the probability of obtaining that award.

Alternatives Before You

Another method of settling your grievance is by alternative dispute resolution (ADR). Mediation and arbitration are two types of ADR, and they are becoming increasingly attractive alternatives to court litigation, because you can usually get quick results at a comparatively low cost. Arbitration of labor disputes, commercial contract disputes, and insurance claims is possible through the American Arbitration Association (AAA), and there are other ADR centers as well (see the "Business Law in Action" near the end of the chapter). You can obtain information on ADR by writing to the Special Committee on Dispute Resolution, American Bar Association, 1800 M Street N.W., Washington, DC 20036. The Yellow Pages in large metropolitan areas usually list agencies and firms that could help you settle your dispute out of court; look under "Mediation" or "Social Service Agencies."

Checklist for Deciding Whether to Sue

☐ 1. Are you prepared to pay for going to court? Make this decision only after you have consulted an attorney to get an estimate of the costs of preparing the lawsuit.

☐ 2. Do you have the patience to follow a court case through the judicial system, even if it takes several years?

☐ 3. Is there a way for you to settle your grievance without going to court? Even if the settlement is less than you think you are owed, in net terms corrected for future expenses, time waiting, time lost, and frustration, you may be better off settling now for the smaller figure.

☐ 4. Can you use some form of alternative dispute resolution? Before you say no, investigate these alternatives—they are usually cheaper and quicker to use than the standard judicial process.

☐ 5. In all cases, only make your decision based on the advice of a competent legal professional. Remember the old adage, "He who does his own legal work has a fool for a client."

❖ Chapter Summary: Courts and Procedures

Types of Jurisdiction	1. *Jurisdiction over persons/property*—Territorial boundaries of a court over the defendant or the defendant's property.
	2. *Jurisdiction over subject matter*—Restriction of a court to hear a particular type of case. a. Limited jurisdiction—Exists when a court is limited to a specific subject matter, such as probate or divorce. b. General jurisdiction—Exists when a court can hear any kind of case.
	3. *Original jurisdiction*—Exists with courts that have authority to first hear a case (trial courts).
	4. *Appellate jurisdiction*—Exists with courts of appeal and review; generally, appellate courts do not have original jurisdiction.
	5. *Federal jurisdiction*—Arises in the following situations: a. When a federal question is involved (when the plaintiff's cause of action is based at least in part on the U.S. Constitution, a treaty, or a federal law). b. In diversity-of-citizenship cases between (1) citizens of different states; (2) a foreign country and citizens of a state or different states; or (3) citizens of a state and citizens or subjects of a foreign country and the amount in controversy exceeds $10,000.
	6. *Concurrent jurisdiction*—Exists when two different courts have authority to hear the same case.
Types of Courts	1. *Trial courts*—Courts of original jurisdiction, where an action is initiated. a. State—Courts of general jurisdiction can hear any case; courts of limited jurisdiction include divorce courts, probate courts, traffic courts, small claims courts, etc. b. Federal—The federal district court is the equivalent of the state trial court. Federal courts of limited jurisdiction include the U.S. Tax Court, the U.S. Bankruptcy Court, and the U.S. Claims Court.
	2. *Intermediate appellate courts*—Courts of appeal and review, generally without original jurisdiction. Many states have an intermediate appellate court; in the federal court system, the U.S. circuit courts of appeals are the intermediate appellate courts.
	3. *Supreme court*—The highest court. Each state has a supreme court, although it may be called by some other name, from which appeal to the U.S. Supreme Court is only possible if a federal question is involved. The U.S. Supreme Court is the highest court in the federal court system and the final arbiter of the Constituion and federal law.
Rules of Procedure	Procedural laws that prescribe the way in which disputes are handled in the courts. Rules differ from court to court, and a separate set of rules exists for federal and state courts, as well as for criminal and civil cases. A sample civil court procedure in a state court would involve the following steps:
	1. *The pleadings*: a. Complaint or petition—A statement of the cause of action and parties involved, filed with the court by the plaintiff's attorney. A summons is then delivered to the defendant. b. Answer—Can take the form of (1) a motion to dismiss; (2) an affirmative defense; (3) a counterclaim; or (4) an answer denying allegations, which could contain both an affirmative defense and a counterclaim.
	2. *Dismissal/judgment before trial*: a. Motion for judgment on the pleadings—May be made by either party; will be granted if no cause of action exists or if the defendant fails to answer. b. Motion for summary judgment—May be made by either party; will be granted if the parties agree on the facts. Judge applies law rendering judgment.

❖ Chapter Summary: Courts and Procedures—Continued

Rules of Procedure (Continued)	3. *Discovery*—The process of gathering evidence concerning the case; involves *depositions* (sworn testimony by the opposing party or any witness) and *interrogatories* (where parties to the action write answers to questions with the aid of their attorneys).
	4. *Pretrial hearing*—Either party or the court can request a pretrial hearing to identify the matters in dispute after discovery has taken place and to plan the course of the trial.
	5. *Trial*—Involves opening statements from both parties' attorneys and then: a. Plaintiff's introduction and direct examination of witnesses and cross-examination by defendant's attorney; possible redirect by plaintiff's attorney and recross-examination by defendant's attorney. b. Defendant's introduction and direct examination of witnesses and cross-examination by plaintiff's attorney; possible redirect by defendant's attorney and recross-examination by plaintiff's attorney. c. Possible rebuttal of defendant's argument by plaintiff's attorney presenting more evidence. d. Possible rejoinder by defendant's attorney to meet that evidence. e. Closing arguments—by both plaintiff's and defendant's attorneys in favor of their respective clients. f. Judge's instructions to the jury. g. Jury verdict.
	6. *Post-trial options:* a. Motion for a new trial—Will be granted if the judge is convinced that the jury was in error. b. Motion for judgment n.o.v. (notwithstanding the verdict)—A second chance to move for directed verdict; will be granted if the judge is convinced that the jury was in error. c. Motion for judgment (made by winner of case). d. Appeal—Either party can appeal the trial court's judgment to an appropriate court of appeals. After posting of bond(s), briefs are filed, a hearing is held, and the court renders a written opinion.
Judicial Review	The process by which the judicial branch determines whether a law is contrary to the mandates of the Constitution. The doctrine of judicial review was first enunciated by the Supreme Court in John Marshall's decision in *Marbury v. Madison* in 1803.
Alternative Dispute Resolution	An increasingly popular alternative to court proceedings. May be accomplished through (1) mediation—where the parties themselves reach an agreement with the help of a third party; or (2) arbitration—where the parties agree to be bound by the decision of a third party (arbitrator).

❖ Questions and Case Problems

2-1. Quite often, trials conclude before they begin. If the parties agree on the facts, the attorneys simply relate these facts to the judge, and then, through a motion for judgment on the pleadings, they ask the judge to decide what the law is and how it applies to this set of facts. How is it possible that two parties can agree on the facts yet disagree as to which party is liable?

2-2. If a judge enters judgment on the pleadings, the losing party can usually appeal but cannot present evidence to the appellate court. Does this seem fair? Explain.

2-3. (a) Before two parties go to trial, there is an involved process called pleadings and discovery. Until recently, pleadings were very formal, and the outcome of trials often turned on elements of surprise. For example, a plaintiff would not necessarily know until the trial what the defendant's defense was going to be. Does this seem like a fair way to conduct a trial?

(b) Within the last twenty years, new rules of pleadings and discovery have substantially changed the situation. Now each attorney can discover practically all the evidence that the other attorney will be presenting at trial. Certain information, however, is still not available to the parties, namely, each attorney's work product. Work product is not a clear concept— basically, it includes all the attorney's thoughts on the case. Can you see any reason why such information should not be made available to the opposing attorney? Explain.

2-4. Sometimes on appeal there are questions of whether the facts presented in the trial court support the conclusion reached by the judge or the jury. The appellate court will reverse on the basis of the facts only when so little evidence was presented at trial that no reasonable person could have reached the conclusion that the judge or jury reached. Appellate courts normally defer to a judge's decision with regard to the facts. Can you see any reason for this?

2-5. The Constitution states that a person cannot be tried twice for the same crime. Does this problem arise when both the federal and the state government try the same person for the same crime? Explain.

2-6. Judicial review allows the courts to decide whether actions of the legislative and executive branches are constitutional. Is this a correct statement? Explain.

2-7. Marya Callais, a citizen of Florida, was walking near a busy street in Tallahassee, Florida, one day when a large crate flew off a passing truck and hit her, resulting in numerous injuries to Callais. She incurred a great deal of pain and suffering plus numerous medical expenses, and she could not work for six months. She wished to sue the trucking firm for $300,000 in damages. The firm's headquarters were in Georgia, although the company did business in Florida. Where can Marya bring her suit—in a Florida state court, a Georgia state court, or a federal court?

2-8. In an arbitration proceeding, the arbitrator need not be a judge or even a lawyer. How, then, can the arbitrator's decision have the force of law and be binding on the parties involved?

Chapter 3

Torts

When the eminent legal scholar William Prosser published *The Law of Torts* in 1941, it was one of the first comprehensive attempts to compile and render understandable the law governing **torts** (wrongful conduct). A definitive treatise on the subject was an impossible task, he felt, as torts are so infinitely various. The field of tort law continues to expand in the late twentieth century, as new ways to commit wrongs are discovered and new conceptions of what is right and wrong in a social or business context emerge.

What this means for anyone involved in business is this: you may be sued. Indeed, to do business is to risk being involved in a lawsuit. Although insurance may handle many of the potential and actual lawsuits that arise, you should learn about how you can be sued so you can understand how to avoid being sued. Employees injured on the job may attempt to sue their employers. Consumers injured on the premises, or when using a product they purchased, may wish to sue a retailer or manufacturer. Lawyers' clients as well as patients of physicians and dentists may sue for malpractice.

At issue in these examples is alleged wrongful conduct by one individual that causes injury to another. Tort law covers a wide variety of injuries. Society recognizes an interest in personal physical safety, and tort law provides remedies for acts causing physical injury or interfering with physical security and freedom of movement. Society recognizes an interest in protecting personal property, and tort law provides remedies for acts causing destruction or damage to property. Society recognizes more intangible interests in such things as personal privacy, family relations, reputation, and dignity. Tort law provides a remedy for invasion of protected interests in these areas.

Tort law is also applied to the area of business. A **business tort** is defined as wrongful interference or wrongful conduct in a business environment. Typical examples of business torts are unfair competition and interfering with the business relations of others. Business torts are discussed later in the chapter.

❖ The Basis of Tort Law

Two notions serve as the basis of all torts: wrongs and compensation. Tort law recognizes that some acts are wrong because they cause injury to a person. Of course,

"Not until yesterday, as legal generations go, did torts achieve recognition as a distinct branch of the law."

William Lloyd Prosser, 1898–1972
(Legal scholar specializing in tort law)

TORT
A wrongful action; a private or civil wrong independent of contract, resulting from a breach of a legal duty.

BUSINESS TORT
A tort occurring within the business context; typical business torts are wrongful interference with the business or contractual relationships of others and unfair competition.

this is not the only type of wrong that exists in the law; crimes involve wrongs also. A crime, however, is an act so reprehensible that it is considered to be a wrong against the state or against society as a whole, as well as against the individual victim. Therefore, the *state* prosecutes a person committing a criminal act. A tort action, however, is a *civil* action in which one person brings a personal suit against another. In some cases, such as assault, a basis could exist for a criminal prosecution as well as a tort action.

❖ Intentional Torts against Persons

INTENTIONAL TORT
A tort in which the actor is expressly or impliedly judged to have injured another intentionally or purposefully.

An **intentional** tort arises from an act that the defendant consciously desired to perform, either in order to harm another or knowing with substantial certainty that injury to another could result. It is the *intent* to perform the original act that is important. The nature of the damage ultimately caused is irrelevant in determining whether there was intent. Because intent is a subjective concept, the law generally assumes that one intends the normal consequences of his or her actions. Thus, an angry push is an intentional tort because the pusher knows or intends for the object of the push to be injured. A playful pat on the shoulder, on the other hand, is not an intentional tort even though, in drawing away suddenly, the person touched may be injured.

Assault and Battery

ASSAULT
Any word or action intended to make another person fearful of immediate physical harm; a reasonably believable threat.

Any intentional, unexcused act that creates in another person a reasonable apprehension or fear of immediate harmful or offensive contact is an **assault**. Apprehension is not the same as fear. If a contact is such that a reasonable person would want to avoid it, and if there is a reasonable basis for believing that the contact will occur, then the plaintiff suffers apprehension whether or not he or she is afraid.

BATTERY
The unprivileged, intentional touching of another.

The interest protected by tort law concerning assault is the freedom from having to expect harmful or offensive contact. The arousal of apprehension is enough to justify compensation. Of course, the *completion* of the act that caused the apprehension, if it results in harm to the plaintiff, is a **battery**, which is defined as an unexcused, harmful or offensive physical contact *intentionally* performed. For example, Ivan threatens Jean with a gun, then shoots her. The pointing of the gun at Jean is an assault; the firing of the gun (if the bullet hits Jean) is a battery. The interest this tort protects is the right to personal security and safety. The contact can be harmful, or it can be merely offensive (such as an unwelcome kiss). Physical injury does not have to occur. The contact can be to any part of the body or anything attached to it—for example, a hat or other item of clothing, a purse, a chair, or an automobile in which one is sitting. Whether the contact is offensive or not is determined by the *reasonable-person* standard.[1] The contact can be made by the defendant or by some force the defendant sets in motion—for example, a rock thrown, food poisoned, or a stick swung.

If the plaintiff shows that there was contact, and the jury agrees that the contact was offensive, the plaintiff has a right to compensation. There is no need to show that the defendant acted out of malice; the person could have been joking or playing

---

1. The reasonable-person standard is an objective test of how a reasonable person would have acted under the same circumstances. See "Breach of the Duty of Care" later in the chapter.

Profile

Melvin M. Belli, Sr. (1907–   )

It could be a scene from a *Perry Mason* episode: a trial lawyer enters the courtroom carrying a large item wrapped in butcher's paper. During the course of the trial, the item is slowly unwrapped by the attorney, who eventually places the unwrapped item, an artificial leg, in the lap of a very startled juror. The ploy worked: the jurors awarded the plaintiff, a woman who had lost her leg in a streetcar accident, damages of $100,000.

In this scene, however, the attorney was not Perry Mason, but Melvin Belli—often called the "king of torts" and certainly one of the most celebrated and successful trial lawyers of our time. Called "flamboyant" so many times he thinks it might as well be his name, Belli has developed an immunity to

critics who refer to him as a "high-priced ambulance chaser." The still-dynamic octogenarian merely has to point to his expensive, lavishly decorated San Francisco law office to indicate that he has no need to chase ambulances.

Belli is widely known not only for his colorful style—which is revealed in his courtroom theatrics as well as in his penchant for an upbeat, jet-set lifestyle—but also for his legal abilities. Born in Sonora, California, on July 29, 1907, Belli received both his bachelor of arts and law degrees from the University of California at Berkeley. Following a brief period of service as an undercover investigator with the National Recovery Administration (NRA) in 1933, Belli turned to private practice and has been with various law firms since, predominantly in California. His specialty is tort law, and during his long career in the courtroom he has won for his clients damage awards totaling more than $100 million. In the 1940 case just mentioned, the $100,000 award was a record for its time, and Belli continued to astonish the public with the six-digit sums he obtained for his clients. Known for his use of "demonstrative evidence"— a technique he pioneered, but which is commonly used in liability lawsuits today—Belli used enlarged X-rays, scale models of traffic intersections, color photos, human skeletons, and other striking devices to demonstrate for the court the nature and extent of his clients' injuries.

Much of Belli's fame has been acquired because of well-known, and sometimes very controversial, clients. The roster includes Mae West, Errol Flynn, Lenny Bruce, and Tony Curtis, among others. He also defended Jack Ruby, who shot President Kennedy's assassin, Lee Harvey Oswald. Among his current clients are residents of Bhopal, India, who were injured in the 1986 Union Carbide chemical accident; relatives of passengers on the Aero Mexico jetliner that crashed in 1986; and a client with lung cancer, who has filed suit against a tobacco firm.

Despite his demanding career, Belli has found time to write more than thirty books, some scholarly and some popular. He is currently updating his six-volume study of modern civil and criminal law procedures, *Modern Trials*. First published in 1954, *Modern Trials* has become a standard reference for many criminal lawyers and students. His most recent publication, *Everybody's Guide to the Law*, co-written by Allen P. Wilkinson, is not as flamboyant as Belli would have liked, he admits, "but the publishers didn't want anyone to smile when they read it."[1]

1. As reported in *USA Today*, December 10, 1986, p. 4D.

or could even have had some benevolent motive. The underlying motive does not matter, only the intent to do the act. In fact, proving a motive is never necessary (but is always relevant). Damages from a battery can be for emotional harm or loss of reputation, as well as for physical harm.

A number of legally recognized defenses can be raised by a defendant who is sued for assault or battery, or both:

1. *Consent*. When a person consents to the act that damages him or her, there is generally no liability for the damage done.
2. *Self-defense*. An individual who is defending his or her life or physical well-being can claim self-defense. In situations of both *real* and *apparent* danger, a person is privileged to use whatever force is *reasonably* necessary to prevent harmful contact.
3. *Defense of others*. An individual can act in a reasonable matter to protect others who are in real or apparent danger.
4. *Defense of property*. Reasonable force may be used in attempting to remove intruders from one's home, although force that is likely to cause death or great bodily injury can never be used just to protect property.

False Imprisonment

False imprisonment is defined as the intentional confinement or restraint of another person's activities without justification. It involves interference with the freedom to move without restraint. The confinement can be accomplished through the use of physical barriers, physical restraint, or threats of physical force. Moral pressure or future threats do not constitute false imprisonment. It is essential that the person being restrained not comply with the restraint willingly. Business people are often confronted with suits for false imprisonment after they have attempted to confine a suspected shoplifter for questioning. Although a merchant can use the defense of probable cause to justify delaying a suspected shoplifter, the delay must be *reasonable*. The following case provides a good example.

Case 3.1
JOHNSON v. K-MART ENTERPRISES, INC.
Court of Appeals of Wisconsin, 1980.
98 Wis.2d 533, 297 N.W.2d 74.

FACTS   Johnson entered defendant's store carrying her small child in an infant seat. When she attempted to leave the store, she was detained in a public place by a security officer who said that another employee had reported seeing her steal the infant seat. To show ownership, Johnson pointed to cat hair, food crumbs, and stains on the seat. After a twenty-minute delay, the security officer apologized to the defendant and permitted her to leave. The trial court dismissed her action for false imprisonment and Johnson appealed.

ISSUE   Did the defendant have probable cause to detain Johnson, and was the twenty-minute detention of Johnson reasonable in these circumstances?

DECISION   Yes, to both. The appellate court upheld the trial court's finding that the defendant acted reasonably and with probable cause.

REASON   The court first addressed the issue of probable cause. Under a Wisconsin statute, it is the shopkeeper's privilege to detain a shopper if, among other things, the merchant has probable cause for believing the shopper stole the merchant's goods. The court held as a matter of law that the merchant, through its security guard, had probable cause to believe the plaintiff had

Case 3.1—Continued

shoplifted because another employee reported that she had seen the theft. The court then turned to Johnson's complaint that her detention was accomplished in an unreasonable manner because she was detained in a public place for an unreasonable period of time. The court balanced the customer's liberty interest against the merchant's need for protection against shoplifting, a need protected by the Wisconsin statute. The court held that

a twenty-minute detention was reasonable. In addition, the court found that the defendant had only stopped the plaintiff, asked her to return to the store, informed her that she was suspected of shoplifting, produced the incriminating witness, apologized to her, and finally released her—none of which was unreasonable. Furthermore, Johnson never asked to go to a more private place.

Infliction of Mental Distress

The tort of infliction of *mental distress* can be defined as an intentional act that amounts to extreme and outrageous conduct resulting in severe emotional distress to another.[2] For example, a prankster telephones an individual and says that the individual's spouse has just been in a horrible accident. As a result, the individual suffers intense mental pain or anxiety. The caller's behavior is deemed to be extreme and outrageous conduct that exceeds the bounds of decency accepted by society and is therefore actionable.

As this is a relatively new tort, it poses some problems. Because it is difficult to prove the existence of mental suffering, a few states (such as Texas) require that the mental disturbance be evidenced by some physical illness.

Defamation

The protection of a person's body is involved in the torts of assault, battery, and false imprisonment. **Defamation** of character involves wrongfully hurting a person's good reputation. The law has imposed a general duty on all persons to refrain from making false, defamatory statements about others. Breaching this duty orally involves the tort of **slander**; breaching it in writing involves the tort of **libel**.

The Publication Requirement   The basis of the tort is the *publication* of a statement or statements that hold an individual up to contempt, ridicule, or hatred. *Publication* here means that the defamatory statements are made to or within the hearing of persons other than the defamed party. If Thompson writes Andrews a private letter accusing him of embezzling funds, the action does not constitute libel. If Peters calls Gordon dishonest, unattractive, and incompetent when no one else is around, the action does not constitute slander. In neither case was the message communicated to a third party. The courts have generally held that even dictating a letter to a secretary constitutes publication, although such publication may fall under a conditional privilege. Moreover, if a third party overhears defamatory statements by chance, the courts usually hold that this also constitutes publication. Note further that any individual who republishes or repeats defamatory statements is liable even if that person reveals the source of such statements. Most radio stations have several-second delays for live broadcasts, such as talk shows, to avoid this kind of liability.

DEFAMATION
Anything published or publicly spoken that causes injury to another's good name, reputation, or character.

SLANDER
An oral defamation of one's character, reputation, business, or property rights.

LIBEL
A written defamation of one's character, reputation, business, or property rights. The First Amendment, to a limited degree, protects the press from libel actions.

2. *Restatement, Second, Torts,* Section 46, Comment d.

"Truth is generally the best vindication against slander."

**Abraham Lincoln, 1809–1865
(Sixteenth president of the
United States, 1861–1865)**

Carol Burnett takes the witness stand in her widely publicized libel suit.

The common law defines four types of false utterances that are considered torts per se (meaning no proof of damages is required before these false utterances become actionable). They are:

1.   A statement that another has a loathsome communicable disease.
2.   A statement that another has committed improprieties while engaging in a profession or trade.
3.   A statement that another has committed or has been imprisoned for a serious crime.
4.   A statement that an unmarried woman is unchaste.

Defenses against Defamation   Truth is normally an *absolute* defense against a defamation charge. Furthermore, there may be a privilege involved. For example, statements made by attorneys and judges during a trial are *privileged* and therefore cannot be the basis for a defamation charge. Members of Congress making statements on the floor of Congress have an absolute privilege. Legislators have complete immunity from liability for false statements made in debate, even if they make such statements maliciously—that is, knowing them to be untrue. In general, false and defamatory statements that are made about public figures and that are published in the press are privileged if they are made without malice.[3]

Notice here the difference between *private individuals* and *public figures*. Public figures include public officers and employees who exercise substantial governmental power and any persons in the public limelight. That is why statements made about public figures, especially when they are made via a public medium, are usually related to matters of general public interest; they are made about people who substantially affect all of us. Public figures generally have some access to a public medium for answering disparaging falsehoods about them; private individuals do not.

In order to prove malice, a plaintiff must show that the defendant acted with either knowledge of falsity or a reckless disregard of the truth. The balance between free speech and the torts of slander and libel is delicate.

The following case illustrates a libel case involving a public figure and the extent of liability that exists when malice is proved.

Case 3.2
BURNETT v. NATIONAL ENQUIRER
California Superior Court, Los Angeles County, 1981.
7 Med.L.Rptr. 1321.

FACTS   Plaintiff Carol Burnett, the famous comedienne, believed that she was libeled by an article in *The National Enquirer,* which stated that Burnett was intoxicated and involved in a "row" with Henry Kissinger in a Washington, D.C., restaurant. She sued the *Enquirer* and was awarded $300,000 in general damages and $1,300,000 in punitive

damages. The *National Enquirer* moved for judgment notwithstanding the verdict and a new trial, claiming that (a) there was no actual malice on its part, (b) it is a news publication and protected from false statements that it has neither time nor opportunity to ascertain, (c) the jury was tainted because three members heard a Johnny Carson "tirade" against the *Enquirer,* and (d) the damages were excessive.

ISSUE   Was there a basis for any or all of the *National Enquirer's* claims?

---

3.   New York Times Co. v. Sullivan, 376 U.S. 254, 84 S.Ct. 710, 11 L.Ed.2d 686 (1964).

Case 3.2—Continued

DECISION   No, to (a), (b), and (c). Yes to (d).

REASON   The court held that Burnett had proved malice beyond a reasonable doubt and that the *Enquirer* as a magazine could not claim the privilege of a newspaper or a radio station's latitude in good-faith reporting of the news. The judge also found that the jury had not been sufficiently tainted by prejudicial trial publicity. The court reduced the amount of general damages to $50,000, however, finding that although Burnett had suffered anxiety, she was able to set it aside "to the point where she was able to function in her profession." The punitive damage award was reduced to $760,000 in order to "bear a reasonable relationship to the compensatory damages." (The punitive damages were further reduced to $150,000 in 1983 by the California State Court of Appeals.)

Slander of Title and Defamation by Computer

There are two torts, typically called business torts, that involve defamation. Defamation arising from a false statement made about a person's product, business, or title to property is called *slander of title* or *disparagement of goods*, depending on the case. Erroneous information from a computer about a person's credit standing or business reputation can impair that person's ability to obtain further credit and is called *defamation by computer*. Defamation by computer is the subject of the following case.

Case 3.3
DUN & BRADSTREET, INC. v. GREENMOSS BUILDERS, INC.
United States Supreme Court, 1985.
464 U.S. 959, 104 S.Ct. 389, 78 L.Ed.2d 334.

FACTS   Dun & Bradstreet, the well-known credit-reporting agency, included false information concerning Greenmoss Builders in a computerized letter sent to several of its subscribers. The false information was that Greenmoss had filed for bankruptcy, when, in fact, it had not. The erroneous report resulted in a loss of business and income for Greenmoss, and, because of these damages, Greenmoss sued Dun & Bradstreet for defamation. The trial court held for Greenmoss and awarded substantial damages. Dun & Bradstreet appealed.

ISSUE   Is a showing of malice on the part of Dun & Bradstreet required before Greenmoss can recover damages for defamation?

DECISION   No, because the plaintiff was not a public figure and the speech did not concern a public matter.

REASON   As in all defamation cases, the Court was required to balance "the State's interest in compensating private individuals for injury to their reputation against the First Amendment interest in protecting . . . expression." In this case, "the State's interest" weighed heavily on the scales because the speech (Dun & Bradstreet's computerized letter) involved no public issue. "There is simply no credible argument," the Court stated, "that this type of credit reporting requires special protection [under the First Amendment] to ensure that 'debate on public issues [will] be uninhibited, robust, and wide-open.' . . . We conclude that permitting recovery of presumed and punitive damages in defamation cases absent a showing of 'actual malice' does not violate the First Amendment when the defamatory statements do not involve matters of public concern."

Invasion of the Right to Privacy

A person's right to solitude and freedom from prying public eyes is the interest protected by the tort of invasion of privacy. Four acts qualify as an invasion of privacy:

1. The use of a person's name or picture for commercial purposes without permission.
2. Intrusion upon an individual's affairs or seclusion.
3. Publication of information that places a person in a false light. This could be a story attributing to the person ideas that are not held or actions that were not taken. (Publishing such a story could involve the tort of defamation as well.)
4. Public disclosure of private facts about an individual that an ordinary person would find objectionable.

Misrepresentation (Fraud, Deceit)

The tort of misrepresentation involves the use of fraud and deceit for personal gain. It includes several elements:

1. Misrepresentation of facts or conditions with knowledge that they are false or are made with reckless disregard for the truth.
2. Intent to induce another to rely on the misrepresentation.
3. Justifiable reliance by the deceived party.
4. Damages suffered as a result of reliance.
5. Causal connection between the misrepresentation and the injury suffered.

Drawing by Chon Day; © 1978, The New Yorker Magazine.

"We find the defendant guilty as charged by the media."

A misrepresentation leads another to believe in a condition that is different from the one that actually exists. This is often accomplished by a false or an incorrect statement. Misrepresentations may be innocently made by someone who is unaware of the existing facts, but a misrepresentation is fraudulent when it is made by a person who knows the facts to be false and intends to mislead another.

In order for fraud to occur, more than mere *seller's talk* must be involved. Fraud exists only when a person represents as a material fact something he or she knows is untrue. For example, it is fraud to claim that a building does not leak when one knows it does. Facts are objectively ascertainable, whereas seller's talk is not. "I am the best accountant in town" is seller's talk. The speaker is not trying to represent something as fact, because the term best is a subjective, not an objective, term.

Normally, the tort of misrepresentation only occurs when there is reliance upon a statement of fact. Sometimes, however, reliance on a statement of opinion may involve the tort of misrepresentation if the individual making the statement of opinion has a superior knowledge of the subject matter. For example, when a lawyer makes a statement of opinion about the law, a court would construe such a statement to be equivalent to a statement of fact.

❖ Intentional Torts against Property

Wrongs against property include (1) trespass to land and (2) trespass to personal property and conversion. The wrong is against the individual who has legally recognized rights with regard to land or personal property. The law distinguishes real property from personal property (see Chapter 34). *Real property* is land and things "permanently" attached thereto. *Personal property* consists of all other items that are basically moveable. Thus, a house and lot are real property, whereas the furniture inside a house is personal property. Money and securities are also personal property.

Trespass to Land

Any time a person enters onto, above, or below the surface of land that is owned by another or causes anything to enter onto the land, or remains on the land or permits anything to remain on it, such action constitutes the civil tort called a **trespass to land**. Note that actual harm to the land is not an essential element of this tort, because the tort is designed to protect the right of an owner to exclusive possession. If no harm is done, usually only nominal damages (such as $1) can be recovered by the landowner. Common types of trespass to land include walking or driving on the land, shooting a gun over the land, throwing rocks or spraying water on a building that belongs to someone else, building a dam across a river that causes water to back up on someone else's land, and placing part of one's building on an adjoining landowner's property.

Trespass Criteria, Rights, and Duties   Before a person can be a trespasser, the real property owner (the person who legally controls the realty) must expressly or impliedly establish that person as a trespasser. For example, "posted" trespass signs expressly establish a person as a trespasser when that person ignores these signs and enters onto the property. A guest in your home is not a trespasser—unless he or she has been

TRESPASS TO LAND
In common law, the intentional or unintentional passing over another person's land uninvited, regardless of whether any physical damage is done to the land. Today a majority of courts find trespass only in cases of intentional intrusion, negligence, or some "abnormally dangerous activity" on the part of the defendant.

asked to leave but refuses. Any person who enters onto your property to commit an illegal act (such as a thief entering a lumberyard at night to steal lumber) is established impliedly as a trespasser, without posted signs. At common law, a trespasser is liable for damages caused to the property and generally cannot hold the owner liable for injuries sustained on the premises. This common-law rule is being abandoned in many jurisdictions in favor of a "reasonable duty" rule that varies depending on the status of the parties. For example, a landowner may have a duty to post a notice that the property is patrolled by guard dogs. Also, trespassers can be removed from the premises through the use of reasonable force without the owner being liable for assault and battery.

Defenses against Trespass to Land   Trespass to land involves wrongful interference with another person's real property rights. But if it can be shown that the trespass was warranted, as when a trespasser enters to assist someone in danger, a complete defense exists. Another defense is to show that the purported owner did not actually have the right to possess the land in question.

Trespass to Personal Property and Conversion

TRESPASS TO PERSONALTY
Any wrongful transgression or offense against the personal property of another.

Whenever any individual unlawfully injures the personal property of another or otherwise interferes with the personal property owner's right to exclusive possession and enjoyment of that property, **trespass to personalty** (or personal property) occurs. Trespass to personal property involves intentional meddling. If a student takes another student's business law book as a practical joke and hides it so that the owner is unable to find it for several days prior to a final examination, the student has engaged in a trespass to personal property.

If it can be shown that trespass to personal property was warranted, then a complete defense exists. Most states, for example, allow automobile repair shops to hold a customer's car (under what is called an artisan's, or possessory, lien) when the customer refuses to pay for repairs already completed.

CONVERSION
Wrongfully taking or retaining possession of personal property that belongs to another.

Whenever personal property is taken from its rightful owner or possessor and placed in the service of another, the act of **conversion** occurs. Conversion is defined as any act depriving an owner of personal property without that owner's permission and without just cause. Conversion is the civil side of crimes related to theft. Theft requires intent, but conversion does not. A store clerk who steals merchandise from the store commits a crime and the tort of conversion at the same time. When conversion occurs, the lesser offense of trespass to personal property usually occurs as well. If the initial taking of the property was unlawful, there is trespass; retention of that property is conversion. If the initial taking of the property was permitted by the owner or for some other reason is not a trespass, failure to return it may still be conversion.

Even if a person mistakenly believed that he or she was entitled to the goods, a tort of conversion may occur. In other words, good intentions are not a defense against conversion; in fact, conversion can be an entirely innocent act. Someone who buys stolen goods, for example, is guilty of conversion even if he or she did not know the goods were stolen. If the true owner brings a tort action against the buyer, the buyer must pay the owner the full value of the property, despite having already paid money to the thief.

A successful defense against the charge of conversion is that the purported owner has no title to the property or does not have a right to possess it that is superior to the right of the holder. Necessity is another possible defense against conversion. If Abrams takes Stephens's cat, Abrams is guilty of conversion. If Stephens sues Abrams, Abrams must return the cat and pay damages. If, however, the cat has rabies and Abrams took the cat to protect the public, Abrams has a valid defense—necessity (and perhaps even self-defense, if he can prove that he was in danger because of the cat).

❖ Unintentional Torts (Negligence)

Intentional torts usually involve a particular mental state. In negligence, however, the actor neither wishes to bring about the consequences of the act nor believes that they will occur. The actor's conduct merely creates a *risk* of such consequences. If there is no risk created, there is no negligence. Moreover, the risk must be foreseeable; that is, it must be such that a reasonable person engaging in some activity would anticipate the risk and guard against it. In determining what is reasonable conduct, courts consider the nature of the possible harm. A very slight risk of a dangerous explosion might be unreasonable, whereas a distinct possibility of burning one's fingers on a stove might be reasonable.

In examining a question of negligence, one should ask six questions:

1. Does (or did) the defendant owe a duty of care to the plaintiff?
2. Was harm done (were damages incurred)?
3. What did the defendant do (what was the nature of the act)?
4. Did the act create a foreseeable risk of harm (breach of duty of care)?
5. Did the act *cause* the harm (causation in fact, or actual cause)?
6. At what point should liability cease (what was the *proximate* cause of the harm)?

Many of the actions discussed in the section on intentional torts would constitute negligence if they were done carelessly, but without intent. For instance, carelessly bumping into someone who falls and breaks an arm constitutes negligence. Likewise, carelessly—as opposed to intentionally—flooding someone's land constitutes negligence. In a sense, negligence is a *way of committing* a tort rather than a distinct *category* of torts.

Negligence involves the allocation of loss between an innocent plaintiff and an innocent, albeit careless, defendant. The extent of duty and liability of both the plaintiff and the defendant is frequently determined by social policy. For example, suppose that Laser Corporation—whose annual sales total $600 million—is sued by Berman for injuries resulting from negligent manufacturing. Berman cannot afford to pay his medical expenses. Laser Corporation, on the other hand, can spread the cost of the damages in its pricing among all its customers. If there is a public policy of spreading such costs, a court may find for the plaintiff. If the defendant is an individual rather than a large corporation, however, the court might decide differently in a similar situation.

The tort of negligence occurs when someone suffers injury because of another's failure to live up to a required duty of care. Three elements must be considered when examining negligence: (1) breach (failure) of the duty of care, (2) injury, and (3) causation.

Breach of the Duty of Care

In determining whether a duty of care has been breached, courts will ask the following two questions:

1. Is there a duty of care? The basic rule of duty is that people are free to act as they please so long as their actions do not infringe on the interests of others. Tort law measures duty by the *reasonable-person standard*, a standard frequently used in law. In determining whether a tort has been committed, the courts ask how a reasonable person would have acted in the same circumstances.
2. Did the defendant's action breach (fail to live up to) that duty? If a person has intentionally harmed another or has failed to comply with the duty of exercising reasonable care, he or she may have committed a tortious act. Failure to live up to a standard of care may be an act (setting fire to a building) or an omission (neglecting to put out a fire). It may be an intentional act, a careless act, or a carefully performed but nevertheless dangerous act that results in injury. Courts consider the nature of the act (whether it is outrageous or commonplace), the manner in which the act is performed (intentional versus accidental), and the nature of the injury (whether it is serious or slight) in determining whether the duty of care has been breached.

Damages or Injury

In order for a tort to have been committed, there must be a *legally* recognizable damage, or injury, to the plaintiff. To recover damages (receive compensation), the plaintiff must have suffered some loss, harm, wrong, or invasion of a protected interest. Essentially, the purpose of tort law is to compensate for legally recognized injuries resulting from wrongful acts, not to punish people for these acts. Because society wants to discourage some torts, the injured person may be given extra compensation as *punitive* damages. But few negligent acts are so reprehensible that punitive damages are available.

Causation

Another element necessary to a tort is causation. If a person fails in a duty of care and someone suffers injury, the wrongful activity must have caused the harm for a tort to have been committed. In deciding whether there is causation, the court must address two questions:

1. Is there *causation in fact*? Did the injury occur because of the defendant's act, or would it have occurred anyway? If an injury would not have occurred without the defendant's act, then there is **causation in fact**. Causation in fact can usually be determined by the use of the *but for* test: "but for" the wrongful act, the injury would not have occurred.
2. Was the act the **proximate cause** of the injury? How far should a defendant's liability extend for a wrongful act that was a substantial factor in causing injury? For example: Ackerman carelessly leaves a campfire burning. The fire not only burns down the forest, but also sets off an explosion in a nearby chemical plant that spills chemicals into a river, killing all the fish for a hundred miles downstream and ruining the economy of a tourist resort. Should Ackerman be liable to the resort owners? To

---

"It makes no difference whether a good man has defrauded a bad man or a bad man defrauded a good man . . . the law can look only to the amount of damage done."

Aristotle, 384–322 B.C.
(Greek philosopher)

CAUSATION IN FACT
An act or omission without which an event would not have occurred.

PROXIMATE CAUSE
The "next" or "substantial" cause; in tort law, a concept used to determine whether a plaintiff's injury was the natural and continuous result of a defendant's negligent act. If the negligent act of a defendant was the sole cause or a substantial cause of injuries to a plaintiff, the defendant is liable.

the tourists whose vacations were ruined? These are questions of proximate cause (sometimes called legal cause). Proximate cause is a question not of fact, but of law and policy. The question is whether the connection between an act and an injury is strong enough to justify imposing liability. Probably the most cited case on proximate cause is the *Palsgraf* case.

Case 3.4
PALSGRAF v. LONG ISLAND R.R. CO.
Court of Appeals of New York, 1928.
248 N.Y. 339, 162 N.E. 99.

FACTS The plaintiff, Palsgraf, was waiting for a train on a station platform. A man carrying a package was rushing to catch a train that was moving away from a platform across the tracks from Palsgraf. As the man attempted to jump aboard the moving train, he seemed unsteady and about to fall. A railroad guard on the car reached forward to grab him, and another guard on the platform pushed him from behind to help him board the train. In the process, the man's package fell on the railroad tracks and exploded because it contained fireworks. There was nothing about the package to indicate its contents. The repercussions of the explosion caused decorative scales to fall from the ceiling and walls around the train platform. One of these scales struck Palsgraf, causing injuries for which she sued the railroad company. At the trial, the jury found that the railroad guards were negligent in their conduct.

ISSUE Was the conduct of the railroad guards the proximate cause of Palsgraf's injuries?

DECISION No. The railroad guards were not negligent with respect to Palsgraf, and the railroad was thus not liable for the injuries that Palsgraf suffered.

REASON The question of whether the guards were negligent with respect to Palsgraf has to do with whether her injury was reasonably foreseeable to the railroad. It is true that the guards may have acted negligently in helping the man board the train and that this conduct may have resulted in injury to that man. This, however, has no bearing on the question of their negligence with respect to Palsgraf. This is not a situation where a person commits an act so potentially harmful (for example, firing a gun at a building) that he or she would be held responsible for any harm that resulted. According to the court, "Here, by concession, there was nothing in the situation to suggest to the most cautious mind that the parcel wrapped in newspaper would spread wreckage through the station."

Since the *Palsgraf* case, the courts have used *foreseeability* as the test for proximate cause. The railroad guards were negligent, but the railroad's duty of care did not extend to Palsgraf because she was an unforeseeable plaintiff. If the consequences of the harm done or the victim of the harm are unforeseeable, there is no proximate cause. Of course, it is foreseeable that people will stand on railroad platforms and that objects attached to the platforms will fall as the result of explosions nearby—however, this is not a chain of events that a reasonable person would usually guard against. It is difficult to predict when a court will say that something is foreseeable and when it will say that something is not. How far a court stretches foreseeability is determined in part by the extent to which the court is willing to stretch the defendant's duty of care.

Defenses to Negligence

The basic defenses in negligence cases are (1) superseding intervening forces, (2) assumption of risk, and (3) contributory and comparative negligence.

Superseding Intervening Forces A superseding or intervening force may break the connection between a wrongful act and injury to another. If so, it cancels out the wrongful act. For example, keeping a can of gasoline in the trunk of one's car creates a foreseeable risk and is thus a negligent act. If lightning strikes the car, exploding the gas tank *and* can as well as injuring passing pedestrians, the lightning supersedes the original negligence as a cause of the damage, since it was not foreseeable.

Assumption of Risk   A plaintiff who voluntarily enters into a risky situation, knowing the risk involved, will not be allowed to recover. This is the defense of **assumption of risk.** For example, a driver entering a race knows there is a risk of being killed or injured in a crash. The driver has assumed the risk of injury.

The requirements of this defense are (1) knowledge of the risk and (2) voluntary assumption of the risk. Risks are not deemed to be assumed in situations involving emergencies. Neither are they assumed where a statute protects a class of people from harm and a member of the class is injured by the harm.

Contributory and Comparative Negligence   All individuals are expected to exercise a reasonable degree of care in looking out for themselves. In some jurisdictions, recovery for injury resulting from negligence is prevented by failure of the injured person to exercise such care over himself or herself. This is the defense of **contributory negligence,** where both parties have been negligent, and their combined negligence has contributed to cause the injury.

The trend is to narrow the scope of the defense of contributory negligence. Instead of allowing contributory negligence to negate a cause of action completely, a majority of states allow recovery based on the doctrine of **comparative negligence.** This doctrine enables both the plaintiff's and the defendant's negligence to be computed, and the liability for damages distributed accordingly. A majority of jurisdictions have adopted a "pure" form of comparative negligence that allows the plaintiff to recover, even if the extent of his or her fault is greater than that of the defendant. If the plaintiff was 80 percent at fault and the defendant 20 percent at fault, the plaintiff may recover 20 percent of his or her damages. Many states' comparative negligence statutes, however, contain a "50 percent" rule by which the plaintiff recovers nothing if he or she was more than 50 percent at fault.

Last Clear Chance   *Last clear chance* is a doctrine that can excuse the effect of a plaintiff's contributory negligence. If applicable, the last-clear-chance rule allows the plaintiff to recover full damages despite failure to exercise care. This rule operates when, through his or her own negligence, the plaintiff is endangered (or his or her property is endangered) by a defendant who has an opportunity to avoid causing damage. For example, if Murphy walks across the street against the light, and Lewis, a motorist, sees her in time to avoid hitting her but hits her anyway, Lewis (the defendant) is not permitted to use Murphy's (the plaintiff's) prior negligence as a defense. The defendant negligently missed the opportunity to avoid injuring the plaintiff. The adoption of the comparative negligence rule has effectively abolished the last-clear-chance doctrine in some jurisdictions.

❖ Strict Liability

Another category of torts is called **strict liability**, or *liability without fault*. Intentional torts and torts of negligence involve acts that depart from a reasonable standard of care and cause injuries. Under the doctrine of *strict liability*, liability for injury is imposed for reasons other than fault. Strict liability for damages proximately caused

---

ASSUMPTION OF RISK
A doctrine whereby a plaintiff may not recover for injuries or damages suffered from risks he or she knows of and assents to. A defense against negligence that can be used when the plaintiff has knowledge of and appreciates a danger and voluntarily exposes himself or herself to the danger.

CONTRIBUTORY NEGLIGENCE
A concept in tort law whereby a complaining party's own negligence contributed to or caused his or her injuries. Contributory negligence is an absolute bar to recovery in some jurisdictions.

COMPARATIVE NEGLIGENCE
A concept in tort law whereby liability for injuries resulting from negligent acts is shared by all persons who were guilty of negligence (including the injured party), on the basis of each person's proportionate carelessness.

STRICT LIABILITY
Liability regardless of fault. Under tort law, strict liability is imposed on a merchant who introduces into commerce a good that is unreasonably dangerous when in a defective condition.

A demolition firm, because of the inherently dangerous nature of its activity, must operate under the law of strict liability.

by abnormally dangerous activities is one application of this doctrine. Strict liability is applied in such cases because of the extreme risk of the activity. For example, even if blasting with dynamite is performed with all reasonable care, there is still a risk of injury. Balancing that risk against the potential for harm, it is fair to ask the person engaged in the activity to pay for injury caused by that activity. Although there is no fault, there is still responsibility because of the dangerous nature of the undertaking.

There are other applications of the strict liability principle, notably in the area of product liability. Liability here is a matter of social policy and is based on two factors: (1) the manufacturing company can better bear the cost of injury because it can spread the cost throughout society by increasing prices of goods and services, and (2) the manufacturing company is making a profit from its activities and therefore should bear the cost of injury as an operating expense. Product liability will be discussed in Chapter 14.

❖ Business Torts

The field of business torts is broad; thus the discussion will be limited to the following causes of action (all of which are normally intentional torts).

1. Wrongful interference with a contractual relationship.
2. Wrongful interference with a business relationship.
3. Wrongfully entering into business.
4. Infringement of trademarks, patents, and copyrights.

Wrongful Interference with a Contractual Relationship

Tort law relating to *intentional interference with a contractual relationship* has expanded greatly in recent years. A landmark case involved an opera singer, Joanna Wagner, who was under contract to sing for a man named Lumley for a specified period of years.[4] A man named Gye, who knew of this contract, nonetheless "enticed" Wagner to refuse to carry out the agreement, and Wagner began to sing for Gye. Gye's action constituted a tort because it interfered with the contractual relationship between Wagner and Lumley. (Wagner's refusal to carry out the agreement also entitled Lumley to sue for breach of contract.)

Three elements are necessary for a wrongful interference with a contractual relationship to occur:

1. A valid, enforceable contract must exist between two parties.
2. A third party must *know* that this contract exists.
3. The third party must *intentionally* cause either of the two parties to break the contract.

The contract may be between a firm and its employees or a firm and its customers. Sometimes a competitor of a firm may draw away a key employee and end up paying damages for breach of contract. If the original employer can show that the competitor induced the breach—that is, that the employee would not normally have broken the contract—damages can be recovered from the competitor.

Wrongful Interference with a Business Relationship

Businesspersons devise countless schemes to attract customers, but they are forbidden by the courts to interfere unreasonably with another's business in their attempts to gain a share of the market. There is a difference between *competition* and *predatory behavior*. The distinction usually depends on whether a business is attempting to attract customers in general or to solicit only those customers who have shown an interest in a similar product or service of a specific competitor. If a shopping center contains two shoe stores, an employee of Store A cannot be positioned at the entrance of Store B for the purpose of diverting customers to Store A. This type of activity constitutes the tort of wrongful interference with a business relationship, or what is commonly considered to be an unfair trade practice. The following case is illustrative.

Case 3.5
AZAR v. LEHIGH CORP.
District Court of Appeal of Florida, Second District, 1978.
364 So. 2d 860.

FACTS   Lehigh Corporation, a developer of real estate, obtained a restraining order against one of its former salespersons, Leroy Azar. Lehigh brought prospective customers to its development, Lehigh Acres, and provided accommodations at its company-owned motel. Azar pursued a practice of following Lehigh purchasers and persuading them to rescind their contracts with Lehigh and purchase less expensive property from him. Azar contended that Lehigh's customers had a right under federal law to rescind their contracts within three days and that he was merely providing them with an oppor-

---

4.   Lumley v. Gye, 118 Eng. Rep. 749 (1853).

Case 3.5—Continued

tunity to be relieved of their contracts and to obtain comparable property for lower prices. Lehigh asserted that Azar was tortiously interfering with the advantageous business relations between Lehigh Corporation and its customers.

ISSUE Did Azar's activities constitute tortious interference with a business relationship?

DECISION Yes. The restraining order against Azar was allowed to stand.

REASON Three basic elements are necessary for the tort of interference with a business relationship to exist: (a) the existence of a relationship where the plaintiff has legal rights, (b) intentional, unjustified interference with that relationship, and (c) resulting damage to the plaintiff. The court held that all three elements were present here. Azar's conduct had been unfair "according to contemporary business standards" and constituted wrongful interference with the relationship between Lehigh Corporation and its customers.

Defenses to Wrongful Interference with a Contractual or Business Relationship Justification is the defense used most often against the accusation of the tort of wrongful interference with a contractual or business relationship. For example, bona fide competitive behavior is a privileged interference even if it results in the breaking of a contract. If Antonio's Meats advertises so effectively that it induces Alex's Restaurant Chain to break its contract with Alvarez Meat Company, Alvarez Meat Company will be unable to recover against Antonio's Meats on a wrongful interference theory. After all, the public policy that favors free competition in advertising outweighs any possible instability that such competitive activity might cause in contractual relations.

Wrongfully Entering into Business

In a freely competitive society it is usually true that any person can enter into any business in order to compete for the customers of existing businesses. Two situations where this notion of free competition does not hold, however, are (1) when entering into business is a violation of the law, and (2) when competitive behavior is predatory.

Any business or profession not subject to regulatory agencies or occupational licensing standards is open to an individual. No one can open a business for the sole purpose of driving another firm out of business, however; such a predatory motive is considered to be *simulated competition*. What the courts consider normal competitive activity is not always easy to ascertain—where does the normal desire to compete and obtain profits end and the tortious action begin?[5] The following landmark case illustrates how a Minnesota court grappled with the question of malicious injury to business.

Case 3.6
TUTTLE v. BUCK
Supreme Court of Minnesota, 1909.
107 Minn. 145, 119 N.W. 946.

FACTS The plaintiff Tuttle, a barber, filed suit against the defendant Buck for malicious interference with his business. The plaintiff had owned and operated a bar-

bershop for the last ten years and had been able to support himself and his family comfortably from the income of the business.

The defendant was a banker in the same community. During the previous twelve months, the defendant had "maliciously" established a competitive barbershop, employed a barber to carry on the business, and used his personal influence to attract customers from the plaintiff's

---

5. Alleged predatory pricing behavior in the international context is the subject of the "Business Law in Action" in Chapter 36.

Case 3.6—Continued

barbershop. Apparently, the defendant had circulated false and malicious reports and accusations about the plaintiff and had personally solicited, urged, threatened, and otherwise persuaded many of the plaintiff's patrons to stop using the plaintiff's services and to use the defendant's shop instead. The plaintiff charged that the defendant undertook this entire plan with the sole design of injuring the plaintiff and destroying his business, and not to serve any legitimate business interest or to practice fair competition.

ISSUE   Did the defendant's activities constitute malicious interference with Tuttle's business?

DECISION   Yes. The defendant was guilty of maliciously interfering with the plaintiff's business.

REASON   Based on the facts presented, the court determined that the defendant's sole purpose in establishing the competing barbershop was to deprive the plaintiff of his livelihood. The court was bound by precedent to preserve competition in the marketplace, but at the same time it was supposed to guard against abusive practices. When a person starts a competing business to drive a competitor out of business rather than to earn profits, that person is guilty of a tort and must answer for the harm done. "To call such conduct competition is a perversion of terms. It is simply the application of force without legal justification, which in its moral quality may be no better than highway robbery."

TRADEMARK
A word or symbol that has become sufficiently associated with a good (in common law) or has been registered with a government agency. Once a trademark is established, the owner has exclusive use of it and has the right to bring a legal action against those who infringe upon the protection given the trademark.

SERVICE MARK
A mark used in the sale or the advertising of services, such as to distinguish the services of one person from the services of others. Titles, character names, and other distinctive features of radio and television programs may be registered as service marks.

TRADE NAME
A name used in commercial activity to designate a particular business, a place where a business is located, or a class of goods. Trade names are not usually affixed to goods sent into the market.

Trademarks, Patents, and Copyrights

Trademark Infringement   A **trademark** is a distinctive mark, motto, device, or implement that a manufacturer stamps, prints, or otherwise affixes to the goods it produces, so that they may be identified on the market and their origin vouched for. In common law, the person who used a symbol or mark to identify a business or product was protected in the use of that trademark. Clearly, if one used the trademark of another, it would lead consumers to believe that one's goods were made by the other. The law seeks to avoid this kind of confusion. Normally, personal names, words, or places that are descriptive of an article or its use cannot be trademarked; they are available to anyone. Words that are used as part of a design or device, however, or words that are uncommon or fanciful may be trademarked.

Consider an example. English leather may not be trademarked to describe leather processed in England. On the other hand, English Leather may be, and is, trademarked as a name for an after-shave lotion, since this constitutes a *fanciful* use of the words. Consider also that even the common name of an individual may be trademarked if that name is accompanied by a picture or some fanciful design that allows for easy identification of the product—for example, Smith Brothers' Cough Drops.

A **service mark** is similar to a trademark but is used to distinguish the services of one person from those of another. For example, each airline has a particular mark or symbol associated with its name. Titles or character names used in radio and television are frequently registered as service marks.

Trademarks are not the same as trade names. The term **trade name** is used to indicate part or all of a business's name, whether the business is a sole proprietorship, a partnership, or a corporation. Generally, a trade name is directly related to a business and its goodwill. As with trademarks, words must be unusual or fancifully used in order to be protected as trade names. The word *Safeway* was held by the courts to

Business Law in Action

Hallmark versus "The Little People"

When does "unfair competition" mean "fair competition"? Apparently, when a leading card-retailing firm such as Hallmark copies and markets the card designs of its minor competitors to draw customers from their businesses. In its defense to an unfair-competition claim brought against it by Blue Mountain Cards, Inc., Hallmark claimed it was merely engaging in fair competitive practices. Unfortunately for Hallmark, a federal judge did not accept Hallmark's definition of fair competition and ruled for Blue Mountain.[1]

1. See *Business Week*, December 8, 1986, p. 42.

The problem arose when Hallmark entered the market for "alternative cards" (cards containing unusual, humorous, or upbeat messages) and met with little success. Its failure led Hallmark to study the competition in the field, including some two hundred Blue Mountain cards, and solicit advice from greeting-card dealers who were contacted by Hallmark for that purpose. Hallmark targeted Blue Mountain as a "formidable competitor," even though the small firm's revenues are estimated to be less than $12 million (compared to Hallmark's $1.5 billion).

In May 1986 Hallmark marketed its "Personal Touch" series, which, according to a Hallmark company memo, "was created . . . to displace Blue Mountain." The owners of Blue Mountain Cards, Inc.; Susan and Stephen Schutz, noted the striking similarity between Hallmark's new series and their own card design and brought suit in federal court under unfair competition laws. In spite of Hallmark's protests that its actions represent nothing more than free-market competition, the judge ruled for Blue Mountain and ordered Hallmark to stop selling 83 card styles. Hallmark let it be known that it will appeal the decision in the $50 million suit and that, although it has never sued a smaller competitor to protect its own designs, it may do so if the ruling is upheld on appeal.

In the meantime, the Schutzes are elated at having won the first round in the battle with the card-industry giant. According to Susan Schutz, "It's a victory for all artists."

---

be sufficiently fanciful to obtain protection as a trade name for a foodstore chain.[6] The decisions of the courts do not give entirely clear guidelines as to when the name of a corporation can be regarded as a trade name. A particularly thorny problem arises when a trade name acquires generic use. For example, Frigidaire, Scotch Tape, Xerox, and Kleenex were originally used only as trade names but today are used generically. Even so, the courts will not allow another firm to use those names in such a way as to deceive a potential consumer. Consider, for example, the following famous case concerning Coca-Cola, decided by the Supreme Court.

Case 3.7
COCA-COLA CO. v. KOKE CO. OF AMERICA ET AL.
United States Supreme Court, 1920.
254 U.S. 143, 41 S.Ct. 113, 65 L.Ed. 189.

FACTS The Coca-Cola Company sought to enjoin other beverage companies from using the words "Koke" or "Dope" for the defendants' products. The defendants contended that the Coca-Cola trademark was a fraudulent representation and that Coca-Cola was therefore not entitled to any help from the courts. By use of the Coca-Cola name, the defendants alleged, the Coca-Cola Company represented that the beverage contained cocaine (from coca leaves).

ISSUE Did the marketing of products called Koke and Dope by the Koke company constitute an infringement on Coca-Cola's trade name?

6. *Safeway Stores v. Suburban Foods*, 130 F.Supp. 249 (E.D.Va. 1955).

Case 3.7—Continued

DECISION Yes for Koke, but no for Dope. The competing beverage companies were enjoined from calling their products Koke, but the Court did not prevent them from calling their products Dope.

REASON Justice Holmes noted that, to be sure, prior to 1900 the Coca-Cola beverage had contained a small amount of cocaine, but this ingredient had been deleted from the formula by 1906 at the latest, and the Coca-Cola Company had advertised to the public that no cocaine was present in its drink. Coca-Cola was a widely popular drink "to be had at almost any soda fountain." Because of the public's widespread familiarity with Coca-Cola, the retention of the name of the beverage (referring to coca leaves and cola nuts) was not misleading. "It hardly would be too much to say that the drink characterizes the name as much as the name the drink. In other words Coca-Cola probably means to most persons the plaintiff's familiar product to be had everywhere rather than a compound of particular substances." The name Coke was found to be so common a term for the trademark name Coca-Cola that the defendants' use of the similar-sounding Koke as a name for their beverages was disallowed. The Court could find no reason to restrain the defendant from using the name "Dope," however.

PATENT
A government grant that gives an inventor the exclusive right or privilege to make, use, or sell his or her invention for a limited time period (currently, seventeen years). The word *patent* usually refers to some invention and designates either the instrument by which patent rights are evidenced or the patent itself.

COPYRIGHT
The exclusive right of "authors" to publish, print, or sell an intellectual production for a statutory period of time (currently, for an identified author, his or her lifetime plus fifty years; for anonymous or pseudonymous authors, seventy-five years from publication or one hundred years from creation). A copyright has the same monopolistic nature as a patent or trademark, but it differs in that it applies exclusively to works of art and literature.

Patent Infringement   A **patent** is a grant from the government that conveys to and secures for an inventor the exclusive right to make, use, and sell an invention for a period of seventeen years. Patents for a lesser period are given for designs, as opposed to inventions. For either a regular patent or a design patent, the applicant must demonstrate to the satisfaction of the patent office that the invention, discovery, or design is genuine, novel, useful, and not obvious in light of current technology. A patent holder gives notice to all that an article or design is patented by placing on it the word "patent" or "pat.," plus the patent number.

Copyright Infringement   A **copyright** is an intangible right granted by statute to the author or originator of certain literary or artistic productions. Works created after January 1, 1978, are automatically given statutory copyright protection for the life of the author plus fifty years. For copyrights owned by publishing houses the term of copyright is seventy-five years from the date of publication or a hundred years from the date of creation, whichever is shorter. For works by one or more authors, the copyright expires fifty years after the death of the last surviving author. It is not possible to copyright an *idea*. What is copyrightable is the particular way an idea is *expressed*. Recent legislation permits the copyright of computer programs. There is a problem, however, regarding how to distinguish an "idea" from its "expression" in the computer context. This issue is currently being addressed by the courts (see the "Landmark in the Law" in this chapter).

Under the "fair use" doctrine, a person or organization can reproduce copyrighted material without paying royalties. Section 107 of the Copyright Act provides:

> Notwithstanding the provisions of section 106, the fair use of a copyrighted work, including such use by reproduction in copies or phonorecords or by any other means specified by that section, for purposes such as criticism, comment, news reporting, teaching (including multiple copies for classroom use), scholarship, or research, is not an infringement of copyright. In determining whether the use made of a work in any particular case is a fair use the factors to be considered shall include—
>
> (1)   the purpose and character of the use, including whether such use is of a commercial nature or is for nonprofit educational purposes;
>
> (2)   the nature of the copyrighted work;

Landmark in the Law

The Computer Software Copyright Act of 1980

Current copyright law is based on the Copyright Reform Act of 1976, which became effective on January 1, 1978. The act grants protection for all "original works of authorship," published or unpublished, from the moment they are "fixed" in a "tangible medium of expression." The content of the work need not be original to be copyrightable. A compilation of preexisting works, for example, can be copyrighted if it is an "original" arrangement or ordering of materials. In 1980 Congress passed the Computer Software Copyright Act, which amended the 1976 act to include computer programs in the list of creative works covered by copyright law. The 1980 statute defines a computer program as a "set of statements or instructions to be used directly or indirectly in a computer in order to bring about a certain result."

The 1980 act has posed some difficult problems for the courts. The first has to do with the fact that computer programs, unlike literary works, interact with machines and are "readable" by machines. Should copyright protection be limited to those parts of a computer program which can be read by humans, such as the high-level language of a source code? Or should it extend to the binary-language object code of a computer program, which is readable only by the computer?

In a 1982 case, a program's source code was held to be copyrightable.[1] In an important 1983 decision, *Apple Computer, Inc. v. Franklin Computer Corp.*, copyright protection was extended to include the binary object code of a computer program.[2] In this decision, the Court of Appeals for the Third Circuit held that "as source code instructions must be translated into object code before the computer can act upon them, only instructions expressed in object code can be used 'directly' by the computer. Thus, a computer program, whether in object code or

source code . . . is protected from unauthorized copying, whether from its object or source code version."

By 1983 it was thus fairly well established—particularly by the *Apple Computer* decision just mentioned—that a program's computer codes were copyrightable. But should copyright protection cover other elements of computer software, such as the overall structure, sequence, and organization of a program? This issue was addressed in a significant 1986 case, *Whelan Associates v. Jaslow Dental Laboratory*.[3] In *Whelan* the court noted that copyrights of other literary works can be infringed upon even when there is no substantial similarity between the works' literal elements. The copyright of a play or a book, for example, can be infringed upon by copying its plot or plot devices. The court applied the same principle to computer programs, which are classified as "literary works" in the Copyright Act, and held that the structure, sequence, and organization of computer programs were copyrightable.

In forming its decision, the court had to deal with the distinction between an "idea," which is not copyrightable, and the "expression of an idea," which is copyrightable. In *Whelan*, the defendant alleged that the structure and organization of the program was the idea, not the expression of the idea. The court responded by saying that the particular structure of the program (designed to aid the business operations of dental laboratories) was not essential to that idea, since other programs on the market perform the same functions but are expressed through different structures and design. The court held that the detailed structure of the plaintiff's program was part of the expression of the idea, not the idea itself.

Because the market for computer programs is highly competitive and because computer copyright legislation is relatively new, the problem of piracy has been significant in the software industry. The nature and extent of protection granted in the 1980 Computer Software Copyright Act is still not entirely clear and is being determined on a case-by-case basis. The judicial decisions mentioned here represent only the first steps toward a definition of what this "landmark" legislation entails.

1. Stern Electronics, Inc. v. Kaufman, 669 F.2d 852 (2d Cir. 1982).
2. 714 F.2d 1240 (3d Cir. 1983).

3. 797 F.2d 1222 (3d Cir. 1986).

(3) the amount and substantiality of the portion used in relation to the copyrighted work as a whole; and

(4) the effect of the use upon the potential market for or value of the copyrighted work.

Unfortunately, the act does not *clearly* define this doctrine, and anyone reproducing copyrighted material may still be subject to a violation.

The act does provide that a copyright owner no longer needs to place a © or ℗ on the work to have the work protected against infringement. Chances are that if somebody created it, somebody owns it.

Whenever the form of expression of an idea is copied, an infringement of copyright occurs. The production does not have to be exactly the same as the original, nor does it have to reproduce the original in its entirety.

Penalties or remedies can be imposed on those who infringe copyrights. These range from actual damages or statutory damages (ranging from $250 to $10,000) imposed at the court's discretion to criminal proceedings for willful violations (which may result in fines and/or imprisonment).

The following case discusses whether recording television broadcasts on home videotape recorders constitutes a copyright infringement.

Case 3.8
SONY CORP. OF AMERICA v. UNIVERSAL CITY STUDIOS, INC.
United States Supreme Court, 1984.
464 U.S. 417, 104 S.Ct. 774, 78 L.Ed.2d 574.

FACTS Universal City Studios alleged that the general public used Betamax videocassette recorders (VCRs), manufactured and marketed by Sony, to record TV broadcasts of Universal's copyrighted television programs, thereby infringing on Universal's copyrights. Claiming that Sony was vicariously liable because it sold the equipment with constructive knowledge that its customers would use Betamax VCRs to make unauthorized copies of copyrighted material, Universal sought money damages, an accounting for profits, and an injunction against the manufacture and marketing of the VCRs. The district court denied relief, but the court of appeals held Sony liable for contributory infringement. Sony appealed to the Supreme Court.

ISSUE Should Sony be held liable for contributory infringement of Universal's copyright?

DECISION No. The Supreme Court concluded that because a substantial number of television broadcast copyright holders would not object to having their broadcasts recorded, and because Universal failed to show that such recording would cause more than minimal harm to the market for or value of their copyrighted works, there were noninfringing uses of the Betamax VCRs. Therefore, Sony was not liable for contributory infringement.

REASON Copyright protection does not "accord the copyright owner absolute control over all possible uses of his work." Rather, Section 106 of the Copyright Act grants the copyright holder certain exclusive rights while Section 107, conversely, allows a noncopyright holder certain "fair uses" of the work. The sale of the VCR "does not constitute contributory infringement if the product is widely used for legitimate purposes, or is even capable of substantial noninfringing uses." Moreover, unless the unauthorized use conflicts with one of the exclusive rights granted under Section 106, the use is not infringing. The court concluded that to challenge a noncommercial use of a copyrighted work, proof is required that either (1) the particular use is harmful, or (2) if such a use should become widespread, it would adversely affect the market for the copyrighted work. Balancing these factors, the Court found that home taping of the copyrighted programs is a "fair use."

Application

Law and the Retailer

Retailers face a potential lawsuit not only any time a customer steps onto the retailer's property, but also any time a customer purchases a product from the retailer. Retailers are faced with potential legal problems every day. Let us consider only a few areas where knowledge of the law can help a retailer prevent a legal problem.

Negligence

Negligence is an important area in tort law. Any retail business firm, whether it be a shoe store or a hamburger stand, must take reasonable care—not be negligent—in providing a safe environment where the customer can examine products or purchase goods and services. The courts have come to conclude that "the customer is always right." Therefore, to believe that customers will take reasonable care in their behavior or in the management of their small children while on your premises is to court disaster. The retailer who assumes that any person on the premises will show a complete lack of common sense is going a long way to prevent being sued for negligence. For example, even though it might be obvious that an employee is washing a section of the sales room floor, there should be signs posted that warn the customer as to what the employee is doing.

Protection of Business Property

The law of trespass may seem clear to the businessperson who has invested his or her life savings in starting a small retail store. But to the courts, the law of trespass and, more specifically, the protection of property against trespassers (i.e., thieves) is not so clear. The usual methods of protecting property against trespassers, such as hiring police protection services and installing alarm systems, are well utilized and accepted, but other methods are not.

In *Katko v. Briney*,[1] for example, a landowner had prepared a "mantrap" to protect an old, abandoned farmhouse from thieves. A spring gun was set so that it would

1.   183 N.W. 2d 657 (Iowa 1971).

Miami innercity shopkeeper Prentice Rasheed poses in front of his variety store. Rasheed's anti-burglary device—an electrified wire grid—caused an intruder to be electrocuted in 1986.

fire when anyone entered the house. A petty thief lost most of his leg when the gun fired at him upon his entry into the building, and the landowner was held liable for both actual and punitive damages—despite the "no trespassing" signs on the property and despite the thief's illegal presence there. In general, courts will hold that a landowner cannot do mechanically what he cannot do in person—that is, use deadly force without sufficient justification. A recent Florida court decision, however, provides an exception to this rule. In October 1986 a Dade County grand jury refused to hold a shopkeeper liable for a death resulting from an electrified wire grid the shopkeeper (Prentice Rasheed) had constructed to deter potential trespassers.[2]

Handling Shoplifters

Shrinkage, the polite word for *shoplifting*, involves both employee theft and customer theft. To what extent can you, the businessperson, detain a suspected shoplifter without being successfully sued for false imprisonment, invasion of privacy, or some other charge—such as defamation or mental duress? Suspected shoplifters can be accosted, accused, and temporarily detained if certain reasonable procedures are used. These procedures differ, depending on the jurisdiction. The word to remember is *reasonable*. Keeping a suspected shoplifter in a locked storeroom for two hours because your manager has not yet gotten around to contacting the police would usually not be considered reasonable if the individual in question sued for false imprisonment.

When apprehending and questioning a suspected shoplifter, choose your words carefully. Using abusive or accusatory words or otherwise subjecting the person to indignity may result in a lawsuit. In one case, for example, the words "A big fat woman like you" served as the basis for the tort of mental duress.[3] If you think

2. See *The Miami Herald*, February 10, 1987, page 2.
3. Haile v. New Orleans Railway & Light Co., 135 La. 229, 65 So. 225 (1914). According to Prosser, this is the mildest insult for which recovery on the grounds of mental duress has been allowed. See Prosser and Keeton on Torts, 5th ed., p. 58.

someone has shoplifted, act on your suspicion before the suspect leaves the store. Usually the courts will allow detention only if the suspected shoplifter is still on your premises. This is not always the case, however. In *Bonkowski v. Arlan's Department Store*,[4] for example, the court allowed detention after the suspect had left the store but was still in the immediate vicinity.

4. 383 Mich. 90, 174 N.W. 2d 765 (1970).

Checklist for the Retailer

☐ 1. Always assume that the worst can happen; therefore, mark all potential hazards no matter how obvious they may be. Always attempt to reason with an individual claiming to have been injured while on your premises. Most important, carry an adequate amount of liability insurance if possible.

☐ 2. Even for the most minor negligence lawsuit, hire an attorney and be willing to consider out-of-court settlement, even if you believe that your customer was 100 percent at fault.

☐ 3. Protect your property through normal means. Any time you decide to exceed "normal" methods, obtain competent legal advice regarding what is considered a reasonable way to protect property in your jurisdiction.

☐ 4. Any employee who may handle shoplifters should be properly schooled on the reasonable steps involved in apprehending a suspect. Print out a short list of rules and have it checked by a local attorney familiar with recent court decisions in your area.

❖ Chapter Summary: Common Torts

Intentional Torts against a Person	1. *Assault and battery*—An unexcused and intentional act that causes another person to be apprehensive or to fear immediate harm. Assault resulting in physical contact is called battery.
	2. *False imprisonment or false arrest*—Intentional confinement or restraint of another person's movement without consent or justification.
	3. *Libel or slander*—A false statement of fact, not made under privilege, which is communicated to a third person, and which causes damage to a person's reputation or a product's reputation. For public figures, the plaintiff must also prove malice.
Intentional Torts against Property	1. *Trespass to land*—Invasion of another's real property without consent or privilege. Specific rights and duties apply once a person is expressly or impliedly established as a trespasser.
	2. *Trespass to personal property or conversion*—Unlawfully damaging or interfering with the owner's right to use, possess, or enjoy his or her personal property. When personal property of the owner is wrongfully converted to the use of the trespasser, conversion occurs.
Unintentional Torts	1. *Negligence*—The careless performance of a legally required duty or the failure to perform a legally required act. Elements that must be proved are that a legal duty exists, that the defendant breached that duty, and that the breach caused damage or injury.
	2. *Strict liability*—A person is held liable, regardless of care exercised, for damages or injuries caused by his or her product or activity. This includes liability for defective products (product liability) and liability for abnormally dangerous activities.
Business Torts	1. *Wrongful interference with a contractual relationship*—Exists only if the following elements are present: (*a*) a valid, enforceable contract exists; (*b*) a third party knows the contract exists; and (*c*) the third party *intentionally* causes one of the parties to break the contract.
	2. *Wrongful interference with a business relationship*—Unreasonable interference with a competing business for the purpose of gaining a greater share of the market. Exists when (*a*) the plaintiff is involved in a business relationship which the plaintiff has a legal right to pursue; (*b*) the defendant intentionally (without justification) interferes with this relationship; and (*c*) the plaintiff suffers damages as a result of this interference.
	3. *Wrongfully entering into business*—Entering into a business in violation of the law (e.g, without an appropriate license if one is required) or engaging in predatory behavior (opening a business for the sole purpose of driving another firm out of business).
	4. *Infringement of trademarks, trade names, patents, and copyrights*—Copying without consent or privilege the trademark, trade name, patented product, or copyrighted material of another firm or individual. Infringement can occur even when trademarks, trade names, and copyrights are not registered.
	5. *Defamation—slander of title or disparagement of goods*—A false statement of a material fact made to a third person about a person's product, business, or title to property.

❖ Questions and Case Problems

3-1. In which of the following situations will the acting party be liable for the tort of negligence? Explain fully.

(a) Mary goes to the golf course on Sunday morning, eager to try out a new set of golf clubs she has just purchased. As she tees off on the first hole, the head of her club flies off and injures a nearby golfer.

(b) Mary's doctor gives her some pain medication and tells her not to drive after she takes it, as the medication induces drowsiness. In spite of the doctor's warning, Mary decides to drive to the store while on the medication. Owing to her lack of alertness, she fails to stop at a traffic light and crashes into another vehicle, in which a passenger is injured.

(c) While driving to the store, Mary suddenly experiences a piercing pain in her head. The pain distracts her to the point that she loses control of the car momentarily, during which time she crashes into a vehicle that has stopped in front of her at a stop sign.

3-2. Professor Haley is teaching a summer seminar in business torts at State University. Several times during the course, he makes copies of relevant sections from business law texts and distributes them to his students. Unbeknownst to Haley, the daughter of one of the textbook authors is a member of his seminar. She tells her father about Haley's copying activities, which has been done without her father's permission. Her father sues Haley for copyright infringement. Haley claims protection under the "fair use" doctrine. Who will prevail? Explain.

3-3. Ruth carelessly parks her car on a steep hill, leaving the car in neutral and failing to engage the parking brake. The car rolls down the hill, knocking down an electric line. The sparks from the broken line ignite a grass fire. The fire spreads until it reaches a barn one mile away. The barn houses dynamite, and the burning barn explodes, causing part of the roof to fall on and injure a passing motorist, Jim. Can Jim recover from Ruth? Why or why not?

3-4. Jennings owns a bakery shop. He has been trying to obtain a long-term contract with the owner of Julie's Tea Salon for some time. Jennings starts a local advertising campaign on radio and television and in the newspaper. The campaign is so persuasive that Julie decides to break the contract she has had for some time with Orley's Bakery so that she can patronize Jennings's bakery. Is Jennings liable to Orley's Bakery for the tort of wrongful interference with a contractual relationship? Is Julie liable for this tort? For anything?

3-5. A grocery cart at Waldbaum's Store was missing the protective flap in the jump seat (or baby seat); this flap can be raised to cover the opening when the seat is not in use by an infant or small child who can dangle his or her feet through the opening. A shopper using the cart placed a large bottle of soda in the jump seat. The bottle fell through the opening and hit Mrs. Gross's foot, causing her injuries. Is Waldbaum's Store liable for these injuries on the ground of negligence? Was the shopper's act of placing heavy or breakable items in the jump seat foreseeable? [Gross v. Waldbaum, Inc., 102 Misc.2d 175, 423 N.Y.S.2d 123 (Civ.Ct.N.Y. 1979)]

3-6. West Publishing Company brought a copyright infringement action against Mead Data Central, Inc. (the owners of LEXIS, a computer-assisted legal research system) when Mead developed a plan for a "star pagination" feature to be used on LEXIS. This feature would incorporate page numbers from West's case reporters into the opinions available on LEXIS and would allow LEXIS users to learn the precise page breaks in a West reporter without ever physically having to refer to a West volume. West claimed that Mead Data's proposed star-pagination system would constitute a copyright infringement of its reporting arrangement. Mead Data contended that "mere page numbers" cannot be copyrighted. Can the use of page numbers, which cannot in themselves be copyrighted, fall under copyright protection in this case? [West Pub. Co. v. Mead Data Cent., Inc., 799 F.2d 1219 (8th Cir. 1986)]

3-7. Felix Contracting Corporation (Felix) was a general contractor responsible for sealing a gas main in a city street. Felix had excavated the site and provided a flagman but did not erect barriers on all sides of the excavation. Derdiarian, an employee of the subcontractor in charge of the actual operation, was working with the hot sealing material when a passing driver had an epileptic seizure, lost control of his car, and ran into him. Derdiarian was severely burned by the sealing material. Is Felix liable for Derdiarian's injuries because of its negligence in not providing adequate protection around the site? Was the epileptic seizure and subsequent accident foreseeable? Explain. [Derdiarian v. Felix Contracting Corp., 51 N.Y.2d 308, 434 N.Y.S.2d 166, 414 N.E.2d 666 (1980)]

3-8. H. E. Butt Grocery Company (HEB) has retail grocery stores scattered throughout Texas. Hawkins went to shop for groceries at one of the HEB stores. A heavy rainstorm and north wind had caused water to be tracked into the store by customers, and to be blown through the door each time the door opened. As Hawkins entered through the automatically opening door, she slipped and fell in the approximately one-half inch of rain water that had accumulated on the floor. The manager knew of the weather conditions and had had employees mop the floor on numerous occasions. There was no sign posted that warned customers of the water hazard. Can Hawkins recover from HEB for injuries sustained when she slipped on the water-covered floor? Explain. [H. E. Butt Grocery Co. v. Hawkins, 594 S.W.2d 187 (Tex.Civ.App. 1980)]

3-9. Yonkers Contracting Co., Inc. (Yonkers) was engaged as the general contractor in the construction of a highway on land owned by defendant State of New York. Plaintiff, an employee of Yonkers, was assisting in preparation for blasting a boulder and was experienced in blasting operations. While the plaintiff was so engaged on October 13, 1980, explosives were detonated and plaintiff was hit in the head by a rock propelled through the air as a result of the blast. He and his wife filed a claim against the state. Given these facts, discuss fully the following questions: Is blasting an inherently dangerous activity? Should liability extend to the landowner, even though an independent contractor directed the blasting? What if an innocent passerby had been injured? [Nagy v. State of New York, 456 N.Y.S.2d 241, 89 A.D.2d 199 (1982)]

Chapter 4

Criminal Law

❖ What Is a Crime?

Crimes are different from other wrongful acts (torts) in a number of ways:

1. Crimes are *offenses against society as a whole* and thus are prosecuted by a public official, not by victims.
2. Those who commit crimes are punished. Tort remedies—remedies for civil wrongs—usually compensate the injured (except when punitive damages are assessed), whereas criminal law punishes (and ideally, rehabilitates) the wrongdoer.
3. The source of criminal law is now primarily statutory, although common law was once the main body of criminal law.

Both crimes and punishments are very specifically set out in statutes. A **crime** can thus be defined as a wrong against society proclaimed in a statute and, if intentionally committed, punishable by society.

❖ Classification of Crimes

Depending on their degree of seriousness, crimes are classified as felonies, misdemeanors, or violations.

Felonies

Felonies are more serious than misdemeanors and are punishable by death or by imprisonment in a federal or state penitentiary for more than a year. The Model Penal Code provides for four degrees of felony: (1) capital offenses, where the maximum penalty is death; (2) first-degree felonies, punishable by a maximum penalty of life imprisonment; (3) second-degree felonies, punishable by a maximum of ten years' imprisonment; and (4) third-degree felonies, punishable by up to five years' imprisonment.

"No state shall make or enforce any law which shall abridge the privileges or immunities of citizens of the United States; nor shall any state deprive any person of life, liberty or property without due process of law, nor deny to any person within its jurisdiction the equal protection of the laws."

Fourteenth Amendment to the U.S. Constitution, July 28, 1868

CRIME
A broad term for violations of law that are punishable by the state and are codified by legislatures. The objective of criminal law is to protect the public.

FELONIES
Crimes—such as arson, murder, rape, and robbery—that carry the most severe sanctions, usually ranging from one year in a state or federal prison to the forfeiture of one's life.

Misdemeanors and Violations

MISDEMEANORS
Lesser crimes than felonies, punishable by a fine or imprisonment in other than a state or federal penitentiary.

Misdemeanors are crimes punishable by a fine or by confinement for up to a year. If incarcerated, the guilty party goes to a local jail instead of a penitentiary. Disorderly conduct and trespass are common misdemeanors. Some states have different classes of misdemeanors. For example, in Illinois misdemeanors are either Class A (confinement for up to a year), Class B (not more than six months), or Class C (not more than thirty days). Whether a crime is a felony or a misdemeanor can also determine whether the case is tried in a magistrate's court (for example, by a justice of the peace) or a general trial court.

Another kind of wrong is termed a petty offense and often is not classified as a crime. Petty offenses include traffic violations and violations of building codes. Even for petty offenses, however, a guilty party can be put in jail for a few days, or fined, or both.

❖ What Constitutes Criminal Liability?

Two elements must exist simultaneously for a person to be convicted of a crime: (1) the performance of a prohibited act, and (2) a specified state of mind or intent on the part of the actor. Even if both elements exist, there are defenses that the law deems sufficient to excuse such actions. These defenses will be discussed later in the chapter.

The Criminal Act

Every criminal statute prohibits certain behavior. Most crimes require an act of *commission;* that is, a person must *do* something in order to be accused of a crime.[1] In some cases an act of *omission* can be a crime, but only when a person has a legal duty to perform the omitted act. Failure to file a tax return is an example of an omission that is a crime.

The *guilty act* requirement is based on one of the premises of criminal law—that a person is punished for *harm done* to society. Thinking about killing someone or stealing a car may be wrong, but the thoughts do no harm until they are translated into action. Of course, a person can be punished for attempting murder or robbery, but only if substantial steps toward the criminal objective were taken. The issue of whether a "substantial step" was taken toward the commission of a crime arises in the following case.

Case 4.1
STATE v. OTTO
Supreme Court of Idaho, 1981.
102 Idaho 250, 629 P.2d 646.

FACTS　The defendant (Otto) hired Watts to kill Allor, a police captain. Otto paid $250 to Watts and agreed to

pay an additional $750 after Allor was killed. Unbeknownst to Otto, Watts was an undercover police officer. Watts did nothing to carry out the crime but instead arrested Otto for attempted first-degree murder. The trial court convicted Otto of attempted first-degree murder, and Otto appealed, claiming insufficient evidence for the charge.

1.　Called the *actus reus,* or guilty act.

Case 4.1—Continued

ISSUE Did the evidence warrant a charge of attempted murder?

DECISION No. The appellate court reversed the lower court's ruling.

REASON The court held that criminal intent alone cannot be the basis for a conviction. Some actual step toward the *commission* of the intended crime must be taken be- fore an "attempt" exists. Although Otto had paid Watts $250, this action was solely a preparatory procedure, not an actual step toward the commission of the crime. Thus the court concluded that, although Otto "solicited" Watts to commit a crime, he did not "attempt" one, as Watts did nothing to carry out Otto's request. The court held that most courts consider such solicitation a crime, but Otto was neither charged nor tried for that offense.

Intent to Commit a Crime

A wrongful mental state [2] is as necessary as a wrongful act in establishing criminal liability. What constitutes such a mental state varies according to the wrongful action. For murder, the act is the taking of a life, and the mental state is the intent to take life. For theft, the guilty act is the taking of another person's property, and the mental state involves both the knowledge that the property belongs to another and the intent to deprive the owner of it. Without the mental state required by law for a particular crime, there is no crime.

> *"It is deliberate purpose that constitutes . . . criminal guilt."*
>
> **Aristotle, 384–322 B.C.**
> **(Greek philosopher)**

❖ Defenses to Criminal Liability

The law recognizes certain conditions that relieve a defendant of criminal liability. These conditions are called defenses, and among the important ones are infancy, intoxication, insanity, mistake, consent, duress, justifiable use of force, entrapment, and the statute of limitations. The burden of proving one or more of these defenses rests on the defendant. A criminal defendant can also be given immunity from prosecution.

Infancy

In the common law, children up to age seven were considered incapable of committing a crime because they did not have the moral sense to understand that they were doing wrong. Children between the ages of seven and fourteen were presumed to be incapable of committing a crime, but this presumption could be rebutted by showing that the child understood the wrongful nature of the act (see Exhibit 4-1).

---

2. Called the *mens rea*, or evil intent.

◆ **Exhibit 4-1**
   Responsibility of Infants for Criminal Acts under Common Law

Age 0–7	Absolute presumption of incompetence.
Age 7–14	Presumption of incompetence, but state may oppose.
Age 14–Adult	Presumption of competence, but infant may oppose.

Intoxication

The law recognizes two types of intoxication, whether from drugs or from alcohol: *involuntary* and *voluntary*. Involuntary intoxication occurs when a person either is physically forced to ingest or inject an intoxicating substance or is unaware that a substance contains drugs or alcohol. Involuntary intoxication is a defense to crime if its effect was to make a person incapable of understanding that the act committed was wrong or incapable of obeying the law.

Using voluntary drug or alcohol intoxication as a defense is based on the theory that extreme levels of intoxication may negate the state of mind that a crime requires. Many courts are reluctant to allow voluntary intoxication as a defense to crime, however. After all, the defendant, by definition, voluntarily chose to put himself or herself into an intoxicated state. Voluntary intoxication as a defense may be effective in cases where the defendant was *extremely* intoxicated when committing the wrong.

Insanity

Just as a child is judged incapable of the state of mind required to commit a crime, so also is someone suffering from mental illness. Thus, insanity is a defense to a criminal charge. The courts have had difficulty deciding what the test for legal insanity should be, and psychiatrists as well as lawyers are critical of the tests used. Almost all federal courts and some states use the relatively liberal standard set forth in the Model Penal Code:

> A person is not responsible for criminal conduct if at the time of such conduct as a result of mental disease or defect he lacks substantial capacity either to appreciate the wrongfulness of his conduct or to conform his conduct to the requirements of the law.

Some states use the *M'Naghten* test,[3] which determines that a criminal defendant is not responsible if, at the time of the offense, he or she did not know the nature

---

3. A rule derived from Daniel M. M'Naghten's case, 8 Eng. Reprint 718 (House of Lords, 1843).

One of the most famous insanity defenses involves John Hinckley, who critically wounded President Ronald Reagan. Hinckley said he was attempting to get actress Jody Foster's attention.

and quality of the act; and if the defendant did know, he or she did not know that the act was wrong. Other states use the irresistible-impulse test. A person operating under an irresistible impulse may know an act is wrong but cannot refrain from doing it. Still other states simply leave it up to the jury to decide.

Mistake

Everyone has heard the saying, "ignorance of the law is no excuse." Ordinarily, ignorance of the law or a mistaken idea about what the law requires is not a valid defense. In some states, however, that rule has been modified. A person who claims that he or she honestly did not know that a law was being broken may have a valid defense if: (1) the law was not published or reasonably made known to the public, or (2) the person relied on an official statement of the law that was erroneous.

A *mistake of fact*, as opposed to a *mistake of law*, operates as a defense if it negates the mental state necessary to commit a crime. If, for example, Oliver Wheaton mistakenly drives off in Julie Tyson's car because he thinks it is his, there is no theft. Theft requires knowledge that the property belongs to another.

Consent

What if a victim consents to a crime or even encourages the person intending a criminal act to commit it? The law allows consent as a defense if the consent cancels the harm that the law is designed to prevent. In each case, the question is whether the law forbids an act that was committed against the victim's will or forbids the act without regard to the victim's wish. The law forbids murder, prostitution, and drug use whether the victim consents to it or not. Also, if the act causes harm to a third person who has not consented, there is no escape from criminal liability. Consent or forgiveness given after a crime has been committed is not really a defense, though it can affect the likelihood of prosecution. Consent operates as a defense most successfully in crimes against property.

Duress

Duress exists when the *wrongful threat* of one person induces another person to perform an act that he or she would not otherwise perform. In such a situation, duress is said to negate the mental state necessary to commit a crime. For duress to qualify as a defense, the threat must be of serious bodily harm or death, the harm threatened must be greater than the harm caused by the crime, the threat must be immediate and inescapable, and the defendants must have been involved in the situation through no fault of their own. One crime that cannot be excused by duress is murder. It is difficult to justify taking a life even if one's own life is threatened.

Justifiable Use of Force

Probably the most well-known defense to criminal liability is *self-defense*. But there are other situations that justify the use of force: the defense of one's dwelling, the defense of other property, and the prevention of a crime. In all of these situations it is important to distinguish between the use of deadly and nondeadly force. Deadly

"Self-defense is nature's oldest law."

John Dryden, 1631–1700
(English poet)

force is likely to result in death or serious bodily harm. Nondeadly force is force that reasonably appears necessary to prevent the imminent use of criminal force.

Generally speaking, people can use the amount of nondeadly force that seems necessary to protect themselves, their dwellings, or other property, or to prevent the commission of a crime. Deadly force can be used in self-defense if there is a *reasonable belief* that imminent death or grievous bodily harm will otherwise result, if the attacker is using unlawful force (an example of lawful force would be that exerted by a police officer), and if the person has not initiated or provoked the attack. Deadly force can be used to defend a dwelling only if the unlawful entry is violent and the person believes deadly force is necessary to prevent imminent death or great bodily harm, or—in some jurisdictions—if the person believes deadly force is necessary to prevent the commission of a felony in the dwelling.

In the following case, the use of force to protect another person from harm was considered by the court to be justifiable.

Case 4.2
STATE v. BERNARDY
Washington Court of Appeals, 1980.
25 Wn.App. 146, 605 P.2d 791.

FACTS The defendant Bernardy came to the defense of his friend Harrison in a fight with Wilson. Wilson started the fight, and after Harrison knocked him down, Bernardy (who was wearing tennis shoes) kicked Wilson several times in the head. Bernardy stated that he did so because he believed an onlooker, Gowens, would join forces with Wilson against Harrison. Bernardy maintained that his use of force was justifiable because he was protecting another (Harrison) from injury. The trial court jury had not been instructed on the defense that force was justifiable

when protecting another from reasonably certain harm, and Bernardy was convicted for assault.

ISSUE Is the use of force to protect another person from harm justified?

DECISION Yes. The trial court's ruling was reversed, and the case was remanded to the lower court for retrial.

REASON The court held that an individual "who acts in the defense of another, reasonably believing him to be the innocent party and in danger of imminent injury, is justified in using force to protect that person. . . . The jury could have found the existence of the privilege if it had been properly instructed."

Entrapment

Entrapment is a defense designed to prevent the police or other government agents from encouraging crimes in order to apprehend persons wanted for criminal acts. In the typical entrapment case, an undercover agent *suggests* that a crime be committed and somehow pressures or induces an individual to commit it. The agent then arrests the individual for the crime. For entrapment to be considered a defense, both the suggestion and the inducement must take place. The defense is not intended to prevent the police from setting a trap for an unwary criminal, but rather, to prevent them from pushing the suspected wrongdoer into it. The crucial issue is whether a person who committed a crime was predisposed to commit the crime or did so because the agent induced it. This is often a question of fact, as illustrated by the following case.

Case 4.3
UNITED STATES v. BOWER
United States Court of Appeals, Fifth Circuit, 1978.
575 F.2d 499.

FACTS This case involves a cocaine transaction that resulted in the defendant's conviction for selling the narcotic to a government Drug Enforcement Administration (DEA) agent, Sylvestri. An informer, Clegg, initiated a relationship with the defendant, Bower. The informer encouraged the defendant to supply a quantity of cocaine to an out-of-town buyer. The defendant agreed to meet the buyer and make the exchange. After the defendant delivered the cocaine to the agent, the agent arrested him. The defendant was subsequently found guilty in trial court on various charges, including possession and distribution of cocaine. The defendant claimed entrapment on the part of the government agents.

ISSUE Did the government agents' actions constitute "entrapment" of Bower?

DECISION No. The appellate court affirmed the defendant's convictions.

REASON The appellate court stated that the "crucial issue in entrapment cases is whether the defendant was predisposed to commit the crime." The court found that the inducement of federal agents did not cause Bower to do something he would never have done otherwise. Therefore, the jury had sufficient evidence to find that Bower was predisposed to commit the crime and was not accordingly entrapped to do so.

Statute of Limitations

An individual can be excused from criminal liability by a statute of limitations. Such statutes provide that the state has only a certain amount of time—which varies from state to state—within which to prosecute a crime. If the state does not do so within the allotted time, it loses its opportunity, and the suspect is free from prosecution. The idea behind this statute is that people should not have to live under the threat of criminal prosecution indefinitely. Also, if prosecution is delayed too long, it becomes difficult to discover the truth because witnesses die or disappear, and evidence is destroyed. Most statutes of limitations do not apply to murder and do not run while the defendant is out of the jurisdiction or in hiding.

Immunity

At times, the state may wish to obtain information from a person accused of a crime. Such accused persons are understandably reluctant to give information if it will be used to prosecute them. The privilege against self-incrimination is granted by the Fifth Amendment to the Constitution, which reads, in part, "nor shall [any person] be compelled in any criminal case to be a witness against himself, . . ." In cases where the state wishes to obtain information from a person accused of a crime, the state can grant immunity from prosecution or agree to prosecute for a less serious offense in exchange for the information. Once immunity is given, the person can no longer refuse to testify on Fifth Amendment grounds, since he or she now has an absolute privilege against self-incrimination. Often a grant of immunity from prosecution for a serious crime is part of the **plea-bargaining** negotiations between defense and prosecution. The defendant may be convicted of the lesser offense, while the state uses his or her testimony to prosecute accomplices for serious crimes carrying heavy penalties.

PLEA BARGAINING
Discussions between a prosecutor and a criminal defendant's lawyer. Typically, the defendant agrees to plead guilty in exchange for the prosecutor's agreement to accept a plea to a less serious charge or to drop some charges or to request a light sentence from the judge for the defendant.

❖ Procedure in Criminal Law

Our criminal justice system operates on the premise that it is far worse for an innocent person to be punished than for a guilty person to go free. A person is innocent until proved guilty, and guilt must be proved beyond a reasonable doubt. The procedure of the criminal legal system is designed to protect the rights of the individual and to preserve the presumption of innocence.

Rights of the Accused

Criminal law brings the weighty force of the state, with all its resources, to bear against the individual. The Constitution provides specific rights to those accused of crimes. The Supreme Court has ruled that most of these rights are actionable not only in federal but also in state courts, by virtue of the due process clause of the Fourteenth Amendment. The basic rights of criminal defendants are as follows. Where appropriate, the constitutional article or amendment on which a right is based is given also. (See the U.S. Constitution in Appendix A.)

Limits on conduct of police and prosecutors

- No unreasonable or unwarranted searches and seizures (Amend. IV)
- No arrest except on probable cause (Amend. IV)
- No coerced confessions or illegal interrogation (Amend. V)
- No entrapment
- Upon questioning, suspect must be informed of rights

Defendant's pretrial rights

- Writ of habeas corpus (Article I, Section 9)[4]
- Prompt arraignment (Amend. VI)
- Legal counsel (Amend. VI)
- Reasonable bail (Amend. VIII)
- Must be informed of charges (Amend. VI)
- Right to remain silent (Amend. V)

Trial rights

- Speedy and public trial before a jury (Amend. VI)
- Impartial jury selected from a cross-section of the community (Amends. VI, VII)
- Trial atmosphere free of prejudice, fear, and outside interference
- Cross-examination of all witnesses (Amend. VI)
- No compulsory self-incrimination (Amend. V)
- Adequate counsel (Amend. VI)
- No cruel or unusual punishment (Amend. VIII)
- Can appeal convictions
- No double jeopardy (Amend. V)

---

4. A writ of habeas corpus (literally, "you have the body") is basically a procedure used to obtain a judicial determination of the legality of an individual's custody.

In recent years the Supreme Court has been active in interpreting these rights. Some cases, such as the *Miranda* decision,[5] are widely known. The right to legal counsel is discussed in the "Landmark" in this chapter.

Criminal Process

A criminal prosecution differs significantly from a civil case in several respects. These differences reflect the desire to safeguard the rights of the individual against the state.

Arrest   Before a warrant for arrest can be issued, there must be probable cause for believing that the individual in question has committed a crime. **Probable cause** can be defined as a substantial likelihood that the person has committed or is about to commit a crime. Note that probable cause involves a likelihood, not just a possibility. Arrests may sometimes be made without a warrant if there is no time to get one, but the action of the arresting officer is still judged by the standard of probable cause.

PROBABLE CAUSE
Reasonable grounds to believe the existence of facts warranting certain actions, such as the search or arrest of a person.

Indictment   Individuals must be formally charged with having committed specific crimes before they can be brought to trial. This charge is called an **indictment** if issued by a grand jury and an **information** if issued by a magistrate. Before a charge can be issued, the grand jury or the magistrate must determine that there is sufficient evidence to justify bringing the individual to trial. The standard used to make this determination varies from jurisdiction to jurisdiction. Some courts use the probable cause standard. Others use the preponderance of evidence standard, which is a belief based on evidence provided by both sides that it is more likely than not that the individual committed the crime. Still other courts use the *prima facie* case standard, which is a belief based on only the prosecution's evidence that the individual is guilty.

INDICTMENT
A charge or written accusation, issued by a grand jury, that a named person has committed a crime.

INFORMATION
A formal accusation or complaint (without an indictment) issued in certain types of actions by a prosecuting attorney or other law officer, such as a magistrate. The types of actions are set forth in the rules of states or in the Federal Rules of Criminal Procedure.

Trial   At the trial the accused person does not have to prove anything; the entire burden of proof is on the prosecutor (the state). Guilt is judged on the basis of the **reasonable doubt** test. The prosecution must show that, based on all the evidence, the defendant's guilt is established beyond all reasonable doubt. Giving a verdict of "not guilty" is not the same as stating that the defendant is innocent. A "not guilty" verdict merely means that not enough evidence was properly presented to the court to prove guilt beyond all reasonable doubt. Courts have complex rules about what types of evidence may be presented and how the evidence may be brought out, especially in jury trials. These rules are designed to ensure that evidence in trials is relevant, reliable, and not prejudicial against the defendant. The defense attorney cross-examines the witnesses who present evidence against his or her client and attempts to show that their evidence is not reliable. The state may cross-examine any witnesses presented by the defendant.

REASONABLE DOUBT
The standard used to determine the guilt or innocence of a person charged with a criminal offense. To be guilty of a crime, one must be proved guilty "beyond and to the exclusion of every reasonable doubt." A reasonable doubt is one that would cause prudent or "reasonable" persons to hesitate before acting in matters important to them.

❖ Crimes Affecting Business

Crimes occur in the business world, just as they do elsewhere. We discuss below the types of crimes that affect business.

---

5.   *Miranda v. Arizona*, 384 U.S. 436, 86 S.Ct. 1602, 16 L.Ed.2d 694 (1966).

Landmark in the Law

Gideon v. Wainwright (1963)

The Sixth Amendment to the U.S. Constitution provides that "in all criminal prosecutions, the accused shall enjoy the right . . . to have the assistance of counsel for his defense." By the passage of the Fourteenth Amendment in 1868, following the Civil War, this and other rights and privileges contained in the Bill of Rights were to be secured for all U.S. citizens, and no state could "deprive any person of life, liberty, or property, without due process of law." Nearly a century passed, however, before the right to counsel was made available to accused persons in state criminal proceedings. Even as late as 1942, the Supreme Court held, in *Betts v. Brady*, that criminal defendants were not automatically guaranteed the right to have a lawyer present when they were tried in court except in capital cases.[1]

In 1963, however, the *Betts v. Brady* precedent was overturned by the decision in *Gideon v. Wainwright*, which became a landmark case in securing the right to counsel for criminal defendants.[2] The case began in 1962 when Clarence Earl Gideon sent a petition to the Supreme

Court to review his most recent conviction—for breaking into a pool hall and stealing money in Panama City, Florida. In his petition, Gideon claimed he could not afford to pay a lawyer to file the petition for him. He also claimed that his conviction and sentencing to a five-year term in prison violated the due process clause of the Fourteenth Amendment to the Constitution. Gideon reported that when he asked for the assistance of a lawyer at the time of his trial, the court refused. The heart of Gideon's petition was his claim that "to try a poor man for a felony without giving him a lawyer was to deprive him of due process of law."

Gideon was successful—with the help of the American Civil Liberties Union (ACLU) and its appointed lawyer, Abe Fortas, whom President Johnson later appointed to the Supreme Court. The Court decided in Gideon's favor, stating that persons accused of felonies who can show they are unable to afford a lawyer must be given one at the government's expense. Represented by an attorney appointed by the court, Gideon was retried and found to be innocent of the charges.

1. 316 U.S. 455, 62 S.Ct. 1252, 86 L.Ed. 1595 (1942).
2. 372 U.S. 335, 83 S.Ct. 792, 9 L.Ed.2d 799 (1963). A biography

of Clarence Earl Gideon and the significance of this case is presented in Anthony Lewis, *Gideon's Trumpet* (New York: Vintage Books, 1964).

Forgery

FORGERY
The false or unauthorized signature of a document, or the false making of a document, with the intent to defraud.

The fraudulent making or altering of any writing that changes the legal rights and liabilities of another is **forgery**. If, without authorization, Pollock signs Bennett's name to the back of a check made out to Bennett, Pollock is committing forgery. Forgery also includes changing trademarks, falsifying public records, counterfeiting, and altering a legal document. Even when a person is authorized to sign another's name, forgery can result, as the following case illustrates.

Case 4.4
UNITED STATES v. McGOVERN
United States Court of Appeals, Third Circuit, 1981.
661 F.2d 27.

FACTS The plaintiff, McGovern, and his friend, Scull, agreed to have McGovern purchase $2,400 worth of traveler's checks in New York. The checks were to be cashed by Scull in Pennsylvania, where he would forge McGovern's name, and then McGovern would report the

checks stolen. According to plan, McGovern purchased the checks, and then he and Scull went to Pennsylvania, where Scull signed McGovern's name to the checks as he cashed them. McGovern reported the checks stolen and requested (and received) $2,400 in reissued checks from the New York bank. McGovern was eventually apprehended and convicted of transporting forged traveler's checks across state lines. Claiming that forgery did not exist because he had authorized Scull to sign the checks, McGovern appealed the decision.

Clarence Earl Gideon

Case 4.4—Continued

ISSUE Does signing a person's name to a traveler's check constitute forgery when the person signing has been authorized to do so by the initial purchaser of the checks?

DECISION Yes. The lower court's ruling was affirmed.

REASON The court held that "not only does the purchaser's agreement [signed by McGovern with the issuing bank in New York when he purchased the checks] deny the purchaser the right to authorize another to sign his name, but such authorization and signature deceives the person cashing it. When a person signs a traveler's check acting as an imposter, his unauthorized signature, accompanied by the intent to defraud, constitutes forgery." McGovern did not have the power to authorize Scull to sign the traveler's checks, so clearly Scull's signatures were unauthorized. The court further stated that an intent to defraud was clear because the checks were signed in accordance with a plan to later report the checks stolen.

Robbery

In common law, **robbery** was defined as forcefully and unlawfully taking personal property of any value from another. The use of force or fear is usually necessary for

ROBBERY
Theft from a person, accompanied by force or fear of force.

an act of theft to be considered a robbery. Thus, pickpocketing is not robbery because the action is unknown to the victim. Typically, states have more severe penalties for *aggravated* robbery—robbery by use of a deadly weapon.

Burglary

BURGLARY
The unlawful entry into a building with the intent to commit theft. (Some state statutes expand this to include the intent to commit any crime.)

In common law, **burglary** was defined as breaking and entering the dwelling of another at night, with the intent to commit a felony. Originally the definition was aimed at protecting an individual's home and its occupants. Most state statutes have eliminated some of the requirements found in the common law definition. The time at which the breaking and entering occurs, for example, is usually immaterial. Some statutes frequently omit the element of breaking, and some states do not require that the building be a dwelling. Aggravated burglary, which is defined as burglary with the use of a deadly weapon or burglary of a dwelling, or both, incurs a greater penalty.

Larceny

LARCENY
The act of taking another person's personal property unlawfully. Some states classify larceny as either grand or petit, depending on the property's value.

Any person who wrongfully or fraudulently takes and carries away another person's personal property is guilty of **larceny**. Larceny includes the fraudulent intent to permanently deprive an owner of property. Many business-related larcenies entail fraudulent conduct.

The place from which physical property is taken is generally immaterial. Statutes usually prescribe a stiffer sentence for property taken from buildings such as banks or warehouses, however. Whereas robbery involves force or fear, larceny does not. Therefore, pickpocketing is larceny, not robbery.

As society becomes more complex, the question often arises as to what is property. In most states, the definition of property that is subject to larceny statutes has expanded. Stealing computer programs may constitute larceny even though the "property" consists of magnetic impulses. Stealing "computer time" can also constitute larceny (see Chapter 37). Trade secrets can be subject to larceny statutes. Stealing the use of telephone wires by the device known as a blue box is subject to larceny statutes. So, too, is the theft of natural gas. These types of larceny are often covered by "theft of services" statutes in many jurisdictions.

The common law distinction between grand and petit larceny depends on the value of the property taken. Many states have abolished this distinction, but in those which have not, grand larceny is a felony and petit larceny a misdemeanor.

Obtaining Goods by False Pretenses

It is a criminal act to obtain goods by means of false pretenses—for example, buying groceries with a check, knowing that one has insufficient funds to cover it. Statutes covering such illegal activities vary widely from state to state.

Receiving Stolen Goods

It is a crime to receive stolen goods. The recipient of such goods need not know the true identity of the owner or the thief. All that is necessary is that the recipient knows or should have known that the goods are stolen, which implies an intent to deprive the owner of those goods.

Embezzlement

When a person entrusted with another person's property or money fraudulently appropriates it, **embezzlement** occurs. Typically, it involves an employee who steals money. Banks face this problem, and so do a number of businesses in which corporate officers or accountants "jimmy" the books to cover up the fraudulent conversion of money for their own benefit. Embezzlement is not larceny because the wrongdoer does not physically take the property from the possession of another, and it is not robbery because force or fear is not used.

It does not matter whether the accused takes the money from the victim or from a third person. If, as the comptroller of a large corporation, Saunders pockets a certain number of checks from third parties that were given to her to deposit into the corporate account, she is embezzling.

The role of intention in establishing whether embezzlement has occurred is emphasized in the following case.

EMBEZZLEMENT
The fraudulent appropriation of money or other property by a person to whom the money or property has been entrusted.

Case 4.5
UNITED STATES v. FAULKNER
United States Court of Appeals, Ninth Circuit, 1981.
638 F.2d 129.

FACTS The defendant (Faulkner), a truck driver, was hauling a load of refrigerators from San Diego to New York for the trucking company that employed him. He departed from his assigned route and stopped in Las Vegas, where he attempted to display and sell some of the refrigerators to a firm. Although the refrigerators never left the truck, in order to display them he had to break the truck's seals, enter the cargo department, and open two refrigerator cartons. The store owner refused to purchase the appliances, and when Faulkner left the store, he was arrested. He was later convicted under federal law for the embezzlement of an interstate shipment. Faulkner appealed, claiming that there were no grounds for the charge since he had never removed any equipment from the truck.

ISSUE Does the charge of embezzlement apply when the property has not been physically removed from the owner's possession?

DECISION Yes. The judgment of the lower court was affirmed.

REASON If a person has possession and control over the property of another and has the *intent* of converting the goods to his or her own use, then embezzlement occurs. By leaving his assigned route in order to sell the refrigerators and keep the proceeds, Faulkner exercised control over the property, with the intent to convert it to his own use.

Arson

The willful and malicious burning of a building (and in some states, personal property) owned by another is the crime of **arson**. In common law, arson applied only to burning down another person's house. The law was designed to protect human life. Today, arson statutes apply to other kinds of buildings.

Every state has a special statute that covers a person burning a building in order to collect insurance. If Allison owns an insured apartment building that is falling apart and sets fire to it himself or pays someone else to do so, he is guilty not only of arson but also of defrauding insurers, which is an attempted larceny. Of course, the insurer need not pay the claim when insurance fraud is proved.

ARSON
The malicious burning of another's dwelling. Some statutes have expanded this to include any real property regardless of ownership, and the destruction of property by other means—for example, by explosion.

Mail Fraud

It is a federal crime to use the mails to defraud the public. Illegal use of the mails must involve: (1) mailing or causing someone else to mail a writing for the purpose of executing a scheme to defraud, and (2) a contemplated or an organized scheme to defraud by false pretenses. If, for example, Johnson advertises by mail the sale of a cure for cancer that he knows to be fraudulent because it has no medical validity, he can be prosecuted for fraudulent use of the mails. Federal law also makes it a crime to use a telegram to defraud.

❖ White-Collar Crime

WHITE-COLLAR CRIME
Nonviolent crimes committed by corporations and individuals. Embezzlement and commercial bribery are two examples of white-collar crime.

Although there is no official definition of **white-collar crime,** the term is popularly used to mean an illegal act or series of acts committed by an individual or corporation using some nonviolent means to obtain a personal or business advantage. Usually this kind of crime is committed in the course of a legitimate occupation. So-called white-collar crimes cost the public $50 billion to $120 billion a year.

Since it is impossible to cover the vast range of white-collar crimes, this chapter will cover four areas: (1) computer crimes, (2) bribery, (3) bankruptcy fraud, and (4) corporate crimes.

Computer Crimes

The age of the computer is now upon us. An increasing percentage of business is carried on via computers. Virtually all the government's and most of large businesses' financial transactions are handled by computer. Many of the money transfers from one business to another business, from an individual to a business, from a business to an individual, and from individuals and businesses to and from government involve not the physical circulation of money but rather the changing of digital information within computer memories.

Clearly, the manipulation of computers for personal or business gain is possible. Detection is often difficult. Certain companies, and even the government, have discovered multimillion-dollar thefts only after a significant amount of time has elapsed. Employees of accounting and computer departments have been known to make extra copies of paychecks, transfer money among accounts, and create fictitious insurance policies that pay out dividends. Although a recent study indicates there may be less computer crime than is generally assumed (see the "Business Law in Action" in this chapter), in fact many such crimes are difficult to detect and often go unreported.

Often laws are inadequate to deal with the various computer crimes. Larceny statutes were originally passed to prohibit the theft of *tangible property*. Computer crimes, however, frequently involve computer software (programs), which are intangible.

As mentioned earlier, some states have expanded their definition of property to allow computer crimes to fall within their larceny statutes. In other states, prosecutors have to rely on other criminal statutes. Computer crimes often result in lenient punishments, which has led lawmakers to put forth various proposals to deal with this new type of crime. Clearly, the law involving computer crime is still in its formative stages.

Business Law in Action

Combating Computer Crime

In the movie *War Games*, a teenage genius accessed a military computer system and almost set off World War III. In 1983, in real life, a group of Milwaukee teenagers (the "414 gang") broke into computer systems across the United States. Two years later, the "New Jersey Seven" reached the headlines of the *New York Post*: "Whiz Kids Zap U.S. Satellites." On investigation it was revealed that, although the satellites were still in their places, the seven New Jersey youths had taken liberties with numerous stolen credit-card numbers and enjoyed the use of free telecommunications with the aid of their computer equipment. How did they do it? According to computer-crime expert Donn Parker of SRI International in Menlo Park, California, "In some cases, penetrating computer systems is extremely difficult and takes a great deal of knowledge. . . . In other cases it's as simple as dialing into bulletins and finding the passwords that other kids have left." [1] The access numbers to remote computer systems were probably gathered by "demon dialers"—programs that search the phone system for on-line computers by calling sequentially every phone number within a given area code. Among the credit-card numbers used by the New Jersey youths, however, at least one was obtained in the old

Neal Patrick, a member of the "414" gang, testifies before a Senate commission investigating how hackers are able to break into supposedly secure computer systems.

familiar way: from a charge-slip carbon found in a trash can.

In contrast to these highly publicized computer-raiding activities, most computer crime is not so dramatic. Nor is it committed by teenagers. According to a 1986 study by the National Center for Computer Crime Data in Los Angeles, most computer crimes are committed by much older people—including well-paid professionals and government employees, as well as computer programmers, computer operators, and airline ticketing clerks.[2] Most of the crimes required little electronic sophistication and most fell into the category of "data diddling"—entering false numbers at a keyboard. One of the surprising results of the study was

how few cases of crime it turned up. Although crime data was gathered from 130 prosecutors' offices in 38 states, only 75 computer crimes were included. The Center concluded that computer crimes are either undetected or unreported.

This conclusion underscores a major issue in the business world today: the problem of secrecy. Although the Counterfeit Access Device and Computer Fraud and Abuse Act of 1984 makes it a federal crime to access a computer without prior authorization, how can such crime be prosecuted if it is not reported? And it seems clear to many people that the full extent of computer crime in the United States is unrevealed because business firms are reluctant to disclose the vulnerability of their systems. Companies adversely affected by such

1. As quoted in *Time*, July 29, 1985, p. 21.

2. Reported in *Time*, February 17, 1986, p. 95.

(continued on next page)

Business Law in Action—Continued

crime do not want to publicize the fact because they are afraid customers will doubt the accuracy and security of computer-generated material—a very legitimate fear.

In combating the problem of computer crime, businesses are thus not looking to the courts but toward increasing the security of their computer systems. Many corporations and government agencies have resorted to using passwords, scrambling devices, dial-back services that require ID numbers, audit systems that identify computer users, and so on. Such protection is costly in terms of both money and convenience of computer use, but given the lack of alternatives, it may be a necessary expense for firms doing business in the computer age.

As discussed in the "Business Law in Action," the full extent of computer crime in our business society is unrevealed. Apprehended perpetrators of computer crimes rarely go to trial. Instead, the affected business usually lets the case be plea bargained. Sometimes, for fear of publicity, the business does not report the crime and may be blackmailed into giving the person who committed the crime a reference for another job.

Bribery

Basically, three types of bribery are considered crimes.

1. **Bribery of Public Officials.** The attempt to influence a public official to act in a way that serves a private interest is a crime. As an element of this crime, intent must be present and proved. The bribe can be anything the recipient considers to be valuable. *The commission of the crime of bribery occurs when the bribe is tendered.* The recipient does not have to agree to perform whatever action is desired by the person tendering the bribe, nor does the recipient have to accept the bribe.
2. **Commercial Bribery.** In some states, so-called kickbacks and payoffs from a person working for one company to an individual or individuals employed by another firm are crimes. No public official need be involved. Typically, people make commercial bribes to obtain proprietary information, cover up an inferior product, or secure new business. Industrial espionage sometimes involves commercial bribes. For example, a person in one firm may offer an employee in a competing firm some type of payoff in exchange for trade secrets and pricing schedules.
3. **Bribery of Foreign Officials.** Bribing foreign officials in order to obtain business contracts is a crime. See the "Landmark" in Chapter 37.

Bankruptcy Fraud

When a business finds itself with an oppressive amount of debt, its creditors may seek to have the court adjudge it a bankrupt company, or the individual or business entity may seek voluntary bankruptcy. Today, individuals or businesses can be relieved of oppressive debt by federal law under the Bankruptcy Reform Act of 1978, as amended by the Bankruptcy Amendments and Federal Judgeship Act of 1984 and by the Bankruptcy Judges, United States Trustees, and Family Farmer Bankruptcy Act of 1986 (see Chapter 20). In short, the act requires that the debtor disclose all assets. Typically, a trustee then takes possession of the assets and follows certain rules and procedures in distributing them to creditors.

Numerous white-collar crimes may be committed during the many phases of a bankruptcy proceeding, including the following.

False Claims of Creditors Creditors are required to file their individual claims against the debtor in bankruptcy proceedings. A creditor who files a false claim commits a crime.

Transfer of Property A debtor sometimes fraudulently transfers assets to favored parties before or after the petition for bankruptcy is filed. For example, a company-owned automobile may be "sold" at a bargain price to a trusted friend or relative. Closely related to the crime of fraudulent transfer of property is the crime of fraudulent concealment of property, such as hiding gold coins.

Scam Bankruptcies In a *scam bankruptcy*, a bankruptcy is planned in advance. The perpetrators buy a legitimate business that sells goods that can be sold rapidly, such as jewelry or electronic home-entertainment equipment. They next purchase numerous items on credit and pay off the creditors within a relatively short period of time. This activity continues until the creditors are willing to offer the new owners larger and larger amounts of credit. Finally, the new owners order a very large amount of merchandise on credit, sell it at whatever price is necessary to unload it quickly for cash, and then close down the business. Of course, creditors file an involuntary petition in bankruptcy against the business. The amount the creditors recover, however, is usually very small, and the scam operators are nowhere to be found.

Corporate Crime

Corporations are "artificial" persons created by law. Clearly, they cannot harbor the criminal intent that is required for conviction of a crime, but their officers can. The modern tendency is to hold corporations criminally responsible for their acts or omissions if the assigned penalty is a fine, and if intent either is not an element of the crime or can be implied.

A corporation cannot commit perjury, nor crimes punishable by imprisonment or corporal punishment. When a statute allows a fine in addition to or in place of these penalties, however, a corporation can be convicted of the crime. If, for example, a statute requires that adequate safety equipment be installed on machines, and a corporation fails to meet that requirement—and if the result is the death of a worker—the corporation can be fined for committing criminal manslaughter. In addition, the corporate officers who were in a position to prevent the wrong may be prosecuted under specific federal and state statutes.

❖ How Much White-Collar Crime Is Prosecuted?

Data from a November 1986 study by the Bureau of Justice Statistics indicate that, contrary to popular belief, white-collar crime is not overlooked by the courts. Eighty-eight percent of those arrested are prosecuted, almost three-fourths are convicted of crimes, and almost two-thirds are sentenced to prison. Although less than twenty percent of people convicted of white-collar crimes are sentenced to more than a year in prison (compared to forty percent of those convicted of violent crimes), criminal justice agencies do not seem to be treating white-collar criminals differently to any significant degree.

Allentown prison is a minimum security prison located in Pennsylvania. Many individuals convicted of white-collar crimes serve their time in these types of prisons.

❖ RICO

In 1970, Congress passed the Organized Crime Control Act. It included the Racketeer Influenced and Corrupt Organizations Act, otherwise known as RICO.[6]

In principle, passage of this act was meant to curb the apparently increasing entry of organized crime into the world of legitimate business. The broad language that Congress decided to use for the RICO statute, however, has allowed law enforcement officials throughout the country to apply RICO to cases that have little or nothing to do with organized crime. Supporters of RICO believe that it has become an effective tool for attacking unethical business practices. Its detractors, however, believe that it is too broad in scope.

There are two aspects of RICO—civil and criminal.

Civil RICO

In the event of a violation, the RICO statute permits the government to seek civil penalties, including the divestiture of a defendant's interest in a business or the dissolution of such a business. Perhaps the most controversial section of RICO has to do with the fact that in some cases private individuals are allowed to recover three times their actual loss, plus attorneys' fees, for business injuries caused by a violation of the statute. Plaintiffs have used the RICO statute in numerous commercial fraud cases because of the lure of trebled damages if they win. The most frequent targets of civil RICO lawsuits are insurance companies, employment agencies, commercial banks, and stock brokerage firms.

---

6. 18 U.S.C. 1961–1968 (1976).

In the following case, decided in 1985, the U.S. Supreme Court rejected the requirement (imposed by lower federal courts) that civil RICO plaintiffs had to "prove a distinct racketeering injury" (an injury resulting from organized illegal operations) as a precondition of recovery. The decision established a precedent.

Case 4.6
SEDIMA, S.P.R.L. v. IMREX CO., INC.
United States Supreme Court, 1985.
473 U.S. 479, 105 S.Ct. 3275, 87 L.Ed.2d 346.

FACTS In 1979 a Belgian corporation, Sedima, entered into a contract with another Belgian firm to supply the latter with electronic components. Sedima also formed a joint venture with a U.S. firm, Imrex Company, whereby Imrex would ship the components to Europe and share the proceeds jointly with Sedima. Approximately $8 million in orders had been shipped by Imrex when Sedima concluded that Imrex was fraudulently claiming extra expenses and inflating its bills accordingly—in order to get more than its fair portion of the proceeds. Sedima brought suit against Imrex, alleging, in part, that Imrex had violated section 1962(c) of RICO. Section 1962(c) requires that a private suit under RICO must be based on an injury brought about by the (1) conduct (2) of an enterprise (3) through a pattern (4) of racketeering activity. Sedima claimed an injury of at least $175,000 (the amount of alleged overbilling) and asked for treble damages. Sedima's RICO claims were dismissed by the district court on the ground that Sedima failed to demonstrate it had suffered any "racketeering injury." The appellate court affirmed, and Sedima appealed to the U.S. Supreme Court.

ISSUE Is it necessary to prove that a "racketeering injury" occurred in order for the plaintiff to recover under RICO?

DECISION No. The judgment of the appellate court was reversed. Sedima could recover.

REASON The Court stated that RICO "is to be read broadly." Justice White wrote that "we perceive no distinct 'racketeering injury' requirement. Given that 'racketeering activity' consists of no more and no less than commission of a predicate act, we are initially doubtful about a requirement of a 'racketeering injury' separate from the harm from the predicate acts. . . . Underlying the Court of Appeals' holding was its distress at the 'extraordinary, if not outrageous' uses to which civil RICO has been put. Instead of being used against mobsters and organized criminals, it has become a tool for everyday fraud cases brought against 'respected and legitimate "enterprises." ' Yet Congress wanted to reach both 'legitimate' and 'illegitimate' enterprises. The former enjoy neither an inherent incapacity for criminal activity nor immunity from its consequences."

Criminal RICO

It is a federal crime (1) to use income obtained from racketeering activity to purchase any interest in an enterprise, (2) to acquire or maintain an interest in an enterprise via racketeering activity, (3) to conduct or participate in the affairs of an enterprise through racketeering activity, or (4) to conspire to do any of the preceding.

Most of the criminal RICO offenses have little, if anything, to do with normal business activities, for they involve gambling, arson, and extortion. But securities fraud (involving the sale of stocks and bonds) and mail fraud are also criminal RICO violations. An aggressive prosecuting attorney may attempt to show that any business fraud constitutes racketeering activity.

An individual found guilty of a criminal RICO violation is subject to a fine of up to $25,000 per violation and imprisonment for up to twenty years.

❖ Chapter Summary: Criminal Law

Definition	Criminal law is concerned with acts against society for which society seeks redress in the form of punishment.
Criminal Liability	Two elements are necessary to establish criminal liability: 1. The performance of a prohibited act (the *actus reus* or "guilty act"), and 2. The intention to commit a prohibited act (the *mens rea* or "evil intent").
Defenses to Criminal Liability	1. Infancy. 2. Intoxication. 3. Insanity. 4. Mistake. 5. Consent. 6. Duress. 7. Justifiable use of force. 8. Entrapment. 9. Statute of limitations. 10. Immunity.
Classification of Crimes	1. *Felonies*—Serious crimes punishable by death or by imprisonment in a federal or state penitentiary. Felonies are classified by degrees of seriousness. Examples of felonies: Homicide, robbery, and arson. 2. *Misdemeanors*—Crimes punishable by a fine or by confinement up to a year. Misdemeanors are sometimes defined as offenses where incarceration takes place in a local jail instead of a penitentiary. Examples of misdemeanors: Public intoxication, prostitution, and trespass. 3. *Violations*—Petty offenses (such as traffic violations) that are often not classified as crimes. Violations may be punishable by fine or imprisonment (for a few days), or both.
Crimes Affecting Business	1. *Forgery*—The fraudulent making or alteration of any writing that changes the legal liability of another. 2. *Robbery*—Forcefully and unlawfully taking personal property of any value from another. 3. *Burglary*—Defined under common law as breaking and entering the dwelling of another at night with the intent to commit a felony. Today, the time of the breaking and entering is usually immaterial, and in some states there need not be a breaking into a building, nor does the building need to be a dwelling. 4. *Larceny*—Wrongfully or fraudulently taking and carrying away the personal property of another. 5. *Obtaining goods by false pretenses*—Such as paying for a purchase with a bad check. 6. *Receiving stolen goods*—This is a crime if the recipient knows or should have known the goods are stolen. 7. *Embezzlement*—The fraudulent conversion of property or money by a person to whom the property or money is entrusted. 8. *Arson*—The willful and malicious burning of a building (and in some states, personal property) owned by another. 9. *Use of the mails to defraud*—Must involve (a) mailing or causing someone else to mail a writing for the purpose of executing a scheme to defraud, and (b) a contemplated or an organized scheme to defraud by false pretenses.
White-Collar Crimes	1. *Computer crimes*—The wrongful manipulation of computers for personal or business gain. 2. *Bribery*—Payment made to a person for the purpose of influencing that person's decisions. 3. *Bankruptcy fraud*—The use of federal bankruptcy laws to defraud creditors.

❖ Questions and Case Problems

4-1. Determine from the facts below what type of crime (larceny, burglary, embezzlement, arson, etc.) has been committed.

    (a) Jerry is walking through an amusement park when his wallet, with $2,000 in it, is "picked" from his pocket.

    (b) Axel and Gordon become involved in a shouting argument. Axel knocks Gordon down, causing a serious head injury to Gordon.

    (c) David continually crosses Martha's back yard without permission, despite Martha's notice to David to stay off her land.

    (d) Harry walks into a camera shop. Without force and without the owner noticing, Harry walks out of the store with a camera.

4-2. The following situations are similar (the theft of Joanne's television set), yet they represent three different crimes. Identify the three crimes, noting the differences among them.

    (a) While passing Joanne's house one night, Sarah sees a portable television set left unattended on Joanne's lawn. Sarah takes the television set, carries it home, and tells everyone she owns it.

    (b) While passing Joanne's house one night, Sarah sees Joanne outside with a portable television set. Holding Joanne at gunpoint, Sarah forces her to give up the set. Then Sarah runs away with it.

    (c) While passing Joanne's house one night, Sarah sees a portable television set in a window. Sarah breaks the front-door lock, enters, and leaves with the set.

4-3. Of the following crimes, which one (or ones) necessarily involves illegal activity on the part of more than one person?

    (a) Bribery

    (b) Forgery

    (c) Embezzlement

    (d) Larceny

    (e) Receiving stolen property

4-4. James, an undercover police officer, stops Laura on a busy street. James offers to sell Laura an expensive wristwatch for a fraction of its value. After some questioning by Laura, James admits that the watch is stolen property, although he says he was not the thief. Laura pays for and receives the wristwatch and is immediately arrested by James for receiving stolen property. At trial, Laura contends entrapment. What is the result of the trial?

4-5. Joe Stahl worked the late shift at a store. The store owner had instructed him that, whenever a certain amount of money accumulated in the cash register, Stahl was to insert all but $50 into a drop-box. The drop-box was always kept locked, and only the owner had a key to it. One night Stahl disappeared, as did the lock-box. When Stahl was convicted of embezzling funds he had taken from the drop-box, he appealed, asserting that he could not have committed the crime of embezzlement since the funds in the drop-box had never been entrusted to him by his employer. Is Stahl correct? [State

v. Stahl, 93 N.M. 62, 596 P.2d 275 (1979)]

4-6. In 1965 Rybicki failed to pay the federal government the total amount of income tax he owed. Attempts by the IRS to collect the tax proved fruitless. Therefore, the IRS obtained (through lawful means) a tax lien on Rybicki's personal property, which included his truck. In February 1967, Rybicki's wife, upon hearing the truck's motor, awakened her sleeping husband. Wielding a shotgun, Rybicki went to his front door and told the two men who were attempting to take his truck to stop. Rybicki claimed that he did not know the two men were IRS agents. Subsequently, the federal government indicted Rybicki for obstructing justice. Can Rybicki be held criminally liable if he did not know that the men were IRS agents performing their duty? [United States v. Rybicki, 403 F.2d 599 (6th Cir. 1968)]

4-7. Seekford rented a car in Utah and drove with some friends to Texas. After they arrived in Texas, Seekford assured his friends he would return the rented car. The car was never returned to the rental agency, however; it was found abandoned several months later in Texas. The state of Utah brought suit against Seekford, who was convicted of larceny. Seekford appealed, alleging that since the criminal act had taken place in Texas, the state of Utah did not have jurisdiction. Under Utah state law, a person is subject to prosecution in Utah for an offense committed either within or outside the state, if the offense is either wholly or partly committed within the state. What element of the offense could have been committed in Utah? (Hint: Remember that two elements are necessary for the commission of a crime—criminal intent and a criminal act.) [State v. Seekford, 638 P.2d 525 (Utah 1981)]

4-8. Khoury went to a department store, spent some time shopping, and eventually filled a large, empty chandelier box with approximately $900 worth of tools. When he went to the check-out counter, the cashier indicated she wanted to look inside the box before accepting Khoury's payment for the chandelier. Khoury then pushed the cart back into the store and departed from the premises. Khoury was convicted of grand larceny by the trial court. On appeal, Khoury alleged that, since he hadn't actually removed any goods from the store, he had not committed larceny. Is Khoury correct? [People v. Khoury, 108 Cal.App.3d Supp. 1, 166 Cal.Rptr. 705 (1980)]

4-9. Lund was working on his doctoral dissertation in statistics at Virginia Polytechnic Institute in Blacksburg, Virginia. He was required to use the computer facilities at the university. His faculty adviser neglected to arrange for the use of the computer. Nonetheless, Lund went ahead and used it without obtaining proper authorization. At trial, Lund was convicted of grand larceny for obtaining approximately $30,000 worth of computer services without authorization. Four faculty members testified during the trial that computer time "probably would have been" or "would have been" assigned to Lund if properly requested. Lund appealed his conviction. What was the result? [Lund v. Commonwealth of Virginia, 217 Va. 688, 232 S.E.2d 745 (1977)]

Unit Two

Contracts

❖ Why We Study Contract Law

Noted legal scholar Roscoe Pound once said that "The social order rests upon the stability and predictability of conduct, of which keeping promises is a large item." [1] Contract law deals with, among other things, the formation and keeping of promises (in Latin, *pacta sunt servanda*—agreement shall be kept). The law encourages competent parties to form contracts for lawful objectives. No aspect of modern life is entirely free of contractual relationships. Indeed, even the ordinary consumer in his or her daily activities acquires rights and obligations based on contract law. You acquire rights and obligations, for example, when you borrow money to make a purchase or when you buy a stereo or house. Contract law is designed to provide stability and predictability, as well as certainty, for both buyers and sellers in the marketplace.

Why do we study contract law? Simply because it is the framework for all commercial law. The law described in the following chapters is the basis for much of the law in more specialized areas, such as the sale of goods. You will learn that transactions governed by statutes, such as the Uniform Commercial Code, can nonetheless be changed by express terms in a contract between parties.

---

1. 3 Pound, Jurisprudence, 162 (1959).

Chapter 5

Nature and Classification

As Arthur Corbin, an eminent scholar in the field of contract law, observed, "new conditions and new interests" continually fashion the law. Like other types of law, contract law reflects our social values, interests, and expectations at a given point in time. It shows, for example, to what extent our society allows people to make promises or commitments that are legally binding. It shows what excuses our society accepts for breaking such promises. And it shows what promises are considered to be contrary to public policy and therefore legally void. If the promise is against the interests of society as a whole, it will be invalidated. Also, if it was made by a child or an insane person, or on the basis of false information, a question will arise as to whether the promise should be enforced. Resolving such questions is the essence of contract law.

In the legal environment of business, questions and disputes concerning **contracts** arise daily. Although aspects of contract law vary from state to state, much of it is based on common law. The Restatement of the Law of Contracts, now in its second edition, is a compilation of the common law relating to contracts. The creation and importance of the Restatement is the subject of the "Landmark" in this chapter.

> *"Life marches on, with new conditions and new interests, causing constant judicial development."*
>
> Arthur L. Corbin, 1874–1967
> *(American legal scholar and educator)*

CONTRACT
An agreement affecting the legal relationships between two or more parties.

❖ The Function of Contracts

Contract law assures the parties to private agreements that the promises they make will be enforceable. Sometimes the promises exchanged create *moral* rather than *legal* obligations. Failure to perform a moral obligation, such as an agreement to take a friend to lunch, does not usually create a legal liability. Some promises may create both a moral and a legal obligation, such as a father's promise to pay for his daughter's college education.

Clearly, many promises are kept because of a sense of duty, or because keeping them is in the mutual self-interest of the parties involved, not because the **promisor** (the person making the promise) or the **promisee** (the person to whom the promise is made) is conscious of the rules of contract law. Nevertheless, the rules of contract law are often followed in business agreements in order to avoid potential problems.

By supplying procedures for enforcing private agreements, contract law provides an essential condition for the existence of a market economy. Without a legal framework for reasonably assured expectations within which to plan and venture, busi-

PROMISOR
A person who makes a promise.

PROMISEE
A person to whom a promise is made.

Landmark in the Law

Restatement (Second) of the Law of Contracts

In the twentieth century, there has been a general movement toward codifying the law through various "uniform" acts. The most significant act is the Uniform Commercial Code or UCC (discussed in other "Landmarks" in the text). When adopted by a state, these acts become the statutory law of that state and replace the common law relating to the transactions covered by the uniform acts.

Notwithstanding this movement toward uniform, statutory laws, the common law remains a significant source of legal authority. To summarize and clarify common-law rules, the American Law Institute (ALI)—consisting of legal scholars and practitioners of the law—drafted and published compilations of the common law. There are Restatements of Law—as these compilations are called—in the areas of contracts, torts, agency, trusts, property, restitution, security, judgments, and conflict of laws. The Restatements follow a similar format: each is divided into sections, with each section presenting a general statement about a legal principle, followed by a discussion. References are made to cases and decisions that illustrate how the point of law under consideration works. The Restatements, which generally summarize the common-law rules followed by most states, do not in themselves have the force of law but are a secondary source of legal analysis and opinion.

The Restatement of the Law of Contracts, published in May 1932, was the first Restatement to be completed by the ALI. It was a highly successful, authoritative exposition on the common law of contracts. Two major legal scholars who participated in the project—Samuel Williston and Arthur L. Corbin (see the "Profile" in this chapter)—helped bring about its success. Williston was the chief reporter in drafting the Restatement, and Corbin acted as a special adviser and the reporter on remedies.

Thirty years later, a second edition of the Restatement was undertaken. This revision—called the Restatement (Second) of the Law of Contracts—was completed in 1979. A number of changes were inspired by the adoption of the UCC by virtually all the states. Like the UCC, the Restatement (Second) reflects the movement from precise rules of law to broader, more flexible legal standards that came about in contract law in the years following the original Restatement's publication. The concept of "good faith," for example, which permeates the UCC, is also embraced by the Restatement (Second). In addition, the Restatement (Second) made numerous style changes. It added extensive commentary explaining the black-letter law, clarified the analysis of points of law where necessary, and included a description and analysis of the development of statutory law since the original Restatement had been issued. Opinions of leading authorities in the various areas of contract law were also included in the Reporters' Notes.

Like its predecessor, the Restatement (Second) does not have the force of law. But because it expresses the reasoning and judgment of some of the leading scholars in contract law, it is frequently used by the courts as a guide in the judicial decision-making process. Since it is a significant source, the Restatement (Second) will be referred to frequently in the following chapters.

nesspersons would be able to rely only on the good faith of others. Duty and good faith are usually sufficient, but when price changes or adverse economic factors make it costly to comply with a promise, these elements may not be enough. Contract law is necessary in order to ensure compliance with a promise or to entitle the innocent party to some form of relief.

The Basic Requirements of a Contract

The following list describes the requirements of a contract. Each will be explained more fully in the chapters indicated.

1. **Agreement.** An agreement includes an *offer* and an *acceptance*. One party must offer to enter into a legal agreement, and another party must accept the terms of the offer. (Chapter 6)

2. **Consideration.** Any promises made by parties must be supported by legally sufficient and bargained-for *consideration* (something of value received or promised, in order to convince a person to make a deal). (Chapter 6)

3. **Contractual Capacity.** Both parties entering into the contract must have the contractual *capacity* to do so; the law must recognize them as possessing characteristics that qualify them as competent parties. (Chapter 7)

4. **Legality.** The contract's purpose must be to accomplish some goal that is *legal* and not against public policy. (Chapter 7)

5. **Genuineness of Assent.** The apparent consent of both parties must be *genuine*. (Chapter 8)

6. **Form.** The contract must be in whatever *form* the law requires; for example, some contracts must be in writing to be enforceable. (Chapter 8)

The first four items in this list are formally known as the *elements of a contract*. The last two are known as *defenses to the formation or the enforcement of a contract*.

❖ Definition of a Contract

A *contract* is an agreement that can be enforced in a court of law or equity. It is formed by two or more parties who agree to perform or refrain from performing some act now or in the future. Generally, contract disputes arise when there is a promise of future performance. A **promise** is a declaration that something either will or will not happen in the future. If the contractual promise is not fulfilled, the party who made it is subject to the sanctions of a court of law or equity (see Chapter 10). That party may be required to pay money damages for failing to perform; in limited instances, the party may be required to perform the promised act.

"A promise made is a debt unpaid."

Robert William Service, 1874–1958
(Canadian writer and poet)

❖ Types of Contracts

There are numerous types of contracts, and each has a legal significance as to formation, enforceability, or performance. The best method of explaining each is to compare one type of contract with another.

Bilateral versus Unilateral Contracts

Every contract involves at least two parties. The **offeror** is the party making the offer. The **offeree** is the party to whom the offer is made. The offeror always promises to do or not to do something and thus is also a promisor. Whether the contract is classified as *unilateral* or *bilateral* depends on what the offeree must do to accept the offer and to bind the offeror to a contract.

If to accept the offer the offeree must only promise to perform, the contract is a **bilateral contract**. Hence, a bilateral contract is a "promise for a promise." If the offer is phrased so that the offeree can accept only by completing the contract performance, the contract is a **unilateral contract**. Hence, a unilateral contract is a "promise for an act." A classic example of a unilateral contract is as follows: Joe says to Celia, "If you walk across the Brooklyn Bridge, I'll give you $10." Joe promises

PROMISE
A declaration that binds the person who makes it (promisor) to do or not to do a certain act. The person to whom the promise is made (promisee) has a right to expect or demand the performance of some particular thing.

OFFEROR
A person who makes an offer.

OFFEREE
A person to whom an offer is made.

BILATERAL CONTRACT
A contract that includes the exchange of a promise for a promise.

UNILATERAL CONTRACT
A contract that includes the exchange of a promise for an act.

Profile

Arthur L. Corbin (1874–1967)

Arthur Linton Corbin was born in 1874 in Cripple Creek, Colorado; he died in 1967 in New Haven, Connecticut. During the course of his long and productive career, Corbin became a foremost scholar and leading authority in the field of American contract law. The fact that "Corbin on Contracts" is now a byword in the halls of law schools throughout the country testifies to his influence.

For nearly fifty years, Corbin was associated with the law school at Yale, first as a student and then as a member of the law faculty. During his many years there, he became widely respected not only for his superb teaching and scholarly abilities, but also for the reforms he implemented to improve Yale's law school. He is credited with introducing the case method of teaching law, as well as creating a full-time law faculty and initiating new recruitment procedures to ensure a better-trained and more mature student body at Yale.

Throughout his life, Corbin fully embraced the view that legal principles, if they were to be appropriate and effective, should be flexible enough to adjust to a changing social context. Corbin didn't abandon legal rules (or *standards*, as he preferred to call them), but he felt such standards should not be regarded as inflexible. Corbin stressed that although the formation and application of general principles are essential to the law, such principles can only be "tentative, working rules, the value of which depends upon the industry and the intelligence of the men who made them, and upon the changes in time and circumstance since they were made." [1]

Corbin's legal pragmatism, or practical approach to the law, is evident in his approach to contract law. The purpose of contract law, according to Corbin, is the "realization of reasonable expectations that have been induced by the making of a promise." What constitutes "reasonable expectations" necessarily depends on the prevailing customs in the society in which the promise was made. For this reason, Corbin felt that when faced with contractual disputes, judges should place the contract in question within its social context and should then look at the intention of the parties within that context before deciding whether a contract exists or has been breached. This "contextualization" of the law—emphasizing what is a reasonable action or expectation in a given set of circumstances—is at the heart of Corbin's methodology. The influence of this approach to contract law is evident in the first and second Restatements of the Law of Contracts and in Article 2 of the Uniform Commercial Code, projects on which he worked in an advisory capacity and which all bear his imprint.

Corbin authored numerous monographs and books on contract law, the most outstanding and widely known being his six-volume treatise on the law of contracts. First published in 1950 and since revised, this opus has become a landmark in the development of American contract law.

1. Arthur L. Corbin, "Principles of Law and Their Evolution," 64 *Yale Law Journal* (December 1954), p. 8.

"What burns me up is that the answer is right here somewhere staring us in the face."

Drawing by Robt. Day; © 1950, 1978, The New Yorker Magazine.

to pay only if Celia walks the entire span of the bridge. Only upon Celia's complete crossing does she accept Joe's offer to pay $10. If she chooses not to undertake the walk, there are no legal consequences.

A problem arises in unilateral contracts when the promisor attempts to revoke (cancel) the offer after the promisee has begun performance but before the act has been completed. The promisee can accept the offer only upon full performance, and offers are normally revocable (capable of being taken back, or canceled) until accepted. The modern-day view, however, is that the offer becomes irrevocable once performance has begun or has been substantially completed. Thus, even though the offer has not yet been accepted, the offeror is prohibited from revoking it for a reasonable time period.

Suppose Roberta offers to buy Ed's sailboat, moored in San Francisco, upon delivery of the boat to Roberta's dock in Newport Beach, 300 miles south of San Francisco. Ed rigs the boat and sets sail. Shortly before his arrival at Newport Beach, Ed receives a radio message from Roberta withdrawing her offer. Roberta's offer is part of a unilateral contract, and only Ed's delivery of the sailboat at her dock is an acceptance. Ordinarily, her revocation would terminate the offer, but since substantial performance—sailing almost 300 miles—had been completed by Ed, under the modern-day view her offer is irrevocable. Ed can deliver the boat and bind Roberta to the contract.

The problem of substantial performance in unilateral contracts often arises in the sale of real estate. A broker, for example, may invest substantial effort in finding a buyer for someone who has listed his or her property for sale and then learn that the seller is canceling the brokerage agreement. The following case illustrates such a situation.

Case 5.1
MARCHIONDO v. SCHECK
Supreme Court of New Mexico, 1967.
78 N.M. 440, 432 P.2d 405.

FACTS   Scheck arranged with Marchiondo, a real-estate broker, for Marchiondo to sell certain property for him. The brokerage agreement, which was in writing, contained a unilateral offer on the part of Scheck that he would pay a commission to Marchiondo if the latter sold the property within six days. Marchiondo found a prospective buyer for the property and, on the afternoon of the sixth day, succeeded in having the buyer sign a purchaser's acceptance of Scheck's offer to sell. On the morning of the sixth day, however, Scheck revoked his offer in writing. Marchiondo sued Scheck for breach of contract. When the trial court dismissed the complaint, Marchiondo appealed.

ISSUE   Given the substantial performance undertaken by Marchiondo, can Scheck revoke his offer, even though a unilateral contract comes into existence only upon the completion of the contemplated act (in this case, the sale of the property)?

DECISION   No. The judgment of the trial court was reversed.

REASON   The court held that partial performance on the part of Marchiondo had transformed this unilateral contract into an option contract or contract with a condition, which made the offer irrevocable during the six-day period. If Marchiondo had not begun the performance invited by the offer, Scheck could have revoked his offer without legal consequence. Since the broker had undertaken substantial performance, however, Scheck could not cancel the brokerage agreement.

Express versus Implied Contracts

EXPRESS CONTRACT
A contract that is oral and/or written (as opposed to an implied contract).

IMPLIED-IN-FACT CONTRACT
A contract formed in whole or in part from the conduct of the parties (as opposed to an express contract).

An **express contract** is one in which the terms of the agreement are fully and explicitly stated in words, oral or written. A signed lease for an apartment or a house is an express written contract. If a classmate calls you on the phone and agrees to buy your textbooks from last semester for $50, an express oral contract has been made.

A contract that is implied from the conduct of the parties is called an **implied-in-fact contract,** or an implied contract. This contract differs from an express contract in that the *conduct* of the parties, rather than their words, creates and defines the terms of the contract. For example, suppose you need a tax consultant or an accountant to fill out your tax return this year. You look through the Yellow Pages and find both an accountant and a tax consultant at an office in your neighborhood, so you drop by to see them. You go into the office and explain your problem, and they tell you what their fees are. The next day you return, giving the secretary all the necessary information and documents, such as canceled checks, W-2 forms, and so on. You say nothing expressly to the secretary; rather, you walk out the door.

Nonetheless, you have entered into an implied-in-fact contract to pay the tax consultant and accountant the usual and reasonable fees for their services. The contract is implied by your conduct and by their conduct. They expect to be paid for completing your tax return. By bringing in the records they will need to do the work, you have implied an intent to pay them.

Steps Necessary for an Implied-in-Fact Contract   The following three steps establish an implied-in-fact contract:

1.   The plaintiff furnished some service or property.
2.   The plaintiff expected to be paid for that service or property, and the defendant knew or should have known that payment was expected (by using the objective-theory-of-contracts test, discussed next).
3.   The defendant had a chance to reject the services or property and did not.

Objective Theory of Contracts   The intent or apparent intent to enter into an express or implied-in-fact contract is of prime importance in the formation of the contract. This intent is determined by what is called the **objective theory of contracts,** not by the personal or subjective intent, or belief, of a party. This is illustrated by the previous tax-preparation example. The theory is that a party's intention to enter into a contract is judged by outward, objective facts as interpreted by a *reasonable* offeree (one to whom the offer is being made), rather than by the party's own secret, subjective intentions. Objective facts include (1) what the party (offeror) said when entering into the contract, (2) how the party (offeror) acted or appeared, and (3) the circumstances surrounding the transaction.

Courts need verifiable evidence in order to determine whether a contract has been made, so they usually rely only on objective factors (facts, conduct, and circumstances) when passing judgment in a contract dispute.

In the following case, which illustrates a court's use of the objective theory of contracts, the court reviewed the conduct and circumstances surrounding a transaction in order to determine whether an express or an implied-in-fact contract existed.

OBJECTIVE THEORY OF CONTRACTS
The view taken by American law that contracting parties shall only be bound by terms that can actually be inferred from promises made. Contract law does not examine a contracting party's subjective intent or underlying motive.

Case 5.2
MOORE v. KUEHN
Missouri Court of Appeals, 1980.
602 S.W.2d 713.

FACTS   James and Margaret Kuehn asked George Moore to submit a written estimate for work needed to repair a damaged building. Moore submitted a proposal for $7,600, but the Kuehns did not sign it, informing Moore that they wanted more time to look over the proposal before agreeing to it. James Kuehn, however, told Moore that the roof should be fixed and to "get on it," whereupon Moore began and subsequently completed the repairs suggested in the proposal, without objection by the Kuehns. The Kuehns never signed the proposal. When Moore requested payment, the Kuehns informed Moore that they

could pay him only $5,500. Moore sued for the balance plus related court costs, and was awarded $2,531. The Kuehns appealed, claiming no contract was ever entered into.

ISSUE   Did a contract exist between Moore and the Kuehns?

DECISION   Yes. The Court of Appeals affirmed the judgment of the trial court and deemed that under the circumstances, an implied-in-fact contract had been created.

REASON   The court based its judgment on the objective theory of contract formation. Under this theory, when one party argues that there was no intent to form a contract, the court will look to what was said, the conduct of the

Case 5.2—Continued

parties, and all the surrounding circumstances. The court began by noting that it is well settled that a written offer may be orally accepted. Since Moore's written proposal was the only offer Kuehn could have accepted when he told Moore to "get on it," the terms of the offer controlled and a contract was established. Further, the Kuehns's silent acquiescence and acceptance of Moore's comple- tion of the other repair work in the proposal constituted an implied acceptance of the contract as it related to those items. Since the Kuehns benefited from Moore's performance, their refusal to sign the proposal did not overcome their implied acceptance of the contract, par- ticularly in light of the fact that they never questioned any of the work, and even cooperated with Moore at one point.

Quasi-Contracts, or Contracts Implied in Law

QUASI-CONTRACT
An obligation or contract imposed by law, in the absence of agreement, to prevent unjust enrichment. Sometimes referred to as an implied-in-law contract (a legal fiction) to distinguish it from an implied-in-fact contract.

Quasi-contracts, or contracts *implied in law,* should be distinguished from contracts *implied in fact.* Quasi-contracts, as their name suggests, are not true contracts. They arise in order to achieve justice rather than from a mutual agreement between the parties. A quasi-contract is imposed on the parties in order to avoid *unjust enrichment.* Unjust enrichment occurs when people profit or enrich themselves inequitably at the expense of others. Quasi-contracts are equitable, rather than contractual, in nature.

The quasi-contract is, in essence, a legal fiction. It is based on neither an express promise by the defendant to pay for the benefit received nor the conduct of the defendant implying such a promise. Indeed, it is possible that a recipient of a benefit (the defendant) is even unaware that any benefit has been conferred upon him or her.

An implied-in-fact contract is a true contract. Through their conduct, both parties have expressed agreement to its terms. The only way an implied-in-fact contract differs from an express contract is in its lack of express words or writings. In an implied-in-law contract (a quasi-contract), the parties have not expressed agreement through words or conduct; thus the court cannot imply that a contract has been formed. Rather, the court creates a fictional contract for reasons of social policy.

Examples of Quasi-Contracts Suppose Diana enters into a contract with Dick, agreeing to work for Dick for one year. At the end of the year, she is to be paid $18,000. Diana works for ten months and then leaves voluntarily, without cause. Dick refuses to pay her for the ten months she worked, so Diana sues in quasi-contract for the value of services rendered. Will the court allow Diana to recover her salary for the ten months worked? Very likely, yes—minus any damages caused to Dick by her early departure.[1]

In another example, a vacationing doctor is driving down the highway and comes upon Emerson lying unconscious on the side of the road. The doctor renders medical aid that saves Emerson's life. Although the injured, unconscious Emerson did not solicit the medical aid and was not aware that the aid had been rendered, Emerson received a valuable benefit and the requirements for a quasi-contract have been fulfilled.

---

1. Britton v. Turner, 6 N.H. 481 (1834).

A Limitation on Quasi-Contracts   Although quasi-contracts exist to prevent unjust enrichment, situations exist where the party obtaining the unjust enrichment is not liable. Basically, the quasi-contractual principle cannot be invoked by the party who has conferred a benefit on someone else unnecessarily or as a result of misconduct or negligence. Consider the following example. You take your car to the local car wash and ask to have it run through the washer and to have the gas tank filled. While it is being washed, you go to a nearby shopping center for two hours. In the meantime, one of the workers at the carwash has mistakenly believed that your car is the one that he is supposed to hand wax. When you come back, you are presented with a bill for a full tank of gas, a wash job, and a hand wax. Clearly, a benefit has been conferred on you. But this benefit has been conferred because of a mistake by the carwash employee. You have not received an *unjust* benefit under these circumstances. People cannot normally be forced to pay for benefits "thrust" upon them.

The doctrine of quasi-contract generally cannot be used when there is a contract that covers the area in controversy. For example, Martinez contracts with Stevenson to deliver a furnace to a building project owned by Richards. Stevenson goes bankrupt without paying Martinez. Martinez cannot collect from Richards in quasi-contract, because Martinez had an existing contract with Stevenson.

The following case illustrates the philosophy behind the creation and enforcement of a quasi-contract and the limitation of its use when there is an express contract covering the area in controversy.

Case 5.3
INDUSTRIAL LIFT TRUCK SERVICE CORP. v. MITSUBISHI INTERNATIONAL CORPORATION

Appellate Court of Illinois, First District, Fourth Division, 1982.
104 Ill. App. 3d 357, 60 Ill. Dec. 100, 432 N.E. 2d 999.

FACTS   In 1973, and again in 1976, an agreement was executed between Industrial Lift (IL) and Mitsubishi calling for IL to purchase forklift trucks from Mitsubishi and to use its best efforts to service and sell the trucks, and allowing Mitsubishi to terminate the agreement without just cause by giving ninety days' notice. From 1973 to 1977, IL allegedly became the nation's largest dealer of Mitsubishi forklift trucks. During this period, IL made design changes in the truck to better suit the American market, design changes that Mitsubishi did not request but later incorporated into the trucks it sold to other dealers. In 1978, Mitsubishi terminated the agreement. IL sued under quasi-contract principles to recover the benefits conferred upon Mitsubishi by the design changes. The suit was dismissed and IL appealed.

ISSUE   Could IL's quasi-contractual claim overcome the written contract attesting to their relationship?

DECISION   No. The appellate court affirmed the lower court's dismissal, holding that the written contract between the parties defined their entire relationship.

REASON   The court reasoned that, absent a valid amendment to the agreement, Mitsubishi had a right to assume that it did not have to compensate IL for any acts performed in relation to the subject matter of the contract except pursuant to the express provisions of the contract. The court characterized a contract implied in law (quasi-contract) as "fictitious and arising by implication of law wholly apart from the usual rules" of contract formation. Sometimes, the court said, when one party benefits another party, and the other party accepts the benefit, and the benefit is not intended as a gift, the law will impose a duty on the benefited party to pay for the services. But when there is already a written contract concerning the same subject matter, the usual rule is that no quasi-contract claim can arise. Further, under the Statute of Frauds,[1] oral evidence that modifies the terms of, and obligations that arise under, a written contract will be permitted by the court only in certain exceptional circumstances—none of which existed here.

1.   See the discussion of the Statute of Frauds in Chapter 8.

Case 5.3—Continued

In this case IL understood the terms of the existing contract, and it knew the risks involved in initiating the design changes it made. The court found that IL, by suing, attempted to unilaterally circumvent the contract it had freely entered into. Consequently, the contract controlled the relationship between the parties, and the suit had to be dismissed.

Formal versus Informal Contracts

FORMAL CONTRACTS
Agreements or contracts that by law require for their validity a specific form, such as executed under seal.

CONTRACTS UNDER SEAL
Formal agreements in which the seal is a substitute for consideration. A court will not invalidate a contract under seal for lack of consideration.

RECOGNIZANCE
A formal obligation to perform a certain act as recorded and required by a court, such as reappearing in court.

INFORMAL CONTRACTS
Contracts that do not require a specified form or formality for their validity.

EXECUTED CONTRACT
A contract that has been completely performed by both parties.

EXECUTORY CONTRACT
A contract that has not as yet been fully performed.

VALID CONTRACT
A properly constituted contract having legal strength or force.

Formal contracts require a special form or method of creation (formation) to be enforceable. They include (1) contracts under seal, (2) recognizances, (3) negotiable instruments, and (4) letters of credit.[2] **Contracts under seal** are formalized writings with a special seal attached.[3] The significance of the seal has lessened, although about ten states require no consideration when a contract is under seal. A **recognizance** is an acknowledgment in court by a person that he or she will pay a certain sum if a certain event occurs or perform some specified obligation. One form of recognizance is the surety bond.[4] Another is the personal recognizance bond used as bail in a criminal matter. Negotiable instruments and letters of credit are special methods of payment designed for use in many commercial settings (they are discussed at length in subsequent chapters). **Negotiable instruments** include checks, notes, drafts, and certificates of deposit. **Letters of credit** are agreements to pay contingent on the purchaser's receipt of invoices and bills of lading (documents evidencing receipt of, and title to, goods shipped).

Informal contracts (also called *simple contracts*) include all other contracts. No special form is required (except for certain types of contracts that must be in writing), as the contracts are usually based on their substance rather than on their form.

Executed versus Executory Contracts

Contracts are also classified according to their state of performance. A contract that has been fully performed on both sides is called an **executed contract**. A contract that has not been fully performed on either side is called an **executory contract**. If one party has fully performed but the other has not, the contract is said to be executed on the one side and executory on the other, but the contract is still classified as executory. For example, assume you agree to buy ten tons of coal from the Western Coal Company. Further assume that Western has delivered the coal to your steel mill, where it is now being burned. At this point, the contract is executed on the part of Western and executory on your part. After you pay Western for the coal, the contract will be executed on both sides.

Valid versus Void, Voidable, and Unenforceable Contracts

A **valid contract** has the necessary elements to entitle at least one of the parties to enforce it in court. Those elements consist of an offer and an acceptance, supported by legally sufficient consideration, for a legal purpose, and made by parties who have

---

2.   Restatement, Second, Contracts, Section 6.
3.   A seal is usually an impression made on a thin wafer of wax firmly affixed to the writing. In some instances, the word *seal* or the letters *L.S.* appear at the end of the document. *L.S.* stands for *locus sigilli* and means "the place for the seal."
4.   An obligation of a party guaranteeing that a second party will be paid if a third party does not perform.

Business Law in Action

Is an Agreement to Form a Contract a Contract?

Sometimes a situation arises where two parties agree to form a contract at some point in the future, and one of the parties assumes that the agreement they have made is itself a "contract." But a contract to form a future contract is not a contract, and even if the other party accepted such an offer, no contract would be formed. Consider, for example, the case of *Seawell v. Continental Casualty Co.*[1]

In 1984 Richard Seawell, a farmer, used on his tobacco crop a fertilizer manufactured by W. R. Grace & Company. Grace later discovered that some of the fertilizer contained a contaminating chemical, and Grace and its insurer,

1.   84 N.C.App. 277, 352 S.E.2d 263 (1987).

Continental Casualty Company, began investigating the problem and adjusting the claims made against them by farmers who had used the fertilizer.

Seawell and several other farmers in his area elected a committee to meet with representatives of Grace and Continental Casualty. At the meeting, which took place on July 30, 1984, Grace and Continental agreed to compensate the farmers for damaged tobacco, according to a formula. Specific damages were to be determined at future meetings between the insurance adjusters and individual farmers. The farmers were assured at the July 30 meeting that they would not suffer any losses resulting from the use of Grace fertilizer.

After the meeting an insurance adjuster came to Seawell's farm, estimated the amount of production, and sampled some of Seawell's tobacco. No agreement was reached during this visit as to the specific amount of damage suffered by

Seawell. When it came time to harvest the tobacco, Seawell did so and sold his crop, later filing suit against Grace and the insurance company for not settling his claim and thus breaching their "contract" of July 30.

But did a contract in fact exist? Are all of the necessary elements to a contract present here? Seawell thought so, and other people in similar situations might agree with him. The trial court, however, held that since no specific amounts of damages were determined for each farmer at the meeting, there could be no contract. The offer made by Grace and the insurance company was too indefinite in its terms to become the basis of a contract. The court concluded that, at best, the July 30 meeting amounted only to an "agreement to agree" in the future with each individual farmer involved. It was thus a proposal by Grace to settle with farmers on an individual basis, and not a contract.

---

the legal capacity to enter into the contract. Each element is discussed in detail in the following chapters.

A **void contract** is no contract at all. The terms *void* and *contract* are contradictory. A void contract produces no legal obligations by any of the parties. For example, a contract can be void because one of the parties was adjudged by a court to be legally insane or because the purpose of the contract was illegal.

A **voidable contract** is a *valid* contract in which one or both of the parties has the option of avoiding his or her legal obligations. The party having the option can elect to avoid any duty to perform or can elect to *ratify* (make valid) the contract. If the contract is avoided, both parties are released from it. If it is ratified, both parties must fully perform their respective legal obligations.

As a general rule, but subject to exceptions, contracts made by minors are voidable at the option of the minor (see Chapter 7). Contracts entered into under fraudulent conditions are voidable at the option of the defrauded party. In addition, contracts entered into because of mistakes and those entered into under legally defined duress or undue influence are voidable.

VOID CONTRACT
A contract having no legal force or binding effect.

VOIDABLE CONTRACT
A contract that may be legally annulled at the option of one of the parties.

UNENFORCEABLE CONTRACT
A valid contract having no legal effect or force in a court action.

    An **unenforceable contract** is one that cannot be enforced because of certain legal defenses against it. It is not unenforceable because a party failed to satisfy a legal requirement of the contract; rather, it is a valid contract rendered unenforceable by some statute or law. For example, certain contracts must be in writing (see Chapter 8), and if they are not, they will not be enforceable except in certain exceptional circumstances.

❖ Chapter Summary: Contracts—Definitions

Contract Requirements	1. Agreement. 2. Consideration. 3. Contractual capacity. } Elements of a contract. 4. Legality. 5. Genuineness of assent. } Defenses to enforcement of a contract 6. Form.
Contract Formation	1. *Bilateral*—A promise for a promise. 2. *Unilateral*—A promise for an act (acceptance is the completed performance of the act). 3. *Express*—Formed by words (oral, written, or a combination). 4. *Implied-in-fact*—Formed by the conduct of the parties. 5. *Quasi-contract* (implied-in-law)—Imposed by law to prevent unjust enrichment. 6. *Formal*—Requires a special form for creation. 7. *Informal*—Requires no special form for creation.
Enforceability	1. *Valid*—The contract has the necessary contractual elements of offer and acceptance, consideration, parties with capacity, and it is made for a legal purpose. 2. *Voidable*—One party has the option of avoiding or enforcing the contractual obligation. 3. *Void*—No contract exists or there is a contract without legal obligations. 4. *Unenforceable*—A contract exists, but it cannot be enforced because of a legal defense.
Performance	1. *Executed*—A fully performed contract. 2. *Executory*—A contract not fully performed.

❖ Questions and Case Problems

5-1. Rosalie, a wealthy widow, invited an acquaintance, Jonathan, to her home for dinner. Jonathan accepted the offer and eager to please Rosalie, spent lavishly preparing for the evening. His purchases included a new blazer, new shoes, an expensive floral arrangement, and champagne. On the appointed evening, Jonathan arrived at Rosalie's house only to find that she had left for the evening. Jonathan wants to sue Rosalie to recover some of his expenses. Can he? Why or why not?

5-2. Jennifer says to her neighbor, Gordon, "If you mow my lawn, I'll pay you $25." Gordon orally accepts her offer. Is there a contract? Is it a bilateral or unilateral contract? What is the legal significance of the distinction?

5-3. Marjorie is sixteen years old. By letter, Marjorie offers to buy Jerry's bicycle for $100. Jerry, an adult, accepts by telegram. Marjorie pays Jerry $100, and Jerry delivers the bicycle to Majorie. How would this contract be classified, and what is the legal effect on Marjorie?

5-4. High-Flying Advertising, Inc. contracted with Big Burger Restaurants to fly an advertisement above the Connecticut beaches. The advertisement offered $5,000 to any person who could swim from the Connecticut beaches to Long Island across

Long Island Sound in less than a day. McElfresh saw the streamer and accepted the challenge. He started his marathon swim that same day at 10 a.m. After he had been swimming for four hours and was about halfway across the Sound, McElfresh saw another plane pulling a streamer that read: "Big Burger revokes." Is there a contract between McElfresh and Big Burger? If there is a contract, what type(s) of contract is (are) formed?

5-5. The city of Blue Haven, which plans to construct a new city hall, sends out invitations to contractors to submit bids on the construction project. Berkeley Construction responds with the lowest bid and gets the job. In this situation, who is the offeror and who is the offeree?

5-6. Engelcke Manufacturing, Inc. planned to design and manufacture Whizball, an electronic game. Engelcke asked Eaton to design the electronic schematic for it. Engelcke told Eaton that he would be paid for the reasonable value of his services, but no written contract was signed. Eaton worked on the project for eleven months. Upon completion, Engelcke contended that there was an express contract; Eaton contended it was an implied-in-fact contract. Who is correct? [Eaton v. Engelcke Mfg., Inc., 37 Wn. App. 677, 681 P.2d 1312 (1984)]

5-7. Financial and Real Estate Consulting Company (Financial) contracted with Regional Properties, Inc. (Regional) to sell to investors limited partnership interests in some ventures being undertaken by Regional. Regional promised to pay Financial for its brokerage services. Financial sold a number of partnership interests and had been paid the stipulated fee for some (but not all) of the sales. Regional later discovered that Financial was not registered with the Securities and Exchange Commission as a broker-dealer, as required by law. Regional brought an action before the court to rescind (nullify) the contract with Financial. Financial counterclaimed for the unpaid fees. Is the contract between Financial and Regional enforceable? Why or why not? [Regional Properties, Inc. v. Financial and Real Estate Consulting Company, 678 F.2d 552 (5th Cir. 1982)]

5-8. Ashton Company, which was engaged in a construction project, leased a crane from Artukovich, Inc. and hired the Reliance Truck Company to deliver the crane to the construction site. Reliance, while the crane was in its possession and without permission from either Ashton or Artukovich, used the crane to install a transformer for a utility company, which paid Reliance for the job. Reliance then delivered the crane to the Ashton construction site at the appointed time of delivery. When Artukovich learned of the unauthorized use of the crane by Reliance, it sued Reliance for damages. What equitable doctrine could be used as a basis for awarding damages to Artukovich? [Artukovich & Sons, Inc. v. Reliance Truck Company, 126 Ariz. 246, 614 P.2d 327 (1980)]

Chapter 6

Agreement and Consideration

"Justice is a fixed and abiding disposition to give to every man his right."

Corpus Juris Civilis
(Roman law code, compiled during the sixth century A.D.)

Although the Roman Empire is centuries distant from the twentieth century, the concept of justice embedded in Roman law is manifest in our own laws as well—including contract law. English and American courts have shown for centuries "a fixed and abiding disposition" to protect the rights of individuals. But, as mentioned in the previous chapter, not all contracts, or promises, are enforced by the courts.

For a contract to be valid and enforceable, six requirements (see pages 108 and 109 in Chapter 5) must be met. We will examine these essential elements to a contract in this and the following two chapters. Although in these three chapters two elements (such as agreement and consideration in this chapter) are linked together, the elements so linked do not have any inherent connection—this ordering is purely arbitrary and is done solely for reasons of space. It is important to realize that each of the six requirements is independently essential to the existence of a valid, enforceable contract.

❖ Agreement

AGREEMENT
A meeting of two or more minds. Often used as a synonym for contract.

OFFER
An offeror's proposal to do something, which creates in the offeree accepting the offer a legal power to bind the offeror to the terms of the proposal.

ACCEPTANCE
In contract law, the offeree's notification to the offeror that the offeree agrees to the terms of the offer and will be bound by them.

Agreement exists when an offer made by one party is accepted or assented to by the other. Ordinarily, agreement is evidenced by an **offer** and an **acceptance.** One party offers a certain bargain to another party, who then accepts that bargain. Because words often fail to convey the precise meaning intended, the law of contracts generally adheres to the objective theory of contracts, as discussed in Chapter 5. Under this theory, a party's words and conduct are held to mean whatever a reasonable person in the offeree's position would think they mean. The court will give words their usual meaning even if "it were proved by twenty bishops that [the] party . . . intended something else." [1]

Problems arise when the offer has missing terms, such as a definite time limit, a specified price, a specified quantity, and so on. Do these "gaps" necessarily mean

---

1. Learned Hand in Hotchkiss v. National City Bank of N.Y., 200 F. 287 (2d Cir. 1911), aff'd 231 U.S. 50, 34 S.Ct. 20, 58 L.Ed. 115 (1913). [The term *aff'd* is an abbreviation for *affirmed*; an appellate court can affirm a lower court's judgment, decree, or order, thereby declaring that it is valid and must stand as rendered.]

that a contract really was not formed? A general maxim of the law is that whenever possible, a contract should be saved, not destroyed. For this reason, the Uniform Commercial Code contains a number of "gap filling" provisions. In cases where it is evident that two parties intended to have a contract, but certain terms or conditions were not specified, the courts will fill in such gaps with "reasonable" terms. For instance, if the place of delivery is left out of a contract, the court will presume the seller's place. Likewise, if the price is omitted, the court will presume a reasonable price. The term *reasonable* appears again and again in the Code.

❖ Requirements of the Offer

As discussed in Chapter 5, the parties to a contract are the *offeror* and the *offeree*. An *offer* is a promise or commitment to perform or refrain from performing some specified act in the future. Three elements are necessary for an offer to be effective:

1. There must be a *serious, objective intention* by the offeror.
2. The terms of the offer must be reasonably *certain* or *definite* so that the parties and the court can ascertain the terms of the contract.
3. The offer must be communicated to the offeree.

Once an effective offer has been made, the offeree has the power to accept the offer. If the offeree accepts, the offer is translated into an agreement (and into a contract, if other essential elements are present).

Intention

The first requirement for an effective offer to exist is a serious, objective intention on the part of the offeror. In other words, the offeror must seriously expect to be bound by the offer. Serious intent is not determined by the *subjective* intentions of the offeror, but rather, by whether the offeree could *reasonably* conclude that a serious offer was being made. Objective intent is therefore inferred from the words and actions of the parties as interpreted by a reasonable person. Offers made in obvious anger, jest, or undue excitement do not meet the serious-and-objective-intent test. Since these offers are not effective, an offeree's acceptance does not create an agreement.

For example, you and three classmates ride to school each day in June's new automobile, which has a market value of $8,000. One cold morning the four of you get into the car, but June cannot get it started. She yells in anger, "I'll sell this car to anyone for $500!" You drop $500 in her lap. A reasonable person, taking into consideration June's frustration and the obvious difference in value between the car's market price and the purchase price, would declare that her offer was not made with serious and objective intent and that you do not have an agreement.

The concept of intention can be further explained by distinguishing between offers and nonoffers.

1. **Expressions of Opinion.** An expression of opinion is not an offer. It does not evidence an intention to enter into a binding agreement. In *Hawkins v. McGee*, for example, Hawkins took his son to McGee, a doctor, and asked McGee to operate on the son's hand. McGee said the boy would be in the hospital three or four days

and that the hand would *probably* heal a few days later. The son's hand did not heal for a month, but the father did not win a suit for breach of contract. The court held that McGee did not make an offer to heal the son's hand in three or four days. He merely expressed an opinion as to when the hand would heal.[2]

2. Statements of Intention. If Joanne says "I *plan* to sell my stock in Novation, Inc. for $150 per share," a contract is not created if John "accepts" and tenders the $150 per share for the stock. Joanne has merely expressed her intention to enter into a future contract for the sale of the stock. No contract is formed because a reasonable person would conclude that Joanne was only *thinking about* selling her stock, not promising to sell, even if John accepts and tenders the $150 per share.

3. Preliminary Negotiations. A request or invitation to negotiate is not an offer; it only expresses a willingness to discuss the possibility of entering into a contract. Examples are statements such as "Will you sell Forest Acres?" or "I wouldn't sell my car for less than $1,000." A reasonable person in the offeree's position would not conclude that these statements evidence an intention to enter into a binding obligation. Likewise, when the government and private firms need construction work done, contractors are invited to submit bids. The *invitation* to submit bids is not an offer, and a contractor does not bind the government or private firm by submitting a bid. (The bids that the contractors submit are *offers*, however, and the government or private firm can bind the contractor by accepting the bid.)

In the following case, the court addressed the question of whether a letter offering a cottage for sale was an offer or merely a preliminary negotiation.

Case 6.1
MELLEN v. JOHNSON
Supreme Judicial Court of Massachusetts, Essex, 1948.
322 Mass. 236, 76 N.E.2d 658.

FACTS Johnson, who owned a small cottage, sent a letter to Mellen saying that he was putting the cottage on the market. Earlier, Mellen had expressed an interest in purchasing it. The letter indicated that several other people, who had also expressed an interest in purchasing the property, were being informed by letter of its availability at the same time. Mellen, interpreting the letter as an offer, promptly accepted. Johnson sold the property to a higher bidder, and Mellen sued.

ISSUE Was Johnson's letter to Mellen an offer?

DECISION No. The court found that the letter was not an offer.

REASON The court held the letter merely expressed Johnson's desire to sell the property and thus was not an offer but an attempt to negotiate. Because the letter announced that Johnson was sending the same letter to other people, Mellen "could not reasonably understand this to be more than an attempt at negotiation. It was a mere request or suggestion that an offer be made to the defendant [Johnson]."

---

4. Advertisements, Catalogues, and Circulars. In general, mail-order catalogues, price lists, and circular letters (meant for the general public) are treated not as offers to contract but as invitations to negotiate. Suppose that Tartop & Co. advertises a used paving machine. The ad is mailed to hundreds of firms and reads, "Used Case Construction Co. paving machine. Builds curbs and finishes cement work all in one process. Price $11,250 firm." If General Paving, Inc. calls Tartop and says, "We

---

2.   Hawkins v. McGee, 84 N.H. 114, 146 A. 641 (1929).

accept your offer," no contract is formed. A reasonable person must conclude that Tartop was not promising to sell the paving machine but rather was soliciting offers to purchase it, because the seller never has an unlimited supply of goods. If advertisements were offers, then everyone who "accepted" after the retailer's supply was exhausted could sue for breach of contract.

Suppose you put an ad in the classified section of your local newspaper offering to sell your guitar for $75. Suppose also that seven people called and "accepted" your "offer" before you could remove the ad from the newspaper. If the ad was truly an offer, you would be bound by seven contracts to sell your guitar. But since *initial* advertisements are treated as *invitations* to make offers rather than offers, you would have seven offers to choose from, and you could accept the best one without incurring any liability for the six you reject. There are occasions, however, when an advertisement contains such definite terms that it can be construed as an offer. One such case is the subject of the "Business Law in Action" in this chapter.

Price lists are another form of invitation to negotiate or trade. A seller's price list is not an offer to sell at that price; it merely invites the buyer to offer to buy at that price. In fact, the seller usually puts "prices subject to change" on the price list. Under certain circumstances, however, a price quotation can be an offer, as the following case shows.

Case 6.2
FAIRMOUNT GLASS WORKS v. GRUNDEN-MARTIN WOODENWARE CO.
Supreme Court of Kentucky, 1899.
106 Ky. 659, 51 S.W. 196.

FACTS Grunden-Martin, interested in purchasing jars from Fairmount Glass Works, wrote to that firm and inquired about prices. Fairmount responded with the following letter: "Gentlemen: Replying to your favor of April 20, we quote you Mason fruit jars, complete, in one-dozen boxes, delivered East St. Louis, Ill.; Pints $4.50, quarts $5.00, half gallons $6.50, per gross, for immediate acceptance, and shipment not later than May 15, 1895; sixty days acceptance, or 2 [percent] off, cash in ten days. Yours truly, Fairmount Glass Works." Grunden-Martin construed the letter as an offer and attempted to accept, but Fairmount refused to sell the jars. Grunden-Martin

sued Fairmount for breach of contract. The trial court found for Grunden-Martin, and the defendant, Fairmount, appealed.

ISSUE Does the letter from Fairmount constitute an offer?

DECISION Yes. The letter is an offer, and Grunden-Martin's acceptance creates a binding contract.

REASON The court reasoned that because this quotation was not addressed to the general public but to a specific party, and because the phrase "for immediate acceptance" was included, indicating the seller's commitment to sell the jars, the letter constituted an offer. The court noted that this was an exception to the general rule that price quotes are not offers.

---

5. Other Nonoffer Situations. An agreement to agree is not an offer because too many terms are indefinite (see the "Business Law in Action" in Chapter 5). Another nonoffer situation is an auction. Although it appears that the auctioneer is "offering" goods for sale on behalf of a seller, the bidder is the one who actually makes the offer. The auctioneer accepts the bid and completes the contract by knocking the hammer. A bidder can retract an offer while the auctioneer sings "going once, going

In this ad, the advertiser is not making an offer to contract but an invitation to negotiate. Note the fine print at the bottom of the ad where it reads "Prices subject to change."

Business Law in Action

When Is an Ad an Offer?

Although most advertisements are treated as invitations to negotiate, this does not mean that an advertisement can never be an offer. If the ad makes a promise so definite in character that it is apparent that the offeror is binding himself or herself to the terms stated, then the ad is treated as an offer. Such was the situation in *Lefkowitz v. Great Minneapolis Surplus Store, Inc.*,[1] a case brought before the Supreme Court of Minnesota in 1957. The case arose when a merchant refused to sell to a customer a fur stole for $1, as promised in a newspaper advertisement. The customer, Lefkowitz, had read the following ad on April 13, 1956, in a Minneapolis newspaper:

"Saturday 9 A.M.
2 Brand New Pastel
Mink 3-Skin Scarfs
Selling for $89.50
Out they go

1. 251 Minn. 188, 86 N.W.2d 689 (1957).

Saturday. Each . . . $1.00
1 Black Lapin Stole
Beautiful,
worth $139.50 . . . $1.00
First Come
First Served"

Lefkowitz was the first to appear at the appropriate counter on the Saturday morning of the sale. He was told, however, that according to a "house rule," the offer was intended for women only and that men could not make the purchase.

Lefkowitz then sued the store for breach of contract, and the trial court awarded him damages. The store appealed the decision, contending that no contract existed because no offer had been made. The advertisement was solely an invitation to customers to make offers to buy the goods on the terms given in the ad—offers which, when forthcoming, could be accepted or rejected by the store.

In evaluating the claim, the court held for Lefkowitz. The court stated that "where the offer is clear, definite, and explicit, and leaves nothing open for negotiation, it constitutes an offer, acceptance of

which will complete the contract. . . . We are of the view on the facts before us that the offer by the defendant of the sale of the Lapin fur was clear, definite, and explicit, and left nothing open for negotiation. The plaintiff having successfully managed to be the first one to appear at the seller's place of business to be served, as requested by the advertisement, and having offered the stated purchase price of the article, was entitled to performance on the part of the defendant." As to the "house rule," the court stated that the defendant did "not have the right, after acceptance, to impose new or arbitrary conditions not contained in the published offer."

In short, the advertisement in this case was sufficiently definite to create an offer. The quantity was specified (one fur stole), as were the price ($1), the value ($139.50), and the person who could accept (first come, first served).[2]

2. Note that today, even if the court had not so held, the surplus store could have been charged with violating Federal Trade Commission (FTC) rules that prohibit deceptive advertising.

twice, third and last call." If the bid is not withdrawn and the hammer falls, the contract is formed.[3]

Definiteness

The second requirement for an effective offer is the definiteness of its terms. An offer must have reasonably definite terms so that a court can determine if a breach has occurred and give an appropriate remedy.[4]

3. See Payne v. Cave, 3 T.R. 148 (1789).
4. Restatement, Second, Contracts, Section 33.

In an auction, the bidder is actually the one making the offer; the auctioneer is only "offering" goods for sale on behalf of the seller.

An offer may invite an acceptance to be worded in such specific terms that the contract is made definite. For example, assume Marcus Business Machines contacts your corporation and offers to sell "from one to ten MacCool copying machines for $1,600 each; state number desired in acceptance." Your corporation agrees to buy two copiers. Since the quantity is specified in the acceptance, the contract is enforceable because the terms are definite.

Is an employment contract that provides for a salary plus "a share of the profits" too vague to enforce? The following case tells the plight of a plaintiff, Victor Petersen, who worked first as construction supervisor and then as manager for the Pilgrim Village Company, the defendant.

Case 6.3
PETERSEN v. PILGRIM VILLAGE
Supreme Court of Wisconsin, 1950.
256 Wis. 621, 42 N.W.2d 273.

FACTS Petersen was employed by Pilgrim Village (Pilgrim) under a contract providing that he was to be paid a stated salary. Petersen claimed that Pilgrim had told him when he began working that he would share in the profits of the corporation and claimed that Pilgrim repeatedly promised him he would be paid. Petersen and Pilgrim, however, never came to any definite agreement as to what the percentage of the profits was to be. When Petersen left Pilgrim's employ, Pilgrim refused to pay Petersen any share of the profits.

ISSUE Did Pilgrim have a contractual obligation to pay Petersen a percentage of the profits?

DECISION No. Pilgrim had no contractual obligation to pay Petersen any percentage of the company's profits because no contract with respect to profits was ever formed.

REASON Pilgrim's offer was too indefinite for a court to determine its terms with any reasonable degree of certainty. In the opinion of the court, "An offer must be so definite in its terms, or require such definite terms in the acceptance, that the promises and performances to be rendered by each party are reasonably certain."

Communication

A third requirement for an effective offer is communication, resulting in the offeree's knowledge of the offer. Suppose Tolson advertises a reward for the return of her lost cat. Hanson, not knowing of the reward, finds the cat and returns it to Tolson. Ordinarily, Hanson cannot recover the reward, because an essential element of a reward contract is that the one who claims the reward must have known it was offered. A few states would allow recovery of the reward, but not on contract principles—Hanson would be allowed to recover on the basis that it would be unfair to deny him the reward just because he did not know about it.

The following case is one of the classic reward suits in common law.

Was a matta yu yella

Case 6.4
GLOVER v. JEWISH WAR VETERANS OF THE UNITED STATES, POST NO. 58
Municipal Court of Appeals for the District of Columbia, 1949.
68 A.2d 233.

FACTS The Jewish War Veterans of the United States placed in the newspaper an offer of a reward of $500 "to the person or persons furnishing information resulting in the apprehension and conviction of the persons guilty of the murder of Maurice L. Bernstein." Mrs. Glover gave police information that led to the arrest and conviction of the murderers, not knowing that a reward had been offered and not learning of it until several days afterward.

ISSUE Does a contract between Mrs. Glover and the Jewish War Veterans exist, given the fact that Mrs. Glover did not know of the reward when she delivered the requested information?

DECISION No. Mrs. Glover's act did not constitute an acceptance since she did not act in response to the offer.

REASON Mrs. Glover was not entitled to the $500 reward because she was not aware of the nongovernmental offer when she gave the police the information. The Restatement of the Law of Contracts says, "It is impossible that there should be an acceptance unless the offeree knows of the existence of the offer."

❖ Termination of the Offer

The communication of an effective offer to an offeree gives the offeree power to transform the offer into a binding, legal obligation (a contract). This power of acceptance, however, does not continue forever. It can be terminated by _action of the parties_ or by _operation of law_.

Termination by Action of the Parties

An offer may be terminated by the action of the parties in any of the following three ways.

1. **Revocation of the Offer. Revocation** is the withdrawal of the offer by the offeror. Unless an offer is irrevocable, the offeror usually can revoke the offer (even if he or she promises to keep the offer open), so long as the revocation is communicated to the offeree before the offeree accepts. Revocation may be accomplished by expressly repudiating the offer (such as, "I withdraw my previous offer of October 17") or by performing acts inconsistent with the existence of the offer, which are made known to the offeree.

REVOCATION
In contract law, the withdrawal of an offer by an offeror; unless the offer is irrevocable, it can be revoked at any time prior to acceptance without liablity.

The general rule followed by most states is that a revocation becomes effective when the offeree or offeree's agent actually receives it. Therefore, a letter of revocation mailed on April 1 and delivered at the offeree's residence or place of business on April 3 becomes effective on April 3.

An offer made to the general public can be revoked in the same manner the offer was originally communicated. Suppose a department store offers a $10,000 reward to anyone giving information leading to the apprehension of the persons who burglarized the store's downtown branch. The offer is published in three local papers and four papers in neighboring communities. In order to revoke the offer, the store must publish the revocation in all seven papers for the same number of days it published the offer. The revocation is then accessible to the general public, even if some particular offeree does not know about it.

Although most offers are revocable, some can be made irrevocable. Increasingly, courts are refusing to allow an offeror to revoke an offer when the offeree has changed position because of justifiable reliance on the offer (under the doctrine of *detrimental reliance* or *promissory estoppel*, discussed later in the chapter). In some circumstances, offers made by merchants may also be considered irrevocable, or "firm offers." Firm offers are discussed in the "Application" in this chapter and in Chapter 11. Another form of irrevocable offer is the "option," used in conjunction with the negotiation of certain real estate sales.

2.   Rejection of the Offer by the Offeree. The offer may be rejected by the offeree, in which case the offer is terminated. Any subsequent attempt by the offeree to accept will be construed as a new offer (or counteroffer), giving the original offeror (now the offeree) the power of acceptance. A rejection is ordinarily accomplished by words or by conduct evidencing an intent not to accept the offer.

As with revocation, rejection of an offer is effective only when it is actually received by the offeror or the offeror's agent. Suppose Growgood Farms mailed a letter to Campbell Soup Company offering to sell carrots at 10 cents a pound. Campbell Soup Company could reject the offer by writing or telephoning Growgood Farms, expressly rejecting the offer, or by mailing the offer back to Growgood, evidencing an intent to reject it. Or Campbell could offer to buy the carrots at 8 cents per pound (a counteroffer), necessarily rejecting the original offer.

Merely inquiring about the offer does not constitute rejection. For example, a friend offers to buy your stereo for $50. If you respond, "Is this your best offer?" or "Will you pay me $75 for it?", a reasonable person would conclude that you did not reject the offer but merely made an inquiry for further consideration of the offer. You can still accept and bind your friend to the $50 purchase price. When the offeree merely inquires as to the firmness of the offer, there is no reason to presume that he or she intends to reject it.

COUNTEROFFER
An offeree's response to an offer in which the offeree rejects the original offer and at the same time makes a new offer.

MIRROR-IMAGE RULE
A common-law rule that requires, for a valid contractual agreement, that the terms of the offeree's acceptance adhere exactly to the terms of the offeror's offer.

3.   Counteroffer by the Offeree. A **counteroffer** is usually a rejection of the original offer and the simultaneous making of a new offer. Suppose Burke offers to sell his home to Lang for $70,000. Lang responds, "Your price is too high. I'll offer to purchase your house for $65,000." Lang's response is termed a counteroffer, since it terminates Burke's offer to sell at $70,000 and creates a new offer by Lang to purchase at $65,000. In common law, the **mirror-image rule** requires that the offeree's acceptance match the offeror's offer exactly—to mirror the offer. If the acceptance contains any material change in, or addition to, the terms of the original offer, it will not be considered an acceptance but a counteroffer—which, of course, need not be accepted. The original offeror can, however, accept the terms of the counteroffer and create a valid contract.

Variance in terms between the offer and the offeree's acceptance, violating the mirror image rule, has caused considerable problems in commercial transactions. This is particularly true in contracts involving the sale of goods where different standardized purchase forms of the seller and buyer are exchanged in the process of offer and acceptance. Seldom do the terms of both purchase forms match each other exactly, but often this fact goes unnoticed until problems arise. Say, for example, that a buyer contracts with a seller over the phone to purchase a certain piece of equipment. All the terms of the sale are orally agreed upon. The buyer then enters the terms of the agreement on the appropriate form and sends it to the seller. The seller does likewise. Because the parties presumed they had reached an oral agreement on the telephone, discrepancies on their respective forms may go unnoticed. The buyer, for example, may not notice that the seller's form says nothing about a warranty—which was a condition of purchase on the buyer's form.

This problem has led to the so-called "battle of the forms," where each party claims that his or her "form" represents the true terms of the agreement. Under common law, the courts tended to resolve this difficulty by holding that the last form to be sent was the final counteroffer. To avoid the battle of the forms, the UCC dispenses with the mirror-image rule. Section 2-207 of the UCC provides that a contract is formed if the offeree makes a definite expression of acceptance (such as signing the form in the appropriate location), even though the terms of the acceptance modify or add to the terms of the original offer.

What happens to these new terms? The answer depends on whether the parties are merchants or nonmerchants. *Between merchants* the new terms automatically become part of the contract unless: (1) the original offer expressly required acceptance of its terms; (2) the new or changed terms materially alter the contract; or (3) the offeror rejects the new or changed terms within a reasonable period of time. If one or both parties are *nonmerchants*, however, the contract is formed according to the terms of the original offer submitted by the original offeror, and not according to the additional terms of the acceptance.

Termination by Operation of the Law

The offeree's power to transform an offer into a binding, legal obligation can be terminated by the operation of the law if any of the following four conditions occur.

1. **Lapse of Time.** An offer terminates automatically by law when the period of time specified in the offer has passed. For example, suppose Jane offers to sell her boat to Jonah if he accepts within twenty days. Jonah must accept within the twenty-day period or the offer will lapse (terminate). The time period specified in an offer normally begins to run when the offer is actually received by the offeree, not when it is sent or drawn up. When the offer is delayed, the period begins to run from the date the offeree would have received the offer, but only if the offeree knows or should know that the offer is delayed.[5] For example, if Jane used improper postage when mailing the offer to Jonah and Jonah knew about the improper mailing, the offer would lapse twenty days after the day Jonah would ordinarily have received the offer had Jane used proper postage.

If no time for acceptance is specified in the offer, the offer terminates at the end of a *reasonable* period of time. A reasonable period of time is determined by the

5. Restatement, Second, Contracts, Section 48.

subject matter of the contract, business and market conditions, and other relevant circumstances. An offer to sell farm produce, for example, will terminate sooner than an offer to sell farm equipment because farm produce is perishable and subject to greater fluctuations in market value.

2. Destruction of the Subject Matter. An offer is automatically terminated if the *specific* subject matter of the offer is destroyed before the offer is accepted. For example, if Bekins offers to sell his cow to Yatsen, but the cow dies before Yatsen can accept, the offer is automatically terminated.

3. Death or Incompetency of the Offeror or Offeree. An offeree's power of acceptance is terminated when the offeror or offeree dies or is deprived of legal capacity to enter into the proposed contract.[6] An offer is personal to both parties and normally cannot pass to the decedent's heirs, guardian, or estate. This rule applies whether or not the one party had notice of the death or incompetency of the other party.

4. Supervening Illegality of the Proposed Contract. A statute or court decision that makes an offer illegal will automatically terminate the offer. If Sue offers to lend Jack $20,000 at 15 percent annually, and a usury statute is enacted prohibiting loans at interest rates greater than 14 percent before Jack can accept, the offer is automatically terminated. (If the statute is enacted after Jack accepts the offer, a valid contract is formed, but the contract may still be unenforceable.)

❖ Acceptance

Acceptance is a voluntary act (either words or conduct) by the offeree that shows assent (agreement) to the terms of an offer. The acceptance must be unequivocal and must be communicated to the offeror.

Who Can Accept?

Generally, a third person cannot be a substitute for the offeree and effectively accept the offer. After all, the identity of the offeree is as much a condition of a bargaining offer as any other term contained therein. Thus, except in special circumstances (to be discussed), only the person to whom the offer is made can accept the offer and create a binding contract. For example, Jean makes an offer to Paul. Paul is not interested, but Paul's friend, José, accepts the offer. No contract is formed.

Unequivocal Acceptance

To exercise the power of acceptance effectively, the offeree must accept unequivocally. This is the *mirror-image rule* previously discussed. If the acceptance is subject to new conditions or if the terms of the acceptance materially change the original offer, the acceptance may be deemed a counteroffer that implicitly rejects the original offer. An acceptance may be unequivocal even though the offeree expresses dissatisfaction with the contract. For example, "I accept the offer, but I wish I could have gotten a better price" is an effective acceptance. So, too, is "I accept, but can you

---

6. Restatement, Second, Contracts, Section 48. If the offer is irrevocable, it is not terminated when the offeror dies. Also, if the offer is such that it can be accepted by the performance of a series of acts, and those acts began before the offeror died, the offeree's power of acceptance is not terminated.

shave the price?" On the other hand, the statement "I accept the offer, but only if I can pay on ninety days' credit" is not an unequivocal acceptance and operates as a counteroffer, rejecting the original offer.

Certain conditions when added to an acceptance will not qualify the acceptance sufficiently to reject the offer. Suppose that in response to a person offering to sell a piano the offeree replies, "I accept; please send written contract." The offeree is requesting a written contract but is not making it a condition for acceptance. Therefore, the acceptance is effective without the written contract. If the offeree replies, "I accept if you send a written contract," however, the acceptance is expressly conditioned on the request for a writing, and the statement is not an acceptance but a counteroffer. (Notice how important each word is!) As noted earlier, under the UCC an acceptance may still be valid even if some terms are added. The new terms are simply treated as proposals for additions to the contract.

Silence as Acceptance

Ordinarily, silence cannot be acceptance, even if the offeror states, "By your silence and inaction you will be deemed to have accepted this offer." This general rule applies because an offeree should not be put under a burden or liability to act affirmatively in order to reject an offer. No consideration—nothing of value—has passed to the offeree to impose such a liability.

In some instances, the offeree does have a duty to speak, in which case his or her silence or inaction will operate as an acceptance. For example, silence may be an acceptance when an offeree takes the benefit of offered services even though he or she had an opportunity to reject them and knew that they were offered with the expectation of compensation. Say Jameson watches while a stranger mows her lawn. The stranger has not been asked to mow the lawn but does so anyway. Jameson knows the stranger expects to be paid and does nothing to stop him. Here, her silence constitutes an acceptance, and an implied-in-fact contract is created. She is bound to pay a reasonable value for the stranger's work. This rule normally applies only when the offeree has received a benefit from the goods or services.

Silence can also operate as acceptance when the offeree has had prior dealings with the offeror. If a merchant, for example, routinely receives shipments from a supplier and in the past has always notified the supplier of rejection of defective goods, then silence constitutes acceptance. Also, if a person solicits an offer specifying that certain terms and conditions are acceptable, and the offeror makes the offer in response to the solicitation, the offeree has a duty to reject. Failure to reject (silence) would operate as an acceptance.

Communication of Acceptance

Whether the offeror must be notified of the acceptance depends on the nature of the contract. Since in a unilateral contract the full performance of some act is called for, acceptance is usually evident and notification is therefore unnecessary. Exceptions do exist. When the offeror requests notice of acceptance or has no adequate means of determining whether the requested act has been performed, or when the law requires such notice of acceptance, then notice is necessary.[7]

An unusual situation is presented in the following case, where performance in a unilateral contract was completed and notice of this performance was mailed (with

---

7. UCC 2-206(2).

proper postage) to the correct address of the offeror. The offeror, however, never received the notification.

Case 6.5
BISHOP v. EATON
Superior Judicial Court of Massachusetts, 1894.
161 Mass. 496, 37 N.E. 665.

FACTS In December 1886, Eaton wrote Bishop a letter in which he offered to reimburse Bishop for any money Bishop would lend Eaton's brother. In January 1887, Bishop signed as surety (a person guaranteeing that another's debt will be paid) a promissory note payable by the brother to a third person and mailed notification of this to Eaton. Eaton, however, claimed that he never received it. In 1891 Bishop paid the promissory note and sought to collect reimbursement from Eaton. Eaton denied that a guarantee (surety) contract existed between them, since he had had no prior notice that Bishop had accepted his offer.

ISSUE Is Eaton bound by his offer to a unilateral guarantee contract with Bishop if Bishop properly mailed notice of his performance but Eaton never received the letter?

DECISION Yes. Bishop fulfilled all that was required when, after assisting Eaton's brother as Eaton had requested, Bishop had seasonably (in a reasonable amount of time) notified Eaton of the performance by mail.

REASON The court ruled that although ordinarily no notice of performance is required in a unilateral contract, in this case Bishop was obliged to notify Eaton of his acceptance because the performance would not otherwise be evident to Eaton and because of the specific nature of the transaction. The court held that since Eaton lived out of the state, Bishop's use of the mail to notify Eaton was reasonable and must have been contemplated by Eaton. Since performance was complete and notification had been sent, even if allegedly not received, the contract was valid.

In a bilateral contract, *communication* of acceptance is necessary because acceptance is in the form of a promise (not performance), and the contract is formed when the promise is made (rather than when the act is performed). The offeree must use reasonable efforts to communicate the acceptance to the offeror. *Communication* of acceptance is not necessary, however, if the offer dispenses with the requirement. Also, if the offer can be accepted by silence, no communication is necessary. Under the UCC an order or other offer to buy goods that are to be promptly shipped may be treated as either a bilateral or a unilateral offer and can be accepted by a promise to ship or by actual shipment.[8]

It is also possible to imply acceptance by conduct, in which case a contract may be formed without verbal or written communication of the acceptance. The following case illustrates such a situation.

Case 6.6
DEECO, INC. v. 3-M CO.
Supreme Court of Alabama, 1983.
435 So.2d 1260.

FACTS Deeco, Inc. owned a campground and had made a three-year lease with 3-M Company in 1976 for advertising Deeco's campsite on a billboard. The lease was renewed in 1979. The billboard was destroyed by a hurricane shortly thereafter, and 3-M wanted to form another contract because the wrong form had been used in 1976. The new 1980 form, which stated that it would not be a binding contract until signed by 3-M, was signed by Deeco but never signed by 3-M, although the 3-M representative told Deeco's president that 3-M would have the new billboard up in sixty days. The billboard was never erected.

---

8.   UCC 2-206(1)(b).

Case 6.6—Continued

3-M did, however, send Deeco monthly bills from January until April 1981 for advertising services on the nonexistent billboard. Deeco sued for breach of contract. 3-M held that no contract existed because it had not signed (accepted) the contract offered by Deeco in 1980. Deeco argued that 3-M had indicated acceptance by its subsequent conduct—especially by the monthly bills sent by 3-M to Deeco, which all indicated that the effective date of the parties' contract was "01-81." 3-M also sent notices to Deeco regarding Deeco's failure to pay the bills, and one notice stated "we have not received payment on your advertising account according to the terms of our contract. . . ." The trial court held for 3-M, and Deeco appealed.

ISSUE Can a contract exist when acceptance is not formally made?

DECISION Yes. The court held that 3-M had breached a valid contract. The judgment was reversed and the case remanded (sent back) to the trial court.

REASON The court concluded that the bills and notices received by Deeco from 3-M referring to their contract, coupled with the fact that Deeco's president had been assured that the billboard would be erected within ninety days, were sufficient evidence of an "objective manifestation" on the part of 3-M to be bound by the agreement. "In our opinion," the court stated, "the rule should be that if the offeree takes steps in furtherance of its contractual obligations which would lead a reasonable businessman to believe that the contract had been accepted, such conduct may, under the circumstances, constitute acceptance of the contract."

Mode and Timeliness of Acceptance

The general rule is that acceptance in a bilateral contract is timely if it is effective within the duration of the offer. Problems arise, however, when the parties involved are not dealing face to face. In such cases, the offeree may use an authorized mode of communication. Acceptance takes effect, thus completing formation of the contract, at the time the communication is sent via the mode expressly or impliedly authorized by the offeror. This is the so-called **mailbox rule,** also called the "deposited acceptance rule," which the majority of courts uphold. Under this rule, if the authorized mode of communication is via the mail, then an acceptance becomes valid when it is dispatched—not when it is received by the offeror. (This is an exception to the rule that acceptance requires a completed communication in bilateral contracts.) The mailbox rule was formed to prevent the confusion that arises when an offeror sends a letter of revocation, but, before it is received by the offeree, the offeree sends a letter of acceptance. Thus, whereas a revocation becomes effective only when it is *received* by the offeree, an acceptance becomes effective upon *dispatch* (even if never received), providing that *authorized* means of communication are used. Authorized means can be either expressly stated in the offer or impliedly authorized by facts or law.[9]

When an offeror specifies how acceptance should be made (for example, by first-class mail or telegram), *express authorization* is said to exist, and the contract is not formed unless the offeree uses that mode of acceptance. Moreover, both offeror and offeree are bound in contract the moment such means of acceptance are employed.

MAILBOX RULE
A rule providing that an acceptance of an offer becomes effective upon dispatch (upon being placed in a mailbox), if mail is, expressly or impliedly, an authorized means of communication of acceptance to the offeror.

---

9. Restatement, Second, Contracts, Section 30 provides that an offer invites acceptance "by any medium reasonable in the circumstances," unless the offer is specific about the means of acceptance. Under Section 65, a medium is reasonable if it is one used by the offeror or one customary in similar transactions, unless the offeree knows of circumstances that would argue against the reasonableness of a particular medium (the need for speed because of rapid price changes, for example).

If telegraph is expressly authorized as the means of dispatch, a contract is established as soon as the offeree gives his or her message to Western Union. Even if Western Union for some reason fails to deliver the message, the contract still exists.

Most offerors do not specify expressly the means by which the offeree is to accept. Thus, common law and statutes recognize what are called implied authorized means of acceptance, as follows:

1.   The means chosen by the offeror in making the offer implies that the offeree is authorized to use the *same* or *faster* means for acceptance.
2.   When two parties are at a distance, *mailing* is impliedly authorized, unless otherwise inferred.[10]
3.   Under the UCC, acceptance of an offer for the sale of goods can be made by any *medium* that is *reasonable* under the circumstances.

There are three basic exceptions to the rule that a contract is formed when acceptance is sent by authorized means:

1.   If the acceptance is not properly dispatched (if a letter is incorrectly addressed, for example, or is without the proper postage), in most states it will not be effective until it is received by the offeror.
2.   The offeror can specifically condition his or her offer upon the receipt of an acceptance by a certain time, in which case, to be effective, the acceptance must be received prior to the end of the time period.
3.   Sometimes an offeree sends a rejection first, then later changes his or her mind and sends an acceptance. Obviously, this chain of events could cause confusion and even detriment to the offeror, depending on whether the rejection or the acceptance arrived first. In such cases, the law cancels the rule of acceptance upon dispatch, and the first communication to be received by the offeror determines whether a contract is formed. If the rejection comes first, there is no contract.[11]

An acceptance given by means not expressly or impliedly authorized is often not effective until it is received by the offeror.

❖ Consideration and Its Requirements

CONSIDERATION
That which motivates the exchange of promises or performance in a contractual agreement. The consideration, which must be present to make the contract legally binding, must result in a detriment to the promisee (something of legal value, legally sufficient, and bargained for) or a benefit to the promisor.

In every legal system, there are promises that will be enforced and promises that will not be enforced. Just because a party has made a promise does not mean it is enforceable. Under common law, a primary basis for the enforcement of promises is **consideration,** which, at a minimum, makes the distinction between gratuitous promises and those which are part of a bargained-for exchange. Therefore, consideration is used to distinguish contracts from gifts.

Consideration is usually defined as the value given in return for a promise. Often consideration is broken down into two parts: (1) something of *legal value* must be given in exchange for the promise, and (2) there must be a *bargained-for* exchange. The "something of legal value" may consist of a return promise that is bargained for. If it consists of performance, that performance may be (1) an act (other than a promise);

10.   See Adams v. Lindsell, 106 Eng. Rep. 250 (K.B. 1818).
11.   Restatement, Second, Contracts, Section 40.

(2) a forbearance (a refraining from action); or (3) the creation, modification, or destruction of a legal relation.[12]

For example, Jerry says to his son, "When you completely finish painting the garage, I will pay you $100." Jerry's son paints the garage. The act of painting the garage is the consideration that creates the contractual obligation of Jerry to pay his son $100. Suppose, however, that Jerry says to his son, "In consideration of the fact that you are not as wealthy as your brothers, I will pay you $500." This promise is not enforceable because Jerry's son has not given any consideration for the $500 promised.[13] Jerry has simply stated his motive for giving his son a *gift*. The fact that the word "consideration" is used does not, alone, make it consideration.

Legal Sufficiency

For a binding contract to be created, consideration not only must exist but also must be legally sufficient. To be *legally sufficient*, consideration for a promise must be legally *detrimental to the promisee* (or, conversely, beneficial to the promisor). Note that *legal* detriment is not synonymous with *actual* (economic) detriment. Legal detriment can be incurred in either of two ways: (1) by doing or promising to do something there was no prior legal duty to do, or (2) by refraining from, or promising to refrain from, doing something there was no prior legal duty to refrain from doing (forbearance).

In this chapter's "Landmark in the Law," where a classic case in the area of consideration is discussed, the question arises as to whether refraining from bad habits at the request of another constitutes a legal detriment to the promisee.

Adequacy of Consideration

Sufficiency of consideration means that consideration must be something of value in the eyes of the law. Adequacy of consideration refers to "how much" consideration is given. Essentially, adequacy of consideration concerns the fairness of the bargain. On the surface, fairness would appear to be an issue when the values of items exchanged are unequal. In general, however, courts do not question the adequacy of consideration if the consideration is legally sufficient. Under the doctrine of freedom of contract, parties are usually free to bargain as they wish. If people could sue merely because they entered into an unwise contract, the courts would be overloaded with frivolous suits. In extreme cases, a court of law may look to the amount or value (the adequacy) of the consideration because apparent inadequate consideration can indicate fraud, duress (unlawful pressure causing someone to do something he or she would not otherwise have done), or undue influence. In cases where the consideration is grossly inadequate, the courts may declare the contract unconscionable and unenforceable.

Preexisting Duty

Under most circumstances, a later promise to do what one already has a legal duty to do is not legally sufficient consideration because no legal detriment or benefit has

---

12.   Restatement, Second, Contracts, Section 71.
13.   See Fink v. Cox, 18 Johns. 145, 9 Am. Dec. 191 (N.Y. 1820).

Landmark in the Law
Hamer v. Sidway (1891)

If, in return for a promise to pay, a person forbears to pursue harmful habits, such as the use of tobacco or alcohol, does such forbearance represent a legal "detriment to the promisee" and thus create consideration for the contract? This was the issue before the court in the landmark case of *Hamer v. Sidway.*[1]

The contract in question was created in 1869 when William Story, Sr., promised his nephew, William Story, II, that if the nephew refrained from drinking alcohol, using tobacco, and playing billiards and cards for money until the age of 21, he would pay him $5,000. The nephew, who indulged occasionally in all of these "vices," agreed to refrain from them and did so for the next six years. Following his twenty-first birthday in 1875, the nephew wrote to his uncle that he had performed his part of the bargain and was thus entitled to the promised $5,000. A few days later, the uncle responded with the following letter:

Buffalo, Feb. 6, 1875

W. E. Story, Jr:

DEAR NEPHEW—Your letter of the 31st ult. came to hand all right, saying that you had lived up to the promise made to me several years ago. I have no doubt but you have, for which you shall have five thousand dollars, as I promised you. I had the money in the bank the day you was 21 years old that I intend for you, and you shall have the money certain. Now, Willie, I do not intend to interfere with this money in any way till I think you are capable of taking care

of it, and the sooner that time comes the better it will please me. . . . This money you have earned much easier than I did besides acquiring good habits at the same time and you are quite welcome to the money; hope you will make good use of it. I was ten long years getting this together after I was your age.

Truly Yours,
W. E. STORY

P.S.—You can consider this money on interest.

The nephew agreed to the terms and conditions and left the money in the care of his uncle, who held it for the next twelve years. When the uncle died in 1887, however, the executor of the uncle's estate refused to pay the $5,000 claim brought by Hamer, a third party to whom the promise had been assigned. The executor, Sidway, contended that the contract was invalid because there was insufficient consideration to support it. He argued that neither a benefit to the promisor (the uncle) nor a detriment to the promisee (the nephew) existed in this case. The uncle had received nothing and the nephew had only benefited by fulfilling the uncle's wishes. Therefore, no contract existed.

Although a lower court upheld Sidway's position, the New York Court of Appeals reversed and ruled in favor of the plaintiff, Hamer. "The promisee used tobacco, occasionally drank liquor, and he had a legal right to do so," the court stated. "That right he abandoned for a period of ten years upon the strength of the promise of the testator that for such forbearance he would give him $5,000. We need not speculate on the effort which may have been required to give up the use of those stimulants. It is sufficient that he restricted his lawful freedom of action within certain prescribed limits upon the faith of his uncle's agreement."

1.   124 N.Y. 538, 27 N.E. 256 (1891).

been incurred.[14] The preexisting legal duty may be imposed by law or may arise out of a previous contract. A sheriff, for example, cannot collect a reward for information leading to the capture of a criminal if the sheriff already has a legal duty to capture the criminal. Likewise, if a party already is bound by contract to perform a certain duty, that duty cannot serve as consideration for a second contract. For example, suppose Bauman-Bache, Inc. begins construction on a seven-story office building and after three months demands an extra $75,000 on its contract or it will stop working. The owner of the land, having no one else to complete construction, agrees to pay the extra $75,000. The agreement is not enforceable because it is not supported

14.   See Foakes v. Beer, 9 App. Cas. 605 (1884).

by legally sufficient consideration; Bauman-Bache was under a preexisting duty to complete the building.

Unforeseen Difficulties   The rule regarding preexisting duty is meant to prevent extortion and the so-called hold-up game. But what happens when an honest contractor, who has contracted with a landowner to build a house, runs into extraordinary difficulties that were totally unforeseen at the time the contract was formed? In the interest of fairness and equity, the courts sometimes allow exceptions to the preexisting-duty rule. In the example just mentioned, if the landowner agrees to pay extra compensation to the contractor for overcoming these unforeseen difficulties, the court may refrain from applying the preexisting-duty rule and enforce the agreement. It should be noted that when the "unforeseen difficulties" that give rise to a contract modification are the type of risks ordinarily assumed in business, the courts usually do not consider this to be a rescission and new contract but instead assert the preexisting-duty rule.

Rescission and New Contract   The law recognizes that two parties can mutually agree to rescind their contract, at least to the extent it is executory (still to be carried out). **Rescission** is defined as the unmaking of a contract in which the parties are returned to the positions they occupied before the contract was made. When rescission and the making of a new contract take place at the same time, the courts frequently are given a choice (as in the earlier Bauman-Bache example) of applying the preexisting-duty rule or allowing rescission and the new contract to stand.[15]

> **RESCISSION**
> A remedy whereby the contract is canceled and the parties are returned to the positions they occupied before the contract was made; may be done through the mutual consent of the parties, by their conduct, or by the decree of a court of equity.

Past Consideration

Promises made in return for actions or events that have already taken place are unenforceable. These promises lack consideration in that the element of bargained-for exchange is missing. In short, you can bargain for something to take place now or in the future, but not for something that has already taken place. Therefore, **past consideration** is no consideration. Suppose Elsie, a real estate agent, does her friend Judy a favor by selling Judy's house and not charging any commission. Later, Judy says to Elsie, "In return for your generous act, I will pay you $3,000." This promise is for past consideration and is thus unenforceable; in effect, Judy is stating her intention to give Elsie a gift. The following case illustrates past consideration.

> **PAST CONSIDERATION**
> An act done before the contract is made, which ordinarily, by itself, cannot be consideration for a later promise to pay for the act.

Case 6.7
LANFIER v. LANFIER
Supreme Court of Iowa, 1939.
227 Iowa 258, 288 N.W. 104.

FACTS   This suit concerned title to certain real property.[1] The plaintiff was a minor bringing suit through his father.

1.   Real property, or *realty,* is defined as land or anything (such as trees or buildings) permanently attached to the land. Personal property, or *personalty,* is all other property. See Chapters 33 and 34.

The defendants were the heirs of August Schultz and the administrators of his estate. The case came to court on the basis of an oral contract allegedly made between Schultz and the plaintiff (through the plaintiff's mother) whereby Schultz agreed to give the plaintiff certain real estate if the plaintiff's mother would name the plaintiff (his grandson) after him. He also agreed to reserve to the plaintiff's parents a life estate (good for their life only) in that real estate. The plaintiff's parents accepted the proposal since they had already named the plaintiff after

15.   Note that under the Uniform Commercial Code, any agreement modifying a contract within Article 2 on Sales needs no consideration to be binding. See UCC 2-209(1).

Case 6.7—Continued

Schultz. Schultz neglected to perform his oral contract and never arranged for the title of the property to pass to the plaintiff. He did, however, deliver possession of the real estate to the plaintiff's parents. The plaintiff wanted the court to adjudge him the absolute owner of the real estate. The trial court awarded the property to the plaintiff based on the alleged oral contract between the decedent and the plaintiff's mother. The heirs of Schultz and the administrators of his estate appealed.

ISSUE Was the contract between Schultz and the plaintiff unenforceable on the grounds of insufficient consideration?

DECISION Yes. Plaintiff was not awarded title to the property. The court found that the consideration was insufficient to support the contract.

REASON The court determined that the consideration in this contract created no detriment to the promisee because it was an event that had happened in the past. The plaintiff was named after his grandfather several months before the oral contract was made. The court stated that "past or moral consideration is not sufficient to support an executory contract. . . ." The plaintiff argued that his love and affection constituted sufficient consideration to support the contract, but the court held that such a mere promise created "at most bare moral obligations."

❖ Problems Concerning Consideration

Problems concerning consideration usually fall into one of the following categories:

1. Promises exchanged where total performance by the parties is uncertain.
2. Settlement of claims.
3. Certain promises enforceable without consideration.

The court's solutions to these types of problems can give you insight into how the law views the complex concept of consideration.

Uncertain Performance

An exchange of promises where performance may never take place suggests that there is no consideration because there is no certain detriment incurred by the promisee or benefit received by the promisor. If the terms of the contract express such uncertainty of performance that the promisor has not definitely promised to do anything, the promise is said to be *illusory*—without consideration and unenforceable. For example, suppose the president of XYZ Corporation says to his employees: "All of you have worked hard, and if profits continue to remain high, a 10-percent bonus at the end of the year will be given—if management thinks it is warranted." The employees continue to work hard, and profits remain high, but no bonus is given. This is an *illusory promise*, or no promise at all, because performance depends solely on the discretion of the president (the management). There is no bargained-for consideration. The statement declares merely that the management may or may not do something in the future. The president is not obligated (incurs no detriment) now or in the future.

The following three types of business contracts have a certain degree of uncertainty as to the amount of performance legally required.

1. **Requirements Contracts.** In a **requirements contract,** the buyer agrees to purchase and the seller agrees to sell all or up to a stated amount of what the buyer *needs* or *requires*. There is implicit consideration in a requirements contract, for the buyer gives up the right to buy from any other seller, and this forfeited right creates a legal detriment. Requirements contracts are common in the business world and are normally enforceable. If, however, the contract terms permit the buyer to purchase only if the buyer *wishes* or *desires* to do so, or if the buyer reserves the right to buy the goods from someone other than the seller, the promise is illusory (without consideration), and the agreement is unenforceable.

2. **Output Contracts.** In an **output contract,** the seller agrees to sell and the buyer agrees to buy all or up to a stated amount of what the seller produces. The UCC imposes a *good-faith limitation* on output and requirements contracts. The quantity under such contracts is the amount of output or the amount of requirements that occur during a *normal* production year. The actual quantity sold or purchased cannot be unreasonably disproportionate to normal or comparable prior output or requirements.[16]

3. **Option to Cancel Clauses.** A term or time contract may include a clause in which one or both parties may reserve the right to cancel the contract prior to the stated period. For example, consider a three-year lease (a term contract) in which the tenant reserves the right to cancel, with notice, at any time after one year's occupancy. The uncertainty of performance is that the contract may or may not last for the entire three-year period. The basic rule of law is that, although it is immaterial if one or both parties have the option, the contract will be enforced if the party having the option must give up an opportunity (legal right or value) to exercise the option. The loss of the opportunity is a detriment and thus constitutes consideration.

Settlement of Claims

An understanding of the enforceability of agreements to settle claims or discharge debts is important in the business world. The following agreements are the most frequent transactions.

1. **Accord and Satisfaction.** The concept of **accord and satisfaction** has to do with a debtor's offer of payment and a creditor's acceptance of a lesser amount of the debt the creditor purports to be owed. The accord is defined as an agreement whereby one of the parties undertakes to give or perform, and the other to accept (in satisfaction of a claim) something other than what was originally agreed upon. Satisfaction may take place when the accord is executed (when the agreed-upon performance is completed), at which point there is an accord and satisfaction. Accord and satisfaction deal with an attempt by the obligor to extinguish an obligation. A basic rule is that there can be no satisfaction unless there is first an accord.

This rule does not apply if the debtor presumably has a preexisting legal obligation to perform according to the contract. In other words, the creditor is owed full performance—payment of the debt as per contract terms. When the amount of money owed is not in dispute, there is a preexisting legal obligation to pay the liquidated debt (the legal term *liquidated* means ascertained, agreed-upon, fixed, settled, and determined). For example, if you sign an installment loan contract with your banker in which you agree to pay a specified rate of interest on a specified sum of money

REQUIREMENTS CONTRACT
An agreement under which a promisor promises to supply the promisee with all the goods and/or services the promisee might require from period to period.

OUTPUT CONTRACT
A binding agreement whereby a seller agrees to deliver/sell the seller's entire output of a good (an unspecified amount at the time of agreement) to a buyer, and the buyer agrees to buy all the goods supplied.

ACCORD AND SATISFACTION
An agreement and payment (or other performance) between two parties, one of whom has a right of action against the other. After the agreement has been made and payment or other performance has been tendered (in a disputed debt, as opposed to a liquidated debt), the "accord and satisfaction" is complete.

---

16. UCC 2-306.

borrowed, at timely monthly intervals in the form of $100 per month for two years, it is a liquidated debt. Reasonable persons do not disagree on the amount owed. In the majority of states, accord (acceptance of a lesser sum) of a liquidated debt is not satisfaction, and the balance of the debt is still legally owed.

Suppose you owe a friend $2,000, and the amount of the debt is not in dispute. One day you meet each other on the street, and your friend asks you for the money. You say, "I don't have $2,000, but I'll give you $1,500. Take it or leave it." Your friend takes it. Can your friend sue you for the remaining portion of the debt? Yes, because you offered no *consideration* for the accord. You were under a preexisting duty to pay $2,000 and suffered no detriment (that is, offered no consideration) for the new agreement.

When the amount of the debt is *disputed*, however, an accord and satisfaction can be created by the creditor accepting a lesser sum than he or she purports is owed. In these circumstances, the accord of the lesser sum is also satisfaction, discharging the purported debt. In the earlier example of your owing a friend $2,000, assume the amount of the debt is in dispute. Suppose you genuinely believe you owe only $1,500 and your friend claims you owe $2,000. You offer to pay $1,750 in return for being released from the entire debt. Your friend agrees and accepts the $1,750. This is a genuine accord and satisfaction, and your friend cannot sue you for the remaining $250.

An accord and satisfaction is common in cases where the debt is in dispute when the debtor sends, and the creditor cashes, a "payment in full" check. In the example just given (where the amount you owe is in dispute), you might send your friend a check on the back of which you write: "Cashing this check acknowledges payment in full of (X's) debt to (Y)." If your friend cashes the check, then your offer of accord is accepted and the debt is satisfied. Even if your friend scratches off "payment in full," cashing the check still represents accord and satisfaction under common law. Note, though, that a good-faith dispute must exist before the payment-in-full check can create an accord and satisfaction. It is also important that the creditor (the person receiving the tendered payment) has *notice* that the payment is intended as full accord and satisfaction for the debt.

In the following case, the tendering of a payment-in-full check by one party and the cashing of it by the other was deemed by the court to have created an accord and satisfaction.

Case 6.8
QUAINTANCE ASSOCIATES, INC. v. PLM, INC.
Appellate Court of Illinois, 1981.
95 Ill.App.3d 818, 51 Ill.Dec. 153, 420 N.E.2d 567.

FACTS PLM, Inc. orally contracted with Quaintance Associates, Inc., an executive recruiting firm, for Quaintance to undertake a search for a new controller for PLM. Quaintance, after a four-month search during which it had not located a controller, billed PLM for search expenses of $808.61 plus a fee of $9,000 for its services. Quaintance alleged that the contract stipulated that PLM would pay a fee plus expenses regardless of whether a successful candidate for the controller position was found. PLM argued that it had agreed to pay a fee only if Quaintance succeeded in finding a controller for PLM. To settle the dispute, PLM sent Quaintance a check for $6,060.48 (a "reasonable fee" of $5,400 plus "reasonable" expenses of $660.48) with a letter stating, in part: "I don't know any other way to handle the situation but I do believe this is fair. I consider this the end of the matter but certainly would be prepared to discuss it if you so desire." PLM wrote on the back of the check: "In full payment of any claims Mr. Simpler [Quaintance's agent] has against PLM, Inc." Quaintance cashed the check, but it wrote on the

Case 6.8—Continued

check that "negotiation does not release claim of payee against PLM, Inc." When Quaintance sued PLM for the remainder of the alleged debt, PLM argued that the cashing of the check by Quaintance constituted an accord and satisfaction. The trial court held for PLM, and Quaintance appealed.

ISSUE Was an accord and satisfaction created by Quaintance's acceptance and cashing of PLM's "payment in full" check?

DECISION Yes. The trial court's ruling was affirmed.

REASON The Court of Appeals noted that the correspondence between the parties showed that the terms of the oral contract concerning the amount of fees due were clearly in dispute. Given this circumstance, an accord and satisfaction was achieved when Quaintance cashed the check from PLM, since the check clearly indicated it was being tendered as payment in full. According to the court, "The acceptance of the check given in full satisfaction of a disputed claim is an accord and satisfaction if the creditor took the check with notice of the condition upon which the check was tendered." Upon receiving PLM's check and the payment-in-full notice, Quaintance "was required to accept the amount proffered in full satisfaction or refuse it. . . . Plaintiff [Quaintance] had no right to cash the check and thereby obtain the benefit of such offer without its corresponding burden of compromise."

---

2. **Release.** A **release** bars any further recovery beyond the terms stated in the release. For example, suppose you are involved in an automobile accident owing to Paul's negligence. Paul offers to give you $500 if you will release him from further liability resulting from the accident. You believe this amount will cover the damages so you agree to the release. Later you discover that the damage to your car is $600. Can you collect the balance from Paul? The answer is normally no; you are limited to the $500 in the release. Why? Because a valid contract existed. You and Paul both assented to the bargain (hence agreement existed), and sufficient consideration was present. The consideration was the legal detriment you suffered (by releasing Paul from liability, you forfeited your right to sue to recover damages, should they be more than $500). Therefore it is important to know the extent of your injuries or damages before signing a release. Releases will generally be binding if they are (1) given in good faith, (2) in a signed writing (required by many states), and (3) accompanied by consideration. Under the UCC, a written, signed waiver or renunciation by an aggrieved party discharges any further liability for a breach, even without consideration.[17]

3. **Covenant Not to Sue.** A **covenant not to sue,** in contrast to a release, does not always bar further recovery. The parties simply substitute a contractual obligation for some other type of action. Suppose (following the earlier example) you agreed with Paul not to sue for damages in a tort action if he would pay for the damage to your car. If Paul fails to pay, you can bring an action for breach of contract.

Promissory Estoppel

Sometimes individuals rely on promises, and such reliance may form a basis for contract rights and duties. Under the doctrine of **promissory estoppel** (also called detrimental reliance), a person who has reasonably relied on the promise of another

RELEASE
The relinquishment, concession, or giving up of a right, claim, or privilege, by the person in whom it exists or to whom it accrues, to the person against whom it might have been enforced or demanded.

COVENANT NOT TO SUE
An agreement to substitute a contractual obligation for some other type of action.

PROMISSORY ESTOPPEL
A doctrine that applies when a promisor reasonably expects a promise to induce definite and substantial action or forbearance by the promisee, and which does induce such action or forbearance in reliance thereon; such a promise is binding if injustice can be avoided only by enforcing the promise.

---

17. UCC 1-107.

"Estoppel rests on the principle that every man is presumed to speak and act according to the truth and facts of the case."

Thomas L. Wharton, 1648–1715
(English politician)

ESTOPPED
Barred, impeded, or precluded.

can often hope to obtain some measure of recovery. For the doctrine of promissory estoppel to be applied, a number of elements are required:

1.   There must be a promise.
2.   The promissee must justifiably rely on the promise.
3.   The reliance normally must be of a substantial and definite character.
4.   Justice will be better served by the enforcement of the promise.[18]

Consider some examples. Your uncle tells you, "I'll pay you $150 a week so you won't have to work anymore." You quit your job but your uncle refuses to pay you. Under the doctrine of promissory estoppel, you may be able to enforce such a promise.[19] Now your uncle makes a promise to give you $10,000 with which to buy a car. If you buy the car and he doesn't pay you, you may once again be able to enforce the promise under this doctrine. The promisor (the offeror) is **estopped** (barred) from revoking the offer.

The following case illustrates a situation where, because of the plaintiff's detrimental reliance on the defendant's promise, the court awarded damages.

Case 6.9
HUNTER v. HAYES
Court of Appeals of Colorado, 1975.
533 P.2d 952.

FACTS   Gordon Hayes and Winslow Construction Company (Hayes) promised to hire Kathleen Hunter as a flag girl on a construction job beginning June 14, 1971. Relying on the offer, Hunter left her position with the telephone company, as Hayes had asked her to do. When Hayes failed to hire her, she was unemployed for two months—in spite of her efforts to find another job. Hunter sued Hayes for damages in the amount of $700, which she would have earned during the two months had she not left the telephone company, where she had been earning $350 a month. The trial court ruled for Hunter, awarding her $700 in damages. Hayes appealed, contending he should not be liable since no valid employment contract existed between the plaintiff and the defendants.

ISSUE   Should Hunter be allowed to recover damages incurred by her reliance on Hayes's offer of employment, even in the absence of a valid employment contract?

DECISION   Yes. The ruling of the trial court was affirmed.

REASON   The Court of Appeals allowed the doctrine of promissory estoppel to be applied in this case because of Hunter's detrimental reliance on Hayes's offer. Since Hayes had asked Hunter to terminate her employment with the telephone company, the consequent detriment (loss of wages) incurred by Hunter should have been foreseen and anticipated by Hayes. The court stated that Hayes's "contention that there was no evidence of a meeting of minds on all the terms of a contract is accurate, but irrelevant in this case. The plaintiff both pleaded and proved her detrimental reliance on defendant Hayes' promise of employment. . . . Having done as she was bidden—as Hayes should have foreseen she would— Hunter was out of work for two months. These circumstances permit the application of the doctrine of promissory estoppel and allow the enforcement of the promise without evidence of a meeting of the minds or consideration. . . . Here, the damages awarded compensated Hunter only for the direct loss she suffered as a result of her reliance on the promised employment. This amount was not unreasonable."

---

18.   Restatement, Second, Contracts, Section 90.
19.   Ricketts v. Scothorn, 57 Neb. 51, 77 N.W. 365 (1898).

Application

Law and the Direct Marketer

Direct marketing is a growing field of business activity. Indeed, it is estimated that 15 percent of all goods are sold through direct-marketing channels, such as through the mails (so-called junk mail), telephone solicitation, and door-to-door sales. The direct marketer faces numerous problems if he or she does not understand the concept of the *firm offer*. Once a firm offer is made, it cannot be revoked. Thus, as a direct marketer, you should never, as a rule, make a firm offer unless you truly plan to keep the offer open. The Uniform Commercial Code specifies that for an offer to be considered a "firm offer," and thus irrevocable, it must (1) concern the purchase and sale of goods; (2) be made by a merchant dealing in those goods; (3) be written and signed by the merchant; and (4) give assurance that it will be held open for some period of time. If an offer you make in the course of your business meets these criteria, it will be a firm offer, and the offeree can accept and bind you to a contract. Most legal scholars hold that even an offeree's rejection or counteroffer does not terminate a firm offer. Even if there is a lack of consideration, the offer cannot be revoked; it will remain open for the period of time specified in the offer, or, if no time is specified, for a reasonable period (although the period of irrevocability without consideration cannot normally exceed three months).

As a direct marketer, you must be able to distinguish between advertisements that the court would hold are merely preliminary negotiations or solicitations to deal with buyers, and advertisements or communications that the court would consider firm offers. Say, for example, that you place the following ad in a magazine: "Classic Hits Compact Discs," $9.95 plus $2.00 shipping and handling; sale ends one month from today." The response is so great that you run out of compact discs (CDs). Are you bound in this situation to a contract with customers who accept your "offer" of the CDs at the price specified? Is this a firm offer? No. Although it contains most of the elements necessary for a firm offer to exist—that is, the ad was placed by a merchant, was for the sale of goods, was in writing (courts could assume the ad sufficed as a writing), and was for a definite time period—the offer was not signed by you, and the recipient of the offer in this case is so vague (the general public) that the courts would conclude the ad represents a solicitation to deal and not an offer.

But be careful. If, in addition to the price ($9.95 plus $2.00 shipping and handling), quantity (one CD), time period (thirty days), and place (your business address), you also specify a particular recipient (such as first come, first served), a court of law may consider your ad an offer.

Let's examine another situation. Say Music Retailing Stores, Inc. writes to you and inquires about the price of CDs. You write back and offer to sell CDs to Music Retailing at $9.95 each (plus $2.00 shipping and handling). You state that Music Retailing can accept your offer within thirty days, after which the CDs may not be available at the same price. In the meantime, increasing sales have decreased your inventory. You call the CD

Checklist for the Direct Marketer

☐ 1. When making a firm offer, clearly indicate the terms—price, quantity, time period, place, intended offeree, etc.

☐ 2. In price quotations, be sure to include a statement such as "prices subject to change"—by doing so, you reserve the right to change the terms of the offer.

☐ 3. Carefully word direct-mail promotional literature and ads in magazines or newspapers to make it clear you are inviting offers, not making an offer.

☐ 4. Think before you speak or before you put any terms in writing. Although firm offers must be in a signed writing, oral agreements to buy or sell your merchandise may be enforced by the courts.

☐ 5. Always remember the "reasonable person" standard when making or accepting offers.

Application—Continued

plant and learn that its price has increased 300 percent since your last order. You send notice of revocation to Music Retailing. Before the thirty-day period has lapsed, however, Music Retailing accepts your offer. Can you revoke your offer to Music Retailing? No—you are committed to a contract of sale with Music Retailing because the terms and conditions specified in your letter were sufficiently definite and met all the requirements of a firm offer under the UCC.

When determining whether an offer is present, the courts generally use the "reasonable person" test. If a recipient of a price quotation, a letter, or a catalogue ad offering goods for sale at a certain price would "reasonably" conclude that he or she is the intended offeree, and if the other terms and conditions of sale are definite enough, then the ad or announcement may be considered an offer.

❖ Chapter Summary: Agreement and Consideration

AGREEMENT	
Offer—Requirements	1. *Intent*—There must be a serious, objective intention by the offeror to become bound by the offer. Nonoffer situations include (a) expressions of opinion, (b) statements of intention, (c) preliminary negotiations, and (d) generally, advertisements, catalogues, and circulars.
	2. *Definiteness*—The terms of the offer must be sufficiently definite to be ascertainable by the parties or by a court.
	3. *Communication*—The offer must be communicated to the offeree.
Offer—Termination	1. *By acts of the parties:* a. Revocation—Unless the offer is irrevocable, it can be revoked at any time before acceptance without liability; not effective until *known* by the offeree or the offeree's agent. Some offers, such as the merchant's firm offer, under UCC 2–205, and option contracts, are irrevocable. b. Rejection—Accomplished by words or actions that demonstrate a clear intent not to accept or consider the offer further; not effective until *known* by the offeror or offeror's agent. c. Counteroffer—A rejection of the original offer and the making of a new offer; under UCC 2–207, a definite acceptance of an offer is not a counteroffer, even if the acceptance terms modify the terms of the original offer.
	2. *By operation of law:* a. Lapse of time—The offer terminates (a) at the end of the time period specified in the offer, or (b) if no time period is stated in the offer, at the end of a reasonable time period. b. Destruction of the specific subject matter of the offer—Automatically terminates the offer. c. Death or insanity—Terminates the offer unless the offer is irrevocable. d. Illegality—Supervening illegality terminates the offer.
Acceptance	1. Can be made only by the offeree or the offeree's agent.
	2. Must be unequivocal. Under common law, if new terms or conditions are added to acceptance, it will be considered a counteroffer (mirror-image rule). Under the UCC, acceptance may be valid even if additional or different terms are stated.
	3. Acceptance of a bilateral offer can be communicated to the offeror by authorized mode of communication and is effective upon dispatch. Unless the mode of communication is expressly specified by the offeror, the following methods are impliedly authorized: a. The same mode used by the offeror, or a faster mode. b. By mail, when the two parties are at a distance. c. In acceptance of offers for the sale of goods, under the UCC, any medium that is reasonable under the circumstances.

❖ Chapter Summary: Agreement and Consideration—Continued

Acceptance (Continued)	4. Acceptance of a unilateral offer is effective upon full performance of the requested act. Generally, no communication is necessary.
CONSIDERATION	
Legal Sufficiency of Consideration	To be legally sufficient, consideration must involve a legal detriment to the promisee—doing (or refraining from doing) something that one had no prior legal duty to do (or refrain from doing). Consideration is not legally sufficient if one is either by law or by contract under a *preexisting duty* to perform the action being offered as consideration for a new contract.
Adequacy of Consideration	Adequacy of consideration relates to "how much" consideration is given and whether a fair bargain was reached. Courts will inquire into the adequacy of consideration (if the consideration is legally sufficient) only when fraud, undue influence, duress, or unconscionability may be involved.
Problem Areas Concerning Consideration	1. *Uncertain performance*—When the nature or extent of performance is uncertain (as can occur with requirements and output contracts and exclusive dealing contracts), too much uncertainty renders the promise illusory (without consideration). 2. *Settlement of claims:* a. Accord and satisfaction—The agreement by one party to a contract to give or perform, and the other party to accept, something less than that which is purportedly owed in satisfaction of a contractual claim; the agreement is the accord, and the execution of the agreement is the satisfaction, if the debt is unliquidated. b. Release—Whereby, for consideration, a party is barred from further recovery beyond the terms specified in the release. c. Covenant not to sue—An agreement not to sue on a present, valid claim.
Promissory Estoppel	An equitable doctrine that applies when a promisor reasonably expects a promise to induce definite and substantial action or forbearance by the promisee, and the promisee does act in reliance thereon; such a promise is binding if injustice can be avoided only by enforcing the promise. Also known as the doctrine of detrimental reliance.

❖ Questions and Case Problems

6-1. On June 1, Jason placed an ad in a local newspaper offering a reward of $100 to anyone who found his wallet. When his wallet had not been returned by June 15, Jason purchased another wallet and took steps to obtain duplicates of his driver's license, credit cards, and other items he had lost. He also placed another ad in the same newspaper revoking his offer. The second ad was the same size as the original. On June 20, Frank, who had seen the first ad but not the second, returned Jason's wallet and requested the $100. Jason did not accept the wallet and refused to pay Frank, claiming he had revoked his offer. Frank sued Jason for the money. Will Jason have to pay the reward?

6-2. On Saturday, Arthur mailed Jane an offer to sell his car to her for $1,000. On Monday, having changed his mind and not having heard from Jane, Arthur sent Jane a letter revoking his offer. On Wednesday, before she had received Arthur's letter of revocation, Jane mailed a letter of acceptance to Arthur. When Jane demanded that Arthur sell his car to her as

promised, Arthur claimed that no contract existed because he had revoked his offer prior to Jane's acceptance. Is Arthur correct?

6-3. Collins purchases widgits produced by Best Manufacturing Company. Best's contract with Collins calls for the delivery of 10,000 widgits at $1 per widgit, in ten equal installments. After delivering two of the installments, Best informs Collins that because of inflation, Best is losing money and will promise to deliver the remaining 8,000 widgits only if Collins agrees to pay $1.20 per widgit. Collins agrees to the higher price in writing. When Best tenders delivery of the next installment of 1,000 widgits to Collins, however, Collins refuses to pay the additional $200. Discuss whether Best can legally collect the extra $200 from Collins.

6-4. Ben hired Lewis to drive his racing car in a race. John, a friend of Lewis, promised to pay Lewis $3,000 if he won the race. Lewis won the race, but John refused to pay the $3,000. John contended that no legally binding contract had been formed since he had received no consideration from Lewis for his promise to pay the $3,000. Lewis sued John for breach of contract, arguing that winning the race was the consideration given in exchange for John's promise to pay the $3,000. What rule of law discussed in this chapter supports John's claim?

6-5. Darrell, a recent college graduate, is on his way home for the Christmas holidays. He gets caught in a snowstorm and is taken in by an elderly couple, who provide him with food and shelter. After the snowplows have cleared the road, Darrell proceeds home. Darrell's father, Bruce, is most appreciative of the elderly couple's action and in a letter promises to pay them $500. The elderly couple, in need of money, accept Bruce's offer. Because of a dispute between Darrell and his father Bruce, Bruce refuses to pay the elderly couple the promised $500. Discuss whether the elderly couple can legally hold Bruce to his promise to pay for the services they rendered to Darrell.

6-6. Kowalsky, a contractor, was required to make periodic payments to a union pension fund administered by Kelly, trustee for the union. Kowalsky and Kelly disagreed over the amount of money Kowalsky owed the union. After a number of heated discussions Kowalsky sent Kelly four checks totaling $8,500 and enclosed them in a letter saying: "These checks are tendered with the understanding that they are full payment of all claims against Kowalsky." Immediately after receiving the checks, Kelly called Kowalsky and told him the checks were not going to be cashed, but would simply be held and that Kowalsky still owed Kelly money because the $8,500 did not cover his late charges on the deposited payments. Kowalsky did not ask for the return of the checks or stop payment. Kelly retained (but did not cash) the checks and sued Kowalsky for the late charges. Kowalsky claimed that the retention of the checks constituted full accord and satisfaction of the debt. Who won and why? [Kelly v. Kowalsky, 186 Conn. 618, 442 A.2d 1355 (1982)]

6-7. John H. Surratt was one of John Wilkes Booth's alleged accomplices in the murder of President Lincoln. On April 20, 1865, the Secretary of War issued and caused to be published in newspapers the following proclamation: "$25,000 reward for the apprehension of John H. Surratt and liberal rewards for any information that leads to the arrest of John H. Surratt." On November 24, 1865, President Johnson revoked the reward and published the revocation in the newspapers. Henry B. St. Marie learned of the reward but left for Rome prior to its revocation. In Rome, St. Marie discovered Surratt's whereabouts. In April 1866, unaware that the reward had been revoked, he reported this information to United States officials. Pursuant to receiving this information, the officials were able to arrest Surratt. Should St. Marie have received the reward? If so, was he entitled to the full $25,000? [Shuey v. United States, 92 U.S. (2 Otto) 73, 23 L.Ed. 697 (1875)]

6-8. The Olivers were planning to sell off some of their ranch land and mentioned this fact to Southworth, a neighbor. Southworth expressed interest in purchasing the property and later notified the Olivers that he had the money available to buy it. The Olivers told Southworth they would let him know shortly about the details concerning the sale. The Olivers later sent a letter to Southworth—and (unknown to Southworth) to several other neighbors—giving information about the sale, including the price, the location of the property, and the amount of acreage involved. When Southworth received the letter, he sent a letter to the Olivers "accepting" their offer. The Olivers stated that the information letter had not been intended as an "offer" but merely as a starting point for negotiations. Southworth brought suit against the Olivers to enforce the "contract." Did a contract exist? [Southworth v. Oliver, 284 Or. 361, 587 P.2d 994 (1978)]

6-9. Maher, a garbage collector, agreed with the city of Newport to collect its garbage for a period of five years. Shortly after the contract was formed, Maher requested that he receive an additional $10,000 per year because of the many additional housing units that had been added to the city, which increased his collection costs beyond what had been anticipated at the time the contract was created. The city council approved Maher's request and for two years paid the additional $10,000 to Maher. A group represented by Angel later sued Murray, a city official, to have Maher repay the city the additional $20,000 he had received under the modified contract. Angel argued that, given the fact Maher had a preexisting duty to collect the garbage, no consideration had been given in exchange for the additional payments. Did Angel prevail? [Angel v. Murray, 113 R.I. 482, 322 A.2d 630 (1974)]

6-10. Joseph Martin, Jr., Delicatessan, leased a store from Schumacher for a period of five years. Under the terms of the lease, the rent would gradually increase from $500 per month to $650 per month. The lease also included a renewal clause, whereby the lease could be renewed at the end of five years at an annual rent "to be agreed upon." When, at the end of the five-year period, Martin informed Schumacher of his intention to renew the lease, Schumacher asked for a rent of $900 per month. Martin, who had learned from an appraiser's report that the fair market rental value of the property was $545 per month, sued Schumacher for breach of contract. Martin wanted the court to compel Schumacher to lease him the property at a more reasonable price. The question before the court was whether the renewal clause in the lease agreement was a "contract" or simply an "agreement to agree" in the future. What did the court decide? [Joseph Martin, Jr., Delicatessan, Inc. v. Schumacher, 52 N.Y.2d 105, 436 N.Y.S.2d 247, 417 N.E.2d 541 (1981)]

Chapter 7

Capacity and Legality

Courts generally want contracts to be enforceable, and much of the law is made to aid in the enforceability of contracts. Nonetheless, as Justice Cardozo indicated in the opening quotation, liberty of contract is not absolute—that is, not all people can make legally binding contracts at all times. Before individuals can enter into a contract, they must have the *contractual capacity* to do so. A person adjudged by a court to be insane, for example, cannot form a legally binding contract with another party. In other situations, contractual capacity takes on a different meaning. Under these circumstances, a party has the capacity to enter into a valid contract but has the right to avoid liability under it. For example, minors usually are not legally bound by contracts. Also, some contracts are prohibited by law. If, for example, the performance of an illegal act is called for, the contract is *illegal* and thus void—it is no contract at all. In this chapter, we examine certain aspects of contractual capacity, as well as the aspects and effects of an illegal bargain.

"Liberty of contract is not an absolute concept. It is relative to many conditions of time and place and circumstance."

Benjamin Cardozo, 1870–1938 (Associate Justice of the U.S. Supreme Court, 1932–1938)

❖ Minors

Under common law, a minor was defined as a male who had not attained the age of twenty-one or a female who was not yet eighteen. Today in most states the age of majority (when a person is no longer a minor) for contractual purposes is eighteen years for both sexes.[1] In addition, some states provide for the termination of minority upon marriage. Subject to certain exceptions, the contracts entered into by a minor are voidable at the option of that minor. The minor has the choice of *ratifying* (accepting and validating) the contract, thus making it enforceable, or *disaffirming* (renouncing) the contract and setting aside the contract and all legal obligations arising from it. On the other hand, an adult who enters into a contract with a minor cannot avoid his or her contractual duties on the ground that the minor can do so. Unless the minor exercises the option to avoid the contract (discussed later), the adult party is bound by it.

Disaffirmance

The general rule is that a minor can enter into any contract an adult can, provided the contract is not one prohibited by law for minors (for example, the sale of alcoholic

---

1. The age of majority may still be twenty-one for other purposes, such as the purchase and consumption of alcohol. The word *infant* is usually used synonymously with the word *minor*.

beverages). Although minors have the right to disaffirm their contracts, there are exceptions (to be discussed later).

DISAFFIRMANCE
The repudiation of an obligation.

Disaffirmance in General   For a minor to exercise the option to avoid a contract, he or she need only manifest an intention not to be bound by it. The minor "avoids" the contract by "disaffirming" it. The technical definition of **disaffirmance** is the legal avoidance, or setting aside, of a contractual obligation. Words or conduct may serve to express this intent. The contract can ordinarily be disaffirmed at any time during minority or for a reasonable time after the minor comes of age. In some states, however, when there is a contract for the sale of land by a minor, the minor cannot disaffirm the contract until he or she reaches majority.

A minor's misrepresentation of his or her age does not usually preclude disaffirmance of the contract (although in some instances, such misrepresentation is the basis for requiring restitution). In some jurisdictions, a minor is held liable for the tort of deceit arising out of misrepresentation of age.

Duty of Restoration   When a contract has been executed, minors cannot disaffirm without returning whatever goods they may have received. Under the majority view, the minor need only return the goods (or other consideration), provided such goods are in the minor's possession or control. Suppose Jim Garrison, a seventeen-year-old, purchases a computer from Radio Shack. While transporting the computer to his home, Garrison negligently drops it, breaking the plastic casement. The next day he returns the computer to Radio Shack and disaffirms the contract. Under the majority view, this return fulfills Garrison's duty even though the computer is now damaged. On the other hand, a few states, either by statute or by court decision, place an additional duty on the minor—the *duty of restitution*. The theory is that the adult should be returned to the position he or she held before the contract was made. In the example just given, Garrison would be required not only to return the computer, but also to pay Radio Shack for the damage done.

If a minor disaffirms a contract, he or she must disaffirm the *entire* contract. The minor cannot decide to keep part of the goods contracted for and return the remainder. When a minor disaffirms, all property that he or she has transferred to the adult as consideration can be recovered, even if it is then in the possession of a third party.[2]

In the following case, a minor's father brought an action on behalf of his son to disaffirm the minor's purchase of an automobile and to recover the money paid for the car from a seller who knew that the purchaser was a minor when the contract was made.

Case 7.1
QUALITY MOTORS, INC. v. HAYS
Supreme Court of Arkansas, 1949.
216 Ark. 264, 225 S.W.2d 326.

FACTS   Johnny Hays, a sixteen-year-old minor, went to Quality Motors, Inc., seeking to purchase a car. The salesperson refused to sell the car unless the purchase was made by an adult. Shortly thereafter, Johnny returned with a young man of twenty-three whom Johnny had met that day for the first time. The sales agent then accepted Hays's cashier's check, and a bill of sale was made out to the twenty-three-year-old. The salesperson recommended a notary public who could prepare the necessary papers to transfer title from the young man to Johnny and then drove the two boys into town for this purpose. The young man transferred title to Johnny, and the salesperson de-

---

2.   The Uniform Commercial Code allows an exception if the third party is a "good faith purchaser for value." See UCC 2–403(1).

Case 7.1—Continued

livered the car to Johnny. Johnny's father attempted to return the car to Quality Motors for a full refund, but Quality Motors refused it. The car was stored while Johnny's father sought to get Quality Motors to take it back, but Johnny found the keys and wrecked the car in an accident. Johnny, by his father, brought suit to disaffirm the contract and recover the purchase price.

ISSUE   Can Johnny disaffirm this contract, since it was nominally made with an adult?

DECISION   Yes. Johnny was able to disaffirm the contract and return the car. He was not held liable for any damages.

REASON   The court reasoned that since the salesperson knew Johnny was a minor, aided Johnny in obtaining the car by selling it to an adult, and assisted in the transfer of title to Johnny, the sale was essentially made to Johnny. When goods—other than necessaries—are sold to a minor, the minor can disaffirm the contract of sale. The loss that Quality Motors suffered was the result of its own act of not accepting the undamaged car when it could have. The presiding justice quoted the law as follows: "The law is well settled . . . that an infant may disaffirm his contracts, except those made for necessaries, without being required to return the consideration received, except such part as may remain in specie in his hands."

The Effect of a Minor's Misrepresentation of Age   Suppose a minor tells a seller she is twenty-one years old when she is really seventeen. Ordinarily, the minor can disaffirm the contract even though she has misrepresented her age. Moreover, the minor is not liable in certain jurisdictions for the tort of deceit for such misrepresentation, the rationale being that such a tort judgment might indirectly force the minor to perform the contract.

Many jurisdictions, however, do find circumstances under which a minor can be bound by a contract when age has been misrepresented. First, several states have enacted statutes for precisely this purpose. In these states, misrepresentation of age is enough to prohibit disaffirmance. Other statutes prohibit disaffirmance by a minor who has engaged in business as an adult.

Second, some courts refuse to allow minors to disaffirm executed (fully performed) contracts unless they can return the consideration received. The combination of the minors' misrepresentation and their unjust enrichment has persuaded several courts to estop (prevent) minors from asserting contractual incapacity.

Third, some courts allow a misrepresenting minor to disaffirm the contract, but they hold the minor liable for damages in tort. Here, the defrauded party may sue the minor for misrepresentation or fraud. A split in authority exists on this point, since some courts, as previously noted, have recognized that allowing a suit in tort is equivalent to the indirect enforcement of the minor's contract.

Basically, a minor's ability to avoid a contractual obligation is allowed by the law as a shield for the minor's defense, not as a sword for his or her unjust enrichment.

In the following case, an Ohio appellate court had to deal with a contract involving a minor's false representation of age. The age of majority in Ohio at the time this case was decided was twenty-one.

 Case 7.2
HAYDOCY PONTIAC, INC. v. LEE
Court of Appeals of Ohio, Franklin County, 1969.
19 Ohio App.2d 217, 250 N.E.2d 898.

FACTS   Jennifer Lee was twenty years old when she contracted to purchase an automobile from Haydocy

Pontiac, Inc., but she represented to the salesperson that she was twenty-one years old. Lee financed most of the purchase price. Immediately following delivery of the automobile, she turned the car over to a third person and never thereafter had possession. She made no further payments on the contract and attempted to rescind it. She made no offer to return the automobile. Haydocy

Case 7.2—Continued

sued for the balance owed. The trial court held for Lee on the rule that permits a minor to avoid a transaction without being required to restore the consideration received.

ISSUE   Could Haydocy recover the balance still owed on the car, given the fact that the purchaser was a minor?

DECISION   Yes. Haydocy was allowed to recover the fair market value of the automobile from Lee on equitable grounds, although the fair market value could not exceed the original purchase price of the automobile. Lee was estopped (precluded) from rescinding (nullifying) the contract on the ground of her infancy since she induced the sale by misrepresenting her age.

REASON   The court reasoned that under the particular circumstances of this case, the disaffirmance of the contract should be determined on the basis of equitable principles. In the words of the presiding judge, "Where [an] infant . . . through falsehood and deceit enters into a contract with another who enters therein in honesty and good faith and, thereafter, the infant seeks to disaffirm the contract without tendering back the consideration, no right or interest of the infant exists which needs protection. The privilege given the infant thereupon becomes a weapon of injustice."

Liability for Necessaries, Insurance, and Loans   A minor who enters into a contract for *necessaries* may disaffirm the contract but remains liable for the reasonable value of the goods. The legal duty to pay a reasonable value does not arise from the contract itself but is imposed by law under a theory of quasi-contract. One theory is that the minor should not be unjustly enriched and should therefore be liable for purchases that fulfill basic needs, such as food, clothing, and shelter. Another theory is that the minor's right to disaffirm a contract has economic ramifications in that a seller is likely to refuse to deal with minors because of it. If minors can at least be held liable for the reasonable value of the goods, a seller's reluctance to enter into contracts with minors will be offset. This theory explains why the courts narrow the subject matter to necessaries—without such a rule, minors might be denied the opportunity to purchase necessary goods.

Traditionally, insurance has not been viewed as a *necessary*, so minors can ordinarily disaffirm their contracts and recover all premiums paid. Some jurisdictions, however, prohibit the right to disaffirm such contracts—for example, when minors contract for life insurance on their own lives.

Financial loans are seldom considered to be necessaries, even if the minor spends the money borrowed on necessaries. If, however, a lender makes a loan to a minor for the express purpose of enabling the minor to purchase necessaries, and the lender personally makes sure the money is so spent, the minor normally is obligated to repay the loan.

Ratification

RATIFICATION
The approval or validation of a previous action; in contract law, giving legal force to an obligation that was previously unenforceable.

In contract law, **ratification** is the act of accepting and giving legal force to an obligation that previously was not enforceable. A minor who has reached the age of majority can ratify a contract in three ways—by express ratification, by conduct, or by a failure to disaffirm the contract within a reasonable period of time. Express ratification takes place when the minor, upon reaching majority, states orally or in writing that he or she intends to be bound by the contract. If a minor manifests an intent to ratify the contract by conduct (by enjoying the benefits of the contract, for example), this may also constitute ratification, particularly if the adult party to the contract has performed his or her part of the bargain. A minor's failure to disaffirm a contract within a reasonable time after reaching the age of majority may also be deemed by the courts to constitute ratification when the contract is executed (performed by both parties). If the contract is still executory (not yet performed, or only partially performed), however, failure to disaffirm the contract will not necessarily imply ratification. Generally, the courts base their determination on whether the minor, after reaching the age of majority, has had ample opportunity to consider the nature of the contractual obligations he or she entered into as a minor and the extent to which the adult party to the contract has performed.

Liability for Torts

Generally, a minor is held personally liable for the torts he or she commits. Therefore, minors cannot disaffirm their liability for their tortious conduct. The parents of the minor can *also* be held liable under certain circumstances. For example, if the minor commits the tort under the direction of, or while performing an act requested by, either or both parents, the injured party can hold the parent liable. In addition, parents are liable in many states up to a statutory amount for malicious torts committed by a minor living in the home of the parents.

❖ Intoxicated Persons

A contract entered into by an intoxicated person can be either voidable or valid. If the person was drunk enough to lack mental capacity, the transaction is voidable at the option of the intoxicated person, even if the intoxication was purely voluntary. For the contract to be voidable, it must be proved that the intoxicated person's reason and judgment were impaired to the extent that he or she did not comprehend the legal consequences of entering into the contract. If the person was intoxicated but understood these legal consequences, the contract is enforceable. Simply because the terms of the contract are foolish or are obviously favorable to the other party does not mean the contract is voidable (unless the other party fraudulently induced the person to become intoxicated). Problems often arise in determining whether a party was drunk enough to avoid legal duties. Many courts prefer looking at objective indications rather than assessing the intoxicated party's mental state. Exhibit 7–1 illustrates a classification of contracts by intoxicated persons.

   The following case shows an unusual business transaction, where boasts and dares "after a few drinks" resulted in a binding sale and purchase transaction. It should be noted that avoidance on the ground of intoxication is rare.

Case 7.3
**W. O. LUCY AND J. C. LUCY v.
A. H. ZEHMER AND IDA S. ZEHMER**
Supreme Court of Appeals of Virginia, 1954.
196 Va. 493, 84 S.E.2d 516.

FACTS Lucy and Zehmer had known each other for fifteen or twenty years. For the last eight years or so, Lucy had been anxious to buy Zehmer's farm. Zehmer had always told Lucy that he was not interested in selling. One night, Lucy stopped in to visit with the Zehmers at a restaurant they operated. Lucy said to Zehmer, "I bet you wouldn't take $50,000 for that place." Zehmer replied, "Yes, I would, too; you wouldn't give fifty." Throughout the evening the conversation returned to the sale of the farm. At the same time, the parties were drinking whiskey. Even-

◆ **Exhibit 7-1   Contract Classification—Intoxicated Persons**

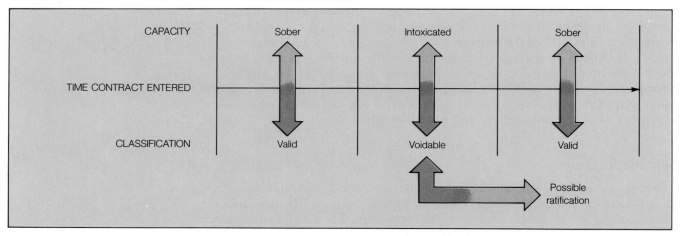

Case 7.3—Continued

tually, Lucy convinced Zehmer to write up an agreement for sale of the farm. Zehmer wrote the agreement on the back of a restaurant check and asked his wife to sign it. She did. When Lucy subsequently tried to enforce the agreement, Zehmer argued that he was "high as a Georgia pine" at the time and that the offer had been made in jest: "two doggoned drunks bluffing to see who could talk the biggest and say the most." Lucy said that although he felt the drinks, he was not intoxicated and, from the way Zehmer handled the transaction, did not think he was either.

ISSUE   Can the Lucy-Zehmer agreement be avoided on the basis of mental incapacity resulting from intoxication?

DECISION   No. The agreement to sell the farm was bind-

ing and the Zehmers could not rescind (undo or nullify) the contract.

REASON   The opinion of the court was that the evidence given about the nature of the conversation, the appearance and completeness of the agreement, and the signing all tended to show that a serious business transaction and not a casual jest was intended. The court had to look into the objective meaning of the words and acts of the Zehmers. "An agreement or mutual assent is of course essential to a valid contract, but the law imputes to a person an intention corresponding to the reasonable meaning of his words and acts. If his words and acts, judged by a reasonable standard, manifest an intention to agree, it is immaterial what may be the real but unexpressed state of mind."

❖ Insane Persons

Contracts made by insane persons can be either void, voidable, or valid. If a person has been adjudged insane by a court of law and a guardian has been appointed, any contract made by the insane person is void—no contract exists. Only the guardian can enter into a binding legal duty on behalf of the insane person.

Insane persons not previously so adjudged by a court may enter into voidable contracts if they do not know they are entering into the contract, or if they lack the mental capacity to comprehend its subject matter, nature, and consequences. In such situations, the contracts are voidable at the option of the insane person but not the other party. Where there is no prior adjudication of insanity or incompetence,

◆ **Exhibit 7-2   Contract Classification—Insane Persons**

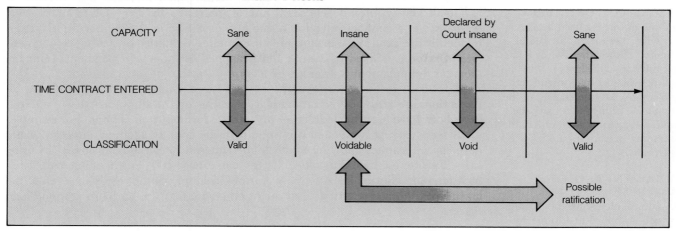

most courts examine whether the party was able to understand the nature, purpose, and consequences of his or her act at the time of the transaction.

The contract may be disaffirmed or ratified. Ratification must occur after the person is mentally competent or after a guardian is appointed and ratifies the contract. Like minors and intoxicated persons, insane persons are liable (in quasi-contract) for the reasonable value of any necessaries they receive.

A contract entered into by an insane person may also be valid, as indicated in Exhibit 7–2. A person can understand the nature and effect of entering into a certain contract yet simultaneously lack capacity to engage in other activities. In such cases the contract is valid, since the person is not legally insane for contractual purposes. Modern courts no longer require that a person be *legally* insane in order to disaffirm contracts.[3]

❖ Illegality—Contracts Contrary to Statute

A contract to do something that is prohibited by federal or state statutory law is illegal and, as such, void from the outset and thus unenforceable. Also, a contract that is tortious or calls for an action counter to public policy is illegal and unenforceable. It is important to note that a contract, or a clause in a contract, may be illegal even in the absence of a specific statute prohibiting the action promised by the contract.

Usury

Every state has statutes setting the maximum rates of interest that can be charged for various types of transactions, including ordinary loans. A lender who gives a loan at an interest rate above the lawful maximum is guilty of **usury**. The maximum rate of interest varies from state to state.

USURY
Charging an illegal rate of interest.

---

3. See Ortelere v. Teachers' Retirement Bd., 25 N.Y.2d 196, 303 N.Y.S.2d 362, 250 N.E.2d 460 (1969). The court determines what tests for mental incompetency are used.

LEGAL RATE OF INTEREST
A rate of interest fixed by statute as either the maximum rate of interest allowed by law, or a rate of interest applied when the parties to a contract intend, but do not fix, an interest rate in the contract. In the latter case, the rate is frequently the same as the statutory maximum rate permitted.

JUDGMENT RATE OF INTEREST
A rate of interest fixed by statute which is applied to a monetary judgment from the moment the judgment is awarded by a court until the judgment is paid or terminated.

This maximum rate should not be confused with either the legal rate or the judgment rate of interest. The **legal rate of interest** is fixed by statute and is what the parties to a contract intend as a rate but do not fix in the contract. This rate is frequently the same as the maximum rate of interest permitted by statute. A **judgment rate of interest** is fixed by statute and is applied to monetary judgments from the moment the judgment is awarded by a court until the judgment is paid.

Exceptions   Because usury statutes place a ceiling on the allowable rates of interest, exceptions have been made in order to facilitate business transactions. For example, many states exempt corporate loans from the usury laws. In addition, almost all states have special statutes allowing much higher interest rates on small loans. In some cases, the interest (including other charges) can exceed 100 percent of the loan. Such high rates are allowed because many borrowers simply cannot get loans even at the lawful maximum interest rate and might otherwise be forced to borrow from "loan sharks."

Installment Loans   Many states have special statutes dealing with allowable charges and interest on installment loans. This is particularly true of retail and motor-vehicle installment sales. Rates vary substantially from state to state. In some states the maximum interest rate allowed may depend on the age of the motor vehicle in question.

Sales agreements often give the purchaser a chance to pay charges through a revolving charge account. The purchaser can make numerous credit purchases (by using a credit card at a department store, for example) and, upon receiving the bill, can either pay it in full or pay a minimum monthly amount, extending the balance to be paid in the future. For the privilege of paying the balance later, the purchaser is charged a monthly interest on the balance. Some courts have interpreted these transactions as not being "loans of money" and therefore not subject to usury laws.

Effects of Usury   The effects of a usurious loan differ from state to state. A number of states allow the lender to recover the principal of a loan along with interest, up to the legal maximum. In effect, the lender is denied recovery of the excess interest. In other states, the lender can recover the principal but not the interest. In a few states, a usurious loan is a void transaction, and the lender cannot recover either the principal or the interest.

Gambling

In general, wagers and games of chance are illegal. All states have statutes that regulate gambling—defined as any scheme that involves distribution of property by chance, among persons who have paid a valuable consideration for the opportunity to receive the property.[4] Gambling is the creation of risk for the purpose of assuming it. A few states do permit gambling, and a number of states have recognized the substantial revenues that can be obtained from legalized, state-operated lotteries.

Sometimes it is difficult to distinguish a gambling contract from the risk-sharing inherent in almost all contracts. Suppose Isaacson takes out a life insurance policy on Donohue, naming himself as beneficiary under the policy. At first glance, this may seem entirely legal; but further examination shows that Isaacson is simply gam-

---

4.   See Wishing Well Club v. Akron, 112 N.E.2d 41 (1951).

bling on how long Donohue will live. To prevent that type of practice, insurance contracts can be entered into only by someone with an **insurable interest.** An insurable interest (discussed in Chapters 12 and 35) is a property or ownership right wherein the insured derives a pecuniary benefit or advantage for its preservation or suffers pecuniary loss or damage for its destruction. Isaacson cannot take out an insurance policy on Donohue's home or auto because Isaacson does not have an insurable interest in Donohue's property. But if Isaacson has a mortgage on Donohue's house, he can take out an insurance policy because he has a property interest.

Futures contracts, or contracts for the future purchase or sale of commodities (such as corn and wheat), are not illegal gambling contracts—although it might appear that a person selling or buying a futures contract is essentially gambling on the future price of the commodity. Since the seller of the futures contract, however, either already has a property interest in the commodity or can purchase the commodity elsewhere and deliver the commodity as required in the futures contract, courts have upheld the legality of such contracts.

INSURABLE INTEREST
An interest either in a person's life (or well-being) or in property which is sufficiently substantial that insuring against injury to the person or damage to the property does not amount to a mere wagering, or betting, contract.

Sabbath Laws

Statutes called Sabbath, or Sunday, laws prohibit the formation or performance of certain contracts on a Sunday. Under common law, such contracts are legal in the absence of this statutory prohibition. Most states, however, have some type of Sunday statute.

Some states have statutes making all contracts entered into on a Sunday illegal. Statutes in other states prohibit only the sale of merchandise, particularly alcoholic beverages, on a Sunday—these are often called blue laws. A number of states have laws that forbid the carrying on of "all secular labor and business on The Lord's Day." Exceptions to Sunday laws permit contracts for necessities (such as food) and works of charity. A fully performed *(executed)* contract entered into on a Sunday cannot be rescinded (canceled). Active enforcement of Sunday laws varies from state to state and even among communities within a particular state. Many states do not enforce the Sunday laws, and some hold these laws to be unconstitutional.

Licensing Statutes

All states require that members of certain professions or callings obtain licenses allowing them to practice. Doctors, lawyers, real estate brokers, architects, electricians, and stockbrokers are but a few of the people who must be licensed. Some licenses are obtained only after extensive schooling and examinations, which indicates to the public that a special skill is involved. Others require only that the particular person be of good moral character.

When a person enters into a contract with an unlicensed individual, the contract may still be enforceable depending on the nature of the licensing statute. Some states expressly provide that the lack of a license in certain occupations bars the enforcement of work-related contracts. If the statute does not expressly state this, one must look to the underlying purpose of the licensing requirements for a particular occupation. If the purpose is to protect the public from unauthorized practitioners, a contract involving an unlicensed individual is illegal and unenforceable. On the other hand, if the underlying purpose of the statute is to raise revenues, a contract entered into with an unlicensed practitioner is enforceable; however, the unlicensed person is usually fined.

"The state . . . has the power to prevent the individual from making certain kinds of contracts, and in regard to them the Federal Constitution offers no protection."

Rufus W. Peckham, 1838–1909
(Associate Justice of the U.S. Supreme Court, 1896–1909)

❖ Illegality—Contracts Contrary to Public Policy

Although contracts involve private parties, some are not enforceable because of the negative impact they would have on society. These contracts are said to be *contrary to public policy.* Examples include a contract to commit an immoral act and a contract that prohibits marriage. For example, suppose Everett offers a young man $500 if he refrains from marrying Everett's daughter. If the young man accepts, the resulting contract is not formed (is void). Thus, if he marries Everett's daughter, Everett can not sue him for breach of contract.

Contracts in Restraint of Trade

Contracts in restraint of trade usually adversely affect the public (which favors competition in the economy) and typically violate one or more federal or state statutes.[5] An exception is recognized when the restraint is reasonable and an integral part of a contract. Many such exceptions are a type of restraint called a covenant not to compete, or a restrictive covenant.

Covenants not to compete are often contained in contracts concerning the sale of an ongoing business. A covenant not to compete is created when a seller agrees not to open a new store in a certain geographical area surrounding the old store. Such agreements enable the seller to sell, and the purchaser to buy, the "good will" and "reputation" of an ongoing business. If, for example, a well-known merchant sells his or her store and opens a competing business a block away, many of the merchant's customers will likely do business at the new store. This, in turn, renders valueless the good name and reputation sold to the new merchant for a price.

When a covenant not to compete is not accompanied by a sales agreement, the contract is void because it unreasonably restrains trade and is contrary to public policy.

Agreements not to compete can also be ancillary to employment contracts. It is common for many people in middle-level and upper-level management positions to agree not to work for competitors or not to start a new business for a specified period of time after terminating employment. Such agreements are legal as long as the specified period of time is not excessive in scope or duration and the geographic restriction is reasonable. Basically, the restriction on competition must be reasonable, that is to say, not any greater than necessary to protect a legitimate business interest. Generally, the courts scrutinize such contracts closely, as the following case indicates.

Case 7.4
ELLIS v. McDANIEL
Supreme Court of Nevada, 1979.
95 Nev. 455, 596 P.2d 222.

FACTS An orthopedic surgeon, Charles Ellis, signed an employment contract with the Elko Clinic in Elko, Nevada, containing the following provision:

In the event that Dr. Ellis's employment by the Elko Clinic terminates for any reason, Dr. Ellis shall not undertake to practice medicine within a distance of five miles from the city limits of Elko, Nevada for a period of two years from the termination date of his employment.

Ellis resigned and told the clinic of his plans to establish a private orthopedic practice in Elko. The clinic alleged

---

5. Such as the Sherman Antitrust Act, the Clayton Act, and the Federal Trade Commission Act (discussed in Chapter 30).

Case 7.4—Continued

that Ellis's plan represented a breach of contract, and the trial court granted a preliminary injunction against Dr. Ellis. Ellis appealed.

ISSUE   At issue in this case is whether or not the covenant not to compete for two years was sufficiently "reasonable" to make this contract enforceable.

DECISION   The court held that the agreement, insofar as it required Dr. Ellis to refrain from practicing his specialty—orthopedic medicine—in the area of Elko for a period of two years, was unreasonable; the court modified the injunction in favor of Dr. Ellis.

REASON   The court considered the fact that Dr. Ellis treated patients who otherwise would have to travel to Reno, Salt Lake City, or elsewhere for orthopedic services. If Dr. Ellis were not allowed to practice in Elko and use the facilities of Elko General Hospital, people would have to travel long distances "at considerable risk and expense" to be treated by an orthopedist. "Thus, in this case, the public interest in retaining the services of the specialist is greater than the interest in protecting the integrity of the contract provision to its outer limits." The court maintained, however, that in regard to the *general practice* of medicine (as opposed to the specialty of orthopedics), the contract provision would be enforced.

Unconscionable Contracts and Exculpatory Clauses

Ordinarily, a court does not look at the fairness or equity of a contract; in other words, it does not inquire into the adequacy of consideration. Persons are assumed to be reasonably intelligent, and the court does not come to their aid just because they have made an unwise or foolish bargain. In certain circumstances, however, bargains are so oppressive that the courts relieve innocent parties of part or all of their duties. Such a bargain is called an **unconscionable contract or clause.**

Recent court decisions distinguish between procedural and substantive unconscionability. The former has to do with how a term becomes part of a contract and relates to factors bearing on a party's lack of knowledge or understanding of the contract terms because of inconspicuous print, unintelligible language ("legalese"), lack of opportunity to read the contract, lack of opportunity to ask questions about its meaning, and other factors. Procedural unconscionability sometimes relates to purported lack of voluntariness because of a disparity in the bargaining power between the two parties.

Substantive unconscionability describes those contracts, or portions thereof, that are oppressive or overly harsh. Courts generally focus on provisions that deprive one party of the benefits of the agreement or leave that party without remedy for nonperformance by the other.

Often closely related to the concept of unconscionability are **exculpatory clauses,** defined as clauses that release a party from liability in the event of monetary or physical injury, *no matter who is at fault.* Indeed, some courts refer to such clauses in terms of unconscionability. In any event, exculpatory clauses that relieve a party from liability for harm caused by simple negligence normally are unenforceable when they are asserted by an employer against an employee. Suppose, for example, that Madison Manufacturing Company hires a laborer and has him sign a contract stating:

> Said employee hereby agrees with employer, in consideration of such employment, that he will take upon himself all risks incident to his position and will in no case hold the company liable for any injury or damage he may sustain, in his person or otherwise, by accidents or injuries in the factory, or which may result from defective machinery or carelessness or misconduct of himself or any other employee in service of the employer.

"Law is the crystallization of the habit and thought of society."

Woodrow Wilson, 1856–1924 (Twenty-eighth president of the United States, 1913–1921)

UNCONSCIONABLE CONTRACT OR CLAUSE A contract or clause that is void as against public policy because one party, as a result of his or her disproportionate bargaining power, is forced to accept terms that are unfairly burdensome and that unfairly benefit the dominating party.

EXCULPATORY CLAUSES Clauses that release a party (to a contract) from liability for his or her wrongful acts.

Business Law in Action

Public Policy and Illegality of Contracts

Public policy is a very nebulous concept. This is because the sources of public policy—the prevailing customs, practices, and ethical and moral norms in a community—are ever changing. Public policy, like society, doesn't stand still, and thus it can never be wholly or permanently explicated. Contracts make up the one area of law most strongly affected by changing opinion concerning public policy. In the business world, however, few contracts are deemed illegal on the basis of public policy. And in those that are, the courts are usually guided by a public policy that is clearly expressed by either statute or a judicial decision. Anticompetitive contracts, for example, are usually held to be counter to the public policy favoring competition. Numerous precedents also exist where contracts, or contract clauses, are held "unconscionable" on the basis of public policy.

Occasionally there is no precedent or statute to guide a court in its determination regarding contract legality. Such situations are inevitable in a changing society that has new customs and practices for which no public policy has yet been legally expressed. Consider, for example, a situation that arose in the last decade because of the changing social views of cohabitation outside marriage: the "palimony" suit.

In the most widely publicized palimony lawsuit, *Marvin v. Marvin*,[1] the court addressed the question of whether an oral contract between Michelle Marvin and Lee Marvin, who cohabited for seven years, was illegal on the basis of public policy. Michelle Marvin alleged that an oral contract existed between her and Lee Marvin and that, according to their agreement, she was entitled to half the property that had been acquired in Lee Marvin's name during the seven years of their cohabitation. She also sought support payments.

The court may have decided differently had this suit been brought even ten years earlier. Traditionally, public policy and the common-law tradition favored marriage, and property rights that arose as a result of cohabitation outside the marital contract were considered to be outside the scope of the law. The year was 1976, however, and the court noted in its decision that in the preceding ten years, the practice of cohabitation had increased eight fold

Lee Marvin

and it was incumbent upon the courts to address the issue of property rights in a nonmarital setting.

Justice Tobriner wrote that "the fact that a man and woman live

1.   18 Cal.3d 660, 134 Cal.Rptr. 815, 557 P.2d 106 (1976).

Michelle Marvin and her attorney Marvin Michelson

Business Law in Action—Continued

together without marriage, and engage in a sexual relationship, does not in itself invalidate agreements between them relating to their earnings, property, or expenses. . . . Of course, they cannot lawfully contract to pay for the performance of sexual services, for such a contract is, in essence, an agreement for prostitution and unlawful for that reason." The court concluded that a contract can exist between nonmarital parties with regard to their earnings and property rights and that such an agreement can be enforced by the courts as long as it is not explicitly founded on the consideration of sexual services. The court thus remanded the case back to the trial

court to determine whether an implied or an express contract existed between the parties.[2]

2. When the case was retried, the court held that no contract in fact existed between Michelle and Lee Marvin, but the court awarded Michelle Marvin $104,000 on "equitable" grounds to allow her to gain sufficient education and skills to become economically independent so that she could "return from her status as companion of a motion picture star to a separate, independent but perhaps more prosaic existence." Lee Marvin appealed this decision, and on appeal the court ruled there was no basis for the award and it was deleted from the judgment. In the end, Michelle Marvin did not receive any monetary award. See 122 Cal. App. 3d 871, 176 Cal. Rptr. 555 (1981).

In the course of history, courts have faced many similar situations where it was necessary to declare for the first time what constitutes public policy on a given issue. In 1986, for example (see the "Landmark" in this chapter), a New Jersey court had to determine public policy on surrogate-parenting contracts. This function of the judiciary is one of its most difficult—and its most creative—because, as stated earlier, public policy is based on a changing social context and is, at times, riddled with uncertainty.

This contract provision attempts to remove Madison's potential liability for injuries occurring to the employee, and it would usually be held contrary to public policy.[6]

Also, exculpatory clauses asserted by a public utility, such as a railroad or an electric company, regarding a harm caused during the public utility's function are usually unenforceable. A railroad, for example, cannot use an exculpatory clause to avoid liability for the negligent maintenance of its trains.

In general, the courts have shown a mixed response to exculpatory clauses used by landlords (regarding a landlord's liability for defective premises), by amusement parks, and by horse-rental and golf-cart concessions.

In the following case, an exculpatory clause releasing a credit-reporting firm from liability resulting from "simple negligence" was enforced by the court. Such enforcement, except in employment contracts and in the other situations just discussed, represents the public policy of allowing parties to contract freely with each other. Note, however, that the credit-reporting firm was held liable for "gross negligence" (the failure to use even *slight* care) and recklessness, because these were not specifically excluded by the exculpatory clause. If they had been included, the court may have held the clause itself to be unconscionable.

---

6. For a case with similar facts, see Little Rock & Ft. Smith Ry. Company v. Eubanks, 48 Ark. 460, 3 S.W. 808 (1887). In such a case, the clause may also be illegal on the basis of a violation of the state workers' compensation law.

Landmark in the Law
The Case of Baby M

The customs and mores of any society change over time. And sooner or later, many such changes result in conflicts not covered by existing law. Such is the case with Baby M, a child born to a surrogate mother who broke her contract with the father. Although surrogate parenting has been practiced for years and more than 500 children have been born to surrogate parents, only a few conflicts arose prior to 1986 and they were all settled out of court. It seemed inevitable, however, that sooner or later such a conflict would appear before the courts. As a lawyer involved in the "Baby M" case remarked, it was "a case waiting to happen, somewhere, sometime." And so it did. The trial in the case of Baby M began in January 1987, and, with no legal precedent or statute to guide it, a New Jersey court had to decide whether a surrogate-parenting contract was legally enforceable and, if not, who in this case should be awarded custody of the child.

The story of Baby M began on February 6, 1985, when Mary Beth Whitehead entered into an agreement with William and Elizabeth Stern to be a surrogate mother for their child. The Sterns both wanted a child but feared that pregnancy and childbirth would be risky for Mrs. Stern, who had been diagnosed as having a mild form of multiple sclerosis, a disease that could be exacerbated by childbirth.

Mary Beth Whitehead, who had applied to be a surrogate parent for them, was considered by the Sterns to represent the ideal solution. Mrs. Whitehead, already married with two children of her own, stated in her application that bearing their child would be more rewarding than working at a conventional job, and the $10,000 she would receive from the Sterns would benefit her and her family. In the six-page contract stating the terms of their agreement, the Sterns agreed to pay all costs and to give Mary Beth Whitehead the $10,000 fee. In addition, they agreed to accept and support the baby, even if it were born with serious defects. In return, Mrs. Whitehead agreed to be artifically inseminated with Mr. Stern's sperm, to have an amniocentesis if the Sterns so desired, and to give the baby to the Sterns following its birth. Mrs. Whitehead acknowledged in the contract that the child would be conceived "for the sole purpose of giving said child to William Stern."

By the time the baby was born, however, the Whiteheads felt differently. Mrs. Whitehead wanted to keep the child and refused to give it up in accordance with the terms of the contract. Although a New Jersey family-court judge awarded temporary custody of the child to the Sterns, the Whiteheads kept the baby and fled to Florida to avoid giving up "Sara"—their name for the child. The Sterns were equally determined to have their baby "Melissa" and paid $20,000 to a private investigator to locate the baby. When the Whiteheads were found three months later, an FBI agent returned the baby to the Sterns, who retained

---

Case 7.5
FIDELITY LEASING CORPORATION v. DUN & BRADSTREET, INC.
United States District Court, Eastern District of Pennsylvania, 1980.
494 F.Supp. 786.

FACTS Fidelity Leasing Corporation purchased credit information from the credit-reporting agency, Dun & Bradstreet, concerning Intercontinental Consulting Corporation. The information was substantially similar to that which had been provided to Fidelity by Intercontinental in its financial statement. Fidelity, on the basis of this information, extended credit to Intercontinental in the amount

of $18,939.84. Over a twenty-month period, Intercontinental made monthly payments to Fidelity but then discontinued payment on the debt, leaving a balance due of $11,442.82. When Fidelity investigated the matter, it discovered that Intercontinental was a sham organization established by another firm in order to obtain credit. Fidelity brought an action against Dun & Bradstreet, accusing the latter of negligence, gross negligence, and recklessness. Dun & Bradstreet moved for summary judgment, contending that it was protected from liability by an exculpatory clause in its contract with Fidelity. The exculpatory clause provided, in part, that Dun & Bradstreet would "not be liable for any loss or injury caused . . . by its negligent acts of omission or commission or

William and Elizabeth Stern

Mary Beth Whitehead

custody pending the results of the trial. Mrs. Whitehead was allowed to visit the girl for two hours twice weekly at a county office building.

On March 30, 1987, the judge ruled that the Stern-Whitehead contract was enforceable, and the Sterns were given permanent custody of "Baby M." In his decision, Judge Sorkow underscored the need for legislatures to address the problem of surrogate parenting: "Unfortunately, the law is slow to react to the rapid advance of science and changing human behavior. . . . As of this date not one state . . . has adopted a law that specifically addresses . . . the concept of surrogate parenting although many studies are in process and legislation has been introduced. . . . While a state could regulate, indeed should and must regulate the circumstances under which parties enter into reproductive contracts, it could not ban or refuse to enforce such transactions altogether without compelling reason." The judge stated that the Whiteheads and the Sterns "clearly understood the terms of the agreement and their obligations," and that no compelling reason existed in this case to bar enforcing the contract.

that of its officers, agents, or employees . . . in procuring, compiling, collecting, interpreting, reporting, communicating or delivering information. . . ."

ISSUE Can Dun & Bradstreet be protected from liability on the basis of the exculpatory clause?

DECISION Yes, to the claim of negligence; no, to the claims of gross negligence and recklessness.

REASON The court reasoned that since the president and co-shareholder of Fidelity was responsible for the transactions with Dun & Bradstreet and freely entered into the contract notwithstanding the exculpatory clause, the clause was enforceable. The clause had specifically stated that Dun & Bradstreet would not be liable for the "negligent acts of omission or commission" on the part of its officers, agents, or employees. The court would enforce the clause because "Pennsylvania courts have uniformly honored contract clauses where entered into freely, so long as they do not contravene public policy." The presiding judge held, however, that the clause did not protect Dun & Bradstreet from liability for gross negligence and recklessness, as the exculpatory clause did not specifically exclude liability from such claims.

Contracts entered into because of one party's vastly superior bargaining power may also be deemed unconscionable. These situations usually involve an adhesion contract, which is a contract drafted by the dominant party and then presented to the other—the adhering party—on a "take it or leave it" basis.[7]

Another example of an unconscionable contract is one where the terms of the agreement "shock the conscience" of the court. Suppose a welfare recipient with a fourth-grade education agrees to purchase a refrigerator for $2,000, signing a two-year, non-usurious installment contract. The same type of refrigerator usually sells for $400 on the market. Some courts have held this type of contract to be unconscionable despite the general rule that the courts will not inquire into the adequacy of the consideration.[8]

Both the Uniform Commercial Code and the Uniform Consumer Credit Code (UCCC) embody the unconscionability concept—the former with regard to the sale of goods and the latter with regard to consumer loans and the waiver of rights.[9]

In the following case, an estate administrator attempted to set aside a contract whereby a nursing home was to provide a woman continuing care in consideration of the transfer of all her present and future assets to the home.

Case 7.6
PIEHL v. NORWEGIAN OLD PEOPLES' HOME SOCIETY OF CHICAGO
Appellate Court of Illinois, 1984.
127 Ill. App. 3d 593, 83 Ill. Dec. 98, 469 N.E. 2d 705.

FACTS In 1981 Mabel Finn signed a document entitled "Continuing Care Contract" with the Norwood Park Home, a nursing facility owned and operated by the Norwegian Old Peoples' Home Society (the Home). The contract provided that the Home would give continuing care in the form of room, board, and nursing and medical services until Finn left the facility voluntarily, involuntarily, or by reason of death. For these services Finn agreed to transfer all her present and future assets. The Home reserved the right to cancel the contract if Finn failed to qualify for old-age assistance benefits once the assets transferred to the Home were exhausted. Five and one-half months later, Finn died while a resident of the Home. The Home paid for Finn's funeral expenses, but, when Finn's administrator demanded an accounting for the assets and funds transferred to the Home, the Home refused to make such an accounting. Piehl, Finn's administrator, filed suit to set aside the contract because mutual agreement to the contract was absent and because the contract terms were oppressive and unconscionable. The trial court granted the Home's petition to dismiss Piehl's action, and Piehl appealed.

ISSUE Could the contract be set aside for lack of mutual agreement to the contract or unconscionability?

DECISION No. The appellate court affirmed the trial court's dismissal of the administrator's petition, and the Home was allowed to keep the assets and funds transferred.

REASON The court addressed Piehl's argument that the "continuing care contract" was void owing to lack of mutual agreement by stating that "a contract does not lack mutuality simply because its obligations appear unequal or because every obligation or right is not met by an equivalent counter-obligation or right in the other party." Further, mutuality exists if each party has made a promise to the other. Here, Finn transferred her assets, and the Home was to provide her with care. Although the contract stipulated that the Home could cancel the agreement under certain circumstances (under an "option to terminate the contract" clause), the Home did not have the absolute right to terminate at any time; it could terminate only in those certain circumstances. Piehl also argued the contract was unconscionable. The court defined an unconscionable contract as a one-sided contract, one that no person in his or her right mind would make, and one that no fair and honest person would accept. The court found the contract not to be so unreasonably favorable to the Home so as to be unconscionable.

---

7. See Henningsen v. Bloomfield Motors, Inc., 32 N.J. 358, 161 A. 2d 69 (1960).
8. Jones v. Star Credit Corp., 59 Misc. 2d 189, 298 N.Y.S. 2d 264 (1969).
9. See, for example, UCC Sections 2-302 and 2-719 and UCCC Sections 5.108 and 1.107.

Case 7.6—Continued

COMMENT The mere fact that the terms of a contract favor one party more than the other is insufficient to claim that unconscionability exists (because of the adequacy of consideration rule), and until the unfairness hurts the consciousness of society, courts will not set aside the contract. The philosophy is that persons must be bound by their legal agreements, even if an agreement turns out to operate as a hardship on one of the parties.

❖ Effect of Illegality

In general, an illegal contract is void: the contract is deemed never to have existed, and the courts will not aid either party. In most illegal contracts, both parties are considered to be equally at fault—*in pari delicto*. If it is executory (not yet fulfilled), neither party can enforce it. If it is executed, there can be neither contractual nor quasi-contractual recovery.

That one wrongdoer in an illegal contract is unjustly enriched at the expense of the other is of no concern to the law—except under certain circumstances (to be discussed shortly). The major justification for this hands-off attitude is that it is improper to place the machinery of justice at the disposal of a plaintiff who has broken the law by entering into an illegal bargain. Another justification is the hoped-for deterrent effect of this general rule. A plaintiff who suffers loss because of an illegal bargain should presumably be deterred from entering into similar illegal bargains in the future.

Exceptions to the General Rule

Some persons are excepted from the general rule that neither party to an illegal bargain can sue for breach and neither can recover for performance rendered.

Justifiable Ignorance of the Facts   When one of the parties is relatively innocent, that party can often obtain restitution or recovery of benefits conferred in a partially executed contract. The courts do not enforce the contract but do allow the parties to return to their original position.

It is also possible for an innocent party who has fully performed under the contract to enforce the contract against the guilty party. For example, Debbie contracts with Tucker to purchase ten crates of goods that legally cannot be bought or sold. Tucker hires a trucking firm to deliver the shipment to Debbie and pays the firm the normal fee of $500. Although the law specifies that the shipment, use, and sale of the goods were illegal, the carrier, being an innocent party, can legally collect the $500 from Tucker.

Members of Protected Classes   When a statute protects a certain class of people, a member of that class can enforce an illegal contract even though the other party cannot. There are also statutes that prohibit certain employees (such as flight attendants) from working more than a specified number of hours per month. An employee who works more than the maximum can recover for those extra hours of service.

Another example of statutes designed to protect a particular class of people are the **Blue Sky laws,** which regulate and supervise investment companies for the protection of the public. Such laws are intended to stop the sale of stock in fly-by-night concerns, such as visionary oil wells and distant gold mines. Investors are protected

BLUE SKY LAWS
Laws that regulate the offer and sale of securities.

as a class and can sue to recover the purchase price of stock issued in violation of such laws.

Most states also have statutes regulating the sale of insurance. If an insurance company violates a statute when selling insurance, the purchaser can nevertheless enforce the policy and recover from the insurer.

Withdrawal from an Illegal Agreement   If the illegal part of a bargain has not yet been performed, the party tendering performance can withdraw from the bargain and recover the performance or its value. For example, suppose Martha and Andy decide to wager (illegally) on the outcome of a boxing match. They each deposit money with a stakeholder, who agrees to pay the winner of the bet. At this point, each party has performed part of the agreement, but the illegal part of the agreement will not occur until the money is paid to the winner. Before such payment occurs, either party is entitled to withdraw from the agreement by giving notice of repudiation to the stakeholder.

Illegal Contract through Fraud, Duress, or Undue Influence   Often illegal contracts involve two blameworthy parties, where one party is more at fault than the other. Whenever a plaintiff has been induced to enter into an illegal bargain as a result of fraud, duress, or undue influence, he or she can either enforce the contract or recover for its value.

Reformation of an Illegal Covenant Not to Compete   On occasion, where the covenant not to compete is unreasonable in its essential terms, the court may *reform* the covenant, converting its terms into reasonable ones. Instead of declaring the covenant illegal and unenforceable, the court applies the rule of reasonableness and changes the contract so that its basic, original intent can be enforced. This presents a problem, however, in that the judge becomes a party to the contract. Consequently, contract reformation is usually carried out by a court only when necessary to prevent undue burdens or hardships.

Application

Law and the Salesperson

Sales personnel, particularly those who are paid on a commission basis, are often eager to make contracts. But sometimes these salespersons must deal with minors or intoxicated persons, both of whom have limited contractual capacity upon entering into such contracts.

A salesperson selling substantial consumer durables, such as console televisions or automobiles, must be careful of contracting with a minor and should heed the adage, "When in doubt, check." Remember that a contract signed with a minor (unless it is for necessaries) is voidable, and the minor may exercise the option to disaffirm the contract, even though the adult who entered into the contract with the minor may not avoid his or her contractual duties. A salesperson should know, therefore, the legal age of majority in his or her state. Proof of legal age should be required of a customer when there is any doubt concerning his or her age.

Little need be said about a salesperson's dealings with obviously intoxicated persons. If the customer, despite intoxication, understands the legal consequences of the contract being signed, it is enforceable. Nonetheless, it is difficult to establish that the intoxicated customer understood the contract if he or she disputes it.

Another potential problem involves installment sales contracts that carry a higher interest rate than the state's legal maximum. Most states have usury laws regulating the maximum rate of interest. Any credit contract that involves a usurious interest rate is contrary to statute and therefore constitutes an illegal bargain. In some states, the contract is considered void. In many states, the lender is simply penalized.

Checklist for the Salesperson

☐ 1. Determine the legal age of majority in your state.

☐ 2. When in doubt about the age of a customer to whom you are about to sell major consumer durable goods or anything other than necessities, require proof of legal age. If such proof is not forthcoming, require that a parent or guardian sign the contract.

☐ 3. Do not sign contracts with intoxicated customers.

☐ 4. If you are involved with retail installment sales contracts or you extend any form of credit to your customers, make sure the interest you charge does not exceed your state's maximum interest rate.

❖ Chapter Summary: Capacity and Legality

CONTRACTUAL CAPACITY	

Minors	A minor is a person who has not yet reached the age of majority. In most states the age of majority is eighteen for contract purposes. Contracts with minors are voidable at the option of the minor. Upon reaching the age of majority, a minor may *disaffirm* or *ratify* contracts made when he or she was a minor.
	
	1. *Disaffirmance:*
	  a. Can take place (in most states) at any time during minority and within a reasonable time after the minor has reached the age of majority.
	  b. When disaffirming executed contracts, the minor has a *duty of restoration*—to return received goods if they are still in the minor's control, or (in some states) to pay their reasonable value.
	  c. If a minor disaffirms a contract, the entire contract must be disaffirmed.
	  d. A minor may disaffirm a contract for necessaries but remains liable for the reasonable value of the goods.
	  e. A minor who has committed an act of fraud (such as misrepresentation of age) will be denied the right to disaffirm by some courts.
	
	2. *Ratification*—May be express or implied.
	  a. Express—Exists when the minor, through a writing or an oral agreement, explicitly assumes the obligations imposed by the contract.
	  b. Implied—Exists when the conduct of the minor is inconsistent with disaffirmance.
	
	3. *Liability for torts*—A minor is liable for his or her torts.

Intoxicated Persons	1. A contract entered into by an intoxicated person is *voidable* at the option of the intoxicated person if the person was drunk enough to lack mental capacity, even if the intoxication was voluntary. 2. A contract with an intoxicated person is *enforceable* if, despite being intoxicated, the person understood the legal consequences of entering into the contract.
Insane Persons	1. A contract made by a person adjudged by a court to be insane is *void*. 2. A contract made by an insane person not adjudged by a court to be insane is *voidable* at the option of the insane person.
LEGALITY	
Contracts Contrary to Statute	1. *Usury*—A lender who makes a loan at an interest rate above the maximum rate of interest mandated by statute is guilty of usury. Some states exempt corporate loans from usury laws; many states have special statutes governing interest on installment loans. 2. *Gambling*—Gambling contracts that contravene (go against) state statutes are deemed illegal and thus void. 3. *Sabbath laws* (Sunday laws)—Laws prohibiting the formation or the performance of certain contracts on Sunday; such laws vary widely from state to state, and most have been abolished. 4. *Licensing statutes*—Contracts entered into by persons who do not have a license, when one is required by statute, will not be enforceable *unless* the underlying purpose of the statute is to raise revenues (and not to protect the public from unauthorized practitioners).
Contracts Contrary to Public Policy	1. *Contracts in restraint of trade*—Contracts whose purpose is to reduce or restrain free competition are illegal unless the restraint is reasonable. Most of these contracts are now prohibited by statutes. An exception is a *covenant not to compete*. It is usually enforced by the courts if the terms are reasonable as to time and area of restraint, especially when the covenant is ancillary to

❖ Chapter Summary: Capacity and Legality—Continued

Contracts Contrary to Public Policy (Continued)	the sale of a business where the goodwill and reputation of the firm are essential to the contract or ancillary to a partnership contract. Courts tend to closely scrutinize a covenant not to compete when it is part of an employment contract. If the covenant is ancillary but unreasonable as to time or area, courts may reform the covenant to be within reasonable constraints and then enforce the reformed contract. 2. *Unconscionable contracts and exculpatory clauses*—When a contract or contract clause is so unfair that it is oppressive to one party, it can be deemed unconscionable by society; as such, it is illegal and cannot be enforced.

Effect of Illegality	1. In general, an illegal contract is void, and the courts will aid neither party when both parties are considered to be equally at fault (in pari delicto). If the contract is executory, neither party can enforce it. If the contract is executed, there can be neither contractual nor quasi-contractual recovery.
	
	2. Exceptions (i.e., situations where recovery is allowed):
	  a. When one party to the contract is relatively innocent.
	  b. When one party to the contract is a member of a group of persons protected by statute.
	  c. When one party was induced to enter into an illegal bargain through fraud, duress, or undue influence.

❖ Questions and Case Problems

7-1. Joseph, who owns the only pizza parlor in Middletown, learns that Giovanni is about to open a competing pizza parlor in the same small town, just a few blocks from Joseph's restaurant. Joseph offers Giovanni $10,000 in return for Giovanni's promise not to open a pizza parlor in the Middletown area. Giovanni accepts the $10,000 but goes ahead with his plans, in spite of the agreement. When Giovanni opens his restaurant for business, Joseph sues to enjoin Giovanni's continued operation of his restaurant or to recover the $10,000. The court denies recovery. On what basis?

7-2. After Katie has several drinks one night, she sells Emily a valuable fur stole for ten dollars. The next day, Katie offers the ten dollars to Emily and requests the return of her stole. Emily refuses, claiming they had a valid contract of sale. Katie explains that she was intoxicated at the time the bargain was made, and thus the contract is voidable at her option. Who is right? Explain.

7-3. Al has been the owner of a car dealership for a number of years. One day, Al sold one of his most expensive cars to Kessler. At the time of the sale, Al thought Kessler acted in a peculiar manner, but he gave the matter no further thought until four months later, when Kessler's court-appointed guardian appeared at his office, tendered back the car, and demanded Kessler's money back. The guardian informed Al that Kessler had been adjudged insane two months previously by a proper court.

(a) Discuss the rights of the parties.
(b) If Kessler had been adjudicated insane at the time of the contract, what would be the legal effect of the contract?

7-4. State X requires that persons be licensed who prepare and serve liquor in the form of drinks at commercial establishments. The only requirement for obtaining a yearly license is that the person be at least eighteen years old. Mickey, age 35, is hired as a bartender for the Southtown Restaurant. Gerald, a staunch alumnus of a nearby university, brings twenty of his friends to the restaurant to celebrate a football victory that afternoon. Gerald orders four rounds of drinks, and the bill is nearly $200. Gerald learns that Mickey failed to renew his bartender's license, and Gerald refuses to pay, claiming the contract is unenforceable. Discuss whether Gerald is correct.

7-5. A famous New York City hotel, Hotel First, is noted for its food as well as its luxury accommodations. Hotel First contracts with a famous chef, Allen Berg, to become its head chef at $7,500 per month. The contract states that should Berg leave the employment of Hotel First for any reason, he will not work as a chef for any hotel or restaurant in New York, New Jersey, or Pennsylvania for one year. During the first six months of the contract, Hotel First substantially advertises Berg as its head chef, and business at the hotel is excellent. Then a dispute arises between the hotel management and Berg, and Berg terminates his employment. One month later, he is hired by a famous New Jersey restaurant just across the New York state line. Hotel First learns of Berg's employment through a large advertisement in a New York City newspaper. It seeks to enjoin Berg from working in that restaurant as a chef for one year. Discuss how successful Hotel First will be in its action.

7-6. In 1982, Webster Street Partnership, Ltd. (Webster) entered into a lease agreement with Matthew Sheridan and Pat Wilwerding. Webster was aware that both Sheridan and Wilwerding were minors. Both tenants were living away from home, apparently with the understanding that they could return home at any time. Sheridan and Wilwerding paid the first month's rent, but then failed to pay the rent for the next month and vacated the apartment. Webster sued them for breach of contract. They claimed that the lease agreement was voidable since they were minors. Who will win, and why? [Webster Street Partnership, Ltd. v. Sheridan, 220 Neb. 9, 368 N.W.2d 439 (1985)]

7-7. Jo Anne Hall's husband induced her to consent to get divorced. She claimed that her former husband represented that the divorce was needed for business reasons. He promised that after the divorce they would continue living together as man and wife, and he would support her as he had in the past. The divorce was granted and they lived together for three months. He then left her so he could marry another woman. Mrs. Hall filed suit, claiming breach of contract, among other allegations. Discuss whether a contract to get a divorce and to cohabitate after the divorce is illegal. [Hall v. Hall, 455 So.2d 813 (Ala. 1984)]

7-8. Roeber and the Swift & Courtney & Beecher Company were both engaged in the business of manufacturing matches. Swift desired to purchase Roeber's business, which was quite lucrative. Pursuant to the sale agreement between Swift and Roeber, Roeber agreed not to engage in the match business in any state in the United States other than Nevada and Montana for ninety-nine years. Was the contract enforceable? [Diamond Match Co. v. Roeber, 106 N.Y. 473, 13 N.E. 419 (1801)]

7-9. Smith purchased a car on credit from Bobby Floars Toyota, Inc. a month before his eighteenth birthday. Smith made regular monthly payments for eleven months, but then returned the car to the dealer and made no further payments on it. The dealer sold the car and sued Smith to recover the difference between the amount obtained by the sale of the car and the money Smith still owed to the dealer. Smith refused to pay on the ground that he had been a minor at the time of purchase and had disaffirmed the contract after he had reached the age of majority. Will the car dealer succeed in its claim that the ten monthly payments made after Smith turned eighteen constituted a ratification of the purchase contract? [Bobby Floars Toyota, Inc. v. Smith, 48 N.C.App. 580, 269 S.E.2d 320 (1980)]

7-10. Arnold entered a stock car race and, along with all the other participants, was required to sign an exculpatory contract by the owner of the fairgrounds where the race was to take place. The contract stated that the drivers assumed the risk for any injuries they may sustain during the race and released the owner from all liability. During the race Arnold's car crashed through a guardrail and hit a telephone pole and a pile of lumber on the other side of the railing. The car caught on fire, and the rescue team sprayed firefighting chemicals on the car without first removing Arnold from the car. This caused Arnold to incur severe brain damage and to become a quadriplegic. Arnold sued the owner of the fairgrounds for damages, claiming that the owner's fire-fighting employees had been negligent in their rescue operations. Can the owner be held liable for Arnold's injuries, notwithstanding the existence of the exculpatory contract? [Arnold v. Schawano County Agricultural Society, 111 Wis.2d 203, 330 N.W.2d 773 (1983)]

Chapter 8

Genuineness of Assent and Form

A contract has been entered into between two parties, each with full legal capacity and for a legal purpose. The contract is also supported by consideration. Nonetheless, the contract may be unenforceable for at least two reasons. First, if the parties do not genuinely assent to the terms of the contract because of fraudulent misrepresentation, duress, undue influence, or mistake (in other words, if there is no true "meeting of the minds"), the contract will not be enforced. As Aristotle stated, the law seeks to ensure that "the citizens of a state will do justice to one another." If the law were to enforce contracts not genuinely assented to by the contracting parties, injustice would result.

Second, a contract may be unenforceable if it is not in the proper form. For example, if the contract is required by law to be in writing, there usually needs to be written evidence of it.

In this chapter we examine problems relating to genuineness of assent; we then look at the kinds of contracts that require a writing under what is called the Statute of Frauds.

> *"Law is a pledge that the citizens of a state will do justice to one another."*
>
> **Aristotle, 384–322 B.C.** *(Greek philosopher)*

❖ Genuineness of Assent

When a mistake, misrepresentation, undue influence, or duress condition a person's acceptance of a contractual obligation, genuine assent to the contract may be lacking and the contract may be unenforceable.

Mistakes

It is important to distinguish between *mistakes as to judgment of value or quality* and *mistakes as to fact*. Only the latter have legal significance. Suppose, for example, that Jane Collins contracts to purchase ten acres of land in Idaho. She believes the land is owned by the Mittens, but it actually belongs to the Krauses. A court may allow this contract to be avoided because Jane has made a mistake of fact. Suppose, however, that Jane contracts to buy ten acres of land and believes it is worth $15,000 when it really is worth only $1,500. Can Jane escape her contractual obligations because of her mistake? Not likely, because her mistake in this instance is one of *value* or *quality*, which normally does not affect the enforceability of the contract.

In contract formation, mistakes can occur in two forms—*unilateral* and *bilateral* (*mutual*). A unilateral mistake is made by only one of the contracting parties; a mutual mistake is made by both.

Unilateral Mistakes   A unilateral mistake involves some *material fact* that is important to the subject matter of the contract. In general, a unilateral mistake does not afford the mistaken party any right to relief from the contract. In other words, the contract is enforceable.[1] For example, Ellen intends to sell her stereo for $550. When she learns that Howard is interested in buying a used stereo, she writes a letter to him and offers to sell her stereo, but she mistakenly types in the price of $500. Howard immediately writes back, accepting Ellen's offer. Even though Ellen intended only to sell her stereo for $550, she has made a unilateral mistake and is bound by contract to sell the stereo to Howard for $500.

There are at least two exceptions: (1) If the *other* party to the contract knows or should have known that a mistake was made; or (2) if the error was due to a mathematical mistake in addition, subtraction, division, or multiplication and was done inadvertently and without gross negligence, the contract may not be enforceable. Consider the following situation. Odell Construction Company made a bid to install the plumbing in an apartment building. When Herbert Odell, the president, added up his costs, his secretary forgot to give him the figures for the pipe fittings. Because of the omission, Odell's bid was $6,500 below that of the other bidders. The prime contractor, Sunspan, Inc., accepted Odell's bid. If Sunspan was not aware of Odell's mistake and could not reasonably have been aware of it, the contract will be enforceable, and Odell will be required to install the plumbing at the bid price. If, however, it can be shown that Odell's secretary mentioned her error to Sunspan, or if Odell's bid was so far below the others that, as a contractor, Sunspan should reasonably have known the bid was a mistake, the contract can be rescinded. Sunspan would not be allowed to accept the offer knowing it was made by mistake.[2] The law of contracts protects only *reasonable* expectations.

In the following case, a stock brokerage firm was unable to recover an overpayment it had mistakenly made to its clients.

Case 8.1
FOSTER & MARSHALL, INC. v. PFISTER
Court of Appeals of Oregon, 1984.
66 Or.App. 685, 674 P.2d 1215.

FACTS   Robert and Wendy Pfister held 100 shares of Tracor Computing Corporation stock, which was no longer being traded on the New York Stock Exchange and which they thought was of little value. They asked a stock brokerage firm, Foster & Marshall, to evaluate it for them.

The brokerage firm advised the Pfisters that Tracor Computing had changed its name to Continuum Co., Inc. and that its stock was worth $49.50 a share; thus, the Pfisters' holdings were valued at $4,950. Robert Pfister suspected there might be an error in the valuation and asked Foster & Marshall to recheck the value, which was done. The Pfisters sold their shares to Foster & Marshall, who paid them the $4,950 for the 100 shares. Later, the brokerage firm discovered that the Tracor Computing stock had been exchanged for Continuum stock at a 10-to-1 ratio, which meant that the Pfisters had owned only 10 shares. The

---

1. Restatement, Second, Contracts, Section 153, liberalizes this rule to take into account the modern trend of allowing avoidance although only one party has been mistaken.
2. Peerless Glass Co. v. Pacific Crockery Co., 121 Cal. 641, 54 P. 101 (1898).

Case 8.1—*Continued*

Pfisters refused to return the $4,466.25 overpayment they had received from the brokerage firm, and Foster & Marshall sued to collect the money. The trial court granted summary judgment to Foster & Marshall, and the Pfisters appealed.

ISSUE Can Foster & Marshall recover the overpayment it made to the Pfisters resulting from Foster & Marshall's unilateral mistake of fact?

DECISION No. The Court of Appeals reversed the decision of the trial court and remanded the case in favor of the Pfisters.

REASON The court stated that a "party making a unilateral mistake of fact is not entitled to restitution unless the mistake is basic to the contract and known to the other party, or circumstances are such that the other party, as a reasonable person, should have known of the mistake." The court found no evidence that the Pfisters had any actual knowledge of the mistaken valuation placed on the stock, nor could it conclude that the Pfisters, as reasonable persons, should have known of the mistake. The court concluded that it was "not inequitable as a matter of law to hold Foster & Marshall to the bad bargain it had made as a result of its own negligent research," especially in light of the fact that the Pfisters contended they had changed their position and had made a commitment to build a new home in reliance on the payment.

Mutual Mistakes When both parties are mistaken about the same material fact, the contract can be rescinded by either party.[3] As stated earlier, the mistake must be about a *material fact* (one that is important and central to the contract). If, instead, a mutual mistake concerns the *value* or *quality* of the object of the contract, the contract can be enforced by either party. This rule is based on the theory that both parties assume certain risks when they enter into a contract. Without this rule, almost any party who did not receive what he or she considered was a fair bargain could argue bilateral mistake. In essence, this would make *adequacy* of consideration a factor in determining whether a contract existed, and, as discussed previously, the courts normally do not inquire into the adequacy of the consideration.

Sometimes courts have difficulty ascertaining whether the mutual mistake is one of identity (fact) or one of value, as occurred in an early Michigan case involving a contract to purchase a cow.[4] Both the owner (seller) and the purchaser thought the cow was barren, and thus the negotiated price was several hundred dollars less than it would have been had the cow been capable of breeding. Just before delivery, the owner discovered the cow had conceived a calf, and he refused to deliver the much more valuable cow to the purchaser, claiming the contract should be rescinded owing to a mutual mistake in identity. In a split decision, the court held that "a barren cow is substantially a different creature than a breeding one." Therefore, the mutual mistake was one of fact because it went to the substance (identity) of the contract rather than the value of the cow.

The classic case on mutual mistake of fact involved a ship named *Peerless* that was to sail from Bombay with certain cotton goods on board. More than one ship named *Peerless* sailed from Bombay that winter, however.

---

3. Restatement, Second, Contracts, Section 152.
4. Sherwood v. Walker, 66 Mich. 568, 33 N.W. 919 (1887).

Case 8.2
RAFFLES v. WICHELHAUS AND ANOTHER
2 H.&C. 908, 1864.

FACTS   Wichelhaus purchased a shipment of cotton from Raffles "to arrive ex 'Peerless' from Bombay." Wichelhaus meant a ship called the *Peerless* sailing from Bombay in October; Raffles meant another ship called the *Peerless* sailing from Bombay in December. When the goods arrived on the December *Peerless,* Raffles delivered them to Wichelhaus. By that time, however, Wichelhaus was no longer willing to accept them.

ISSUE   Was there a bilateral mistake of fact, which would release Wichelhaus from the contract?

DECISION   Yes. The court adjudged that a bilateral mistake in fact had occurred, and hence there was no contract.

REASON   When both parties contract under the mistaken, but reasonable, belief that a certain fact is true from an objective viewpoint, neither one is bound by the contract. The British court hearing the case stated, "There is nothing on the face of the contract to show that any particular ship called the 'Peerless' was meant."

Fraudulent Misrepresentation

Although fraud is a tort, it also affects the genuineness of the innocent party's consent to the contract. Thus, the transaction is not voluntary in the sense required by "mutual assent." When an innocent party consents to a contract with fraudulent terms, the contract usually can be voided because he or she has not *voluntarily* consented.[5] Normally, the innocent party can either rescind the contract and be restored to the original position or enforce the contract and seek damages for injuries resulting from the fraud.

Typically, there are four elements of fraud:

1.   A misrepresentation of a material fact has occurred.
2.   There is an intent to deceive.
3.   The innocent party has justifiably relied on the misrepresentation.
4.   The innocent party has been injured.

Misrepresentation Must Occur   The first element of proving fraud is to show that misrepresentation of a material fact has occurred. This misrepresentation can be in words or actions. For example, the statement "This painting is a Picasso" is an express misrepresentation of fact if the painting was done by another artist.

A statement of opinion is generally not subject to a claim of fraud. For example, claims such as "this computer will never break down" or "this car will last for years and years" are statements of opinion, not fact, and contracting parties should recognize them as such and not rely on them. A fact is objective and verifiable; an opinion is usually subject to debate. Therefore, a seller is allowed to "huff and puff his wares" without being liable for fraud.

In certain cases, however, particularly when a naïve purchaser relies on a so-called expert's opinion, the innocent party may be entitled to rescission or reformation. This occurred in the following case.

---

5.   Restatement, Second, Contracts, Sections 163 and 164.

Case 8.3
VOKES v. ARTHUR MURRAY, INC.
District Court of Appeal of Florida, Second District, 1968.
212 So. 2d 906.

FACTS   Audrey Vokes was a fifty-one-year-old widow. While she was attending a dance party at Davenport's School of Dancing, an instructor sold her eight half-hour dance lessons for the sum of $14.50. Thereafter, over a period of less than sixteen months, she was sold a total of fourteen dance courses, which amounted to 2,302 hours of dancing lessons for a total cash outlay of $31,090.45. All of these lessons were sold to her by salespersons who continually assured her that she was very talented, that she was progressing in her lessons, that she had great dance potential, and that they were "developing her into a beautiful dancer." Vokes contended that, in fact, she was not progressing in her dancing ability, had no "dance aptitude," and had difficulty even "hearing the musical beat." She finally attempted to terminate her contract for unused dance lessons.

ISSUE   Could Vokes's contract be rescinded because salespersons misrepresented her dancing ability?

DECISION   Yes. Vokes could avoid her contractual obligations since her agreement to purchase lessons from the studio was procured by false representations of her talents and abilities.

REASON   To be grounds for rescission of a contract, a misrepresentation must usually be one of fact rather than opinion, but there are exceptions to the rule. The court held, "A statement of a party having . . . superior knowledge may be regarded as a statement of fact although it would be considered as opinion if the parties were dealing on equal terms. It could be reasonably supposed here that defendants had 'superior knowledge' as to whether plaintiff had 'dance potential.' . . . " According to the court, "it would be a reasonable inference from the undenied averments of the complaint that the flowery eulogiums heaped upon her by defendants as a prelude to her contracting for . . . additional hours of instruction . . . proceeded as much or more from the urge to 'ring the cash register' as from any honest or realistic appraisal of her dancing prowess or a factual representation of her progress."

Misrepresentation by Conduct   Misrepresentation need not be expressly made through the words or writings of another; it can also occur by conduct. For example, if a seller, by his or her actions, prevents a buyer from learning of some fact that is material to the contract, such an action constitutes misrepresentation by conduct. Suppose, for example, Cummings contracts to purchase a racehorse from Garner. The horse is blind in one eye, but when Garner shows the horse, he skillfully conceals this fact by keeping the horse's head turned so that Cummings does not see the defect. The concealment constitutes fraud.[6] Another example of misrepresentation by conduct is the false denial of knowledge or information concerning facts that are material to the contract, when such knowledge or information is requested.

Misrepresentation of Law   Misrepresentation of law does not *ordinarily* entitle the party to be relieved of a contract. For example, Debbie has a parcel of property that she is trying to sell to Barry. Debbie knows that a local ordinance prohibits building anything higher than three stories on the property. Nonetheless, she tells Barry, "You can build a condominium fifty stories high if you want to." Barry buys the land and later discovers that Debbie's statement is false. Normally, Barry cannot avoid the contract, because under common law, people are assumed to know state and local laws.

---

6.   Restatement, Second, Contracts, Section 160.

Also, a layperson should not rely on a nonlawyer's statement about a point of law. Exceptions to this rule occur, however, when the misrepresenting party is in a profession known to require greater knowledge of the law than the average citizen possesses.

In the following case, a party brought an action against a hotel owner for his misrepresentation of state law.

Case 8.4
TWO, INC. v. GILMORE
Colorado Court of Appeals, 1984.
679 P.2d 116.

FACTS   Gilmore owned the Jerome Hotel in Aspen. Two, Inc. contacted Gilmore about the possibility of operating a disco in the hotel. Gilmore represented to Two that if they agreed to a "management agreement," by law Two could share Gilmore's liquor license. Shortly thereafter, Gilmore discovered that the agreement did not conform with state liquor codes and was therefore illegal. After Gilmore threatened to notify the liquor distributors that Two did not have a liquor license, Two abandoned the premises and sued for damages on the grounds of fraud. The trial court entered a judgment for Gilmore, and Two appealed.

ISSUE   Does Gilmore's misrepresentation of law entitle Two, Inc. to damages on the grounds of fraudulent misrepresentation?

DECISION   No. The trial court's judgment was affirmed.

REASON   Gilmore's representation to Two, Inc. that the "management agreement" would allow the sharing of the liquor-license privileges was a representation of law. Because a representation of law is only an expression of opinion and can be tested for truthfulness by ordinary vigilance and attention, the party to whom such a representation is made has no right to rely on it. Consequently, an incorrect representation of law cannot void a contract or support an action for damages.

Misrepresentation by Silence   Ordinarily, neither party to a contract has a duty to come forward and disclose facts, and a contract normally will not be set aside because certain pertinent information is not volunteered. For example, suppose you are selling a car that has been in an accident and repaired. You do not need to volunteer this information to a potential buyer. If, however, the purchaser asks you if the car has had extensive body work and you lie, you have committed a fraudulent misrepresentation. Generally, if a *serious* defect or a *serious* potential problem is known to the seller but cannot reasonably be suspected by the buyer, the seller may have a duty to speak. For example, if a city fails to disclose to bidders subsoil conditions that will cause great expense in constructing a sewer, the city is guilty of fraud.[7] Also, when the parties are in a fiduciary relationship (one of trust, such as partners, doctor and patient, and attorney and client), there is a duty to disclose material facts; failure to do so may constitute fraud.

SCIENTER
Knowledge by the misrepresenting party that material facts have been falsely represented or omitted with an intent to deceive.

Intent to Deceive   The second element of fraud is knowledge on the part of the misrepresenting party that facts have been falsely represented. This element, normally called **scienter**, or "guilty knowledge," normally signifies that there was an *intent to*

---

7.   *City of Salinas v. Souza & McCue Constr. Co.,* 66 Cal.2d 217, 57 Cal.Rptr. 337, 424 P.2d 921 (1967). Normally, the seller must disclose only "latent" defects—that is, defects that would not readily be discovered even by an expert. Thus, termites in a house would not be a latent defect, since an expert could readily discover their presence.

deceive. Proof of intent is not necessary if the circumstances surrounding a transaction are such that one can *infer* the intent.

Reliance on the Misrepresentation   The third element of fraud is reasonably *justifiable reliance* on the misrepresentation of fact. The deceived party must have a justifiable reason for relying on the misrepresentation, and the misrepresentation must be an important factor (but not necessarily the sole factor) in inducing the party to enter into the contract.

Reliance is not justified if the innocent party knows the true facts or relies on obviously extravagant statements. Suppose a used-car dealer tells you, "This old Cadillac will get fifty miles to the gallon." You would not normally be justified in relying on this statement. But suppose Merkel, a bank director, induces O'Connell, a co-director, into signing a guarantee that the bank's assets will satisfy its liabilities by stating, "We have plenty of assets to satisfy our creditors." If O'Connell knows the true facts, he is not justified in relying on Merkel's statement. If O'Connell does not know the true facts, however, *and has no way of finding them out*, he is justified in relying on the statement. The same rule applies to defects in property sold. If the defects are obvious, the buyer cannot justifiably rely on the seller's representations. If the defects are hidden or latent (that is, not appearing on the surface), the buyer is justified in relying on the seller's statements.

Injury to the Innocent Party   The final element of fraud is injury to the innocent party. The courts are divided on this issue. Some do not require a showing of injury when the action is to *rescind* or *cancel* the contract—these courts hold that since rescission returns the parties to the position they were in prior to the contract, a showing of injury to the innocent party is unnecessary.[8]

For a person to *recover damages* caused by fraud, proof of an injury is universally required. The measure of damages is ordinarily equal to the property's value had it been delivered as represented, less the actual price paid for the property. In actions based on fraud, courts often award **punitive** or **exemplary damages,** which are granted to a plaintiff over and above the proved, actual compensation for the loss. Punitive damages are based on the public-policy consideration of *punishing* the defendant or setting an example for similar wrongdoers.

PUNITIVE OR EXEMPLARY DAMAGES
Compensation in excess of actual or consequential damages, for the purpose of punishing the wrongdoer. Awarded only in cases involving willful or malicious misconduct.

Undue Influence

Undue influence arises from relationships in which one party can greatly influence another party, thus overcoming that party's free will. Minors and elderly people are often under the influence of guardians. If a guardian induces a young or elderly ward to enter into a contract that benefits the guardian, undue influence is probably being exerted. Undue influence can arise from a number of confidential or fiduciary relationships: attorney-client, doctor-patient, guardian-ward, parent-child, husband-wife, and trustee-beneficiary. The essential feature of undue influence is that the party being taken advantage of does not, in reality, exercise free will in entering into a contract. A contract entered into under excessive or undue influence lacks genuine assent and is therefore voidable.[9]

---

8.   See, for example, Kaufman v. Jaffe, 244 App.Div. 344, 279 N.Y.S. 392 (1935).
9.   Restatement, Second, Contracts, Section 177.

Business Law in Action

In Search of Wisdom

In 1959, a case involving alleged misrepresentation came before the appellate division of the Superior Court of New Jersey: *Trustees of Columbia University v. Jacobsen.*[1] After attending Dartmouth for his freshman year, Roy Jacobsen attended Columbia from 1951 to 1954, but he failed to graduate because of poor scholastic standing. When Columbia sued Jacobsen for $1,000 in tuition still owed by him, Jacobsen countered with the allegation that the august institution of higher learning had failed to impart the wisdom promised—by its motto, its brochures, the inscriptions over its buildings, in its presidential addresses, and so on. Because Columbia had promised something it could not deliver, it was guilty of misrepresentation and deceit and should return to Jacobsen all the tuition he had paid—$7,016.

Jacobsen's counterclaim consisted of fifty counts, which alleged that Columbia had promised to teach him

1. 53 N.J.Super. 574, 148 A.2d 63 (1959), affirmed 31 N.J. 221, 156 A.2d 251 (1959).

"wisdom, truth, character, enlightenment, understanding, justice, liberty, honesty, courage, beauty, and similar virtues and qualities; that it would develop the whole man, maturity, well-roundedness, objective thinking, and the like." At the heart of these fifty counts was a single complaint, according to Jacobsen:

> I have really only one charge against Columbia: that it does not teach Wisdom as it claims to do. From this charge ensues an endless number of charges, of which I have selected fifty at random . . . though the central issue is that of Columbia's pretense of teaching Wisdom.

Jacobsen went on to define wisdom, drawing from Webster's dictionary, the Bhagavad Gita, the Analects of Confucius, the Koran, Plato, the Bible, and countless other sources.

The court delved into the problem with proper judicial rigor. After commenting on the "inartistic" character of the defendant's counterclaim, the court noted that Jacobsen cited no legal authority for his position. Also, during his years at Columbia Jacobsen was a difficult student and became increasingly critical of his professors. He shifted

his academic interests a number of times—from physics to social work to creative writing and other areas. In his last year, he attended classes only as he chose, and he rejected the university's regimen requiring examinations and term papers. "I want to learn," Jacobsen said in a letter to the dean of students, "but I must do it my own way. I realize my behavior is non-conforming, but in these times when there are so many forces that demand conformity I hope I will find Columbia willing to grant some freedom to a student who wants to be a literary artist."

The court's heartstrings were largely untouched by the claims of the defendant—who acted as his own counsel during the trial. The court found no cause of action. The judges felt that Jacobsen simply "chose to judge Columbia's educational system by the shifting standards of his own fancy, and now seeks to place his failure at Columbia's door on the theory that it had deliberately misrepresented that it taught wisdom." The court concluded that if the defendant's "pleadings, affidavit and exhibits demonstrate anything, it is indeed the validity of what Pope said in his *Moral Essays:* 'A little learning is a dangerous thing. . . .' "

Duress

DURESS
Unlawful pressure brought to bear on a person, overcoming that person's free will and causing him or her to do what he or she would not otherwise have done.

Assent to the terms of a contract is not genuine if one of the parties is *forced* into the agreement. Recognizing this, the courts allow that party to rescind the contract. Forcing a party to enter into a contract under the fear of threats is legally defined as **duress.**[10] For example, if Sharkside Loan Company threatens to harm you or your family unless you sign a promissory note for the money you owe, Sharkside is guilty of exerting duress. In addition, blackmail or extortion to induce consent to an informal contract constitutes duress. Duress is both a defense to the enforcement of a contract

10. Restatement, Second, Contracts, Sections 174 and 175.

and a ground for rescission or cancellation of a contract. Therefore, the party upon whom the duress is exerted can choose to carry out the contract or to avoid the entire transaction. (The wronged party usually has this choice in cases where assent is not real or genuine.)

Economic need is generally not sufficient to constitute duress, even when one party exacts a very high price for an item the other party needs. If the party exacting the price also creates the need, however, economic duress may be found. For example, the Internal Revenue Service assessed a large tax and penalty against Sam Thompson. Thompson retained Earl Eyman to resist the assessment. The last day before the deadline for filing a reply with the IRS, Eyman declined to represent Thompson unless he signed a very high contingency-fee agreement for his services. The agreement was unenforceable.[11] Although Eyman had threatened only to withdraw his services, something that he was legally entitled to do, he was responsible for delaying his withdrawal until the last day. Since it would have been impossible at that late date to obtain adequate representation elsewhere, Thompson was forced into either signing the contract or losing his right to challenge the IRS assessment.

In the following case, the court examines whether the consent obtained in an agreement resulted from economic duress.

Case 8.5
SELMER CO. v. BLAKESLEE-MIDWEST CO.
United States Court of Appeals, Seventh Circuit, 1983.
704 F.2d 924.

FACTS Selmer Co. agreed with Blakeslee-Midwest to be a subcontractor for Blakeslee in a project to build a prestressed concrete structure. The contract stated that Blakeslee would provide Selmer with the necessary materials and that Selmer would do the construction for $210,000. When Blakeslee did not supply Selmer with the materials on time, Selmer, instead of canceling the contract, orally agreed to go ahead with the work on the condition that Blakeslee pay Selmer for the added costs it incurred because of Blakeslee's breach. On completion of the project, Selmer billed Blakeslee for $120,000, the extra costs incurred. Blakeslee offered $67,000 instead and refused to pay more. According to Selmer, Blakeslee effectively said "give up $53,000 on your claim for extras ($120,000 minus $67,000), or you will get nothing." Selmer, in desperate need of the money, agreed to accept the $67,000 and release Blakeslee from further liability on the $120,000 debt. Several years later Selmer brought suit against Blakeslee for the extra costs, contending that its agreement to accept the $67,000 offer was the result

of economic duress. The trial court held for Blakeslee, and Selmer appealed.

ISSUE Can Selmer's acceptance of the agreement to settle for $67,000 be set aside on the grounds of economic duress?

DECISION No. The judgment of the trial court was affirmed.

REASON Since Selmer claimed duress on the basis of a desperate need for money, the court focused on whether "financial difficulty can by itself justify setting aside a settlement on grounds of duress." The court concluded that it cannot. "The adverse effect on the finality of settlements and hence on the willingness of parties to settle their contract disputes without litigation would be great if the cash needs of one party were alone enough to entitle him to a trial on the validity of the settlement." The court noted, however, that "matters stand differently when the complaining party's financial distress is due to the other party's conduct." In this case, there was no evidence that Blakeslee was the cause of Selmer's financial distress.

The court reasoned that even given the fact that Selmer claimed its financial crisis occurred as a result of Blakeslee's breach of contract (the company's failure to provide the necessary materials), Selmer had been under

---

11.   Thompson Crane & Trucking Co. v. Eyman, 123 Cal.App.2d 904, 267 P.2d 1043 (1954).

Case 8.5—Continued

no obligation to provide the materials at its own expense. Selmer "could have walked away from the contract without loss or penalty" but instead chose to continue construction. Selmer assumed this responsibility voluntarily, and Blakeslee could not be held liable for Selmer's con-

sequent financial difficulties. In the eyes of the court, "a vast number of contract settlements would be subject to being ripped open upon an allegation of duress" if financial difficulties (not caused by the other party) were alone sufficient to claim duress.

> *"Ignorance of the law is no excuse in any country. If it were, the laws would lose their effect, because ignorance can always be pretended."*
>
> **Thomas Jefferson, 1743–1826**
> *(Third president of the United States, 1801–1809)*

❖ The Statute of Frauds—Requirement of a Writing

The term *Statute of Frauds* is misleading, as it neither applies to fraud nor invalidates any type of contract. Rather, the statute denies enforceability to contracts that do not comply with its requirements. Under the Statute of Frauds, there are at least five types of contracts that must be evidenced by a writing:

1. Contracts involving interests in land.
2. Contracts that cannot *by their terms* be performed within one year from the date of formation.
3. Collateral contracts, such as promises to answer for the debt or duty of another.
4. Promises made in consideration of marriage.
5. Contracts for the sale of goods priced at $500 or more.

Contracts Involving Interests in Land

Sale of Land   Land is real property and includes all physical objects that are permanently attached to the soil, such as buildings, plants, trees, and the soil itself. A contract calling for the sale of, or transfer of an interest in, land is not enforceable unless it is in writing or evidenced by a written memorandum.[12] If Carol, for example, contracts orally to sell Seaside Shelter to Arnold but later decides not to sell, Arnold cannot enforce the contract. Likewise, if Arnold refuses to close the deal, Carol cannot force Arnold to pay for the land by bringing a lawsuit. The Statute of Frauds is a *defense* to the enforcement of this type of oral contract.

An exception exists in some jurisdictions: if a buyer is in possession of the property and has made permanent improvements thereon, the contract will be enforced. In other jurisdictions, the contract will be enforced even if only minor improvements have been made by a buyer in possession if the buyer has begun performance under the contract (has paid part of the purchase price).

Frequently it is necessary to distinguish between real property and personal property. A contract for the sale of land ordinarily involves the entire interest in the real property, including buildings, growing crops, vegetation, minerals, timber, and anything else affixed to the land. Therefore, a fixture (personal property so affixed or so used as to become a part of the realty) is treated as real property. But anything else, such as a couch, is treated as personal property.

Other Interests   The Statute of Frauds requires written contracts not just for the sale of land but also for the transfer of other interests in land. These interests include life estates, real estate mortgages, easements, and leases.

---

12. The contract will be enforced, however, if each party admits to the existence of the oral contract in court or admits to its existence pursuant to discovery before trial.

Landmark in the Law
The Statute of Frauds

On April 12, 1677, the English Parliament passed "An Act for the Prevention of Frauds and Perjuries." Four days later, the act was signed by King Charles II and became the law of the land. The act contained twenty-five sections and required that certain types of contracts, in order to be enforceable by the courts, would henceforth have to be in writing or evidenced by a written memorandum.[1]

The intention of the act was to prevent harm to innocent parties by requiring written evidence of agreements concerning important transactions. Although it was acknowledged that the requirements of the act would render commercial transactions more cumbersome, it was felt that the benefits would far outweigh the costs. In the United States, nearly every state has a Statute of Frauds modeled after the British act. Some of the statute's provisions have also been incorporated into the Uniform Commercial Code.

The British act was created specifically to prevent further perpetration of the many frauds caused by witnesses giving perjured testimony in cases involving breached oral agreements, where no written evidence of the agreement existed. Although in the early history of common law in England, oral contracts were generally not enforced by the courts, they began to be so in the fourteenth century in certain *assumpsit* actions.[2] These actions, to which the origins of modern contract law are traced, allowed a party to sue and obtain relief in cases where a promise or contract had been breached. Enforcement of oral promises in actions in *assumpsit* became a common practice in the King's Court during the next two centuries.

Because courts enforced oral contracts on the strength of oral testimony by witnesses, it was not too difficult to evade justice by alleging that a contract had been breached and then procuring "convincing" witnesses to support the claim. The possibility of fraud in such actions was enhanced by the fact that in seventeenth-century England,

1.   These contracts are discussed in the text of this chapter.
2.   *Assumpsit* is Latin for *he undertook* or *he promised*; the emergence of remedies on the basis of breached promises dates to these actions. One of the earliest occurred in 1370, when the court allowed an individual to sue a person who, in trying to cure the plaintiff's horse, had acted so negligently that the horse died. Another such action was permitted in 1375, when a plaintiff obtained relief for having been maimed by a surgeon hired to cure him.

courts did not allow oral testimony to be given by the parties to a lawsuit—or by any parties with an interest in the litigation, such as husbands or wives. Defense against breach-of-contract actions was thus limited to written evidence or the testimony given by third parties.

Essentially, the Statute of Frauds offers a defense against oral contracts that fall under the statute. If a contract is oral when it is required to be in writing, it can be deemed void (that is, no contract at all) by the courts. Since its inception three hundred years ago, the statute has been criticized by some because, although it was created to protect the innocent, it can also be used as a technical defense by a party breaching a genuine oral contract—if the contract falls within the Statute of Frauds. For this reason, some legal scholars believe the act has caused more fraud than it has prevented. Nevertheless, the courts are slow to apply the Statute of Frauds in cases where its application will result in obvious injustice. In some instances, this has required a good deal of inventiveness on the part of the courts.[3]

3.   See, for example, Bader v. Hiscox, 188 Iowa 986, 174 N.W. 565, 10 A.L.R. 316 (1919), where, according to Corbin, the court "worked indefatigably to prevent the defendant from using the statute to defeat the enforcement of his promise."

King Charles II

LIFE ESTATE
An interest in land that exists only for the duration of the life of some person, usually the holder of the estate.

MORTGAGE
A written instrument giving a creditor (the mortgagee) an interest (lien) in the debtor's (mortgagor's) property as security for a debt.

EASEMENT
A nonpossessory right to use another's property in a manner established by either express or implied agreement.

1. *Life estates.* A **life estate** is an ownership interest in land that lasts for a person's lifetime. For example, if John Merrick conveys his farm to Barbara Johnson "for life, then after Johnson's death, to Deborah Pyron," Johnson has a life estate in the farm. This means that Johnson can live on and farm the land during her lifetime, but when Johnson dies Pyron will have a full estate in the farm—that is, she will own it entirely.[13]

2. *Mortgages.* A real estate **mortgage** is a conveyance of an interest in land as a security for repayment of a loan. If Deborah Pyron, now full owner of the farm in the example just given, wants to borrow money from State Bank and Trust Company, State Bank will require *collateral* for the loan. By giving conditional title of the farm to the bank, Pyron can get the loan. When Pyron pays off the debt, the farm will be hers once again in total ownership.

3. *Easements.* An **easement** is a legal right to use land without owning it. Easements are created expressly or impliedly. An express easement arises when the owner of land expressly agrees to allow another person to use the land. To be enforceable, the agreement must be in writing. Implied easements can arise from the past conduct of the parties. For example, when a farmer has used a certain path to reach the back forty acres of his farm for twenty years, and the path goes across a neighbor's property, the farmer has an *implied* easement to cross the neighbor's property. Implied easements need not be in writing and rarely are, because of the way they are created.

4. *Leases.* A lease is a transfer without title of real property for a certain period of time.[14] Most states have statutes dealing specifically with leases apart from the Statute of Frauds; leases of one year or less are exempt from the writing requirements. Thus, any lease lasting more than one year must normally be in writing.

The One-Year Rule

Contracts that cannot, *by their own terms*, be performed within one year from the date the contract is formed must be in writing to be enforceable. Since disputes over such contracts are unlikely to occur until some time after the contracts are made, resolution of these disputes is difficult unless the contract terms have been put in writing. The idea behind this rule is that a witness's memory is not to be trusted for longer than a year.

For a particular contract to fall into this category, contract performance must be objectively impossible to perform within a year from the date of contract formation. If the contract, by its terms, makes performance within the year *possible* (even if not probable), the contract is not within the Statute of Frauds and need not be in writing.

The one-year period begins to run *the day after the contract is made*.[15] Suppose you graduate from college on June 1. An employer orally contracts to hire you immediately (June 1) for one year at $2,000 per month. Under the Statute of Frauds, this contract need not be in writing to be enforceable because the one-year period to measure performance begins on June 2. Since your performance of one year can begin immediately, it would take you exactly one year from the date of entering the contract to complete the performance.

The test to determine whether an oral contract is enforceable under the one-year rule of the statute is not whether an agreement is *likely* to be performed within one

---

13.   Full ownership like that of Deborah Pyron is called a fee simple absolute. See Chapter 34.
14.   Although a lease is technically a conveyance of an interest in land, it is usually accompanied by a contract rather than a deed.
15.   Corbin on Contracts, Section 444.

◆ **Exhibit 8-1   Contracts Impossible to Perform within One Year**

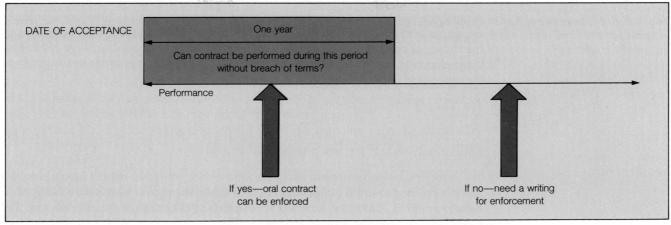

year from the date of making the contract, but whether the performance within a year is *possible*. Conversely, when performance of a contract is impossible during a one-year period, this provision of the Statute of Frauds will bar recovery on an oral contract. Exhibit 8-1 illustrates the one-year rule.

The following case involves the application of the Statute of Frauds one-year rule. Note that even though the parties did not anticipate performance within one year, the oral contract was enforceable because performance was *possible* within one year.

Case 8.6
**CHESAPEAKE FINANCIAL
CORPORATION v. LAIRD**
Supreme Court of Maryland, 1981.
289 Md. 594, 425 A.2d 1348.

FACTS   Donald Laird and Joseph Martin, land developers, orally contracted with Chesapeake Financial Corporation to undertake a joint venture to develop some real estate. According to the agreement, Chesapeake was to provide the financing for the venture. Chesapeake later refused to provide the necessary funding, and Laird and Martin sued for damages as a result of Chesapeake's alleged misrepresentation. Chesapeake asserted the Statute of Frauds as a defense, claiming that the oral contract was unenforceable because they had not anticipated completing the project within one year's time. Under the Maryland Statute of Frauds, "any agreement that is not to be performed within the space of one year from the making thereof" is required to be in writing. The trial court held for Laird and Martin and awarded damages. Chesapeake appealed.

ISSUE   The issue before the court was whether the contract could be performed within one year. If it could, it would fall outside the Statute of Frauds and thus be enforceable. If it could not be performed within one year, it would fall under the Statute of Frauds requirement that such contracts be in writing, and Chesapeake could avoid the obligations of the contract.

DECISION   The Supreme Court of Maryland held that the contract terms could have been performed within one year, and thus the oral contract was enforceable. The trial court's decision was affirmed.

REASON   The court reasoned that although the parties anticipated that the project would take at least two, and possibly three, years to complete, there was no evidence that it was *impossible* to perform the contract within one year. The court stated that it had historically "interpreted 'literally and very narrowly' the words of the statute [regarding the one-year rule]. . . . [Chesapeake has] not clearly demonstrated that, under the terms of the alleged oral contract, as contrasted with the expectations of the parties, it could not be performed within one year."

Collateral Promises

Among the collateral promises covered by the Statute of Frauds is the express promise to pay the debt of another. Promises made by one person to pay the debts or discharge the duties of another if the latter fails to perform must be in writing. The following three elements, as illustrated in Exhibit 8-2, must be present in order to require that the agreement be in writing.

1. Three parties are involved.
2. Two promises are involved.
3. The secondary, or collateral, promise is an express promise to pay a debt or fulfill a duty only if the first promisor fails to do so.

Sometimes a party steps in as a guarantor or a surety for a debt. Guarantors and sureties promise to fulfill obligations or pay a debt if the person who has the obligation fails to fulfill it. Only the promise between the guarantor (or the surety) and the creditor falls under the Statute of Frauds. The key point here is that the debt of the guarantor or surety is secondary; the debtor's obligation is primary. The Statute of Frauds applies if, and only if, the guarantor's or surety's obligation is contingent upon the debtor's refusal or inability to pay the creditor.

Suppose Jennings Petroleum signs an agreement with Marvin Oil Company to ship 40,000 barrels of crude oil to Marvin for a specified price. In other words, Marvin incurs an initial, or primary, obligation to Jennings. The president of European Petrochemical, Ltd., a major distributor for Marvin, makes a *collateral* promise to Jennings that European will pay for the oil in the event Marvin does not. If this collateral promise is not in writing, it is not enforceable. The nature of European's liability is secondary (European is liable only if Marvin does not pay).

◆ **Exhibit 8-2**
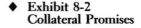
Collateral Promises

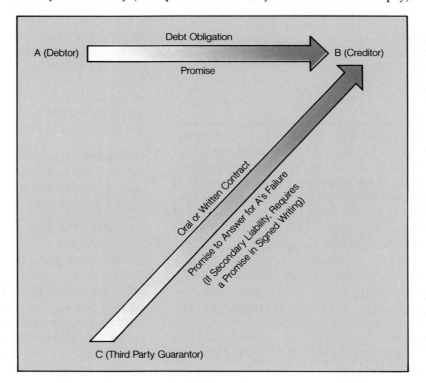

Or suppose that Kenneth orally contracts with Joanne's Floral Boutique to send his mother a dozen roses for Mother's Day. Kenneth's oral contract with Joanne's Floral Boutique provides that he will pay for the roses if his mother does not do so. Is the contract enforceable against Kenneth? The answer is yes. Kenneth's mother is not a debtor, nor is she obligated to pay the florist. Kenneth's obligation is primary, not secondary, because his mother has no obligation as a promisor under the contract. Kenneth's oral contract is supported by legally sufficient consideration and is enforceable.[16]

Now suppose Kenneth's mother owes $1,000 to the Medford Trust Company on a promissory note payable on June 1. Kenneth knows that his mother cannot pay on the due date. He orally contracts with Medford Trust for the bank to extend the note payment for six months. Should Kenneth's mother not pay the note by the end of that period, Kenneth agrees to pay it. Does this oral contract fall within the Statute of Frauds? Yes, the contract is express, made between the guarantor, Kenneth, and the creditor, Medford Trust, and Kenneth's obligation is secondary (he is obligated to pay only if his mother does not pay on her primary obligation). Therefore, this contract is not enforceable unless it is supported by a writing. Had Kenneth secured his mother's release from the debt (the release being a discharge of her primary obligation to pay) or co-signed the note, Kenneth's promise to pay would have become the *primary* liability. Thus it would have fallen outside the Statute of Frauds and would not have needed to be in writing in order to be enforceable.

The "Main Purpose" Rule   The oral promise to answer for the debt of another is covered by the Statute of Frauds unless the guarantor's main purpose in accepting secondary liability is to secure a personal benefit. This type of contract need not be in writing.[17] The assumption is that a court can infer from the circumstances of a case whether the "leading objective" of the promisor was to secure a personal benefit and thus, in effect, to answer for his or her own debt.

Consider an example. Southtown Construction Corporation agrees to build a home for Garrison. Southtown subcontracts part of its work to Quick Construction Company. After several weeks, Quick Construction refuses to supply more labor or materials because Southtown's financial condition is shaky, and Quick Construction is worried about being paid. Garrison wants to inhabit the house soon so that his children can start school on time in their new neighborhood. Therefore, Garrison orally agrees to pay Quick Construction's debts if Southtown fails to pay. Garrison's oral promise is enforceable because the main purpose in making the guarantee is to get the house built.[18]

Another typical application of the so-called main-purpose doctrine is where one creditor guarantees the debtor's debt to another creditor in order to forestall litigation. This allows the debtor to remain in business long enough to generate profits sufficient to pay *both* creditors.

Promises Made in Consideration of Marriage

A unilateral promise to pay a sum of money or to give property in consideration of a promise to marry must be in writing. If Mr. Baumann promises to pay Joe Villard

---

16. Restatement, Second, Contracts, Section 112.
17. Restatement, Second, Contracts, Section 116.
18. See Kampman v. Pittsburgh Contracting and Engineering Co., 316 Pa. 502, 175 A. 396 (1934).

$10,000 if Villard promises to marry Baumann's daughter, the promise must be in writing. The same rule applies to *prenuptial agreements* (agreements made before marriage), which define each partner's ownership rights in the other partner's property. For example, a prospective husband may wish to limit the amount his prospective wife could obtain if the marriage ends in divorce. Prenuptial arrangements must be in writing to be enforceable, and in most cases there must be consideration. (Some states, such as Florida, do not require consideration.)

Contracts for the Sale of Goods

The UCC contains several Statute of Frauds provisions that require written evidence of a contract. Section 2-201 contains the major provision, which generally requires a writing or memorandum for the sale of goods priced at $500 or more. A writing that will satisfy the Code requirement need only state the quantity term; other terms agreed upon need not be stated "accurately" in the writing, so long as they adequately reflect both parties' intentions. The contract will not be enforceable, however, for any quantity greater than that set forth in the writing. In addition, the writing must be signed by the person to be charged—that is, by the person who refuses to perform or the one being sued. Beyond these two requirements, the writing need not designate the buyer or the seller, the terms of payment, or the price.

Section 2-201 of the UCC defines three exceptions to the Statute of Frauds. Oral contracts for the sale of goods priced at $500 or more will be enforced if: (1) the goods are specially manufactured for the buyer, not suitable for sale to others, and a substantial beginning of their manufacture or commitment for their procurement has begun; (2) there is an admission under oath of the existence of an oral contract; or (3) there has been partial performance through the buyer's payment or possession, in which case the contract will be enforced to the extent the goods have been paid for or possessed by the buyer. Also, as between merchants, when one sends a written confirmation and the receiver does not object in writing within ten days, this constitutes an exception to the Statute of Frauds (see Chapter 11 for details).

❖ The Statute of Frauds—Sufficiency of the Writing

To be safe, all contracts should be fully set forth in a writing signed by all the parties. This assures that if any problems arise concerning performance of the contract, a written agreement fully specifying the performance promised by each party can be introduced into court. The Statute of Frauds and the UCC require either a written contract or a *written memorandum* signed by the party against whom enforcement is sought. A written memorandum can consist of any confirmation, invoice, sales slip, check, or telegram—such items, singly or in combination, may constitute a writing sufficient to satisfy the Statute of Frauds.[19] The signature need not be placed at the end of the document but can be anywhere in the writing; it can even be initials rather than the full name.

A memorandum evidencing the oral contract need only contain the essential terms of the contract. Under the UCC, for the sale of goods the writing need only

---

19.   Even if the Statute of Frauds is satisfied, however, the existence and terms of the contract must be proved in court.

name the quantity term and be signed by the party being charged. Under most provisions of the Statute of Frauds, the writing must name the parties, subject matter, consideration, and quantity. Contracts for the sale of land, in some states, require that the memorandum also state the *essential* terms of the contract, such as location and price, with sufficient clarity to allow the terms to be determined from the memo itself, without reference to any outside sources.[20]

Only the party to be held liable on the contract need sign the writing. Therefore, a contract may be enforceable by one of its parties but not by the other. Suppose Devlin and Rock contract for the sale of Devlin's lake house and lot for $50,000. Devlin writes Rock a letter confirming the sale by identifying the parties and the essential terms of the sales contract—price, method of payment, and legal address—and signs the letter. Devlin has made a written memorandum of the oral land contract. Since she signed the letter, she can be held to the oral contract by Rock. Rock, however, since he has not signed or entered into a written contract or memorandum, can plead the Statute of Frauds as a defense, and Devlin cannot enforce the contract against him.

The following classic case illustrates what may be construed to be a "signed writing" by the court.

Case 8.7
DRURY v. YOUNG
Supreme Court of Maryland, 1882.
58 Md. 546.

FACTS The plaintiff, Young, formed an oral agreement with the defendant, Drury, to buy several carloads of tomatoes. Subsequent to the agreement, Drury wrote a memorandum concerning the agreement and all its terms for his own records and put it in his safe. The memo, which Drury did not sign, was created using Drury's letterhead (which is a sufficient signing in the eyes of the court) and contained Young's name in the text. Subsequently, Drury wrote a letter to Young stating he was not going to sell Young the tomatoes as agreed. On the date of the scheduled delivery, however, Young tendered payment and requested Drury to keep his part of the bargain—but Drury again refused to sell. When Young sued Drury for breach of contract, Drury used the Statute of Frauds as a defense, alleging that since his memo had

never been delivered to Young, no written confirmation of the oral contract existed. The trial court held in Young's favor, claiming that Drury's memo (even if it had not been delivered to Young) combined with the subsequent letter satisfied the writing requirement of the Statute of Frauds. Drury appealed.

ISSUE Does the memo written by Drury satisfy the writing requirement under the Statute of Frauds?

DECISION Yes. The judgment of the trial court was affirmed.

REASON The court stated that the Statute of Frauds is not concerned with whether or not a writing has been delivered, or with the custody of a writing, but just with the *existence* of a writing evidencing the agreement. Drury's memo with the terms of the agreement, kept in his own safe, in conjunction with the subsequent letter to Young denying delivery, provided sufficient evidence to the court that the Statute of Frauds had been satisfied.

❖ The Parol Evidence Rule

The **parol evidence rule** prohibits the introduction at trial of evidence of the parties' prior negotiations or agreements or contemporaneous oral agreements that contradicts or varies the terms of written contracts.[21] The written contract is ordinarily assumed

PAROL EVIDENCE RULE
A substantive rule of contracts under which a court will not admit at trial evidence of prior negotiations or agreements or contemporaneous oral agreements that contradicts or varies the terms of a written contract.

---

20. Rhodes v. Wilkins, 83 N.M. 782, 498 P.2d 311 (1972).
21. Restatement, Second, Contracts, Section 213.

to be the complete embodiment of the parties' agreement. Courts are reluctant to recognize evidence of prior negotiations or agreements or contemporaneous oral agreements that conflict with the terms of the written agreement. Therefore, courts assume that all such negotiations and agreements are embodied in the written contract. Because of the rigidity of the parol evidence rule, however, courts make several exceptions.

First, evidence of *subsequent modification* of a written contract can be introduced into court. Courts assume all prior negotiations and agreements and contemporaneous oral agreements are merged in the written contract, but changes in the written contract can occur after the writing. Keep in mind that the oral modifications may not be enforceable if they come under the Statute of Frauds—for example, if they increase the price of the goods for sale to $500 or more or increase the term for performance to more than one year. Also, oral modifications will not be enforceable if the original contract provides that any modification must be in writing.[22]

Second, oral evidence can be introduced in all cases to show that the contract was voidable or void (for example, induced by mistake, fraud, or misrepresentation). In this case, if deception led one of the parties to agree to the terms of a written contract, oral evidence attesting to fraud should not be excluded. Courts frown upon bad faith and are quick to allow such evidence when it establishes fraud.

Third, when the terms of a written contract are ambiguous, extraneous evidence is admissible in order to show the meaning of the terms.

Fourth, extraneous evidence is admissible when the written contract is incomplete in that it lacks one or more of the essential terms. The courts allow extraneous evidence to "fill in the gaps."

Fifth, under the UCC, extraneous evidence can be introduced to explain or supplement a written contract by showing a prior course of dealing or usage of trade.[23] When buyers and sellers deal with each other over extended periods of time, certain customary practices develop. These practices are often overlooked when writing the contract, so courts allow the introduction of extraneous evidence to show how the parties have acted in the past.

Sixth, the parol evidence rule does not apply if the existence of the entire written contract is subject to an orally agreed upon condition. Proof of the condition does not *alter* or *modify* the written terms but involves the *enforceability* of the written contract. Suppose, for example, you agree with your friend Amy to buy her car for $4,000, but only if your brother, Frank, inspects it and approves of your purchase. Amy agrees to this condition, but because she is leaving town for the weekend and you want to use the car (if you buy it) before she returns, you write up a contract of sale, and both of you sign it. Frank does not approve of the purchase, and when you do not buy the car, Amy sues you, alleging that you breached the contract. In this case, your oral agreement did not alter or modify the terms of your written agreement, but concerned whether or not the contract would exist at all. This example parallels the leading case concerning this exception, *Pym v. Campbell*, in which the court stated that "evidence to vary the terms of an agreement in writing is not admissible, but evidence to show that there is not an agreement at all is admissible."[24]

Seventh, when an *obvious* or *gross* clerical (or typographic) error exists that clearly would not represent the agreement of the parties, parol evidence is admissible

---

22. UCC 2-209(2)(3).
23. UCC 1-205, 2-202.
24. 6 El. & Bl. 370 (Q.B. 1856).

in order to correct the error. For example, Sharon agrees to lease 1,000 square feet of office space at the current monthly rate of $3 per square foot from Stone Enterprises. The signed written lease provides for a monthly lease payment of $30 rather than the $3,000 agreed to by the parties. Since the error is obvious, Stone Enterprises would be allowed to admit evidence to correct the mistake.

The key in determining whether evidence will be allowed basically depends on whether the written contract is intended to be a complete and final embodiment of the terms of the agreement. If it is so intended, it is referred to as an integrated contract, and extraneous evidence is excluded. If it is only partially integrated, evidence of consistent additional terms is admissible to supplement the written agreement.[25]

---

25.   Restatement, Second, Contracts, Section 216.

Application

Law and the Businessperson— The Problem with Oral Contracts

As a general rule, most business contracts should be in writing even when the contract falls outside the Statute of Frauds requirement. Oral contracts are frequently made over the telephone, however, particularly when the parties have done business with each other in the past.

Any time an oral contract is made, it is advisable for one of the parties to send either a written memorandum or a confirmation of the oral agreement to the other party. Two purposes are accomplished by this: (1) It demonstrates a party's clear intention to form a contract, and (2) it provides the terms that at least one of the parties believed were agreed upon. If the party receiving the memorandum or confirmation then disagrees with the terms or the intent, the issue can be addressed before performance begins.

What about the sale of goods between merchants? A written confirmation received by one merchant removes the Statute of Frauds requirement of a writing unless the merchant receiving the confirmation objects in writing within ten days of its receipt. This law points out clearly the need for the merchant receiving the confirmation to review it carefully to ascertain that the confirmation conforms to the oral contract. If the writing does not so conform, the merchant can object in writing (the Statute of Frauds still applies), and the parties can resolve misunderstandings without legal liability. If the merchant fails to object, the written confirmation can be used as evidence to prove the terms of the oral contract. Note, however, that this ten-day rule does not apply to contracts for services and interests in realty.

Checklist for Oral Contracts

- [ ] 1. When feasible, use written contracts.
- [ ] 2. If you enter into an oral contract over the telephone, send a written confirmation outlining your understanding of the oral contract.
- [ ] 3. If you receive the other party's written memorandum or confirmation, read it carefully to make sure that its terms agree with what you believed was already agreed on in the oral contract.
- [ ] 4. If you have any objections, put them in writing within ten days.

❖ Chapter Summary: Genuineness of Assent and Form

PROBLEMS OF ASSENT	
Mistakes	1. *Bilateral*—When both parties' mistake goes to a material fact, such as identity, either party can avoid the contract. If the mistake goes to value or quality, either party can enforce the contract.
	2. *Unilateral*—Generally, the mistaken party is bound by the contract *unless* (a) the other party knows or should have known of the mistake, or (b) in some states, the mistake is an inadvertent mathematical error—such as an error in addition, subtraction, etc.—committed without gross negligence.
Misrepresentation	1. *Fraud*—When fraud occurs, usually the innocent party can enforce or avoid the contract. The four elements necessary to establish fraud are: a. A misrepresentation of a material fact must have occurred. b. There must be an intent to deceive.

❖ Chapter Summary: Genuineness of Assent and Form—Continued

Misrepresentation (Continued)	c. The innocent party must justifiably rely on the misrepresentation. d. For damages, the innocent party must have been injured. 2. *Other*—Intent to deceive need not be shown. Usually, the innocent party can rescind the contract but cannot seek damages. A misrepresentation of law generally does not permit a person to avoid the contract.
Influence/Coercion	1. *Undue influence*—Arises from special relationships, such as fiduciary or confidential relationships, in which one party's free will has been overcome by the undue influence exerted by the other party. Usually, the contract is voidable. 2. *Duress*—Defined as forcing a party to enter a contract under the fear of a threat; for example, the threat of violence or economic pressure. The party forced to enter the contract can rescind the contract.
VALID BUSINESS CONTRACTS UNDER THE STATUTE OF FRAUDS	
Contracts to Guarantee the Debt of Another	1. *Application*—Applies only to express contracts made between the guarantor and the creditor, whose terms make the guarantor secondarily liable. 2. *Exception*—Main-purpose rule.
Contracts Involving an Interest in Realty	1. *Application*—Applies to any contract for an interest in realty, such as sale, lease, mortgage, and real estate broker contracts. 2. *Exceptions:* a. Statute—Most states permit short-term leases (usually of a year or less) formed by an oral agreement to be enforceable. b. Partial performance—Principle in equity where parties cannot be restored to status quo.
Contracts Whose Terms Cannot Be Performed within One Year	1. *Application*—Applies only to contracts objectively impossible to perform fully within one year from the date of the contract's formation. 2. *Exception*—None. (Some courts ignore option-to-cancel clauses in terms contracts for Statute of Frauds purposes.)
Contracts for the Sale of Goods Priced at $500 or More	1. *Application*—Applies only to the sale of goods, and where the purchase price (excluding taxes) is $500 or more. UCC 2-201(1) 2. *Exceptions:* a. Between merchants, where one sends a written confirmation and the recipient does not object in writing within ten days. b. Specially ordered goods where the seller has made a substantial beginning of manufacture or commitment for procurement. c. Admission under oath of an oral contract. d. Partial performance by buyer's payment or possession, at least to the extent paid or quantity possessed. UCC 2-201(2)(3)
Exceptions to All Statute of Frauds Contracts	*Memorandum*—Written evidence of an oral contract signed by the party against whom enforcement is sought. Generally, the writing must name the parties, identify the subject matter of the contract, and, in the sale of goods, the quantity; in the sale of land, it must name essential terms, such as land description and price.

❖ Questions and Case Problems

8-1. On January 1, 1988, Dominic, for consideration, orally promised to pay Francis $300 a month for as long as Francis lived, with the payments to be made on the first day of every month. Dominic made the payments regularly for nine months and then made no further payments. Francis claimed that Dominic had breached the oral contract and sued Dominic for damages. Dominic contended that the contract was unenforceable because, under the Statute of Frauds, contracts that cannot be performed within one year must be in writing. Will Dominic succeed in this defense?

8-2. The Public Works Department of the city of Rivertown invited bids for a new construction project. Bartlett Construction Corporation offered to do the work for $130,000 and, since this was the lowest bid, was awarded the contract. The next highest bid was $185,000. Later, Bartlett discovered that it had made a mathematical error in its calculations, and the contract would actually cost $185,000 to perform. Bartlett now requests more money or release from the contract. Will he obtain either? Explain.

8-3. Discuss which of the following contracts are fully enforceable:

(a) Simington finds a stone in his pasture that he believes to be quartz. Jackson, who also believes that the stone is quartz, contracts to purchase it for $10. Just before it is delivered, the stone is discovered to be a diamond worth $1,000.

(b) Allen's barn is burned to the ground. He accuses Garrison's son of arson and threatens to bring criminal action unless Garrison agrees to pay him $5,000. Garrison agrees to pay.

(c) McCumber is a new salesperson and innocently tells Burroughs that a particular lawnmower has a five-year manufacturer's warranty. Burroughs contracts to purchase the lawnmower in reliance on McCumber's statement about the warranty. Burroughs and McCumber are transacting business for the first time. At the time of delivery, it is discovered that the manufacturer warrants the lawnmower for only one year.

8-4. Larry offers to sell Stanley his car and tells Stanley that the car has been driven only 25,000 miles and has never been in an accident. Stanley hired Cohen, a mechanic, to appraise the condition of the car, and Cohen said that the car probably had at least 50,000 miles on it and probably had been in an accident. In spite of this information, Stanley still thought the car would be a good buy for the price, so he purchased it. Later, when the car developed numerous mechanical problems, Stanley sought to rescind the contract on the basis of Larry's fraudulent misrepresentation of the auto's condition. Will Stanley be able to rescind his contract?

8-5. Rimshot, the director of a local basketball camp, wished to increase his business by advertising his camp. He discussed with Lyal, a local printer, the possibility of having flyers printed up about the camp. Rimshot told Lyal that he wanted him not only to print the flyers, but also to distribute them to local merchants. Lyal said that he usually distributed about 20 flyers to each merchant and charged a small publication fee. Subsequently, Lyal and Rimshot entered into a written agreement under which Lyal agreed to print 1,000 flyers for Rimshot and to "publish the same locally." Lyal printed the flyers but distributed them to only four merchants, giving 250 to each. After the poorest turnout in his basketball camp's history, Rimshot sued Lyal for breach of contract. Can he introduce parol evidence concerning Lyal's statements about how he normally distributed flyers? [See similar fact pattern in Stoops v. Smith, 100 Mass. 63, 97 Am. Dec. 76 (1868).]

8-6. Fernandez orally promised Pando that if Pando helped her win the New York state lottery, she would share the proceeds equally with him. Pando agreed to purchase the tickets in Fernandez's name, select the lottery numbers, and pray for the divine intervention of a saint to help them win. Fernandez won $2.8 million in the lottery, which was to be paid over a ten-year period. When Fernandez failed to share the winnings equally, Pando sued for breach of her contractual obligation. Fernandez countered that their contract was unenforceable under the Statute of Frauds, since the contract could not be performed within one year. Could the contract be performed within one year? [Pando by Pando v. Fernandez, 127 Misc. 2d 224, 485 N.Y.S. 2d 162 (1984)]

8-7. Bloom sold Messerly a three-unit apartment building without telling Messerly that he had installed an illegal septic tank on the property. Later, Messerly sold the land to the Pickles. The Messerly-Pickles sales contract included a clause stating that the buyers agreed to accept the property in its present condition ("as is"). Subsequently, when the Pickles visited the premises, they noted sewage seeping out of the ground. The county health board condemned the property and obtained a permanent injunction against further human habitation of the premises. The Pickles sought to have the purchase contract rescinded on the basis of mutual mistake on the part of both the buyer and seller as to the condition of the property. Will the court allow the contract to be rescinded? [Lenawee County Board of Health v. Messerly, 417 Mich. 17, 331 N.W. 2d 203 (1982)]

8-8. The plaintiff publishes a directory entitled *New York Yellow Pages*, which is strikingly similar in color and format to the *New York Telephone Company Yellow Pages*, but which in fact is part of an independent business enterprise. In addition, the *New York Yellow Pages* has on its cover the legend "Let your fingers do the walking!," along with the familiar logo of walking fingers that appears on the *New York Telephone Company Yellow Pages*. The plaintiff's representative, stating that this publication would replace the bulkier *New York Telephone Company Yellow Pages*, sold advertising space to Grossman for $1,492.80. Grossman made a down payment of $118.40 and one installment payment of $65.20 and thereafter refused to make any payments. The plaintiff sued. Grossman claimed that the plaintiff fraudulently induced him to enter into the contract by leading him to believe that the plaintiff's book was a new, improved version of the *New York Telephone Company Yellow Pages*. Can Grossman rescind the contract on grounds of fraudulent inducement? [New York Yellow Pages, Inc. v. Growth Personnel Agency, Inc., 98 Misc.2d 541, 414 N.Y.S.2d 260 (Civ.Ct. 1979)]

8-9. Nosrat, a citizen of Iran, owned a hardware store with his brother-in-law, Edwin. Edwin induced Nosrat to sign a promissory note for $11,400, payable to a third party, telling Nosrat that the document was a credit application for the hardware store. Although Nosrat could read and write English, he failed to read the note or to notice that the document was clearly entitled "PROMISSORY NOTE (SECURED) and Security Agreement." The money received from the third party in exchange for the note was spent by Edwin and others. When the third party sued for payment, Nosrat sought to void the note on the basis of Edwin's fraudulent inducement. Will Nosrat succeed in his attempt? [Waldrep v. Nosrat, 426 So.2d 822 (Ala. 1983)]

Chapter 9

Third-Party Rights and Discharge

PRIVITY OF CONTRACT
The relationship that exists between the promisor and the promisee of a contract.

ASSIGNMENT OF RIGHTS
The act of transferring to another all or part of one's rights arising under a contract.

DELEGATION OF DUTIES
The act of transferring to another all or part of one's duties arising under a contract.

THIRD-PARTY-BENEFICIARY CONTRACT
A contract between two or more parties, the performance of which is intended to directly benefit a third party, thus giving the third party a right to file suit for breach of contract by either of the original contract parties.

Once it has been determined that a valid and legally enforceable contract exists, attention can turn to the rights and duties of the parties to the contract. Since a contract is a private agreement between the parties who have entered into it, it is fitting that these parties alone should have rights and liabilities under the contract. This is referred to as **privity of contract,** and it establishes the basic concept that third parties have no rights in a contract to which they are not a party.

Suppose I offer to sell you my watch for $100, and you accept. Later, I refuse to deliver the watch to you, even though you tender the $100. You decide to overlook my breach, but your close friend, Ann, is unhappy with my action and files suit. Can she receive a judgment? The answer is no, as she was not a party to the contract. You, as a party, have rights under the contract and could file a successful suit, but Ann has no *standing to sue* (right to sue).

You are probably convinced by now that for every rule of contract law there is an exception. Exceptions exist because, as former Chief Justice Stone remarked (see the chapter's opening quotation), law is a human institution, created for human ends. When the "end" of justice cannot be served by adhering to a rule of law, exceptions to the rule must be, and are, made. There are two exceptions to the rule of privity of contract. One exception allows a party to a contract to transfer the rights arising from the contract to another and/or to free himself or herself from the duties of a contract by having another person perform them. Legally, such an action is referred to as an **assignment of rights** and/or a **delegation of duties**. A second exception to the rule of privity of contract involves a **third-party-beneficiary contract**. Here, the rights of a third party against the promisor (the party making a promise) arise from the original contract, as the parties to the original contract normally make it with the intent to benefit the third party. The law relating to assignments, delegations, and third-party-beneficiary contracts is discussed in the first half of this chapter.

At some point, parties to the contract must know when their duties are at an end. In other words, when is a contract terminated? The second part of this chapter deals with the **discharge** of a contract, which is normally accomplished after both parties have performed the acts promised in the contract. We will look at the degree of **performance** required and the ways that discharge can occur, such as by agreement or by impossibility of performance.

❖ Assignments and Delegations

When third parties acquire rights or assume duties arising from a contract to which they were not parties, the rights are transferred to them by *assignment* and the duties are transferred by *delegation*. Assignment and delegation occur *after* the original contract is made, when one of the parties transfers to another party an interest or duty in the contract.

Assignments

In a bilateral contract, the two parties have corresponding rights and duties. One party has a *right* to require the other to perform some task, and the other has a *duty* to perform it. The transfer of *rights* to a third person is known as an *assignment*. When rights under a contract are assigned unconditionally, the rights of the assignor (the party making the assignment) are extinguished.[1] The third party (the assignee, or party receiving the assignment) has a right to demand performance from the other original party to the contract (the obligor). This is illustrated in Exhibit 9-1.

Once Ackerman has assigned to Cramer her rights under the original contract with Barlow, Cramer can enforce the contract against Barlow if Barlow fails to perform. The assignee takes only those rights which the assignor originally had. For example, suppose Barlow owes Ackerman $50, and Ackerman assigns to Cramer the

---

1. Restatement, Second, Contracts, Section 317.

DISCHARGE
The termination of one's obligation. In contract law, discharge occurs when the parties have fully performed their contractual obligations or when events, conduct of the parties, or operation of the law release the parties from further performance.

PERFORMANCE
In contract law, the fulfillment of one's duties arising under a contract with another; the normal way of discharging one's obligations in a contract.

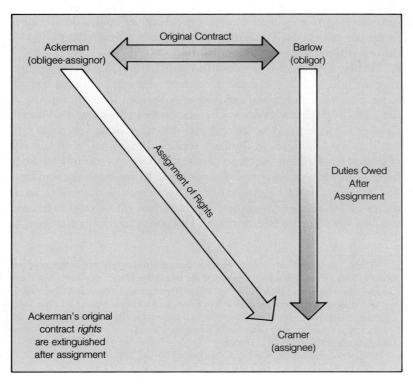

◆ **Exhibit 9-1**
Assignment Relationships

right to receive the $50. Here, a valid assignment of a debt exists. Cramer is entitled to enforce payment in a court of law if Barlow does not pay her the $50.

Furthermore, the assignee's rights are subject to the defenses that the obligor has against the assignor. Suppose Barlow contracts to sell her boat to Ackerman for $40,000. The contract calls for delivery of the boat to Ackerman or her assignee upon presentation of a receipt of payment signed by Barlow. Ackerman fraudulently gives Barlow a worthless check, and Barlow signs the receipt, noting thereon "payment by check." Ackerman is in debt to Cramer and in satisfaction of the debt assigns to Cramer the contract rights for the delivery of the boat. Barlow, upon discovery of the worthless check, has a legal right to avoid the contractual obligation to deliver the boat to Ackerman. Since the assignee Cramer's rights are subject to this same defense, Cramer also cannot require that Barlow transfer the boat, even though she is an innocent party to these events.

Rights That Can Be Assigned   As a general rule, all rights can be assigned, except in special circumstances. The following is a list of these special circumstances.

1.   If a statute expressly prohibits assignment, the particular right in question cannot be assigned. Suppose Mary is a new employee of Computer Future, Inc. Computer is an employer under workers' compensation statutes in this state, and thus Mary is a covered employee. Mary has a relatively high-risk job. In need of a loan, Mary borrows some money from Stark, assigning to Stark all workers' compensation benefits due her should she be injured on the job. The assignment of *future* workers' compensation benefits is prohibited by state statute and thus such rights cannot be assigned.

2.   If a contract stipulates that the rights cannot be assigned, then *ordinarily* they cannot be assigned.[2] Suppose Barlow agrees to build a house for Ackerman. The contract between Barlow and Ackerman states: "The contract cannot be assigned by Ackerman. Any assignment renders this contract void, and all rights hereunder will thereupon terminate." Ackerman then attempts to assign her rights to Cramer. Cramer cannot enforce the contract against Barlow.

3.   When a contract is *personal* in nature, the rights under the contract cannot be assigned unless all that remains is a money payment.[3] Suppose Barlow signs a contract to be a tutor for Ackerman's children. Ackerman then attempts to assign to Cramer her right to Barlow's services. Cramer cannot enforce the contract against Barlow. Cramer's children may be more difficult to tutor than Ackerman's; thus if Ackerman could assign her rights to Barlow's services to Cramer, it would change the nature of Barlow's obligation. Because personal services are unique to the person rendering them, rights to receive personal services are likewise unique and cannot be assigned.

4.   A right cannot be assigned if assignment will materially increase or alter the duties of the obligor.[4] Assume Ackerman has a hotel and to insure it she takes out a policy with Northwest Insurance. The policy insures against fire, theft, floods, and

---

2.   There are several exceptions. First, a contract cannot prevent assignment of the right to receive money. This exception exists to encourage the free flow of money and credit in modern business settings. Second, the assignment of rights in real estate often cannot be prohibited because it is contrary to public policy. Such prohibitions are called restraints against alienation. Third, the assignment of negotiable instruments cannot be prohibited. Fourth, in a contract for the sale of goods, the right to receive damages for breach of contract or for payment of an account owed may be assigned even though the sales contract prohibits assignment [UCC 2-210(2)].

3.   Restatement, Second, Contracts, Sections 317 and 318.

4.   See UCC 2-210(2).

vandalism. Ackerman attempts to assign the insurance policy to Cramer, who also owns a hotel. The assignment is ineffective because it substantially alters Northwest Insurance's *duty of performance*. Insurance companies evaluate the particular risk of a certain party and tailor their policies to fit that risk. If the policy is assigned to a third party, the insurance risk is materially altered. Therefore, the assignment will not operate to give Cramer any rights against Northwest Insurance.

In the following case, the central issue was whether a seller of a spa could assign membership contracts that included an exculpatory clause limiting liability for personal injuries.

Case 9.1
PETRY v. COSMOPOLITAN SPA INTERNATIONAL, INC.
Court of Appeals of Tennessee, Eastern Section, 1982.
641 S.W.2d 202.

FACTS Petry signed a contract with Cosmopolitan Spa providing for spa membership. The contract contained an exculpatory clause, which stated in pertinent part: "Member fully understands and agrees that in participating in one or more of the courses, or using facilities maintained by Cosmopolitan, there is the possibility of accidental or other physical injury. Member further agrees to assume the risk of such injury and further agrees to indemnify Cosmopolitan from any and all liability to Cosmopolitan by either the Member or third party as the result of the use by the Member of the facilities and instructions as offered by Cosmopolitan." About eighteen months later, Cosmopolitan sold the spa to Holiday Spas. Soon thereafter, Petry was injured when an exercise machine collapsed under her. She sued both Cosmopolitan and Holiday for damages arising out of negligent maintenance of the machine. Both Cosmopolitan and Holiday asserted that the exculpatory clause negated their liability. Petry argued that the exculpatory clause was unenforceable, and, even if it were enforceable, it could not be assigned by Cosmopolitan to Holiday. The trial court granted summary judgment to the defendants. Petry appealed.

ISSUE The issue in this case is twofold: (1) Is the exculpatory clause in the Cosmopolitan-Petry contract enforceable? (2) Is the contract containing the exculpatory clause assignable to Holiday?

DECISION Yes, to both. The appellate court held that the exculpatory clause was clearly enforceable and that the contract was assignable to Holiday. Thus the summary judgment granted by the trial court was proper.

REASON The court relied on an earlier decision of the Supreme Court of Tennessee that upheld an exculpatory clause almost exactly like the one in this case. In regard to Petry's claim that the contract was unassignable, the court stated that contract rights can be assigned unless the assignment (a) would "materially change the duty of the obligor, or materially increase the burden of risk imposed on him by the contract, or materially impair his chance of obtaining return performance, or reduce its value to him," or (b) is illegal or against public policy, or (c) is precluded by contract. The court found none of these exceptions to be applicable. Further, the court disagreed with Petry's claim that the contract was of a personal nature; rather, the contract was primarily for the use of spa facilities.

Notice of Assignment One wishing to assign his or her rights in a contract to another party may indicate that intention by any communication to the other party or the other party's representative. There is no requirement that the communication be in writing, even though the most obvious form of assignment is a writing signed by the assignor and delivered to the assignee, stating explicitly that the assignor assigns to the assignee his or her rights against a third person. The rights being assigned, of course, must be described in the writing, and both the rights and the third person have to be identifiable. But remember that assignment is the transfer of an already existing subject matter, and thus the rights must have been specific and identified in the *original* agreement. An assignment can be effective between the assignor and the assignee without any notice to the third party. It is effective as to the third party so long as there is no change in his or her position because he or she has not been given notice.

The party accepting an assignment of rights should notify the third person of the assignment. Until the obligor has notice of assignment, the obligor can discharge his or her obligation by performance to the assignor, and this performance constitutes a discharge to the assignee. Once the obligor receives proper notice, only performance to the assignee can discharge the obligor's obligations.

Suppose Barlow owes Ackerman $1,000 on a contract obligation. Ackerman assigns this monetary claim to Cramer. No notice of assignment is given to Barlow. Barlow pays Ackerman the $1,000. Although the assignment was valid, Barlow's payment to Ackerman was a discharge of the debt, and Cramer's failure to give Barlow notice of the assignment caused Cramer to lose the right to collect the money from Barlow. If Cramer had given Barlow notice, Barlow's payment to Ackerman would not have discharged the debt, and Cramer would have had a legal right to require payment from Barlow.

Delegations

Just as a party can transfer rights through an assignment, a party can also transfer duties. Duties are not assigned, however; they are *delegated*. (Delegation relationships are graphically illustrated in Exhibit 9-2.) Normally, a delegation of duties does not relieve the party making the delegation (the delegator) of the obligation to perform in the event that the party to whom the duty has been delegated (the delagatee) fails to perform. No special form is required to create a valid delegation of duties. As long as the delegator expresses an intention to make the delegation, it is effective; the delegator need not even use the word *delegate*.

Duties That Can Be Delegated   As a general rule, any duty can be delegated. There are, however, some exceptions to this rule. Delegation is prohibited:

1.   When performance depends on the *personal* skill or talents of the obligor.
2.   When special trust has been placed in the obligor.
3.   When performance by a third party will vary materially from that expected by the obligee (the one to whom performance is owed) under the contract.
4.   When the contract expressly prohibits delegation.

Suppose Barlow contracts with Ackerman to tutor Ackerman in the various aspects of financial underwriting and investment banking. Barlow, an experienced businessperson known for her expertise in finance, wants to delegate her duties to a third party, Cramer. This delegation is ineffective since Barlow contracted to render a service that is founded on Barlow's *expertise*. It is a change from Ackerman's expectancy under the contract. Therefore, Cramer cannot perform Barlow's duties.

Suppose Barlow, an attorney, contracts with Ackerman, a banker, to advise Ackerman on a proposed merger with a savings and loan association. Barlow wishes to delegate her duty to Cramer, a law firm across town. Attorney services are *personal* in nature; Barlow's delegation is thus ineffective.

Assume that Barlow contracts with Ackerman to pick up and deliver heavy construction machinery to Ackerman's property. Barlow delegates this duty to Cramer, who is in the business of delivering heavy machinery. The delegation is effective.

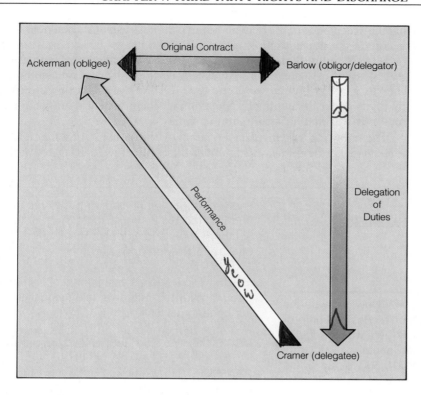

◆ **Exhibit 9-2**
Delegation Relationships

The performance required is of a *routine* and *nonpersonal* nature and does not change Ackerman's expectancy under the contract.

Effect of a Delegation   If a delegation of duties is enforceable, the obligee must accept performance from the delegatee. The obligee can legally refuse performance from the delegatee only if the duty is one that cannot be delegated. A valid delegation of duties does not relieve the delegator of obligations under the contract.[5] If the delegatee fails to perform, the delegator is still liable to the obligee.

Liability of the Delegatee to the Obligee   If the delegatee fails to perform, whether the obligee can hold the delegatee liable comes into issue. If the delegatee has made a promise of performance that will directly benefit the obligee, there is an "assumption of duty." Breach of this duty makes the delegatee liable to the obligee.

Suppose, for example, that Barlow contracts to build Ackerman a house according to Ackerman's blueprint. Barlow becomes seriously ill and contracts to have Cramer build the house for Ackerman (the obligee). Cramer fails to build the house. Since the delegatee Cramer contracted with Barlow (the obligor) to build the house for the benefit of Ackerman (the obligee), Ackerman can sue Barlow, or Cramer, or both. Although there are many exceptions, the general rule today is that the obligee can sue both the delegatee and the obligor.

When a contract provides for "assignment of all rights," this wording may also be treated as an "assumption of duties." The traditional view was that under this type of assignment, Cramer did not assume any duties. This view was based on the theory

---

5.   Crane Ice Cream Co. v. Terminal Freezing & Heating Co., 147 Md. 588, 128 A. 280 (1925).

that the acceptance of the benefits of the contract was not sufficient to imply a promise to assume the duties of the contract.

Modern authorities, however, take the view that the probable intent in using such general words is to create both an assignment of rights and an assumption of duties.[6] Therefore, when general words are used (for example, "I assign the contract" or "all my rights under the contract"), the contract is construed as implying both an assignment of rights and an assumption of duties.

The following case involves a conflict over whether, when the rights in a contract were assigned, the duties arising under the contract were delegated at the same time.

Case 9.2
NEWTON v. MERCHANTS & FARMERS BANK OF DUMAS

Arkansas Court of Appeals, 1984.
11 Ark.App. 167, 668 S.W.2d 51.

FACTS Kenneth Rogers agreed with Newton to do the plumbing work as a subcontractor on a construction project. Their contract stipulated that Rogers was to receive $22,100 in three installments. Rogers secured a loan from the Merchants & Farmers Bank for $15,500 to pay for the necessary expenses when he began work and before he had received his first installment from Newton. In return for the borrowed money, Rogers assigned to the bank his rights in the contract he had formed with Newton. On February 11, the bank sent Newton notice of the assignment and asked Newton to make his payment checks payable to Rogers and the bank *jointly*. Newton agreed in a letter to the bank to do this. On March 12, however, Newton wrote a check for $7,085 payable to Rogers only.

Rogers completed the work for Newton and had paid all his expenses except for that owed to one of his suppliers, Southern Pipe and Supply Company. Rogers eventually defaulted on his payments to the bank, and the bank sued Newton for the balance on the note. Newton could not avoid his obligation to the assignee of the note (the bank), but he claimed that he should not be responsible for the bill to Southern Pipe and Supply. He claimed that Rogers's assignment of his contract with Newton to the bank obligated the bank to assume Rogers's duties under the contract (including payments to all suppliers) and that the bank should therefore pay the bill owed to Southern Pipe and Supply. The trial court held for the bank, and Newton appealed.

ISSUE Did Rogers's assignment of his rights in his contract with Newton include a delegation of the duties under the contract as well?

DECISION No. The judgment for the bank was affirmed.

REASON The court quoted the rule of the Restatement (Second) of Contracts, Section 328(1), where it states: "Unless the language or the circumstances indicate to the contrary, as in an assignment for security, an assignment of 'the contract' or of 'all my rights under the contract' or an assignment in similar general terms is an assignment of the assignor's rights and a delegation of his unperformed duties under the contract." In the case at bar, the court concluded that "the language of the consumer note and security agreement Rogers signed to get the loan from the Bank describes the assignment as a 'security interest' to secure the . . . loan." In the bank's letter to Newton, notifying Newton of the assignment, the bank had explicitly stated that the assignment of the contract was to secure the loan, and "there is no evidence showing the Bank intended to perform Rogers's duties under the contract." The court concluded that Rogers had assigned his right to payments on his contract only, and not his duty to pay Southern Pipe.

❖ Third-Party Beneficiaries

To have contractual rights, a party normally must be a party to the contract. As mentioned earlier in this chapter, however, an exception exists when the original

---

6.   UCC 2-210(1)(4) (where there is a general assignment of a contract for the sale of goods); Restatement, Second, Contracts, Section 328.

parties to the contract intend at the time of contracting that the contract performance directly benefit a third person. The third person becomes a beneficiary of the contract and has legal rights.

A classic case where a third-party beneficiary was allowed to bring suit against a promisor is *Lawrence v. Fox* (see the "Landmark"). This case established the rule that a *creditor beneficiary* can sue the promisor directly. A creditor beneficiary is one who benefits from a contract in which one party (the promisor) promises another party (the promisee) to pay a third party (the creditor beneficiary). When a contract is made for the express purpose of giving a gift to a third party, the third party is called a *donee beneficiary*. In a 1918 landmark case, a donee beneficiary was allowed to bring an action against the promisor.[7]

Traditionally, only creditor beneficiaries and donee beneficiaries could sue the promisor directly if a contract was breached. As the law concerning third-party beneficiaries evolved, however, numerous cases arose that did not fit readily into either category. Thus the modern view, and the one adopted by the Restatement (Second) of Contracts, does not draw such clear lines and distinguishes only between *intended beneficiaries* (those who can sue) and *incidental beneficiaries* (those who cannot). The rationale behind the law providing that intended third-party beneficiaries can sue the promisor directly is that it decreases the number of lawsuits. Without such a law, a third party would sue the promisee, who would then sue the promisor. Allowing a third party to sue the promisor directly, thus circumventing the "middle person" (the promisee), reduces the burden on the courts.

Intended Beneficiaries

An **intended beneficiary** is one who can sue the promisor directly for breach of a contract made for the beneficiary's benefit. But who is the promisor? In bilateral contracts, both parties to the contract are promisors since they both make promises that can be enforced. The courts determine the promisor by asking which party made the promise that benefits the third-party beneficiary—that person is the "promisor."

In determining whether a third-party beneficiary is an intended or an incidental beneficiary, the courts generally use the *reasonable person* test. That is, a beneficiary will be considered an *intended* beneficiary if a reasonable person in the position of the third-party beneficiary would believe that the promisee *intended* to confer upon him or her the right to bring suit to enforce the contract. Intended third-party beneficiaries can include, but are not limited to, creditor and donee beneficiaries. Although the Restatement (Second) of the Law of Contracts has replaced the terms *creditor beneficiary* and *donee beneficiary* with *intended beneficiaries*, courts still use them occasionally, so the traditional terms will be used here.

Creditor Beneficiaries   If a promisee's main purpose in making a contract is to discharge a duty or debt he or she already owes to a third party, the third party is a *creditor beneficiary*. A debtor-creditor relationship must be established between the parties to the contract. The debtor then makes a contract with another person, which is intended to discharge the debt of the debtor and at the same time confer a benefit on the debtor's creditor. The creditor, although not a party to the contract between the debtor and the other person, becomes the *intended beneficiary* and can thus enforce the promisor's promise to pay the debt.

INTENDED BENEFICIARY
A third party for whose benefit a contract is formed; intended beneficiaries can sue the promisor if such a contract is breached.

---

7.   Seaver v. Ransom, 224 N.Y. 233, 120 N.E. 639 (1918).

Landmark in the Law

Lawrence v. Fox (1859)

In 1859, a landmark decision was handed down by the New York Court of Appeals in *Lawrence v. Fox*.[1] The decision held that a third-party beneficiary to a contract could sue the promisor to enforce the contract. At the time, this was a novel idea and represented a radical departure from contract law. Prior to that time, contractual liability had always been limited to the parties to the contract.

As one might suspect, given the exceptional outcome of this case, the circumstances surrounding it were also somewhat novel. In its simplest outline, the background to *Lawrence v. Fox* was as follows: On or about November 15, 1854, Holly borrowed $300 from Lawrence. Shortly thereafter, Holly loaned $300 to Fox, who in return promised Holly he would pay Holly's debt to Lawrence on the following day. Lawrence therefore was the creditor beneficiary of the contract between Holly and Fox. When Lawrence failed to obtain the $300 from Fox after several attempts, he brought suit against Fox to recover the money. The trial court held for Lawrence, as did, ultimately, the New York Court of Appeals (the highest court in the New York state system).

The case is puzzling for two reasons. First, given the large sum of money involved (about a year's wages back then), why wasn't a promissory note of some kind created and indorsed over to Lawrence by Fox as a means of repayment of the debt, in accordance with the commercial practice of the times? And second, why didn't Lawrence sue Holly directly, rather than pursue the highly unusual and more circuitous route of suing Fox, whereby his chances at recovery were much slimmer? The answers to both questions have to do with the apparent fact [2] that the

1.   20 N.Y. 268 (1859).
2.   See Antony Jon Waters, "The Property in the Promise: A Study of the Third Party Beneficiary Rule," *Harvard Law Review* 98 (1985), pp. 1109–1168.

"Holly" in this case was one Merwin Spencer Hawley, a prominent Buffalo, New York, merchant and president of the Buffalo Board of Trade, of which the defendant, Arthur Wellesley Fox, was also a member. Evidence at trial suggested that the debt Hawley owed Lawrence was a gambling debt. Since gambling was illegal under New York law, Lawrence could not recover from Hawley directly in court, as the contract would have been deemed illegal and thus void.

The Court of Appeals in a sense followed the "gambler's law" in deeming that Fox was in the wrong. Although citing numerous precedents, mostly relating to agency and trust law, the court based its decision ultimately on equitable grounds: It was manifestly "just" to allow Lawrence to recover the money from Fox. The principle of law enunciated was that "[In the case of] a promise made for the benefit of another, he for whose benefit it is made may bring an action for its breach." The dissenting justices vigorously opposed the ruling and expressed their concern about privity of contract and the ability of the promisor and the promisee to rescind or modify a contract. They stressed that Lawrence had had nothing to do with the contract. "It was not made to him, nor did the consideration proceed from him. If Lawrence can maintain the suit, it is because an anomaly has formed its way into the law on this subject."

The third-party-beneficiary rule is unique to this country. In all other common-law countries, privity of contract is required before a party can sue to have a contract enforced—unless a statutory exception exists to counter common law. This legal precedent of 1859 went largely unnoted in the courts for more than fifty years, and privity of contract remained the guiding principle until after the turn of the century. In *MacPherson v. Buick Motor Company* (1916) and in *Seaver v. Ransom* (1918), the New York Court of Appeals cited *Lawrence v. Fox* in justifying its departure from the privity-of-contract principle. Since then, the third-party-beneficiary rule has been continuously expanded in scope, and today any "intended beneficiary" to a contract will likely be entitled to sue in order to have the contract enforced.

The assumption of a real estate mortgage is a type of third-party creditor-beneficiary contract. Suppose some years ago your parents purchased their home. Unable to pay cash, they contracted to borrow the money from Applegate Savings & Loan at a rate of 8.5 percent interest, with Applegate taking a mortgage on the home purchased.

Today your parents decide to sell their home to Levy. Levy is interested in the 8.5-percent rate of interest and agrees (1) to pay your parents the difference between the selling price and what they still owe on the mortgage loan, and (2) to pay the mortgage-loan installment payments to Applegate Savings & Loan, the creditor beneficiary. Even though Applegate is not a party to the present contract for the sale of the home to Levy, does Applegate have any rights in this contract?

The answer is yes, if the assumption of the mortgage by a third party is not prohibited in the mortgage contract. When your parents purchased the home through a mortgage, they became debtors and Applegate Savings & Loan a creditor. When your parents sold the home to Levy, Levy's assumption of their mortgage created a benefit for Applegate in that Applegate could then hold Levy personally liable on the loan—in addition to holding your parents liable or repossessing the property should there be a default. Thus, Applegate is a creditor beneficiary of certain terms of the contract between your parents and Levy and can enforce the monthly mortgage payments against Levy.

Donee Beneficiaries   If a promisee's main purpose in making a contract is to confer a benefit upon a third party in the form of a gift, the third party is a *donee beneficiary*. A donee beneficiary can enforce the promise of a promisor just as a creditor beneficiary can. Suppose Ackerman goes to her attorney, Barlow, and enters into a contract whereby Barlow promises to draft a will naming Ackerman's son, John, as an heir. John is a donee beneficiary, and if Barlow does not prepare the will properly, John can sue Barlow.[8] Or suppose Ackerman offers to put in a swimming pool in Barlow's backyard if Barlow pays $2,000 to John, Ackerman's son. Ackerman wants to give the money to John as a gift. John is a donee beneficiary and can enforce Barlow's promise to pay the $2,000.

The most common donee-beneficiary contract is a life insurance contract. In a typical contract, Ackerman (the promisee) pays premiums to Standard Life, a life insurance company, and Standard (the promisor) promises to pay a certain amount of money upon Ackerman's death to anyone Ackerman designates as a beneficiary. The designated beneficiary, John, is a donee beneficiary under the life insurance policy and can enforce the promise made by the insurance company to pay John upon Ackerman's death.

When the Rights of a Third Party Vest   A third party cannot enforce a contract against the original parties until the rights of the third party have *vested*, which means the rights have taken effect and cannot be taken away. Until these rights have vested, the original parties to the contract—the promisor and the promisee—can modify or rescind the contract without consent of the third party. When do the rights of third parties vest? Generally, the rights of an *intended* beneficiary (incidental beneficiaries have no rights to vest) vest when either of the following occurs:

1.   When the third party demonstrates *manifest assent* to the contract, such as sending a letter or note acknowledging awareness of and consent to a contract formed for his or her benefit.
2.   When the third party materially alters his or her position in *detrimental reliance* on the contract.

---

8.   Lucas v. Hamm, 56 Cal.2d 583, 15 Cal.Rptr. 821, 364 P.2d 685 (1961).

If the contract expressly reserves the right to cancel, rescind, or modify the contract, the rights of the third-party beneficiary are subject to any changes that result. In such a case, the vesting of the third party's rights does not terminate the power of the original contracting parties to alter their legal relationships.[9] This is particularly true in most life insurance contracts, where the right to change the beneficiary is reserved.

Incidental Beneficiaries

INCIDENTAL BENEFICIARY
A third party who incidentally benefits from a contract but whose benefit was not the reason the contract was formed; incidental beneficiaries have no rights in a contract and cannot sue the promisor if the contract is breached.

The benefit that an **incidental beneficiary** receives from a contract between two parties is unintentional. Therefore, an incidental beneficiary cannot enforce a contract to which he or she is not a party. Several factors must be examined to determine whether a party is an incidental beneficiary. The presence of one or more of the factors listed here strongly indicates an *intended* (rather than an incidental) benefit to a third party.

1. Performance rendered directly to the third party.
2. The right of the third party to control the details of performance.
3. Express designation in the contract.

The following are examples of incidental beneficiaries. The third party has no rights in the contract and cannot enforce it against the promisor.

1. Jules contracts with Vivian to build a cottage on Vivian's land. Jules's plans specify that Super Insulation Company's insulation materials must be used when constructing the house. Super Insulation Company is an incidental beneficiary and cannot enforce the contract against Jules by attempting to require that Jules purchase its insulation materials.
2. Ed contracts with Raymond to build a recreational facility on Raymond's land. Once the facility is constructed, it will greatly enhance the property values in the neighborhood. If Ed subsequently refuses to build the facility, Fred, a neighboring property owner, cannot enforce the contract against Ed by attempting to require that Ed build the facility.
3. Ellison works for Roberts. Ellison has been promised a promotion if his employer obtains a contract with Lattimore. Roberts is unable to obtain the contract with Lattimore. Ellison is an incidental beneficiary to that contract. Ellison has no right to sue Lattimore for being the cause of his nonpromotion to a better-paying position. Indeed, Ellison cannot sue Lattimore even if Ellison loses his job as a result of the failure of Roberts and Lattimore to reach an agreement.

❖ Conditions of Performance

In most contracts, promises of performance are not *expressly* conditioned or qualified. They are called *absolute promises*. They must be performed, or the party promising the act will be in breach of contract. For example, I contract to sell you my radio

---

9. Defenses raised against third-party beneficiaries are given in Restatement, Second, Contracts, Section 309.

for $50. Our promises are unconditional: my transfer of the radio to you and your payment of $50 to me. The $50 does not have to be paid if the radio is not transferred.

In some cases, however, performance may be beneficial only if a certain event either does or does not occur. Therefore, a *condition* is inserted into the contract, either expressly by the parties or impliedly by courts. If this condition is not satisfied, the obligations of the parties are discharged.

Suppose I offer to purchase a tract of your land on the condition that your neighbor to the south agrees to sell me her land. You accept my offer. Our obligations (promises) are conditioned upon your neighbor's willingness to sell her land. Should this condition not be satisfied (for example, if your neighbor refuses to sell), our obligations to each other are discharged and cannot be enforced.

Thus, a **condition** is a possible future event, the occurrence or nonoccurrence of which will trigger the performance of a legal obligation or terminate an existing obligation under a contract.

Although there is a fundamental distinction between the breach of an absolute promise and the failure or nonoccurrence of an express condition, both can occur in a single contract. For example, suppose you promise to buy a futures contract for corn from a brokerage firm *if the price of yellow corn reaches $2.25 per bushel.* The condition to your promise to buy is that the price of yellow corn reaches $2.25 per bushel. If there is a failure of that condition—if that price is never reached—then you do not breach the contract by not buying. Once the price of corn does reach $2.25, your promise to buy becomes absolute; if at that point you do not buy, the contract is breached.

Three types of conditions can be present in any given contract: precedent, subsequent, and concurrent.

1.   Conditions Precedent. A condition that must be fulfilled before a party's promise becomes absolute is called a **condition precedent.**[10] The condition precedes the absolute duty to perform. For example, James promises to contribute $2,000 to Friends Church if Jonathan completes college. James's promise is subject to the (express) condition precedent that Jonathan complete college. Until the condition is fulfilled or satisfied, James's promise to donate to the church is not absolute.

2.   Conditions Subsequent. When a condition operates to terminate a party's absolute promise to perform, it is called a **condition subsequent.**[11] The condition follows, or is subsequent to, the absolute duty to perform. If the condition occurs, the party need not perform any further. For example, if you promise an employer you will continue to work at your job unless you are admitted to the Yale Law School, your absolute duty to work is conditioned upon not being admitted. Your promise to work for your employer continues to be absolute. Once you are officially admitted to Yale Law School, the absolute duty to work for your employer ends, and you are released from the contract.

3.   Concurrent Conditions. When each party's absolute duty to perform is conditioned on the other party's absolute duty to perform, there are **concurrent conditions.** These conditions exist only when the parties expressly or impliedly are to perform their respective duties *simultaneously.* For example, if a buyer promises to pay for goods when they are delivered by the seller, each party's absolute duty to perform is

CONDITION
A qualification, provision, or clause in a contractual agreement, the occurrence of which creates, suspends, or terminates the obligations of the contracting parties.

CONDITION PRECEDENT
In a contractual agreement, a condition that must be met before the other party's obligations arise.

CONDITION SUBSEQUENT
A condition in a contract which, if not met, discharges an existing obligation of the other party.

CONCURRENT CONDITIONS
Conditions that must occur or be performed at the same time; they are mutually dependent. No obligations arise until these conditions are simultaneously performed.

---

10.   Restatement, Second, Contracts, Section 224, eliminates the terms *condition precedent* and *condition subsequent.*

11.   Restatement, Second, Contracts, Section 224. A condition may be subsequent in form but precedent in fact.

conditioned upon the other party's absolute duty to perform. The buyer's duty to pay for the goods does not become absolute until the seller either delivers or attempts to deliver the goods. Accordingly, the seller's duty to deliver the goods does not become absolute until the buyer tenders or actually makes payment. Therefore, neither can recover from the other for breach without first tendering performance.

❖ Ways to Discharge a Contract

The most common way to discharge (terminate) one's contractual duties is by performance of those duties. But there are numerous other ways a contract can be discharged, including discharge by agreement of the parties and by impossibility of performance.

Discharge by Performance

TENDER
A timely offer, or expression of willingness, to pay a debt or perform an obligation.

The contract comes to an end when both parties fulfill their respective duties by performance of the acts they have promised. Performance can also be accomplished by tender. **Tender** is an unconditional offer to perform by a person who is ready, willing, and able to do so. Therefore, a seller who places goods at the disposal of a buyer has tendered delivery and can demand payment according to the terms of the agreement. A buyer who offers to pay for goods has tendered payment and can demand delivery of the goods. Once performance has been tendered, the party making the tender has done everything possible to carry out the terms of the contract. If the other party then refuses to perform, the party making the tender can consider the duty discharged and sue for breach of contract.

It is important to distinguish among three types of performance: (1) complete (or strict), (2) substantial, and (3) inferior (constituting a material breach of contract).

Complete (or Strict) Performance   Although in most contracts the parties fully discharge their obligations by complete performance, sometimes a party fulfills most (but not all) of the duties or completes the duties in a manner contrary to the terms of the contract. The issue then arises as to whether this failure of complete performance acts as a discharge of performance for the other party.

For example, a couple contracts with a construction company to build them a house. The contract specifies Brand X plasterboard be used for the walls. The builder cannot secure the Brand X brand and installs Brand Y instead. All other aspects of construction conform to the contract. Does this deviation discharge the buyer from paying for the house upon completion?

To determine the answer, courts usually ask the following questions:

1.   Does the term in dispute constitute an express condition of the contract? In other words, was the use of Brand X plasterboard expressly required by the contract?
2.   Can only "complete performance" discharge the promise?

If the answer to both questions is yes, then only *complete* performance constitutes a discharge of performance. If the terms of the contract do not fit both these categories, *substantial* (not complete) performance is required. In this case, it must be determined whether the performance is substantial. If it is not, the party is then in *material* breach.

Substantial Performance Most terms or promises are not made or construed as conditions. Human nature dictates that performance will not always fully satisfy the parties. Therefore, for the sake of justice and fairness, the courts hold that a party's obligation is not discharged as long as the other party has fulfilled the terms of the contract by *substantial performance*. To qualify as substantial, the performance must not vary greatly from the performance promised in the contract, and it must create substantially the same benefits as those promised in the contract. If performance is substantial, the other party's duty to perform remains absolute (less damages, if any, for the minor deviations).

In the following case, substantial performance by a contractor is at issue.

Case 9.3
WARREN v. DENISON
Court of Appeals of Texas, 1978.
563 S.W.2d 299.

FACTS Denison was a building contractor hired by the Warrens to construct a house on their property. The parties formed a written contract in which it was stated that the Warrens would pay Denison $73,400 for the work. Further writings gave Denison the right to foreclose on the house if the Warrens refused to make payments. After the Warrens took possession of the house, they noted several flaws in the construction of the home and refused to pay the $48,400 still owed to Denison. Denison initiated foreclosure proceedings, and the Warrens sued Denison, alleging that Denison had breached their contract by his poor workmanship. The trial court ruled for Denison and the Warrens appealed.

ISSUE Had Denison, despite his poor workmanship, discharged his duty to the contract?

DECISION Yes. The judgment for Denison was affirmed.

REASON The court noted that "literal performance of each and every particular of such [construction] contracts is virtually impossible. Rather than require perfect performance . . . substantial performance is regarded as full performance in allowing the builder to recover on the contract. . . . A job can be substantially performed with some breaches of workmanlike construction preventing perfect performance." The Warrens were thus ordered to pay the $48,400 still owed to Denison, minus $2,161.50—which the Warrens felt was necessary to undertake repairs on the house necessitated by Denison's "construction flaws."

Performance to the Satisfaction of Another Contracts often state that completed work must personally satisfy one of the parties or a third person. The question arises as to whether this satisfaction becomes a condition precedent, requiring actual personal satisfaction or approval for discharge, or whether the test of satisfaction is an absolute promise requiring such performance as would satisfy a "reasonable person" (substantial performance).

When the subject matter of the contract is personal, a contract to be performed to the satisfaction of one of the parties is conditioned, and performance must actually satisfy that party. For example, contracts for portraits, works of art, medical or dental work, and tailoring are considered personal. Therefore, only the personal satisfaction of the party is sufficient to fulfill the condition—unless a jury finds the party is expressing dissatisfaction only to avoid payment or otherwise is not acting in good faith.

Contracts that involve mechanical fitness, utility, or marketability need only be performed to the satisfaction of a reasonable person unless they *expressly state otherwise*. When contracts require performance to the satisfaction of a third party (for example, "to the satisfaction of Robert Ames, the supervising engineer"), the courts are divided. A majority of courts require the work to be satisfactory to a reasonable person, but some courts hold that the personal satisfaction of the third party (Robert Ames) must be met. Again, the personal judgment must be made honestly, or the condition will be excused.

BREACH OF CONTRACT
Failure, without legal excuse, of a promisor to perform the obligations of a contract.

Inferior Performance (Material Breach of Contract)   A **breach of contract** is the nonperformance of a contractual duty. When the breach is *material*[12] or when performance is not substantial, the nonbreaching party is excused from the performance of contractual duties and has a cause of action to sue for damages caused by the breach. If the breach is *minor* (not material), the nonbreaching party's duty to perform can sometimes be suspended until the breach is remedied but is not entirely excused. Once the minor breach is cured, the nonbreaching party must resume performance of the contractual obligations undertaken. A breach entitles the non-breaching party to sue for damages, but only a material breach discharges the non-breaching party from the contract. The policy underlying these rules allows contracts to go forward when only minor problems occur but terminates them if major problems arise.[13]

The difference between substantial performance and performance so inferior as to constitute a material breach of contract is illustrated in the following case. Note here how the defendant failed to follow *express* contractual conditions (instructions) in performing construction work, and the significance of these express instructions in the court's determination as to whether the contract had, or had not, been substantially performed.

Case 9.4
BUTKOVICH & SONS, INC. v. STATE BANK OF ST. CHARLES
Appellate Court of Illinois, Second District, 1978.
62 Ill. App. 3d 810, 20 Ill. Dec. 4, 379 N.E. 2d 837.

FACTS   Grane, a homeowner, contracted with Butkovich & Sons to enlarge Grane's basement and build a new room over the new basement area. Butkovich was also to lay a new garage floor and construct a patio area. The parties agreed to a price of $19,290 for the work. When the construction was completed, Grane refused to pay the contractor the $9,290 balance he still owed, claiming that Butkovich had failed to install water stops and reinforcing wire in one concrete floor as Grane had specified, and that the main floor of the addition was 8⅞ inches lower than the plans had called for. As a mortgage holder on the property, the State Bank of St. Charles was named co-defendant, as its interests would be affected by a judgment against Grane if the latter could not pay. The trial court ruled that, notwithstanding the defects, Butkovich

had substantially performed the contract. Grane and the bank appealed.

ISSUE   Has the contract been substantially performed by Butkovich, notwithstanding his deviations from the specifications made by Grane?

DECISION   No. The appellate court reversed the trial court's judgment and ruled that the contract had not been substantially performed. The case was remanded to the trial court for further proceedings.

REASON   The appellate court concluded that the trial court had been in error when it accepted Butkovich's argument that the plans did not call for the water stops or the reinforcing wire. Both had been specifically indicated by the plans drawn up by Grane and submitted to the trial court as evidence. Because these plans constituted express conditions of performance, and because the main floor was 8⅞ inches lower than the plans called for, "it is clear that plaintiff did *not* substantially perform the contract."

---

12.   Restatement, Second, Contracts, Section 241.
13.   See UCC 2-612 dealing with installment contracts for the sale of goods.

Anticipatory Repudiation   Before either party to a contract has a duty to perform, one of the parties may refuse to perform his or her contractual obligations. This is called **anticipatory breach** or **anticipatory repudiation**.[14] When anticipatory repudiation occurs, it is treated as a material breach of contract and the nonbreaching party is permitted to bring an action for damages immediately, even though the scheduled time for performance under the contract may still be in the future.[15]

There are two reasons for treating an anticipatory breach as a present, material breach:

1.   The nonbreaching party should not be required to remain ready and willing to perform when the other party has already repudiated the contract.
2.   The nonbreaching party should have the opportunity to seek a similar contract elsewhere.

It is important to note that until the nonbreaching party treats this early repudiation as a breach, the breaching party can retract his or her anticipatory repudiation by proper notice and restore the parties to their original obligations.[16]

Quite often an anticipatory breach occurs when a sharp fluctuation in market prices causes the contract, if performed, to be extremely unfavorable to one of the parties. For example, Shasta Manufacturing Company contracts to manufacture and sell 100,000 personal computers to New Age, Inc., a computer retailer with 500 outlet stores. Delivery is to be made eight months from the date of the contract. The contract price is based on the seller's present costs of acquiring inventory parts purchased from others. One month later, three inventory suppliers raise their prices to Shasta. Based on these prices, if Shasta manufactures and sells the computers to New Age at the contract price, Shasta stands to lose $500,000. Shasta immediately writes a letter to New Age stating that Shasta cannot deliver the 100,000 computers at the agreed-upon contract price. Even though you might feel sorry for Shasta, its letter is an anticipatory repudiation of the contract, allowing New Age the option of treating the repudiation as a material breach and proceeding immediately to pursue remedies, even though the actual contract delivery date is still seven months away.[17]

Discharge by Agreement

Any contract can be discharged by the agreement of the parties. The agreement can be contained in the original contract, or the parties can form a new contract for the express purpose of discharging the original contract.

Discharge by Rescission   **Rescission** is the process whereby the parties cancel the contract and are returned to the positions they occupied prior to the contract's formation. For *mutual rescission* to take place, the parties must make another agreement that also satisfies the legal requirements for a contract—there must be an *offer*, an *acceptance*, and *consideration*. Ordinarily, if the parties agree to rescind the original

ANTICIPATORY BREACH OR ANTICIPATORY REPUDIATION
An assertion or action by a party indicating that he or she will not perform an obligation that the party is contractually obligated to perform at a future time.

RESCISSION
A remedy whereby a contract is canceled and the parties are returned to the positions they occupied before the contract was made; may be effected through the mutual consent of the parties, by their conduct, or by the decree of a court of equity.

---

14.   Restatement, Second, Contracts, Section 253, and UCC 2-610.
15.   The doctrine of anticipatory breach first arose in the landmark case of Hochster v. De La Tour, 2 Ellis and Blackburn Reports 678 (1853), when the English court recognized the delay and expense inherent in a rule requiring a nonbreaching party to wait until the time of performance before suing on an anticipatory breach.
16.   See UCC 2-611.
17.   Another illustration can be found in Reliance Cooperage Corp. v. Treat, 195 F.2d 977 (8th Cir. 1952).

contract, their promises not to perform those acts promised in the original contract will be legal consideration for the second contract. This occurs when the performance of each is executory (not yet completed).

The rescission agreement is generally enforceable even if made orally and even if the original agreement was in writing. There are two basic exceptions: one applies to transfers of realty, and the other has to do with the sale of goods under the UCC, where the sales contract requires written rescission.[18]

When one party has fully performed, however, an agreement to call off the original contract is not usually enforceable. Because the performing party has received no consideration for the promise to call off the original bargain, additional consideration is necessary. Generally, contracts that are *executory* on *both* sides (contracts where neither party has performed) can be rescinded solely by agreement.[19] But contracts that are *executed* on *one* side (contracts where one party has performed) can be rescinded only if the party who has performed receives consideration for the promise to call off the deal.

NOVATION
The substitution, by agreement, of a new contract for an old one, with the rights under the old one being terminated. Typically, there is a substitution of a new person who is responsible for the contract and the removal of the original party's rights and duties under the contract.

Discharge by Novation or Substituted Agreement The process of **novation** substitutes a new party for one of the original parties. Essentially, the parties to the original contract and one or more new parties all get together and agree to the substitution. A *substituted* agreement is a new contract between the same parties that expressly or impliedly revokes and discharges a prior contract.[20] The parties involved may simply want a new agreement with somewhat different terms, so they expressly state in a new contract that the old contract is now discharged. They can also make the new contract without expressly stating that the old contract is discharged. If the parties do not expressly discharge the old contract, it will be *impliedly* discharged owing to the different terms of the new contract.

The requirements of a novation are:

1. The existence of a previous, valid obligation.
2. Agreement by all the parties to a new contract.
3. The extinguishing of the old obligation (discharge of the prior party).
4. A new, valid contract.

A novation differs from an assignment or delegation in that it is an agreement entered into by *all* the parties concerned to substitute one party to the contract for another. In a novation the dismissed party is no longer liable under the contract, whereas in an assignment or delegation the original party remains liable.

Suppose you contract with A. Logan Enterprises to sell it your office-equipment business. Logan later learns that it should not expand at this time, but knows of another party, MBI Corporation, interested in purchasing your business. All three of you get together and agree to a novation. As long as the new contract is supported by consideration, the novation discharges the original contract between you and Logan and replaces it with the new contract between you and MBI Corporation.

---

18. UCC 2-209(2)(4).
19. Note, however, that certain contracts made by a consumer in his or her home can be rescinded by the consumer within three days for no reason at all. This three-day "cooling-off" period is designed to aid consumers who are susceptible to high-pressure door-to-door sales tactics. See U.S.C., Section 1635(a).
20. This immediate discharge of the prior contract distinguishes a substituted contract from an accord and satisfaction, discussed in the next section.

Logan prefers the novation because it discharges all the contract liabilities stemming from its contract with you. Suppose an installment sales contract was involved, requiring twelve monthly payments. A mere assignment of the contract to MBI Corporation would have retained Logan's liability to you for the payments if MBI Corporation defaulted.

A *compromise,* or settlement agreement, that arises out of a bona fide dispute over the obligations in an existing contract will be recognized by law. Such an agreement is substituted as a new contract, and it either expressly or impliedly revokes and discharges the obligations in any prior contract.

Discharge by Accord and Satisfaction   As discussed in Chapter 6, for a contract to be discharged by **accord and satisfaction,** the parties must agree to accept performance different from the performance originally promised. An **accord** is defined as an executory contract (one that has not yet been performed) to perform some act in order to satisfy an existing contractual duty.[21] The duty is not yet discharged. A **satisfaction** is the performance of the accord agreement. An *accord* and its *satisfaction* (performance) discharge the original contractual obligation.

Once the accord has been made, the original obligation is merely suspended unless the accord agreement is breached. Thus, the obligor can discharge the obligation by performing the obligation agreed to in the accord. Likewise, if the obligor refuses to perform the accord, the obligee can bring action on the original obligation.

Suppose Bill obtains a judgment against Martha for $4,000. Later both parties agree that the judgment can be satisfied by Martha transferring her automobile to Bill. This agreement to accept the auto in lieu of $4,000 in cash is the accord. If Martha transfers her automobile to Bill, the accord agreement is fully performed and the $4,000 debt is discharged. If Martha refuses to transfer her car, the accord is breached. Since the original obligation is merely suspended, Bill can bring action to enforce the judgment for $4,000 in cash.

Discharge by Impossibility of Performance

After a contract has been made, performance may become impossible in an objective sense. This is known as **impossibility of performance** and may discharge a contract.[22] This *objective impossibility* ("It can't be done") must be distinguished from *subjective impossibility* ("I simply can't do it"). Examples of subjective impossibility include contracts in which goods cannot be delivered on time because of freight car shortages [23] and contracts in which money cannot be paid on time because the bank is closed.[24] In effect, the party in these cases is saying "It is impossible for *me* to perform," not "It is impossible for *anyone* to perform." Accordingly, such excuses do not discharge a contract, and the nonperforming party is normally held in breach of contract.

Objective Impossibility   Four basic types of situations generally qualify under the objective impossibility-of-performance rules that discharge contractual obligations: [25]

ACCORD AND SATISFACTION
A method of discharging a claim in which the parties agree to give and accept something different from the performance originally promised in settlement of the claim. The accord is the agreement, and the satisfaction is its execution, or performance. Normally, an accord and satisfaction results in a full release, that is, the discharge of the original contractual obligation.

ACCORD
An agreement between two persons, one of whom has a right of action against the other, to settle a contractual obligation.

SATISFACTION
The tender of substitute performance in return for the relinquishing of the right of action on a prior obligation.

IMPOSSIBILITY OF PERFORMANCE
A doctrine under which a party to a contract is relieved of his or her duty to perform when performance becomes impossible or totally impracticable (through no fault of either party).

---

21. Restatement, Second, Contracts, Section 281.
22. Restatement, Second, Contracts, Section 261.
23. Minneapolis v. Republic Creosoting Co., 161 Minn. 178, 201 N.W. 414 (1924).
24. Ingham Lumber Co. v. Ingersoll & Co., 93 Ark. 447, 125 S.W. 139 (1910).
25. Restatement, Second, Contracts, Sections 262–266, and UCC 2-615.

1.   When one of the parties to a personal contract *dies or becomes incapacitated prior to performance*. For example, Fred, a famous dancer, contracts with Ethereal Dancing Guild to play a leading role in its new ballet. Before the ballet can be performed, however, Fred becomes ill and dies. His personal performance was essential to the completion of the contract. Thus his death discharges the contract and his estate's liability for his nonperformance.

2.   When the *specific* subject matter of the contract is destroyed. For example, A-I Farm Equipment agrees to sell Gudgel the green tractor on its lot and promises to have it ready for Gudgel to pick up on Saturday. On Friday night, however, a truck veers off the nearby highway and smashes into the tractor, destroying it beyond repair. Because the contract was for this specific tractor, A-I's performance is rendered impossible owing to the accident.

3.   When a change in *law* renders performance illegal. Examples include a contract to loan money at 20 percent, but the usury rate is changed to make loans in excess of 12 percent illegal; and a contract to build an apartment building, but the zoning laws are changed to prohibit the construction of residential rental property. Both changes render the contracts impossible to perform.

4.   When performance becomes *commercially impracticable*. This type of impossibility results from a growing trend to allow parties to discharge contracts in which the originally contemplated performance turns out to be more difficult or expensive than anticipated. This is known as the *doctrine of commercial impracticability*.

For example, the California Supreme Court held that a contract was discharged because a party would have to pay ten times more than the original estimate to excavate a certain amount of gravel.[26] On the other hand, a court did not find commercial impracticability in a case where a carrier of goods was to deliver wheat from the West Coast of the United States to a safe port in Iran.[27] The Suez Canal, the usual route, was nationalized by Egypt and closed, forcing the carrier to travel around Africa and the Cape of Good Hope, through the Mediterranean, and on to Iran. The added expense was approximately $42,000 above and beyond the contract price of $306,000, and the original journey of 10,000 miles was extended by an additional 3,000 miles. Nevertheless, the court held that performance could not be excused on the grounds of commercial impracticability, because the closing of the Suez Canal was foreseeable. Therefore, caution should be used in invoking the doctrine of commercial impracticability. The added burden of performing must be *extreme* and, more important, must *not* be within the cognizance of the parties at the time the contract is made.

Temporary Impossibility   An occurrence or event that makes it temporarily impossible to perform the act for which a party has contracted operates to *suspend* performance until the impossibility ceases. Then, ordinarily, the parties must perform the contract as originally planned. If, however, the lapse of time and the change in circumstances surrounding the contract make it substantially more burdensome for the parties to perform the promised acts, the contract is discharged.

The leading case on the subject, *Autry v. Republic Productions*, involved an actor who was drafted into the army in 1942.[28] Being drafted rendered his contract temporarily impossible to perform, and it was suspended until the end of the war. When the actor got out of the army, the value of the dollar had so changed that performance of the contract would have been substantially burdensome to him. Therefore, the contract was discharged.

26.   Mineral Park Land Co. v. Howard, 172 Cal. 289, 156 P. 458 (1916).
27.   Transatlantic Financing Corp. v. United States, 363 F.2d 312 (D.C. Cir. 1966).
28.   30 Cal.2d 144, 180 P.2d 888 (1947).

Application

Law and the Debtor

An understanding of the enforceability of agreements to settle claims or discharge debts is important in the business world. As discussed in Chapter 6 and reinforced in this chapter, one of the most often used agreements in such settlement transactions is accord and satisfaction—a debtor's offer to pay and a creditor's acceptance of a lesser amount of the debt owed. If you are the debtor, for you to be able to discharge a debt by accord and satisfaction, the amount owed must be in bona fide dispute. If such is the case, you can generally relieve yourself from any further obligation on the debt by offering a check for the amount that you believe is owed, with a note on the back of it stating it is complete payment for the debt. The old adage "a bird in the hand is worth two in the bush" leads many creditors to cash the check—at which point your obligation usually is completely discharged.

Suppose you are the creditor. If a check is offered to you in discharge of an obligation, you must decide whether to accept it or not. If the amount of the obligation is *not* in dispute, then in the majority of states you can still cash the check, no matter what is written on the back of it, and still sue for the difference. A word of caution is in order. Just because you think the amount of the obligation is not in dispute does not necessarily mean that such is the case. The other party, acting as a "reasonable" person, has to know how much is owed for it to be undisputed in amount. As long as he or she has a good-faith claim, the amount is, in fact, in dispute, and by your cashing the check you agree that the obligation is discharged.

Checklist for Discharging a Debt by Accord and Satisfaction

□ **1.** The amount owed must be in bona fide dispute.

□ **2.** If you are the debtor and write on the back of your check that the amount is in complete payment for the debt obligation, and the check is cashed, your obligation is normally discharged.

□ **3.** In the majority of cases, if the debt amount is not in dispute, the creditor can cash the check and still sue for the difference.

❖ Chapter Summary: Third-Party Rights and Discharge

THIRD-PARTY RIGHTS	
Assignment	1. An assignment is the transfer of *rights* under a contract to a third party whereby the rights of the assignor (the person making the assignment) may be extinguished, and the assignee (the person to whom the rights are assigned) has a right to demand performance from the other original party to the contract (the obligor).
	2. Notice of the assignment should be given by the assignee to the obligor. Unless so notified, an obligor can tender performance to the assignor and, if performance is accepted by the assignor, the obligor's duties under the contract are discharged without benefit to the assignee.
	3. Generally, all rights can be assigned, except in the following circumstances: a. When assignment is expressly prohibited by statute (e.g., workers' compensation benefits). b. When the contract itself stipulates that the rights cannot be assigned (except a money claim). c. When a contract calls for the performance of personal services. d. When the assignment will materially increase or alter the duties of the obligor.
Delegation	1. A delegation is the transfer of *duties* under a contract to a third party whereby the delegatee (the third party) assumes the obligation of performing the contractual duties previously held by the delegator (the one making the delegation).
	2. As a general rule, any duty can be delegated, except in the following circumstances: a. When performance depends on the personal skill or talents of the obligor. b. When special trust has been placed in the obligor. c. When performance by a third party will vary materially from that expected by the obligee (the one to whom the duty is owed) under the contract. d. When the contract expressly prohibits delegation.
	3. A valid delegation of duties does not relieve the delegator (the one making the delegation) of obligations under the contract. If the delegatee fails to perform, the delegator is still liable to the obligee.
Third-Party- Beneficiary Contract	A third-party-beneficiary contract is one made for the purpose of benefiting a third party. 1. *Intended beneficiary*—One for whose benefit a contract is created. When the promisor (the one making the contractual promise) fails to perform as promised, the third party can sue the promisor directly. Examples of third-party beneficiaries are creditor and donee beneficiaries. 2. *Incidental beneficiary*—A third party who indirectly (incidentally) benefits from a contract, but for whose benefit the contract was not specifically intended. Incidental beneficiaries have no rights to the benefits received and cannot sue the promisor to have them enforced.
CONDITIONS OF PERFORMANCE	

1. *Condition precedent*—A condition that must be fulfilled before a party's promise becomes absolute. The condition precedes the absolute duty to perform (Example: A promises to buy B a Cadillac on the condition that B complete college. B's completing college is a *condition precedent*.)

2. *Condition subsequent*—A condition that operates to terminate a party's absolute promise to perform. (Example: A promises to work for B *unless* A is admitted to Yale. A's promise to work is absolute *until* A is admitted to Yale. Admission to Yale is a *condition subsequent*.)

3. *Concurrent conditions*—Exist when each party's absolute duty to perform is conditioned on the other party's absolute duty to perform and only when the parties expressly or impliedly are to perform their respective duties simultaneously. (Example: A promises B to pay for B's used car only upon delivery of the car; B promises A to deliver his used car only upon tender of payment by A. These are *concurrent conditions* of performance, because each promise is conditioned on the other party's simultaneous performance.)

❖ Chapter Summary: Third-Party Rights and Discharge—Continued

WAYS TO DISCHARGE A CONTRACT

1. *Performance*—Complete or substantial (if terms are construed as promises).

2. *Breach*—Material nonperformance discharges the nonbreaching party's performance.

3. *Mutual rescission*—An enforceable agreement to restore parties to their precontract positions.

4. *Novation*—By valid contract, a new party is substituted for an original party, thereby terminating the old contract.

5. *Accord and satisfaction*—An agreement whereby the original contract can be discharged by performance different from that originally agreed upon.

6. *Objective impossibility of performance owing to one of the following*:
   a. The death or incapacity of a person whose performance is essential to the completion of the contract.
   b. The destruction of the specific subject matter of the contract prior to transfer.
   c. A declaration that the performance called for by the contract is illegal—supervening illegality.
   d. The commercial impracticability of performance.

❖ Questions and Case Problems

9-1. Terry is a college student. She signs a one-year lease agreement for September 1 through August 31. The agreement specifies that the lease cannot be assigned without the landlord's consent. Terry decides not to go to summer school and assigns the balance of the lease (three months) to a close friend, Richard. The landlord objects to the assignment and denies Richard access to the apartment. Terry claims that Richard is financially sound and should be allowed the full rights and privileges of an assignee. Discuss fully whether the landlord or Terry is correct.

9-2. Five years ago, Jeannette purchased a house. At that time, being unable to pay the full purchase price, she borrowed money from Heart Savings and Loan, which in turn took a 9-percent mortgage on the house. The mortgage contract did not prohibit the assignment of the mortgage. Jeannette gets a job in another city and sells the house to Darlene. The purchase price includes payment to Jeannette of the value of her equity and the assumption of the mortgage held by Heart. Heart did not know of or consent to the sale at the time it occurred. On the basis of these facts, if Darlene defaults in making house payments to Heart, what are Heart's rights?

9-3. Doug owes creditor Cartwright $1,000, which is due and payable on June 1. Doug has a car accident, misses several months of work, and consequently does not have the money on June 1. Doug's father, Bert, offers to pay Cartwright $1,100 in four equal installments if Cartwright will discharge Doug from any further liability on the debt. Cartwright accepts. Discuss the following: (a) Is the transaction a novation, or is it an accord and satisfaction? Explain. (b) Does the contract between Bert and Cartwright have to be in writing to be enforceable? (Review the Statute of Frauds.) Explain.

9-4. Nate sold his sporting-goods business to Barry. Included in the written sales contract was a provision whereby Barry agreed to pay all of Nate's business debts that were outstanding at the time of the sale. Carlton, a creditor, requested payment of $2,200 for equipment he had delivered to the store while it was still owned by Nate and for which he had never been paid. Barry, the new owner, refused payment, claiming that he was not responsible for the debt as he (Barry) had no contract with Carlton. Given this set of circumstances, discuss the following questions: (a) Can Barry be held liable for the debt to Carlton, if Carlton brings suit? Explain. (b) Can Carlton sue Nate to recover the amount of the debt? Explain.

9-5. Millie contracted to sell Frank 1,000 bushels of corn to be grown on Millie's farm. Owing to drought conditions during the growing season, Millie's yield was much less than anticipated, and she could only deliver 250 bushels to Frank. Frank accepted the lesser amount but sued Millie for breach of contract. Can Millie defend successfully on the basis of objective impossibility of performance? Explain.

9-6. Rensselaer Water Company was under contract to the city of Rensselaer, New York, to provide water to the city, including water at fire hydrants. A warehouse owned by H. R. Moch Company was totally destroyed by a fire which could not be extinguished because of inadequate water pressure at the fire hydrants. Moch brought suit against Rensselaer Water Company for damages, claiming that Moch was a third-party beneficiary to the city's contract with the water company. Will Moch be able to recover damages from the water company on the basis that the water company breached its contract with the city? Explain. [H. R. Moch Co. v. Rensselaer Water Co., 247 N.Y. 160, 159 N.E. 896 (1928)]

9-7. Allegheny Ludlum Industries contracted with Louisiana Power & Light to supply the light company with stainless-steel condenser tubing for use in a nuclear power plant. The contract price for the tubing was $1,127,387. Prior to delivery, Allegheny's costs for supply and labor increased approximately 38 percent over what they had been when its contract with Louisiana Power & Light was formed. Allegheny informed the light company that it might not be able to perform at the agreed price, and when the light company demanded assurance that Allegheny would perform at the contract price, Allegheny failed to give such assurance. The light company then purchased the tubing from another supplier for $1,729,278, and sued Allegheny for breach of contract and damages in the amount of $601,891—the extra amount the light company had been forced to pay for the tubing because of Allegheny's failure to supply it. Allegheny claimed that the 38-percent increase in its supply and labor costs made it commercially impracticable to perform at the agreed-upon price. Will the court agree with Allegheny? Explain. [Louisiana Power & Light v. Allegheny Ludlum Industries, Inc., 517 F.Supp. 1319 (E.D.La. 1981)]

9-8. O. W. Grun Roofing and Construction Company (Grun) contracted to put a new brown roof on Cope's house. Some of the shingles used by Grun, however, were yellow and created an appearance unsatisfactory to Cope. When Cope complained about this to Grun, Grun replaced many of the yellow shingles, but the replacements still did not match the color of the roof. Cope remained dissatisfied and refused to pay Grun for the work. Grun claimed it had substantially performed the contract and placed a mechanic's lien on Cope's house to recover the price of the roof. Cope sued to have the mechanic's lien set aside and to recover damages for the inferior work. Did Grun materially breach the contract with Cope, or was substantial performance rendered? Explain. [O. W. Grun Roofing and Construction Co. v. Cope, 529 S.W.2d 258 (Tex.Civ.App. 1975)]

9-9. Zilg is the author of *DuPont: Behind the Nylon Curtain*, a historical account of the role played by the DuPont family in America's social, political, and economic affairs. Prentice-Hall signed Zilg to a contract for the exclusive publication of the book. There was no provision to have Prentice-Hall use its best efforts to promote the book, but rather it was left up to the publisher to use its discretion as to the number of volumes printed and the level of promotion to be undertaken. Prentice-Hall printed 13,000 volumes, authorized an advertising budget of $5,500, distributed more than 600 copies to reviewers, and purchased ads in major newspapers. Zilg claims that Prentice-Hall cut its first printing by 5,000 copies and its advertising budget by $9,500, and these cuts were evidence that Prentice-Hall had not made a "best effort" to promote fully the book. Prentice-Hall claimed that its reduction came after careful review and was based on sound and valid business decisions. Based on these facts only, discuss whether Prentice-Hall has fulfilled its contractual duty to Zilg. [Zilg v. Prentice-Hall, Inc., 717 F.2d 671 (2d Cir. 1983)]

9-10. Clement was seriously injured in a car accident with King. When Clement sued King, King retained Prestwich as her attorney. Due to the alleged negligence of Prestwich, Clement was able to obtain a $21,000 judgment on her claim against King. Clement received from King a purported written assignment of King's malpractice claim against Prestwich as settlement for the judgment against her. Can King assign her cause of action against Prestwich to Clement? [Clement v. Prestwich, 114 Ill.App.3d 479, 70 Ill.Dec. 161, 448 N.E.2d 1039 (1983)]

Chapter 10

Breach and Remedies

Normally, the reason a person enters into a contract with another is to secure benefits. And normally, as the Greek lawgiver Solon instructed centuries ago, a contract will not be broken as long as "it is to the advantage of both" parties not to break it. However, when it is no longer advantageous for a party to fulfill his or her contractual obligations, breach of contract may result. *Breach of contract* occurs when a party fails to perform part or all of the required duties under a contract.[1] Once a party fails to perform or performs inadequately, the other party—the nonbreaching party—can choose one or more of several remedies. A **remedy** is the relief provided for an innocent party when the other party has breached the contract. It is the means employed to enforce a right or to redress an injury. Technically, the "remedy" is not a part of a lawsuit, but the result thereof, the object for which the lawsuit is presented and the end to which all litigation is directed. The most common remedies available to a nonbreaching party are damages, rescission and restitution, specific performance, and reformation.

In the past, a distinction was made between **remedies at law** and **remedies in equity.** The emergence of equitable remedies and the granting of equitable relief by equity courts in the early history of English common law is the subject of the "Landmark" in this chapter.

❖ Damages

A breach of contract entitles the nonbreaching party to sue for money damages. **Damages** are designed to compensate the nonbreaching party for the loss of the bargain. Often, courts say that innocent parties are to be placed in the position they would have occupied had the contract been fully performed.[2]

Types of Damages

There are basically four kinds of damages: compensatory, consequential, punitive, and nominal.

---

1. Restatement, Second, Contracts, Section 235(2).
2. Restatement, Second, Contracts, Section 347, and UCC 1–106(1).

"Men keep their engagements when it is to the advantage of both not to break them."

Solon, sixth century B.C. (Athenian legal reformer)

REMEDY
Refers to the relief given to innocent parties, by law or by contract, when a contract is breached.

REMEDY AT LAW
A remedy available under the particular circumstances of a case in a court of law.

REMEDY IN EQUITY
A remedy allowed by courts in situations where remedies at law are not appropriate. Based on settled rules of fairness, justice, and honesty.

DAMAGES
Money sought as a remedy for a breach of contract action or for tortious acts.

COMPENSATORY DAMAGES
A money award equivalent to the actual value of injuries or damages sustained by the aggrieved party.

Compensatory Damages   Damages compensating the nonbreaching party for the *loss* of the bargain are known as **compensatory damages.** These damages compensate the injured party only for injuries actually sustained and proved to have arisen directly from the loss of the bargain due to the breach of contract. They simply replace the loss caused by the wrong or injury. Suppose you contract with Marinot Industries to perform certain services exclusively for Marinot during August for $3,000. Marinot cancels the contract and is in breach. You are able to find another job during August but can only earn $500. You can sue Marinot for breach and recover $2,500 as compensatory damages.

The measurement of compensatory damages varies by type of contract. Certain types of contracts deserve special mention—those for the sale of goods, land contracts, and construction contracts.

1.   **Sale of Goods.** In a contract for the sale of goods, the usual measure of compensatory damages is an amount equal to the difference between the contract price and the market price.[3] Suppose MediQuick Laboratories contracts with Cal Computer Industries to purchase ten model X-15 computer terminals for $8,000 each. If Cal Computer fails to deliver the ten terminals, and the current market price of the terminals is $8,150, MediQuick's measure of damages is $1,500 (10 × $150). In cases where the breach is by the buyer and the seller has not as yet produced the goods, compensatory damages normally equal the lost profits on the sale, not the difference between the contract price and the market price.

2.   **Sale of Land.** The measure of damages in a contract for the sale of land is ordinarily the same as it is for contracts involving the sale of goods—that is, the difference between the contract price and the market price of the land. The majority of states follow this rule regardless of whether it is the buyer or seller who breaches the contract. A minority of states, however, follow a different rule when the seller breaches the contract and the breach is not deliberate. An example of a nondeliberate breach of contract to sell land is when an unknown easement renders title to the land unmarketable. In such a case, these states allow the prospective purchaser to recover any down payment plus any expenses incurred (such as fees for title searches, attorneys, and escrows). This minority rule effectively places purchasers in the position they occupied prior to the contract of sale.

3.   **Construction Contracts.** With construction contracts, the measure of damages often varies depending upon which party breaches and at what stage the breach occurs. See Exhibit 10-1 for illustrations.

CONSEQUENTIAL DAMAGES
Special damages, which compensate for a loss that is not direct or immediate (i.e., lost profits). The special damages must have been reasonably foreseeable at the time the breach or injury occurred in order for the plaintiff to collect them.

Consequential (Special) Damages   **Consequential damages** are foreseeable damages that result from a party's breach of contract. They differ from compensatory damages in that they are caused by special circumstances beyond the contract itself. When a seller does not deliver goods, knowing that a buyer is planning to resell those goods immediately, consequential damages are awarded for the loss of profits from the planned resale. For a nonbreaching party to recover consequential damages, the breaching party must know (or have reason to know) that special circumstances will cause the nonbreaching party to suffer an additional loss. [See UCC 2-715(2)]

For example, Gilmore contracts to have a specific item shipped to her—one that she desperately needs to repair her printing press. In contracting with the shipper, Gilmore tells him that she must receive it by Monday or she will not be able to print her paper and will lose $750. If the shipper is late, Gilmore can recover the consequential damages caused by the delay (that is, the $750 in lost profits).

---

3.   At the time and place where the goods were to be delivered or tendered. See UCC 2–708 and UCC 2–713.

PARTY IN BREACH	TIME OF BREACH	MEASUREMENT OF DAMAGES
Owner	Before construction begins	Profits (contract price less cost of materials and labor)
Owner	After construction begins	Profits plus costs incurred up to time of breach
Owner	After construction is completed	Contract Price
Contractor	Before construction is completed	Generally all costs incurred by owner to complete construction

◆ Exhibit 10-1
Measurement of Damages—
Breach of Construction
Contracts

Likewise, when a bank wrongfully dishonors a check, the drawer of the check (customer of the bank) may recover consequential damages (such as those resulting from slander of credit or reputation) if he or she is arrested or prosecuted.[4] Another example of consequential damages is when an ice company fails to deliver ice to keep a butcher's meat cold. The ice company can be held liable for meat spoilage if it does not deliver the ice on time.

A leading case on the necessity of giving notice of "consequential" circumstances is *Hadley v. Baxendale*, decided in 1854. This case involved a broken crankshaft used in a mill operation. In the mid-1800s, it was very common for large mills, such as the one the plaintiffs operated, to have more than one crankshaft in case the main one broke and had to be repaired, as it did in this case. Also, in those days it was common knowledge that flour mills had spares. It is against this background that the parties argued whether or not the damages resulting from lost profits while the crankshaft was out for repair were "too remote" to be recoverable.

Case 10.1
HADLEY v. BAXENDALE
9 Exch. 341, 156 Eng.Rep. 145, 1854.

FACTS The Hadleys owned a flour mill. A crankshaft in the mill's steam engine broke, causing the mill to shut down. The owners of the mill took the shaft to Baxendale, a common carrier, for shipment to another city, where a duplicate shaft was to be made. Baxendale collected the freight charges and promised to deliver the shaft the following day. It was not delivered for several days, however, and the reopening of the mill was delayed. The owners sued the common carrier to recover the profits they lost while the mill was closed. The trial court held for the plaintiffs (the mill owners).

ISSUE If Baxendale was unaware that failure to deliver the crankshaft on time would result in lost profits to the mill owners, should he nonetheless be held liable for lost profits as damages?

DECISION No. The Court of Exchequer ruled that the special circumstances must be known by the breaching party before the nonbreaching party can recover lost profits. The judgment was reversed and a new trial ordered.

REASON According to the court, the special circumstances that caused the lost profits had never been sufficiently communicated by the plaintiffs to the defendant. Compensation is given only for those injuries which the defendant could reasonably have foreseen as a probable result of the usual course of events following a breach. If the injury is outside the usual and foreseeable course of events, the plaintiffs must show specifically that the defendant had reason to know the facts and foresee the injury. "Where two parties have made a contract which one of them has broken, the damages which the other

4. Weaver v. Bank of America Nat. Trust & Sav. Ass'n, 59 Cal.2d 428, 30 Cal.Rptr. 4, 380 P.2d 644 (1963). A checking account is a contractual arrangement; see UCC 4–402.

Case 10.1—Continued

party ought to receive in respect of such breach of contract should be such as may fairly and reasonably be considered either arising naturally, i.e., according to the usual course of things, from such breach of contract itself, or such as may reasonably be supposed to have been in the contemplation of both parties, at the time they made the contract, as the probable result of the breach of it."

PUNITIVE, OR EXEMPLARY, DAMAGES
Compensation in excess of actual or consequential damages. Awarded in order to punish the wrongdoer; awarded only in cases involving willful or malicious misconduct.

Punitive Damages   **Punitive,** or **exemplary, damages** are generally not recoverable in a breach of contract action. Punitive damages are designed to punish and make an example of a guilty party in order to deter similar conduct in the future. Such damages have no legitimate place in contract law since they are, in essence, penalties, and a breach of contract is not unlawful in a criminal or societal sense. A contract is simply a civil relationship between the parties. The law may compensate one party for the loss of bargain—no more and no less.

In a few situations, a person's actions can cause both a breach of contract and a tort. For example, the parties can establish by contract a certain reasonable standard or duty of care. Failure to live up to that standard is a breach of contract, and the act itself may constitute negligence.

A review of Chapter 3, dealing with torts, indicates that an intentional tort (such as fraud) may also be tied to a breach of contract. In such a case, it is possible for the nonbreaching party to recover punitive damages for the tort in addition to compensatory and consequential damages for breach of contract.

NOMINAL DAMAGES
A small monetary award (often one dollar) granted to a plaintiff when no actual damage was suffered.

"Nominal damages are, in effect, only a peg to hang costs on."

Sir William Henry Maule, 1788–1858
(British jurist)

Nominal Damages   **Nominal damages** are awarded to an innocent party when only a technical injury is involved and no actual damage (no financial loss) has been suffered. Nominal-damage awards are often small, such as a dollar, but they do establish that the defendant acted wrongfully. For example, suppose that Parrott contracts to buy potatoes at 50 cents a pound from Lentz. Lentz breaches the contract and does not deliver the potatoes. Meanwhile, the price of potatoes falls. Parrott is able to buy them in the open market at half the price he contracted for with Lentz. He is clearly better off because of Lentz's breach. Thus, in a breach of contract suit, Parrott may be awarded only nominal damages for the technical injury he sustained, since no monetary loss was involved. Most lawsuits for nominal damages are brought as a matter of principle under the theory that a breach has occurred and some damages must be imposed regardless of actual loss.

Mitigation of Damages

MITIGATION OF DAMAGES
The rule requiring the party suing to have done whatever was reasonable to minimize damages caused by the defendant.

In most situations when a breach of contract occurs, the injured party is held to a duty to mitigate, or reduce, the damages that he or she suffers. Under this **mitigation of damages** doctrine, the required action depends on the nature of the situation. For example, some states require that a lessor use reasonable means to find a new tenant if the lessee abandons the premises and fails to pay rent. If an acceptable tenant becomes available, the landlord is required to lease the premises to this tenant to mitigate the damages recoverable from the former lessee. The former lessee is still liable for the difference between the amount of the rent under the original lease and

Landmark in the Law

Courts of Equity and Equitable Maxims

The distinction between law and equity is primarily of historical interest, but it has special relevance for students of business law. In the early king's courts of England, the kinds of remedies the courts could grant were severely restricted. If one person wronged another, the king's courts could award as compensation one or more of the following: (1) land, (2) items of value, or (3) money. These courts became known as *courts of law*, and the three remedies were called *remedies at law*. Even though such a system introduced uniformity in the settling of disputes, when plaintiffs wanted a remedy other than economic compensation, the courts of law could do nothing, so "no remedy, no right."

Courts of Equity

When individuals could not obtain an adequate remedy in a court of law because of strict technicalities, they petitioned the king for relief. Most of these petitions were decided by an adviser of the king, called a *chancellor*. The chancellor was said to be the "keeper of the king's conscience." When the chancellor thought that the claim was a fair one, new and unique remedies were granted. In this way, a new body of chancery rules and reliefs (or remedies) came into being, and eventually formal chancery courts were established. These became known as *courts of equity*, granting *remedies in equity*.

Equity is that branch of unwritten law, founded in justice and fair dealing, that seeks to supply a more equitable and adequate remedy than any available remedy at law. Thus, two distinct systems were created, each having a different set of judges. Two bodies of rules and remedies existed at the same time—remedies at law and remedies in equity.

Plaintiffs had to specify whether they were bringing an "action at law" or an "action in equity," and they chose their courts accordingly. For example, a plaintiff might ask a court of equity to order a defendant to perform within the terms of a contract. A court of law could not issue such an order because its remedies were limited to payment of money or property as compensation for damages.

A court of equity, however, could issue a decree for *specific performance*—an order to perform what was promised.

Likewise, a court of equity could issue an *injunction*, directing that a party *refrain* from engaging in a particular act. In certain cases, when the legal remedy of the payment of money for damages was unavailable or inadequate, a court of equity might have allowed for the *rescission* of the contract, that is, the undoing of the agreement, to return the parties to the positions they held prior to the contract's formation.

Courts of equity had the responsibility of using discretion in supplementing the common law. Even today, when the same court can award both legal and equitable remedies, such discretion is often guided by what are known as *equitable principles and maxims*. These principles or maxims are propositions or general statements of rules of law that courts often invoke. Some of them are listed here.

Equitable Principles and Maxims

1. Whoever seeks equity must do equity.
2. Equity treats as done what ought to be done.
3. Where there is equal equity, the law must prevail.
4. One seeking the aid of an equity court must come to the court with clean hands.
5. Equity will not suffer a wrong to be without a remedy.
6. Equality is equity.
7. Equity regards substance rather than form.
8. Equity imputes an intent to fulfill an obligation.
9. Equity delights to do justice and not by halves.
10. Equity aids the vigilant, not those who rest on their rights.

The last maxim means that individuals who fail to look out for their rights until after a reasonable time has passed will not be helped. This maxim has become known as the *equitable doctrine of laches*. The doctrine of laches can be used as a defense. It arose to encourage people to bring lawsuits while the evidence is fresh. What constitutes a reasonable time, of course, varies according to the circumstances of the case. Time periods for different types of cases are now usually fixed by *statutes of limitations*. After the time allowed under a statute of limitations has expired, no action can be brought, no matter how strong the case was originally.

(continued on next page)

Landmark in the Law—Continued

The Merging of Law and Equity

Today the courts of law and equity are merged, and thus the distinction between the two courts has largely disappeared. A plaintiff may now request both legal and equitable remedies in the same action, and the trial-court judge may grant either form—or both forms—of relief.

Yet the merging of law and equity does not diminish the importance of distinguishing legal remedies from equitable remedies. To request the proper remedy, one must know what remedies are available. Therefore, students of business law should be aware of the various equitable as well as legal remedies.

---

the rent received from the new lessee. If the lessor does not take reasonable means to find a new tenant, presumably a court could reduce the award by the amount of rent the lessor could have received by using such reasonable means.

In the majority of states, wrongfully terminated employees owe the duty to mitigate damages suffered by their employer's breach. The damages awarded are their salaries less the incomes they would have received in similar jobs obtained by reasonable means. It is the employer's burden to prove the existence of such a job and to prove that the employee could have been hired. The employee is, of course, under no duty to take a job that is not of the same type and rank. This is illustrated in the following case.

Case 10.2
PARKER v. TWENTIETH-CENTURY FOX FILM CORPORATION

Supreme Court of California, 1970.
3 Cal. 3d 176, 89 Cal. Rptr. 737, 474 P. 2d 689.

FACTS Twentieth-Century Fox planned to produce a musical, *Bloomer Girl,* and contracted with Shirley MacLaine Parker to play the leading female role. According to the contract, Fox was to pay Parker $53,571.42 per week for fourteen weeks, for a total of $750,000. Fox later decided not to produce *Bloomer Girl* and tried to substitute the existing contract with another contract whereby Parker would play the leading role in a western movie for the same amount of money guaranteed by the first contract. Fox gave Parker one week in which to accept the new contract. Parker filed suit against Fox to recover the amount of compensation guaranteed in the first contract because, she maintained, the two roles were not at all equivalent. The *Bloomer Girl* production was a musical, to be filmed in California, and could not compare to a "western type" production that was tentatively planned to be produced in Australia. When the trial court held for Parker, Fox appealed.

ISSUE May Fox's substitute offer of the western-movie contract be used in mitigating the damages ensuing from the breach of the first contract?

DECISION No. The judgment for Parker was affirmed.

REASON The court noted that the "measure of recovery by a wrongfully discharged employee is the amount of salary agreed upon for the period of service, less the amount which the employer affirmatively proves the employee has earned or with reasonable effort might have earned from other employment. Before projected earnings from other employment opportunities not sought or accepted by the discharged employee can be applied in mitigation, however, the employer must show that the other employment was comparable, or substantially similar, to that of which the employee has been deprived. . . ." The court held that the two roles were substantially dissimilar—that is, one called for Parker's dancing and acting abilities and the other for simply an acting role in a western movie. The court asserted that "by no stretch of the imagination" could the western-style movie "be considered the equivalent of or substantially similar to the lead in a song-and-dance production."

Liquidated Damages versus Penalties

A **liquidated damages** provision in a contract specifies a certain amount to be paid in the event of a future default or breach of contract. (Liquidated means determined, settled, or fixed.) For example, a provision requiring a construction contractor to pay $100 for every day he or she is late in completing the construction project is a liquidated damages provision. Liquidated damages differ from penalties. A **penalty** specifies a certain amount to be paid in the event of a default or breach of contract and is *designed to penalize* the breaching party. Liquidated damage provisions are enforceable; penalty provisions are not. [See UCC 2-718(1)]

To determine whether a particular provision is for liquidated damages or for a penalty, the court must answer two questions. First, were the potential damages that would be incurred if the contract were not performed on time difficult to estimate when the contract was entered into? Second, was the amount set as damages a reasonable estimate of those potential damages, and not excessive?[5] If both answers are yes, the provision will be enforced. If either answer is no, the provision will normally not be enforced. In a construction contract, it is difficult to estimate the amount of damages that might be caused by a delay in completing construction, so liquidated damage clauses are often used.

❖ Rescission and Restitution

Rescission is essentially an action to undo, or cancel, a contract—to return the nonbreaching parties to the positions they occupied prior to the transaction.[6] When fraud, mistake, duress, or failure of consideration is present, rescission is available. The failure of one party to perform entitles the other party to rescind the contract. The rescinding party must give prompt notice to the breaching party. To rescind a contract, both parties must make **restitution** to each other by returning goods, property, or money previously conveyed.[7] If the goods or property can be restored *in specie*—that is, if they can be returned—they must be. If the goods or property have been consumed, restitution must be an equivalent amount of money.

Essentially, restitution refers to the recapture of a benefit conferred on the defendant through which the defendant has been unjustly enriched. For example, Andrea conveys $10,000 to Miles in return for Miles's promise to design a house for Andrea. The next day Miles calls Andrea and tells her that he has taken a position with a large architectural firm in another state and cannot design the house. Andrea decides to hire another architect that afternoon. Andrea can get restitution of $10,000 because an unjust benefit of $10,000 was conferred on Miles.

❖ Specific Performance

The equitable remedy of **specific performance** calls for the performance of the act promised in the contract. This remedy is quite attractive to the nonbreaching party

LIQUIDATED DAMAGES
An amount, stipulated in the contract, which the parties believe to be a reasonable estimation of the damages that will occur in the event of a breach.

PENALTY
A sum inserted into a contract, not as a measure of compensation for its breach, but rather as punishment for a default. The agreement as to the amount will not be enforced, and recovery will be limited to actual damages.

RESCISSION
A remedy whereby the contract is canceled and the parties are returned to the positions they occupied before the contract was made. This may be done through the mutual consent of the parties, by their conduct, or by the decree of a court of equity.

RESTITUTION
An equitable remedy under which a person is restored to his or her original position prior to loss or injury, or placed in the position he or she would have been, had the breach not occurred.

SPECIFIC PERFORMANCE
A remedy requiring *exactly* the performance that was specified in a contract.

---

5.   Restatement, Second, Contracts, Section 356(1).
6.   The rescission discussed here refers to unilateral rescission, where only one party wants to undo the contract. In mutual rescission, both parties agree to undo the contract. Mutual rescission discharges the contract; unilateral rescission is generally available as a remedy for breach of contract.
7.   Restatement, Second, Contracts, Section 370.

In contracts for the sale of unique goods such as rare coins, money damages are inadequate. Therefore, courts will often require specific performance as a remedy.

"Specific performance is a remedy of grace and not a matter of right, and the test of whether or not it should be granted depends on the particular circumstances of each case."

George Bushnell, 1887–1965 (American jurist)

since it provides the exact bargain promised in the contract. It also avoids some of the problems inherent in a suit for money damages, such as the following: First, the nonbreaching party need not worry about collecting the judgment.[8] Second, the nonbreaching party need not look around for another contract. Third, the actual performance may be more valuable than the money damages. Although the equitable remedy of specific performance is often preferable to other remedies, it is not granted unless the party's legal remedy (money damages) is inadequate.[9]

For example, contracts for the sale of goods rarely qualify for specific performance. Money damages ordinarily are adequate in such situations because substantially identical goods can be bought or sold in the market. If the goods are unique, however, a court of equity will decree specific performance. For example, paintings, sculptures, or rare books or coins are so unique that money damages will not enable a buyer to obtain substantially identical substitutes in the market.

The same principle applies to contracts relating to sales of land or interests in land—since each parcel of land is unique. Specific performance as a remedy in such contracts is discussed in the "Business Law in Action" in this chapter.

Contracts for Personal Services

Personal-service contracts require that one party work personally for another party. Courts of equity normally refuse to grant specific performance of personal-service contracts. Sometimes the remedy at law may be adequate if substantially identical service is available from other persons (for example, if you hire someone to mow your lawn). Even for individually tailored personal-service contracts, courts are very hesitant to order specific performance by a party because public policy strongly

---

8. As final dispositions of cases, courts enter judgments that must be collected. Collection, however, poses problems—such as when the judgment debtor is insolvent or has only a small net worth.
9. Restatement, Second, Contracts, Section 359.

Business Law in Action

Specific Performance and Land Sales Contracts

Owing to its very nature, real estate possesses the characteristics of uniqueness. Each parcel of land is different from another. Because of this, the remedy at law (monetary compensation or the substitution of other property) for breach of a land sales contract is inadequate, and the courts grant the equitable remedy of specific performance instead. This is so even though performance may cause the seller to incur substantial unanticipated expense.

Consider, for example, the case of *Mohrlang v. Draper*.[1] Here, the plaintiff, Mohrlang, agreed to purchase a tract of land from Draper for $14,875. Mohrlang planned to build a solar home, and this particular lot was desirable because of its southern exposure. The only problem was the existence of a buried gas line on the property, which prevented any construction on the lot, but Draper promised in the sales contract to have the gas line removed at his expense so that Mohrlang could begin construction.

1. 219 Neb. 630, 365 N.W.2d 443 (1985).

Shortly after the contract was signed, Draper called the gas company to obtain an estimate for moving the gas line. To his surprise—and consternation—he learned it would cost $10,000 to have the gas line relocated. Because of this, he refused to transfer the title to Mohrlang as promised in the contract. In the meantime, Mohrlang had hired an architect to draw up plans for the home, and so on. When Draper refused to perform on the contract, Mohrlang sued for specific performance. Draper contended that, given the circumstances and the expenses he would incur if required to perform on the contract, the appropriate remedy was monetary damages. Mohrlang argued that no other available lot had the unique characteristics or the southern exposure of the Draper lot, and thus specific performance should be allowed.

The case eventually came before the Supreme Court of Nebraska, which granted a decree of specific performance compelling Draper to go through with the sale, notwithstanding the burden it would put on him. But, given the expense to Draper in performing the contract, doesn't the "equitable" remedy of specific performance seem "inequitable" in these circumstances?

According to the court, no. Its reasoning was that Draper *could* have obtained the estimate of the cost of relocating the gas line prior to signing the contract, instead of later, and thus could have spared himself the surprise and consequent burden. In the words of the court, "The inescapable inference is that complete information about relocating the gas line was available when Draper entered the contract to sell his lot." Relocating the gas line was a burden voluntarily undertaken by Draper when the contract was formed, and "Draper's belated realization that his financial burden under the contract was greater than initially anticipated at origination of the agreement does not constitute hardship excusing specific performance of his contract with Mohrlang. . . . It was Draper's neglect which increased his burden, not an unforeseeable circumstance."

The moral of this story is that whenever a seller enters into a contract regarding a land interest, the nature of any burden he or she voluntarily assumes should be thoroughly explored. The court presumes that individuals will look after their own interests when making contracts and, if they fail to do so, will not excuse them from their obligations to other parties with whom they contract.

discourages involuntary servitude.[10] Moreover, the courts do not want to monitor a personal service contract. For example, if you contract with a brain surgeon to perform brain surgery on you, and the surgeon refuses to perform, the court would not compel

10. The Thirteenth Amendment to the U.S. Constitution prohibits involuntary servitude, but *negative* injunctions (that is, prohibiting rather than ordering certain conduct) are possible. Thus, whereas you may not be able to compel a person to perform under a personal-service contract, you may be able to restrain that person from engaging in similar contracts for a period of time.

(and you certainly would not want) the surgeon to perform under these circumstances. There is no way the court can assure meaningful performance in such a situation.[11]

❖ Reformation

REFORMATION
A court-ordered correction of a written contract so that it reflects the true intentions of the parties.

Reformation is an equitable remedy used when the parties have *imperfectly* expressed their agreement in writing. Reformation allows the contract to be rewritten to reflect the parties' true intentions. It applies most often when fraud or mutual mistake (for example, a clerical error) occurs. If Keshkekian contracts to buy a certain piece of equipment from Shelley, but both parties are mistaken about what piece of equipment is to be sold, a mutual mistake has occurred. Accordingly, a court of equity could reform the contract so that Keshkekian and Shelley can agree on which piece of equipment is being sold.

Two other examples deserve mention. The first involves two parties who have made a binding oral contract. They further agree to reduce the oral contract to writing, but in doing so, they make an error in stating the terms. Universally, the courts allow into evidence the correct terms of the oral contract, thereby reforming the written contract.

The second example has to do with written agreements (covenants) not to compete (see Chapter 7). If the covenant is for a valid and legitimate purpose (such as the sale of a business), for example, but the area or time restraints of the covenant are unreasonable, some courts reform the restraints by making them reasonable and enforce the entire contract as reformed. Other courts, however, throw the entire restrictive covenant out as illegal.

❖ Recovery Based on Quasi-Contract

As stated in Chapter 5, a quasi-contract is not a true contract but an equitable theory *imposed* on the parties in order to obtain justice and prevent unjust enrichment. Hence, a quasi-contract becomes an equitable basis for relief. The legal obligation, or duty, arises because the law *implies* a promise to pay for the benefits received by a party. Generally, when one party confers a benefit on another, justice requires that the party receiving the benefit pay a reasonable value for it in order not to be unjustly enriched at the other party's expense.

Quasi-contractual recovery is useful when one party has *partially* performed under a contract that is unenforceable. It can be an alternative to suing for damages and allows the party to recover the reasonable value of the partial performance.

For quasi-contractual recovery to occur, the party seeking recovery must show that:

1. A benefit was conferred on the other party.
2. The benefit was conferred with the expectation of being paid.
3. The party seeking recovery did not act as a volunteer in conferring the benefit.

---

11.   Similarly, courts often refuse to order specific performance of construction contracts, because courts are not set up to operate as construction supervisors or engineers.

4. Retaining the benefit without being paid would result in unjust enrichment of the party receiving the benefit.

For example, suppose Ericson contracts to build two oil derricks for Petro Industries. The derricks are to be built over a period of three years, but the parties do not make a written contract. Enforcement of the contract will therefore be barred by the Statute of Frauds.[12] If Ericson completes one derrick before Petro Industries informs him that it will not pay for the derrick, Ericson can sue in quasi-contract because: First, a benefit has been conferred on Petro Industries, since one oil derrick has been built. Second, Ericson built the derrick (conferred the benefit), expecting to be paid. Third, Ericson did not volunteer to build the derrick; he built it under an unenforceable oral contract. Fourth, allowing Petro Industries to retain the derrick would enrich the company unjustly. Therefore, Ericson should be able to recover the reasonable value of the oil derrick (under the theory of *quantum meruit*—"as much as he deserved"). The reasonable value is ordinarily equal to the fair market value.

❖ Election of Remedies

In many cases, a nonbreaching party has several remedies available, but they may be inconsistent with each other. Therefore, the party must choose which remedy to pursue. For example, a person who buys a fraudulently represented car can either cancel (rescind) the sales contract or sue to recover damages. Obviously, these remedies are inconsistent. An action to rescind undoes the contract; an action for damages affirms it.

The purpose of the *election of remedies* doctrine is to prevent double recovery. Suppose Jefferson agrees to sell his land to Adams. Then Jefferson changes his mind and repudiates the contract. Adams can sue for compensatory damages or for specific performance. If she receives damages caused by the breach, she should not be able to get specific performance of the sales contract, since failure to deliver possession of the land was the cause of the injury for which she received damages. If Adams could seek compensatory damages in addition to specific performance, she would recover twice for the same breach of contract. The doctrine of election of remedies requires that Adams choose the remedy she wants, and it eliminates any possibility of double recovery.

Unfortunately, the doctrine has been applied in a rigid and technical manner, leading to some harsh results. For example, in a Wisconsin case, a man named Carpenter was fraudulently induced to buy a piece of land for $100.[13] He spent $140 moving onto the land and then discovered the fraud. Instead of suing for damages, Carpenter sued to rescind the contract. The court denied recovery of the $140 because the seller, Mason, did not receive the $140 and was therefore not required to reimburse Carpenter for his moving expenses. So Carpenter suffered a net loss of $140 on the transaction. If Carpenter had sued for damages, he could have recovered the $100 purchase price and the $140.

---

12. Contracts which by their terms cannot be performed within one year must be in writing to be enforceable. See Chapter 8.
13. See Carpenter v. Mason, 181 Wis. 114, 193 N.W. 973 (1923).

Because of the harsh results of the doctrine, the UCC expressly rejects it. Remedies under the UCC (see UCC 2-703 and UCC 2-711) are essentially cumulative in nature.

❖ Waiver of Breach

WAIVER
An intentional, knowing relinquishment of a legal right.

Under certain circumstances, a nonbreaching party may be willing to accept a defective performance of the contract. This knowing relinquishment of a legal right (that is, the right to require satisfactory and full performance) is called a **waiver**.[14] When a waiver of a breach of contract occurs, the party waiving the breach cannot take any later action for damages caused by the breach. In effect, the waiver operates to keep the contract going. The waiver prevents the nonbreaching party from calling the contract to an end or rescinding the contract. The contract continues, but the nonbreaching party can recover damages caused by defective or less-than-full performance.

Of course, the waiver of breach of contract extends only to the matter waived and not to the whole contract. Businesspersons often waive breaches of contract by the other party in order to get whatever benefit possible out of the contract. For example, a seller contracts with a buyer to deliver to the buyer 10,000 tons of coal on or before November 1. The contract calls for the buyer making payment by November 10 for coal delivered. Because of a coal miners' strike, coal is unavailable. The seller breaches the contract by not tendering delivery until November 5. The buyer may well be advised to waive the seller's breach, accept delivery of the coal, and pay as contracted. The seller still remains liable for any damages to the coal buyer caused by the five-day delay in shipping the coal.

Ordinarily, the waiver by a contracting party does not operate to waive future breaches of contract. This is always true when the subsequent breaches are unrelated to the first breach. For example, an owner who waives the right to sue for late completion of a stage of construction does not waive the right to sue for failure to comply with engineering specifications.

A waiver can be extended to subsequent defective performance if a reasonable person would conclude that similar defective performance in the future would be acceptable. Therefore, a *pattern of conduct* that waives a number of successive breaches operates as a continued waiver. To change this result, the nonbreaching party should give notice to the breaching party that full performance will be required in the future.

For example, suppose a construction project was to be completed in six stages, each two months apart, spanning a period of one year. The question is whether the waiver of the right to object to lateness of performance of stage 1 operates as a waiver of the time requirements of performance for stages 2 through 6. If only the time requirements for stage 1 are waived, the waiver does not extend to the other five stages. If the first five stages were all late, however, and the right to object to the lateness was always waived, the waivers would extend to stage 6 unless the owner gave proper notice that future performance was to be on time.

Does the acceptance of mortgage payments that are consistently late constitute a waiver of the mortgage holder's right to prompt payment? This issue is addressed in the following case.

---

14. Restatement, Second, Contracts, Sections 84, 246, and 247. The Restatement uses the term *promise* rather than *waiver*. See also UCC 1-107.

Case 10.3
SANSON v. GONZALES
Court of Appeals of Arizona, 1984.
142 Ariz. 30, 688 P.2d 676.

FACTS   Benny and Lupe Gonzales, the defendants, purchased an office building from Joseph Sanson. The defendants signed a promissory note whereby they agreed to pay Sanson the balance due on the purchase price in monthly payments. A clause was included in the deed of trust stating that Sanson, "by accepting payment of any sum secured hereby after its due date" did not "waive his right either to require prompt payment when due of all other sums so secured or to declare default for failure to pay." After accepting eighteen late payments, Sanson declared that the debt was in default and brought an action to sell the property. The defendants claimed that, since Sanson had accepted eighteen late payments, he was required to give them notice before taking such action. Sanson argued that no notice was required, given the terms of the deed of trust. The trial court ruled for Sanson, and the defendants appealed.

ISSUE   Does Sanson's consistent acceptance of late mortgage payments waive his right to prompt payment, notwithstanding the existence of the nonwaiver clause in the deed of trust?

DECISION   No. The appellate court affirmed the judgment of the lower court.

REASON   The court adopted the rule that "the repeated acceptance of late payments constitutes a waiver as a matter of law." Further, the court did "not need to determine here how many accepted late payments it takes to constitute a waiver. Eighteen is enough." Absent a nonwaiver clause in the deed of trust, this repeated acceptance of late payments would waive Sanson's right to prompt payment *unless* notice of the reinstatement of this right was given by Sanson to the defendants. Since the nonwaiver clause was included in the deed of trust, however, the defendants were deemed to have had sufficient notice of Sanson's right to prompt payment, and Sanson, notwithstanding the repeated acceptance of late payments, was under no obligation to notify the defendants that he was going to enforce that right.

❖ Provisions Limiting Remedies

A contract may include provisions stating that no damages can be recovered for certain *types* of breaches or that damages must be limited to a *maximum amount*. The contract may also provide that the only remedy for breach is replacement, repair, or refund of the purchase price. Provisions stating that no damages can be recovered are called *exculpatory clauses* (see Chapter 7). Provisions that affect the availability of certain remedies are called *limitation-of-liability clauses*.

The Requirement of Mutual Assent

Initially, a court must determine whether the provision has been made a part of the contract by offer and acceptance. For a term or provision to become part of a contract, both parties must consent to it. Therefore, courts analyze whether the provision was noticed by the parties—whether, for example, it was in fine print or on the back of a lengthy contract. If either party did not know about the provision, it is not a part of the contract and cannot be enforced.[15]

For example, motorists often park their cars in lots and receive small ticket stubs that exclude liability for damages to cars parked in the lot. If a reasonable person would have noticed such an exculpatory clause, it will be enforced. If the clause is

---

15.   Refer, for example, to the provisions of the Magnuson-Moss Warranty Act, discussed in Chapter 14.

not conspicuous and a reasonable person would not have noticed it, the clause will not be enforced, and the motorist can sue for damage caused to his or her car.[16]

Type of Breach Covered

Once the court determines that the provision or clause is part of the contract, the analysis must focus on the type of breach that is exculpated. For example, a provision excluding liability for fraudulent or intentional injury will not be enforced. Likewise, a clause excluding liability for illegal acts or violations of law will not be enforced. On the other hand, a clause excluding liability for negligence may be enforced in appropriate cases. When an exculpatory clause for negligence is contained in a contract made between parties who have roughly equal bargaining positions, the clause usually will be enforced.

For example, suppose Delta Airlines buys six DC-9s from Douglas Aircraft. In the contract for sale, a clause excludes liability for errors in design and construction of the aircraft. The clause will be upheld because both parties are large corporations with roughly equal bargaining positions. The equality of bargaining power assures that the exculpatory clause was not dictated by one of the parties and forced on the other.

Limited Remedies—UCC

The UCC provides that in a contract for the *sale of goods*, remedies can be limited. If only a certain remedy is desired, the contract must state that the remedy is exclusive. Suppose you buy an automobile and the sales contract limits your remedy to the repair or replacement of defective parts. Under the UCC, the sales contract must state that the *sole* and *exclusive* remedy available to the buyer is repair and/or replacement of the defective parts.[17] If the contract states that the remedy is exclusive, then the specified remedy will be the only one ordinarily available to the buyer (provided that the contract is not unconscionable).

When circumstances cause an exclusive remedy to fail in its essential purpose, it is not exclusive.[18] Continuing with the preceding example, suppose your car breaks down several times, and the dealer is unable to fix or replace the defective parts. The exclusive remedy thus has failed in its essential purpose, and all the other remedies under the UCC become available.

Under the UCC, a sales contract may also limit or exclude consequential damages, provided the limitation is not unconscionable. When the buyer is purchasing consumer goods, the limitation of liability for personal injury is *prima facie* ("on its face" or "at first view") unconscionable and will not normally be enforced. When the buyer is purchasing goods for commercial use, the limitation of liability for personal injury is not necessarily unconscionable.[19]

Suppose you purchase a small printing press as a birthday present for your teenage son. He will be using it to print leaflets and pamphlets for his social club. The contract

---

16. See California State Auto Ass'n Inter-Insurance Bureau v. Barrett Garages, Inc., 257 Cal. App. 2d 71, 64 Cal. Rptr. 699 (1967).
17. UCC 2-719(1).
18. See UCC 2-719(2).
19. See UCC 2-719(3).

for purchase states that consequential damages, arising from personal injury as a result of a defect in the small printing press, are excluded. This exclusion or limitation of liability is *prima facie* unconscionable (illegal). It will not be enforced. On the other hand, if you buy a printing press for your business, the limitation will not necessarily be unconscionable and may be enforceable.

In the following case, a sales contract contained a clause excluding consequential damages in the event of breach.

Case 10.4
LEWIS REFRIGERATION CO. v. SAWYER FRUIT, VEGETABLE & COLD STORAGE CO.
United States Court of Appeals, Sixth Circuit, 1983. 709 F.2d 427.

FACTS Sawyer Fruit, Vegetable & Cold Storage Co. (Sawyer) purchased a machine for producing quick-frozen fruit from Lewis Refrigeration Company (Lewis). Lewis warranted that the machine would process 6,000 pounds of fruit per hour. In the sales contract it was provided that if the machine failed to perform as warranted, Lewis had the right to repair or replace promptly any parts required in order for the machine to function properly. If Lewis was unable to correct the problem through repair or replacement of parts, Sawyer's sole remedy under the contract was limited to rescission; consequential damages were excluded.

When the machine did not process the volume warranted, Sawyer had trouble meeting its contracts to supply its customers with frozen fruit. Sawyer did not want to rescind the contract and return the faulty machine, because this would cause the company to fall even further behind in filling its orders. When Sawyer failed to pay the amount still owing on the purchase price of the machine, Lewis sued Sawyer to recover the balance. Sawyer counterclaimed for consequential damages (lost profits). The trial-court jury found that the repair and rescission remedies had failed their essential purpose under UCC

2-719(2) and awarded Sawyer damages in the amount of $25,823 for lost profits. Lewis appealed.

ISSUE Is Sawyer entitled to consequential damages, notwithstanding the clause in the sales contract excluding consequential damages as a remedy?

DECISION Only if the clause excluding consequential damages was found to be unconscionable. The appellate court reversed the trial court's judgment and remanded the case to the trial court, with directions to the trial judge to determine whether the clause was unconscionable.

REASON The Court of Appeals held that the enforceability of the damages limitation was controlled by UCC 2-719(3), which states, "Consequential damages may be limited or excluded unless the limitation or exclusion is unconscionable. Limitation of consequential damages for injury to the person in the case of consumer goods is prima facie unconscionable but limitation of damages where the loss is commercial is not." Thus, even though the repair and rescission remedies had failed their essential purpose, this did not mean that the clause excluding consequential damages was necessarily inapplicable. Only if the clause was found to be unconscionable could the buyer have recourse to consequential damages. Hence, the case was remanded to the trial court for determination as to whether unconscionability was present.

Application

Law and the Contractor Who Cannot Perform

Not every contract can be performed. If you are a contractor, you may take on a job which, for one reason or another, you cannot or do not wish to perform. Simply walking away from the job and hoping for the best is not normally the best way to avoid litigation—which can be costly, time consuming, and emotionally draining. Indeed, avoidance of litigation through *compromise* should usually be considered.

For example, suppose you are a building contractor who signs a contract to custom-build a home for the Andersons. Performance is to begin on June 15. On June 1, Central Enterprises offers you a position that will yield you two and a half times the amount of net income you could earn as an independent builder. To take the job, however, you have to start on June 15. You cannot be in two places at the same time, so to accept the new position you must breach the contract with the Andersons.

What to do? An attempt at negotiating with the Andersons for a *release* should be made. You can offer to find another qualified builder who will build a house of the same quality at the same price. Or you can offer to pay any additional costs if another builder takes the job and is more expensive. In any event, this additional cost would be the measure of damages that a court would impose on you if you were sued by the Andersons for breach of contract and the Andersons prevailed. Thus, by making the offer, you might be able to avoid the expense of litigation—if the Andersons accept your offer.

Often parties are reluctant to propose compromise settlements because they fear that what they say will be used against them in court if litigation ensues. The general rule, however, is that offers for settlement cannot be used in court to prove that you are liable for a breach of contract.

Checklist for the Contractor Who Cannot Perform

☐ 1. Consider a compromise.

☐ 2. Offer to find an alternative source to fulfill your obligation.

☐ 3. Subcontract out the work and oversee it.

☐ 4. Make a cash offer in order to "buy" a release from your contract. If anything other than an insignificant amount of money is involved, however, work with an attorney in making the offer.

❖ Chapter Summary: Breach of Contract and Remedies

COMMON REMEDIES AVAILABLE TO NONBREACHING PARTY	

Damages	A legal remedy designed to compensate the nonbreaching party for the loss of the bargain. By awarding money damages, the court tries to place the parties in the position they would have occupied had the contract been fully performed. The nonbreaching party frequently has a duty to *mitigate* (lessen or reduce) the damages incurred as a result of the contract's breach. There are five broad categories of damages:
	
	1. *Compensatory damages*—Compensate the nonbreaching party for injuries actually sustained and proved to have arisen directly from the loss of the bargain resulting from the breach of contract.
	   a. In breached contracts for the sale of goods, the usual measure of compensatory damages is an amount equal to the difference between the contract price and the market price.
	   b. In breached contracts for the sale of land, the measure of damages is ordinarily the same as in contracts for the sale of goods.
	   c. In breached construction contracts, the measure of damages depends on which party breaches and at what stage of construction the breach occurs.
	
	2. *Consequential damages*—Damages resulting from special circumstances beyond the contract itself; they flow only from the consequences of a breach. For a party to recover consequential damages, the damages must be the foreseeable result of a breach of contract, and the breaching party must have known at the time the contract was formed that special circumstances existed and that the nonbreaching party would incur additional loss upon breach of the contract. Also called *special* damages.
	
	3. *Punitive damages*—Damages awarded to punish the breaching party. Not awarded in a breach-of-contract action unless a tort is involved.
	
	4. *Nominal damages*—Damages small in amount (such as one dollar) awarded when a breach has occurred but no actual damages have been suffered. Awarded only to establish that the defendant acted wrongfully.
	
	5. *Liquidated damages*—May be specified in a contract as the amount to be paid to the nonbreaching party in the event the contract is breached. Liquidated-damage clauses are enforced if the damages were difficult to estimate at the time the contract was formed and if the amount estimated is reasonable. If construed as a penalty, the clause cannot be enforced.

Rescission and Restitution	1. *Rescission*—An action by prompt notice to cancel the contract and return the parties to the positions they occupied prior to the transaction. Available when fraud, a mistake, duress, or failure of consideration is present. 2. *Restitution*—When a contract is rescinded, both parties must make restitution to each other by returning goods, property, or money previously conveyed. Restitution prevents the unjust enrichment of the defendant.
Specific Performance	An equitable remedy calling for the performance of the act promised in the contract. Only available in special situations—such as contracts for the sale of unique goods, including land, and where monetary damages would be an inadequate remedy. Specific performance is not available as a remedy in breached contracts for personal services.
Reformation	An equitable remedy allowing a contract to be "reformed" or rewritten to reflect the parties' true intentions. Available when an agreement is imperfectly expressed in writing.
Quasi-Contractual Recovery	An equitable theory imposed by the courts to obtain justice and prevent unjust enrichment in a situation where no enforceable contract exists. The party seeking recovery must show that: a. A benefit was conferred on the other party. b. The benefit was conferred with the expectation of being paid. c. The benefit was not volunteered. d. Retention of the benefit without being paid would result in unjust enrichment of the party receiving the benefit.
ELECTION OF REMEDIES, WAIVER OF BREACH, AND CONTRACT PROVISIONS LIMITING REMEDIES	
Election of Remedies	1. *Under common law*—A doctrine to prevent double recovery. A nonbreaching party must choose one remedy from those available. 2. *Under the UCC*—In contracts for the sale of goods, the doctrine of election of remedies has been eliminated; remedies are cumulative.

❖ Chapter Summary: Breach of Contract and Remedies—Continued

Waiver of Breach	A waiver is a knowing relinquishment of a legal right. If a party repeatedly accepts defective performance from the other party to the contract, this pattern of conduct operates as a waiver of the right to full performance—unless notice is given that full performance is expected in the future. The waiver prevents the nonbreaching party from calling the contract to an end or rescinding the contract, but the non-breaching party can recover damages caused by defective performance.
Contract Provisions Limiting Remedies	1. *Exculpatory clause*—A clause stating that no damages (or only a limited amount of damages) can be recovered in the event the contract is breached. Exculpatory clauses excluding liability for fraudulent or intentional injury or for illegal acts cannot be enforced. Clauses excluding liability for negligence may be enforced if both parties hold roughly equal bargaining power. 2. *Exclusive remedy clause*—Under the UCC, in contracts for the sale of goods, contract provisions may be included that limit the nonbreaching party to a sole or exclusive remedy (such as repair and replacement of parts). Such clauses are enforceable *unless* the exclusive remedy fails in its essential purpose or the clause is unconscionable. 3. *Provisions excluding consequential damages*—Under the UCC, a sales contract may limit or exclude consequential damages, providing the limitation is not unconscionable.

❖ Questions and Case Problems

10-1. Fulbright purchases an automobile from Hanford Motors, paying $1,000 down and agreeing to pay off the balance in thirty-six monthly payments of $200 each. The terms of the agreement call for Fulbright to make each payment on or before the first of each month. During the first six months, Hanford receives the $200 payments before the first of each month. During the next six months, Fulbright's payments are never made until the fifth of each month. Hanford accepts and cashes the payment check each time. When Fulbright tenders the thirteenth payment on the fifth of the next month, Hanford, claiming that Fulbright is in breach of contract, refuses to accept the check and demands the entire balance owed. Fulbright claims that Hanford cannot hold her in breach. Discuss the result in detail.

10-2. Discuss fully which of the following breach-of-contract situations warrant specific performance as a remedy:

(a) Tarrington contracts to sell her house and lot to Rainier. Then, on finding another buyer willing to pay a higher purchase price, she refuses to deed the property to Rainier.

(b) Alice contracts to sing and dance in Horace's nightclub for one month, beginning June 1. She then refuses to perform.

(c) Harold contracts to purchase a rare coin owned by Edmund, as Edmund is breaking up his coin collection. At the last minute, Edmund decides to keep his coin collection intact and refuses to deliver the coin to Harold.

(d) There are three shareholders of Astro Computer Corporation: Ronald, who owns 48 percent of the stock; De Valle, who owns 48 percent; and Cary, who owns 4 percent. Cary contracts to sell his 4 percent to De Valle but later refuses to transfer the shares to him.

10-3. Alioto Painting & Roofing Corporation contracted to paint Jameson's house, beginning May 1, for $2,500. Alioto estimated it would require four days to complete the painting. On April 15, Jameson changed his mind and canceled the contract with Alioto. Alioto then contracted with Baker to paint Baker's house for $2,300, beginning May 1. Alioto painted Baker's house, and the work took him four days to complete. Alioto then sued Jameson for $2,500 for breach of contract. Discuss the extent, if any, of Jameson's liability to Alioto.

10-4. Ben owns and operates a famous candy store. He makes most of the candy sold in the store, and business is particularly heavy during the Christmas season. Ben contracts with Sweet, Inc. to purchase 10,000 pounds of sugar, to be delivered on or before November 15. Ben informs Sweet that this particular order is to be used for the Christmas season business. Because of production problems the sugar is not tendered to Ben until December 10, at which time Ben refuses the order because it is so late. Ben has been unable to purchase the quantity of sugar needed to meet the Christmas orders and has had to turn down numerous regular customers, some of whom indicated they would purchase candy elsewhere in the future. The sugar Ben was able to purchase cost him 10 cents per pound above Sweet's price. Ben sues Sweet for breach of contract, claiming as damages the higher price paid for the sugar from others, lost profits from this year's lost Christmas sales, future lost profits from customers who indicated they would discontinue doing business with him, and punitive damages for failure to meet the contracted delivery date. Sweet claims Ben is limited to compensatory damages only. Discuss who is correct.

10-5. Johnson contracted to lease a house to Fox for $700 a month, beginning October 1. Fox stipulated in the contract that before he moved in, the interior of the house had to be completely repainted. On September 9, Johnson hired Keever to do the required painting for $1,000. He told Keever that the painting had to be finished by October 1 but did not explain why. On September 28, Keever quit for no reason, having completed approximately 80 percent of the work. Johnson then paid Sam $300 to finish the painting, but Sam did not finish until October 4. Fox, when the painting had not been completed as stipulated in his contract with Johnson, leased another home. Johnson found another tenant who would lease the property at $700 a month, beginning October 15. Johnson then sued Keever for breach of contract, claiming damages of $650 (which included the $300 Johnson had paid Sam to finish the painting and $350 for rent for the first half of October that he had lost as a result of Keever's breach). Johnson had not yet paid Keever anything for Keever's work. Can Johnson collect the $650 from Keever? Explain.

10-6. Ballard was working for El Dorado Tire Company. He was discharged, and he sued El Dorado for breach of the employment contract. The trial court awarded damages to Ballard, and El Dorado Tire appealed. In the appeal, El Dorado claimed that the trial court failed to reduce Ballard's damages by the amount that he might have earned in other employment during the remainder of the breached contract. El Dorado introduced as evidence the fact that there was an extremely low rate of unemployment for professional technicians and managers with Ballard's qualifications. The implication was that Ballard had not taken advantage of the opportunity to mitigate his damages. Was El Dorado correct? Explain. [Ballard v. El Dorado Tire Co., 512 F.2d 901 (5th Cir. 1975)]

10-7. Kerr Steamship Company delivered to RCA a twenty-nine-word coded message to be sent to Kerr's agent in Manila. The message included instructions on loading cargo onto one of Kerr's vessels. Kerr's profits on the carriage of the cargo were to be about $6,600. RCA mislaid the coded message, and it was never sent. Kerr sued RCA for the $6,600 in profits that it lost because RCA never sent the message. Can Kerr recover? Explain. [Kerr Steamship Co. v. Radio Corp. of America, 245 N.Y. 284, 157 N.E. 140 (1927)]

10-8. Hurdis Realty, Inc., the owner of a commercial building in North Providence, Rhode Island, noted that sewage was backing up in the building. A plumber hired by Hurdis determined that the backup was caused by a blocked sewer line under the city street in front of the building. Hurdis requested that the Town of North Providence remedy the problem. When the city refused to do so, Hurdis hired a private contractor to take care of the matter. Hurdis then sued the Town of North Providence to recover the $4,800 it had paid the contractor to clear the sewer line. On what basis might Hurdis recover? [Hurdis Realty, Inc. v. North Providence, 121 R.I. 275, 397 A.2d 896 (1979)]

10-9. Dewerff was a teacher and basketball coach for Unified School District No. 315. The employment contract included a clause that read, in part: "Penalty for breaking contracts: . . . In all cases where a teacher under contract fails to honor the full term of his or her contract, a lump sum of $400 is to be collected if the contract is broken before August 1." Dewerff resigned on June 28, 1978, and he was told that the school would accept his resignation upon his payment of the $400 stipulated in the contract. When Dewerff refused to make the $400 payment, the school district sued for $400 as "liquidated damages" on the basis of the contract clause. Dewerff argued that the contract provision was a "penalty" clause and unenforceable in this situation. Is Dewerff correct? [Unified School District No. 315, Thomas County v. Dewerff, 6 Kan.App.2d 77, 626 P.2d 1206 (1981)]

10-10. Westinghouse entered into a contract with New Jersey Electric to manufacture and install a turbine generator for producing electricity. The contract price was over $10 million. The parties engaged in three years of negotiations and bargaining before they agreed on a suitable contract. The ultimate contract provided, among other things, that Westinghouse would not be liable for any injuries to the property belonging to the utility or to its customers or employees. Westinghouse warranted only that it would repair any defects in workmanship and materials appearing within one year of installation. After installation, part of New Jersey Electric's plant was damaged and several of its employees were injured because of a defect in the turbine. New Jersey Electric sued Westinghouse, claiming that Westinghouse was liable for the damages because the exculpatory provisions in the contract were unconscionable. What was the result? [Royal Indem. Company v. Westinghouse Elec. Corp., 385 F.Supp. 520 (S.D.N.Y. 1974)]

Unit Three

Commercial Transactions, Sales, and the Uniform Commercial Code

❖ Why We Study the Uniform Commercial Code

This unit deals exclusively with the Uniform Commercial Code (UCC), whose official text (with comments) embodies more than 700 pages. It is probably the most sweeping in scope of any law codification in the United States. To understand the importance of the UCC, we need merely to examine the Code's concept that "commercial transactions" is a single subject of the law. Consider the following:

1. One transaction might involve a contract for the sale of goods followed by the actual sale. Article 2 of the UCC examines all the facets of this transaction.
2. A single transaction might involve the giving of a check for the entire purchase price of the goods. The check will be negotiated and pass through one or more banks for collection. Article 3 on commercial paper and Article 4 on bank deposits and collections cover this part of the transaction.
3. Suppose that the goods purchased and paid for by check are shipped or stored. Then they may be covered by a warehouse receipt. Article 7 on documents of title deals with this subject.
4. Suppose further that the transaction involves the acceptance of some form of security for a remaining balance owed. Article 9 on secured transactions covers this part of the transaction.

Quite clearly, all four of these phases of the transaction are part of one transaction—the sale of, and payment for, a good. The UCC was therefore written to deal with all the phases that ordinarily arise in the handling of a commercial transaction. Because just about anyone contemplating a career in business will at one time or another be involved in commercial transactions, an understanding of the fundamental rules governing such transactions is imperative. Since the Uniform Commercial Code is the general and inclusive group of laws adopted by virtually all the states, it is impossible for a person to be in the business world without coming into contact with some aspect of the UCC.

Chapter 11

Introduction to Sales Contracts and Their Formation

When we focus on sales contracts, we move away from common-law principles and into the area of statutory law. As discussed in the Unit introduction, the statutory law governing sales transactions is the Uniform Commercial Code. It qualifies as the most "voluminous" legal codification ever created in this nation, but, contrary to Hamilton's belief that a voluminous code of laws is an "inconvenience," the UCC is in fact just the opposite. It facilitates, rather than hinders, commercial transactions by making the laws governing the purchase and sale of goods clearer, simpler, and readily applicable to the numerous difficulties that can arise during such transactions.

"It has been frequently remarked, with great propriety, that a voluminous code of laws is one of the inconveniences necessarily connected with the advantages of a free government."

Alexander Hamilton, 1755–1804
(American lawyer and revolutionary leader; first U.S. Secretary of the Treasury, 1789–1795)

❖ The Sale of Goods

No body of law operates in a vacuum. A **sales contract** is governed by the common-law principles applicable to all contracts—offer, acceptance, consideration, capacity, and legality—and you should reexamine these principles when studying sales. The law of sales, found in Article 2 of the UCC, is part of the law of contracts, and the relevant common law is often changed by the UCC.

Keep in mind two things. First, Article 2 deals with the sale of *goods*; it does not deal with real property (real estate), services, or intangible property such as stocks and bonds. Second, in some cases, the rules may vary quite a bit, depending on whether the buyer or the seller is a *merchant*.

It is always a good idea to note the subject matter of a dispute and the kind of parties involved. If the subject is goods, the UCC governs. If it is real estate or services, common law applies. Although the majority of rules under Article 2 apply to all sellers and buyers of goods, some rules apply only if the seller or buyer, or both, are merchants.

SALES CONTRACT
A contract by means of which the ownership of goods is transferred from a seller to a buyer for a fixed price in money, paid or agreed to be paid by the buyer.

What Is a Sale?

Section 2-102 of the Code states that Article 2 "applies to transactions in goods." This implies a broad scope—covering leases, gifts, bailments (temporary delivery of

237

SALE
The passing of title from the seller to the buyer for a price, where title refers to the formal right of ownership of property.

TANGIBLE PROPERTY
Property that has physical existence and can be apprehended by the senses of touch, sight, and so on. A car is tangible property; a patent right is intangible property.

personal property), and purchases of goods. In this chapter, however, we treat Article 2 as being applicable only to an actual sale (as would most authorities and courts).[1] A **sale** is officially defined as "the passing of title from the seller to the buyer for a price," where title refers to the formal right of ownership of property.[UCC 2-106(1)] The price may be payable in money or in other goods, services, or realty (real estate).

What Are Goods?

To be characterized as a *good*, the item of property must be *tangible*, and it must be *movable*. **Tangible property** has physical existence—it can be touched or seen. Intangible property—such as corporate stocks and bonds, promissory notes, bank accounts, patents and copyrights, and ordinary contract rights—have only conceptual existence and thus do not come under Article 2. A *movable* item can be carried from place to place. Hence, real estate is excluded from Article 2.

Two areas of dispute arise in determining whether the object of the contract is goods and thus whether Article 2 is applicable. One problem concerns *goods associated with realty*, such as crops or timber, and the other concerns contracts involving a combination of *goods and services*.

Goods associated with real estate often fall within the scope of Article 2. Section 2-107 provides the following rules:

1. A contract for the sale of minerals or the like (including oil and gas) or a structure (such as a building) is a contract for the sale of goods *if severance is to be made by the seller*. If the buyer is to sever (separate) them from the land, the contract is considered to be a sale of real estate governed by the principles of real-property law, not the UCC.
2. A sale of growing crops or timber to be cut is a contract for the sale of goods *regardless of who severs them*.
3. Other "things attached" to realty but capable of severance without material harm to the land are considered goods *regardless of who severs them*.[2]

Examples of "things attached" that are severable without harm to realty are a heater, a window air-conditioner in a house, and counters and stools in a restaurant. The test is whether removal will cause *material harm* to the realty to which the item is attached. Removal of a window air conditioner would be considered a sale of goods, but removal of a central air-conditioning system would probably do a great deal of damage to the realty and would be treated as a sale of real estate. When the parties do not envision any items being removed (severed) from the realty, such as in the sale of "ten acres with corn standing," then the transaction is characterized as the sale of real estate.

In cases where goods and services are combined, courts disagree. For example, is the blood furnished to a patient during an operation a "sale of goods" or the

---

1. Note that the Permanent Editorial Board of the UCC has recently approved a codification of the law with respect to leases of goods. This codification, entitled Article 2A of the UCC, is now ready for final editing and then adoption by the states. When adopted, Article 2 will thus cover (in Article 2A) leases as well as sales of goods.
2. The Code avoids the term *fixtures* here because of the numerous definitions of the word. A fixture is anything so firmly or permanently attached to land or to a building so as to become a part of it. Once personal property becomes a fixture, it is governed by real estate law. See Chapter 34.

Landmark in the Law

The Uniform Commercial Code

Of all the attempts in the United States to produce a uniform body of laws relating to commercial transactions, none has been as comprehensive or successful as the Uniform Commercial Code (UCC). The Code was the brainchild of William A. Schnader, president of the National Conference of Commissioners on Uniform State Laws (NCC).

The UCC was not the first effort to create more uniformity in the law. Since its founding in 1892, the NCC drafted a number of uniform acts, many of which were accepted in whole or in part by various states. The first was the Negotiable Instruments Law of 1896, followed by the Uniform Sales Act (1906) and a number of others. In the early 1920s, the NCC was joined in its efforts by the American Law Institute, which was formed for a similar purpose.

The drafting of the Uniform Commercial Code began in 1945. The most significant individual involved in the project was its chief reporter, Karl N. Llewellyn (see the "Profile" in this chapter), of the Columbia University Law School. Llewellyn's intellect, continuous efforts, and ability to compromise made the first draft of the Code (1949) a legal landmark. Yale scholar Grant Gilmore said of Llewellyn:

> It was, I believe, Karl's non-systematic, particularizing cast of mind and his case-law orientation which gave to the

statutes he drafted . . . their profound originality. His instinct appeared to be to draft in a loose, opened-ended style; his preferred solutions turned on questions of fact (reasonableness, good faith, usage of trade) rather than on rules of law. He had clearly in mind the idea of a case-law Code: one that would furnish guide-lines for a fresh start, would accommodate itself to changing circumstances, would not so much contain the law as free it for a new growth.[1]

Over the next several years, the Code was reviewed and substantially accepted by every state in the Union (except Louisiana, which accepted only part of it). The Code attempts to provide a consistent and integrated framework of rules to deal with all phases *ordinarily arising* in a commercial sales transaction from start to finish.

Two articles of the UCC seemingly do not address the "ordinary" commercial sales transaction, however. Article 6 on bulk transfers has to do with merchants who sell off the major part of their inventory. Such bulk sales are not part of the ordinary course of business. Article 8, investment securities, deals with negotiable securities (stocks and bonds), transactions that do not involve the sale of or payment for *goods*. The subject matter of Articles 6 and 8, however, was considered by the Code's drafters to be related *sufficiently* to commercial transactions to warrant their inclusion in the UCC.

1. Grant Gilmore, "In Memoriam: Karl Llewellyn," 71 *Yale Law Journal* 813 (1962).

"performance of a medical service"? Some courts say it is a good; others say it is a service. Since the Code does not provide the answer, the courts try to determine which factor is predominant—the good or the service.

The Code does stipulate, however, that serving food or drink to be consumed either on or off restaurant premises is the "sale of goods," at least for the purpose of an implied warranty of merchantability. [UCC 2-314(1)] Other special cases are also explicitly characterized as goods by the Code, including the unborn young of animals and rare coins. Whether the transaction in question involves the sale of goods or services is important because the majority of courts treat services as being excluded by the UCC.

The following case shows the criteria used by a court in determining whether a contract is for goods or services.

Case 11.1
COLORADO CARPET INSTALLATION, INC. v. PALERMO
Colorado Supreme Court, 1983.
668 P.2d 1384.

FACTS Fred and Zuma Palermo contacted Colorado Carpet for a price quotation on providing and installing new carpeting and tiling in their home. In response, Colorado Carpet submitted a written proposal to provide and install the carpet at a certain price per square foot of material, *including* labor. The total was in excess of $500. The proposal was never accepted in writing by the Palermos, and the parties disagreed over how much of the proposal had been agreed to orally.

Once the installation of the carpet and tiling was under way, Mrs. Palermo became dissatisfied and sought the services of another contractor. Colorado Carpet then sued the Palermos for breach of the oral contract. The trial court held that the contract was one for services and was thus enforceable (that is, it didn't fall under the Statute of Frauds [UCC 2-201], which requires contracts for the sale of *goods* in the amount of $500 or more to be in writing in order to be enforceable). The court of appeals reversed the trial court's decision and ruled that the contract had been for the sale of *goods;* it was thus unenforceable

under the Statute of Frauds. Colorado Carpet appealed the decision.

ISSUE Was the contract between the Palermos and Colorado Carpet primarily for the sale of goods or for the sale of services?

DECISION The Supreme Court of Colorado ruled that the contract was for the sale of goods and hence fell under the Statute of Frauds and was unenforceable. The judgment for the Palermos was affirmed.

REASON In determining that the contract was primarily for the sale of goods, the court considered several "useful factors." These factors included: the contractual language used by the parties; whether the agreement involved one overall price that included both goods and labor or, instead, called for separate and discrete billings for goods on the one hand and labor on the other; the ratio that the cost of goods bore to the overall contract price; and the nature and reasonableness of the purchaser's contractual expectations of acquiring a property interest in goods (goods being defined as things that are movable at the time of identification in the contract). The court concluded that the contract, in respect to all these factors, appeared to be predominantly for a sale of goods "with labor or service only incidentally involved."

Who Is a Merchant?

Article 2 governs the sale of goods in general. It applies to sales transactions between all buyers and sellers. In a limited number of instances, however, the Code presumes that in certain phases of sales transactions involving *merchants*, special business standards ought to be imposed because of the merchants' relatively high degree of commercial expertise.[3] Such standards do not apply to the casual or inexperienced ("consumer") seller or buyer. Section 2-104 defines three ways that *merchant* status can occur:

1. A merchant is a person who *deals in goods of the kind* involved in the sales contract. Thus, a retailer, a wholesaler, or a manufacturer is a merchant of those goods sold in the business. A merchant for one type of goods is not necessarily a merchant for another type. For example, a sporting-equipment retailer is a merchant when selling tennis equipment but not when selling stereo equipment.

---

3. The provisions that apply only to merchants deal principally with the Statute of Frauds, firm offers, confirmatory memoranda, warranties, and contract modification. These special rules reflect expedient business practice commonly known to merchants in the commercial setting. They will be discussed later in this chapter.

Profile

Karl N. Llewellyn (1893–1962)

Karl Nickerson Llewellyn was born on May 22, 1893, in Seattle and became one of the nation's most significant legal scholars. He died in his sleep on February 13, 1962, in Chicago, Illinois. Upon his death, Arthur Corbin said:

The world is poorer that he is gone; it is richer that he has lived. So quick of mind, so blithe of spirit, so ardent of effort, so kind and affectionate of heart, and yet so understanding and essentially so unprideful of opinion, we shall not soon see his like again. To this ancient he was not merely a student; he was a son and comrade. His very name bore omens for the future; Life and Love and Learning and Law—each beckoned him to a shining goal, a goal that he attained.[1]

1. Arthur L. Corbin, "A Tribute to Karl Llewellyn," 71 *Yale Law Journal* 805, p. 812.

Like Corbin, Llewellyn had strong attachments to the law school at Yale. Educated in the home of a German schoolteacher, Llewellyn decided at an early age to become an educator. He received his legal training at Yale and became editor-in-chief of the *Yale Law Journal*. He hoped to join the faculty upon graduation, and he was, in fact, offered a teaching post there—a post that was held open, according to Corbin, for a good ten years should he wish to accept it. Because of his marital circumstances, however, he accepted a position on the Columbia University law faculty in 1924 and remained a professor there until his death.

One of Llewellyn's greatest undertakings was the drafting of the Uniform Commercial Code. As Chief Reporter for the UCC, he was instrumental in its final format and was responsible for reviewing and revising all of its provisions, as well as establishing its scope, objectives, and style. According to William Schnader, in a 1967 article discussing the preparation and enactment of the UCC, "the outstanding man in the United States to undertake this task" was Llewellyn. This was because Llewellyn was "the type of law professor who was never satisfied unless he knew exactly how commercial transactions were carried on in the market place. He insisted that provisions of the Code should be drafted from the standpoint of what actually takes place from day to day in the commercial world rather than

from the standpoint of what appeared in statutes and decisions."[2]

From 1937 to 1952, Llewellyn devoted most of his energies to this project, and the creation of the UCC is considered by many to be one of his most far-reaching achievements. Llewellyn was noted for his diplomatic and democratic approach. He constantly sought consensus among the various authors of the Code, and this open—and disarming—democratic process played an important role in the UCC's final acceptance by the various states.

The "selling" of the UCC after it was drafted in 1949 became his wife's task, owing to Llewellyn's ill health. His wife and long-time chief assistant, Soia Mentschikoff, was also a legal scholar and the Associate Reporter for the UCC. She had been Llewellyn's student, a practicing attorney, and Harvard Law School's first woman faculty member.

Although Llewellyn is most remembered for his work on the UCC, his work as an educator should not go unnoticed. As a professor at Columbia, he influenced a tremendous number of future attorneys. He also authored several books, most important being *The Bramble Bush* (a novel), *Sales*, and *The Common Law Tradition*—as well as countless articles on commercial law.

2. William Schnader, "A Short History of the Preparation and Enactment of the Uniform Commercial Code," 22 *U. Miami Law Review* 1 (1967), p. 4.

2. A merchant is a person who, by occupation, *holds himself or herself as having knowledge and skill peculiar to the practices or goods involved in the transaction*. This broad definition may include banks or universities as merchants.

3. A person who employs a merchant as a broker, agent, or other intermediary has the status of merchant in that transaction. Hence, if a "gentleman farmer" who ordinarily does not run the farm hires a broker to purchase or sell livestock, the farmer is considered a merchant in the transaction.

In summary, a person is a merchant when he or she, acting in a mercantile capacity, possesses or uses an expertise specifically related to the goods being sold. This basic distinction, however, is not always clear-cut. For example, there is disagreement as to whether a farmer is a merchant. The answer depends on the goods involved, the transaction, and whether, in the particular situation, the farmer has special knowledge concerning the goods.

❖ The Sales Contract

The policy of the UCC is to recognize that the law of sales is part of the general law of contracts. The Code often restates general principles. In cases where the Code is silent, the common law of contracts and applicable state statutes govern. The following sections summarize the ways that UCC provisions *change* the effect of the general law of contracts.

The Offer

In general contract law, the moment a definite offer is met by an unqualified acceptance, a binding contract is formed. In commercial sales transactions, the verbal exchanges, the correspondence, and the actions of the parties may not reveal exactly when a binding contractual obligation arises. The Code states that an agreement sufficient to constitute a contract can exist even if the moment of its making is undetermined. [UCC 2-204(2)]

Open Terms According to contract law, an offer must be definite enough for the parties (and the courts) to ascertain its essential terms when it is accepted. The UCC states that a sales contract will not fail for indefiniteness even if one or more terms are left open as long as (1) the parties intended to make a contract, and (2) there is a reasonably certain basis for the court to grant an appropriate remedy. [UCC 2-204(3)]

The Code provides numerous *open term* provisions that can be used to fill the gaps in a contract. Two facts should be kept in mind. First, the more terms left open, the less likely the courts will find that the parties intended to form a contract. Second, as a general rule, if the *quantity* term is left open, the courts will have no basis for determining a remedy, and the sales contract will fail unless the contract is either an output or a requirements contract. [UCC 2-306]

1. Open Price Term. If the parties have not agreed on a *price*, the court will determine a "reasonable price *at the time for delivery*." [UCC 2-305(1)] If either the buyer or the seller is to determine the price, it means a price fixed in good faith. [UCC 2-305(2)]

Sometimes the price fails to be fixed through the fault of one of the parties. In that case, the other party can treat the contract as canceled or fix a reasonable price. For example, Johnson and Merrick enter into a contract for the sale of goods and agree that Johnson will fix the price. The agreement becomes economically burdensome to Johnson, and Johnson refuses to fix the price. Merrick can either treat the contract as canceled or set a reasonable price. [UCC 2-305(3)]

2. Open Payment Term. When parties do not specify *payment terms*, payment is due at the time and place at which the buyer is to receive the goods. [UCC 2-310(a)] Generally, cash, not credit, is used. The buyer can tender payment using any commercially normal or acceptable means, such as a check or credit card. If the seller demands payment in cash, however, the buyer must be given a reasonable time to obtain it. [UCC 2-511(2)] This is especially important when a definite and final time for performance is stated in the contract.

Although the UCC has radically lessened the requirements for definiteness of essentials in contracts of sale, it has not removed the common-law requirements that the contract be at least definite enough for the court to identify the agreement, in order to either enforce the contract or award appropriate damages in the event of breach.

3. Open Delivery Term. When no delivery terms are specified, the buyer normally takes delivery at the seller's place of business. [UCC 2-308(a)] If the seller has no place of business, the seller's residence is used. When goods are located in some other place and both parties know it, delivery is made there. If the time for shipment or delivery is not clearly specified in the sales contract, the court infers a "reasonable" time for performance. [UCC 2-309(1)]

4. Duration of an Ongoing Contract. A single contract might specify successive performances but not indicate how long the parties are required to deal with one another. Although either party may terminate the ongoing contractual relationship, principles of good faith and sound commercial practice call for reasonable notification before termination so as to give the other party reasonable time to seek a substitute arrangement. [UCC 2-309(2)(3)]

5. Options and Cooperation Regarding Performance. When specific shipping arrangements have not been made but the contract contemplates shipment of the goods, the *seller* has the right to make these arrangements in good faith, using commercial reasonableness in the situation. [UCC 2-311]

When terms relating to the assortment of goods are omitted from a sales contract, the *buyer* can specify the assortment. For example, Marconi's Dental Supply and Powers contract for the sale of 1,000 toothbrushes. The toothbrushes come in a variety of colors, but the contract does not specify color. Powers, the buyer, has the right to take 600 blue toothbrushes and 400 green ones if he wishes. Powers must make the selection in good faith, however, and use commercial reasonability. [UCC 2-311]

Merchant's Firm Offer   The **firm offer** is in the category of rules applicable only to *merchants*. Under regular contract principles, an offer can be revoked any time before acceptance. The major common-law exception is an option contract, where the offeree pays consideration for the offeror's irrevocable promise to keep the offer open for a stated period.

FIRM OFFER
An offer (by a merchant) that is irrevocable without consideration for a period of time. A firm offer by a merchant must be in writing, must be signed by the offeror, and must state that the offer is to remain open for a stated or a reasonable period of time (not more than three months).

The UCC has another exception that applies only to *firm offers* for the sale of goods made *by a merchant* (regardless of whether or not the offeree is a merchant). If the merchant-offeror gives *assurances* in a *signed writing* that the offer will remain open for the stated period or, if no definite period is specified, for a reasonable period (neither to exceed three months), the *merchant's firm offer* is irrevocable without the necessity of consideration.[4] [UCC 2-205]

It is necessary, however, that the offer be both *written and signed* by the offeror.[5] When a firm offer is contained in a form contract prepared by the offeree, a *separate* firm offer assurance must be signed also. The purpose of the merchant's firm-offer rule is to give effect to a merchant's deliberate intent to be bound to a firm offer. If the firm offer is buried amid copious language, in one of the pages of the offeree's form contract, the offeror might inadvertently sign the contract without realizing there is a firm offer, thus defeating the purpose of the rule.

Acceptance

Methods of Acceptance   The general common-law rule is that an offeror can specify, or authorize, a particular means of acceptance, making that means the only one effective for the contract. The rule has been altered recently, however, so that even unauthorized means of communication are effective as long as the acceptance is received by the specified deadline. For example, suppose the offer states, "Answer by telegraph within five days." If the offeree sends a letter, and it is received by the offeror within five days, a valid contract is formed.

When the offeror does not specify a means of acceptance, the Code provides that acceptance can be made by any means of communication reasonable under the circumstances, even if the acceptance is not received within the designated time. [UCC 2-206(1)] For example, Anodyne Corporation writes Bethlehem Industries a letter offering to sell $1,000 worth of goods. The offer states that Anodyne will keep the offer open for only ten days from the date of the letter. Before the ten days have lapsed, Bethlehem sends Anodyne a telegram of acceptance. The telegram is misdirected by the telegraph company and does not reach Anodyne until after the ten-day deadline. Is a valid contract formed? The answer is probably yes, since acceptance by telegram appears to be a commercially reasonable medium of acceptance under the circumstances. Acceptance would be effective upon Bethlehem's delivery of the message to the telegraph office, which occurred before the offer lapsed.

The UCC permits acceptance of an offer to buy goods for current or prompt shipment by either a *promise* to ship or *prompt shipment* of the goods to the buyer. [UCC 2-206(1)(b)] This provision of the Code retains the common-law acceptance of an offer (performance by delivery of conforming goods to the carrier) and adds as acceptance the commercial practice of sellers who send promises to ship conforming goods. These promises are effective when sent, if they are sent by a medium that is commercially reasonable under the circumstances.

---

4.   If the offeree pays consideration, then an option contract (not a merchant's firm offer) is formed.
5.   "Signed" includes any symbol executed or adopted by a party with present intention to authenticate a writing. [UCC 1-201(39)] A complete signature is not required. Therefore, initials, a thumbprint, a trade name, or any mark used in lieu of a written signature will suffice, regardless of its location on the document.

The Code goes one step further and provides that if the seller does not promise to ship conforming goods but instead ships *nonconforming goods*, this shipment constitutes both an *acceptance* (contract) and a *breach*. This rule does not apply if the seller seasonably (within a reasonable amount of time) notifies the buyer that the nonconforming shipment is offered only as an accommodation, or a favor. The notice of accommodation must clearly indicate to the buyer that the shipment does not constitute an acceptance and that, therefore, no contract has been formed.

For example, McIntosh orders 5,000 *blue* widgets from Halderson. Halderson ships 5,000 *black* widgets to McIntosh, notifying McIntosh that since Halderson only has black widgets in stock, these are sent as an accommodation. The shipment of black widgets is not an acceptance, but an offer (usually a counteroffer), and a contract will be formed only if McIntosh accepts the black widgets.

If, however, Halderson ships 5,000 black widgets instead of blue widgets *without* notifying McIntosh that the goods are being shipped *as an accommodation*, Halderson's shipment acts as both an acceptance of McIntosh's offer and a *breach* of the resulting contract. McIntosh may sue Halderson for any appropriate damages.

Under common law, since a unilateral offer invites acceptance by a performance, the offeree need not notify the offeror of performance unless the offeror would not otherwise know about it. The UCC is more stringent than common law, stating that "[w]here the beginning of requested performance is a reasonable mode of acceptance an offeror who is not notified of acceptance within a reasonable time may treat the offer as having lapsed before acceptance." [UCC 2-206(2)]

For example, Lee writes Pickwick Book Store on Monday, "Please send me a copy of *West's Best Law Text* for $40, C.O.D.," and signs it, "Lee." Pickwick receives the request on Tuesday and immediately prepares the book for shipment—but does not ship it for four weeks. When the book arrives, Lee rejects it, claiming that it has arrived too late to be of value. In this case, since Lee heard nothing from Pickwick for a month, he was justified in assuming that the store did not intend to deliver *West's Best Law Text*. Lee could consider that the offer lapsed because of the length of time.

Additional Terms   Under traditional common law, if Alderman makes an offer to Beale, and Beale in turn accepts but adds some slight qualification, there is no contract. The so-called "mirror-image rule" of offer-to-acceptance (see Chapter 6) makes Beale's action a rejection of, and a counteroffer to, Alderman's offer.

The UCC generally takes the position that if the offeree's response indicates a *definite* acceptance of the offer, a contract is formed, even if the acceptance includes terms in addition to or different from the original offer. [UCC 2-207(1)] The Code, however, provides that the offeree's expression cannot be construed as an acceptance if the modifications are subject to (conditional upon) the offeror's "assent."

For example, Philips offers to sell Hundert 650 pounds of turkey thighs at a specified price and with specified delivery terms. Hundert responds, "I accept your offer for 650 pounds of turkey thighs, *as evidenced by a city scale weight certificate*, at the price and delivery terms stated in your offer." Hundert's response constitutes a contract even though the acceptance adds the words "as evidenced by a city scale weight certificate." If, however, Hundert says, "I accept your offer for 650 pounds of turkey thighs *on the condition* that the weight be evidenced by a city scale weight certificate," there is no contract unless Philips so agrees.

If it is determined that a contract exists, the issue then becomes one of determining under whose terms performance is measured—the offeror's or the offeree's (with modifications). The Code addresses this issue in an attempt to solve the so-called battle of the forms between commercial buyers and sellers (referred to in Chapter 6).

1.   Rules That Apply When the Seller or the Buyer Is a Nonmerchant. When the seller or buyer is a nonmerchant, or when both are nonmerchants, the additional terms are construed as mere proposals (suggestions), and the modified terms do not become part of the contract. Thus, the contract is formed on the offeror's terms. [UCC 2-207(2)]

For example, Tolsen offers to sell his personal computer to Valdez for $1,500. Valdez replies, "I accept your offer to purchase your computer for $1,500. I *would like* a box of computer paper and ten diskettes to be included in the purchase price." Valdez has given Tolsen a definite expression of acceptance (creating a contract) even though Valdez's acceptance also suggests an added term for the offer. Since Tolsen is not a merchant, the additional term is merely a proposal (suggestion), and Tolsen is not legally obligated to comply. On the other hand, if Valdez made the requested computer supplies a definite *condition* of acceptance, such as "I will accept your offer *only* if it includes a free box of paper and ten diskettes," then Valdez would be making a counteroffer and rejecting the original offer.

2.   Rules That Apply between Merchants. The Code rule for *additional* terms in the acceptance is a little different when the transaction occurs between merchants (that is, when *both* buyer and seller are merchants). Between merchants, the additional proposed terms *automatically* become part of the contract unless:

a.   They *materially alter* the original contract.
b.   The *offer expressly states* that no terms other than those in the offer will be accepted.
c.   The offeror timely objects to the modified terms. [UCC 2-207(2)]

Suppose Hanky and Willaby are merchants. Hanky offers to sell Willaby 500 leather wallets at a price of $5 per wallet, *plus* freight. Willaby responds, "I accept your offer. Price is $5.02 per wallet, *including* freight." There is a contract between Hanky and Willaby because Willaby made a definite expression of acceptance. Unless Hanky objects to the freight modification within a reasonable time after receiving notice of the change, Hanky is bound to the $5.02 price per wallet, including freight.

Such is not the case, however, if the modification materially alters the contract. What constitutes a material alteration is frequently a question only a court can decide. Generally, if the modification involves no unreasonable element of surprise or hardship for the offeror, the court will hold that it did not materially alter the contract. If, in the example just presented, the actual freight charge and the two cents per wallet are within a reasonable range of each other, the modification will *probably* not be considered material.

Now suppose that Hanky's offer states, "500 leather wallets at a price of $5 per wallet, plus freight. Your acceptance on these terms and these terms only." Willaby's definite expression of acceptance with the modified freight terms still constitutes a contract, but because Hanky's offer specifically restricts his obligations to the terms of his offer, the contract is formed on Hanky's terms of "$5 per wallet, plus freight."

Exhibit 11-1 is an example of a purchase order. The front of the form constitutes the actual order for particular goods. The back contains standard contract clauses and terms governing the sale. These clauses are sometimes modified to meet a particular purchase requirement.

◆ **Exhibit 11-1   An Example of a Purchase Order (Front)**

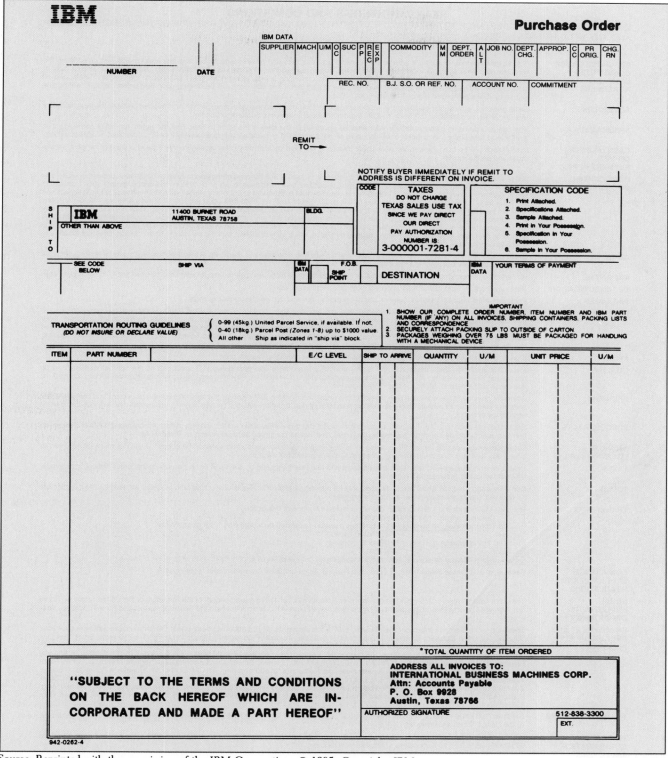

Source: Reprinted with the permission of the IBM Corporation. © 1985. Copyright: IBM.

(Continued on next page)

◆ **Exhibit 11-1—Continued   An Example of a Purchase Order (Back)**

STANDARD TERMS AND CONDITIONS

IBM EXPRESSLY LIMITS ACCEPTANCE TO THE TERMS SET FORTH ON THE FACE AND REVERSE SIDE OF THIS PURCHASE ORDER AND ANY ATTACHMENTS HERETO:

PURCHASE ORDER CONSTITUTES COMPLETE AGREEMENT
This Purchase order, including the terms and conditions on the face and reverse side hereof and any attachments hereto, contains the complete and final agreement between International Business Machines Corporation (IBM) and Seller. Reference to Seller's bids or proposals, if noted on this order, shall not affect terms and conditions hereof, unless specifically provided to the contrary herein, and no other agreement or quotation in any way modifying any of said terms and conditions will be binding upon IBM unless made in writing and signed by IBM's authorized representative.

ADVERTISING
Seller shall not, without first obtaining the written consent of IBM, in any manner advertise, publish or otherwise disclose the fact that Seller has furnished, or contracted to furnish to IBM, the material and/or services ordered hereunder.

APPLICABLE LAW
The agreement arising pursuant to this order shall be governed by the laws of the State of New York. No rights, remedies and warranties available to IBM under this contract or by operation of law are waived or modified unless expressly waived or modified by IBM in writing.

CASH DISCOUNT OR NET PAYMENT PERIOD
Calculations will be from the date an acceptable invoice is received by IBM. Any other arrangements agreed upon must appear on this order and on the invoice.

CONFIDENTIAL INFORMATION
Seller shall not disclose to any person outside of its employ, or use for any purpose other than to fulfill its obligations under this order, any information received from IBM pursuant to this order, which has been disclosed to Seller by IBM in confidence, except such information which is otherwise publicly available or is publicly disclosed by IBM subsequent to Seller's receipt of such information or is rightfully received by Seller from a third party. Upon termination of this order, Seller shall return to IBM upon request all drawings, blueprints, descriptions or other material received from IBM and all materials containing said confidential information. Also, Seller shall not disclose to IBM any information which Seller deems to be confidential, and it is understood that any information received by IBM, including all manuals, drawings and documents will not be of a confidential nature or restrict, in any manner, the use of such information by IBM. Seller agrees that any legend or other notice on any information supplied by Seller, which is inconsistent with the provisions of this article, does not create any obligation on the part of IBM.

GIFTS
Seller shall not make or offer gifts or gratuities of any type to IBM employees or members of their families. Such gifts or offerings may be construed as Seller's attempt to improperly influence our relationship.

IBM PARTS
All parts and components bailed by IBM to Seller for incorporation in work being performed for IBM shall be used solely for such purposes.

OFF-SPECIFICATION
Seller shall obtain from IBM written approval of all off-specification work.

PACKAGES
Packages must bear IBM's order number and show gross, tare and net weights and/or quantity.

PATENTS
Seller will settle or defend, at Seller's expense (and pay any damages, costs or fines resulting from), all proceedings or claims against IBM, its subsidiaries and affiliates and their respective customers, for infringement, or alleged infringement, by the goods furnished under this order, or any part or use thereof of patents (including utility models and registered designs) now or hereafter granted in the United States or in any country where Seller, its subsidiaries or affiliates, heretofore has furnished similar goods. Seller will, at IBM's request, identify the countries in which Seller, its subsidiaries or affiliates, heretofore has furnished similar goods.

PRICE
If price is not stated on this order, Seller shall invoice at lowest prevailing market price.

QUALITY
Material is subject to IBM's inspection and approval within a reasonable time after delivery. If specifications are not met, material may be returned at Seller's expense and risk for all damages incidental to the rejection. Payment shall not constitute an acceptance of the material nor impair IBM's right to inspect or any of its remedies.

SHIPMENT
Shipment must be made within the time stated on this order, failing which IBM reserves the right to purchase elsewhere and charges Seller with any loss incurred, unless delay in making shipment is due to unforeseeable causes beyond the control and without the fault or negligence of Seller.

SUBCONTRACTS
Seller shall not subcontract or delegate its obligations under this order without the written consent of IBM. Purchases of parts and materials normally purchased by Seller or required by this order shall not be construed as subcontracts or delegations.

(NON-U.S. LOCATIONS ONLY)
Seller further agrees that during the process of bidding or production of goods and services hereunder, it will not re-export or divert to others any IBM specification, drawing or other data, or any product of such data.

TAXES
Unless otherwise directed, Seller shall pay all sales and use taxes imposed by law upon or on account of this order. Where appropriate, IBM will reimburse Seller for this expense.

TOOLS
IBM owned tools held by Seller are to be used only for making parts for IBM. Tools of any kind held by Seller for making IBM's parts must be repaired and renewed by Seller at Seller's expense.

TRANSPORTATION
Routing—As indicated in transportation routing guidelines on face of this order.
F.O.B.—Unless otherwise specified, ship collect, F.O.B. origin.
Prepaid Transportation (when specified)—Charges must be supported by a paid freight bill or equivalent.
Cartage   ) No charge allowed
Premium Transportation   ) unless authorized
Insurance   ) by IBM.
Consolidation—Unless otherwise instructed, consolidate all daily shipments to one destination on one bill of lading.

COMPLIANCE WITH LAWS AND REGULATIONS
Seller shall at all times comply with all applicable Federal, State and local laws, rules and regulations.

EQUAL EMPLOYMENT OPPORTUNITY
There are incorporated in this order the provisions of Executive Order 11246 (as amended) of the President of the United States on Equal Employment Opportunity and the rules and regulations issued pursuant thereto with which the Seller represents that he will comply, unless exempt.

EMPLOYMENT AND PROCUREMENT PROGRAMS
There are incorporated in this order the following provisions as they apply to performing work under Government procurement contracts: Utilization of Small Business Concerns (if in excess of $10,000) (Federal Procurement Regulation (FPR) 1-1.710-3(a)); Small Business Subcontracting Program (if in excess of $500,000) (FPR 1-1.710-3 (b)); Utilization of Labor Surplus Area Concerns (if in excess of $10,000) (FPR 1-1.805-3(a)); Labor Surplus Area Subcontracting Program (if in excess of $500,000) (FPR 1-1.805-3 (b)); Utilization of Minority Enterprises (if in excess of $10,000) (FPR 1-1.1310-2 (a)); Minority Business Enterprises Subcontracting Program (if in excess of $50,000) (FPR 1-1.1310-2(b)); Affirmative Action for Handicapped Workers (if $2,500 or more) (41 CFR 60-741.4); Affirmative Action for Disabled Veterans and Veterans of the Vietnam Era (if $10,000 or more) (41 CFR 60-250.4); Utilization of Small Business Concerns and Small Business Concerns Owned and Controlled by Socially and Economically Disadvantaged Individuals (if in excess of $10,000) (44 Fed. Reg. 23610 (April 20, 1979)); Small Business and Small Disadvantaged Business Subcontracting Plan (if in excess of $500,000) (44 Fed. Reg. 23610 (April 20, 1979)).

WAGES AND HOURS
Seller warrants that in the performance of this order Seller has complied with all of the provisions of the Fair Labor Standards Act of 1938 of the United States as amended.

WORKERS' COMPENSATION, EMPLOYERS' LIABILITY INSURANCE
If Seller does not have Workers' Compensation or Employer's Liability Insurance, Seller shall indemnify IBM against all damages sustained by IBM resulting from Seller's failure to have such insurance.

Consideration

The UCC radically changes the common-law rule that contract modification must be supported by new consideration. Section 2-209(1) states that "an agreement modifying a contract needs no consideration to be binding." Of course, contract modification must be sought in good faith. [UCC 1-203] Modifications *extorted* from the other party are in bad faith and, therefore, unenforceable.

For example, Jim agrees to manufacture and sell certain goods to Louise for a stated price. Subsequently, a sudden shift in the market makes it difficult for Jim to sell the items to Louise at the given price, without suffering a loss. Jim tells Louise of the situation, and Louise agrees to pay an additional sum for the goods. Later Louise reconsiders and refuses to pay more than the original price. Under Section 2-209(1) of the UCC, Louise's promise to modify the contract needs no consideration to be binding. Hence, Louise is bound by the modified contract.

In this example, a shift in the market is a *good faith* reason for contract modification. In fact, Section 1-203 states, "Every contract or duty within this act imposes an obligation of good faith in its performance or enforcement." Good faith in the case of a merchant is defined to mean honesty in fact and the observance of reasonable commercial standards of fair dealing in the trade. [UCC 2-103(1)(b)] But what if there really were no shift in the market, and Jim knew that Louise needed the goods immediately but refused to deliver unless Louise agreed to pay an additional sum of money? This sort of extortion of a modification without a legitimate commercial reason would be ineffective, as it would violate the duty of good faith. Jim would not be permitted to enforce the higher price.

When Modification without Consideration Requires a Writing   In some situations, modification without consideration must be written in order to be enforceable. For example, the contract itself may prohibit any modification or rescission of the contract unless such is in a signed writing. Therefore, only those changes agreed to in the signed writing are enforceable. [UCC 2-209(2)] If a consumer (nonmerchant buyer) is dealing with a merchant, *and* the merchant supplies the form that contains a prohibition against oral modification, the consumer must sign a separate acknowledgment of such a clause.

Also, any modification that brings the contract under the Statute of Frauds will usually require that the modification be in writing to be enforceable. Thus, if an oral contract for the sale of goods priced at $400 is modified so that the contracted goods are now priced at $600, the modification must be in writing to be enforceable. [UCC 2-209(3)] If, however, the buyer accepts delivery of the goods after the modification, he or she is bound to the $600 price. [UCC 2-201(3)(c)]

Statute of Frauds

Section 2-201(1) of the UCC contains a Statute of Frauds provision that applies to contracts for the sale of goods. The provision requires that if the price is $500 or more, there must a writing in order for the contract to be enforceable. The parties can have an initial oral agreement, however, and satisfy the Statute of Frauds by having a subsequent written memorandum of their oral agreement. In each case, the writing must be signed by the party against whom enforcement is sought.

Written Confirmation between Merchants   Once again the UCC provides a special rule for a contract for the sale of goods between merchants. Merchants can satisfy the requirements of a writing for the Statute of Frauds if, after the parties have agreed orally, one of the merchants sends a signed written confirmation to the other merchant. The communication must indicate the terms of the agreement, and the merchant receiving the confirmation must have reason to know of its contents. Unless the merchant who receives the confirmation gives written notice of objection to its contents within ten days after receipt, the writing is sufficient against the receiving merchant, even though he or she has not signed anything.

For example, Alfonso is a merchant buyer in Cleveland. He contracts over the telephone to purchase $4,000 worth of goods from Goldstein, a New York City merchant seller. Two days later Goldstein sends written confirmation detailing the terms of the oral contract, and Alfonso subsequently receives it. If Alfonso wishes to use the Statute of Frauds as a defense against enforcement of the contract against him, Alfonso must give Goldstein written notice of objection to the contents of the written confirmation within ten days of receipt.

What happens if a seller's writing in confirmation of a purchase order is received in the buyer's mailroom but is never brought to the buyer's attention by the buyer's company staff? Will such a memo satisfy the Statute of Frauds? This situation is addressed in the following case.

Case 11.2
THOMSON PRINTING MACHINERY CO. v. B. F. GOODRICH CO.

United States Court of Appeals, Seventh Circuit, 1983.
714 F.2d 744.

FACTS   Ingram Meyers, a B. F. Goodrich Company employee and agent, made an oral agreement with James Thomson of Thomson Printing Machinery Company to sell Thomson some printing machinery. Four days later, Thomson sent a "writing in confirmation" to the Goodrich Company. The writing consisted of (1) a purchase order, which contained Thomson Printing's name, address, telephone number, and some details concerning the purchase of the machinery; and (2) a check which, by its notations, was specifically connected with the purchase order.

Several weeks later, when Thomson called Goodrich about the machinery, it was revealed that the machinery had been sold to someone else. Thomson then brought suit against Goodrich to enforce the oral contract. Goodrich, however, contended that the oral contract was not enforceable because the "writing" sent to Goodrich by Thomson had never been received by Ingram Meyers. Thus Goodrich could not be held liable for the contract because it could not repudiate a writing it did not receive. Goodrich alleged that the written confirmation had never

been received by its agent/seller because the envelope had not been properly sent to the attention of Meyers or to the surplus equipment department where Meyers worked. Goodrich further contended that it made several attempts to "find a home" for the purchase order and check by sending copies of its contents to various divisions. Meyers stated he did not learn of the purchase order until several weeks later, when Thomson called to arrange for removal of the machines. The trial court ruled for Goodrich, holding that the "between merchants" receipt requirement of the Statute of Frauds had not been met and thus the contract was unenforceable. Thomson appealed.

ISSUE   Does the writing (the purchase order and check) sent by Thomson to Goodrich and received in Goodrich's mailroom satisfy the requirements of the Statute of Frauds, thus making the oral contract enforceable?

DECISION   Yes. The trial court's judgment for Goodrich was reversed and the case remanded for further proceedings.

REASON   The court reasoned that "if Goodrich had exercised due diligence in handling Thomson Printing's purchase order and check, these items would have reasonably promptly come to Ingram Meyers' attention. First, the

Case 11.2—Continued

purchase order on its face should have alerted the mailroom that the documents referred to a purchase of used printing equipment. Since Goodrich had only one surplus machinery department, the documents' 'home' should not have been difficult to find. Second, even if the mailroom would have had difficulty in immediately identifying the kind of transaction involved, the purchase order had Thomson Printing's phone number printed on it and we think a 'reasonable routine' in these particular circumstances would have involved at some point in the process a simple phone call to Thomson Printing." The court thus concluded that Goodrich's mailroom had mishandled the confirmatory writings and that such "failure should not permit Goodrich to escape liability by pleading nonreceipt."

Relaxed Requirements　The UCC has greatly relaxed the requirements for the sufficiency of a writing to satisfy the Statute of Frauds. A written contract or a memorandum will be sufficient as long as a sales contract (agreement) is indicated and as long as it is signed by the party (or agent) against whom enforcement is sought. The single term that must be included in the writing is the quantity (except in the case of output and requirements contracts). All other terms can be proved in court by oral testimony. Often, terms that are not agreed on can be supplied by the open-term provisions of Article 2.

Exceptions　Section 2-201 defines three other exceptions to the Statute of Frauds requirement. A contract, if proved to exist, will be enforceable despite the absence of a writing even if it involves a sale of goods for $500 or more if:

1.　*The oral contract is for (a) specially manufactured goods for a particular buyer, (b) these goods are not suitable for resale to others in the ordinary course of the seller's business, and (c) the seller has substantially started to manufacture the goods or made commitments for the manufacture of the goods.* In this situation, once the seller has taken action, the buyer cannot repudiate the agreement claiming the Statute of Frauds as a defense.

For example, suppose Womach orders custom-made draperies for her new boutique. The price is $1,000, and the contract is oral. When the merchant seller finishes the draperies and tenders delivery to Womach, Womach refuses to pay for them even though the job has been completed on time. Womach claims she is not liable because the contract is oral. Clearly, if the unique style of the draperies makes it improbable that the seller can find another buyer, Womach is liable to the seller. Also, the seller must have made a substantial beginning in manufacturing the specialized item prior to Womach's repudiation. (Here, the drapery manufacture was completed.) Of course, the court must still be convinced that there was an oral contract.

2.　*A party to a contract admits in pleadings* (written answers), *testimony, or other court proceedings that a contract for sale was made.* In this case, the contract will be enforceable even though it was oral, but enforceability is limited to the quantity of goods admitted.

For example, Lane and Sugg negotiate an agreement over the telephone. During the negotiations, Lane requests a delivery price for 500 gallons of gasoline and a separate price for 700 gallons of gasoline. Sugg replies that the price would be the same, $1.10 per gallon. Lane orally orders 500 gallons. Sugg honestly believes that

Lane ordered 700 gallons and tenders that amount. Lane refuses the shipment of 700 gallons, and Sugg sues for breach. Lane's answer and testimony admit an oral contract was made, but only for 500 gallons. Since Lane admits the existence of the oral contract, Lane cannot plead the Statute of Frauds as a defense. The contract is enforceable, however, only to the extent of the quantity admitted (500 gallons).

3. *Payment has been made and accepted or to the extent that goods have been received and accepted.* This is the "partial performance" exception. The oral contract will be enforced at least in terms of the amount of performance that *actually* took place.

Suppose Allan orally contracts to sell Opus ten chairs at $100 each. Before delivery, Opus sends Allan a check for $600, which Allan cashes. Later, when Allan attempts to deliver the chairs, Opus refuses delivery, claiming the Statute of Frauds as a defense, and he demands the return of his $600. Under the UCC's partial-performance rule, Allan can enforce the oral contract by tender of delivery of six chairs for the $600 accepted. Similarly, if Opus had made no payment but had accepted the delivery of six chairs from Allan, the oral contract would have been enforceable against Opus for $600, the price of the six chairs delivered.

Parol Evidence

If the parties to a contract set forth its terms in a confirmatory memorandum (a writing expressing offer and acceptance of the deal) or in a writing intended as their final expression, the terms of the contract cannot be contradicted by evidence of any prior agreements or contemporaneous oral agreements. The terms of the contract may, however, be explained or supplemented by consistent additional terms, or by *course of dealing, usage of trade, or course of performance.* [UCC 2-202]

Consistent Additional Terms   If the court finds an ambiguity in a writing that is supposed to be a complete and an exclusive statement of the agreement between the parties, it may accept evidence of consistent additional terms to clarify or remove the ambiguity. The court will not, however, accept evidence of contradictory terms. This is the rule under both the Code and the common law of contracts.

Course of Dealing and Usage of Trade   The Code has determined that the meaning of any agreement, evidenced by the language of the parties and by their actions, must be interpreted in light of commercial practices and other surrounding circumstances. In construing a commercial agreement, the court will assume that the *course of prior dealing* between the parties and the *usage of trade* were taken into account when the agreement was phrased. [UCC 2-202 and 1-201(3)] A **course of dealing** is a sequence of previous actions and communications between the parties to a particular transaction that establishes a common basis for their understanding. [UCC 1-205(1)] Course of dealing is restricted, literally, to the sequence of actions and communications between the parties that has occurred prior to the agreement in question. The Code states, "A course of dealing between the parties and any usage of trade in the vocation or trade in which they are engaged or of which they are or should be aware give particular meaning to [the terms of the agreement] and supplement or qualify the terms of [the] agreement." [UCC 1-205(3)]

Usage of trade is defined as any practice or method of dealing having such regularity of observance in a place, vocation, or trade as to justify an expectation that

---

"Usage is one of the great master-keys which unlocks the meaning of words."

Sir John Eardley Wilmot, 1647–1680
(Second Earl of Rochester; British court wit and poet)

COURSE OF DEALING
A sequence of previous conduct between the parties to a particular transaction that establishes a common basis for their understanding.

USAGE OF TRADE
Any practice or method of dealing having such regularity of observance in a place, vocation, or trade as to justify an expectation that it will be observed with respect to the transaction in question.

it will be observed with respect to the transaction in question. [UCC 1-205(2)] Further, the express terms of an agreement and an applicable course of dealing or usage of trade will be construed to be consistent with each other whenever reasonable. When such construction is *unreasonable*, however, the expressed terms in the agreement will prevail. [UCC 1-205(4)]

In the following case, the court permitted the introduction of evidence of usage and custom in the trade to explain the meaning of quantity figures that the parties took for granted when the contract was formed.

Case 11.3
HEGGBLADE-MARGULEAS-TENNECO, INC. v. SUNSHINE BISCUIT, INC.

Court of Appeals of California, Fifth District, 1976.
59 Cal.App.3d 948, 131 Cal.Rptr. 183.

FACTS Heggblade-Marguleas-Tenneco (HMT) contracted with Sunshine Biscuit to supply potatoes to be used in the production of potato-snack foods. HMT had never marketed processing potatoes before. The quantity mentioned in its contract negotiations was 100,000 sacks of potatoes. The parties agreed that the amount of potatoes to be supplied would vary somewhat with Sunshine Biscuit's needs. Subsequently, a decline in demand for Sunshine Biscuit's products severely reduced its need for potatoes, and it prorated the reduced demand among its suppliers, including HMT, as fairly as possible. Sunshine Biscuit was able to take only 60,105 sacks out of the 100,000 previously estimated. In HMT's suit for breach of contract, Sunshine Biscuit attempted to introduce evidence that it is customary in the potato-processing industry for the number of potatoes specified in sales contracts to be reasonable estimates rather than exact

numbers that a buyer intends to purchase. The trial court held for Sunshine Biscuit.

ISSUE Could evidence of custom in the potato-processing trade be admissible?

DECISION Yes. The trial court's ruling was affirmed.

REASON UCC Section 2-202 states that even though evidence of prior agreements or contemporaneous oral agreements that contradicts a written contract is inadmissible, evidence of course of dealing or of trade usage is admissible to explain or supplement a written contract. The fact that specific numbers were used to designate quantities of potatoes that Sunshine Biscuit thought it needed does not dispose of the issue. In its statement that evidence of trade usage was admissible, the court quoted the UCC: "[I]n order that the true understanding of the parties as to the agreement may be [reached, such] writings are to be read on the assumption that . . . the usages of trade were taken for granted when the document was phrased. Unless carefully negated they have become an element of the meaning of the words used." HMT was held to have sufficient knowledge of the "trade custom."

Course of Performance **Course of performance** is the conduct that occurs under the terms of a particular agreement. Presumably, the parties themselves know best what they meant by their words, and the course of performance actually undertaken under their agreement is the best indication of what they meant. [UCC 2-208]

For example, suppose Janson's Lumber Company contracts with Barrymore to sell Barrymore a specified number of "2 by 4s." The lumber in fact does not measure 2 inches by 4 inches but rather 1⅞ inches by 3¾ inches. If Barrymore objects to the lumber delivered, Janson's can prove that 2 by 4s are never exactly 2 inches by 4 inches, by applying usage of trade or course of prior dealings, or both. Janson's can show that in previous transactions Barrymore took 1⅞-inch by 3¾-inch lumber without objection. In addition, Janson's can show that in the trade, 2 by 4s are commonly 1⅞ inches by 3¾ inches. Both usage of trade and course of prior dealings are relevant in determining and explaining what the parties meant by 2 by 4s.

COURSE OF PERFORMANCE
The conduct that occurs under the terms of a particular agreement; such conduct indicates what the parties to an agreement intended it to mean.

Suppose that Janson's agrees to deliver the lumber in five deliveries. The fact that Barrymore has without objection accepted lumber in the first three deliveries under the agreement (course of performance) is relevant in determining that the words 2 *by* 4 actually mean 1⅞ *by* 3¾.

The Code provides *rules of construction*. Express terms, course of performance, course of dealing, and usage of trade are to be construed together when they do not contradict one another. When such construction is unreasonable, however, the following order of priority controls: (1) express terms, (2) course of performance, (3) course of dealing, and (4) usage of trade. [UCC 1-205(4) and 2-208(2)]

In the following case, the court held that the express terms of a contract had priority over course of performance (described in this case, however, as a "course of dealings") in settling a dispute between a debtor and creditor.

Case 11.4
FLAGSHIP NATIONAL BANK v. GRAY DISTRIBUTION SYSTEMS, INC.
District Court of Appeal of Florida, Third District, 1986. 485 So.2d 1336.

FACTS In October of 1976 Samuel and Marilyn Gray, principals of GDS Drugs, Gray Distribution Systems, Inc., and other related companies (Gray), signed personal guarantees for a loan of $375,000 from Flagship National Bank of Miami. In May of 1978 the Grays, owing to a deterioration in their business, defaulted on their payments and agreed with Flagship to a "workout" agreement. Under the terms of this agreement, Gray sold its Atlanta store and applied the proceeds to its debt, Flagship took control of Gray's inventory and accounts receivable, and the loan was increased to $400,000. A demand note was executed, by which the bank had authority to demand full payment of the loan at any time from Gray. From time to time during the following months, Flagship provided Gray's suppliers with letters of credit. As a result of the additional extensions of credit, Gray's indebtedness grew to about $600,000—well beyond the amount stated in the demand note.

In November of 1978, Flagship demanded payment in full on the note. Litigation ensued, and one of Gray's several counterclaims asserted that Flagship had failed to exercise good faith when it refused to continue extending credit to Gray and had therefore breached its loan agreement. The trial court held that Flagship's conduct over the several months prior to its demand of payment in full constituted a course of dealings, which mod-

ified the original agreement and bound Flagship to continue extending credit beyond the amount of the loan agreed to in the note. Since Flagship failed to continue to extend credit to Gray, it had breached the loan contract. Flagship appealed.

ISSUE Of the several issues involved in this case, the one of concern here is whether Flagship's conduct constituted a course of performance that modified the express loan agreement.

DECISION The appellate court reversed the trial court's ruling on this issue and held that no breach of contract had occurred.

REASON The court noted that "under some circumstances, a written agreement may be modified by a course of dealings . . . ; however, when a course of dealings and the express terms of an agreement appear to conflict, the practice of the parties and the agreement must be construed, wherever reasonable, as consistent with each other. . . . If no reasonable consistent construction can be drawn, the express terms of the agreement control." Thus the court held that the express terms of the loan agreement—the $400,000 amount and the fact that it was a demand instrument—overrode "any inconsistent interpretation of the parties' agreement which might be inferred from their dealings."

As to Gray's allegation that the bank had not acted in good faith in calling in its loan, the appellate court found that the good-faith obligation of the UCC "may not be imposed to override express terms in the contract."

Unconscionability

As discussed in Chapter 7, an unconscionable contract is one that is so unfair and one-sided that it would be unreasonable to enforce it. Section 2-302 allows the court to evaluate a contract or any clause in a contract, and if the court deems it to be unconscionable *at the time it was made,* the court can (1) refuse to enforce the contract, or (2) enforce the remainder of the contract without the unconscionable clause, or (3) limit the application of any unconscionable clauses to avoid an unconscionable result.

The inclusion of Section 2-302 in the UCC reflects an increased sensitivity to certain realities of modern commercial activities. Classical contract theory holds that a contract is a bargain in which the terms have been worked out *freely* between parties that are equals. In many modern commercial transactions, this premise is invalid. Standard form contracts are often signed by consumer-buyers who understand few of the terms used and who often do not even read them. Virtually all the terms are advantageous to the parties supplying the standard form contract. With Section 2-302, the courts have a powerful weapon for policing such transactions, as the next case illustrates.

Case 11.5
JONES v. STAR CREDIT CORP.
Supreme Court of New York, Nassau County, 1969.
59 Misc. 2d 189, 298 N.Y.S.2d 264.

FACTS   The Joneses, plaintiffs, were welfare recipients who agreed to purchase a freezer for $900 as the result of a salesperson's visit to their home. Tax and financing charges raised the total price to $1,234.80. At trial, the freezer was found to have a maximum retail value of approximately $300. The plaintiffs, who had made payments totaling $619.88, sued to have the purchase contract declared unconscionable under the UCC.

ISSUE   Can this contract be denied enforcement on the ground of unconscionability?

DECISION   Yes. The court held that the contract was not enforceable as it stood, and the contract was "reformed" so that no further payments were required.

REASON   The court relied on UCC 2-302(1), which states that if "the court as a matter of law finds the contract or any clause of the contract to have been unconscionable at the time it was made the court may . . . so limit the application of any unconscionable clause as to avoid any unconscionable result." The court then examined the disparity between the $900 purchase price and $300 retail value, as well as the fact that the credit charges alone exceeded the retail value. These excessive charges were exacted despite the seller's knowledge of the plaintiff's limited resources. The court reformed the contract so that the plaintiffs' payments amounting to more than $600 were regarded as payment in full.

❖ Chapter Summary: The Formation of Sales Contracts

Offer and Acceptance	1. The acceptance of unilateral offers can be made by a promise to ship or by shipment itself. UCC 2-206(1)(b)
	2. Not all terms have to be included for a contract to result. UCC 2-204
	3. Particulars of performance can be left open. UCC 2-311(1)
	4. Firm written offers by a *merchant offeror* for three months or less cannot be revoked. UCC 2-205
	5. Acceptance by performance requires notice within a reasonable time; otherwise, the offer can be treated as lapsed. UCC 2-206(2)
	6. The price does not have to be included to have a contract. UCC 2-305
	7. Variations in terms between the offer and the acceptance may not be a rejection but may be an acceptance. UCC 2-207
	8. Acceptance may be made by any reasonable means of communication; it is effective when dispatched. UCC 2-206(1)(a)
Consideration	1. A modification of a contract for the sale of goods does not require consideration. UCC 2-209(1)
Requirements under the Statute of Frauds	1. All contracts for the sale of goods priced at $500 or more must be in writing. A writing (either a contract or a memorandum) is sufficient so long as the quantity of the goods purchased is stated and it is signed by the party (or agent) against whom enforcement is sought. UCC 2-201(1)
	2. Exceptions to the requirement of a writing exist in the following situations: a. When written confirmation of an oral contract *between merchants* is not objected to in writing by the receiver within ten days. UCC 2-201(2) b. When the oral contract is for specially manufactured goods not suitable for resale to others, and the seller has substantially started to manufacture the goods. UCC 2-201(3)(a) c. When the defendant admits in pleadings, testimony, or other court proceedings that an oral contract for the sale of goods was made. In this case the contract will be enforceable to the quantity of goods admitted. UCC 2-201(3)(b) d. When payment has been made and accepted under the terms of an oral contract. The oral agreement will be enforceable to the extent that such payment has been received and accepted or to the extent that goods have been received and accepted. UCC 2-201(3)(c)
Parol Evidence	1. The terms of a clearly and completely worded written contract cannot be contradicted by evidence of prior agreements or contemporaneous oral agreements.
	2. Evidence is admissible to clarify the terms of a writing: a. If the contract terms are ambiguous. b. If evidence of course of dealing, usage of trade, or course of performance is necessary to learn or to clarify the intentions of the parties to the contract.
Unconscionability	An unconscionable contract is one that is so unfair and one-sided that it would be unreasonable to enforce it. If the court deems a contract to be unconscionable at the time it was made, the court can (1) refuse to enforce the contract; (2) refuse to enforce the unconscionable clause of the contract; or (3) limit the application of any unconscionable clauses to avoid an unconscionable result. UCC 2-302.

❖ Questions and Case Problems

11-1. Fresher Foods, Inc. *orally* agreed to purchase from Dale Vernon, a farmer, 1,000 bushels of corn for $1.25 per bushel. Fresher Foods paid $125 down and agreed to pay the remainder of the purchase price upon delivery, which was scheduled for one week later. When Fresher Foods tendered the balance of $1,125 on the scheduled day of delivery and requested the corn, Vernon refused to deliver it. Fresher Foods sued Vernon for damages, claiming Vernon had breached their oral contract. Can Fresher Foods recover, and, if so, to what extent?

11-2. On September 1, Jennings, a used-car dealer, wrote a letter to Wheeler in which he stated: "I have a 1955 Thunderbird convertible in mint condition which I will sell you for $13,500 at any time before October 9. [signed] Peter Jennings." By September 15, having heard nothing from Wheeler, Jennings sold the Thunderbird to another party. On September 29, Wheeler accepted Jennings's offer and tendered the $13,500. When Jennings told Wheeler he had sold the car to another party, Wheeler claimed Jennings had breached their contract. Is Jennings in breach? Explain.

11-3. If, in problem 11-2, Jennings had been a student instead of a used-car dealer, would the answer to the question be different? In what way?

11-4. M. M. Salinger, Inc., a retailer of television sets, orders 100 Model Color-X sets from manufacturer Fulsom. The order specifies the price and that the television sets are to be shipped via Interamerican Freightways on or before October 30. The order is received by Fulsom on October 5. On October 8 Fulsom writes Salinger a letter indicating that the order was received and that the sets will be shipped as directed, at the specified price. This letter is received by Salinger on October 10. On October 28 Fulsom, in preparing the shipment, discovers it has only 90 Color-X sets in stock. Fulsom ships the 90 Color-X sets and 10 television sets of a different model, stating clearly on the invoice that the 10 are being shipped only as an accommodation. Salinger claims Fulsom is in breach of contract. Fulsom claims the shipment was not an acceptance, and therefore no contract was formed. Explain who is correct and why.

11-5. Carol Levine, an architect, contracted orally with Hallendale Cabinet Makers to custom-build for her a cabinet that would fit a niche in her study. The cabinet had to contain numerous wide, shallow drawers where she could keep oversized sketches, drawings, and blueprints. The price of the cabinet was $1,500. Hallendale completed the cabinet within the time specified and delivered it to Levine. Levine refused to accept or pay for it, stating that she had accepted a job in another city and would have no use for the specially designed cabinet. Hallendale claimed that Levine breached their contract and was liable for damages. Levine contended that the oral contract was unenforceable under the Statute of Frauds. Who is correct and why?

11-6. Loeb & Company entered into an oral agreement with Schreiner, a farmer, whereby Schreiner was to sell Loeb 150 bales of cotton, each weighing 480 pounds. Shortly thereafter, Loeb sent Schreiner a letter confirming the terms of the oral contract. Schreiner neither acknowledged receipt of the letter nor objected to its terms. When delivery came due, Schreiner ignored the oral agreement and sold his cotton on the open market because the price of cotton had more than doubled (from 37 cents to 80 cents per pound) since the oral agreement had been made. In the lawsuit by Loeb & Company against Schreiner, did Loeb recover? [Loeb & Co. v. Schreiner, 294 Ala. 722, 321 So.2d 199 (1975)]

11-7. McNabb agreed to sell soybeans to Ralston Purina Company. Severe weather damaged a significant portion of all soybean crops that year. When McNabb was unable to meet the November 30 delivery deadline, Ralston Purina modified the contracts monthly without additional consideration to allow delivery as late as February 28 of the following year. Between November and February, the price of soybeans rose substantially. If Ralston Purina's extensions of the delivery date were intended to *maximize* damages in the event of McNabb's breach, would the modifications to the contract be enforceable? [Ralston Purina Co. v. McNabb, 381 F.Supp. 181 (W.D.Tenn. 1974)]

11-8. Riegel Fiber Corporation contracted in writing with Anderson Gin Company to purchase at 32 cents per pound all the cotton produced on specified acreage. Some of the designated acreage was owned by Anderson Gin Company itself, and some was owned by independent farmers who had separate contracts with Anderson. Prior to the harvest, however, the market price of cotton rose to 81 cents per pound and Anderson refused to deliver the cotton at the contract price of 32 cents per pound. When Riegel sued for specific performance on its contract with Anderson as well as on the contracts between Anderson and the independent farmers, Anderson claimed that the contract did not contain a quantity term sufficiently definite to satisfy the Statute of Frauds. Is Anderson correct? Explain. [Riegel Fiber Corp. v. Anderson Gin Co., 512 F.2d 784 (5th Cir. 1975)]

11-9. Gates Engineering Company contracted with the Mennonite Deaconess Home and Hospital, Inc. to supply the hospital with a "one-ply roofing system." The roofing system was to be installed by a subcontractor and approved by Gates. When the work was substantially completed, the hospital paid the subcontractor 90 percent of the price, withholding the remaining 10 percent of the purchase price pending approval by Gates. Gates withheld approval. The roof leaked badly, and the hospital had to completely replace it at its own expense. The hospital brought suit against Gates, claiming that he was subject to the provisions of the UCC concerning product warranties and that he had breached these warranties. Gates contended that the sale of the roofing system was a sale of services, not of goods, and thus the sale was not covered by the UCC. Will Gates succeed in this defense? [Mennonite Deaconess Home & Hospital, Inc. v. Gates Engineering Co., Inc., 219 Neb. 303, 363 N.W.2d 155 (1985)]

11-10. Leonard Palmer contracted with Safe Auto Sales, Inc. to purchase a 1980 Toyota Tercel at a price of $5,822.04. When the new Toyota arrived from the manufacturer, the car dealer told Palmer that he would have to pay an additional $250 owing to an increase in the cost of the car to the dealer, which had occurred after they formed their sales contract. Palmer needed the car and paid the additional $250. Later, however, Palmer brought suit to recover the $250 from the dealer, claiming that it was an unenforceable modification of their contract. Discuss Palmer's possibilities for recovery. [Palmer v. Safe Auto Sales, Inc., 114 Misc.2d 964, 452 N.Y.S.2d 995 (Civ.Ct.City of N.Y. 1982)]

Chapter 12

Title, Risk, and Insurable Interest

Before the creation of the UCC, *title*—the right of ownership—was the central concept in sales law. The numerous problems attending this concept and the need to define more precisely the stages concerning passage of title and risk of loss from a seller to a buyer are discussed in this chapter's "Landmark." In most situations, the Code has replaced the concept of title by three other concepts: (1) identification, (2) risk of loss, and (3) insurable interest. By breaking down the transfer of ownership into these three components, the drafters of the UCC have essentially followed Aristotle's advice and created greater precision in the law governing sales—leaving as few points of law as possible "to the decision of the judges."

> *"Now, it is of great moment that well-drawn laws should themselves define all the points they possibly can and leave as few as may be to the decision of the judges."*
>
> **Aristotle, 384–322 B.C. (Greek philosopher and politician)**

❖ Identification

Before any interest in specific goods can pass from the seller to the buyer, two conditions must prevail: (1) the goods must be in existence, and (2) they must be identified to the contract. If either condition is lacking, only a contract to *sell* (not a sale) exists. [UCC 2-105(2)] Goods that are not both existing and identified to the contract are called "future goods." For example, a contract to purchase next year's crop of hay would be a contract for future goods, a crop yet to be grown.

For passage of title, the goods must be identified in a way that will distinguish them from all other similar goods. **Identification** is a designation of goods as the subject matter of the sales contract.

In many cases, identification is simply a matter of specific designation. For example, you contract to purchase a fleet of five cars by the serial numbers listed for the cars, or you agree to purchase all the wheat in a specific bin at a stated price per bushel. Usually, problems only occur when a quantity of goods is purchased from a larger mass, such as 1,000 cases of beans from a 10,000-case lot.

There is a general rule that when a purchaser buys a quantity of goods to be taken from a larger mass, identification can be made only by separating the contracted goods from the mass. Therefore, until the seller separates the 1,000 cases of beans from the 10,000-case lot, title and risk of loss remain with the seller.

A few exceptions exist. For example, a seller owns approximately 55,000 chickens (hens and roosters). A buyer agrees to purchase all the hen chickens at a stated price.

IDENTIFICATION
Proof that a thing is what it is purported or represented to be. In the sale of goods, the express designation of the goods as provided in the contract.

Most courts would hold that "all the hen chickens" is a sufficient identification, and title and risk can pass to the buyer without the goods identified in the contract being physically separated from the other goods (the hens from the roosters). The reasoning is that the contract identification serves as sufficient separation.

The most common exception deals with fungible goods. [UCC 1-201(17)] Fungible goods are goods that are alike naturally, by agreement or trade usage. Typical examples are wheat, oil, and wine. If these goods are held or intended to be held by tenants in common (owners have an undivided share of the entire mass), a seller-tenant can pass title and risk of loss to the buyer without an actual separation. The buyer replaces the seller as a tenant in common. [UCC 2-105(4)]

For example, Anselm, Braudel, and Carpenter are farmers. They deposit, respectively, 5,000 bushels, 3,000 bushels, and 2,000 bushels of the same grade of grain in a bin. The three become tenants in common, with Anselm owning 50 percent of the 10,000 bushels, Braudel 30 percent, and Carpenter 20 percent. Anselm could contract to sell 5,000 bushels of grain to Tareyton and, since the goods are fungible, pass title and risk of loss to Tareyton without physically separating 5,000 bushels. Tareyton now becomes a tenant in common with Braudel and Carpenter.

Identification is significant because it gives the buyer the right to obtain insurance on (an insurable interest in) the goods and the right to recover from third parties who damage the goods. In certain circumstances, identification allows the buyer to take the goods from the seller.

In their contract, parties can agree on when identification will take place. But if they do not so specify, the following additional rules apply: [UCC 2-501(1)]

1. Identification takes place at the time the contract is made *if the contract calls for the sale of specific and ascertained goods already existing.*

2. If the sale involves unborn young animals that will be born within twelve months from the time of the contract, or if it involves crops to be harvested within twelve months (or the next harvest season occuring after contracting, whichever is longer), identification will take place, in the first case, when the young are conceived and, in the second case, when the crops are planted or begin to grow.

3. In other cases, identification takes place when the goods are marked, shipped, or somehow designated by the seller as the particular goods to pass under the contract. The seller can delegate the right to identify goods to the buyer.

Passage of Title

Once goods exist and are identified, the provisions of UCC 2-401 apply to the passage of title. In virtually all subsections of UCC 2-401, the words "unless otherwise explicitly agreed" appear, meaning that any explicit understanding between the buyer and the seller determines when title passes. Unless an agreement is explicitly made, title passes to the buyer at the time and the place the seller performs the *physical* delivery of the goods. [UCC 2-401(2)] The delivery arrangements determine when this occurs.

Shipment and Destination Contracts   Under shipment contracts (where the seller is required or authorized to ship goods by carrier), the seller is required only to deliver the goods into the hands of a carrier (such as a trucking company), and title passes to the buyer at the time and place of shipment. [UCC 2-401(2)(a)]

Landmark in the Law

Passage of Title—The UCC Compared with the Uniform Sales Act of 1906

The transporting of goods between contracting parties is often an uncertain event. Many things can go wrong, owing to accident or wrongdoing, to destroy or lessen the value or usefulness of the goods. Such loss results in hardship to one of the contracting parties. It is therefore important for the law to provide a remedy for the injured party.

Under the Uniform Sales Act of 1906, which governed passage of title in all thirty-four states that had adopted it prior to the UCC, the remedy was to allocate the risk of loss to the party that possessed title—and thus had a legal right—to the goods. Thus, if the seller had title when the loss occurred, he or she would be liable for the buyer's damages; conversely, if the buyer had title, then the buyer would remain liable to the seller for payment, despite the fact that the goods were destroyed.

In theory, the Uniform Sales Act's reliance on the passage-of-title concept is simple, but in application it was very impractical and resulted in widespread controversy and a tremendous amount of litigation. The problem was that determining when title actually passed was difficult and often resulted in seemingly bizarre applications. Consider the following example: A shoe retailer contracts with a wholesaler of shoes to purchase 100 pairs of shoes per month for the next ten months. The wholesaler thus sets aside in his warehouse a total of 1,000 shoes. The warehouse is destroyed by fire. Who is liable for the 1,000 shoes? Under the Uniform Sales Act, probably the buyer-retailer would be. This is because once the wholesaler set the shoes aside pursuant to the contract, title for those shoes passed from the wholesaler to the retailer, even though the retailer had no control over the goods.

Recognizing the many problems stemming from the Uniform Sales Act, the drafters of the Uniform Commercial Code, and Karl Llewellyn in particular, all but eliminated the concept of title in Article 2 of the UCC. Instead, the UCC uses a three-part checklist for determining risk of loss. First, one must look at the contract itself, asking whether the parties to the contract included any provision allocating risk. If they did, then it is binding and applied. Second, if the contract is silent as to risk, then one must look at whether either party breached the contract. If so, the party in breach is liable. Finally, if there is no breach, the Code looks to when the loss occurred in the context of the transaction, and who had possession of, or control over, the goods. Under the Code, the party who had control of the goods (or last had control, if an independent shipper is used) is liable for any loss. The rationale behind the Code's provisions is that the party in control is mostly likely to insure and otherwise protect the goods from loss.

Now let's return to our shoe merchant and apply the UCC provisions to this situation. Assuming the contract did not allocate risk and that neither party was in breach, the wholesaler would be liable for the loss of the shoes caused by the warehouse fire. Since it was the wholesaler's warehouse, the wholesaler was in control of the goods and was in the best position to protect the goods from loss and to insure them.

In general, as a result of the UCC, conflicts in this area—and, consequently, the number of cases that have come before the courts—have been greatly reduced. What was once, according to Llewellyn and many others, a highly "mysterious" area of the law to lawyers and judges alike has been rendered logical and commercially practicable under the UCC.

With destination contracts for the sale of goods, the seller is required to deliver the goods to a particular destination, usually directly to the buyer but sometimes to the buyer's designate. Title passes to the buyer when the goods are *tendered* at that destination. [UCC 2-401(2)(b)]

Delivery without Movement of the Goods   When the contract of sale does not call for the seller's shipment or delivery (buyer to pick up), the passage of title depends on whether the seller must deliver a document of title, such as a bill of lading or a warehouse receipt, to the buyer. When a document of title is required, title passes to the buyer *when and where the document is delivered*. Thus, if the goods are stored in a warehouse, title passes to the buyer when the appropriate documents are delivered to the buyer. The goods never move. In fact, the buyer can choose to leave the goods at the same warehouse for a period of time, and the buyer's title to those goods will be unaffected.

When no documents of title are required, and delivery is made without moving the goods, title passes at the time and place the sales contract was made, if the goods have already been identified. If the goods have not been identified, title does not pass until identification occurs. Consider an example. Rogers sells lumber to Kimble. It is agreed that Kimble will pick up the lumber at the yard. If the lumber has been identified (segregated, marked, or in any other way distinguished from all other lumber), title will pass to Kimble when the contract is signed. If the lumber is still in storage bins at the mill, however, title will not pass to Kimble until the particular pieces of lumber to be sold under this contract are identified. [UCC 2-401(3)]

❖ Risk of Loss

Under the UCC, several concepts replace the concept of title in determining the rights and remedies of parties to a sales contract. For example, risk of loss does not necessarily pass with title. The question of who suffers a financial risk if goods are damaged, destroyed, or lost is resolved primarily under Sections 2-509 and 2-319. Risk of loss may depend on whether a sales contract has been breached at the time of loss. [UCC 2-510]

Risk of loss can be assigned through an agreement by the parties, preferably in writing. In this way, the parties can generally control the exact moment that risk of loss passes from the seller to the buyer. Of course, at the time so agreed, the goods must be in existence and identified to the contract for this contract provision to be enforceable.

Carrier Cases

When there is no specification in the agreement, the following rules apply to so-called carrier cases.

Shipment Contracts   In a shipment contract, if the seller is required or authorized to ship goods by carrier (not required to deliver them to a particular destination), risk of loss passes to the buyer when the goods are duly delivered to the carrier. [UCC 2-509(1)(b)]

For example, a seller in Texas sells 500 cases of grapefruit to a buyer in New York, F.O.B. Houston (free on board in Houston—that is, buyer pays the transportation charges from Houston). The contract authorizes a shipment by carrier; it does not require that the seller tender the grapefruit in New York. Risk passes to the buyer when the conforming goods are properly placed in the possession of the carrier. If the goods are damaged in transit, the risk of loss is the buyer's. (Actually, buyers have recourse against carriers, subject to tariff rule limitations, and they usually insure the goods from the time the goods leave the seller.) Generally, all contracts are assumed to be shipping contracts if nothing to the contrary is stated in the contract.

It is important for buyers and sellers to have a provision written into their contract concerning risk of loss in order to avoid disputes when goods are destroyed by accident or for other reasons.

Destination Contracts   In a destination contract, the seller is required to deliver the goods at a particular destination. The risk of loss passes to the buyer when the goods are *tendered* to the buyer at that destination. In the preceding example, if the contract had been F.O.B. New York, risk of loss during transit to New York would have been the seller's.

Contract Terms   Specific *terms* in the contract, even though used in connection with a stated price, assist one in determining when risk of loss passes to the buyer. These terms are listed in Exhibit 12-1.

◆ **Exhibit 12-1   Contract Terms—Definitions**

F.O.B. (free on board) indicates that the selling price of goods includes transportation cost (and that the seller carries risk of loss) to the F.O.B., which is a specific place named in the contract. The place can be either at place of shipment (for example, seller's city or place of business) or at place of destination (for example, buyer's city or place of business). [UCC 2-319(1)]
F.A.S. (free alongside) vessel requires that the seller at his or her own expense and "risk" deliver the goods alongside the vessel before risk passes to the buyer. [UCC 2-319(2)]
CIF or C&F (cost, insurance, and freight, or just cost and freight) requires, among other things, that the seller "put the goods in possession of a carrier" before risk passes to the buyer. [UCC 2-320(2)] (These are basically pricing terms and remain shipment contracts, not destination contracts.)
Delivery ex-ship (from the carrying vessel) means that risk of loss does not pass to the buyer until the goods leave the ship or are otherwise properly unloaded. [UCC 2-322]

In the following case, the court reviewed UCC 2-509(1) as it relates to passage of the risk of loss. Under the Code, an F.O.B. term indicates whether the contract is a "shipment" contract or a "destination" contract, with the risk of loss passing at different times in each of these contracts. The F.O.B. terminology controls. In this case a "shipment" contract shifted the risk of loss to the buyer when the goods were delivered to a carrier. The fact that there was a "ship to" address had no significance in changing the UCC presumption that the contract was a "shipment" contract.

Case 12.1
PESTANA v. KARINOL CORP.
District Court of Appeals of Florida, Third District, 1979. 367 So.2d 1096.

FACTS Defendant Karinol Corporation contracted "to ship" watches to the plaintiff in Chetumal, Mexico. The contract contained no delivery terms, such as F.O.B., nor specific terms for allocation of loss while goods were in transit. The plaintiff-buyer, Pestana, had made a deposit. The watches were shipped by Karinol, but they were lost in transit. Pestana sought a refund for the deposit, claiming risk of loss was the seller's. Karinol claimed that Pestana suffered the risk of loss and owed the balance of the purchase price. The trial court held for the defendant, Karinol Corporation, and ruled that the buyer, Pestana, was liable for the loss.

ISSUE Who should bear the risk of loss when no provision concerning risk allocation or delivery terms is included in the sales contract?

DECISION The buyer. The appellate court upheld the trial court's decision.

REASON After discussing risk of loss under both shipment and destination contracts, the court held that where the contract has "(a) no explicit provisions allocating the risk of loss while the goods are in the possession of the carrier and (b) no delivery terms such as F.O.B. place of destination . . . such a contract, without more, constitutes a shipment contract wherein the risk of loss passes to the buyer when the seller duly delivers the goods to the carrier. . . ." Thus, "[w]here the risk of loss falls on the buyer at the time the goods are lost or destroyed, the buyer is liable to the seller for the purchase price of the goods sold."

BAILEE
One to whom goods or property owned by another (a bailor) are entrusted. The bailee is obligated to return the bailed goods or property to the bailor or dispose of them as directed by the bailor.

Delivery without Movement of Goods The Code also addresses situations where the seller is required neither to ship nor to deliver the goods. Frequently, the buyer is to pick up the goods from the seller, or the goods remain in a warehouse, or they are held by a **bailee** (the person to whom they are entrusted). [UCC 2-509(2)(3)]

When the goods are held by a bailee, they are usually represented by a negotiable or nonnegotiable document of title (a bill of lading or a warehouse receipt—see Exhibits 12-2 and 12-3). If the goods are held by the seller, a document of title is usually not used. This distinction is important in applying the rules on passage of risk of loss to the buyer. [UCC 2-509(2)(3)]

If the seller is a merchant, risk of loss to goods held by the seller passes to the buyer when the buyer *actually takes physical possession of the goods*. [UCC 2-509(3)] If the seller is not a merchant, the risk of loss to goods held by the seller passes to the buyer upon *tender of delivery*. [UCC 2-509(3)] A tender of delivery is the seller's placing or holding of conforming goods at the buyer's disposition (with any necessary notice), enabling the buyer to take delivery. [UCC 2-503(1)]

◆ **Exhibit 12-2 A Sample Negotiable Bill of Lading**

UNIFORM MOTOR CARRIER ORDER BILL OF LADING

Original—Domestic

1st Sheet

Shipper's No._____

Agent's No._____

CENTRAL FREIGHT LINES INC.

RECEIVED, subject to the classifications and tariffs in effect on the date of the issue of this Bill of Lading,

From _____, Date _____ 19____

At _____ Street, _____ City, _____ County, _____ State

the property described below, in apparent good order, except as noted (contents and condition of contents of packages unknown) marked, consigned and destined as shown below, which said company (the word company being understood throughout this contract as meaning any person or corporation in possession of the property under the contract) agrees to carry to its usual place of delivery at said destination, if within the scope of its lawful operations, otherwise to deliver to another carrier on the route to said destination. It is mutually agreed, as to each carrier of all or any of said property over all or any portion of said route to destination, and as to each party at any time interested in all or any of said property, that every service to be performed hereunder shall be subject to all the conditions not prohibited by law, whether printed or written, herein contained, including the conditions on back hereof, which are hereby agreed to by the shipper and accepted for himself and his assigns.

The surrender of this Original ORDER Bill of Lading properly indorsed shall be required before the delivery of the property. Inspection of property covered by this bill of lading will not be permitted unless provided by law or unless permission is indorsed on this original Bill of lading or given in writing by the shipper.

Consigned to Order of _____

Destination _____ Street, _____ City, _____ County, _____ State

Notify _____

At _____ Street, _____ City, _____ County, _____ State

I. C. C. No. _____ Vehicle No. _____

Routing _____

No. Pack-ages	Description of Articles, Special Marks, and Exceptions	*Weight (Subject to Correction)	Class or Rate	Check Column	
					Subject to Section 7 of Conditions, if this shipment is to be delivered to the consignee without recourse on the consignor, the consignor shall sign the following statement: The carrier shall not make delivery of this shipment without payment of freight and all other lawful charges.
					(Signature of consignor.)
					If charges are to be prepaid write or stamp here, "To be Prepaid."
					Received $_____ to apply in prepayment of the charges on the property described hereon.
					Agent or Cashier.
					Per_____ (The signature here acknowledges only the amount prepaid.)

*If the shipment moves between two ports by a carrier by water, the law requires that the bill of lading shall state whether it is "carrier's or shipper's weight."

Note—Where the rate is dependent on value, shippers are required to state specifically in writing the agreed or declared value of the property.

The agreed or declared value of the property is hereby specifically stated by the shipper to be not exceeding

_____ per _____

Charges advanced:

$_____

Shipper _____ Agent.

Per _____ Per _____

Permanent address of Shipper _____ Street, _____ City, _____ State

MOORE BUSINESS FORMS, INC., WACO, TEX. U

Source: Reprinted with permission of Central Freight Lines Inc. © 1985 Central Freight Lines, Inc.
Note: This form is printed in yellow to warn holders that it is an order bill of lading. The back of the form permits negotiation by indorsement.

◆ **Exhibit 12-3   A Sample Nonnegotiable Warehouse Receipt**

HART

Warehouse Receipt – Not Negotiable

Agreement No. _____   Vault No. _____ _____ _____ _____ _____

Service Order _____   _____ _____ _____ _____ _____

Receipt and
Lot Number_____   Date of Issue_____19_____

Received for the account of and deliverable to *_____

whose latest known address is _____ **SAMPLE**

_____ the goods enumerated on the inside or attached schedule to be

stored in Company warehouse, located at _____
which goods are accepted only upon the following conditions set forth below:

READ CAREFULLY ▶ That the value of all goods stored, including the contents of any container, and all goods hereafter stored for Depositor's account to be not over $ _____ per pound † per article unless a higher value is noted in the schedule, for which an additional monthly storage charge of _____ ¢ on each $_____ valuation in excess of $ _____ per pound † per article or fraction thereof will be made.

If there are any items enumerated in this receipt valued in excess of the above limitations per pound per article and not so noted in the schedule, return this receipt within 10 days with proper values so indicated in writing in order that the receipt may be re-issued and proper higher storage rates assessed.

OWNERSHIP. The Customer, Shipper, Depositor, or Agent represents and warrants that he is lawfully possessed of goods to be stored and/or has the authority to store or ship said goods. (If the goods are mortgaged, notify the Company the name and address of the mortgagee.)

PAYMENT OF CHARGES. Storage bills are payable monthly in advance for each month's storage or fraction thereof. Labor charges, cartage and other services rendered are payable upon completion of work. All charges shall be paid at the warehouse location shown hereon, and if delinquent, shall incur interest monthly at the rate of _____ per cent ( ) per year.
The Depositor will pay reasonable attorney's fee incurred by The Company in collecting delinquent accounts.

LIABILITY OF COMPANY. The company shall be liable for any loss or injury to the goods caused by its failure to exercise such care as a reasonably careful man would exercise under like circumstances. The company will not be liable for loss or damage to fragile articles not packed, or articles packed or unpacked by other than employees of this company. Depositor specifically agrees that the warehouse will not be liable for contamination of or for insect damage to articles placed in drawers of furniture by the depositor. Periodic spraying of the warehouse premises shall constitute ordinary and proper care, unless the depositor requests in writing and pays for anti-infestation treatment of articles in drawers and compartments of stored furniture.

CHANGE OF ADDRESS. Notice of change of address must be given the Company in writing, and acknowledged in writing by the Company.

TRANSFER OR WITHDRAWAL OF GOODS. The warehouse receipt is not negotiable and shall be produced and all charges must be paid before delivery to the Depositor, or transfer of goods to another person; however, a written direction to the Company to transfer the goods to another person or deliver the goods may be accepted by the Company at its option without requiring tender of the warehouse receipt.

ACCESS TO STORAGE, PARTIAL WITHDRAWAL. A signed order from the person in whose name the receipt is issued is required to enable others to remove or have access to goods. A charge is made for stacking and unstacking, and for access to stored goods.
BUILDING—FIRE—WATCHMAN. The Company does not represent or warrant that its building cannot be destroyed by fire or that the contents of said buildings including the said property cannot be destroyed by fire. The Company shall not be required to maintain a watchman or sprinkler system and its failure to do so shall not constitute negligence.
CLAIMS OR ERRORS. All claims for non-delivery of any article or articles and for damage, breakage, etc., must be made in writing within ninety (90) days from delivery of goods stored or they are waived. Failure to return the warehouse receipt for correction within ( ) days after receipt thereof by the depositor will be conclusive that it is correct and delivery will be made only in accordance therewith.
FUTURE SERVICE. This Contract shall extend and apply to future services rendered to the Depositor by the Company and to any additional goods deposited with the Company by the Depositor.
WAREHOUSEMAN'S LIEN. The Company reserves the right to sell the goods stored, in accordance with the provisions of the Uniform Commercial Code (Business and Commerce Code if stored in Texas), for all lawful charges in arrears.
TERMINATION OF STORAGE. The Company reserves the right to terminate the storage of the goods at any time by giving to the Depositor thirty (30) days' written notice of its intention so to do, and, unless the Depositor removes such goods within that period, the Company is hereby empowered to have the same removed at the cost and expense of the Depositor, or the Company may sell them at auction in accordance with state law.

DEPOSITOR WILL PAY REASONABLE LEGAL FEES INCURRED BY WAREHOUSE IN COLLECTING DELINQUENT CHARGES.

THIS DOCUMENT CONTAINS THE WHOLE CONTRACT BETWEEN THE PARTIES AND THERE ARE NO OTHER TERMS, WARRANTIES, REPRESENTATIONS, OR AGREEMENTS OF EITHER DEPOSITOR OR COMPANY NOT HEREIN CONTAINED.

Storage per month or fraction thereof	$_____
Warehouse labor	$_____
Cartage	$_____
Packing at residence . . .	$_____
Wrapping and preparing for storage	$_____
Charges advanced	$_____
	$_____
	$_____

By_____

*Insert "Mr. and/or Mrs." or, if military personnel, appropriate rank or grade.
†Delete the words "per pound" if the declared value is per article.
For goods stored for military personnel under PL 245, the contractor's liability for care of goods is as provided in Basic Agreement with U.S. Government.

THIS PROPERTY HAS NOT BEEN INSURED BY THIS COMPANY FOR FIRE OR ANY OTHER CASUALTY
SCHEDULE OF GOODS ON FOLLOWING PAGE OR ATTACHED

W-1 (4/81) Approved by SH H T4 ©   Re-order from Hart Graphics, Austin, Texas

Source: Reprinted with permission of Hart Graphics, Inc. of Austin, Texas. © 1985 Hart Graphics, Inc.

Cases Involving Bailees   When a bailee is holding goods for a person who has contracted to sell them and the goods are to be delivered without being moved, the risk of loss passes to the buyer when (1) the buyer receives a negotiable document of title for the goods, or (2) the bailee acknowledges the buyer's right to possess the goods, or (3) the buyer receives a nonnegotiable document of title *and* has had a *reasonable time* to present the document to the bailee and demand the goods. Obviously, if the bailee refuses to honor the document, the risk of loss remains with the seller. [UCC 2-509(2) and 2-503(4)(b)]

In the following case, the court concluded that although title to goods in the possession of a bailee had passed from seller to buyer, risk of loss had not yet passed when the goods were destroyed by fire. Note that the court looks beyond the literal instructions of the UCC to the intention of the framers of the Code in order to arrive at a fair decision.

Case 12.2
JASON'S FOODS, INC. v. PETER ECKRICH & SONS, INC.
United States Court of Appeals, Seventh Circuit, 1985.
774 F.2d 214.

FACTS   In December of 1982, Peter Eckrich & Sons contracted to buy from Jason's Foods 38,000 pounds of "St. Louis style" pork ribs. It was arranged that the ribs would be transferred from Jason's account in an independent warehouse to Eckrich's account in the same warehouse—without any actual movement of the ribs. In its confirmation of the agreement, Jason's notified Eckrich that the transfer would be effected between January 10 and January 14. On January 13, Jason's telephoned the warehouse and requested that the transfer be made. The transfer was entered on the warehouse books immediately, but no warehouse receipt was sent to Eckrich until January 17 or 18, and Eckrich did not receive the receipt—and thus did not know the transfer had occurred—until January 24.

The warehouse burned down on January 17, and Jason's subsequently sued Eckrich to recover the contract price. The trial court held that Eckrich was not liable because risk of loss had not passed to Eckrich prior to the fire. The trial court judge thus granted summary judgment for Eckrich, and Jason's appealed.

ISSUE   Who should bear the risk of loss of the goods—Jason's or Eckrich?

DECISION   The trial court ruling was affirmed, and Jason's had to bear the risk of loss of the goods.

REASON   The court had little difficulty establishing that title had passed when the transfer was entered into the warehouse accounts. But when did risk of loss pass? Under the UCC, the relevant rule covering this situation is that risk of loss passes to the buyer "on acknowledgment by the bailee of the buyer's right to possession of the goods." [UCC 2-509(2)(b)] But this section does not indicate to whom acknowledgment must be made—the buyer or the seller. The court indicated that, according to the official comments on this section of the UCC, it was not intended to change the corresponding section of the Uniform Sales Act, Section 43(3), which had expressly required acknowledgment to the buyer.

This case troubled the court a great deal, and in arriving at its conclusion it looked toward the intention of the framers of the UCC. One of the primary policy choices built into the UCC is to create incentives for the parties in order to minimize the adverse consequences of untoward events such as fires. This can be done in one of two ways: by determining which party is best able or most likely to insure the goods, or by determining which party is best able to prevent the event. In this case, both parties could insure the ribs, although arguably Jason's was in the better position to do so since Eckrich did not know when actual delivery was to occur and Jason's did. Similarly, both parties were in the same position in regard to their ability to protect the goods from untoward loss—neither had any more control over the goods than the other. Arguably, however, Jason's might have been in the best position to protect the goods since it was the party making the critical decisions as to the exact date of transfer. The court also noted that Jason's could have requested that the warehouse notify Eckrich of the transfer

Case 12.2—Continued

by telephone, rather than by letter, but Jason's failed to do so.

Because the scales were thus slightly tipped in Eckrich's favor, the court ruled that, although the title to the ribs passed to Eckrich when the warehouse made the transfer on its books, the risk of loss did not pass until Eckrich received "acknowledgment" from the bailee.

Sale-on-Approval and Sale-or-Return Contracts

SALE ON APPROVAL
A type of conditional sale that becomes absolute only when the buyer approves or is satisfied with the good(s) sold. Besides express approval of goods, approval may be inferred if the buyer keeps the goods beyond a reasonable time, or uses the goods in any way that is inconsistent with the seller's ownership.

SALE OR RETURN
A type of conditional sale wherein title and possession pass from the seller to the buyer; however, the buyer retains the option to rescind or return the goods during a specified period even though the goods conform to the contract.

A **sale on approval** is not a sale until the buyer accepts (approves) the offer. A **sale or return** is a sale that can be rescinded by the buyer without liability.

Sale on Approval When a seller offers to sell goods to a buyer and permits the buyer to take the goods on a trial basis, a sale on approval is made. The term *sale* here is a misnomer, since only an *offer* to sell has been made, along with a bailment created by the buyer's possession.[1]

Therefore, title and risk of loss (from causes beyond the buyer's control) remain with the seller until the buyer accepts (approves) the offer. Acceptance can be made expressly, by any act inconsistent with the *trial* purpose or seller's ownership, or by the buyer's election not to return the goods within the trial period. If the buyer does not wish to accept, the buyer may notify the seller of such fact within the trial period, and the return is at the seller's expense and risk. [UCC 2-327(1)] Goods held on approval are not subject to the claims of the buyer's creditors until acceptance.

Sale or Return Sale or return (sometimes called *sale and return*) is a species of contract by which the seller delivers a quantity of goods to the buyer, on the understanding that if the buyer wishes to retain any portion of those goods (for use or resale), the buyer will consider the portion retained as having been sold to him or her and will pay accordingly. The balance will be returned to the seller or will be held by the buyer as a bailee subject to the seller's order. When the buyer receives possession at the time of sale, the title and risk of loss pass to the buyer. Both remain with the buyer until the buyer returns the goods to the seller within the time period specified. If the buyer fails to return the goods within this time period, the sale is finalized. The return of the goods is at the buyer's risk and expense. The goods held on a sale-or-return contract are subject to the claims of the buyer's creditors while they are in the buyer's possession.

Under a contract of sale or return, the title vests immediately in the buyer, who has the privilege of rescinding the sale. [UCC 2-326] It is often difficult to determine from a particular transaction which exists—a contract for sale on approval or a contract for sale or return. The Code states that (unless otherwise agreed) if the goods are for the buyer to use, the transaction is a sale on approval; if the goods are for the buyer to resell, the transaction is a sale or return.[UCC 2-326(1)]

---

1. A bailment is an agreement to entrust goods or personal property of one person (bailor) to another (bailee), with the obligation of the bailee to return the bailed property to the bailor or dispose of the property as directed. See Chapter 33.

Risk of Loss in a Breached Sales Contract

There are many ways to breach a sales contract, and the transfer of risk operates differently depending on whether the seller or the buyer breaches. Generally, the party in breach bears the risk of loss.

When the Seller Breaches   If the goods are so nonconforming that the buyer has the right to reject them, the risk of loss does not pass to the buyer until the defects are cured or until the buyer accepts the goods in spite of their defects (thus waiving the right to reject). For example, a buyer orders blue widgets from a seller, F.O.B. seller's plant. The seller ships black widgets, giving the buyer the right to reject. The widgets are damaged in transit. The risk of loss falls on the seller (although the risk would have been on the buyer if blue widgets had been shipped under a shipment contract). [UCC 2-510(2)]

If a buyer accepts a shipment of goods and later discovers a defect, acceptance can be revoked. Revocation allows the buyer to pass the risk of loss back to the seller, at least to the extent that the buyer's insurance does not cover the loss. [UCC 2-510(2)] This situation is illustrated in the following case.

Case 12.3
GRAYBAR ELECTRIC CO. v. SHOOK
Supreme Court of North Carolina, 1973.
283 N.C. 213, 195 S.E.2d 514.

FACTS   Harold Shook agreed with Graybar Electric Co. to purchase three reels of burial cable for use in Shook's construction work. When the reels were delivered, each carton was marked "burial cable," although two of the reels were in fact aerial cable. Shook accepted the conforming reel of cable and notified Graybar that he was rejecting the two reels of aerial cable. Because of a trucker's strike, Shook was unsuccessful in arranging for the return of the reels to Graybar, and stored the reels in a well-lighted space near a grocery store owner's dwelling, which was close to Shook's work site. About four months later, Shook noticed that one of the reels had been stolen. On the following day he notified Graybar of the loss and, worried about the safety of the second reel, Shook arranged to have it transported to a garage for storage. Before the second reel was transferred, however, it was also stolen, and Shook notified Graybar of the second theft. Graybar sued Shook for the purchase price, claiming that Shook had agreed to return to Graybar the nonconforming reels and had failed to do so. Shook contended that he agreed only to contact a trucking company

to return the reels, and, since he had contacted three trucking firms to no avail (owing to the strike) his obligation had been fulfilled. The trial court ruled for Shook, and Graybar appealed.

ISSUE   Who should bear the risk of loss for the two stolen reels?

DECISION   Graybar. The Supreme Court of North Carolina affirmed the lower court's judgment in Shook's favor.

REASON   The court relied on UCC 2-510(1), which states, "Where tender or delivery of goods so fails to conform to the contract as to give a right of rejection, the risk of their loss remains on the seller until cure or acceptance." The court held that Shook had formed no contract with Graybar to return the nonconforming goods, although Shook had attempted to facilitate the cable's return at the owner's request. Graybar, on the other hand, "with full notice of the place of storage which was at the place of delivery did nothing but sleep on its rights for more than three months." Thus, Graybar had evidenced neither the promptness of action nor the good faith required by the UCC.

When the Buyer Breaches   The general rule is that when a buyer breaches a contract, the risk of loss *immediately* shifts to the buyer. There are three important limitations with this rule:

1.   The seller must have already identified the goods under the contract. (Regardless of the delivery arrangements, the risk shifts.)
2.   The buyer bears the risk for only a *commercially reasonable time* after the seller learns of the breach.
3.   The buyer is liable only to the extent of any *deficiency* in the seller's insurance coverage. [UCC 2-510(3)]

❖ Insurable Interest

"When the praying does no good, insurance does help."

Bertolt Brecht, 1898–1956 (German playwright and poet)

Buyers and sellers often obtain insurance coverage to protect against damage, loss, or destruction of goods. But any party purchasing insurance must have a "sufficient interest" in the insured item to obtain a valid policy. Insurance laws—not the Code— determine "sufficiency" (see Chapter 35). The Code is helpful, however, because it contains certain rules regarding the buyer's and seller's insurable interest in goods.

Buyer's Insurable Interest

INSURABLE INTEREST
An interest either in a person's life or well-being or in property which is sufficiently substantial that insuring against injury to the person or damage to the property does not amount to a mere wagering (betting) contract.

Buyers have an **insurable interest** in *identified* goods. The moment the goods are identified in the contract by the seller, the buyer has a "special" property interest that allows the buyer to obtain necessary insurance coverage for those goods even before the risk of loss has passed. [UCC 2-501(1)]

Consider an example: In March a farmer sells a cotton crop he hopes to harvest in October. After the crop is planted, the buyer insures it against hail damage. In September a hailstorm ruins the crop. When the buyer files a claim under her insurance policy, the insurer refuses to pay the claim, asserting that the buyer has no insurable interest in the crop. The insurer is not correct. The buyer acquired an insurable interest in the crop when it was planted, since she had a contract to buy it. The rule in UCC 2-501(1)(c) states that a buyer obtains an insurable interest in the goods by identification, which occurs "when the crops are planted or otherwise become growing crops . . . if the contract is . . . for the sale of crops to be harvested within twelve months or the next normal harvest season after contracting, whichever, is longer."

Seller's Insurable Interest

A seller has an insurable interest in goods as long as he or she retains title to the goods. Even after title passes to a buyer, however, a seller who has a "security interest" in the goods (a right to secure payment) still has an insurable interest and can insure the goods. [UCC 2-501(2)]

Hence, both a buyer and a seller can have an insurable interest in identical goods at the same time. In all cases, one must sustain an actual loss in order to have the right to recover from an insurance company.

❖ Bulk Transfers

Special problems arise when a major portion of a business's assets are transferred. This is the subject matter of UCC Article 6 on bulk transfers.[2] A bulk transfer is defined as any transfer of a major part of the material, supplies, merchandise, or other inventory *not made in the ordinary course of the transferor's business.* [UCC 6-102(1)] Difficulties may occur, for example, when a business that owes debts to numerous creditors sells a substantial part of its equipment and inventories to a buyer. The business should use the proceeds to pay off the debts. But what if the merchant instead spends the money on a trip, leaving the creditors without payment? Can the creditors lay any claim to the goods that were transferred in bulk to the buyer?

To prevent this situation, UCC 6-104 and 6-105 establish certain requirements for bulk transfers. All four of the following steps must be undertaken in order to comply with the statutory requirements:

1. The seller must furnish to the buyer a sworn list of his or her existing creditors. The list must include those whose claims are disputed, and state names, business addresses, and amounts due.
2. The buyer and the seller must prepare a schedule of the property to be transferred.
3. The buyer must preserve the list of creditors and the schedule of property for six months and permit inspection of the list by any creditor of the seller, or file the list and the schedule of property in a designated public office.
4. The buyer must give notice of the proposed bulk transfer to each of the seller's creditors at least ten days before the buyer takes possession of the goods or makes payments for them, whichever happens first.

If these requirements are met, the buyer acquires title to the goods free of all claims by the seller's creditors. If the requirements are not met, goods in the possession of the buyer continue to be subject to the claims of the unpaid creditors of the seller for six months. [UCC 6-111]

❖ Sales by Nonowners

Problems also occur when persons who acquire goods with imperfect titles attempt to resell them. UCC 2-402 and 2-403 deal with the rights of two parties who lay claim to the same goods, sold with imperfect titles.

Void Title

A buyer acquires at least whatever title the seller has to the goods sold. A buyer may unknowingly purchase goods from a seller who is not the owner of the goods. If the seller is a thief, the seller's title is *void*—legally, no title exists. Thus, the buyer acquires no title, and the real owner can reclaim the goods from the buyer.

For example, if Jim steals goods owned by Margaret, Jim has *void title* to those goods. If Jim sells the goods to Sandra, Margaret can reclaim them from Sandra even though Sandra acted in good faith and honestly was not aware that the goods were stolen.

---

2. Recently, the National Conference of Commissioners on Uniform State Laws recommended that those states that have adopted Article 6 repeal it. For states disinclined to do so, Article 6 has been revised to provide creditors with better protection while reducing the burden imposed on good faith purchasers.

Business Law in Action

Grounds for Suspicion

In early September of 1984, Barry Hyken saw an ad in a St. Louis newspaper for the sale of a 1980 Rolls Royce Corniche for $62,000. Hyken was a businessperson and the owner of Landshire Food Service, Inc., and as a hobby he collected and traded expensive, imported cars. Hyken called a friend and dealer of imported automobiles and asked whether $62,000 was a good price for a 1980 Rolls Royce Corniche. The friend thought the asking price was on the low side of fair market value and that Hyken "could not go wrong" if he bought the car for that amount.

Hyken then arranged a meeting with the seller, which took place at a hotel near the St. Louis airport. The seller said his name was J. A. Coghill, and when Hyken requested identification, the seller produced a New Hampshire driver's license with a New Hampshire address and an air-carrier crew card with an Illinois address. Hyken did not question the disparity between the addresses or Coghill's "explanation" of the disparity, which was that he was in the process of moving from Illinois to the St. Louis area. When Hyken asked Coghill why the newspaper ad read 1980 Rolls Royce when in fact the car was a 1979 model, Coghill attributed the error to a newspaper misprint.

Hyken later agreed to purchase the auto, and the two parties met at Hyken's office to complete the sale. Coghill produced an Illinois certificate of title which was signed by J. A. Coghill as seller, dated August

25, 1984, and showed the transferee as Executive Jet Leasing. Coghill explained that this assignment was an attempted transfer to his company, which he had not completed on the advice of his accountants. Coghill crossed out Executive Jet Leasing and wrote in "Landshire Foods and B. J. Hyken" as the transferees, without correcting the date. Coghill also signed an affidavit stating that the first transferee had been inserted by mistake. Hyken then gave Coghill a cashier's check for $58,500 and a check from Landshire Foods for $3,500. On September 17, Hyken registered the title and paid the sales tax.

Two weeks later, the St. Louis County Police took possession of the vehicle at the request of Illinois authorities and placed it in a police garage. It turned out that the seller was not J. A. Coghill. J. A. Coghill was in fact an Illinois resident who had sold his 1979 Rolls Royce

Corniche in August of 1984 to a person who claimed to be Daniel Bellman. Bellman had given Coghill a cashier's check in the amount of $94,500 and requested that the transferee on the Illinois certificate of title be listed as his business firm, Executive Jet Leasing. When Coghill learned from his bank that the cashier's check was forged, he reported the vehicle as stolen.

As noted in the text, when goods are obtained by fraud, the person obtaining the goods has voidable title. If the fraudulently obtained goods are then sold to a good-faith purchaser, the buyer can claim valid title against the original owner. Thus, if Hyken could demonstrate he was a good-faith purchaser, he could claim valid title to the vehicle. To be a good-faith purchaser, Hyken would have had to have purchased the auto "without knowledge of the circumstances that would make a person of ordinary prudence inquire

A 1979 Rolls Royce Corniche

Business Law in Action—Continued

about the title of the seller of the goods." Were the irregularities attending the sale of the Rolls Royce sufficient to have caused a "person of ordinary prudence" to be suspicious about the seller's rights in the vehicle?

The Missouri Court of Appeals, which heard the case in the spring of 1986,[1] concluded that, given the

1. Landshire Food Service, Inc. v. Coghill, 709 S.W.2d 509 (Mo.App. 1986).

circumstances of the sale, a reasonable person would have had grounds for suspicion. The contradictory addresses given by the seller, the vehicle's low price, and the existence of a prior transferee on the title (indicating a prior assignment) should have, according to the court, put a reasonable person on notice that inquiry into the seller's title rights was warranted. Since Hyken failed to make any such inquiry, he was not a good-faith purchaser in the eyes of the law. "A buyer will not be

protected," the court stated, "where he is put on notice of the irregularities in a seller's title either by defects in the face of the certificate or by other circumstances. The requisite notice 'may be imparted to a prospective purchaser by actual or constructive notice of facts which would place a reasonably prudent person upon inquiry as to the title he is about to purchase.' "

Voidable Title

A seller has a *voidable title* if the goods that he or she is selling were obtained by fraud; paid for with a check that is later dishonored; purchased on credit, when the seller was insolvent; or purchased from a minor. Purchasers of such goods acquire all title that their transferors either had or had the power to transfer.

In contrast to a seller with *void* title, a seller with *voidable title* has the power to transfer a good title to a **good-faith purchaser** for value. This chapter's "Business Law in Action" concerns a sale of an automobile that had been fraudulently obtained by the seller. Note the importance of the "good faith purchaser" rule in the court's determination as to whether the buyer received valid title to the Rolls Royce.

The Entrustment Rule

According to Section 2-403(2), entrusting goods to a merchant *who deals in goods of that kind* gives the merchant the power to transfer all rights to a *buyer in the ordinary course of business*. Entrusting includes both delivering the goods to the merchant and leaving the purchased goods with the merchant for later delivery or pickup. [UCC 2-403(3)] A "buyer in the ordinary course" is a person who buys in good faith from a person who deals in goods of that kind. The buyer cannot have knowledge that the sale violates the ownership rights of a third person.

For example, Jan leaves her watch with a jeweler to be repaired. The jeweler sells both new and used watches. The jeweler sells Jan's watch to Kim, a customer, who does not know that the jeweler has no right to sell it. Kim gets *good title* against Jan's claim of ownership.

The good-faith buyer, however, obtains only those rights held by the person entrusting the goods. For example, Jan's watch is stolen by Greg. Greg leaves the watch with a jeweler for repairs. The jeweler sells the watch to Bonnie, who does not know that the jeweler has no right to sell it. Bonnie gets good title against Greg, the entrustor, but not against Jan, who neither entrusted the watch to Greg nor authorized Greg to entrust it.

GOOD-FAITH PURCHASER
A purchaser who buys without notice of circumstance, which would put a person of ordinary prudence on inquiry as to the title, or as to an impediment on the title, of a seller. Sometimes used interchangeably with a "buyer in the ordinary course of business."

Application

Law and the Shipper or Buyer—Who Has the Risk of Loss?

A major aspect of commercial transactions involves the shipment of goods. Many issues arise when the unforeseen occurs, such as fire, theft, or other forms of damage to goods in transit.

Recall from the "Landmark" discussion that the UCC uses a three-part checklist to determine risk of loss:

1.   If the contract includes terms allocating risk of loss, those terms are binding and must be applied.
2.   If the contract is silent as to risk, and either party breaches the contract, the breaching party is liable for risk of loss.
3.   When a contract makes no reference to risk and neither party breaches, risk of loss is borne by the party having control over the goods.

As a seller of goods to be shipped, realize that, absent any explicit agreement in the contract or any breach on the buyer's part, as long as you have control over the goods, you are liable for any loss.

When there is no explicit agreement, the Uniform Commercial Code uses the delivery terms in your contract as a basis for determining control. Thus a shipment "F.O.B. buyer's business" is a destination-delivery term, and risk of loss would not pass to the buyer until there was a tender of delivery at the point of destination. Any loss or damage in transit falls on the seller because the seller has control until proper tender has been made.

From the buyer's point of view, it is important to remember that most sellers prefer "F.O.B. seller's business" delivery terms. Once the goods are delivered to the carrier, the buyer has the risk of loss. Thus if conforming goods are completely destroyed or lost in transit, the buyer not only suffers the loss, but is legally obligated to pay the seller the contract price.

At the time of contract negotiation, both the seller and buyer should determine the importance of risk of loss. In some cases, risk is relatively unimportant (such as when ten boxes of mimeograph paper are being sold) and the delivery terms should simply reflect costs and price. In other cases, risk is extremely important (such as when a fragile piece of equipment is being sold), and the parties will need an express agreement as to the moment risk is to pass so they can insure accordingly. The important point is that risk should be considered before the loss, not after it.

Checklist for the Shipment of Goods

☐ 1.   Prior to entering a contract, determine the importance of risk of loss for a given sale.

☐ 2.   If risk is extremely important, the contract should expressly state the moment risk of loss will pass from the seller to the buyer. This clause could even provide that risk does not pass until the goods are "delivered, installed, inspected, and tested (or in running order for a period of time)."

☐ 3.   If an express clause cannot be agreed upon, delivery terms determine passage of risk of loss.

☐ 4.   When appropriate, either or both parties should consider the need to procure insurance.

❖ Chapter Summary: Title, Risk, and Insurable Interest

PASSAGE OF TITLE AND RISK OF LOSS	
Shipment Contracts	In absence of agreement, title and risk pass upon seller's delivery of conforming goods to the carrier. UCC 2-401(2)(a), UCC 2-509(1)(a)
Destination Contracts	In absence of agreement, title and risk pass upon seller's *tender* of delivery of conforming goods to the buyer at the point of destination. UCC 2-401(2)(b), UCC 2-509(1)(b)

Goods That Are to Be Delivered Without Physical Movement	1. In absence of agreement, if the goods are not represented by a document of title—
	   a. Title passes upon the formation of the contract. UCC 2-401(3)(b)
	   b. Risk passes to the buyer, if seller is a merchant, upon buyer's *receipt* of the goods; if the seller is a nonmerchant, upon seller's *tender* of delivery of the goods. UCC 2-509(3)
	
	2. In absence of agreement, if the goods are represented by a document of title—
	   a. If negotiable, title and risk pass upon the buyer's *receipt* of the document. UCC 2-401(3)(a), UCC 2-509(2)(a)
	   b. If nonnegotiable, title passes upon the buyer's receipt of the document, but risk does *not* pass until the buyer, after receipt of the document, has had a reasonable time to present the document to demand the goods. UCC 2-401(3)(a), UCC 2-509(2)(c), UCC 2-503(4)(b)

Sale-on-Approval Contracts	Title and risk of loss (from causes beyond the buyer's control) remain with the seller until the buyer approves (accepts) the offer. UCC 2-327(1)
Sale-or-Return Contracts	When the buyer receives possession of the goods, title and risk of loss pass to the buyer, with buyer's option to return both to seller upon return of the goods. UCC 2-327(2)

Passage of Risk of Loss in a Breached Sales Contract	1. If the seller breaches by tendering nonconforming goods which are rejected by the buyer, the risk of loss does not pass to the buyer until the defects are cured (unless the buyer accepts the goods in spite of their defects, thus waiving the right to reject). UCC 2-510(1)
	
	2. If the buyer breaches the contract, the risk of loss to identified goods immediately shifts to the buyer. Limitations to this rule are as follows—
	   a. The buyer bears the risk for only a commercially reasonable time after the seller learns of the breach.
	   b. The buyer is liable only to the extent of any deficiency in the seller's insurance coverage. UCC 2-510(3)

Bulk Transfers	In a bulk transfer of assets, the buyer acquires title to the goods free of all claims of creditors of the seller if the following statutory requirements are met— 1. The transferor (seller) furnishes to the transferee a sworn list of existing creditors, listing the names, business addresses, amounts due, and any disputed claims. UCC 6-104(1)(a) 2. The buyer and seller prepare a schedule of the property transferred. UCC 6-104(1)(b) 3. The buyer preserves the list of creditors and the schedule of property for six months, allowing any creditor of the seller to inspect it, or files the list and schedule of property in a designated public office. UCC 6-104(1)(c) 4. Notice of the proposed bulk transfer is given by the buyer to each creditor of the seller at least ten days before the buyer takes possession of the goods or pays for them, whichever happens first. UCC 6-105

Sales by Nonowners	1. Between the owner and a good-faith purchaser—
	   a. Void title—Owner prevails. UCC 2-403(1)
	   b. Voidable title—Buyer prevails. UCC 2-403(1)
	   c. Entrusting to a merchant—Buyer prevails. UCC 2-403(2)(3)

INSURABLE INTEREST	
Buyer's Insurable Interest	Buyers have an insurable interest in goods the moment the goods are identified in the contract by the seller. UCC 2-501(2)
Seller's Insurable Interest	Sellers have an insurable interest in goods as long as they have (1) title to the goods, or (2) a security interest in the goods. UCC 2-501(2)

❖ Questions and Case Problems

12-1. On April 1, Adams agreed to sell Fenimore a 1964 VW Beetle. Fenimore was to pick up the VW on April 10 and pay for it at that time. The terms of the sale were all expressed in a written contract between Adams and Fenimore on April 1. On April 6, a judgment creditor (a creditor enabled by court judgment to seize property in satisfaction of a debt) of Adams had the sheriff seize the VW under a valid writ of execution. Both Adams and Fenimore claimed the seizure was illegal because Adams no longer owned the car. Nothing had been mentioned in the contract as to when title would pass to the buyer. Are Adams and Fenimore correct in their contention that the seizure was illegal? Why or why not?

12-2. Julian Makepeace, who had been declared insane by a court, sold his diamond ring to Golding for value. Golding later sold the ring to Carmichael for value. Neither Golding nor Carmichael knew that Makepeace had been adjudged to be insane by a court. Farrel, who had been appointed as Makepeace's guardian, subsequently learned that the diamond ring was in Carmichael's possession and demanded its return from Carmichael. Who has legal ownership of the ring? Why?

12-3. On May 1, Beringford goes into Jackson's retail clothing store to purchase a suit. Beringford finds a suit he likes for $190 and buys it. The suit needs alteration, so Beringford agrees to pick up the altered suit at Jackson's store on May 10. Assume (separately) the following:

    (a) One of Jackson's major creditors has a judgment against Jackson and levies execution on that judgment against all clothing in Jackson's possession.

    (b) On May 9, through no fault of Jackson, his store burns down, and all the merchandise is destroyed.

Discuss Beringford's rights to the suit on which the major creditor has levied. Between Jackson and Beringford, who suffers the loss of the suit destroyed by fire? Explain.

12-4. Alberto's Food Stores contracts to purchase from Giant Food Distributors, Inc. 100 cases of Golden Rod corn to be shipped F.O.B. seller's warehouse by Janson Truck Lines. Giant Food Distributors, by mistake, delivers 100 cases of Gold Giant corn to Janson Truck Lines. While in transit, the Gold Giant corn is stolen. Between Alberto's and Giant Food Distributors, who suffers the loss? Explain.

12-5. Chi Moy, a student, contracted to buy a television set from Ted's Electronics. Under the terms of the contract, Moy was to try out the set for thirty days, and, if he liked it, he was to pay for the set at the end of the thirty-day period. If he did not want to purchase the set after thirty days, he could return the TV to Ted's Electronics with no obligation. Ten days after Moy took the set home, the set was stolen from Moy's apartment, although Moy had not been negligent in his care of the set in any way. Ted's Electronics claimed that Moy had to pay for the stolen set. Moy argued that the risk of loss fell on Ted's Electronics. Which party prevailed?

12-6. Tony Mangum contracted to purchase a 580C Case backhoe and loader from Liles Brothers & Son on November 25, 1977. The sales price was $20,561. Mangum wrote two checks in payment for the machine, one for $3,000 dated November 25 and one for $17,561 postdated to December 2. Liles checked with Mangum's bank and learned that there were sufficient funds to cover the $3,000 check, and Mangum assured Liles that by December 2 there would be sufficient funds in his account to cover the second check. Three days later, Mangum, posing as a heavy-equipment sales representative, sold the equipment for $11,000 to Carl Wright, who operated a septic-tank service. Wright had been looking for a backhoe and knew the market price for this equipment was around $20,000. Wright paid for the equipment with a certified check. On December 2, Liles learned that Mangum did not have sufficient funds in his bank account to cover the check dated December 2 and that Mangum was in jail. When Liles discovered that the backhoe was in Wright's possession, he sought the return of the backhoe from Wright. Does Wright have valid title to the backhoe? Explain. [Liles Bros. & Son. v. Wright, 638 S.W.2d 383 (Tenn. 1982)]

12-7. Israel Martin contracted to purchase a truck and attached haystack mover for $35,389 from Melland's, Inc., a farm implement dealer. Martin was given a trade-in allowance of $17,389 on his purchase price, leaving a balance due of $18,000, plus $720 sales tax. Martin mailed Melland's the title to the old unit being traded in, but Melland's allowed Martin to continue to use the old unit until the new one was ready for delivery. While the old unit was still in Martin's possession, but after Melland's had received title to it, the equipment was destroyed by fire. There was no provision in the contract concerning insurance or risk of loss on the unit. Who bears the risk of loss, Martin or Melland's? [Martin v. Melland's, Inc., 283 N.W.2d 76 (N.D. 1979)]

12-8. Crump, a television fanatic, purchased a television antenna and antenna tower from Lair Distributing Company, with a ten-year conditional sales contract that obligated him to make monthly payments. The contract provided that Lair Company would retain title until Crump had completed all payments. The contract stated, among other things, that Crump was not to move or tamper with the antenna during the ten-year payment period. About a year later, lightning struck and destroyed Crump's antenna. At Crump's request, Lair Company performed extensive repairs on it. Crump refused to pay for the repairs, claiming that risk of loss or damage resulting from the lightning should be borne by Lair. Was Lair successful in suing for the cost of its repairs? [Lair Distributing Co. v. Crump, 48 Ala.App. 72, 261 So.2d 904 (1972)]

12-9. Isis Foods, Inc., located in St. Louis, wanted to purchase a shipment of food from Pocasset Food Sales, Inc. The sale of food was initiated by a purchase order from Isis stating that the shipment was to be made "F.O.B. St. Louis." Pocasset made the shipment by delivery of the goods to the carrier. Pocasset's invoices contained a provision stating: "Our liability ceases upon delivery of merchandise to carrier." The shipment of food was destroyed in transit before reaching St. Louis. Discuss which party has the risk of loss and why. [In re Isis Foods, Inc., 38 B.R. 48 (Bktcy.W.D.Mo. 1983)]

12-10. A new car owned by a New Jersey car rental agency was stolen in 1967. The agency collected the full price of the car from its insurance company, Home Indemnity Company, and assigned all its interest in the automobile to the insurer. Subsequently, the thief sold the car to an automobile wholesaler, who in turn sold it to a retail car dealer. Schrier purchased the car from the dealer without knowledge of the theft. Home Indemnity Insurance Company sued Schrier to recover the car. Can Home Indemnity recover? [Schrier v. Home Indemnity Co., 273 A.2d 248 (D.C. 1971)]

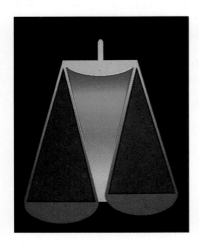

Chapter 13

Performance and Breach

Most sales contracts involve virtually no problems. There are billions of such contracts carried out every year without any difficulties in the United States. As Cicero stated centuries ago, the law is a "silent magistrate" governing the actions of individuals. Most people are aware of, and try to fulfill, their contractual obligations. The first part of this chapter deals with performance of contractual obligations under the Uniform Commercial Code.

Sometimes circumstances make it difficult for a person to carry out the performance promised, in which case the contract may be breached. When breach occurs, the aggrieved party looks for remedies—dealt with in the second half of the chapter.

❖ Good Faith and Commercial Reasonableness

To understand the performance required of a seller and buyer, one needs to know the duties and obligations each party has assumed under the terms of the contract. Keep in mind that "duties and obligations" under the terms of the contract include those specified in the agreement, those which are customary in the trade, and those required under the Code.

Sometimes the sales contract leaves open some particulars of performance and permits one of the parties to specify them. The obligations of "good faith" and "commercial reasonableness," however, underlie every sales contract within the UCC. They are obligations that can form the basis for a breach of contract suit later on. These standards are read into every contract, and they provide a framework in which the parties can specify particulars of performance. "Any such specification must be made in good faith and within limits set by commercial reasonableness." [UCC 2-311(1)]

GOOD FAITH
Honesty in fact; for a merchant, the observance of reasonable commercial standards of fair dealing.

These obligations must be read along with the Code's **good faith** provision, which can never be disclaimed. In all contracts, honesty in fact is a condition *precedent* to a contract, and good faith exists if a party can meet the subjective test of innocence—sometimes called the "white heart and empty head" test—when entering the contract. Merchants, however, are also held to an objective standard of observing reasonable commercial practices, and "good faith" in the case of a merchant means honesty in fact *and* the observance of reasonable commercial standards of fair dealing in the trade. [UCC 2-103(1)(b)]

Thus, when one party delays specifying particulars of performance for an unreasonable period of time or fails to cooperate with the other party, the innocent party is excused from any resulting delay in performance. In addition, the innocent party can proceed to perform in any reasonable manner. If the innocent party has performed as far as is reasonably possible under the circumstances, the other party's failure to specify particulars or to cooperate can be treated as a breach of contract.

Good faith can mean that one party must not take advantage of another party by manipulating contract terms. Good faith applies to both parties, even the nonbreaching party. The principle of good faith applies through both the performance and the enforcement of all agreements or duties within the contract. Good faith is a question of fact for the jury.

The following case illustrates an application of the "good faith" principle in business transactions.

Case 13.1
MASSEY-FERGUSON, INC. v. HELLAND
Appellate Court of Illinois, Second District, 1982.
105 Ill.App.3d 648, 61 Ill.Dec. 142, 434 N.E.2d 295.

FACTS Bennie Helland was a partner in Newark Trucking and Implement Company, a partnership dealing in the purchase of new and used farm equipment for resale to the public. In the course of his business, Helland bought about thirty pieces of new and used equipment from Colusa Farm Equipment, Inc. in the spring of 1981. Colusa had the previous year contracted with Massey-Ferguson, a farm-implement manufacturer, to become its dealer, and much of the equipment Colusa sold to Helland had been supplied to Colusa by Massey-Ferguson. Massey-Ferguson retained a security interest in each piece of equipment until Colusa paid for it. That is to say, Massey-Ferguson retained a right in the property in order to be sure that the full purchase price was paid by Colusa. According to the contract between Colusa and Massey-Ferguson, the latter would make bi-monthly inspections of Colusa's sales lot, and Colusa would have to account to Massey for any missing equipment. In the course of one such inspection, Massey's agent noted that $200,000 worth of equipment had been sold to Helland, but Colusa had not made any payment to Massey. Massey sought to collect from Colusa, and when Colusa would not pay, the dealership was terminated and Massey brought an action against Helland. Massey argued that its security interest in the goods entitled it to recovery of the equipment in question. The trial court ruled in Helland's favor, and Massey-Ferguson appealed.

ISSUE Can Massey-Ferguson recover the property from Helland, an innocent party who purchased the equipment in the ordinary course of his business and in good faith?

DECISION No. The trial court's judgment was affirmed. Massey-Ferguson was not entitled to recover the property from Helland.

REASON The court reasoned that, as Massey-Ferguson's authorized dealer, Colusa was expected to sell the equipment, and any buyer in the ordinary course of business could normally take the equipment free of Massey-Ferguson's security interest—as long as the purchase is made in good faith. Under the UCC, merchants are required to observe reasonable commercial standards of fair dealing in addition in honesty in fact. The court noted that Helland "had been in business for a period of more than twenty years and had dealt in, purchased and sold farm equipment and industrial equipment, and that his experience had given him an understanding of financing arrangements common to a manufacturer-dealership agreement." The court could find no evidence of bad faith or dishonesty on Helland's part or that he had acted at all unreasonably for a merchant.

❖ Performance of a Sales Contract

A seller has the basic obligation to *transfer and deliver conforming goods*. The buyer has the basic obligation to *accept and pay for conforming goods* in accordance with the contract. [UCC 2-301] Overall performance of a sales contract is controlled by the agreement between the buyer and the seller. When the contract is unclear and disputes arise, the courts look to the Code.

❖ Seller's Obligations

Tender of Delivery

Tender of delivery requires that the seller have and hold *conforming* goods at the buyer's disposal and give the buyer whatever notification is reasonably necessary to enable the buyer to take delivery. [UCC 2-503(1)]

Tender must occur at a *reasonable hour* and in a *reasonable manner*. In other words, a seller cannot call the buyer at 2:00 A.M. and say, "The goods are ready. I'll give you twenty minutes to get them." Unless the parties have agreed otherwise, the goods must be tendered for delivery at a reasonable time and kept available for a reasonable period of time to enable the buyer to take possession of them. [UCC 2-503(1)(a)]

All goods called for by a contract must be tendered in a single delivery unless the parties agree otherwise [UCC 2-612] or the circumstances are such that either party can rightfully request delivery in lots. [UCC 2-307] Hence, an order for 1,000 shirts cannot be delivered two at a time. If seller and buyer contemplate that the shirts be delivered in four orders of 250 each, as they are produced (for summer, winter, fall, and spring stock) and the price can be apportioned accordingly, it may be commercially reasonable to do so.

Place of Delivery

Noncarrier Cases If the contract does not designate where the goods are to be delivered, and the buyer is expected to pick them up, the place of delivery is the *seller's place of business* or, if the seller has none, the *seller's residence*. [UCC 2-308] If the contract involves the sale of *identified goods*, and the parties know when they enter into the contract that these goods are located somewhere other than at the seller's place of business (such as at a warehouse or in the possession of a bailee), then the *location of the goods* is the place for their delivery. [UCC 2-308]

For example, Rogers and Simonson live in San Francisco. In San Francisco, Rogers contracts to sell Simonson five used trucks, which both parties know are located in Chicago. If nothing more is specified in the contract, the place of delivery for the trucks is Chicago. Assume further that the trucks are stored in a warehouse and that Simonson will need some type of document to show the warehouse (bailee) in Chicago that Simonson is entitled to take possession of the five trucks. The seller "tenders delivery" without moving the goods. The seller may "deliver" by either giving the buyer a *negotiable document of title* or obtaining the *bailee's* (warehouse's) *acknowledgement* that the buyer is entitled to possession.[1]

Carrier Cases   In many instances, attendant circumstances or delivery terms in the contract make it apparent that the parties intend that a carrier be used to move the goods. There are two ways a seller can complete performance of the obligation to deliver the goods in carrier cases—through a shipment contract or through a destination contract.

1.   Shipment Contracts. A shipment contract requires or authorizes the seller to ship goods by a carrier. The contract does not require that the seller deliver the goods at a particular destination. [UCC 2-509 and 2-319] Unless otherwise agreed, the seller must:

(a) Put the goods into the hands of the carrier.
(b) Make a contract for their transportation that is reasonable according to the nature of the goods and their value. (For example, certain types of goods need refrigeration in transit.)
(c) Obtain and promptly deliver for tender to the buyer any documents necessary to enable the buyer to obtain possession of the goods from the carrier.
(d) Promptly notify the buyer that shipment has been made. [UCC 2-504]

If the seller fails to notify the buyer that shipment has been made or fails to make a proper contract for transportation, and a *material loss* of the goods or a *delay* results, the buyer can reject the shipment. Of course, the parties can agree that a lesser amount of loss or a delay will be grounds for rejection.

2.   Destination Contracts. Under a destination contract, the seller agrees to see that the goods will be duly tendered to the buyer at a particular destination. Once the goods arrive, the seller must tender the goods at a reasonable hour and hold conforming goods at the buyer's disposal for a reasonable length of time, giving appropriate notice. The seller must also provide the buyer with any documents of title necessary to enable the buyer to obtain delivery from the carrier. This is often done by tendering the documents through ordinary banking channels. Although not a part of the seller's tender, unless otherwise agreed, the buyer must furnish facilities reasonably suited for the receipt of the goods. [UCC 2-503]

The Perfect-Tender Rule

As previously noted, the seller has an obligation to ship or tender *conforming goods*, and this entitles the seller to acceptance by and payment from the buyer according to the terms of the contract. Under common law, the seller was obligated to deliver goods in conformity with the terms of the contract in every detail. This was called the *perfect tender* doctrine. The UCC (in Section 2-601) preserves the perfect-tender doctrine by stating that "if goods or tender of delivery fail *in any respect* to conform

---

1.   If the seller delivers a nonnegotiable document of title or merely writes instructions to the bailee to release the goods to the buyer without the bailee's *acknowledgment* of the buyer's rights, this is also a sufficient tender, unless the buyer objects. [UCC 2-503(4)] But risk of loss does not pass until the buyer has a reasonable amount of time in which to present the document or the instructions.

to the contract" (emphasis added), the buyer has the right to accept the goods, reject the entire shipment, or accept part and reject part.

For example, a buyer contracts to purchase 200 cases of Brand X carrots to be delivered at the buyer's place of business on or before October 1. On September 28 the seller discovers that there are only 180 cases of Brand X in inventory, but there will be another 500 cases within the next two weeks. So the seller tenders delivery of the 180 cases of Brand X on October 1, with the promise that the other cases will be delivered within three weeks. Since the seller failed to make a perfect tender of 200 cases of Brand X, the buyer has the right to reject the entire shipment and hold the seller in breach. (Such a rigid rule, however, seems uncharacteristic of the Code's philosophy of finding and preserving a contract whenever possible and inconsistent with the idea of good faith that permeates the Code generally.)

Exceptions to the Perfect-Tender Rule

There are several exceptions to the rule of perfect tender, some of which are discussed here.

Agreement of the Parties   If the parties have agreed, for example, that defective goods or parts will not be rejected if the seller is able to repair or replace them within a reasonable period of time, the perfect-tender rule does not apply.

CURE
The right of a party who tenders nonconforming performance to correct, without liability, his or her performance within the contract period.

Cure   The term **cure** is not specifically defined in the Code, but it refers to the seller's right to repair, adjust, or replace defective or nonconforming goods. [UCC 2-508] When any tender or delivery is rejected because of *nonconforming goods* and the time for performance has *not yet expired*, the seller can notify the buyer promptly of the intention to cure and can then do so *within the contract time for performance*. [UCC 2-508(1)] Once the time for performance under the contract has *expired*, the seller can still exercise the right to cure if the seller had *reasonable grounds to believe that the nonconforming tender would be acceptable to the buyer*. [UCC 2-508(2)]

Frequently, a seller will tender nonconforming goods with some type of price allowance, which serves as the "reasonable grounds" to believe the nonconforming tender will be acceptable to the buyer. Other reasons may also serve as the basis for a seller's assumption that a buyer may accept a nonconforming tender. For example, if in the past a buyer frequently allowed a particular substitute for a good when the good ordered was not available, the seller has reasonable grounds to believe the buyer will again accept such a substitute. If the buyer rejects the substitute good on this particular occasion, the seller nonetheless had "reasonable grounds to believe" that the substitute would be acceptable. Therefore, the seller can cure within a reasonable time, even though conforming delivery will occur after the actual time limit for performance allowed under the contract.

The seller's right to cure substantially restricts the buyer's right to reject. If the buyer refuses a tender of goods as nonconforming but does not disclose the nature of the defect to the seller, the buyer cannot later assert the defect as a defense if the defect is one that the seller could have cured. The buyer must act in good faith and state specific reasons for refusing to accept the goods. [UCC 2-605]

In the following case, a buyer rejected nonconforming goods but was held liable because the seller's "reasonable and timely offer to cure" was improperly rejected.

Case 13.2
T. W. OIL, INC. v. CONSOLIDATED EDISON COMPANY

Court of Appeals of New York, 1982.
57 N.Y.2d 574, 457 N.Y.S.2d 458, 443 N.E.2d 932.

FACTS In January 1974, T. W. Oil, Inc., the plaintiff, purchased fuel oil that was still at sea on the tanker *M. T. Khamsin.* The oil company then contracted to sell to Consolidated Edison (Con Ed), the defendant, this cargo of oil, with delivery to take place between January 24 and January 30. When the plaintiff purchased the oil shipment, it received a certificate from the foreign refinery that stated the sulfur content of the oil was .52 percent. When the oil company then contracted with Con Ed to sell the oil to the latter, the oil company specified that the sulfur content was .5 percent, rounding off the .52 percent, as was the custom in the trade. During the negotiations with Con Ed, the oil company learned that Con Ed was authorized to buy and burn oil with a sulfur content of up to 1 percent and would mix oils containing more and less than that to maintain that figure.

When the *Khamsin* oil shipment arrived, its sulfur content tested out to be .92 percent. On February 14 Con Ed rejected the shipment. The oil company offered a reduced price, which was rejected by Con Ed on February 20. The next day, T. W. Oil offered to cure with a substitute shipment of conforming oil on a tanker due to arrive on February 28. On February 21, Con Ed rejected the offer to cure. T. W. Oil sued for breach of contract, and the trial court held for the plaintiff T. W. Oil in the sum of $1,285,512.83, holding that the plaintiff's "reasonable and timely offer to cure" was improperly rejected. The defendant, Con Ed appealed.

ISSUE Was Con Ed required to accept the substitute shipment tendered by T. W. Oil?

DECISION Yes. The trial court's ruling was affirmed.

REASON The court focused on UCC 2-508(2) which states, "Where the buyer rejects a non-conforming tender which the seller had reasonable grounds to believe would be acceptable with or without money allowance the seller may if he seasonably notifies the buyer have a further reasonable time to substitute a conforming tender." There was no question that the buyer had rejected a nonconforming shipment—the .92 percent sulfur content of the *Khamsin* oil did not conform to the .5 percent specified in the contract. Although the tender was non-conforming, T. W. Oil had reason to believe Con Ed would accept it, with a money allowance being made, because of knowledge acquired during contract negotiations to the effect that Con Ed burned fuel with a content of up to 1 percent. Further, T. W. Oil had seasonably notified the buyer (the day after Con Ed had rejected the *Khamsin* oil) that it would substitute a conforming tender as soon as the tanker at sea arrived. In view of these facts, the court concluded that "it is almost impossible, given the flexibility of the Uniform Commercial Code definitions of 'seasonable' and 'reasonable' . . . to quarrel with the finding that the . . . requirements of the statute had been met and that Con Ed was obligated to accept the substitute shipment tendered by T. W. Oil."

Substitution of Carriers When an agreed manner of delivery (berthing, loading, or unloading facilities) becomes impracticable or unavailable through no fault of either party, but a commercially reasonable substitute is available, this substitute performance is sufficient tender to the buyer. [UCC 2-614(1)]

For example, a sales contract calls for the delivery of a large piece of machinery to be shipped by Roadway Trucking Corporation on or before June 1. The contract terms clearly state the importance of the delivery date. The employees of Roadway Trucking go on strike. The seller will be entitled to make a reasonable substitute tender, perhaps by mail. Note that the seller here is responsible for any additional shipping costs, unless contrary arrangements have been made in the sales contract.

Installment Contracts An **installment contract** is a single contract that requires or authorizes delivery in two or more separate lots to be accepted and paid for separately.

INSTALLMENT CONTRACT
A contract whereby payments due are made periodically. Also may allow for delivery of goods in separate lots with payment made for each.

In an installment contract, a buyer can reject an installment *only if the nonconformity substantially impairs the value* of the installment and cannot be cured. [UCC 2-612(2) and 2-307] Notice, then, how this is a substantial limitation on the perfect tender rule.

The entire installment contract is breached only when one or more nonconforming installments *substantially* impair the value of the *whole contract*. If the buyer subsequently accepts a nonconforming installment and fails to notify the seller of cancellation, the contract is reinstated, however. Also, if the buyer brings an action with respect only to past installments or demands performance as to future installments, the aggrieved party has reinstated the contract. [UCC 2-612(3)]

A major issue to be determined is what constitutes substantial impairment of the "value of the whole." For example, consider an installment contract for the sale of twenty carloads of plywood. The first carload does not conform to the contract because 9 percent of the plywood deviates from the thickness specifications. The buyer cancels the contract, and immediately thereafter the second and third carloads of plywood arrive at the buyer's place of business. The court would have to grapple with the question of whether the 9 percent of nonconforming plywood substantially impaired the value of the whole.[2]

The point to remember is that the UCC substantially alters the right of a buyer to reject the entire contract in installment sales contracts. Such contracts are broadly defined in the UCC, which strictly limits rejection to cases of substantial nonconformity.

Commercial Impracticability   Whenever occurrences unforeseen by either party when the contract was made make performance commercially impracticable, the rule of perfect tender no longer holds. According to UCC 2-615(a), delay in delivery or nondelivery in whole or in part is not a breach when performance has been made impracticable "by the occurrence of a contingency the nonoccurrence of which was a basic assumption on which the contract was made. . . ." The seller must, however, notify the buyer as soon as practicable that there will be a delay or nondelivery.

The notion of commercial impracticability is derived from contract-law theories of impossibility and frustration of purpose.[3] An increase in cost resulting from inflation does not in and of itself excuse performance, since this kind of risk is ordinarily assumed by a seller conducting business. The unforeseen contingency must be one that would have been impossible to contemplate in a given business situation.

For example, a major oil company that receives its supplies from the Middle East has a contract to supply a buyer with 100,000 gallons of oil. Because of an oil embargo by the Organization of Petroleum Exporting Companies (OPEC), the seller is prevented from securing oil supplies to meet the terms of the contract. Because of the same embargo, the seller cannot secure oil from any other source. This situation comes fully under the commercial-impracticability exception to the perfect-tender doctrine.

Sometimes the unforeseen event only *partially* affects the seller's capacity to perform, and the seller is thus able to fulfill the contract *partially* but cannot tender total performance. In this event, the seller is required to allocate in a fair and

---

2.   Continental Forest Products, Inc. v. White Lumber Sales, Inc., 256 Or. 466, 474 P.2d 1 (1970). The court held that the deviation did not substantially impair the value of the whole contract. Additionally, the court stated that the nonconformity could be cured by an adjustment in the price.

3.   See "Discharge by Impossibility of Performance" in Chapter 9.

reasonable manner any remaining production and deliveries among the contracted customers. The buyer must receive notice of the allocation, with the obvious right to accept or reject the allocation.

For example, a Florida orange grower, Best Citrus, Inc., contracts to sell this season's production to a number of customers, including Martin's grocery chain. Martin's contracts to purchase 2,000 crates of oranges. Best Citrus has sprayed *some* of its orange groves with a chemical called Karmoxin. The Department of Agriculture discovers there is a potential danger that persons who eat products sprayed with Karmoxin may develop cancer. An order prohibiting the sale of these products is effected. Best Citrus picks all the oranges not sprayed with Karmoxin, but the quantity does not fully meet all the contracted-for deliveries. In this case, Best Citrus is required to allocate its production, notifying Martin's that it cannot deliver the full quantity agreed upon in the contract and specifying the amount it will be able to deliver under the circumstances. Martin's can either accept or reject the allocation, but Best has no further contractual liability.

Can unanticipated increases in a seller's costs, which make the seller's performance "impracticable," constitute a valid defense to performance on the basis of commercial impracticability? The court deals with this question in the following case.

Case 13.3
MAPLE FARMS, INC. v. CITY SCHOOL DISTRICT OF ELMIRA
Superior Court of New York, 1974.
76 Misc.2d 1080, 352 N.Y.S.2d 784.

FACTS   In June of 1973, Maple Farms, Inc. formed an agreement with the school district to supply the school district with milk for the 1973–1974 school year. The agreement was in the form of a requirements contract, whereby Maple Farms would sell to the school district all the milk the district required at a fixed price—which was the June market price of milk. By December of 1973, however, the price of raw milk had increased by 23 percent over the price specified in the contract. This meant that if the terms of the contract were fulfilled, Maple Farms would lose $7,350. Because it had similar contracts with other school districts, Maple Farms stood to lose a great deal if it was held to the price stated in the contracts. When the school district would not agree to release Maple Farms from its contract, Maple Farms brought an action for a declaratory judgment. It contended that the price of raw milk was an event not contemplated by the parties when the contract was formed, and that, given the in-

creased price, performance of the contract was commercially impracticable.

ISSUE   Can Maple Farms be released from the contract on the grounds of commercial impracticability?

DECISION   No. The court ruled that performance in this case was not impracticable.

REASON   The court reasoned that commercial impracticability arises when an event occurs that is totally unexpected and unforeseeable by the parties. The increased price in raw milk was not totally unexpected, given the fact that in the previous year the price of milk had risen 10 percent and that the price of milk had traditionally varied. Also, the general inflation of prices in the United States should have been anticipated. Maple Farms had reason to know these facts and could have placed a clause in its contract with the school district to protect itself from its present situation. The court also noted that the primary purpose of the contract, on the part of the school district, was to protect itself (for budgeting purposes) against price fluctuations.

Destruction of Identified Goods   The Code provides that when a casualty totally destroys *identified goods* under a sales contract through no fault of either party and *before risk passes to the buyer*, the seller and buyer are excused from performance. [UCC 2-613(a)] If the goods are only partially destroyed, however, the buyer can inspect them and either treat the contract as void or accept the damaged goods with a reduction of the contract price.

Consider an example. Atlas Appliances has on display six Model X dishwashers, a model that has been discontinued. Five are white, and one is harvest gold. No others of that model are available. Rivers, who is not a merchant, clearly specifies that she needs the harvest-gold dishwasher because it fits her kitchen's color scheme, and she buys it. Before Atlas can deliver the dishwasher, it is destroyed by a fire. In such a case, under Section 2-613, Atlas Appliances is not liable to Rivers for failing to deliver the harvest-gold dishwasher. The goods suffered a casualty without fault of either party, before the risk of loss passed to the buyer. The loss was total, so the contract is avoided. Clearly, Atlas has no obligation to tender that dishwasher and Rivers has no obligation to pay for it.

❖ Buyer's Obligations

Once the seller has adequately tendered delivery, the buyer is obligated to accept the goods and pay for them according to the terms of the contract. In the absence of any specific agreements, the buyer must:

1. Furnish facilities reasonably suited for receipt of the goods. [UCC 2-503(1)(b)]
2. Make payment at the time and place the buyer *receives* the goods, even if the place of shipment is the place of delivery. [UCC 2-310(a)]

Payment

When a sale is made on credit, the buyer is obliged to pay according to credit terms (for example, 60, 90, or 120 days), *not* when the goods are received. The credit period usually begins on the *date of shipment*. [UCC 2-310(d)]

Payment can be made by any means agreed upon between the parties—cash or any other method generally acceptable in the commercial world. If the seller demands cash when the buyer offers a check, credit card, or the like, the seller must permit the buyer reasonable time to obtain legal tender. [UCC 2-511]

Right of Inspection

Unless otherwise agreed, or for C.O.D. (collect on delivery) goods, the buyer's right to inspect the goods is absolute. This right allows the buyer to verify, before making payment, that the goods tendered or delivered are what are contracted for or ordered. If the goods are not what the buyer ordered, there is no duty to pay. *An opportunity for inspection is therefore a condition precedent to the seller's right to enforce payment.* [UCC 2-513(1)]

Unless otherwise agreed, inspection can take place at any reasonable place and time and in any reasonable manner. Generally, what is reasonable is determined by custom of the trade, past practices of the parties, and the like. The Code also provides for inspection after arrival when goods are to be shipped. Costs of inspecting conforming goods are borne by the buyer unless agreed otherwise. [UCC 2-513(2)]

C.O.D. Shipments If a seller ships goods to a buyer C.O.D. (or under similar terms) and the buyer has not agreed to a C.O.D. shipment in the contract, the buyer can rightfully *reject* them. This is because C.O.D. does not permit inspection before payment, which is a denial of the buyer's right of inspection. But when the buyer has agreed to a C.O.D. shipment in the contract or has agreed to pay for the goods upon the presentation of a bill of lading, no right of inspection exists because it was negated by the agreement. [UCC 2-513(3)]

Payment Due—Documents of Title Under certain contracts, payment is due on the receipt of the required documents of title even though the goods themselves may not have arrived at their destination. With C.I.F. and C.&F. contracts (see Exhibit 12-1 in Chapter 12), payment is required upon receipt of the documents unless the parties have agreed otherwise. Thus, payment is required prior to inspection, and it must be made unless the buyer knows that the goods are nonconforming. [UCC 2-310(b) and 2-513(3)]

Acceptance

The buyer can manifest assent to the delivered goods in the following three ways, each of which constitutes acceptance.

1.   The buyer can expressly accept the shipment by words or conduct. For example, there is an acceptance if the buyer, after having reasonable opportunity to inspect, signifies agreement to the seller that either the goods are conforming or they are acceptable despite their nonconformity. [UCC 2-606(1)(a)]
2.   Acceptance is presumed if the buyer has had a reasonable opportunity to inspect the goods and has failed to reject them within a reasonable period of time. [UCC 2-606(1)(b) and 2-602(1)]
3.   The buyer accepts the goods by performing any act inconsistent with the seller's ownership. For example, any use or resale of the goods generally constitutes an acceptance. Limited use for the sole purpose of testing or inspecting the goods is not an acceptance, however. [UCC 2-606(1)(c)]

Revocation of Acceptance

Acceptance of the goods by the buyer precludes the buyer from exercising the right of rejection. Acceptance does not in and of itself impair the right of the buyer to pursue remedies (discussed later in this chapter). But if the buyer accepts the non-conforming goods and fails to notify the seller of the breach when it is discovered (or when it should have been discovered), the buyer is barred from pursuing any remedy against the seller. In other words, the buyer must inform the seller of the breach within a reasonable time. The burden is on the buyer to establish the existence of a breach of contract once the goods are accepted. [UCC 2-607(3)]

After a buyer accepts a lot or a commercial unit, acceptance can still be revoked if the nonconformity *substantially* impairs the value of the unit or lot and if one of the following factors is present:

1.   If acceptance was predicated on the reasonable assumption that the nonconformity would be cured, and it has not been cured within a reasonable period of time. [UCC 2-608(1)(a)]

2. If the buyer does not discover the nonconformity, either because it is difficult to discover before acceptance or because the seller's assurance that the goods are conforming kept the buyer from inspecting the goods. [UCC 2-608(1)(a)]

Revocation of acceptance is not effective until notice is given to the seller, which must occur within a reasonable time after the buyer either discovers *or should have discovered* the grounds for revocation. Also, revocation must occur before the goods have undergone any substantial change not caused by their own defects (such as spoilage). [UCC 2-608(2)]

The requirements for revocation of acceptance are summarized in *Inniss v. Methot Buick-Opel, Inc.*, a case presented on pages 13–15 in Chapter 1.

If some of the goods delivered do not conform to the contract, and the seller has failed to cure, the buyer can make a *partial* acceptance. [UCC 2-601(c)] The same is true if the nonconformity was not reasonably discoverable before acceptance. A buyer cannot accept less than a single *commercial unit*, however. According to Section 2-105, *commercial unit* means a unit of goods that, by commercial usage, is viewed as a "single whole" for purposes of sale, division of which would materially impair the character of the unit, its market value, or its use. A commercial unit can be a single article (such as a machine), or a set of articles (such as a suite of furniture or an assortment of sizes), or a quantity (such as a bale, a gross, or a carload), or any other unit treated in the trade as a single whole.

❖ Anticipatory Repudiation

The buyer and seller have *concurrent* conditions of performance. But what if, before the time for either performance, one party clearly communicates to the other the intention not to perform? Such an action is a breach of the contract by *anticipatory repudiation*—the focus of the "Landmark" in this chapter. When anticipatory repudiation occurs, the aggrieved party can, according to UCC 2-610:

1. For a commercially reasonable time, await performance by the repudiating party.
2. Resort to any remedy for breach even if the aggrieved party has notified the repudiating party that he or she awaits the latter's performance and has urged retraction.
3. In either case, *suspend performance* or proceed in accordance with the provisions of this Article on the seller's right to identify goods to the contract notwithstanding breach or to salvage unfinished goods. [Emphasis added.]

The key to anticipatory breach is that the repudiation takes place *prior* to the time the party is required under contract to tender performance. The nonbreaching party has a choice of two responses. He or she can treat the repudiation as a final breach by pursuing a remedy; or he or she can wait, hoping that the repudiating party will decide to honor the obligations required by the contract despite the avowed intention to renege.

Should the latter course be pursued, the Code permits the breaching party (subject to some limitations) to "retract" his or her repudiation. The retraction can be by any

Landmark in the Law

Hochster v. De La Tour (1853)

When, prior to the time for performance, one party to a contract clearly communicates to the other the intention not to perform, this action is an *anticipatory repudiation* or *anticipatory breach* of the contract. As discussed in the text, both in this chapter and earlier in Chapter 9, when this occurs, the nonbreaching party is permitted to sue for damages immediately, instead of waiting until the time that performance is due to begin.

The leading case on anticipatory repudiation, *Hochster v. De La Tour*, was decided in England in 1853.[1] The facts were as follows: De La Tour made an employment contract with Hochster in April of 1852 to employ Hochster as a courier for the months of June, July, and August. Hochster's performance was to begin on June 1. On May 11, De La Tour told Hochster, "I am going abroad this summer and will not need a courier." In view of De La Tour's anticipatory breach of their employment contract, Hochster, on May 22, brought an action against De La Tour for damages.

De La Tour's attorney maintained that Hochster could not sue for damages as no "breach" could possibly occur before the scheduled time for performance—June 1. According to De La Tour's attorney, Hochster had two choices: He could agree to rescind (cancel) the contract, therefore forfeiting his right to damages; or he could wait until June 1, standing "ready and willing" to work for De La Tour, and then bring an action for breach. Hochster was thus caught in a conflict: He could either forgo employment

with anyone else until June 1 (and he had been offered a job elsewhere, to begin on May 22) so he could sue for damages, *or* agree to rescind the contract and forfeit his cause of action against De La Tour.

According to legal scholar Arthur Corbin, it was this rigid set of exclusive alternatives posed by De La Tour's attorney that caused the court to enunciate the doctrine of anticipatory repudiation. It would have been in keeping with the legal practice of the time had Hochster been given a third alternative by De La Tour: that of being legally free to look for and accept other work prior to June 1 *without* at the same time forfeiting a potential suit for damages.[2] In any event, given these circumstances, Lord Chief Justice Campbell made the following decision:

> If it should be held that, upon a contract to do an act on a future day, a renunciation of the contract by one party dispenses with a condition to be performed in the meantime by the other, there seems no reason for requiring that other to wait till the day arrives before seeking his remedy by action. And the only ground on which the condition can be dispensed with seems to be that the renunciation may be treated as a breach of the contract.

The doctrine of anticipatory repudiation creates efficiency in the sense that the nonbreaching party is free to sue for damages on the breached contract and at the same time to look for another contract whereby the damages may be mitigated. *Hochster v. De La Tour* became a precedent in contract law. Also, remedies for anticipatory breach of contract have been incorporated into the Uniform Commercial Code.[3] The aggrieved party's rights in situations where the other party has breached a contract by anticipatory repudiation are discussed in this chapter.

1. 2 Ellis and Blackburn Reports 678 (1853).

2. 6 Corbin on Contracts, Section 960.
3. UCC 2-610, 2-611.

method that clearly indicates an intent to perform. Once retraction is made, the rights of the repudiating party under the contract are reinstated. [UCC 2-611]

❖ Remedies of the Seller

There are numerous remedies available to a seller when the buyer is in breach under the UCC, many of which follow.

"Want of right and remedy are in one equipage."

Sir Edward Coke, 1552–1634
(British jurist and legal scholar)

The Right to Withhold Delivery

In general, sellers can withhold or discontinue performance of their obligations under a sales contract when buyers are in breach. If the breach results from the buyer's insolvency, the seller can refuse to deliver the goods unless the buyer pays in cash. [UCC 2-702(1)]

Consider an example. On September 1, Barton receives an order from Caruthers for ten cases of copier paper, to be shipped on September 13. Caruthers wants the goods put on his thirty-day open account. On September 6, Caruthers files involuntary bankruptcy. On September 9, Barton learns of the buyer's bankruptcy and therefore refuses to ship the goods on September 13. The court-appointed trustee of Caruthers's assets now claims that Barton has breached his contract with Caruthers by not shipping the goods on September 13 as agreed. The trustee will not prevail because Barton was under no obligation to ship goods on credit to an insolvent buyer. The trustee, of course, could still obtain the goods for the benefit of Caruthers's bankrupt estate by paying cash for them.

If a buyer has wrongfully rejected or revoked acceptance, failed to make proper and timely payment, or repudiated a part of the contract, the seller can withhold delivery of the goods in question. Furthermore, the seller can withhold the entire undelivered balance of the goods if the buyer's breach is material. [UCC 2-703]

The Right to Stop Delivery of Goods in Transit

If the seller has delivered the goods to a carrier or a bailee, but the buyer has not as yet received them, the goods are said to be *in transit*. If the seller learns of the buyer's insolvency while the goods are in transit, the seller can stop the carrier or bailee from delivering the goods to the buyer on the basis of the buyer's insolvency, regardless of the quantity shipped. A person is insolvent under the UCC when that person ceases to pay "his debts in the ordinary course of business or cannot pay his debts as they become due or is insolvent within the meaning of the federal bankruptcy law." [UCC 1-201(23)]

If the buyer is not insolvent but repudiates the contract or gives the seller some other right to withhold or reclaim the goods, the seller can stop the goods in transit only if the quantity shipped is at least a carload, a truckload, a planeload, or a larger shipment. In order to stop delivery, the seller must *timely notify* the carrier or other bailee that the goods are to be returned or held for the seller. If the carrier has sufficient time to stop delivery, the goods must be held and delivered according to the instructions of the seller, who is liable to the carrier for any additional costs incurred. A carrier that fails to act properly is liable to the seller for any loss. [UCC 2-705(3)]

The right of the seller to stop delivery of goods in transit is lost when:

1. The buyer obtains possession of the goods.
2. The carrier acknowledges the buyer's rights by reshipping or storing the goods for the buyer.
3. A bailee of the goods other than a carrier acknowledges that he or she is holding the goods for the buyer.
4. A negotiable document of title covering the goods has been negotiated to the buyer. [UCC 2-705(2)]

The Right to Reclaim Goods in the Possession of an Insolvent Buyer

If a seller discovers that the buyer has *received* goods on credit and is insolvent, the seller can demand return of the goods, if such demand is made within ten days of the buyer's receipt of the goods. The seller can demand and reclaim the goods at any time if the buyer misrepresented his or her solvency in writing within three months prior to the delivery of the goods. [UCC 2-702(2)]

The seller's right to reclaim, however, is subject to the rights of a good-faith purchaser or other buyer in the ordinary course of business who purchases the goods from the buyer before the seller reclaims.[4]

Successful reclamation of goods under the UCC constitutes preferential treatment as against the buyer's other creditors—the seller need only demand the return of the goods within ten days after the buyer has received them.[5] Because of this preferential treatment, the Code provides that reclamation *bars* the seller from pursuing any other remedy as to these goods. [UCC 2-702(3)]

The Right to Identify and/or Resell Goods after the Buyer's Breach

Sometimes a buyer breaches or repudiates a sales contract while the seller is still in possession of finished or partially manufactured goods. In this event, the seller can identify to the contract the conforming goods that are still in his or her possession or control, even if they were not identified at the time of the breach. Then the seller can resell the goods, holding the buyer liable for any loss. [UCC 2-704]

When the goods contracted for are unfinished at the time of breach, the seller can do one of two things: (1) cease manufacturing the goods and resell them for scrap or salvage value, or (2) complete the manufacture, identify the goods to the contract, and resell them—holding the buyer liable for any deficiency. In choosing between these two alternatives, the seller must exercise reasonable commercial judgment in order to mitigate the loss and obtain maximum realization of value from the unfinished goods. [UCC 2-704(2)]

When a seller possesses or controls the goods at the time of the buyer's breach, or rightfully reacquires the goods by stopping them in transit, the seller has the right to resell the goods. The resale must be made in good faith and in a commercially reasonable manner. The seller can recover any deficiency between the sales price and the contract price, along with **incidental damages,** defined as those costs to the seller resulting from the breach. [UCC 2-706(1) and UCC 2-710]

The resale can be private or public, and the goods can be sold as a unit or in parcels. The seller must give the original buyer reasonable notice of the resale, unless the goods are perishable or will rapidly decline in value. [UCC 2-706(2) and 2-706(3)] In the latter case, the seller has a duty to resell the goods as rapidly as possible in order to mitigate damages. A bona fide purchaser in a resale takes the goods free of

INCIDENTAL DAMAGES
Damages resulting from a breach of contract, including all reasonable expenses incurred because of the breach.

---

4.   A *buyer in the ordinary course of business* is a person who, in good faith and without knowledge that the sale violates the ownership rights or security interest of a third party, buys in ordinary course from a person (other than a pawnbroker) in the business of selling goods of that kind. [UCC 1-201(9)]

5.   This remedy is extemely important should the buyer go through bankruptcy. The 1978 Bankruptcy Reform Act as amended provides that the rights of the trustee are "subject to any statutory right or common law right of a seller . . . if the debtor has received such goods while insolvent."

any of the rights of the original buyer, even if the seller fails to comply with these requirements of the Code. [UCC 2-706(5)]

In the following case, after the buyer repudiated a contract, the seller sold the goods and sued the buyer on the original contract for the difference between the contract price and the price received from the sale.

Case 13.4
SERVBEST FOODS, INC. v. EMESSEE INDUSTRIES, INC.
Appellate Court of Illinois, 1980.
82 Ill. App. 3d 662, 37 Ill. Dec. 945, 403 N.E.2d 1.

FACTS   Servbest Foods had a contract with Emessee whereby Emessee was to purchase 200,000 pounds of beef trimmings from Servbest at 52.5 cents per pound. Servbest delivered to Emessee the warehouse receipts and invoices for the beef trimmings. The price of beef trimmings then fell significantly, and Emessee returned the documents to Servbest and canceled the contract. Servbest then sold the beef trimmings for 20.25 cents per pound and sued Emessee for damages (the difference between the contract price and the market price at which it had been forced to sell the trimmings) for breach of

contract, plus incidental damages. The trial court ruled for Servbest, and Emessee appealed.

ISSUE   Should Emessee be required to pay damages in this case?

DECISION   Yes. The judgment of the trial court was affirmed.

REASON   The court concluded that one of the options open to a seller when a buyer wrongfully repudiates a contract is to sell the goods at the most reasonable price attainable and collect from the repudiating party the difference between this price and the price stated in the contract. Since the seller had made a timely and commercially reasonable resale in this case, it was entitled to the damages awarded by the trial court.

The Right to Recover the Purchase Price Plus Incidental Damages

Before the UCC was adopted, a seller could not sue for the purchase price of the goods unless title had passed to the buyer. Under the Code, an unpaid seller can bring an action to recover the purchase price and incidental damages, but only under one of the following unusual circumstances:

1.   When the buyer has accepted the goods and has not revoked acceptance, in which case title would have passed to the buyer.
2.   When conforming goods have been lost or damaged after the risk of loss has passed to the buyer.
3.   When the buyer has breached after the goods have been identified to the contract and the seller is unable to resell the goods. [UCC 2-709(1)]

An action to recover the purchase price and incidental damages, available to the seller only under the circumstances just described, is different from an action to recover damages for breach of the sales contract. If a seller sues for the contract price of goods that he or she has been unable to resell, the goods must be held for the buyer. The seller can resell at any time prior to collection (of the judgment) from the buyer, but the net proceeds from the sale must be credited to the buyer. This is an example of the duty to mitigate damages.

For example, suppose Southern Realty contracts with Gem Point, Inc. to purchase 1,000 pens with Southern Realty's name inscribed on them. Gem Point delivers the 1,000 pens, but Southern Realty refuses to pay. Or suppose Gem Point tenders the 1,000 pens to Southern Realty, but Southern Realty refuses to accept them. In either case, Gem Point has, as a proper remedy, an action for the purchase price. In the first situation, Southern Realty accepted conforming goods, but by failing to pay, it is in breach. In the second case, the goods have been identified to the contract, but it is obvious that Gem Point could not sell to anyone else the pens inscribed with the buyer's realty name. Thus, both situations fall under UCC 2-709.

The Right to Recover Damages for the Buyer's Wrongful Repudiation

If a buyer repudiates a contract or wrongfully refuses to accept the goods, a seller can maintain an action to recover the damages that were sustained. Ordinarily, the amount of damages equals the difference between the contract price and the market price (at the time and place of tender of the goods) plus incidental damages. [UCC 2-708(1)] The time and place of tender are frequently given by such terms as F.O.B., F.A.S., C.I.F., and the like, which determine whether there is a shipment or destination contract.

If the difference between the contract price and the market price is too small to place the seller in the position that he or she would have been in if the buyer had fully performed, the proper measure of damages is the seller's lost profits, including a reasonable allowance for overhead and other incidental expenses. [UCC 2-708(2)]

The Right to Cancel the Sales Contract

A seller can cancel a contract if the buyer wrongfully rejects or revokes acceptance of conforming goods, fails to make proper payment, or repudiates the contract in part or in whole. The contract can be canceled with respect to the goods directly involved, or the entire contract can be canceled if the breach is material. A material breach is one that substantially impairs the value of the entire contract. [UCC 2-703]

The seller must *notify* the buyer of the cancellation, and at that point all remaining obligations of the seller are discharged. The buyer is not discharged from all remaining obligations but is in breach and can be sued under any of the subsections mentioned in UCC 2-703 and UCC 2-106(4).

If the seller's cancellation is not justified, the seller is in breach of the contract, and the buyer can sue for appropriate damages.

❖ Remedies of the Buyer

Under the UCC, there are numerous remedies available to the buyer. We treat many of them here.

The Right to Reject
Nonconforming or Improperly Delivered Goods

If either the goods or the seller's tender of the goods fails to conform to the contract *in any respect*, the buyer can reject the goods. If some of the goods conform to the contract, the buyer can keep the conforming goods and reject the rest. [UCC 2-601]

Timeliness and Reason for Rejection Required   Goods must be rejected within a reasonable amount of time and the seller must be seasonably notified. [UCC 2-602] Furthermore, the buyer must designate defects that are ascertainable by reasonable inspection. Failure to do so precludes the buyer from using such defects to justify rejection or to establish breach when the seller could have cured the defects if they had been stated seasonably. [UCC 2-605] After rejecting the goods, the buyer cannot exercise any right of ownership over them. If the buyer acts inconsistently with the seller's ownership rights, the buyer is deemed to have accepted the goods. [UCC 2-606]

Merchant Buyer's Duties When Goods Are Rejected   If a *merchant buyer* rightfully rejects goods, and the seller has no agent or business at the place of rejection, the buyer is required to follow any reasonable instructions received from the seller with respect to the goods controlled by the buyer. The buyer is entitled to reimbursement for the care and cost entailed in following the instructions. [UCC 2-603] The same requirements hold if the buyer rightfully revokes his or her acceptance of the goods at some later time. [UCC 2-608(3)]

   If no instructions are forthcoming and the goods are perishable or threaten to decline in value quickly, the buyer can resell the goods in good faith, taking the appropriate reimbursement from the proceeds. [UCC 2-603(1)] If the goods are not perishable, the buyer may store them for the seller's account or reship them to the seller. [UCC 2-604]

The Right to Recover
Identified Goods from an Insolvent Seller

If a buyer has made a partial or full payment for goods that remain in the possession of the seller, the buyer can recover the goods if the seller becomes insolvent within ten days after receiving the first payment and if the goods are identified to the contract. To exercise this right, the buyer must tender to the seller any unpaid balance of the purchase price. [UCC 2-502]

The Right to Obtain Specific Performance

A buyer can obtain specific performance when the goods are unique or when the buyer's remedy at law is inadequate. [UCC 2-716(1)] Ordinarily, a suit for money damages is sufficient to place a buyer in the position he or she would have occupied if the seller had fully performed. When the contract is for the purchase of a particular work of art, a patent, a copyright, or a similarly unique item, however, money damages may not be sufficient. Under these circumstances, equity will require that the seller perform exactly (a remedy of specific performance) by delivering the particular goods identified to the contract.

   For example, Sutherlin contracts to sell his antique car to Fenwick for $30,000, with delivery and payment due on June 14. Fenwick tenders payment on June 14, but Sutherlin refuses to deliver. Since the antique car is unique, Fenwick can probably obtain specific performance of the contract from Sutherlin.

The Right to Replevy Goods

Replevin is an action to recover specific goods in the hands of a breaching party who is unlawfully withholding them from the other party. The buyer can replevy goods *identified* to the contract if the seller has repudiated or breached the contract. *Additionally,* buyers must usually show that they are *unable to cover* for the goods after a reasonable effort; that is, unable to buy what is needed from another seller when the original one does not make good on a sale. [UCC 2-716(3)]

Consider the following example. On July 1, Woods contracts to sell her tomato crop to Creighton, with delivery and payment due on August 10. By August 1, it is clear that the local tomato crop will be bad and that the price of tomatoes is going to rise. Woods contracts to sell her tomato crop to De Valle for a higher price and then informs Creighton that she will not deliver on August 10 as agreed. Creighton indicates that cover is unavailable and that he is therefore going to bring a replevin action against Woods to force her to deliver the tomatoes to Creighton on August 10.

This replevin action will succeed. Although a tomato crop is not unique, a buyer of scarce goods for which no cover is available has a right to replevin. In a more typical season (when tomato crops thrive) cover would probably have been available and Creighton would have been limited to an action for damages.

REPLEVIN
An action in equity brought in order to recover possession of personal property unlawfully held by another.

The Right to Retain and
Enforce a Security Interest in the Goods

Buyers who rightfully reject goods or who justifiably revoke acceptance of goods that remain in their possession or control have a security interest in the goods (basically, a lien to recover expenses, costs, and the like). The security interest encompasses any payments the buyer has made for the goods as well as any expenses incurred with regard to inspection, receipt, transportation, care, and custody of the goods. [UCC 2-711(3)] A buyer with a security interest in the goods is a "person in the position of a seller." This gives the buyer the same rights as an unpaid seller. Thus, the buyer can resell, withhold delivery, or stop delivery of the goods. A buyer who chooses to resell must account to the seller for any amounts received in excess of the security interest. [UCC 2-711 and 2-706(6)]

The Right to Cancel the Contract

When a seller fails to make proper delivery or repudiates the contract, the buyer can cancel or rescind the contract. In addition, a buyer who has rightfully rejected or revoked acceptance of the goods can cancel or rescind that portion of the contract directly involved in the breach. If the seller's breach is material and substantially impairs the value of the whole contract, the buyer can cancel or rescind the whole contract. Upon notice of cancellation, the buyer is relieved of any further obligations under the contract but still retains all remedy rights that can be assessed against the seller.

The Right of Cover

In certain situations, buyers can protect themselves by obtaining *cover*, that is, by substituting goods for those which were due under the sales contract. This option is available to a buyer who has rightfully rejected goods or revoked acceptance. It is also available where the seller repudiates the contract or fails to deliver the goods. In obtaining cover, the buyer must act in good faith and without unreasonable delay. [UCC 2-712] After purchasing substitute goods, the buyer can recover from the seller the difference between the cost of cover and the contract price, plus incidental and consequential damages less the expenses (such as delivery costs) that were saved as a result of the seller's breach. [UCC 2-712 and 2-715] Consequential damages are any loss suffered by the buyer that the seller could have foreseen (had reason to know about) at the time of contract and any injury to the buyer's person or property proximately resulting from a breach of warranty. [UCC 2-715(2)]

Buyers are not required to cover, and failure to do so will not bar them from using any other remedies available under the UCC. [UCC 2-712(3)] But a buyer who fails to cover may *not* be able to collect the consequential damages that could have been avoided had he or she purchased substitute goods. [UCC 2-715(2)(a)] Thus the UCC encourages buyers to cover in order to mitigate damages.

The Right to Recover Damages for Nondelivery or Repudiation

If a seller repudiates the sales contract or fails to deliver the goods, the buyer can sue for damages. The measure of recovery is the difference between the contract price and the market price of the goods at the time the buyer *learned* of the breach. The market price is determined at the place where the seller was supposed to deliver the goods. In appropriate cases, the buyer can also recover incidental and consequential damages less the expenses that were saved as a result of the seller's breach. [UCC 2-713] Note that the damages here are based on the time and place a buyer would normally obtain cover.

Consider an example. Schilling orders 10,000 bushels of wheat from Valdone for $5 a bushel, with delivery due on June 14 and payment due on June 20. Valdone does not deliver on June 14. On June 14 the market price of wheat is $5.50 per bushel. Schilling chooses to do without the wheat. He sues Valdone for damages for nondelivery. Schilling can recover $5,000 plus any expenses the breach may have caused him to incur. Here the measure of damages is the market price less the contract price on the day Schilling was to have received delivery. (Any expenses Schilling saved by the breach would be deducted from the damages.)

The Right to Recover Damages for Breach in Regard to Accepted Goods

A buyer who has accepted nonconforming goods must notify the seller of the breach within a reasonable time after the defect was or should have been discovered. Otherwise, the buyer cannot complain about defects in the goods. [UCC 2-607(3)] In addition, the parties to a sales contract can insert a provision requiring that the buyer give notice of any defects in the goods within a prescribed period. Such a requirement is ordinarily binding.

When the seller breaches a warranty, the measure of damages equals the difference between the value of the goods as accepted and their value if they had been delivered as warranted. For other types of breaches where the buyer has accepted the goods, the buyer is entitled to recover for any loss "resulting in the ordinary course of events . . . as determined in any manner which is reasonable." [UCC 2-714(1)] The UCC also permits the buyer, with proper notice to the seller, to deduct all or any part of the damages from the price still due and payable to the seller. [UCC 2-717]

❖ Statute of Limitations

An action brought by a buyer or seller for breach of contract must be commenced under the Code *within four years after the cause of action accrues*. In addition to filing suit within the four-year period, an aggrieved party usually must notify the breaching party of a defect within a reasonable time. [UCC 2-607(3)(a)] By agreement in the contract, the parties can reduce this period to not less than one year but cannot extend it beyond four years. [UCC 2-725(1)]

A cause of action accrues for breach of warranty when the seller makes *tender* of delivery. This is the rule even if the aggrieved party is unaware that the cause of action has accrued. [UCC 2-725(2)] The one-year limitation in these cases may have a tremendous impact if the goods purchased are going to be stored primarily for future use. To avoid this impact, a purchaser can include a clause in the sales contract to delay the time at which the cause of action accrues until a future date, such as at the time of first performance of the goods.

When a buyer or seller brings suit on a legal theory unrelated to the Code, the limitation periods just specified do not apply, even though the claim relates to goods. Rather, such suits are governed by the state's statute of limitations.

❖ Limitation of Remedies

The parties to a sales contract can vary their respective rights and obligations by contractual agreement. For example, a seller and buyer can expressly provide for remedies in addition to those provided in the Code. They can also provide remedies in lieu of those provided in the Code, or they can change the measure of damages. The seller can provide that the buyer's only remedy upon breach of warranty be repair or replacement of the item, or the seller can limit the buyer's remedy to return of the goods and refund of the purchase price. Such a remedy is in addition to those provided in the Code unless the parties expressly agree that the remedy is exclusive of all others. [UCC 2-719(1)]

If the parties state that a remedy is exclusive, then it is the sole remedy. But when circumstances cause an exclusive remedy to fail in its essential purpose, it is no longer exclusive. [UCC 2-719(2)] For example, a sales contract that limits the buyer's remedy to repair or replacement fails in its essential purpose if the item cannot be repaired and no replacements are available.

A contract can limit or exclude consequential damages, provided the limitation is not unconscionable. When the buyer is a consumer, the limitation of consequential damages for personal injuries resulting from a breach of warranty is *prima facie* unconscionable. The limitation of consequential damages is not necessarily unconscionable when the loss is commercial in nature—for example, lost profits and property damage. [UCC 2-719(3)] Most sellers' forms limit a buyer's right to receive consequential damages.

Application

Law and the Businessperson— Breach of Contract

A contract for the sale of goods has been breached. Can such a breach be settled without going to court? The answer depends on the willingness of the parties to agree on an appropriate remedy. First, the parties by contract may have already agreed on the remedy applicable in the event of a breach. This may be in the form of liquidated damages [UCC 2-718] or a contract restricting or expanding remedies provided for under the Uniform Commercial Code [UCC 2-719].

Consider an example. When defective goods are delivered and accepted, usually it is preferable for the buyer and seller to reach an agreement on a reduced purchase price. Practically speaking, the buyer may be unable to obtain a partial refund from the seller. The UCC in Section 2-717 allows the buyer in such circumstances to give notice of intention to do so and to deduct the damages from any part of the purchase price not yet paid. If you are a buyer who has accepted defective goods and have not yet paid in full, it may be appropriate for you to exercise your rights under UCC 2-717 and not pay in full when you make your final payment.

If there is nothing in your agreement to cover a breach of contract, and you are the nonbreaching party, the UCC gives you a variety of alternatives. What you need to do is analyze the remedies available if you were to go to court, put these remedies in order of priority, and then predict how successful you might be in pursuing each remedy. Next, look at the position of the breaching party to determine the basis for negotiating a settlement, including whether it is actually worth your trouble to go to court. Remember that most breaches of contract do not end up in court—they are settled beforehand.

Checklist for the Nonbreaching Party to a Contract

- ☐ 1. Ascertain what remedy is explicitly written into your contract. Use it, if possible, to avoid litigation.

- ☐ 2. If no specific remedy is available, look to the UCC.

- ☐ 3. Assess how successful you might be in pursuing a remedy if you went to court.

- ☐ 4. Analyze the position of the breaching party.

- ☐ 5. Determine whether a negotiated settlement is preferable to a lawsuit.

❖ Chapter Summary: Performance and Breach

REQUIREMENTS OF PERFORMANCE	
Good Faith and Commercial Reasonableness	Good faith is a basic requirement of performance under the UCC. In the case of a merchant, good faith means honesty in fact *and* the observance of reasonable commercial standards of fair dealing in the trade. UCC 2-103(1)(b)
Seller's Obligations	1. The seller must ship or tender *conforming* goods to the buyer. Tender must be at a *reasonable hour* and in a *reasonable manner*. Under the perfect-tender doctrine, the seller must tender goods that exactly conform to the terms of the contract. UCC 2-301, UCC 2-503(1), UCC 2-601
	2. If the seller tenders nonconforming goods and the buyer rejects them, the seller may *cure* (repair or replace the goods) within the contract time for performance. UCC 2-508(1)
	3. If the seller tenders nonconforming goods, but the seller has reasonable grounds to believe the buyer would accept them, upon buyer's rejection the seller has a reasonable time to substitute conforming goods without liability. UCC 2-508(2)
	4. If the agreed means of delivery become impracticable or unavailable, the seller must substitute an alternative available means (such as a different carrier) if such is available. UCC 2-614(1)
	5. If a seller tenders nonconforming goods (in any one installment) under an installment contract, the buyer may reject the installment only if its value is substantially impaired and as such cannot be cured. The entire installment contract is breached when one or more installments *substantially* impair the value of the *whole* contract. UCC 2-612
	6. When performance becomes commercially impracticable owing to circumstances unforeseen when the contract was formed, the perfect-tender rule no longer holds. UCC 2-615(a)
Buyer's Obligations	1. Upon tender of delivery by the seller, the buyer must furnish facilities reasonably suited for receipt of the goods. UCC 2-503(1)(b)
	2. The buyer must pay for the goods at the time and place the buyer *receives* the goods, even if the place of shipment is the place of delivery, unless the sale is made on credit. Payment may be by any method generally acceptable in the commercial world. UCC 2-310, UCC 2-511
	3. Unless otherwise agreed, the buyer has an absolute right to inspect the goods before acceptance. UCC 2-513(1)
	4. The buyer can manifest acceptance of delivered goods expressly in words or by conduct, by failing to reject the goods after a reasonable period of time after inspection or after the buyer has had a reasonable opportunity to inspect them, or by performing any act inconsistent with the seller's ownership. UCC 2-606(1)
	5. Following acceptance of delivered goods, the buyer may revoke acceptance only if the nonconformity *substantially* impairs the value of the unit or lot and if one of the following factors is present: (a) Acceptance was predicated on the reasonable assumption that the nonconformity would be cured and it was not cured within a reasonable time. UCC 2-608(1)(a) (b) The buyer does not discover the nonconformity, either because it was difficult to discover before acceptance or because the seller's assurance that the goods were conforming kept the buyer from inspecting the goods. UCC 2-608(1)(b)
Anticipatory Repudiation	If, before the time for performance, either party clearly indicates to the other an intention not to perform, under UCC 2-610 the aggrieved party may: 1. Await performance by the repudiating party for a commercially reasonable time. 2. Resort to any remedy for breach. 3. In either case, *suspend performance*.
REMEDIES FOR BREACH OF CONTRACT	
Seller's Remedies for Buyer's Breach	1. If the goods are in the seller's possession, the seller may: (a) Withhold delivery. UCC 2-703(a) (b) Identify goods to the contract. UCC 2-704 (c) Resell the goods. UCC 2-706 (d) Sue for breach of contract. UCC 2-708 (e) Cancel (and rescind). UCC 2-703

(continued)

❖ Chapter Summary: Performance and Breach—Continued

Seller's Remedies for Buyer's Breach (Continued)	2. If the goods are in transit, the seller may stop the carrier or bailee from delivering the goods. UCC 2-705 3. If the goods are in the buyer's possession, the seller may: (a) Sue for the purchase price. UCC 2-709 (b) Reclaim goods received by an insolvent buyer if the demand is made within ten days of receipt (excludes all other remedies on reclamation). UCC 2-702
Buyer's Remedies for Seller's Breach	1. If the seller refuses to deliver or the seller tenders nonconforming goods and the buyer rejects them, the buyer may: (a) Cancel and, with notice, rescind. UCC 2-711 (b) Cover. UCC 2-712 (c) Sue for breach of contract. UCC 2-713 2. If the seller tenders nonconforming goods and the buyer accepts them, the buyer with notice, may: (a) Sue for ordinary damages. UCC 2-714(1) (b) Sue for breach of warranty. UCC 2-714(2) (c) Deduct damages from the price of the goods. UCC 2-717 3. If the seller refuses delivery and the buyer wants the goods, the buyer may: (a) Sue for specific performance. UCC 2-716(1) (b) Replevy the goods. UCC 2-716(3) (c) Recover goods from the seller on the seller's insolvency within ten days, if the buyer has paid part or all of the purchase price. UCC 2-502

❖ Questions and Case Problems

13-1. Cummings ordered two Model-X Super Fidelity speakers from Jamestown Wholesale Electronics, Inc. Jamestown shipped the speakers via United Parcel Service, C.O.D. (collect on delivery), although Cummings had not requested or agreed to C.O.D. shipment of the goods. When the speakers were delivered, Cummings refused to accept them, since he was unable to inspect them before payment. Jamestown claimed that Cummings had breached their contract because Jamestown had shipped conforming goods. Had Cummings breached the contract? Explain.

13-2. Moore contracted in writing to sell her 1986 Olds Cutlass to Hammer for $5,500. Moore agreed to deliver the car on Wednesday, and Hammer promised to pay the $5,500 on the following Friday. On Tuesday, Hammer informed Moore that he would not be buying the car after all. By Friday, Hammer had changed his mind again and tendered $5,500 to Moore. Moore, although she had not sold the car to another party, refused the tender and refused to deliver. Hammer claimed Moore had breached their contract. Moore contended that Hammer's repudiation released her from her duty to perform under the contract. Who is correct, and why?

13-3. In June, Redmond Machinery contracted in writing to construct a custom-built machine for Jolson Manufacturing for $6,000. Delivery was to be made on August 1. On July 15, Jolson told Redmond that it would be unable to accept or pay for the equipment. Redmond searched for another buyer for the machine, but the equipment was so unique that there was no market for it. Redmond therefore sued Jolson for $6,000 in damages. Will Redmond succeed in recovering the entire contract price? Explain.

13-4. Kraus, a farmer, contracts to deliver to the Cartwright cannery 1,000 bushels of corn at the market price. Delivery and payment are to be made on October 1. On September 10, Cartwright informs Kraus that because of financial reverses it cannot pay on October 1. Kraus immediately notifies Cartwright that he is holding Cartwright in breach of contract. On September 15, Kraus files suit for breach of contract. On October 3, Cartwright files an answer to Kraus's lawsuit. Cartwright claims that had Kraus tendered delivery on October 1, it would have paid for the corn. Cartwright claims that since no delivery was tendered, it cannot be held liable. Discuss whether Kraus can hold Cartwright liable.

13-5. Rodriguez is an antique car collector. He contracts to purchase spare parts for a 1938 engine from Gerrard. These parts are not made anymore and are scarce. To get the contract with Gerrard, Rodriguez has to pay 50 percent of the purchase price in advance. On May 1, Rodriguez sends the payment, which is received on May 2. On May 3, Gerrard, having found another buyer willing to pay substantially more for the parts, informs Rodriguez that he will not deliver as contracted. That same day Rodriguez learns that Gerrard is insolvent. Gerrard has the parts, and Rodriguez wants them. Discuss fully any available remedies that would allow Rodriguez to obtain these car parts.

13-6. In November of 1975 Sun Maid Raisin Growers of California contracted to purchase 1,900 tons of raisins from Victor Packing Company. The first 100 tons were priced at 39 cents per pound and the remainder at 40 cents per pound. No delivery date was specified in the contract. On August 10, 1976, Victor informed Sun Maid that it would not complete performance as it was unable to deliver the last 610 tons. Sun Maid was able to purchase 200 tons of raisins at 43 cents per pound from another supplier. In September of 1976, heavy rains damaged the new crop of raisins, causing the price of raisins to increase dramatically. Sun Maid sued Victor for damages, including lost profits (consequential damages). Victor claims it should not be liable for lost profits because the disastrous rain was not foreseeable. Discuss Victor's claim. [Sun Maid Raisin Growers of California v. Victor Packing Company et al, 146 Cal.App.3d 787, 194 Cal.Rptr. 612 (1983)]

13-7. On July 20, 1978, Mr. and Mrs. Ramirez contracted to purchase a camper van from Autosport, to be delivered August 3. Under the terms of the contract, Autosport was to give them an allowance of $4,700 for their old van as a trade-in, and the Ramirezes agreed to pay an additional $9,900 for the new vehicle. Mr. and Mrs. Ramirez left their old van with Autosport. On August 3, the Ramirezes tendered payment, but the new van showed several defects, including scratched paint, missing electrical and sewer hookups, and missing hubcaps. Autosport told the Ramirezes that it would cure all the problems, and later notified them that the van was ready. The Ramirezes went to Autosport to pick up their van on August 14. The workers were still touching up the paint, however, so the Ramirezes left. Later Autosport notified them that the van would be ready on September 1, but when they arrived, they were asked to wait. After waiting an hour and a half, they left. On October 5, they returned with their attorney and requested return of the old van that they had traded in. Autosport had already sold it to a third party. On November 20, the Ramirezes sued Autosport, seeking rescission of the contract and recovery of the value of the old van. Will they succeed? [Ramirez v. Autosport, 88 N.J. 277, 440 A.2d 1345 (1982)]

13-8. In August of 1979, A. B. Parker purchased a Ford-manufactured F-100 pickup truck from Bell Ford, Inc. for $6,155.40. Parker made several complaints of excessive tire wear to Bell Ford, and Bell Ford gave Parker a purchase order to have the vehicle aligned at an independent alignment shop. Though the problem was not cured, Parker never returned the vehicle to Bell Ford, nor did he complain further. A later inspection of the vehicle disclosed a defective wheel housing, which was causing the tires to wear excessively. Parker sued Bell Ford and Ford Motor Company for breach of warranty. Bell Ford and Ford Motor Company claimed that Parker's continued acceptance of the vehicle under the circumstances precluded Parker's action. Discuss Bell Ford and Ford Motor Company's contention. [A. B. Parker v. Bell Ford, Inc., 425 So.2d 1101 (Ala. 1983)]

13-9. In a contract between Associated Metals & Minerals Corporation and Kaiser Trading Company, Associated promised to deliver to Kaiser 4,000 tons of cryolite over the following sixteen months. After Associated had delivered about one-eighth of the cryolite to Kaiser, it repudiated the contract. Kaiser sought to enforce the contract and requested that the court grant it specific performance against Associated. Kaiser presented convincing proof at trial that only a few hundred tons of cryolite were available on the open market and that Kaiser needed the 4,000 tons that Associated had promised to deliver in order to fulfill its contractual obligations to a number of other industries. Should the court grant specific performance in this case? Explain. [Kaiser Trading Co. v. Associated Metals and Minerals Corp., 321 F.Supp. 923 (N.D.Cal. 1970)]

13-10. Mishara, a construction company, negotiated with Transit-Mixed Concrete Corporation (Transit) for the supply of ready-mixed concrete to be used on a housing project. Under the agreement, transit was to supply all the necessary concrete for $13.25 a cubic yard, with deliveries to be made at the times and in the amounts ordered by Mishara. Both parties performed under the contract for several months. Then labor difficulties arose, and a picket line was maintained on the site until the project was completed. Throughout the period of labor difficulties, despite frequent requests by Mishara, Transit made no shipments. Mishara purchased the rest of the concrete from another supplier at a higher price and sued Transit for breach of contract and damages for the higher price it had had to pay to obtain the replacement concrete. Transit argued that the picket line had made its performance on the contract commercially impracticable and thus it was not liable for damages. Who will prevail? [Mishara Constr. Co., Inc. v. Transit-Mixed Concrete Corp., 365 Mass. 122, 310 N.E.2d 363 (1974)]

Chapter 14

Warranties and Product Liability

Warranty is an age-old concept. In sales law, a warranty is an assurance by one party of the existence of a fact upon which the other party can rely. Just as Shakespeare warranted his friend "heart-whole" in *As You Like It,* so sellers warrant to buyers that their goods are as represented or will be as promised.

The Uniform Commercial Code has numerous rules governing the concept of product warranty as it occurs in a sales contract. That will be the subject matter of the first part of this chapter. A natural addition to the discussion is product liability— who is liable to consumers, users, and bystanders for physical harm and property damage caused by a particular good or the use thereof? Product liability encompasses the contract theory of warranty, as well as the tort theories of negligence and strict liability (discussed in Chapter 3).

❖ Warranty of Title

Title warranty arises automatically in most sales contracts. UCC 2-312 imposes three types of warranties of title.

Good Title

In most cases, sellers warrant that they have good and valid title to the goods sold and that transfer of the title is rightful. [UCC 2-312(1)(a)] For example, Stan steals goods from Lloyd and sells them to Cordelia, who does not know they are stolen. If Lloyd discovers that Cordelia has the goods, Lloyd has the right to reclaim them from her. Under this Code provision, however, Cordelia can then sue Stan for breach of warranty, because a thief has no title to stolen goods and thus cannot give good title in a subsequent sale. When Stan sold Cordelia the goods, Stan *automatically* warranted to her that the title conveyed was valid and that its transfer was rightful. Since this was not in fact the case, Stan has breached the warranty of title imposed by UCC 2-312(1)(a), and Stan becomes liable to the buyer for the appropriate damages.

No Liens

A second warranty of title provided by the Code protects buyers who are *unaware* of any encumbrances—claims, charges or liabilities, usually called liens—against goods at the time the contract was made. [UCC 2-312(1)(b)] This warranty protects buyers who, for example, unknowingly purchase goods that are subject to a creditor's security interest (see Chapter 19). If a creditor legally repossesses the goods from a buyer who *had no actual knowledge of the security interest*, the buyer can recover from the seller for breach of warranty. (The buyer who has *actual knowledge* of a security interest has no recourse against a seller.)

For example, Harvey buys a used color television set from Suarez for cash. A month later, Roper repossesses the set from Harvey, proving that she, Roper, has a valid security interest in the set. She proves that Suarez is in default, having missed five payments. Harvey demands his money back from Suarez. Under Section 2-312(2)(b), Harvey can recover because the seller of goods warrants that the goods shall be delivered free from any security interest or other lien of which the buyer has no knowledge.

No Infringements

A third type of title warranty is warranty against infringement. A merchant is deemed to warrant that the goods delivered are free from any patent, trademark, or copyright claims of a third person.[1] [UCC 2-312(3)] If this warranty is breached and the buyer is sued by the claim holder, the buyer *must notify the seller* of litigation within a reasonable time to enable the seller to decide whether to defend the lawsuit. If the seller states in writing that he or she has decided to defend and agrees to bear all expenses, including that of an adverse judgment, then the buyer must let the seller undertake litigation; otherwise, the buyer loses all rights against the seller if any infringement liability is established. [UCC 2-607(3)(b) and (5)(b)]

For example, Gleason buys a machine from Baker, a manufacturer of such machines, for use in his factory. Three years later, Parker sues Gleason for damages for patent infringement. Parker claims that he has a patent on the machine and that it cannot be used without his permission. At once, Gleason informs Baker of this suit and demands that Baker take over the defense. Baker refuses to do so, claiming that Parker has no case. Gleason goes to court and loses. Parker obtains a judgment against Gleason, which Gleason pays off. Gleason now demands that Baker reimburse him for this amount. Baker must reimburse Gleason because merchant sellers of goods warrant to buyers that the goods they regularly sell are free of infringement claims by third parties.

Disclaimer of Title Warranty

In an ordinary sales transaction, the title warranty can be disclaimed or modified only by *specific language* in a contract. For example, sellers assert that they are transferring only such rights, title, and interest as they have in the goods.

---

1. Recall from Chapter 11 that a merchant is defined in UCC 2-104(1) as a person who deals in goods of the kind involved in the sales contract or who, by occupation, presents himself or herself as having knowledge or skill peculiar to the goods involved in the transaction.

In certain cases, the circumstances of the sale are sufficient to indicate clearly to a buyer that no assurances as to title are being made. The classic example is a sheriff's sale, where buyers know that the goods have been seized to satisfy debts, and it is apparent that the goods are not the property of the person selling them. [UCC 2-312(2)]

❖ Express Warranties

EXPRESS WARRANTY
A promise, ancillary to an underlying sales agreement, that is included in the written or oral terms of the sales agreement under which the promisor assures the quality, description, or performance of the goods.

A seller can create an **express warranty** by making representations concerning the quality, condition, description, or performance potential of the goods. Under UCC 2-313, express warranties arise when a seller indicates that:

1.   The goods conform to any *affirmation or promise* of fact that the seller makes to the buyer about the goods. Such affirmations or promises are usually made during the bargaining process. Statements such as "These drill bits will *easily* penetrate stainless steel—and without dulling" are express warranties.
2.   The goods conform to any *description* of them. For example, "Crate contains one 150-horsepower diesel engine," or the contract calls for delivery of a "camel's-hair coat."
3.   The goods conform to any *sample or model*.

In the following case, a warranty on the label of a hair-bleaching product was breached when a user suffered damages after using the product.

Case 14.1
ROTH v. RAY-STEL'S HAIR STYLISTS, INC.
Court of Appeals of Massachusetts, 1984.
18 Mass.App. 975, 470 N.E.2d 137.

FACTS   On March 13, 1980, Judith Roth went to the hairdresser she had been using for the last seven years to have her hair bleached. The hair stylist used a new bleaching product, manufactured by Roux Laboratories, on Mrs. Roth's hair. Although other Roux products had been used previously with excellent results, the use of the new product resulted in damage to Mrs. Roth's hair which caused her embarrassment and anguish for the next several months as her hair grew back. The product's label had guaranteed it would not cause damage to a user's hair. Roth sued Ray-Stel's Hair Stylists and Roux Laboratories, Inc, alleging negligence and breach of express and implied warranties (discussed later in this chapter) resulting in personal injuries to her.

The trial court found liability on the part of Roux on the basis of negligence and breach of express warranty and assessed damages in the amount of $5,000. The jury found no liability on the part of Ray-Stel Hair Stylists. Roux appealed the judgment.

ISSUE   Did the product's performance breach an express warranty?

DECISION   Yes. The Court of Appeals affirmed the trial court's ruling.

REASON   When a product's label says that the product will (or will not) perform in a certain manner and it fails to (or does) do so, it violates an express warranty. As a result, the manufacturer is liable for the damage caused by the unfulfilled promise. According to the court, "the jury had before them all of the required elements for a claim of breach of express warranty."

Basis of the Bargain

The Code requires that for an express warranty to be created, the affirmation, promise, description, or sample must become part of the "basis of the bargain." Just what constitutes the basis of the bargain is hard to say. The Code does not define the concept, and it is a question of fact in each case whether a representation came at such a time and in such a way that it induced the buyer to enter the contract.

Statements of Opinion

According to Section 2-313(2), "It is not necessary to the creation of an express warranty that the seller use formal words such as 'warrant' or 'guarantee' or that he has a specific intention to make a warranty. . . . " It is necessary only that a reasonable buyer would regard the representation as part of the basis of the bargain.

On the other hand, if the seller merely makes a statement that relates to the value or worth of the goods, or makes a statement of opinion or recommendation about the goods, the seller is not creating an express warranty. [UCC 2-313(2)] For example, a seller claims, "This is the best used car to come along in years; it has four new tires and a 350-horsepower engine just rebuilt this year." The seller has made several *affirmations of fact* that can create a warranty: The automobile has an engine; it has a 350-horsepower engine; it was rebuilt this year; there are four tires on the automobile; the tires are new. But the seller's *opinion* that the vehicle is "the best used car to come along in years" is known as "puffing" and creates no warranty. (Puffing is the expression of a seller's opinion that is not made as a representation of fact.) A statement relating to the value of the goods, such as "it's worth a fortune" or "anywhere else you'd pay $10,000 for it," does not usually create a warranty.

A seller's opinion relating to the value of the merchandise does not usually create a warranty. This sales representative's pitch that this car is an "excellent buy" and a "well manufactured machine" is an example of puffing.

The ordinary seller can give an *opinion* that is not a warranty. If the seller is an expert and gives an opinion as an expert, however, then a warranty can be created. For example, Stevens is an art dealer and an expert in seventeenth-century paintings. If Stevens states to Boller, a purchaser, that in his opinion a particular painting is a Rembrandt, and Boller buys the painting, Stevens has warranted the accuracy of his opinion.

What constitutes an express warranty and what constitutes puffing is not easy to determine. Merely recognizing that some statements are not warranties does not tell us where one should draw the line between puffs and warranties. The reasonableness of the buyer's reliance appears to be the controlling criterion in many cases. For example, a salesperson's statements that a ladder "will never break" and will "last a lifetime" are so clearly improbable that no reasonable buyer should rely on them. Also, the context within which a statement is made might be relevant in determining the reasonableness of the buyer's reliance. For example, a statement made in a written advertisement is more likely to be relied on by a reasonable person than a statement made orally by a salesperson.

❖ Implied Warranties

IMPLIED WARRANTY
A warranty that the law implies either through the situation of the parties or the nature of the transaction.

An **implied warranty** is one that *the law derives* by implication or inference from the nature of the transaction or the relative situation or circumstances of the parties.

For example, Joplin buys an axe at Gershwin's Hardware Store. There are no express warranties made. The first time she chops wood with it, the axe handle breaks, and Joplin is injured. She immediately notifies Gershwin. Examination shows that the wood in the handle was rotten but that the rottenness could not have been noticed by either Gershwin or Joplin. Nonetheless, Joplin notifies Gershwin that she will hold him responsible for the medical bills. Gershwin is responsible because a merchant seller of goods warrants that the goods he or she sells are fit for normal use. This axe was obviously not fit for normal use.

Implied Warranty of Merchantability

IMPLIED WARRANTY OF MERCHANTABILITY
A promise by a merchant seller of goods that the goods are reasonably fit for the general purpose for which they are sold, are properly packaged and labeled, and are of proper quality.

An **implied warranty of merchantability** automatically arises in every sale of goods made *by a merchant* who deals in goods of the kind sold. [UCC 2-314] Thus, a retailer of ski equipment makes an implied warranty of merchantability every time the retailer sells a pair of skis, but a neighbor selling his or her skis at a garage sale does not.

Goods that are *merchantable* are "reasonably fit for the ordinary purposes for which such goods are used." They must be of at least average, fair, or medium-grade quality. The quality must be comparable to quality that will pass without objection in the trade or market for goods of the same description. To be merchantable, the goods must also be adequately packaged and labeled as provided by the agreement, and they must conform to the promises or affirmations of fact made on the container or label, if any.

Some examples of nonmerchantable goods are light bulbs that explode when switched on, pajamas that burst into flames upon slight contact with a stove burner, high heels that break off shoes under normal use, and shotgun shells that explode prematurely.

A sale is also accompanied by an implied warranty of merchantability that imposes on the merchant liability for the safe performance of the product. It makes no difference whether the merchant knew of or could have discovered a defect that makes the product unsafe. (Of course, merchants are not absolute insurers against *all* accidents arising in connection with the goods. For example, a bar of soap is not unmerchantable merely because a user could slip and fall by stepping on it.) In an action based on breach of implied warranty, it is necessary to show:

1. The existence of the implied warranty.
2. That the warranty was broken.
3. That the breach of warranty was the proximate cause of the damage sustained.

The serving of food or drink to be consumed on or off the premises is recognized as a sale of goods subject to the warranty of merchantability. [UCC 2-314(1)] "Merchantable" food means food that is fit to eat. Therefore, any object within the food that a buyer would ordinarily expect sometimes to be in the food would not render the food nonmerchantable. Thus, a pearl swallowed by a buyer eating oysters would not subject the merchant seller to liability, but a nail would.

The following classic case deals with a court's determination of whether a fish bone in chowder is a foreign substance rendering the chowder unfit for consumption.

Case 14.2
WEBSTER v. BLUE SHIP TEA ROOM, INC.

Supreme Judicial Court of Massachusetts, 1964.
347 Mass. 421, 198 N.E. 2d 309.

FACTS   Blue Ship Tea Room was located in Boston in an old building overlooking the ocean. Webster, who had been born and raised in New England, went to the restaurant and ordered fish chowder. The chowder was milky in color. After three or four spoonfuls, she felt something lodged in her throat. As a result she underwent two esophagoscopies; in the second, a fish bone was found and removed. Webster brought suit for breach of implied warranty of merchantability against the restaurant.

ISSUE   Does serving fish chowder that contains a bone constitute the breach of an implied warranty of merchantability on the part of the restaurant?

DECISION   No. Webster could not recover against Blue Ship Tea Room, because no breach of warranty had occurred.

REASON   The court, citing UCC Section 2-314, stated that "a warranty that goods shall be merchantable is implied in a contract for their sale if the seller is a merchant with respect to goods of that kind. Under this section, the serving for value of food or drink to be consumed either on the premises or elsewhere is a sale. Goods to be merchantable must at least be . . . fit for the ordinary purposes for which such goods are used. . . . " The question here is whether a fish bone made the chowder unfit for eating. In the judge's opinion, "the joys of life in New England include the ready availability of fresh fish chowder. We should be prepared to cope with the hazards of fish bones, the occasional presence of which in chowders is, it seems to us, to be anticipated, and which, in the light of a hallowed tradition, do not impair their fitness or merchantability."

Implied Warranty of Fitness for a Particular Purpose

The implied warranty of fitness for a particular purpose arises when *any seller* (merchant or nonmerchant) knows the particular purpose for which a buyer will use the goods *and* knows that the buyer is relying on the seller's skill and judgment to select suitable goods. [UCC 2-315]

A "particular purpose of the buyer" differs from the "ordinary purpose for which goods are used" (merchantability). Goods can be merchantable but unfit for a buyer's particular purpose. Say, for example, that you need a gallon of paint to match the color of your living room walls—a light shade somewhere between coral and peach. You take a sample to your local hardware store and request a gallon of paint of that color. Instead, you are given a gallon of bright blue paint. Here, the salesperson has not breached any warranty of implied merchantability—the bright blue paint is of high quality and suitable for interior walls—but he or she has breached an implied warranty of fitness for a particular purpose.

A seller does not need actual knowledge of the buyer's particular purpose. It is sufficient if a seller "has reason to know" the purpose. The buyer, however, must have *relied* on the seller's skill or judgment in selecting or furnishing suitable goods in order for an implied warranty to be created.

For example, Bloomberg buys a shortwave radio from Radio Shop, telling the salesperson that she wants a set strong enough to pick up Radio Luxembourg, which is 8,000 miles away. Radio Shop sells Bloomberg a Model X set. The set works, but it does not pick up Radio Luxembourg. Bloomberg wants her money back. Here, since Radio Shop is guilty of a breach of implied warranty of fitness for the buyer's particular purpose, Bloomberg will be able to recover. The salesperson knew specifically that she wanted a set that would pick up Radio Luxembourg. Furthermore, Bloomberg relied on the salesperson to furnish a radio that would fulfill this purpose. Since Radio Shop did not do so, the warranty was breached.

An interesting situation arose in the following case, where a purchaser specified to the seller a particular design for a product, and the seller then created it. When the purchaser later alleged the seller had breached the implied warranty of fitness for a particular purpose, the court had to decide whether such a warranty existed.

Case 14.3
SAM'S MARINE PARK ENTERPRISES, INC. v. ADMAR BAR & KITCHEN EQUIPMENT CORP.

Civil Court, Kings County, New York, 1980.
103 Misc.2d 276, 425 N.Y.S.2d 743.

FACTS Sam's Marine Park Enterprises, Inc., the plaintiff, sold frankfurters, ice cream, and other food items from picturesque pushcarts in Brooklyn's Marine Park. The business being successful, Sam's wished to expand and thus ordered from Admar Bar & Kitchen Equipment Corporation two additional carts at a cost of $6,480. Sam's gave detailed instructions to Admar concerning the carts: They were to be equipped with insulated and refrigerated compartments and a cabinet for housing two cylinders of bottled gas. Another design requirement of Sam's was that the pushcart have one of the two large classic wheels

reduced in size and hidden from view. Admar prepared a blueprint, affirmed by Sam's, and Sam's gave the seller $3,300 on account. Subsequently, Sam's inspected the pushcarts being prepared by the seller and approved the design, paid the full balance, and accepted delivery.

The new carts, however, did not "push" well, according to Sam's, who then sued the seller for breach of implied warranty of fitness for a particular purpose.

ISSUE Had Admar Bar & Kitchen breached an implied warranty of fitness for a particular purpose in this case?

DECISION No. The complaint was dismissed with judgment for the defendant, Admar Bar & Kitchen.

REASON The court noted that under both common law and the UCC, a seller was required to furnish goods suitable to meet a buyer's particular use, especially when

Case 14.3—Continued

the buyer was relying on the expertise of the seller. In this case, however, the court concluded that "the seller attempted to fulfill buyer's own design mandates and produced 'very good wagons,' according to the testimony of the buyer's president. The only item of dissatisfaction stems from the claimed lack of mobility. . . . If the buyer cannot use these carts in the particular manner it had intended, that is not a sufficient basis on which to charge defendant with a breach of warranty." In a case where a product whose design specifications, submitted by the buyer, were met by the manufacturer/seller, the buyer could not claim the seller breached a warranty if the design was unsuitable to the buyer's needs. The expertise of the seller, in

this instance, lay in its ability to manufacture a cart that met the buyer's design requirements. This duty was performed satisfactorily in the eyes of the buyer. Therefore, the seller had not breached an implied warranty of fitness for a particular purpose.

The court, in conclusion, advised that, "Since this Court was able to move the wagon in front of the courthouse without physical difficulty or discomfort the buyer should perhaps look toward more hearty and different personnel, motorization or installation in the conventional location of the larger traditional wheel that has successfully served such vehicles for generations."

Other Implied Warranties

The Code recognizes in Section 2-314(3) that implied warranties can arise (or be excluded or modified) from course of dealing, course of performance, or usage of trade. [UCC 2-316(3)(c)] In the absence of evidence to the contrary, when both parties to a sales contract have knowledge of a well-recognized trade custom, the courts will infer they both intended for that custom to apply to their contract. For example, if an industrywide custom is to lubricate a new car before it is delivered, and a dealer fails to do so, the dealer can be held liable to a buyer for resulting damages, under breach of implied warranty. This, of course, would also be negligence on the part of the dealer.

❖ Overlapping Warranties

Sometimes two or more warranties are made in a single transaction. An implied warranty of merchantability or fitness for a particular purpose, or both, can exist in addition to an express warranty. For example, when a sales contract for a new car states that "this car engine is warranted to be free from defects for 12,000 miles or twelve months, whichever occurs first," there is an express warranty against all defects and an implied warranty that the car will be fit for normal use.

The rule of UCC 2-317 is that express and implied warranties are construed as *cumulative* if they are consistent with one another. If the warranties are *inconsistent*, the courts usually hold that:

1.   *Express* warranties displace inconsistent *implied* warranties, except implied warranties of fitness for a particular purpose.
2.   Samples take precedence over inconsistent general descriptions.
3.   Technical specifications displace inconsistent samples or general descriptions.

Suppose that when Bloomberg buys the shortwave radio at Radio Shop, the contract expressly warrants radio receivership to a maximum range of 4,000 miles. She tries to pick up Radio Luxembourg—the stated purpose of her purchase—which is 8,000 miles away. The set cannot perform that well. Bloomberg claims that Radio

Shop is guilty of breach of warranty of fitness. The express warranty takes precedence over any implied warranty of merchantability that a shortwave set should pick up a station anywhere in the world. Bloomberg does have a good claim for the breach of implied warranty of fitness for a specific purpose, however, because she had made it clear that she was buying the set to pick up Radio Luxembourg. In cases of inconsistency between an express warranty and a warranty of fitness for a buyer's particular purpose, the warranty of fitness for the buyer's purpose normally prevails. [UCC 2-317(c)]

❖ Third-Party Beneficiaries of Warranties

One of the general principles of contract law is that unless you are one of the parties to a contract, you have no rights under the contract. (Notable exceptions are assignments and third-party-beneficiary contracts; see Chapter 9.) In short, common law established that **privity** must exist between a plaintiff and a defendant with respect to the matter under dispute in order to maintain any action based on a contract.

PRIVITY
The relationship that exists between the promisor and the promisee of a contract.

For example, I purchase a ham from retailer Bill. I invite you to my house that evening. I prepare the ham properly. You are served first, since you are my guest, and you become severely ill because the ham is spoiled. Can you sue retailer Bill for breach of the implied warranty of merchantability? Since warranty is based on a contract for the sale of goods, under common law you would normally have warranty rights only if you were a party to the purchase of the ham. Therefore, the warranty would extend only to me, the purchaser.

In the past, this hardship was sometimes resolved by court decisions removing privity as a requirement in order to hold manufacturers and sellers liable for certain defective products (notably food, drugs, and cosmetics) that were sold. The UCC, reflecting some of these decisions, has addressed the problem of privity, at least to the extent of giving the state of the option of determining with whom privity is no longer required.

There is sharp disagreement over how far warranty liability should extend. In order to satisfy opposing views of the various states, the drafters of the UCC proposed three alternatives for liability under UCC 2-318. All three alternatives are intended to eliminate the privity requirement with respect to certain enumerated types of injuries (personal versus property) for certain beneficiaries (for example, household members or bystanders).

❖ Warranty Disclaimers

Since each warranty is created in a special way, the manner in which each one can be disclaimed or qualified by the seller varies.

Express Warranties

Any affirmation of fact or promise, description of the goods, or use of samples or models by a seller creates an express warranty. Obviously, then, express warranties can be excluded if the seller has carefully refrained from making any promise or

FRANK & ERNEST

Reprinted by permission of Newspaper Enterprises Association, Inc.

affirmation of fact relating to the goods, or describing the goods, or selling by means of a sample model. [UCC 2-313]

The Code does permit express warranties to be negated or limited by specific and unambiguous language, provided this is done in a manner that protects the buyer from surprise. Therefore, a written disclaimer in language that is clear and conspicuous, and called to a buyer's attention, could negate all oral express warranties not included in the written sales contract. This allows the seller to avoid false allegations that oral warranties were made, and it ensures that only representations by properly authorized individuals are included in the bargain.

Note, however, that a buyer must be made aware of any warranty disclaimers or modifications at the time the sales contract is formed. In other words, any oral or written warranties—or disclaimers—made during the bargaining process cannot be modified at a later time by the seller.

Implied Warranties

Generally speaking, and unless circumstances indicate otherwise, implied warranties (merchantability and fitness) are disclaimed by the expressions "as is," "with all faults," or other similar expressions that in common understanding for *both* parties call the buyer's attention to the fact that there are no implied warranties. [UCC 2-316(3)(a)]

The Code also permits a seller to specifically disclaim the implied warranty either of fitness or of merchantability. [UCC 2-316(2)] To disclaim the implied warranty of fitness for a particular purpose, the disclaimer *must* be in writing and conspicuous. The word "fitness" does not have to be mentioned in the writing; it is sufficient if, for example, the disclaimer states, "There are no warranties that extend beyond the description on the face hereof."

A *merchantability disclaimer* must be more specific; it must mention *merchantability*. It need not be written; but if it is, the writing must be conspicuous. According to UCC 1-201(10):

A term or clause is conspicuous when it is so written that a reasonable person against whom it is to operate ought to have noticed it. A printed heading in capitals is conspicuous. Language in the body of a form is conspicuous if it is in larger or other contrasting type or color.

For example, Forbes, a merchant, sells Maves a particular lawnmower selected by Forbes with the characteristics clearly requested by Maves. At the time of the sale,

Forbes orally tells Maves that he does not warrant the merchantability of the mower, as it is last year's model. The mower proves to be defective and does not work. Maves wants to hold Forbes for breach of implied warranty of merchantability and of fitness for a particular purpose.

Maves can hold Forbes for breach of warranty of fitness, but not of warranty of merchantability. Forbes's oral disclaimer mentioning the word *merchantability* is a proper disclaimer. But for Forbes to have disclaimed the implied warranty of fitness, a conspicuous writing would have been required. Since no written disclaimer was made, Forbes can still be held liable.

Buyer's Refusal to Inspect

If a buyer actually examines the goods (or a sample or model) as fully as desired before entering a contract, or if the buyer refuses to examine the goods, *there is no implied warranty with respect to defects that a reasonable examination will reveal.*

Suppose, in the illustration concerning Joplin's purchase of an axe from Gershwin's hardware store, the defect in Joplin's axe could have been spotted easily by normal inspection. Joplin, even after Gershwin asks, refuses to inspect the axe before buying it. After being hurt by the defective axe, she cannot hold Gershwin for breach of warranty of merchantability because she could have spotted the defect during an inspection. [UCC 2-316(3)(b)]

Failing to examine the goods is not a *refusal* to examine them; a refusal occurs only when the seller *demands* that the buyer examine the goods. The seller remains liable for any latent (hidden) defects that ordinary inspection would not reveal. What the examination ought to reveal depends on a buyer's skill and method of examination. For example, an auto mechanic purchasing a car should be responsible for discovering defects that a nonexpert would not be expected to find. The circumstances of each case determine what defects a so-called reasonable inspection should reveal.

Warranty Disclaimers and Unconscionability

The Code sections dealing with warranty disclaimers do not refer specifically to unconscionability as a factor. Eventually, however, the courts will test warranty disclaimers with reference to the unconscionability standards of Section 2-302. Such things as lack of bargaining position, "take it or leave it" choices, and a buyer's failure to understand or know of a warranty-disclaimer provision will become relevant to the issue of unconscionability. Note in the following pre-UCC landmark decision the court's recognition of the consumer's "bargaining" position with respect to large auto manufacturers.

Case 14.4
HENNINGSEN v. BLOOMFIELD MOTORS, INC.

Supreme Court of New Jersey, 1960.
32 N.J. 358, 161 A.2d 69.

FACTS Henningsen purchased a new Chrysler from Bloomfield Motors for his wife. Subsequently, his wife suf-

fered severe injuries as a result of an apparent defect in the steering wheel mechanism. The standard-form purchase order used in the transaction contained an express ninety-day/4,000-mile warranty. In addition, the purchase order contained a disclaimer, in fine print, of any and all other express or implied warranties. Thus, Bloomfield Motors and Chrysler Corporation refused to pay for Mrs. Henningsen's injuries, asserting that the sales contract,

Case 14.4—Continued

which warranted that Bloomfield would repair defects at no charge, disclaimed warranty liabilities for injuries suffered. A lawsuit followed, based in part on breach of the implied warranty of merchantability. The trial court held for the Henningsens and Bloomfield appealed.

ISSUE   Can the Henningsens recover from Bloomfield Motors and Chrysler despite the disclaimer contained in the sales contract?

DECISION   Yes. The judgment of the trial court was affirmed.

REASON   The liability of Bloomfield Motors and Chrysler Corporation was based on an implied warranty of merchantability contained in the Uniform Sales Act (now included in the UCC) for the sale of goods. The court stated that the implied warranty of merchantability is "a general incident of sale of an automobile by description. The warranty does not depend upon the affirmative intention of the parties" or a finding of fault. The legislature's purpose in implying a warranty in the sale of goods was to protect buyers and "not to limit the liability of the seller or manufacturer."

In the opinion of the court, "The disclaimer of the implied warranty and exclusion of all obligations except those specifically assumed by the express warranty signify a studied effort to frustrate the protection. True, the Sales Act authorizes agreements between buyer and seller qualifying the warranty obligations. But quite obviously the Legislature contemplated lawful stipulations [which are determined by the circumstances of a particular case] arrived at freely by parties of relatively equal bargaining strength. The lawmakers did not authorize the automobile manufacturer to use its grossly disproportionate bargaining power [and the unfair surprise of fine print] to relieve itself from liability and to impose on the ordinary buyer, who in effect has no real freedom of choice, the grave danger of injury to himself and others that attends the sale of such a dangerous instrumentality as a defectively made automobile. In the framework of this case, illustrated as it is by the facts and the many decisions noted, we are of the opinion that Chrysler's [and Bloomfield's] attempted disclaimer of an implied warranty of merchantability and of the obligations arising therefrom is so inimical to the public good as to compel an adjudication of its invalidity."

❖ Magnuson-Moss Warranty Act

The Magnuson-Moss Warranty Act was designed to prevent deception in warranties by making them easier to understand.[2] The act is mainly enforced by the Federal Trade Commission (FTC). Additionally, the attorney general or a consumer who has been injured can enforce the act if informal procedures for settling disputes prove to be ineffective. The act modifies UCC warranty rules to some extent when *consumer* sales transactions are involved. The UCC, however, remains the primary codification of warranty rules for industrial and commercial transactions.

No seller is *required* to give a written warranty for consumer goods sold under this act. But if a seller chooses to make an express written warranty, and the cost of the consumer goods is more than $10, the warranty must be labeled as "full" or "limited." In addition, if the cost of the goods is more than $15 (FTC regulation), the warrantor must make certain disclosures fully and conspicuously in a single document in "readily understood language." This disclosure states the names and addresses of the warrantor(s), what specifically is warranted, procedures for enforcement of the warranty, any limitations on warranty relief, and that the buyer has legal rights.

---

2.   15 U.S.C., Sections 2301–12.

Although a *full warranty* may not cover every aspect of the consumer product sold, what it covers ensures some type of buyer satisfaction in case the product is defective. Full warranty requires free repair or replacement of any defective part; if the product cannot be repaired within a reasonable time, the consumer has the choice of either a refund or a replacement without charge. The full warranty frequently does not have a time limit on it. Any limitation on consequential damages must be *conspicuously* stated. Also, the warrantor need not perform warranty services if the problem with the product was caused by damage to the product or unreasonable use by the consumer.

A *limited warranty* arises when the written warranty fails to meet one of the minimum requirements of a full warranty. The fact that a seller is giving only a limited warranty must be conspicuously designated. If it is only a time limitation that distinguishes a limited warranty from a full warranty, the Warranty Act allows the seller to indicate it as a full warranty by such language as "full twelve-month warranty."

Creating an express warranty under the Warranty Act differs from creating one under the UCC.[3]

1. An express warranty is *any written promise or affirmation of fact* made by the seller to a consumer indicating the quality or performance of the product and affirming or promising that the product is either free of defects or will meet a specific level of performance over a period of time. For example, "this watch will not lose more than one second a year."
2. An express warranty is a written agreement to refund, repair, or replace the product if it fails to meet written specifications. This is typically a service contract.

Implied warranties are not covered under the Magnuson-Moss Warranty Act; they continue to be created according to UCC provisions. When an express warranty is made in a sales contract or a combined sales and service contract (where the service contract is undertaken within ninety days of the sale), the Magnuson-Moss Warranty Act prevents sellers from disclaiming or modifying the implied warranties of merchantability and fitness for a particular purpose. Sellers, however, can impose a time limit on the duration of an implied warranty, but it has to correspond to the duration of the express warranty.[4]

❖ Product Liability Based on Negligence

"*Negligence is the omission to do something which a reasonable man . . . would do, or doing something which a prudent and reasonable man would not do.*"

B. Alderson (in *Hadley v. Baxendale,* 1854)

Chapter 3 defined *negligence* as failure to use the degree of care that a reasonable, prudent person would have used under the circumstances. If a seller fails to exercise such reasonable care and an injury results, he or she may be sued for negligence. Thus, a manufacturer must exercise "due care" to make a product safe. Due care must be exercised in designing the product, in selecting the materials, in using the

---

3. For example, express warranties created by description or sample or model are still governed under UCC provisions because only written promises or affirmations of fact are covered by the Magnuson-Moss Warranty Act.
4. The time limit on an implied warranty occurring by virtue of the seller's express warranty must, of course, be reasonable, conscionable, and set forth in clear and conspicuous language on the face of the warranty.

Landmark in the Law

Lemon Laws

Beginning in 1963 when Chrysler Corporation initiated a five-year/50,000-mile "power train warranty," the auto industry discovered that warranties attracted consumers. In fact, the Chrysler warranty increased its new-car sales by 40 percent. For consumers, however, the warranty was not a panacea for all the problems arising from automobile purchases. Dealers and manufacturers frequently failed to live up to their express or implied warranties, with the result that unsatisfactory warranty service became the most frequent and significant complaint of consumers buying new cars.

The Magnuson-Moss Warranty Act aided consumers to some extent. Since much of the act applies only to "full" or comprehensive warranties, however, and since most automobile dealers and manufacturers do not offer such warranties (offering "limited" warranties instead), the act is rarely applicable to auto sales contracts.

To help consumers who have had the bad luck of purchasing a "lemon," the majority of states now have "lemon laws." These laws generally allow a purchaser to rescind a sales contract for the purchase of a new automobile should the vehicle need servicing four or more times for the same problem, or if the vehicle cannot be used for thirty business days within the first year. If such a situation develops, the consumer is entitled to obtain a replacement auto or a cash refund (with minor adjustments for normal vehicle use) from the manufacturer. State laws also require a complaining consumer to go through informal settlement procedures before suing in court. So far, the states are fairly evenly divided on what type of defect can trigger the law. Half of the states with lemon laws follow Connecticut's lead and require that the defect *substantially* impair the use and the value of the vehicle. The other half follow the California statute, which requires that the defect impair the use, value, or safety of the vehicle in any way.

The steady increase in lemon laws has greatly benefited consumers and represents a growing recognition of the need to balance the bargaining scales between the individual consumer and the "giant" corporation. Currently, more than thirty states have lemon laws covering the sale of new automobiles.[1] In nearly all the states that do not yet have them, proposals have been introduced and are being considered for adoption.

1. As of January 1, 1986, the following thirty-three states and the District of Columbia had passed lemon laws: Alaska, Arizona, California, Colorado, Connecticut, Delaware, Florida, Hawaii, Illinois, Iowa, Louisiana, Maine, Maryland, Massachusetts, Minnesota, Missouri, Montana, Nebraska, Nevada, New Hampshire, New Jersey, New York, Oregon, Pennsylvania, Rhode Island, Tennessee, Texas, Vermont, Virginia, Washington, West Virginia, Wisconsin, and Wyoming.

Not all states have passed lemon laws, and some consumers have resorted to creative measures to fight back.

A technician runs tests on a commercial drug for a large pharmaceutical company. Failure to exercise due care to make its product safe would be negligence.

appropriate production process, in assembling and testing the product, and in placing adequate warnings on the label informing the user of dangers of which an ordinary person might not be aware. The duty of care extends to the inspection and testing of purchased products used in the final product sold by the manufacturer. The failure to exercise due care is negligence.

In the following landmark case, the New York Court of Appeals dealt with the liability of a manufacturer that failed to exercise reasonable care in manufacturing a finished product.

Case 14.5
MacPHERSON v. BUICK MOTOR CO.
Court of Appeals of New York, 1916.
217 N.Y. 382, 111 N.E. 1050.

FACTS The MacPherson case is the classic product-liability case. Its subject matter, defectively manufactured wooden wheels for automobiles, is dated, but the principles involved are not. MacPherson purchased a new Buick from a Buick Motor Company dealer. Later, he was injured when the car ran into a ditch after one of its wheels collapsed because the spokes were made from defective wood. The wheel itself had been made by another manufacturer. MacPherson brought suit against Buick directly, instead of against the retailer from whom he purchased the car. The evidence presented at the trial showed

that the defects could have been discovered by reasonable inspection by the manufacturer and that inspection had not been made. The trial court held for MacPherson. Buick appealed.

ISSUE Can Buick be held liable for the injuries sustained by MacPherson owing to the defective wheel?

DECISION Yes. MacPherson was able to recover for his injuries from Buick Motor Company.

REASON Buick Motor Company's duty to exercise reasonable care extended to MacPherson even though MacPherson and the company were not in privity of contract. (The sales contract was between MacPherson and the retailer.) Buick Motor Company's duty of care lay in

Case 14.5—Continued

tort and extended to any person who could foreseeably be injured as a result of a defect in an automobile it manufactured. The duty arises because of the potential danger a defectively manufactured automobile poses to those who ride in it.

After a survey of prior decisions, Justice Cardozo stated, "Beyond all question, the nature of an automobile gives warning of probable danger if its construction is defective. This automobile was designed to go fifty miles an hour. Unless its wheels were sound and strong, injury was almost certain . . . . The defendant [Buick Motor Company] knew the danger. . . . The maker of this car supplied it for the use of purchasers from the dealer. . . . It is true that . . . an automobile is not an inherently dangerous vehicle. The meaning, however, is that danger is not to be expected when the vehicle is well constructed. . . . If danger was to be expected as reasonably certain, there was a duty of vigilance, and this whether you call the danger inherent or imminent."

"We think the defendant was not absolved from a duty to inspect because it bought the wheels from a reputable manufacturer. It was not merely a dealer in automobiles. It was responsible for the finished product. It was not at liberty to put the finished product on the market without subjecting the component parts to ordinary and simple tests. . . . The obligation to inspect must vary with the nature of the thing to be inspected. The more probable the danger, the greater the need of caution."

COMMENT This case has been interpreted to cover all articles that imperil life whenever negligently made. Prior to *MacPherson*, manufacturers escaped liability to consumers whenever their contractual dealings were with "middle people" or retailers. Since *MacPherson*, that is no longer the case.

Privity of Contract Not Required

An action based on negligence does not require privity of contract between the injured plaintiff and the negligent defendant-manufacturer. Section 395 of the Restatement, Second, Torts states:

A manufacturer who fails to exercise reasonable care in the manufacture of a chattel [movable good] which, unless carefully made, he should recognize as involving an unreasonable risk of causing substantial bodily harm to those who lawfully used it for a purpose for which it was manufactured and to those whom the supplier should expect to be in the vicinity of its probable use, is subject to liability for bodily harm caused to them by its lawful use in a manner and for a purpose for which it is manufactured.

Simply stated, a manufacturer is liable for its failure to exercise due care to any person who sustained an injury proximately caused by a negligently made (defective) product, regardless of whether there was a sale or a contract to sell.

Misrepresentation

When a fraudulent misrepresentation has been made to a user or consumer, and that misrepresentation ultimately results in an injury, the basis of liability may be the tort of **fraud**. Examples are the intentional mislabeling of packaged cosmetics or the intentional concealment of a product's defects. A more interesting basis of liability is nonfraudulent misrepresentation, which occurs when a merchant *innocently* misrepresents the character or quality of goods.

A famous example involved a drug manufacturer and a person who became addicted to a prescription medication called Talwin. The manufacturer, Winthrop Laboratories, a division of Sterling Drug, Inc., innocently indicated to the medical profession that the drug was not physically addictive. Using this information, a

FRAUD
Any misrepresentation, either by misstatement or omission of a material fact, knowingly made with the intention of misrepresentation to another and on which a reasonable person would and does rely, to his or her detriment.

physician prescribed the drug for his patient, who developed an addiction that turned out to be fatal. Even though the addiction was a highly unusual reaction resulting from the victim's highly unusual susceptibility to this product, the drug company was still held liable.[5]

❖ The Doctrine of Strict Liability

"In Burma an elephant is . . . but a domestic animal, no more a subject for strict liability than a horse, but the same elephant, transported to England in a circus, becomes an abnormal danger to that community."

William L. Prosser, 1898–1972
(American legal scholar and educator)

A fairly recent development of tort law is the revival of the old doctrine of strict liability. Under this doctrine, people are liable for the results of their acts regardless of their intentions or their exercise of reasonable care. For example, a company that uses dynamite to blast for a road is strictly liable for any damages that it causes, even if it takes reasonable and prudent precautions to prevent such damages. In essence, the blasting company becomes liable for any personal injuries it causes and thus is an absolute insurer.

The English courts accepted the doctrine of strict liability for many years. Often persons whose conduct resulted in the injury of another were held liable for damages, even if they had not intended to injure anyone and had exercised reasonable care. This approach was abandoned around 1800 in favor of the *fault* approach, in which an action was considered tortious only if it was wrongful or blameworthy in some respect.

Strict liability was reapplied to manufactured goods in several landmark cases in the 1960s and has since become a common method of holding manufacturers liable. Basically, if the purchaser of a product is injured through the use of the product, that person can show a cause of action against the manufacturer by proving that (1) the product was defective, (2) the defect made the product unreasonably dangerous, and (3) the defect was the proximate cause of the injury.

The Restatement of Torts

The Second Restatement of Torts designates how the doctrine of strict liability should be applied. It is a precise and widely accepted statement of the liabilities of sellers of goods (including manufacturers) and deserves close attention. Section 402A of the Restatement, Second, Torts states:

> (1) One who sells any product in a defective condition unreasonably dangerous to the user or consumer or to his property is subject to liability for physical harm thereby caused to the ultimate user or consumer or to his property, if
> (a) the seller is engaged in the business of selling such a product, and
> (b) it is expected to and does reach the user or consumer without substantial change in the condition in which it is sold.
>
> (2) The rule stated in Subsection (1) applies although
> (a) the seller has exercised all possible care in the preparation and sale of his product, and
> (b) the user or consumer has not bought the product from or entered into any contractual relation with the seller.

---

5.   Crocker v. Winthrop Laboratories, Div. of Sterling Drugs, Inc., 514 S.W.2d 429 (Tex. 1974).

Thus, liability is imposed by law as a matter of public policy. It does not depend on privity of contract or on proof of negligence. The manufacturer's liability to an injured party is virtually unlimited.[6] In fact, courts extend the manufacturer's liability to bystanders as well as to consumers and users.

The injured party does not have to be the buyer or a third-party beneficiary, as required under contract warranty theory. [UCC 2-318] Indeed, this type of liability in law is not governed by the provisions of the UCC.

The following case started an important trend toward strict liability.

Case 14.6
GREENMAN v. YUBA POWER PRODUCTS, INC.
Supreme Court of California, 1962.
59 Cal. 2d 57, 27 Cal. Rptr. 697, 377 P. 2d 897.

FACTS California was the first state to impose strict liability in tort on manufacturers. In this landmark case, the plaintiff, Greenman, wanted a Shopsmith—a combination power tool that could be used as a saw, drill, and wood lathe—after seeing a Shopsmith demonstrated by a retailer and studying a brochure prepared by the manufacturer. The plaintiff's wife bought and gave him one for Christmas. More than a year later, a piece of wood flew out of the lathe attachment of the Shopsmith while the plaintiff was using it, inflicting serious injuries on him. About ten and a half months later, the plaintiff sued both the retailer and the manufacturer for breach of warranties and negligence. The trial court jury found for the plaintiff.

ISSUE Can the manufacturer and retailer be held liable for Greenman's injuries?

DECISION Yes. The jury verdict for the plaintiff was upheld.

REASON The plaintiff had successfully proved that the design and construction of the Shopsmith were defective, that statements in the manufacturer's brochure constituted express warranties and were untrue, and that the plaintiff's injuries were caused by their breach. The manufacturer argued that the plaintiff had waited too long to give notice of the breach of warranty, but the court, in imposing strict liability upon the manufacturer, held that it was not necessary for the plaintiff to establish an express warranty, or breach thereof. The court stated that "a manufacturer is strictly liable in tort when an article he places on the market, knowing that it is to be used without inspection for defects, proves to have a defect that causes injury to a human being." The court stated that the "purpose of such liability is to insure that the costs of injuries resulting from defective products are borne by the manufacturers . . . rather than by the injured persons who are powerless to protect themselves."

Requirements of Strict Product Liability

The six basic requirements of strict product liability are:

1. The defendant must sell the product in a defective condition.
2. The defendant must normally be engaged in the business of selling that product.
3. The product must be unreasonably dangerous to the user or consumer because of its defective condition.[7]

---

6. Some states have enacted what are called statutes of repose. Basically, these statutes provide that after a specific statutory period of time from date of manufacture or sale, a plaintiff is precluded from pursuing a cause of action for injuries or damages sustained from a product, even though the product is defective. States such as Illinois, Indiana, Alabama, Tennessee, Florida, and Nebraska are illustrative.
7. This element is no longer required in some states, for example, in California.

Business Law in Action

Even "Stricter" Strict Liability

As mentioned earlier, in recent years a strict-liability standard for product-defect cases has evolved rapidly. In its most general form, the strict-liability rule states that the manufacturer of a product is subject to liability for harm caused to the user if the product as sold was unreasonably dangerous because of its defective condition. In other words, under the strict-liability standard, there is no legal defense for placing a product on the market that is dangerous to the consumer or user because of a known or knowable defect.

In the 1980s, courts in several states have extended the relatively tough standard of strict liability to a much stronger one called *absolute liability*. The most important case was handed down by the New Jersey Supreme Court in 1982, *Beshada v. Johns-Manville Products Corp.*[1] *Beshada* is one of numerous cases brought by plaintiffs who have suffered health injuries from asbestos

exposure. Since early in this century, asbestos was the material of choice for home insulation and was so widely used that thousands upon thousands of individuals were harmfully affected by it. Manville, being the major manufacturer of the product, was the target of so many liability lawsuits that in 1982 it applied for bankruptcy-law protection.

What distinguishes the *Beshada* case from similar asbestos cases was the judge's reasoning that a manufacturer could be strictly liable for failure to warn of a product hazard, even if the hazard was scientifically unknowable at the time of manufacture. Under this reasoning, a company can no longer use as a defense the assurance that it did its best according to the state of the art in its industry at the time of manufacture. Under the rule of absolute liability, that defense is irrelevant. The producer is always liable for damages later caused by a product, even if the producer had no way of knowing—and no matter how much the producer was willing to spend at the time—that the product could cause a problem later on.

The absolute-liability standard is not always applied, and laws on

liability and available defenses vary widely among the states and in courts within each state. This has injected a large amount of uncertainty into the business process, because manufacturers of products sold nationwide cannot determine the standards of conduct to which they will be held. Federal product-liability legislation was introduced into Congress in 1984, but, as of 1987, had not yet passed. The proposed federal law is, in many ways, similar to the strict-liability standard of Chief Justice Cardozo, as expressed in the MacPherson case described earlier. Under the proposed law, a product would be held to be unreasonably dangerous if "the manufacturer knew, or, through the exercise of reasonable prudence, should have known about the danger which allegedly caused the claimant's harm" and if "a reasonably prudent person in the same or similar circumstances would not have manufactured the product or used the design or formulation that the manufacturer used." The proposed legislation would also require that the courts consider whether "the benefits and usefulness of the product to the public outweighed the likelihood and probable seriousness of the harm."

1.   90 N.J. 191, 447 A.2d 539 (1982).

4.   The plaintiff must incur physical harm to self or property by use or consumption of the product.

5.   The defective condition must be the proximate cause of the injury or damage.

6.   The goods must not have been substantially changed from the time the product was sold to the time the injury was sustained.

Thus, in any action against a manufacturer or seller, the plaintiff does not have to show why or in what manner the product became defective. The plaintiff does, however, have to show that at the time the injury was sustained, the condition of the product was essentially the same as it was when it left the hands of the defendant manufacturer or seller.

Defenses

Assumption of Risk   Assumption of risk can be used as a defense in an action based on strict liability in tort. Whenever consumers or users use goods improperly under unreasonable circumstances, they assume the risk of injury. For such a defense to be established, the defendant must show that:

1.   The plaintiff voluntarily engaged in the risk while realizing the potential danger.
2.   The plaintiff knew and appreciated the risk created by the defect.
3.   The plaintiff's decision to undertake the known risk was unreasonable.

Product Misuse   Similar to the defense of voluntary assumption of risk is that of misuse of the product. Here the injured party does not know that the product is dangerous for a particular use, but that use is not the one for which the product was designed. (Contrast this with assumption of risk.) This defense has been severely limited by the courts, however. Even if the injured party does not know about the inherent danger of using the product in a wrong way, if the misuse is foreseeable, the seller must take measures to guard against it.

Contributory Negligence   As pointed out in Chapter 3, under common law, in any action based on negligence, contributory negligence of the injured party either completely barred recovery or reduced the amount of recovery under the rule of comparative negligence. In principle, negligence and contributory negligence are immaterial in any action based on the theory of strict liability in tort.

Recent developments in the area of comparative negligence are affecting the doctrine of strict liability. Whereas previously the plaintiff's conduct was not a defense to strict liability, today a growing number of jurisdictions consider the negligent or intentional actions of the plaintiff in the apportionment of liability and damages. This "comparing" of the plaintiff's conduct to the defendant's strict liability results in an application of the doctrine of comparative negligence. Some states that have adopted this doctrine are Texas, California, Oregon, Florida, and Hawaii. Although comparative negligence in strict liability is the minority view, its recent growth may indeed have a pervasive effect on this area of tort law.

Strict Liability to Bystanders

All courts extend the strict liability of manufacturers and other sellers to injured bystanders, although the drafters of Restatement, Second, Torts, Section 402A did not take a position on bystanders. For example, in one case, an automobile manufacturer was held liable for injuries caused by the explosion of a car's motor. A cloud of steam that resulted from the explosion caused multiple collisions because other drivers could not see well.[8]

Other Applications of Strict Liability

Under the rule of strict liability in tort, the basis of liability has been expanded to include suppliers of component parts and lessors of movable goods. Thus, if General

---

8.   Giberson v. Ford Motor Co., 504 S.W.2d 8 (Mo. 1974).

Motors buys brake pads from a subcontractor and puts them in Chevrolets without changing their composition, and those pads are defective, both the supplier of the brake pads and General Motors will be held strictly liable for the damages caused by the defects.

Liability for personal injuries caused by defective goods extends also to those who lease such goods. Section 408 of the Restatement, Second, Torts states that:

> One who leases a chattel as safe for immediate use is subject to liability to those whom he should expect to use the chattel, or to be endangered by its probable use, for physical harm caused by its use in a manner for which and by a person for whose use it is leased, if the lessor fails to exercise reasonable care to make it safe for such use or to disclose its actual condition to those who may be expected to use it.

Some courts have held that a leasing agreement gives rise to a contractual *implied warranty* that the leased goods will be fit for the duration of the lease. Under this view, if Hertz Rent-a-Car leases a Chevrolet that has been improperly maintained, and a passenger is injured in an accident, the passenger can sue Hertz. (Liability is based on the contract theory of warranty, not tort.)

Application

Law and the Salesperson— The Creation of Warranties

Warranties are important in both commercial and consumer purchase transactions. There are three types of product warranties: express warranties, implied warranties of merchantability, and implied warranties of fitness for a particular purpose. If you are a seller of products, you can make or create any one of these warranties, which are available to consumers and commercial purchasers.

First and foremost, sellers and buyers need to know whether warranties have been created. Express warranties do not have to be labeled as such, but statements of opinion generally do not constitute express warranties. Express warranties can be made by descriptions of the goods. Express warranties can be found in a seller's advertisement, brochure, or promotional materials, or can be made orally or in an express writing. A sales representative should use care in describing the merits of a product; otherwise the seller could be held to an express warranty. If an express warranty is not intended, the sales pitch should not promise too much.

In most sales, because the seller is a merchant, the purchased goods carry the implied warranty of merchantability. As a seller, you also must be aware of the importance of the implied warranty of fitness for a particular purpose. Assume a customer comes to your sales representative and says, "I really need something that can do the job." (The "job" has been described in detail by the customer.) Your sales representative replies, "This product will do the job." An implied warranty that the product is fit for that particular purpose has been created.

Many sellers, particularly in commercial sales, try to limit or disclaim warranties. The Uniform Commercial Code permits all warranties, including express warranties, to be excluded or negated. Conspicuous statements such as "THERE ARE NO WARRANTIES WHICH EXTEND BEYOND THE DESCRIPTION ON THE FACE HEREOF" or "THERE ARE NO IMPLIED WARRANTIES OF FITNESS NOR MERCHANTABILITY WHICH ACCOMPANY THIS SALE" disclaim the implied warranties of fitness and/or merchantability. Used goods sometimes are sold "as is" or "with all faults" so that any implied warranties of fitness or merchantability that accompany the sale are disclaimed. Thus, a purchaser should be aware that his or her expectations of an average-quality product will not be enforced.

Checklist for the Salesperson

☐ 1. If you wish to limit warranties, do so by means of a carefully worded and prominently placed provision that a reasonable person would think is fair.

☐ 2. As seller, you might wish to have the buyer sign a statement certifying that he or she has read all of your warranty disclaimer provisions.

☐ 3. If you do not intend to make an express warranty, do not make a promise or an affirmation of fact concerning the performance or quality of a product you are selling.

❖ Chapter Summary: Warranties and Product Liability

WARRANTIES		
TYPE	**HOW CREATED**	**POSSIBLE DEFENSES**
Warranty of Title UCC 2-312	Upon transfer of title, the seller warrants— 1. The right to pass good and rightful title. 2. That the goods are free from unstated liens or encumbrances. 3. If a merchant, that the goods are free from infringement claims.	1. Exclusion or modification only by specific language or circumstances. UCC 2-312(2)
Express Warranty UCC 2-313	As part of a sale or bargain— 1. An affirmation of fact or promise. 2. A sale by description. 3. A sample shown as conforming to bulk. Under the Magnuson-Moss Warranty Act, express written warranties covering consumer goods priced at more than $10, *if* made, must be labeled as one of the following— 1. "Full" warranty—free repair or replacement of defective parts; refund or replacement for goods if cannot be repaired in a reasonable time. 2. "Limited" warranty—when less than full warranty is being offered.	1. Opinion. 2. Exclusion or limitation. UCC 2-316(1) 3. No statement by seller.
Warranty of Merchantability UCC 2-314	1. Where the seller is a merchant, and 2. Goods are properly packaged and labeled, are of proper quality, and are fit for ordinary use or resale.	1. Specified disclaimer—can be oral or in writing, but must mention "merchantability" and if in writing must be conspicuous. UCC 2-316(2) 2. Sales stated "as is" or "with all faults." UCC 2-316(3)(a) 3. If there is an examination by the buyer, the buyer is bound by all defects found, or that should have been found, or if the buyer refuses or fails to examine, the buyer is bound by obvious defects. UCC 2-316(3)(b) 4. Course of dealing, performance, or usage of trade. UCC 2-316(3)(c)
Warranty of Fitness for a Particular Purpose UCC 2-315	1. The buyer's purpose or use must expressly or impliedly be known by the seller, and 2. The buyer must purchase in reliance on the seller's selection.	1. Specific disclaimer—must be in writing and be conspicuous. "There are no warranties which extend beyond the description on the face hereof." UCC 2-316(2) 2. Same as merchantability above (numbers 2 through 4).
Implied Warranty Arising from Course of Dealing or Trade Usage UCC 2-314(3)	1. By prior dealings and/or custom of trade	1. Exclusion by specific language or as provided under UCC 2-316.

❖ Chapter Summary: Warranties and Product Liability—Continued

PRODUCT LIABILITY	
Liability Based on Negligence or Fraud	1. Due care must be used by the manufacturer in designing the product, selecting materials, using the appropriate production process, assembling and testing the product, and placing adequate warnings on the label or product. 2. Privity of contract is not required. A manufacturer is liable for failure to exercise due care to any person who sustains an injury proximately caused by a negligently made (defective) product. 3. Fraudulent misrepresentation of a product may result in the tort of fraud. A manufacturer may also be liable for nonfraudulent (innocent) misrepresentation of a product to a user.
Requirements of Strict Product Liability	1. The defendant must sell the product in a defective condition. 2. The defendant must normally be engaged in the business of selling that product. 3. The product must be unreasonably dangerous to the user or consumer because of its defective condition (in most states). 4. The plaintiff must incur physical harm to self or property by use or consumption of the product. (Courts will also extend strict liability to include injured bystanders.) 5. The defective condition must be the proximate cause of the injury or damage. 6. The goods must not have been substantially changed from the time the product was sold to the time the injury was sustained.
Possible Defenses to Negligence and Strict Liability	1. Assumption of risk on the part of the user or consumer. 2. Misuse of the product by the user or consumer in a way unforeseeable by the manufacturer. 3. Contributory negligence on the part of the user/consumer. If allowed, liability may be distributed between plaintiff and defendant under the doctrine of comparative negligence.

❖ Questions and Case Problems

14-1. Epstein contracted to purchase a used car from Martin's Auto Sales. During the oral negotiations for the sale, Martin told Epstein that this used car was in "A-1 condition" and would get sixteen miles to the gallon. Epstein asked if the car used oil. Martin replied that he had personally checked the car, and in his opinion the car did not use oil. After delivery, Epstein used the car for one month (400 miles of driving) and was unhappy with its performance. The car needed numerous repairs, did not get sixteen miles to the gallon, and had used two quarts of oil. Epstein claims Martin is in breach of express warranties as to the condition of the car, gas mileage, and oil use. Martin claims no express warranties were made. Discuss who is correct.

14-2. Griggs was hospitalized with a serious illness and, while in the hospital, received a blood transfusion. Griggs's illness was complicated by serum hepatitis which he contracted from the blood. Griggs subsequently brought suit against both the hospital and the blood bank from which the hospital had purchased the blood, claiming damages for breach of implied warranty of merchantability on the ground that the blood had been unfit for use in a transfusion. Can Griggs recover?

14-3. Laura Hollingsworth purchased a washing machine from Marshall Appliances. The sales contract included a provision explicitly disclaiming all express or implied warranties, including the implied warranty of merchantability. The disclaimer was printed in the same size and color type as the rest of the contract. The machine turned out to be a "lemon," and never functioned properly. Hollingsworth sought a refund of the purchase price, claiming Marshall had breached the implied warranty of merchantability. Can Hollingsworth recover her money, notwithstanding the warranty disclaimer in the contract? Explain.

14-4. Appleton was driving on an interstate highway when one of his tires blew out. The blow-out caused Appleton to lose control of his car, which collided with another vehicle and injured its driver. Appleton had not been driving negligently. When it was later discovered that a defect in the tire had caused the blowout, Appleton sued Good-Rubber Tires, Inc., the manufacturer of the tire, for damages caused by the accident. Will Appleton succeed in his suit? Explain.

14-5. Sam is a farmer who needs to place a 2,000-pound piece of equipment in his barn. The equipment must be lifted

30 feet up into a hayloft. Sam goes to Durham Hardware and tells Durham that he needs some heavy-duty rope to be used on his farm. Durham recommends a one-inch-thick nylon rope, and Sam purchases 200 feet of it. Sam ties the rope around the piece of equipment, puts it through a pulley, and with the aid of a tractor lifts the equipment off the ground. Suddenly the rope breaks. In the crash to the ground, the equipment is severely damaged. Sam files suit against Durham for breach of implied warranty of fitness for a particular purpose. Discuss how successful Sam will be with his suit.

14-6. Barton sells plastic auxiliary fuel tanks for diesel-powered passenger cars. Barton approaches Tra-Mo, Inc., a plastic manufacturer, about the possibility of Tra-Mo producing tanks from a less expensive material than Barton has used in the past. Tra-Mo suggests using high-density polyethylene and demonstrates the strength by using water tanks made of the material. Tra-Mo also produced five to eight tanks from Barton's molds and subjected them to strength tests. Barton, impressed by Tra-Mo's demonstration, entered into an agreement to purchase more than 2,000 tanks. After delivery, approximately 600 of these tanks bulged, split, or shattered under normal use. Is Tra-Mo liable for breach of express warranty by sample or model? Explain. [Barton v. Tra-Mo, Inc., 69 Or.App. 295, 686 P.2d 423 (1984)]

14-7. Mobley bought a new car from Century Dodge. The contract of sale contained a provision disclaiming all warranties, express or implied. Although the contract described the car as "new," Mobley later discovered that the car had been involved in an accident. Mobley brought suit against Century Dodge for damages, claiming that Century Dodge had breached its express warranty that the car was "new." Century Dodge argued that it had disclaimed any express warranty. Who will prevail, and why? [Century Dodge, Inc. v. Mobley, 155 Ga.App. 712, 272 S.E.2d 502 (1980)]

14-8. Larry Colvin, an iron worker, was setting a steel truss on a concrete column while he was in a squatting position. He reached above his head to pull himself up and grabbed an I-beam, known as a purlin, which was eight or ten feet long and was not yet welded into place. The purlin failed to support Colvin's weight, and he fell. The plans for the building called for the purlins to be over forty feet long, but only seven were

that length. The remaining purlins were substantially shorter and were welded together to serve their purpose as spacers between the trusses and the roof. The purlins were supplied by Red Steel Company. Explain whether Red Steel is strictly liable for Colvin's injury resulting from the short length of the purlins. [Colvin v. Red Steel Company, 682 S.W.2d 243 (Tex. 1984)]

14-9. A two-year-old child lost his leg when he became entangled in a grain auger on his grandfather's farm. The auger had a safety guard that prevented any item larger than 4⅝ inches from coming into contact with the machine's moving parts. The child's foot was smaller than the openings in the safety guard. Was such an injury reasonably foreseeable? [Richelman v. Kewanee Machinery & Conveyor Co., 59 Ill.App.3d 578, 16 Ill.Dec. 778, 375 N.E.2d 885 (1978)]

14-10. On April 24, 1985, Lawrence Bouchard purchased a 1970 Datsun 280 ZX automobile from Robert Savoca, a car dealer, for $10,178.95. Between April 25 and May 9, 1985, the car broke down six times, and on each occasion Bouchard returned the car to the dealer for repairs—all of which were unsuccessful. On May 9, Bouchard returned the car to the dealer and demanded the return of the purchase price. The dealer, sure that the defect could be cured, refused to comply with Bouchard's demand, and Bouchard brought suit to recover his money. Under the "Lemon Law" adopted by the New York Legislature, when an automobile malfunction has been the subject of three or more unsuccessful attempts at repair within the warranty period, the seller is required, upon the purchaser's request, to return the purchase price of the vehicle. The trial court granted summary judgment for the plaintiff, Bouchard, on the basis that the dealer had violated the New York Lemon Law by not returning the purchase price to Bouchard. The dealer appealed, claiming that the Lemon Law should not apply as the dealership had attempted, in good faith and at its own expense, to repair the vehicle on each occasion and had indeed, by the time of the trial in August (three months later), succeeded in correcting the defect and restoring the auto to a superior condition. Given these circumstances, discuss fully whether the dealer should be required to return the purchase price to Bouchard. [Bouchard v. Savoca, 129 Misc.2d 506, 493 N.Y.S.2d 417 (1985)]

Chapter 15

Commercial Paper— Basic Concepts

The "chief business of the American people," as President Coolidge defined it, is business. And the vast number of commercial transactions that take place daily in the modern business world would be inconceivable without commercial paper. **Commercial paper** is any written promise or order to pay a sum of money. Drafts, checks, and promissory notes are typical examples. Commercial paper is transferred more readily than ordinary contract rights, and persons who acquire it are normally subject to less risk than the ordinary assignee of a contract right.

The law concerning commercial paper has a long history, and, as is noted in the "Landmark" in this chapter, grew out of commercial necessity. In turn, the development of laws regulating the exchange of commercial paper aided the growth of commerce. Today, the purchase and sale of commercial paper has become an industry itself, as discussed in this chapter's "Business Law in Action."

> *"The chief business of the American people is business."*
>
> **Calvin Coolidge, 1872–1933**
> *(Thirtieth president of the United States, 1923–1929)*

> **COMMERCIAL PAPER**
> Under UCC Article 3, negotiable instruments, which are signed writings that contain an unconditional promise or order to pay an exact sum of money, either when demanded or at an exact future time. Includes bills of exchange (i.e., drafts), promissory notes, certificates of deposits, and checks.

❖ The Functions of Commercial Paper

Commercial paper functions in two ways—as a substitute for money and as a credit device.

A Substitute for Money

Debtors sometimes use currency, but for convenience and safety they often use commercial paper instead. For example, commercial paper is being used when a debt is paid by check. The substitute-for-money function of commercial paper developed in the Middle Ages. Merchants deposited their precious metals with bankers in order to avoid the dangers of loss or theft. When they needed funds to pay for the goods they were buying, they gave the seller a written order addressed to the bank. This authorized the bank to deliver part of the precious metals to the seller. These orders, called *bills of exchange*, were sometimes used as a substitute for money. Today people use checks in the same way. They also use drafts, promissory notes, and certificates of deposit that are payable either on demand or on some specified date in the future. Commercial paper as a substitute for money is further indicated by the Federal Reserve's official definition of what is called the "narrow" money supply—

327

currency (dollar bills and coins) in the hands of the public and checking-account balances (and the like) held in all financial institutions.

A Credit Device

Commercial paper may represent an extension of credit. When a buyer gives a seller a promissory note, the terms of which provide that it is payable within sixty days, the seller has essentially extended sixty days of credit to the buyer. The credit aspect of commercial paper was developed in the Middle Ages soon after bills of exchange began to be used as substitutes for money. Merchants were able to give to sellers bills of exchange that were not payable until a future date. Since the seller would wait until a maturity date to collect, this was a form of extending credit to the buyer.

Discounting   The holder of a promissory note payable in sixty or ninety days who wishes to sell this instrument to a third party may do so for immediate cash. Typically, banks buy these instruments and wait until their maturity date to receive payment. In order to induce a bank to buy a promissory note, the holder of the instrument accepts a discount of, say, 5, 10, or 15 percent of the face amount. In effect, the bank pays less than the amount it will eventually collect as a way of charging interest.

Collectibility   For commercial paper to operate *practically* as either a substitute for money or a credit device, or both, it is essential that the paper be easily transferable without danger of being uncollectible. This is the function that characterizes negotiable commercial paper. Each rule studied in this chapter can be examined in light of this function.

❖ Parties to Commercial Paper

A note (or certificate of deposit—CD) has two original parties: the maker and the payee. A draft, or check, has three original parties—the drawer, the drawee, and the payee. Sometimes two of the parties to a draft can be the same person (drawer-drawee or drawer-payee). Once an instrument is issued, additional parties can become involved. **Issue** is defined as the "first delivery of an instrument to a holder." [UCC 3-102(1)(a)] The liability of these parties is discussed in Chapter 17.[1]

ISSUE
The first transfer, or delivery, of an instrument to a holder.

Makers

MAKER
One who issues a promissory note or certificate of deposit (*i.e.*, one who promises to pay a certain sum to the holder of the note or CD).

A **maker** is the person who issues a promissory note or a CD, promising to pay a certain sum of money to a payee or bearer. The maker's signature must appear on the face of the promissory note or CD for the maker to be liable on the note.

---

1.   One can also refer to primary and secondary parties. Primary parties are makers of notes and acceptors of drafts. These parties promise to pay the instrument according to its terms. A signature of a person other than the maker or the acceptor makes that person a secondary party.

Landmark in the Law

The Law Merchant and the Bills of Exchange Act of 1882

Today we take for granted the role that commercial paper plays in our lives and in our economy. A check is a form of commercial paper and was designed to be a substitute for money. It is a drawer's order to the drawee to pay the holder upon demand. Were it not for commercial paper, all transactions would have to occur face to face, with physical exchange of goods for actual dollars and cents or other goods.

The history of commercial paper began when I.O.U.s began to be used instead of coinage during the late Middle Ages when merchants, particularly in port towns, developed their own customs and courts to hear disputes arising out of commercial transactions. Disputes were settled quickly by courts set up at the traveling fairs and were decided by juries of other merchants. Decisions were originally not written down and were based on the customs of the par-

ticular time and place. Eventually, these decisions became a distinct set of laws known as the *Lex Mercantoria* (Law Merchant).

By the end of the seventeenth century, the principles of the Law Merchant were widely accepted and quite naturally became a part of common law. In 1878 Judge M.D. Chalmers codified the Law Merchant into a digest of law that was then reviewed and adopted by the British Empire in 1882 as the Bills of Exchange Act. In England and in some of the other nations of the British Commonwealth, such as Canada, the 1882 act is still used—although it has been greatly amended.

In the United States, the Bills of Exchange Act of 1882 became the basis for the Uniform Negotiable Instruments Law of 1896, which was the first "uniform" law (adopted by all the states) drafted by the National Conference of Commissioners on Uniform State Laws. The Uniform Negotiable Instruments Law of 1896, which has since been superceded by Article 3 of the Uniform Commercial Code, is the topic of the "Landmark" in Chapter 16.

Drawers, Drawees, and Payees

When a check or other draft is issued, the person who issues it, known as the **drawer,** orders the **drawee** (who is a bank, in the case of a check) to pay a certain sum of money to a **payee** (or to the bearer of the instrument).

For example, George has a checking account with Citizens Bank. At the end of the month, George receives his electric bill for $120 from the Power Plus Corporation. George writes a check payable to the order of the utility, signing it in the lower right-hand corner. George is the *drawer* of the check. Citizens Bank, which has been ordered to pay the check, is the *drawee.* Power Plus Corporation, to which George has issued the check, is the *payee.*

Indorsers

The payee of a note or draft may transfer it by signing (indorsing) it and delivering it to another person. By doing this, the payee becomes an **indorser.** For example, Martha receives a graduation check for $100. She can transfer the check to her mother (or to anyone) by signing it on the back. Martha is an indorser.

Indorsees

The person who receives the indorsed instrument is the **indorsee.** In the example just given, Martha's mother is the indorsee. She is entitled to the $100 payment by

DRAWER
A person who initiates a draft (including a check) ordering the drawee to pay.

DRAWEE
The person who is ordered to pay a draft or check. With a check, the bank is always the drawee.

PAYEE
A person to whom an instrument is made payable.

INDORSER
One who, being the payee or holder of a negotiable instrument, signs by indorsement on the back of it.

INDORSEE
The one to whom a negotiable instrument is transferred by indorsement.

Business Law in Action

The Commercial-Paper Industry

As noted in the text, commercial paper is broadly defined in the Uniform Commercial Code as consisting of promissory notes, drafts, checks, and certificates of deposit. One of the most fundamental of these types of commercial paper is the promissory note, which serves as documentary evidence of a debt. Certain types of promissory notes, such as corporate bonds, are sold at a discount—below their face value—and can be redeemed on the date of maturity for the entire face value of the note. The difference between the purchase price and the redemption price is the "interest" earned on the investment.

The purchase and sale of promissory notes represents the commercial paper "industry," which is booming in the United States. With about $350 billion in commercial paper outstanding in the United States, these notes now account for about 25 percent of

corporate debt. The participants in this market range from giants like General Motors Acceptance Corporation (GMAC) to municipalities like Oshkosh, Wisconsin.

Commercial-paper markets provide a way for corporations to borrow funds at lower rates than they would pay at banks by bypassing the banking system. Institutional investors, such as mutual funds and pension funds, also benefit from circumventing commercial banks when they receive higher rates of return by purchasing these notes. Commercial banks can also take advantage of this market to borrow short-term funds and to avoid the restrictions of time deposits, and bank commercial paper represents a large part of the total market.

Large corporations, such as General Motors and Sears, Roebuck & Company, and commercial banks can place directly (issue and sell themselves) their commercial paper. Direct placements are used by only 10 percent of issuers in the market but account for 50 percent of the

market's volume. Most issuers, however, go through a financial intermediary, such as an investment bank, which acts as an agent or underwriter (purchases the issue itself to then distribute). In the past, commercial banks (banks that accept demand deposits) were prohibited from underwriting most types of securities by the Glass-Steagall Act of 1933, which restricted such activities to investment banks. In recent years, however, commercial banks have been trying to move into the lucrative market for commercial paper.

The keen competition in the commercial-paper industry is a mark of the 1980s, a decade that has witnessed increasing deregulation of the banking industry. In the wake of this competition, the commercial-paper industry—which has been continuous in the United States for over a century—is thriving. Prompted by the success and great expansion of the U.S. market in recent years, commercial-paper markets are currently opening in several European countries as well.

---

virtue of Martha's indorsement. Martha's mother can indorse the check to someone else and thus become an indorser as well.

Bearers

BEARER
A person in the possession of an instrument payable to bearer or indorsed in blank.

A **bearer** is any person who has physical possession of an instrument that either is payable to anyone without specific designation or is indorsed in blank. If a note is expressly made "payable to bearer," the person who possesses that note is the bearer. A person possessing a note or check payable to "cash" is also a bearer. A check payable to the order of a named person and indorsed by that named person in blank on the back makes its possessor a bearer also.

Holders

The term **holder** includes any person in the possession of an instrument drawn, issued, or indorsed to him or her or to his or her order or to bearer or in blank.[2] For example, a check made payable to the order of John Doe, in his possession, makes John Doe a holder. A promissory note written by Jane Johnson promises to pay a sum of money to the order of Broderick Fisher. While the note is in Fisher's possession, Fisher is a holder. If Fisher signs (indorses) the back of the note and transfers (negotiates) it to Alistair Adams, the note becomes bearer paper, and Adams becomes the holder.

The holder and the owner of negotiable paper is often the same person, but not necessarily. For example, a thief who steals a bearer instrument is a *holder* under commercial law principles, but obviously is not the owner. Nonetheless, the thief can legally transfer (negotiate) the bearer instrument to another person, who then becomes a *holder*.

Holder in Due Course   Under UCC 3-302, a **holder in due course** (HDC) is a person who acquires an instrument for value in a good-faith transaction, without notice that it is defective or overdue. It is easier for an HDC to collect payment on an instrument than it is for an assignee of a contract to collect payment. The assignee is subject to all outstanding defenses of prior parties; the HDC is protected from all but a few defenses.[3]

Holder through a Holder in Due Course   An ordinary holder whose manner of acquisition fails to meet the requirements of a holder in due course can still be afforded HDC protection by proving that any prior holder qualified as a holder in due course. [UCC 3-201(1)]

Acceptors

An **acceptor** is a *drawee* of a draft or check who has, by signing the instrument, manifestly agreed to pay the draft when due. For example, when the buyer "agrees" to pay the trade acceptance (a promise by a company to pay a certain amount at a future date) of the seller, drawn on the buyer (drawee), the buyer becomes an acceptor of the draft. The same result takes place when a drawee bank certifies a check drawn on that bank.

Accommodation Parties

An **accommodation party** is one who signs an instrument in any capacity to lend "his name to another party to it." [UCC 3-415(1)] The accommodation party actually lends his or her credit to the party to whom the accommodation is made and is classified accordingly.

HOLDER
A person "who is in possession of a document of title or negotiable instrument or a certificated investment security drawn, issued, or indorsed to him or his order or to bearer or blank."
[UCC 1-201(20)]

HOLDER IN DUE COURSE
Any holder who acquires a negotiable instrument for value, in good faith, and without notice that the instrument is defective or overdue.

ACCEPTOR
A drawee who accepts a draft and who engages to be primarily responsible for its payment.

ACCOMMODATION PARTY
A person who signs an instrument for the purpose of lending that person's credit to another party on that instrument.

---

2.   UCC 1-201(20) defines *holder* as "a person who is in possession of a document of title or an instrument or a certificated investment security drawn, issued, or indorsed to him or to his order or to his bearer or in blank."

3.   As will be discussed in Chapter 17, the HDC is subject to real defenses. These generally involve the validity of the instrument—for example, legal capacity or certain sorts of forgery or alteration. [UCC 3-305] An HDC is free from all personal defenses between prior parties—for example, breach of contract.

For example, Grant seeks a loan from Citizens Bank. The bank will make the loan only if Grant will get a third party with a good credit rating to co-sign the note. Ashley qualifies and agrees to accommodate Grant by signing the note below Grant's signature. Grant is the *maker*, and Ashley is the *accommodation maker*.

❖ Types of Commercial Paper

UCC 3-104 specifies four types of instruments—drafts, checks, notes, and certificates of deposit.

Drafts

DRAFT
Any instrument drawn on a drawee (including a bank) which orders the drawee to pay a certain sum of money.

A **draft** (bill of exchange) is an unconditional written order. The party creating it (the drawer) orders another party (the drawee) to pay money, usually to a third party (the payee). Exhibit 15-1 shows a typical draft. The drawee must be obligated to the drawer either by agreement or through a debtor-creditor relationship before the drawee is obligated to the drawer to honor the order.

Time and Sight Drafts   A time draft is payable at a definite future time. A sight (or demand) draft is payable on sight, that is, when the holder presents it for payment.[4] A draft can be both a time and a sight draft; such a draft is one payable at a stated time after sight.

◆ **Exhibit 15-1 A Typical Time Draft—A Bill of Exchange**

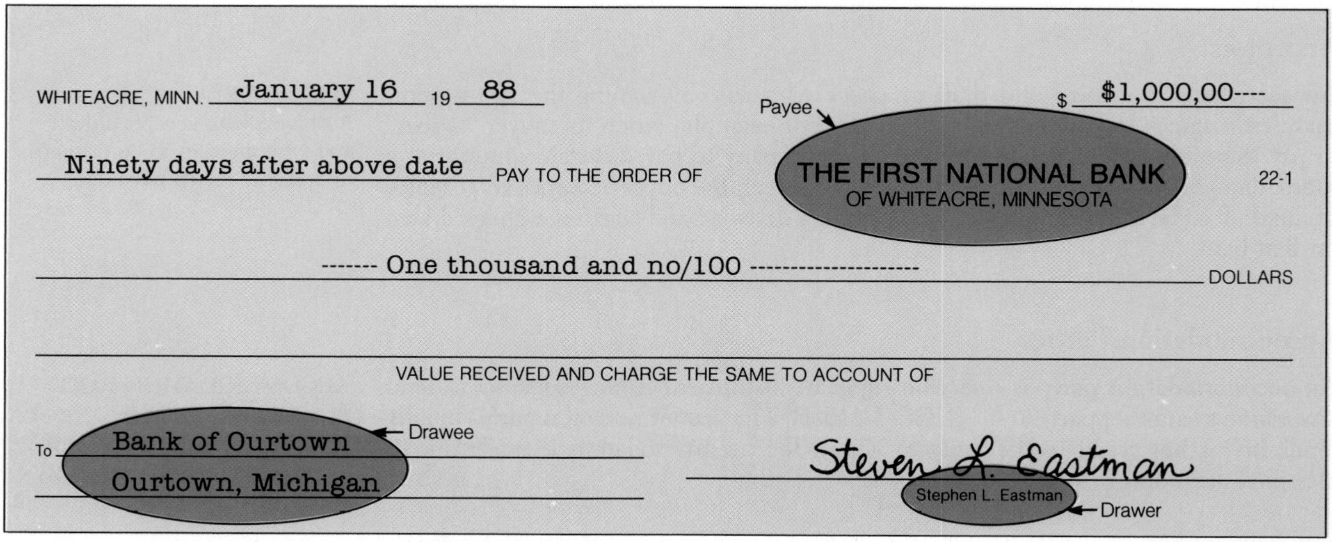

WHITEACRE, MINN. _January 16_ 19 _88_   Payee → $ _$1,000,00----_

Ninety days after above date PAY TO THE ORDER OF   **THE FIRST NATIONAL BANK**   22-1
                                                                      OF WHITEACRE, MINNESOTA

------- One thousand and no/100 --------------------   DOLLARS

VALUE RECEIVED AND CHARGE THE SAME TO ACCOUNT OF

To _Bank of Ourtown_   ← Drawee
   Ourtown, Michigan   *Steven L. Eastman*
                                                Stephen L. Eastman   ← Drawer

---

4.   Or a sight draft is payable on acceptance. Acceptance is the drawee's written promise (engagement) to pay the draft when it comes due. The usual manner of accepting is by writing the word *accepted* across the face of the instrument, followed by the date of acceptance and the signature of the drawee.

◆ **Exhibit 15-2   A Typical Time Draft—A Trade Acceptance**

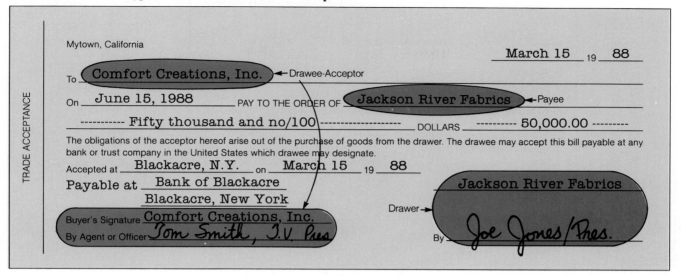

Trade Acceptances   A **trade acceptance** is a draft frequently used with the sale of goods. The seller is both the drawer and the payee on this draft. Essentially, the draft orders the buyer to pay a specified sum of money to the seller, usually at a stated time in the future.

For example, Jackson River Fabrics sells $50,000 worth of fabric to Comfort Creations, Inc. each fall on terms requiring payment to be made in ninety days. One year Jackson River needs cash, so it draws a *trade acceptance* that orders Comfort Creations to pay $50,000 to the order of Jackson River Fabrics ninety days hence. Jackson River presents the paper to Comfort Creations. Comfort Creations *accepts* by signing the face of the paper and returns it to Jackson River Fabrics. Comfort Creations' acceptance creates an enforceable promise to pay the instrument when it comes due in ninety days. Jackson River can sell the trade acceptance in the commercial money market more easily than it can assign the $50,000 account receivable. Trade acceptances are the standard credit instruments in sales transactions (see Exhibit 15-2).

TRADE ACCEPTANCE
A bill of exchange/draft drawn by the seller of goods on the purchaser and accepted by the purchaser's written promise to pay the draft. Once accepted, the purchaser becomes primarily liable to pay the draft.

Checks

A **check** is a distinct type of draft, *drawn* on a *bank* and payable on *demand*. Checks are discussed more fully in Chapter 18. Note here, however, that with certain types of checks the bank is both the drawer and the drawee. For example, cashier's checks drawn by the bank on itself are payable on demand when issued. In addition, a check can be drawn by a bank on another bank. This instrument is known as a bank draft.

When traveler's checks are drawn on a bank, they are checks, but they require the purchaser's authorized signature before becoming payable. (Technically, most traveler's checks are not checks but drafts, because the drawee—for example, American Express—is usually not a bank).

CHECK
A draft drawn on a bank, signed by the drawer, and payable on demand.

◆ **Exhibit 15-3**   **A Typical Promissory Note**

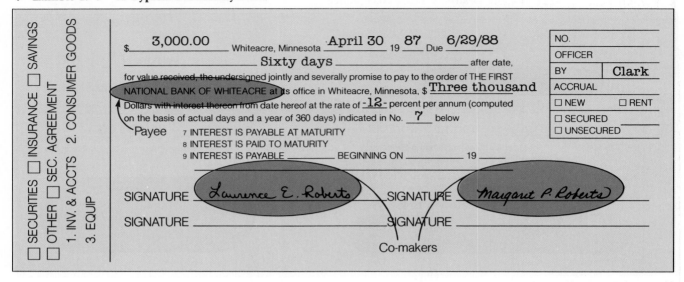

Promissory Notes

PROMISSORY NOTE
A written instrument signed by a maker unconditionally promising to pay a certain sum in money to a payee or a holder on demand or on a specified date.

The **promissory note** is a written promise between two parties. One party is the maker of the promise to pay, and the other is the payee, or the one to whom the promise is made. A promissory note, commonly referred to simply as a *note*, can be made payable at a definite time or on demand. It can name a specific payee or merely be payable to bearer. A sample promissory note is shown in Exhibit 15-3.

Notes are used in a variety of credit transactions and often carry the name of the transaction involved. For example, in real estate transactions, promissory notes for the unpaid balance on a house, secured by a mortgage on the property, are called *mortgage notes*. A note that is secured by personal property is called a *collateral note*, where collateral is property pledged as security for the satisfaction of a debt. And a note payable in installments, such as for payment of a television set over a twelve-month period, is called an *installment note*.

Certificates of Deposit

CERTIFICATE OF DEPOSIT
An instrument evidencing a promissory acknowledgment by a bank of a receipt of money with an engagement to repay it.

A **certificate of deposit** (CD) is an acknowledgment by a bank of the receipt of money with an engagement to repay it. [UCC 3-104(2)(c)] Certificates of deposit in small denominations are often sold by savings and loan associations, savings banks, and commercial banks. They are called small CDs and are for amounts up to $100,000. Certificates of deposit for amounts over $100,000 are called large CDs.[5] Exhibit 15-4 shows a typical small CD.

---

5.   Large CDs are included in certain definitions of the money supply because they are fully negotiable.

♦ **Exhibit 15-4   A Typical Small CD**

THE FIRST NATIONAL BANK OF WHITEACRE   22–1/960   NUMBER 332
NEGOTIABLE CERTIFICATE OF DEPOSIT

WHITEACRE, MINN. __February 15__ 19 __88__

THIS CERTIFIES to the deposit in the Bank the sum of $ __5,000.00__

-------- Five thousand and no/100 ----------------------- DOLLARS

Payee (Bearer)
which is payable to bearer on the __15th__ day of __July__ 19 __88__ , against presentation and surrender of this certificate and bears interest at the rate of **9 3/4** % per annum, to be computed (on the basis of 360 days and actual days elapsed) to, and payable at, maturity. No payment may be made prior to, and no interest runs after, that date. Payable at maturity in federal funds, and if desired, at Manufacturers Hanover Trust Company, New York.

THE FIRST NATIONAL BANK OF WHITEACRE

By ___John Doe___
                                           Signature
                                           Maker

❖ Letters of Credit

A **letter of credit** is neither a draft nor a note. It is an agreement that the issuer will pay drafts drawn by the creditor. Letters of credit are made by a bank or other person at the request of a customer and can be revocable or irrevocable commitments. Letters of credit are frequently used by buyers in the purchase of goods in commerce.

For example, a corporate buyer in New Mexico wishes to purchase manufacturing equipment from a Parisian firm. The buyer goes to its bank and through a loan agreement gets the bank to issue and to send a letter of credit to the seller in Paris. The letter of credit provides that upon the seller's presentation of certain documents evidencing tender of goods (**bills of lading,** invoices, **customs receipts,** and the like) to the bank, the bank will pay any drafts drawn by the seller on the buyer up to a stated amount. As the drafts are presented to the bank for payment, the bank remits the funds to the seller. The bank then collects the amount from the buyer under the terms of the loan agreement (see Exhibit 15-5).

Today, letters of credit are used for a variety of lending arrangements (such as the development of real estate) for both domestic and foreign commercial purposes. Much of the law governing letters of credit is found in Article 5 (Letters of Credit) in the UCC. Letters of credit are discussed further in Chapter 36.

❖ Other Ways of Classifying Commercial Paper

The preceding classifications of commercial paper follow the language of the UCC. There are numerous other ways to classify commercial paper, some of which follow.

LETTER OF CREDIT
A written instrument, usually issued by a bank on behalf of a customer or other person, in which the issuer promises to honor drafts or other demands for payment by third persons in accordance with the terms of the instrument.

BILL OF LADING
A document of title given by a carrier, such as a shipping company, that lists the goods accepted for transport. Additionally, the bill of lading lists the terms of the shipping agreement.

CUSTOMS RECEIPTS
Receipts evidencing payment of taxes due on goods imported from other countries.

◆ **Exhibit 15-5**
Events and Relationships in a Typical Letter-of-Credit Transaction

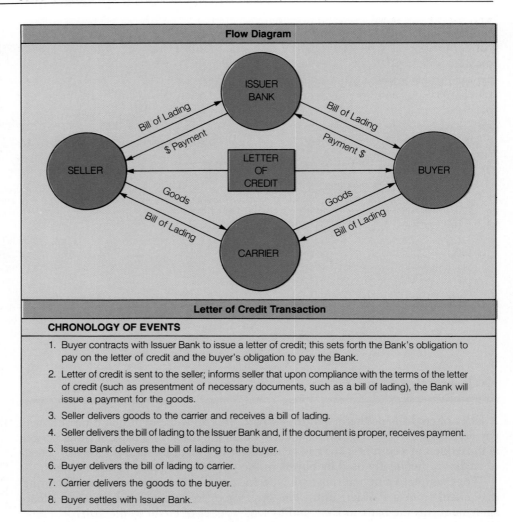

Flow Diagram

Letter of Credit Transaction

CHRONOLOGY OF EVENTS

1. Buyer contracts with Issuer Bank to issue a letter of credit; this sets forth the Bank's obligation to pay on the letter of credit and the buyer's obligation to pay the Bank.

2. Letter of credit is sent to the seller; informs seller that upon compliance with the terms of the letter of credit (such as presentment of necessary documents, such as a bill of lading), the Bank will issue a payment for the goods.

3. Seller delivers goods to the carrier and receives a bill of lading.

4. Seller delivers the bill of lading to the Issuer Bank and, if the document is proper, receives payment.

5. Issuer Bank delivers the bill of lading to the buyer.

6. Buyer delivers the bill of lading to carrier.

7. Carrier delivers the goods to the buyer.

8. Buyer settles with Issuer Bank.

Demand Instruments and Time Instruments

Commercial paper can be classified as demand instruments or time instruments. A demand instrument is payable on demand, that is, whenever the holder—a possessor *to whom the instrument runs*—chooses to present it to the maker (in the case of a note) or to the drawee (in the case of a draft). (Instruments payable on demand include those payable on sight or on presentation, and in which no time for payment is stated.) [UCC 3-108] All checks are demand instruments because, by definition, they must be payable on demand; therefore, checking accounts are called **demand deposits.** Time instruments are payable at a future date.

DEMAND DEPOSIT
Funds (accepted by a bank) subject to immediate withdrawal, in contrast to a time deposit which requires that a depositor wait a specific time before withdrawing or pay a penalty for early withdrawal.

Orders to Pay and Promises to Pay

Commercial paper involving the payment of money can be classified as either a *promise* to pay or an *order* to pay. Checks and drafts are orders to pay; certificates of deposit and promissory notes are promises to pay.

Negotiable and Nonnegotiable Instruments

All commercial paper is either *negotiable* or *nonnegotiable*. This serves as another means of classification. Both its form and its content determine whether commercial paper is a **negotiable instrument**. All the elements listed in UCC 3-104 must be present for negotiability. When an instrument is negotiable, its transfer from one person to another is governed by Article 3 of the UCC. Indeed, UCC 3-102(e) defines *instrument* as a "negotiable instrument." For that reason, wherever the term *instrument* is used in this book, it refers to a negotiable instrument. Transfers of nonnegotiable instruments are governed by rules of assignment of contract rights (see Chapter 9).

NEGOTIABLE INSTRUMENT
A written and signed unconditional promise or order to pay a specified sum of money on demand or at a definite time payable to order or bearer.

❖ Chapter Summary: Commercial Paper—Basic Concepts

Functions of Commercial Paper	1. As a substitute for money. 2. As a credit device.
Parties to Commercial Paper	1. *Maker:* The person who issues a promissory note or a CD promising to pay a certain sum of money to a payee or bearer. 2. *Drawer, Drawee, Payee:* When a check or other draft is issued, the person who issues it, the *drawer,* orders the *drawee* (a bank, in the case of a check) to pay a sum of money to a *payee* (or to the bearer of the instrument). 3. *Indorser:* A payee or holder of a negotiable instrument who transfers the instrument by signing (indorsing) it and delivering it to another person. 4. *Indorsee:* The person who receives an indorsed instrument. 5. *Bearer:* Any person who has physical possession of an instrument that is either payable to anyone without specific designation or indorsed in blank. 6. *Holder:* Any person in possession of an instrument drawn, issued, or indorsed to him or her or to his or her order or to bearer or in blank. (a) A holder in due course (HDC) is a person who acquires an instrument for value in a good-faith transaction without notice that it is defective or overdue. UCC 3-302 (b) A holder through a holder in due course is an ordinary holder who acquires the rights of a holder in due course by proving that any prior holder qualified as a holder in due course. 7. *Acceptor:* A drawee of a draft or check who has, by signing the instrument, manifestly agreed to pay the draft when due. 8. *Accommodation party:* One who signs an instrument in any capacity to lend "his name to another party to it"; one who lends his or her credit to the party to whom the accommodation is made.
Types of Commercial Paper	1. *Draft (bill of exchange):* An unconditional written order by a drawer to a drawee to pay money, usually to a third party (the payee). Drafts include: (a) Time and sight drafts: A time draft is payable at a definite future time; a sight (demand) draft is payable on sight (when the holder presents it for payment). (b) Trade acceptances: A trade acceptance is a draft on which the seller is both the drawer and the payee. The draft orders the buyer to agree (written acceptance) to pay a specified sum of money usually at a specified future time. 2. *Check:* A draft drawn on a bank and payable on demand. A bank may draw a check on itself (cashier's check) or on another bank (bank draft).

(Continued)

❖ Chapter Summary: Commercial Paper—Basic Concepts—Continued

Types of Commercial Paper (Continued)	3. *Promissory note:* A written promise whereby the maker of the note promises to pay the payee or bearer.
	4. *Certificate of deposit (CD):* A written acknowledgment by a bank for the deposit of money with an engagement to repay it plus interest.
Other Ways of Classifying Commercial Paper	1. *Demand instruments and time instruments:* A demand instrument is payable on demand (when the holder presents it to the maker or drawee). Time instruments are payable at a future date.
	2. *Orders to pay and promises to pay:* Commercial paper may be classified as either promises to pay or orders to pay. A check or a draft is an *order* to pay. A CD or a promissory note is a *promise* to pay.
	3. *Negotiable and nonnegotiable instruments:* Transfers of negotiable instruments are governed by Article 3 of the UCC. Transfers of nonnegotiable instruments are governed by rules of assignment of contract rights.
Letter of Credit	A written instrument, usually issued by a bank on behalf of a customer or other person, in which the issuer promises to honor drafts and other demands for payment by third persons in accordance with the terms of the instrument.

❖ Questions and Case Problems

15-1. A partnership called Bowers & Wolfe is a law firm. Wolfe won a case for her client, Donnelly, against Phillip Barnes. When Wolfe collected the judgment from Barnes, Barnes wrote out a check that read: "Pay to the order of Bowers & Wolfe $50,000 [signed] Phillip Barnes." On the top of the check was printed "First Bank & Trust Company of Colusa." When Wolfe deposited the check in the trust account that she had set up for her client, she signed the back of the check, "J. Wolfe." How are each of these parties designated in commercial paper law?

15-2. Often when two parties to a sale are strangers, and the sale is for a substantial amount of money, the selling party insists that the purchaser make payment with a cashier's check. A cashier's check is a check on which the bank is both the drawer and the drawee. To purchase a cashier's check, a person goes to a bank teller, tenders the amount of money for which the check is to be payable, and supplies the teller with the name of the person who is to be the payee of the check. Once the payee's name is inscribed on the check, only the payee (or a person to whom the payee negotiates the check) will be able to receive money for the check. What problem might arise if a seller asks a prospective buyer of goods to make payment with a cashier's check, and the buyer purchases the check, naming the seller as the payee? How can this problem be avoided?

15-3. Identify the following types of commercial paper *or* parties involved in commercial paper.

(a) A draft drawn on a bank payable to a payee on demand.

(b) A written acknowledgment by a bank of a receipt of money with an obligation to repay it.

(c) A written promise to pay another (or holder) a certain sum of money.

(d) An instrument drawn by a bank on itself, payable on demand.

(e) Any person who acquires the instrument as a payee, by indorsement, or by delivery.

(f) A person who issues a promissory note payable to a named payee.

(g) A payee who transfers an order instrument by signing the instrument.

(h) A person who indorses a check on behalf of the payee upon the payee's transfer to an indorsee.

15-4. Harley Babcock, a college student, wished to purchase a new stereo from Horowitz Fidelity Sound, Inc. Since Babcock did not have the cash to pay for the entire stereo system, he offered to sign a note promising to pay $150 per month for the next six months. Horowitz Fidelity Sound, anxious to sell the system to Babcock, agreed to accept the promissory note if Babcock would have one of his professors sign it. Babcock did this and tendered a note to Horowitz Fidelity Sound that stated, "I, Harley Babcock, promise to pay Horowitz Fidelity Sound or its order the sum of $150 per month for the next six months." The note was signed by Harley Babcock and his business law professor. About a week later, Horowitz Fidelity Sound, badly in need of cash, signed the back of the note and sold it to Central Bank. Give the specific designation of the four parties on this note.

15-5. In which of the following situations is Abel a holder of a negotiable instrument?

(a) Adam writes a check on the Bank of Eden payable

to Eve. Eve writes on the back of the check, "Pay to the order of Cain." Eve then asks Abel to hold the check for her until Cain returns from the fields.

(b) Instead of indorsing the above check to Cain, Eve simply writes her name on the back and gives the check to Abel.

(c) Eve writes a check on the Bank of Eden payable to "cash" and gives the check to Abel.

(d) Eve writes a check on the Bank of Eden payable to bearer, and Abel steals it.

15-6. Negotiable instruments play an important part in commercial transactions. Different needs can be fulfilled by using different instruments. For instance, many insurance companies use a form of draft instead of a check to remit insurance benefits. The insurance company is both the drawer and the drawee; the beneficiary (the person receiving the money) is the payee; and the draft is made payable through a bank (called a pay-through draft—see UCC 3-120) where the insurance company has a large account. What are the advantages of using such a draft?

Chapter 16

Commercial Paper—
The Negotiable Instrument,
Transferability, and
Negotiation

In the complicated, fast-paced environment of business, commercial paper must be generally accepted as money and thus be freely transferable. The law that creates and governs negotiable instruments is primarily designed, therefore, to urge their use as a substitute for money. Leland Stanford's observation that money is of little value to an individual unless it is of value to others is true also of commercial paper. In order for commercial paper to be valuable to people, they must be confident when they accept a check, promissory note, or other item of commercial paper that all parties involved with the paper will be required by law to meet their responsibilities.

In this chapter, we examine not only the elements of a negotiable instrument, but the way in which commercial-law principles of negotiation come into play once a negotiable instrument circulates beyond the original parties. As we will see, the method of transfer that is used to pass a negotiable instrument from person to person determines the rights and duties that are passed with it.

❖ What Is a Negotiable Instrument?

In order for an instrument to be negotiable, it must meet certain criteria specified in UCC 3-104(1) and discussed here.

Written Form

Negotiable instruments must be in written form. Clearly, an oral promise can create the danger of fraud or make it difficult to determine liability. Negotiable instruments must possess the quality of certainty that only formal, written expression can give.

There are certain practical limitations concerning the writing and the substance on which it is placed:

1. The writing must be on material that lends itself to *permanence*. Instruments have been carved in blocks of ice and recorded on other impermanent surfaces. Suppose Suzanne writes in the sand, "I promise to pay $500 to the order of Jack."

This is not a negotiable instrument because, although it is in writing, it lacks permanence.

2. The writing must have *portability*. Though this is not a spelled-out legal requirement, if an instrument is not movable, it obviously cannot meet the requirement that it be freely transferable. For example, Charles writes on the side of a cow, "I promise to pay Paul $500." Technically, this meets the requirements of a negotiable instrument, but since a cow cannot easily be transferred in the ordinary course of business, the "instrument" is nonnegotiable.

Signatures

For an instrument to be negotiable, it must be signed by (1) the maker if it is a note or a certificate of deposit or (2) the drawer if it is a draft or a check. [UCC 3-104(1)(a)]

Extreme latitude is granted in determining what constitutes a **signature**. UCC 1-201(39) defines the word *signed* as "[including] any symbol executed or adopted by a party with present intention to authenticate a writing." UCC 3-401(2) expands upon this: "A signature is made by use of any name, including any trade or assumed name, upon an instrument, or by any word or mark used in lieu of a written signature." Thus, initials, an X, or a thumbprint will suffice. A trade name or an assumed name is sufficient even if it is false. A so-called rubber stamp bearing a person's signature is permitted and frequently used in the business world. If necessary, parol evidence (see Chapter 8) is admissible in identifying the signer. When the signer is identified, the signature becomes effective.

SIGNATURE
The name or mark of a person, written by that person or at his or her direction. In commercial law, any name, word, or mark used with the intention to authenticate a writing constitutes a signature.

Placement of the Signature   The location of the signature on the document is unimportant, though the usual place is the lower right-hand corner. A *handwritten* statement on the body of the instrument, such as, "I, Louise Ackerman, promise to pay John Grant," is sufficient to act as Louise's signature.

There are virtually no limitations on the manner in which a signature can be made, but one should be careful about receiving an instrument that has been signed in an unusual way since the burden of proving the genuineness of a signature rests on the recipient. Furthermore, an unusual signature clearly decreases the *marketability* of an instrument because it creates uncertainty.

Signature by Authorized Representative   If a person signs an instrument as the agent for the maker or drawer, the maker or drawer has effectively signed the instrument, provided the agent has *authority* to do so. No particular form of appointment as an agent is necessary to show authority; all that is needed is proof that the agent has such authority. [UCC 3-403]

If the agent has authority, the maker or drawer is liable on the instrument, just as if he or she had actually signed it. If the agent has authority and clearly has signed the instrument in a representative capacity, he or she will not be personally liable. If the agent has no such authority, or if the agent did not clearly sign in a representative capacity, the agent is personally liable. This situation arose in the following case. The importance of which parties have liability in these situations will be discussed in detail in Chapter 22.

Case 16.1
HILL v. CONSUMER NATIONAL BANK
Supreme Court of Mississippi, 1986.
482 So.2d 1124.

FACTS On March 29, 1982, Cary Hill, President of C&H Distributors, executed a ninety-day promissory note for $17,600 with the Consumer National Bank. When the note came due, Hill failed to pay. The bank then sought judicial enforcement. Hill claimed he should not be held personally liable on the note because, although the promissory note in no way indicated his representative capacity, he indicated verbally to the bank when the loan was made that he was obtaining it for C&H Distributors. The trial court granted the bank's request for summary judgment, and Hill was held liable for the amount of the loan plus attorneys' fees—a total of $28,968.04. Hill appealed.

ISSUE Is Hill personally liable on the promissory note to the bank?

DECISION Yes. The trial court's ruling was affirmed.

REASON The court noted that, under Mississippi statute, "An authorized representative who signs his own name to an instrument is personally obligated if the instrument neither names the person represented nor shows that the representative signed in a representative capacity." Since the statute was, according to the court, "plain and simple," it ruled that "there is no reason to think it to mean other than just what it says." If Hill had shown any evidence of his verbal explanations to the bank concerning his argument that the loan was taken out for C&H Distributors, he might have had a defense against the bank. But Hill could produce no such evidence.

Unconditional Promise or Order to Pay

The terms of a promise or order must be included in the writing on the face of a negotiable instrument. These terms must not be conditioned upon the occurrence or nonoccurrence of some other event or agreement or state that the instrument is to be paid only out of a particular fund. [UCC 3-105(2)]

Promise or Order In order for an instrument to be negotiable, it must contain an express order or promise to pay. A mere acknowledgment of the debt, which might logically *imply* a promise, is not sufficient under the UCC because the promise must be an *affirmative* undertaking. [UCC 3-102(1)(c)]

For example, the traditional I.O.U. is only an acknowledgment of indebtedness. Therefore, it is not a negotiable instrument. But if such words as "to be paid on demand" or "due on demand" are added, the need for an affirmative promise is satisfied. For example, if a buyer executes a promissory note using the words, "I promise to pay $1,000 to the order of the seller for the purchase of goods X," then the requirement for a negotiable instrument is satisfied.

A certificate of deposit is different. Here, the requisite promise is satisfied because the bank's acknowledgment of the deposit and the other terms of the instrument clearly indicate a promise.

An order is associated with three-party instruments, such as trade acceptances, checks, and drafts. An order directs a third party to pay the instrument as drawn. In the typical check, for example, the word "pay" (to the order of a payee) is a command to the drawee bank to pay the check when presented, and thus it is an order. The order is mandatory even if it is written in a courteous form with words like "Please pay" or "Kindly pay." Generally, precise language must be used. An order stating, "I wish you would pay," does not fulfill the requirement of precision.

In addition to being precise, an effective order must specifically identify the drawee (the person who must pay). [UCC 3-102(1)(b)] A bank's name printed on the face of a check, for example, sufficiently designates the bank as drawee.

Landmark in the Law

The Uniform Negotiable Instruments Law

The early history of American commercial law was strongly influenced by several conditions—the instability of the monetary system, the large number of separate jurisdictions, and the diversity of nationalities among settlers in America. Although English common law was influential, each state generally adopted statutory rules governing the use of commercial paper. Thus, unlike in England prior to 1882, commercial-paper law in the early years of the United States was regulated by written law.

Although statutes governing the use of commercial paper had been created in the various states for the purpose of facilitating commerce, in fact, they produced as many problems as they solved. The variance of statutes from one state to the next often impeded commerce, particularly the interstate commerce that was rapidly developing in the nineteenth century. Consequently, when the American Bar Association was first formed, in 1878, one of its major goals was the establishment of some degree of uniformity of law among the states to avoid the problems created by conflicting state statutes. This concern eventually led to the creation of the National Conference of

Commissioners on Uniform State Laws (discussed in the "Landmark in the Law" in Chapter 11), and it was a committee of this conference that drafted the Uniform Negotiable Instruments Law.

Modeled on the English Bills of Exchange Act of 1882, the law was drafted primarily by John J. Crawford of New York, who submitted it to the National Conference in 1896. Having approved the draft, the Conference urged its enactment by the states. Twenty-eight years later, all the states had adopted the new law.

Although uniformity and certainty of negotiable instruments were to some extent achieved by the Uniform Law, the long-term result was even greater uncertainty, because the courts rarely applied the act uniformly. Some did not use it at all but relied on the common law instead; others relied on the Uniform Law solely. In general, its application depended upon the particular judge's view in a particular state. By 1940 it was apparent that the original goal of the Conference to create a uniform law governing negotiable instruments was far from realized. The Conference, in studying solutions to this problem—and to similar problems stemming from uniform acts enacted in other areas of commercial law—eventually formed the Uniform Commercial Code (UCC), Article 3 of which replaced the Uniform Negotiable Instruments Law.

Unconditionality of Promise or Order A negotiable instrument's utility as a substitute for money or as a credit device would be dramatically reduced if it had conditional promises attached to it. It would be expensive and time-consuming to investigate conditional promises, and, therefore, the transferability of the negotiable instrument would be greatly restricted. Substantial administrative costs would be required to process conditional promises. Furthermore, the payee would risk the possibility of the condition not occurring.

If Andrew promises in a note to pay Frances $10,000 only if a certain ship reaches port, no one could safely purchase the promissory note without first investigating whether the ship had arrived. Even then, the facts disclosed by the investigation might be incorrect. To avoid such problems, the UCC provides that only unconditional promises or orders can be negotiable. [UCC 3-104(1)(b)]

The Code expands the definition of *unconditional*, however, in order to prevent certain necessary conditions commonly used in business transactions from rendering an otherwise negotiable instrument nonnegotiable. These conditions, resolved by UCC 3-105, are discussed here.

1. *Statements of consideration.* Many instruments state the terms of the underlying agreement as a matter of standard business practice. Somewhere on its face, the

instrument refers to the transactions or agreement for which it is being used in payment. The policy of the UCC is to integrate standard trade usages into its provisions. For example, the words "as per contract" or "This debt arises from the sale of goods X and Y" do not render an instrument nonnegotiable.

2.   *Reference to other agreements.* The UCC provides that mere reference to another agreement does not affect negotiability. If, on the other hand, the instrument is made subject to the other agreement, it is rendered nonnegotiable. [UCC 3-105(2)(a)] A reference to another agreement is normally inserted for the purpose of keeping a record or giving information to anyone who may be interested. Notes frequently refer to separate agreements that give special rights to a creditor for an acceleration of payment or to a debtor for prepayment. References to these rights do not destroy the negotiability of the instrument. For example, the statement that an instrument's payment is secured by collateral will not render an otherwise negotiable instrument nonnegotiable. Rather, this statement adds to the salability and marketability of the instrument.

3.   *Payments out of a particular fund.* UCC 3-105(2)(b) states that a promise or order renders the instrument nonnegotiable if the terms provide that payment can be made only out of a particular fund or source. Thus, for example, terms in a note that condition payment out of next year's cotton crop would make the note nonnegotiable. Because such a rule would operate as a hardship for certain entities and organizations, the UCC specifically states that government entities can issue negotiable instruments, even if payment is to come only from a particular fund or source. [UCC 3-105(1)(g)] Also, partnerships, unincorporated associations, and trusts or estates can issue negotiable instruments even though payment is to come from the entire assets of the organization or the estate. [UCC 3-105(1)(h)]

In the following case, a promissory note that incorporated another agreement was rendered nonnegotiable.

Case 16.2
HOLLY HILL ACRES, LTD. v. CHARTER BANK OF GAINESVILLE

District Court of Appeal of Florida, Second District, 1975.
314 So.2d 209.

FACTS Holly Hill Acres was the maker of a promissory note that named Rogers and Blythe as payees. Holly Hill gave the note to Rogers and Blythe as payment for certain property, and they retained a mortgage (lien) on the property. The note stated in part: "This note is secured by a mortgage on real estate. . . . The terms of said mortgage are by this reference made part hereof." Subsequently, Rogers and Blythe assigned the promissory note and the mortgage to Charter Bank of Gainesville. Holly Hill defaulted on the note, and, when the bank sued to recover, Holly Hill claimed that Rogers and Blythe had fraudulently induced it to purchase land. Holly Hill refused to pay on the note. The bank argued that it was a special type of assignee called a *holder in due course* because the promissory note was a negotiable instrument. This being so, the bank claimed an unhampered right to recover on the note despite any underlying disputes between Holly Hill and Rogers and Blythe. (A holder in due course takes a negotiable instrument free of most claims of other parties. This is the rule only when a negotiable instrument is involved.) The trial court held that the promissory note was negotiable and that the bank, as a holder in due course, could recover. Holly Hill appealed, claiming that, because the note was made subject to the mortgage agreement, the note was rendered nonnegotiable.

ISSUE Does the fact that the note was made subject to the mortgage agreement render the note nonnegotiable?

DECISION Yes. The appellate court reversed the trial court's decision and held the note to be nonnegotiable.

Case 16.2—Continued

REASON For the note to be negotiable, the "[m]ere reference to a note being secured by mortgage . . . does not impede the negotiability of the note." The court held, however, that when the instrument provides that the terms of a mortgage are by reference made a part thereof, the note is conditional, being governed by the mortgage, and "the note is rendered nonnegotiable." Because the note was nonnegotiable, the bank was not a holder in due course, and Holly Hill Acres could assert fraud as a defense.

Sum Certain in Money

Negotiable instruments must state the amount to be paid in a *sum certain in money*, a requirement that promises clarity and certainty in determining the value of the instrument. [UCC 3-104(1)(b)] Any promise to pay in the future is risky, because the value of money (purchasing power) fluctuates. Nonetheless, the present value of such an instrument can be estimated with a reasonable degree of accuracy by financial experts. If the instrument's value were stated in terms of goods or services, it would be too difficult to ascertain the market value of those goods and services at the time the instrument was to be discounted.

The UCC mandates that the negotiable commercial paper be paid wholly in money. A promissory note that provides for payment in diamonds, or in 1,000 hours of services, would not be payable in money and thus would be nonnegotiable.

Sum Certain The term *sum certain* means an amount that is ascertainable from the instrument itself without reference to an outside source. A demand note payable with 12 percent interest meets the requirement of sum certain because its amount can be determined at the time it is payable. [UCC 3-106(1)] The basic test is whether any holder who receives the instrument can determine by calculation the amount required to be paid when the instrument is due. Instruments that provide simply for payment of interest at prevailing bank rates are generally nonnegotiable, because bank rates fluctuate. A mortgage note tied to a variable rate of interest that fluctuates as a result of market conditions would not be negotiable. When, however, an instrument is payable at the legal rate of interest, or at a judgment rate of interest, or as fixed by state law, the instrument is negotiable (if it meets other criteria).

Money and No Other Promise UCC 3-104(1)(b) provides that a sum certain is to be payable in "money and no other promise." The Code defines money as "a medium of exchange authorized or adopted by a domestic or foreign government as a part of its currency." [UCC 1-201(24)]

Suppose that the maker of a note promises "to pay on demand $1,000 in U.S. gold." Since gold is not a medium of exchange adopted by the U.S. government, the note is not payable in money. The same result would occur if the maker promises "to pay $1,000 and fifty liters of 1964 Chateau Lafite-Rothschild wine," as the instrument is not payable *entirely* in money.

The statement, "Payable in $1,000 U.S. currency or an equivalent value in gold," would render the instrument nonnegotiable if the maker reserved the option of paying in money or gold. If the option were left to the payee, some legal scholars argue that the instrument would be negotiable.

If an instrument is payable in a foreign currency, the UCC has a special provision. [UCC 3-107(2)] Any instrument payable in the United States with a face amount stated in a foreign currency can be paid in the equivalent in U.S. dollars at the due date, unless the paper expressly requires payment in the foreign currency.

To summarize, only instruments payable in money are negotiable. An instrument payable in government bonds or in shares of IBM stock is not negotiable because neither bonds nor stock are a medium of exchange recognized by the U.S. government.

Payable on Demand or at a Definite Time

UCC 3-104(1)(c) requires that a negotiable instrument "be payable on demand or at a definite time." Clearly, in order to ascertain the value of a negotiable instrument, it is necessary to know when the maker, drawee, or acceptor is required to pay. It is also necessary to know when the obligations of secondary parties—drawers, indorsers, and accommodation parties—will arise. Furthermore, it is necessary to know when an instrument is due in order to calculate when the statute of limitations may apply. And, finally, with an interest-bearing instrument, it is necessary to know the exact interval during which the interest will accrue in order to determine the present value of the instrument.

Payable on Demand   Instruments that are payable on demand include those that contain the words "Payable at sight" or "Payable upon presentment" and those that say nothing about when payment is due. The very nature of the instrument may indicate that it is payable on demand. For example, a check, by definition, is payable on demand. [UCC 3-104(2)(b)] If no time for payment is specified, and if the person responsible for payment must pay upon the instrument's presentment, the instrument is payable on demand. [UCC 3-108]

Payable at a Definite Time   If an instrument is not payable on demand, it must be payable at a definite time specified on the face of the instrument, in order to be negotiable. The maker or drawee is under no obligation to pay until the specified time has elapsed.

Often instruments contain additional terms that seem to conflict with the definite-time requirement. UCC 3-109 attempts to clear up some of these potential problems as follows:

(1) An instrument is payable at a definite time if by its terms it is payable:

    (a) on or before a stated date or at a fixed period after a stated date; or

    (b) at a fixed period after sight; or

    (c) at a definite time subject to any acceleration; or

    (d) at a definite time subject to extension at the option of the holder, or to extension to a further definite time at the option of the maker or acceptor, or automatically upon or after a specified act or event.

(2) An instrument which by its terms is otherwise payable only upon an act or event uncertain as to time of occurrence is not payable at a definite time even though the act or event has occurred.

Suppose an instrument dated June 1, 1988, states, "One year after the death of my grandfather, Henry Adams, I promise to pay to the order of James Harmon $500.

[Signed] Jacqueline Wells." This instrument is nonnegotiable. Because the date of the grandfather's death is uncertain, the maturity date is uncertain, even though the event is bound to occur.

When an instrument is payable on or before a stated date, it is clearly payable at a definite time, although the maker has the option of paying before the stated maturity date. This uncertainty does not violate the definite-time requirement. If Levine gives Hirsch an instrument dated May 1, 1988, that indicates on its face that it is payable on or before May 1, 1989, it satisfies the requirement. On the other hand, an instrument that is undated and made payable "one month after date" is clearly nonnegotiable. There is no way to determine the maturity date from the face of the instrument.

Acceleration Clause An **acceleration clause** is one that allows a payee or other holder of a time instrument to demand payment of the entire amount due, with interest, if a certain event occurs, such as a default in payment of an installment when due. There must be, of course, a good-faith belief that payment will not be made before an acceleration clause is invoked.

Assume that Martin lends $1,000 to Ruth. Ruth makes a negotiable note promising to pay $100 per month for eleven months. The note may contain a provision that permits Martin or any holder to accelerate all the payments plus interest if Ruth fails to pay an installment in any given month. If, for example, Ruth fails to make the third payment, the note will be due and payable in full. If Martin accelerates the unpaid balance, Ruth will owe Martin the remaining principal plus interest.

Under UCC 3-109(1)(c), instruments that include acceleration clauses are negotiable because (1) the exact value of the instrument can be ascertained and (2) the instrument will be payable on a fixed date if the event allowing acceleration does not occur. Thus, the fixed date is the outside limit used to determine the value of the instrument.

Extension Clauses The reverse of an acceleration clause is an extension clause, which allows the date of maturity to be extended into the future. To keep the instrument negotiable, the interval of the extension must be specified if the right to extend is given to the maker of the instrument. If, on the other hand, the holder of the instrument can extend it, the maturity date does not have to be specified.

Suppose a note reads, "The maker [obligor] has the right to postpone the time of payment of this note beyond its definite maturity date of January 1, 1988. This extension, however, shall be for no more than a reasonable time." Any note with this language is not negotiable because it does not satisfy the definite-time requirement. The right to extend is the maker's, and the maker has not indicated when the note will become due after the extension.

If a note reads, "The holder of this note at the date of maturity, January 1, 1989, can extend the time of payment until the following June 1 or later, if the holder so wishes," it is a negotiable instrument. The length of the extension does not have to be specified because the option to extend is solely that of the holder. After January 1, 1989, the note is, in effect, a demand instrument.

Payable to Order or to Bearer

Since one of the functions of a negotiable instrument is to serve as a substitute for money, freedom to transfer is an essential requirement. To assure a proper transfer,

ACCELERATION CLAUSE
A clause in a contract for installment payments that provides for all future payments to become due immediately upon the failure to tender timely payments or upon the occurrence of a specified event.

the instrument must be "Payable to order or to bearer." [UCC 3-104(1)(d)] These required words indicate that at the time of issuance it is expected that future unknown persons—not just the immediate party—will eventually be the owners. If either of these words is not present, the instrument is nonnegotiable and therefore only assignable and governed by contract law.

Order Instruments   UCC 3-110(1) defines an instrument as an order to pay "when by its terms it is payable to the order . . . of any person therein specified with reasonable certainty. . . ." This section goes on to state that an order instrument can be payable to the order of

    (a) the maker or drawer; or
    (b) the drawee; or
    (c) a payee who is not maker, drawer, or drawee; or
    (d) two or more payees together or in the alternative; or
    (e) the representative of an estate, trust, or fund, or [the representative's] successor; or
    (f) an office or officer by title [such as a tax assessor]; or
    (g) a partnership or unincorporated association.

The purpose of order paper is to allow the maker or drawer to transfer the instrument to a specific person. This in turn allows that person to transfer the instrument to whomever he or she wishes. Thus, the maker or drawer is agreeing to pay either the person specified or whomever that person might designate. In this way, the instrument retains its transferability.

Suppose an instrument states, "Payable to the order of Rocky Reed," or, "Pay to Rocky Reed or order." Clearly, the maker or drawer has indicated that a payment will be made to Reed or to whomever Reed designates. The instrument is negotiable.

If, however, the instrument states, "Payable to Rocky Reed," or, "Pay to Rocky Reed only," the instrument loses its negotiability. (The maker or drawer indicates only that Reed will be paid.)

In addition, except for bearer paper, the person specified must be named with *certainty* because the transfer of an order instrument requires an indorsement. If an instrument states, "Payable to the order of my kissing cousin," the instrument is nonnegotiable, as a holder could not be sure which cousin was intended to indorse and properly transfer the instrument.

BEARER INSTRUMENT
In the law of commercial paper, any instrument that runs to the bearer, including instruments payable to the bearer or to "cash."

Bearer Instrument   UCC 3-111 defines a **bearer instrument** as one that does not designate a specific payee. The term *bearer* means the person in possession of an instrument that is payable to bearer or indorsed in blank. [UCC 1-201(5)] This means that the maker or drawer agrees to pay anyone who presents the instrument for payment, and complete transferability is implied.

Any instrument containing the following terms is a bearer instrument:

● "Payable to the order of bearer."
● "Payable to Rocky Reed or bearer."
● "Payable to bearer."
● "Pay cash."
● "Pay to the order of cash."

In addition, an instrument that contains "any other indication which does not purport to designate a specific payee" is bearer paper. [UCC 3-111(c)] The use of such designations can cause problems and should be avoided. Therefore, a check made payable to the order of "Uncle Sam" would probably be to a designated payee, the United States government, and be an order instrument. An instrument "payable to the order of a bucket of milk" would not designate a specific payee, and the instrument would be a bearer instrument.

Where an instrument is made payable both to order and to bearer, if the bearer words are handwritten or typewritten, the instrument is a bearer instrument. But if the bearer words are in a printed form, it is an order instrument. [UCC 3-110(3)]

❖ Factors Not Affecting Negotiability

There are other factors that do not affect the negotiability of an instrument, and the UCC provides rules for clearing up ambiguous terms. Some of these rules follow:

1. Unless the date of an instrument is necessary to determine a definite time for payment, the fact that an instrument is undated does not affect its negotiability. A typical example is an undated check. [UCC 3-114(1)]
2. Postdating or antedating an instrument does not affect negotiability. [UCC 3-114(1)]
3. Handwritten terms outweigh typewritten and printed terms. [UCC 3-118(b)] For example, if your check is printed, "Pay to the order of," and in handwriting you insert in the blank, "Jerry Adams or bearer," the check is a bearer instrument.
4. Words outweigh figures unless the words are ambiguous. [UCC 3-118(c)] This is important where the numerical amount and written amount on a check differ.
5. Where a particular interest rate is not specified but the instrument simply states "with interest," the interest rate is the judgment rate, not the legal rate. [UCC 3-118(d)]

In the following case, the numerical amount and written amount on a check differed. When the bank paid the numerical amount (which was in excess of the written amount), the plaintiff brought suit for the difference.

Case 16.3
YATES v. COMMERCIAL BANK & TRUST COMPANY
District Court of Appeal of Florida, Third District, 1983.
432 So.2d 725.

FACTS While acting as the personal representative of Marion Cahill's estate, Emmett McDonald wrote a check to himself drawn on the estate checking account at Commercial Bank & Trust Company and then absconded with the funds. The payee and amount on the check read as follows: "Pay to the order of *Emmett E. McDonald $10075.00 Ten hundred seventy-five . . . Dollars.*" The bank paid McDonald $10,075.00 and debited Marion Cahill's estate for that amount. McDonald's successor as personal representative of Cahill's estate, William Yates, brought suit against the bank to recover $9,000—the difference between $10,075.00 and $1,075.00, claiming that the bank should have paid the amount written in words on the check. The complaint was dismissed by the trial court, and Yates appealed.

Case 16.3—Continued

ISSUE Should the bank be held liable to Yates for the $9,000?

DECISION Yes. The appellate court ordered the bank to replace the $9,000 taken from the estate's account.

REASON The court stated that under UCC 3-118(c), words will control figures unless the words are ambiguous, in which case figures will control. The court thus concluded that "[u]nder this provision of the UCC, it was clearly improper for the bank to have paid the larger sum stated in numbers, rather than the smaller one unambiguously stated by McDonald's words. It is, therefore, prima facie liable to the estate for the excess."

❖ Transfer by Assignment or Negotiation

Once issued, a negotiable instrument can be transferred by *assignment* or by *negotiation*.

Transfer by Assignment

Recall from Chapter 9 that under general contract principles, a transfer by assignment to an assignee gives the assignee only those rights that the assignor possessed. Assignment is a transfer of rights under a contract. Any defenses that can be raised against an assignor can be raised against the assignee (unless there is an enforceable waiver-of-defense clause). Article 3 applies only to negotiable instruments; obviously, there can be no negotiation of a nonnegotiable instrument. Furthermore, when a transfer fails to qualify as a negotiation, it becomes an assignment. The transferee is then an *assignee* rather than a *holder*.

Transfer by Negotiation

NEGOTIATION
The transferring of a negotiable instrument to another in such form that the transferee becomes a holder.

Negotiation is the transfer of an instrument in such form that the transferee becomes a holder. [UCC 3-202(1)] Under UCC principles, a transfer by negotiation creates a holder who, at the very least, receives the rights of the previous possessor. [UCC 3-201(1)] Unlike an assignment, a transfer by negotiation can make it possible for a holder to receive more rights in the instrument than the prior possessor. [UCC 3-305] (A holder who receives greater rights is known as a *holder in due course*. See Chapter 17.) There are two methods of negotiating an instrument so that the receiver becomes a holder. The method used depends on whether the instrument is order paper or bearer paper.

ORDER PAPER
A negotiable instrument that is payable to a specific payee or to any person the payee by indorsement designates.

Negotiating Order Paper **Order paper** contains the name of a payee capable of indorsing, as in, "Pay to the order of Lloyd Sorenson." Order paper is also paper that has as its last or only indorsement a *special* indorsement, as in, "Pay to Sorenson. [Signed] Adams." If the instrument is order paper, it is negotiated by delivery with any necessary indorsements. For example, National Express Corporation issues a payroll check "to the order of Lloyd Sorenson." Sorenson takes the check to the supermarket, signs his name on the back (an indorsement), gives it to the cashier (a delivery), and receives cash. Sorenson has negotiated the check to the supermarket. [UCC 3-202(1)]

In the following case, a party intended to assign her rights in a promissory note payable to her to another party. Because she indorsed the note, however, with a special indorsement, the court held that the note had been not assigned, but negotiated, to the other party.

Case 16.4
ALVES v. BALDAIA
Court of Appeals of Ohio, Third District, 1984.
14 Ohio App. 3d 187, 470 N.E. 2d 459.

FACTS   In January of 1973, Keith and Joyce Alves loaned Joyce Alves's parents, Beatrice and William Baldaia, $15,000. In return, the Baldaias executed a promissory note payable to Joyce Alves. In February of 1978, Keith and Joyce Alves divorced. The separation agreement contained the following provision: "Wife agrees to assign to Husband any and all right, title, and interest she may have in a certain note, executed by her parents, dated January 3, 1973 on or before date of final hearing." Joyce Alves later wrote on the promissory note, "Pay to the order of Keith R. Alves. [Signed] Joyce Ann Alves."

Some time later, Keith Alves tried to collect payment on the note from the Baldaias, who refused to pay it. Alves then sought payment from his former wife, who had since remarried and taken the name of Schaller. Schaller claimed that her transfer of the promissory note to Alves, pursuant to the separation agreement, constituted an "assignment" of her rights and interests in the note, and not a formal "negotiation" of the note. The trial court held that Schaller's signature on the note operated as an indorsement. Schaller and her parents, the Baldaias, then appealed the decision, claiming the trial court had been in error by dismissing their motion for summary judgment.

ISSUE   Was the transfer of the promissory note an assignment or a negotiation?

DECISION   The appellate court confirmed the trial court's judgment that the transfer had been a negotiation and, hence, Joyce Alves Schaller was secondarily liable (liable in the event her parents failed to pay the note) on the instrument.

REASON   The court reasoned that if Joyce Alves Schaller had wished only to "assign" the note, she should not have indorsed it. As it stood, the indorsement of the note technically gave Keith Alves the rights of a holder. Although the divorce agreement made it clear that Joyce Alves had intended an assignment of the note, as a matter of law such collateral evidence could not be used to determine the intent of the parties. The decision had to rest on what the *instrument itself* stated or reflected, and parol evidence was inadmissible in this case. The court stated that an "indorser may disclaim his liability on the contract of indorsement, *but only if the indorsement itself so specifies. . . . The customary manner of disclaiming the indorser's liability . . . is to indorse 'without recourse.'*" Since no disclaimer was written on the instrument, Joyce Alves Schaller's signature on the note meant that "she contracted to pay the instrument, according to its tenor, to the holder thereof if the maker dishonored the note at maturity."

Negotiating Bearer Paper   If an instrument is payable to bearer, it is negotiated by delivery—that is, by transfer into another person's possession. Indorsement is not necessary. [UCC 3-202(1)] The use of *bearer paper* involves more risk through loss or theft than the use of order paper.

Assume Richard Kraychek writes a check "Payable to cash" and hands it to Jessie Arnold (a delivery). Kraychek has issued the check (a bearer instrument) to Arnold. Arnold places the check in her wallet, which is subsequently stolen. The thief has possession of the check. At this point, negotiation has not occurred, because delivery must be voluntary on the part of the transferor. If the thief "delivers" the check to an innocent third person, however, negotiation will be complete. All rights to the check will be passed *absolutely* to that third person, and Arnold will lose all right to recover the proceeds of the check from him or her. [UCC 3-305] Of course, she can recover her money from the thief if the thief can be found.

Converting Order Paper to Bearer Paper and Vice Versa   The method used for negotiation depends upon the character of the instrument at the time the negotiation takes place. For example, a check originally payable to "cash" but subsequently indorsed, "Pay to Arnold," must be negotiated as order paper (by indorsement and delivery) even though it was previously bearer paper. [UCC 3-204(1)]

An instrument payable to the order of a named payee and indorsed in blank (blank indorsements will be discussed shortly) becomes a bearer instrument. [UCC 3-204(2)] To illustrate, a check made payable to the order of Jessie Arnold is issued to Arnold, and Arnold indorses her name on the back of it. The instrument can now be negotiated by delivery only. Arnold can negotiate the check to whomever she wishes by delivery, and that person in turn can negotiate by delivery without indorsement. If Arnold, after such indorsement, loses the check, then a finder can negotiate it further.

❖ Indorsements

Indorsements are required whenever the instrument being negotiated is classified as an order instrument. (Many transferees of bearer paper require indorsement for identification purposes, even though the UCC does not require it.) An **indorsement** is a signature with or without additional words or statements. It is most often written on the back of the instrument itself. If there is no room on the instrument, indorsements can be written on a separate piece of paper called an **allonge.** The allonge must be "so firmly affixed [to the instrument] as to become a part thereof." [UCC 3-202(2)] Pins or paper clips will not suffice. Some courts hold that staples are sufficient.

One purpose of an indorsement is to effect the negotiation of order paper. Sometimes the transferee of bearer paper will request the holder-transferor to indorse. This is done to impose liability on the indorser. The liability of indorsers will be discussed later, in Chapter 17.

Once an instrument qualifies as a negotiable instrument, the form of indorsement will have no effect on the character of the underlying instrument. Indorsement relates to the right of the holder to negotiate the paper and the manner in which it must be done.

Types of Indorsements

We will examine four categories of indorsements: blank, special, qualified, and restrictive.

Blank Indorsements   A **blank indorsement** specifies no particular indorsee and can consist of a mere signature. [UCC 3-204(2)] Hence, a check payable "to the order of Jennifer Hill" can be indorsed in blank simply by having her signature written on the back of the check. Exhibit 16-1 shows a blank indorsement.

INDORSEMENT
A signature placed on an instrument or a document of title for the purpose of transferring one's ownership in the instrument or document of title.

ALLONGE
A piece of paper firmly attached to a negotiable instrument, upon which transferees can make indorsements if there is no room left on the instrument itself.

BLANK INDORSEMENT
One made by the mere writing of the indorser's name on the back of an instrument. Such indorsement causes an instrument, otherwise payable to order, to become payable to bearer and negotiated only by delivery.

Jennifer Hill

An instrument payable to order and indorsed in blank becomes payable to bearer and can be negotiated by delivery alone. [UCC 3-204(2)] In other words, a blank indorsement converts an order instrument to a bearer instrument, which anybody can cash. If Jennifer Hill indorses a check payable to her order in blank and then loses it on the street, Reed can find it and sell it to Hollander for value without indorsing it. This constitutes a negotiation because Reed has made delivery of a bearer instrument (which was an order instrument until it was indorsed).

Special Indorsements   A **special indorsement** indicates the specific person to whom the indorser intends to make the instrument payable; that is, it names the indorsee. [UCC 3-204(1)] No special words of negotiation are needed. Words such as "Pay to the order of Jones" or "Pay to Jones" followed by the signature of the indorser are sufficient. When an instrument is indorsed in this way, it is order paper. Had the words "Pay to Jones" been used on the face of the instrument to indicate the payee, the instrument would not have been negotiable.

SPECIAL INDORSEMENT
An indorsement of an instrument specifying to whom or to whose order the instrument is payable.

To avoid the risk of loss from theft, one may convert a blank indorsement to a special indorsement. This changes the bearer paper back to order paper. UCC 3-204(3) allows a holder to "convert a blank indorsement into a special indorsement by writing over the signature of the indorser in blank any contract consistent with the character of the indorsement."

For example, a check is made payable to Arthur Rabe. He indorses his name by blank indorsement on the back of the check and negotiates the check to Ted Sheppard. Ted, not wishing to cash the check immediately, wants to avoid any risk should he lose the check. He therefore writes, "Pay to Ted Sheppard," above Arthur's blank indorsement. In this manner, Ted has converted Arthur's blank indorsement into a special indorsement. Further negotiation now requires Ted Sheppard's indorsement plus delivery. (See Exhibit 16-2.)

Pay to Ted Sheppard
Arthur Rabe

Qualified Indorsements   Generally, an indorser, *merely by indorsing*, impliedly promises to pay the holder, or any subsequent indorser, the amount of the instrument in the event that the drawer or maker defaults on the payment. [UCC 3-414(1)] A qualified indorsement is used by an indorser to disclaim or limit this contract liability on the instrument. In this form of indorsement, the notation "without recourse" is commonly used. A sample of such an indorsement is shown in Exhibit 16-3.

◆ **Exhibit 16-3**
A Qualified Indorsement

Pay to Holly Hughes without recourse, Bridgett Cage

QUALIFIED INDORSEMENT
An indorsement on a negotiable instrument under which the indorser disclaims to subsequent holders secondary liability on the instrument; the most common qualified indorsement is "without recourse."

A qualified indorsement is often used by persons acting in a representative capacity. For instance, insurance agents sometimes receive checks payable to them that are really intended as payment to the insurance company. The agent is merely indorsing the payment through to the principal and should not be required to make good on the check if it is later dishonored. The "without recourse" indorsement absolves the agent. If the instrument is dishonored, the holder cannot obtain recovery from the agent who indorsed "without recourse" unless the indorser has breached one of the warranties listed in UCC 3-417(2) and (3), which relate to good title, authorized signature, no material alteration, and so forth. Usually, blank and special indorsements are *unqualified indorsements*. That is, the blank or special indorser is guaranteeing payment of the instrument in addition to transferring title to it. The qualified indorser is not guaranteeing such payment. Nonetheless, the qualified indorsement ("without recourse") still transfers title to the indorsee; an instrument bearing a qualified indorsement can be further negotiated.

Qualified indorsements are accompanied by either a special or a blank indorsement that determines further negotiation. Therefore, a special qualified indorsement makes the instrument an order instrument, and it requires an indorsement plus delivery for negotiation. A blank qualified indorsement makes the instrument a bearer instrument, and only delivery is required for negotiation.

Assume that a check is made payable to the order of Bridgett Cage and that Bridgett wants to negotiate the check specifically to Holly Hughes with a qualified indorsement. Bridgett would indorse the check, "Pay to Holly Hughes, without recourse. [Signed] Bridgett Cage." For Holly to further negotiate the check to Chad Everett, Holly would have to indorse and deliver the check to Chad.

Restrictive Indorsements   Prior to the existence of the UCC, a restrictive indorsement was thought to prohibit the further negotiation of an instrument. Although some who indorse in this manner still believe the restrictive indorsement prevents any further transfer, the Code holds to the contrary. UCC 3-206(1) states that "no restrictive indorsement prevents further transfer or negotiation of the instrument."

RESTRICTIVE INDORSEMENT
Any indorsement of a negotiable instrument that purports to condition or prohibit further transfer of the instrument. As against payor and intermediary banks, such indorsements are usually ineffective.

The **restrictive indorsement** requires indorsees to comply with certain instructions regarding the funds involved. Restrictive indorsements come in many forms. UCC 3-205 gives four separate categories:

1. *Conditional indorsements.* When payment is dependent on the occurrence of some specified event, the instrument has a conditional indorsement. [UCC 3-205(a)] Exhibit 16-4 illustrates a conditional indorsement. Except against intermediary banks

(defined in Chapter 18), the indorsement is enforceable, and neither Roberts nor any subsequent holder has the right to enforce payment against Arrowsmith on the note before the condition is met. [UCC 3-206(3)]

It is important to note that a conditional indorsement does not prevent further negotiation of the instrument. If the conditional language had appeared on the face of the instrument, however, it would not have been negotiable because it would not have met the requirement that the note contain an unconditional promise to pay.

2. *Indorsements prohibiting further indorsement.* An indorsement such as, "Pay to Samuel Mead only. [Signed] X," does not destroy negotiability. Mead can negotiate the paper to a holder just as if it had read, "Pay to Samuel Mead. [Signed] X." [UCC 3-206(1)] This type of restrictive indorsement has the same legal effect as a special indorsement. It is rarely used. [UCC 3-205(b)]

3. *Indorsement for deposit or collection.* A common type of restrictive indorsement is one that makes the indorsee (almost always a bank) a collecting agent of the indorser. (See Exhibit 16-5 for an illustration where the check is payable and issued to Geraldine Sellers.)

In particular, a "Pay any bank or banker" or "For deposit only" indorsement has the effect of locking the instrument into the bank collection process. Only a bank can acquire rights of a holder following this indorsement until the item has been specially indorsed by a bank to a person who is not a bank. [UCC 4-201(2)] A bank's liability for payment of an instrument with a restrictive indorsement is discussed in Chapter 18.

4. *Trust, or agency, indorsements.* Indorsements that are for the benefit of the indorser or a third person are trust, or agency, indorsements. Samples are shown in Exhibit 16-6.

◆ **Exhibit 16-6**
Trust Indorsements

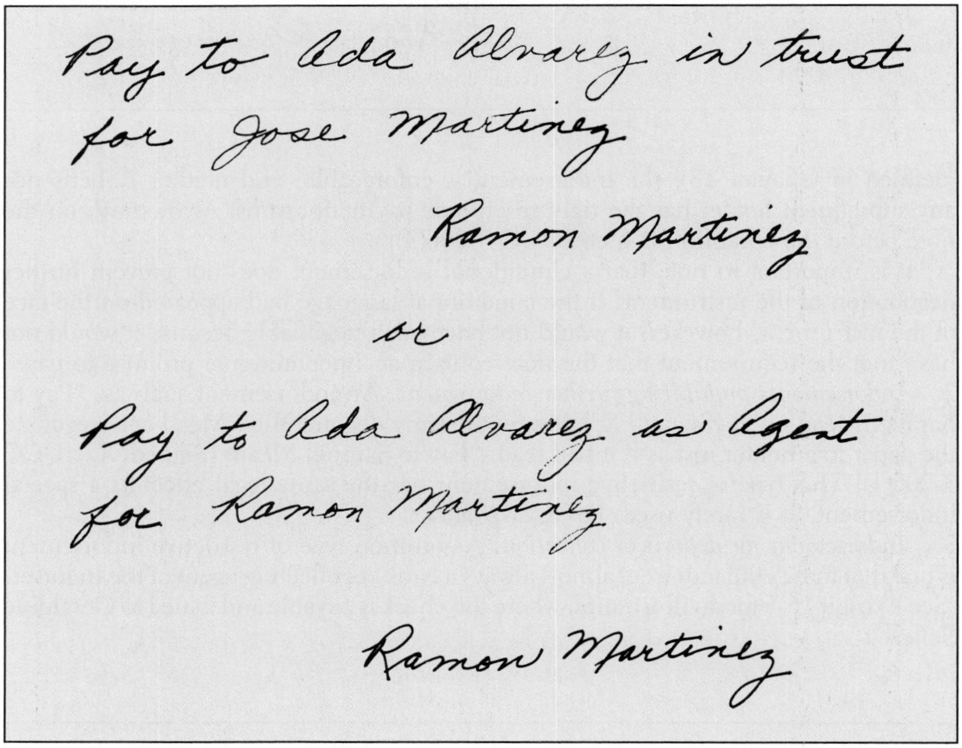

The indorsement results in legal title vesting in the original indorsee. To the extent that the original indorsee pays or applies the proceeds consistently with the indorsement (for example, "in trust for Jose Martinez"), the indorsee is a holder and can become a holder in due course (see Chapter 17). [UCC 3-205(d) and 3-206(4)]

The fiduciary restrictions on the instrument do not reach beyond the original indorsee.[1] Any subsequent purchaser can qualify as a holder in due course unless he or she has actual notice that the instrument was negotiated in breach of the fiduciary duty.[2]

---

1.   Compare this to the rule governing conditional indorsements. A conditional indorsement obligates all subsequent indorsers (except certain banks) and primary parties to see that the money is applied consistently with the condition. Agency or trust indorsements limit this responsibility to the original indorsee.

2.   See Quantum Dev. v. Joy, 397 F.Supp. 329 (D. Virgin Is. 1975).

Unauthorized Signatures

People are not normally liable to pay on negotiable instruments unless their signatures appear on the instruments. Hence, an unauthorized signature is wholly inoperative and will not bind the person whose name is forged.[3]

There are exceptions to this rule, found in UCC 3-404(1). If the person whose unauthorized signature was used ratifies that signature or is in some way precluded from denying it, then the unauthorized signature will operate as "the signature of the unauthorized signer in favor of any person who in good faith pays the instrument or takes it for value." [UCC 3-404(1)]

Generally, when there is a forged or unauthorized indorsement, the burden of loss falls on the first party to take the instrument with the forged indorsement. Two situations are possible, however, in which the loss falls on the maker or drawer:

1.   When an imposter induces the maker or drawer of an instrument to issue it to the imposter.

2.   When a person signs as or on behalf of a maker or drawer, intending that the payee will have no interest in the instrument, or when an agent or employee of the maker or drawer has supplied him or her with the name of the payee, also *intending* the payee to have no such interest. [UCC 3-405(1)] Such a situation often involves an employee who wishes to swindle an employer by padding bills or payrolls.

Imposters

An **imposter** is one who, by use of the mails, telephone, or personal appearance, induces a maker or drawer to issue an instrument in the name of an impersonated payee. If the maker or drawer believes the imposter to be the named payee at the time of issue, the indorsement by the imposter is not treated as unauthorized when transferred to an innocent party. This is because the maker or drawer *intended* the imposter to receive the instrument.

IMPOSTER
One who, with the intent to deceive, pretends to be somebody else.

In these situations, the unauthorized indorsement of a payee's name can be as effective as if the real payee had signed. The *imposter rule* of UCC 3-405 provides that an imposter's indorsement will be effective—that is, not considered a forgery—insofar as the drawer goes.

For example, a man walks into Harry Marsh's paint store and purports to be Jerry Lewis soliciting contributions for his annual fund raising for muscular dystrophy. Marsh has heard of the Lewis Telethon but has never met or seen Jerry Lewis. Wishing to support a worthy cause, Marsh writes out a check for $250 payable to Jerry Lewis and hands it to the imposter. The imposter forges the signature of Jerry Lewis and negotiates the check to a Stop and Shop convenience store. Marsh discovers the fraud and stops payment on the check, claiming the payee's signature is forged. Since the imposter rule is in effect, Marsh cannot claim a forgery against Stop and Shop but must seek redress from the imposter instead. If Marsh had sent the check to the real Jerry Lewis, but the check had been stolen and negotiated to the store by a forged indorsement, the imposter rule would not apply, and Stop and Shop would have to seek redress against the forger.

---

3.   On the other hand, a drawee is charged with knowledge of the drawer's signature. The drawee cannot recover money it pays out to a holder in due course on a negotiable instrument bearing a forged drawer's signature. See UCC 3-418.

Business Law in Action

The $800,000 Getaway

The agent of Bradford Trust Company saw nothing unusual or unduly suspicious in the document before him. It was a properly signed letter by one of Bradford's mutual fund account holders, Frank Rochefort, authorizing Bradford to liquidate $800,000 worth of mutual funds in his account and wire the proceeds to his account in the Texas American Bank of Houston. The account number of the Houston bank was included. The agent did as directed and arranged for the $800,000 to be transferred by wire to the Texas bank.

The matter went unnoted by the agent's superiors in the firm until an astonished Frank Rochefort noted the withdrawal on his statement and informed Bradford Trust that he had not authorized the transfer. Bradford reinstated Rochefort's account and

turned to the Texas bank for a hoped-for recovery. When the Texas bank refused, Bradford sued the bank, and the true story began to unfold as the legal proceedings commenced.

It was revealed that Bradford Trust was the victim of an ingenious scheme perpetrated by two con artists, aliases Hank and David Friedman. The Friedmans had arranged to buy $800,000 worth of rare gold coins and bullion from Colonial Coins, Inc., in Houston. They said they would arrange to have the funds transferred from their Boston bank to Colonial's account at the Texas-American Bank, and Colonial agreed. The Friedmans then forged the letter to Bradford Trust, signing Rochefort's name and authorizing Bradford to liquidate the stock and transfer the money. In the letter, they directed Bradford to wire the funds to the account of "Frank S. Rochefort" at the Texas-American Bank, but gave Colonial's account number with

Rochefort's name. When the money arrived at Texas-American, the bank failed to investigate the discrepancy between the account number and the account holder's name. Instead, since it had been advised by Colonial to expect the transfer, it immediately deposited the funds into the account number given on the wire and telephoned Colonial to let the merchant know the funds had been received. At that point, the Friedmans received the gold and coins and left.

Bradford never did retrieve its money. The court would not agree that the Texas bank had been more at fault than Bradford Trust—which had dealt directly with the imposter and thus had been in the best position to avoid the loss.[1] Bradford was thus left holding the proverbial bag—in this case, a very empty one.

1. Bradford Trust Co. v. Texas American Bank-Houston, 790 F.2d 407 (5th Cir. 1986).

Fictitious Payees

FICTITIOUS PAYEE
A payee on a negotiable instrument whom the maker or drawer does not intend to have an interest in the instrument and whose name is supplied by an agent or employee of the drawer or maker. Indorsements by fictitious payees are not forgeries under negotiable instruments law.

The so-called **fictitious-payee** rule deals with the intent of the maker or drawer to issue an instrument to a payee who has *no interest* in the instrument. This most often takes place when (1) a dishonest employee deceives the employer-maker or drawer into signing an instrument payable to a party with no right to receive the instrument, or (2) a dishonest employee or agent has the authority to so issue the instrument on behalf of the maker or drawer. In these situations, the payee's indorsement is not treated as a forgery, and the maker or drawer is held liable on the instrument by an innocent holder.

Assume that Flair Industries, Inc., gives its bookkeeper, Axel Ford, general authority to issue checks in the company name drawn on First State Bank so that Ford can pay employees and pay other corporate bills. Ford decides to cheat Flair Industries out of $10,000 by issuing a check payable to Erica Nied, an old acquaintance of his. Ford does not intend Nied to receive any of the money, and Nied is not an employee or creditor of the company.

Ford indorses the check in Nied's name, naming himself as indorsee. He then cashes the check with a local bank, which collects payment from the drawee bank, First State Bank. First State Bank charges Flair Industries' account $10,000.

Flair Industries discovers the fraud and demands that the account be recredited. Who bears the loss? The rule of UCC 3-405 provides the answer. Neither the local bank that first accepted the check nor First State Bank is liable. Since Ford's indorsement in the name of a payee with no interest in the instrument is "effective," there is no "forgery." Hence, the collecting bank is protected in paying on the check, and the drawee bank is protected in charging Flair's account. It is the employer-drawer, Flair Industries, that bears the loss.[4]

Whether a dishonest employee actually signs the check or merely supplies his or her employer with names of fictitious creditors (or with true names of creditors having fictitious debts), the Code makes no distinction in result. Assume that Nathan Knudson draws up the payroll list from which employee checks are written. He fraudulently adds the name Sally Slight (a fictitious person) to the payroll, thus causing checks to be issued to her. Again, it is the employer-drawer who bears the loss because the employer is in the best position to prevent such fraud.

Correction of Name

An indorsement should be identical to the name that appears on the instrument. The payee or indorsee whose name is misspelled can indorse with the misspelled name or the correct name, or both. [UCC 3-203] For example, if Sheryl Kruger receives a check payable to the order of Sherill Krooger, she can indorse the check either "Sheryl Kruger" or "Sherrill Krooger." The usual practice is to indorse the name as it appears on the instrument and follow it by the correct name.[5]

---

4. May Dept. Stores Co. v. Pittsburgh Nat. Bank, 374 F.2d 109 (3d Cir. 1967).
5. Watertown Federal Sav. and Loan v. Spanks, 346 Mass. 398, 193 N.E.2d 333 (1963).

Application

Law and the Consumer— Indorsing Checks

As a consumer or as a businessperson, you will certainly be writing and receiving checks. There are pitfalls involved in both activities.

The danger in signing a blank check is clear. Anyone can write in an unauthorized amount and cash the check. While you may be able to assert lack of authorization against the person who filled in the unauthorized amount, subsequent holders of the properly indorsed check may be able to enforce the check as completed. While you are haggling with the person who inserted the unauthorized figure and who may not be able to repay the excess amount, you will have had to honor the check for the unauthorized amount to any subsequent holder in due course.

Just as a check signed in blank may be dangerous, a negotiable instrument with a blank indorsement also has

dangers, because it is easily transferred as cash. When you make a bank deposit, therefore, you should sign (indorse) the back of the check in blank only in the presence of a teller. If you choose to sign it ahead of time, make sure you insert the words "For deposit only" before you sign your name.

Checklist for the Use of Negotiable Instruments

☐ **1.** A good rule of thumb is never to sign a blank check.

☐ **2.** Another good rule of thumb is never to indorse in blank a negotiable instrument unless a bank teller is simultaneously giving you a receipt for your deposit.

❖ Chapter Summary: The Negotiable Instrument, Transferability, and Negotiation

EIGHT REQUIREMENTS FOR NEGOTIABLE INSTRUMENTS	
Requirements	**Basic Rules**
Must be in Writing UCC 3-104(1)	1. A writing can be on anything readily transferable that has a degree of permanence.
Must Be Signed by the Maker or Drawer UCC 3-104(1)(a) UCC 3-401(2) UCC 1-201(39) UCC 3-403(1)	1. The signature can be any place on the instrument. 2. It can be in any form (such as a word, mark, or rubber stamp) that purports to be a signature and authenticates the writing. 3. It can be signed in a representative capacity.
Must Be a Definite Promise or Order UCC 3-104(1)(b)	1. A promise must be more than a mere acknowledgment of a debt. 2. The words "I/We promise" or "Pay" meet this criterion.

❖ Chapter Summary: The Negotiable Instrument, Transferability, and Negotiation—Continued

Requirements	Basic Rules
Must Be Unconditional UCC 3-104(1)(b) UCC 3-105	1. Payment cannot be expressly conditional upon the occurrence of an event. 2. Payment cannot be made subject to or governed by another agreement. 3. Payment cannot be paid only out of a particular fund (except, for example, a government-issued instrument).
Must Be an Order or Promise to Pay a Sum Certain UCC 3-104(1)(b) UCC 3-106	1. An instrument is a sum certain even if paid in installments, with interest, at a stated discount, or at an exchange rate.
Must Be Payable in Money UCC 3-104(1)(b) UCC 3-107	1. Any medium of exchange recognized as the currency of a government is money. 2. The maker or drawer cannot retain the option to pay the instrument in money or something else.
Must Be Payable on Demand or at a Definite Time UCC 3-104(1)(c) UCC 3-108 UCC 3-109	1. Any instrument payable on sight, presentation, or issue is a demand instrument. 2. An instrument is still payable at a definite time even though payable on or before a stated date, within a fixed period after sight, or even though the drawer or maker has an option to extend time for a definite period.
Must Be Payable to Order or Bearer UCC 3-104(1)(d) UCC 3-110 UCC 3-111	1. An order instrument must name the payee with reasonable certainty. 2. An instrument whose terms intend payment to no particular person is payable to bearer.

TYPES OF INDORSEMENTS AND THEIR CONSEQUENCES		
Words Comprising the Indorsement	Type of Indorsement	Indorser's Signature Liability
"Jennifer Hill"	Blank	Unqualified signature liability upon proper presentment and notice of dishonor.
"Pay to Ted Sheppard, Arthur Rabe"	Special	Unqualified signature liability upon proper presentment and notice of dishonor.
"Without recourse, Bridgett Cage"	Qualified (Blank for further negotiation)	No signature liability. Transfer warranty liability if breach. [See UCC 3-417(2)(3) and Chapter 17.]
"Pay to Holly Hughes, without recourse, Bridgett Cage"	Qualified (Special for further negotiation)	No signature liability. Transfer warranty liability if breach. [See UCC 3-417(2)(3) and Chapter 17.]
"Pay to Michael Roberts, provided he completes landscaping my yard at 808 South Hyatt Ave. by July 30, 1988, Esther Arrowsmith"	Restrictive-Conditional (Special for further negotiation)	Qualified signature liability only to condition being met. If condition is met, unqualified upon proper presentment and notice of dishonor.

(continued on next page)

❖ Chapter Summary: The Negotiable Instrument, Transferability, and Negotiation—Continued

"Pay to Samuel Mead only, Jennifer Hill"	Restrictive-Prohibition (Special for further negotiation)	Qualified only to Samuel Mead receiving payment. If Mead receives payment, unqualified upon proper presentment and notice of dishonor.
"For Deposit, Geraldine Sellers"	Restrictive-Agency (Blank for further negotiation)	Qualified only to Sellers having amount deposited in her account. If deposit is made, unqualified upon proper presentment and notice of dishonor.
"Pay to Ada Alvarez in trust for Jose Martinez, Ramon Martinez"	Restrictive-Trust (Special for further negotiation)	Qualified to payment to Ada Alvarez for Jose Martinez's benefit. If restriction is met, unqualified upon proper presentment and notice of dishonor.
UNAUTHORIZED SIGNATURES		
Unauthorized Signatures	An unauthorized signature will not bind the person whose name is forged. Exceptions: (a) The person whose unauthorized signature was used will be bound by the signature if he or she ratifies the signature or is in some way precluded from denying it. [UCC 3-404, 3-406] (b) An unauthorized signature will operate as "the signature of the unauthorized signer in favor of any person who in good faith pays the instrument or takes it for value." [UCC 3-404(1)]	
Unauthorized Indorsements	In cases of forged or unauthorized indorsements, the burden of loss falls on the first party to take the forged instrument, *except* in the following situations in which the resulting loss falls on the drawer or maker: (a) When an imposter induces the maker or drawer of an instrument to issue it to the imposter. (b) When a person signs as or on behalf of a maker or drawer, intending that the payee will have no interest in the instrument, or an agent or employee of the maker or drawer has supplied him or her with the name of the payee, also intending the payee to have no such interest (fictitious-payee rule). [UCC 3-405(1)]	

❖ Questions and Case Problems

16-1. The following note is written by Murial Evans on the back of an envelope: "I, Murial Evans, promise to pay Karen Marvin or bearer $100 on demand." Discuss fully if this constitutes a negotiable instrument.

16-2. A check drawn by David for $500 is made payable to the order of Matthew and issued to Matthew. Matthew owes his landlord $500 in rent and transfers the check to his landlord with the following indorsement: "For rent paid. [Signed] Matthew." Matthew's landlord has contracted to have Juarez do some landscaping on the property. When Juarez insists on immediate payment, the landlord transfers the check to Juarez without indorsement. Later, in order to pay for some palm trees purchased from Green's Nursery, Juarez transfers the check with the following indorsement: "Pay to Green's Nursery, without recourse. [Signed] Juarez." Green's Nursery sends the check to its bank indorsed "For deposit only. [Signed] Green's Nursery."

(a) Classify each of these indorsements.

(b) Was the transfer from Matthew's landlord to Juarez, without indorsement, an assignment or a negotiation? Explain.

16-3. The following instrument was written on a sheet of paper by Jeff Nolan: "I, the undersigned, do hereby acknowledge that I owe Stephanie Craig one thousand dollars, with interest, payable out of the proceeds of the sale of my horse, Swiftfoot, next month. Payment is to be made on or before six months from date." Discuss specifically why this instrument is nonnegotiable.

16-4. Which of the following are order instruments and which are bearer instruments?

(a) A note payable to the order of Jean Cranston and indorsed "Pay to Carlo Capezio. [Signed] Jean Cranston." Below this indorsement is another indorsement reading "Carlo Capezio."

(b) A check payable to "cash."

(c) A note payable to bearer with the following indorsement: "Pay to Paul Hirsch. [Signed] Jean Cranston."

(d) A note payable to Mark Stevens indorsed as follows: "Mark Stevens."

16-5. Rolf Cahill ordered a set of luggage from a catalog seller. Rolf sent the seller a check for $150 with the order. The seller cashed the check. When the seller learned that the luggage ordered by Rolf was out of stock and no longer being produced, she drew and sent a refund check payable to Ralph Cahill. Rolf needs to negotiate the check to pay an overdue bill. Will the fact that the check is made payable to Ralph, instead of Rolf, prohibit Rolf from negotiating the check under any circumstances? Explain.

16-6. First National Bank collected debts owed to Rock Island Bedding Company and Berry Industries, Inc., and in turn paid those two firms the amount collected by remitting checks to them drawn on First National Bank. On several occasions Johns, an employee of First National, asked the bank's accounting department to prepare cashier's checks payable to Rock Island Bedding Company and to Berry Industries, Inc. The requests appeared to be normal, because the bank had been making regular payments to the two firms. Johns, however, forged the payees' indorsements on eighteen of the checks so issued and deposited them into an account at First City Bank. Johns fraudulently obtained $903,300 in this way. First City indorsed the checks "P.E.G." (prior indorsements guaranteed) and presented them to First National for payment. First National paid the checks and later recovered from its insurer, Fidelity & Casualty Company. Fidelity sought recovery from First City Bank, claiming that Johns's forged signature did not authorize First City to pay the checks and that First City should bear the loss. Do you agree? Why or why not? [Fidelity & Casualty Co. v. First City Bank of Dallas, 675 S.W.2d 316 (Tex.App.-Dallas 1984, no writ.)]

16-7. Briggs signed a note that read in part: "Ninety days after date, I, we, or either of us, promise to pay to the order of Three Thousand Four Hundred Ninety-Eight and 45/100 Dollars." The underlined words and symbols were typed out. The remainder of the words in the quote were printed. No blanks had been left on the face of the instrument; any unused space had been filled in with hyphens. The note contained several clauses that permitted acceleration in the event the holder deemed itself insecure. When the note was not paid at maturity, Broadway Management Corporation brought suit on the note for full payment, claiming it was a holder. Is this order or bearer paper? What changes, if any, would have to be made on the note for it to be a negotiable instrument? [Broadway Management Corp. v. Briggs, 30 Ill.App.3d 403, 332 N.E.2d 131 (1975)]

16-8. A life insurance policy was taken out on the life of Robert Agaliotis by Louis Agaliotis, his father. A provision in the policy allowed Louis to request $1,852 be paid to him as the owner of the policy. Through a clerical error, the insurance company made the check payable to Robert, but it was correctly delivered to Louis. If Louis indorses Robert's name and cashes the check, will he be liable for wrongfully indorsing the check? [Agaliotis v. Agaliotis, 38 N.C.App. 42, 247 S.E.2d 28 (1978)]

16-9. Wilson was the bookkeeper for Palmer and Ray Dental Supply. He was to deposit several checks into the Palmer and Ray account. Using a rubber stamp with the company's name and address, he instead indorsed the checks and then cashed them.

(a) Did Wilson effectively change the checks from order paper to bearer paper?

(b) If the checks were effectively changed to bearer paper, could Palmer and Ray recover the money from the bank that cashed the checks?

[Palmer and Ray Dental Supply of Abilene, Inc. v. First National Bank of Abilene, 477 S.W.2d 954 (Tex.Civ.App.-Eastland 1972, no writ.)]

16-10. Dynamics Corporation and Marine Midland Bank had a long-standing agreement under which Marine Midland received checks payable to Dynamics and indorsed and deposited them into Dynamics' account. Dynamics never saw the checks. They were made out to the order of Dynamics and delivered directly to Marine Midland. Marine Midland stamped the backs of the checks with Dynamics' name and insignia and transferred them. Within the meaning of the UCC, is the act of sending checks to Marine Midland Bank a negotiation? If Marine Midland transfers the checks to other parties, is this a negotiation? [Marine Midland Bank—New York v. Graybar Electric Co., Inc., 41 N.Y.2d 703, 395 N.Y.S.2d 403, 363 N.E.2d 1139 (1977)]

Chapter 17

Commercial Paper —Holder in Due Course, Liability, and Defenses

HOLDER IN DUE COURSE
The holder of an instrument who took it in good faith, for value, and without notice that the instrument is overdue or has been dishonored or that any defense or claim exists against it.

REAL DEFENSES
Defenses that can be used to avoid payment to all holders of a negotiable instrument, including an HDC or a holder through an HDC (the shelter principle).

PERSONAL DEFENSES
Defenses that can be used to avoid payment to an ordinary holder of a negotiable instrument. Personal defenses cannot be used to avoid payment to an HDC or a holder through an HDC (the shelter principle).

Although it is used as a substitute for money, commercial paper, in a broad sense, is actually a form of credit. Any note promising to pay another creates a debtor (the one promising) and a creditor (the one to be paid). As the eminent British politician Disraeli indicated in the opening quotation, for credit to "arrive at maturity" is a long and gradual historical process. The extensive exchange of commercial paper that takes place daily in the United States is predicated, ultimately, on the existence of commercial paper law and a government capable of enforcing that law.

Issues of litigation concerning commercial paper usually turn on which party can obtain payment on an instrument when it is due, or on whether or not some defense can be asserted to discharge or to cancel liability on an instrument. For these reasons, a person seeking payment prefers to have the rights of a **holder in due course** (HDC)— meaning one who takes a negotiable instrument free of all claims and most defenses of other parties. The holder in due course has the right to collect payment on that instrument, and this right will take priority over the claims of other parties.

The first part of this chapter will deal exclusively with the issue of the holder in due course. The second part of the chapter deals with the liability associated with negotiable instruments. There is liability derived from the UCC rules relating to the signature on the instrument, and there is liability based on warranty liability, which extends to both signers and nonsigners.

The remainder of the chapter considers the defenses available to prevent liability and, briefly, the ways that a person can be discharged from an obligation on a negotiable instrument. Defenses fall into two general categories—**real** (or universal) **defenses** and **personal defenses**. Real defenses are used to avoid payment to *all holders* of a negotiable instrument, including an HDC or a holder through an HDC (explained in this chapter). [UCC 3-305(2)] Personal defenses are used to avoid payment to an *ordinary holder* of a negotiable instrument. [UCC 3-306] A holder in due course thus takes commercial paper free from personal (as opposed to real) defenses.

❖ Holder versus Holder in Due Course (HDC)

As pointed out in Chapter 15, a holder is a person who possesses a negotiable instrument "drawn, issued, or indorsed to him or his order or to bearer or in blank."

[UCC 1-201(20)] In other words, the holder is the person who, by the terms of the instrument, is legally entitled to payment. The holder of an instrument need not be its owner in order to transfer it, negotiate it, discharge it, or enforce payment of it in his or her own name. [UCC 3-301]

A holder has the status of an assignee of a contract right. A transferee of a negotiable instrument who is characterized merely as a holder (as opposed to a holder in due course) obtains only those rights that the predecessor-transferor had in the instrument. In the event that there is a conflicting, superior claim or defense to the instrument, an ordinary holder will not be able to collect payment.

A holder in due course is a special-status transferee of a negotiable instrument who, by meeting certain acquisition requirements, takes the instrument *free* of most defenses or adverse claims to it. Stated another way, an HDC can normally acquire a higher level of immunity to defenses against payment on the instrument or claims of ownership to the instrument by other parties.

❖ Requirements for HDC Status

The basic requirements for attaining HDC status are set forth in UCC 3-302. An HDC must first be a holder of a negotiable instrument and must take the instrument (1) for value, (2) in good faith, and (3) without notice that it is overdue or that it has been dishonored, or that any person has a defense against it or a claim to it.

The underlying requirement of "due course" status is that a person must first be a holder on that instrument. Regardless of other circumstances surrounding acquisition, only a holder has a chance to become an HDC.

Taking for Value

An HDC must have given *value* for the instrument. [UCC 3-303] A person who receives an instrument as a gift or who inherits it has not met the requirement of value. In these situations, the person becomes an ordinary holder and does not possess the rights of an HDC.[1]

The concept of *value* in the law of negotiable instruments is not the same as the concept of *consideration* in the law of contracts. An *executory promise* (a promise to give value in the future) is a clearly valid consideration to support a contract. [UCC 1-201(44)] It does not, however, normally constitute value sufficient to make one an HDC. UCC 3-303 provides that a holder takes the instrument for value only to the extent that the agreed-upon consideration has been performed. Therefore, if the holder plans to pay for the instrument later or plans to perform the required services at some future date, the holder has not yet given value. In that case, the holder is not yet a holder in due course.

Suppose Marcia Morrison draws a $500 note payable to Reinhold Niebuhr in payment for goods. Niebuhr negotiates the note to Judy Larson, who promises to pay Niebuhr for it in thirty days. During the next month, Larson learns that Niebuhr

---

1. There is one way an ordinary holder who fails to meet the value requirement can have the rights of a holder in due course. The *shelter provision* of the Code allows an ordinary holder to succeed to HDC status if any prior holder was an HDC. This exception is discussed later in the chapter. [UCC 3-201(1)]

breached the contract by delivering defective goods and that Morrison will not honor the $500 note. Niebuhr has left town. Whether Larson can hold Morrison liable on the note will depend on whether Larson is a holder in due course. Since Larson had given no value at the time she learned of Morrison's defense, Larson is a mere holder, not a holder in due course. Thus, Morrison's defense is valid not only against Niebuhr but also against Larson. If Larson had paid Niebuhr for the note on the transfer (which would mean the agreed-upon consideration had been performed), she would be a holder in due course and could hold Morrison liable on the note even though Morrison had a valid breach-of-contract or warranty defense against Niebuhr.

The Code provides for a holder to take the instrument for value in one of three ways. Basically, a holder gives value:

1. To the extent that the agreed-upon consideration has been paid or a security interest or lien acquired.
2. By taking an instrument in payment of or as security for an antecedent debt.
3. By giving a negotiable instrument or irrevocable commitment as payment.

In the following case, the court takes up the question of value, as well as good faith and taking without notice, in determining whether a bank had acquired HDC status in regard to certain negotiable instruments it had received.

Case 17.1
IN RE WILLIAMS BROTHERS ASPHALT PAVING COMPANY

United States Bankruptcy Court, Western District of Michigan, 1986.
59 B.R. 71.

FACTS In the fall of 1980 the Williams Brothers Asphalt Paving Company contracted with two local communities in Michigan to resurface some of their streets. During the course of the jobs, Williams incurred debts to its supplier, Rieth-Riley Construction Company, in the amount of $45,960. When the work was completed, Williams received a total of $188,433 from the two communities and deposited the funds into its checking account at First Security Bank.

Although the amount owed to Rieth-Riley ($45,960) was to have been set aside by the communities in a special trust (the Michigan Builders' Trust Fund), it was not. Williams owed a secured debt to First Security Bank, so immediately paid to the bank the entire amount it had received. The payment was in the form of checks drawn on Williams's checking account at the bank and made payable to the bank's order. Williams later filed for bankruptcy, and Rieth-Riley sought to get its money from the bank, contending that Williams Brothers had no right to the $45,960 still owed to Rieth-Riley and thus could not

negotiate it (via checks Williams Brothers had made payable to the bank) to the bank.

ISSUE Is the bank a holder in due course in this instance?

DECISION Yes. The court held, in pertinent part, that the bank was a holder in due course under Michigan law, and thus the supplier was not entitled to recover the payments.

REASON Under Article 3 of the UCC, a holder in due course takes an instrument free from all claims to it on the part of any person. A holder in due course is a holder who takes an instrument for value, in good faith, and without notice of a claim against it by any person. The central issue in determining whether the bank was a holder in due course was whether the bank had taken the checks "for value." The court noted that under the common law, "payments of property received in satisfaction of pre-existing indebtedness are not received for value." This common-law rule, however, is supplanted by UCC 3-303(b), which states that a holder takes an instrument for value "when he takes the instrument in payment of or as security for an antecedent claim against any person whether or not the claim is due."

Case 17.1—Continued

The court applied this rule to the bank. The bank gave Williams value for the money it received by extinguishing a pre-existing debt owed to the bank by Williams. The bank also accepted Williams's checks in good faith and did not know some of the money it was receiving from Williams belonged to Rieth-Riley, nor should it have known of this claim. The bank was thus a holder in due course.

Taking in Good Faith

The second requirement for HDC status is that the holder take the instrument in *good faith.* [UCC 3-302(1)(b)] This means that the purchaser-holder must have acted honestly in the process of acquiring the instrument. As discussed previously, *good faith* is defined by the Code as "honesty in fact in the conduct or transaction concerned."

The good-faith requirement *applies only to the holder.* It is immaterial whether the transferor acted in good faith. Thus, a person who in good faith takes a negotiable instrument from a thief can be an HDC. The reason is simple. An inherent characteristic of negotiable paper is that any person in possession of an instrument that runs to him or to her by its terms is a holder. Also, anyone can deal with the possessor as a holder.

Because of the good-faith requirement, one must ask whether the purchaser, when acquiring the instrument, honestly believed the instrument was not defective. If a person purchases a $10,000 note for $100 from a stranger on a street corner, the issue of good faith can be raised on the grounds of the suspicious circumstances as well as the grossly inadequate consideration. The Code does not provide clear guidelines to determine good faith, so each situation must be examined separately.

Taking without Notice

The third requirement for HDC status involves *notice.* [UCC 3-304] A person will not be afforded HDC protection if he or she acquires an instrument knowing, or having reason to know, that it is defective in any one of the following ways: [UCC 3-302(1)(c)]

1. It is overdue.
2. It has been dishonored.
3. There is a defense against it.
4. There is another claim to it.

The main provisions of UCC 3-304 spell out the common circumstances that, as a matter of law, constitute notice of a claim or defense and notice of an overdue instrument. UCC 3-304(4) specifies, however, certain facts that a purchaser might know about an instrument but that do not constitute notice of a defense or claim. These facts do not disqualify the purchaser from HDC status.

Notice of a fact involves (1) actual knowledge of it, (2) receipt of a notice about it, and (3) reason to know that a fact exists, given all the facts and circumstances known at the time in question.

In the following case, a holder of a check was denied due-course status on the ground that he had sufficient reason to know the check was very likely defective.

Case 17.2
E. BIERHAUS & SONS v. BOWLING
Court of Appeals of Indiana, First District, 1985.
486 N.E.2d 598.

FACTS   Dennis Bowling was a friend and neighbor of David Dabney. Bowling had no indication that Dabney was financially troubled. Indeed, by all evidence, Dabney was quite well off: He owned four grocery stores, he drove a Cadillac, his wife owned a new sports car, he had race horses, lived in an expensive home, and he also (Bowling had been led to believe) owned real estate in other areas. In the fall of 1983 Dabney admitted to Bowling that he had "cash flow" problems and borrowed $40,000 from Bowling. At the same time, Dabney proposed they become partners in his grocery business, and discussions concerning this prospect ensued over the following weeks. At one point, Dabney asked Bowling for a signed blank check which would be deposited with a new grocery supplier as "security" and which would never be used without Bowling's consent. If it were, Dabney promised to reimburse Bowling's account appropriately.

Shortly thereafter, Dabney dated and filled out Bowling's blank check for $10,606.79 and gave the check to his major supplier and creditor, Bierhaus & Sons. Dabney owed Bierhaus more than $400,000 for past deliveries, and, after receiving ten to twenty bad checks from Dabney, Bierhaus required cash or cashier's checks from Dabney for any deliveries. Dabney had told Bierhaus about the supposedly imminent partnership with Bowling, and, under those circumstances, Bierhaus's agent accepted the $10,606.79 check from Bowling in payment for a delivery of groceries.

Bowling's check was returned to Bierhaus as there were insufficient funds in Bowling's account to cover it. Dabney had filed for bankruptcy protection. Bierhaus sought to collect the amount of the check from Bowling. The trial court held in Bowling's favor, and Bierhaus appealed.

ISSUE   The central issue here is whether Bierhaus meets the requirements of holder-in-due-course status. If so, Bowling will have no defense against Bierhaus. If Bierhaus is not an HDC, however, Bowling can assert as a defense the material and fraudulent alteration of the check by Dabney. [UCC 3-407(2)(3)]

DECISION   The court affirmed the trial court's ruling in Bowling's favor. Bierhaus was not a holder in due course on this instrument.

REASON   The court reasoned that, although "signing and delivering a blank check is such negligence which can expose the maker to liability to a holder in due course," [UCC 3-406] Bierhaus was not an HDC. In order to be accorded HDC status, the "holder has the burden of proving that he was acting in accordance with reasonable commercial standards, or that he was acting in good faith *and* he was without notice." The previous bad checks from Dabney, the fact that Bierhaus's agent had never met Bowling and only knew about him from Dabney's representations, and the fact that he never contacted Bowling concerning the check, even though Bowling's name, address, and phone number were given on the face of the check, should have been sufficient notice to Bierhaus that the status of the check was problematic.

Overdue Instruments   All negotiable paper is either payable at a definite time (*time instrument*) or payable on demand (*demand instrument*). What constitutes notice that an instrument is overdue will vary depending upon whether a person takes time or demand paper.

Time Instruments   A holder of a time instrument who takes the paper the day after its expressed due date is *on notice* that it is overdue. Nonpayment by the due date should indicate to any purchaser who is obligated to pay that the primary party has a defense to payment. Thus, a promissory note due on May 15 must be acquired

Business Law in Action

Three Important Letters—HDC

Charles Lawton, a retired welder, engaged in his "first try" at purchasing commercial paper in April of 1980. Lawton was pleased with his purchase—which included a promissory note worth $7,050 for which he had paid $5,000. He had acquired it from an acquaintance, Martin Swersky, who had sold a car to Emily Walker in 1976 and in return had accepted Walker's promissory note for the price of the car plus interest. The amount of the note, signed by Walker, was $12,000, and the terms were that Walker would pay Swersky $100 a month for 120 months. By the time Lawton purchased the note from Swersky, the balance still owing on the note was $7,050. Swersky also transferred to Lawson a title certificate issued to Emily V. Walker for a 1976 Ford.

All went well for over a year, and Walker made monthly payments to Lawton regularly. In October of 1981, however, the situation

changed. Walker refused to make any further payments to Lawton on the balance due of $4,950, and it took nearly six years of litigation before Lawton was able to recover the balance.

What went wrong? Why did Walker cease paying on the bill? According to Walker, she had never agreed to pay Swersky $12,000, and she had never signed the $12,000 note. She stated at trial that she had agreed to pay Swersky $7,250 for the vehicle over a period of five years, and she had fulfilled that commitment by making payments through October of 1981. Lawton had no claim to the alleged "balance" because he should have known of the "rotten" deal, as Ms. Walker called it, and the exorbitant interest charges that brought the total due to $12,000.

Should Lawton have known of the forged signature? Should he have noticed that the amount of the note ($12,000) was unreasonably high for a 1976 Ford, when the market price in 1976 for the type of automobile purchased by Walker was about half that amount? These were key

questions before the court, and the court's answers were important to Lawton. They would determine whether Lawton was a holder in due course or simply a holder, and it was Lawton's status in this case that was the deciding factor. The court concluded that Lawton had taken the note for value and in good faith, and that there was no evidence to indicate that he had been aware of any irregularity in the note when he purchased it from Swersky. Lawton was therefore a holder in due course in the eyes of the court and, as an HDC, was entitled to recover the $4,950 still owing on the note.[1]

What would have resulted if Lawton had not been deemed an HDC of the instrument? As an ordinary holder, Lawton would have been subject to the personal defense of fraud in the inducement raised by Walker, and, very likely, Lawton would not have been able to recover the balance.

1. Lawton v. Walker, 231 Va. 247, 343 S.E.2d 335 (1986).

before midnight on May 15. If it is purchased on May 16, the purchaser will be an ordinary holder, not an HDC. Sometimes instruments read, "Payable in thirty days." A note dated December 1 that is payable in thirty days is due by midnight on December 31. If the payment date falls on a Sunday or holiday, the instrument is payable on the next business day.

In the case of an installment note, notice that the maker has defaulted on any installment of principal (but not interest) payments will prevent a purchaser from becoming an HDC. [UCC 3-304(3)(a)] Also, when a series of notes, each with successive maturity dates, is issued at the same time for a single indebtedness, an uncured default in payment of any one note of the series will constitute overdue notice for the entire series. In this way, prospective purchasers know that they cannot qualify as HDCs.

Suppose a note reads, "Payable May 15, but may be accelerated if the holder feels insecure." A purchaser, unaware that a prior holder has elected to accelerate the due date on the instrument, buys the instrument prior to May 15. UCC 3-304(3)(b) provides that such a purchaser can be an HDC unless he or she has reason to know that the acceleration has occurred.

Demand Instruments   A purchaser has notice that a demand instrument is overdue if he or she takes the instrument knowing that demand has been made or takes it an unreasonable length of time after its issue. "A reasonable time for a check drawn and payable within the states and territories of the United States and the District of Columbia is *presumed* to be 30 days" (emphasis added). [UCC 3-304(3)(c)]

Payee As an HDC   Under certain circumstances, a payee may qualify as an HDC; the payee must exercise good faith, give value, and take the instrument without notice of a defense against it or claim to it. [UCC 3-302(2)]

To illustrate: Manfred Rubens is an attorney for Don Adams. Rubens recently had minor outpatient surgery performed by Dr. Paulson in his office and owes Dr. Paulson $500. Rubens has agreed to draft a land sales contract for Adams next week, on the condition that Adams issue a check payable to Dr. Paulson for $500. Adams sends the check to Dr. Paulson with a note, "In payment of medical services rendered to Manfred Rubens." Rubens leaves town and never performs the legal services for Adams. Adams stops payment on the check. Can Dr. Paulson enforce payment as an HDC? The answer is yes. Although Dr. Paulson is the payee, he gave value (medical services), took the check in good faith, and took it without notice of dishonor, defense or claim, or that the check was overdue.

❖ Holder through an HDC

A person who does not qualify as an HDC but who derives his or her title through an HDC can acquire the rights and privileges of an HDC. According to UCC 3-201(1):

> Transfer of an instrument vests in the transferee such rights as the transferor has therein, except that a transferee who has himself been a party to any fraud or illegality affecting the instrument or who as a prior holder had notice of a defense or claim against it cannot improve his position by taking from a later holder in due course.

SHELTER PRINCIPLE
The principle that the holder of a negotiable instrument who cannot qualify as a holder in due course, but who derives his or her title through a holder in due course, acquires the rights of a holder in due course.

This rule, sometimes called the **shelter principle**, seems counter to the basic HDC philosophy. It is, however, in line with the concept of marketability and free transferability of commercial paper, as well as with contract law, which provides that assignees acquire the rights of assignors. The transfer rule extends the HDC benefits, and it is designed to aid the HDC in disposing of the instrument readily. Since any instrument in the hands of an HDC is free from personal defenses (by definition), an HDC should reasonably have the privilege of transferring all rights in the instrument.

Anyone, no matter how far removed from an HDC, who can trace his or her title ultimately back to an HDC, comes within the shelter principle. Normally, a person who acquires an instrument from an HDC or from someone with HDC rights receives HDC rights on the principle that the transferee of an instrument receives at least the rights that the transferor had.

Limitations on the Shelter Principle

UCC 3-201(1) explicitly indicates, however, that certain persons who formerly held instruments cannot improve their positions by later reacquiring them from HDCs. Thus, if a holder was a party to fraud or illegality affecting the instrument, or if, as a prior holder, he or she had notice of a claim or defense against an instrument, that holder is not allowed to improve his or her status by repurchasing from a later HDC. In other words, a person is not allowed to "launder" the paper by passing it into the hands of an HDC and then buying it back.

Suppose Barry and Sheila collaborate to defraud Helen. Helen is induced to give Sheila a negotiable note payable to Sheila's order. Sheila then specially indorses the note for value to Joseph, an HDC. Barry and Sheila split the proceeds. Joseph negotiates the note to Paul, another HDC. Paul then negotiates the note for value to Barry. Barry, even though he got the note through an HDC, is not a holder through an HDC, for he participated in the original fraud and can never acquire HDC rights in this note.

❖ Signature Liability of Parties to Commercial Paper

The key to liability on a negotiable instrument is a *signature*, which is defined in UCC 3-401(2) as "any name, including any trade or assumed name, upon an instrument, or . . . any word or mark used in lieu of a written signature." A signature can be handwritten, typed, or printed; or it can be made by mark, by thumbprint, or in virtually any manner. According to UCC 1-201(39), "signed" means any symbol executed or adopted by a party with the "present intention to authenticate a writing."

The requirement of a signature has its origin in the Law Merchant and is based simply on the need to know whose obligation the instrument represents. The critical element with any signature is a "present intention to authenticate a writing." Parol evidence can be used to identify the signer, and, once identified, the signature is effective against the signer no matter how it is made. UCC 3-401(1) states the general rule: "No person is liable on an instrument unless his signature appears thereon."

The only two exceptions to the general rule are contained in UCC 3-404, covering unauthorized signatures:

1.   Any unauthorized signature is wholly inoperative unless the person whose name is signed ratifies it or is precluded from denying it. [UCC 3-404(1)] For example, a signature made by an agent exceeding the scope of actual, implied, or apparent authority can be ratified by the principal. A Pennsylvania court held that a wife's acceptance and retention of benefits from a promissory note constituted ratification of an otherwise unauthorized signature made by her husband.[2] Moreover, a person who writes and signs a check, leaving blank the amount and the name of the payee, and who then leaves the check in a place available to the public can be estopped (prevented), on the basis of negligence, from denying liability for its payment. [UCC 3-115, 3-406, and 4-401(2)(b)]

---

2.   Rehrig v. Fortunak, 39 D.&C.2d 20 (Pa. 1966).

2.   An unauthorized signature operates as the signature of the unauthorized signer in favor of an HDC. For example, a person who forges a check can be held personally liable by an HDC. [UCC 3-404 and 3-401(2)]

Agents' Signatures

The general law of agency covered in Chapter 22 applies to negotiable instruments. Agents can sign negotiable instruments and thereby bind their principals. [UCC 3-403(1)] Without such a rule, all corporate commercial business would stop. As Chapter 27 will show, every corporation can and must act through its agents. Because of the critical function the signature plays in determining liability on a negotiable instrument, however, this chapter will go into some detail concerning the potential problems of agents' signatures.

Generally, an authorized agent does not bind a principal on an instrument unless the agent *clearly names* the principal in his or her signature (by writing, mark, or some symbol). The agent may or may not add his or her own name. [3]

For example, any of the following signatures by Collingsworth as agent for Peterson would bind Peterson on the instrument:

1.   Peterson, by Collingsworth, agent.
2.   Peterson.
3.   Peterson, Collingsworth. (This signature would bind Peterson only by parol evidence, as will be discussed shortly.)

If the authorized agent (Collingsworth, in this case) signed just his or her own name, however, the principal would not be bound on the instrument. The agent would be personally liable. In these situations, form prevails over intent. Under UCC 3-403(2)(a), this holds true even when the parties know of the agency relationship. In addition, the parol-evidence rule precludes the introduction of evidence to establish that the signature was made for a principal (see Chapter 8).

Under UCC 3-403(2)(b), two other situations in which an agent is held personally liable on a negotiable instrument can arise. If the instrument is signed in both the agent's name and the principal's name—"John Collingsworth, Bob Peterson" or, as shown in Number 3 in the earlier list of signatures that would bind a principal, "Peterson, Collingsworth"—but nothing on the instrument indicates the agency relationship (so the agent cannot be distinguished from the principal), the form of the signature binds the agent (and it can also bind the principal). Since inclusion of both the agent's and the principal's names without indicating their relationship is ambiguous, parol evidence is admissible *as between the original parties* to prove the agency relationship.

Also, when an agent indicates agency status in signing a negotiable instrument but fails to name the principal—for example, "John Collingsworth, agent"—the agent is personally liable against any subsequent holder, and the unnamed principal cannot be held on the instrument. But, since the indication of agency status without naming the principal is ambiguous, parol evidence is admissible *as between the*

---

3.   If the agent signs the principal's name, the Code presumes that the signature is authorized and genuine. [UCC 3-307(1)(b)]

original parties to prove the agency relationship and to establish the liability of the unnamed principal. [UCC 3-403(2)(b)]

The following case illustrates the personal liability of an agent who signed a check without disclosing that he was signing in a representative capacity.

Case 17.3
GRIFFIN v. ELLINGER
Supreme Court of Texas, 1976.
538 S.W.2d 97.

FACTS Griffin issued three checks to Ellinger, drawn on the account of the Greenway Building Company. Griffin, the president of the company, signed his name to the checks without revealing his representative capacity. The name of the company was on the face of each check, and Griffin was authorized to sign checks as president of the company. At the time the checks were issued, neither Ellinger (the payee) nor Griffin discussed who was responsible for paying the checks. The drawee bank refused to honor the checks because of insufficient funds in the Greenway account, and Ellinger sought recovery from Griffin personally.

ISSUE Can Griffin be held personally liable for the debt to Ellinger?

DECISION Yes. Griffin was individually liable on the three checks.

REASON Under UCC Section 3-403, "An authorized representative who signs his own name to an instrument . . . is personally obligated if the instrument names the person represented but does not show that the representative signed in a representative capacity, or if the instrument does not name the person represented but does show that the representative signed in a representative capacity." In the three checks at issue, Greenway Building Company was named, but Griffin's representative capacity was not indicated. Thus, Griffin was individually liable. The court stated, "Under Section 3-413, any person who signs a draft engages that, upon dishonor, he will pay the amount thereof to the holder. . . . [O]ne signing an instrument is personally liable thereon even though he is authorized to and does in fact bind his principal, if he does not disclose that he is signing only in a representative capacity. In short, the burden is on the signer to relieve himself of personal liability by disclosing his agency."

When a negotiable instrument is signed in the name of an organization, and the organization's name is preceded or followed by the name and office of an authorized individual, the organization is bound; the individual who has signed the instrument in the representative capacity is not bound. [UCC 3-403(3)]

If the agent had no authority, either apparent or implied, to sign the principal's name, the "unauthorized signature is wholly inoperative as that of the person whose name is signed." [UCC 3-404(1)] Assume that Maria Ortega is the principal and Justin Cohen is her agent. Cohen, without authority, signs a promissory note as follows: "Maria Ortega, by Justin Cohen, agent." Since Maria Ortega's "signature" is unauthorized, she cannot be held liable on the note, but Cohen is liable. This would be true even if Cohen had merely signed the note "Maria Ortega," without indicating any agency. In either case, the unauthorized signer, Cohen, is liable on the instrument.

Signature Liability

Primary and Secondary Liability   Every party, except a *qualified indorser*,[4] who signs a negotiable instrument is either primarily or secondarily liable for payment of that instrument when it comes due. If primarily liable, then the person is absolutely required to pay the instrument, subject to certain real defenses. [UCC 3-305] Only makers and acceptors are primarily liable. [UCC 3-413(1)]

Secondary liability on a negotiable instrument is similar to that of a guarantor in a simple contract. Drawers and indorsers have secondary liability. Secondary liability is *contingent liability*. In the case of notes, an indorser's secondary liability does not arise until the maker, who is primarily liable, has defaulted on the instrument. [UCC 3-413(1) and 3-414]

With regard to drafts and checks, a drawer's secondary liability does not arise until the drawee fails to pay or to accept the instrument, whichever is required. Note, however, that a drawee is not primarily liable. Makers of notes promise to pay, but drawees are ordered to pay. Therefore, drawees are not primarily liable unless they promise to pay—for example, by certifying a check. Nor are drawees even secondarily liable on an instrument. As stated in UCC 3-409, "a check or draft does not of itself operate as an assignment of any funds in the hands of the drawee available for its payment." Thus, unless a drawee accepts the instrument, the drawee's only obligation is to honor the drawer's orders.

Primary Liability of the Maker or Acceptor   The maker of a note promises to pay the note. The words "I promise to pay" embody the maker's obligation to pay the instrument according to the terms as written at the time of the signing. If the instrument is incomplete when the maker signs it, then the maker's obligation is to pay it according to the terms written when it is completed, assuming that the instrument is properly completed. [UCC 3-413(1) and 3-115]

A maker guarantees that certain facts are true by signing a promissory note. In particular, Section 3-413(3) specifies that a maker admits to all subsequent parties that the payee in fact exists and that the payee has current capacity to indorse the note (for example, that the payee is not a minor at the time the note is signed). Primary liability is unconditional. The primary party's liability is immediate when the note becomes due. No action by the holder of the instrument is required.

The drawee/acceptor is in virtually the same position as the maker of a note. [UCC 3-413(1)(3)] A drawee who does not accept owes a contractual duty to the drawer to pay in accordance with the drawer's orders, but a drawee owes no duty to either the payee or any holder.

For example, Braun buys from Stanley goods costing $2,000. The goods will be shipped to arrive on September 1. Instead of giving Stanley cash, Braun draws a draft on a finance company for $2,000 payable to Stanley on September 1. At this point, the finance company is not liable on the draft, and it will not become liable on the draft unless and until it accepts the draft.

Three situations under which a holder must present the instrument to a drawee for acceptance are:

---

4.   A qualified indorser—one who indorses "without recourse"—undertakes no obligation to pay. A qualified indorser merely assumes warranty liability, which is discussed later in this chapter.

1. Where the instrument requires such presentation (see trade acceptances, discussed in Chapter 15).
2. Where the draft is to be payable at an address different from that of the drawee.
3. Where the draft's payment date is dependent on such presentment [UCC 3-501(1)(a)]—for example, if the draft is payable thirty days after acceptance or sight.

Presentment in these situations is required to charge the drawer and indorsers with secondary liability.

If the drawee accepts the instrument as presented, the drawee becomes an acceptor and is primarily liable to all subsequent holders. A drawee who refuses to accept such a draft has dishonored the instrument.

A check is a special type of draft that is drawn on a bank and is payable on demand. Acceptance of a check is called *certification*. Certification is not necessary on checks, and a bank is under no obligation to certify. Upon certification, however, the drawee bank occupies the position of an acceptor and is primarily liable on the check to holders. [UCC 3-411]

Secondary Liability Dishonoring an instrument triggers the liability of secondarily liable parties on the instrument—that is, the drawer, unqualified indorsers, and **accommodation indorsers**. Parties who are secondarily liable on a negotiable instrument promise to pay on that instrument only if:

1. The instrument is properly and timely presented.
2. The instrument is dishonored.
3. Timely notice of dishonor is given to the secondarily liable party.[5]

ACCOMMODATION INDORSER
An indorser who signs an instrument for the purpose of lending his or her credit to another indorser.

These requirements are necessary for a secondarily liable party to have signature liability on a negotiable instrument, but they are not necessary to hold a secondarily liable party to warranty liability (to be discussed later). [UCC 3-414, 3-501, and 3-502]

UCC 3-413(2) provides that "upon dishonor of the draft and any necessary notice of dishonor . . . [the drawer] will pay the amount of the draft to the holder or to any indorser who takes it up." For example, Nina Lee writes a check on her account at Universal Bank payable to the order of Stephen Miller. If Universal Bank does not pay the check when Miller presents it for payment, then Nina is liable to Stephen on the basis of her secondary liability. Drawers are secondarily liable on drafts unless they disclaim their liability by drawing the instruments "without recourse." [UCC 3-413(2)]

Since drawers are secondarily liable, their liability does not arise until presentment and notice of dishonor have been made *properly* and in a *timely* way. If a draft (or check) is payable at a bank, improper presentment or notice relieves the drawer from secondary liability only when the drawee bank is insolvent.

An unqualified indorser promises that in the event of presentment, dishonor, and notice of dishonor, the indorser will pay the instrument. Thus, the liability of an indorser is much like that of a drawer, with one major exception: Indorsers are relieved of their contractual liability to the holder of the instrument by (1) improper (late)

---

5. An instrument can be drafted to provide a waiver of the presentment, dishonor, and notice of dishonor requirements. Presume for simplicity's sake that such waivers have not been incorporated into the instruments described in this chapter.

presentment or (2) late notice or failure to notify the indorser of dishonor. [UCC 3-414, 3-501, and 3-502]

Proper Presentment   The Code spells out what constitutes a proper presentment. Basically, presentment by a holder must be to the proper person, must be made in a proper manner, and must be timely. [UCC 3-503 and 3-504]

A note or CD must be presented to the maker for payment. A draft is presented by the holder to the drawee for acceptance or payment, or both, whichever is required. A check is presented to the drawee for payment. [UCC 3-504]

The proper manner for presentment can be in any one of the following three ways, depending on the type of instrument: [UCC 3-504(2)]

1.   By mail (but presentment is not effective until receipt of the mail).
2.   Through a clearinghouse procedure, such as deposited checks.
3.   At the place specified in the instrument for acceptance or payment—or, if the instrument is silent as to place, at the place of business or the residence of the person required to accept or pay.

One of the most crucial criteria for proper presentment is timeliness. [UCC 3-503] Failure to present on time is the most prevalent reason for improper presentment and consequent discharge of unqualified indorsers from secondary liability. See Exhibit 17-1, bearing in mind that its contents are oversimplified.

Proper Notice   Once the instrument has been dishonored, proper notice must be given to hold secondary parties liable. The rules of proper notice are basically as follows: [UCC 3-508]

1.   Notice must be given to the party to be held secondarily liable, but such notice can come from any person who could be liable on the instrument. Once proper notice is received, it is effective for all subsequent holders. In other words, notice once given operates for the benefit of all parties who have rights on the instruments against the party notified. [UCC 3-508(8)]
2.   Except for dishonor of foreign drafts, notice may be given in any reasonable manner. This includes oral or written notice and notice written or stamped on the instrument itself. [UCC 3-508(3)] To give notice of dishonor of a foreign draft (a draft drawn in one country and payable in another country), a formal notice called a *protest* is required. [UCC 3-509]

◆ **Exhibit 17-1**
Time for Proper Presentment [UCC 3-503]

TYPE OF INSTRUMENT	FOR ACCEPTANCE	FOR PAYMENT
Time	On or before due date	On due date
Demand	Within a reasonable time (after date or issue, or after secondary party becomes liable thereon)	
Check (domestic)	Not applicable	Presumed to be: Within thirty days (of date or issue) to hold drawer secondarily liable Within seven days (of indorsement) to hold indorser secondarily liable

3. Any necessary notice must be given by a bank before its midnight deadline (midnight of the next banking day after receipt). [UCC 4-104(1)(h)] Notice by any party other than a bank must be given before midnight of the third business day after either dishonor or receipt of notice of dishonor [UCC 3-508(2)]. Written notice is effective when sent, even though it is never received.

4. Notice to a partner is notice to a partnership. Similarly, when a party is deceased, incompetent, or bankrupt, notice may be given to that party's representative.

Accommodation Party   An **accommodation party** is one who signs an instrument for the purpose of lending his or her name as credit to another party on the instrument. [UCC 3-415(1)] Accommodation parties are one form of security against nonpayment on a negotiable instrument. For example, a bank about to lend money, a seller taking a large order for goods, or a creditor about to extend credit to a prospective debtor all want some reasonable assurance that the debts will be paid. A party's uncertain financial condition or the fact that the parties to a transaction are complete strangers can make a creditor reluctant to rely solely on the prospective debtor's ability to pay. To reduce the risk of nonpayment, the creditor can require the joining of a third person as an accommodation party on the instrument.

If the accommodation party signs on behalf of the maker, he or she is an *accommodation maker* and is primarily liable on the instrument. If the accommodation party signs on behalf of a payee or other holder (usually to make the instrument more marketable), he or she is an *accommodation indorser* and is secondarily liable. Any indorsement not in the ordinary chain of title is notice of its accommodation character. [UCC 3-415(2)(4)]

ACCOMMODATION PARTY
A person who signs an instrument for the purpose of lending that person's credit to another party on that instrument.

❖ Warranty Liability of Parties

In addition to the signature liability discussed in the preceding sections, transferors make certain implied warranties regarding the instruments that they are negotiating. Liability under these warranties is not subject to the conditions of proper presentment, dishonor, and notice of dishonor. These warranties arise even when a transferor does not indorse the instrument (as in delivery of bearer paper). [UCC 3-417] Sometimes it is more expedient to compel a transferor to take back an instrument on the basis of breach of warranty than it is to prove a case of signature liability as a holder in due course against the maker or drawer. Warranties fall into two categories, those that arise from the *transfer* of a negotiable instrument and those that arise upon *presentment*.

Transfer Warranties

The five *transfer warranties* are described in UCC 3- 417(2). They provide that any person who indorses an instrument and receives consideration warrants to all subsequent transferees and holders who take the instrument in good faith that:

1. The transferor has good title to the instrument or is otherwise authorized to obtain payment or acceptance on behalf of one who does have good title.

2. All signatures are genuine or authorized.

3. The instrument has not been materially altered.
4. No defense of any party is good against the transferor.
5. The transferor has no knowledge of any insolvency proceedings against the maker, the acceptor, or the drawer of an unaccepted instrument.

A qualified indorser who indorses an instrument "without recourse" limits the fourth warranty to a warranty that he or she has "no knowledge" of such a defense rather than that there is no defense. [UCC 3-417(3)]

The manner of transfer and the negotiation that is used determine how far and to whom a transfer warranty will run. Transfer by indorsement and delivery of order paper extends warranty liability to any subsequent holder who takes the instrument in good faith. The warranties of a person who transfers without indorsement (by delivery of bearer paper), however, will extend only to the immediate transferee. [UCC 3-417(2)]

Suppose Abrams forges Peter's name as a maker of a promissory note. The note is made payable to Abrams. Abrams indorses the note in blank and negotiates it to Carla, then leaves the country. Carla, without indorsement, delivers the note to Bob. Bob, in turn without indorsement, delivers the note to Shirley. Upon Shirley's presentment of the note to Peter, the forgery is discovered. Shirley can hold Bob (the immediate transferor) liable for breach of warranty that all signatures are genuine. Shirley cannot hold Carla liable, because Carla is not Shirley's immediate transferor but is a prior non-indorsing transferor. This example shows the importance of the distinction between (1) transfer by indorsement and delivery of order paper and (2) transfer by delivery of bearer paper without indorsement.

Presentment Warranties

Any person who seeks payment or acceptance of a negotiable instrument impliedly warrants to any other person who in good faith pays or accepts the instrument that:

PRESENTMENT WARRANTY
A warranty impliedly made by any person who seeks payment or acceptance of a negotiable instrument to any other person who in good faith pays or accepts the instrument that (1) the party presenting has good title to the instrument, or is authorized to obtain payment or acceptance on behalf of a person who has good title, and (2) the party presenting has no knowledge that the signature of a maker or the drawer is unauthorized, and (3) the instrument has not been materially altered.

1. The party presenting has good title to the instrument or is authorized to obtain payment or acceptance on behalf of a person who has good title.
2. The party presenting has no knowledge that the signature of the maker or the drawer is unauthorized.
3. The instrument has not been materially altered.

These warranties exist under UCC 3-417(1) and are often referred to as **presentment warranties** because they protect the person to whom the instrument is presented.

The second and third warranties in the preceding list do not apply in certain cases (to certain persons) where the presenter is a holder in due course. It is assumed, for example, that a drawer or a maker will recognize his or her own signature and that a maker or an acceptor will recognize whether an instrument has been materially altered.

Both transfer and presentment warranties attempt to shift liability back to a wrongdoer or to the person who dealt face to face with a wrongdoer and thus was in the best position to prevent the wrongdoing.

❖ Defenses

Depending upon whether a holder or an HDC (or a holder through an HDC) makes the demand for payment, certain defenses can bar collection from persons who would otherwise be primarily or secondarily liable on the instrument. As discussed in the introduction to this chapter, there are two general categories of defenses—real defenses and personal defenses.

Real Defenses

Real (universal) defenses are valid against all holders, including HDCs or holders who take through an HDC.

Forgery   Forgery of a maker's or drawer's signature cannot bind the person whose name is used (unless that person ratifies the signature or is precluded from denying it). [UCC 3-401 and 3-404(1)] Thus, when a person forges an instrument, the person whose name is used has no liability to pay any holder or any HDC the value of the forged instrument. In addition, a principal can assert the defense of unauthorized signature against any holder or HDC when an agent exceeds his or her authority to sign negotiable paper on behalf of the principal. [UCC 3-403]

Fraud in the Execution or Inception   If a person is deceived into signing a negotiable instrument, believing that he or she is signing something other than a negotiable instrument (such as a receipt), fraud in execution is committed against the signer. For example, a consumer unfamiliar with the English language signs a paper presented by a salesperson as a request for an estimate when in fact it is a promissory note. Even if the note is negotiated to an HDC, the consumer has a valid defense against payment. This defense cannot be raised, however, if a reasonable inquiry would have revealed the nature and terms of the instrument.[6] Thus, the signer's age, experience, and intelligence are relevant, since they frequently determine whether the signer should have known the nature of the transaction before signing.

The following case concerns a farmer who signed a negotiable instrument under the mistaken assumption that he was signing a receipt for funds received. As you read the case, try to determine what the outcome might have been had the plaintiff been an ordinary holder instead of a holder in due course.

Case 17.4
FEDERAL DEPOSIT INSURANCE CORPORATION v. CULVER
United States District Court, District of Kansas, 1986.
640 F.Supp. 725.

FACTS   Gary Culver, a Missouri farmer, made a business arrangement in 1984 with Nasib Ed Kalliel. Kalliel was to manage the business end of the farming enter-

prise, while Culver did the actual farming. Culver was to receive a salary and a percentage of the profits. In the summer of 1984 Culver notified Kalliel that he urgently needed money to prevent foreclosure. One week later Culver received $30,000 from the Rexford State Bank of Rexford, Kansas. Culver thought that the money had come from Kalliel and that Kalliel was responsible for repayment. About a week later, a representative from the Rexford Bank, Jerry Gilbert, approached Culver and re-

---

6.   Burchett v. Allied Concord Financial Corp., 74 N.M. 575, 396 P.2d 186 (1964).

Case 17.4—Continued

quested Culver's signature on a blank promissory note form, stating that "Rexford State Bank wanted to know where the $30,000.00 went, . . . for their records." Apparently, Gilbert led Culver to believe that the document was merely a receipt for the $30,000. The maturity date, interest rate, and the amount of the promissory note were later filled in, only the amount read $50,000 instead of $30,000. It was later verified that $50,000 had been deposited into Kalliel's Rexford Bank account, from which the $30,000 sent to Culver had been drawn.

Subsequent to these events, the Rexford Bank became insolvent, and the Federal Deposit Insurance Corporation (FDIC) purchased the bank's outstanding notes, including the one signed by Culver. The FDIC sought recovery on the note, since the note had matured and no money had ever been paid on it, and moved for summary judgment against Culver. Culver claimed that he should not be liable on the note because Gilbert's misrepresentations of the nature of the note constituted fraud in the execution.

ISSUE Can Culver successfully raise the real defense of fraud in the execution to avoid liability on the note?

DECISION No. The court granted the FDIC's request for summary judgment against Culver.

REASON The court had little difficulty in establishing that the FDIC was a holder in due course (HDC) in this instance. The FDIC had purchased Culver's note, along with others, in good faith, for value, and without notice that it was defective. Under the UCC, a holder in due course "takes the instrument free from all defenses of any party to the instrument with whom the holder has not dealt except . . . such misrepresentation as has induced the party to sign the instrument *with neither knowledge nor reasonable opportunity to obtain knowledge of its character or its essential terms*" (emphasis added). [UCC 3-305(2)(c)] The court found that, because Culver could read and understand English, he had had a "reasonable opportunity" to discover the "character" of the note.

Culver argued that, while this may have been so, there was no way he could have had a reasonable opportunity to learn the "essential terms" of the note since they were not included on the form when he signed it. In response to this argument, the court ruled that Culver's negligence in signing a blank promissory note was inexcusable and precluded him from asserting fraud as a real defense against the claim of a holder in due course. Culver had, in effect, signed a "blank check" that could be enforced by any subsequent holder in due course according to any terms added by an intervening holder. [UCC 3-407(3)]

Material Alteration An alteration is material if it changes the contract terms between any two parties in any way. Examples of material alterations follow: [UCC 3-407(1)]

1. Changing the number or relations of the parties.
2. Completing an instrument in an unauthorized manner.
3. Adding to the writing as signed or removing any part of it.

Thus, cutting off part of the paper of a negotiable instrument, adding clauses, or making any change in the amount, the date, or the rate of interest—even if the change is only one penny, one day, or 1 percent—is material. But it is not a material alteration to correct the maker's address, to have a red line drawn across the instrument to indicate that an auditor has checked it, or to correct the total final payment due when a mathematical error is discovered in the original computation. If the alteration is not material, any holder is entitled to enforce the instrument according to its original terms.

Material alteration is a *complete defense* against an ordinary holder but is at best only a *partial defense* against an HDC. An ordinary holder can recover nothing on an instrument if it has been materially altered. [UCC 3-407(2)]

If the original terms have been altered, such as the monetary amount payable, the HDC can enforce the instrument against the maker or drawer according to the original terms (tenor). If the instrument was incomplete and later completed in an unauthorized manner, alteration no longer can be claimed as a defense against an HDC, as the HDC can enforce the instrument as completed. [UCC 3-407(2)(3)] If the alteration is readily apparent, then obviously the holder has notice of some defect or defense and therefore cannot be an HDC. [UCC 3-302(1)(c) and 3-304(1)(a)]

Discharge in Bankruptcy   Discharge in bankruptcy is an absolute defense on any instrument regardless of the status of the holder because the purpose of bankruptcy is to settle finally all of the insolvent party's debts. [UCC 3-305(2)(d)]

Minority   Minority, or infancy, is a real defense only to the extent that state law recognizes it as such. [UCC 3-305(2)(a)] Thus, this defense renders the instrument voidable rather than void.

Illegality   When the law declares that an instrument is void because it has been executed in connection with illegal conduct, then the defense is absolute against both an ordinary holder and an HDC. If the law merely makes it voidable, as in the personal (rather than real) defense of illegality, discussed later, then it is still a defense against a holder, but not against an HDC. The courts are sometimes prone to treat the word *void* in a statute as meaning *voidable* in order to protect a holder in due course. [UCC 3-305(2)(b)]

Mental Incapacity   If a person is adjudicated mentally incompetent by state proceedings, then any instrument issued by that person thereafter is null and void. The instrument is *void ab initio* (from the beginning) and unenforceable by any holder or any HDC. [UCC 3-305(2)(b)]

Extreme Duress   When a person signs and issues a negotiable instrument under such extreme duress as an immediate threat of force or violence (for example, at gunpoint), the instrument is void and unenforceable by any holder or HDC. (Ordinary duress is a personal, not real, defense.) [UCC 3-305(2)(b)]

Personal Defenses

As mentioned before, personal defenses are used to avoid payment to an ordinary holder of a negotiable instrument.

Breach of Contract   When there is a breach of the underlying contract for which the negotiable instrument was issued, the maker of a note can refuse to pay it or the drawer of a check can stop payment. Breach of the contract can be claimed as a defense to liability on the instrument. For example, Rhodes purchases several sets of imported china from Livingston. The china is to be delivered in four weeks. Rhodes gives Livingston a promissory note for $1,000, which is the price of the china. The china arrives, but many of the pieces are broken, and several others chipped or cracked. Rhodes refuses to pay the note on the basis of breach of contract and breach of warranty. (Under sales law, a seller impliedly promises that the goods are at least merchantable; see Chapter 14.) If the note is no longer in the hands of the payee seller but is presented for payment by an HDC, the maker-buyer will not be able to plead breach of contract as a defense against liability on the note.

Landmark in the Law

The FTC Rule of 1976

On May 14, 1976, the Federal Trade Commission (FTC) issued a rule[1] that has severely limited the preferential position enjoyed by a holder in due course in certain circumstances. This FTC rule limits the rights of an HDC over an instrument that evidences a debt arising out of a *consumer credit* transaction. The rule, entitled "Preservation of Consumers' Claims and Defenses," is an attempt to prevent a situation in which a consumer is required to make payment for a defective product to a third party who is a holder in due course of a promissory note that formed part of the contract with the dealer who sold the defective good.

To illustrate: A consumer purchases a used car under express warranty from an automobile dealer, paying $500 down and signing a promissory note to the dealer for the remaining $2,000 due on the car. The dealer then sells to the bank this promissory note, which is a negotiable instrument, and the bank then becomes the creditor, to whom the consumer makes payments. The car does not perform as warranted, and the consumer returns the car, requesting the down payment back and cancellation of the contract. Even if the dealer did return the $500, however, the consumer would normally still owe the remaining $2,000, because the consumer's claim of breach of

1.   Volume 16 of the Code of Federal Regulations, Section 433.2. The rule was enacted pursuant to the FTC's authority under the Federal Trade Commission Act, Title 15, U.S.C. Section 41 *et seq.*

warranty is a personal defense, and the bank is a holder in due course. Thus, the traditional HDC rule left consumers who purchased defective products liable to the holder for the debt.

The rule makes the following provision for any seller or lessor of goods or services who takes or receives a consumer credit contract or who accepts as full or partial payment for such sale or lease the proceeds of any purchase money loan made in connection with any consumer credit contract:

NOTICE
ANY HOLDER OF THIS CONSUMER CREDIT CONTRACT IS SUBJECT TO ALL CLAIMS AND DEFENSES WHICH THE DEBTOR COULD ASSERT AGAINST THE SELLER OF GOODS OR SERVICES OBTAINED PURSUANT HERETO OR WITH THE PROCEEDS HEREOF. RECOVERY HEREUNDER BY THE DEBTOR SHALL NOT EXCEED AMOUNTS PAID BY THE DEBTOR HEREUNDER.

A consumer who is party to a consumer credit transaction can now bring any defense he or she would normally have against the seller of a product against the subsequent holder also. In essence, the FTC rule places a holder in due course of the paper or of the negotiable instrument in the position of a contract assignee and has made the buyer's duty to pay conditional upon the seller's full performance of the contract. It also has made both the seller and the creditor responsible for seller misconduct. Finally, it clearly reduces the degree of transferability of commercial paper resulting from consumer credit contracts.

Fraud in the Inducement   A person who issues a negotiable instrument based on false statements by the other party will be able to avoid payment on that instrument. To illustrate: Jerry agrees to purchase Howard's used tractor for $2,000. Howard, knowing his statements to be false, tells Jerry that the tractor is in good working order and that it has been used for only one harvest. In addition, he tells Jerry that he owns the tractor free and clear of all claims. Jerry pays Howard $500 in cash and issues a negotiable promissory note for the balance. As it turns out, Howard still owes the original seller $500 on the purchase of the tractor, and the tractor is subject to a filed security interest (see Chapter 19). In addition, the tractor is three years old and has been used in three harvests. Jerry can refuse to pay the note if it is held by an ordinary holder; but if Howard has negotiated the note to an HDC, Jerry must pay the HDC. Of course, Jerry can then sue Howard.

Illegality   Certain types of illegality constitute personal defenses. Other types constitute real defenses. Some transactions are prohibited under state statutes or ordinances, and some of these applicable statutes fail to provide that the prohibited transactions are void. If a statute provides that an illegal transaction is voidable, the defense is personal. If a statute makes an illegal transaction void, the defense is a real defense and can successfully be asserted against an HDC. For example, a state may make gambling contracts illegal and void but be silent on payments of gambling debts. Thus, the payment of a gambling debt becomes voidable and is a personal defense.

The following case presents a situation where, although a transaction was illegal (in violation of a court order), state law did not prevent the enforcement of a promissory note issuing from the illegal transaction.

Case 17.5
**NEW JERSEY MORTGAGE &
INVESTMENT CORPORATION
v. BERENYI**

Superior Court of New Jersey, Appellate Division, 1976.
140 N.J. Super 406, 356 A.2d 421.

FACTS   On May 25, 1964, Kroyden Industries, Inc., a New Jersey corporation, was prohibited by court order from making certain representations to its customers in connection with the sale of carpeting. In August of 1964, in violation of this order, one of Kroyden's employees offered to give Anna Berenyi and her husband carpeting free of charge if they referred prospective buyers to Kroyden Industries. Mr. and Mrs. Berenyi agreed to this condition and, relying upon the employee's offer, Anna Berenyi signed a promissory note for $1,521, from which "finder's fees" would be deducted when prospective buyers were referred to Kroyden Industries. Kroyden subsequently negotiated the note to the plaintiff in this case, New Jersey Mortgage and Investment Corporation. When Berenyi refused to pay the note, the plaintiff brought this legal action against her to recover the debt. Berenyi claimed that she was not liable on the note because the contract with Kroyden was illegal, having been prohibited by court order. The trial court held for the plaintiff, and Berenyi appealed.

ISSUE   Can Berenyi avoid her obligations on the note on the basis of illegality?

DECISION   No. The appellate court affirmed the trial court's judgment.

REASON   In addressing the question of Berenyi's liability on the note, the court stated that the "controlling issue presented is whether the defense here asserted is a 'real' defense or a 'personal' defense. Real defenses are available against even a holder in due course of a negotiable instrument; personal defenses are not available against such a holder." It was undisputed that the plaintiff was a holder in due course. The New Jersey Mortgage and Investment Corporation had taken the note in good faith, for value, and with no notice of the court order against Kroyden or of its violation by Kroyden's employee. Under New Jersey law, "a holder in due course takes free and clear of the defense of illegality, unless the statute which declares the act illegal also indicates that payment thereunder is void." The court concluded that, since no New Jersey statute ordained "that a note obtained in violation of an injunction is void and unenforceable," the illegality involved did not qualify as a real defense but only as a personal defense. As such, it was ineffective against the claim of a holder in due course.

Mental Incapacity   There are various types and degrees of mental incapacity. Ordinarily it is only a personal defense; but if a maker or drawer is so extremely incapacitated that the transaction becomes a nullity, then the instrument is void. In that case, the defense becomes real, and it is good against an HDC as well as an ordinary holder. [UCC 3-305(2)(b)]

If the maker drafts a negotiable instrument while insane, but before a formal court hearing declares (adjudicates) him or her to be insane, many courts declare the obligation thereon to be voidable. If, however, the maker has been declared by a court as being insane and a guardian has been appointed before the note is written, many courts will hold the obligation to be null and void.

Other Personal Defenses A number of other personal defenses can be used to avoid payment to an ordinary holder of a negotiable instrument, including:

1. Discharge by payment or cancellation. [UCC 3-601(1)(a) and 3-602]
2. Unauthorized completion of an incomplete instrument. [UCC 3-115, 3-407, 3-304(4)(d), and 4-401(2)(b)]
3. Nondelivery. [UCC 1-201(14), 3-305, 3-306(c)]
4. Ordinary duress or undue influence. [UCC 3-305]

❖ Discharge

Discharge from liability on an instrument can come from payment, cancellation, or material alteration, as previously discussed. Discharge can also occur if a party reacquires an instrument, if a holder impairs another party's right of recourse, or if a holder surrenders collateral without consent. [UCC 3-601]

Application

Law and the Purchaser of a Negotiable Instrument

Negotiable instruments are transferred on virtually every business day of the year. Most purchasers of negotiable instruments do not encounter any problems in further negotiation and transfer of the instruments or in collection if such instruments are time instruments. Potential problems exist, however, against which precautions should be taken.

For example, suppose that you wish to purchase a demand instrument. By definition, such an instrument has no stated time for payment and therefore may be overdue. That is to say, payment has been demanded but not made, or a reasonable amount of time has passed. (With checks, a reasonable amount of time is often presumed to be thirty days.) In any event, if you have any doubt about whether a demand instrument is overdue, you should investigate.

With any negotiable instrument, as a prospective purchaser, you cannot afford to ignore a defect in the instrument. If one exists and you have not made a reasonable inquiry, you may be unable to obtain payment. In other words, it is prudent to determine whether the instrument is complete and in some cases to determine whether the transferor has engaged in questionable business dealings in the past.

Checklist for the Purchase of Negotiable Instruments

☐ 1. Make sure, by contacting the obligor, that a demand instrument is not overdue prior to purchase.

☐ 2. Make sure that the negotiable instrument has no defects—make a good-faith attempt to determine whether the maker or drawer of the instrument might have a valid reason for refusing to pay.

❖ Chapter Summary: Holder in Due Course, Liability, and Defenses

REQUIREMENTS FOR HOLDER-IN-DUE-COURSE STATUS	
Must Be a Holder	A holder is defined as a person who is in possession of an instrument "drawn, issued or indorsed to him or his order or to bearer or in blank." UCC 1-201(20)
Must Take for Value	Value is: 1. To the extent agreed-upon consideration has been paid or a security interest or lien is acquired, or 2. Payment of or as security for an antecedent debt, or 3. Giving a negotiable instrument or irrevocable commitment as payment. UCC 3-303
Must Take in Good Faith	Good faith is defined as "honesty in fact in the conduct or transaction concerned." UCC 1-201(19)

Must Take without Notice	1. *That the instrument is overdue:*
	  a. Time instruments are overdue the moment after due date for payment.
	  b. Demand instruments are overdue after demand has been made or a reasonable time has lapsed from issue.
	  c. Domestic checks are *presumed* to be overdue after thirty days from issue. UCC 3-304

❖ Chapter Summary: Holder in Due Course, Liability, and Defenses—Continued

Must Take without Notice (Continued)	2. *That the instrument has been previously dishonored:*
	   a. Actual knowledge or knowledge of facts that would lead a person to suspect instrument has been dishonored. UCC 3-302(1)(c)
	
	3. *Knowledge that a claim or a defense exists:*
	   a. Actual knowledge—The instrument is so incomplete, bears such visible evidence of forgery or alteration, or is so irregular that a reasonable person would be put on notice from examination or from facts surrounding the transaction. UCC 3-304(1)

The Shelter Principle (Holder through a Holder in Due Course)	Under transfer and assignment law, a holder who cannot qualify as a holder in due course has the *rights* of a holder in due course if he or she derives title through a holder in due course. UCC 3-201
SIGNATURE LIABILITY OF PARTIES TO COMMERCIAL PAPER	
Primary Liability of Maker or Acceptor	1. The maker or acceptor is obligated to pay a negotiable instrument according to "its tenor at the time of his engagement" or as properly completed. UCC 3-413(1) 2. The drawee is primarily liable to the drawer to pay a negotiable instrument in accordance with the drawer's orders but owes no duty to the payee or any holder.
Secondary Liability	Parties other than the maker who can be secondarily liable on a negotiable instrument are the drawer, unqualified indorsers, and accommodation indorsers. These parties promise to pay on the instrument only if: 1. The instrument is properly and timely presented. 2. The instrument is dishonored. 3. Timely notice of dishonor is given to the secondarily liable party. UCC 3-413(2), 3-414
Liability for Agents' Signatures	An agent can sign negotiable instruments and thereby bind the principal if the agent indicates he or she is signing on behalf of a clearly named and identified principal or if he or she signs the principal's name (and is authorized by the principal to do so). UCC 3-403(1)(2)
TRANSFER AND PRESENTMENT WARRANTIES	
Transfer Warranties	*General indorsers*—The following five transfer warranties extend to all subsequent holders: 1. Transferor has good title or is otherwise authorized to obtain payment or acceptance on behalf of one who does have good title. 2. All signatures are genuine or authorized. 3. Instrument has not been materially altered. 4. No defense of any party is good against transferor. 5. Transferor has no knowledge of insolvency proceedings against the maker, acceptor, or drawer of an unaccepted instrument. UCC 3-417(2) *Non-indorsers*—Same as for the general indorser, but *warranties extend only to the immediate transferee.* UCC 3-417(2) *Qualified indorsers*—The same five transfer warranties as the general indorser except that a qualified indorsement ("without recourse") limits the fourth warranty to a warranty of "no knowledge" of such a defense (as opposed to no defense). These warranties extend to all subsequent holders. UCC 3-417(2)(3)
Presentment Warranties	The following *presentment warranties* are impliedly made by any person who seeks payment or acceptance of a negotiable instrument to any other person who in good faith pays or accepts the instrument: 1. The party presenting has good title to the instrument or is authorized to obtain payment or acceptance on behalf of a person who has good title. 2. The party presenting has no knowledge that the signature of the maker or the drawer is unauthorized. 3. The instrument has not been materially altered.

❖ Chapter Summary: Holder in Due Course, Liability, and Defenses—Continued

VALID DEFENSES AGAINST HOLDERS OF NEGOTIABLE INSTRUMENTS	
Real Defenses (**Valid against all holders, including HDCs or holders with the rights of HDCs.**) UCC 3-305	1. Forgery. 2. Fraud in the execution. 3. Material alteration. 4. Discharge in bankruptcy. 5. Minority—if the contract is voidable. 6. Illegality, mental incapacity, or extreme duress—if the contract is void.
Personal Defenses (**Valid against mere holders; not valid against HDCs or holders with rights of HDCs.**) UCC 3-306	1. Breach of contract. 2. Fraud in the inducement. 3. Illegality, ordinary duress or undue influence, and mental incapacity—if the contract is voidable. 4. Previous payment of the instrument. 5. Unauthorized completion of the instrument. 6. Nondelivery of the instrument.
Discharge by Payment	Under UCC 3-601(1)(a) and 3-603, all parties to a negotiable instrument will be discharged when the party primarily liable on it pays to a holder the amount due in full. By contrast, such payment made by any other party (such as an indorser) will discharge only the indorser and subsequent parties on the instrument. The party making such a payment still has the right to recover on the instrument from any prior parties.

❖ Questions and Case Problems

17-1. Charles is a well-known industrialist in the community. He has agreed to purchase a rare coin from Joy's Coin Shop. The purchase price is to be determined by independent appraisal. Payment is to be by Charles's check. Charles is going out of town and informs Joy that his agent will bring her a check during his absence. Charles draws up a check payable to Joy, leaving the amount blank, and gives the check to his agent, Paul. Paul, without authority, fills in the amount for $10,000 and presents the check to Joy, who now has the appraisal. The appraisal price is $7,000. Paul tells Joy that Charles wanted to be sure the check would cover the appraisal and that he (Paul) is authorized to receive the coin plus the balance in cash. Joy gives Paul the coin plus $3,000. When Charles discovers Paul's fraud, Charles stops payment on the check and offers Joy $7,000 for the coin. Joy claims she is a holder in due course and is entitled to the face value of the check, $10,000. Discuss whether Joy is an HDC and can therefore successfully pursue her claim.

17-2. Jules sold Alfred a small motorboat for $1,500, maintaining to Alfred that the boat was in excellent condition. Alfred gave Jules a check for $1,500, which Jules gave to Sherry for value with indorsement. When Alfred took the boat for a trial run, he discovered that the boat leaked, needed to be painted, and needed a new motor. Alfred stopped payment on his check, which had not yet been cashed. Jules has disappeared. Can Sherry recover from Alfred as holder in due course?

17-3. Fox purchased a used car from Emerson for $1,000. Fox paid for the car with a check, written in pencil, payable to Emerson for $1,000. Emerson, through careful erasures and alteration, changed the amount on the check to read $10,000 and negotiated the check to Sanderson. Sanderson took the check for value, in good faith, and without notice of the alteration and thus met the Code requirements for holder-in-due-course status. Can Fox successfully raise the real defense of material alteration to avoid payment on the check? Explain.

17-4. Marion makes out a negotiable promissory note payable to the order of Perry. Perry indorses the note, "without recourse, Perry," and transfers the note for value to Steven. Steven, in need of cash, negotiates the note to Harriet by indorsing it, "Pay to Harriet, Steven." On the due date, Harriet presents the note to Marion for payment, only to learn that Marion has filed for bankruptcy and will have all debts (including the note) discharged in bankruptcy. Discuss fully whether Harriet can hold Marion, Perry, and Steven liable on the note.

17-5. Jerry Sims issues a ninety-day negotiable promissory note payable to the order of David Johnson. The amount of the note is left blank, pending a determination of the amount of money Johnson will need to purchase a bull for Sims. Sims authorizes any amount not to exceed $2,000. Johnson, without authority, fills in the note in the amount of $5,000 and thirty days later sells the note to Sunset Bank for $4,500. Johnson not only does not buy the bull but has left the state. Sunset Bank had no knowledge that the instrument was incomplete when issued or that Johnson had no authority to complete the instrument in the amount of $5,000.

(a) Does the bank qualify as a holder in due course, and, if so, for what amount? Explain.

(b) If Johnson had sold the note to a stranger in a bar for $500, would the stranger qualify as a holder in due course? Explain.

17-6. Cook was the treasurer of Arizona Auto Auction, Inc. In her capacity as treasurer, she issued three corporate checks to Central Motors, signing each check on the signature line at the bottom of the check, just under the corporate name. She did not indicate that she was signing as treasurer or in any representative capacity. Central Motors deposited the checks into its account at the Valley National Bank. When the checks were dishonored, Valley National sued both the corporation and Cook. Was Cook personally liable on the check? Explain. [Valley National Bank, Sunnymead v. Cook, 136 Ariz. 232, 665 P.2d 576 (App. 1983)]

17-7. One day, while Ort, a farmer, was working alone in his field, a stranger approached him. The stranger said he was the state agent for a manufacturer of iron posts and wire fence. The two men conversed for some time, and eventually the stranger persuaded the farmer to accept a township-wide agency for the same manufacturer. The stranger then completed two documents for Ort to sign, telling Ort that they were identical copies of an agency agreement. Because the farmer did not have his glasses with him and could read only with great difficulty, he asked the stranger to read what the document said. The stranger then purported to read the document to Ort, not mentioning that it was a promissory note. Both men signed each document, the farmer assuming that he was signing a document of agency. The stranger later negotiated the promissory note he had fraudulently obtained from Ort to an HDC. When the HDC brought suit against the farmer, the farmer attempted to defend on the basis of fraud in the execution. Did Ort succeed in the real defense of fraud? Explain. [Ort v. Fowler, 31 Kan. 478, 2 P. 580 (1884)]

17-8. An employee of Epicycle Corporation cashed a payroll check at Money Mart Check Cashing Center. Money Mart deposited the check, with others, into its bank account. When the check was returned marked "payment stopped," Money Mart sought to recover from Epicycle for the value of the check. Money Mart claimed that it was a holder in due course on the instrument because it had accepted the check for value, in good faith, and without notice that a stop-payment order had been made. Epicycle argued that Money Mart was not a holder in due course because it had failed to verify that the check was good before it cashed the check. Did Money Mart's failure to inquire into the validity of the check preclude it from being a holder in due course? Explain. [Money Mart Check Cashing Center, Inc. v. Epicycle Corp., 667 P.2d 1372 (Colo. 1983)]

17-9. A bank sued an accommodation indorser for payment of a note. The indorser asserted illegality as a defense, claiming that the bank could not collect because the purpose of the loan was to purchase the bank's own stock—a transaction that is prohibited under federal banking law. The federal statute does not make this type of loan void. Was the indorser's defense of illegality successful? Explain. [Pan American Bank of Tampa v. Sullivan, 375 So.2d 338 (Fla.App. 4th Dist. 1979)]

17-10. Mecham signed a note payable to Munson for a brokerage fee on a mortgage Munson's firm was obtaining for him. Munson gave the note to his bank as security for a debt. Mecham maintained that Munson did not obtain the type of mortgage on which they had agreed, and he refused to make payment on the note. Was the bank able to recover from Mecham as an HDC? Explain. [Mecham v. United Bank of Arizona, 107 Ariz. 437, 489 P.2d 247 (1971)]

Chapter 18

Commercial Paper—Checks and the Banking System

While money may or may not be all Carl Sandburg claims, it is most certainly a valuable commodity. As legal tender, it is continuously used in the purchase and sale of goods and services. Most exchanges of money today are made by means of checks, credit cards, and charge accounts, which are rapidly replacing currency as a means of payment in almost all transactions for goods and services. Checks are the most common form of commercial paper regulated by the Uniform Commercial Code. It is estimated that approximately 57 billion personal and commercial checks are written each year in the United States. Checks are more than a daily convenience; checkbook money is an integral part of the American economic system.

This chapter will identify the legal characteristics of checks and the legal duties and liabilities that arise when a check is issued. Then it will consider the check deposit and collection process—that is, the actual procedure by which checkbook money moves through banking channels, causing the underlying cash dollars to be shifted from one bank account to another.

> *"Money is power, freedom, a cushion, the root of all evil, the sum of all blessings."*
>
> **Carl Sandburg, 1878–1967 (American poet and biographer)**

❖ Checks

A **check** is a special type of draft that is drawn on a bank, ordering it to pay a sum of money on demand. [UCC 3-104(2)(b)] A check does not, in and of itself, operate as an assignment of funds [UCC 3-409(1)], because it does not show an intention to make immediate transfer of the right to the specified sum. Thus, the drawee bank[1] is not liable to a payee or holder who presents the check for payment, even though the drawer has sufficient funds to pay the check. The payee's, or holder's, only recourse is against the drawer. (The drawer, however, may subsequently hold the bank liable for its wrongful refusal to pay.)

CHECK
A draft drawn by a drawer ordering the drawee bank to pay a certain amount of money to the holder on demand.

Cashier's Check

Checks are usually three-party instruments, but on certain types of checks, the bank can serve as both the drawer and the drawee. For example, when a bank draws a

---

1. See Chapter 15 for definitions of the parties to commercial paper, such as drawee, drawer, and payee.

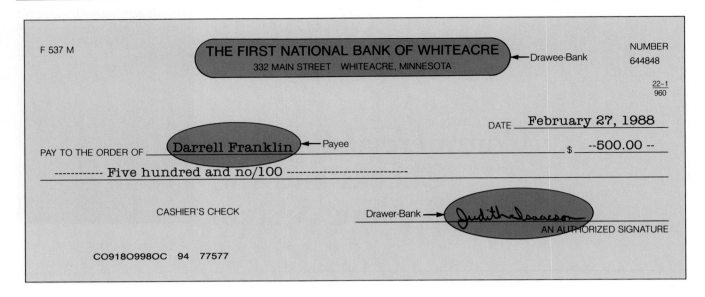

F 537 M

THE FIRST NATIONAL BANK OF WHITEACRE ← Drawee-Bank
332 MAIN STREET   WHITEACRE, MINNESOTA

NUMBER
644848

22–1
960

DATE **February 27, 1988**

PAY TO THE ORDER OF ___ Darrell Franklin ___ ← Payee $ __--500.00 --__

------------ Five hundred and no/100 --------------------------

CASHIER'S CHECK   Drawer-Bank → *Judith Isaacson*

AN AUTHORIZED SIGNATURE

CO918O998OC 94 77577

♦ **Exhibit 18-1
Cashier's Check**

CASHIER'S CHECK
A draft drawn by a bank on
itself.

TRAVELER'S CHECK
An instrument purchased from a
bank, express company, or the
like, in various denominations,
that can be used as cash upon a
second signature by the
purchaser. It has the
characteristics of a cashier's
check.

CERTIFIED CHECK
A check drawn by an individual
on his or her own account but
bearing a guarantee (acceptance)
by a bank that the bank will pay
the check regardless of whether
the drawer's account contains
adequate funds at the time the
check is presented.

check upon itself, the check is called a **cashier's check** and is a negotiable instrument
upon issue (see Exhibit 18-1). In effect, with a cashier's check, the bank lends its
credit to the purchaser of the check, thus making it available for immediate use in
banking circles. (The drawee is treated similar to an acceptor.) A cashier's check is
therefore an acknowledgment of a debt drawn by the bank upon itself.

Traveler's Check

A **traveler's check** is generally not a true check, but a straight draft. It is an instrument
on which a financial institution is both the drawer and the drawee. (It is most often
a regular draft since a bank is seldom the drawee.) A traveler's check, however, entails
the additional requirement that the purchaser must provide his or her authorized
signature in order for it to become a negotiable instrument. Drawn by the issuer
upon itself, a traveler's check has the characteristics of a cashier's check from the
issuing bank (see Exhibit 18-2).

Certified Check

When a person writes a check, it is assumed that he or she has money on deposit
to cover that check when it is presented for payment. To ensure against dishonor for
insufficient funds, a check may be certified by the drawee bank. A **certified check**
is recognized and accepted by a bank officer as a valid appropriation of the specified
amount that is drawn against the funds held by the bank (see Exhibit 18-3). The
usual method of certification is for the cashier or teller to write across the face of the
check, over the signature, a statement that it is good (certified) when properly indorsed.
    The certification should contain the date, the amount being certified, and the
name and title of the person certifying. Certification prevents the bank from denying
liability. It is a promise that sufficient funds are on deposit and *have been set aside*
to cover the check. Not only are certified checks used in many business dealings,
especially when the buyer and seller are strangers, but sometimes they are the required

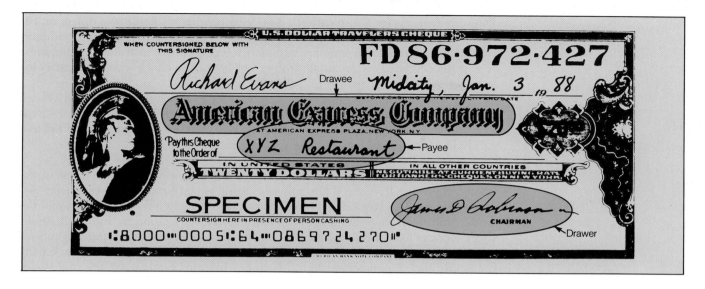

form of payment under state law—for example, in purchases at a sheriff's sale, which is commonly done by an auction conducted by a sheriff or other court officer to carry out a decree of foreclosure ordered by a court.

A drawee bank is not obligated to certify a check, and failure to do so is not a dishonor of the check. [UCC 3-411(2)] When a bank agrees to certification, it immediately charges the drawer's account with the amount of the check and transfers those funds to its own certified check account. In effect, the bank is agreeing in advance to accept that check when it is presented for payment and to make payment from those funds reserved in the certified check account. [UCC 3-411(1)]

◆ Exhibit 18-2
Traveler's Check

◆ Exhibit 18-3
Certified Check

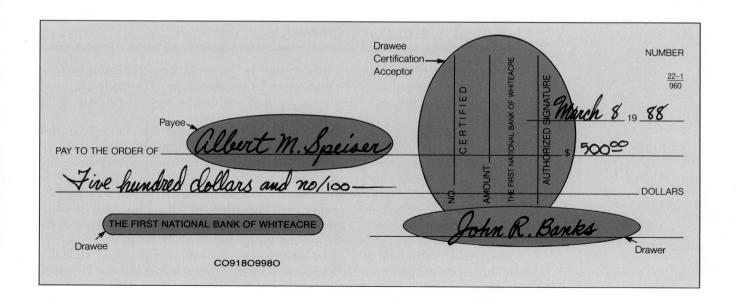

Drawer's Request for Certification   The legal liability of the drawer differs on the basis of whether the certification is requested by the drawer or the holder. The drawer who obtains certification remains *secondarily liable* on the instrument if for some reason the certifying bank cannot or does not honor the check when it is presented for payment.

For example, Martinez buys Waldstein's car for $500. Martinez writes out a check for that amount and takes it to the bank, where it is certified. In the unlikely event that the bank fails to honor the check when it is presented for payment, Waldstein can hold Martinez liable for payment of the $500.

Holder's Request for Certification   If the check is certified at the request of the holder, then the drawer and any indorsers prior to certification are completely discharged. A holder's request for certification is viewed as an affirmative choice for the bank's promise to pay over the drawer's and any indorser's promises. In this situation, the holder can look only to the bank for payment. In the preceding example, Martinez writes a $500 check to Waldstein, but Waldstein takes the check to the drawee bank for certification. Upon certification, Martinez is released from all liability, and Waldstein can look only to the bank for his $500. [UCC 3-411(1)]

Revocation of Certification   The bank's ability to revoke certification is extremely limited. If a good-faith holder has changed position in reliance on that certification, the bank cannot revoke. Furthermore, since certification constitutes *acceptance* of an instrument under the UCC, a bank can never revoke certification against an HDC regardless of whether the HDC has changed position in reliance on the certification. [UCC 3-418]

Alteration of a Certified Check   A bank is liable for payment of an altered check only if the check was altered prior to certification. Upon certification, the drawee bank becomes an acceptor and becomes liable for the instrument according to its tenor at the time of certification. Alterations after certification are not binding on the bank.

❖ Bank-Customer Relationship

The bank-customer relationship begins when the customer opens a checking account and deposits money that will be used to pay for checks written. The rights and duties of the bank and the customer are contractual and depend upon the nature of the transaction.

Article 4 of the UCC is a statement of the principles and rules of modern bank deposit and collection procedures. It governs the relationships of banks with one another as they process checks for payment, and it establishes a framework for deposit and checking agreements between a bank and its customers.

Article 3 of the UCC, dealing with the use of commercial paper, sets forth the requirements for negotiable instruments. The extent to which any party is either charged with or discharged from liability on a check is established according to the provisions of this article. Note that a check can fall within the scope of Article 3 as a negotiable instrument and yet be subject to the provisions of Article 4 while it is in the course of collection. In the case of a conflict between Article 3 and Article 4, Article 4 controls. [UCC 4-102(1)]

Profile

John Marshall (1755–1835)

It is often said that John Marshall was probably the greatest chief justice ever to head the U.S. Supreme Court. During his thirty-four-year tenure as chief justice, he penned many decisions of lasting impact on the course of American history and the American judicial system. He is most renowned for having enunciated the doctrine of judicial review (see *Marbury* v. *Madison*, in the "Landmark" in Chapter 2) and for establishing the Supreme Court as the final arbiter and authority in matters concerning constitutional interpretation.

Marshall was born in 1755 in a log cabin on the Virginia frontier, the first of fifteen children born to Thomas Marshall, a descendant of Welsh immigrants, and his wife, who was the daughter of a Scottish clergyman. According to John Marshall, his father had only a "limited education," but in spite of this he educated his son as best he

could in English literature and in Blackstone's *Commentaries on the Law*. The elder Marshall eventually became a member of the Virginia House of Burgesses and a landowner of some substance. Apart from what he learned from his father, John Marshall's education was also limited—to two years of formal schooling. His legal education took even less time and consisted of six weeks of lectures given by George Wythe, American's first law professor, at the College of William and Mary. When he first began practicing law, six months after attending Wythe's lectures, Marshall's legal library consisted solely of notes he had taken while reading a borrowed copy of Francis Bacon's *Abridgement* of English law. Three years later he was elected to the Virginia legislature and eventually participated in Virginia's constitutional convention as one of the state's leading Federalists.

Among the many far-reaching decisions authored by Chief Justice Marshall was one that was to have great significance for the American banking industry. The case was *McCulloch* v. *Maryland* (1819),[1] and the issue concerned the constitutionality of the Second National Bank.

The issue of constitutionality had been raised when the First Bank of the United States was chartered, for a period of twenty years, in 1791. That bank was sufficiently successful that, when its charter expired in 1811, the cry went up for a second bank. The Second Bank of the United States, chartered in 1816 for a twenty-year period, had a less illustrious fate than

the First Bank, however. The Second Bank was characterized by mismanagement and corruption and became the target of much criticism. In this context, the issue of the bank's constitutionality was again raised.

Maryland was one of many states that opposed the existence of the Second Bank of the United States, claiming that it represented unfair competition against state banks and an extension of centralized political power. Yielding to pressure from its state banks, the government of Maryland imposed a tax on the Second Bank's Baltimore branch. The branch's cashier, James William McCulloch, refused to pay the Maryland tax. Maryland took McCulloch to its state court. In that suit the state of Maryland won. Since similar taxes were being levied in other states, the national government appealed the case to the Supreme Court.

The central question before the Court was whether Congress had the power to establish a national bank, even though the Constitution did not specify any such power. In his decision, Marshall admitted that the power to establish a national bank was not expressed in the Constitution. In Article I, Section 8, of the Constitution, however, Congress was granted the general power "to make all laws which shall be necessary and proper" for carrying out "all other powers" vested in the national government. If establishing such a national bank aided the national government in the exercise of its designated powers, then the authority to set up such a bank was implied. To Marshall, the "necessary and proper" clause embraced "all means which are appropriate" to

---

1. 17 U.S. (4 Wheat.) 316, 4 L.Ed. 579 (1819).

Profile—Continued

carry out "the legitimate ends" of the Constitution. The national bank was necessary in order to carry out the government's powers that were enumerated in the Constitution, and hence the Second Bank could not be declared unconstitutional.

By refusing to bind the national government by the literal limits of its expressed powers, the Marshall Court enabled the national government to grow and to meet problems that the Founding Fathers were unable to foresee. The creation of a permanent, viable national banking system was yet to come and only emerged in 1913 when the Federal Reserve System was established. The issue of the constitutionality of a national banking system, however, had been resolved nearly a century before by Marshall's decision. Without that decision, the history of U. S. banking might have taken an entirely different course.

A creditor-debtor relationship is created between a customer and a bank when, for example, the customer makes cash deposits into a checking account or when final payment is received for checks drawn on other banks.

A principal-agent relationship underlies the check-collection process. A check does not operate as an immediate legal assignment of funds between the drawer and the payee. [UCC 3-409] The money in the bank represented by that check does not move from the drawer's account to the payee's account; nor is any underlying debt discharged until the drawee bank honors the check and makes final payment. To transfer checkbook dollars among different banks, each bank acts as the agent of collection for its customer. [UCC 4-201(1)]

❖ Honoring Checks

When a commercial bank provides checking services, it agrees to honor the checks written by its customers with the usual stipulation that there be sufficient funds available in the account to pay each check. When a drawee bank *wrongfully* fails to honor a check, it is liable to its customer for damages resulting from its refusal to pay. The Code does not attempt to specify the theory under which the customer may recover for wrongful dishonor; it merely states that the drawee is liable. Thus, the drawer customer does not have to prove that the drawee bank breached its contractual commitment, or slandered the customer's credit, or was negligent. [UCC 4-402] When the bank properly dishonors a check for insufficient funds, it has no liability to the customer.

On the other hand, a bank may charge against a customer's account a check that is payable from that account even though the account contains insufficient funds to cover the check. [UCC 4-401(1)] Once a bank makes special arrangements with its customer to accept overdrafts on an account, the payor bank can become liable to its customer for damages proximately caused by its wrongful dishonor of overdrafts. The charging of overdrafts will be discussed later in this chapter.

The customer's agreement with the bank includes a general obligation to keep sufficient money on deposit to cover all checks written. The customer is liable to the payee or to the holder of a check in a civil suit if a check is not honored. If intent to defraud can be proved, the customer can also be subject to criminal prosecution for writing a "hot" check.

Stale Checks

The bank's responsibility to honor its customers' checks is not absolute. A bank is not obliged to pay an uncertified check presented more than six months from its date. [UCC 4-404] Commercial banking practice regards a check outstanding for longer than six months as a **stale check.** UCC 4-404 gives a bank the option of paying or not paying on such a check without liability. The usual banking practice is to consult the customer, but if a bank pays in good faith without consulting the customer, it has the right to charge the customer's account for the amount of the check.

STALE CHECK
A check, other than a certified check, that is presented for payment more than six months after its date.

Missing Indorsements

Depositary institutions are allowed to supply any necessary indorsements of a customer. This rule does not apply if the item expressly requires the payee's indorsement. The depositary bank places a statement on the item to the effect that it was deposited by a customer or credited to that customer's account. [UCC 4-205(1)]

Death or Incompetence of a Customer

UCC 4-405 provides that if, at the time a check is issued or its collection has been undertaken, a bank does not know of an adjudication of incompetence, an item can be paid and the bank will not incur liability. Neither death nor incompetence revokes the bank's authority to pay an item until the bank knows of the situation and has had reasonable time to act. Even when a bank knows of the death of its customer, for ten days after the date of death, it can pay or certify checks drawn on or prior to the date of death—unless a person claiming an interest in that account, such as an heir or an executor of the estate, orders the bank to stop payment. Without this provision, banks would constantly be required to verify the continued life and competency of their drawers.

Stop-Payment Orders

Only a customer can order his or her bank to pay a check, and only a customer can order payment of a check to be stopped. This right does not extend to holders—that is, payees or indorsees—because the drawee bank's contract is not with them, but only with its drawers. However, a customer has no right to stop payment on a check that has been certified or accepted by a bank. Also, a **stop-payment order** must be received within a reasonable time and in a reasonable manner to permit the bank to act on it. [UCC 4-403(1)]

 Although a stop-payment order can be given orally, usually by phone, it is binding on the bank for only fourteen calendar days unless confirmed in writing.[2] A written

STOP-PAYMENT ORDER
An order by the drawer of a draft or check directing the drawer's bank not to pay the check.

---

2. Some states do not recognize oral stop-payment orders; they must be in writing.

TO THE FIRST NATIONAL BANK
OF SOUTH MIAMI
SOUTH MIAMI, FLORIDA

DATE OF ORDER

ACCOUNT NUMBER

Please STOP PAYMENT on my (or our) check drawn on your bank, described as follows:

NO.: DATED: PAYABLE TO: AMOUNT $

REASON: DUPLICATE ISSUED?

THIS REQUEST IS MADE WITH THE UNDERSTANDING THAT THE BANK WILL USE REASONABLE PRECAUTION IN FOLLOWING YOUR INSTRUCTION BUT IN CONSIDERATION OF THE ACCEPTANCE OF THIS REQUEST IT IS EXPRESSLY AGREED THAT THE BANK WILL IN NO WAY BE LIABLE IN THE EVENT THE CHECK IS PAID IF PAID THE SAME DAY YOUR ORDER IS RECEIVED OR IF PAID BY OVERSIGHT OR INADVERTENCE OR IF BY REASON OF SUCH PAYMENT OTHER CHECKS DRAWN BY THE UNDERSIGNED ARE RETURNED FOR INSUFFICIENT FUNDS AND THE UNDERSIGNED FURTHER AGREES TO INDEMNIFY THE BANK AGAINST ALL EXPENSES AND COSTS THAT IT MIGHT INCUR BY REASON OF REFUSING PAYMENT ON SAID CHECK.

EXPIRATION DATE

IT IS HEREBY AGREED AND UNDERSTOOD THAT THIS ORDER WILL REMAIN IN EFFECT FOR A SIX-MONTH PERIOD UNLESS OTHERWISE DIRECTED AND THE BANK WILL CHARGE $5.00 FOR EACH SIX-MONTH PERIOD OR PORTION THEREOF THAT THIS ORDER IS IN EFFECT. THE BANK MAY CHARGE MY ACCOUNT WITH THIS AMOUNT.

ORDER RECEIVED BY   IN PERSON   BY LETTER   SIGNATURE OF MAKER

BANK NOT LIABLE IF CHECK HAS BEEN CASHED IN THE SAME DAY THIS ORDER WAS ACCEPTED.

◆ **Exhibit 18-4
Stop-Payment Order**

stop-payment order (see Exhibit 18-4) or oral order confirmed in writing is effective for six months, at which time it must be renewed in writing. [UCC 4-403(2)]

Should the drawee bank pay the check over the customer's properly instituted stop-payment order, the bank will be obligated to recredit the account of the drawer customer. The bank, however, is liable for no more than the actual loss suffered by the drawer because of such wrongful payment.

Assume that Arlene Drury orders six bamboo palms from Waverly's Nursery at $25 each. Drury pays in advance for the trees with her check for $150. Later that day, Waverly's Nursery tells Drury that they will not deliver the palms as arranged. Drury immediately calls her bank and stops payment on the check. Two days later, in spite of this stop-payment order, the bank inadvertently honors Drury's check to Waverly's Nursery for the undelivered palms. The bank will be liable to Drury for the full $150.

The result would be different if Waverly's had delivered five palms. Since Drury would have owed Waverly's $125 for the goods delivered, she would have been able to establish actual losses of only $25 resulting from the bank's payment over her stop-payment order. Consequently, the bank would be liable to Drury for only $25.

A stop-payment order has its risks for a customer. The drawer must have a *valid legal ground* for issuing such an order; otherwise, the holder can sue the drawer for payment. Moreover, defenses sufficient to refuse payment against a payee may not be valid grounds to prevent payment against a subsequent holder in due course. [UCC 3-305]

A person who wrongfully stops payment on a check will not only be liable to the payee for the amount of the check, but might also be liable for special damages resulting from the wrongful order. These special damages must be separately pleaded and proved at trial.

The following case confirms the bank's duty to honor in a timely fashion a customer's stop-payment order.

Case 18.1
THOMAS v. MARINE MIDLAND TINKERS NATIONAL BANK
Civil Court of the City of New York, 1976.
86 Misc.2d 284, 381 N.Y.S.2d 797.

FACTS On December 8, 1973, the plaintiff (Thomas) gave Ralph Gallo a check for $2,500 as a down payment on two rugs Thomas was purchasing from Gallo. The check was postdated to December 10 and drawn on the Marine Midland Tinkers National Bank. Having changed his mind about the purchase, Thomas went to the Marine Midland bank on the morning of December 10 and arranged with a bank officer whom he knew to have a stop-payment order placed on the check. Thomas gave the bank officer all the required information, but the check was described as #22 instead of #221, the correct number. On the afternoon of the following day, the check was presented for payment at the same bank, and the bank cashed it and debited the plaintiff's account in the amount of the $2,500. When Thomas called Gallo, demanding the return of the $2,500, Gallo refused to pay and threatened to enforce the purchase agreement. Thomas then brought an action against the bank for wrongful payment. The bank moved for dismissal of the charge on the basis of the incorrect information (the erroneous check number) given by Thomas on the stop-payment order.

ISSUE Can Thomas recover the $2,500 from the bank?

DECISION Yes. The bank was held responsible for its act of improperly making payment upon the check.

REASON The court held that "[a] day and a half is more than reasonable notice to enforce a stop order on a check presented at the very same branch, and payment of the item by the bank thereafter constitutes a breach of its obligations to honor the stop order. The normal problem of reasonable computer lag when dealing with a great number of other branches of a large bank has no relevancy to the facts at bar, where all transactions occurred in a single branch." As to the error regarding the check number, the court stated, "The single digital mistake in describing the check in the stop order is deemed trivial, and insignificant. Enough information was supplied to the bank to reasonably provide it with sufficient information to comply with the stop payment order. The bank is therefore held responsible for its act of improperly making payment upon the check."

Overdrafts

When the bank receives an item properly payable from its customer's checking account, but there are insufficient funds in the account to cover the amount of the check, the bank can either dishonor the item or it can pay the item and charge the customer's account, creating an overdraft. [UCC 4-401(1)] The bank can subtract the difference from the customer's next deposit because the check carries with it an enforceable implied promise to reimburse the bank.

When a check "bounces," a holder can resubmit the check, hoping that at a later date sufficient funds will be available to pay it. The holder must notify any indorsers on the check of the first dishonor; otherwise, they will be discharged from their signature liability.

Payment on Forged Signature of Drawer

A forged signature on a check has no legal effect as the signature of a drawer. [UCC 3-404(1)] Banks require signature cards from each customer who opens a checking account. The bank is responsible for determining whether the signature on a customer's check is genuine. The general rule, illustrated in the following case, is that the bank must recredit the customer's account when it pays on a forged signature.

Case 18.2
SCCI, INC. v. UNITED STATES NATIONAL BANK OF OREGON
Court of Appeals of Oregon, 1986.
78 Or.App. 176, 714 P.2d 1113.

FACTS   Susan Wolf, who was employed as a secretary and bookkeeper for SCCI, Inc., a construction contractor, forged her employer's name on more than ninety checks drawn on SCCI's account at the U. S. National Bank of Oregon. The bank cashed the checks and debited SCCI's account, and Susan Wolf wrongfully received a total of approximately $22,600. The plaintiff, SCCI, brought a criminal action against Wolf when the forgeries were discovered but later dropped the charges and settled out of court. SCCI also demanded that the bank credit its account for the $22,600 worth of forged checks. The bank, however, refused to credit SCCI's account for the amount of the forged checks, claiming that the out-of-court settlement between SCCI and Wolf undermined its ability to collect from Wolf (which, of course, it would attempt to

do if it were to credit SCCI's account). SCCI argued that it was the bank's duty, under its contractual responsibilities to SCCI, to cash checks only when they were authorized by SCCI. The trial court granted the bank's request for summary judgment, and SCCI appealed the decision.

ISSUE   Can the bank be held liable for cashing the forged checks?

DECISION   Yes. The trial court's ruling was reversed and the case remanded to the trial court.

REASON   The court reasoned that since there was no evidence that "plaintiff's negligence substantially contributed to the forgery, plaintiff was not obligated for the forged checks that the bank had honored . . . and the bank lacked authority to debit plaintiff's account for the checks. Plaintiff was entitled to have the bank credit its account."

Customer Negligence   When the customer's negligence substantially contributes to the forgery, the bank will not normally be obliged to recredit the customer's account for the amount of the check. Suppose Gemco Corporation uses a mechanical check-writing machine to write its payroll and business checks. Gemco discovers that one of its employees used the machine to write himself a check for $10,000 and that the bank subsequently honored it. Gemco requests the bank to recredit $10,000 to its account for incorrectly paying on a forged check. If the bank can show that Gemco failed to take reasonable care in controlling access to the check-writing equipment, Gemco cannot require the bank to recredit its account for the amount of the forged check. [UCC 3-406]

Timely Examination Required   A customer has an *affirmative duty* to examine monthly statements and canceled checks promptly and with reasonable care and to report any forged signatures promptly. [UCC 4-406(1)] This includes forged signatures of indorsers, to be discussed later. [UCC 4-406] Failure to so examine and report, or any carelessness by the customer that results in a loss to the bank, makes the customer liable for the loss. [UCC 4-406(2)(a)] Even if the customer can prove that reasonable care was taken against forgeries, the Code provides that discovery of such forgeries and notice to the bank must take place within specific time frames, or the customer cannot require the bank to recredit his or her account.

When a series of forgeries by the same wrongdoer takes place, the Code provides that the customer, in order to recover for all the forged items, must discover and report the forgery to the bank within fourteen calendar days of the receipt of the bank statement and canceled checks that contain the forged item. [UCC 4-406(2)(b)]

Failure to notify within this period of time discharges the bank's liability for all similar forged checks prior to notification.

For example, Jamestown Bank sends out monthly statements and canceled checks on the last day of each month. Barker, owner of a small store, unknowingly has had a number of his blank checks stolen by employee Sam. On April 20, Sam forges Barker's signature and cashes check #1. On April 22, Sam forges and cashes check #2. The checks canceled in April (including the forged ones) and the April statement from the Jamestown Bank are received on May 1. Barker sets aside the statement and does not reconcile his checking account. On May 20 Sam forges check #3. The checks canceled in May and the May statement are received by Barker on June 1. Immediately thereafter, Barker examines both statements and discovers the forgeries.

Can Barker demand that the bank recredit his account for all forged checks? The answer is no, assuming the bank was not negligent in paying the forged checks. [UCC 4-406(3)] A series of forgeries by the same wrongdoer has been committed. The two forged checks in April were made available to Barker for inspection on May 1. Liability for any forged check in the series falls on Barker after May 15 (fourteen days after receipt of the April statement). In addition, if Barker's negligence in failing to examine his April statement promptly results in a loss to the Jamestown Bank, the bank's liability to recredit Barker's account for any forged item would be reduced by the amount of any loss the bank suffered by reason of Barker's delay in notifying the bank.

Had Barker examined his April statement immediately upon receipt and reported the two April forgeries, the bank would have been obligated to recredit fully Barker's account. If the bank could have proved that Barker's carelessness in permitting the blank checks to be stolen substantially contributed to the forgery, however, Barker, not the bank, would have been liable. [UCC 3-406 and 4-406]

Regardless of the degree of care exercised by the customer or the bank, the Code has placed an absolute time limit on the liability of a bank for forged customer signatures. UCC 4-406(4) provides that a customer who fails to report his or her forged signature one year from the date that the statement and canceled checks were made available for inspection loses the legal right to have the bank recredit his or her account.

The importance of exercising due care in controlling access to check-writing equipment and in examining monthly statements is emphasized in the following case, where the bank was released from liability for honoring forged checks.

Case 18.3
READ v. SOUTH CAROLINA NATIONAL BANK.
Supreme Court of South Carolina, 1985.
286 S.C. 534, 335 S.E.2d 359.

FACTS In July of 1979 Read & Read, Inc., a corporation owned by Thomas and Emerson Read, hired Judy Bode as a sales secretary. She was promoted to executive secretary shortly thereafter and worked primarily for Emerson Read. Judy Bode eventually assumed responsibility for overseeing nearly all of Read's checking accounts, including his personal account. She also reviewed the bank statements for each account and reconciled them to the corresponding checkbooks. As a result of a hunting accident, Mr. Read lost his hand and, to facilitate check signing, had a rubber signature stamp made. Ms. Bode had easy access to the stamp.

From September 1980 until January 1981, Ms. Bode used the rubber stamp to forge a total of fourteen checks for her own purposes on Read's accounts, including one check for over $8,000. Read, who did not review any bank

Case 18.3—Continued

statements during this entire period of time, was unaware of the forgeries. When the forgeries were discovered in January of 1981, Read sued his bank, the South Carolina National Bank, to recover the amount of the forged checks that he alleged had been wrongfully honored by the bank. The trial court held for the bank, and Read appealed.

ISSUE Can Read recover from the bank the funds lost as a result of Judy Bode's forgeries?

DECISION No. The Supreme Court of South Carolina affirmed the lower court's ruling. The bank was released from liability due to Read's negligence and failure to examine his statements in a timely manner.

REASON The bank acknowledged its duty to discover unauthorized or forged signatures and its potential liability in this case for the forged checks. The bank raised as a defense, however, the fact that Read, by his negligence, substantially contributed to the making of the unauthorized signatures and that he failed in his duty to discover and promptly notify the bank of the forgeries. The law imposes upon a bank's customer the duty of exercising reasonable care and promptness in examining bank statements and reporting any forgeries or alterations. Read's failure to do this precluded his recovery from the bank.

Payment on Forged Indorsement

A bank that pays a customer's check bearing a forged indorsement must recredit the customer's account or be liable to the customer-drawer for breach of contract. Suppose Brian issues a $50 check "to the order of Antonio." Jimmy steals the check, forges Antonio's indorsement, and cashes the check. When the check reaches Brian's bank, the bank pays it and debits Brian's account. Under UCC 4-401 the bank must recredit Brian's account $50 because it failed to carry out Brian's order to pay "to the order of Antonio." (Brian's bank will in turn recover—under breach-of-warranty principles—from the bank that cashed the check.) [UCC 4-207(1)(a)]

By comparison, the bank has no right to recover from a holder who, without knowledge, cashes a check bearing a *forged drawer's signature*. The holder merely guarantees that he or she has no knowledge that the signature of the drawer is unauthorized. Unless the bank can prove such knowledge, its only recourse is against the forger. [UCC 3-418 and 4-207(1)(b)] The customer, however, has a duty to examine the returned checks and statements received from the bank and to report forged indorsements promptly upon discovery or notice. Failure to report forged indorsements within a three-year period after such forged items are made available to the customer relieves the bank of liability. [UCC 4-406(4)]

Payment on Altered Check

The customer's instruction to the bank is to pay the exact amount on the face of the check to the holder. The bank must examine each check before making final payment. If it fails to detect an alteration, it is liable to its customer for the loss because it did not pay as the drawer customer ordered. The loss is the difference between the original amount of the check and the amount actually paid. Suppose a check written for $11 is raised to $111. The customer's account will be charged $11 (the amount the customer ordered it to pay). The bank will normally be responsible for the $100. [UCC 4-401(2)(a)]

The bank is entitled to recover the amount of loss from the transferor who, by presenting the check for payment, warrants that the check has not been materially

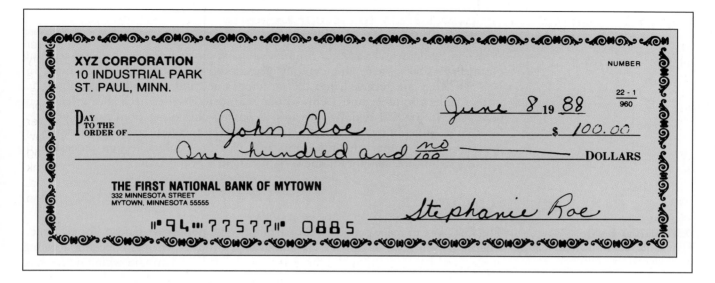

XYZ CORPORATION
10 INDUSTRIAL PARK
ST. PAUL, MINN.

NUMBER

22 - 1
960

June 8 19 88

PAY
TO THE
ORDER OF _____ *John Doe* _____ $ *100.00*

One hundred and $\frac{no}{100}$ _____ DOLLARS

THE FIRST NATIONAL BANK OF MYTOWN
332 MINNESOTA STREET
MYTOWN, MINNESOTA 55555

Stephanie Roe

⑴94⑾77577⑾ 0885

◆ **Exhibit 18-5**
Poorly Filled-Out Check

altered. No customer or collecting bank or other holder in due course who acts in good faith gives this warranty to:

1. The maker of a note.
2. The drawer of a draft.
3. The acceptor of an item with respect to an alteration made prior to the acceptance if the holder in due course took the item after the acceptance.
4. The acceptor of an item with respect to an alteration made after the acceptance. [UCC 4-207(1)(c) and 3-417(1)(c)]

A customer's negligence can shift the risk of loss. A common example is when a person carelessly writes a check, leaving large gaps around the numbers and words so that additional numbers and words can be inserted (see Exhibit 18-5).

Similarly, a person who signs a check and leaves the dollar amount for someone else to fill in is barred from protesting when the bank unknowingly and in good faith pays whatever amount is shown. [UCC 4-401(2)(b)] Finally, if the bank can trace its loss on successive altered checks to the customer's failure to discover the initial alteration, then the bank can alleviate its liability for reimbursing the customer's account.[3] [UCC 4-406] The law governing the customer's *duty* to examine monthly statements and canceled checks, and to discover and report alterations to the drawee bank, is the same as that applied to forged customer signatures.

In every situation involving a forged drawer's signature or alteration, a bank must observe reasonable commercial standards of care in paying on a customer's checks. [UCC 4-406(3)] The customer's contributory negligence can be asserted only if the bank has exercised ordinary care.

---

3. The bank's defense is the same whether the successive payments were made on a forged drawer's signature or on an altered check. The bank must prove that prompt notice would have prevented its loss. For example, notification might have alerted the bank to stop paying further items or might have enabled it to catch the forger.

❖ Bank's Duty to Accept Deposits

A second fundamental service a commercial bank provides for its checking-account customers is that of accepting deposits of cash and checks. Cash deposits made in U.S. currency are received into the customer's account without being subject to further collection procedures. This section will focus on the check after it has been deposited. In the vast majority of cases, deposited checks are from parties who do business at different banks, but sometimes checks are written between customers of the same bank. Either situation brings into play the bank collection process as it operates within the statutory framework of Article 4 of the UCC.

Definitions

DEPOSITARY BANK
The first bank to which an item is transferred for collection, even though it may also be the payor bank.

PAYOR BANK
A bank on which an item is payable as drawn (or is payable as accepted).

COLLECTING BANK
Any bank handling an item for collection, except the payor bank.

INTERMEDIARY BANK
Any bank to which an item is transferred in the course of collection, except the depositary or payor bank.

The first bank to receive a check for payment is the **depositary bank.**[4] For example, when a person deposits an IRS tax-refund check into a personal checking account at the local bank, that bank is the depositary bank. The bank on which a check is drawn (the drawee bank) is called the **payor bank.** Any bank except the payor bank that handles a check during some phase of the collection process is a **collecting bank.** Any bank except the payor bank or depositary bank to which an item is transferred in the course of this collection process is called an **intermediary bank.**

The Collection Process

During the collection process, any bank can take on one or more of the various roles of depositary, payor, collecting, or intermediary bank. To illustrate: A buyer in New York writes a check on her New York bank and sends it to a seller in San Francisco. The seller deposits the check in her San Francisco bank account. The seller's bank is both a *depositary bank* and a *collecting bank*. The buyer's bank in New York is the *payor bank*. As the check travels from San Francisco to New York, any collecting bank (other than the ones already acting as depositary bank and payor bank) handling the item in the collection process is also called an *intermediary bank*.

Bank's Liability for Restrictive Indorsements   As just stated, banks handling commercial paper in the normal course of collection are called *intermediary banks* [UCC 4-105(c)], and banks paying on commercial paper are called *payor banks*. [UCC 4-105(b)] Neither type of bank is bound by any restrictive indorsements of any person except the immediate holder who transfers or presents the instrument for payment. [UCC 3-206(2)] This means that only the first bank to which the item is presented for collection must pay in a manner consistent with any restrictive indorsement. [UCC 3-206(3)] This bank is called the depositary bank [UCC 4-105(a)] even if it is also the payor bank (that is, where only one bank is involved).

To illustrate: Charles writes a check on his San Francisco bank account and sends it to Leota. Leota indorses the check with a restrictive indorsement that reads, "For deposit into Account #4012 only." A Dallas bank is the first bank to which this check is presented for payment (the depositary bank), and it must act consistently with the terms of the restrictive indorsement. Therefore, it must credit account #4012

---

4.   All definitions in this section are found in UCC 4-105.

with the money or be liable to Leota for conversion. Charles's check leaves the Dallas bank indorsed "for collection." As the check moves through the collection network of intermediary banks to Charles's San Francisco bank for payment, each intermediary bank is bound only by the preceding bank's indorsement to collect.

The division of responsibility between types of banks is necessary. Collecting banks process huge numbers of commercial instruments, and there is no practical way for them to examine and comply with the effect of each restrictive indorsement. Therefore, the only reasonable alternative is to charge the depositary bank with the responsibility of examining and complying with any restrictive indorsements.

Check Collection between Customers of Same Bank An item that is payable by the depositary bank (also the payor bank) that receives it is called an "on-us item." If the bank does not dishonor the check by the opening of the second banking day following its receipt, it is considered paid. [UCC 4-213(4)(b)] For example, Williams and Merkowitz each have a checking account at State Bank. On Monday morning, Merkowitz deposits into his own checking account a $300 check from Williams. That same day, State Bank issues Merkowitz a "provisional credit" for $300. When the bank opens on Wednesday, Williams's check is considered honored, and Merkowitz's provisional credit becomes a final payment.

Check Collection between Customers of Different Banks Millions of checks circulate throughout the United States each day, and every check must be physically transported to its payor bank before final payment is made. Once a depositary bank receives a check, it must arrange to present it either directly or through intermediary banks to the appropriate payor bank. Each bank in the collection chain must pass the check on or before midnight of the next banking day following its receipt. [UCC 4-202(2)]

The bank has a duty to use ordinary care in performing its collection functions. [UCC 4-202(1)] This duty requires banks to conform to general banking usage as established in the Uniform Commercial Code, Federal Reserve regulations, clearinghouse rules, and so on.[5] [UCC 4-103(1)] Banks also have a duty to act seasonably, meaning that they should take appropriate action before the midnight deadline following the receipt of a check, a notice, or a payment. [UCC 4-104(1)(h)] So, for example, a collecting bank that receives a check on Monday must forward it to the next collection bank prior to midnight on Tuesday.

Upon receipt of a check by a payor bank through the collection process, the midnight deadline for action becomes extremely important. Unless the payor bank dishonors the check or returns it by midnight on the next banking day following receipt, the payor bank is accountable for the face amount of the check. [UCC 4-302]

Because of this and because of the need for an even work flow of the many items handled by banks daily, the Code permits what is called *deferred posting*, or delayed return, in which checks received after a certain time (say, 2:00 P.M.) can be deferred until the next day. Thus, a check received by a payor bank at 3:00 P.M. on Monday would be deferred for posting until Tuesday. In this case, the payor bank's deadline would be midnight Wednesday. [UCC 4-301(1)]

---

5. The Code is explicit that "the obligations of good faith, diligence, reasonableness and care . . . may not be disclaimed." [UCC 1-102(3)]

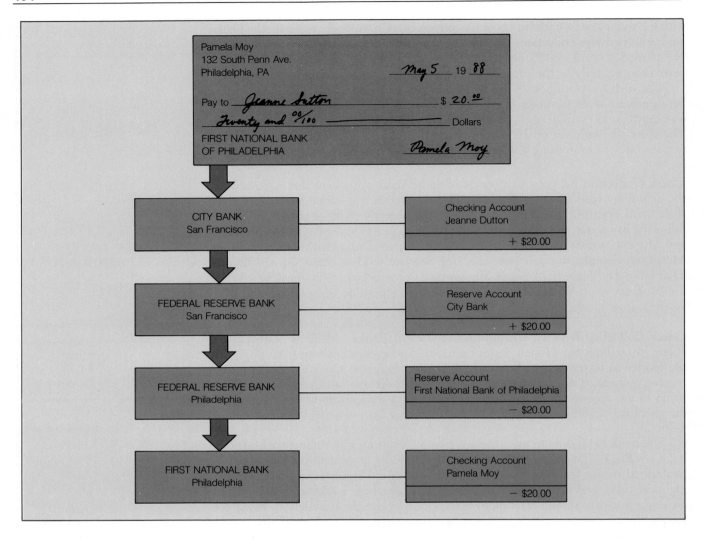

Pamela Moy
132 South Penn Ave.
Philadelphia, PA   May 5   19 88

Pay to _Jeanne Sutton_____ $ 20.00

_Twenty and 00/100_____ Dollars

FIRST NATIONAL BANK
OF PHILADELPHIA   Pamela Moy

CITY BANK
San Francisco

Checking Account
Jeanne Dutton
+ $20.00

FEDERAL RESERVE BANK
San Francisco

Reserve Account
City Bank
+ $20.00

FEDERAL RESERVE BANK
Philadelphia

Reserve Account
First National Bank of Philadelphia
− $20.00

FIRST NATIONAL BANK
Philadelphia

Checking Account
Pamela Moy
− $20.00

◆ **Exhibit 18-6**
How a Check Is Cleared

How the Federal Reserve System Clears Checks   The Federal Reserve System has greatly simplified the clearing of checks—that is, the method by which checks deposited in one bank are transferred to the banks on which they were written. Suppose Pamela Moy of Philadelphia writes a check to Jeanne Sutton in San Francisco. When Jeanne receives the check in the mail, she deposits it in her bank. Her bank then deposits the check in the Federal Reserve Bank of San Francisco, which transfers it to the Federal Reserve Bank of Philadelphia. That Federal Reserve Bank then sends the check to Moy's bank, where the amount of the check is deducted from Moy's account. Exhibit 18-6 illustrates this process.

Expedited Funds Availability Act

Congress recently passed an act to improve the check-processing system and to shorten the time period before deposited funds are made available to a customer. The major problem Congress addressed in this legislation was the practice of depository insti-

Landmark in the Law

The Electronic Fund Transfer Act (1978)

With the widespread use of checks and credit cards, America has become well nigh a "cashless society." With the advent of electronic fund transfer systems (EFTS), it may soon become a "checkless" society as well. It is estimated that over $65 trillion are moved between the Federal Reserve and its member banks each year via the electronic fund transfer networks. Automated teller machines (ATMs) are now commonplace features at banks, shopping malls, airports, and supermarkets; and countless dollars are transferred daily by means of point-of-sale systems, consumer terminals, and pay-by-phone systems—such as those described in this chapter.

This new development of electronic fund transfers has not gone unregulated by the government. A decade and a half ago, Congress established the National Commission of Electronic Fund Transfers to "conduct a thorough study and investigation and recommend appropriate administrative action and legislation necessary in connection with the possible development of public or private electronic fund transfer systems, taking into account, among other things . . . the need to protect the legal rights of users and consumers." [1] On October 28, 1977, the commission issued its final report, and in 1978 Congress passed the Electronic Fund Transfer Act, which became effective in 1980.

In addition to providing a basic framework for the rights, liabilities, and responsibilities of participants in EFTS, the Federal Reserve Board was given authority to issue rules and regulations to help implement the act. The Federal Reserve Board's implemental regulation is called "Regulation E—Electronic Funds Transfers."

Some of the major rules that apply to the use of EFTS are:

1. 12 U.S.C. 2401 (October 28, 1974).

1.   If a customer's debit card is lost or stolen and used without his or her permission, the customer has to pay only $50. The customer, however, must notify the bank of the loss or theft within two days of learning about it. Otherwise, the liability increases to $500. The customer is liable for more than $500 if the unauthorized use is not reported within sixty days after it appears on the customer's statement. (Even the $50 limit does not apply if the customer gives his or her card to someone who uses it improperly or if fraud is committed.)

2.   Any error on the monthly statement must be picked up by the customer within sixty days, and the bank must be notified. The bank then has ten days to investigate and must report its conclusions to the customer in writing. If the bank takes longer than ten days, it must return the disputed amount of money to the customer's account until the error is found. If there is no error, the customer has to give the money back to the bank.

3.   The bank must furnish receipts for transactions made through computer terminals, but it is not obliged to do so for telephone transfers.

4.   A monthly statement must be made for every month in which there is an electronic transfer of funds. Otherwise, statements must be made every quarter. The statement must show the amount and date of the transfer, the names of the retailers involved, the location or identification of the terminal, and the fees. Additionally, the statement must give an address and a phone number for inquiries and error notices.

5.   Any authorized prepayment for utility bills and insurance premiums can be stopped three days before the scheduled transfer.

All of the preceding information must be given to the customer who opens an EFTS account.

---

tutions (depositary banks) placing a "hold" on deposited checks—that is, not allowing the depositor to draw on (either as cash or by means of a check) these funds until the check has been honored (paid) by the payor bank. Many "hold" periods were lengthy, and even deposited government checks had a hold placed on the funds by many institutions for a week or longer.

The act, known as the Expedited Funds Availability Act, required that a temporary "availability" schedule became effective on September 1, 1988, and that a permanent schedule be implemented by the Federal Reserve on or before September 1, 1990. Basically, under the temporary "availability" schedule, any local check deposited must be available for withdrawal by check or as cash within two business days from the date of deposit. The Federal Reserve Board designated "check processing regions," and if the depositary and payor banks are located within the same region, the check is classified as a local check. For nonlocal checks, the availability period for withdrawal shall not be more than six business days. By September 1, 1990, these time periods are to be reduced to one business day (for local checks) and four business days (for nonlocal checks).

In addition, the act requires the following:

1.   That funds be available on the *next business day* for cash deposits and wire transfers, government checks, the first $100 of a day's check deposit, cashier's checks, certified checks, and checks where the depositary and payor banks are branches of the same institution.

2.   That, for cash withdrawals, the first $100 of any deposit will be available on the opening of the next business day after deposit. The next $400 will be available for withdrawal by no later than 5:00 P.M. the next business day. The remainder would be available as provided in the schedule. If, for example, you deposit a local check for $500 on Monday, you can withdraw $100 in cash at the opening of the business day on Tuesday, and an additional $400 must be available for withdrawal by no later than 5:00 P.M. on Wednesday.

There is a different availability schedule for deposits made at *nonproprietary* automated teller machines (ATMs). These machines are not owned or operated by the depository institution. Basically, there is a six-day hold permitted on all deposits, including cash deposits, made at nonproprietary ATMs.

❖ Electronic Fund Transfer Systems

The present basis of the payment-collection process is the check, but banks are finding it increasingly difficult to cope with the trillions of pieces of paper that evidence funds. New systems of automatic payment and direct deposits, known as electronic fund transfer systems (EFTS) (see this chapter's "Landmark"), promise to rid banks of the burden of having to move mountains of paper in order to transfer money.

The benefits of EFTS are obvious. Transferring of funds electronically enormously reduces the task of handling masses of information. Not surprisingly, it also poses difficulties on occasion. One such difficulty is explored in "Business Law in Action." The new technology has also aroused some serious consumer concerns, including the following:

1.   It is difficult to issue stop-payment orders.
2.   Fewer records are available.
3.   The possibilities for tampering (with a resulting decrease in privacy) are increased.
4.   The time between the writing of a check and its deduction from an account (*float* time) is lost.

Business Law in Action

Can a Machine Tell a Lie?

Mrs. Judd and her husband had a joint checking account at a Citibank branch in New York. They also had Citicards that gave them access to the computer via the bank's automatic teller machines (ATMs) located throughout the city. Each card, before it could access the computer, had to be first "validated" by the bank. Although Mrs. Judd had gone into the bank to receive her "personal identification number" (PIN) and have her card validated, her husband had not yet done so. Thus, only Mrs. Judd's card could be used to obtain cash or make any other transaction via the ATM, and then only if the user knew her PIN—which she said she had given to no one and which

she had not even written down, but memorized.

The Judds were thus stunned to learn that $800 had been charged to their checking account as a result of two transactions, one made on February 26, 1980, between 2:13 and 2:14 P.M., and the other on March 28, 1980, between 2:30 and 2:32 P.M. The bank maintained that there was no way the funds could have been withdrawn without the use of Mrs. Judd's card and PIN. But Mrs. Judd was convinced the bank had made an error—or, rather, that the computer had. She could not have withdrawn the funds at those times, she contended, because she had been at work on both days at those times; a letter from her employer confirmed her statement.

Eventually, the case came before the Civil Court of New York City,

and Judge John Marmarellis was faced with the problem of deciding the issue. Whom was he to believe? Mrs. Judd, whom he described as a "credible witness"? Or the bank's computer printout, which, as "translated" by the bank's manager, verified that the amounts could have been withdrawn from her account only by the use of her card and PIN? He opted to believe Mrs. Judd and awarded her $800 plus interest and disbursements, having stated in his opinion the following: "It is too commonplace in our society that when faced with the choice of man or machine, we readily accept the 'word' of the machine every time. This, despite the tales of computer malfunctions that we hear daily."[1]

1. Judd v. Citibank, 107 Misc.2d 526, 435 N.Y.S.2d 210 (1980).

Funds can be transferred electronically by (1) automated teller machines, (2) point-of-sale systems, (3) consumer terminals, (4) automated clearinghouses, and (5) wire transfers. These and other aspects of electronic transfer systems are discussed here.

Automated Teller Machines

Automated teller machines (ATMs), which are also called *customer bank communications terminals* or *remote services units*, are located either on the bank's premises or at convenient locations such as stores, supermarkets, drugstores, and shopping centers. Automated teller machines receive deposits, dispense funds from checking or savings accounts, make credit card advances, and receive payments. The devices are connected on-line to the bank's computers. Customers usually have a *debit card*, or *EFTS card*, which is similar to a plastic credit card and allows a customer to use a computer banking system. In order to make a withdrawal from an ATM, the customer uses his or her debit card in addition to punching a *personal identification number (PIN)*. The PIN protects the customer from someone else's use of a lost or stolen credit card.

Point-of-Sale Systems

Point-of-sale systems allow the consumer to transfer funds to merchants in order to make purchases. On-line terminals are located at checkout counters in the merchant's

Automated teller machines (ATMs) are now commonplace in our society.

store. When making a purchase, the customer's card is inserted into the terminal, which reads the data encoded on it. The computer at the customer's bank verifies that the card and identification code are valid and that there is enough money in the customer's account. After the purchase is made, the customer's account is debited for the amount of purchase.

Consumer Terminals

Some institutions allow consumers to perform routine transactions by using electronic terminals in their homes or offices. Home banking, a recent EFTS development, is part of a growing network of financial and home information services to which you can gain access with a telephone and a personal or desktop computer (or, more recently, with what is known as a pocket terminal). A typical home banking system allows you to transfer funds between linked accounts, find out your account balances, and pay bills or schedule payments in advance to businesses and services participating in your home banking system.

Automated Clearinghouses

Automated clearinghouses are similar to ordinary clearinghouses in which checks are cleared between banks. The main difference is that entries are made in the form of electronic signals; no checks are used. Funds are electronically transferred between banks and between accounts. Rather than further automating the handling of paper checks, these systems eliminate the checks. The electronic transfer of funds is convenient, and the service can be performed at less cost than the actual clearing of checks.

Direct Deposit and Payment Arrangements   Bank customers often find it useful to have the bank pay routine expenses, such as utility bills or insurance premiums, directly from their account through electronic transfers. Businesspersons often have recurrent payments, such as payroll, social security, or pension fund payments, made in this manner. Likewise, customers may arrange with their banks to have certain income, such as social security checks or government benefits, deposited directly into their accounts routinely each month.

Pay-by-Telephone Arrangements   Customers can also arrange with their banks in many cases to authorize certain payments and transfers by telephone. Funds may be transferred between accounts upon telephone request, or a customer may authorize a bank by telephone to pay a certain sum to a third party. This is a useful service to individuals who routinely make a payment to another party, particularly where the amount of each payment varies.

Unauthorized Transfers

Unauthorized transfers of funds by means of EFT systems are one of the hazards of electronic banking. A paper check leaves highly visible evidence of a transaction, and a customer can easily detect a forgery or an altered check with ordinary vigilance. But the highly unsatisfactory evidence of an electronic transfer is in many cases only a computer printout of the various debits and credits made to a particular account during a specified time period.

Because of the vulnerability of EFT systems to fraudulent activities, the Electronic Fund Transfer Act (EFTA) of 1978 clearly defined what constitutes an unauthorized transfer. Under the act, a transfer is unauthorized if (1) it is initiated by a person other than the consumer and without actual authority to initiate such transfer; (2) the consumer receives no benefit from it; and (3) the consumer did not furnish such person "with the card, code, or other means of access" to his or her account. The respective liabilities of the bank and the customer in cases of unauthorized transfers are presented in this chapter's "Landmark."

In the following case, the court had to determine whether an account holder had authorized an imposter to withdraw funds from the customer's account. The first two parts of the definition of an unauthorized transfer just cited were obviously not relevant—the customer had not initiated or given actual authority for the transfer, nor had he benefited from it. He had, however, unwittingly furnished the imposter with his EFTS card and bank code. The case contains a lesson for all ATM users.

Reprinted by permission of Newspaper Enterprises Association, Inc.

Case 18.4
OGNIBENE v. CITIBANK, N.A.
Civil Court of New York City, 1981.
112 Misc. 2d 219, 446 N.Y.S. 2d 845.

FACTS   On August 16, 1981, Frederick Ognibene stopped at a Citibank automatic teller machine (ATM), located outside the bank, to make a $20 withdrawal from his checking account. There were two ATMs located close together, and in between them was a public telephone. While Ognibene made his withdrawal, a man was talking on the phone and appeared to be telling the bank's customer service that one of the machines was not working. The man then turned to Ognibene and said that the bank's customer service department had asked if Ognibene might try his card in the malfunctioning machine to see if it would activate it. Ognibene, the good samaritan in this case, complied with the request and inserted his card in the ATM in question. The man on the telephone then punched in a personal identification code (which, unbeknownst to Ognibene, was Ognibene's own PIN that had been observed by the other man when Ognibene made his $20 withdrawal a few seconds earlier) and continued talking on the telephone, supposedly to bank personnel. Again, the man turned to Ognibene and asked him to insert his card once more, because the customer service department wanted to make sure the machine would continue to function properly, and this Ognibene did. The man reported to the fictitious person on the other end of the phone line that the machine was now functioning, hung up, thanked Ognibene, took his cash and left.

Later, when Ognibene realized $400 had been withdrawn from his account at that same time of that same day, he brought an action against the bank to recover the $400.

ISSUE   At issue was whether the stranger's withdrawal from Ognibene's account had been "authorized" by Ognibene given the circumstances. Ognibene had permitted the stranger to use his card and had allowed, albeit unwittingly, the stranger to view his personal identification code number as Ognibene punched it in for his $20 withdrawal. Thus, while Ognibene contended he in no way authorized the stranger to withdraw cash from Ognibene's account, the bank argued that technically Ognibene did give that authority by his negligent actions.

DECISION   The court held for Ognibene and ordered the bank to reinstate the $400 into Ognibene's account.

REASON   Under the Electronic Fund Transfer Act (EFTA), a consumer's liability is limited in cases where "unauthorized" access to his or her account was made. It was undisputed that the first two requirements for an unauthorized transfer under the EFTA had been met. Ognibene had clearly not initiated the transfer himself and had not given "actual authority" to the imposter to use his card, nor had he benefited from the transaction. As to the third requirement, the fact that Ognibene had handed the stranger his access card, while a voluntary act, did not mean Ognibene intended to authorize the stranger's withdrawal of funds from Ognibene's account. Nor was Ognibene's act negligent—he innocently believed he was assisting a bank employee. The court further noted that Ognibene was aware of the fact that his code number as well as his card was necessary to provide "access" to his account, and he had not volunteered his code number to the stranger and was unaware that the stranger had observed it.

When a fraud is committed, a court will often determine liability on the basis of which party was in the best position to prevent the fraud. In this case, evidence at trial indicated that the bank had received several reports of fraudulent withdrawals conducted by imposters posing as bank employees and gaining access to accounts in the same manner as in the Ognibene case. The court held that "[s]ince the bank had knowledge of the scam and its operational details (including the central role of the customer service telephone), it was negligent in failing to provide plaintiff-customer with information sufficient to alert him to the danger." Although the bank had posted a notice in its ATM areas "containing a red circle approximately 2½ inches in diameter" on which was written, "Do Not Let Your Citicard Be Used For Any Transaction But Your Own," the court found that this printed admonition was not sufficient as a security measure since it failed to state the reason for the admonition. The court thus concluded that "the responsibility for the fact that plaintiff's code, one of the two necessary components of the 'access device' . . . to his account, was observed and utilized as it was must rest with the bank."

Error Resolution and Damages

Error-resolution procedures prescribed by the EFTA are discussed in the "Landmark." These rules must be followed strictly by a bank. If the bank fails to investigate the error and report its conclusion promptly to the customer, and in the specific manner designated by the EFTA, it will be in violation of the act and subject to civil liability. Its liability extends to any actual damages sustained by a customer and to all the costs of a successful action brought against the bank by a customer, including attorneys' fees. In addition, the bank is liable for statutory damages ranging from $100 to $1,000 in an individual action. Even when a customer has sustained no actual damage, the bank, if it fails to follow the proper procedures outlined by the EFTA in regard to error resolution, may be liable for legal costs and statutory damages. This point is illustrated clearly by the following case.

Case 18.5
BISBEY v. D. C. NATIONAL BANK

United States Court of Appeals, District of Columbia, 1986.
253 U.S.App.D.C. 244, 793 F.2d 315.

FACTS Sandra Bisbey opened a checking account with the District of Columbia National Bank in January of 1981. Subsequently, she authorized the bank to debit her checking account for fund transfer directives submitted monthly by the New York Life Insurance Company (NYLIC) for payment of her insurance premiums. In September of 1981, Bisbey's account lacked sufficient funds to cover the NYLIC payment, and no transfer was made. In October, the September request was resubmitted by NYLIC, in addition to the October directive. Although Bisbey's account still lacked sufficient funds to cover the requests, the bank honored them anyway and sent Bisbey two overdraft notices, each in the amount of her monthly insurance premium. Bisbey, having forgotten her nonpayment of the September premium, believed that the bank had erroneously made two payments in October. She thus wrote a letter to the bank, requesting the bank to look into the matter.

Approximately ten days later, a bank official telephoned Bisbey and explained that there had been no improper duplication of her premium payments. Bisbey, still convinced there had been an error, filed suit against the bank for damages on the ground that the bank had not met the requirements of the Electronic Fund Transfer Act (EFTA). Under the EFTA the bank was required to give a written, rather than an oral, explanation of the re-

sults of its investigation of Bisbey's inquiry concerning the allegedly duplicated payments. Any bank that failed to do this incurred civil liability to its customer, including an award for attorneys' fees. The district court held that although the bank had violated the EFTA in its resolution of Bisbey's inquiry about her account, the EFTA did not contemplate a finding of civil liability for this type of procedural mistake. Bisbey appealed.

ISSUE Can the bank be held liable for a violation of the EFTA, even though the bank's customer had incurred no damage as a result of this violation?

DECISION Yes. The lower court's judgment was reversed and the case remanded for a determination of civil liability and attorneys' fees.

REASON The court noted the seeming injustice that the bank should be held "liable for a transaction that benefited the plaintiff. Ms. Bisbey's account contained insufficient funds to cover either of the premium requests submitted by NYLIC. Though she had no overdraft agreement, the bank did not charge an overdraft fee. Thus, the effect of the bank's payments was to provide her, at no cost, with insurance coverage she would not have had otherwise." The only error on the part of the bank was that it had failed to notify its customer in writing of its conclusions, using the telephone instead. Nonetheless, the bank clearly did fail to comply with the requirements of the EFTA, "and the statute compels a finding that the Bank is liable."

Commercial Wire Transfers

The transfer of funds "by wire" between commercial parties is another way in which funds are transferred electronically. Trillions of dollars are transferred every year on private wire transfer systems operated by banks and businesses, as well through public networks such as the telex service provided by ITT.

Unauthorized wire transfers are obviously possible and, indeed, have become a problem. If an imposter, for example, succeeds in having funds wired from another's account, the other party will bear the loss (unless he or she can recover from the imposter). Such a situation arose in the case discussed in "Business Law in Action" in Chapter 16. At present, any disputes arising as a result of unauthorized or incorrectly made transfers are settled by the courts under the common-law principles of tort law or contract law. In the future, however, problems arising in this area will likely be covered by the UCC.

Application

Law and the Businessperson and the Consumer— Stop-Payment Orders

Stop-payment orders should not be misused by a drawer for a variety of reasons. One reason is monetary; bank charges for stop-payment orders are not small in relation to checks written for small amounts. Another reason is the risk attached to the issuing of a stop-payment order for any drawer-customer. The bank is entitled to take a reasonable amount of time to enforce your stop order before it has liability for improper payment. Hence, it is possible that the payee or holder may be able to cash the check despite your stop order if he or she acts quickly. Indeed, you could be writing out a stop order in the bank lobby while the payee or holder cashes the check in the drive-in facility next door.

Remember that each drawer must have a legal reason for issuing a stop-payment order. Any wrongful stop order subjects the drawer to liability to the payee or a holder, and this liability may include special damages that resulted because of the order. When all is considered, it may be unwise to hastily order a stop payment on a check because of a minor dispute with the payee.

Checklist for Stop Payments

☐ 1. Compare the stop-payment fee with the disputed sum to make sure it is worthwhile to issue a stop-payment order.

☐ 2. Make sure that your stop-payment order will be honored by your bank prior to the payee's cashing the check.

☐ 3. Make sure that you have a legal reason for issuing the stop-payment order.

❖ Chapter Summary: Checks and the Banking System

CHECKS—DEFINITIONS	
Check	A special type of draft that is drawn on a *bank*, ordering the bank to pay a sum of money on *demand*. The maker of the check is the *drawer*, the bank is the *drawee*, and the person to whom the check is payable is the *payee*.
Cashier's Check	A check drawn by a bank on itself (the bank is both the drawer and the drawee) and purchased by a customer. In effect, the bank lends its credit to the purchaser of the check, thus making the funds available for immediate use in banking circles.
Traveler's Check	A draft (generally not a check) on which a financial institution is both the drawer and the drawee. The payee must provide his or her signature in order for a traveler's check to become a negotiable instrument.
Certified Check	A check for which the drawee bank certifies that it will set aside funds in the drawer's account to ensure payment of the check upon presentation. The usual method of certification is for a bank cashier or teller to write across the face of the check, over the signature, a statement that it is certified and will be paid when properly indorsed. 1. When certification is requested by the drawer, the drawer remains secondarily liable on the instrument if the bank dishonors the check. 2. When certification is requested by a holder, the drawer and all prior indorsers are completely discharged from liability on the check. 3. If a certified check is *altered*, a bank will be liable for full payment only if the check was altered prior to certification.

❖ Chapter Summary: Checks and the Banking System—Continued

BANK-CUSTOMER RELATIONSHIPS	
Bank's Charge against Customer's Account UCC 4-401	The bank has the right to charge a customer's account for any item properly payable, even if the charge results in an overdraft.
Wrongful Dishonor UCC 4-402	The bank is liable to its customer for actual damages proved due to wrongful dishonor. Damages can include those proximately caused for arrest or prosecution, or other consequential damages.
Stop-Payment Orders UCC 4-403	The customer must make a stop-payment order in time for the bank to have a reasonable opportunity to act. Oral orders are binding for only fourteen days unless they are confirmed in writing. Written orders are effective for only six months unless renewed in writing. The bank is liable for wrongful payment over a timely stop-payment order.
Stale Check UCC 4-404	The bank is not obligated to pay an uncertified check presented more than six months after its date, but it may do so in good faith without liability.
Death or Incompetence of a Customer UCC 4-405	So long as the bank does not know of the death or incompetence of a customer, the bank can pay an item without liability to the customer's estate. Even with knowledge of a customer's death, a bank can honor or certify checks (in the absence of a stop-payment order) for ten days after the date of the customer's death.
Unauthorized Signature or Alteration UCC 4-406	The customer has a duty to examine account statements with reasonable care upon receipt and to notify the bank promptly of any unauthorized signatures or alterations. On a series of unauthorized signatures or alterations by the same wrongdoer, examination and report must be given within fourteen calendar days of receipt of the statement. Failure to comply releases the bank from any liability unless the bank failed to exercise reasonable care. Regardless of care or lack of care, the customer is estopped from holding the bank liable after one year for unauthorized customer signatures or alterations, and after three years for unauthorized indorsements.
Bank's Liability under EFTS—Major Rules **(Under the Electronic Fund Transfer Act of 1978)**	1. If a customer's debit card is lost or stolen and used without his or her permission, the maximum amount the customer has to pay is $50, as long as the loss or theft is reported to the bank within two days. Otherwise, the customer's liability increases to $500. If the loss or theft is not reported within sixty days, the customer is liable for more than $500. 2. Any error on the monthly statement must be reported to the bank within sixty days. The bank then has ten days to investigate. If the bank's investigation requires more time, the bank must return the disputed amount to the customer's account until the dispute is resolved. 3. The bank must furnish receipts for transactions made through computer terminals, but it is not required to do so for telephone transfers. 4. A monthly statement must be made for every month in which there is an electronic transfer of funds. Otherwise, statements must be made every quarter. 5. Any authorized direct prepayment from the customer's account made by the bank (such as for utility bills or insurance premiums) can be stopped three days before the scheduled transfer.
CHECK COLLECTION	
Definitions	1. *Depository bank:* The bank accepting a check for deposit into a customer's account. 2. *Payor bank:* The bank on which a check is drawn. 3. *Collecting bank:* Any bank except the payor bank that handles a check during the collecting process. 4. *Intermediary bank:* Any bank except the payor bank or the depositary bank to which an item is transferred in the course of the collection process.
The Collection Process	1. *Liability for restrictive indorsements:* Only the depositary bank must pay in a manner consistent with any restrictive indorsement. UCC 3-206(3)

❖ Chapter Summary: Checks and the Banking System—Continued

The Collection Process (Continued)	2. *Check collection between customers of the same bank:* A check payable by the depositary bank that receives it is an "on-us" item; as such, if the bank does not dishonor the check by the opening of the second banking day following its receipt, the check is considered paid. UCC 4-213(4)(b)
	3. *Check collection between customers of different banks:* Each bank in the collection process must pass the check on to the next appropriate bank before midnight of the next banking day following its receipt. UCC 4-202(2)
	4. *The Role of the Federal Reserve System:* The Federal Reserve System facilitates the check-clearing process by serving as a clearinghouse for checks.

❖ Questions and Case Problems

18-1. Clemson had a rubber stamp made with which he signed his checks. One day, Clemson's daughter used the stamp to sign a check she had written on her father's account. The check was for $300 and payable to a friend to whom she owed money. First Federal, Clemson's bank, honored the check. When Clemson's bank statement arrived and he noticed the check, he promptly notified the bank that the check was a forgery and requested that the bank return the funds to his account. Must the bank restore the funds to Clemson's account? Explain.

18-2. Marco owed Dick $300 and wrote a check payable to Dick in this amount, drawn on First Bank. Dick deposited the check into his account with Midland State Bank but failed to indorse the check. Midland State Bank supplied an indorsement stating that the funds were to be credited to Dick's account and sent the check to First Bank for payment. First Bank honored the check. When Marco learned this, he claimed the bank had wrongfully honored the check, because Dick had not indorsed it. Is Marco correct? Explain.

18-3. Dora drafts a check for $2,000 payable to Peter and drawn on the Western City Bank. After issue of the check, Peter, by blank indorsement, negotiates the check to Gregory. Gregory finds an ideal real estate lot for sale, but to close the deal he needs to make a $2,000 down payment by certified check. Gregory takes the check to Western City Bank and requests Western to certify Dora's check.

    (a) If Western City Bank refuses to certify Dora's check, can either Dora or Gregory hold the bank liable? Explain.

    (b) If Western City Bank certifies the check, explain fully the liability of Dora as drawer to Gregory and to Peter as indorser.

18-4. Gary goes grocery shopping and carelessly leaves his checkbook in his shopping cart. His checkbook, with two blank checks remaining, is stolen by Susan. On May 5 Susan forges Gary's name on a check for $10 and cashes the check at Gary's bank, Citizens Bank of Middletown. Gary has not reported the theft to his bank. On June 1 Gary receives his monthly bank statement and cancelled checks from Citizens Bank, including the forged check. Gary does not reconcile his checkbook balance with the bank statement. On June 20 Susan forges Gary's last check. This check is for $1,000 and is cashed at the Eastern City Bank, a bank with which Susan has previously done business. The Eastern City Bank puts the check through the collection process, and the Citizens Bank honors it. On July 1, upon receipt of his bank statement and cancelled checks, Gary discovers both forgeries and immediately notifies Citizens Bank. Susan cannot be found. Gary claims that Citizens Bank must recredit his account for both checks, as his signature was forged. Discuss fully Gary's claim.

18-5. On January 5 Brian drafts a check for $3,000 drawn on the Southern Marine Bank and payable to his assistant, Georgette. Brian puts last year's date on the check by mistake. On January 7, before Georgette has had a chance to go to the bank, Brian is killed in an automobile accident. The Southern Marine Bank is aware of Brian's death. On January 10 Georgette presents the check to the bank, and the bank honors the check by payment to Georgette. Brian's widow, Joyce, claims that the bank wrongfully paid Georgette since it knew of Brian's death and also paid a check that was by date over one year old. Joyce, as executrix of Brian's estate and sole heir by his will, demands that Southern Marine Bank recredit Brian's estate for the check paid to Georgette. Discuss fully Southern Marine's liability in light of Joyce's demand.

18-6. In September of 1976 Edward and Christine McSweeney opened a joint checking account with the United States Trust Company of New York. Between April of 1978 and July of 1978, 195 checks totaling $99,063 were written. In July of

1978 activity in the account ceased. Ninety-five of the 195 checks were written by Christine, totaling $16,811, and the rest of the checks were written by Edward. After deposits were credited for that period, the checks amounted to a cumulative overdraft of $75,983. Can a bank knowingly honor a check when payment creates an overdraft, or must the bank dishonor the check? If the bank pays a check creating an overdraft, can the bank collect the amount of the overdraft from its customer? [United States Trust Company of New York v. McSweeney, 91 A.D.2d 7, 457 N.Y.S.2d 276 (1982)]

18-7. Reinhard purchased a cashier's check made payable to The Patchworks Company from Marine Midland Bank. The check was delivered to The Patchworks in exchange for goods purchased by Reinhard. Because he was dissatisfied with the goods, Reinhard told the bank that he had lost the check and asked that payment be stopped. Can Reinhard stop payment? Explain. [Moon Over the Mountain, Ltd. v. Marine Midland Bank, 87 Misc.2d 918, 386 N.Y.S.2d 974 (1976)]

18-8. Ossip-Harris Insurance, Inc. (Ossip) maintained a checking account with Barnett Bank of South Florida, N.A. (Barnett). From May 1980 through June 1981, Ossip's book-keeper used a facsimile signature stamp to forge the name of Ossip's president, Harris, to ninety-nine checks totaling $19,711.90. When the cancelled checks came back to Ossip, the bookkeeper would replace the payee name with one of a legitimate Ossip business expense. Although Harris periodically reviewed the monthly statement and cancelled checks, he did not detect the forgeries until June of 1981. At that time, Harris notified Barnett, and Barnett paid no further forged checks. Ossip alleged that Barnett wrongfully paid the forged checks drawn on Ossip's account. Discuss fully to what extent, if any, Barnett can be held liable for its payment of the forged checks. [Ossip-Harris Insurance, Inc. v. Barnett Bank of South Florida, N.A., 428 So.2d 363 (Fla.App. 1983)]

18-9. On September 14 Parr sent a check to Champlin Oil Company in payment of a bill she owed them. On September 15 she called the bank and requested that payment on the check be stopped. She gave the bank her account number and the check number, the date the check was written, the payee on the check, and the amount. All information was correctly given to the bank except for the amount, which was substantially different than what she had actually written on the check. On September 16 she went to the bank and executed a written stop-payment order. The written order also contained the erroneous amount. On September 17, the bank paid the check. Parr sued the bank for wrongfully paying the check over her stop-payment order. The bank claimed that Parr's error on the stop-payment request concerning the amount of the check relieved it of liability. Will the bank succeed in this defense? Explain. [Parr v. Security Nat. Bank, 680 P.2d 648 (Okl.App. 1984)]

18-10. Sanford was fired from his job in a restaurant owned by Vickrey. Vickrey gave Sanford a number of checks for wages due to him, plus a stock refund check for $720 that Sanford had invested in Vickrey's other businesses. Sanford told Vickrey that he needed the money to pay his bills and to get to Las Vegas where he could get another job. Vickrey gave him a check for $720 on which he wrote, "Refund for stock deposit." After depositing the checks in his bank, Sanford returned to the restaurant where he cursed and threatened Vickrey and then set out for Las Vegas. Vickrey stopped payment on the $720 check. Sanford's bank got in touch with Sanford a few days later and asked him to sign a note for the $720. Sanford made two trips back to Texas to straighten out the matter. He sought recovery from Vickrey for the amount of the check and, as special damages, the expenses he had incurred in making the two trips to Texas. Discuss fully Sanford's chances of success. [Vickrey v. Sanford, 506 S.W.2d 270 (Texas Civ.App. 1974)]

Chapter 19

Secured Transactions

The concept of a secured transaction is as basic to modern business practice as the concept of credit. Few purchasers (manufacturers, wholesalers, retailers, consumers) have the resources to pay cash for goods being purchased, yet lenders are reluctant to lend money to a debtor solely upon the debtor's promise to repay the debt. Logically enough, sellers and lenders do not want to risk nonpayment, so they will not sell goods or lend money unless the promise of payment is somehow guaranteed. When payment is guaranteed, or *secured*, by personal property owned by the debtor, or in which the debtor has a legal interest, the transaction becomes known as a **secured transaction.**

The importance of being a secured creditor cannot be overemphasized. Secured creditors are generally not hampered by **state exemption laws** favorable to debtors, and they have a favored position should the debtor become bankrupt. Indeed, business as we know it could not exist without secured transaction law.

The underlying philosophy of secured transaction law deals with two major concerns of the creditor should the debtor default on the obligation:

1. Can the debt be satisfied from some specific property offered as security—that is, **collateral**—by the debtor?
2. Will satisfaction of that particular debt from that collateral be given priority over the claims of other creditors?

The answers form the basis for the law of secured transactions.

❖ Article 9 of the UCC

Prior to adoption of the UCC, a great number of security devices were used by creditors, such as chattel mortgages, conditional sales contracts, assignment of accounts, and trust receipts. Each had separate rules, and each had different terminology. Article 9 of the UCC has eliminated these distinctions among the various forms of financing, simplified the terminology, and provided a framework for the law of secured transactions.

> " '[S]ecure' means that which is presently reduced to possession, or that of which payment is made sure."
>
> **Edward W. Hatch, 1851–1924 (New York jurist)**

SECURED TRANSACTION
Any transaction, regardless of its form, that is intended to create a security interest in personal property or fixtures, including goods, documents, and other intangibles.

STATE EXEMPTION LAWS
Laws passed by individual states describing the property of the debtor that cannot be attached by a judgment creditor or trustee in bankruptcy to satisfy a debt.

COLLATERAL
In a broad sense, any property used as security for a loan. Under the UCC, property in which a debtor has an interest or a right.

CHATTEL PAPER
Any writing or writings that show both a debt and the fact that the debt is secured by personal property. In many instances, chattel paper consists of a negotiable instrument coupled with a security agreement.

MECHANIC'S LIEN
A statutory lien upon the real property of another, created to ensure priority of payment for work performed and materials furnished in erecting or repairing a building or other structure.

SECURITY INTEREST
Every interest "in *personal property or fixtures* [emphasis added] which secures payment or performance of an obligation." [UCC 1-201(37)]

SECURED PARTY
A lender, seller, or any other person in whose favor there is a security interest, including a person to whom accounts or chattel paper have been sold.

SECURITY AGREEMENT
The agreement that creates or provides for a security interest between the debtor and a secured party.

Article 9 applies to any transaction that is intended to create a security interest in personal property, the sale of accounts, **chattel paper,** and fixtures. Transactions excluded from Article 9 include real estate mortgages, landlords' liens, **mechanics' liens,** claims arising from judicial proceedings, and so on. [UCC 9-104] In general, these transactions do not deal with personal property and are excluded because they are extensively treated in other areas of the law.

As will become evident, the law of secured transactions tends to favor the rights of creditors; but, to a lesser extent, it offers debtors some protection, too.

❖ The Terminology of Secured Transactions

The terminology used under the Code is now uniformly adopted in all documents drawn in a secured transaction situation. A brief summary of the UCC's definition of terms follows:

1.   A **security interest** is every interest "in personal property or fixtures which secures payment or performance of an obligation." [UCC 1-201(37)]
2.   A **secured party** is a lender, a seller, or any person in whose favor there is a security interest, including a person to whom accounts or chattel paper have been sold. [UCC 9-105(1)(m)]
3.   A *debtor* is the party who owes payment or performance of the secured obligation, whether or not that party actually owns or has rights in the collateral. When the debtor and the owner of *collateral* are not the same person, the term *debtor* refers to the actual owner of the collateral or describes the obligor on an obligation, or both, depending upon the context in which the term is used. [UCC 9-105(1)(d)]
4.   A **security agreement** is the agreement that creates or provides for a security interest between the debtor and a secured party. [UCC 9-105(1)(*l*)]
5.   *Collateral* is the property subject to a security interest, including accounts and chattel paper that have been sold. [UCC 9-105(1)(c)]

These basic definitions form the concept under which a debtor-creditor relationship becomes a secured transaction relationship (see Exhibit 19-1).

◆ **Exhibit 19-1**
Secured Transactions—
Concept and Terminology

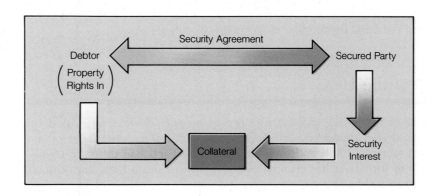

❖ Creating a Security Interest

Before a creditor can become a secured party, the creditor must have a security interest in the collateral of the debtor. Three requirements, which will be explained here in detail, must be met in order for a creditor to have an enforceable security interest. Once they are met, the creditor's rights are said to *attach* to the collateral. This means that the creditor has a security interest against the debtor that is enforceable. *Attachment* ensures that the security interest between the debtor and the secured party is effective. [UCC 9-203]

Written Security Agreement

Unless the collateral is in the possession of the secured party (the creditor), there must be a written security agreement describing the collateral and signed by the debtor. See Exhibit 19-2 for a detailed sample security agreement. The security agreement creates, or provides for, a security interest. For example, it might read, "Debtor hereby grants to secured party a security interest in the following goods." In order for a security agreement to be valid, it must (1) be signed by the debtor,

"Article 9 is clearly the most novel and probably the most important article of the Code. . . . and covers the entire range of transactions in which the debts are secured by personal property."

Walter D. Malcolm, 1904– 1979
(President of the National Conference of Commissioners on Uniform State Laws, 1963– 1966)

◆ **Exhibit 19-2
Sample Security Agreement**

_____
Date

_____
Name   No. and Street   City   County   State

(hereinafter called "Debtor") hereby grants to _____
Name

_____
No. and Street   City   County   State

(hereinafter called "Secured Party") a security interest in the following property (hereinafter called the "Collateral"): _____

_____

to secure payment and performance of obligations identified or set out as follows (hereinafter called the "Obligations"): _____

_____

    Default in payment or performance of any of the Obligations or default under any agreement evidencing any of the Obligations is a default under this agreement. Upon such default Secured Party may declare all Obligations immediately due and payable and shall have the remedies of a secured party under the _____ Uniform Commercial Code.
    Signed in (duplicate) triplicate.

_____   _____
Debtor   Secured Party
By _____   By _____

(2) contain a description of the collateral, and (3) reasonably identify the collateral. [UCC 9-203(1) and 9-110]

Secured Party Must Give Value

The secured party must give *value*, which, according to UCC 1-201(44), is any consideration that supports a simple contract. In addition, value can be security given for a preexisting (antecedent) obligation or any binding commitment to extend credit. Normally, the value given by a secured party is in the form of a direct loan, or it involves a commitment to sell goods on credit.

Debtor's Rights in Collateral

The debtor must have *rights* in the collateral; that is, the debtor must have some ownership interest or right to obtain possession of that collateral. The debtor's rights can represent either a current or a future legal interest in the collateral. For example, a retail seller-debtor can give a secured party a security interest not only in existing inventory owned by the retailer, but also in future inventory to be acquired by the debtor.

❖ Purchase Money Security Interest

PURCHASE MONEY SECURITY INTEREST
A security interest to the extent that it is (1) taken or retained by a seller of the collateral to secure all or part of its price; or (2) taken by a creditor who, by making advances or incurring an obligation, gives value to enable the debtor to acquire rights in or use of collateral, if such value is in fact so used.

Often sellers of consumer durable goods, such as stereos and television sets, agree to extend credit for part of the purchase price of those goods.[1] Also, lenders not necessarily in the business of selling such goods often agree to lend much of the purchase price for them. There is a special name for the security interest that the seller or the lender obtains when such a transaction occurs. It is called a **purchase money security interest.** Formally, such an interest exists when one or the other of the following conditions occurs:

1.   A security interest is retained in, or taken by the seller of, the collateral in order to secure part or all of its price.
2.   A security interest is taken by a person who, by making advances or incurring an obligation, gives something of value that enables the debtor to acquire rights in the collateral or to use it. [UCC 9-107]

In either case, a lender or seller has essentially provided a buyer with the "purchase money" to buy goods. Suppose Jamie wants to purchase a combination color television–stereo set from ABC Appliances. The purchase price is $900. Not being able to pay cash, Jamie signs a purchase agreement to pay $100 down and $50 per month until the balance plus interest is fully paid. ABC Appliances is to retain a security interest

---

1.   Under the FTC's "unfair credit practices" rules, it is a violation of Section 5 of the FTC Act for a lender or retail seller to take or receive a *nonpossessory, nonpurchase* money security interest in household goods.

In recent years, due to strong competition from Japan, Detroit auto manufacturers have begun to extend credit at below-market interest rates for the purchase of new cars.

in the purchased set until full payment has been made. Since the security interest was created as part of the purchase agreement, it is a purchase money security interest.

The same result would occur if Jamie went to Midtown Bank and borrowed the $900 to buy the combination set from ABC Appliances. After Jamie signs a loan agreement with Midtown Bank, with the to-be-purchased set as collateral, Midtown Bank has a purchase money security interest the moment the set is purchased from the appliance store. Obviously, if Jamie used the money for other purposes, Midtown Bank would not have a security interest. For this reason, Midtown Bank might arrange to pay the $900 directly to ABC Appliances.

The importance of a purchase money security interest is basically twofold:

1. It allows for an automatic **perfection** of a purchase money security in consumer goods without the secured party's possession or filing (to be discussed shortly).
2. It ordinarily gives a secured party priority over a nonpurchase money security interest in the same collateral (to be discussed later).

PERFECTION
A process in which certain steps are legally required to give a secured party a priority interest over the debtor's collateral against other parties with claims to the same collateral.

❖ Perfecting a Security Interest

A creditor has two main concerns if the debtor defaults: (1) satisfaction of the debt out of certain predesignated property and (2) priority over other creditors. The concept of *attachment*, which establishes the criteria for creating an enforceable security interest, deals with the former concern; the concept of *perfection* deals with the latter.

Even though a security interest has attached, the secured party must nevertheless take steps in order to protect its claim to the collateral over claims that third parties may have, such as other secured creditors, general creditors, trustees in bankruptcy,

Landmark in the Law

The Roman Pledge

Secured transactions date back at least to Roman times, where the most commonly employed security device was the *pledge* (in Latin, *pignus*). What the Romans meant by this word is not too clear because it was used variously to mean "pledge," "bet" (or "forfeit"), and "promise"—words that represent three different legal concepts today. According to one scholar, however, the word *pignus* was used most frequently in the modern sense of "forfeit." That is, personal property pledged as security for a loan was entirely forfeited to the creditor until the loan was paid off. In other words, the property was itself regarded as payment for the debt, so the debt was legally extinguished by the pledge—the debt did not exist. If the debtor defaulted on the loan, the creditor kept the property permanently. If the loan was repaid in full, the property was returned to the debtor.[1]

With this early form of pledge, if the value of the property was greater or less than the amount of the loan, and the debtor defaulted, the creditor suffered the detriment or reaped the benefit. To illustrate: Peter borrows fifty denarii from Marcus, offering his chariot (the market

value of which is fifty denarii) as security. Peter defaults on the loan, and Marcus sells the chariot to recover his fifty denarii. But in the meantime, the market value of Peter's chariot has fallen dramatically—to only twenty-five denarii. Marcus has no recourse against Peter for the remainder of the debt, as the debt no longer exists. Likewise, if the market value of the chariot increases to seventy-five denarii, Peter cannot recover the twenty-five denarii difference, or surplus, over the amount of the loan. This is retained by the creditor.

In the later Roman Empire, the pledge evolved into an arrangement that more closely resembled a modern form of secured transaction. A contractual relationship existed between the debtor and the creditor whereby the pledged property was regarded as collateral—security—for a loan, with title to (and, generally, possession of) the property being conditionally entrusted to the creditor. If the debtor defaulted on the loan under the terms of the agreement, the property was sold, the debt paid, and any surplus returned to the debtor. If the proceeds from the sale were insufficient to cover the amount of the debt, the debtor was liable for the deficit.

The pledge concept, as developed in Roman law, eventually evolved, centuries later, into the modern law governing secured transactions that you will read about in this chapter. As you will note, today taking possession of a debtor's collateral (the essential feature of the pledge) is only one of several ways in which a creditor can perfect a security interest in a debtor's personal property.

1. John H. Wigmore, "The Pledge-Idea: A Study in Comparative Legal Systems," 11 *Harvard Law Review* 1 (April 1897), pp. 18–39.

and purchasers of the collateral that is the subject matter of the security agreement. Perfection represents the legal process by which a secured party protects itself against the claims of third parties who may wish to have their debts satisfied out of the same collateral.

Methods of Perfection

There are basically three methods of perfection, to which we now turn.

1. *By transfer of collateral.* The debtor can transfer possession of the collateral itself to the secured party. This occurs, for example, when the debtor gives the secured party stocks or bonds, or even a piece of jewelry, provided that it is collateral securing the debt. For most collateral, possession by the secured party is impractical as it denies the debtor the right to use, sell, or derive income from the property to pay off the debt. With respect to instruments (negotiable as per UCC 3-104) or a certif-

icated security (as defined in UCC 8-102), except for a few cases of temporary perfections, the only way for proper perfection is by possession by the secured party. This type of transfer is called a **pledge**. [UCC 9-302(1)(a), 9-304(1), 9-305]

2. *By attachment of a purchase money security interest in consumer goods.* In certain circumstances, the security interest can be perfected automatically at the time of a credit sale—that is, at the time that the security interest is created under a written security agreement. Note that this *automatic perfection rule* with regard to purchase money security interests applies only when the goods are consumer goods (defined as goods bought or used by the debtor primarily for personal, family, or household purposes). The seller in this situation need do nothing more to protect his or her interest. There are exceptions to this rule, however, that cover security interests in fixtures and in motor vehicles. [UCC 9-302(1)(d)] For those states that have not adopted the 1972 UCC amendments,[2] a purchase money security interest in farm equipment under a certain statutory value is also automatically perfected by attachment.

3. *By filing.* The third and most common method of perfection is by filing a *financing statement,* a sample of which is shown in Exhibit 19-3. The UCC requires a financing statement to have (1) the signature of the debtor, (2) the addresses of both the debtor and the creditor, and (3) a description of the collateral by type or item.[3] [UCC 9-402(1)] Filing is generally the means of perfection to use—unless, of course, the collateral is the kind that a secured party can take possession of, or is required to take possession of, in order to perfect (such as chattel paper), or unless the creditor has a purchase money security interest in consumer goods.

Both the security agreement and the financing statement must contain a description of the collateral in which the secured party has a security interest. The UCC requires that the security agreement include a description of the collateral because no security interest in goods could exist unless the parties agree on which goods are subject to the security interest and then describe these goods in writing. On the other hand, the purpose of including a description of collateral in a financing statement is to put persons who might later wish to lend to the debtor on notice that certain goods in the debtor's possession are already subject to a security interest.

Sometimes the descriptions in the two documents vary, with the description in the security agreement being more precise and the description in the financing statement more general. For example, a security agreement for a commercial loan to a manufacturer may list all the manufacturer's equipment (subject to the loan) by serial number, whereby the financing statement may simply state "all equipment owned or hereafter acquired."

To avoid problems arising from such variations in descriptions, a secured party may repeat exactly the security agreement's description in the financing statement, or file the security agreement as a financing statement assuming such meets the previously discussed criteria, or, where permitted, file a combination security agreement–financing statement form. If the financing statement is too general or vague, a court may find it insufficient to perfect a security interest. This occurred in the following case.

PLEDGE
The bailment of personal property to a creditor as security for the payment of a debt.

---

2. The following states have not adopted the 1972 amendments in whole or in part: Louisiana, Missouri, South Carolina, and Vermont.

3. Certain types of collateral—crops, timber to be cut, minerals, accounts, or goods that are to become fixtures—require more than mere description, i.e., a description of the real estate concerned. [UCC 9-402(1)(5), 9-103(5), and 9-313]

◆ **Exhibit 19-3   Sample Financing Statement**

This FINANCING STATEMENT is presented for filing pursuant to the California Uniform Commercial Code.

| 1. DEBTOR   (LAST NAME FIRST—IF AN INDIVIDUAL) | | 1A. SOCIAL SECURITY OR FEDERAL TAX NO. | |

| 1B. MAILING ADDRESS | 1C. CITY, STATE | 1D. ZIP CODE |

| 2. ADDITIONAL DEBTOR   (IF ANY)   (LAST NAME FIRST—IF AN INDIVIDUAL) | | 2A. SOCIAL SECURITY OR FEDERAL TAX NO. | |

| 2B. MAILING ADDRESS | 2C. CITY, STATE | 2D. ZIP CODE |

| 3. DEBTOR'S TRADE NAMES OR STYLES   (IF ANY) | 3A. FEDERAL TAX NUMBER |

4. SECURED PARTY
  NAME
  MAILING ADDRESS
  CITY   STATE   ZIP CODE

4A. SOCIAL SECURITY NO., FEDERAL TAX NO. OR BANK TRANSIT AND A.B.A. NO.

5. ASSIGNEE OF SECURED PARTY   (IF ANY)
  NAME
  MAILING ADDRESS
  CITY   STATE   ZIP CODE

5A. SOCIAL SECURITY NO., FEDERAL TAX NO. OR BANK TRANSIT AND A.B.A. NO.

6. This FINANCING STATEMENT covers the following types or items of property **(include description of real property on which located and owner of record when required by Instruction 4).**

As security for and in consideration of all present and any future advances or other obligations debtor hereby grants United California Bank a security interest in all of the following types or items of property ("Collateral" herein) in which the debtor now has or hereafter acquires any right, title, or interest, or rights present and future, wheresoever located and whether in the possession of the debtor, a warehouseman, bailee, trustee or any other person, and all increases, therein and replacements, products, and proceeds thereof. Proceeds include but are not limited to inventory, returned merchandise, accounts, chattel paper, general intangibles, insurance proceeds, documents, money, goods, equipment, instruments, and any other tangible or intangible property arising under the sale, lease or other disposition of collateral:

7. CHECK IF APPLICABLE [X]   7A. □ PRODUCTS OF COLLATERAL ARE ALSO COVERED

7B. DEBTOR(S) SIGNATURE NOT REQUIRED IN ACCORDANCE WITH INSTRUCTION 5(c) ITEM:
□ (1)   □ (2)   □ (3)   □ (4)

8. CHECK IF APPLICABLE [X]   □ DEBTOR IS A "TRANSMITTING UTILITY" IN ACCORDANCE WITH UCC § 9105 (1) (n)

9.   DATE:

▶
SIGNATURE(S) of DEBTOR(S)

TYPE OR PRINT NAME(S) OF DEBTOR(S)

▶
SIGNATURE(S) OF SECURED PARTY(IES)

TYPE OR PRINT NAME(S) OF SECURED PARTY(IES)

11. *Return copy to:*

  NAME
  ADDRESS
  CITY
  STATE
  ZIP CODE

CODE: 1 2 3 4 5 6 7 8 9 0

10. THIS SPACE FOR USE OF FILING OFFICER (DATE, TIME, FILE NUMBER AND FILING OFFICER)

(1) FILING OFFICER COPY   FORM UCC-1—FILING FEE $3.00
Approved by the Secretary of State

MS-336 10-78

Case 19.1
IN RE BECKER
United States District Court, Western
District of Wisconsin, 1985.
53 B.R. 450.

FACTS   On September 5, 1974, Dwight and Irene Becker entered into a loan agreement with the Bank of Barron. To secure the loan, the agreement provided the bank with a security interest in all the Beckers' assets. On September 11, 1974, the bank filed a financing statement with the Barron County Register of Deeds, as was the custom. But the statement filed was a very general one, claiming an interest in all the Becker farm's personal property and "feed now owned and hereafter acquired. 25% dairy assignment." When the Beckers later filed for bankruptcy, the bank claimed that its filed statement gave it the status of a perfected secured creditor in the bankruptcy proceedings. The Beckers claimed that the statement filed by the bank was much too general and therefore was insufficient to give the bank a perfected security interest.

ISSUE   Did the bank have a perfected security interest in the Beckers' farm assets?

DECISION   No, for the most part. To the extent the statement filed had been specific—that is, concerning the feed and the 25 percent milk assignment—the bank had perfected its security interest. In respect to all other farm assets, the statement had been too general, so the security interest had not been perfected.

REASON   The reason that security interests are filed is to put other potentially interested parties on notice of already present claims on the property. To do this, the filed statement must adequately describe the collateral. This means that some specificity must be employed in the description. In the present case, the court found the bank's statement to be too vague and ambiguous in its description to suffice in perfecting the security interest in all of the Beckers' assets.

Where to File   It is important to know where to file because an improper filing reduces a secured party's claim in bankruptcy to that of an unsecured creditor. Depending upon the classification of collateral, filing is with either the secretary of state or the county clerk or other official, or both, according to state law. According to UCC 9-401, a state may choose one of these alternatives.[4] In general, financing statements for consumer goods should be filed with the county clerk.[5] Other kinds of collateral require filing with the secretary of state. [UCC 9-401]

When the secured party obtains a security interest in *unissued* shares of stock, UCC 9-302(1) prevails, because unissued securities are categorized as general intangibles under UCC 9-106: "General intangibles means any personal property (including things in action) other than goods, accounts, chattel paper, documents, instruments, and money." Under UCC 9-301(1), a security interest in unissued stock is perfected by filing a financing statement with the secretary of state.

Classification by Collateral   The classification of collateral is important also in determining where to file. Exhibit 19-4 summarizes the various classifications of collateral and the methods of perfecting a security interest.

---

4.   Approximately half the states have adopted the second alternative. Filing fees range from as low as $2 to as high as $15.

5.   On December 23, 1985, Congress passed the Food Security Act. In this act were provisions that protected a purchaser in the ordinary course of business of farm products from a prior perfected security interest, *unless* the secured party has perfected *centrally* and the buyer has received proper notice. Prior to this act, most states required local filing for perfection of security interests in farm-related collateral.

◆ **Exhibit 19-4   Types of Collateral and Methods of Perfection**

TYPE OF COLLATERAL	DEFINITIONS	PERFECTION METHOD	UCC SECTIONS
Tangible Goods	All things which are *movable* at the time the security interest attaches or which are *fixtures* (emphasis added) [UCC 9-105(1)(h)]. This includes timber to be cut, growing crops, and unborn young animals.		
1. Consumer Goods	Goods used or bought primarily for personal, family, or household purposes—for example, household furniture [UCC 9- 109(1)].	For purchase money security interest, attachment is sufficient; for boats, motor vehicles, and trailers, there is a requirement of filing or compliance with a certificate of title statute; for other consumer goods, general rules of filing or possession apply.	9-302(1)(d); 9-302(3); 9-302(4); 9-305
2. Equipment	Goods bought for or used primarily in business—for example, a delivery truck [UCC 9-109(2)].	Filing or possession by secured party.	9-302(1); 9-305
3. Farm Products	Crops, livestock, and supplies used or produced in a farming operation in the possession of a farmer debtor. This includes products of crops or livestock—for example, milk, eggs, maple syrup, and ginned cotton [UCC 9-109(3)].	Filing or possession by secured party.	9-302(1); 9-305
4. Inventory	Goods held for sale or lease, and materials used or consumed in the course of business—for example, raw materials or floor stock of a retailer [UCC 9-109(4)].	Filing or possession by secured party.	9-302(1); 9-305
5. Fixtures	Goods which become so affixed to realty that an interest in them arises under real estate law—for example, a central air conditioning unit [UCC 9-313(1)(a)].	Filing only.	9-313(1)
Indispensable Paper			
1. Chattel Paper	Any writing(s) that evidences both a *monetary obligation and a security interest*—for example, a thirty-six-month-payment retail security agreement and note signed by a buyer to purchase a car [UCC 9-105(1)(b)].	Filing or possession by secured party.	9-304(1); 9-305
2. Documents of Title	Paper which entitles the person in possession to hold, receive, or dispose of the paper or goods the document covers—for example, bills of lading, warehouse receipts, and dock warrants [UCC 9-105(1)(f), 1-201(15), 7-201].	Filing or possession by secured party.	9-304(1)(3); 9-305
3. Instruments	Any writing(s) which evidences a right to payment of money which is not a security agreement or lease, and any negotiable instrument or certificated security, which in the ordinary course of business is transferred by delivery with any necessary indorsement or assignment—for example, stock certificates, promissory notes, and certificates of deposit [UCC 9-105(1)(i), 3-104, 8-102(1)(a)].	Unless temporary perfected status, possession only.	9-304(1), (4), (5); 9-305

◆ **Exhibit 19-4   Types of Collateral and Methods of Perfection—Continued**

TYPE OF COLLATERAL	DEFINITIONS	PERFECTION METHOD	UCC SECTIONS
Intangible Collateral			
1. Accounts	Any right(s) to payment of goods sold or leased or services *rendered* that are not evidenced by an instrument or chattel paper—for example, accounts receivable, contract right payments [UCC 9-106].	Filing required (with exceptions).	9-302(1)(e), (g)
2. General Intangibles	Any personal property other than that defined above—for example, a patent, copyright, goodwill, or trademark [UCC 9- 106].	Filing only.	9-302(1)

❖ Range of Perfection and the Floating-Lien Concept

A security agreement can cover various types of property in addition to collateral already in the debtor's possession—the proceeds of the sale of collateral, after-acquired property, and future advances.

Proceeds

Proceeds include whatever is received when collateral is sold, exchanged, collected, or disposed of. A secured party has an interest in the proceeds of the sale of collateral. For example, suppose a bank has a perfected security interest in the inventory of a retail seller of refrigerators. The retailer sells a refrigerator out of this inventory to you, a buyer in the ordinary course of business. You cannot pay cash, so have agreed to a retail security agreement whereby you pay monthly payments for a period of twenty-four months. If the retailer should go into default on the loan from the bank, the bank is entitled to the remaining payments you owe to the retailer as proceeds.

Perfection of the proceeds is available automatically upon perfection of the secured party's security interest and remains perfected for ten days after receipt of the proceeds by the debtor. After that time, the interest becomes unperfected unless perfection takes place before the expiration of the ten-day period. Such perfection may take place if the secured party takes possession of the proceeds or files as to proceeds before the end of the ten-day period. Another way to extend the ten-day automatic period is to provide for such extended coverage in the original security agreement. This is typically done when the collateral is the type that is likely to be sold.

The UCC provides that in the following circumstances the security interest in proceeds remains perfected for longer than ten days after the receipt of the proceeds by the debtor.

1.   When a filed financing statement covers the original collateral, and the proceeds are collateral in which a security interest may be perfected by filing in the office or offices where the financing statement has been filed. Furthermore, if the proceeds are acquired with cash proceeds, the description of collateral in the financing statement must indicate the types of property constituting the proceeds. [UCC 9-306(3)(a)]
2.   Whenever there is a filed financing statement that covers the original collateral, and the proceeds are identifiable cash proceeds. [UCC 9-306(3)(b)]

PROCEEDS
In secured transactions law, whatever is received when the collateral is sold, exchanged, collected, or otherwise disposed of, such as insurance payments for destroyed or lost collateral. Money, checks, and the like are *cash proceeds*, while all other proceeds received are *noncash proceeds*.

3. Whenever the security interest in the proceeds is perfected before the expiration of the ten-day period. [UCC 9- 306(3)(c)]

After-Acquired Property

AFTER-ACQUIRED PROPERTY
Property of the debtor that is acquired after a secured transaction with a secured party is created.

After-acquired property of the debtor is property acquired after the execution of the security agreement. The security agreement itself may provide for coverage of after-acquired property. [UCC 9-204(1)] This is particularly useful for inventory financing arrangements, because a secured party whose security interest is in existing inventory knows that the debtor will sell that inventory, thereby reducing the collateral subject to the security interest. Generally, the debtor will purchase new inventory to replace the inventory sold. The secured party wants this newly acquired inventory to be subject to the *original* security interest. Thus, the after-acquired property clause continues the secured party's claim to any inventory acquired thereafter. This is not to say that such original security interest will be superior to the rights of all other creditors with regard to this after-acquired inventory, as will be discussed later.

An after-acquired property clause normally does not allow for attachment of a security interest in consumer goods "unless the debtor acquires rights in them within 10 days after the secured party gives value." [UCC 9-204(2)] Presumably, this protects consumers from encumbering all their present and future property.

Consider a typical example. Amato buys factory equipment from Bronson on credit, giving as security an interest in all of her equipment—both what she is buying and what she already owns. The security interest with Bronson contains an after-acquired property clause. Six months later, Amato pays cash to another seller for more equipment. Six months after that, Amato goes out of business before she has paid off her debt to Bronson. Bronson has a security interest in all of Amato's equipment, even the equipment bought from the other seller.

Future Advances

Often, a debtor will have a continuing *line of credit* under which the debtor can borrow intermittently. This is often arranged with a *letter of credit* (sometimes called *line of credit*)—an agreement in which the issuer of the letter agrees to pay drafts drawn on it by the creditor (as explained in Chapter 15). It is an advance arrangement of financing with the maximum amount of advance that the debtor can obtain. A letter of credit, typically issued by a bank, has three parties: the issuer, the customer, and a beneficiary who will draw the drafts under it. Letters of credit typically specify not only a maximum amount but a specified time duration. They can be subject to a security interest in certain properly perfected collateral.

The security agreement may provide that any future advances made against that line of credit are also subject to the security interest in the same collateral. For example, Stroh is the owner of a small manufacturing plant with equipment valued at $1 million. Being in immediate need of $50,000 working capital, he secures a loan from Midwestern Bank and signs a security agreement putting up his entire equipment as security. In the security agreement, Stroh can borrow up to $500,000 in the future, using the same equipment as collateral (future advances). In such cases, it is not necessary to execute a new security agreement and perfect a security interest in the collateral each time an advance is made to the debtor. [UCC 9-204(3)]

The Floating-Lien Concept

When a security agreement provides for the creation of a security interest in proceeds of the sale of the collateral that was the subject matter of the secured transaction—after-acquired property or future advances, or both—it is referred to as a **floating lien.** Floating liens commonly arise in the financing of inventories, for example. A creditor is not interested in specific pieces of inventory, because they are constantly changing.

Suppose that Cascade Sports, Inc., a cross-country ski dealer, has a line of credit with Portland First Bank to finance an inventory of cross-country skis. Cascade and Portland First enter into a security agreement that provides for coverage of proceeds, after-acquired inventory, present inventory, and future advances. This security interest in inventory is perfected by filing centrally (with the secretary of state). One day, Cascade sells a new pair of the latest cross-country skis, for which it receives a used pair in trade. That same day, it purchases two new pairs of skis from a local manufacturer with an additional amount of money obtained from Portland First. Portland First gets a perfected security interest in the used pair of skis under the proceeds clause, has a perfected security interest in the two new pairs of skis purchased from the local manufacturer under the after-acquired property clause, and has the new amount of money advanced to Cascade secured by the future-advance clause.

All of this is accomplished under the original perfected security agreement. The various items in the inventory have changed, but Portland First still has a perfected security interest in Cascade's inventory, and hence it has a floating lien on the inventory.

The concept of a floating lien can also apply to a shifting stock of goods. Under Section 9-205, the lien can start with raw materials and follow them as they become finished goods and inventories and as they are sold, turning into accounts receivable, chattel paper, or cash.

FLOATING LIEN
A security interest retained in collateral even when the collateral changes in character, classification, or location.

Collateral Moved to Another Jurisdiction

Obviously, collateral may be moved by the debtor from one jurisdiction (state) to another. This produces a problem when it occurs, because a secured party's perfection by filing serves as notice only to the third parties who check the records in the county (local filing) or state (central filing) where the perfection properly took place. Frequently, the secured party is not even aware of the collateral being moved out of the jurisdiction.

The Code addresses this problem and at the same time furthers the concept of the floating lien. In general, a properly perfected security interest in collateral moved into a new jurisdiction continues to be perfected in the new jurisdiction for a period of up to four months from the date it was moved, or for the period of time remaining under the perfection in the original jurisdiction, whichever expires first. [UCC 9-103(1)(d) and 9-103(3)(e)] Collateral moved from county to county within a state (where local filing is required), rather than from one state to another, however, may not have a four-month limitation, and the original filing would have continuous priority. [UCC 9-403(3)]

To illustrate: Suppose that on January 1 Wheeler secures a loan from a Nebraska bank by putting up all his wheat-threshing equipment as security. The Nebraska bank files the security interest centrally with the secretary of state. In June Wheeler has an opportunity to harvest wheat crops in South Dakota and moves his equipment into that state on June 15. The law just mentioned means that the Nebraska bank's perfection remains effective in South Dakota for a period of four months from June 15. If the Nebraska bank wishes to retain its perfection priority, the bank must perfect properly in South Dakota during this four-month period. Should the bank fail to do so, its perfection is lost after four months, and subsequent perfected security interests in the same collateral in South Dakota would prevail.

In the area of mobile goods, automobiles pose one of the biggest problems. If either the new or the original jurisdiction requires a certificate of title as part of its perfection process in regard to an automobile, perfection does not automatically end after four months. Instead, perfection ends as soon as the automobile is registered again (after the end of the four-month period) and a "clean" certificate of title is obtained. [UCC 9- 103(2)]

Effective Time of Perfection

The Code furthers the floating-lien concept with provisions affecting the time period during which a properly perfected security interest has priority. A filing statement is effective for five years from the date of filing. [UCC 9-403(2)] If a continuation statement is filed *within six months* prior to the expiration date, the effectiveness of the original statement is continued for another five years, starting with the expiration date of the first five-year period. [UCC 9-403(3)] The effectiveness of the statement can be continued in the same manner indefinitely.

❖ Priorities

The consequences of perfection and nonperfection are important in determining priorities among parties having conflicting interests in the same collateral. Perfection is important because the Code makes it clear that an unperfected security interest is of little value when challenged by a third party. Assuming a party has an enforceable security interest, his or her priority will depend upon the time when the security interest *attached* (became enforceable) or the time when it became perfected, or both, according to the following rules:

1. *Conflicting perfected security interests.* When two or more secured parties have perfected security interests in the same collateral, generally the first to perfect (file or take possession of collateral) has priority. [UCC 9-312(5)(a)]
2. *Conflicting unperfected security interests.* When two conflicting security interests are unperfected, the first to attach has priority. [UCC 9-312(5)(b)]
3. *Conflicting perfected security interests in commingled or processed goods.* When goods, with two or more perfected security interests, are so manufactured or commingled that they lose their identity into a product or mass, the perfected parties' security interests attach to the new product or mass "according to the ratio that the cost of goods to which each interest originally attached bears to the cost of the total product or mass." [UCC 9-315(2)]

Under certain circumstances, the perfection of a security interest will not protect a secured party against certain other third parties having claims to the collateral. For example, the Code provides that under certain conditions a purchase money security interest, properly perfected, will prevail over a nonpurchase money security interest in after-acquired collateral, even though the nonpurchase money security interest was perfected first. [UCC 9-312]

Since buyers should not be required to find out if there is an outstanding security interest on a merchant's inventory, the Code also provides that a person who buys "in the ordinary course of business" will take the goods free from any security interest in the merchant's inventory. This is so even if the security interest is perfected and even if the buyer knows of its existence. [UCC 9-307(1)] A *buyer in the ordinary course of business* is defined as any person who in good faith, and without knowledge that the sale is in violation of the ownership rights or security interest of a third party in the goods, buys in ordinary course from a person in the business of selling goods of that kind. [UCC 1-201(9)] The priority of claims to a debtor's collateral is detailed in Exhibit 19-5.

❖ Rights and Duties of Debtor and Creditor

The security agreement itself determines most of the rights and duties of the debtor and creditor. The UCC, however, imposes some rights and duties that are applicable in the absence of a security agreement to the contrary.

Information Request by Creditors

Under UCC 9-407(1), a creditor has the option, when making the filing, of asking the filing officer to make a note of the file number, the date, and the hour of the original filing on a copy of the financing statement. The filing officer must send this copy to the person making the request. Under UCC 9-407(2), a filing officer must also give information to a person who is contemplating obtaining a security interest from a prospective debtor. The filing officer must give a certificate that provides information on possible perfected financing statements with respect to the named debtor. The filing officer will charge a fee for the certification and for any information copies provided.

Assignment, Amendment, and Release

Whenever desired, a secured party of record can release part or all of the collateral described in a filed financing statement. This ends his or her security interest in the collateral. [UCC 9-406] A secured party can assign part or all of the security interest to another, called the *assignee*. That assignee becomes the secured party of record if, for example, he or she either makes a notation of the assignment somewhere on the financing statement or files a written statement of assignment. [UCC 9-405(2)]

It is also possible to amend a financing statement that has already been filed. *The amendment must be signed by both parties.* The debtor signs the security agreement, the original financing statement, and the amendments. [UCC 9-402] All other secured transaction documents, such as releases, assignments, continuations of perfection,

"Let us live in a small circle as we will, we are either debtors or creditors before we have had time to look round."

Johann Wolfgang von Goethe, 1749–1832
(German poet and dramatist)

◆ **Exhibit 19-5   Priority of Claims to a Debtor's Collateral**

PARTIES	PRIORITY
Unperfected Secured Party	Prevails over unsecured creditors and unlevied judgment creditors. UCC 9-301.
Purchasers of Debtor's Collateral	1. Goods purchased in the ordinary course of business prevail over a secured party's security interest, even if perfected and even if the purchaser knows of the security interest. UCC 9-307(1) 2. Consumer goods purchased out of the ordinary course of business prevail over a secured party's interest, even if perfected, providing purchaser purchased— a. For value. b. Without actual knowledge of the security interest. c. For use as a consumer good. d. Prior to secured party's perfection by *filing*. UCC 9-307(2) 3. The chattel paper purchaser prevails over a perfected secured party providing the purchaser— a. Gave new value. b. Took possession. c. Took in the ordinary course of business. d. Took without *actual* knowledge of secured party's perfection. UCC 9-308 4. Purchasers of negotiable instruments, documents, and securities prevail over a perfected secured party, particularly if the purchaser is a holder in due course, a holder to whom the document has been duly negotiated, or a bona fide purchaser of a security. UCC 9-308, UCC 9-309
Perfected Secured Parties to Same Collateral	As between two perfected secured parties in the same collateral, the general rule is that first in time of perfection is first in right to the collateral. UCC 9-312(5). Exceptions are— 1. Crops—New value to produce crops given within three months of planting has priority over prior six-month perfected interest. UCC 9-312(2) 2. Purchase money security interest—Even if second in time of perfection (first in time of perfection is a nonpurchase money security interest), it has priority providing— a. Inventory—Purchase money security interest is perfected and proper written notice is given to nonpurchase money perfected security interest holder *on* or *before* debtor takes possession. UCC 9-312(3) b. Other collateral—Purchase money security interest has priority providing such is perfected within ten (10) days after debtor receives possession. UCC 9-312(4)

perfections of collateral moved into another jurisdiction, or termination statements, need only be signed by the secured party.

Reasonable Care of Collateral

If a secured party is in possession of the collateral, he or she must use reasonable care in preserving it. Otherwise, the secured party is liable to the debtor. [UCC 9-207(1) and 9-207(3)] If the collateral increases in value, the secured party can hold this increased value or profit as additional security unless it is in the form of money, which must be remitted to the debtor or applied toward reducing the secured debt. [UCC 9-207(2)(c)] Additionally, the collateral must be kept in identifiable condition unless it is fungible. [UCC 9-207(2)(d)] Finally, the debtor must pay for all reasonable charges incurred by the secured party in preserving, operating, and taking care of the collateral in possession. [UCC 9-207(2)(a)]

The Status of the Debt

During the time that the secured debt is outstanding, the debtor may wish to know the status of the debt. If so, the debtor need only sign a statement that indicates the aggregate amount of the unpaid debt at a specific date (and perhaps a list of the collateral covered by the security agreement). The secured party must then approve or correct this statement in writing. The creditor must comply with the request within two weeks of receipt; otherwise, the creditor is liable for any loss caused to the debtor by the failure to do so. [UCC 9-208(2)] One such request is allowed without charge every six months. For each additional request, the secured party can require a fee not exceeding $10 per request. [UCC 9-208(3)]

❖ Default

Article 9 defines the rights, duties, and remedies of a secured party and of the debtor upon a debtor's default. Should the secured party fail to comply with its duties, the debtor is afforded particular rights and remedies.

The topic of default is one of great concern to secured lenders and to the lawyers who draft security agreements. What constitutes default is not always clear. In fact, Article 9 does not define the term. Consequently, parties are encouraged in practice and by the Code to include in their security agreements certain standards to be applied should default occur. In so doing, parties can stipulate the conditions that will constitute a default. [UCC 9-501(1)]

Typically, because of the unusual disparity in the bargaining position between a debtor and creditor, these critical terms are shaped with exceeding breadth by the creditor in an attempt to provide the maximum protection possible. The ultimate terms, however, are not allowed to go beyond the limitations imposed by the good-faith requirement of UCC 1-203 and the unconscionability doctrine.

Although any breach of the terms of the security agreement can constitute default, default occurs most commonly when the debtor fails to meet the scheduled payments that the parties have agreed upon or when the debtor becomes bankrupt. If the security agreement covers equipment, however, the debtor may have warranted that he or she is the owner of the equipment or that no liens or other security interests are pending on that equipment. Breach of any of these representations can result in default.

Basic Remedies

According to UCC 9-501, upon default, a secured creditor can reduce a claim to judgment, foreclose, or enforce a security interest by any available judicial process. Where the collateral consists of documents of title, a secured party can proceed against either the documents or the underlying goods.

A secured party's remedies can be divided into two basic categories:

EXECUTION
An action to carry into effect the directions in a decree or judgment; otherwise stated, an official carrying out of a court's order or judgment.

LEVY
The obtaining of money by legal process through seizure and sale of property, usually done after an execution has been issued.

1. A secured party can relinquish a security interest and proceed to judgment on the underlying debt, followed by **execution** and **levy.** This is rarely done unless the value of the secured collateral has been reduced greatly below the amount of the debt, and the debtor has other nonexempt assets available to satisfy the debt. [UCC 9-501(1)]

2. A secured party can take possession of the collateral covered by the security agreement. [UCC 9-503] Upon taking possession, the secured party can retain the collateral covered by the security agreement for satisfaction of the debt [UCC 9-505(2)] or can resell the goods and apply the proceeds toward the debt. [UCC 9-504]

The rights and remedies under UCC 9-501(1) are *cumulative.* Therefore, if a creditor is unsuccessful in enforcing rights by one method, another method can be pursued. The UCC does not require election of remedies between an action on the obligation or the repossession of the collateral.[6]

When a security agreement covers both real and personal property, the secured party can proceed against the personal property in accordance with the remedies of Article 9. On the other hand, the secured party can proceed against the entire collateral under procedures set down by local real estate law, in which case the Code does not apply. [UCC 9-501(4)]

For example, this situation occurs when the security interest on a corporate loan applies to the manufacturing plant (real property) and also to the inventory (personal property). Determining whether particular collateral is personal or real property can prove difficult, especially when dealing with fixtures—things affixed to real property. Under certain circumstances, the Code allows the removal of fixtures upon default; such removal, however, is subject to the provisions of Article 9. [UCC 9-313]

Secured Party's Right to Take Possession

The secured party has the right to take possession of the collateral upon default unless the security agreement states otherwise. As long as there is no *breach of the peace,* (which is undefined by the Code and must be determined by state law), the secured party can simply repossess the collateral. Otherwise, the secured party must resort to the judicial process. [UCC 9-503] What constitutes a breach of the peace is of prime importance to both parties, for such an act can open the secured party to tort liability.

Generally, the creditor or the creditor's agent cannot enter a debtor's home, garage, or place of business without permission. Consider a situation where an automobile is collateral. If the repossessing party walks onto the debtor's premises, proceeds up the driveway, enters the vehicle without entering the garage, and drives off, it probably will not amount to a breach of the peace. In some states, however, an action for wrongful trespass could start a cause of action for breach of the peace. (Most car repossessions occur when the car is parked on a street or in a parking lot.) In the following Florida case, a bank repossessed an automobile from an open carport and was sued for committing a trespass on the debtor's property.

---

6.   See White and Summers, *Uniform Commercial Code,* 2d ed. (St. Paul: West Publishing Co., 1980), pp. 1093–1094.

Case 19.2
MARINE MIDLAND BANK-CENTRAL v. COTE
District Court of Appeal of Florida, 1977.
351 So. 2d 750.

FACTS The defendant, Cote, had purchased an automobile in which Marine Midland Bank had a purchase money security interest. When Cote defaulted on the payments, Marine Midland's agent entered Cote's open carport and removed the car. Later, Cote sued the bank for trespass. The trial court awarded Cote $2,500 in compensatory damages and $2,500 in punitive damages. The bank appealed the judgment.

ISSUE Was the bank's agent committing a trespass by entering onto the property of Cote to repossess the automobile?

DECISION No. The court reversed the decision of the trial court in the bank's favor.

REASON The court reasoned that since the security agreement authorized repossession of the car, and since it had been repossessed without threatening the debtor or otherwise breaching the peace, the entry by the creditor's agent onto the debtor's property was not in this case a trespass.

Disposition of Collateral

Once default has occurred, the secured party may sell, lease, or otherwise dispose of the collateral in any commercially reasonable manner. [UCC 9-504(1)] Any sale is always subject to procedures established by state law.

Retention of Collateral by Secured Party The Code recognizes that parties are sometimes better off if they do not sell the collateral. Therefore, a secured party can retain collateral, but this general right is subject to several conditions. The secured party must send written notice of the proposal to the debtor if the debtor has not signed a statement renouncing or modifying his or her rights after default. In the case of consumer goods, no other notice need be given. In all other cases, notice must be sent to any other secured party from whom the secured party has received written notice of a claim of interest in the collateral in question.

If within twenty-one days after the notice is sent, the secured party receives an objection in writing from a person entitled to receive notification, then the secured party must dispose of the collateral under UCC 9-504. If no such written objection is forthcoming, the secured party can retain the collateral in full satisfaction of the debtor's obligation. [UCC 9-505(2)]

Consumer Goods When the collateral is consumer goods with a purchase money security interest, and the debtor has paid 60 percent or more of the cash price, or loan, then the secured party must dispose of the collateral under UCC 9-504 within ninety days. Failure to comply opens the secured party to an action for conversion or other liability under UCC 9-507(1) unless the consumer-debtor signed a written statement *after default* renouncing or modifying the right to demand the sale of the goods. [UCC 9-505(1)]

Disposition Procedures A secured party who does not choose to retain the collateral must resort to the disposition procedures prescribed under UCC 9-504. The Code allows a great deal of flexibility with regard to disposition. The only real limitation is that it must be accomplished in a commercially reasonable manner. UCC 9-507(2) supplies some examples of what does or does not meet the standard of commercial reasonableness.

> The fact that a better price could have been obtained by a sale at a different time or in a different method from that selected by the secured party is not of itself sufficient to establish that the sale was not made in a commercially reasonable manner. If the secured party either sells the collateral in the usual manner in any recognized market therefor or if he sells at the price current in such a market at the time of sale or if he has otherwise sold in conformity with reasonable commercial practices among dealers in the type of property sold, he has sold in a commercially reasonable manner.

A secured party is not compelled to resort to public sale to dispose of the collateral. The party is given latitude under the Code to seek out the best terms possible in a private sale. Generally, no specific time requirements must be met; however, the time must ultimately meet the standard of commercial reasonableness.

Notice must be sent by the secured party to the debtor if the debtor has not signed a statement renouncing or modifying the right to notification of sale after default. For consumer goods, no other notification need be sent. In all other cases, notification must be sent to any other secured party from whom the secured party has received written notice of claim of an interest in the collateral. [UCC 9-504(3)] Such notice is not necessary, however, when the collateral is perishable or threatens to decline speedily in value, or when it is of a type customarily sold on a recognized market. To be classified as a sale conducted in a commercially reasonable manner, generally notice of the place, time, and manner of sale is required.

What happens when a secured creditor sends a notice of repossession and sale to a debtor but the debtor does not receive the notice? This situation arose in the following case.

Case 19.3
CALCOTE v. CITIZENS & SOUTHERN NATIONAL BANK
Court of Appeals of Georgia, 1986.
179 Ga.App. 132, 345 S.E.2d 616.

FACTS Ms. Calcote obtained an automobile loan from Citizens & Southern National Bank, with the bank maintaining a security interest in the car. On March 28, 1984, after Ms. Calcote had defaulted on the loan, the bank repossessed the vehicle. On the following day, the bank sent a certified letter, return receipt requested, to Ms. Calcote informing her of the repossession, of the bank's plans to sell the auto at a private sale in May of 1984, and of her right to demand a public sale of the vehicle. Although the letter was sent to the address on the bank's records and at which the bank had repossessed the car, Ms. Calcote never received the letter. On April 19, 1984, it was returned to the bank stamped "unclaimed." On May

11, 1984, the car was sold at a private sale to which over 150 dealers had been invited. When Ms. Calcote learned that the car had been sold, she brought this action against the bank, claiming she had not been properly notified of the repossession and sale and that the private sale was not a commercially reasonable method of disposition. The trial court entered a judgment in favor of the bank, and Calcote appealed.

ISSUE Was sufficient notice given to Ms. Calcote, and was the private sale "commercially reasonable"?

DECISION Yes to both questions. The Court of Appeals affirmed the trial court's judgment.

REASON The court found that the bank's procedure for providing notice complied with the minimum state law in that the bank had promptly sent the notice, to the appro-

Case 19.3—Continued

priate address, via certified mail. Although in some cases merely mailing a letter may not be sufficient notice, particularly if the letter is unclaimed, in this case the court found the notice to be reasonable and sufficient. As to the sale, the law allows the debtor to require a public sale of collateral. If there is no demand, the secured party may sell the collateral in any commercially reasonable manner. Here the private sale was found to be reasonable.

Proceeds from Disposition   Proceeds from the disposition must be applied in the following order:

1.   Reasonable expenses stemming from the retaking, holding, or preparing for sale are covered first. When authorized by law and if provided for in the agreement, these can include reasonable attorneys' fees and legal expenses.
2.   Satisfication of the balance of the debt owed to the secured party must then be made.
3.   Subordinate security interests whose written demands have been received prior to the completion of distribution of the proceeds are covered third. [UCC 9-504(1)]
4.   Any surplus generally goes to the debtor.

Deficiency Judgment   Often, after proper disposition of the collateral, the secured party does not collect all that is still owed by the debtor. Unless otherwise agreed, the debtor is liable for any deficiency. On the other hand, if the underlying transaction was a sale of accounts or of chattel paper, the secured party can collect a deficiency judgment only if the security agreement so provides. [UCC 9-504(2)]

Redemption Rights   Any time before the secured party disposes of the collateral or enters into a contract for its disposition, or before the debtor's obligation has been discharged through the secured party's retention of the collateral, the debtor or any other secured party can exercise the right of *redemption* of the collateral. The debtor can do this by tendering performance of all obligations secured by the collateral, by paying the expenses reasonably incurred by the secured party, and by retaking the collateral and maintaining its care and custody. [UCC 9-506]

❖ Termination

When a debt is paid, the secured party generally must send a termination statement to the debtor or file such a statement with the filing officer to whom the original financing statement was given. If the financing statement covers consumer goods, the termination statement must be filed by the secured party within one month after the debt is paid, or if the debtor requests the termination statement in writing, it must be filed within ten days of receipt of such request, whichever is earlier. [UCC 9-404(1)] In all other cases, the termination statement must be filed or furnished to the debtor within ten days after a written request is made by the debtor. If the affected secured party fails to file such a termination statement, as required by UCC 9-404(1), or fails to send the termination statement within ten days after proper demand, the secured party will be liable to the debtor for $100. Additionally, the secured party will be liable for any loss caused to the debtor.

Application

Law and the Businessperson— Perfecting Your Security Interest

The importance of perfecting your security interest cannot be overemphasized, particularly when the debt is large and you wish to maximize your priority over the debtor's collateral covered by your security interest. Failure to perfect or to perfect properly may result in your becoming the equivalent of an unsecured creditor.

The filing of a financing statement, either locally or centrally with the secretary of state, is the most common method of perfection. Generally, the moment the filing takes place, your priority over the other creditors is established, as well as over some purchasers of the collateral and a subsequent trustee in bankruptcy.

We have noted that as a secured party, you do not have to file to perfect a purchase money security interest in consumer goods. Nonetheless, you are advised to do so. A filing can often save an interest that would otherwise be lost if the debtor sells a good to another consumer.

When you make a financing statement, describe the collateral, not necessarily in detailed terms, but, then again, not in too general a way. If your description is too general, your security interest will not be perfected. For example, instead of stating, "All equipment located at (address)," state specifically the equipment that will serve as the collateral.

Sometimes credit transactions occur outside normal business relationships. You may be asked, for example, to aid an associate, a relative, or a friend. At that moment, you should reflect on your need for security for any debt that will be owed to you. If there is a need for security, then your security interest should be perfected, even if you believe this is an unnecessary action because the debtor is a friend or a relative. That particular relationship is irrelevant should he or she ever be forced into bankruptcy. Bankruptcy law does not allow friends or relatives to be paid ahead of nonfriends or nonrelatives. You will end up standing in line with the other unsecured creditors if you have not perfected your security interest in the collateral. The best method to protect your security interest by perfection is to have your friend, relative, or associate transfer to your possession the collateral—stocks, bonds, jewelry, or whatever. Possession of such collateral by the secured party is a method of perfection that permits the transaction to be kept private, but still allows you to have security for the loan.

Checklist for Perfecting Your Security Interest

☐ 1. File a financing statement promptly.

☐ 2. Describe the collateral well—it is better to err on the side of too much detail rather than too little detail.

☐ 3. Even with friends, relatives, or associates, be sure to perfect your security interest, perhaps by having the debtor transfer the collateral to your possession.

❖ Chapter Summary: Secured Transactions

Requirements for a Security Interest under Article 9	1. Unless the creditor has possession of the collateral, there must be an agreement in writing, signed by the debtor, describing and reasonably identifying the collateral. 2. The secured party must give value to the debtor. 3. The debtor must have rights in the collateral—some ownership interest or rights to obtain possession of the specified collateral.
Property That May Be Secured by a Creditor	1. *Collateral* in the present possession of the debtor. 2. *Proceeds* from a sale, exchange, or disposition of secured collateral. 3. *After-acquired property*: A security agreement may provide that property acquired after the execution of the security agreement will also be secured by the agreement. This provision often accompanies security agreements covering a debtor's inventory. 4. *Future advances*: A security agreement may provide that any future advances made against a line of credit will be subject to the security interest in the same collateral.

Methods of Perfecting a Security Interest	1. *By transfer of collateral*: The debtor can transfer possession of the collateral itself to the secured party. This type of transfer is called a *pledge*.
	
	2. *By attachment of a purchase money security interest in consumer goods*: If the secured party has a purchase money security interest in consumer goods (goods bought or used by the debtor for personal, family, or household purposes), the secured party's security interest is perfected automatically. Exceptions: security interests in fixtures or motor vehicles—under UCC 9- 302(1)(d).
	
	3. *By filing*: The most common method of perfection is by filing a financing statement containing the names and addresses of the secured party and the debtor and describing the collateral by type or item. The financing statement must be signed by the debtor.
	   a. State laws determine where the financing statement is to be filed—with secretary of state, county clerk (or other official), or both.
	   b. Classification of collateral determines the place of filing. (See Exhibit 19-4)

Priorities among Parties with Claims to the Same Collateral	(See Exhibit 19-5)
Rights and Duties of Creditors and Debtors under the UCC	1. *Information request by creditors*: Upon request by any person, the filing officer must send a statement listing the file number, the date, and the hour of original filing of financing statements covering collateral of a particular debtor. A fee is charged. 2. *Reasonable care of collateral*: If a secured party is in possession of the collateral, he or she must use reasonable care in preserving it and (unless the collateral is fungible) in maintaining its identifiable condition. The debtor must pay all reasonable charges incurred by the secured party in doing so. 3. *The status of the debt*: If a debtor wishes to know the status of a secured debt, he or she may sign a descriptive statement of the amount of the unpaid debt (and could include a list of the covered collateral) at a specific date. The creditor must then approve or correct this statement in writing within two weeks of receipt or be liable for any loss caused to the debtor by failure to do so. Only one request without charge is permitted per six-month period.

❖ Chapter Summary: Secured Transactions—Continued

Remedies of the Secured Party upon Debtor's Default	1. Relinquish the security interest and proceed to judgment on the underlying debt, followed by execution and levy on the nonexempt assets of debtor. This remedy is rarely pursued.
	2. Take possession (peacefully or by court order) of the collateral covered by the security agreement and either:
	a. Retain the collateral (unless the secured party has a purchase money security interest in consumer goods and the debtor has paid 60 percent or more of the selling price or loan), in which case the creditor:
	(1) Must give written notice to debtor if debtor has not signed a statement renouncing or modifying his or her rights after default. With consumer goods, no other notice is necessary.
	(2) Must send notice to any other secured party with an interest in the same collateral. If an objection is received from the debtor or any other secured party within twenty-one days, in writing, the creditor must dispose of the collateral according to the requirements of UCC 9-504. Otherwise, the creditor may retain the collateral in full satisfaction of the debt.
	b. Sell the collateral, in which case the creditor:
	(1) Must notify the debtor and other secured parties (except in sales of consumer goods) having claims to the collateral of the sale (unless the collateral is perishable or will decline rapidly in value).
	(2) Must sell the goods in a commercially reasonable manner at a public or private sale.
	(3) Must apply the proceeds in the following order:
	(a) Expenses incurred by the sale (which may include reasonable attorneys' fees and other legal expenses).
	(b) Balance of the debt owed to the secured party.
	(c) Subordinate security interests whose written demands have been received prior to the completion of the distribution of the proceeds.
	(d) Surplus to the debtor.
Termination Statement	When a debt is paid, the secured party generally must send to the debtor or file with the filing officer to whom the original financing statement was given a *termination statement*. Failure to comply results in the secured party's liability to the debtor for $100 plus any loss caused to the debtor.
	1. If the financing statement covers consumer goods, the termination statement must be *filed* by the secured party within one month after the debt is paid, or if the debtor requests the termination statement in writing, it must be filed within ten days after the debt is paid—whichever is earlier.
	2. In all other cases, the termination statement must be *filed* or *furnished to the debtor* within ten days after a written request is made by the debtor.

❖ Questions and Case Problems

19-1. Frank agreed to purchase Janet's used computer from Janet for $450. He paid $200 down and promised to pay the balance of the purchase price within thirty days. Both parties orally agreed that if Frank failed to pay, Janet could repossess the computer. When two months later Frank still had not paid the remaining $250, Janet threatened to repossess the com- puter. Frank claimed that she had no security interest in the computer as their entire agreement had been oral. Is Frank correct? Explain.

19-2. Edward owned a retail sporting goods shop. A new ski resort was being created in his area, and to take advantage of the potential business, Edward decided to expand his operations. He borrowed a large sum of money from his bank, which took a security interest in his present inventory and any after-acquired inventory as collateral for the loan. The security interest was properly perfected by the bank by filing properly a financing statement. A year later, just a few months after the ski resort had opened, an avalanche destroyed the ski slope and lodge. Edward's business consequently took a turn for the worse, and he defaulted on his debt to the bank. The bank sought possession of his entire inventory, even though the inventory was now twice as large as it had been when the loan was made. Edward claimed that the bank only had rights to half his inventory. Who prevailed?

19-3. Andy is a seller of electric generators. He purchases a large quantity of generators from manufacturer Oberlin Corporation by making a down payment and signing a security agreement to make the balance of payments over a period of time. The security agreement gives Oberlin Corporation a security interest in the generators sold and the proceeds. Oberlin Corporation files a financing statement on its security interest centrally. Andy receives the generators and immediately sells one of them to Williamson on an installment contract, with payment to be made in twelve equal installments. At the time of the sale, Williamson knows of Oberlin's security interest. Two months later Andy defaults on his payments to Oberlin. Discuss Oberlin's rights against purchaser Williamson in this situation.

19-4. Marsh has a prize horse named Arabian Knight. Marsh is in need of working capital. She borrows $5,000 from Mendez, with Mendez taking possession of Arabian Knight as security for the loan. No written agreement is signed. Discuss whether, in the absence of a written agreement, Mendez has a security interest in Arabian Knight. Also, is Mendez a perfected secured party?

19-5. Sweeney is a retail seller of television sets. He sells a color television set to Cummings for $600. Cummings cannot pay cash, so she signs a security agreement, paying $100 down and agreeing to pay the balance is twelve equal installments of $50 each. The security agreement gives Sweeney a security interest in the television set sold. Cummings makes six payments on time; then she goes into default because of unexpected financial problems. Sweeney repossesses the set and wants to keep it in full satisfaction of the debt. Discuss Sweeney's rights and duties in this matter.

19-6. In 1969 Jones and Percell executed a promissory note and a security agreement covering a converted military aircraft built in the 1950s. Upon default, the Bank of Nevada repossessed the aircraft. After providing the required notice to Jones and Percell, the bank placed advertisements in several trade journals as well as in major newspapers in several large cities. In addition, the bank sent 2,000 brochures to 240 sales organizations. A sales representative was hired to market the aircraft. The plane was later sold for $71,000 to an aircraft broker, who in turn resold it for $123,000 after spending $33,000 on modifications. Since the price obtained on the sale of the plane was about $75,000 less than the amount Jones and Percell

owed the bank, the bank initiated a lawsuit to obtain the amount of the deficiency. Can Jones and Percell object to the bank's manner of resale? Why or why not? [Jones v. Bank of Nevada, 91 Nev. 368, 535 P.2d 1279 (1975)]

19-7. Elite Boats, Division of Glasco, Inc., financed the purchase of some marine engines by a loan obtained from the Citizens Bank of Perry. Although the boating firm's legal corporate name was Glasco, Inc., it did business under the name of Elite Boats, Division of Glasco, Inc., and its stationery, checks, and bank account all bore the latter name. The longer name was also used in its bills, contracts, and telephone listing. The bank executed a promissory note for the amount of the loan and a security agreement. Both documents bore the name "Elite Boats, Division of Glasco, Inc.," as did the financing statement filed by the bank with the secretary of state. The financing statement was indexed by the filing clerk under "Elite Boats, Division of Glasco, Inc.," and no cross-reference was made on the index to "Glasco, Inc." When Glasco later filed for bankruptcy, the trustee in bankruptcy could not locate any financing statements filed under "Glasco, Inc.," and the bank's financing statement was never disclosed. The trustee sold the marine engines. Upon learning of Glasco's bankruptcy action and the trustee's sale of the engines, the bank brought an action against the trustee for the sale proceeds. Did the bank succeed in its action? [Matter of Glasco, Inc., 642 F.2d 793 (5th Cir. 1981)]

19-8. In 1977 the Marcuses sold their drugstore business to Mistura, Inc. Mistura made a down payment on the purchase price, and the Marcuses took a security interest in the fixtures and personal property of the business for the unpaid portion of the debt. Arizona law requires that financing statements relating to security interests in personal property be filed with the secretary of state. Since the Marcuses had filed their statement with the Maricopa County Recorder, only their security interest in the fixtures was properly perfected. Mistura later obtained a loan from McKesson, using the same property secured by the Marcuse transaction as collateral. McKesson properly perfected a security interest in this same collateral by filing with the secretary of state. McKesson had actual knowledge at the time of the loan that the Marcuses had not properly perfected their security interest in the personal property of Mistura's business. A few days after McKesson's filing, the Marcuses filed a financing statement with the secretary of state. Which party had a superior security interest in the collateral, McKesson or the Marcuses? Explain. [In re Mistura, Inc., 705 F.2d 1496 (9th Cir. 1983)]

19-9. Mueller bought a thirty-two-foot motor boat for a cash sale price of $29,000. Part of the sale was financed by Chemical Bank. The retail installment contract security agreement was assigned to Chemical Bank on June 15, 1976. Ten days after the assignment, Chemical Bank filed a financing statement. Approximately a year later, Mueller, now representing himself as Lawrence J. Miller, traded the thirty-two-foot boat in on a thirty-six-foot boat at Miller Yacht Sales. Mueller made a down payment of $2,000. He was given a trade-in allowance of

$22,500. The balance due was financed with another bank. When Miller Yacht Sales took possession of the thirty-two-foot boat traded in by Mueller, it resold it to someone else. Then Mueller defaulted on his payments on the original retail installment contract to Chemical Bank and disappeared. Chemical Bank notified Miller Yacht Sales that it had a security interest. Since Miller Yacht Sales had already resold the boat, Chemical brought suit against Miller Yacht Sales. What was the result? [Chemical Bank v. Miller Yacht Sales, 173 N.J. Super. 90, 413 A.2d 619 (1980)]

19-10. In July of 1978 Dr. Jose B. Namer executed to Citizens & Southern National Bank a note in the amount of $35,000 with an accompanying security agreement in the following property: "All equipment of the debtor of every description used or useful in the conduct of the debtor's business, now or hereafter existing or acquired. . . . The listed assets held for collateral are presently located at 4385 Hugh Howell Rd, Tucker, Ga." In July of 1980 Dr. Namer moved some of his equipment to a new office owned by Hudson Properties, Inc., in Fairburn, Georgia. In order to finance this move, Dr. Namer procured a loan from a Fairburn bank, and Hudson co-signed the note. The Fairburn bank prepared a security agreement covering the same equipment as the 1978 security agreement. In September of 1980 Dr. Namer defaulted on the first note and absconded with the equipment in the Fairburn office. Hudson received an insurance payment as cash proceeds for the missing equipment. Citizens & Southern National Bank claimed priority rights to the missing equipment or proceeds even though the equipment was moved to Fairburn. Did Citizens & Southern National Bank recover this insurance money from Hudson? [Hudson Properties, Inc. v. Citizens & Southern National Bank, 168 Ga. App. 331, 308 S.E.2d 708 (1983)]

Chapter 20

Creditors' Rights and Bankruptcy

America's font of practical wisdom, Ben Franklin, observed a truth known to all debtors—that creditors do observe "set days and times" and will expect to recover their money at the agreed-upon time. Normally, creditors have no problem collecting the debts owed to them. But when disputes arise over the amount owed, or when the debtor simply cannot or will not pay, what happens then? What remedies are available to creditors when debtors default? And what laws assist and protect debtors? The first part of this chapter provides the answers to these questions. It deals with the various rights and remedies available through statutory laws, common law, and contract law to assist the debtor and creditor in resolving their disputes without the debtor having to resort to bankruptcy. The second part of this chapter discusses bankruptcy as a last resort to resolve debtor-creditor problems.

"Creditors are . . . great observers of set days and times."

Benjamin Franklin, 1706–1790
(American diplomat, author, and scientist)

❖ Laws Assisting Creditors

Numerous laws create rights and remedies for creditors. We discuss many of them in this section.

Mechanic's Lien on Real Property

When a person contracts for labor, services, or material to be furnished for the purpose of making improvements on real property but does not immediately pay for the improvements, a creditor can place a **mechanic's lien** on the property. This creates a special type of debtor-creditor relationship wherein the real estate itself becomes security for the lien (debt).

For example, a painter agrees to paint a house for a homeowner for an agreed-upon price to cover labor and materials. If the homeowner cannot pay or pays only a portion of the charges, a mechanic's lien against the property can be created. The painter is the lienholder, and the real property is encumbered with a mechanic's lien

MECHANIC'S LIEN
A statutory lien filed against the entire realty for labor, services, or materials performed in improving or repairing the realty.

443

for the amount owed. If the homeowner does not pay the lien, the property can be sold to satisfy the debt. Note that the law governing mechanics' liens is state law. State law determines the time period within which a mechanic's lien must be filed. Usually, the period is within 60 to 120 days from the last date labor or materials were provided.

Artisan's and Innkeeper's Liens on Personal Property

ARTISAN'S LIEN
A possessory lien given to a person who has made improvements and added value to another person's personal property as security for payment for services performed.

INNKEEPER'S LIEN
A possessory or statutory lien allowing the innkeeper to take the personal property of a guest, brought into the hotel, as security for nonpayment of the guest's bill (debt).

An **artisan's lien** and an **innkeeper's lien** are security devices, created at common law, similar to a mechanic's lien but used to charge personal property with the payment of a debt for labor done, for value added, or for caring for the personal property (bailee or warehousing costs).

For example, Cindy leaves her diamond ring at the jewelers to be repaired and to have her initials engraved on the band. In the absence of an agreement, the jeweler can keep the ring until Cindy pays for the services that the jeweler provides. Should Cindy fail to pay, the jeweler has a lien on Cindy's ring for the amount of the bill and can sell the ring in satisfaction of the lien.

An artisan's lien is a *possessory lien*. The lienholder ordinarily must have retained possession of the property and have expressly or impliedly agreed to provide the services on a cash, not a credit, basis. Usually, the lienholder retains possession of the property. When this occurs, the lien remains in existence as long as the lienholder maintains possession and is terminated once possession is voluntarily surrendered— unless the surrender is only temporary. If it is a temporary surrender, there must be an agreement that the property will be returned to the lienholder. Even with such an agreement, if a third party obtains rights in that property while it is out of the possession of the lienholder, the lien is lost. The only way a lienholder can protect a lien and surrender possession at the same time is to record notice of the lien in accordance with state lien and recording statutes.

Modern statutes permit the holder of an artisan's lien to foreclose and sell the property subject to the lien in order to satisfy payment of the debt. As with the mechanic's lien, the lienholder is required to give notice to the owner of the property prior to foreclosure and selling. The sale proceeds are used to pay the debt and the costs of the legal proceedings, and the surplus, if any, is paid to the former owner.

An innkeeper's lien is placed on the baggage of guests for the agreed-upon hotel charges that remain unpaid. If no express agreement is made on those charges, then the lien will be the reasonable value of the accommodations furnished. The innkeeper's lien is terminated either by the guest's payment of the hotel's charges or by surrender of the baggage to the guest, unless such surrender is temporary. Also, the lien is terminated by conversion of the guest's baggage by the innkeeper. Although state statutes permit such conversion by means of a public sale, there is a trend toward requiring that the guest first be given an impartial judicial hearing.[1]

In the following case, a creditor with a purchase money security interest in an automobile tried to repossess the property but failed to do so because an artisan's lien had also been placed on the car.

---

1. Klim v. Jones, 315 F.Supp. 109 (N.D.Cal. 1970).

Case 20.1
NATIONAL BANK OF JOLIET v. BERGERON CADILLAC, INC.
Appellate Court of Illinois, 1977.
66 Ill.2d 140, 5 Ill.Dec. 588, 361 N.E.2d 1116.

FACTS In February of 1973 Gladys Schmidt borrowed $4,120 from the National Bank of Joliet to finance the purchase of a Cadillac. The bank held a security interest in the automobile and had perfected this interest by filing in the office of the secretary of state. In August of 1973 Schmidt took the car to Bergeron Cadillac for repairs, which cost approximately $2,000. When Schmidt failed to pay for the repairs, Bergeron Cadillac retained possession of the car and placed an artisan's lien upon it. In September Schmidt defaulted on her payments to the bank, and the bank later filed an action to gain possession of the Cadillac from Bergeron. The trial court held for Bergeron Cadillac.

ISSUE Which party has a right to possession of the vehicle—Bergeron Cadillac or the National Bank?

DECISION Bergeron Cadillac. The judgment of the trial court was affirmed.

REASON The court looked to both the common law and to the UCC in its determination: "The plain language of Section 9-310 gives the lien of persons furnishing services or materials upon goods in their possession priority over a perfected security interest unless the lien is created by statute and the statute expressly provides otherwise." In response to the bank's contention that the common law possessory lien had been superseded in Illinois by two statutes providing for repairmen's liens, the court ruled that in both cases "the statutes expressly provide that the liens created shall be in addition to, and shall not exclude, any lien existing by virtue of the common law."

Writ of Execution

A debt must be past due in order for a creditor to commence legal action against a debtor. If the creditor is successful in such a legal action, the court awards the creditor a judgment against the debtor (usually for the amount of the debt plus any interest and legal costs incurred in obtaining the judgment). Attorneys' fees are not included in this amount unless provided for by statute or contract.

Frequently, the creditor finds it easy to secure a judgment against the debtor but nevertheless fails to collect the awarded amount. If the debtor will not or cannot pay the judgment, the creditor is entitled to go back to the court and obtain a **writ of execution,** which is an order, usually issued by the clerk of the court, directing the sheriff to seize (levy) and sell any of the debtor's nonexempt real or personal property that is within the court's geographic jurisdiction (usually the county in which the courthouse is located). The proceeds of the sale are used to pay off the judgment and the costs of the sale. Any excess is paid to the debtor. The debtor can pay the judgment and redeem the nonexempt property any time before the sale takes place. Because of exemption and bankruptcy laws, however, many judgments are virtually uncollectible.

WRIT OF EXECUTION
A writ that puts in force a court's decree or judgment.

Attachment

Attachment is a court-ordered seizure and taking into custody of property prior to the securing of a judgment for a past-due debt. Attachment rights are created by state statutes. Normally a *prejudgment* remedy, attachment occurs either at the time of or immediately after the commencement of a lawsuit and before the entry of a final judgment. By statute, the restrictions and requirements for a creditor to attach before

ATTACHMENT
In a secured transaction, the process by which a security interest in the property of another becomes enforceable; the legal process of seizing another's property in accordance with a writ or judicial order for the purpose of securing satisfaction of a judgment yet to be rendered.

"By no means run in debt: take thine own measure. Who cannot live on twenty pound a year, cannot on forty."

George Herbert, 1593–1633 (English poet)

WRIT OF ATTACHMENT
A writ employed to enforce obedience to an order or judgment of the court. The writ may take the form of taking or seizing property to bring it under the control of the court.

GARNISHMENT
A legal process whereby a creditor appropriates the debtor's property or wages that are in the hands of a third party.

judgment are very specific and limited. The due-process clause of the Fourteenth Amendment to the Constitution limits the courts' power to authorize seizure of a debtor's property without notice to the debtor or a hearing on the facts. In recent years, a number of state attachment laws have been held to be unconstitutional.

In order to use attachment as a remedy, the creditor must have an enforceable right to payment of the debt under law, and the creditor must follow certain procedures. Otherwise, the creditor can be liable for damages for wrongful attachment. He or she must file with the court an affidavit stating that the debtor is in default and stating the statutory grounds under which attachment is sought. A bond must be posted by the creditor to cover at least court costs, the value of the loss of use of the good suffered by the debtor, and the value of the property attached. When the court is satisfied that all the requirements have been met, it issues a **writ of attachment**, which is similar to a writ of execution in that it directs the sheriff or other officer to seize nonexempt property. If the creditor prevails at trial, the seized property can be sold to satisfy the judgment.

Garnishment

Garnishment is similar to attachment except that it is a collection remedy that is directed not at the debtor but at the debtor's property or rights held by a third person. The third person, the garnishee, owes a debt to the debtor or has property that belongs to the debtor, such as wages or a bank account. The typical garnishee is an employer. The wages an employer owes to the debtor-employee are subject to garnishment. Both state and federal laws, however, permit only a limited portion of the debtor's wages to be garnished.[2]

Federal and state laws limit the amount of money that can be garnished from a debtor's weekly take-home pay. Typically, a garnishment judgment will be served on a person's employer so that part of the person's usual paycheck will be paid to the creditor. Federal law provides a minimal framework to protect debtors from losing all their income in order to pay judgment debts.[3]

State laws also provide dollar exemptions, and these amounts are often larger than those provided by federal law. State and federal statutes can be applied together to help create a pool of funds sufficient to enable a debtor to continue to provide for family needs while also reducing the amount of the judgment debt in a reasonable way.

Garnishment of an employee's wages by a creditor cannot be grounds for dismissal of an employee. Federal law prohibits any employer from discharging an employee who has been involved in a single garnishment proceeding.

The legal proceeding for a garnishment action is governed by state law. As a result of a garnishment proceeding, the debtor's employer is ordered by the court to turn over a portion of the debtor's wages to pay the debt. Garnishment operates differently from state to state, however. According to the laws in some states, the judgment creditor needs to obtain only one order of garnishment that will then continuously apply to the judgment debtor's weekly wages until the entire debt is paid. In other states, the judgment creditor must go back to court for a separate order of garnishment for each pay period.

---

2.   Some states (for example, Texas) do not usually permit garnishment of wages by private parties.
3.   For example, the federal Consumer Credit Protection Act, 15 U.S.C., Section 1601 *et seq.*, provides that a debtor can retain either 75 percent of the disposable earnings per week or the sum equivalent to thirty hours of work paid at federal minimum wage rates, whichever is greater.

Creditors' Composition Agreements

Creditors may contract with the debtor for discharge of the debtor's liquidated debts upon payment of a sum less than that owed. These agreements are called *composition agreements* or **creditors' composition agreements** and are usually held to be enforceable.

Suretyship and Guaranty

When a third person promises to pay a debt owed by another in the event the debtor does not pay, either a *suretyship* or *guaranty* relationship is created. Exhibit 20-1 illustrates these relationships. The third person's credit becomes the security for the debt owed.

Surety   A contract of strict suretyship is a promise made by a third person to be responsible for the debtor's obligation. It is an express contract between the surety and the creditor. The surety in the strictest sense is *primarily* liable for the debt of the principal. The creditor can demand payment from the surety from the moment that the debt is due. A suretyship is not a form of indemnity; that is, it is not merely a promise to make good any loss that a creditor may incur as a result of the debtor's failure to pay. The creditor need not exhaust all legal remedies against the principal debtor before holding the surety responsible for payment. Moreover, a surety agreement does not have to be in writing to be enforceable, although it usually is.

For example, Robert Delmar wants to borrow money from the bank to buy a used car. Because Robert is still in college, the bank will not lend him the money unless his father, Joseph Delmar, who has dealt with the bank before, will co-sign

CREDITORS' COMPOSITION AGREEMENT
An agreement formed between a debtor and his or her creditors whereby the creditors agree to accept a lesser sum than that owed by the debtor in full satisfaction of the debt.

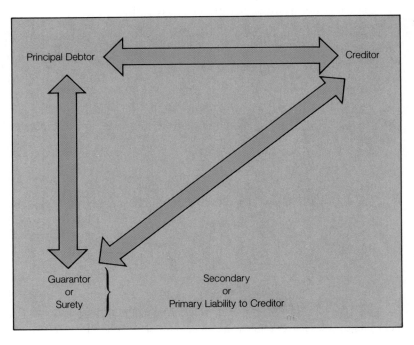

◆ **Exhibit 20-1 Suretyship and Guaranty Parties**

the note. When Mr. Delmar co-signs the note, he becomes primarily liable to the bank. On the note's due date the bank has the option to seek payment from either Robert or Joseph Delmar, or both jointly.

Guaranty A guaranty contract is similar to a suretyship in that it includes a promise to answer for the debt or default of another. With suretyship, however, the surety is primarily liable for the debtor's obligation of the principal. With a guaranty arrangement, the guarantor—the third person making the guaranty—is *secondarily* liable. The guarantor can be required to pay the obligation only after the debtor defaults, and then usually only after the creditor has made an attempt to collect from the principal debtor.

For example, a closely held corporation, BX Enterprises, needs to borrow money to meet its payroll. The bank is skeptical about the creditworthiness of BX and requires Dawson, its president, who is a wealthy businessperson and owner of 70 percent of BX Enterprises, to sign an agreement making himself personally liable for payment if BX does not pay off the loan. As a guarantor of the loan, Dawson cannot be held liable until BX Enterprises is in default.

A guaranty contract between the guarantor and creditor must be in writing to be enforceable unless the *main-purpose* exception applies. Briefly, this exception provides that if the main purpose of the guaranty agreement is to benefit the guarantor, then the contract need not be in writing to be enforceable. (See Chapter 8 for a more detailed discussion of this exception.)

The guaranty contract terms determine the extent and time of the guarantor's liability. For example, a guaranty can be *continuing*, designed to cover a series of transactions by the debtor. Also, the guaranty can be *unlimited* or *limited* as to time and amount. In addition, the guaranty can be *absolute*, wherein the guarantor becomes liable immediately upon the debtor's default, or *conditional*, wherein the guarantor becomes liable only upon the happening of a certain event.

Defenses of the Surety (and Guarantor) The defenses of the surety and guarantor are basically the same. Therefore, the following discussion applies to both. A creditor is obligated to try to prevent certain actions that would release the surety from the obligation. For example, any material change made in the terms of the original contract between the principal debtor and the creditor, including the awarding of a *binding* extension of time for making payment without first obtaining the consent of the surety, will discharge the surety either completely or to the extent that the surety suffers a loss.

When a creditor discharges the principal debtor (or any one of the principal debtors), the surety is released from any obligation unless the surety agrees to the discharge. Naturally, if the principal obligation is paid by the debtor or by another person on behalf of the debtor, the surety is discharged from the obligation. Similarly, if valid tender of payment is made, and the creditor for some reason rejects it with knowledge of the surety's existence, then the surety is released from any obligation on the debt.

Generally, any defenses available to a principal debtor can be used by the surety to avoid liability on the obligation to the creditor; the defenses that cannot be used are incapacity, bankruptcy, and the statute of limitations. The ability of the surety to assert any defenses the debtor may have against the creditor is the most important concept in suretyship, since most of the defenses available to the surety are those of the debtor.

Obviously, a surety may have his or her own defenses—for example, incapacity or bankruptcy. Another defense is when the creditor fraudulently induced the surety to guaranty the debt of the debtor. In most states, the creditor has a legal duty to inform the surety, prior to the formation of the suretyship contract, of material facts known by the creditor that would materially increase the surety's risk. Failure to so inform is fraud and makes the suretyship obligation voidable.

In addition, if a creditor surrenders or impairs the debtor's collateral while knowing of the surety and without the surety's consent, the surety is released to the extent of any loss that would be suffered from the creditor's actions. The primary reason for this is to protect the surety who agreed to become obligated only because the debtor's collateral was in the possession of the creditor.

Rights of the Surety (and Guarantor)   The rights of the surety and guarantor are basically the same. Therefore, the following discussion applies to both. When the surety pays the debt owed to the creditor, the surety is entitled to certain rights. First is the legal **right of subrogation.** Simply stated, this means that any right the creditor had against the debtor now becomes the right of the surety. Included are creditor rights in bankruptcy, rights to collateral possessed by the creditor, and rights to judgments secured by the creditor. In short, the surety now stands in the shoes of the creditor and may pursue any remedies that were available to the creditor against the debtor.

Second, the surety has a **right of reimbursement** from the debtor. This right either stems from the suretyship contract or from equity. Basically, the surety is entitled to receive from the debtor all outlays made on behalf of the suretyship arrangement. Such outlays can include expenses incurred as well as the actual amount of the debt paid to the creditor.

Third, in the case of **co-sureties** (two or more sureties on the same obligation owed by the debtor), a surety who pays more than his or her proportionate share upon a debtor's default is entitled to recover from the co-sureties the amount paid above the surety's obligation. This is the **right of contribution.** Generally, a co-surety's liability either is determined by agreement or, in absence of agreement, is set at the maximum liability under the suretyship contract.

Assume that two co-sureties are obligated under a suretyship contract to guarantee the debt of a debtor. One surety's maximum liability is $15,000, and the other's is $10,000. The debtor owes $10,000 and is in default. The surety with the $15,000 maximum liability pays the creditor the entire $10,000. In the absence of agreement, this surety can recover $4,000 from the other surety ($10,000/$25,000 × $10,000 = $4,000, this co-surety's obligation).

Foreclosure

Mortgage holders have the right to foreclose on mortgaged property in the event of a debtor's default. In regard to the latter, the usual method of foreclosure is by judicial sale of the property, although the statutory methods of foreclosure vary from state to state. If the proceeds of the foreclosure sale are sufficient to cover both the costs of the foreclosure and the mortgaged debt, any surplus is received by the debtor. If the sale proceeds are insufficient to cover the foreclosure costs and the mortgaged debt,

RIGHT OF SUBROGATION
The right of a person to substitute one person in the place of another, giving the substituted party the same legal rights that the original party had. Subrogation appears most frequently in construction contracts, insurance contracts, suretyship, and negotiable instruments law.

RIGHT OF REIMBURSEMENT
The legal right of a person to be restored, repaid, or indemnified for costs, expenses, or losses incurred or expended on behalf of another.

CO-SURETIES
Joint sureties; two or more sureties to the same obligation.

RIGHT OF CONTRIBUTION
The act of any one or several of a number of co-sureties in reimbursing one of their number who has paid the whole debt, each to the extent of his or her proportionate share.

however, the mortgagee (the creditor/lender) can seek to recover the difference from the mortgagor (the debtor) by obtaining a *deficiency judgment* representing the difference between the mortgaged debt and the amount actually received from the proceeds of the foreclosure sale. A deficiency judgment is obtained in a separate legal action that is pursued subsequent to the foreclosure action. It entitles the creditor to recover from other nonexempt property owned by the debtor.

Other rights of creditors include those of secured creditors under Article 9 of the UCC (discussed in Chapter 19).

❖ State Exemption Laws

HOMESTEAD EXEMPTION
A law allowing an owner to designate his or her house and adjoining land as a homestead and thus exempt it from liability for his or her general debt.

In most states, certain types of real and personal property are exempt from levy of execution or attachment. Probably the most familiar of these exemptions is the **homestead exemption.** Each state permits the debtor to retain the family home, either in its entirety or up to a specified dollar amount, free from the claims of unsecured creditors or trustees in bankruptcy. The purpose is to ensure that the debtor will retain some form of shelter.

Suppose that Van Cleave owes Goodwin $40,000. The debt is the subject of a lawsuit, and the court awards Goodwin a judgment of $40,000 against Van Cleave. The homestead of Van Cleave is valued at $50,000. There are no outstanding mortgages or other liens on his homestead. To satisfy the judgment debt, Van Cleave's family home is sold at public auction for $45,000. Assume the homestead exemption is $25,000. The proceeds of the sale are distributed as follows:

1. Van Cleave is given $25,000 as his homestead exemption.
2. Goodwin is paid $20,000 toward the judgment debt, leaving a $20,000 deficiency judgment (that is, "leftover debt") that can be satisfied (paid) from any other nonexempt property (personal or real) that Van Cleave may have, if allowed by state law.

In a few states, statutes permit the homestead exemption only if the judgment debtor has a family. The policy behind this type of statute is to protect the family. If a judgment debtor does not have a family, a creditor may be entitled to collect the full amount realized from the sale of the debtor's home.

State exemption statutes usually include both real and personal property. Personal property that is most often exempt from satisfaction of judgment debts includes:

1. Household furniture up to a specified dollar amount.
2. Clothing and certain personal possessions, such as family pictures or a Bible.
3. A vehicle (or vehicles) for transportation (at least up to a specified dollar amount).
4. Certain classified animals, usually livestock but including pets.

❖ Laws Providing Special Protection for Consumer-Debtors

Numerous consumer protection statutes and rules apply to the debtor-creditor relationship. Although most of these are discussed in detail in Chapter 31, a brief listing and discussion here will illustrate the breadth and importance of these consumer-oriented protection laws.

Consumer Credit Protection Act (CCPA)

Commonly known as the *Truth-in-Lending Act*, the Consumer Credit Protection Act (CCPA) is basically a *disclosure law*, administered by the Federal Reserve Board. This law requires sellers and lenders to disclose credit terms on loans so that a consumer-debtor can shop around for the best financing arrangements. Essentially, it requires that the creditor clearly indicate to the consumer-debtor what charges are being made for the privilege of paying the debt over a period of time, including what the total annual interest percentage rate is.

Uniform Consumer Credit Code (UCCC)

In an attempt to make consumer credit laws at the state level uniform, the National Conference of Commissioners on Uniform State Laws proposed legislation called the Uniform Consumer Credit Code (UCCC). Its essential points are as follows:

1.   To place statutory ceilings on interest rates and other charges.
2.   To require disclosure similar to that required by the truth-in-lending law.
3.   To limit garnishment actions against take-home wages to a certain amount and to prohibit discharge of an employee solely because of garnishment proceedings.
4.   To allow cancellation of a contract solicited by a seller in the consumer-debtor's home within three business days of the solicitation.
5.   To limit the holder-in-due-course concept to the acceptance of a check, rather than any other type of negotiable instrument, from the consumer-debtor.
6.   To prohibit referral sales, which are sales in which a seller offers a rebate or discount to a buyer for furnishing the names of other prospective purchasers.
7.   To provide criminal as well as civil penalties for violations.

Only a handful of states have adopted the UCCC, even though it has undergone numerous drafts. Some other states have passed laws similar to some of the provisions of the UCCC, such as laws concerning home-solicitation sales.

Federal Trade Commission Rule—Holder in Due Course (HDC)

As discussed in the "Landmark" in Chapter 17, as part of the consumer-protection movement, the Federal Trade Commission (FTC) promulgated a rule that limited the rights of a holder in due course (HDC) where the debtor-buyer executes a negotiable promissory note as part of a consumer transaction. This rule provides basically that any personal defenses the buyer can assert against the seller can also be asserted against an HDC. The seller must disclose this rule clearly on the sales agreement.

The HDC rule basically eliminates the use of a buyer's waiver-of-defense clause in a consumer transaction. These clauses in security agreements, otherwise permitted under UCC 9-206, waive any claim or defense the debtor might have against a good-faith assignee for value of a security interest.

Landmark in the Law

The Bankruptcy Reform Act of 1978 and Its Amendments

The U. S. Constitution, Article I, Section 8, states "The Congress shall have the power . . . to establish . . . uniform laws on the subject of bankruptcies throughout the United States." The inclusion of this clause in the Constitution reflects the early conviction of our nation's leaders that debtors should be given a second chance and not have to spend months, and sometimes years, in debtors' prisons—which were anathema to the founding fathers.

Congress first exercised this power in 1800, when the first bankruptcy law was enacted due to the business crisis created by restraints imposed on American trade by the British and French. In 1803, the law was repealed, and during the rest of the century—always in response to some crisis—periodically Congress enacted (and later repealed) other bankruptcy legislation. The National Bankruptcy Act of 1898, however, was not repealed, and since that time the United States has had ongoing federal statutory laws concerning bankruptcy. The 1898 act allowed only for liquidation in bankruptcy proceedings. Some relief through reorganization was allowed, beginning with amendments to the 1898 act in the 1930s.

Modern bankruptcy law is based on the Bankruptcy Reform Act of 1978, which repealed the 1898 act as amended and represented a major overhaul of federal bankruptcy law. A major organizational change in the 1978 act was the establishment of a new system of bankruptcy courts, whereby each federal judicial district would have an adjunct bankruptcy court with exclusive jurisdiction over bankruptcy cases. The 1978 act also empowered bankruptcy court judges to consider and decide issues "arising in or related to" bankruptcy cases. Critics assailed this provision in the 1978 act, claiming that the bankruptcy judges had excessively broad jurisdiction. The judges, appointed for fourteen-year terms, had most of the authority of federal district court judges but not the life tenure or salary protection of the latter. In 1982 this provision was declared unconstitutional.[1]

The controversy arising over the 1978 act caused Congress to review the law, and in doing so, Congress passed the Bankruptcy Amendments and Federal Judgeship Act of 1984. These amendments created 232 bankruptcy judgeships in various judicial districts throughout the United States. The bankruptcy judges still have fourteen-year terms, but they are now under the authority of the U. S. district courts and no longer have authority to decide nonbankruptcy issues affecting debtors. The 1984 amendments also remedied apparent abuses, misuses, delays, and ambiguous provisions resulting from the 1978 act.

The Bankruptcy Act of 1978 was further amended in 1986 by the Bankruptcy Judges, United States Trustees, and Family Farmer Bankruptcy Act. This amendment created 52 additional bankruptcy judgeships, extended the bankruptcy trustee system nationally and granted more power to *bankruptcy trustees* in the handling of bankruptcy matters, and created a new chapter in bankruptcy to aid financially troubled farmers.

The Bankruptcy Reform Act of 1978, as amended, is the basis for the description within this chapter of existing bankruptcy law. The Bankruptcy Code is contained in the U. S. Code as Title 11 and has nine chapters. Chapters 1, 3, and 5 include general definitional provisions and provisions governing case administration, creditors, the debtor,[2] and the estate. These three chapters apply generally to all kinds of bankruptcies. The next five chapters set forth the different types of relief that debtors may seek. Chapter 7 provides for liquidations. Chapter 9 governs the adjustment of debts of a municipality. Chapter 11 governs reorganizations. Chapter 12 (family farmers) and Chapter 13 (individuals) provide for adjustment of debts by parties with regular income. Chapter 15 sets up a U. S. Trustee system.

1. See Northern Pipeline Co. v. Marathon Pipeline Co., 458 U.S. 50, 102 S.Ct. 2858, 73 L.Ed.2d 598 (1982).
2. It is noteworthy that the term *bankrupt* no longer exists under the Bankruptcy Code. Those who were formerly bankrupts under the old Bankruptcy Act are now merely *debtors*.

Business Law in Action

How to Collect Debts—in Bogota

Creditors trying to collect unpaid bills in Bogota, Colombia, no longer have to rely solely on attorneys or the court system to get their money from debtors who refuse to pay. Certain collection agencies in Bogota, such as *Universal de Cobranzas* or *Organizacion Juridica de Cobranzas*, will, if the standard form letters and telephone calls are ineffective, send *chepitos* to the debtor's premises. Loosely translated as "harassers," *chepitos* are men dressed in tuxedos and top hats, carrying canes and black briefcases, who stand in front of a debtor's home or business advertising the fact (by the lettering on their briefcases) that a *deudor moroso* (debtor in default) dwells therein. No words are said, but the *chepitos* remain on the site until the debt is paid.

It is an extremely effective technique and, for creditors trying to collect unpaid debts, an increasingly popular alternative to attorneys or court proceedings. Although the city's population has nearly tripled in the last twenty years, the size of the court system has remained the same during that time period. The result is that the courts are overcrowded, and lawsuits to collect debts usually take at least two years.

The Colombian National Association of Litigation Lawyers (ANDAL), however, maintains that using *chepitos* to collect debts is the equivalent of extortion or debt collection by intimidation. ANDAL would like to see the *chepitos* outlawed. "They are a plague," according to ANDAL's executive director. "They are displacing lawyers, and taking justice in their own hands."[1] Executives of the collection agencies retort that ANDAL's fury could be due to the fact that the *chepitos* were sent to visit ANDAL offices when the lawyers' association—which fell behind in its debts due to an expensive banquet—would not pay one of its bills.

1. As quoted in *The Miami Herald*, December 9, 1986, p. 2A.

❖ Bankruptcy and Reorganization

Bankruptcy law in the United States has two goals—to protect a debtor by giving him or her a fresh start, free from creditors' claims, and to ensure equitable treatment to creditors who are competing for a debtor's assets. As discussed in the "Landmark," bankruptcy legislation was first enacted in 1898 and since then has undergone several modifications—both major and minor—the most recent being the 1986 amendments to the 1978 Bankruptcy Reform Act. The remaining sections in this chapter deal with the most frequently used bankruptcy plans: Chapter 7 liquidations, Chapter 11 reorganizations, and Chapter 12 and Chapter 13 plans. The latter three chapters are sometimes referred to as *rehabilitation chapters*. As you read the following sections on bankruptcy, be sure to keep in mind that references to Chapter 7, Chapter 9, Chapter 12, and Chapter 13 are references to chapters contained in the Bankruptcy Code, not references to chapters within this textbook.

"Bankruptcy is one of those words like 'war' that you have heard all your life and think that you understand until you actually become involved with the process the word is intended to identify."

Jerome Weidman, 1913–
(Novelist and playwright)

❖ Chapter 7 Liquidations

Liquidation is the most familiar type of bankruptcy proceeding and is often referred to as an *ordinary* or *straight bankruptcy*. Put simply, debtors in a straight bankruptcy state their debts and turn their assets over to a trustee. The trustee sells the assets and distributes the proceeds to creditors. With certain exceptions, the balance of the debts is then discharged (extinguished), and the debtors are relieved of their obligation to pay the debts. Any "person"—defined as including individuals, partnerships, and corporations[4]—may be a debtor under Chapter 7. Railroads, insurance companies, banks, savings and loan associations, and credit unions cannot be Chapter 7 debtors. Rather, other chapters of the Bankruptcy Act, as amended (hereinafter, the Code), or federal or state statutes, apply to them.

Filing the Petition

A straight bankruptcy may be commenced by the filing of either a voluntary or an involuntary petition.

Voluntary Bankruptcy   A voluntary petition is brought by the debtor, who files official forms designated for that purpose in the bankruptcy court. The 1984 amendments require a consumer-debtor who has selected Chapter 7 to state in the petition, at the time of filing, that he or she understands the relief available under other chapters and has chosen to proceed under Chapter 7. If the consumer-debtor is represented by an attorney, the attorney must file an affidavit stating that the attorney has informed the debtor of the relief available under each chapter. Anyone who is liable on a claim held by a creditor can do this. The debtor does not even have to be insolvent to file a petition.

The voluntary petition contains the following schedules:

1.   A list of both secured and unsecured creditors, their addresses, and the amount of debt owed to each.
2.   A statement of the financial affairs of the debtor.
3.   A list of all property owned by the debtor, including property claimed by the debtor to be exempt.
4.   A listing of current income and expenses. (This schedule was added by the 1984 amendments to provide creditors and the court with relevant information on the debtor's ability to pay creditors a reasonable amount from future income. This information could possibly lead a court, on its own motion, to dismiss a consumer-debtor's Chapter 7 petition after a hearing,[5] encouraging a Chapter 13 petition where such would result in a substantial improvement of a creditor's receipt of payment.)

The official forms must be completed accurately, sworn to under oath, and signed by the debtor. To conceal assets or knowingly supply false information on these schedules is a crime under the bankruptcy laws. If the voluntary petition for bankruptcy is found to be proper, the filing of the petition will itself constitute an *order for relief*. Once a consumer-debtor's voluntary petition has been filed, the clerk of the court (or person directed) must give the trustee and creditors mailed notice of the order of relief not more than twenty days after entry of said order.

A new feature allows a husband and wife to file jointly for bankruptcy under a single petition. As mentioned previously, debtors do not have to be insolvent (when

---

4.   The definition of *corporation* includes unincorporated companies and associations. It also covers labor unions.
5.   The law does give the debtor a presumption in favor of granting an order of relief for whatever chapter in the Bankruptcy Act is requested by the debtor.

debts exceed fair market value of assets exclusive of exempt property) to file for voluntary bankruptcy.

Involuntary Bankruptcy   An involuntary bankruptcy occurs when the debtor's creditors force the debtor into bankruptcy proceedings. Such a case cannot be commenced against a farmer[6] or a charitable institution, however. Nor can it be filed unless the following requirements are met: If the debtor has twelve or more creditors, three or more of those having unsecured claims aggregating at least $5,000 must join in the petition. If a debtor has fewer than twelve creditors, one or more creditors having a claim of $5,000 may file.

If the debtor challenges the involuntary petition, a hearing will be held, and the bankruptcy court will enter an *order for relief* if it finds that:

1.   The debtor is generally not paying debts as they become due.[7]
2.   A custodian was appointed to take charge of or took possession of substantially all the debtor's property within 120 days before the filing of the petition.

If the court grants an order for relief, the debtor will be required to supply the information in the bankruptcy schedules discussed previously.

An involuntary petition should not be used as an everyday debt-collection device, and the Code provides penalties for the filing of frivolous petitions against debtors. Judgment may be granted against the petitioning creditors for the costs and attorneys' fees incurred by the debtor in defending against an involuntary petition that is dismissed by the court. If the petition is filed in bad faith, damages can be awarded for injury to the debtor's reputation. Punitive damages may also be awarded.

Automatic Stay

The filing of a petition, either voluntary or involuntary, operates as an *automatic stay*, or a suspension of virtually all litigation and other action by creditors against the debtor or the debtor's property. In other words, once a petition is filed, creditors cannot commence or continue most legal actions against the debtor to recover claims. Nor can creditors take any action to repossess property in the hands of the debtor. A secured creditor, however, may petition the bankruptcy court for relief from the automatic stay in certain circumstances.

Underlying the Code's automatic-stay provision for a secured creditor is a concept known as *adequate protection*, which holds, among other things, that secured creditors are protected from losing their security as a result of the automatic stay. The bankruptcy court can provide adequate protection by requiring the debtor or trustee to

---

6.   The definition of *farmer* stipulates persons who receive more than 80 percent of their gross income from farming operations, such as tilling the soil, dairy farming, ranching, or the production or raising of crops, poultry, or livestock. Corporations and partnerships can be *farmers* as well as individuals.
7.   The inability to pay debts as they become due is known as *equitable* insolvency. A balance-sheet insolvency, which exists when a debtor's liabilities exceed assets, is not the test. Thus, it is possible for debtors to be thrown into involuntary bankruptcy even though their assets far exceed their liabilities. This situation may occur when a debtor's cash-flow problems become severe.

make periodic cash payments, or a one-time cash payment (or provide additional collateral or replacement liens) to the extent that the stay causes the value of the property involved to decrease. Or the court may grant other relief that is the "indubitable equivalent" of the secured party's interest in the property, such as a guaranty by a solvent third party to cover losses suffered by the secured party as a result of the stay.

For example, G&M Trucking owns two trucks in which Middleton Bank has a security interest. G&M Trucking has failed to make its monthly payments for two months. It files a petition in bankruptcy, and the automatic stay prevents Middleton Bank from repossessing the trucks. Meanwhile, the trucks (whose collective value is already less than the balance due) are depreciating at a rate of several hundred dollars a month. Middleton Bank's inability to repossess and immediately resell the trucks is harming the bank to the extent of several hundred dollars per month. The bankruptcy court may prevent Middleton Bank from being harmed by requiring G&M Trucking to make a one-time cash payment or periodic cash payments (or provide additional collateral or replacement liens) to the extent that the trucks are depreciating in value. If the debtor is unable to provide adequate protection, the court may vacate the stay and allow Middleton Bank to repossess the trucks.

A creditor's failure to abide by an automatic stay imposed by the filing of a petition could be costly. The 1984 amendments provide that if a creditor *knowingly* violates the automatic stay (a willful violation), any party injured is entitled to recover actual damages, costs, and attorneys' fees and may also be entitled to recover punitive damages.

In the following case, a creditor petitioned the bankruptcy court for, and received relief from, the automatic-stay provision of the Bankruptcy Code.

Case 20.2
IN RE McNEELY
United States Bankruptcy Court, District of Utah, 1985.
51 B.R. 816.

FACTS Max McNeely owed Western States Petroleum, Inc., over $130,000. Western sought and received writs of attachment on all of McNeely's real and personal property. Western also caused a writ of garnishment to be directed to McNeely's bank accounts. Because McNeely's total assets amounted to less than $75,000, McNeely sought protection from Western's collection attempts by filing for Chapter 7 bankruptcy. By filing for bankruptcy, McNeely was able to prevent Western's execution of its writs of attachment. Because of the bankruptcy filing, Western was unable to execute the writs by having McNeely's property seized and sold in satisfaction of the debt. Western petitioned the bankruptcy court to vacate the automatic stay as to the property subject to the writs on the ground that the writs created a valid lien

against the property, giving Western the status of a secured creditor.

ISSUE Should the automatic stay be removed in this case?

DECISION The court granted Western relief from the automatic-stay provision, thus making it a secured creditor in the subsequent bankruptcy action.

REASON The court, because it concluded the writs of attachment were valid, realized that if Western were not allowed to execute the attachments, it would not attain the status of a secured creditor during the bankruptcy proceedings.

COMMENT This case illustrates the importance of being a secured creditor, particularly in the case of a bankruptcy proceeding.

The Trustee

Promptly after the order for relief has been entered, an interim, or provisional, trustee is appointed to preside over the debtor's property until the first meeting of creditors.[8] At this first meeting, either a permanent trustee is elected or the interim trustee becomes the permanent trustee. As will be discussed later in this chapter, the trustee's principal duty is to collect and reduce to money the "property of the estate" for which he or she serves, and to close up the estate as expeditiously as is compatible with the best interests of the parties. Trustees are entitled to compensation for services rendered, plus reimbursement for expenses.

Creditors' Meeting

Within a reasonable time after the order of relief is granted (not less than ten days or more than thirty days), the bankruptcy court must call a meeting of creditors listed in the schedules filed by the debtor. The bankruptcy judge does not attend or preside at this meeting. A permanent trustee[9] is elected (by 20 percent or more of the unsecured creditors with fixed claims), and the interim trustee's duties are discharged, or more typically, in the absence of election the interim trustee becomes the permanent trustee. The debtor is required to attend this meeting (unless excused by the court) and to submit to examination under oath by the creditors and the trustee. Failure to appear when required or false statements made under oath may result in the debtor being denied a discharge of bankruptcy.

Proof of claims by creditors must normally be filed within ninety days of this meeting.

Property of the Estate

Upon commencement of a Chapter 7 proceeding, an *estate in property* is created. The estate consists of all the debtor's legal and equitable interests in property presently held, wherever located, together with community property, property transferred in a transaction voidable by the trustee, proceeds and profits from the property of the estate, and certain after-acquired property. Interests in certain property, such as gifts, inheritances, property settlements (divorce), or life insurance death proceeds, to which the debtor becomes entitled *within 180 days after filing* may also become part of the estate. Thus, the filing of a bankruptcy petition generally fixes a dividing line: Property acquired prior to the petition becomes property of the estate, and property acquired after the filing of the petition, except as just noted, remains the debtor's.

Exemptions

Any individual debtor is entitled to exempt certain property from the property of the estate. Prior to the enactment of the Code, state law exclusively governed the extent

---

8. The Bankruptcy Judges, United States Trustees, and Family Farmer Bankruptcy Act of 1986 provides for a national trustee system. Once completely operational, one of these trustees will be assigned to preside over the debtor's property and administer the debtor's estate.
9. See Footnote 8.

of the exemptions. The Code, however, establishes a federal exemption scheme. An individual debtor (or husband and wife who file jointly) now has the option of choosing between the exemptions provided under the applicable state law or the federal exemptions.[10] The Code exempts the following property:

1. Up to $7,500 in equity in the debtor's residence and burial plot.
2. Interest in a motor vehicle up to $1,200.
3. Interest, up to $200 for any particular item, in household goods and furnishings, wearing apparel, appliances, books, animals, crops, or musical instruments (the 1984 amendments limit, however, an aggregate total of all items to $4,000).
4. Interest in jewelry up to $500.
5. Any other property worth up to $400, plus any unused part of the $7,500 homestead exemption up to an amount of $3,750.[11]
6. Up to $750 interest in any tools of the debtor's trade.
7. Any unmatured life insurance contract owned by the debtor.
8. Certain interests in accrued dividends or interest under life insurance contracts owned by the debtor.
9. Professionally prescribed health aids.
10. The right to receive social security and certain welfare benefits, alimony and support, and certain pension benefits.
11. The right to receive certain personal injury and other awards.

Trustee's Powers

The basic duty of the trustee is to collect the debtor's available estate and reduce it to money for distribution, preserving the interests of both the debtor and unsecured creditors. In other words, the trustee is accountable for administering the debtor's estate. To enable the trustee to accomplish this duty, the Code gives him or her certain powers, stated in both general and specific terms.

General powers are vouchsafed by the statement that the trustee occupies a position *equivalent* in rights to that of other parties. For example, the trustee has the same rights as a *lien creditor* on a simple contract who could have obtained a judicial lien on the debtor's property or who could have levied execution on the debtor's property. This means that a trustee has priority over an unperfected secured party to the debtor's property. A trustee also has power equivalent to that of a *bona fide purchaser* of real property from the debtor. Thus, the trustee would prevail in priority over a secured party's *unperfected* fixture security interest.

In addition, the trustee has specific powers of avoidance. These powers include any voidable rights available to the debtor, preferences, certain statutory liens, and fraudulent transfers by the debtor. Each will be discussed in more detail in this chapter.

With these powers, persons holding the debtor's property at the time the petition is filed are required to deliver the property to the trustee. The following case illustrates the trustee's rights and powers in a dispute with a secured party over the collateral

---

10. Individual states are given the power to pass legislation precluding the use of the federal exemptions by debtors in their states. Approximately half of the states permit a debtor to use only state (not federal) exemptions.

11. The 1984 amendments placed a cap of $3,750 on the unused part of the homestead exemption to prevent some debtors from receiving a complete $7,500 windfall.

of the debtor and shows the importance for the secured party of properly filing in order to perfect a security interest.

Case 20.3
IN RE KARACHI CAB CORP.
United States Bankruptcy Court, Southern District of New York, 1982.
21 B.R. 822.

FACTS The Karachi Cab Company negotiated a loan from Ruth Wapnick. Ms. Wapnick wanted her loan to be secured, so she asked Karachi to put up two of its medallions (licenses to operate a cab in the city of New York) as collateral. Karachi signed the property security agreement, and Wapnick attempted to perfect her security interest by filing the financing statement (often called simply a UCC-1) in the office of the county clerk of New York. Later, Karachi filed for bankruptcy. The trustee attempted to avoid Wapnick's security interest, arguing to the bankruptcy court that it was not properly perfected because the filing was improper. Given the nature of the collateral, the trustee claimed that the security interest should have been filed with the secretary of state instead of the county clerk.

ISSUE Was Wapnick's security interest perfected?

DECISION No. The court adjudged Wapnick's security interest to be unperfected and allowed the trustee to avoid it as inferior to the rights of the trustee as a lien creditor.

REASON Because the collateral medallions were used or bought for use primarily in the debtor's business, under UCC 9-109(2) the medallions are classified as equipment. UCC 9-401 explicitly mandates that a financing statement must be filed with the secretary of state for a security interest in equipment to be properly perfected. Wapnick filed her financing statement in the county clerk's office. Thus, the court concluded that Wapnick's security interest was not properly perfected. In bankruptcy, the trustee has the status of a lien creditor without notice under section 544(a) of the Bankruptcy Code. Moreover, UCC 9-301 makes the unperfected security interest subordinate to one who "becomes a lien creditor before the security interest is perfected." Consequently, the trustee in bankruptcy, as a constructive lien creditor under Section 544(a), has priority over the unsecured (unperfected) creditor with respect to the collateral. Wapnick's unsecured claim, therefore, was disallowed and reclassified as wholly unsecured.

COMMENTS This case illustrates the importance of a proper perfection of a secured party's security interest in the collateral of a debtor. A secured party with a properly perfected security interest generally prevails as to the debtor's property over all unsecured creditors, secured parties who have not perfected properly, some purchasers of the debtor's collateral, and a trustee in bankruptcy.

Voidable Rights A trustee steps into the shoes of the debtor. Thus, any reason that a debtor can use to obtain the return of his or her property can be used by the trustee as well. These grounds (for recovery) include fraud, duress, incapacity, and mutual mistake.

For example, Rob sells his boat to Inga. Inga gives Rob a check, knowing that there are insufficient funds in the bank account to cover the check. Inga has committed fraud. Rob has the right to avoid that transfer and recover the boat from Inga. Once an order for relief has been entered for Rob, the trustee can exercise the same right to recover the boat from Inga.

Preferences A debtor should not be permitted to transfer property or to make a payment that favors one creditor over others. Thus, the trustee is allowed to recover such property or payments, whether made voluntarily or involuntarily.

To constitute a preference that can be recovered, an *insolvent* debtor generally (though not always, since exceptions exist) must have transferred property for a *preexisting* debt within ninety days of filing the petition in bankruptcy. The transfer must give the creditor more than would have been received had the case been a Chapter 7 liquidation proceeding. The trustee does not have to prove insolvency, as the Code provides that the debtor is presumed to be insolvent during this ninety-day period.

Sometimes the creditor receiving the preference is an *insider*, meaning an individual, partner, partnership, officer, or director of a corporation (or relative of these) who has a close relationship with the debtor. If such is the case, the avoidance power of the trustee is extended from transfer preferences made within ninety days to those made within one year of filing the petition; however, the presumption of insolvency is confined to the ninety-day period, so the trustee must prove insolvency before that period.

Not all transfers and conveyances are preferences, but only those involving something other than current consideration. Therefore, it is generally assumed by most courts that payment for services rendered within forty-five days prior to the petition for current consideration is not a preference. If a creditor receives payment in the ordinary course of business, such as payment of last month's telephone bill, the payment cannot be recovered by the trustee in bankruptcy. To be recoverable, a preference must be a transfer for an antecedent debt, such as a year-old telephone bill. In addition, the 1984 amendments permit a consumer-debtor to transfer any property to a creditor up to a total value of $600 without the transfer constituting a preference.

If a preferred creditor has sold the property to an innocent third party, the property cannot be recovered from the innocent party, but in such circumstances, the creditor generally can be held accountable for the value of the property.

Liens on Debtor's Property   The trustee is permitted to avoid the fixing of certain statutory liens, such as a landlord's lien, on property of the debtor. Liens that first become effective at the time of the bankruptcy or insolvency of the debtor are voidable by the trustee. Liens that are not perfected or enforceable on the date of the petition against a bona fide purchaser are also voidable.

Fraudulent Transfers   The trustee may avoid fraudulent transfers or obligations if they were made within one year of filing the petition and/or if they were made with actual intent to hinder, delay, or defraud a creditor. Transfers made for less than a reasonably equivalent consideration are also vulnerable if the debtor thereby became insolvent, was left engaged in business with an unreasonably small amount of capital, or intended to incur debts that would be beyond his or her ability to pay.

The debtor shares most of the trustee's avoiding powers. Thus, if the trustee does not take action to enforce one of his or her rights (for example, to recover a preference), the debtor in a Chapter 7 bankruptcy would nevertheless be able to enforce that right.[12]

---

12.   Under Chapter 11 (to be discussed later), for which no trustee generally exists, the debtor has the same avoiding powers as a trustee under Chapter 7. Under Chapters 12 and 13 (also to be discussed later) a trustee must be appointed.

Claims of Creditors

Generally, any legal obligation of the debtor is a claim. In the case of disputed or unliquidated claims, the bankruptcy court will estimate the value of the claim. Any creditor holding a debtor's obligation can file a claim against the debtor's estate.

These claims are automatically allowed unless contested by the trustee, debtor, or another creditor. The Code, however, does not allow claims for breach of employment contracts or real estate leases for terms longer than one year. Such claims are limited to one year's rent or wages, despite the remaining length of either contract in breach. Therefore, an employee who has a three-year employment contract that is breached during the first year by the employer's bankruptcy would be limited to damages accruing during one year from the filing of the petition, or from the date the employment contract was repudiated, whichever is earlier.

Property Distribution

Creditors are either secured or unsecured. (The rights of secured creditors were discussed in Chapter 19.) A *secured* creditor has a security interest in collateral that secures the debt. Before the 1984 amendments, secured parties were frequently put on hold for months concerning the disposition of the secured collateral held by the debtor because of the automatic-stay provisions. Today, the law provides that a consumer-debtor, within thirty days of the filing of a Chapter 7 petition, or before the date of the first meeting of the creditors (whichever is first), must file with the clerk a statement of intention with respect to the secured collateral. That intent must state whether the debtor will retain the collateral or surrender it to the secured party.[13]

The trustee is obligated to enforce the debtor's intent within forty-five days after the intent is filed. If the secured collateral is surrendered to the secured party, the secured creditor can enforce the security interest either by accepting the property in full satisfaction of the debt or by foreclosing on the collateral and using the proceeds to pay off the debt. In this way, the secured party has priority over unsecured parties to the proceeds from the disposition of the secured collateral. Indeed, the Code provides that if the value of the secured collateral exceeds the secured party's claim, the secured party also has priority to the proceeds in an amount that will cover reasonable fees and costs incurred because of the debtor's default. Any excess over this amount is used by the trustee to satisfy the claims of unsecured creditors. Should the secured collateral be insufficient to cover the secured debt owed, the secured creditor becomes an unsecured creditor for the difference.

Bankruptcy law establishes an order or priority for classes of debts owed to *unsecured* creditors, and they are paid in the order of their priority. Each class of debt must be fully paid before the next class is entitled to any of the proceeds—if there are sufficient funds to pay the entire class. If not, the proceeds are distributed *proportionately* to each creditor in a class, and all classes lower in priority on the list receive nothing. The order of priority among classes of unsecured creditors is as follows:

1. All costs and expenses for preserving and administering the estate, including such items as court costs and trustee and attorneys' fees and costs incurred by the

---

13. Also, if applicable, the debtor must specify whether the collateral will be claimed as exempt property, and whether the debtor intends to redeem the property or reaffirm the debt secured by the collateral.

trustee during the administration of the estate, such as rental fees and appraisal fees.

2.   Unsecured claims in an involuntary proceeding arising in the ordinary course of the debtor's business after commencement of the case but before the appointment of a trustee or issuance of an order for relief.

3.   Claims for wages, salaries, and commissions up to an amount of $2,000 per claimant, provided that they were earned within ninety days of the filing of the petition in bankruptcy. Any claims in excess of $2,000 are treated as the "claims of general creditors" (listed as Number 8 in this list).

4.   Unsecured claims for contributions to employee benefit plans arising under services rendered within 180 days before filing the petition and limited to the number of employees covered by the plan multiplied by $2,000.

5.   Farm producers and fishermen, up to $2,000 against debtors who own or operate grain-storage facilities or a fish-produce storage or processing facility (1984 amendments).

6.   Unsecured claims for money deposited (up to $900) with the debtor before the filing of the petition in connection with the purchase, lease, or rental of property or services that were not delivered or provided. Any claim in excess of $900 is treated as a "claim of a general creditor" (listed as Number 8 in this list).

7.   Certain taxes and penalties legally due and owing various government units (rules vary depending on type of tax owed).

8.   Claims of general creditors. These debts have the lowest priority and are paid on a pro rata basis if, and only if, funds remain after all the debts having priority are paid in full.

9.   Any remaining balance is returned to the debtor.

Discharge

From the debtor's point of view, the primary purpose of a Chapter 7 liquidation is to obtain a fresh start through the discharge of debts.[14] The primary effect of a discharge is to void any judgment on a discharged debt and enjoin any action to collect it. (A discharge does not affect the liability of a co-debtor.) There are circumstances, however, in which, either because of the nature of the claim or the conduct of the debtor, a claim will not be discharged.

Exceptions to Discharge   Exceptions to discharge include the following (the 1984 amendments added the exceptions in Numbers 9 through 11 in the following list):

1.   Claims for back taxes accruing within three years prior to bankruptcy.

2.   Claims against property or money obtained by the debtor under false pretenses or by false representations.

3.   Unscheduled claims.

4.   Claims based on fraud or misuse of funds while the debtor was acting in a fiduciary capacity, or claims involving the debtor's embezzlement or larceny.

5.   Alimony and child support.

6.   Claims based on willful or malicious injury by the debtor to another or to the property of another.

---

14.   Discharges are granted only to "individuals" who are debtors under Chapter 7, not to corporations or partnerships. The latter may use Chapter 11 or (where appropriate) Chapter 12, or they may liquidate under state law.

7. Certain fines and penalties payable to government units.

8. Certain student loans, unless such imposes an undue hardship on the debtor and the debtor's dependents.

9. Consumer debts of more than $500 for luxury goods or services owed to a single creditor incurred within forty days of the order of relief. This denial of discharge is a rebuttable presumption, and any debts reasonably acquired to support or maintain the debtor or dependents are not classified as luxury goods or services.

10. Cash advances aggregating more than $1,000 as an extension of open-end consumer credit obtained by the debtor within twenty days of the order of relief. This is also a rebuttable presumption.

11. Judgments or consent decrees awarded against a debtor for liability incurred as a result of the debtor's operation of a motor vehicle while legally intoxicated.

In the following case, the question of the discharge of a student loan was at issue.

Case 20.4
BAKER v. UNIVERSITY OF TENNESSEE AT CHATTANOOGA (IN RE BAKER)

United States Bankruptcy Court, Eastern District of Tennessee, 1981.
10 B.R. 870.

FACTS Baker, while a student, received a number of educational loans. Some time after graduation Baker filed for bankruptcy and sought a discharge of these loans in the bankruptcy decree, claiming that it would be an undue hardship on her to repay the loans. At the time of her filing, Baker asserted that her husband had deserted her, that she had been ill, and that two of her children had physical problems.

ISSUE Would paying the debt pose an undue hardship for Baker?

DECISION Yes. The debtor's student loans were discharged.

REASON The purpose of the prohibition against discharge was designed "to remedy an abuse by students who, immediately upon graduation, would file bankruptcy to secure a discharge of educational loans." In this case, Baker did not file bankruptcy to secure a discharge only from her educational loans. The bankruptcy court found that Baker could reduce her expenses somewhat, but that her reasonable expenses each month far exceeded her income. Given Baker's circumstances, the court found that forcing payment of Baker's debts would create an undue hardship, and that the Bankruptcy Code was drafted to provide a fresh start for those such as Baker "who have truly fallen on hard times."

Objections to Discharge   In addition to the exceptions to discharge previously listed, the following circumstances will cause a discharge to be denied.

1. Debtor's concealment or destruction of property with the intent to hinder or delay or defraud a creditor.

2. Debtor's fraudulent concealment or destruction of records, or failure to keep adequate records, of his or her financial condition.

3. Debtor's refusal to obey a lawful order of a bankruptcy court.

4. Debtor's failure to satisfactorily explain the loss of assets.

5. Grant of a discharge to debtor within six years of the filing of the petition.[15]
6. Debtor's written waiver of discharge approved by the court.

When a discharge is denied under these circumstances, the assets of the debtor are still distributed to the creditors, but the debtor remains liable for the unpaid portions of all claims.

Prior to the 1984 amendments, creditors were reluctant to challenge and object to the granting of a discharge to a debtor. If the challenge was denied, the creditor was liable in judgment to the debtor for all costs and reasonable attorneys' fees. To encourage legitimate objections, the amendments provide that even if the creditor loses on the challenge, the creditor is liable for costs and attorneys' fees *only if the challenge was not substantially justified.*

Revocation of Discharge   The Code provides that a debtor may lose his or her bankruptcy discharge by *revocation.* The bankruptcy court may within one year revoke the discharge decree if it is discovered that the debtor was fraudulent or dishonest during the bankruptcy proceedings. The revocation renders the discharge null and void, allowing creditors not satisfied by the distribution of the debtor's estate to proceed with their claims against the debtor.

Reaffirmation of Debt   A debtor may voluntarily wish to pay off a discharged debt. This is called a *reaffirmation* of the debt. The 1984 amendments completely revised the procedure and rules concerning reaffirmation agreements. To be enforceable, such agreements now must be made before a debtor is granted a discharge, and they must be filed with the court. If the debtor is represented by an attorney, court approval is not required if the attorney files a declaration or affidavit stating that (1) the debtor has been fully informed of the consequences of the agreement, (2) the agreement is voluntarily made, and (3) the agreement does not impose a hardship on the debtor or the debtor's dependents. If the debtor is not represented by an attorney, court approval is required, and the agreement will be approved only if the court finds no undue hardship and if the agreement is in the best interest of the debtor.

In addition, the debtor will now have the ability to rescind the agreement at any time prior to discharge or within sixty days[16] of filing the agreement, whichever is later. This rescission period must be stated *clearly* and *conspicuously* in the reaffirmation agreement.

❖ Chapter 11 Reorganizations

The type of bankruptcy proceeding used most commonly by a corporate debtor is a Chapter 11 reorganization. In this reorganization, the creditors and the debtor formulate a plan under which the debtor pays a portion of his or her debts and is discharged of the remainder. Then the debtor is allowed to continue in business. Although this type of bankruptcy is commonly a corporate reorganization, any debtor

---

15.   A discharge under Chapter 13 of the Code within six years of the filing of the petition does not bar a subsequent Chapter 7 discharge where a good-faith Chapter 13 plan paid at least 70 percent of all allowed unsecured claims.
16.   Formerly, the time limit was thirty days.

who is eligible for Chapter 7 relief is eligible for Chapter 11 relief. In addition, railroads are also eligible for Chapter 11 relief.

The same principles that govern the filing of a Chapter 7 petition apply to Chapter 11 proceedings. The case may be brought either voluntarily or involuntarily. The same principles govern the entry of the order for relief. The automatic-stay and adequate-protection provisions previously discussed are applicable in reorganizations. The automatic-stay provisions and use of a plan to discharge unsecured debts and obligations have engendered controversy by being used to prevent injured parties from securing judgments in lawsuits and to prevent unions from enforcing collective-bargaining agreements. The courts and the 1984 amendments have attempted to clarify some of these issues, particularly as regards collective-bargaining agreements.

In some instances, creditors may prefer private, negotiated adjustments of creditor-company relations, also known as **workouts,** to bankruptcy proceedings. Quite frequently, these out-of-court workouts are much more flexible and thus more conducive to a speedy settlement. Speed is critical, since delay is one of the most costly elements in any bankruptcy proceeding.

Another advantage of workouts is that they avoid the various administrative costs of bankruptcy proceedings. Thus, under Section 305(a) of the Bankruptcy Code, a court, after notice and a hearing, may dismiss or suspend all proceedings in a case at any time if such a dismissal or suspension would better serve the interests of the creditors of the debtor. Section 1112 also allows a court, at the request of a party in interest, and after notice and a hearing, to dismiss a case under Chapter 11 for cause. *Cause* includes an absence of a reasonable likelihood of rehabilitation, the inability to effectuate a plan, and an unreasonable delay by the debtor that is prejudicial to creditors.[17] In the following case, creditors of Johns-Manville Corporation sought to dismiss, under Section 1112, a voluntary Chapter 11 petition filed by Manville.

WORKOUTS
A common law or bankruptcy out-of-court negotiation with creditors whereby a debtor enters into an agreement with a creditor or creditors for a payment or plan to discharge the debtor's debt(s).

Case 20.5
IN RE JOHNS-MANVILLE CORP.
United States Bankruptcy Court, Southern District of New York, 1984.
36 B.R. 727

FACTS On August 26, 1982, Johns-Manville Corporation, a highly successful industrial enterprise, filed for protection under Chapter 11 of the Bankruptcy Code. This filing came as a surprise to some of Manville's creditors, as well as to some of the other corporations that were also being sued, along with Manville, for injuries caused by asbestos exposure. Manville asserted that the approximately 16,000 lawsuits pending as of the filing date and the potential lawsuits of people who had been exposed but who would not manifest the asbestos-related diseases until some time in the future necessitated its filing. The creditors of Manville, on motion to the bank-

ruptcy court, contended that Manville did not file in good faith, that Manville was not insolvent, and thus the voluntary Chapter 11 petition should be dismissed under Section 1112 of the Bankruptcy Code.

ISSUE Was Manville eligible to file a voluntary petition for Chapter 11 reorganization under the Bankruptcy Code?

DECISION Yes. The court held that bankruptcy proceedings were appropriate in this situation and denied the motions to dismiss Manville's petition.

REASON With respect to voluntary petitions, the court noted that "it is no longer necessary for a petitioner for reorganization to allege or show insolvency or inability to pay debts as they mature." Manville clearly met all of the threshold eligibility requirements for filing a voluntary pe-

---

17. See 11 U.S.C., Section 1112(b).

Case 20.5—Continued

tition. Furthermore, in determining whether to dismiss under Section 1112(b), a court is not necessarily required to consider the debtor's good faith in filing because "good faith" is not a specified predicate for filing under the Code. Rather, good faith emerges as a requirement for confirmation of the plan; that is, good faith is required to come out of Chapter 11, but not to get into it. A "principal goal" of the Code is to provide open and easy access into the bankruptcy process. Here, liquidation would be inefficient and wasteful, destroying the utility of Manville's assets as well as jobs; and, more important, would preclude compensation of future asbestos claimants. Ultimately, the court concluded that Manville needed the protection of the Bankruptcy Code and should not be required to wait until its economic picture deteriorated beyond salvation to file for reorganization.

Debtor-in-Possession

Upon entry of the order for relief, the debtor generally continues to operate his or her business as a *debtor-in-possession*. The court, however, may appoint a trustee to operate the debtor's business if gross mismanagement of the business is shown, or if it is in the best interests of the estate. As soon as practicable after the entry of the order for relief, a creditors' committee of unsecured creditors is appointed. The committee may consult with the trustee or the debtor-in-possession concerning the administration of the case or the formulation of the plan.

Creditors' Committees

Additional creditors' committees may be appointed to represent special interest creditors. The creditors' committee is, in a sense, a party in interest in the proceedings. Orders affecting the estate generally will not be entered without either (1) the consent of the committee or (2) a hearing by the judge of the position of the creditors' committee.

Filing the Plan

Only the debtor may file a plan within the first 120 days after the date of the order for relief. If the debtor does not meet the 120-day deadline, however, or if the debtor fails to obtain the required creditor consent within 180 days, any party may propose a plan.

Contents of Plan

A Chapter 11 plan must be "fair and equitable" and must:

1. Designate classes of claims and interests under the plan.
2. Specify the treatment to be afforded the classes. Also, the plan must provide the same treatment for each claim in a particular class.
3. Provide an adequate means for the plan's execution.

Acceptance of Plan

Once the plan has been developed, it is submitted to each class of creditors for acceptance. Acceptance of a plan is required by each class unless the class is not impaired. [11 U.S.C., Section 1129(8)] A class of claims has accepted the plan when a majority of the number of creditors, representing two-thirds of the amount of the total claim, vote to approve it.

Confirmation of Plan

Each plan submitted is almost a case history in itself, and each plan varies. The plan must be "in the best interests of the creditors." Even when all classes of claims accept the plan, the court may refuse to confirm it if it fails to meet this requirement. Also, even if only one class of claims has accepted the plan, the court may still confirm it under the Code's so-called *cram-down* provision. The plan is binding upon confirmation. Upon confirmation, the debtor is given a Chapter 11 discharge from all claims not protected under the plan. This discharge, however, does not apply to any claims denied discharge under Chapter 7 (as previously discussed).

❖ Chapter 13 Plans

The former Bankruptcy Act provided for the formulation of *wage-earner plans* as a means of allowing wage earners to pay off their debts free from the harassment of creditors. Under these plans, the wage earner avoided the stigma of being adjudicated a "bankrupt." Chapter 13 of the Bankruptcy Code provides for "Adjustment of Debts of an Individual with Regular Income."

Individuals (not partnerships or corporations) with regular income who owe non-contingent, liquidated, unsecured debts of less than $100,000 or similar secured debts of $350,000 may take advantage of Chapter 13. Individual proprietors and individuals on welfare, social security, fixed pensions, or investment income are included.[18] There are several advantages in filing a Chapter 13 plan when eligible. One of these advantages is that it is less expensive and less complicated than a Chapter 11 proceeding, or even a Chapter 7 liquidation.

Filing the Petition

A Chapter 13 case can be initiated only by the filing of a voluntary petition by the debtor. Certain Chapter 7 and Chapter 11 cases may be converted to Chapter 13 cases with the consent of the debtor. A trustee must be appointed.

Automatic Stay

Upon the filing of a Chapter 13 petition, the automatic stay previously discussed takes effect. It enjoins creditors from taking action against co-obligors of the debtor. Although it applies to all or part of a consumer debt, it does not apply to any business debt incurred by the debtor.

---

18. Prior to the new Bankruptcy Act, self-employed persons could not file under Chapter 13.

Drawing by Ross; © 1984, The New Yorker Magazine.

A creditor has the right to seek relief from the automatic stay. A 1984 amendment was enacted to save the creditor time and money in seeking court approval to vacate the stay and recover from the co-obligor. The new law provides that upon the creditor's request to vacate the stay against the co-debtor, unless written objection is filed, twenty days later the stay against the co-debtor is automatically terminated without a hearing.

Filing the Plan

Only the debtor may file a plan under Chapter 13. This plan may provide either for the payment of all obligations in full or for payment of an amount less than 100 percent.

Contents of Plan

A Chapter 13 plan must:

1.   Provide for the turnover of such future earnings or income of the debtor to the trustee as is necessary for execution of the plan.
2.   Provide for full payment in deferred cash payments of all claims entitled to priority.
3.   Provide for the same treatment of each claim within a particular class. (The 1984 amendments permit the debtor to list co-debtors, such as guarantors or sureties, as a separate class.)

The time for payment under the plan may not exceed three years unless the court approves an extension. The term, with extension, may not exceed five years.

The 1984 amendments require the debtor to make "timely payments," and the trustee is required to "insure" these payments. The law now provides that the debtor shall commence making payments under the proposed plan within thirty days after the plan has been filed. If the plan has not been confirmed, the trustee is instructed to retain the payments until the plan is confirmed and then distribute accordingly. If the plan is denied, the trustee will return the payments to the debtor less any costs. Failure of the debtor to make timely payments or to commence payments within the thirty-day period will allow the court to convert the case to a Chapter 7 bankruptcy or to dismiss the petition.

Confirmation of Plan

After the plan is filed, the court holds a confirmation hearing at which interested parties may object to the plan. The court will confirm a plan with respect to each claim of a secured creditor:

1. If the secured creditors have accepted the plan.
2. If the plan provides that creditors retain their liens and if the value of the property to be distributed to them under the plan is not less than the secured portion of their claims.
3. If the debtor surrenders the property securing the claim to the creditors.

Prior to the 1984 amendments, unsecured creditors had little protection under a debtor's plan filed under Chapter 13. The court was required to confirm the plan providing:

1. The plan conformed to the requirements (including payments of fees) of Chapter 13.
2. The plan was proposed in "good faith."
3. The value of the property to be distributed would not be less than that paid if the estate were to be liquidated under Chapter 7.
4. The debtor would be able to make all payments under the plan.[19]

Some courts interpreted these criteria as permitting the confirmation of zero plans (unsecured creditors receive nothing). These courts found no statutory requirement suggesting that a Chapter 13 debtor pay more than what a creditor would get in a straight liquidation proceeding. If the creditor would receive nothing under Chapter 7, there was no requirement to pay the unsecured creditor anything to obtain a Chapter 13 discharge.

Other courts interpreted the criteria much differently. These courts held that the very title of Chapter 13 requires that the petitioner have "regular income" and assumes that the debtor will use future income to make payments to creditors. In addition, a prerequisite to confirmation is that the debtor be able to make "all payments" under the plan. This very section anticipates that a debtor must live within a proposed

---

19. 11 U.S.C., Section 1325(a).

budget to make some payments to an unsecured creditor. Lastly, these courts held that the "good-faith" test requires the court to ensure that all parties are treated fairly. Therefore, if "no meaningful repayment can be proposed, the debtor is not entitled to Chapter 13 relief."[20]

Objection to the Plan

Unsecured creditors do not have a vote to confirm a Chapter 13 plan. The 1984 amendments, however, attempted to address zero plans and to give the trustee and unsecured creditors a meaningful right of objection to a plan submitted by a debtor. The amendments forbid the court to approve a plan over the objection of the trustee or any unsecured creditor unless either of the following situations exist:

1. The value of the property to be distributed under the plan is at least equal to the amount of the claim.
2. All the debtor's projected disposable income to be received during the three-year plan period will be applied to making payments. Disposable income is all income received *less* amounts needed to support the debtor and dependents and/or amounts needed to meet ordinary expenses to continue the operation of a business.

Modification of the Plan

Prior to completion of payments, the plan may be modified upon the request of the debtor, the trustee, or an unsecured creditor. If there is an objection by any interested party to the modification, the court must hold a hearing to determine approval or disapproval of the modified plan.

Denial or Loss of Discharge

After completion of all payments under a Chapter 13 plan, the court grants a discharge of all debts provided for by the plan. The exemptions to discharge are for certain long-term debts. Except for claims constituting a priority debt and except for alimony and child support, all other debts are dischargeable. Priority debts must be paid because the priority claims are a minimum requirement of what must be included in a plan. That means that the present status of the law allows a Chapter 13 discharge to include fraudulently incurred debts and claims resulting from malicious or willful injury. Therefore, a Chapter 13 discharge is much more beneficial to the debtor than a Chapter 7 discharge.

Even if the debtor does not complete the plan, a "hardship" discharge may be granted if the failure to complete the plan was due to circumstances beyond the

---

20. In re Iacovoni, 2 B.R. 256 (Bkrtcy.D.Utah 1980). The court in its opinion cited Justice Douglas in Bank of Marin v. England, 385 U.S. 99, 103, 87 S.Ct. 274, 277, 17 L.Ed.2d 197, 201 (1966): "Yet we do not read these statutory words with the ease of a computer. There is an overriding consideration that equitable principles govern the exercise of bankruptcy jurisdiction."

debtor's control and if the property distributed with the plan was of greater value than would have been paid in a Chapter 7 liquidation. A discharge can be revoked within one year if it was obtained by fraud.

❖ Chapter 12 Plans

On November 27, 1986, the Family Farmer Bankruptcy Act became law. In order to help relieve economic pressure on small farmers, Congress created a new chapter in the Bankruptcy Code. The new law defines a family farmer as one whose gross income is at least 50 percent farm-dependent and whose debts are at least 80 percent farm-related. The total debt must not exceed $1,500,000. A partnership or closely held corporation (at least 50 percent owned by the "farm family") can also take advantage of this new law.

A Chapter 12 filing is very similar in procedure to a Chapter 13 filing. The farmer debtor must file a plan not later than ninety days after the order of relief. The filing of the petition acts as an automatic stay against creditors and co-obligor actions against the estate.

A secured creditor can petition for adequate protection to lift the automatic stay. The Fourth and Ninth Circuits have held that adequate protection under Chapter 11 requires the debtor to compensate the secured creditor for so-called "lost-opportunity costs" where the value of the collateral is less than the amount of the debt secured. Because farmland values have dropped substantially, farmers could not possibly pay lost-opportunity costs. Chapter 12 adds a different means for providing adequate protection—payment of reasonable market rental payments—while keeping the family farmer from paying the lost-opportunity costs.

In order to help relieve economic pressure on small farmers and to avoid auctions of this sort, Congress created a new chapter in the Bankruptcy Code in 1986.

The content of the plan is basically the same as a Chapter 13 filing. The plan can be modified by the farmer-debtor but, except for cause, must be confirmed or denied within forty-five days of the filing of the plan.

Court confirmation of the plan is the same as for a Chapter 13 plan. In summary, the plan must provide for payment of secured debts at the value of the collateral. If the secured debt exceeds the value of the collateral, the remaining debt is unsecured. For unsecured debtors, the plan must be confirmed if either the value of the property to be distributed under the plan equals the amount of the claim, or if the plan provides that all of the debtor-farmer's disposable income received in a three-year period (longer by court approval) will be applied to making payments.

Disposable income is all income received less amounts needed to support the farmer-debtor and family and continue the farming operation. Completion of payments under the plan is a discharge of all debts provided for by the plan.

The new law also allows a farmer who has already filed under Chapter 11 or Chapter 13 to convert to Chapter 12. Chapter 12, like Chapters 11 and 13, allows for the farmer-debtor to convert to liquidation under Chapter 7.

Application

Law and the Businessperson— Voluntary versus Involuntary Bankruptcy

Chapter 7 and Chapter 11 bankruptcies can be entered into voluntarily or involuntarily. A Chapter 13 (for adjustment of the debts of an individual) bankruptcy and a Chapter 12 (family farmer) bankruptcy can be initiated only by a voluntary petition. Most experts believe that involuntary bankruptcies should rarely occur. Indeed, it is only when a debtor is completely uncooperative that creditors may wish to use involuntary bankruptcy as a last resort.

Remember that even when a petition for involuntary bankruptcy has been filed against you, as a debtor you may continue to use, acquire, and dispose of your property until the moment that the court orders otherwise. Creditors will often convince the court to appoint a temporary trustee to prevent you, the debtor, from disposing of your property nonetheless. As a debtor, you can oppose any involuntary bankruptcy petition by filing an answer. If you prevail, the petitioning creditors must pay you for legal expenses and reasonable attorneys' fees. And in cases where a petitioning creditor was found to have acted in bad faith, that creditor can be ordered by the court to pay damages to you.

Most debtors, particularly owners of businesses, know about their financial troubles well before creditors need to force the debtor into bankruptcy. As an owner of a business, it would be up to you to analyze your financial position and ask yourself some questions when considering which chapter in bankruptcy is preferable and deciding whether there is no other solution to your financial problems.

For example, if you are relieved of some of your debts, could you continue making a business profit in the future, or would your financial troubles continue? If you believe that your business could operate at a profit by reorganizing, readjusting, and eliminating some debts,

you probably would want to voluntarily ask for relief under Chapter 11, Chapter 12, or Chapter 13. These chapters will allow you to continue to stay in business, with some relief from the claims of your creditors.

Alternatively, if you realize that even with debt elimination your financial problems will not be resolved, perhaps because of changing markets and economic conditions, you may wish to voluntarily file a Chapter 7 petition and liquidate your business. If so, you have the choice of when to liquidate, rather than having it forced upon you. Later you will have a "fresh start" in pursuing another business venture if you so choose.

In many cases, particularly with small businesses, the individual has become personally liable for many if not all of the debts of the business. As an insolvent debtor, you still may be able to use state and federal exemptions to shelter many of your personal assets from creditor claims in bankruptcy. Assuming no fraud on creditors exists, there are legal means to exchange nonexempt assets for exempt assets before you voluntarily or involuntarily go into bankruptcy. For example, a number of states have homestead exemptions. In Florida and Texas, the equity that you have in your personal residence is normally untouchable by creditors in a bankruptcy proceeding. That means that prior to bankruptcy, you may wish to make relatively expensive improvements to your home (but not buy expensive furniture, which may not be exempt).

Checklist for Bankruptcy

☐ 1.   Don't wait until you are forced into bankruptcy; plan ahead, and if it is inevitable, do it voluntarily.

☐ 2.   Consult with a bankruptcy attorney to see how you may exchange nonexempt assets for exempt assets in a legal manner that will not be disallowed during bankruptcy court proceedings.

❖ Chapter Summary: Creditors' Rights and Bankruptcy

REMEDIES AVAILABLE TO CREDITORS	
Mechanic's Lien	A nonpossessory, filed lien on an owner's real estate for labor, services, or materials furnished to or made on the realty.
Artisan's Lien/ Innkeeper's Lien	A possessory lien on an owner's personal property for labor performed, value added, or care of said personal property that was not paid for.
Writ of Execution	In cases of unsatisfied judgments, a court order directing the sheriff to seize and sell sufficient nonexempt property of the judgment debtor to satisfy the judgment.
Attachment	A court-ordered seizure of property (generally prior to full resolution of the creditor's rights resulting in judgment). Attachment is available only upon posting bond and in strict compliance with the applicable state statutes.
Garnishment	A collection remedy that allows the creditor to attach a debtor's money (such as wages owed or bank accounts) and property that is held by a third person.
Suretyship or Guaranty	Under contract, a third person agrees to be primarily or secondarily liable for the debt owed by the principal debtor. A creditor can turn to this third person for satisfaction of the debt.
Secured Transaction UCC Article 9	Upon the debtor's default, a secured party has the right to repossess collateral subject to the secured party's security interest and either keep or sell the collateral to satisfy the debt.
Mortgage Foreclosure	Upon the debtor's default, the entire mortgage debt is due and payable, allowing the creditor to foreclose on the realty by selling it or taking title to it to satisfy the debt.
Creditors' Composition Agreement	A contract between a debtor and his or her creditors whereby the debtor's debts are discharged by payment of a sum less than that owed in the original debt.
Fraudulent Conveyance (Express or Implied)	If a conveyance is fraudulent, the creditor may set aside the transfer to a third party and proceed against the property conveyed.
LAWS ASSISTING DEBTORS	
Exemption Laws	State laws exempting certain types of real and personal property from levy of execution or attachment. 1. *Real property:* Each state permits a debtor to retain the family home, either in its entirety or up to a specified dollar amount, free from the claims of unsecured creditors or trustees in bankruptcy (homestead exemption). 2. *Personal property:* Personal property that is most often exempt from satisfaction of judgment debts includes: a. Household furniture up to a specified dollar amount. b. Clothing and certain personal possessions. c. Transportation vehicles up to a specified dollar amount. d. Certain classified animals, such as livestock and pets.
Consumer Credit Protection Act (CCPA) (Truth-in-Lending Act)	A disclosure law, administered by the Federal Reserve Board, requiring sellers and lenders to disclose credit terms on loans, including the total annual percentage rate of interest and finance charges.
Uniform Consumer Credit Code (UCCC)	The essential points of the UCCC are: 1. To place statutory ceilings on interest rates and other charges. 2. To require disclosure similar to that required by the truth-in-lending law. 3. To limit garnishment actions against take-home wages to a certain amount and to prohibit discharge of an employee solely because of a single garnishment proceeding. 4. To allow cancellation of a contract solicited by a seller in the consumer-debtor's home within three business days of the solicitation.

❖ Chapter Summary: Creditors' Rights and Bankruptcy—Continued

Uniform Consumer Credit Code (UCCC) (Continued)	5. To limit the holder-in-due-course (HDC) concept to the acceptance of a check, rather than any other type of negotiable instrument, from the consumer-debtor. 6. To prohibit referral sales. 7. To provide criminal as well as civil penalties for violations.
FTC Rule Limiting the Rights of an HDC	A rule limiting the rights of an HDC where the debtor-buyer executes a negotiable promissory note as part of a consumer transaction. The rule provides that any personal defenses the buyer could assert against the seller can also be asserted against an HDC who has purchased the buyer's note from the seller. The seller must disclose this rule clearly on the sales agreement.

BANKRUPTCY—A COMPARISON OF CHAPTERS 7, 11, 12, AND 13

Issues	Chapter 7	Chapter 11	Chapters 12 and 13
Purpose	Liquidation.	Reorganization.	Adjustment.
Who Can Petition	Debtor voluntary or creditors involuntary.	Debtor voluntary or creditors involuntary.	Debtor voluntary only.
Who Can Be a Debtor	Any "person" (including partnerships and corporations) except railroads, insurance companies, banks, savings and loan institutions, and credit unions. Farmers and charitable institutions cannot be involuntarily petitioned.	Any debtor eligible for Chapter 7 relief, except that railroads are also eligible.	*Chapter 12*—Any family farmer whose gross income is at least 50 percent farm-dependent and whose debts are at least 80 percent farm-related, or any partnership or closely held corporation at least 50 percent owned by a farm family, where total debt does not exceed $1,500,000. *Chapter 13*—Any individual (not partnerships or corporations) with regular income who owes noncontingent, liquidated, unsecured debt of less than $100,000 and secured debt of less than $350,000.
Procedure Leading to Discharge	Nonexempt property sold with proceeds to be distributed (in order) to priority groups. Dischargeable debts are terminated.	Plan is submitted and, if approved, debts are discharged if plan is followed.	Plan is submitted (must be approved if debtor turns over disposable income for three-year period), and upon approval, all debts are discharged if plan is followed.
Advantages	Upon liquidation and distribution, most debts are discharged, and debtor has opportunity for fresh start.	Debtor continues in business, and creditors can either accept plan, or it can be "crammed down" on them. Plan allows for reorganization and liquidation of debts over plan period.	Debtor continues in business or possession of assets. If plan is approved, most debts are discharged after a three-year pay-out period.

❖ Questions and Case Problems

20-1. Jeannie takes her car to Bob's Auto Shop for repairs. A sign in the window states that all repairs must be paid for in cash unless credit is approved in advance. Jeannie and Bob agree that Bob will repair Jeannie's car engine and put in a new transmission. No mention is made of credit. Because Bob is not sure how much engine repair will be necessary, he refuses to give Jeannie an estimate. He repairs the engine and puts in a new transmission. When Jeannie comes to pick up her car, she learns that the bill is $895. Jeannie is furious, refuses to pay Bob that amount, and demands possession of her car. Bob demands payment. Discuss the rights of the parties in this matter.

20-2. Meredith, a farmer, borrowed $5,000 from Farmer's Bank and gave the bank $4,000 in bearer bonds to hold as collateral for the loan. Meredith's neighbor, Peterson, who had known Meredith for years, signed as surety on the note. Due to a drought, Meredith's harvest that year was only a fraction of what it normally was, and he was forced to default on his payments to Farmer's Bank. The bank did not immediately sell the bonds but instead requested $5,000 from Peterson. Peterson paid the $5,000 and then demanded that the bank give him the $4,000 in securities. Can Peterson enforce this demand? Explain.

20-3. Sabrina is a student at Sunnyside University. In need of funds to pay tuition and books, she attempts to secure a short-term loan from University Bank. The bank agrees to make a loan if Sabrina will have someone financially responsible guarantee the loan payments. Abigail, a well-known businessperson and a friend of Sabrina's family, calls the bank and agrees to pay the loan if Sabrina cannot. Because of Abigail's reputation, the loan is made. Sabrina makes several payments on the loan, but because of illness she is not able to work for one month. She requests that University Bank extend the loan for three months. The bank agrees, raising the interest rate for the extended period. Abigail has not been notified of the extension (and therefore has not consented to it). One month later, Sabrina drops out of school. All attempts to collect from Sabrina have failed. University Bank wants to hold Abigail liable. Will the bank succeed? Explain.

20-4. Delmondo is a retail seller of television sets. He sells Maria a $900 set under a retail installment-loan agreement in which she pays $100 down and agrees to pay the balance in equal installments. Delmondo retains a security interest in the set sold, and he perfects that security interest by filing a financing statement locally. Two months later Maria is in default on her payments to Delmondo and is involuntarily petitioned into bankruptcy by her creditors. Delmondo wants to repossess the television set as provided for in the security agreement, and he wants to have priority over the trustee in bankruptcy to any proceeds from the disposal of the set. Discuss fully Delmondo's right to repossess the set and whether he has priority over the trustee in bankruptcy to any proceeds from disposal of the set.

20-5. Runyan petitions himself into voluntary bankruptcy. He has three major claims against his estate. One is by Calvin, a friend who holds Runyan's negotiable promissory note for $2,500; one is by Ellis, an employee who is owed three months' back wages of $4,500; and one is by the First Bank of Sunny Acres on an unsecured loan of $5,000. In addition, Martinez, an accountant retained by the trustee, is owed $500, and property taxes of $1,000 are owed to Micanopa County. If Runyan's nonexempt property has been liquidated, with the proceeds totaling $5,000, what amount will be received by the First Bank of Sunny Acres? Explain.

20-6. On July 6, 1982, Henry Wilson filed a voluntary petition for Chapter 7 bankruptcy. In October of that year, one of Wilson's creditors, John Milam, filed a complaint with the bankruptcy court objecting to the discharge of a debt owed to him by Wilson. The debt was incurred in 1978 when Wilson had purchased Milam's accounting practice. Wilson made a down payment, and under the terms of their written agreement Wilson was obligated to make monthly payments to Milam until the balance of the debt was paid. When Wilson failed to make the June 1978 payment, Milam brought suit against Wilson and, as a result of the suit, was awarded a judgment against Wilson in the amount of $57,569. This was one of the debts that Wilson sought to discharge in bankruptcy. Milam contended that the debt should not be discharged, because Wilson failed to keep adequate records on the accounting business from which the financial condition of the business could be ascertained. Wilson admitted that the only business record he maintained for the account practice for 1980, 1981, and 1982 was a single checking account from which both business and personal expenses were paid. Was Wilson's debt to Milam discharged by the bankruptcy court? Explain. [Matter of Wilson, 33 B.R. 689 (Bkrtcy.M.D.Ga. 1983)]

20-7. In 1974 Gonzales defaulted on a student loan that had been assigned to the Commerce Bank of Kansas City, Missouri (Commerce). In 1976, the United States (U.S.) repaid the note under a federal program of student loan insurance. Approximately five years later, the U.S. filed suit in district court for recovery from Gonzales. On guarantees of student loans, there is a six-year statute of limitations from the date the action accrues. Gonzales claimed the U.S. was a mere assignee of Commerce and that the statute of limitations on the defaulted debt barred the action against him. The U.S. argued that it was a guarantor and that the statute began to run on the date of its repayment to Commerce of the loan. Discuss fully whether the U.S. is an assignee or a guarantor in this case. [United States v. Gonzales, 541 F.Supp. 783 (D.Kan.1982)].

20-8. A. J. Kellos Construction Company was the general contractor for the construction of a building in Georgia. Kellos entered into a subcontract with Roofing Specialists, Inc., for the construction of the roof of this project. A performance bond was executed by Balboa Insurance Company in favor of

Kellos that Roofing Specialists would faithfully perform its contract. A performance bond is a type of contract bond that protects against loss due to the inability or refusal of a contractor to perform his contract. Such bonds are often required on public construction projects. When the roofing was condemned by the state architect, Kellos sued Balboa on the bond for damages resulting from the subcontractor's default on the contract. Was the bond executed by Balboa in favor of Kellos a contract of liability insurance or a suretyship? [A. J. Kellos Const. Co., Inc. v. Balboa Ins. Co., 495 F.Supp. 408 (S.D.Ga. 1980)]

20-9. Tracey Service Company, Inc., filed a petition for a Chapter 11 reorganization. Acar Supply Company, one of Tracey's creditors, filed a motion to convert the case to a Chapter 7 liquidation. The court found that the debtor corporation had no place of business, no inventory, no equipment, no employees, and no business phone. Was Tracey Service permitted to reorganize under Chapter 11? [In re Tracey Service Co., Inc., 17 B.R. 405 (Bkrtcy.E.D.Pa. 1982)]

Unit Four

Business Organizations

❖ Why We Study Business Organizations

Every business activity involves—implicitly or explicitly—a form of business organization, whether it be a sole proprietorship, a partnership, a corporation, or some hybrid form. Each form provides different degrees of flexibility and different rights and liabilities, and it is important to be aware of these differences when choosing and structuring one's business organization.

This unit begins with Chapter 21 introducing the various forms of business organization available to entrepreneurs (those who risk going into business for themselves). The law of agency, which governs relationships that exist within partnerships and corporations, is then discussed in Chapter 22. An agent is a person authorized by another (the principal) to act for him or her, and the law of agency applies to that relationship. A description of the formation and operation of partnerships, including limited partnerships, is offered in Chapters 23 and 24, and Chapters 25 through 29 deal with corporations, including the financial regulation of corporations in the United States.

The goal of this unit is to provide a fundamental understanding of those laws that affect the most important entities existing in the United States. The corporation is emphasized because the modern corporation is perhaps the most important form of business organization in the history of the world. Some even argue that without it, the tremendous economic growth of the western world in the past several centuries would have been impossible.

Chapter 21

The Entrepreneur's Options

Every **entrepreneur** needs to decide what would be the best form of business organization for his or her business endeavor. In this chapter, we will examine the features of sole proprietorships, partnerships, corporations, and private franchises. We will also touch on joint ventures, syndicates, joint stock companies, business trusts, and cooperatives.

"Entrepreneur: A person who organizes, operates, and assumes the risk for business ventures."

The American Heritage Dictionary

ENTREPRENEUR
One who initiates and assumes the financial risks of a new enterprise and one who undertakes to provide or control its management.

❖ Types of Business Organizations

Sole Proprietorship

The simplest form of business is a *sole proprietorship*. In this form, the owner is the business; thus, anyone who does business without creating an organization has a sole proprietorship. The advantages and disadvantages of a sole proprietorship are discussed later in this chapter; but for now suffice it to say that such enterprises are often, though not always, small, and the owner's personal estate is liable for all business debts.

Partnership

A *partnership* arises from an agreement, express or implied, between two or more persons to carry on a business for profit. Partners are co-owners of a business and have joint control over its operation and the right to share in its profits. No particular form of partnership agreement is necessary for its creation, although it is desirable that it be in writing. Both partnerships and sole proprietorships are creatures of common law rather than of statute, although the Uniform Partnership Act (UPA), adopted in forty-eight states,[1] governs the operation of partnerships in the absence of express agreements. Basically, the partners may agree to almost any terms when establishing the partnership so long as they are not illegal or contrary to public policy.

---

1. Only the states of Louisiana and Georgia have not adopted the UPA. Guam, the District of Columbia, and the Virgin Islands have adopted it. See Appendix C for its complete text.

The UPA comes into play only if the partners have neglected to include a necessary term. In a sense, then, the UPA is a gap-filler rather than a code that must be followed in order to create the legal entity called a partnership.

Moreover, a partnership is a legal entity only for limited purposes such as the partnership name and title of ownership and property. The personal net worth of the partners is subject to partnership obligations, and the partnership itself is not subject to levy for federal income taxes, although an information return must be filed. A partner's profit from the partnership (whether or not distributed) is taxed as individual income to the individual partner.

Limited Partnership

A special and quite popular form of partnership is the *limited partnership*, which consists of at least one general partner and one or more limited partners. One of the major benefits of becoming a limited partner is limited liability, both with respect to lawsuits brought against the partnership and money at risk. The maximum money at risk is defined by the limited partnership agreement, which specifically states how much each limited partner must contribute to the partnership.

The limited partnership is created by an agreement; but, unlike a general partnership, the limited partnership does not come into existence until a certificate of partnership is filed appropriately in a state. Furthermore, unlike a general partnership, a limited partnership is completely a creature of statute. If the statute is not followed almost to the letter, the courts will hold that a general partnership exists instead. Then those who thought their liability was limited by their investment in a limited partnership will be held generally liable to the full extent of their personal net worth.

All states permit limited partnerships. Twenty-seven states have adopted the Uniform Limited Partnership Act (ULPA), and twenty-two have adopted its revision, the Revised Uniform Limited Partnership (RULPA). This act and its revision govern the organization and operation of limited partnerships.

Corporation

The most important form of business organization is the *corporation*. A corporation comes into existence by an act of the state, and therefore it is a legal entity. It typically has perpetual existence. One of the key features of a corporation is that the liability of its owners is limited to their investments. Their personal estates are usually not liable for the obligations of the corporation.

Corporations consist of shareholders, who are the owners of the business. A board of directors, elected by the shareholders, manages the business. The board of directors normally employs officers to oversee day-to-day operations.

Joint Venture

When two or more persons or entities combine their interests in a particular business enterprise and agree to share in losses or profits jointly or in proportion to their contributions, they are engaged in a *joint venture*. The joint venture is treated much like a partnership, but it differs in that its creation is in contemplation of a limited activity or a single transaction.

Profile

Steven Jobs (1955–   )

Economists, sociologists, psychologists, and others have long pondered the question of just what combination of characteristics makes a successful entrepreneur. Willingness to take risks is certainly one characteristic. Personal ambition, a desire to succeed, the wish for status or riches, business acumen, and talent are obviously others. And an element of luck is often present. Whatever the formula, Steven Jobs—the history-making entrepreneur of the computer industry—obviously possesses the correct, if elusive, combination. Although his role in designing the Apple computer was minimal, it was Job's entrepreneurial abilities that developed the Apple computer firm—first formed in 1975 and housed in the bedroom and garage of Jobs's parents' house—into a $200 million business by 1980, the

year the firm sold shares of common stock to the public.

Both Steven Jobs and Stephen Wozniak, the co-founder of Apple Computers, were sons of the high-tech culture of California's Silicon Valley. Jobs and Wozniak became friends while attending Homestead High School in Los Altos and became kindred spirits in their attachment to electronic gadgetry. After graduating from high school, Jobs attended Reed College in Portland, Oregon, for two years, while Wozniak studied at Berkeley. By 1974 they had both returned to the Bay Area. Jobs took a job as a designer for Atari—then a small firm of ten employees—and Wozniak was employed by Hewlett-Packard. Wozniak spent his off hours designing a computer. By 1976 he had succeeded in designing the prototype of what was to become the Apple computer—a computer smaller than a portable typewriter but capable of the feats of much larger computers. For Wozniak the computer was a fascinating plaything. Jobs, though, saw its commercial potential as a computer for small businesses and home use. Jobs persuaded Wozniak to leave Hewlett-Packard and start a business together with him.

The new business was a from-scratch operation in the first stages. Jobs sold his VW microbus, and Wozniak contributed the proceeds from the sale of his Hewlett-Packard scientific calculator. Together, they raised $1,300. The name "Apple" was contributed by Jobs, who had once spent a pleasant summer in the Oregon apple orchards and enjoyed recalling the experience.

Although Wozniak had designed

the computer, it was Jobs who created the business. He succeeded in convincing Regis McKenna, the foremost public-relations specialist in the area, to take on Apple as a client. Through his connections with Atari, Jobs was able to interest A. C. Markkula, a marketing agent formerly with Intel, a computer-chip manufacturer, in the potential of the new computer business. Markkula was impressed sufficiently to invest $250,000 in the undertaking and became an equal partner in the firm. Markkula helped arrange for a line of credit with the Bank of America and persuaded others to invest in Apple. The rest is history. Within a year, sales had reached $2.7 million. By 1980, as mentioned earlier, they had soared to $200 million. By 1984 Jobs was predicting $40 billion in sales by the end of the decade.

By the age of thirty, in 1985, Jobs had attained stardom in the computer world and success in a measure few even dream of. Disagreements with others at Apple resulted in his departure from that firm in 1985. His entrepreneurial talents are still being exercised, however, in the establishment of a new business for the purpose of creating and marketing another computer. The new firm, called NeXT, had thirty-five other employees in 1987 and is housed in an attractive, two-story building in Palo Alto, California. According to Jobs, the NeXT computer is designed with the needs of the scientific community in mind and will have ten times the computing capacity of the Apple Macintosh. Given the past feats of this entrepreneur, one can only wonder what will be next—after NeXT.

Landmark in the Law

The Small Business Administration

Public policy in the United States has long favored the small business enterprise and healthy competition among businesses for profits. In today's world, however, the handicaps faced by small firms are sometimes too enormous to overcome. Lack of sufficient management skills and lack of financial depth ("deep purses") are two of the greatest causes of small business failure. In addition, the lower per-unit costs of production often obtainable by large corporate enterprises, due to more efficient production facilities, are not available to small businesses, placing them at a competitive disadvantage.

In the interests of protecting small business, Congress passed the Small Business Act of 1953, which created the Small Business Administration (SBA). The primary aims of the SBA are given in the U. S. Government Manual:

> The fundamental purposes of the Small Business Administration . . . are to aid, counsel, assist, and protect the interests of small business; ensure that small business concerns receive a fair portion of Government purchases, contracts and subcontracts, as well as of the sales of Government

property; make loans to small business concerns, State and local development companies, and the victims of floods or other catastrophes, or of certain types of economic injury; and license, regulate, and make loans to small business investment companies.

The SBA also derives its authority from the Small Business Investment Act of 1958 and other legislation that has delegated certain functions to the SBA. Since 1976 farming enterprises have been included in the category of "small business concerns."

The SBA assists small business firms in a variety of ways. Generally its activities fall into the following four categories: [1]

Financial Assistance

The SBA occasionally loans money directly to those entering small business ventures in order to help them finance equipment, plant construction, supplies, and other essentials. More typically, the SBA guarantees loans offered by commercial banks to small businesses. The SBA also lends assistance to those wishing to expand existing small business enterprises. In the event of a natural dis-

1.   Details of these and other SBA programs can be obtained from the Office of Public Affairs, Small Business Administration, 1441 L St., N.W., Washington, D.C. 20416 [(202) 653-6832].

For example, Abel and Cain pool their resources to buy an old boat, remodel it, and sell it, dividing the profits. This creates not a partnership but a joint venture. The same is true if Abel, owning a piece of land, and Cain, owning an adjoining piece of land, agree to sell both parcels together as one unit to the highest bidder and then divide the proceeds proportionately to the value of each parcel of land held.

Members of a joint venture usually have limited powers to bind their co-venturers. A joint venture is normally not a legal entity and therefore cannot be sued as such, but its members can be sued individually. Usually joint ventures are taxed like partnerships. They range in size from very small activities to huge, multimillion-dollar joint actions engaged in by some of the world's largest corporations.

Syndicate

A group of individuals getting together to finance a particular project, such as the building of a shopping center or the purchase of a professional basketball franchise, is called a *syndicate* or an *investment group*. The form of such groups varies considerably. They may exist as corporations or as general or limited partnerships. In some cases, the members merely own property jointly and have no legally recognized business arrangement.

aster, such as a flood or other catastrophe, loans are provided to help small business firms that have been damaged substantially by the disaster.

In addition to this direct and indirect financial assistance, the SBA also licenses, regulates and financially assists small business investment companies, whose purpose is to provide venture capital to small business concerns. The SBA also aids small businesses in obtaining long-term financing of pollution-control equipment.

Procurement Assistance

The SBA works closely with the purchasing agencies of the U. S. Government and sets aside appropriate purchases for competitive bidding by small business firms. It also develops subcontract opportunities for small businesses through major contractors. Through its Procurement Automated Source System (PASS), the SBA makes available a master list of the names and addresses of small firms capable of performing work on federal contracts and subcontracts. This computerized list is used by federal procurement officials in awarding contract and subcontract work to small businesses. Any small business wishing to participate in PASS can obtain appropriate forms at any regional or local SBA office.

Minority Assistance

The SBA has numerous programs that have been established to create opportunities for minority groups. It is authorized to make special loans to handicapped individuals and to nonprofit organizations employing handicapped people in the production of goods or services. It also assures that women are given equal access to the small business opportunities it offers in the areas of financial assistance and procurement contracts. The SBA lends management and financial assistance to small businesses owned, or majority-controlled, by veterans, and it attempts to coordinate its efforts with existing state and local veterans' programs that have been established for the benefit of veterans.

Information and Advocacy Services

The SBA also acts as an information service center for small businesses by means of conferences, informational booklets, and special courses offered to small business representatives.

The Office of Advocacy is the lobbying arm of the SBA and represents small business interests at national, state, and local levels. This office does research on matters affecting small businesses, including the effects of federal laws and programs.

Joint Stock Company

A *joint stock company* or *association* is a true hybrid of a partnership and a corporation. It has many characteristics of a corporation in that (1) its ownership is represented by transferable shares of stock, (2) it is usually managed by directors and officers of the company or association, and (3) it can have a perpetual existence. Most of its other features, however, are more characteristic of a partnership, and it is usually treated like a partnership. As with a partnership, it is formed by agreement (not statute), property is usually held in the names of the members, shareholders have personal liability, and generally the company is not treated as a legal entity for purposes of a lawsuit. In a joint stock company, however, shareholders are not considered to be agents of each other, as would be the case if the company were a true partnership.

Business Trust

A *business trust* is created by a written trust agreement that sets forth the interests of the beneficiaries and the obligations and powers of the trustees. With a business trust, legal ownership and management of the property of the business stay with one or more of the trustees, and the profits are distributed to the beneficiaries.

The business trust was started in Massachusetts in an attempt to obtain the limited-liability advantage of corporate status while avoiding certain restrictions on a corporation's ownership and development of real property. The business trust resembles a corporation in many respects. Death or bankruptcy of a beneficiary, for example, does not terminate the trust, and beneficiaries are not personally responsible for the debts or obligations of the business trust. In fact, in a number of states business trusts must pay corporate taxes.

Cooperative

A *cooperative* is an association, either incorporated or not, that is organized to provide an economic service without profit to its members (or shareholders). An incorporated cooperative is subject to state laws governing nonprofit corporations. It will make distributions of dividends, or profits, to its owners on the basis of their transactions with the cooperative rather than on the basis of the amount of capital they contributed.

Cooperatives that are unincorporated are often treated like partnerships. The members have joint liability for the cooperative's acts. This form of business is generally adopted by groups of individuals who wish to pool their resources in order to gain some advantage in the marketplace. Consumer purchasing co-ops are formed to obtain lower prices through quantity discounts. Seller marketing co-ops are formed to control the market and thereby obtain higher sale prices from consumers. Often cooperatives are exempt from certain federal laws—for example, antitrust statutes—because of their special status.

❖ Sole Proprietorships— Advantages and Disadvantages

"Small business is more than a form of business activity; it is a veritable way of life."

Rudolph L. Weissman, 1900– *(American financial editor and writer)*

A major advantage of the sole proprietorship is that the proprietor receives all the profits (because he or she takes all the risk). In addition, it is often easier and less costly to start a sole proprietorship than to start any other kind of business. Few legal forms must be completed, and since the proprietor makes all the decisions, the problem of reaching agreement among all the people involved is avoided. The sole proprietor is also free from corporate income taxes, paying only personal income taxes on profits. These taxes are not necessarily lower than those for a corporation, however.

A major disadvantage of the sole proprietorship is that, as sole owner, the proprietor alone bears the risk of losses. In addition, the proprietor's opportunity to raise capital is limited to personal funds and the funds of those who are willing to make loans. Also, the sole proprietorship has the disadvantage of lacking continuity of business upon the death of the proprietor. Generally, when the owner dies, the business ceases to survive. Additionally, and perhaps more importantly for many potential entrepreneurs, the sole proprietor has unlimited liability, or legal responsibility, for all obligations incurred in doing business.

❖ Partnerships and Corporations—A Comparison

Exhibit 21-1 is an abbreviated comparison between a partnership and a corporation, giving the essential advantages and disadvantages of each. Other points of comparison concern the liability of owners, tax considerations, and the need for capital.

◆ **Exhibit 21-1 Partnerships and Corporations—A Comparison**

CHARACTERISTIC	PARTNERSHIP	CORPORATION
1. Method of Creation	Created by agreement of the parties.	Charter issued by state—created by statutory authorization.
2. Legal Position	Not a separate legal entity in many states.	Always a legal entity separate and distinct from its owners—a legal fiction for the purposes of owning property and being a party to litigation.
3. Liability	Unlimited liability (except for limited partners in a limited partnership).	Limited liability of shareholders—shareholders are not liable for the debts of the corporation.
4. Duration	Terminated by agreement of the partners, by the death of one or more of the partners, by withdrawal of a partner, by bankruptcy, etc.	Can have perpetual existence.
5. Transferability of Interest	Although partnership interest can be assigned, assignee does not have full rights of a partner.	Shares of stock can be transferred.
6. Management	Each general partner has a direct and equal voice in management unless expressly agreed otherwise in the partnership agreement. (Limited partner has no rights in management in a limited partnership.)	Shareholders elect directors who set policy and appoint officers.
7. Taxation	Each partner pays pro rata share of income taxes on net profits, whether or not they are distributed.	Double taxation—corporation pays income tax on net profits, with no deduction for dividends, and shareholders pay income tax on disbursed dividends they receive.
8. Organizational Fees, Annual License Fees, and Annual Reports	None.	All required.
9. Transaction of Business in Other States	Generally no limitation.[a]	Normally must qualify to do business and obtain certificate of authority.

[a]A few states have enacted statutes requiring that foreign partnerships qualify to do business there—for example, 3 N.H.Rev.Stat.Ann. Chapter 305-A in New Hampshire.

Liability of Owners

The form of the organization does not always in and of itself determine the liability of the owners. Generally, sole proprietorships and general partners have personal liability, while the liability of limited partners and shareholders of corporations is limited to their investment. The issue of liability is an important one for creditors in deciding whether to extend credit to a business. For example, a bank may be unwilling to lend money to a corporation that is relatively small and has only a few shareholders.

Just because the business is a corporation does not guarantee that it is a better credit risk than, say, a sole proprietor. Typically, in corporations with relatively few shareholders, the shareholders must personally sign for any loans made to the corporation. That is, the shareholders agree to become personally liable for the loan if the corporation goes under or cannot meet its debts. In essence, the shareholders become guarantors for the corporation's debt. Hence, the corporate form of business does not prevent them from having personal liability in such a case, because they have assumed the liability voluntarily.

Tax Considerations

Various tax considerations must be taken into account when one compares a partnership with a corporation. These considerations are listed in Exhibit 21-2.

◆ **Exhibit 21-2 Tax Aspects of Partnerships and Corporations**

TAX ASPECT	PARTNERSHIP	CORPORATION
1. Federal Income Tax	Partner is taxed on proportionate share of partnership income, even if not distributed; the partnership files information returns only.	Income of the corporation is taxed; stockholders are also taxed on distributed dividends. Must file corporate income tax forms.
2. Accumulation	Partners taxed on accumulated as well as distributed earnings.	Corporate stockholders not taxed on accumulated earnings. There is, however, a penalty tax, in some instances, that the corporation must pay for unreasonable accumulations of income.
3. Capital Gains	All partners taxed on their proportionate share of capital gains which are taxed at ordinary income rate.	Corporation taxed on capital gains and losses.
4. Exempt Interest	Partners are not taxed on exempt interest received from the firm.	Any exempt interest distributed by a corporation is fully taxable income to the stockholders. Exempt interest can come, for example, from municipal bonds.
5. Pension Plan	Partners can adopt a Keogh Plan, an IRA, or a 401-K Plan.	Employees and officers who are also stockholders can be beneficiaries of a pension trust. The corporation can deduct its payments to the trust.
6. Social Security	Partners must pay a self-employment tax (13.3 percent by 1990).	All compensation to officers and employee stockholders subject to social security taxation up to the maximum.
7. Death Benefits (excluding those provided by insurance)	There is no exemption for payments to partners' beneficiaries.	Benefits up to $5,000 can be received tax-free by employees' beneficiaries.
8. State Taxes	The partnership is not subject to taxes. State income taxes are paid by each partner.	The corporation is subject to state income taxes (although these taxes can be deducted on federal returns).

Need for Capital

One of the most common reasons for changing from a sole proprietorship to a partnership or a corporation is the need for additional capital to finance expansion. A sole proprietor can seek partners who will bring capital with them. The partnership might be able to secure more funds from potential lenders than could the sole proprietor. But when a firm wants to expand greatly, simply increasing the number of partners can lead to too many partners and make it difficult for the firm to operate effectively. Therefore, incorporation might be the best choice for an expanding business organization. There are many possibilities for obtaining more capital by issuing shares of stock. The original owners will find that, although their proportion of the company is reduced, they are able to expand much more rapidly by selling shares in the company.

❖ Private Franchises

About 25 percent of all retail sales and an increasing part of the gross national product of the United States are generated by private franchises. A **franchise** is any arrangement in which the owner of a trademark, a trade name, or a copyright has licensed others to use the trademark, trade name, or copyright in selling goods or services. As a **franchisee** (a purchaser of a franchise), you are generally legally independent, but economically dependent on the integrated business system of the **franchisor** (the seller of the franchise). In other words, you can operate as an independent businessperson but still obtain the advantages of a regional or national organization. Well-known franchises are Hilton Hotels, McDonald's, Kentucky Fried Chicken, and Burger King.

FRANCHISE
A written agreement whereby an owner of a trademark, trade name, or copyright licenses another to use that trademark, trade name, or copyright in selling goods and services.

FRANCHISEE
One receiving a license to use another's (the franchisor's) trademark, trade name, or copyright in the sale of goods and services.

FRANCHISOR
One licensing another (the franchisee) to use his or her trademark, trade name, or copyright in the sale of goods or services.

Types of Franchises

There are three types of franchises, which we now discuss.

1. *Distributorship.* Occurs when a manufacturing concern (franchisor) licenses a dealer (franchisee) to sell its product. Often, a distributorship covers an exclusive territory. An example of this type of franchise is an automobile dealership.

2. *Chain-style business operation.* Occurs when a franchise operates under a franchisor's trade name and is identified as a member of a select group of dealers that engages in the franchisor's business. The franchisee is generally required to follow standardized or prescribed methods of operations. Often, the franchisor requires that minimum prices and standards of operation be maintained. In addition, sometimes the franchisee is obligated to deal exclusively with the franchisor to obtain materials and supplies. An example of this type of franchise is McDonald's or most other fast-food chains.

3. *Manufacturing or processing-plant arrangement.* Occurs when the franchisor transmits to the franchisee the essential ingredients or formula to make a particular product. The franchisee then markets it either at wholesale or at retail in accordance with the franchisor's standards. Examples of this type of franchise are Coca-Cola and other soft-drink corporations.

McDonald's is an example of a chain-style business operation. Owners of these franchises are required to meet McDonald's high quality standards.

Franchise Agreement

The franchise relationship is defined by a contract between the franchisor and the franchisee. Each franchise relationship and each industry has its own characteristics, so it is difficult to describe the broad range of details a franchising contract may include. The following sections, however, will define the essential characteristics of the franchise relationship.

Entering the Franchise Relationship   Prospective franchisees must initially decide on the type of business they wish to undertake. Then they must obtain information about the business from the franchisor. Usually, franchisors have numerous statistics and market studies available for prospective franchisees to examine. Of course, people who acquire franchised businesses vary greatly in their degree of business acumen. Some are experienced business people with a firm grasp of the economic realities of how to operate a franchise. Others have no business experience. Obviously, the inexperienced franchisee must rely heavily on the franchisor in evaluating and setting up the initial business organization.

Paying for the Franchise   The franchisee ordinarily pays an initial fee or lump-sum price for the franchise license (the privilege of being granted a franchise). This fee is separate from the various products that the franchisee purchases from or through the franchisor. In some industries, the franchisor relies heavily on the initial sale of the franchise for realizing a profit. In other industries, the continued dealing between the parties brings profit to both.

In most situations, the franchisor will receive a stated percentage of the annual sales or annual volume of business done by the franchisee. The franchise agreement may also require the franchisee to pay a percentage of advertising costs and certain administrative expenses incurred under the franchise agreement.

Location and Business Organization of the Franchise   Typically, the franchisor will determine the territory to be served. The franchise agreement may specify whether the premises for the business must be leased or purchased outright. In some cases, construction of a building is necessary to meet the terms of the franchise agreement.

Certainly the agreement will specify whether the franchisor supplies equipment and furnishings for the premises or whether this is the responsibility of the franchisee. When the franchise is a service operation, such as a motel, the contract often provides that the franchisor will establish certain standards for the facility and will make inspections to ensure that the standards are being maintained in order to protect the franchise name and reputation.

The business organization of the franchisee is of great concern to the franchisor. Depending on the terms of the franchise agreement, the franchisor may specify particular requirements for the form and capital structure of the business. The franchise agreement can provide that standards of operation, such as sales quotas, quality standards, or record keeping, be conducted by the franchisor. Furthermore, a franchisor may wish to retain stringent control over the training of personnel involved in the operation and over administrative aspects of the business. Although the day-to-day operation of the franchise business is normally left up to the franchisee, the franchise agreement may provide for whatever amount of supervision and control the parties agree upon.

One area of franchises that causes a great deal of conflict is the territorial exclusivity of the franchise. Many franchise agreements, while they do define the territory allotted to a particular franchise, specifically state that the franchise is nonexclusive. The ramifications of nonexclusivity can be severe because it allows the franchisor to establish additional franchises in the same territory as the existing franchisee. This problem is illustrated by the following case.

Case 21.1
IMPERIAL MOTORS, INC. v. CHRYSLER CORPORATION

United States District Court, District of
Massachusetts, 1983.
559 F.Supp. 1312.

FACTS   In 1976 Imperial Motors, Inc., entered into direct dealer agreements for Chrysler and Plymouth dealerships with the Chrysler Corporation. The direct dealer agreements explicitly provided that Imperial would not have an exclusive dealership right for a four-town area of South Carolina. The Chrysler district manager orally assured Imperial, however, that Imperial's Chrysler-Plymouth dealership would be the only one in these four towns. In August of 1976 Chrysler allowed another Chrysler-Plymouth dealer, Carroll Motors, to move to a new showroom seven miles from Imperial's location. Imperial claimed that Chrysler, by approving the relocation of Carroll Motors, had violated the Automobile Dealers' Franchise Act of 1956. This federal statute gives to an auto dealer a federal cause of action against an automobile manufac-

turer who fails to act in good faith in complying with the terms and provisions of the franchise or in terminating the franchise. Chrysler moved in district court for summary judgment, claiming that the Automobile Dealers' Franchise Act covered written franchise agreements only.

ISSUE   Had Chrysler violated the Automobile Dealers' Franchise Act by disregarding its oral promise to Imperial?

DECISION   No. The court upheld Chrysler's motion for summary judgment and ruled that Chrysler, by allowing a franchise to Carroll in the same area, had not violated the Automobile Dealers' Franchise Act.

REASON   The court noted that the Automobile Dealers' Franchise Act covers only those actions of a franchisor that amounts to a "failure . . . to act in good faith in performing or complying with any of the terms or provisions of the franchise, or in terminating, cancelling, or not renewing the franchise with a dealer." Good faith is narrowly

Case 21.1—Continued

defined as "the duty of each party . . . to act in a fair and equitable manner toward each other so as to guaranty the other party freedom from coercion, intimidation, or threats of coercion or intimidation by the other party. . . . The failure to abide by the terms of a franchise agreement cannot by itself constitute a violation of the act." The court said the act explicitly defines a franchise as a "written agreement," and thus oral promises are not part of a franchise agreement and do not form the basis of a claim of bad faith. Thus, Imperial was left unprotected by the franchise agreement as far as territorial exclusivity was concerned.

COMMENTS The same denial of relief has been the result under the Unfair Trade Practices Act, when a Ford automobile dealer (with a nonexclusive franchise agreement) filed suit after Ford Motor Company granted another Ford dealership in close proximity to his own. [See McLaughlin Ford, Inc. v. Ford Motor Company, 192 Conn. 558, 473 A.2d 1185 (1984).]

Price and Quality Controls of the Franchise Franchises provide the franchisor with an outlet for the firm's goods and services. Depending upon the nature of the business, the franchisor may require the franchisee to purchase certain supplies from the franchisor at an established price.[2] Of course, a franchisor cannot set the prices at which the franchisee will resell the goods, as this is a violation of state or federal antitrust laws, or both. A franchisor can suggest retail prices but cannot insist on them.

As a general rule, the validity of a provision permitting the franchisor to enforce certain quality standards is unquestioned. Since the franchisor has a legitimate interest in maintaining the quality of the product or service in order to protect its name and reputation, it can exercise greater control in this area than would otherwise be tolerated.

Termination of the Franchise Arrangement The duration of the franchise is a matter to be determined between the parties. Generally, a franchise will start out for a short period, such as a year, so that the franchisee and the franchisor can determine whether they want to stay in business with one another. Usually the franchise agreement will specify that termination must be "for cause," such as death or disability of the franchisee, insolvency of the franchisee, breach of the franchise agreement, or failure to meet specified sales quotas. Most franchise contracts provide that notice of termination must be given. If no set time for termination is given, then a reasonable time with notice will be implied. A franchisee must be given reasonable time to wind up the business—that is, to do the accounting and return the copyright or trademark or any other property of the franchisor.

Much franchise litigation has arisen over termination provisions. Since the franchise agreement is normally a form contract drawn and prepared by the franchisor, and since the bargaining power of the franchisee is rarely equal to that of the franchisor, the termination provisions of contracts are generally more favorable to the franchisor. It is in this area that the lack of statutory law and case law is felt most

---

2. Although a franchisor can require franchisees to purchase supplies from it, requiring a franchisee to purchase exclusively from the franchisor may violate federal antitrust laws. For two landmark cases in these areas, see United States v. Arnold, Schwinn & Co., 388 U.S. 365, 87 S.Ct. 1856, 18 L.Ed.2d 1249 (1967), and Fortner Enterprises, Inc. v. U.S. Steel Corp., 394 U.S. 495, 89 S.Ct. 1252, 22 L.Ed.2d 495 (1969).

Business Law in Action

A Case of Disfranchisement

One of the major problems faced by franchisees arises when the franchisor decides to terminate the franchise arrangement. Typically, there is a wide disparity in the bargaining power of the two parties to the franchise contract, with the franchisor holding most of the bargaining chips. This situation is particularly characteristic of dealership franchises in the oil and gas industry, where the economic and legal power of a large oil company such as Shell or Amoco could easily be used to overwhelm an individual operating one of its service stations through a franchise agreement. A leading commentator in the area of franchise law wrote in 1971 that

> the major oil firms have the gasoline station dealers in virtual bondage, hinged on the constant threat that their short-term contracts will not be renewed unless they submit to burdensome franchisor-imposed practices. . . . It is generally conceded that the gasoline station situation is almost hopeless and offers a prime example of the worst abuses in franchising.[1]

Such franchising abuses led Congress to enact the Petroleum Marketing Practices Act (PMPA), which regulates the conditions and grounds for which a franchise relationship between franchisors and franchisees in the oil and gas industry can be terminated. The act requires that the franchisor give the franchisee

1. Roberts v. Amoco Oil Co., 740 F.2d 602 (8th Cir. 1984).

reasonable notice of nonrenewal of the contract, and it provides that a franchisor may sell a service station or otherwise withdraw from a market area so long as the determination is "made in good faith and in the normal course of business." If a franchisor decides to sell the station, however,

> in the case of leased marketing premises such franchisor, during the 90-day period after notification [of nonrenewal to the franchisee must] either (1) [have] made a bona fide offer to sell, transfer, or assign to the franchisee such franchisor's interest in such premises; or (2) if applicable, offered the franchisee a right of first refusal of at least 45 days duration of an offer, made by another, to purchase such franchisor's interest in such premises. [Section 2802(b)(3)(D)(iii)]

The PMPA thus addressed the disparity in bargaining power between franchisors and franchisees in this industry by establishing certain rights for the franchisee in cases where the franchisor wants to terminate the relationship. But people and business firms do circumvent the law on occasion (or try to), especially if they have the legal resources of a firm such as Amoco at their disposal—as Don Roberts of Des Moines, Iowa, learned first-hand.

Roberts had operated an Amoco station in Des Moines for fifteen years, leasing the premises under a franchise arrangement with Amoco. His last lease had been for five years, due to expire January 31, 1982. In late August of 1981 Amoco sent Roberts a letter notifying Roberts that Amoco was not going to renew the lease and that it intended to sell

the premises. Soon thereafter, Amoco sent Roberts the offer to sell him the premises—in accordance with PMPA requirements—for $66,500. But there was a catch: The offer specifically excluded "the gasoline pumps, dispensers, storage tanks, and piping or other equipment"—in short, the essence of the business.

Roberts vacated the premises on October 1, 1981, and brought suit against Amoco for violating the PMPA. Roberts alleged that Amoco had violated the PMPA's requirement that the franchisor make a "bona fide offer to sell" the leased premises to the franchisee. Amoco, Roberts argued, had not made a "bona fide" offer because the offer excluded equipment essential to the leased premises. The district court did not agree. Instead, it concluded that "nothing in the plaintiff's brief or the exhibits indicates that defendant's decision to sell the premises and not renew the lease was less than a good faith business decision." The court accepted Amoco's argument that the replacement cost of the pumps and tanks had been deducted from the selling price in the offer and granted Amoco's request for summary judgment.

"Trial courts search for truth, and appellate courts search for error"—so goes the anonymous saying. In this case, the appellate court found what it considered to be an error in the trial court's reading of the pertinent clause in the PMPA. In Section 2801(9) of the PMPA, the term "leased marketing premises" is defined as "marketing premises owned, leased, or in any way controlled by a franchisor and which the franchisee is authorized or

(continued on next page)

Business Law in Action—Continued

permitted, under the franchise, to employ in connection with the sale, consignment, or distribution of motor fuel." The appellate court felt the language of the act was quite clear and that it clearly applied to this case. "When Congress required a franchisor to make a bona fide offer to sell the leased marketing premises to its franchisee, Congress certainly intended the offer to include more than the real property. It explicitly required that the offer include the property controlled by the franchisor and used by the franchisee to distribute motor fuel. . . . We thus conclude that the district court erred in granting summary judgment for Amoco on Roberts' claim."

keenly by the franchisee. Automobile dealerships and gasoline stations subject to franchise contracts have some statutory protection, however (see Case 21.1 and the "Business Law in Action").

The franchisee normally invests a substantial amount of time and money in the franchise operation to make it successful. Despite this fact, the franchisee may receive little or nothing for the business upon termination. The franchisor owns the trademark and hence the business. The courts, however, have often struggled to offer a terminated franchisee some kind of relief.

Application

Law and the Franchisee

A franchise arrangement appeals to many prospective businesspersons who want independence, yet feel more comfortable with an established product or service and a management network that is regional or national in scope and that has been in place for some time. Franchise agreements and operations may, nonetheless, lead to difficulties, as well as financial loss to the actual or prospective franchisee.

Consider the franchise fee. Virtually all franchise contracts require a franchise fee payable up front or in installments. Some franchise arrangements hide franchise-fee payments as part of the price charged to the franchisee for goods or services that have to be purchased from the franchisor. In other words, if you as a franchisee are required to purchase paper napkins with a logo from the franchisor at a 20 percent premium over the bona fide wholesale price, then you are implicitly paying a franchise fee. Additionally, your required contribution to advertising monies administered by the franchisor may be in excess of your bona fide pro rata share. The difference again is an implicit franchise fee.

A major economic consequence, usually of a negative nature, will occur if your franchise agreement is terminated by the franchisor. The courts have not made a clear statement as to what a franchisee's rights are upon termination. Some courts, for example, have held that if a franchise investment is substantial and the relationship between the parties has been established, it cannot be terminated until after a reasonable period of time has elapsed. What is considered to be a reasonable time period depends on the circumstances in each case, such as the amount of preliminary promotional expenditures made, the length of time in operation, the prospects of forfeiting profits, and the actual profitability of the franchise during its operation.

In order to avoid many economic, as well as legal, problems, it is imperative that you as a potential franchisee, before paying for the franchise, obtain all of the relevant details of the business and of the franchise agreement.

Checklist for the Franchisee

1. Find out all you can about the franchisor: How long has the franchisor been in business? How profitable is the business? Is there a healthy market for the product?

2. Obtain the most recent financial statement from the franchisor and a complete description of the business.

3. Obtain a clear and complete statement of all fees that you will be required to pay.

4. Will the franchisor help you in training management and employees? With promotion and advertising? By supplying capital or credit? In finding a good location for your business?

5. Visit other franchisees in the same business. Ask them about their experiences with the product, the market, and the franchisor.

6. Evaluate your training and experience in the business you are about to embark upon. Are they sufficient to ensure success as a franchisee?

7. Carefully examine the franchise contract provisions relating to termination of the franchise agreement. Are they specific enough to allow you to sue for breach of contract in the event the franchisor wrongfully terminates the contract? Find out how many franchises have been terminated in the past several years.

8. Have an attorney familiar with franchise law examine the contract before you sign it.

9. Will you be required to open additional outlets according to a fixed schedule?

10. Will you have an exclusive geographical territory and, if so, for how many years?

11. Finally, what can the franchisor do for you that you cannot do for yourself?

❖ Chapter Summary: Forms of Business Organization

FORM	ESSENTIAL CHARACTERISTICS
Sole Proprietorship	1. The simplest form of business; used by anyone who does business without creating an organization. The owner is the business. 2. The owner pays personal income taxes on all profits. 3. The owner is personally liable for all business debts.
General Partnership	1. Created by agreement of the parties. 2. Not treated as an entity except for limited purposes. 3. Partners have unlimited liability for partnership debts. 4. Each partner has an equal voice in management, unless otherwise provided for in the partnership agreement. 5. Capital contribution of each partner is determined by agreement. 6. Each partner pays a pro rata share of income taxes on the net profits of the partnership, whether or not they are distributed; the partnership files an information return only. 7. Terminated by agreement, or can be dissolved by action of partner (withdrawal), operation of law (death or bankruptcy), or court decree.
Limited Partnership	1. Must be formed in compliance with statutory requirements. 2. Consists of one or more general partners, and one or more limited partners. 3. Only general partners can participate in management. Limited partners have no voice in management; if they do participate in management activities, they risk having general-partner liability. 4. General partners have unlimited liability for partnership losses; limited partners are liable only to the extent of their contribution.
Corporation	1. Created by state-issued charter. 2. A legal entity separate and distinct from its owners. 3. Shareholders have limited liability—that is, they are not personally liable for the debts of the corporation. 4. Shareholders elect directors who set policy and appoint officers to manage corporate affairs. 5. The corporation pays income tax on net profits; shareholders pay income tax on disbursed dividends (double taxation). 6. Can have perpetual existence.
Other Business Forms	1. *Joint venture*—An organization created by two or more persons in contemplation of a limited activity or a single transaction. Otherwise, similar to a partnership. 2. *Syndicate*—An investment group that undertakes to finance a particular project; may exist as a corporation or as a general or limited partnership. 3. *Joint stock company*—A business form similar to a corporation in some respects (perpetual existence, transferable shares of stock, management by directors and officers) but otherwise resembles a partnership.

❖ Chapter Summary: Forms of Business Organization—Continued

Other Business Forms (Continued)	4. *Business trust*—Created by a written trust agreement that sets forth the interests of the beneficiaries and obligations and powers of the trustee(s). Similar to a corporation in many respects. Beneficiaries are not personally liable for the debts or obligations of the business trust.
	5. *Cooperative*—An association organized to provide an economic service, without profit, to its members. May take the form of a corporation or a partnership.
Private Franchises	1. *Types of franchises:* a. Distributorship (e.g., an automobile dealership). b. Chain-style operation (e.g., fast-food chains). c. Manufacturing/processing plant arrangement (e.g., soft-drink corporations such as Coca-Cola). 2. *The franchise agreement:* a. Ordinarily requires the franchisee (purchaser) to pay a price for the franchise license. b. Specifies the territory to be served by the franchisee's firm. c. May require the franchisee to purchase certain supplies from the franchisor at an established price. d. May require the franchisee to abide by certain standards of quality relating to product or service offered, but cannot set retail resale price. e. Usually provides for the date and/or conditions of termination of the franchise arrangement.

❖ Questions and Case Problems

21-1. In each of the following situations, determine whether Georgio's Fashions is a sole proprietorship, a partnership, or a corporation.

(a) Georgio's defaulted on a payment to supplier Donovan Creations. Donovan sued Georgio's and each of the owners of Georgio's personally for payment of the debt.

(b) Georgio's raised $200,000 through the sale of shares of its stock.

(c) It is tax time. Georgio's files an information return to the IRS declaring the tax liability of the owners of the business but does not pay taxes directly to the IRS on the business profits.

(d) It is tax time. Georgio's files a tax return with the IRS, and the business pays taxes on the net profits of the firm.

21-2. Suppose George, Martha, and Jocelyn are college graduates, and George has come up with an idea for a new product that he believes could make the three of them very rich. His idea is to manufacture beer dispensers for home use and market them to consumers throughout the Midwest. George's personal experience qualifies him to be both first-line supervisor and general manager of the new firm. Martha is a born salesperson. Jocelyn has little interest in sales or management but would like to invest a large sum of money that she has inherited from her aunt. What should George, Martha, and Jocelyn consider in deciding which form of business organization to adopt?

21-3. In the situation described in Question 21-2, assume that Jocelyn is willing to put her inherited money in the business, but she does not want any further liability should the beer dispenser manufacturing business fail. The bank is willing to lend the capital to George and Martha at a 14 percent interest rate, but it will do so only if certain restrictions are placed on management decisions. This is not satisfactory to George or Martha, and the two decide to bring Jocelyn into the business. Under these circumstances, discuss which types of business organizations are best suited to meet Jocelyn's needs.

21-4. The limited-liability aspect of the corporation is one of the most important reasons that firms choose to organize as corporations rather than as partnerships or sole proprietorships. Limited liability means that if a corporation is not able to meet its obligations with corporate assets, creditors will not be allowed to look to the owners (stockholders) of the corporation to satisfy their claims. Assume that George and Martha (from Question 21-2) do not have a wealthy friend like Jocelyn who wishes to go into business with them and that they therefore must borrow money to start their business. George and Martha decide to incorporate. What do you think a lender will require from them when they seek a loan? What effect does this have on the "advantage" of limited liability under incorporation?

21-5. Assume that Faraway Corporation is considering entering into two contracts, one with a joint stock company that distributes home products east of the Mississippi River, and the other with a business trust formed by a number of sole proprietors who were sellers of home products on the West Coast. Both contracts involve large capital outlays for Faraway Corporation in supplying each business with beer dispensers. In both business organizations, at least two shareholders or beneficiaries are personally wealthy, but each business organization has limited financial resources. The owner-managers of Faraway Corporation are not familiar with either form of business organization. Since each form resembles a corporation, they are concerned with the possibility of liability in the event that either business organization breaches the contract by failing to make the deferred payments. Discuss fully Faraway Corporation's concern.

21-6. The H. C. Blackwell Company was a truck dealership owned by the Blackwell family. In 1961 they purchased a franchise from Kenworth Truck Company to sell Kenworth trucks. The franchise agreement had been renewed several times. In November of 1975 the Blackwells began negotiations with Kenworth to renew the recently expired franchise, and disagreements arose concerning the franchise. On February 4, 1976, Kenworth wrote to Blackwell that the franchise would be terminated in ninety days unless Blackwell met twelve specific demands made by Kenworth. In trying to meet these demands—which included increased sales, a better method of keeping business records, and capital improvements at their dealership—Blackwell spent approximately $90,000. By the end of the ninety-day period, however, the demands had not been met, so Kenworth terminated the franchise. Blackwell sued Kenworth for damages on the ground that Kenworth had wrongfully terminated the franchise agreement and, in so doing, had violated the Automobile Dealers' Franchise Act. During the trial, Kenworth's own regional sales manager stated that the demands imposed by Kenworth upon Blackwell would have taken at least a year to meet. Has Kenworth wrongfully ter-

minated the franchise under the Automobile Dealers' Franchise Act? [H. C. Blackwell Co., Inc. v. Kenworth Truck Co., 620 F.2d 104 (5th Cir. 1980)]

21-7. In 1981 the Huangs entered into a franchise agreement with Holiday Inns, Inc., whereby the Huangs agreed to adhere to the quality standards established by Holiday Inns and to comply in every respect with the Holiday Inns Standards Manual. In November of 1983 the district director of Holiday Inns made a courtesy inspection which revealed cracked windows, damaged and discolored walls, inoperative smoke detectors, broken light fixtures, poultry being stored at room temperature, and numerous other indications that the Huangs were not maintaining the established Holiday Inn quality standards in accordance with the franchise agreement. A formal inspection in February of 1984 revealed no significant improvement in quality standards, and the hotel was given an official rating of "unacceptable." The Huangs, who had been given detailed reports concerning the findings of both inspections, were advised that if the noted deficiencies were not remedied within sixty days, Holiday Inns would have grounds to terminate the franchise. When an inspection in April of 1984 revealed that the deficiencies had not been cured, Holiday Inns notified the Huangs that the franchise would be terminated on July 30 unless the deficiencies were remedied by June 28. The Huangs, who in May had begun renovations on the hotel costing $55,000, requested a ninety-day extension to the June 28 deadline, which Holiday Inns refused to grant. The Huangs then petitioned the court for a preliminary injunction against Holiday Inns' termination of the franchise, claiming that Holiday Inns had acted "capriciously and arbitrarily" by (1) not stating precisely the nature of the deficiencies and what was required to make repairs and improvements, and (2) not giving the Huangs a reasonable time in which to remedy the deficiencies. Discuss fully whether Holiday Inns should be enjoined from terminating the franchise, given these circumstances. [Huang v. Holiday Inns, Inc., 594 F.Supp. 352 (C.D.Cal.1984)]

Chapter 22

Agency

One of the most common, important, and pervasive legal relationships is that of **agency**. In an agency relationship between two parties, one of the parties, called the **agent**, agrees to represent or act for the other, called the **principal**. The principal has the right to control the agent's conduct in matters entrusted to the agent. More formally, the Restatement, Second, Agency,[1] defines *agency* as "the fiduciary relation which results from the manifestation of consent by one person to another that the other shall act in his behalf and subject to his control, and consent by the other so to act." The term **fiduciary** is at the heart of the "universal principle" of agency law that Justice Story referred to in the opening quotation. The term can be used both as a noun and as an adjective. When used as a noun, it refers to a person having a duty created by his or her undertaking to act primarily for another's benefit in matters connected with the undertaking. When used as an adjective, as in "fiduciary relationship," it means that the relationship is one involving trust and confidence.

❖ The Nature of Agency

An agent acts for his or her principal. By using agents, a principal can conduct multiple business operations simultaneously in various locations. Thus, for example, contracts that bind the principal can be made at different places with different persons at the same time. A familiar example of an agent is a corporate officer who serves in a representative capacity for the owners of the corporation. In this capacity, the officer has the authority to bind the principal (the corporation) to a contract. Indeed, agency law is essential to the existence and operation of a corporate entity, because only through its agents can a corporation function and enter into contracts.

A business world without agents is hard to imagine. Picture Henry Ford trying to sell all of the cars that Ford Motor Company manufactured. Obviously, other people must be appointed to fill in—act as agents—for the owner of a large company (the principal). Since agency relationships permeate the business world, an understanding of the law of agency is crucial to understanding business law.

> "[I]t is a universal principle in the law of agency, that the powers of the agent are to be exercised for the benefit of the principal only, and not of the agent or of third parties."
>
> **Joseph Story, 1779–1845**
> *(Associate Justice of the U. S. Supreme Court, 1811–1844)*

AGENT
A person authorized by another to act for or in place of him or her.

PRINCIPAL
In agency law, a person who, by agreement or otherwise, authorizes an agent to act on his or her behalf in such a way that the acts of the agent become binding on the principal.

AGENCY
A relationship between two persons where, by agreement or otherwise, one (the principal) is bound by the words and acts of the other (the agent).

---

1. Restatement, Second, Agency, Section 1(1). The Restatement is an authoritative summary of the law of agency, which is often referred to by jurists in decisions and opinions.

FIDUCIARY
As a noun, a person having a duty created by his or her undertaking to act primarily for another's benefit in matters connected with the undertaking. As an adjective, a relationship founded upon trust and confidence.

❖ Types of Agency Relationships

The first step in analyzing an agency relationship is to determine whether such a relationship exists. Traditional analysis in the law of agency focuses on three categories of relationships: (1) principal and agent, (2) master and servant, and (3) principal or employer and independent contractor. Note, however, that the principal-and-agent relationship can also be found within a master-servant or a principal-or-employer/ independent-contractor relationship.

Principal-Agent

In a principal-agent relationship, the parties have agreed that the agent will act *on behalf of and instead of* the principal in negotiating and transacting business with third persons. This relationship will affect the principal's rights and duties. Thus, an agent is empowered to perform legal acts that are binding on the principal. For example, an agent can bind a principal in a contract with a third person.

An agent has *derivative authority* in carrying out the principal's business. For example, Bruce is hired as a booking agent for a rock group—The Crash. As the group's agent, Bruce can negotiate and sign contracts for the rock group to appear at concerts. The contracts will be binding and thus legally enforceable against the group.

Master-Servant

Today's law defines *servant* as an employee—one employed by a master to perform services; the servant's physical conduct is controlled or is subject to control by the master. A servant can be a species of agent. However, the term *master-servant relationship* has been supplanted by *employer-employee relationship*. The term *employee*, of course, had no significance for common-law rules of agency but came into prominence with the industrial revolution and recent social legislation. Today an employee (other than an independent contractor) can be an agent if he or she has an appointment or contract for hire with authority to represent the employer.

For example, Donna owns a dress shop. She employs Myra, Roxanne, and Nita as salespeople, and Kari as a janitor. Donna is the employer (master), the other women are the employees (servants). The key feature of the employer-employee relationship is that the employer controls, or at least has the right to control, the employee in the performance of the tasks involved in the employment. The employees do not have *independent* business discretion. The dress shop salespeople not only can be told to sell the dresses but also can be told how to sell them. In selling the dresses, however, they are agents as well as employees. They have been given the authority by Donna to contract for and represent Donna in creating sales with customers. On the other hand, Kari is merely an employee and not an agent. Donna completely controls Kari's workplace and work habits, and Kari has no authority to represent Donna in dealings with others.

All employment laws (state and federal) apply only to the employer-employee relationship. Statutes governing social security, withholding taxes, workers' compensation, unemployment compensation, workplace safety laws, and the like, are applicable only if there is an employer-employee status. These laws do not apply to the independent contractor.

Principal/Employer–Independent Contractor

Independent contractors are not employees (servants), because their employers have no control over the details of their physical performance. The Restatement, Second, Agency, Section 2, defines an independent contractor as

> [A] person who contracts with another to do something for him but who is not controlled by the other nor subject to the other's right to control with respect to his physical conduct in the performance of the undertaking. He may or may not be an agent.

The following factors are relevant in determining the status of independent contractors:

1. What is the extent of control that the employer can exercise over the details of the work?
2. Is the employed person engaged in an occupation or business distinct from that of the employer?
3. Is the work usually done under the employer's direction, or is it done by a specialist without supervision?
4. Does the employer supply the tools at the place of work?
5. For how long is the person employed?
6. What is the method of payment—by time period or at the completion of the job?
7. What is the degree of skill required by the person employed?

Building contractors and subcontractors are independent contractors, and a property owner does not control the acts of either of these professionals. Truck drivers who own their equipment and hire out on an *ad hoc* basis are independent contractors; however, truck drivers who drive company trucks on a regular basis are usually employees (servants). A collection agent and a real estate broker are other examples of independent contractors.

In the following case, the question arises as to whether a builder of a prefabricated structure is the agent of the manufacturer of the component materials or an independent contractor.

Case 22.1
HERMAN v. BONANZA BUILDINGS, INC.
Supreme Court of Nebraska, 1986.
223 Neb. 474, 390 N.W.2d 536.

FACTS In 1980 Albert and Mildred Herman responded to an advertisement for a prefabricated "Bonanza" steel building. They called the long-distance number listed in the ad and were given the name and telephone number of a dealer in Kearney, Nebraska. Soon thereafter, they were visited by Kurt Lauer, a sales representative of Big Valley, a business firm located in Kearney. Lauer showed the Hermans a brochure on which the name "Bonanza" was prominently featured and in which various types of Bonanza homes were described. The ad guaranteed a "worry-free" home and "a Written Warranty to repair or replace defective material or workmanship." The Hermans selected the building they wanted, and agreed to pay Big Valley a total price of $9,707 for the materials and the construction of the building. Big Valley then purchased the components from Bonanza and completed the construction within a month, by which time the Hermans had paid fully the price of the structure. Later, during a rainstorm, the Hermans noticed that the rain leaked through the windows, doors, and skylights of the building. They also noticed that fifteen to twenty nails in the roof had missed the rafters. Lauer came back several times in the fall of 1980 to take care of the problem, but the

Case 22.1—Continued

leaks were never fully repaired. When the Hermans learned that Big Valley had gone out of business in 1981, they contacted Bonanza, which sent a representative to the Herman's home to do some caulking. Still the leaks persisted. The Hermans then brought suit against Bonanza for damages, claiming that Big Valley had been Bonanza's agent in its sale and construction of the home. The trial court granted Bonanza's motion for dismissal.

ISSUE   Is Big Valley an agent of Bonanza or an independent contractor in this case?

DECISION   The Nebraska Supreme Court ruled that Big Valley was an independent contractor, but the court remanded the case to the trial court to determine the extent to which the warranty statements in the Bonanza brochure formed the basis of the bargain between Big Valley and the Hermans.

REASON   The relationship between Big Valley and Bonanza was defined by a written agreement (of which the Hermans were unaware) providing that Big Valley was an independent contractor and that neither party to the agreement would act as the agent of the other. The court stated, "It is true that Bonanza referred Big Valley to Mr. Herman, that Big Valley used a brochure prepared by Bonanza in negotiating its contract with Mr. Herman, that Bonanza offered training sessions and presumably trained Big Valley, and that Big Valley used a warranty form prepared by Bonanza. Those facts, however, do not make Big Valley an agent of Bonanza." The court concluded that the agreement concerning the structure had been one solely between Big Valley and the Hermans and did not include Bonanza. Big Valley had purchased the materials, determined the price, done the construction work, and in so doing no intention to benefit Bonanza was present.

Commingling of the Relationships

It is important to note that the employer-employee (master-servant) relationship may or may not involve an agency relationship. The same holds true for the relationship between a principal or employer and an independent contractor. To illustrate: An employer who hires a traveling salesperson as an employee has created not only an employer-employee relationship but one of agency as well. A seller-owner of real estate who hires a real estate broker to negotiate a sale of property has not only contracted with an independent contractor (the real estate broker) but has also established an agency relationship for the specific purpose of assisting in the sale of the property. On the other hand, an employer who hires someone exclusively as a delivery person has created only an employer-employee relationship, and the delivery person is not an agent.

❖ Formation of Agency Relationships

The following discussions will emphasize the usual form taken by agency relationships. Such relationships are *consensual*; that is, they come about by voluntary consent and agreement between the parties. Generally, the agreement need not be in writing, and consideration is not required.[2]

A principal must have legal capacity to enter into contracts. A person who cannot legally enter into contracts directly should not be allowed to do it indirectly through

---

2.   There are two main exceptions to oral agency agreements: (1) Whenever agency authority empowers the agent to enter into a contract that the Statute of Frauds requires to be in writing, then the agent's authority from the principal must likewise be in writing (this is called *equal-dignity rule*, to be discussed later in this chapter). (2) A power of attorney, which confers authority to an agent, must be in writing.

an agent. Since an agent derives the authority to enter into contracts from the principal, and a contract made by an agent is legally viewed as a contract of the principal, it is immaterial whether the agent personally has the legal capacity to make that contract. Thus, a minor can be an agent but in some states cannot be a principal appointing an agent.[3] Where permitted, however, any resulting contracts will be voidable by the minor principal, but not by the adult third party.

In sum, any person can be an agent, regardless of whether he or she has the capacity to contract. Even a person who is legally incompetent can be appointed an agent if that person is capable of performing the required functions.

An agency relationship can be created for any legal purpose. One created for an illegal purpose or contrary to public policy is unenforceable. If Sharp (as principal) contracts with Blesh (as agent) to sell illegal narcotics, the agency relationship is unenforceable because selling narcotics illegally is a felony and is contrary to public policy. It is also illegal for medical doctors and other licensed professionals to employ unlicensed agents to perform professional actions.

Generally, no formalities are required to create an agency. The agency relationship can arise by acts of the parties in one of the four ways discussed below.

Agency by Agreement

Because agency is a consensual relationship, it must be based on some *affirmative* indication that the agent agrees to act for the principal and the principal agrees to have the agent so act. An agency agreement can take the form of an express written contract. For example, Ann enters into a written agreement with Troy, a realtor, to sell Ann's house. An agency relationship exists between Ann and Troy for the sale of the house and is detailed in a written document that both parties sign.

Many express agency agreements are oral. If Ann asks Cary, a gardener, to contract with others for the care of her lawn on a regular basis, and Cary agrees, an agency relationship exists between Ann and Cary for the lawn care.

An agency agreement can also be implied from conduct. For example, a hotel expressly allows only Jonathan Adams to park cars, but Jonathan has no employment contract there. The hotel's manager tells Jonathan when to work and where and how to park the cars. The hotel's conduct amounts to a manifestation of its willingness for Jonathan to park its customers' cars, and Jonathan can infer from the hotel's conduct that he has authority to act as a parking valet. It can be implied that he is an agent for the hotel, his purpose being to provide valet parking services for hotel guests.

Agency by Ratification

On occasion, a person who is in fact not an agent (or who is an agent acting outside the scope of his or her authority) may make a contract on behalf of another (a principal). If the principal approves or affirms that contract by word or by action, an agency relationship is created by **ratification.** Ratification is a question of intent, and intent can be expressed by either words or conduct. The basic requirements for ratification are discussed later in this chapter.

RATIFICATION
In contract law, the act of adopting or confirming a previous act that without ratification would not be an enforceable contractual obligation; or the act of confirming an obligation by a person who did not have the authority to make the obligation (or who was incompetent at the time the contract was made). The act of ratification causes the obligation to be binding as if such were valid and enforceable in the first instance.

---

3. Exceptions have been granted by some courts to allow a minor to appoint an agent for the limited purpose of contracting for the minor's necessities of life. See Casey v. Kastel, 237 N.Y. 305, 142 N.E. 671 (1924).

Agency by Estoppel

When a principal causes a third person to believe that another person is his or her agent, and the third person deals with the supposed agent, the principal is "estopped to deny" the agency relationship. In such a situation, the principal's actions create the *appearance* of an agency that does not in fact exist.

Suppose Andrew accompanies Charles to call on a customer, Steve, the proprietor of the General Seed Store. Andrew has done sales work but is not employed by Charles at this time. Charles boasts to Steve that he wishes he had three more assistants "just like Andrew." Steve has reason to believe from Charles's statements that Andrew is an agent for Charles. Steve then places seed orders with Andrew. If Charles does not correct the impression that Andrew is an agent, Charles will be bound to fill the orders just as if Andrew were really Charles's agent. Charles's representation to Steve created the impression that Andrew was Charles's agent and had authority to solicit orders.

Agency by estoppel does not extend to all acts under all circumstances. For example, the acts or declarations of the purported agent in and of themselves do not create an agency by estoppel. It is the deeds or statements of the principal, not the agent, that create an agency. Suppose Alice walks into Dru's Dress Boutique and claims to be a sales agent for an exclusive Paris dress designer, Pierre Dumont. Dru has never had business relations with Pierre Dumont. Based on Alice's claim, however, Dru gives Alice an order and prepays 15 percent of the sales order. Alice is not an agent, and the dresses are never delivered. Dru cannot hold Pierre Dumont liable. Alice's acts and declarations, in and of themselves, do not create an agency by estoppel.

In addition, the third person must prove that he or she *reasonably* believed that an agency relationship existed and that the agent had authority. Facts and circumstances must show that an ordinary, prudent person who is familiar with business practice and custom would be justified in concluding that the agent had authority.

Agency by Operation of Law

In some cases, the courts have found it desirable to find an agency relationship in the absence of a formal agreement. This may occur in family relationships. For example, suppose one spouse purchases certain basic necessaries and charges them to the other spouse's charge account. The courts will often rule that the latter is liable for payment of such necessaries either because of a social policy of promoting the general welfare of the spouse or because of a legal duty to supply necessaries to family members. Sometimes agency by *operation of law* is created, giving an agent emergency power to act under unusual circumstances that are not covered by the agreement when failure to act would cause the principal substantial loss. If the agent is unable to contact the principal, the courts will often grant this emergency power.

❖ Duties of Agents and Principals

Once the principal-agent relationship has been created, both parties have duties that govern their conduct. As discussed previously, the principal-agent relationship is *fiduciary*—one of trust. In a fiduciary relationship, each party owes the other the duty to act with the utmost good faith. Neither party may keep from the other information that has any bearing on their agency relationship.

Agent's Duties to Principal

The duties that an agent owes to a principal are set forth in the agency agreement or arise by operation of law. They are implied from the agency relationship *whether or not the identity of the principal is disclosed to a third party*. When an agent employs or appoints a *subagent*, a fiduciary duty exists between the subagent and the principal as well as between the subagent and the agent. Subagents owe the same duties to agents and to principals as agents owe to principals. Generally, the agent owes the principal the following five duties:

Performance   An implied condition in every agency contract is the agent's agreement to use reasonable diligence and skill in performing the work. When an agent fails to perform his or her duties entirely, liability for breach of contract generally will occur. The degree of skill or care required of an agent is usually that expected of a reasonable person under similar circumstances. Although in most cases this is interpreted to mean ordinary care, an agent may have presented himself or herself as possessing special skills (such as those that an accountant or attorney possesses). In these situations, the agent is expected to exercise the skill or skills claimed. Failure to do so constitutes a breach of the agent's duty.

Not all agency relationships are based on contract. In some situations, an agent acts gratuitously, that is, not for money. A gratuitous agent cannot be liable for breach of contract since there is no contract; he or she is subject only to tort liability. Once a gratuitous agent has begun to act in an agency capacity, though, he or she has the duty to continue to perform in that capacity in an acceptable manner and is subject to the same standards of care and duty to perform as other agents. Consider an example: Peterson's friend, Stendhof, is a real estate broker. Stendhof gratuitously offers to sell Peterson's farm. If Stendhof never attempts to sell the farm, Peterson has no legal cause of action to force Stendhof to do so. If Stendhof does find a buyer and keeps promising a sales contract, but fails to provide one within a reasonable period of time, causing the buyer to seek other property, then Peterson has a cause of action in tort for negligence.

Notification   It is a maxim in agency law that all the agent knows, the principal knows. Thus, it is only logical that the agent be required to notify the principal of all matters that come to his or her attention concerning the subject matter of the agency. This is the duty of notification. What the agent actually tells the principal is not relevant; what the agent *should have told* the principal is crucial. Under the law of agency, notice to the agent is notice to the principal.

Loyalty   Loyalty is one of most fundamental duties in a fiduciary relationship. Basically stated, the agent has the duty to act solely for the benefit of his or her principal and not in the interest of the agent or a third party. For example, an agent cannot represent two principals in the same transaction unless both know of the dual capacity and consent to it. Thus, a real estate agent cannot represent both the seller and the buyer in collecting commissions, unless the seller and the buyer so agree. The duty of loyalty also means that any information or knowledge acquired through the agency relationship is considered confidential. It would be a breach of loyalty to disclose such information both during the agency relationship and after its termination. Typical examples of confidential information are trade secrets and customer lists compiled by the principal.

Furthermore, an agent employed by a principal to buy cannot buy from himself or herself, and an agent employed to sell cannot become the purchaser without the principal's consent. In short, the agent's loyalty must be undivided. The agent's actions must be strictly for the benefit of the principal and must not result in any secret profit for the agent.

In the following case, an agent sued the principal for promised compensation that he never received. The court ruled the agent could not recover because he had not fulfilled his duty of loyalty to the principal.

Case 22.2
DOUGLAS v. AZTEC PETROLEUM CORP.
Court of Civil Appeals of Texas, 1985.
695 S.W.2d 312.

FACTS Aztec Petroleum Company arranged to have Douglas buy oil and gas leases for Aztec. In return for his services, Douglas was to receive an initial $5,000 plus a royalty interest in the leases he obtained. Douglas obtained a number of leases for Aztec but represented to Aztec that the prices paid for the leases were higher than they actually were. By sending Aztec photocopies of altered checks, both as to payee and amount, and forged receipts, Douglas was able to keep for himself a substantial amount of the money that Aztec had entrusted to him for payment of the leases. This money was used by Douglas for the purchase of personal items, including two new cars, a boat, and other personal items. When Aztec refused to grant Douglas the promised royalty interest in the leases, Douglas brought suit to obtain it.

ISSUE In view of Douglas's deceptive activities, is Aztec required to grant the royalty interest?

DECISION No. Douglas had breached his fiduciary duty to Aztec, and, for this reason, Aztec was not required to fulfill its earlier promise.

REASON The court cited the Restatement, Second, Agency, Section 469, which reads, in part: "An agent is entitled to no compensation for conduct which is disobedient or which is a breach of his duty of loyalty." The court judged that the royalty interest "represented compensation for Douglas for 'honest and forthright' performance of his agency, a duty imposed on every fiduciary. . . . The court's denial of the [royalty interest] to Douglas is a proper legal consequence of his established infidelity."

Obedience When an agent is acting on behalf of the principal, a duty is imposed on that agent to follow all lawful and clearly stated instructions of the principal. Any deviation from such instructions is a violation of this duty. During emergency situations, however, when the principal cannot be consulted, the agent may deviate from such instructions without violating this duty if the circumstances so warrant. Whenever instructions are not clearly stated, the agent can fulfill the duty of obedience by acting in good faith and in a reasonable manner under the circumstances.

Accounting Unless an agent and a principal agree otherwise, the agent has the duty to keep and make available to the principal an account of all property and money received and paid out on behalf of the principal. This includes gifts from third persons in connection with the agency. For example, a gift from a customer to a salesperson for prompt deliveries made by the principal belongs to the principal. The agent has a duty to maintain separate accounts for the principal's funds and for the agent's personal funds, and no intermingling of these accounts is allowed. Whenever a licensed professional violates this duty to account, he or she may be subject to disciplinary proceedings by the appropriate regulatory institution. Such proceedings would be in addition to the agent's liability to the principal for failure to account.

Principal's Duties to Agent

The principal also has certain duties to the agent, either expressed or implied by law. The following four duties are included:

Compensation   Except in a gratuitous agency relationship, where an agent does not act for money, the principal must pay the agreed-upon value for an agent's services. Whenever the amount of compensation is agreed upon by the parties, the principal owes the duty to pay it upon completion of the agent's specified activities. If no amount is expressly agreed upon, then the principal owes the agent the customary compensation for such services.

In general, when a principal requests certain services from an agent, the agent reasonably expects payment. A duty is therefore implied for the principal to pay the agent for services rendered. For example, when an accountant or an attorney is asked to act as an agent, an agreement to compensate the agent for such service is implied. The principal also has the duty to pay that compensation in a timely manner.

In the following case, a real estate agent sued her broker/principal to obtain what she felt was her rightful commission, given the usual practices and customs of the brokerage firm with which she worked.

Case 22.3
TARVER v. LANDERS
Court of Appeals of Louisiana, Third Circuit, 1986.
486 So.2d 294.

FACTS   Brenda Tarver worked as an independent contractor with Dianne Landers's real estate agency. The agents in the firm worked on a commission basis, and Tarver's contract read that she would receive 30 percent of the agency's commissions for sales for which she was "entitled as either listing and/or selling agent." In the spring of 1984 Charles Smith and his wife contacted the agency concerning some property for sale listed by the agency and advertised in the local newspaper. The Smiths were referred to Tarver, who showed them the property, handled their offer to purchase the property, and the seller's counteroffer. In all, Tarver negotiated three offers and three counteroffers between the seller and the buyer. Later, however, the Smiths returned to the agency and, because Tarver was out of the office, negotiated with Dianne Landers concerning the last counteroffer they had rejected. After some modifications were made, they reached an agreement with the seller and purchased the property. Landers would not pay Tarver a commission for the sale

because Tarver had not negotiated the final purchase. Tarver sued to recover her commission on the grounds that it was customary in the real estate office that the initial selling agent would be paid the commission and that when the initial selling agent was absent from the office, another agent would handle negotiations—but not receive the commission if a sale resulted. The trial court held for Tarver, and Landers appealed.

ISSUE   The question of whether Landers had a duty to compensate Tarver rested on the issue of whether Tarver was the "selling agent" in this case. If so, by their contract terms, Tarver would be entitled to her commission.

DECISION   The appellate court affirmed the trial court's holding that Tarver was the selling agent and entitled to her commission as stipulated by the contract.

REASON   Lacking any written definition of what constituted the "selling agent" in the sales conducted through the real estate agency, the court based its decision on the practices that had customarily been followed in the office. Tarver was undoubtedly the selling agent, in the court's eyes, because she had done all the negotiating

Case 22.3—Continued

with the Smiths and written up the offers and counteroffers. When the Smiths paid their final visit to the office,
they were apparently ready to buy but with minor modi-

fications to the agreement—modifications penciled in by
Landers. Landers therefore had a duty to compensate
Tarver, as agreed upon by the parties.

Reimbursement and Indemnification   Whenever an agent disburses sums of money
at the request of the principal, and whenever the agent disburses sums of money to
pay for necessary expenses in the course of a reasonable performance of his or her
agency duties, the principal has the duty to reimburse. Agents cannot recover for
expenses incurred by their own misconduct or negligence, however.

Subject to the terms of the agency agreement, the principal has the duty to
reimburse an agent for authorized payments or *indemnify* (compensate) an agent for
liabilities incurred because of authorized and lawful acts and transactions and also
for losses suffered because of the principal's failure to perform any duties. Additionally,
the principal must indemnify the agent for the value of benefits that the agent confers
upon the principal unofficially. The amount of indemnification is usually specified
in the agency contract. If it is not, the courts will look to the nature of the business
and the type of loss in order to determine the amount.

Cooperation   A principal has a duty both to cooperate with and to assist an agent
in performing his or her duties. The principal must do nothing to prevent such
performance. For example, when a principal grants an agent an exclusive territory,
the principal cannot compete with the agent or appoint or allow another agent to so
compete in violation of the *exclusive agency*. Such competition would expose the
principal to liability for the agent's lost sales or profits.

Safe Working Conditions   The common law requires the principal to provide safe
working premises, equipment, and conditions for all agents and employees. The
principal has a duty to inspect working conditions and to warn agents and employees
about any unsafe areas. If the agency is one of employment, the employer's liability
is frequently covered by workers' compensation insurance, which is the primary
remedy for an employee's injury on the job.

❖ Rights and Remedies in Agency Relationships

In general, for every duty of the principal, the agent has a corresponding right, and
vice versa. When one party to the agency relationship violates his or her duty to the
other party, the remedies available to the party not in breach arise out of contract
and tort law. These remedies include monetary damages, termination of the agency
relationship, injunction, and required accountings.

❖ Scope of Agent's Authority

An agent's authority to act can be either actual (express or implied) or apparent (by
estoppel). If an agent contracts outside the scope of his or her authority, the principal
may still become liable by ratifying the contract.

Express Authority

Express authority is embodied in that which the principal has engaged the agent to do. It can be given orally or in writing. For example, giving an agent a *power of attorney* confers express authority.[4] The power of attorney is a written document and is usually notarized. Like all agency relationships, a power of attorney can be special—permitting the agent to do specified acts only—or it can be general—permitting the agent to transact all business dealings for the principal. A sample power of attorney is shown in Exhibit 22-1.

An agent holding a power of attorney for a client is expressly authorized to act *only* on the principal's behalf when exercising that power. In the following case, a lawyer was held liable for damages when he breached his duty of loyalty to his principal.

Case 22.4
KING v. BANKERD
Supreme Court of Maryland, 1985.
303 Md. 98, 492 A.2d 608.

FACTS   Howard and Virginia Bankerd were having marital difficulties. In 1968 Howard decided to leave "for the west," but before he did so, he executed a power of attorney to his lawyer, Arthur King. Virginia continued to reside in their home in Maryland and assumed all expenses for the home. In 1975 Howard gave King an updated power of attorney and asked King to sell the property "on such terms as to him [King] seem best." In 1977 Virginia asked the lawyer to exercise his power of attorney and transfer her husband's interest in the property to her. She wished to sell the property and retire. After three letters failed to elicit any response from Howard, King concluded Howard "didn't give a damn" about the property. King therefore transferred the property to Virginia by deed in 1978. Virginia paid no consideration for the transfer. Howard subsequently sued King, claiming that King had breached his duty of loyalty and trust by transferring the property gratuitously to Virginia. King argued that he

had acted reasonably under the circumstances. The trial court held for Howard Bankerd, and King appealed.

ISSUE   Had King breached his fiduciary duty of loyalty and trust by transferring the property gratuitously to Virginia?

DECISION   Yes. The trial court's judgment was affirmed.

REASON   The court cited the Restatement, Second, Agency, Section 387, which reads: "Unless otherwise agreed, an agent is subject to a duty to his principal to act solely for the benefit of the principal in all matters connected with his agency." When King was granted a power of attorney to act for Howard, the attorney was bound to act for the benefit, and not to the detriment, of his principal. Although Howard had requested King to "convey, grant, bargain and/or sell" the property "on such terms as to him may seem best," the court concluded that these words "did not expressly authorize a gratuitous transfer of property. Because an agent must act for the benefit of his principal, we decline to interpret this broad, all-encompassing language as authority for the agent to make a gift of the principal's property."

The **equal dignity rule** in most states requires that if the contract being executed is or must be in writing, then the agent's authority must also be in writing.[5] Failure to comply with the equal dignity rule can make a contract voidable *at the option of*

EQUAL DIGNITY RULE
In most states, express authority given to an agent must be in writing if the contract to be made on behalf of the principal is required to be in writing.

---

4.   An agent who holds the power of attorney is called an *attorney-in-fact* for the principal. The holder does not have to be an attorney-at-law.
5.   An exception to the equal dignity rule exists in modern business practice. An executive officer of a corporation, when acting for the corporation in an ordinary business situation, is not required to obtain written authority from the corporation.

◆ **Exhibit 22-1 Power of Attorney**

POWER OF ATTORNEY

GENERAL

Know All Men by These Presents: That I, _____

_____

the undersigned (jointly and severally, if more than one) hereby make, constitute and appoint _____

_____

as a true and lawful Attorney for me and in my name, place and stead and for my use and benefit:

(a) To ask, demand, sue for, recover, collect and receive each and every sum of money, debt, account, legacy, bequest, interest, dividend, annuity and demand (which now is or hereafter shall become due, owing or payable) belonging to or claimed by me, and to use and take any lawful means for the recovery thereof by legal process or otherwise, and to execute and deliver a satisfaction or release therefor, together with the right and power to compromise or compound any claim or demand;

(b) To exercise any or all of the following powers as to real property, any interest therein and/or any building thereon: To contract for, purchase, receive and take possession thereof and of evidence of title thereto; to lease the same for any term or purpose, including leases for business, residence, and oil and/or mineral development; to sell, exchange, grant or convey the same with or without warranty; and to mortgage, transfer in trust, or otherwise encumber or hypothecate the same to secure payment of a negotiable or non-negotiable note or performance of any obligation or agreement;

(c) To exercise any or all of the following powers as to all kinds of personal property and goods, wares and merchandise, choses in action and other property in possession or in action: To contract for, buy, sell, exchange, transfer and in any legal manner deal in and with the same; and to mortgage, transfer in trust, or otherwise encumber or hypothecate the same to secure payment of a negotiable or non-negotiable note or performance of any obligation or agreement;

(d) To borrow money and to execute and deliver negotiable or non-negotiable notes therefor with or without security; and to loan money and receive negotiable or non-negotiable notes therefor with such security as he shall deem proper;

(e) To create, amend, supplement and terminate any trust and to instruct and advise the trustee of any trust wherein I am or may be trustor or beneficiary; to represent and vote stock, exercise stock rights, accept and deal with any dividend, distribution or bonus, join in any corporate financing, reorganization, merger, liquidation, consolidation or other action and the extension, compromise, conversion, adjustment, enforcement or foreclosure, singly or in conjunction with others of any corporate stock, bond, note, debenture or other security; to compound, compromise, adjust, settle and satisfy any obligation, secured or unsecured, owing by or to me and to give or accept any property and/or money whether or not equal to or less in value than the amount owing in payment, settlement or satisfaction thereof;

(f) To transact business of any kind or class and as my act and deed to sign, execute, acknowledge and deliver any deed, lease, assignment of lease, covenant, indenture, indemnity, agreement, mortgage, deed of trust, assignment of mortgage or of the beneficial interest under deed of trust, extension or renewal of any obligation, subordination or waiver of priority, hypothecation, bottomry, charter-party, bill of lading, bill of sale, bill, bond, note, whether negotiable or non-negotiable, receipt, evidence of debt, full or partial release or satisfaction of mortgage, judgment and other debt, request for partial or full reconveyance of deed of trust and such other instruments in writing of any kind or class as may be necessary or proper in the premises.

Giving and Granting

unto my said Attorney full power and authority to do and perform all and every act and thing whatsoever requisite, necessary or appropriate to be done in and about the premises as fully to all intents and purposes as I might or could do if personally present, hereby ratifying all that my said Attorney shall lawfully do or cause to be done by virtue of these presents. The powers and authority hereby conferred upon my said Attorney shall be applicable to all real and personal property or interests therein now owned or hereafter acquired by me and wherever situate.

My said Attorney is empowered hereby to determine in his sole discretion the time when, purpose for and manner in which any power herein conferred upon him shall be exercised, and the conditions, provisions and covenants of any instrument or document which may be executed by him pursuant hereto; and in the acquisition or disposition of real or personal property, my said Attorney shall have exclusive power to fix the terms thereof for cash, credit and/or property, and if on credit with or without security.

The undersigned, if a married woman, hereby further authorizes and empowers my said Attorney, as my duly authorized agent, to join in my behalf, in the execution of any instrument by which any community real property or any interest therein, now owned or hereafter acquired by my spouse and myself, or either of us, is sold, leased, encumbered, or conveyed.

When the contest so requires, the masculine gender includes the feminine and/or neuter, and the singular number includes the plural.

WITNESS my hand this _____ day of _____, 19____

_____   _____

_____   _____

State of California,

    County of _____ } SS.

On _____, before me, the undersigned, a Notary Public in and for said

State, personally appeared _____

_____

known to me to be the person _____ whose name _____ subscribed

to the within instrument and acknowledged that _____ executed the same.

Witness my hand and official seal.   (Seal) _____

                                                              Notary Public in and for said State.

the principal. The law regards the contract at that point as a mere offer. If the principal decides to accept the offer, acceptance must be ratified in writing. Assume that Shubb (the principal) orally asks Parkinson (the agent) to sell a ranch that Shubb owns. Parkinson finds a buyer and signs a sales contract (a contract for an interest in realty must be in writing) on behalf of Shubb to sell the ranch. The buyer cannot enforce the contract unless Shubb subsequently ratifies Parkinson's agency status *in writing*. Once the contract is ratified, either party can enforce rights under the contract.

The equal dignity rule does not apply when an agent acts in the presence of a principal or when the agent's act of signing is merely perfunctory. Thus, if Dickens (the principal) negotiates a contract but is called out of town the day it is to be signed, and authorizes Dirkson to sign, the oral authorization is sufficient.

Implied Authority

Implied authority can be (1) conferred by custom, (2) inferred from the position the agent occupies, or (3) inferred as being reasonably necessary to carry out express authority. For example, Mueller is employed by Al's Grocery to manage one of its stores. Al has not specified (expressly stated) that Mueller has authority to contract with third persons. In this situation, authority to manage a business implies authority to do what is reasonably required (as is customary or can be inferred from a manager's position) to operate the business. Such actions include participating in contracts for employee help, for buying merchandise and equipment, and even for advertising the products sold in the store.

When implied authority is conferred on the basis of custom, the third person must be familiar with the custom of the trade. Thus, a traveling salesperson normally may have implied authority to solicit orders for the principal but may not have implied authority to collect for the goods unless the salesperson is in possession of the goods.

The list of basic principles of implied authority based on custom or on the agent's position is extensive. It suffices to state that implied authority is always authority customarily associated with the position occupied by the agent, or authority that can be inferred from the express authority given to the agent to perform fully his or her duties. The test is whether it was reasonable for the agent to believe that he or she had the authority to enter the contract in question.

Apparent Authority—Estoppel

Apparent authority, or authority by estoppel, exists when the principal, by either word or action, causes a third party reasonably to believe that an agent has authority to act, even though the agent has no express or implied authority. To illustrate: a traveling saleswoman (the agent) has no express authority to collect payments for orders solicited from customers. (Since she neither possesses the goods ordered nor delivers them, she also has no implied authority to collect.) A customer, Carter, pays this agent, Anderson, for a solicited order. Anderson then takes the payment to the principal's accounting department, where an accountant accepts the payment and sends Carter a receipt. This procedure is thereafter followed for other orders solicited and paid for by Carter.

Later Anderson solicits an order, and Carter pays her as before. This time, however, Anderson absconds with the money. Can Carter claim that the payment to the saleswoman was authorized and thus, in effect, a payment to the principal? The answer is yes, because the principal's *repeated* acts of accepting Carter's payment led him reasonably to expect that Anderson had authority to receive payments for goods solicited. Although Anderson did not have express or implied authority, the principal's conduct gave her *apparent* authority to collect. The principal cannot claim the agent had no authority to collect in this particular case; the principal would be estopped from such a claim.

Sometimes a principal will go beyond mere statements or actions that convince a third party that a certain person is the principal's agent. If, for example, the principal has "clothed the agent" with both possession and apparent ownership of the principal's property, the agent will have very broad powers and can deal with the property as if he or she were the true owner.

For example, to deceive certain creditors, Blake (the principal) and Howard (the agent) agree verbally that Howard will hold certain stock certificates for Blake. Howard's possession and apparent ownership of the stock certificates are such strong indications of ownership that a reasonable person would conclude that Howard was the actual owner. If Howard negotiates the stock certificates to a third person, Blake will be estopped from denying Howard's authority to transfer stock.

Where land is involved, courts have held that possession alone is not a sufficient indication of ownership. Therefore, if an agent has mere possession of realty, a reasonable person should realize that possession alone is not an adequate assurance of ownership. If, on the other hand, the agent also possesses the deed to the property and sells the property against the principal's wishes to an unsuspecting buyer, the principal cannot cancel the sale or assert a claim to title.

The next case illustrates the issue of whether there is apparent authority to bind a principal when the principal allows the agent to use the principal's corporate name as part of the agent's corporate name and in the agent's advertising.

Case 22.5
CITY OF DELTA JUNCTION v. MACK TRUCKS, INC.

Supreme Court of Alaska, 1983.
670 P.2d 1128.

FACTS The City of Delta Junction (Delta) decided to purchase a fire tanker and sought bids from several truck dealers. The city eventually purchased a truck from Alaska Mack, Inc., a Mack truck dealer. Alaska Mack modified a Mack chassis to carry a 5,000 gallon tank, but the truck exceeded the manufacturer's specified weight limits and was dangerously unbalanced and difficult to drive. When subsequent modifications failed to remedy these problems, the city brought suit for breach of warranty against Alaska Mack, and Mack Trucks, Inc., as principal, under the theory of apparent agency (authority).

Mack Trucks, Inc., the manufacturer of Mack trucks, claimed that Alaska Mack was not its agent and that it was not responsible for any actions undertaken by Alaska Mack. Delta argued that Alaska Mack was listed in trade journals and the Fairbanks telephone directory under the heading "Mack Trucks" and that its advertisements carried the familiar Mack bulldog trademark. On the basis of these representations, both Delta's mayor and fire chief, at the time of the purchase, believed that Alaska Mack was an agent for the manufacturer of Mack trucks. Alaska Mack's bid was accepted by the city council, even though it was the highest bid received for the truck, because of the manufacturer's reputation. The trial court granted a directed verdict for Mack Trucks, Inc.; and Delta appealed.

ISSUE Did an apparent agency exist between Alaska Mack and Mack Trucks, Inc.?

Case 22.5—Continued

DECISION The Alaska Supreme Court remanded the case to the trial court for the jury to decide whether an apparent agency existed in this case.

REASON The court stated that apparent authority for an act exists when the written or spoken words, or other conduct, of the principal, reasonably interpreted, cause a third person to believe that the principal consents to have the act done on his or her behalf by the person purporting to act for the principal. Whether the franchisor's acquiescence in a franchisee's use of a corporate logo or name incorporating a trade name creates apparent authority is a question of fact for determination by a jury. In this case, the mayor, the fire chief, and the city council of Delta Junction all assumed they were dealing with Mack Trucks, Inc. The court further noted that the Mack trademark and name have become "part of the American scene." In the words of the court: "The average citizen, who couldn't name five vice-presidents to save himself from eternal damnation, will recognize a Mack advertisement as far as the eye can see." The court believed it could be reasonably inferred from the evidence that Alaska Mack's use of the name and trademark was with Mack Trucks, Inc.'s knowledge and approval, but whether its acquiescence was sufficient to bind Mack Trucks, Inc., under Delta's theory of apparent authority was a jury question.

Ratification

As mentioned previously in this chapter, ratification is the affirmation of a previously unauthorized contract or act. It can be either express or implied. If the principal does not ratify, there is no contract binding on the principal, and the third-party agreement with the agent is viewed merely as an unaccepted offer. The principal's acceptance (ratification) is binding only if the principal *knows* all the terms of the contract, because under contract law one cannot accept terms that one does not know about. If a principal ratifies a contract and later realizes the full terms were not known to him or her—whether due to the agent's fraud or simply because of a mistake on the principal's part—the ratification can be repudiated, unless the third party has changed position in reliance on the principal. In this case, the unauthorized contract remains an offer.

Because the third party's agreement is treated as an unaccepted offer, the third party can revoke an offer at any time prior to the principal's ratification without liability. Death or incapacity of the third party before ratification will void an unauthorized contract. Most courts also recognize intervening and extraordinary change of circumstances as a basis for setting aside a principal's ratification to permit a third party to revoke.

The requirements for ratification can be summarized as follows:

1.   The presumptive agent must have acted on behalf of a principal who subsequently ratifies, although some states permit ratification by an undisclosed principal.
2.   The principal must know of all material facts involved in the transaction.
3.   The agent's act must be affirmed in its entirety by the principal.
4.   The principal must have the legal capacity to authorize the transaction at the time the agent engages in the act and at the time the principal ratifies.
5.   The principal's affirmance must occur prior to the withdrawal of the third party from the transaction or prior to a changing of the circumstances in such a way that it would be unjust to hold the third party to the transaction.
6.   The principal must observe the same formalities when he or she approves the act purportedly done by the agent on his or her behalf as would have been required to authorize it initially.

In the following case, an agent for a corporation purchased supplies in the name of the corporate president, chairman of the board, and sole stockholder of the corporation, rather than in the corporation's name. The question as to whether the agent's actions were ratified by the principal—and thus whether he is personally liable for the debt incurred—is considered by the court.

Case 22.6
SUTTON'S STEEL & SUPPLY, INC. v. VAN STAVERN
Court of Appeals of Louisiana, Third Circuit, 1986.
496 So.2d 1360.

FACTS B. D. Van Stavern is the chairman of the board of directors, president, and sole stockholder of the Van Stavern Construction Company (the corporation). One of the corporation's employees, Fred Hash, was a field supervisor in charge of constructing a new plant. As part of his duties, Hash entered into a contract with Sutton's Steel Company to purchase steel for use in the constructing the plant. Sutton delivered steel to the plant site from June 1983 through January 1984. Employees at the plant site received the materials and approved the invoices. The invoices were made out not to the corporation but to B. D. Van Stavern, the name given to Sutton by Hash as the person responsible for payment. Invoices for materials delivered through December 2, 1983, were all paid by corporate check by a corporate employee. Van Stavern was unaware that the materials had been purchased in his name and not in the name of the corporation. When Sutton later sued Van Stavern personally for payment of $40,437.91 for deliveries made after December 2, the trial court held for Sutton's Steel, concluding that Van Stavern had ratified Hash's unauthorized agreement with Sutton that Van Stavern would be personally responsible for payment of the steel supplies. The court held that payment by the corporation of the invoices made out to Van Stavern personally evidenced Van Stavern's ratification of his agent's unauthorized action.

ISSUE Had Van Stavern ratified (by paying Sutton's invoices) Hash's unauthorized arrangement with Sutton to bill Van Stavern personally for the supplies, notwithstanding Van Stavern's lack of knowledge that he was being personally billed for the supplies?

DECISION No. The trial court's finding was reversed by the appellate court. Van Stavern had not ratified the unauthorized arrangement and was thus not subject to personal liability for the debt.

REASON The court noted that Hash did not have authority to make an agreement with Sutton to bill Van Stavern personally for the steel. Crucial to the determination of whether Van Stavern ratified his agent's unauthorized instructions was whether or not Van Stavern knew of the instructions. In order to ratify an act of an agent, a principal must have knowledge of all the necessary material facts. In this case, Van Stavern was unaware of the fact he was being billed personally for the materials and honestly believed that he was operating at the new plant site without personal liability for obligations incurred in constructing the plant. Van Stavern alleged he had not seen the invoices that had been paid, and the court held that the fact the invoices had been paid by corporate checks attested to the fact that Van Stavern considered the plant site expenses to be corporate expenses.

❖ Liability of Principals and Agents for Contracts

DISCLOSED PRINCIPAL
A principal whose identity and existence as a principal is known by a third person at the time a transaction is conducted by an agent.

The Restatement, Second, Agency, Section 4, classifies principals as disclosed, partially disclosed, or undisclosed. A **disclosed principal** is one whose identity is known by the third party at the time the contract is made by the agent. For example, a purchasing agent signing a contract for the purchase of office supplies will probably sign his or her name as purchasing agent for a specific company (for which he or she works), whose identity is well known to the office supply store owner.

A **partially disclosed principal** is one whose identity is not known by the third party, but the third party knows that the agent is or may be acting for a principal at the time the contract is made. For example, a seller of real estate may wish to keep his or her identity a secret, yet the agent with whom the seller has contracted can make it perfectly clear to the purchaser of the real estate that the agent is acting in an agency capacity for a principal.

An **undisclosed principal** is one whose identity is totally unknown by the third party, and the third party has no knowledge that the agent is acting in an agency capacity at the time the contract is made. For example, Albright agrees to sell two truckloads of apples to Zimmer. Zimmer believes that he is buying the apples from Albright; but actually Albright is the agent for Henderson, who legally owns the apples. In this case, Henderson is an undisclosed principal.

If an agent acts within the scope of his or her authority, a disclosed or partially disclosed principal is liable to a third party for a contract made by the agent. In these situations, an agent has no contractual liability for the nonperformance of the principal or the third party. If the agent exceeds the scope of authority, and the principal fails to ratify the contract, the principal cannot be held liable in a contract by a third party. The agent is generally liable, however, unless the third party knew of the agent's lack of authority.

When neither the fact of agency nor the identity of the principal is disclosed, a third party is deemed to be dealing with the agent personally, and the agent is liable as a party on the contract. If an agent has acted within the scope of authority, the undisclosed principal is bound to perform fully just as if the principal had been fully disclosed at the time the contract is made. Conversely, the undisclosed principal can hold the third party to the contract unless (1) the undisclosed principal was expressly excluded as a party in the contract, (2) the contract is a negotiable instrument signed by the agent with no indication of signing in a representative capacity, or (3) the performance of the agent is personal to the contract, allowing the third party to refuse the principal's performance.

❖ Liability of Principals and Agents for Torts of Agent

Obviously, an agent is liable to third persons for his or her own torts and crimes. A principal becomes liable for an agent's torts if the torts are committed within the scope of the agency or the scope of employment. The theory of liability used here involves the doctrine of ***respondeat superior*** (see this chapter's "Landmark").

The Restatement, Second, Agency, Section 229, indicates the general factors that courts will consider in determining whether or not a particular act occurred within the course and scope of employment. They are:

1. Whether the act was authorized by the employer.
2. The time, place, and purpose of the act.
3. Whether the act was one commonly performed by employees on behalf of their employers.
4. The extent to which the employer's interest was advanced by the act.
5. The extent to which the private interests of the employee were involved.

PARTIALLY DISCLOSED PRINCIPAL
A principal whose identity is unknown by a third person, but the third person knows that the agent is or may be acting for a principal at the time the contract is made.

UNDISCLOSED PRINCIPAL
A principal whose identity is unknown by a third person, and the third person has no knowledge that the agent is acting in an agency capacity at the time the contract is made.

RESPONDEAT SUPERIOR
In Latin, "Let the master respond." The employer is responsible for acts of an employee that are committed during the course of employment.

Landmark in the Law

The Doctrine of *Respondeat Superior*

The idea that a master must respond to third persons for losses negligently caused by the master's servant first appeared in Lord Holt's opinion in *Jones* v. *Hart* (1698).[1] By the early nineteenth century, this maxim was adopted by most courts and referred to as the doctrine of *respondeat superior*—Latin for "let the master respond" or "let the master serve."

The vicarious liability of the master for the acts of the servant has been supported primarily by two theories. The first rests on the issue of *control*, or *fault*: the master has control over the acts of the servant and is thus responsible for injuries arising out of such service. The second theory is economic in nature: since the master takes the benefits or profits of the servant's service, he or she should also suffer the losses; moreover, the master is better able than the servant to absorb such losses.

The *control* theory is clearly recognized in the Restatement, Second, Agency, wherein the master is defined as "a principal who employs an agent to perform service in his affairs and who controls, or has the right to control, the physical conduct of the other in the performance of the service." Conversely, a servant is defined as "an agent employed by a master to perform service in his affairs whose physical conduct in his performance of the service is controlled, or is subject to control, by the master."

It is important to note that there are limitations on the master's liability for the acts of the servant. An employer (master) is only responsible for the wrongful conduct of an employee (servant) that occurs in "the scope of the employment." Actions that are normally considered to be within the scope of employment by the Restatement, Second, Agency, are listed in the text. Generally, the act must be of a kind the servant was employed to do. Second, it must have occurred within "authorized time and space

limits." And third, it must have been "activated, at least in part, by a purpose to serve the master."

A useful insight into the "scope of employment" concept may be gained by examining Baron Parke's classic distinction between a "detour" and a "frolic" in the case of *Joel* v. *Morison* (1834):

> If the servants, being on their master's business took a *detour* . . . , the master will be responsible. . . . The master is only liable where the servant is acting in the course of his employment. If he was going out of his way, against his master's implied commands, when driving on his master's business, he will make his master liable; but if he was going on a *frolic of his own*, without being at all on his master's business, the master will not be liable.[2]

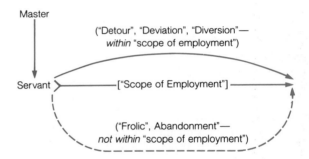

The doctrine of *respondeat superior* has been accepted by the courts for nearly two centuries. This theory of vicarious liability is laden with practical implications in all situations where an principal-agent (master-servant, employer-employee) relationship exists. The small-town grocer with one clerk, as well as the multinational corporation with thousands of employees, are equally subject to the doctrinal demand of "let the master respond."

1. K.B. 642, 90 Eng. Reprint 1255.
2. Car. & P., 501, 503, 172 Eng. Reprint 1338, 1339 (1834).

6. Whether the employer furnished the means or instrumentality (for example, a truck or a machine) by which the injury was inflicted.

7. Whether the employer had reason to know that the employee would do the act in question and whether the employee had ever done it before.

8. Whether the act involved the commission of a serious crime.

A principal or employer will also be liable for an agent's or employee's torts if he or she participates by conspiracy or other action. A principal is liable for an employee's torts if:

1. The principal directs the agent to do the act.

2. There is a negligent entrustment.

3. The principal fails to supervise properly the agent-employee.

In the following case, the question arose as to whether the employer could be held liable for the intentional tort of its employee.

Case 22.7
JOHNSON v. DIXON
Court of Appeals of Louisiana, 1984.
457 So.2d 79.

FACTS   Amax Nickel Refining Company, Inc., hired Louisiana Industrial Coatings (LIC), an independent contractor, to do some painting at the Amax plant. LIC was instructed that the painting was a high priority and that it should not stop painting in any given work area unless instructed to do so by an Amax supervisor. At one point, a LIC employee, Gregory Dixon, was spray painting the surface above the work area of an Amax employee, Kenneth Johnson, and accidentally sprayed coal tar on Johnson. An argument ensued when Johnson told Dixon to stop painting in Johnson's work area. Johnson believed that Amax employees had priority and could stop LIC painters if they interfered with Amax work. Dixon said that he had been told that the LIC work took priority and that he would not stop unless a supervisor told him to. Words and threats ensued, including racial slurs against Dixon, and eventually Johnson was injured when Dixon shoved him against a steel beam.

Johnson sued Dixon and LIC for injuries caused by Dixon's battery under the doctrine of *respondeat superior.* LIC argued that it could not be held liable for Dixon's tort because it was committed outside the scope of Dixon's employment. According to LIC, the argument was personal in nature and stemmed from Dixon's desire to punish Johnson for racial taunts and to "appease his own machismo." The trial court held for Johnson, and LIC appealed.

ISSUE   The central issue to be decided was whether Dixon was acting within the scope of his employment when he injured Johnson. If he was, then LIC would be liable for Dixon's tort under the doctrine of *respondeat superior.*

DECISION   The Court of Appeals held that Dixon was acting within the scope of his employment when he injured Johnson, thus affirming the decision of the trial court.

REASON   The court rejected LIC's argument that Dixon was not acting within the course and scope of his employment at the time the incident occurred. All of the evidence indicated that the dispute arose over the question of which worker had priority to perform his job in the area. The court thus concluded that "[a]lthough racial slurs and some personal bravado were undoubtedly involved, it is clear that this argument between these workers was primarily employment-rooted and reasonably incidental to the performance of each worker's duties in furtherance of his employer's business." Accordingly, the court found "no error in the trial judge's conclusion that Dixon acted in the course and scope of his employment, thereby making LIC . . . liable under the doctrine of *respondeat superior* for his tortious conduct."

Misrepresentation

A principal is exposed to tort liability whenever a third person sustains loss due to the agent's misrepresentation. The key to a principal's liability is whether or not the agent was actually or apparently authorized to make representations, and whether such representations were made within the scope of the agency.

An interesting series of cases has arisen on the theory that when a principal has placed an agent in a position to defraud a third party, the principal is liable for the agent's fraudulent acts. Suppose a bank loan officer, Pruitt, falsely represents to a customer, Hawkins, that additional collateral, such as stocks and bonds, is needed for a loan. Hawkins turns over to Pruitt numerous stock certificates to satisfy Pruitt's request. Pruitt keeps Hawkins's stock certificates in her own possession and later uses them to make personal investments. The bank will be liable to Hawkins for losses sustained on the stocks even though the bank had no direct role in or knowledge of the fraudulent scheme.

The principal is always directly responsible for an agent's misrepresentation made within the scope of the agent's authority, whether the misrepresentation was made fraudulently or simply by the agent's mistake or oversight.

Negligence

Principals are liable only for the negligence of their agents that causes physical harm to third persons provided that the act takes place within the scope of the agent's employment. Therefore, the liability of a principal for an agent's negligence is dependent upon whether the agent is also an employee (and whether the employer has control of the conduct of the agent).

Generally, the principal is not liable for physical harm caused to a third person by the negligent act of an independent contractor in the performance of the contract, since in this situation the employer does not have the *right to control* the details of performance. An exception to this doctrine prevails when exceptionally hazardous activities are involved, such as blasting operations, the transportation of highly volatile chemicals, or the use of poisonous gases. In these cases an employer cannot be shielded from liability merely by using an independent contractor. Strict liability is imposed upon the employer as a matter of law and, in some states, by statute.

❖ Termination of Agency

Agency law is similar to contract law in that both an agency and a contract terminate by an act of the parties or by operation of law. Once the relationship between the principal and agent has ended, the agent no longer has the right to bind the principal. Third persons may also need to be notified, however, when the agency has been terminated, in order to terminate an agent's apparent authority.

Termination by Act of the Parties

An agency may be terminated by act of the parties in several ways:

Lapse of Time   An agency agreement may specify the time period during which the agency relationship will exist. If so, the agency ends when that time period expires. Thus, if Allen signs an agreement of agency with Proust "beginning January 1, 1984, and ending December 31, 1989," the agency is automatically terminated on December 31, 1989. Of course, the parties can agree to continue the relationship, in which case the same terms will apply.

If no definite time is stated, then the agency continues for a reasonable time and can be terminated at will by either party. What constitutes a "reasonable time" depends upon the circumstances and the nature of the agency relationship. Suppose Proust asks Allen to sell Proust's car. After two years, if Allen has not sold Proust's car and there has been no communication between Proust and Allen, it is safe to assume that the agency relationship has terminated. Allen no longer has the authority to sell Proust's car.

Purpose Achieved   An agent can be employed to accomplish a particular objective, such as the purchase of stock for a cattle rancher. In that case, the agency automatically ends after the cattle have been purchased.

If more than one agent is employed to accomplish the same purpose, such as the sale of real estate, the first agent to complete the sale automatically terminates the agency relationship for all the others.

Occurrence of a Specific Event   An agency can be created to terminate upon the happening of a certain event. If Proust appoints Allen to handle his business affairs while he is away, when Proust returns, the agency automatically terminates.

Sometimes one aspect of the agent's authority terminates on the occurrence of a particular event, but the agency relationship itself does not terminate. Suppose Proust, a banker, permits Allen, the credit manager, to grant a credit line of $2,000 to certain depositors who maintain $2,000 in a savings account. If any customer's savings account falls below $2,000, Allen can no longer continue making the credit line available to that customer. But Allen's right to extend credit to the other customers maintaining the minimum balance will continue.

Mutual Agreement   Recall from basic contract law that parties can cancel (rescind) a contract by mutually agreeing to terminate the contractual relationship. The same holds true in agency law regardless of whether the agency contract is in writing or whether it is for a specific duration. Assume that Proust no longer wishes Allen to be her agent, and Allen does not want to work for Proust anymore. Either party can communicate to the other the intent to terminate the relationship. Agreement to terminate effectively relieves each of the rights, duties, and powers inherent in the relationship.

Termination by One Party   As a general rule, either party can terminate the agency relationship. The agent's act is said to be a renunciation of authority. The principal's act is a revocation of authority. But although both parties may have the *power* to terminate, they may not each possess the *right*. Wrongful termination can subject the canceling party to a suit for damages.

For example, Allen has a one-year employment contract with Proust to act as an agent for $25,000. Proust can discharge Allen before the contract period expires (Proust has the *power* to breach the contract); however, Proust will be liable to Allen for money damages because Proust has no *right* to breach the contract.

Even in an agency at will, the principal who wishes to terminate must give the agent reasonable notice, that is, at least sufficient notice to allow the agent to recoup his or her expenses and, in some cases, to make a normal profit.

Agency Coupled with an Interest   An agency *coupled with an interest* is a relationship created for the benefit of the agent. The agent actually acquires a beneficial interest in the subject matter of the agency. Under these circumstances, it is not equitable to permit a principal to terminate at will. Hence, this type of agency is *irrevocable*.

To illustrate: Sally Rather (the principal) owns Green Hills. She needs some immediate cash, so she enters into an agreement with Jack Harrington that Harrington will lend her $10,000, and she agrees to grant Harrington a one-half interest in Green Hills and "the exclusive right to sell" it for $35,000 if she fails to repay the $10,000. The loan is to be repaid out of the sale's proceeds. Harrington's power to sell Green Hills is coupled with a beneficial interest of one-half ownership in Green Hills created at the time of the loan for the purpose of supporting it and securing its repayment. Harrington's agency power is irrevocable.

An agency coupled with an interest should not be confused with situations where the agent merely derives proceeds or profits from the sale of the subject matter. For example, an agent who merely receives a commission from the sale of real property does not have a beneficial interest in the property itself. Likewise, an attorney whose fee is a percentage of the recovery (a contingency fee) merely has an interest in the proceeds. These agency relationships are revocable by the principal, subject to any express contractual arrangements that the principal has with the agent.

Since, in an agency coupled with an interest, the interest is not created for the benefit of the principal, it is not really an agency in the usual sense. Therefore, any attempt by the principal to revoke an agency coupled with an interest normally has no legal force or effect and is not terminated by the death of either the principal or the agent.

Termination by Operation of Law

Termination of an agency by operation of law takes place in the following circumstances:

Death or Insanity   The general rule is that death or insanity of either the principal or the agent automatically and immediately terminates the ordinary agency relationship. Knowledge of the death is not required.[6] Suppose Proust sends Allen to the Far East to purchase a rare book. Before Allen makes the purchase, Proust dies. Allen's agent status is terminated at the moment of death, even though Allen does not know that Proust has died. Some states, however, have changed this common law by statute.

Agents' transactions that occur after the death of the principal are not binding on the principal's estate.[7] Assume Allen is hired by Proust to collect a debt from Thomas (a third party). Proust dies, but Allen still collects the money from Thomas, not knowing of Proust's death. Thomas's payment to Allen is no longer legally sufficient to discharge Thomas's debt to Proust because Allen no longer has Proust's authority to collect the money. If Allen absconds with the money, Thomas must again pay the debt to Proust's estate.

---

6.   An exception to virtually all notice and termination rules occurs in an agency coupled with an interest, which is not automatically terminated by death or incapacity.

7.   There is an exception to this rule in banking whereby the bank as the agent can continue to exercise specific types of authority even after the customer's death or insanity unless it has knowledge of the death or insanity [UCC 4-405]. Even with knowledge of the customer's death, the bank has authority for ten days following the customer's death to honor checks in absence of a stop-payment order.

Impossibility   When the specific subject matter of an agency is destroyed or lost, the agency terminates. If Proust employs Allen to sell Proust's house, but prior to the sale, the premises are destroyed by fire, then Allen's agency and authority to sell Proust's house terminate. When it is impossible for the agent to perform the agency lawfully, the agency terminates.

Changed Circumstances   When an event occurs that has such an unusual effect on the subject matter of the agency that the agent can reasonably infer that the principal will not want the agency to continue, the agency terminates. For example, Proust hires Allen to sell a tract of land for $20,000. Subsequently, Allen learns that there is oil under the land and that the land is therefore worth $1 million. The agency and Allen's authority to sell the land for $20,000 are terminated.

Bankruptcy   Bankruptcy of the principal or the agent usually, but not always, terminates the agency relationship (*insolvency* will not necessarily terminate the relationship). Some situations, such as a serious financial loss, might indicate that future contracts should not be made.

War   When the principal's country and agent's country are at war with each other, the agency is terminated or at least suspended.

Notice of Termination Required

When an agency terminates by operation of law because of the preceding reasons or some other unforeseen circumstance, there is no duty to notify third persons, unless the agent's authority is coupled with an interest. If the parties themselves have terminated the agency, however, it is the principal's duty to inform any third parties who know of the existence of the agency that it has been terminated (although notice may be given by others).

An agent's authority continues until the agent receives some notice of termination. Notice to third parties, however, follows the general rule that an agent's *apparent* authority continues until the third person is notified (from any source of information) that such authority has been terminated.

The principal is expected to notify directly any third person who the principal knows has dealt with the agent. For third persons who have heard about the agency but have not dealt with the agency, *constructive notice* is sufficient.[8]

No particular form of notice of agency termination is required to be effective. The principal can actually notify the agent, or the agent can learn of the termination through some other means. For example, Manning bids on a shipment of steel, and Stone is hired as an agent to arrange transportation of the shipment. When Stone learns that Manning has lost the bid, Stone's authority to make the transportation arrangement terminates.

If the agent's authority is written, it must be revoked in writing, and the writing must be shown to all people who saw the original writing that established the agency relationship. Sometimes a written authorization (like that granting power of attorney) contains an expiration date. The passage of the expiration date is sufficient notice of termination for third parties.

---

8.   Constructive notice is information or knowledge of a fact imputed by law to a person if he or she could have discovered the fact by proper diligence. Constructive notice is often accomplished pursuant to a statute by newspaper publication.

Application

Law and the Employer— Using Independent Contractors

One reason for using an independent contractor is that it may reduce your susceptibility to tort liability. If, however, an independent contractor's words or conduct lead another party to believe that he or she is your employee, you may not escape liability for the worker's tort. To minimize the possibility of your being legally liable for negligence on the part of an independent contractor, you should, prior to hiring that contractor, inquire about his or her qualifications. The degree to which you should investigate depends, of course, on the nature of the work. A more thorough investigation is necessary when there is a potential danger to the public from the contractor's activities (as in delivering explosives).

Another reason for hiring an independent contractor is that you need not pay or deduct social security and unemployment taxes on behalf of such individuals. The independent contractor is the responsible party for paying these taxes. Additionally, the independent contractor is not eligible for any retirement or medical plans, or other fringe benefits that you have for yourself and other employees; and this is a cost saving to you.

A word of caution, though: Simply designating a person as an independent contractor does not make him or her one. Under Internal Revenue Service rules, an individual will be treated as an employee if he or she is "in fact" an employee, regardless of any classification that you might have made. For example, a secretary will not be treated by the IRS as an independent contractor simply because you designate him or her as such. If, however, you contract with a secretarial service, the secretary is an employee of the service and not your employee directly. In this case, even though you are utilizing an independent contractor (the secretarial service), you still retain the right to supervise and inspect work to make sure that it meets your contract specifications. Just be-

cause you utilize this right does not change the worker's status from that of an independent contractor to an employee.

If you improperly designate an employee as an independent contractor, the penalty may be high. Usually you would be liable for back social security and unemployment taxes, plus interest and penalty. In addition, if you have a pension plan, it might be disqualified. When in doubt, seek professional assistance in such matters.

Checklist for Using Independent Contractors

☐ 1. Check the qualifications of any independent contractor you plan to use to reduce the potential for his or her negligent actions.

☐ 2. It is best to require in any contract with an independent contractor that the contractor must assume liability for harm to a third person because of the contractor's negligence.

☐ 3. Require that independent contractors working for you carry liability insurance. Examine the policy to make sure that it is current, particularly when actions that are more than normally hazardous to the public are going to be undertaken by the contractor.

☐ 4. Make sure that independent contractors do not represent themselves as your employees to the rest of the world.

☐ 5. Regularly inspect the work of the independent contractor to make sure that it is being performed in accordance with contract specifications. Such supervision on your part will not change the worker's status as an independent contractor.

❖ Chapter Summary: Agency

Types of Agency Relationships	1. *Principal-agent*—Where an agent acts on behalf of and instead of the principal, using a certain degree of his or her own discretion. 2. *Master-servant (employer-employee)*—The so-called servant is an employee whose physical conduct is controlled or subject to control by an employer. A servant (employee) can also be an agent. 3. *Principal (employer)–independent contractor*—The contractor is not an employee, and the employer or principal has no control over the details of physical performance. Except for real estate and collection agencies, the independent contractor is not usually an agent.
Formation of the Principal-Agent Relationship	1. *By agreement*—Through express consent (oral or written), or implied by conduct. 2. *By ratification*—Principal either by act or agreement ratifies the conduct of an agent who acted outside the scope of authority or the conduct of a person who is in fact not an agent. 3. *By estoppel*—When the principal causes a third person to believe that another person is his or her agent. 4. *By operation of law*—Based on a social duty (such as the need to support family members), or in emergency situations where the agent is unable to contact the principal.

Duties of Agents and Principals	1. *Duties of the agent:*
	  a. Performance—The agent must use reasonable diligence and skill in performing his or her duties.
	  b. Notification—The agent is required to notify the principal of all matters that come to his or her attention concerning the subject matter of the agency.
	  c. Loyalty—The agent has a duty to act solely for the benefit of his or her principal and not in the interest of the agent or a third party.
	  d. Obedience—The agent must follow all lawful and clearly stated instructions of the principal.
	  e. Accounting—The agent has a duty to make available to the principal records of all property and money received and paid out on behalf of the principal.
	
	2. *Duties of the principal:*
	  a. Compensation—Except in a gratuitous agency relationship, the principal must pay the agreed-upon value (or reasonable value) for an agent's services.
	  b. Reimbursement and indemnification—The principal must reimburse the agent for all sums of money disbursed at the request of the principal and for all sums of money the agent disburses for necessary expenses in the course of reasonable performance of his or her agency duties.
	  c. Cooperation—A principal must cooperate with and assist an agent in performing his or her duties.
	  d. Safe working conditions—A principal must provide safe working conditions for the agent-employee.

Scope of Agent's Authority	1. *Express authority*—Can be oral or in writing. Must be in writing if a power of attorney or if the agent is to execute a contract that must be in writing (Statute of Frauds). 2. *Implied authority*—Authority customarily associated with the position of the agent or authority that is deemed necessary in order for the agent to carry out expressly authorized tasks. 3. *Apparent authority (authority by estoppel)*—Exists when the principal, by word or action, causes a third party reasonably to believe that an agent has authority to act, even though the agent has no express or implied authority.

❖ Chapter Summary: Agency—Continued

Scope of Agent's Authority (Continued)	4. *Ratification*—The affirmation by the principal of an agent's unauthorized action or promise; can be either express or implied. For the ratification to be effective, the principal must be aware of all material facts.
Principal's and Agent's Liability for Contract	1. *Disclosed principals and partially disclosed principals*—Principal is liable to a third party for a contract made by the agent, if the agent acted within the scope of his or her authority. 2. *Undisclosed principals*—Agent is liable to a third party for a contract made by the agent. If agent acted within scope of authority, principal is fully bound by contract. If agent is forced to pay the third party and the agent has contracted within the scope of authority, the agent is entitled to indemnification by the principal.
Principal's and Agent's Liability for Torts of an Agent	1. Under the doctrine of *respondeat superior* the principal is liable for any harm caused to another through the agent's negligence if the agent was acting within the scope of his or her employment at the time the harmful act occurred.

Termination of an Agency	1. *By act of the parties:*
	  a. Lapse of time (when a definite time for the duration of the agency was agreed upon when agency established).
	  b. Purpose achieved.
	  c. Mutual rescission (requires mutual consent of principal and agent).
	  d. Termination by act of either the principal (revocation) or the agent (renunciation). (A principal cannot revoke an agency coupled with an interest.)
	
	2. *By operation of law:*
	  a. Death or insanity of either the principal or the agent (except in an agency coupled with an interest).
	  b. Impossibility (when the purpose of the agency cannot be achieved due to an event beyond the parties' control).
	  c. Changed circumstances (where it would be inequitable to require that the agency be continued).
	  d. Bankruptcy (but not insolvency) of the principal or the agent.
	  e. War between the principal's and agent's countries.
	
	3. *Notification of termination:*
	  a. When agency is terminated by act of the parties, all third persons who have previously dealt with the agency must be directly notified; constructive notice will suffice for all other third parties.
	  b. When agency is terminated by operation of law, no notice to third parties is required.

❖ Questions and Case Problems

22-1. Springer was a political candidate running for congressional office. He was operating on a tight budget and instructed his campaign staff not to purchase any campaign materials without his explicit authorization. In spite of these instructions, one of his campaign workers ordered Johnson Printing Company to print some promotional materials for Springer's campaign. When the printed materials were received, Springer did not return them but instead used them during his campaign. When Johnson failed to obtain payment from Springer for the materials, he sued for recovery of the price. Springer contended that he was not liable on the sales contract because he had not authorized his agent to purchase the printing services. Johnson argued that Springer's use of the materials constituted ratification of his agent's unauthorized purchase. Is Johnson correct? Explain.

22-2. Moore managed a hardware store for Atchison and was authorized by Atchison to sell goods on credit. Moore normally checked with the local credit bureau to obtain credit ratings on any customers wishing to buy on credit. One Saturday afternoon when the store was unusually busy, Moore was approached by a customer, Albert, who needed a lawn mower right away and asked if he could buy one on credit. Moore agreed to extend the credit and did not bother to run the usual credit check because he was busy and the credit application looked good. On the following Monday, Moore requested routine credit information from the credit bureau on Albert and was astonished to learn that Albert's credit rating was very poor. Albert had failed to pay numerous debts to other retail stores in the area, and Moore realized, too late, that he should not have extended credit to Albert. When Albert failed to make payments on the equipment, Moore tried to reach him, but the address and phone number on the application were false. Atchison, the owner of the hardware, claimed that Moore was liable to him for the price of the lawn mower. Moore argued that he should not be liable because he was Atchison's agent and Atchison had authorized him to sell goods on credit. Who will prevail?

22-3. Brooks is a traveling sales agent. Brooks not only solicits orders but delivers the goods and collects payments from her customers. Brooks places all payments in her private checking account and at the end of each month draws sufficient cash from her bank to cover the payments made. Giberson, Brooks's employer, is totally unaware of this procedure. Because of a slowdown in the economy, Giberson tells all his salespeople to offer 20 percent discounts on orders. Brooks solicits orders, but she offers only 15 percent discounts, pocketing the extra 5 percent paid by customers. Brooks has not lost any orders by this practice, and she is rated as one of Giberson's top salespersons. Giberson now learns of Brooks's actions. Discuss fully Giberson's rights in this matter.

22-4. Paul Everett is a purchasing agent-employee for Peterson Coal Supply, a partnership. Everett has authority to purchase the coal needed by Peterson to satisfy the needs of its customers. While Everett is leaving a coal mine from which he just purchased a large quantity of coal, his car breaks down. He walks into a small roadside grocery store for help. While there, he runs into Wiley, who owns 360 acres back in the mountains with all mineral rights. Wiley, in need of money, offers to sell Everett the property at $1,500 per acre. Upon inspection, Everett believes the subsurface contains valuable coal deposits. Everett contracts to purchase the property for Peterson, signing the contract, "Peterson Coal Supply, Paul Everett, agent." The closing date is set for August 1. Everett takes the contract to the partnership. The managing partner is furious, as Peterson is not in the property business. Later, just before August 1, both Wiley and the partnership learn that the value of the land is at least $15,000 per acre. Discuss the rights of Peterson and Wiley concerning the land contract.

22-5. Ruth owes Carla $1,000, and the debt is due and payable. Ruth does not have the cash to pay the debt, but she has a diamond ring valued at $1,800. She gives Carla authority to sell the diamond ring to satisfy the debt, with any surplus being paid back to Ruth. Later Ruth and Carla have a severe disagreement over another matter, and Ruth sends a letter to Carla terminating her authority and agency to sell the ring. Notwithstanding her receipt of the letter, Carla contracts to sell the ring to Philip for $1,200. Philip pays Carla, but Ruth refuses to turn over the ring to Philip or accept the $1,200 from Carla. Ruth claims that at the time the contract with Philip was made, no agency existed between Ruth and Carla. Discuss fully Ruth's contention.

22-6. L.M.T. Steel Products contracted with a school to install numerous room partitions. To accomplish this work, L.M.T. hired a man by the name of Webster. Webster was not a regular employee of L.M.T., and it was stipulated that he was to be paid by the number of feet of partitions installed. Webster did not have a contractor's license. He hired other workers to do the installing, and these workers were paid by L.M.T. Webster was given blueprints by L.M.T., but he was not otherwise at any time actively supervised by L.M.T. on the job. Needing to place a telephone call to L.M.T., Webster drove his own personal vehicle to a public telephone. On the way, he negligently collided with another car, and an occupant of that car, Ms. Peirson, was injured. Peirson sued L.M.T., claiming that Webster was an employee. L.M.T. claimed Webster was an independent contractor. Who was correct? Explain. [L.M.T. Steel Products, Inc. v. Peirson, 47 Md.App. 633, 425 A.2d 242 (1981)]

22-7. Hunter Farms purchased a supply of Sencor, an herbicide, from a seller located in Canada. Hunter had been advised by the seller that an "import specialist" had estimated that the import duties would probably be about 5 percent but that the final determination would be based on an examination conducted by U.S. customs agents when the shipment crossed the border. Hunter hired an import broker, F.W. Myers & Company, to see the Sencor through customs and take care of the necessary paperwork. As Hunter's agent, Myers was also authorized to pay the import duties levied by the customs officials. The actual import duty turned out to be much higher than Hunter had been advised. Instead of approximately $30,000, it was over $128,000. Myers paid the $128,000 and requested reimbursement from Hunter. Hunter refused to reimburse, claiming that Myers had failed in his agency duty to notify Hunter of the fact that the import duty was substantially more than the estimated 5 percent. Myers defended on the ground that it was customary in the import business for the estimated import duty to vary from the actual duty, and that import brokers customarily do not notify their principals when such variance occurs. Myers also stated that he was unaware that Hunter was inexperienced in the importation of goods. Did Hunter have to reimburse Myers for the $128,000? Explain. [F.W. Myers & Co. v. Hunter Farms, 319 N.W.2d 186 (Iowa, 1982)]

22-8. Pastor John Rich sought to expand and beautify his church. The church bylaws provided that all business affairs and property transactions of the church were under the "general charge" of a committee of parish members. The pastor, however, gradually exercised control over more and more church business matters and over time borrowed large sums of money from local banking institutions on behalf of the church, offering church property as collateral without the committee's approval. The money was used to do extensive landscaping, to install two swimming pools and construct parking lots, to renovate the interior of the church, to establish an art gallery, and to fund other highly visible projects. When the church found it difficult to meet the loan payments and eventually defaulted, a new committee was elected by the church members. The new committee brought suit against the pastor and the two banking firms that had lent money to the pastor, contending that the pastor had no authority to borrow money and mortgage church property without the committee's explicit approval and that the church was therefore not liable for payment of the loans. A special master appointed by the trial court held that the committee's long silence in regard to the pastor's financial undertakings constituted ratification of the pastor's actions. The committee appealed. What was the result? [Perkins v. Rich, 11 Mass. App. 317, 415 N.E. 2d 895 (1981)]

22-9. Beverly Baumann took her mother to Memorial Hospital, where the mother was placed in the intensive care unit for a serious heart condition. Baumann was asked by a nurse to sign a number of documents, including an authorization for the hospital to receive the mother's insurance benefits directly in payment of hospital expenses for her mother's care. The authorization, which Baumann signed, included the clause, "I understand I am financially responsible to the hospital for charges not covered by this authorization." Baumann's mother died while still in the hospital. Later, the hospital sought recovery of $19,013.42 in unpaid hospital charges from Baumann, claiming that by signing the authorization form Baumann had guaranteed payment of her mother's hospital expenses. Baumann contended that she was not liable because she signed the form as an agent for a disclosed principal, her mother. Was Baumann acting as an agent for her mother when she signed the authorization form? Explain. [Memorial Hospital v. Baumann, 100 A.D. 2d 701, 474 N.Y.S. 2d 636 (1984)]

22-10. Sam Kademenos was about to sell a $1 million life insurance policy to a prospective customer when he resigned from his position with Equitable Life. Before resigning from the company, he had expended substantial amounts of company money and had utilized Equitable's medical examiners in order to procure the $1 million sale. After resigning, Kademenos joined a competing insurance firm, Jefferson Life Insurance Company, and made the sale through it. Has he breached any duty to Equitable? [Kademenos v. Equitable Life Assur. Soc'y, 513 F. 2d 1073 (3d Cir. 1975)]

Chapter 23

Partnerships—Creation and Termination

As we pointed out in the introduction to this unit, agency law governs relationships arising in both partnerships and corporations. Partnership law derives from agency law because each partner is considered an agent of every other partner. Therefore, the agency concepts outlined in Chapter 22 apply; specifically, the imputation of knowledge of and responsibility for acts done within the scope of the partnership relationship. In Justice Cardozo's words, partners are bound by "fiduciary ties" in their relationship to one another.

Differences exist, however, between partnership relationships and agency relationships. A partnership is based on a voluntary contract between two or more competent persons agreeing to place money, labor, and skill in a business with the understanding that profits and losses will be proportionately shared. In an agency relationship, the agent usually does not have an ownership interest in the business, nor is he or she obliged to bear a portion of the any business losses.

The Uniform Partnership Act (UPA) (discussed in the "Landmark" in Chapter 24) is a codification of partnership law in the United States and has done much to reduce controversies in the law relating to partnerships. Except for Georgia and Louisiana, the UPA has been adopted in all of the states, as well as the District of Columbia. The UPA defines **partnership** as "an association of two or more persons to carry on as co-owners a business for profit."[1] Therefore, the essential elements of a partnership are (1) a common ownership interest in a business, (2) the sharing of the profits and losses of the business, and (3) the right to manage the operations of the partnership.

A special type of partnership, called a **limited partnership** (examined in the latter part of this chapter) involves one or more **general partners** who assume the management of the partnership and also therefore assume full liability for all debts of the partnership. In addition, there are **limited partners,** who may contribute cash or other property and own an interest in the firm but are not allowed to involve themselves in any management responsibilities. The limited partners are not personally liable for partnership debts beyond the amount that they have agreed to invest. An early form of the limited partnership, the *commenda* of the Middle Ages, is the subject of this chapter's "Landmark."

"Many forms of conduct permissible in a workaday world for those acting at arm's length, are forbidden to those bound by fiduciary ties."

Benjamin Cardozo, 1870–1938 (Associate Justice of the U. S. Supreme Court, 1932–1938)

PARTNERSHIP
An association of two or more persons to carry on, as co-owners, a business for profit. [UPA Section 6(1)]

LIMITED PARTNERSHIP
A partnership consisting of one or more general partners, who carry on the business and who are liable to the full extent of their personal assets for debts of the partnership, and of one or more limited partners, who contribute only assets and who are liable only up to the amount contributed by them.

GENERAL PARTNER
In a limited partnership, a partner who assumes responsibility for the management of the partnership and liability for all partnership debts.

---

1. UPA Section 6(1).

LIMITED PARTNER
In a limited partnership, a partner who contributes capital to the partnership but has no right to participate in the management and operation of the business. The limited partner assumes no liability for partnership debts beyond the capital contributed.

Current law governing limited partnerships is contained in the Uniform Limited Partnership Act (ULPA) of 1916 and the Revised Uniform Limited Partnership Act (RULPA) of 1976. All of the states except Louisiana have adopted either the ULPA (twenty-seven states) or the RULPA (twenty-two states).

❖ Partnership Characteristics

A partnership is sometimes called a *firm* or a *company*, terms that connote an entity separate and apart from its aggregate members. Sometimes the law of partnership recognizes the independent entity, but for certain other purposes, the law treats it as an aggregate of individual partners. At common law, a partnership was never treated as a separate legal entity. Thus, at common law a suit could never be brought by or against the firm in its own name; each individual partner had to sue or be sued. Today, most states provide specifically that the partnership can be treated as an entity for certain purposes. This usually includes the capacity to sue or be sued, to collect judgments, and to have all accounting procedures in the name of the partnership. In addition, the Uniform Partnership Act recognizes that partnership property may be held in the name of the partnership rather than in the names of the individual partners. Finally, federal procedural laws frequently permit the partnership to be treated as an entity in such matters as suits in federal courts, bankruptcy proceedings, and filing of informational federal tax returns.

When the partnership is not regarded as a separate legal entity, it is treated as an *aggregate* of the individual partners. For example, for federal income tax purposes, a partnership is not a tax-paying entity. The income or losses incurred by it are "passed through" the partnership framework and attributed to the partners on their individual tax returns. The partnership as an entity has no tax identity or liability, other than for the filing of an informational return indicating the profit and loss that each partner will report on his or her individual tax return.

❖ Partnership Formation

A partnership is ordinarily formed by an explicit agreement among the parties, although the law recognizes another form of partnership—*partnership by estoppel*—in which persons who are not partners represent themselves as partners when dealing with third parties. The liability of partners by estoppel is covered later in this chapter.

This section will describe the requirements for the creation of a true partnership, including references to the liability of *alleged partners*. The next section will deal with the process by which partnerships are terminated.

A true partnership is a voluntary association of individuals and, as such, is generally based on an agreement among the parties that reflects their intention to create a partnership, contribute capital, share profits and losses, and participate in management. The true partnership relationship involves a high degree of trust and reliance. Each partner is an agent for the other partners.

Parties cannot avoid partnership liability, even by expressly designating themselves as some other business form, if the evidence establishes the essential elements of a partnership.

Formalities of Partnership Formation

As a general rule, agreements to form a partnership can be oral, written, or implied by conduct. Some partnership agreements, however, must be in writing to be legally enforceable within the Statute of Frauds. (See Chapter 8 for details.) For example, a partnership agreement that, by its terms, is to continue for more than one year, or one that authorizes the partners to deal in real property transfers, must be evidenced by a sufficient writing. A sample partnership agreement is shown in Exhibit 23-1.

Practically speaking, the provisions of any partnership agreement should always be in writing. One disadvantage of an oral agreement is that its terms are difficult to prove, because a court must evaluate oral testimony given by persons with an interest in the eventual decision. In addition, potential problems that would have been detected in the course of drafting a written agreement may go unnoticed in an oral agreement.

To illustrate: Terrence and Frank plan to enter into a partnership agreement to sell tires. Among the provisions to be included is that Terrence provide two-thirds of the capital to start up the business and receive two-thirds of the profits in return. The agreement is made orally. Terrence now sues because Frank claims that one-half of the profits should be his. Without a writing, Terrence may have a hard time overcoming the presumption that he is entitled to only one-half of the profits of a two-person partnership.[2] A partnership agreement, called **articles of partnership,** usually specifies each partner's share of the profits and is binding regardless of how uneven the distribution appears to be.

ARTICLES OF PARTNERSHIP
A written agreement that sets forth each partner's rights in, and obligations to, the partnership.

Partnership Duration

The partnership agreement can specify the duration of the partnership in terms of a date or the completion of a particular project. This is called a *partnership for a term.* A dissolution without the consent of all the partners prior to the expiration of the partnership term constitutes a breach of the agreement, and the responsible partner can be liable for any losses resulting from it.

If no fixed duration is specified, the partnership is a *partnership at will.* This type of partnership can be dissolved at any time by any partner without violating the agreement and without incurring liability for resulting losses to other partners because of the termination. Normally, reasonable notice of the dissolution of the partnership is given to all partners in order to inform them of what is about to happen.

Capacity of Partners

Any person having the capacity to enter a contract can become a partner. A partnership contract entered into with a minor as a partner is voidable and can be disaffirmed by the minor. (See Chapter 7 for details.)

Lack of legal capacity due to insanity at the time of the agreement likewise allows the purported partner either to avoid the agreement or to enforce it. If a partner becomes insane and is adjudicated mentally incompetent during the course of the partnership, the partnership is not automatically dissolved, but dissolution can be decreed by a court upon petition.

---

2. The law assumes that members of a partnership share profits and losses equally unless a partnership agreement provides otherwise [UPA Section 18(a)].

◆ **Exhibit 23-1 Partnership Agreement**

PARTNERSHIP AGREEMENT

This agreement, made and entered into as of the _____, by and among _____
_____ (hereinafter collectively sometimes referred to as "Partners").

WITNESSETH:

Whereas, the Parties hereto desire to form a General Partnership (hereinafter referred to as the "Partnership"), for the term and upon the conditions hereinafter set forth;

Now, therefore, in consideration of the mutual covenants hereinafter contained, it is agreed by and among the Parties hereto as follows:

Article I
BASIC STRUCTURE

Form. The Parties hereby form a General Partnership pursuant to the Laws of _____
_____.

Name. The business of the Partnership shall be conducted under the name of _____
_____.

Place of Business. The principal office and place of business of the Partnership shall be located at _____, or such other place as the Partners may from time to time designate.

Term. The Partnership shall commence on _____, and shall continue for _____years, unless earlier terminated in the following manner: (a) By the completion of the purpose intended, or (b) Pursuant to this Agreement, or (c) By applicable _____law, or (d) By death, insanity, bankruptcy, retirement, withdrawal, resignation, expulsion, or disability of all of the then Partners.

Purpose—General. The purpose for which the Partnership is organized is _____

Article II
FINANCIAL ARRANGEMENTS

Each Partner has contributed to the initial capital of the Partnership property in the amount and form indicated on Schedule A attached hereto and made a part hereof. Capital contributions to the Partnership shall not earn interest. An individual capital account shall be maintained for each Partner. If at any time during the existence of the Partnership it shall become necessary to increase the capital with which the said Partnership is doing business, then (upon the vote of the Managing Partner(s)): each party to this Agreement shall contribute to the capital of this Partnership within _ days notice of such need in an amount according to his then Percentage Share of Capital as called for by the Managing Partner(s).

The Percentage Share of Profits and Capital of each Partner shall be (unless otherwise modified by the terms of this Agreement) as follows:

Names	Initial Percentage Share of Profits and Capital

No interest shall be paid on any contribution to the capital of the Partnership. No Partner shall have the right to demand the return of his capital contributions except as herein provided. Except as herein provided, the individual Partners shall have no right to any priority over each other as to the return of capital contributions except as herein provided.

Distributions to the Partners of net operating profits of the Partnership, as hereinafter defined, shall be made at _____. Such distributions shall be made to the Partners simultaneously.

For the purpose of this Agreement, net operating profit for any accounting period shall mean the gross receipts of the Partnership for such period, less the sum of all cash expenses of operation of the Partnership, and such sums as may be necessary to establish a reserve for operating expenses. In determining net operating profit, deductions for depreciation, amortization, or other similar charges not requiring actual current expenditures of cash shall *not* be taken into account in accordance with generally accepted accounting principles.

◆ **Exhibit 23-1 Partnership Agreement—Continued**

No Partner shall be entitled to receive any compensation from the Partnership, nor shall any Partner receive any drawing account from the Partnership.

Article III
MANAGEMENT

The Managing Partner(s) shall be _____.

The Managing Partner(s) shall have the right to vote as to the management and conduct of the business of the Partnership as follows:

Names   **Vote**

Article IV
DISSOLUTION

In the event that the Partnership shall hereafter be dissolved for any reason whatsoever, a full and general account of its assets, liabilities and transactions shall at once be taken. Such assets may be sold and turned into cash as soon as possible and all debts and other amounts due the Partnership collected. The proceeds thereof shall thereupon be applied as follows:

(a) To discharge the debts and liabilities of the Partnership and the expenses of liquidation.

(b) To pay each Partner or his legal representative any unpaid salary, drawing account, interest or profits to which he shall then be entitled and in addition, to repay to any Partner his capital contributions in excess of his original capital contribution.

(c) To divide the surplus, if any, among the Partners or their representatives as follows: (1) First (to the extent of each Partner's then capital account) in proportion to their then capital accounts. (2) Then according to each Partner's then Percentage Share of [*Capital//Income*].

No Partner shall have the right to demand and receive property in kind for his distribution.

Article V
MISCELLANEOUS

The Partnership's fiscal year shall commence on January 1st of each year and shall end on December 31st of each year. Full and accurate books of account shall be kept at such place as the Managing Partner(s) may from time to time designate, showing the condition of the business and finances of the Partnership; and each Partner shall have access to such books of account and shall be entitled to examine them at any time during ordinary business hours. At the end of each year, the Managing Partner(s) shall cause the Partnership's accountant to prepare a balance sheet setting forth the financial position of the Partnership as of the end of that year and a statement of operations (income and expenses) for that year. A copy of the balance sheet and statement of operations shall be delivered to each Partner as soon as it is available.

Each Partner shall be deemed to have waived all objections to any transaction or other facts about the operation of the Partnership disclosed in such balance sheet and/or statement of operations unless he shall have notified the Managing Partner(s) in writing of his objectives within thirty (30) days of the date on which such statement is mailed.

The Partnership shall maintain a bank account or bank accounts in the Partnership's name in a national or state bank in the State of _____. Checks and drafts shall be drawn on the Partnership's bank account for Partnership purposes only and shall be signed by the Managing Partner(s) or their designated agent.

Any controversy or claim arising out of or relating to this Agreement shall only be settled by arbitration in accordance with the rules of the American Arbitration Association, one Arbitrator, and shall be enforceable in any court having competent jurisdiction.

Witnesses   **Partners**

_____   _____

_____   _____

Dated: _____

The Corporation As Partner

Disagreement exists on whether a corporation can become a partner. After all, general partners are personally liable for the debts incurred by the partnership. But if one of the general partners is a corporation, then what does personal liability mean?

One view is that a corporation cannot be a partner unless the corporation's articles of incorporation specifically empower it to enter into a partnership as a partner. The opposite view, which prevails today, is contained in the Model Business Corporation Act and allows corporations generally to make contracts and incur liabilities. Basically, then, the capacity of corporations to contract is a question of corporation law. The UPA, on the other hand, specifically permits a corporation to be a partner. By definition, "a partnership is an association of two or more persons," and the UPA defines a person as including corporations.[3]

Many states have restrictions on corporations becoming partners, though such restrictions have become less common over the years. Many decisions in jurisdictions that do not permit corporate partners nevertheless validate the arrangements by characterizing them as joint ventures rather than as partnerships.

"The partner of my partner is not my partner."

Roman Legal Maxim

Mutual Consent of Partners

A partnership is a voluntary association of co-owners. The *intent* to associate is a key element of a partnership, and one cannot join a partnership unless all other partners consent.[4]

Indications of Partnership

Parties commonly find themselves in conflict over whether their business enterprise is a legal partnership, especially in the absence of a formal written contract. To answer this question, the UPA and the courts have developed broad guidelines for interpreting partnership status. A partnership is created by three factors:

1. A sharing of profits or losses.
2. A joint ownership of the business.
3. An equal right in management of the business.

A problem arises when evidence is insufficient to establish all three factors. The UPA provides a set of guidelines in this event. For example, the sharing of profits from a business is considered *prima facie* evidence that a partnership exists. No such inference is made, however, if the profits were received as payment of any of the following:

1. A debt by installments or interest on a loan.
2. Wages of an employee.
3. Rent to a landlord.
4. An annuity to a widow or representative of a deceased partner.
5. A sale of goodwill of a business or property.[5]

---

3. UPA Section 2.
4. UPA Section 18(g).
5. UPA Section 7(4).

Business Law in Action

Never Jump to Conclusions

Occasionally cases come before the court in which parties assume they are implied partners in a business endeavor when in fact they are not. This was the situation with Richard and Ola Circo, who assumed that they had a partnership arrangement with the Spanish Garden Food Manufacturing Company. Richard's father, Tom Circo, had sold and delivered food products manufactured by the owner of Spanish Gardens for nearly thirty years. When the owner of Spanish Gardens died in 1976, the food manufacturing business was operated by the court-appointed administrator of the owner's estate, who continued the arrangement with Tom Circo. When the elder Circo died a year later, Richard and Ola took over the business.

Richard and Ola distributed the food products to some sixteen grocery stores and warehouses in the Kansas City, Missouri, area. In most cases, the grocers would place their orders with the Circos directly, who would then purchase the goods from Spanish Gardens, at a discount of 15 percent below wholesale price, and deliver the goods to the grocery stores. No written agreement of any sort ever existed between the manufacturing house and the Circos, nor was any verbal agreement made as to the specific terms of their arrangements. The younger Circos simply continued to perform as Richard's father had.

The arrangement between the younger Circos and Spanish Gardens went smoothly until the business was sold in 1981. The new ownership advised the Circos that it would no longer continue to give the Circos the discount and, in fact, planned to begin to deal directly with the grocers instead of, as had previously been the case, indirectly through the Circos. By 1983 this plan was implemented, and the Circos lost their business.

The Circos believed that, even though they had no written partnership agreement with Spanish Gardens, the continuous course of dealing over three decades between the Circo family and Spanish Gardens had established an implied partnership agreement. They thus brought suit against Spanish Gardens for breach of an implied partnership contract.

But were the factors determining partnership status present here? They were not. And so the court noted in its opinion: "[T]he evidence makes it clear that plaintiffs did not have, and were not intended by the parties to have, any voice in the management of defendant's affairs in connection with the distribution of its products; that the parties did not share, or intend to share, risks, profits or losses with respect to the distribution of those products; and that the parties did not exercise, or intend to exercise, joint control or ownership of any assets. The necessary indicia of a joint venture or partnership of any kind are thus entirely lacking. [1]

1. Circo v. Spanish Gardens Food Manufacturing Co., Inc., 643 F.Supp. 51 (W.D.Mo. 1985).

To illustrate: A debtor businessperson owes a creditor $5,000 on an unsecured debt. To repay the debt, the debtor agrees to pay (and the creditor to accept) 10 percent of the debtor's monthly profits until the loan with interest is paid. Although the creditor is sharing profits from the business, the debtor and creditor are not presumed to be partners.

As a further example, consider a young college graduate who wants to start a retail dress shop. The graduate leases a building from the landlord. Both the landlord and the graduate know that it will take time to establish a clientele, and standard equal rental payments could severely restrict the graduate's ability to purchase inventory. Thus, the lease calls for a minimum low rental payment plus a percentage of the monthly profits for the term of the lease. This sort of arrangement does not make the landlord and the tenant partners, even though there is a sharing of profits.

Joint ownership of property, obviously, does not in and of itself create a partnership. Therefore, the fact that Allen and Burke own real property as joint tenants or as tenants-in-common (a form of joint ownership) does not establish a partnership. In fact, the sharing of gross returns and even profits from such ownership is usually not enough to create a partnership.[6] Thus, if Allen and Burke jointly own a piece of rural property and lease the land to a farmer, the sharing of the profits from the farming operation by the farmer in lieu of set rental payments would ordinarily not make Allen, Burke, and the farmer partners. In sum, the sharing of profits in itself does not prove the existence of a partnership, but sharing both profits and losses does.

Partnership by Estoppel

Parties who are not partners sometimes represent themselves as such and cause third persons to rely on representations made by the alleged partners. The law of partnership does not confer any partnership rights on these persons, but it may impose liability on them. This is true also when a true partner represents, expressly or impliedly, that a non-partner is a member of the firm. When this occurs, the non-partner is regarded as an agent whose acts are binding on the partnership. In such cases *partnership by estoppel* is deemed to exist, provided a third person has reasonably and detrimentally relied on the representation that a non-partner was part of the partnership. This theory is applied in the following case.

Case 23.1
PARAMOUNT PETROLEUM CORPORATION v. TAYLOR RENTAL CENTER

Court of Appeals of Texas, Fourteenth District, 1986.
712 S.W.2d 534.

FACTS During June and July of 1981 Taylor Rental Center rented pumps and sandblasting equipment for use on the *M/V Courtney D,* a seagoing vessel. Apparently, the vessel was owned by Paramount Petroleum Corporation. When the request for rental was submitted, Taylor checked the authorization to rent by telephoning the number given. The phone was answered by a business calling itself "Paramount," and Taylor was instructed by phone to send invoices for the rental charges to the Houston post office box of the company. The identification of the employees picking up the equipment was also checked by Taylor. A second request to rent equipment was made by a captain claiming to represent Paramount Steamship Company, Ltd. Since the equipment was to be used on the *Courtney D,* and since the invoices were to be sent to the same address as the earlier rental, Taylor assumed the two Paramount firms were a single enterprise, or a partnership. The invoices went unpaid, and Taylor learned that Paramount had apparently gone out of business. Taylor then sought payment from Paramount Petroleum, claiming that it was liable for the bill and, if it was not the same corporation as Paramount Steamship, it was at least its partner. When the trial court held for Taylor, Paramount Petroleum appealed.

ISSUE Was a partnership between Paramount Petroleum and Paramount Steamship implied by the fact that they shared telephone facilities and a post office box and were both involved in operations on the *Courtney D?*

DECISION Yes. The appellate court affirmed the trial court's judgment that a partnership by estoppel existed.

REASON A finding of partnership by estoppel requires (1) a representation that the one sought to be bound is a member of a partnership and (2) a reliance by one to whom the representation is made by giving credit to the partnership. Thus, when the employees of Paramount Steamship rented the equipment from Taylor, Taylor reasonably assumed they were also employees of Paramount Petroleum because all indications led to that conclusion. Taylor relied in good faith upon a partnership relationship between the two Paramount firms.

---

6. UPA Section 7(2)(3).

❖ Partnership Termination

Any change in the relations of the partners that demonstrates unwillingness or inability to carry on partnership business dissolves the partnership, resulting in termination.[7] If any of the partners wishes to continue the business, he or she is free to reorganize into a new partnership with the remaining members.

The termination of a partnership has two stages—dissolution and winding up. Both must take place before termination is complete. *Dissolution* occurs when any partner (or partners) indicates an intention to disassociate from the partnership. *Winding up* is the actual process of collecting and distributing the partnership assets. Dissolution of a partnership can be brought about by the acts of the partners, by the operation of law, and by judicial decree, each of which events will be discussed here.

Dissolution by Acts of Partners

Dissolution of a partnership may come about through the acts of the partners in several ways. First, the partnership can be dissolved by the partners' agreement. For example, when a partnership agreement expresses a fixed term or a particular business objective to be accomplished, the passing of the date or the accomplishment of the objective dissolves the partnership. Second, since a partnership is a voluntary association, a partner has the power to disassociate himself or herself from the partnership at any time and thus dissolve the partnership. Any change in the partnership, whether by the withdrawal of a partner or by the admission of a new partner, results in dissolution. In practice, this is modified by providing that the remaining or new partners continue in the firm's business. Nonetheless, a new partnership arises. Finally, although the UPA provides that voluntary transfer or involuntary sale of a partner's interest for the benefit of creditors does not by itself dissolve the partnership, either occurrence can ultimately lead to judicial dissolution of the partnership, as will be discussed.[8]

Dissolution by Operation of Law

If one of the partners dies, the partnership is dissolved by operation of law, even if the partnership agreement provides for carrying on the business with the executor of the decedent's estate. Any change in the composition among partners results in a new partnership. The bankruptcy of a partner will also dissolve a partnership, and, naturally, the bankruptcy of the firm itself will result in dissolution. Additionally, any event that makes it unlawful for the partnership to continue its business or for any partner to carry on in the partnership will result in dissolution. Note, however, that even if the illegality of the partnership business is a cause for dissolution, the partners can decide to change the nature of their business and continue in the partnership. When the illegality applies to an individual partner, then dissolution is mandatory. For example, if an attorney in a law firm is appointed a magistrate, the partnership must be dissolved, because a judge cannot remain part of a law firm due to possible conflict-of-interest problems.

---

7. UPA Section 29.
8. UPA Sections 27 and 28.

Dissolution by Judicial Decree

For dissolution of a partnership by judicial decree to occur, an application or petition must be made in an appropriate court. The court then either denies the petition or grants a decree of dissolution. The UPA, Section 32, cites situations in which a court can dissolve a partnership. One situation occurs when a partner is adjudicated insane or is shown to be of unsound mind. This action often involves a series of complex tests and standards. Another situation arises when a partner appears incapable of performing his or her duties under the partnership agreement. If the incapacity is likely to be permanent and to substantially affect the partner's ability to discharge his or her duties to the firm, a court will dissolve the partnership by decree. Judicial dissolution may also be ordered by a court when it becomes obviously impractical for the firm to continue—for example, if the business can only be operated at a loss. Additionally, a partner's impropriety involving partnership business (for example, fraud perpetrated upon the other partners) or improper behavior reflecting unfavorably upon the firm will provide grounds for a judicial decree of dissolution. Finally, if dissension between partners becomes so persistent and harmful as to undermine the confidence and cooperation necessary to carry on the firm's business, dissolution may also be granted.

In the following case, the court granted a petition for judicial dissolution to enable a withdrawing partner to receive his fair share of the assets that had been refused him by the partnership.

Case 23.2
FELTON INVESTMENT GROUP v. TAURMAN

Supreme Court of Montana, 1986.
722 P.2d 1135.

FACTS Wayne Taurman was an employee of John Felton's Felton Construction Company. In 1969 Mr. Felton formed Felton Investment Group (FIG) as a general partnership consisting of deserving employees of Felton Construction Company. Each member of FIG made weekly contributions—deducted from the employee's paycheck—to the investment fund. The money was then placed in investments agreed upon by all the partners. Taurman was a charter member of FIG. In 1974 Felton began to promote the idea that FIG should become a limited partnership with Felton in charge as general partner. Taurman opposed Felton's idea. Taurman's employment by the company was later terminated on the grounds that Taurman had refused to renounce his union membership to work on a nonunion job.

Shortly after his termination, Taurman received a check for $21,448.98 from FIG. The check represented Taurman's contributions to FIG, plus 4 percent annual interest. In the FIG partnership agreement, this was the amount payable in cases where employees were discharged for misconduct. Taurman did not feel he had been guilty of misconduct and wanted his full share of the partnership assets upon withdrawing from the partnership. Felton disagreed. Taurman then brought an action to have the partnership dissolved, its assets sold, and the proceeds distributed to its partners. The trial court granted the dissolution, and Felton appealed to the Supreme Court of Montana.

ISSUE Is Taurman entitled to have the partnership dissolved by judicial decree?

DECISION Yes. The appellate court affirmed the trial court's judgment.

REASON The court found that Taurman's termination was wrongful; that is, he should not have been fired for refusing to renounce his union membership. Therefore, the portion of the partnership agreement concerning dispersal of contributions when termination is due to misconduct was inapplicable. The agreement did not cover wrongful discharge, so the court applied standard partnership law and ordered that Taurman was entitled to repayment of contributions and a pro rata share of partnership assets.

Landmark in the Law

The Medieval *Commenda*

It goes without saying that all businesses require capital. But often those who have capital may not wish to assume responsibility for the management of a business or for business liabilities that extend beyond the amount of the original investment. The need for an organization allowing a right to share in the profits without management responsibilities, and with limited liability for losses, was felt keenly in the later Middle Ages when trade and commerce were expanding and merchants were accumulating capital.

During the twelfth and thirteenth centuries, most commerce was typically undertaken by individual merchants who traveled from market to market or from fair to fair. But as the scope of commerce widened and the volume of transactions increased, more complex forms of business arose. One of these was the *commenda*, a partnership normally involving a short-term agreement between a merchant with capital and a traveler trading overseas. In this arrangement, the resident party would supply capital but no management, and the traveling party would supply management but no capital. In this partnership, in practice if not in theory, liability to the resident was usually limited to the amount of the investment, as it is in modern limited partnerships. It was by means of *commenda* agreements that many merchants, particularly in northern Italy, accumulated vast profits and the excess capital that eventually led to the creation of banking firms. The problem with the *commenda* partnership was its short-term nature. Usually the contract would only cover one voyage at a time, as merchants were apparently reluctant to invest funds on a longer-term basis.

The *commenda* was included as a form of business organization in the French Commercial Code of 1807, in Sections 23–25. Over a century later, the first limited partnership acts were adopted in New York (in 1822) and in Connecticut and Pennsylvania (in 1836). By 1916, as mentioned earlier, the Uniform Limited Partnership Act was promulgated and eventually adopted by most of the states. Limited liability and lack of management responsibility for limited partners remain the essential features of limited partnership law today.

During the fifteenth century in Italy, many merchant shipping voyages were financed through a short-term agreement between a resident merchant who supplied capital but remained in the home port and a traveling party who supplied management but no capital.

Notice of Dissolution

The intent to dissolve or to withdraw from a firm must be communicated clearly to each partner. This notice of intent can come from either the actions or the words of a partner. All partners will share liability for the acts of any partner who continues conducting business for the firm without knowing that the partnership has been dissolved.

Dissolution of a partnership by the act of a partner requires notice to all affected third persons as well. The manner of giving notice depends upon the third person's relationship to the firm. Any third person who has extended credit to the firm must receive *actual notice* (given to the party directly and personally). For all others, *constructive notice* (a newspaper announcement or similar public notice) is sufficient. Dissolution resulting from operation of law generally requires no notice to third parties.[9]

Winding Up and Distribution of Assets

Once dissolution occurs and partners have been notified, they cannot create new obligations on behalf of the partnership. Their only authority is to complete transactions begun but not finished at the time of dissolution and to wind up the business of the partnership. Winding up includes collecting and preserving partnership assets, discharging liabilities (paying debts), and accounting to each partner for the value of his or her interest in the partnership.

Both creditors of the partnership and creditors of the individual partners can make claims on the partnership's assets. In general, creditors of the partnership have priority over creditors of individual partners in the distribution of partnership assets; the converse priority is usually followed in the distribution of individual partner assets, except under the new Bankruptcy Act. The distribution of a partnership's assets is made after third-party debts are paid. The priorities, after third-party debts, are as follows:

1. Refund of advances (loans) made to or for the firm by a partner.
2. Return of capital contribution to a partner.
3. Distribution of the balance, if any, to partners in accordance with their respective share in the profits.

Partners continue in fiduciary relationship to one another until the winding-up process is completed. In the following case, the question arose as to whether one of the partners had breached this fiduciary duty by purchasing for his own future business the partnership assets.

Case 23.3
CUDE v. COUCH
Supreme Court of Tennessee, 1979.
588 S.W.2d 554.

FACTS   In 1965 Cude and Couch formed a partnership for the purpose of operating a laundromat. The business was located in a building owned by Couch, which also housed Couch's car dealership. The laundromat rented space for the business on a month-to-month basis from Couch. Couch, from the beginning of the partnership, stated that he did not want to lease the property because he might need the space for his car dealership and did not want the laundromat to interfere with his plans in that respect. After the partnership was dissolved in 1973, a

---

9.   Childers v. United States, 442 F.2d 1299 (5th Cir. 1971).

Case 23.3—Continued

public sale of the partnership assets, which consisted of the laundry equipment, was held. During the sale, Couch let it be known that he would not lease the premises to anyone who purchased the equipment, and thus the buyer would have to remove the equipment from the premises. Ultimately, the equipment was sold at a low price to a person named Platkin. Although it was unknown to others at the time of the sale, Platkin was an agent for Couch. Couch and his son then continued to operate the laundromat business at the same location.

Cude moved to have the court set aside the sale on the grounds that Couch's refusal to lease the premises to others artificially depressed the price of the equipment and that Couch had purchased the equipment clandestinely. Cude claimed that these actions breached Couch's fiduciary duty to Cude. Cude's motion was denied by the trial court, and Cude appealed.

ISSUE Did Couch's actions during the sale breach his fiduciary duty to Cude?

DECISION No. The Supreme Court of Tennessee affirmed the trial court's decision.

REASON The court did not question the fiduciary duty that all partners owe to one another, and it stressed "that this duty continues while the partnership is being liquidated." But it did not agree that Couch had breached his fiduciary duty in this case. Couch had possessed an inherent advantage over Cude throughout the partnership's duration because of his ownership of the property on which the laundromat was located. The court could find no evidence, however, that Couch had used this advantage to force Cude out of the partnership, and "[a]bsent such a showing, neither Couch's refusal to permit others to lease the premises, nor the manner and price of his purchase of the equipment—which together form the basis of the petitioner's complaint—can be termed improper." Couch had made it clear from the beginning of the partnership that he did not wish to lease the premises to others, and the court could not "conceive that Couch's admitted duty to his partner would require that he lease the premises against his own best interests, despite the fact that the laundry could not be sold as a going business without a lease." As to Couch's manner of purchasing the equipment at the sale, the court concluded that "while we agree with the petitioner that it would have been better had Platkin disclosed his agency, there is no suggestion in the record that his failure to do so, of itself, prejudiced either the partnership or Cude."

❖ Limited Partnership

Definition of Limited Partnership

Limited partnerships consist of at least one general partner and one or more limited partners.[10] The general partner (or partners) assumes management responsibility of the partnership and, as such, has full responsibility for the partnership and for all debts of the partnership. The limited partner (or partners) contributes cash (or other property) and owns an interest in the firm but does not undertake any management responsibilities and is not personally liable for partnership debts beyond the amount of his or her investment. A limited partner can forfeit limited liability by taking part in managing the business. In many ways, limited partnerships are like general partnerships. They are sometimes referred to as *special partnerships*, in contrast to *general partnerships*. A comparison of the basic characteristics of general partnerships and limited partnerships is given in Exhibit 23-2.

---

10. Originally, limited partnerships were conceived to accommodate only a few limited partners. There seems to be no statutory limit to their numbers today, however, and in some cases very large groups have been assembled.

◆ **Exhibit 23-2 Basic Comparison of Types of Partnerships**

CHARACTERISTIC	GENERAL PARTNERSHIP	LIMITED PARTNERSHIP	REVISED LIMITED PARTNERSHIP
Creation	By agreement of two or more persons to carry on a business as co-owners for profit.	By agreement of two or more persons, under the laws of the state, having one or more general partners and one or more limited partners to carry on a business as co-owners for profit. Filing of certificate in appropriate state office is required.	Same as limited partnership, except filing of certificate with Secretary of State is required.
Sharing of profits and losses	By agreement, or in absence thereof, profits are shared equally by partners and losses are shared in same ratio as profits.	Profits are shared as required in certificate agreement, and losses shared likewise, except limited partners share losses only up to their capital contribution.	Same as limited partnership, except in absence of provision in certificate agreement, profits and losses are shared on basis of percentages of capital contributions.
Liability	Unlimited personal liability of all partners.	Unlimited personal liability of all general partners; limited partners only to extent of capital contributions.	Same as limited partnership.
Capital contribution	No minimal or mandatory amount; set by agreement.	Set by agreement; may be cash, property, or any obligation except services.	Same as limited partnership; except contribution of services is allowed.
Management	By agreement, or in absence thereof, all partners have an equal voice.	General partners by agreement, or else each has an equal voice. Limited partners have no voice, or else subject to liability as a general partner.	Same as limited partnership, except limited partner involved in partnership management is liable as a general partner *only* if third party has knowledge of such involvement. Limited partner may act as agent or employee of partnership, and vote on amending certificate or sale or dissolution of partnership.
Duration	By agreement, or can be dissolved by action of partner (withdrawal), operation of law (death or bankruptcy), or court decree.	By agreement in certification, or by withdrawal, death, or insanity of general partner in absence of right of other general partners to continue the partnership. Death of a limited partner, unless he or she is only remaining limited partner, does not terminate partnership.	Same as limited partnership, except it enlarges class of activities by general partner that result in termination.

◆ Exhibit 23-2 Basic Comparison of Types of Partnerships—Continued

CHARACTERISTIC	GENERAL PARTNERSHIP	LIMITED PARTNERSHIP	REVISED LIMITED PARTNERSHIP
Assignment	Interest can be assigned, although assignee does not have rights of substituted partner, without consent of other partners.	Same as general partnership. If partners consent to assignee becoming a partner, certificate must be amended.	Same as limited partnership. Upon assignment of all interest, partner ceases to be a partner.
Priorities (order) upon liquidation	1. Outside creditors. 2. Partner creditors. 3. Capital contribution of partners. 4. Profits of partners.	1. Outside creditors. Limited partner creditors. 2. Profits to limited partners. 3. Limited partner capital contributions. 4. General partner creditors. 5. Profits to general partners. 6. Capital contributions of general partners.	1. Outside creditors. Partner creditors. 2. Amounts before withdrawal to which partners are entitled. 3. Capital contributions—limited and general partners. 4. Profits—limited and general partners.

Limited Partnership— Formation and Dissolution

Compared with the informal, private, and voluntary agreement that usually suffices for a general partnership, the formation of a limited partnership is a public and formal proceeding that must follow statutory requirements.

A limited partnership must have two or more partners, as mentioned previously, and the partners must sign a certificate of limited partnership (see Exhibit 23-3), which requires information similar to that found in a corporate charter. The certificate must be filed with the designated state official—normally in the county where the principal business of the firm will be conducted or with the secretary of state. It is usually open to public inspection. In essence, the content of the certificate and the method of filing are similar to those for the corporate charter.

A limited partnership is dissolved in much the same way as an ordinary partnership. The retirement, death, or insanity of a general partner can dissolve the partnership, but not if the business can be continued by one or more of the other general partners in accordance with their certificate or by consent of all members. The death or assignment of interest of a limited partner does not dissolve the limited partnership. A limited partnership can also be dissolved by court decree.

Illegality, expulsion, and bankruptcy of the general partners dissolve a limited partnership. Bankruptcy of a limited partner, however, does not dissolve the partnership unless it causes the bankruptcy of the firm. The retirement of a general partner causes a dissolution unless the members consent to a continuation by the remaining general partners or unless this contingency is provided for in the certificate.

◆ Exhibit 23-3 Certificate of Limited Partnership

CERTIFICATE OF LIMITED PARTNERSHIP

The undersigned, desiring to form a Limited Partnership under the Uniform Limited Partnership Act of the State of _____ , make this certificate for that purpose.

§ 1. Name. The name of the Partnership shall be "_____
_____ ".

§ 2. Purpose. The purpose of the Partnership shall be to [*describe*].

§ 3. Location. The location of the Partnership's principal place of business is _____County, _____ .

§ 4. Members and Designation. The names and places of residence of the members, and their designation as General or Limited Partners are:

_____	[*Address*]	General Partner
_____	[*Address*]	General Partner
_____	[*Address*]	Limited Partner
_____	[*Address*]	Limited Partner

§ 5. Term. The term for which the Partnership is to exist is indefinite.

§ 6. Initial Contributions of Limited Partners. The amount of cash and a description of the agreed value of the other property contributed by each Limited Partner are:

[*Name*]	[*Describe*]
[*Name*]	[*Describe*]

§ 7. Subsequent Contributions of Limited Partners. Each Limited Partner may (but shall not be obliged to) make such additional contributions to the capital of the Partnership as may from time to time be agreed upon by the General Partners.

§ 8. Profit Shares of Limited Partners. The share of the profits which each Limited Partner shall receive by reason of his contribution is:

[*Name*]	_____ %
[*Name*]	_____ %

Signed _____ , 19_____

_____
_____
_____
_____

Signed and sworn before me, the undersigned authority, this _____
_____ , 19_____ .

Notary Public
_____County, _____

Upon dissolution, creditors' rights to assets precede partners' rights, and, under the ULPA, limited partners' rights precede general partners' rights. Limited partners take both their share of the profits and of contributed capital before general partners receive anything.

The following case involves the dissolution of a limited partnership by judicial decree.

Case 23.4
BLOCK v. DARDANES
Supreme Court of Illinois, 1980.
83 Ill.App.3d 819, 39 Ill.Dec. 216, 404 N.E.2d 807.

FACTS Dardanes was the general partner of a limited partnership. The partnership had purchased a restaurant, and Dardanes, as general partner, managed the restaurant. Block, a limited partner, was concerned that Dardanes was not fulfilling his managerial duties to the partnership. Dardanes rarely appeared at the restaurant, had placed others in charge of restaurant operations, and did not involve himself in the day-to-day business of the restaurant. Block wanted to review the business records and asked Dardanes for income statements and an accounting, but Dardanes refused to cooperate. Block petitioned the court for an accounting and for dissolution of the partnership by judicial decree. When the trial court granted the petition, Dardanes appealed.

ISSUE Can a limited partnership be dissolved by judicial decree when the general partner fails to render to a limited partner an accounting when the limited partner has reasonable grounds to request an accounting?

DECISION Yes. The Supreme Court of Illinois ruled that a general partner's failure to render an accounting of the business upon reasonable demand is grounds for dissolution of the partnership.

REASON One of the rights of limited, as well as general, partners is the right to an accounting of business assets and liabilities. Such an accounting, and all business records of the partnership, must be made available to a partner when reasonably requested. The court found that Block had a reasonable basis for requesting an accounting, and Dardanes's failure to cooperate created grounds for judicial dissolution of the partnership.

Application

Law and the Partner— Arranging for a Buyout

Most partnerships are entered into when the partners are getting along with each other. But what happens if the situation changes, and they can no longer work together—who buys out whom, and at what price? Explicit arrangements (usually called *buy-and-sell* agreements) need to be made during the formation of the partnership rather than when the partners are at each other's throats.

Each partnership agreement should be written in such a way as to allow for the smooth operation of a business through a period when the partners disagree sufficiently to require a dissolution of the partnership (as distinguished from the dissolution of the business itself). Partnership agreements for small partnerships generally require the unanimous consent of the partners to do just about anything. Hence, it is wise initially to set up the partnership agreement so that one partner has principal management authority and therefore has the ability to pay employees (but not give raises), the ability to order new supplies, and, in general, the ability to ensure that business will continue on a day-to-day basis. Even in times of dispute, then, the business will continue while the partners have time to cool off and make arrangements for one group to buy out the other.

When a partnership has to be dissolved because the partners can no longer get along, it is difficult for them to agree on who buys and who sells and at what price. One way out of this dilemma is to divide the disputing factions into two groups (which is easy if there are only two partners), whereby one group can decide on the value of the business and the other group can decide whether to buy or sell. It is not nearly as complicated as it sounds: One group tells the other, "The business is worth $36,000. You buy us out, or we'll buy you out." Each side gets to make a decision on either the price or whether to buy or sell, but not both simultaneously.

Checklist for a Partnership Buyout

☐ 1. Include in your original partnership arrangement a buy-and-sell agreement.

☐ 2. Each partner should use independent counsel to examine and approve the buyout agreement so that no one can later succeed in claiming that the agreement itself lacked impartiality.

❖ Chapter Summary: Partnerships—Creation and Termination

GENERAL PARTNERSHIPS	

Legal Characteristics of a Partnership	1. A partnership is an association of two or more persons to carry on, as co-owners, a business for profit.
	
	2. *Partnership as an entity:*
	   a. Legal capacity—In some states, partnerships can be a party in a legal suit. Federal courts follow state laws except when a constitutional question is involved—then the partnership is treated as an entity.
	   b. Bankruptcy—An adjudication of bankruptcy applies only to the partnership entity; it does not constitute bankruptcy for the partners.
	   c. Conveyance of property—The partnership can own and transfer property as an entity, without individual partners joining in the transaction.
	
	3. *Aggregate theory of partnership:* When the partnership is not regarded as a separate legal entity, it is treated as an aggregate of the individual partners.

Partnership Formation	1. *Agreement*—A partnership is formed by explicit agreement (oral, written, or implied by contract) of the parties. 2. *Duration*—The partnership agreement can specify the duration of the partnership (partnership for a term); otherwise, the partnership can be dissolved at any time by any partner (partnership at will). 3. *Capacity*—Any person having the capacity to enter a contract can become a partner. 4. Under the MBCA and the UPA, a corporation can be a partner. 5. *Mutual consent*—Partners must consent to the partnership; the *intent* to associate is a key element of partnership. 6. *Indications of partnership*—Generally, if a business organization shares profits and losses, jointly owns the business, and all owners have an equal right in the management of the business, it will be deemed a partnership. 7. *Partnership by estoppel*—Exists when parties who are not partners represent themselves as partners with the result that third persons rely on the representation.

Partnership Termination	1. *Dissolution by acts of the partners:*
	   a. By agreement.
	   b. By the withdrawal of a partner.
	   c. By the admission of a new partner.
	
	2. *Dissolution by operation of law:*
	   a. Death of a partner.
	   b. Bankruptcy (but not insolvency) of a partner.
	   c. Illegality of partnership business.
	
	3. *Dissolution by judicial decree:*
	   a. A court's adjudication of the insanity of a partner.
	   b. Permanent incapacity of a partner to perform his or her duties.
	   c. Business impracticality—if the firm can be operated only at a loss.
	   d. Improper conduct of one or more of the partners.
	
	4. *Notice of dissolution (when partnership dissolved by acts of partners):*
	   a. The intent to dissolve or to withdraw from a firm must be communicated clearly, by words or conduct, to each partner.

❖ Chapter Summary: Partnerships—Creation and Termination—Continued

Partnership Termination (Continued)	b. Notice of dissolution must be given to all affected third persons. Any third person who has dealt with the firm must receive *actual notice*; for all others, *constructive notice* (e.g., a newspaper announcement) is sufficient.
	5. *Winding up*—Includes collecting and preserving partnership assets, discharging liabilities, and accounting to each partner for his or her interest in the partnership.
	6. *Distribution of assets*—After third-party debts are paid, partnership assets are distributed to the partners. Partners' loans first, and then capital contributions, are returned to the partners; any remaining assets are distributed to the partners on the basis of their respective shares in the partnership.
LIMITED PARTNERSHIPS	
Formation	Formed by statute; formal filing procedure must be followed, as with a corporation.
Termination	A limited partnership is dissolved in much the same way as a general partnership. 1. *Causes*—Completion of the undertaking; expiration of the partnership term; retirement, death, or insanity of a general partner (where no other general partner or partners can take over the management of the firm's business).
	2. *Distribution of assets*—Creditors' rights to assets precede partners' rights; relative priority of limited and general partners' rights to assets varies, depending on whether ULPA or RULPA is used.

❖ Questions and Case Problems

23-1. Jackson, Bright, Romanovski, and Palance were partners in a small publishing enterprise. They had a written partnership agreement that the partnership would endure for five years. For the first two years, the business ran smoothly, and the firm was profitable. In the third year, however, disagreements among the partners arose concerning a potential investment in a new printing process. Jackson and Bright were opposed to the investment as it would place the firm heavily in debt. Romanovski and Palance believed that if the investment were not made, the firm would lose profits in the long run. Eventually, the disagreement escalated into bitter hostility between the two factions, and it became difficult to perform the necessary day-to-day tasks of the business. Jackson wants to withdraw from the partnership, but the other partners will not consent to his withdrawal. Discuss Jackson's options under these circumstances.

23-2. Broderick is the owner of a chain of shoe stores. He hires Marvin as a manager of a new store, which is to open in Grand Rapids, Michigan. Broderick, by written contract, agrees to pay Marvin a monthly salary. In addition, Broderick and Marvin have agreed to an 80-20 percent split in profits. Without Broderick's knowledge, Marvin represents himself to Carrington as Broderick's partner, showing Carrington the agreement to share profits. Carrington extends credit to Mar-

vin. Marvin defaults. Discuss whether Carrington can hold Broderick liable as Marvin's partner.

23-3. Arlington, Benton, and Collins have formed a twenty-year partnership to purchase land, develop it, manage it, and then sell the property. The partnership agreement calls for the partners to devote their full time to the business. Assume one of the following events takes place:

    (a) After two years, Benton and Collins agree that the working hours of the partnership will be from 8:00 A.M. to 6:00 P.M. rather than the previously established schedule of 9:00 A.M. to 5:00 P.M. Arlington refuses to come to work before 9:00 A.M. and quits promptly at 5:00 P.M.

    (b) After two years, Arlington walks out, quitting the partnership.

    (c) After two years, Arlington becomes insolvent.

    (d) After two years, Arlington dies.

Discuss fully which of these acts constitutes a dissolution of the partnership and whether there is any ensuing liability on the part of Arlington.

23-4. Inniss borrowed $4,000 from Crawford to establish a small copying and instant-printing business. Under the loan agreement, Inniss promised to pay Crawford $100 each month plus 15 percent of the monthly profits until the debt was paid.

Are Inniss and Crawford partners? Explain.

23-5. Allen and Becker form a limited partnership with Allen as the general partner and Becker as the limited partner. Becker puts up $15,000, and Allen contributes some office equipment that he owns. A certificate of limited partnership is properly filed, and business is begun. One month later, Allen becomes ill. Instead of hiring someone to manage the business, Becker takes over the complete management of the firm himself. While Becker is in control, he makes a contract with Schilling involving a large sum of money. Allen returns to work. Because of other commitments, the Schilling contract is breached. Schilling contends that she can hold Allen and Becker personally liable if her judgment cannot be satisfied out of the assets of the limited partnership. Discuss her contention.

23-6. Alvin and Carol Volkman negotiated with David McNamee, a construction contractor, to have a house built. McNamee informed the Volkmans that he was going into business with Phillip Carroll. On several occasions when the Volkmans went to McNamee's offices, Carroll was present, and by all indications he was a partner in the decisions concerning the construction of their house. On one occasion, when McNamee had to make a decision about which contractor's form to use, McNamee left the room stating, "I will ask Phil." On other occasions, Carroll made the following statements: "I hope we'll be working together," and "I am happy that we will be working with you." Correspondence to the Volkmans from McNamee was written on stationery carrying the letterhead "DP Associates," and the Volkmans assumed the "DP" represented David and Phillip. When the construction contract was not performed as agreed, the Volkmans brought suit against DP Associates, McNamee, and Carroll. Carroll petitioned the trial court to dismiss the suit against him since he was not a partner of DP Associates. Given these facts, did the court find Carroll to be a partner by estoppel? Explain. [Volkman v. DP Associates, 48 N.C.App. 155, 268 S.E.2d 265 (1980)]

23-7. Jebeles and Costellos were partners in "Dino's Hot Dogs," doing business on the Montgomery Highway in Alabama. From the outset, Costellos had worked at the business full time, while Jebeles involved himself only to a small extent in the actual running of the business. Jebeles was married to Costellos's sister, and when marital difficulties developed between Jebeles and his wife, Costellos barred Jebeles from the premises. Jebeles sued for an accounting of the partnership's profits and for dissolution of the partnership, claiming that the partnership was a partnership at will and the relationship between the partners made it impossible to conduct partnership business. Did the court grant the petition? Explain. [Jebeles v. Costellos, 391 So.2d 1024 (Ala. 1980)]

23-8. Carola and Grogan were partners in a law firm. The partnership began business in 1974 and was created by an oral agreement. On September 6, 1976, Carola withdrew from the partnership some of its files, furniture, books, and various other items of office equipment. The next day, Carola informed Grogan he had withdrawn from the partnership. Were Carola's actions on September 6, 1976, deemed effective notice of dissolution to Grogan? [Carola v. Grogan, 102 A.D.2d 934, 477 N.Y.S.2d 525 (1984)]

23-9. On September 28, 1958, Reid and three others entered into a written partnership agreement for the purpose of leasing for profit certain real property located in Montgomery County, Pennsylvania. Reid was to manage the property, and the others were to perform the physical labor necessary to maintain the premises in good condition. One year later, Reid notified the others that she was dissolving the partnership and requested that the partnership assets be liquidated by the remaining partners as soon as possible. Had dissolution occurred? Assuming dissolution had occurred, were the other partners able to recover damages for breach of partnership agreement on the ground that the partnership was a partnership for a particular undertaking and hence not terminable at will? [Girard Bank v. Haley, 460 Pa. 237, 332 A.2d 443 (1975)]

23-10. Lynne, Ernest, and Stanley Timmermann established a partnership in 1965 for the purpose of engaging in farming activities. In January 1969 Lynne stated to the other two partners that he no longer wished to be involved in the partnership. It was not until August 31, 1970, however, that Lynne ceased to participate in the farming activities of the partnership. In January 1972 Lynne attempted to bring about a forced liquidation of the partnership through a lawsuit. In January 1969 the value of the partnership was approximately $50,000. On August 31, 1970, the value of the partnership was slightly less than $10,000; and in January 1972 the value of the partnership was in excess of $300,000. Lynne had a one-third interest in the partnership. Approximately how much was he deemed due to receive when he withdrew? Explain your answer. [Timmermann v. Timmermann, 272 Or. 613, 538 P.2d 1254 (1975)]

Chapter 24

Partnerships— Operation and Duties

"All partners have equal rights in the management and conduct of the partnership business."

Uniform Partnership Act, Section 18(c)

The rights and duties of partners are governed largely by the specific terms of their partnership agreement. In the absence of provisions to the contrary in the partnership agreement, the law imposes the rights and duties discussed in this chapter. As indicated in the UPA quotation, one such right is the right of partners to participate in the management of the partnership. The character and nature of the partnership business generally influence the application of these rights and duties.

❖ Rights among Partners

The rights held by partners in a partnership relate to the following areas: management, interest in the partnership, compensation, inspection of books, accounting, and property rights.

Management of Partnership

Under the Uniform Partnership Act, all partners have equal rights in managing the partnership. Each partner in an ordinary partnership[1] has one vote in management matters *regardless of the proportional size of his or her interest in the firm*. Often, in a large partnership, partners will agree to delegate daily management responsibilities to a management committee made up of one or more of the partners.

The majority rule controls decisions in ordinary matters connected with partnership business, unless otherwise specified in the agreement. Unanimous consent of the partners is required, however, to bind the firm in any of the following actions:

1. To alter the essential nature of the firm's business as expressed in the partnership agreement or to alter the capital structure of the partnership.[2]

---

1. Compare the management rights of partners in ordinary partnerships to those in limited partnerships, discussed in Chapter 23 and later in this chapter. The absence of management responsibility and the concomitant liability limitations are distinguishing characteristics of limited partnerships.
2. UPA Section 18(h).

2. To admit new partners or to enter a wholly new business.
3. To assign partnership property into a trust for the benefit of creditors.
4. To dispose of the partnership's good will.
5. To confess judgment against the partnership or to submit partnership claims to arbitration.
6. To undertake any act that would make further conduct of partnership business impossible.[3]

Each of these matters significantly affects the nature of the partnership.

> *"Of legal knowledge I acquired such a grip, that they took me into the partnership."*
>
> **William S. Gilbert, 1836–1911**
> *(English playwright; Sullivan's collaborator in comic opera)*

Interest in Partnership

Each partner is entitled to the proportion of business profits and losses designated in the partnership agreement. If the agreement does not apportion profits or losses, the UPA provides that profits shall be shared equally and losses shall be shared in the same ratio as profits.[4]

To illustrate: The partnership agreement for Alderson and Brent provides for capital contributions of $6,000 from Alderson and $4,000 from Brent, but it is silent as to how Alderson and Brent will share profits or losses. In this case, Alderson and Brent would share both profits and losses equally. Had the partnership agreement provided for profits to be shared in the same ratio as capital contributions, the profits would be shared 60 percent for Alderson and 40 percent for Brent; and had it been silent as to losses, losses would be shared in the same ratio as the profits (60-40 percent).

Compensation from Partnership

A partner's time, skill, and energy on behalf of the partnership business is a duty and generally not a compensable service. Partners can, of course, agree otherwise. For example, the managing partner of a law firm often receives a salary in addition to his or her share of profits for performing special administrative duties in office and personnel management. UPA Section 18(f) provides that when a partnership must be terminated because a partner dies, a surviving partner is entitled to reasonable compensation for services in winding up partnership affairs (and reimbursement for expenses incurred in the process) above and apart from his or her share in the partnership profits.

Each partner impliedly promises to subordinate his or her economic interests to those of the partnership. Assume that Hall, Banks, and Porter enter into a partnership. Porter undertakes independent consulting for an outside firm without the consent of Hall and Banks. Porter's compensation from the outside firm is considered partnership income.[5] A partner cannot engage in any independent competitive activities that involve the partnership's time unless expressly agreed upon by the partnership.

If Porter engages in an activity that competes with the partnership, then Porter has breached the fiduciary duty that he owes it. Even with a noncompetitive activity, Porter can breach his fiduciary duty if the partnership suffers a loss from his efforts.

---

3. UPA Section 9(3), various subsections.
4. UPA Section 18(a).
5. UPA Section 21.

Landmark in the Law

The Uniform Partnership Act (1914)

The National Conference of Commissioners on Uniform State Laws (NCC)[1] first discussed the desirability of a uniform act on partnership law in 1902 at their annual meeting. The Committee on Commercial Law was instructed at that time to oversee the preparation of a draft on partnership law, and during the following decade a number of drafts were prepared.

A major problem for the drafters of the act was determining which theory of partnership should be employed. Under common law, the partnership was interpreted as an *aggregate* of individuals associated in business—this was the theory commonly used in most of the states. An alternate theory regarded the partnership as an *entity*. In order to make the best determination, the committee invited to a 1910 conference in Philadelphia "all the teachers of, and writers on, partnerships, besides several other lawyers known to have made a special study of the subject"[2]—

1. See the "Landmark" and the "Profile" in Chapter 11 for details concerning the NCC.
2. "Commissioners' Prefatory Note, Uniform Partnership Act," in *Uniform Laws Annotated* (St. Paul: West Publishing Co., 1969), p. 6.

something which, needless to say, would be inconceivable today! At the conclusion of this meeting, the assembled experts recommended that the act be based on the aggregate, or common law, theory. Thus, the committee requested that the partnership act be drafted on this basis.

At the 1914 meeting of the NCC, the eighth and final draft of the act was reported to the conference, which passed a resolution recommending the act for adoption by the legislatures of all the states. Thus, after a decade of drafting and deliberation, the Uniform Partnership Act (UPA) became a reality.

The UPA contains forty-five sections and is divided into seven parts. Its laws are applied by the courts whenever a partner or a partnership is involved in a dispute in an area not covered by the express agreement of the partners. All of the law affecting partnerships is not contained in the UPA; it therefore provides that the law of agency and the law of estoppel be followed where applicable, and it further states that in situations not covered by the act, common law and equity will govern.

The first state to adopt the UPA was Pennsylvania, which did so in 1914; other states followed, and today all of the states except Georgia and Louisiana have adopted the UPA. The UPA can be found in its entirety in Appendix C of this text.

Of course, the partnership agreement or the unanimous consent of the partners can permit a partner to engage in any activity.

Inspection of Partnership Books

Partnership books and records must be kept accessible to all partners. Each partner has the right to receive (and each partner has the corresponding duty to produce) full and complete information concerning the conduct of all aspects of partnership business.[6] Each firm retains books in which to record and secure such information. Partners contribute the information, and a bookkeeper typically has the duty to preserve it. The books must be kept at the firm's principal business office and cannot be removed without the consent of all the partners.[7] Every partner, whether active or inactive, is entitled to inspect all books and records upon demand and can make

6. UPA Section 20.
7. UPA Section 19.

copies of the materials. The personal representative of a deceased partner's estate has the same right of access to partnership books and records that the decedent would have had.

Accounting of Partnership Assets

An accounting of partnership assets or profits is required to determine the value of each partner's share in the partnership. An accounting can be performed voluntarily, or it can be compelled by the order of a court in equity.[8] Formal accounting occurs by right in connection with dissolution proceedings, but, under UPA Section 22, a partner also has the right to a formal accounting in the following situations:

1.   When the partnership agreement provides for a formal accounting.
2.   When a partner is wrongfully excluded from the business, from access to the books, or both.
3.   When any partner is withholding profits or benefits belonging to the partnership in breach of the fiduciary duty.
4.   When circumstances "render it just and reasonable."

Property Rights in Partnership

A partner has three basic property rights:

1.   An interest in the partnership.
2.   A right in specific partnership property.
3.   A right to participate in the management of the partnership, as previously discussed.[9]

An important legal distinction exists between a partner's rights in specific property that belongs to the firm and is used for business purposes, as opposed to a partner's right to share in the firm's earned profits to the extent of his or her interest in the firm. No individual partner has an absolute right to specific property of the firm. A partner is a co-owner with his or her partners of specific partnership property, holding as a tenant in partnership.

UPA Section 8(1) provides that "all property originally brought into the partnership's stock or subsequently acquired, by purchase or otherwise, on account of the partnership, is partnership property." For example, in the formation of a partnership, a partner may bring into the partnership property he or she owns as a part of his or her capital contribution. This property becomes partnership property even though title to it may still be in the name of the contributing partner. Indications that the assets were acquired with the intention that they be partnership assets is the heart of the phrase "on account of the partnership." Thus, the more closely an asset is

---

8.   The principal remedy of a partner against co-partners is an equity suit for dissolution, an accounting, or both. With minor exceptions, a partner cannot maintain an action against other firm members for damages until partnership affairs are settled and an accounting is done. This rule is necessary because legal disputes between partners invariably involve conflicting claims to shares in the partnership. Logically, the value of each partner's share must first be determined by an accounting.
9.   UPA Section 24.

associated with the business operations of the partnership, the more likely it is to be a partnership asset.

Partner's Interest in Firm   A partner's interest in the firm is a personal asset consisting of a proportionate share of the profits earned [10] and a return of capital after dissolution and winding up. A partner's interest is susceptible to assignment or to a judgment creditor's lien. Judgment creditors can attach a partner's interest by petitioning the court that entered the judgment to grant the creditors a *charging order*. This order entitles the creditors to profits of the partner and to any assets available to the partner upon dissolution.[11] Neither an assignment nor a court's charging order entitling a creditor to receive a share of the partner's money will cause dissolution of the firm.[12]

Partnership Property   Partners are *tenants in partnership* of all firm property.[13] Tenancy in partnership has several important effects. If a partner dies, the surviving partners, not the heirs of the deceased partner, have the right of survivorship to the specific property. Although surviving partners are entitled to possession, they have a duty to account to the decedent's estate for the *value* of the deceased partner's interest in said property.[14]

A partner has no right to sell, assign, or in any way deal with a particular item of partnership property as an exclusive owner.[15] Nor is a partner's personal credit related to partnership property; therefore, creditors cannot use partnership property to satisfy the personal debts of a partner. Partnership property is available only to satisfy partnership debts, to enhance the firm's credit, or to achieve other business purposes.

Every partner is a co-owner with all other partners of specific partnership property, such as office equipment, paper supplies, and vehicles. Each partner has equal rights to possess partnership property for business purposes or in satisfaction of firm debts, but not for any other purpose without the consent of all the other partners.

The following case deals with an attempt by the surviving brothers of a partnership to breach their duty to account to their deceased brother's estate for the value of his interest in partnership property.

Case 24.1
STROTHER v. STROTHER
Supreme Court of Alabama, 1983.
436 So.2d 847.

FACTS   Three brothers, James, John, and Claude, purchased several parcels of land, taking title to the land either in their names or in their partnership name, Strother Brothers. The brothers never executed a written partner-

ship agreement. After James died, John and Claude, along with their mother Minnie, brought suit to have Minnie declared owner of a one-fourth interest in the lands. This would leave James's heirs with only a one-fourth interest in the partnership instead of a one-third interest. Before trial Minnie died, leaving all her property to John and Claude. The trial court held that Minnie Strother was not a partner with her sons and thus did not own a one-fourth interest in the lands. The case was appealed to the state supreme court.

---

10.   UPA Section 26.
11.   UPA Section 28.
12.   UPA Section 27.
13.   UPA Section 25(1).
14.   UPA Section 25(2)(d)(e).
15.   UPA Section 25(2)(a)(b).

Case 24.1—Continued

ISSUE Was Minnie an equal partner with her sons, thus owning a one-fourth interest in the lands? The issue turned primarily on whether Minnie contributed part of the purchase price for the lands so as to be entitled to a resulting trust. If she did contribute funds for the purchase, the heirs of James would take only a one-fourth interest in the lands; if she did not, his heirs would take a one-third share.

DECISION The Supreme Court of Alabama upheld the trial court's finding that Minnie did not own a one-fourth interest in the lands. Each brother was thus given a one-third interest in the partnership property.

REASON Since no facts were presented to support the contention that Minnie was an equal partner with her sons, there was nothing to indicate that she had any interest in the land. Additionally, no partnership agreement was ever executed. Deeds to the land, in the three sons' names, were the only written evidence of the partnership. Thus, the court found that the partnership consisted only of the three brothers, defeating the attempt by John and Claude to enlarge their partnership share.

❖ Duties and Powers of Partners

The duties and powers of partners consist of a fiduciary duty of each partner to the other and the general agency powers discussed here.

Fiduciary Duty

Partners stand in a fiduciary relationship to one another the way that principals and agents do (see Chapter 22). It is a relationship of extraordinary trust and loyalty. The fiduciary duty imposes a responsibility upon each partner to act in good faith for the benefit of the partnership. It requires that each partner subordinate his or her personal interests in the event of conflict to the mutual welfare of the partners.

General Agency Powers

Each partner is an *agent* of every other partner and acts as both a principal and an agent in any business transaction within the scope of the partnership agreement. Each partner is a general agent of the partnership in carrying out the usual business of the firm. Thus, every act of a partner in every contract and in every contract signed in the partnership name, concerning partnership business, binds the firm.[16]

The UPA affirms general principles of agency law that pertain to the authority of a partner to bind a partnership in contract or tort. When a partner is apparently carrying on partnership business with third persons in the usual way, both the partner and the firm share liability. It is only when third persons are aware that the partner has no such authority that the partnership is not liable.

For example, Paula, a partner in Firm X, applies for a loan on behalf of the partnership without authorization from the other partners. The bank manager knows Paula has no authority. If the bank manager grants her the loan, Paula will be personally bound, but the firm will not be liable.

---

16. UPA Section 9(1).

Joint Liability   Partners have only *joint liability* on all partnership debts and contracts. Partners are jointly and severally (each on his or her own) liable for tort actions and breaches of trust to third persons.[17] Joint liability means that the group of partners wins or loses as a group. One partner cannot be singled out to be sued. Unless the partnership is treated as an entity, every partner's name must be listed in the suit, and the individual assets of each partner are equally exposed to potential liability (although the actual contribution in the event of a judgment is calculated on each partner's proportionate share of the firm). If the court awards the claimant a judgment, the claimant is barred from further suits against the partners and against the firm once satisfaction (that is, payment) of the judgment is made.

In states that allow a firm to be sued in its own name, a contract claimant or a creditor claimant can sue the firm as an *entity* without joining each partner. A judgment against the partnership binds only partnership assets. In such states, the better practice is to sue both the firm as an *entity* and all partners *jointly*. Then, judgment is enforceable against the assets of the partnership and the assets of the individual partners. The judgment rendered in such a case must be internally consistent. For example, if Cal sues the partnership firm Apex and all its partners jointly for breach of contract, and the court finds the firm liable, then it must hold the partners liable (and vice versa).

Joint and several liability means that a claimant can sue one partner without joining the others. Moreover, regardless of the outcome of the suit against the first partner, *res judicata* (a matter or thing settled by judgment in the courts) does not protect the other partners in subsequent suits filed against them.

Liability of Incoming Partner   A newly admitted partner to an existing partnership has limited liability for whatever debts and obligations the partnership incurred prior to the new partner's admission. UPA Section 17 provides that the new partner's liability can be satisfied only from partnership assets. This means that the new partner has no personal liability for these debts and obligations, but any capital contribution made by him or her is subject to these debts. This principle is illustrated in the following case.

RES JUDICATA
A rule that prohibits the same factual dispute between two parties to be retried by a court after final judgment has been entered by a trial court and all appeals have been exhausted (or the time for appeal has passed).

Case 24.2
MOSELEY v. COMMERCIAL STATE BANK
Supreme Court of Alabama, 1984.
457 So.2d 967.

FACTS   Southern Distilleries was a general partnership created in 1980 for the purpose of producing and selling gasohol. The partnership agreement contained a provision stating that any three partners having a combined 60 percent interest in the partnership could borrow money on behalf of the partnership, thereby binding the other partners to liability on the loan. In December of 1980 Southern Distilleries, through the action of three of its partners, borrowed $140,184 from Commercial State Bank and executed two promissory notes, which were due on March 19, 1981. In July of 1981 Southern Distilleries paid the interest on its overdue notes held by Commercial State Bank and executed a new promissory note in the amount of $140,000. The bank marked the notes dated December 19 as "paid."

Southern Distilleries failed to pay the July 21 note when it came due, and the bank sued the partnership as an entity and each of the partners jointly and severally. The trial court held that the partnership and the partners were

---

17.   UPA Section 15.

Case 24.2—Continued

jointly and severally liable on the note. One of the partners, Julius Moseley, had joined the partnership in April of 1981. Moseley appealed, claiming he was not personally liable on the note of July 1981 because the note represented the renewal of a preexisting obligation of the partnership. Under the UPA, an incoming partner assumes liability for preexisting obligations of the partnership, but his or her liability can be satisfied only out of partnership assets; the incoming partner cannot be held *personally* liable for such obligations.

ISSUE   Did the obligation owed by the partnership to the bank arise before Moseley's admission into the partnership?

DECISION   No. The Supreme Court of Alabama affirmed the trial court's decision.

REASON   The court did not accept Moseley's argument that the note being sued on represented a renewal of a preexisting debt. In the eyes of the court, it was "clear that the obligation created by the old note terminated when the bank accepted the new note" and marked the December 19, 1981, note as "paid." Although Moseley had no knowledge of the note until the bank sued for payment, he had nonetheless "signed an agreement granting him all the rights of a general partner in the firm and authorizing the other partners to obligate him as a general partner, which they did." According to the court, no "fraud or overreaching" existed here. The court held that the parties were "competent business men dealing at arm's length, who presumably have ample access to counsel. If Moseley had wished to limit his exposure to liability he should have taken steps to do so when he chose to become involved in the enterprise."

Trading versus Non-Trading Partnerships—A Digression   At common law, prior to the UPA, a distinction was drawn between trading and non-trading partnerships. Essentially, any partnership business that had goods in inventory and made profits in buying and selling those goods was considered a trading partnership. All other partnerships were non-trading. This distinction is important in discussing the apparent authority of the partnership and of its individual members. The UPA does not expressly adopt the distinction between these two types of partnerships, but many cases decided under the UPA have nonetheless followed it.

Authority of Partners   Agency concepts relating to apparent authority, actual authority, and ratification are also applicable to partnerships. The extent of *implied authority* is generally broader for partners than for ordinary agents. The character and scope of the partnership business and the customary nature of the particular business operation determine the scope of implied powers. For example, the usual course of business in a trading partnership involves buying and selling commodities. Consequently, each partner in a trading partnership has a wide range of implied powers to borrow money in the firm name and to extend the firm's credit in issuing or indorsing negotiable instruments.

In an ordinary partnership, firm members can exercise all implied powers reasonably necessary and customary to carry on that particular business. Some customarily implied powers include the authority to make warranties on goods in the sales business, the power to convey real property in the firm name where such conveyances are part of the ordinary course of partnership business, the power to enter contracts consistent with the firm's regular course of business, and the power to make admissions and representations concerning partnership affairs.[18]

If a partner acts within the scope of authority, the partnership is bound to third parties. For example, a partner's authority to sell partnership products carries with it

---

18.   UPA Section 11.

the implied authority to transfer title and to make usual warranties. Hence, in a partnership that operates a retail tire store, any partner negotiating a contract with a customer for the sale of a set of tires can warrant that "each tire will be warranted for normal wear for 40,000 miles."

This same partner, however, would not have the authority to sell office equipment, fixtures, or the partnership office building without the consent of all of the other partners. In addition, since partnerships are formed to create profits, a partner does not generally have the authority to make charitable contributions without the consent of the other partners. Any such actions are not binding on the partnership unless they are ratified by all of the other partners.

As in the law of agency, the law of partnership imputes one partner's knowledge to all other partners, because members of a partnership stand in a fiduciary relationship to one another. Such a fiduciary relationship implies that each partner will fully disclose to every other partner all relevant information pertaining to the business of the partnership. The same rule applies to members of a joint venture.

In the following case, the issue was raised as to whether a promise made by one partner in an accounting firm to an employee of the firm was binding on the partnership.

Case 24.3
HOFNER v. GLENN INGRAM & CO.

Appellate Court of Illinois,
First District, Fourth Division, 1985.
140 Ill. App. 3d 874, 95 Ill. Dec. 90, 489 N.E. 2d 311.

FACTS Glenn Ingram & Company is an accounting firm organized as a partnership. James Hofner, a certified public accountant, signed a partnership agreement with Ingram on May 4, 1978. The agreement stated that Hofner's salary would be based on an estimation of the future year's earnings by the firm. After signing the agreement, Hofner told William Gifford, a senior partner involved in the firm's management, that he would leave the firm if he (Hofner) did not make at least $40,000 that year in salary. Gifford reassured Hofner that he would make that amount and orally guaranteed the salary. When Hofner did not make the $40,000 as promised, he left the firm and initiated this action for the difference between the actual salary he received and the promised $40,000. The trial court dismissed Hofner's case for failure to state a cause of action. Hofner then appealed.

ISSUE Is Hofner entitled to bring suit against the partnership to recover the balance of the promised salary?

DECISION Yes. The appellate court judged that Hofner did have a cause of action and remanded the case to the trial court for factual determination.

REASON At the heart of the case is the question of whether Ingram is bound by Gifford's promise. The answer turns on whether Gifford had the authority to change the signed partnership agreement, and on whether a reasonable person in Hofner's position would have assumed that Gifford had the authority to make promises concerning salary. If Gifford did not have the authority to counter the express written agreement between Ingram and Hofner, a further question arises as to whether the firm had knowledge of Gifford's promise and ratified by its conduct the misrepresentation. These were questions that the appellate court left for the trial court to decide.

❖ Limited Partners—Rights and Liabilities

General partners, unlike limited partners, are personally liable to the partnership's creditors; thus, at least one general partner is necessary in a limited partnership, so that someone has personal liability. This policy can be circumvented in states that allow a corporation to be the general partner in a partnership. Since the corporation has limited liability by virtue of corporate laws, no one in the limited partnership in this case has personal liability.

Rights of Limited Partner

Subject to the limitations that will be discussed here, limited partners have essentially the same rights as general partners, including the right of access to partnership books and the right to an accounting of partnership business. Upon dissolution, they are entitled to a return of their contributions in accordance with the partnership certificate.[19] They can also assign their interests subject to specific clauses in the certificate.[20]

In some jurisdictions, courts have recognized fully the limited partner's right to sue, either individually or on behalf of the firm, for economic injury to the firm by the general partners or by outsiders. In addition, investor protection legislation, such as securities laws (discussed in Chapter 29), may give some protection to limited partners.

Liabilities of Limited Partner

A limited partner is liable to creditors to the extent of any contribution that had been promised to the firm or any part of a contribution that was withdrawn from the firm.[21] If the firm is organized in an improper manner, and the limited partner fails to renunciate (withdraw from the partnership) on discovery of the defect, the partner can be held personally liable by the firm's creditors. Note, though, that the ULPA and the revised ULPA allow people to remain limited partners regardless of whether they comply with statutory technicalities. Decisions on liability for false statements in a partnership certificate run in favor of persons relying on the false statements and against members who sign the certificate knowing of the falsity.[22] A limited partnership is formed by good-faith compliance with the requirements for signing and filing the certificate, even if it is incomplete or defective. When a limited partner discovers a defect in the formation of the limited partnership, he or she can obtain shelter from future liability by renouncing an interest in the profits of the partnership, thereby avoiding any future reliance by third parties.[23]

The liability of a limited partner is limited to the capital that he or she contributes or agrees to contribute to the partnership. By contrast, the liability of a general partner for partnership indebtedness is virtually unlimited. In a recent case, the general partner of a limited partnership remained personally liable for partnership debts after the limited partnership went through a Chapter 7 bankruptcy proceeding.[24]

Limited Partners and Management

The exemptions from personal liability of the limited partners rest on their not participating in management.[25] First, under the ULPA the contribution of a limited

19. ULPA Section 10.
20. ULPA Section 19.
21. See Kittredge v. Langley, 252 N.Y. 405, 169 N.E. 626 (1930).
22. See Walraven v. Ramsay, 335 Mich. 331, 55 N.W.2d 853 (1953) and ULPA Section 6.
23. ULPA Section 11.
24. Rohdie v. Washington, 641 S.W.2d 317 (Tex.Ct.App. 1982).
25. ULPA Section 7.

Business Law in Action

Partnerships Can Be Harmful to Your Health

A study undertaken by the Harvard Business School of 450 entrepreneurs (30 percent of whom were members of partnerships) resulted in the following findings:[1]

1. About 60 percent work more than fifty hours per week.
2. About 67 percent work nights, and 55 percent work on Saturdays.
3. About 57 percent have back problems and indigestion problems at least once a week.
4. Over 60 percent have chronic insomnia and/or chronic headaches.
5. Over 33 percent have chest pains at least once a week.

[1] Pierre Mornell, "Anatomy of a Law Firm," *Legal Administrator*, Spring 1986, p. 27.

It does not require psychiatric training to recognize the symptoms of stress denoted by these findings. Surprisingly, however, the same study revealed that only 7 percent of the 450 under study felt that they should reduce their workload. Even more surprisingly, the few in the study who explored the reasons for their stress symptoms did not blame their ills on long hours or work-related tension, but on their partners.

Dr. Pierre Mornell, a psychiatrist, concluded after reviewing these data that the reason partnerships are "falling apart at an alarming rate" is that business and law students are never given any training in how to deal with either the physical or psychological demands that arise on a day-to-day basis within the partnership context. A key ingredient in such training is to develop an awareness of the need for consensus among partners if headaches are to be

avoided and, in some cases, if the partnership is to endure at all. Whether it be a new telephone system or a new policy proposed by the leading partners in a firm, consensus is necessary to make it "work" and to satisfy all partners that it is a joint decision. Policymaking in a partnership is the same as policymaking at the government level: It involves a lot of discussion and a lot of compromise if the result is to be a policy endorsed by the entire firm. And, according to one member of a large legal partnership, "[b]uilding a consensus is . . . the policymaker's primary goal."[2]

[2] Harding A. Orren, "Who Decides 'Policy' in a Large Law Firm?" *Law Off. Econ. & Mgmt.* (1986–87), p. 25.

partner cannot be in his or her services as manager—it has to be in cash or other property.[26] Second, the surname of a limited partner cannot be included in the partnership name.[27] A violation of either of these provisions renders the limited partner just as liable as a general partner to any creditor who does not know that he or she is a limited partner. Note that no law expressly bars the participation of limited partners in the management of the partnership. Rather, the threat of personal liability normally deters their participation.

The revised ULPA does restrict a limited partner's liability. Only if the third party had knowledge of the limited partner's management activities is the limited partner liable as a general partner. How much actual review and advisement a limited partner can engage in before being exposed to liability is an unsettled question.[28]

An interesting problem arose in the following case when three limited partners in a limited partnership sought to compel the general partner to distribute partnership profits. But, as limited partners with no control over management responsibilities, were they entitled to make such a decision?

---

26. ULPA Section 4. RULPA Section 101(2), however, permits services rendered as a contribution.
27. ULPA Section 5.
28. See Plasteel Products Corp. v. Helman, 271 F.2d 354 (1st Cir. 1959) (interpreting Massachusetts law).

Case 24.4
BROOKE v. MT. HOOD MEADOWS OREG., LTD.
Court of Appeals of Oregon, 1986.
81 Or.App. 387, 725 P.2d 925.

FACTS Mt. Hood Meadows, Oregon, Ltd., is a limited partnership established to carry on the business of constructing and operating a winter sports development in the Hood River area of Oregon. Elizabeth Brooke and two of the other limited partners were dissatisfied because, for all the years in which profits were earned after 1974, the general partner distributed only 50 percent of the limited partners' taxable profits. The remaining profits were retained and reinvested in the business. Each of the limited partners was taxed on their distributable share of the profits, however, regardless of whether the cash was actually distributed. Brooke and the others brought this action to compel the general partner to distribute all of the limited partnership's profits. The trial court held for Brooke and the limited partners, and the limited partnership appealed.

ISSUE Do the limited partners have a right to compel the general partner to distribute to the limited partners all the profits allocated to them under the provisions of the partnership agreement?

DECISION No. The trial court's decision was reversed.

REASON The Court of Appeals held that because the limited partnership agreement gave the general partner managerial authority and did not include within the agreement a provision requiring full distribution of the profits, the limited partners could not compel distribution. The court pointed out that one of the essential characteristics of the limited partnership was the limited liability of the limited partner who had no control over the management of the firm. If the limited partner does take part in the management of the business, he or she may be held liable as a general partner.

The decision to reinvest profits is strictly a managerial one, according to the court, and thus should be made by the general partner. Absent a provision in the partnership agreement concerning the distribution of profits, and absent misconduct or violation of fiduciary duty on the part of the general partner, the general partner's decision regarding distribution of profits is binding on the limited partnership.

❖ Chapter Summary: Partnerships—Operation and Duties

GENERAL PARTNERSHIP	
Rights of Partners	1. *Management*—Each partner has one vote in management regardless of the proportional size of his or her interest in the firm, unless otherwise specified in the partnership agreement. Unanimous agreement is necessary for decisions significantly affecting the partnership (such as admitting a new partner, altering the firm's business, etc.); otherwise, majority rule controls decisions.
	2. *Interest in the partnership*—Unless otherwise agreed, all partners share equally in the profits of the firm, and losses are shared in the same ratio as profits.
	3. *Compensation*—Unless otherwise agreed, partners are not entitled to compensation for services (except for winding up a dissolved partnership), and compensation from a partner's outside activities (apart from the partnership) is considered to be partnership income.
	4. *Inspection of books*—Each partner has the right to receive (and the duty to produce for other partners) full and complete information concerning the conduct of all aspects of partnership business.
	5. *Accounting*—An accounting of partnership assets or profits is required to determine the value of each partner's proportionate share in the partnership. An accounting can be performed voluntarily or ordered by a court in equity. It occurs automatically by right in connection with dissolution proceedings.

❖ Chapter Summary: Partnerships—Operation and Duties—Continued

Rights of Partners (Continued)	6. *Property rights*—A partner has three basic property rights:
	   a. An interest in the partnership (the right to share profits and to the return of capital upon termination).
	   b. An interest in specific personal and real property of the partnership (called a *tenancy in partnership*).
	   c. A right to participate in management (see #1 in this list).

Duties and Powers of Partners	1. *Fiduciary duty*—The partnership relationship is one of trust and loyalty. Each partner must act in good faith for the benefit of the partnership.
	
	2. *General agency powers*—Each partner is an *agent* of every other partner and acts as both a principal and an agent in any business transaction within the scope of the partnership agreement.
	   a. Joint liability—Partners are jointly liable for partnership debts and obligations. Partners are jointly and severally liable for tort actions and breaches of trust to third persons.
	   b. Liability of incoming partner—A newly admitted partner to an existing partnership does not have personal liability for preexisting partnership debts or obligations; such debts and obligations must be paid from partnership assets, including any capital contribution made by the incoming partner.
	   c. Authority of partners—Similar to agency concepts relating to apparent authority, actual authority, and ratification except the extent of *implied authority* is generally broader for partners than for ordinary agents. The character and scope of the partnership business and the customary nature of the particular business operation determine the scope of implied powers. If the partner acts within the scope of authority, the partnership is bound to third parties.

LIMITED PARTNERSHIP	
Rights and Duties of Limited Partners	Limited partnerships are subject to the same rules as general partnerships with the following exceptions: 1. Only general partners (in a limited partnership) are exposed to unlimited liability. 2. Limited partners are liable for partnership losses only up to the amount they contributed to the partnership. 3. Only general partners can participate in management of the limited partnership. Limited partners are excluded from management affairs; if they do participate, they risk incurring the liability of a general partner for partnership losses.

❖ Questions and Case Problems

24-1. Schwartz and Kenilworth were partners in an accounting firm. Since business was booming and profits were better than they had been in years, they decided to invest some of the firm's profits in some Municifent Corporation stock. The investment turned out to be a good one as Munificent Corporation stock continued to increase in value. On Schwartz's death several years later, Kenilworth assumed full ownership of the business, including the Municifent Corporation stock, a partnership asset. Schwartz's daughter Rosalie, however, claimed a 50 percent ownership interest in the Municifent Corporation stock as Schwartz's sole heir. Can Rosalie enforce her claim? Explain.

24-2. Johnson and Mendoza operate as partners a car dealership. The partnership has existing debts of $300,000 with

General Motors. Johnson and Mendoza take in a new partner, Xavier. Xavier contributes to the partnership land valued at $100,000 to be used by the partnership as a used car lot. Xavier is new to the car dealership business and, in making his first sale, warrants to a customer that the partnership will repair the car at no cost for a period of two years regardless of mileage. General Motors sues the partners jointly on the debt and obtains a judgment. Johnson and Mendoza insist that Xavier's warranty to the customer is not binding on the partnership.

    (a) Discuss Xavier's liability to General Motors.

    (b) Discuss Johnson's and Mendoza's claim that Xavier's warranty is not binding on the partnership.

24-3. Byerly, Samms, and Berg were partners in a business firm. The firm's business equipment included several expensive computers. One day Byerly borrowed one of the computers for use in his home but never bothered to return it. When the other partners asked him about it, Byerly claimed that since the computer represented less than one-third of the computers owned by the partnership, and since he owned one-third of the business, he had a right to keep the equipment. Was he right? Explain.

24-4. Abelard, Heloise, and Thomas form a partnership to operate a window washing service. Abelard contributes $10,000 to the partnership, and Heloise and Thomas contribute $1,000 each. The partnership agreement is silent on how profits and losses will be shared. One month after the partnership is in operation, Heloise and Thomas vote, over Abelard's objection, to purchase another truck for the firm's operation. Abelard believes that since he contributed $10,000 to the business, a major commitment to purchase by the partnership cannot be made over his objection. In addition, Abelard claims that, in absence of agreement, profits must be divided in the same ratio as each partner's capital contribution. Discuss Abelard's contentions.

24-5. Betts, Grove, and Sanderson form a partnership to operate a hairstyling salon. After one year's operation, the salon has become very busy and profitable. Most customers prefer one of the partners to perform the various services offered. Betts becomes very ill, and Grove and Sanderson start working sixty-hour weeks. It appears that Betts will not return to work for at least two months. Grove and Sanderson want to bring in Donovan as a new partner. Betts objects to Donovan and refuses to consent to Donovan's admission into the partnership. Grove and Sanderson insist that they be paid extra compensation for having to work additional hours because of Betts's illness. Discuss whether Grove and Sanderson are entitled to the compensation claimed and whether Donovan can be admitted as a new partner by majority vote.

24-6. Birch and DeLong formed Birch-DeLong Construction Company in 1972 as a partnership. They agreed that all proceeds from the sale of houses would be deposited in a bank, and that disbursement of the funds would be only by mutual agreement or authorization. Initially, both men signed all the checks, but in 1974 DeLong agreed that Birch would take over the accounting and disburse funds for the business. In 1980 the business was suffering, and DeLong realized Birch had been paying some personal expenses out of partnership funds. Did DeLong have a valid claim to an accounting of the funds Birch used to cover his personal expenses? [State of Washington v. Birch, 36 Wn.App. 405, 675 P.2d 246 (1984)]

24-7. Elaine Zuckerman and her infant son, Daniel Zuckerman, sued Dr. Joseph Antenucci and Dr. Jose Pena for medical malpractice. The mother had been treated by both doctors during her pregnancy. Evidence at trial proved that the alleged malpractice occurred during the course of the doctors' partnership business. The trial court held that Dr. Pena was guilty of malpractice but that Dr. Antenucci was not. Damages of $4 million were awarded to Elaine Zuckerman. When Mrs. Zuckerman moved for a judgment against Antenucci and Pena in the amount of $4 million, Antenucci claimed that he should not be held liable for his partner's malpractice because the partnership itself had not been named on the summons and Antenucci had not been designated as a partner on the summons. Was Antenucci liable in this case for the malpractice (tort) of his partner? [Zuckerman v. Antenucci, 124 Misc.2d 971, 478 N.Y.S.2d 578 (1984)]

24-8. Oddo and Ries entered into a partnership agreement in March 1978 to create and publish a book describing how to restore F-100 pickup trucks. Oddo was to write the book, and Ries was to provide the capital. Oddo supplied Ries with the manuscript, but Ries was dissatisfied and hired someone else to revise the manuscript. Ries published the book containing substantial amounts of Oddo's work. Was Oddo able to require Ries to account formally for the profits on the book? [Oddo v. Ries, 743 F.2d 630 (9th Cir. 1984)]

24-9. The Sports Factory, Inc., executed a lease with Ridley Park Associates, a limited partnership, to operate a health and racquetball club. William Chanoff was the general partner of Ridley Park Associates. Over several months Ridley Park failed to meet the original agreement with Sports Factory, Inc., including the altering of architectural plans for the racquetball courts and the acquisition of zoning changes needed for operation of a health spa. Sports Factory sued Ridley Park for breach of the agreement. Who was liable? [Sports Factory, Inc. v. Chanoff, 586 F.Supp. 342 (E.D.Pa. 1984)]

24-10. Herman McCloud was the executor of his mother's estate. He retained Husted and Husted, a law firm, to help him with estate matters. Edgar Husted, one of the firm's partners, determined the tax liability of the McCloud estate to be $18,800 and told McCloud to issue a check in that amount payable to the Husted and Husted Trust Account. Edgar was to pay the Internal Revenue Service from the trust account. Edgar, however, deposited the check into his own personal bank account and did not pay the estate taxes. Later, the IRS requested payment of the taxes from McCloud, and McCloud paid the taxes, plus interest. McCloud then brought suit against

Edgar Husted and his father, Selwyn Husted, the only other partner in the partnership, and the partnership for compensatory and punitive damages for Edgar's wrongful conversion of the tax funds. Were the partnership entity and Edgar's father also held liable for compensatory damages? For punitive damages? Explain. [Husted v. McCloud, 450 N.E.2d 491 (Ind. 1983)]

Chapter 25

Corporations—Formation and Classification

The corporation is a creature of statute. As John Marshall noted, a corporation is an "artificial being," existing in law only and neither tangible nor visible. Its existence depends generally upon state law, although some corporations, especially public organizations, can be created under federal law. Each state has its own body of corporate law, and these laws are not entirely uniform. The Model Business Corporation Act (MBCA) is a codification of modern corporation law. The MBCA and the revised MBCA (RMBCA) are discussed in detail in the "Landmark" in Chapter 26.

As stated in the introduction to this unit, the corporation is the most important form of business organization in the United States and has been for over one hundred years. In this chapter, after a brief look at the history of the corporation, we will examine the nature of this form of business enterprise and the various classifications of corporations. We will then discuss the formation of today's corporation.

> "A corporation is an artificial being, invisible, intangible, and existing only in law."
>
> **John Marshall, 1755–1835**
> **(Chief Justice of the U. S. Supreme Court, 1801–1835)**

❖ The Corporation—A Brief History

A corporation can be owned by a single person, or it can have hundreds, thousands, or even millions of shareholders. The shareholder form of business organization developed in Europe at the end of the seventeenth century. Called *joint stock companies*, they frequently collapsed because their organizers absconded with the funds or proved to be incompetent.

The most famous collapse involved the South Sea Company, which assumed England's national debt in 1711 and obtained in return a monopoly over British trade with the South Sea Islands in South America plus an annual interest payment. The shares of the company were driven up by speculation, fraud was exposed, and a collapse followed. The event came to be known as the South Sea Bubble, and it led to the Bubble Act of 1720, a law that curtailed the use of joint stock companies in England for over a hundred years. Because of this history of fraud and collapse, organizations resembling corporations were regarded with suspicion in the United States during its early years.

In the eighteenth century, a typical U.S. corporation was a municipality. Although several business corporations were formed after the Revolutionary War, it was not until the nineteenth century that the corporation came into common use for private business. In 1811 the state of New York passed a general incorporation law allowing businesses to incorporate. Incorporation was permissible by five or more persons for the manufacture of textiles, glass, metals, and paint. A corporation could have maximum capital of $100,000 (about $750,000 in today's dollars) and a life of twenty years.

The significance of the New York law was that it allowed voluntary incorporation using standard bureaucratic procedures rather than special acts of the legislature, which were usually available only to businesspersons with political influence. By the mid-nineteenth century, railroads predominated among corporations; and after the Civil War, manufacturing corporations became numerous.

❖ Nature of the Corporation

CORPORATION
A legal entity created under the authority of the laws of a state or the federal government. The entity exists distinctly from its several members.

A **corporation** is a legal entity created and recognized by state law. It can consist of one or more *natural* persons (as opposed to the artificial "person" of the corporation) identified under a common name.

The Corporation as a Legal "Person"

A corporation is recognized under state and federal law as a "person," and it enjoys many, but not all, of the same rights and privileges that U. S. citizens enjoy. The Bill of Rights guarantees a "person," as a citizen, certain protections; and corporations are considered persons in most instances. Accordingly, a corporation has the same right as a natural person to equal protection of the laws under the Fourteenth Amendment. It has the right of access to the courts as an entity that can sue or be sued. It also has the right of due process before denial of life, liberty, or property, as well as freedom from unreasonable search and seizures and from double jeopardy.

Under the First Amendment, corporations are entitled to freedom of speech; [1] however, only the corporation's individual officers and employees possess the Fifth Amendment right against self-incrimination. [2] In addition, the privileges and immunities clause of the Constitution (Article IV, Section 2) does not protect corporations, nor does it protect an unincorporated association. [3] This clause requires each state to treat citizens of other states equally with respect to access to courts, travel rights, and so forth.

An unsettled area of corporation law has to do with the criminal acts of a corporation. Since obviously a corporation cannot be sent to prison—even though, under law, it is a person—most courts hold a corporation that has violated the criminal statutes liable for fines. Where criminal conduct can be attributed to corporate officers or agents, those individuals, as *natural* persons, are held liable and can be imprisoned for their acts.

---

1. See First National Bank of Boston v. Bellotti, 435 U.S. 765, 98 S.Ct. 1407, 55 L.Ed.2d 707 (1978).
2. United States v. Barth, 745 F.2d 184 (2d Cir. 1984).
3. W. C. M. Window Co., Inc. v. Bernardi, 730 F.2d 486 (7th Cir. 1984).

Characteristics of the Corporate Entity

A corporation is an artificial person, with its own corporate name, owned by individual shareholders. It is a legal entity with rights and responsibilities. The corporation substitutes itself for its shareholders in conducting corporate business and in incurring liability, yet its authority to act and the liability for its actions are separate and apart from the individuals who own it. (In certain limited situations the "corporate veil" can be pierced; that is, liability for the corporation's obligations can be extended to shareholders, a topic to be discussed later in this chapter.) Responsibility for the overall management of the corporation is entrusted to a board of directors, which is elected by the shareholders. Corporate officers and other employees are hired by the board of directors to run the daily business operations of the corporation.

When an individual purchases a share of stock in a corporation, that person becomes a shareholder and an owner of the corporation. Unlike the members in a partnership, the body of shareholders can change constantly without affecting the continued existence of the corporation. A shareholder can sue the corporation, and the corporation can sue a shareholder. A **derivative suit,** for example, is an action brought by a shareholder to enforce a corporate cause of action that is based upon a primary right the corporation has failed, deliberately or not, to act upon. The shareholder thus asserts this primary right of the corporation on behalf of the corporation.

DERIVATIVE SUIT
A suit by a shareholder to enforce a corporate cause of action against a third person.

The rights and duties of all corporate personnel are discussed in the following chapters. Since a corporation is a separate legal entity, corporate profits are taxed by state and federal governments. Corporations can do one of two things with corporate profits—retain them or pass them on to shareholders in the form of dividends. The corporation receives no tax deduction for dividends distributed to shareholders. Div-

Drawing by W. B. Park; © 1984, The New Yorker Magazine.

"Two lone corporate lawyers sitting down to do battle. Don't you find something rather thrilling about that?"

Landmark in the Law

The Dartmouth College Case (1819)

In 1819 the U. S. Supreme Court heard the case of *The Trustees of Dartmouth College* v. *Woodward*.[1] The decision by the Court in that case determined not only the continued private existence of the small college in New Hampshire, but also the continued existence of private corporations in the United States.

Dartmouth College, named in honor of one of its wealthy patrons, the Earl of Dartmouth, had been founded by Reverend Eleazar Wheelock, a young Connecticut minister who sought to establish a school to train both missionaries and native Americans. In 1769 a corporate charter was obtained from the royal governor of New Hampshire. The charter made Wheelock and his English patrons who had donated capital to the college a self-perpetuating board of trustees for the project. When Wheelock died, his son became president of the college. Under the new, less experienced leadership, many disputes arose over the running of the institution, with the participants eventually dividing along the prevailing political party lines of New Hampshire.

The Republican group believed that the college ought to be under the control of the state and become a public rather than a sectarian institution. The Republicans persuaded the Republican-controlled New Hampshire Congress to pass legislation that significantly altered the com-

position of the board of trustees and added a board of overseers that had virtual authority to control the college. The Federalist board of trustees wanted to preserve the conservative, congregational character of the school and wanted to continue to govern the college without interference. They brought suit against William Woodward, the secretary-treasurer of the state-appointed board of overseers, alleging that the legislation violated the college's original charter. The trustees argued that the original grant of the charter, with its self-perpetuating board of trustees, was effectively a contract between the king and the board. Thus, the U. S. Constitution, which in Article I, Section 10, forbids states to pass legislation that would impair the obligations of contracts, prohibited the state from legislating changes in the self-governing structure of the board. The New Hampshire legislature was, therefore, without power to add trustees to the board, to create a board of overseers, or to alter the original charter in any manner.

Chief Justice Marshall delivered the opinion of the Court. He stated that the grant of the charter was a contract regarding private property within the meaning of Article I, Section 10, and that the legislative acts of New Hampshire, passed without the board of trustees' assent, were not binding upon them. Justice Story, in a separate opinion, distinguished between public and private corporations. He stated that if the shareholders of a corporation were municipal or other public officials, then the corporation was a public corporation and therefore subject to continual public regulation. If the shareholders were private individuals, however, quite a contrary situation obtained. The corporation was private, regardless of whether it served some public interest. The private corporation was

1. 17 U.S. (4 Wheaton) 518, 4 L.Ed. 629 (1819).

idends are again taxable (except when they represent distributions of capital) as ordinary income to the shareholder receiving them. This double-taxation feature of the corporation organization is one of its major disadvantages. Retained earnings, if invested properly, will yield higher corporate profits in the future and thus cause the price of the company's stock to rise. Individual shareholders can then reap the benefits of these retained earnings in the gains they receive when they sell their shares.

❖ Classification of Corporations

The classification of a corporation depends upon its purpose, ownership characteristics, or location.

consequently bound only by the terms of its original charter. Had the state reserved regulatory rights in the original grant of the charter, then the college would be subject to such control. In the absence of such reservations, the state of New Hampshire's legislative acts clearly impaired the original charter and thus violated the U. S. Constitution.

Story's opinion opened an avenue for the future regulation of new corporations, while at the same time creating vested rights in "private" corporations. Marshall and Story both made it clear that the Supreme Court would afford the property rights of private corporations the same protection as afforded to other forms of property.

Daniel Webster, standing, argues the Dartmouth College *case before the Supreme Court in a twentieth century painting by Robert Burns. Chief Justice John Marshall, fourth from the left, presides over the Court.*

"THIS, SIR, IS MY CASE! IT IS THE CASE NOT MERELY OF THAT HUMBLE INSTITUTION, IT IS THE CASE OF EVERY COLLEGE IN OUR LAND!...IT IS, SIR, AS I HAVE SAID, A SMALL COLLEGE. AND YET..."

Domestic, Foreign, and Alien Corporations

A corporation is referred to as a **domestic corporation** by its home state (the state in which it incorporates). A corporation formed in one state but doing business in another is referred to in that other state as a **foreign corporation.** A corporation formed in another country, say Mexico, but doing business within the United States is referred to in the United States as an **alien corporation.**

A foreign corporation does not have an automatic right to do business in a state other than its state of incorporation. It must obtain a *certificate of authority* in the states where it plans to do business. Once the certificate has been issued, the powers conferred upon a corporation by its home state generally can be exercised in the other state.

DOMESTIC CORPORATION
In a given state, a corporation that does business in, and is organized under the laws of, that state.

FOREIGN CORPORATION
In a given state, a corporation that does business in the state without being incorporated therein.

Profile

Joseph Story (1779–1845)

Joseph Story has been described as one of the most "elusive" major figures in the legal history of nineteenth-century America. A brief look at his life and career confirm this characterization. Born in Marblehead, Massachusetts, on September 18, 1779, Story graduated from Harvard College in 1798, read law with Samuel Sewell, and began his practice in Salem, Massachusetts, in 1801. His Salem practice marked the beginning of his great professional and public career. Although he was

for a time affiliated with the Federalist party, in 1808 he was elected to the U. S House of Representatives as a Republican. In 1811 President Madison, a fellow Republican, appointed Story to the post of associate justice of the U. S. Supreme Court.

In appointing Story to the bench of the high court, Madison and his political allies undoubtedly believed that Story would help shift the balance of the court—then dominated by the great Federalist John Marshall—to a more Republican ("democratic") direction. Much to their surprise and chagrin, however, Marshall and Story became strong allies in the protection of property rights and of other predominantly Federalist, conservative interests.

Story's opinions clearly reflected his firm belief in the legal values of stability, continuity, and the protection of private property rights. His opinion in the *Dartmouth College* case (see the "Landmark" in this chapter) placed Story squarely within the Federalist camp. For all his Federalist tendencies, however, Story was not insensitive to democratic pressures for change in the common law. In 1837, when

asked by the Massachusetts legislature whether the common-law rules could be codified, Story replied that setting forth the detailed application of common-law rules might result in a stultification of the law. He further suggested that a legal principle, before it can be codified, must be applied over a long period of time, in differing circumstances, as a test of its validity. Thus, while his approach was conservative in some instances, Story nonetheless felt that doctrinal law should be formed in a manner consistent with the needs of expansive, orderly, and predictable economic development.

Story codified his jurisprudence in a series of commentaries. His treatises included, among others, *Bailments* (1832), *The Federal Constitution* (1833), *Conflict of Laws* (1834), *Equity Jurisprudence* (1836), *Equity Pleading* (1838), *Bills of Exchange* (1843), and *Promissory Notes* (1845). Story's treatises soon came to exert some of the same powerful authority over the development of U. S. law that had previously been accorded the works of Sir William Blackstone and Sir Edward Coke. In fact, by the time of his death in 1845, he was often referred to as the "U. S. Blackstone."

ALIEN CORPORATION
A corporation formed in another country but doing business in the United States.

Before a state court can hear a dispute in which a foreign corporation is the defendant, the state court must have *jurisdiction* over the defendant; and this requires that the foreign corporation have sufficient *contacts* with the state. A foreign corporation that has its home office within the state or has manufacturing plants in the state meets this *minimum-contacts* requirement. A foreign corporation whose only contact with the state is the fact that one of its directors resides there does not have sufficient contact with the state for the state court to exercise jurisdiction over it. This modern view that jurisdiction over foreign corporations is determined by a minimum-contacts standard was established in the following landmark case.

Case 25.1
INTERNATIONAL SHOE CO. v. WASHINGTON, OFFICE OF UNEMPLOYMENT COMPENSATION AND PLACEMENT

United States Supreme Court, 1945.
326 U.S. 310, 66 S.Ct. 154, 90 L.Ed. 95.

FACTS   The state of Washington sought to collect unemployment contributions from International Shoe based on commissions paid by the corporation to its sales representatives who lived in Washington. International Shoe asserted that its activities within the state of Washington were not sufficient to manifest its "presence" there and thus the state courts could not constitutionally exercise jurisdiction over it. It argued that (1) it had no office in the state of Washington; (2) although it employed eleven to thirteen Washington sales representatives to market its product in Washington, no actual sales or purchase contracts were made in that state; and (3) it maintained no stock of merchandise in Washington. Consequently, it was a denial of due process for the state to subject it to suit. The Supreme Court of Washington held for the state, and International Shoe appealed to the U. S. Supreme Court.

ISSUE   Does International Shoe have sufficient contacts with the state of Washington to enable the state of Washington to claim jurisdiction over International Shoe?

DECISION   Yes. The U. S. Supreme Court affirmed the Supreme Court of Washington's decision and found that International Shoe had sufficient contacts with the state of Washington to allow the state to constitutionally exercise jurisdiction over the foreign corporation.

REASON   The Court found that the activities of the Washington salespeople were "systematic and continuous," resulting in a large volume of business for International Shoe. The company, by conducting its business within the state, received the benefits and protections of the laws of Washington and was entitled to have its rights enforced in Washington courts. Thus, International Shoe's operations established "sufficient contacts or ties with the state . . . to make it reasonable and just according to our traditional conception of fair play and substantial justice to permit the state to enforce the obligation" that the company incurred there.

COMMENTS   The Supreme Court established in this case a new test for jurisdiction over foreign corporations. In order for a state to exercise jurisdiction constitutionally over a foreign corporation, the corporation must have minimum contacts with the foreign state. Several subsequent Supreme Court cases have dealt with the limits of "minimum contacts." (See, for example, McGee v. International Life Insurance Co., 355 U.S. 220, 78 S.Ct. 199, 2 L.Ed.2d 223 [1957]; and Hanson v. Denckla, 357 U.S. 235, 78 S.Ct. 1228, 2 L.Ed.2d 1283 [1958].)

Public and Private Corporations

A public corporation is one formed by the government to meet some political or governmental purpose. Cities and towns that incorporate are common examples. In addition, many federal government organizations, such as the U. S. Postal Service, the Tennessee Valley Authority, and Amtrak, are public corporations. Private corporations, on the other hand, are created either wholly or in part for private benefit. Most corporations are private. Although they may serve a public purpose, such as a public utility does, they are owned by private persons rather than by the government.

Nonprofit Corporations

Corporations formed without a profit-making purpose are called *nonprofit, not-for-profit,* or *eleemosynary* (charitable) corporations. Usually (although not necessarily) private corporations, they can be used in conjunction with an ordinary corporation to facilitate making contracts with the government. Private hospitals, educational

Many government organizations, such as Amtrak, are public corporations.

institutions, charities, religious organizations, and the like are frequently organized as nonprofit corporations. The nonprofit corporation is a convenient form of organization that allows various groups to own property and to form contracts without the individual members being personally exposed to liability.

Close Corporations

A **close corporation** is one whose shares are closely held by members of a family or by relatively few persons. Close corporations are often referred to as *closed, closely held, family,* or *privately held* corporations. Usually, the members of the small group that is involved in a close corporation are personally known to each other. Because the number of shareholders is so small, there is no trading market for the shares. In practice, a close corporation is often operated like a partnership. A few states recognize this in special statutory provisions that cover close corporations.

CLOSE CORPORATION
A corporation whose shareholders are limited to a small group of persons, often including only family members. The rights of shareholders of a close corporation usually are restricted regarding the transfer of shares to others.

Statutes for Close Corporations   In order to be eligible for close-corporation status, a corporation has to have a limited number of shareholders, the transfer of corporation stock must be subject to certain restrictions, and the corporation must not make any public offering of its securities.[4] Close corporation statutes provide greater flexibility by expressly permitting electing corporations to vary significantly from those subject to traditional corporation law.[5]

---

4.   See, for example, 8 Del. Code Annotated, Section 342, which section provides that close corporations must have a maximum limitation on the number of shareholders, not exceeding thirty.
5.   For example, in some states (such as Maryland), the close corporation need not have a board of directors.

Management of Close Corporations   The close corporation has a single shareholder or a closely knit group of shareholders who usually hold the positions of directors and officers. Management of a close corporation resembles that of a sole proprietorship or a partnership, although, as a corporation, the firm must meet the same legal requirements as other corporations—except where special statutes have been enacted, as mentioned previously. In states without such special statutes, close corporations have sometimes found it difficult to meet the requirements of state corporation law.

Consider a case where a state law requires that a corporation have two directors, but the close corporation has only one shareholder. One way of satisfying this law is to set two as the number of directors in the articles of incorporation and operate the corporation with a permanent vacancy on the board of directors. Alternatively, a disinterested person, usually a friend, might be convinced to put his or her name down as director.

Transfer of Shares in Close Corporations   Since, by definition, a close corporation has a small number of shareholders, the transfer of shares of one shareholder to someone else can cause serious management problems. In other words, the other shareholders can find themselves required to share control with someone they may not know or like. To avoid this problem, it is usually advisable for the close corporation with several shareholders to specify restrictions on the transferability of stock in its articles of incorporation.

Consider an example: Three brothers, Terry, Damon, and Henry Johnson, are the only shareholders of Johnson's Car Wash, Inc. Terry and Damon do not want Henry to sell his shares to an unknown third person. The articles of incorporation might therefore restrict the transferability of shares to outside persons by stipulating that shareholders offer their shares to the corporation or other shareholders before selling them to an outside purchaser.

Another way that control of a close corporation can be stabilized is through the use of a shareholder agreement. Agreements among shareholders to vote their stock in a particular way are generally upheld.[6] Shareholder agreements can also provide that when one of the original shareholders dies, his or her shares of stock in the corporation will be divided in such a way that the proportionate holdings of the survivors, and thus their proportionate control, will be maintained. The court evaluated such a shareholder agreement in the following case.

Case 25.2
RENCH v. LEIHSER
Appellate Court of Illinois, Fifth District, 1986.
139 Ill.App.3d 889, 94 Ill.Dec. 324, 487 N.E.2d 1201.

FACTS   In February of 1955 Robert Leihser, Albert Rench, and Claude Mullen purchased Loyd Trucking Corporation. They divided the fifty corporate shares equally and signed an agreement in 1956 that should any of them die or wish to sell his shares, the remaining stockholder(s) would purchase the shares. A specific procedure was described in the agreement for transferring the shares in such an event. In 1961 Claude Mullen sold his stock, and Leihser and Rench each bought half of Mullen's shares. The specific procedural details outlined in the 1956 agreement were not followed by Mullen, however, when he sold his shares. Also in violation of the 1956 agreement, Leihser and Rench each assigned one share of

---

6. An important case upholding the validity of shareholders' agreements is Ringling Bros.–Barnum and Bailey Combined Shows v. Ringling, 29 Del.Ch. 610, 53 A.2d 441 (1947).

Case 25.2—Continued

stock to their respective spouses. Then in 1981 Rench died. Leihser sought to buy Rench's shares from Rench's wife, in accordance with the shareholder agreement. Mrs. Rench was willing to sell, but they could not agree on a price. Finally, Leihser initiated this action to compel Mrs. Rench to sell him the shares. The trial court granted Leihser specific performance and ordered Mrs. Rench to sell the stocks to Leihser. Mrs. Rench appealed.

ISSUE   Should the 1956 shareholder agreement, which had not been followed by the shareholders in 1961 at the time Mullen sold his shares, be binding in 1981 on Mrs. Rench?

DECISION   No. The appellate court reversed the finding of the trial court and ruled that the 1956 agreement was no longer binding on the shareholders.

REASON   The court stated that "[a]s a general matter, restrictions upon the right to transfer shares of corporate stock are permissible provided that those restrictions are reasonable and not contrary to any law or public policy. Where, as here, the shares are not available on the open market and have no market value, agreements imposing permissible restrictions on their transfer or sale may be enforced by specific performance." The court went on to state, however, that because such agreements impose a restraint on the "otherwise free alienation of the parties' shares," courts must closely scrutinize such agreements. Here the court noted that the 1956 agreement had been violated (1) when Mullen sold his shares and did not follow some of the exact procedural details stipulated in the shareholder agreement and (2) when the purchasing shareholders assigned a share of stock to their respective spouses. These violations testified to the fact that the shareholders themselves no longer considered the 1956 agreement to be binding in 1961. The court therefore ruled that Leihser could not enforce the agreement against Mrs. Rench.

S Corporations

Certain corporations can choose to qualify under Subchapter S of the Internal Revenue Code to avoid the imposition of income taxes at the corporate level while retaining all the advantages of a corporation, particularly limited liability. In 1982 Congress enacted the Subchapter S Revision Act, the purpose of which was "to minimize the effect of federal income taxes on choices of the form of business organizations and to permit the incorporation and operation of certain small businesses without the incidence of income taxation at both the corporate and shareholder level."[7]

Additionally, Congress decreed that all corporations are divided into two groups: **S corporations** (formerly *Subchapter S corporations*), which have elected Subchapter S treatment, and *C corporations*, which are all other corporations.

While the S corporation has the advantages of the corporate form without the double taxation of income (corporate income is generally not taxed separately), it does have some disadvantages. One of the most important disadvantages relates to the fact that an S corporation's fringe-benefit payments for employee-shareholders who own more than 2 percent of the stock are nondeductible.

Qualification Requirements for S Corporations   Among the numerous requirements for S-corporation qualification are the following, more important ones:

1.   The corporation must be a domestic corporation.
2.   The corporation must not be a member of an affiliated group of corporations.

S CORPORATION
A close business corporation, which has met certain requirements as set out by the Internal Revenue Code, that qualifies for special income-tax treatment. Essentially, an S corporation is taxed the same as a partnership but its owners enjoy the privilege of limited liability.

---

7.   Senate Committee Report No. 97-640.

3. The shareholders of the corporation must be either individuals, estates, or certain trusts. Corporations, partnerships, and nonqualifying trusts cannot be shareholders.
4. The corporation must have thirty-five or fewer shareholders.
5. The corporation can have only one class of stock. Not all shareholders need have the same voting rights.
6. No shareholder of the corporation can be a nonresident alien.

Benefits of S Corporations At times it is beneficial for a regular corporation to elect S-corporation status, as detailed in the following checklist.

1. When the corporation has losses, the S election allows the shareholders to use such losses to offset other income.
2. Whenever the stockholders are in a lower tax bracket than the corporation, the S election causes their entire income to be taxed in the shareholders' bracket, whether or not it is distributed. This is particularly attractive when the corporation wants to accumulate earnings for some future business purpose.
3. Each shareholder reports, for income-tax purposes, a pro-rata share of income based on stock ownership and the number of days the stock was held.

Professional Corporations

Professional corporations are relatively new in corporate law. In the past, professional persons such as physicians, lawyers, dentists, and accountants could not incorporate. Today they can, and their corporations are typically called *professional service associations* or *professional corporations*. They can be identified by the letters S.C. (service corporation), P.C. (professional corporation), Inc. (incorporated), or P.A. (professional association). In general, a professional corporation is formed similar to the way in which an ordinary business corporation is formed.

The professional corporation equalized the tax burden on professionals who, due to their ethical principles, could not incorporate their businesses. By 1981, however, this form of enterprise had come to be widely viewed as permitting unacceptable tax avoidance through many tax-deductible investments, including certain kinds of pension plans. Since 1981 stringent limitations enacted by Congress have helped stop the growth of professional corporations and eliminate the tax loopholes available through them.

Liability of Shareholders Subject to certain exceptions, the shareholders of a professional corporation have limited liability. Three basic areas of liability deserve brief attention. First, a shareholder in a professional association may be liable for the malpractice liability of a member. Under normal corporate law, no member of a corporation is liable for the malpractice of another member. A court, however, might, for liability purposes, regard the professional corporation as a partnership in which each partner is unlimitedly liable for whatever malpractice liability is incurred by the others within the scope of the partnership. Second, a shareholder in a professional corporation is protected from the liability imposed because of torts (unrelated to malpractice) committed by other members. Third, although any shareholder of a professional corporation who engages in a negligent action and who is guilty of

Business Law in Action

Partnership or Corporation?

Because the professional corporation is so similar to a partnership, courts often have difficulty in making decisions concerning this form of business organization. Should partnership or corporate law apply? Sometimes courts will disregard the corporate form and find that the shareholders are in fact partners.[1] At other times, courts will acknowledge the corporate form and apply corporate law. Which determination is made can often be very significant for the parties involved in litigation.

In a case heard by the U. S. Court of Appeals, Second Circuit, in 1986,[2] the determination of whether a professional corporation was a partnership or a corporation was crucial to the outcome of the lawsuit. The case was *Hyland v. New Haven Radiology Associates, P.C.*, in which the plaintiff, Dr. Hyland, brought suit against a professional corporation, alleging his forced resignation from the firm violated anti-age-discrimination statutes. When the P.C. had been formed in 1972, Hyland and four other radiologists each contributed the same

1. See EEOC v. Dowd & Dowd, Ltd., 736 F.2d 1177 (7th Cir. 1984).
2. Hyland v. New Haven Radiology Associates, P.C., 794 F.2d 793 (2d Cir. 1986).

amount of capital for equal shares in the corporation and an equal voice in management; they each served as a corporate officer or director. They divided the profits and losses of the business evenly among themselves. Stock was held only by shareholder-members, who were required to be licensed physicians.

In 1980, after hearing numerous complaints about Dr. Hyland's services—that he was often unavailable, uncooperative, and indulged in abusive conduct, and so on—the corporation requested his resignation from the firm. Hyland, then fifty-one years old, brought suit against the corporation on the grounds that his requested resignation violated the Age Discrimination in Employment Act, which makes it unlawful for an employer to discharge an employee between ages forty and seventy because of the individual's age.

Courts have found that there is no necessary incompatibility in major stockholders or directors and officers of corporations also being "employees" of the corporation. That is, a corporate director can be both an employer and an employee at the same time. Thus, if Hyland's professional corporation were deemed by the court to be a corporation, Hyland, as an employee of that corporation, could benefit from the age-discrimination statutes. If the organization were deemed by the

court to be a partnership, however, Hyland, as a partner, would not be considered an "employee" and thus would not come under the protection of age-discrimination legislation.

In this case, the district court applied an "economic realities" test—that is, it looked at how the business actually was operated—and concluded that the professional corporation amounted to a partnership, and, as a partner, Hyland could not claim protection under the Age Discrimination in Employment Act. The appellate court, in reversing the trial court's ruling, held that the professional corporation was a corporation. In justifying its conclusion, the court stated that "the use of the corporate form precludes any examination designed to determine whether the entity is in fact a partnership. . . . The fact that certain modern partnerships and corporations are practically indistinguishable in structure and operation is no reason for ignoring a form of business organization freely chosen and established. Having made the election to incorporate, the professional corporation should not now be heard to say that it is essentially a medical partnership among co-equal radiologists."

Given the plausibility of both arguments, it is not surprising that courts vary in their conclusions.

malpractice is *personally* liable for the damage caused, many professional corporation statutes retain personal liability of professional persons for their acts and the professional acts performed under their supervision.

❖ Formation of Corporations—Promoters' Activities

Before a corporation becomes a reality, people invest in the proposed corporation as subscribers, and contracts are frequently made by **promoters** on behalf of the future corporation. Promoters are those who, for themselves or others, take the preliminary steps in organizing a corporation. They issue the prospectus [8] for the proposed organization and secure a charter.

Promoter's Liability

It is not unusual for a promoter to purchase or lease property with a view to selling it to the corporation when the corporation is formed. In addition, the promoters enter into contracts with attorneys, accountants, architects, or other professionals whose services will be needed in planning for the proposed corporation. Finally, they induce people to purchase stock in the corporation.

Some interesting legal questions arise in regard to promoters' activities, the most important centering on whether the promoter is personally liable for contracts made on behalf of a corporation that does not yet have any legal existence. In addition, once the corporation is formed, does it assume liability on these contracts, or is the promoter still personally liable?

As a general rule, a promoter is held personally liable on pre-incorporation contracts. Courts simply hold that promoters are not agents where a corporation has yet to come into existence. If, however, the promoter secures the contracting party's agreement to hold only the corporation (not the promoter) liable on the contract, the promoter will not be liable in the event of any breach of contract.

Basically, the same rule of personal liability of the promoter continues even after incorporation unless the third party *releases* the promoter. In most states, this rule is applied whether or not the promoter made the agreement in the name of, or with reference to, the proposed corporation.

Once the corporation is formed (the charter issued), the promoter remains personally liable until the corporation assumes the pre-incorporation contract by *novation* (see Chapter 9). Novation releases the promoter and makes the corporation liable for performing the contractual obligations. In some cases the corporation *adopts* the promoter's contract by undertaking to perform it. Most courts hold that adoption in and of itself does not discharge the promoter from contractual liability. Obviously, a corporation cannot normally *ratify* a pre-incorporation contract, as there was no principal in existence at the time the contract was made.

Incorporation does not make the corporation automatically liable for pre-incorporation contracts. Until the newly formed corporation consents, the third party

PROMOTER
An entrepreneur who participates in the organization of a corporation in its formative stage, usually by issuing a prospectus, procuring subscriptions to the stock, making contract purchases, securing a charter, and the like.

---

8. A prospectus is a document required by federal or state securities laws and regulations (see Chapter 29) that contains material facts concerning the financial operations of the corporation, thus allowing an investor to make an informed decision.

cannot enforce the promoter's contract against the corporation. The liability of the promoter for pre-incorporation contracts was addressed in the following case.

Case 25.3
SKANDINAVIA, INC. v. CORMIER
Supreme Court of New Hampshire, 1986.
128 N.H. 215, 514 A.2d 1250.

FACTS Skandinavia, Inc., manufactured and sold polypropylene underwear. In 1981, following two years of poor sales, Skandinavia entered into negotiations to sell the business to Odilon Cormier, an experienced textile manufacturer. On June 15, 1981, Skandinavia and Cormier agreed that Cormier would take Skandinavia's polypropylene underwear inventory and use it in a new corporation, which would be called Polypro, Inc. In return, Skandinavia would receive a commission on future sales from Polypro, Inc. Polypro was established and began selling the underwear. Skandinavia, however, never received any commissions from the sales. It therefore brought suit against Polypro, Inc., and Cormier to recover its promised commissions. The suit against Polypro, Inc., was dismissed by the trial court. In the suit against Cormier, the trial court found Cormier to be personally liable for the commissions owed. Cormier appealed to the Supreme Court of New Hampshire.

ISSUE Is Cormier personally liable for the contract he signed in the course of setting up a new corporation?

DECISION Yes. The appellate court found Cormier personally liable for the debt as a promoter; the judgment of the trial court was affirmed.

REASON As a general rule, promoters are personally liable on contracts which they have entered into personally, even though they have contracted for the benefit of a projected corporation. The promoter is not discharged from liability until (1) the corporation's board of directors expressly adopts or ratifies the promoter's contract, thus assuming liability for the contract; or (2) the promoter assigns his or her rights and liabilities under the contract, assuming another party accepts; or (3) the pre-incorporation contract is transferred to the corporation by novation. Since Cormier undertook none of these alternatives with regard to his contract with Skandinavia, Cormier retained personal liability on the contract.

Subscribers and Subscriptions

Prior to the actual formation of the corporation, the promoter can contact potential individual investors and they can agree to purchase capital stock in the future corporation. This agreement is often called a *subscription agreement*, and the potential investor is called a *subscriber*. Depending on state law, subscribers become shareholders as soon as the corporation is formed or as soon as the corporation accepts the agreement. This way, if Corporation X becomes insolvent, the trustee in bankruptcy can collect the consideration for any unpaid stock from a pre-incorporation subscriber.

Most courts view pre-incorporation subscriptions as continuing offers to purchase corporate stock. On or after its formation, the corporation can choose to accept the offer to purchase stock. Many courts also treat a subscription as a contract between the subscribers, making it irrevocable except with the consent of all of the subscribers. The Model Business Corporation Act allows that a subscription is irrevocable for a period of six months unless otherwise provided in the subscription agreement or unless all the subscribers agree to the revocation of the subscription. In some courts and jurisdictions, the pre-incorporation subscriber can revoke the offer to purchase before acceptance without liability, however.

❖ Incorporation

Exact procedures for incorporation differ among states, but the basic requirements are similar.

Procedures and Requirements

State Chartering Since state incorporation laws differ, individuals have found some advantage in looking for the states that offer the most advantageous tax or incorporation provisions. Delaware has historically had the least restrictive laws. Consequently, many corporations, including a number of the largest, have incorporated there. Delaware's statutes permit firms to incorporate in Delaware and carry out business and locate operating headquarters elsewhere. (Most other states now permit this.) On the other hand, closely held corporations, particularly those of a professional nature, generally incorporate in the state where their principal stockholders live and work.

Articles of Incorporation The primary document needed to begin the incorporation process is called the *articles of incorporation* (see Exhibit 25-1). The articles include

ARTICLE ONE
The name of this corporation is _____ .

ARTICLE TWO
The period of its duration is perpetual (may be a number of years or until a certain date).

ARTICLE THREE
The purpose (purposes) for which the corporation is organized is (are) _____
_____ .

ARTICLE FOUR
The aggregate number of shares that the corporation shall have authority to issue is _____ of the par value of _____ dollar(s) each (or without par value).

ARTICLE FIVE
The corporation will not commence business until it has received for the issuance of its shares consideration of the value of $1,000 (can be any sum not less than $1,000).

ARTICLE SIX
The address of the corporation's registered office is _____ , New Pacum, and the name of its registered agent at such address is _____ . (Use the street or building or rural route address of the registered office, not a post office box number.)

ARTICLE SEVEN
The number of initial directors is _____ , and the names and addresses of the directors are _____
_____
_____ .

ARTICLE EIGHT
The name and address of the incorporator is _____
_____ .

(signed) _____
Incorporator
Sworn to on _____ by the above-named incorporator.
(date)

_____
Notary Public _____ County, New Pacum
(Notary Seal)

◆ **Exhibit 25-1**
Articles of Incorporation

basic information about the corporation and serve as a primary source of authority for its future organization and business functions. The person or persons who execute the articles are called *incorporators* and are discussed below. Generally, the following should be included in the articles of incorporation:

1. *Corporate name*: Choice of a corporate name is subject to state approval to ensure against duplication or deception. Fictitious-name statutes usually require that the secretary of state run a check on the proposed name in the state of incorporation. Some states require that the incorporators, at their own expense, run a check on the proposed fictional name for the newly formed corporation. Once cleared, a name can be reserved for a short time, for a fee, pending the completion of the articles of incorporation. All corporate statutes require the corporation name to include the word *Corporation, Incorporated,* or *Limited,* or abbreviations of these terms.

A corporate name is prohibited from being the same as, or deceptively similar to, the name of an existing corporation doing business within the state. For example, if an existing corporation is named General Dynamics, Inc., the state will not allow another corporation to be called General Dynamic, Inc., because that name is deceptively similar to the first, and it impliedly transfers a part of the good will established by the first corporate user to the second corporation.

2. *Nature and purpose*: The intended business activities of the corporation must be specified in the articles, and, naturally, they must be lawful. A general statement of corporate purpose is usually sufficient to give rise to all of the powers necessary or convenient to the purpose of the organization. The corporate charter can state, for example, that the corporation is organized "to engage in the production and sale of agricultural products." There is a trend toward allowing corporate charters to state that the corporation is organized for "any legal business," with no mention of specifics, in order to avoid unnecessary future amendments to the corporate charter.

Some states prohibit the incorporation of certain professionals, such as doctors or lawyers, except pursuant to a professional incorporation statute. Also, in some states, certain industries, such as banks, insurance companies, or public utilities, cannot be operated in the general corporate form and are governed by special incorporation statutes.

3. *Duration*: A corporation can have perpetual existence under most state corporate statutes. A few states, however, prescribe a maximum duration after which the corporation must formally renew its existence.

4. *Capital structure*: The capital structure of the corporation is generally set forth in the articles. A few state statutes require a relatively small capital investment (for example, $1,000) for ordinary business corporations but a greater capital investment for those engaged in insurance or banking. The number of shares of stock authorized for issuance, their par value, the various types or classes of stock authorized for issuance, and other relevant information concerning equity, capital, and credit must be outlined in those provisions of the articles.

5. *Internal organization*: Whatever the internal management structure of the corporation, it should be described in the articles, although it can be included in bylaws adopted after the corporation is formed. The articles of incorporation commence the corporation; the bylaws are formed after commencement by the board of directors. Bylaws are subject to and cannot conflict with the incorporation statute or the corporation's charter. Section 27 of the Model Business Corporation Act (MBCA), for example, provides that "the power to alter, amend, or repeal the bylaws or adopt new bylaws shall be vested in the board of directors unless reserved to the shareholders

by the articles of incorporation." That section further requires that bylaws be consistent with the articles of incorporation. Typical bylaw provisions describe the quorum and voting requirements for shareholders, the election of the board of directors, the methods of replacing directors, and the manner and time of scheduling shareholder and board meetings.

6. *Registered office and agent*: The corporation must indicate the location and address of its registered office within the state. Usually, the registered office is also the principal office of the corporation. The corporation must give the name and address of a specific person who has been designated as an *agent* and who can receive legal documents on behalf of the corporation. These legal documents include service of process (the delivery of a court order requiring an appearance in court).

7. *Incorporators*: Each incorporator must be listed by name and must indicate an address. An incorporator is a person (or persons) who applies to the state on behalf of the corporation to obtain its corporate charter. The incorporator need not be a subscriber and need not have any interest at all in the corporation. Many states do not impose residency or age requirements for incorporators. States vary on the required number of incorporators; it can be as few as one or as many as three. Incorporators are required to sign the articles of incorporation when they are submitted to the state; often this is their only duty. In some states, they participate at the first organizational meeting of the corporation.

Certificate of Incorporation   Once the articles of incorporation have been prepared, signed, and authenticated by the incorporators, they are sent to the appropriate state official, usually the secretary of state, along with the appropriate filing fee. In many states, the secretary of state then issues a *certificate of incorporation* representing the state's authorization for the corporation to conduct business. (This may be called the *corporate charter*.) The certificate and a copy of the articles are returned to the incorporators, who then hold the initial organizational meeting that completes the details of incorporation.

First Organizational Meeting   The first organizational meeting is provided for in the articles of incorporation but is held after the charter is actually granted. At this meeting, the incorporators elect the first board of directors and complete the routine business of incorporation (pass bylaws, issue stock, and so forth). Sometimes, the meeting is held after the election of the board of directors, and the business to be transacted depends upon the requirements of the state's incorporation statute, the nature of the business, the provisions made in the articles, and the desires of the promoters.

Adoption of bylaws—the internal rules of management for the corporation—is probably the most important function of the first organizational meeting. The shareholders, directors, and officers must abide by bylaws in conducting corporate business; but corporation employees and third persons dealing with the corporation are not bound by them unless they have reason to be familiar with them.

Corporate Financing   Corporations are financed by the issuance and sale of corporate securities—bonds and stock. A detailed description of the types of securities that can be issued and the difference between stocks and bonds is given in Chapter 29.

Corporate Status

The procedures for incorporation are very specific. If they are not followed precisely, others may be able to challenge the existence of the corporation.

Improper Incorporation   Errors in the incorporation procedures can become important when, for example, a third person who is attempting to enforce a contract or bring suit for a tort injury fortuitously learns of them. On the basis of improper incorporation, the plaintiff could seek to make the would-be shareholders personally liable.

Also, when the corporation seeks to enforce a contract against a defaulting party, if the defaulting party learns of a defect in the incorporation procedure, he or she may be able to avoid liability on that ground. Courts have developed three theories to prevent the windfall that would occur in giving a contracting party the benefit of the stockholders' personal liability. The theories are *de jure* corporation, *de facto* corporation, and corporation by estoppel.

De Jure and De Facto Corporations   In the event of substantial compliance with all conditions precedent to incorporation, the corporation is said to have *de jure* existence in law. In most states the certificate of incorporation is viewed as evidence that all mandatory statutory provisions have been met. This means that the corporation is properly formed, and neither the state nor a third party can attack its existence. If for example, an incorporator's address was incorrectly listed, this would mean that the corporation was improperly formed; but the law does not regard such inconsequential procedural defects as detracting from substantial compliance, and courts will uphold the *de jure* status of the corporate entity.

Sometimes there is a defect in complying with statutory mandates—for example, the corporation charter may have expired. Under these circumstances, the corporation may have a *de facto* status, meaning that its existence cannot be challenged by third persons (except for the state). The following elements are required for *de facto* status:

1.   There must be a state statute under which the corporation can be incorporated validly.
2.   The parties must have made a good-faith attempt to comply with the statute.
3.   The enterprise must have already undertaken to do business as a corporation.

Corporation by Estoppel   If an association that is neither an actual corporation nor a *de facto* or *de jure* corporation holds itself out as being a corporation, it will be estopped from denying corporate status in a lawsuit by a third party. This usually occurs when a third party contracts with an association that claims to be a corporation but does not hold a certificate of incorporation. When the third party brings suit naming the so-called corporation as the defendant, the association may not escape from liability on the ground that no corporation exists. When justice requires, the courts treat an alleged corporation as if it were an actual corporation for the purpose of determining the rights and liabilities involved in a particular situation. Corporation by estoppel is thus determined by the situation. It does not extend recognition of corporate status beyond the resolution of the problem at hand.

❖ Disregarding the Corporate Entity

In some unusual situations, a corporate entity is used by its owners to perpetuate a fraud, circumvent the law, or in some other way accomplish an illegitimate objective.

In these cases, the court will ignore the corporate structure by "piercing the corporate veil," exposing the shareholders to personal liability.

Some of the factors that frequently cause the court to pierce the corporate veil are:

1. A party is tricked or misled into dealing with the corporation rather than the individual.
2. The corporation is set up to never make a profit or always be insolvent, or it is too "thinly" capitalized.
3. The shareholder or director unconditionally guarantees to be personally liable for corporate obligations and/or debts.
4. Statutory corporate formalities, such as calling required corporation meetings, are not followed.
5. Personal and corporate interests are commingled.

To elaborate on the fifth factor in the preceding list, commingling of personal and corporate interests, consider the corporations that are formed according to law by a single person or by a few family members. In these cases, the corporate entity and the sole stockholder (or family-member stockholders) must carefully preserve the separate status of the corporation and its owners. Certain practices invite trouble for the one-person or family-owned corporation: the commingling of corporate and personal funds, the failure to hold and record minutes of board of directors' meetings, or the shareholders' continuous, personal use of corporate property (for example, vehicles). When the corporate privilege is abused for personal benefit and the corporate business is treated in such a careless manner that the corporation and the shareholder in control are no longer separate entities, the court will require an owner to assume personal liability to creditors for the corporation's debts. In short, where the facts show that great injustice would result from the use of a corporation to avoid individual responsibility, a court of equity will look behind the corporate structure to the individual stockholder.

General corporation law has no specific prohibition against a stockholder lawfully lending money to his or her corporation. When an officer or director lends the corporation money and takes back security in the form of corporate assets, however, the courts will scrutinize the transaction closely. Any such transaction must be made in good faith and for fair value.

The following case illustrates a situation in which the funds of the corporation and its sole shareholder were so intermingled that the shareholder was held personally liable for unpaid corporate taxes.

Case 25.4
WOLFE v. UNITED STATES
United States Court of Appeals, Ninth Circuit, 1986.
798 F.2d 1241.

FACTS Charles Wolfe was the sole shareholder and president of Wolfe & Company, a firm that leased tractor-trailers. The corporation had no separate bank account. Banking transactions were conducted through Wolfe's personal accounts, and employees were paid from them. Wolfe never consulted with any other corporate directors. During the tax years 1974–1976, the corporation incurred $114,472.91 in federal tax liabilities for employment, fuel, and highway-use taxes, and for penalties, fees, and interest. The government held Wolfe personally liable. Wolfe paid the tax bill and then brought this action against the government for disregarding his corporate entity. The trial court held that the corporation was merely an "alter ego"

Case 25.4—Continued

of the sole shareholder, Wolfe, and granted the government's motion for summary judgment. Wolfe appealed to the U. S. Court of Appeals.

ISSUE Can the government disregard the corporate entity in Wolfe's case and hold Wolfe personally liable for corporate taxes?

DECISION Yes. The trial court's ruling was affirmed, and Wolfe was held personally liable for the taxes on the grounds that the corporation was merely his alter ego.

REASON The alter-ego doctrine holds that if an individual does not keep separate his corporate and personal finances and activities, clearly delineating what belongs to the corporation, then the corporate entity may be disregarded. In this case, the court found the evidence overwhelmingly sufficient to indicate that the corporation was Wolfe's alter ego.

Application

Law and the Entrepreneur—
How to Incorporate

Incorporation generally involves a very modest investment in legal fees and filing fees. Indeed, just about anybody can form a corporation for any lawful purpose in any state in the union. The requirements differ from state to state. But you do not have to form a corporation in the state in which you live or the state in which you are doing business. In fact, a large number of individuals form their corporations, or obtain a corporate charter, from the state of Delaware because it has the least legal restrictions on corporate formation and operation. More recently, Delaware also has limited the liability of directors, so a number of large companies are moving their corporate charters into that state.

Delaware is also the state most often chosen by the "mail-order incorporation" type of company. Perhaps you have even seen the ad—"You, too, can incorporate"—in various national and regional magazines. Those ads are usually generated by organizations in Delaware that have preprinted incorporation forms for you to fill out and send back with a small fee. The employees of said organization send or take your forms to the appropriate state office in Delaware to obtain your certificate of incorporation. While such "do-it-yourself" incorporating may be sufficient for those interested in starting a small business without serious aspirations of growing, if you believe that the business in which you are going to engage has growth potential and may require significant financing in the future, you are best advised to contact a local lawyer to take you through the necessary steps in incorporating your business.

Checklist of Factors to Discuss with an Attorney Concerning Incorporation

☐ 1. Tax considerations.

☐ 2. The initial cost of incorporation and any continuing costs.

☐ 3. The formalities that are necessary.

☐ 4. The amount of record-keeping that will be required.

☐ 5. What should be included in the bylaws.

❖ Chapter Summary: Corporations—Formation and Classification

Legal Characteristics of Corporations	1. Formal statutory requirements must be followed in forming a corporation. Corporate law varies from state to state, but statutory incorporation requirements that have been adopted to some degree in every state are embodied in the Model Business Corporation Act (MBCA) and the revised MBCA.
	2. The corporation is a legal entity distinct from its owners.
	3. The shareholders own the corporation. They elect a board of directors to govern the corporation. The board of directors hires corporate officers and other employees to run the daily business of the firm.
	4. The corporation pays income tax on net profits; shareholders pay income tax on disbursed dividends they receive from the corporation (double-taxation feature).
	5. The corporation can have perpetual existence or be chartered for a specific period of time.
Classification of Corporations	1. *Domestic, foreign, and alien corporations:* a. A corporation is referred to as a *domestic corporation* within its home state (the state in which it incorporates). b. A corporation is referred to as a *foreign corporation* by any state that is not its home state. c. A corporation is referred to as an *alien corporation* if it originates in another country but does business in the United States.
	2. *Public and private corporations:* a. A public corporation is one formed by the government (e.g., cities, towns, and public projects). b. A private corporation is one formed wholly or in part for private benefit (most corporations are private).
	3. *Nonprofit corporations*—Corporations formed without a profit-making purpose (e.g., charitable, educational, and religious organizations or hospitals).
	4. *Close corporations*—Corporations owned by a family or a relatively small number of individuals; transfer of shares is usually restricted, and the corporation cannot make a public offering of its securities.
	5. *S corporations*—Small domestic corporations (must have thirty-five or fewer U.S. citizens as members) that, under Subchapter S of the Internal Revenue Code, are given special tax treatment. These corporations allow shareholders to enjoy the limited legal liability of the corporate form but avoid its double-taxation feature (taxes are paid by shareholders as personal income, and the S corporation is not taxed separately).
	6. *Professional corporations*—Corporations formed by professionals (e.g., doctors, lawyers) to obtain the benefits of incorporation (pension plans, tax benefits, limited liability); in most cases the professional corporation is treated like a corporation, but sometimes the courts will disregard the corporate form and treat the shareholders as partners.
Formation of the Corporation	1. *Promoters*—Those who take the preliminary steps in organizing a corporation (issue prospectus, secure charter, interest investors in the purchase of corporate stock, form subscription agreements, etc.). Until the new corporation assumes pre-incorporation contracts made by the promoter by novation, the promoter remains personally liable for all obligations incurred on behalf of the future corporation.
	2. *Incorporation—basic requirements:* a. Preparation and filing of the articles of incorporation; the articles generally should include the following information concerning the corporation: name, nature and purpose, duration, capital structure, internal organization, registered office and agent, and incorporators.

❖ Chapter Summary: Corporations—Formation and Classification—Continued

Formation of the Corporation (Continued)	b. Certificate of incorporation—Charter received from appropriate state office (usually the secretary of state) after articles of incorporation have been filed. Authorizes the corporation to conduct business. d. First organizational meeting—Provided for in the articles of incorporation but held after the charter is granted. Board of directors elected and other business completed (bylaws passed, stock issued, etc.).
Corporate Status	If a corporation has been improperly incorporated, courts will sometimes impute corporate existence to the firm by holding that the firm is a *de jure* corporation (cannot be challenged by the state or third persons) or a *de facto* corporation (can be challenged by the state but not by third persons). If a firm is neither an actual nor a *de jure* nor *de facto* corporation but represents itself to be a corporation and is sued as such by a third party, it may be held to be a corporation by estoppel.
Disregarding the Corporate Entity	Where equity demands, courts may "pierce the corporate veil" and hold a shareholder or shareholders personally liable for a judgment against the corporation. This usually occurs only when the corporation was established to circumvent the law or when it is used for an illegitimate or fraudulent purpose, or when the controlling shareholder commingles his or her own interests with those of the corporation to such an extent that the corporation no longer has a separate identity.

❖ Questions and Case Problems

25-1. Sam and Irvin were a computer consulting team doing business under the name SI Corporation. Although they had "SI Corporation" printed on their invoices, stationery, business cards, and checks, Sam and Irvin had never taken any actual steps to incorporate the business, and they knew that SI Corporation had no legal existence. When they began doing business together, Sam and Irvin leased an office in the name of SI Corporation from Harvey. At the time the lease was formed, Harvey had no idea that SI Corporation did not exist. Due to increasing competition in their line of business, Sam and Irvin saw reduced profits and could not meet the payments due under the lease contract with Harvey. Harvey then learned that SI Corporation had no legal existence, so he sued Sam and Irvin personally for damages arising from the breach of the lease contract. Can Sam and Irvin be held personally liable for breaching the lease contract? Explain.

25-2. Jerry, Ted, and Andrew Denton inherited a small paper-supply business from their father, who had operated the business as a sole proprietorship. The Denton Brothers decided to incorporate under the name of Denton Corporation and retained an attorney by the name of Gentry to draw up the necessary documents. All of the proper papers were drawn up by Gentry, and he had the brothers sign them. Gentry neglected, however, to send the application for a corporate charter to the secretary of state's office. The Denton brothers assumed that all necessary legal work had been taken care of, and they proceeded to do business as Denton Corporation. One day, a Denton Corporation employee was delivering a carton of paper supplies to one of Denton's customers. On the way to the

customer's office, the employee negligently ran a red light and caused a car accident. Baxter, the driver of the other vehicle involved in the accident, was injured as a result and sued Denton Corporation for damages. Baxter then learned that no state charter had ever been issued to Denton Corporation, so he sued Jerry, Ted, and Andrew Denton personally for damages. Can the Denton brothers avoid personal liability for the tort of their employee? Explain.

25-3. Albright, Bond, and Cripps form a corporation. The state laws governing incorporation require that the articles of incorporation be signed by three incorporators. A charter is issued, and the corporation begins to do business. Thompson extends credit to the corporation. Because of a national recession, the corporation becomes insolvent. At this time Thompson learns that Albright failed to sign the articles of incorporation. Thompson claims that the corporation's formation was improper and that Albright, Bond, and Cripps are personally liable. Discuss Thompson's claim.

25-4. Cuthbert and Simons decided to form a corporation for the production and sale of electronic games. The secretary of state refused to issue a corporate charter in the name of Electronic Gametime, their proposed name, because the name did not include the words *Incorporated* or *Corporation* or any word or abbreviation indicating that it was a corporation. Is this a legitimate action on the part of the secretary of state?

25-5. Christy, Briggs, and Dobbs are recent college graduates who want to form a corporation to manufacture and sell personal computers. Perez tells them he will set in motion the formation of their corporation. Perez first makes a contract for the purchase of a piece of land for $25,000 with Oliver. Oliver does not know of the prospective corporate formation at the time of the signing of the contract. Perez then makes a contract with Barth to build a small plant on the property being purchased. Barth's contract is conditional on the corporation's formation. Perez secures all necessary subscription agreements and capitalization, and he files the articles of incorporation. A charter is issued.

    (a) Discuss whether the newly formed corporation or Perez, or both, are liable on the contracts with Oliver and Barth.

    (b) Discuss whether the corporation is automatically liable to Barth upon being formed.

25-6. Pacific Development, Inc., was incorporated in the District of Columbia for the purpose of international brokerage consulting. Pacific's founder, president, and sole shareholder was Tongsun Park, a South Korean who was on close terms with South Korea's president, Park Chung Hee. The U.S. government alleged that Park's main purpose was to influence Congress to give economic and military aid to South Korea. There was initially no board of directors, and later, when appointed by Park, the board rarely met. The IRS assessed $4.5 million in back taxes against Park in 1977. It then seized the assets of Pacific Development, Inc., claiming that the company was a mere alter ego of Park. Valley Finance, Inc., was another corporation wholly owned by Park. It had loaned money to Pacific Development, and it held a second deed of trust on the real property that the IRS had seized. Both Pacific Development and Valley Finance attempted to obtain the return of Pacific Development's assets that the IRS had seized. The plaintiffs claimed that the IRS had improperly pierced the corporate veil of Pacific. Do you agree? [Valley Finance, Inc. v. United States, 629 F.2d 162 (D.C. Cir. 1980)]

25-7. On December 3, 1974, William J. Brunetti sent the certificate of incorporation for his new corporation, Sunshine Greenery, Inc., to the secretary of state's office for filing. The filing was completed on December 18, 1974. Brunetti, as president of the new corporation, leased a building from Edward Cantor and Leo Masin. The lease agreement was signed on December 16, 1974, two days before the certificate of incorporation was filed by the state. When the corporation failed to meet its payments under the lease, Cantor and Masin sued Brunetti, alleging that Brunetti should be personally liable for the lease because the corporation had no legal existence at the time the lease was signed. Since all of the technical requirements for *de jure* corporate status had not been met at the time

the lease was signed, is there any way Brunetti could successfully claim that the corporation was liable for the debt? [Cantor v. Sunshine Greenery, Inc., 165 N.J.Super. 411, 398 A.2d 571 (1979)]

25-8. Harvey's is a group of New York corporations. Five of these entered into an agreement with Flynt Distributing Company for Flynt to distribute their magazines. Following this agreement, Harvey's failed to pay Flynt or to ship the magazines to Flynt, causing Flynt injury. Two of Harvey's shareholders converted the assets of the five corporations to their own use, which left the corporations undercapitalized. Discuss whether this conduct amounted to an abuse of corporate business, allowing Flynt to pierce the corporate veil to obtain recovery. [Flynt Distributing Co., Inc. v. Harvey, 734 F.2d 1389 (9th Cir. 1984)]

25-9. Leslie R. Barth was president of five corporations. During the course of an IRS investigation for failure to file corporate and personal income tax returns, the IRS served an administrative summons for Barth to turn over prescribed corporate records. Barth only partially complied, and the IRS took Barth to district court. The court ordered the corporations to furnish the requested information and to designate an agent to testify for the corporations "without revoking their personal privileges against self-incrimination." Barth appealed the order, claiming that such an order violated the "agent's" (his) constitutional right against self-incrimination, and that Fifth Amendment protection against self-incrimination extended to the corporations. Discuss whether the corporations did possess Fifth Amendment privileges against self-incrimination, and whether Barth's individual officer self-incrimination privilege was denied by the district court's order. [United States v. Barth, 745 F.2d 184 (2d Cir. 1984)]

25-10. Pointer formed a corporation with $1,000 capital and later loaned over $400,000 to the corporation. Six days after he was notified that Tigrett had filed suit against his corporation, Pointer transferred corporate assets amounting to $400,000 to himself as repayment of the loans. Pointer then transferred these assets to another corporation, of which he was the sole shareholder. The second corporation took over all the business and duties of the original corporation. At the time that Pointer undertook these transfers, Tigrett had not obtained a judgment against the corporation and so was not one of its creditors. By the time Tigrett was awarded a judgment against the original corporation, it had no assets. Was there any way for Tigrett to collect the amount of her judgment? Explain. [Tigrett v. Pointer, 580 S.W.2d 375 (Tex.Civ.App. 1978)]

Chapter 26

Corporations—Corporate Powers and Management

Sir Edward Coke's comment, obvious though it may be, drives home the point well that a corporation is not a person. It is a legal fiction, a creature of statute. It is important to keep in mind, however, its status as a "legal person." Under modern law, except as limited by charters, statutes, or constitutions, *a corporation can engage in all acts and enter into any contract available to a natural person in order to accomplish the purposes for which it was created.*

When a corporation is created, the express and implied powers necessary to achieve its purpose also come into existence. These powers do not give the men and women who run the corporations unlimited management discretion, however. In this chapter, we will discuss these corporate powers, as well as the responsibilities of corporate directors and officers.

> *"They [corporations] cannot commit treason, nor be outlawed nor excommunicated, because they have no soul."*
>
> **Sir Edward Coke, 1552–1634 (British jurist and legal scholar)**

❖ Corporate Powers

Express Powers

The express powers of a corporation are found in its articles of incorporation, in the law of the state of incorporation, and in the state and federal constitutions. The order of priority used when conflicts arise among documents involving corporations follows:

1. The U. S. Constitution.
2. State constitutions.
3. State statutes.
4. The certificate of incorporation (charter).
5. Bylaws.
6. Resolutions of the board of directors.

Implied Powers

Certain inherent powers attach when a corporation is created. Barring express constitutional, statutory, or charter prohibitions, the corporation has the implied power to perform all acts reasonably appropriate and necessary to accomplish its corporate purposes. For this reason, a corporation has the implied power to borrow money within certain limits, to lend money, or to extend credit to those with whom it has a legal or contractual relationship, and to make charitable contributions.[1]

To borrow money, the corporation acts through its board of directors to authorize the execution of negotiable paper. Most often, the president or chief executive officer of the corporation will execute the necessary papers on behalf of the corporation. In so doing, corporate officers have the implied power to bind the corporation in matters directly connected with the *ordinary* business affairs of the enterprise. A corporate officer does not have the authority to bind the corporation in matters of great significance to the corporate purpose or undertaking, however, as is illustrated in the following case.

Case 26.1
BOSTON ATHLETIC ASSOCIATION v. INTERNATIONAL MARATHONS, INC.
Supreme Judicial Court of Massachusetts, 1984.
392 Mass. 356, 467 N.E.2d 58.

FACTS William T. Cloney was the president of the Boston Athletic Association (BAA), a nonprofit corporation whose principal purpose is to present the annual Boston Marathon. At a 1981 BAA board of directors' meeting, Cloney was "authorized and directed to negotiate and to execute in the name of and in behalf of [the BAA] such agreements as he deems in the best interest of the Association for the perpetuation, sponsorship, or underwriting of the Boston A. A. Marathon." For past marathons, Cloney himself had undertaken to secure contracts with individual sponsors, and the BAA had full control over the presentation of the Marathon. This time, however, Cloney contracted with International Marathons, Inc. (IMI) for IMI to be the exclusive promoter of the race. Under the terms of the contract, (1) BAA transferred all rights to use the Boston Marathon name and logos to IMI, (2) the agreement was to be automatically renewable from year to year, and (3) IMI was entitled to keep any profits beyond the first $400,000, which would be paid to BAA. In short, the contract with IMI prevented the BAA from having any significant control over the sponsorship or presentation of the race, which was essentially the reason for its corporate existence.

When the board of directors learned of Cloney's agreement with IMI, it brought an action to have the agreement set aside on the ground that Cloney had exceeded the authorization vested in him by the board. IMI claimed that Cloney had been given the authority to make the contract, and therefore it should be enforced. The trial court held for BAA, and IMI appealed.

ISSUE Had Cloney exceeded his authorization by granting IMI excessive, and perpetual, control over the Boston Marathon?

DECISION Yes. The trial court's judgment was affirmed.

REASON The Supreme Judicial Court of Massachusetts stated that under "the traditional principles of corporate governance, the board of governors of the BAA does not have the power to delegate to an individual officer authority to enter into a contract which so totally encumbers the most significant purpose of the BAA, the presentation of the Marathon. . . . It is the obligation of the board of governors to oversee the presentation of the Marathon, not to surrender virtually complete control of the event to another organization." The court also concluded that the contract was inconsistent with the nonprofit nature of the BAA, because IMI's primary goal in promoting the marathon was to secure profits for itself from the promoting activities. For these reasons, the court deemed that Cloney was not empowered to make the contract with IMI, and the contract was thus unenforceable.

---

1. The right of a corporation to make political contributions in federal elections is prohibited by the Federal Elections Campaign Act. [18 U.S.C. Section 321] Early law held that a corporation had no implied authority to make charitable contributions, because charitable activities were contrary to the primary purpose of the corporation to make a profit. Modern law, by statutes and court decisions, now holds that a corporation has such implied authority.

Ultra Vires Doctrine

The term **ultra vires** means "beyond the powers." In corporate law, acts of a corporation that are beyond the authority given to it under its charter or under the statutes by which it was incorporated are *ultra vires* acts. In other words, acts in furtherance of the corporation's expressed purposes are within the corporate power; acts beyond the scope of corporate business as described in the charter are *ultra vires* acts. Thus, *ultra vires* acts can be understood only within the context of the particular stated purpose for which the corporation was organized.

The stated purposes in the articles of the corporation set the limits of the activities the corporation can legally pursue. Any time the corporation takes on activities outside the stated purpose(s), the corporation can be charged with committing an *ultra vires* act. Because of this, corporations are increasingly aware of the benefit of adopting a very broad statement of purpose in their articles of incorporation to include virtually all conceivable activities. Corporate statutes in many states permit the expression "any lawful purpose" to be a legally sufficient stated purpose in the articles of incorporation.

A majority of cases dealing with *ultra vires* acts have involved contracts made for unauthorized purposes. For example, it is difficult to see how a contract made by a plumbing company for the purchase of 6,000 cases of vodka is reasonably related to the conduct and furtherance of the corporation's stated purpose of providing plumbing installation and services. Hence, such a contract would probably be held *ultra vires*.

Corporate acts can be *ultra vires* simply in the sense of being beyond corporate powers. Such acts are not necessarily illegal; however, all illegal acts are inherently *ultra vires*. Modern areas of *ultra vires* concern include whether a corporation has the power to make charitable or political contributions, to grant employee fringe benefits, to make loans to directors or officers, or to acquire shares of other corporations. The prudent corporate executive will always check applicable statutes and the articles of incorporation before taking these actions.

In certain cases, the law recognizes the right of a shareholder to sue the board of directors for its alleged wrongful action of pursuing *ultra vires* acts. A stockholder can bring what is called a *derivative suit* (discussed in Chapter 25) against the corporation after first demanding that the directors correct the wrong. If the directors fail to act, the stockholder can ask the court to enforce the corporate right.

Certain acts of the board of directors can be unauthorized at the time they first occur but ratified later by a majority vote of the stockholders. Such ratification of the board of directors' actions by a majority of shareholders will ordinarily cure an otherwise voidable wrong. Certain acts, however, such as the waste of corporate assets, usually require unanimous shareholder action for ratifying or condoning the wrong.

Judicial Treatment of *Ultra Vires* Contracts

The courts have treated *ultra vires* contracts in a variety of ways. One treatment is based upon the common-law principle of *agency*, whereby an unauthorized contract made by an agent is void, meaning no rights or duties arise for either party. Early decisions often held that *ultra vires* contracts were void.

The more modern approach is to uphold the validity of contracts that have been performed (executed). In some states, when a contract is entirely executory, neither party having performed, a defense of *ultra vires* can be used by either party to prevent

ULTRA VIRES
Activities of a corporation's managers that are outside the scope of the power granted them by its charter or the laws of the state of incorporation.

Landmark in the Law

The Model Business Corporation Act

The Model Business Corporation Act (MBCA) is a codification of modern corporation law. A "model" statute is created with the understanding that it may need amendments or changes in order to reflect local interests, needs, or problems, but it is presented for various jurisdictions to draw upon in forming their decisions concerning corporate law.

The MBCA was first published in its complete form in 1933 by the Committee on Corporate Laws of the American Bar Association. It was patterned after the Illinois Business Corporation Act of 1933. The act was drafted, in part, in response to the tumultous history of corporations in the United States prior to that time. While the corporate form of business organization is common today, it was rare until after the Civil War. Until the late 1800s the corporate privilege was granted sparingly, and only when the grant seemed necessary to procure some specific benefit for the community.

The reason the corporate form was limited was because people feared that the sheer size of a corporate enterprise, along with its concentration of economic power and its separation of ownership from control, would have disastrous effects on the economic life of the community. It was felt that corporations could easily swallow up individual businesspersons and could virtually enslave labor and thus dominate the state. Even when the use of the corporate structure was eventually permitted for more general business purposes, the states placed severe restrictions upon the size and scope of its use. The states also limited the scope of the business corporation's powers and activities, established a maximum duration for corporate franchises, and required state residence as a prerequisite to incorporation.

Because of the growing interest in the corporate form of business by the turn of the century, however, a number of states removed these safeguards from their incorporation statutes in order to capture the significant revenue to be obtained by granting corporate charters. For example, a New York corporation would be permitted to incorporate under the more permissive laws of New Jersey and yet continue to operate principally in New York. The consequent rivalry between states vying for revenues and control incident to domestic incorporation created notable inconsistencies in corporate law among the states and substantial confusion in the courts.[1] The need for some kind of uniformity in corporate law was evident—a need filled by the Model Business Corporation Act (MBCA), published in its complete form in 1933 by the Committee on Corporate Laws of the American Bar Association. Since 1933 the act has undergone several changes and was last revised and renumbered in 1969.

The Revised Model Business Corporation Act (RMBCA), as approved in June of 1984, was drafted as a convenient guide for revision of state business corporation acts. It was designed for use by both publicly held and closely held corporations and includes provisions for the rights and duties of shareholders, management, and directors. Already a number of states have amended their corporation laws, to a limited degree, based on the RMBCA.

Neither the revised and renumbered 1969 act nor the 1984 act has been totally adopted by any state in its current form. The 1969 act, however, has been influential in the codification of corporate statutes in more than thirty-seven states and in the District of Columbia. It should be kept in mind that there is considerable variation among the state statutes based on the MBCA; therefore, those individual statutes should be relied upon rather than the MBCA.

1. The intense competition among the states to attract corporate charters is vividly described by Justice Brandeis in *Louis K. Liggett Co. v. Lee*, 288 U.S. 517, 548–564, 53 S.Ct. 483, 490–496, 77 L.Ed. 929 (1933).

enforcement of the contract. In cases where an *ultra vires* contract is only partially executed at the time of challenge, courts may nevertheless enforce the contract if the circumstances are such that it would be inequitable to allow a party to assert the defense of *ultra vires*.

The current trend in dealing with *ultra vires* contracts is embodied in statutory enactments similar to Section 7 of the Model Business Corporation Act, which upholds the validity and enforceability of an *ultra vires* contract as between the parties involved. The right of shareholders on behalf of the corporation, the right of the corporation itself to recover damages from the officers and directors who caused the transactions, and the right of the attorney general of the state to institute an injunction against the transaction or to institute dissolution proceedings against the corporation for *ultra vires* acts, however, have been upheld.

The following case illustrates a court's willingness to embrace the Model Business Corporation Act's policy of denying to a corporation the right to avoid an *ultra vires* contract.

Case 26.2
JAMES v. J.F.K. CARWASH, INC.
Supreme Court of Arkansas, 1982.
275 Ark. 141, 628 S.W.2d 299.

FACTS Mansell, Grubbs, and James each owned a one-third interest in J.F.K. Carwash, Inc., an Arkansas corporation. James wanted out of the corporation, and all three agreed that the corporation would repurchase his shares. A corporate promissory note for the amount of the repurchase was issued by Carwash and secured by the personal guarantees of Mansell and Grubbs. At the time the note was issued, Carwash had a deficit of $16,184.36 and had no unrestricted earned surplus (i.e., retained earnings—net profit minus the dividends paid out—that are not owed). Arkansas law requires that a corporation repurchase its stock out of unrestricted earned surplus. Carwash was unable to make its payments on the note, and James filed suit to recover the unpaid principal. Mansell and Grubbs maintained that the note was void because it was *ultra vires*. The trial court entered a judgment for the defendants, and James appealed.

ISSUE Could Mansell and Grubbs escape liability on the promissory note on the basis that it was an *ultra vires* contract?

DECISION No. The trial court's judgment was reversed.

REASON Although the note was executed in violation of the Arkansas statute governing corporate repurchase of stock, and was therefore *ultra vires,* the court would not allow the doctrine to be used by the corporation to an inequitable end. The court began by noting that Arkansas statutes provide that when a corporation acts outside its powers, such an "action will not be invalid solely because the corporation was without either the capacity or the power to do such act." Lack of capacity or power, under the statute, can be asserted only (1) by a shareholder suing to enjoin the performance of an *ultra vires* contract, (2) by a shareholder bringing a derivative suit for damages against the officials who diverted business by *ultra vires* acts, or (3) by the attorney general. Since none of these conditions was present, an assenting shareholder could not assert the defense of *ultra vires,* and so the note was valid. Because the note was valid, the personal guarantees were valid.

COMMENTS The *ultra vires* doctrine is generally not available to release a corporation from its commitments when there is an execution of those commitments. Often, if an *ultra vires* transaction is partially executed, elements of fairness, unjust enrichment, or estoppel will prevent courts from releasing the corporation from its obligations.

Torts and Criminal Acts

A corporation is liable for the torts committed by its agents or officers within the course and scope of their employment. A corporation can act only through its agents and servants. This principle applies to a corporation exactly as it applies to the ordinary agency relationships discussed in Chapter 22. It follows the doctrine of *respondeat superior*.

At common law, a corporation could not be held liable for a crime, particularly one that required intent. Under modern criminal law, however, a corporation can sometimes be held liable for the criminal acts of its agents and employees, provided the punishment can be applied to the corporation.[2] The following case illustrates an instance of a corporation being convicted on a charge of manslaughter, which was punishable by a $20,000 fine.

Case 26.3
COMMONWEALTH v. FORTNER LP GAS CO., INC.
Court of Appeals of Kentucky, 1980.
610 S.W.2d 941.

FACTS Fortner LP Gas Co., Inc., a Kentucky corporation, was sued by the commonwealth of Kentucky when a Fortner truck struck two schoolchildren, injuring one and killing the other. The children had just gotten off a school bus and were walking across the street when the truck, unable to stop because the brakes failed to work, hit them. Later inspection of the brakes revealed them to be defective. The Commonwealth of Kentucky prosecuted the corporation, and a grand jury indicted the corporation for manslaughter in the second degree, a felony punishable by a $20,000 fine. Fortner brought a motion for dismissal of the indictment on the ground that it was a corporation and, as such, could not commit manslaughter. The trial court held for the corporation, and the Commonwealth of Kentucky appealed.

ISSUE Can a corporation commit manslaughter?

DECISION Yes. The appellate court reversed the trial court's judgment and held in favor of the Commonwealth of Kentucky.

REASON The court stated that, although in the past corporations were deemed by Kentucky courts to be unable by their very nature to commit crimes, the intent of the legislature to hold corporations liable for crimes of their agents or employees in certain instances is manifest in the Kentucky Penal Code. Under the Code, "A corporation is guilty of an offense when . . . . (c) the conduct constituting the offense is engaged in by an agent of the corporation acting within the scope of his employment and in behalf of the corporation; and the offense is a misdemeanor or violation; or the offense is one defined by a statute which clearly indicates a legislative intent to impose such criminal liability on a corporation." The court also cited the commentaries to the Kentucky Penal Code, which state, in part: "The major difficulty with corporate responsibility under the criminal law has been the obvious fact that corporations cannot be imprisoned for commission of crimes. This difficulty should be eliminated through the creation in Section 534.050 of a penalty structure that provides corporate fines for commission of all classes of crimes." Section 534.050 provides for a corporate fine of $20,000 for the commission of a felony, such as manslaughter. Because the legislature obviously intended that corporations could be liable for criminal offenses, if they were punishable by fines, the court reversed the trial court's decision and held that Fortner was liable for the death of the child.

❖ Corporate Management—Shareholders

The acquisition of a share of stock makes a person an owner and shareholder in a corporation. As a shareholder, that person acquires certain powers in the corporation that are discussed here, along with the relationship of the shareholders to the corporation.

---

2. Obviously, a corporation cannot be imprisoned; it can be fined, however, and possibly dissolved.

Shareholders' Powers

Shareholders must approve fundamental changes affecting the corporation before the changes can be effected. Hence, shareholders are empowered to amend the articles of incorporation (charter) and bylaws, approve merger or dissolution of the corporation, and approve the sale of all or substantially all of the corporation's assets. Some of these powers are subject to prior board approval.

Election and removal of the board of directors are accomplished by a vote of the shareholders. The first board of directors is either named in the articles of incorporation or chosen by the incorporators to serve until the first shareholders' meeting. From that time on, selection and retention of directors are exclusively a shareholder function.

Directors usually serve their full term; if they are unsatisfactory, they are simply not reelected. Shareholders have the inherent power, however, to remove a director from office *for cause* (breach of duty or misconduct) by a majority vote.[3] Some state statutes even permit removal of directors *without cause* by the vote of a majority of the holders of outstanding shares entitled to vote.[4] Some corporate charters expressly provide that shareholders, by majority vote, can remove a director at any time *without cause*.

Relationship between Shareholders and Corporation

As a general rule, shareholders have no responsibility for the daily management of the corporation, although they are ultimately responsible for choosing the board of directors, which does have such control. Ordinarily, corporate officers and other employees owe no direct duty to individual stockholders. Their duty is to the corporation as a whole. A director, however, is in a fiduciary relationship to the corporation and therefore serves the interests of the shareholders as a whole.

Generally, there is no legal relationship between shareholders and creditors of the corporation. Shareholders can, in fact, be creditors of the corporation and have the same rights of recovery against the corporation as any other creditor. The rights and liabilities of shareholders are discussed in detail in the following chapter.

Shareholders' Forum

Shareholders' meetings must occur at least annually, and additional, special meetings can be called to take care of urgent matters. Since it is usually not practical for owners of only a few shares of stock of publicly traded corporations to attend the shareholders' meetings, they normally give third persons a written authorization to vote their shares at the meeting. This authorization, called a **proxy**, is often solicited by management, as will be discussed later.

Notice of Meetings The notice and time of meetings, including the day and the hour, is announced in writing to each shareholder at a reasonable length of time

PROXY
In corporation law, a written agreement between a stockholder and another under which the stockholder authorizes the other to vote the stockholder's shares in a certain manner.

---

3. A director can often demand court review of removal for cause.
4. Most states allow *cumulative voting* for directors, meaning that no individual director can be removed if the number of votes cast against his removal would be sufficient to elect him if cumulatively voted at an election of the entire board of directors. See, for example, California Corporate Code, Section 303A. Also see Section 39 of the MBCA.

Shareholders' meetings must occur at least annually.

prior to the date of the shareholders' meeting.[5] Special-meeting notices must include a statement of the purpose of the meeting; business transacted at a special meeting is limited to that purpose.

In the following case, shareholders objected to the fact they had not been properly notified as to the purpose of a shareholder meeting and to the fact that a director participated, as a shareholder, in a vote to determine whether the business should be sold.

Case 26.4
SOLOMON v. ATLANTIS DEVELOPMENT, INC.
Supreme Court of Vermont, 1986.
145 Vt. 349, 516 A.2d 132.

FACTS Dennis Solomon was one of four shareholders of Atlantis Development, Inc. All shareholders held an equal number of shares. Initially, there were only three shareholders, but poor sales required Atlantis to take on an additional one, Malloy, who supplied additional capital. Malloy's role was at first that of financier, but because of continued mismanagement of the firm, he assumed active control over business operations. In spite of Malloy's efforts, however, Atlantis continued to suffer financially until finally the shareholders considered bankruptcy. Bankruptcy was eventually rejected in favor of selling the company to Malloy for one dollar. The deal was voted on and approved by the shareholders in a three-to-one vote. Malloy assumed Atlantis's liabilities with the intention to liquidate the firm. He managed to turn the business around and make a profit, however, after changing the firm's name and investing a considerable amount of his money into the business.

---

5. The shareholder can waive the requirement of written notice by signing a waiver form. A shareholder who does not receive written notice, but who learns of the meeting and attends without protesting the lack of notice, is said to have waived notice by such conduct. State statutes and corporate bylaws typically set forth a minimum allowance notice requirement. Both the MBCA and the RMBCA have advance-notice requirements ranging from ten to sixty days.

Case 26.4—Continued

Solomon brought this action against Malloy and Atlantis, claiming that the vote to sell the corporation to Malloy should be invalidated because proper notification of the purpose of the meeting had not been given to the shareholders. Solomon further claimed that Malloy had breached his fiduciary duty to the corporation by voting to sell the firm to himself. The trial court held for Solomon, and Malloy appealed.

ISSUES (1) Could the shareholder's vote to sell the firm to Malloy be invalidated on the basis of improper notification to the shareholders as to the purpose of the meeting they attended? (2) Did Malloy breach his fiduciary duty to the other shareholders by his actions?

DECISION No, to both issues. The Supreme Court of Vermont reversed the decision of the trial court.

REASON The sale of all, or substantially all, of a corporation's assets must be authorized at a shareholders' meeting duly called for that purpose by a vote of two-thirds of outstanding shares entitled to vote thereon. Even though the shareholder meeting was not called for the purpose of selling Atlantis, the court ruled that by attending the meeting and accepting decisions thereof, the shareholders had waived their right to object.

As to Solomon's claim that Malloy, as a director of the corporation, breached his duty when he voted at the shareholders' meeting to sell the business to himself, the court held that Malloy should have abstained from the vote because he was an interested party. The court noted that Malloy was also a stockholder, however, and as such he was not automatically disqualified from voting on matters affecting his self-interest. Although in a close corporation shareholders owe each other a duty of loyalty and good faith, such a duty is fulfilled by voting for legitimate business purposes. The court concluded that Malloy had, in this case, acted for a legitimate business purpose and in good faith and had not breached his fiduciary duty.

The court further stated that a shareholder who opposes a sale of corporate assets must express his or her objection in writing, vote against the proposed action, and demand an appraisal of the corporate assets. Since Solomon failed to follow this procedure, he foreclosed upon his opportunity to have a future appraisal made of the value of the shares.

Shareholder Voting In order for shareholders to act, a minimum number of them (in terms of number of shares held) must be present at a meeting. This minimum number, called a *quorum*, is generally more than 50 percent. Corporate business matters are presented in the form of *resolutions*, which shareholders vote to approve or disapprove. Some state statutes have set forth voting limits, and corporations' articles or bylaws must remain within these statutory limitations. Some states provide that the unanimous written consent of shareholders is a permissible alternative to holding a shareholders' meeting.

Once a quorum is present, a majority vote of the shares represented at the meeting is usually required to pass resolutions. Assume that Novo Pictures, Inc., has 10,000 outstanding shares of voting stock. Its articles set the quorum at 50 percent of outstanding shares and provide that a majority vote of the shares present is necessary to pass on ordinary matters. At the shareholders' meeting, a quorum of stockholders representing 5,000 outstanding shares must be present to conduct business, and a vote of at least 2,501 of those shares represented at the meeting is needed to pass ordinary resolutions. If more than 5,000 are present, a larger vote will be needed.

At times, a larger-than-majority vote will be required either by statute or by corporate charter. Extraordinary corporate matters, such as merger, consolidation, or dissolution of the corporation (to be discussed in Chapter 28), require a higher percentage of the representatives of all corporate shares entitled to vote, not just a majority of those present at that particular meeting.

Voting Lists   Voting lists are prepared by the corporation prior to each shareholders' meeting. Persons whose names appear on the corporation's stockholder records as owners are the ones ordinarily entitled to vote.[6] The voting list contains the name and address of each shareholder as shown on the corporate records on a given cutoff date, or record date. (The Revised MBCA, Section 7.07, allows a record date to be as much as seventy days before the meeting.) It also includes the number of voting shares held by each owner. The list is usually kept at the corporate headquarters and is available for shareholder inspection.

Voting Techniques   Most states permit or require shareholders to elect directors by *cumulative voting*, a method of voting designed to allow minority shareholders representation on the board of directors.[7] Cumulative voting operates as follows: The number of members of the board to be elected is multiplied by the total number of voting shares held. The result equals the number of votes a shareholder has, and this total can be cast for one or more nominees for director. All nominees stand for election at the same time. Where cumulative voting is not required either by statute or under the articles, the entire board can be elected by a majority of shares at a shareholders' meeting.

To illustrate: A corporation has 10,000 shares issued and outstanding. The minority shareholders hold only 3,000 shares, and the majority shareholders hold the other 7,000 shares. Three members of the board are to be elected. The majority shareholders' nominees are Adams, Barkley, and Cranston. The minority shareholders' nominee is Drake. Can Drake be elected by the minority shareholders?

If cumulative voting is allowed, the answer is yes. The minority shareholders have 9,000 votes among them (the number of directors to be elected times the number of shares equals 3 times 3,000, which equals 9,000 votes). All of these votes can be cast to elect Drake. The majority shareholders have 21,000 votes (3 times 7,000 equals 21,000 votes), but these votes have to be distributed among their three nominees. The principle of cumulative voting is that no matter how the majority shareholders cast their 21,000 votes, they will not be able to elect all three directors if the minority shareholders cast all of their 9,000 votes for Drake, as illustrated in Exhibit 26-1.

Shareholder Agreements   A group of shareholders can agree in writing prior to the meeting to vote their shares together in a specified manner. Voting agreements are usually held to be valid and enforceable.

Proxy Voting   A shareholder can appoint a voting agent. A *proxy* is a written authorization to cast the shareholder's vote, and a person can solicit proxies from a number of shareholders in an attempt to concentrate voting power.

VOTING TRUST
The transfer of title by stockholders of shares of a corporation to a trustee who is authorized to vote the shares on their behalf.

Voting Trust   Shareholders can enter into a **voting trust,** which is an agreement (a trust contract) whereby legal title (record ownership on the corporate books) is transferred to a trustee who is responsible for voting the shares. The agreement can specify how the trustee is to vote, or it can allow the trustee to use his or her discretion.

---

6.   Where the legal owner is deceased, bankrupt, incompetent, or in some other way under a legal disability, his or her vote can be cast by a person designated by law to control and manage the owner's property.
7.   See, for example, the California Corporate Code, Section 708. The RMBCA, Section 7.28, however, states that no cumulative voting rights exist unless the articles of incorporation so provide.

◆ **Exhibit 26-1**
Results of Cumulative Voting

BALLOTS	MAJORITY SHAREHOLDERS' VOTES			MINORITY SHAREHOLDERS' VOTES	DIRECTORS ELECTED
	Adams	Barkley	Cranston	Drake	
1	10,000	10,000	1,000	9,000	Adams/Barkley/Drake
2	9,001	9,000	2,999	9,000	Adams/Barkley/Drake
3	6,000	7,000	8,000	9,000	Barkley/Cranston/Drake

The trustee takes physical possession of the actual stock certificate and in return gives the shareholder a *voting trust certificate*. The shareholder retains all of the rights of ownership (for example, the right to receive dividend payments) except for the power to vote.

A voting trust is not the same thing as a proxy, for the latter can be revoked more easily. The holder of a proxy has neither legal title to the stock nor possession of the certificates, whereas voting trustees have both.[8]

❖ Corporate Management—Directors

Every corporation is governed by directors. Subject to statutory limitations, the number of directors is set forth in the corporation's articles or bylaws. Historically, the minimum number of directors has been three, but today many states permit fewer. Indeed, the Revised Model Business Corporation Act, in Section 8.01, permits corporations with fewer than fifty shareholders to eliminate the board of directors.

Directors' Election and Term of Office

The first board of directors is normally appointed by the incorporators upon the creation of the corporation, or directors are named by the corporation itself in the articles. The first board serves until the first annual shareholders' meeting. Subsequent directors are elected by a majority vote of the shareholders.

The term of office for a director is usually one year—from annual meeting to annual meeting. Longer and staggered terms are permissible under most state statutes. A common practice is to elect one-third of the board members each year for a three-year term. In this way, there is greater management continuity.

A director can be removed *for cause*, either as specified in the articles or bylaws or by shareholder action. Even the board of directors itself may be given power to remove a director for cause, subject to shareholder review. In most states, unless the shareholders have reserved the right at the time of election, a director cannot be removed without cause.

When vacancies occur on the board of directors due to death or resignation, or when a new position is created through amendment of the articles or bylaws, either the shareholders or the board itself can fill the position, depending on state law or on the provisions of the bylaws.

---

8.   Under Section 34 of the MBCA, the term of a voting trust cannot exceed ten years.

Directors' Qualifications and Compensation

Few legal qualifications exist for directors. Only a handful of states retain minimum age and residency requirements. A director is sometimes a shareholder, but this is not a necessary qualification unless, of course, statutory provisions, corporate articles, or bylaws require ownership.

Compensation for directors is ordinarily specified in the corporate articles or bylaws. Because directors have a fiduciary relationship to the shareholders and to the corporation, an express agreement or provision for compensation is necessary for them to receive money from the funds they control or for which they have responsibilities.

Directors' Management Responsibilities

Directors have responsibility for all policymaking decisions necessary to the management of all corporate affairs. Just as shareholders cannot act individually to bind the corporation, the directors must act as a body in carrying out routine corporate business. One director has one vote, and generally the majority rules.

The general areas of responsibility of the board of directors include the following:

1. Declaration and payment of corporate dividends to shareholders.
2. Authorization for major corporate policy decisions—for example, the initiation of proceedings for the sale or lease of corporate assets outside of the regular course of business, the determination of new product lines, and the overseeing of major contract negotiations and major management-labor negotiations.
3. Appointment, supervision, and removal of corporate officers and other managerial employees and the determination of their compensation.
4. Financial decisions such as the issuance of authorized shares or bonds.

Directors' Liability

BUSINESS JUDGMENT RULE
A rule that immunizes corporate management from liability for actions that are undertaken in good faith, when the action was within both the power of the corporation and the authority of management.

Honest mistakes of judgment and poor business actions on the part of the directors do not make them liable to the corporation for damages sustained. After all, directors are not insurers of the business success of the corporation. Usually, the **business judgment rule** applies to the actions of directors. In general, this rule sustains corporate transactions and immunizes management (the directors) from liability where the transaction is within the powers of the corporation and within the authority of management, as long as that transaction involves the exercise of due care and compliance with the duties of management.

Of course, directors must be loyal, honest, and reasonably careful at all times. If directors (and their officers) hire employees carefully, they are not personally liable for the willful wrongs and negligent acts of such employees; rather, the corporation is liable.

When a director neither attends board meetings nor examines records and books, however, he or she can be held liable for losses resulting from unsupervised acts of officers and employees. Also, when directors (and officers) allow the assets of the corporation to be diverted to objectives outside the charter or statutory powers, they may be held liable for damages to the corporation, to a trustee appointed for the corporation, or to the shareholders in a derivative suit.

Business Law in Action

The Uses and Abuses of the "Business Judgment Rule"

As discussed in the text, the common-law business judgment rule provides that directors of a corporation will not be held liable for a breach of their fiduciary duty to the corporation or its shareholders for their actions, as long as the actions were made in good faith and were based on business judgments that seemed reasonable. Unless fraud, bad faith, gross overreaching, or abuse of discretion is present, the judgment of directors is conclusive, and courts are reluctant to interfere, even if a bad decision harms the corporation. The rationale for this rule is that directors are in a better position than either the courts or the shareholders to make business judgments concerning their corporations and that a certain flexibility is necessary if directors are to fulfill their responsibility as the ultimate managers of a corporate enterprise.

Consider, for example, the case of *Shlensky* v. *Wrigley*,[1] where the question before the court was whether the director and controlling shareholder of the corporation that owned the Chicago Cubs major league baseball team had exercised sound business judgment when he decided not to install lights for nighttime baseball games. Shlensky, a minority shareholder of the corporation, sued Wrigley and other directors on behalf of the corporation and asked the court to force the board

1.   95 Ill.App.2d 173, 237 N.E.2d 776 (1968).

of directors to install lights at Wrigley Field and to hold night games because the Cubs were supposedly losing profits by not doing so, to the detriment of shareholders in the corporation. The reason Wrigley had refused to install the lights and initiate night games was because he felt such a step would result in a deterioration of the surrounding neighborhood and thus a reduction in the property value of Wrigley Field. In this case, the court stated that it was "not the function of courts to resolve for a corporation questions of policy and business management. The directors are chosen to pass upon such question. Their judgment, unless shown to be tainted with fraud, is accepted as final."

Other courts, however, will not accept a director's judgment as final, even though it is not "tainted with fraud." Such courts maintain that the business judgment rule, in some

circumstances, can be used as a defensive tool by directors to avoid their responsibilities to stockholders. Those who share this attitude feel that there are times when directors' decisions should be closely scrutinized according to the benefit or detriment they cause to the stockholders and the specific conflict of interest involved.

The court took this position in *Koenings* v. *Joseph Schlitz Brewing Company*.[2] In this case, Schlitz, in the midst of a takeover struggle with another firm, entered into *golden-parachute* employment contracts with its key employees. The contracts stated that if any employee's workload dropped significantly, he or she could consider the contract terminated and collect the rest of the salary due

(continued on next page)

2.   123 Wis.2d 490, 368 N.W.2d 690 (1985).

Business Law in Action—Continued

under the contract as liquidated damages. Among the key employees involved in the contracts was Koenings, who was Schlitz's attorney. After the contracts had been formed, Schlitz was acquired by Stroh. When Koenings experienced a drop in his workload, he demanded the remainder of his salary due under the golden-parachute provision in the contract, but Schlitz refused to pay.

Koenings then sued for breach of contract.

The Wisconsin Court of Appeals eventually heard the case and had to determine whether the golden-parachute provision was a reasonable exercise of the board of directors' business judgment and thus enforceable. The appellate court decided that the damages clause was an unreasonable penalty and invalid

as a matter of public policy. In this instance, the court regarded "the business judgment rule" as "archaic and unresponsive to fair treatment of stockholders" and ruled that it should not be a basis for upholding contracts that "bear the taint of conflict of interest in favor of the management-beneficiaries to the detriment of the stockholders' interest."

Board of Directors' Forum

The board of directors conducts business by holding formal meetings with recorded minutes. The date upon which regular meetings are held is usually established in the articles and bylaws or by board resolution, and no further notice is customarily required. Special meetings can be called with notice sent to all directors.

Quorum requirements can vary among jurisdictions. Many states leave the decision to the corporate articles or bylaws. In the absence thereof, most states provide that a quorum is a majority of the number of directors authorized in the articles or bylaws. Voting is done *in person* (unlike voting at shareholders' meetings, which can be done by proxy).[9] The rule is one vote per director. Ordinary matters generally require a majority vote; certain extraordinary issues may require a greater-than-majority vote.

Delegation of Board of Directors' Powers

The board of directors can delegate some of its functions to an executive committee or to corporate officers. In doing so, the board is not relieved of its overall responsibility for directing the affairs of the corporation, but corporate officers and managerial personnel are empowered to make decisions relating to ordinary, daily corporate affairs within well-defined guidelines.

Executive Committee   Most states permit the board of directors to elect an executive committee from among the directors to handle the interim management decisions between board of directors' meetings, as provided in the bylaws. The executive committee is limited to making management decisions about ordinary business matters.

Corporate Officers   The officers and other executive employees are hired by the board of directors or, in rare instances, by the shareholders. In addition to carrying

---

9. Except in Louisiana, where a director can vote by proxy under certain circumstances. Some states, such as Michigan and Texas (and Sections 43 and 44 of the MBCA), permit telephone conferences and unanimous voting for board of director meetings.

out the duties articulated in the bylaws, corporate and managerial officers act as agents of the corporation, and the ordinary rules of agency apply or have been applied to their employment (unlike the board of directors, whose powers are conferred by the state).

Qualifications are determined at the discretion of the corporation and are included in the articles or bylaws. In most states, a person can hold more than one office and can be both an officer and a director of the corporation. Corporate officers can be removed by the board of directors at any time with or without cause and regardless of the terms of the employment contract, although it is possible for the corporation to be liable for breach-of-contract damages.

❖ Chapter Summary: Corporate Powers and Management

CORPORATE POWERS	
Express Powers	The express powers of a corporation are granted by the following laws and documents (listed according to their priority): federal constitution, state constitutions, state statutes, certificate of incorporation (charter), bylaws, and resolutions of the board of directors.
Implied Powers	Barring express constitutional, statutory, or charter prohibitions, the corporation has the implied power to do all acts reasonably appropriate and necessary to accomplish its corporate purposes.
Ultra Vires Doctrine	1. Any act of a corporation that is beyond the authority given to it under its charter or under the statutes by which it was incorporated is an *ultra vires* act ("beyond the powers" of the corporation). 2. *Ultra vires* contracts may or may not be enforced by the courts, depending on whether the contract is executed or executory and on whether its enforcement would lead to an inequitable result. 3. In certain cases, shareholders, on behalf of the corporation, have the right to recover damages for *ultra vires* acts of corporate officers or directors. In addition, the state attorney general may also bring an action either to institute an injunction against the transaction or to institute dissolution proceedings against the corporation for *ultra vires* acts. 4. The corporation is liable for the torts committed by its agents or officers within the course and scope of their employment (under the doctrine of *respondeat superior*). In some cases, a corporation can be held liable (and be fined) for criminal acts of its agents and employees.
CORPORATE MANAGEMENT	

Shareholders	1. *Shareholder powers include:*
	  a. Approval of all fundamental changes affecting the corporation (e.g., amendment of charter or bylaws, merger, dissolution).
	  b. Election of the board of directors.
	
	2. *Shareholder meetings must comply with the following rules:*
	  a. Meetings must occur at least annually; special meetings can be called when necessary.
	  b. Notice of time and place of meeting (and purpose of meeting if the meeting is specially called) must be sent to shareholders.
	  c. A minimum number of shareholders (a quorum—generally 50 percent of shares held) must be present at a meeting; resolutions are passed (usually) by majority vote.
	  d. Voting lists of shareholders on record must be prepared by the corporation prior to each shareholders' meeting.
	  e. Cumulative voting may or may not be required or permitted so as to give minority shareholders a better chance to be represented on the board of directors.

❖ Chapter Summary: Corporate Powers and Management—Continued

Shareholders (Continued)	f. Shareholders' voting agreements to vote their shares together are usually held to be valid and enforceable. g. A shareholder may appoint a proxy (substitute) to vote his or her shares. h. A shareholder may enter into a voting trust agreement whereby title (record ownership) of his or her shares is given to a trustee, and the trustee votes the shares in accordance with the trustee agreement.
Directors	1. *Election and term of office*: a. The first board of directors is usually appointed by the incorporators; thereafter, directors are elected by shareholders. b. Directors usually serve a one-year term, although it can be longer. 2. *Qualifications and compensation*: a. Few qualifications are required; a director can be a shareholder but is not required to be. b. Compensation is usually specified in the corporate articles or bylaws. 3. *Management responsibilities include*: a. All policymaking decisions necessary to the management of corporate affairs. b. Appointment, supervision, and removal of corporate officers and other managerial employees; determination of their compensation. c. Authorization for major corporate decisions. d. Declaration and payment of corporate dividends to shareholders. 4. *Liability*: a. The *business judgment rule* immunizes directors from liability in corporate transactions as long as the transaction was within the powers of the corporation and within the authority of director management, and as long as due care was exercised by the director. b. Directors may be liable for any damage caused to the corporation by allowing the assets of the corporation to be diverted to objectives outside of the charter or statutory powers or by neglecting to supervise properly acts of officers and employees. 5. *Directors' meetings*: a. The date of regular directors' meetings is usually established in the corporate articles or bylaws; special meetings can be called with notice sent to all directors. b. Quorum requirements vary from state to state; usually, a quorum is the majority of corporate directors. c. Voting is usually required *in person*, and in ordinary matters only a majority vote is required. 6. *Delegation of board of directors' powers*: a. Executive committee—directors elected to handle interim management decisions between board of directors' meetings. b. Corporate officers—usually hired by the board of directors.

❖ Questions and Case Problems

26-1. Feldman owned an electronics store. Business had been going downhill for some time, so Feldman sold the store to Kennedy Corporation. Under Kennedy's articles of incorporation, the stated purpose of the corporation was to operate a drug store. The articles had never been amended to reflect its expansion into the electronics business, and none of the shareholders had ever objected to Kennedy's purchase and operation of Feldman's store. Under the management of Kennedy Corporation, the electronics firm began to prosper, and Feldman had second thoughts about having sold it. Feldman learned that Kennedy's articles of incorporation did not include running an electronics business as a purpose, and thus the directors, in purchasing the firm, had committed an *ultra vires* act. Feldman seeks to have the contract of sale rescinded on this ground. Can he? Explain.

26-2. Krieger Corporation notified its shareholders that its annual shareholders' meeting would be held on October 15, and that all Krieger Corporation shareholders of record as of October 1 would be entitled to vote. Sherry sold her 30 shares of Krieger stock to Darrell on September 28. On October 2, Darrell sent in the old certificate in order to have a new certificate issued, and the newly issued certificate was received by Darrell on October 13. Both Sherry and Darrell came to the October 15 meeting, each planning to vote the 30 shares of stock. Which party is legally entitled to vote the shares? Explain.

26-3. Abigail owns 10 shares of Major Corporation. Major Corporation has 100,000 outstanding issued common shares. Abigail believes that many decisions of the board of directors do not consider the preservation of the environment. Two pending proposals approved by the board deal with the purchase of timberland for conversion into condominiums. Both proposals require an amendment to the corporate charter and thus need a two-thirds shareholder vote. Abigail knows other shareholders who she believes would oppose these proposals. Unfortunately, most shareholders live a considerable distance from the site of the shareholders' meeting and will be unable to attend. Discuss any techniques Abigail can use to oppose these proposals.

26-4. Algonquin Corporation has issued and has outstanding 100,000 shares of common stock. Four stockholders own 60,000 of these shares, and for the past six years they have nominated a slate of people for membership on the board, all of whom get elected. Walter and twenty other shareholders, owning 20,000 shares, are dissatisfied with corporate management and want a representative on the board who shares their views. Explain under what circumstances Walter and the minority shareholders can elect their representative to the board.

26-5. Trudy is elected to the board of directors of a corporation. The board consists of nine members. The articles and bylaws are silent as to what constitutes a quorum. The bylaws do permit the board itself, by majority vote, to elect board members to fill vacancies created by death or resignation. The bylaws also require majority votes for ordinary corporate decisions made at regular corporate board meetings. Just prior to a regular meeting, a board member dies. At the scheduled regular meeting a proposal is to be made that Trudy opposes. She cannot attend the meeting so sends her proxy. The meeting takes place with five members in attendance. By a vote of three to two, Harold is elected to fill the board vacancy, and the proposal is passed. Trudy's proxy is declared invalid by the chairman of the board. Trudy challenges both votes. Discuss whether her challenges will be successful.

26-6. Herbert and Emile Carp were president and executive vice-president, respectively, of Carps, Inc. The Carps wished to obtain a personal loan from a bank for $267,000, but the bank required the note to be guaranteed by a third party. The

Carps co-signed the note in the name of the corporation. Later, the note was assigned by the bank to Molasky Enterprises. When the Carps defaulted on the note, Molasky sued the corporation for payment. The corporation asserted as a defense that Herbert and Emily Carp had exceeded their authority when they co-signed the note on behalf of the corporation. Had they? Explain. [Molasky Enterprises, Inc. v. Carps, Inc., 615 S.W.2d 83 (Mo.App. 1981)]

26-7. Hamfab Credit Union (HCU) borrowed from the Ohio Central Credit Union, Inc. (OCCU) over $550,000. This amount exceeded 25 percent of HCU's capital and surplus, which was in violation of Ohio state law. The statute in question provided that "[a] credit union may not borrow money in excess of twenty-five per cent of its unimpaired capital and surplus, without prior specific authorization by the supervisor." HCU had not received any such authorization. When HCU became insolvent, Wagner was appointed as the liquidator. Wagner refused to pay OCCU the full amount of the debt owed to OCCU, claiming that some of the loans had been made in violation of state law and therefore OCCU had acted *ultra vires* in making the loans. Did Wagner succeed in this defense? Explain. [Ohio Central Credit Union, Inc. v. Wagner, 67 Ohio App.2d 138, 426 N.E.2d 198 (1980)]

26-8. A stockholder learned that the corporation had paid over $11 million in kickbacks and bribes. The board of directors investigated the allegations and determined that they were true but decided not to file suit. The directors decided that the corporation's actions were excused by the business judgment doctrine (or rule). The stockholder then brought a *derivative suit*, which is a lawsuit by a stockholder against a person who is usually an officer of the company in order to enforce certain rights that the shareholder believes the corporation has against that person. The directors maintained that the business judgment rule was a complete defense to their payment of bribes and sought immediate dismissal of the suit. Was the business judgment rule judged a complete defense to this type of corporate activity? Explain. [Auerbach v. Bennett, 64 A.D.2d 98, 408 N.Y.S.2d 83 (1978)]

26-9. The Midtown Club, Inc., was a nonprofit corporation whose certificate of incorporation stated that the sole purpose of the club was "to provide facilities for the serving of luncheon or other meals to members." Samuel Cross, a member of the club, brought a female guest to lunch at the club, but he and his friend were both refused seating. On several occasions, Cross made application on behalf of females for their admission to the club, but the club would either ignore or reject them. Cross brought an action against the club, alleging that the club's actions were *ultra vires*. Did he succeed? Explain. [Cross v. Midtown Club, Inc., 33 Conn.Supp. 150, 365 A.2d 1227 (1976)]

26-10. Mohawk Rubber Company was a corporation organized under the laws of the state of Ohio. Fawcett and Ernst were the principle executives of Mohawk. The board of directors included Fawcett and Ernst and five outside directors. The board directed Ernst to consider a new stock option plan, as

Mohawk was profiting nicely and would likely be the target of a takeover bid. On January 4, 1983, sixteen days before the regularly scheduled board of directors meeting at which Ernst was to present his stock option plan, Ernst telephoned each of the directors individually to obtain their approval for the plan. No prior written notice was given to the directors, nor did they see a written version of the plan. Each director orally approved the plan as it was described to him on the telephone. "Minutes of the Board of Directors Meeting" were prepared that outlined the events of January 4, 1983, as if it had been a formal meeting. Later a proxy statement was issued urging the share-holders to give prompt attention to the plan and indicating that the board of directors had unanimously recommended a vote for the plan. Fradkin, a Mohawk shareholder, filed a derivative suit to stop the plan. To cure the omission of the formal meeting, Ernst and Fawcett presented a document entitled "Approval of Directors of the Mohawk Rubber Company to Action without a Meeting" at a subsequent board meeting. All of the directors signed the document. Was Fradkin successful in his derivative suit? Explain. [Fradkin v. Ernst, 571 F.Supp. 829 (N.D. Ohio 1983)]

Chapter 27

Corporations—Rights and Duties of Directors, Managers, and Shareholders

Although Ambrose Bierce's definition of a corporation has a facetious ring to it, it nonetheless is true—to an extent. A corporation joins the efforts and resources of a large number of individuals for the purpose of producing greater returns than those individuals could have obtained individually. No one individual shareholder or director bears sole responsibility for the corporation and its actions.

Sometimes actions that benefit the corporation as a whole do not coincide with the separate interests of the individuals comprising the corporation. In such situations, it is important to know the rights and duties of all participants in the corporate enterprise. This chapter focuses on the rights and duties of directors, managers, and shareholders and the ways in which conflicts among them are resolved.

"Corporation: An ingenious device for obtaining individual profit without individual responsibility."

Ambrose Bierce, 1842–1914
(American writer)

❖ Role of Officers and Directors

A director occupies a position of responsibility unlike that of other corporate personnel. Directors are sometimes inappropriately characterized as *agents* because they act for and on behalf of the corporation. No *individual* director, however, can act as an agent to bind the corporation, and, as a group, directors collectively control the corporation in a way that no agent can control a principal. Directors are often incorrectly characterized as *trustees* because they occupy positions of trust and control over the corporation. Unlike trustees, however, they do not own or hold title to property for the use and benefit of others.

Directors manage the corporation through the officers who are selected by the board; these officers are agents of the corporation. Directors and officers are deemed fiduciaries of the corporation. Their relationship with the corporation and its shareholders is one of trust and confidence. The fiduciary duties of the directors and officers include the duty of care and the duty of loyalty.

Duty of Care

Directors are obligated to be honest and to use prudent business judgment in the conduct of corporate affairs. The business judgment rule does not require directors to ensure the success of every venture that the corporation undertakes. The test most often used is objective—the directors must exercise the same degree of care that reasonably prudent people use in the conduct of their own personal business affairs. Thus, corporate losses resulting merely from poor business judgment or an honest mistake in judgment will not normally impose legal liability on directors.

Directors can be held answerable to the corporation and to the shareholders for breach of their duty of care. When directors delegate work to corporate officers and employees, they are expected to use a reasonable amount of supervision. Otherwise, they will be held liable for *negligence* or *mismanagement* of corporate personnel.

For example, a corporate bank director failed to attend any board of directors' meetings in five and one-half years and never inspected any of the corporate books or records. Meanwhile, the bank president made various improper loans and permitted large overdrafts. The corporate director was held liable to the corporation for losses of nearly $20,000 resulting from the unsupervised actions of the bank president and the loan committee.

The standard of *due care* has been variously described and codified in many corporation codes and by judicial decisions.[1] The impact of the standard is to require that directors carry out their responsibilities in an informed, businesslike manner.

Depending on the nature of the business, directors and officers are often expected to act in accordance with their own knowledge and training. Most states (and Section 35 of the MBCA), however, allow a director to make decisions in reliance on information furnished by competent officers or employees, professionals such as attorneys and accountants, or even an executive committee of the board, without being accused of acting in bad faith or failing to exercise due care if such information turns out to be faulty.

Directors are expected to attend board of directors' meetings, and their votes should be entered into the minutes of corporate meetings. Unless a dissent is entered, the director is presumed to have assented. Directors who dissent rarely are held individually liable for mismanagement of the corporation. For this reason, a director who is absent from a given meeting sometimes registers with the secretary of the board a dissent to actions taken at the meeting.

Directors are expected to be informed on corporate matters and to understand legal and other professional advice rendered to the board. A director who is unable to carry out such responsibilities must resign. Even when the required duty of care has not been exercised, directors and officers are liable only for the damages caused to the corporation by their negligence.

In the following case, a group of shareholders of Texaco Corporation alleged that a buy-back of Texaco stock held by a third party represented a violation of the directors' fiduciary duties to the shareholders.

---

1. See, for example, Section 35 of the Model Business Corporation Act, which provides that "a director shall perform his duties as a director, including his duties as a member of any committee of the board upon which he may serve, in good faith, in any manner he reasonably believes to be in the best interest of the corporation, and with such care as an ordinarily prudent person in a like position would use under similar circumstances." See also the Revised Model Business Corporation Act, Section 8.30. Some courts require the standard of care to be that which an ordinarily prudent person would use in the exercise of his or her personal affairs.

Case 27.1
POLK v. GOOD

Supreme Court of Delaware, 1986.
507 A.2d 531.

FACTS Howard Good represented Texaco, Inc. Polk represented a set of shareholders seeking the rescission of a share buy-back agreement made by Texaco and the Bass Group—an investment group that, between December 1983 and January 1984, acquired 9.9 percent of Texaco's outstanding stock. The Bass Group had indicated that it would purchase up to 20 percent of Texaco's stock, but Texaco—because of its involvement in a dispute with Pennzoil over the purchase of Getty Oil Company—decided it would be better not to sell any further shares to the Bass Group. Furthermore, it sought to buy back shares previously sold to the Bass Group, and an agreement was reached whereby Texaco paid the Bass Group 3 percent over their market price for half of the stock, and the Bass Group agreed to vote the remaining stock in accordance with the Texaco board of directors' desires. This agreement was voted on by the board. Texaco's decision to repurchase the stock from the Bass Group was recommended by legal and financial counsel on the basis of research by outside, independent organizations.

The trial court approved the agreement as not conflicting with the Texaco directors' fiduciary duty to its shareholders, and summary judgment was granted to Texaco/Good. Polk appealed.

ISSUE Did the board of directors breach their fiduciary duty to the corporation and to its shareholders by repurchasing the Bass Group's shares?

DECISION No. The appellate court could find no breach; the buy-back was a benefit to the company and to most of its stockholders.

REASON In performing its duties of managing a corporation, the board of directors owes a fundamental duty of care and loyalty to the corporation and its shareholders. A board is protected by the business judgment rule in discharging its responsibilities. This rule creates a presumption that in making a business decision, if the directors acted in good faith and in the honest belief that the action was in the corporation's best interests, they have not breached their duty to the shareholders. As part of managing a corporation, the board may buy back shares, provided the purchase is free from fraud, unfairness, or the personal interests of the directors. Such repurchases are permissible when there is a reasonable threat to the corporate entity. Determining the reasonableness of a threat is a business judgment and thus protected by the business judgment rule. In this case, the court found that the Bass Group's ownership of Texaco shares during the latter's sensitive dealings with Pennzoil did constitute a threat to the corporation's welfare, thereby making the buy-back of the shares a reasonable business decision. The fact that the price paid for the shares was also reasonable supported the conclusion that the directors had not breached their fiduciary duty.

Duty of Loyalty

One can define *loyalty* as faithfulness to one's obligations and duties. The essence of the fiduciary duty requires subordination of self-interest to the interest of the entity to which the duty is owed. It presumes constant loyalty to the corporation on the part of the directors and officers. In general, the duty of loyalty prohibits directors from using corporate funds or confidential corporate information for their personal advantage. It requires officers and directors to disclose fully any corporate opportunity or any possible conflict of interest that might occur in a transaction involving the directors of the corporation.

Cases dealing with fiduciary duty typically involve one or more of the following:

1. Competing with the corporation.
2. Usurping a corporate opportunity.
3. Having an interest that conflicts with the interest of the corporation.

> *"It is not within the lawful powers of a board of directors to shape and conduct the affairs of a corporation for the merely incidental benefit of shareholders."*
>
> **Russell C. Ostrander,**
> **1851–1919**
> *(Michigan jurist)*

4. Engaging in insider trading (using information that is not public in order to make a profit trading securities).
5. Authorizing some corporate transaction that is detrimental to minority shareholders.
6. Selling control over the corporation.

In the following case, the Alabama Supreme Court reviewed a situation in which officers, directors, and shareholders attempted to secure advantages for themselves at the expense of the corporation.

Case 27.2
MORAD v. COUPOUNAS
Supreme Court of Alabama, 1978.
361 So.2d 6.

FACTS Morad, Thomson, and Morad's wife were officers, directors, and shareholders of Bio-Lab, Inc. Coupounas was a shareholder. While serving as officers and directors of Bio-Lab, Morad, Thomson, and Morad's wife incorporated and operated a competing business, Med-Lab, Inc. Thereupon, Coupounas sued individually and derivatively (on behalf of the corporation), alleging that the directors of Bio-Lab had breached their fiduciary duty (by usurping a corporate opportunity) to him and to Bio-Lab by opening the competing business.

ISSUE Had the directors of Bio-Lab breached their fiduciary duty to the corporation by opening a competing business, thereby usurping a corporate opportunity?

DECISION Yes. The Bio-Lab directors were guilty of misappropriating a corporate opportunity.

REASON Officers and directors of a corporation may in some instances seize upon an opportunity that they discover as a result of their positions. If, however, the opportunity is available both to the corporate officer or director personally and to the corporation, the officer or director must make others in the company aware of the opportunity and may not surreptitiously exploit it. The court concluded that "[i]t is well settled that directors and other governing members of a corporation are so far agents of the corporation that in their dealings respecting corporate interests, they are subject to the rules which apply generally to persons standing in fiduciary relations and which forbid such persons to secure an advantage for themselves which fidelity to the trust reposed in them would carry to others whose interests they ought to represent." The Alabama Supreme Court determined that the appropriate remedy for the defendants' breach of their duty of loyalty was for the court to impose a "constructive trust," which would require all profits of Med-Lab to be paid to Bio-Lab.

Conflicts of Interest

Corporate directors often have many business affiliations, and they can even sit on the board of more than one corporation. Of course, they are precluded from entering into or supporting any business that operates in direct competition with the corporation. The fiduciary duty requires them to make a full disclosure of any potential conflicts of interest that might arise in any corporate transaction.

Contracts between Director and Corporation   Sometimes a corporation enters into a contract or engages in a transaction in which an officer or director has a material interest. The director or officer must make a *full disclosure* of that interest and must abstain from voting on the proposed transaction.

For example, Sunwood Corporation needs office space. Lambert Alden, one of its five directors, owns the building adjoining the corporation. He negotiates a lease with Sunwood for the space, making a full disclosure to Sunwood and the other four board directors. The lease arrangement is fair and reasonable, and it is unanimously approved by the corporation's board of directors. In such a case, the contract is valid. The rule is one of reason; otherwise, directors would be prevented from ever giving financial assistance to the corporations they serve.

The various state statutes contain different standards, but a contract will generally not be voidable if:

1. It was fair and reasonable to the corporation at the time the contract was made.
2. There was a full disclosure of the interest of the officers or directors in the transaction.
3. The contract is approved by a majority of the disinterested directors or shareholders.[2]

Contracts between Corporations Having Common Directors   Often contracts are negotiated between corporations having one or more directors who are members of both boards. Such transactions require great care, as they are closely scrutinized by courts. Section 8 of the Clayton Act of 1914 specifically indicates that no person shall be a director in any two or more competing corporations if any one of them has capital surplus and undivided profits aggregating more than $1 million (other than banks, banking associations, trust companies, and common carriers).

❖ Rights of Directors

A director of a corporation has a number of rights, including the rights of participation, inspection, indemnification, and compensation.

Participation

Among the rights that a corporate director must have in order to function properly in that position, the main right is one of participation—meaning that the director must be notified of board of directors' meetings so as to participate in them. As pointed out in Chapter 26, regular board meetings are usually established by the bylaws or by board resolution, and no notice of these meetings is required. If special meetings are called, however, notice is required unless waived by the director.

Inspection

A director must have access to all corporate books and records in order to make decisions and to exercise the necessary supervision. This right is virtually absolute and cannot be restricted.

---

2.   See Section 41 of the Model Business Corporation Act.

Business Law in Action

A Conflict of Interests

It is not always easy for a director of a corporation to observe the duty of loyalty when a conflict of interests arises. Consider, for example, the situation of Arthur Modell, who was president of a corporation involved in a business transaction with another corporation of which he was a director and major shareholder.[1]

The corporation of which he was president was the Cleveland Stadium Corporation (CSC). Modell also owned 80 percent of the stock in CSC. The other corporation was the Cleveland Browns Football Co., Inc., in which Modell was a 53-percent shareholder and a member of the board. Aside from Modell, several

1. Gries Sports Enterprises, Inc. v. Cleveland Browns Football Co., Inc., 26 Ohio St. 3d 15, 496 N.E. 2d 959 (1986).

other members of the board of directors of the Browns served also on the CSC board. At a March 16, 1982, meeting of the Browns' board of directors, the board voted to purchase all of the stock of CSC for $6,000,000. Note that, in this situation, the sellers and the buyers were the same people, and that Modell had the controlling interest in both cases.

The one person who did not stand to benefit by the purchase of CSC by the Browns was Robert Gries, who, jointly with his business firm, Gries Sports Enterprises, owned 43 percent of the Browns and was also a director on the board. Gries had objected to the sale, but was outvoted at the March meeting mentioned above. Gries felt the purchase price was far too high, based on other appraisals that valued CSC at no more than $2,000,000. Not only did the purchase for the price of $6,000,000

increase the debt load of the Browns to a point higher than necessary, the sale of CSC also directly, and, according to Gries, unfairly, benefited Modell.

Gries took his argument to court. He filed a shareholder's derivative action seeking the rescission of the CSC acquisition. After a four-week trial in 1984, the trial court ruled in favor of Gries. The appellate court, however, reversed. Gries appealed to the Ohio Supreme Court. The high court, in its determination, held for Gries. It stated that "rather than serving the best interests of the Browns and all of the Browns' stockholders, the effect of this transaction was to benefit the majority stockholder of the Browns . . . at the expense of the principal minority shareholder. . . . The judgment of the court of appeals is reversed, and the judgment of the trial court is reinstated."

Indemnification

It is not unusual for corporate directors to become involved in lawsuits by virtue of their position and their actions as directors. Most states (and the MBCA, Section 5) permit a corporation to indemnify a director for legal costs, fees, and judgments involved in defending corporation-related suits.

At common law, a director had no right to be indemnified; however, there was little objection to indemnification if the director was absolved of liability. Today, statutes and court decisions allow indemnification even if the director is not absolved of liability, as long as his or her actions were made in good faith and based on a reasonable belief that such actions were in the best interests of the corporation.

Criminal convictions usually require evidence of bad faith, but bad faith is not presumed merely because the director settles the litigation, pleads *nolo contendere* (no contest), or even is found liable civilly. Many states specifically permit a corporation to purchase liability insurance for the directors and officers to cover indemnification. Where the statutes are silent on this matter, the power to purchase such insurance is usually considered to be part of the corporation's implied power.

Compensation

Historically, directors have had no inherent right to compensation for their services as directors. Officers receive compensation, and nominal sums are often paid as honoraria to directors. In many cases, directors are also chief corporate officers and receive compensation in their managerial positions. Most directors, however, gain through indirect benefits, such as business contacts, prestige, and other rewards.

There is a trend toward providing more than nominal compensation for directors, especially in large corporations where directorships can be enormous burdens in terms of time, work, effort, and risk. Many states permit the corporate articles or bylaws to authorize compensation for directors, and in some cases the board can set its own compensation unless the articles or bylaws provide otherwise.

❖ Rights of Officers and Management Employees

As noted earlier, corporate officers' duties are the same as the duties of directors because their respective corporate positions involve both of them in decision making and place them in similar positions of control. Hence, they are viewed as having the same fiduciary duty of care and loyalty in their conduct of corporate affairs.

The rights of corporate officers and other high-level managers are defined by employment contracts, since they are employees of the company.

❖ Rights of Shareholders

As stated in Chapter 26, the acquisition of a share of stock makes a person an owner and shareholder in a corporation. Shareholders thus own the corporation. Although they have no legal title to corporate property vested in the corporation, such as buildings and equipment, they do have an *equitable* interest in the firm. The rights of shareholders are established in the articles of incorporation and under the state's general incorporation law.

Stock Certificates

A stock certificate evidences ownership, and shareholders have the right to demand that the corporation issue a certificate and record their names and addresses in the corporate stock record books. Stock is *intangible* personal property—the ownership right exists independently of the certificate itself. A stock certificate may be lost or destroyed, but ownership is not destroyed with it.

A new certificate can be issued to replace one that has been lost or destroyed.[3] Notice of shareholder meetings, dividends, and operational and financial reports are

---

3. For a lost or destroyed certificate to be reissued, a shareholder normally must furnish an indemnity bond to protect the corporation against potential loss should the original certificate reappear at some future time in the hands of a bona fide purchaser. [UCC 8-302 and 8-405(2)]

Landmark in the Law

The Death of D&O Insurance

Directors and officers in the corporate world of today are exposed to the possibility of extensive liability. Because of this, as mentioned in the preceding text, most states allow corporations to indemnify directors for expenses and judgments resulting from lawsuits relating to the defense of corporate interests. The extent to which corporations can indemnify its directors is determined by state statute. Generally, states require that a corporation reimburse a director for all expenses if the director successfully defends himself or herself. Corporations are permitted (but not required) to indemnify its directors even in cases where a judgment is made against the director. Usually, such indemnification is allowed when the director acted reasonably and with the assurance that he or she was acting in the best interests of the corporation.

Corporations protect themselves from indemnification expenses by obtaining D&O (directors' and officers') insurance. Typically, D&O insurance has a twofold function. First, it reimburses corporations for indemnification costs, and, second, it offers liability coverage for directors and officers for situations not covered by the corporation's indemnification policy.

In the litigious world of today, the need for extensive D&O insurance coverage is obvious, particularly in large firms where directors and officers engage in multimillion-dollar transactions that entail a huge potential liability for an erroneous judgment or a mistake of any sort. In *Smith v. Van Gorkom*, for example, a corporation's directors were held to have breached their fiduciary duty to the company by approving a cash-out merger of the business for $55 per share. When the case came before the Delaware Supreme Court, the court held that the directors were personally liable "to the extent that the fair value of Trans Union [the firm in question] exceed[ed] $55 per share."[1] The action was ultimately settled for $23.5 million. The D&O insurance carrier provided $10 million, which was the maximum reimbursement under the policy.

As the need for broad D&O coverage has expanded, the willingness of insurance companies to provide it has decreased substantially. D&O insurance has obviously not escaped the general "crisis" occurring in all areas of liability insurance. A Directors and Officers Liability Survey

1.   488 A.2d 858 (Del. 1985).

---

all distributed according to the recorded ownership listed in the corporation's books, not on the basis of possession of the certificate.

Assume that Barbara Ames's certificate showing ownership of corporate stock in R&A Corporation is destroyed in a fire on September 1. The corporation declares a dividend on September 5. According to corporate records, Barbara Ames is the "record owner" and receives the dividend even though she no longer has the certificate.

Of course, to sell or otherwise transfer the shares, indorsement and delivery of the actual certificate to the transferee are required.

PREEMPTIVE RIGHT
A shareholder's right to purchase newly issued stock of a corporation before it is offered to any outside buyers, equal in percentage to shares presently held, enabling the shareholder to maintain proportionate ownership and voice in the corporation.

Preemptive Rights

A **preemptive right** is a common-law concept in which a preference is given to a shareholder over all other purchasers to subscribe to or purchase a prorated share of a new issue of stock. This allows the shareholder to maintain his or her portion of control, voting power, or financial interest in the corporation. Most statutes either (1) grant preemptive rights but allow them to be negated in the corporation's articles of 1984[2] concluded that in the ten preceding years, not only had the number of companies who had experienced claims against their directors risen, but also the average cost of defending a claim rose from approximately $180,000 per claim to approximately $460,000 per claim. In addition, the percentage of claims paying over $1 million nearly doubled (from 4.8 to 8.3 percent).

As a result of the higher claims payments, insurers have been excluding more and more claims, particularly those brought by corporations against their own directors and officers, which in the mid-1980s became increasingly frequent—and expensive. In one case, insurance companies paid Chase Manhattan Bank $32.5 million in a settlement resulting from the bank's lawsuit against six of its officers.[3] An increasing number of insurance companies are no longer even issuing D&O insurance. Those who do issue it offer reduced coverage at often prohibitive premiums and with high deductibles.

This places directors and officers of corporations in an increasingly cautious position. As one observer noted,

Directors already have a bias toward being more cautious than is optimal for society—that is, they take less risk than owner-managers would. Directors have nothing personal to gain from risky behavior. It is, therefore, in the interest of society not to force on directors an added incentive to be too cautious. These undesirable effects are greatest on new, growing companies.[4]

In many cases, when a corporation loses a substantial part of its D&O insurance, directors have little choice but to leave the corporation, simply to protect themselves from potentially ruinous liability claims. In 1985, for example, when a Houston firm lost its $2 million D&O insurance coverage, four of its five directors left the firm.[5] Such instances of sudden exodus due to the D&O insurance crisis are numerous.

Although several solutions to the problem have been posed—including self-insurance programs and legislative proposals—none have so far provided a workable answer to the problem. How this may affect the growth and leadership of corporations in the future is a major question of the late 1980s.

2. The study was conducted by the Wyatt Company, a consulting firm; see D. J. Block et al., "Advising Directors on the D&O Insurance Crisis," *Securities Regulation Law Journal* 14:130 (1986), pp. 146–147.
3. Sloane, "Insurer-Management Liability Rift Seen Growing," *New York Times*, December 19, 1985, p. D8.
4. Herzel, "Law Should Allow Indemnity for Derivative Suits," *Legal Times*, March 31, 1986, p. 11.
5. Hilder, "Liability Insurance Is Difficult to Find Now for Directors, Officers," *The Wall Street Journal*, July 10, 1985, p. 1.

or (2) deny preemptive rights except to the extent that they are granted in the articles. The result is that the articles of incorporation determine the existence and scope of preemptive rights. Generally, preemptive rights apply only to additional, newly issued stock sold for cash and must be exercised within a specified time period (usually thirty days).

For example, Detering Corporation authorizes and issues 1,000 shares of stock, and Pat Southern purchases 100 shares, making her the owner of 10 percent of the company's stock. Subsequently, Detering, by vote of its shareholders, authorizes the issuance of another 1,000 shares (amending the articles of incorporation). This increases its capital stock to a total of 2,000 shares. If preemptive rights have been provided, Pat Southern can purchase one additional share of the new stock being issued for each share currently owned—100 additional shares. Thus, she can own 200 of the 2,000 shares outstanding, and her relative position as a shareholder will be maintained. If preemptive rights are not reserved, her proportionate control and voting power will be diluted from that of a 10-percent shareholder to that of a 5-percent shareholder because of the issuance of the additional 1,000 shares.

Preemptive rights are far more significant in a close corporation because of the relatively few number of shares and the substantial interest each shareholder controls.

Stock Warrants

STOCK WARRANT
A certificate granting a transferable option to buy a given number of shares of stock, usually within a set time period.

When preemptive rights exist and a corporation is issuing additional shares, each shareholder is usually given **stock warrants,** which are transferable options to acquire a given number of shares from the corporation at a stated price. Warrants are often publicly traded on securities exchanges. When the warrant option is for a short period of time, the stock warrants are usually referred to as *rights*.

Dividends

DIVIDEND
A distribution to corporate shareholders, disbursed in proportion to the number of shares held.

A **dividend** is a distribution of corporate profits or income *ordered by the directors* and paid to the shareholders in proportion to their respective shares in the corporation. Dividends can be paid in cash, property, stock of the corporation that is paying the dividends, or stock of other corporations.[4]

State laws vary, but every state determines the general circumstances and legal requirements under which dividends are paid. State laws also control the sources of revenue to be used; only certain funds are legally available for paying dividends. Once declared, a cash dividend becomes a corporate debt enforceable at law like any other debt.[5]

Dividends payable from limited funds are prescribed by various state statutes as current net earnings, net profits, or surplus. Dividends can be paid only from the following sources of funds:

1. *Retained earnings:* All states allow dividends to be paid from the undistributed net profits earned by the corporation, including capital gains from the sale of fixed assets. The undistributed net profits are called *earned surplus* or *retained earnings*.
2. *Net profits:* A few state statutes allow dividends to be issued from current net profits without regard to deficits in prior years.
3. *Surplus:* A number of state statutes allow dividends to be paid out of any kind of surplus.

When directors fail to declare a dividend, shareholders can ask a court of equity for an injunction to compel the directors to meet and to declare a dividend. For the injunction to be granted, it must be shown that the directors have acted so unreasonably in withholding the dividend that their conduct is an abuse of their discretion.

Often large money reserves are accumulated for a bona fide purpose, such as expansion, research, or other legitimate corporate goals. The mere fact that sufficient corporate earnings or surplus are available to pay a dividend is not enough to compel directors to distribute funds that, in the board's opinion, should not be paid. The courts are circumspect about interfering with corporate operations and will not compel directors to declare dividends unless abuse of discretion is clearly shown. Thus, directors are not ordinarily forced to declare dividends to shareholders. A striking exception to this rule was made in the following classic case.

---

4. Technically, dividends paid in stock are not dividends. They maintain each shareholder's proportional interest in the corporation. On one occasion a distillery declared and paid a "dividend" in bonded whiskey.
5. An insolvent corporation cannot declare a dividend.

Case 27.3
DODGE v. FORD MOTOR CO.
Supreme Court of Michigan, 1919.
204 Mich. 459, 170 N.W. 668.

FACTS   Henry Ford was the president and major share-holder of Ford Motor Company. In the company's early years, business expanded rapidly, and, in addition to regular quarterly dividends, special dividends were often paid. By 1916 surplus above capital was still $111,960,907. That year, however, Henry Ford declared that the company would no longer pay special dividends, but would put back into the business all the earnings of the company above the regular dividend of 5 percent. The court quoted Ford: "My ambition," declared Mr. Ford, "is to employ still more men, to spread the benefits of this industrial system to the greatest possible number, to help them build up their lives and their homes. To do this, we are putting the greatest share of our profits back into the business." The minority shareholders of Ford (who owned 10 percent of the stock) brought a suit to force the declaration of a dividend.

ISSUE   Was Ford's refusal to pay a dividend an abuse of managerial discretion?

DECISION   Yes. Because of the special circumstances of this case, the court compelled Ford to pay a dividend.

REASON   The undisputed facts were that Ford had a surplus of $112 million—approximately $54 million in cash on hand. It had made profits of $59 million in the past year and expected to make $60 million in the coming year. The board of directors gave no reason to justify withholding a dividend. Thus, in doing so, it violated the stated purpose of the corporation's existence. "Courts of equity will not interfere in the management of the directors unless it is clearly made to appear that they are guilty of fraud or misappropriation of the corporate funds, or refuse to declare a dividend when the corporation has a surplus of net profits which it can, without detriment to its business, divide among its stockholders, and when a refusal to do so would amount to such an abuse of discretion as would constitute a fraud, or breach of that good faith which they are bound to exercise towards the stockholders."

Whenever a dividend is paid while the corporation is *insolvent*, it is automatically an illegal dividend, and shareholders may be liable for returning the payment to the corporation or its creditors. Dividends are generally required by statute to be distributed only from certain authorized corporate accounts representing profits. Sometimes dividends are improperly paid from an unauthorized account, or their payment causes the corporation to become insolvent. Generally, in this case, shareholders must return illegal dividends only if they knew that the dividends were illegal when they received them.

In all cases of illegal and improper dividends, the board of directors can be held personally liable for the amount of the payment. When directors can show that a shareholder knew a dividend was illegal when it was received, however, the directors are entitled to reimbursement from the shareholder.

Voting Rights

Shareholders exercise ownership control through the power of their votes. In the early development of corporate law, each shareholder was entitled to one vote per share. This rule still holds today, but the voting techniques discussed in Chapter 26 (including shareholder agreements, voting trusts, and cumulative-voting methods) all enhance the power of the shareholder's vote.

The articles can exclude or limit voting rights, particularly to certain classes of shares. For example, owners of preferred shares are usually denied the right to vote. Treasury shares, held by the corporation, cannot be voted until they have been reissued by the corporation. (See Chapter 29 for a description of the different classes of stock.)

Inspection Rights

Shareholders in a corporation enjoy both common-law and statutory inspection rights.[6] Shareholders at common law enjoyed qualified rights to inspect and copy corporate books and records, such as the bylaws and minutes of the board of directors' meetings and the shareholders' meetings, as well as documents such as contracts, correspondence, and tax returns. They even had the right to inspect the corporate headquarters. The shareholder's right of inspection is limited, however, to inspection and copying of corporate books and records for a *proper purpose*, provided the request is made in advance. Either the shareholder can inspect in person, or an attorney, agent, accountant, or other type of assistant can do so.

The power of inspection is fraught with potential abuses, and the corporation is allowed to protect itself from them. For example, a shareholder can properly be denied access to corporate records to prevent harassment or to protect trade secrets or other confidential corporate information. Section 52 of the MBCA imposes various standard requirements on the shareholder's inspection right:

> Any person who shall have been a holder of record shares . . . at least six months immediately preceding his [or her] demand or [who is] the holder of . . . at least 5 percent of all the outstanding shares of the corporation, upon written demand stating the purpose thereof, shall have the right to examine, in person, or by agent or attorney, at any reasonable time or times, for any proper purpose its relevant books and records of accounts, minutes, and record of shareholders and to make extracts therefrom.

A corporation's improper refusal to allow access to its records can result in severe and costly liability. Under Section 52 of the MBCA, the penalty is 10 percent of the value of the shares owned by the shareholder who has been denied access to the books.[7]

The MBCA, Section 31, as well as the RMBCA, Section 7.20, require the corporation to maintain an alphabetical voting list of shareholders with addresses and number of shares owned. This list must be kept open at the annual meeting for inspection by any shareholder of record.

The following case illustrates a court's dilemma in determining whether a stockholder-competitor could inspect the corporate books for limited purposes.

Case 27.4
ULDRICH v. DATASPORT, INC.
Court of Appeals of Minnesota, 1984.
349 N.W.2d 286.

FACTS Uldrich, the plaintiff, was a shareholder and former director, officer, and employee of Datasport, Inc., a Minnesota corporation. Datasport, the defendant, terminated Uldrich's employment, directorship, and office. Aside from maintaining his status as shareholder, Uldrich was also a competitor of Datasport. While Uldrich was still a director and an officer, he was prohibited from marketing his competing product for one year by a court order upon Datasport's request. After his dismissal, Uldrich was de-

---

6. See, for example, Schwartzman v. Schwartzman Packing Co., 99 N.M. 436, 659 P.2d 888 (1983).
7. The Revised Model Business Corporation Act, Section 16.02, however, eliminates the six-month, 5-percent requirement. Also, Section 16.04 dilutes the penalty and liability provisions of the MBCA.

Case 27.4—Continued

nied access to Datasport's records and books. Uldrich was concerned about the fact that other shareholders of Datasport were running other businesses using Datasport assets, such as leasing office space to, and sharing it with, Datasport. Uldrich felt that Datasport's revenues were being eaten up by operating expenses. He filed for a *writ of mandamus* (an order issued from a court and directed to a private or municipal corporation or any of its officers commanding the performance of a particular act) which, in this case, would permit Uldrich's inspection. His purpose was to place a monetary value on his shares and to evaluate the conduct and affairs of the other shareholders, directors, and officers. The trial court awarded Uldrich a writ of mandamus compelling Datasport to permit inspection. Although the writ enjoined Uldrich from making competitive use of such information, Datasport appealed the order.

ISSUE Should Uldrich, as a competitor to Datasport, be entitled to exercise his shareholder's right to inspect Datasport books and records, and does he have a legitimate purpose for wanting to inspect the corporate records?

DECISION Yes, in both cases. The Court of Appeals affirmed Uldrich's writ of mandamus commanding Datasport to allow Uldrich to exercise his shareholder's right of inspection.

REASON In Minnesota, shareholders are granted the statutory right to examine the "books of account" and records of the corporation "for any proper purpose." To enforce this right, a writ of mandamus is available. The shareholder, however, must show a proper purpose to prevail; curiosity will not suffice. The court held that, since other shareholders were conducting other business activities using Datasport assets, Uldrich's concern over their conduct was legitimate, and he thus had a sufficient and proper reason for wanting to inspect the books. In particular, the court noted that the return on Uldrich's original investment in Datasport ($1,000) was "trivial" when compared to Datasport's substantial sales record ($1.5 million). Consequently, equity required a broad scope be given to the concept of shareholder access. As long as Uldrich refrained from making competitive use of any information obtained from Datasport records, he was entitled to inspect the books.

Transfer of Shares

Corporate stock represents an ownership right in intangible personal property. The law generally recognizes the right of an owner to transfer property to another person unless there are valid restrictions on its transferability. Although stock certificates are negotiable and freely transferable by indorsement and delivery, transfer of stock in closely held corporations is generally restricted by contract, the bylaws, or a restriction stamped on the stock certificate. The existence of any restrictions on transferability must always be noted on the face of the stock certificate, and these restrictions must be reasonable.

Right of First Refusal Sometimes corporations or their shareholders restrict transferability by reserving the option to purchase any shares offered for resale by a shareholder. This *right of first refusal* remains with the corporation or the shareholders for only a specified time or reasonable time. Variations on the purchase option are possible. For example, a shareholder might be required to offer the shares to other shareholders or to the corporation first.

Corporate Records When shares are transferred, a new entry is made in the corporate stock book to indicate the new owner. Until the corporation is notified and the entry is complete, voting rights, notice of shareholders' meetings, dividend distribution, and so forth, are all held by the current record owner.

Rights on Dissolution

When a corporation is dissolved and its outstanding debts and the claims of its creditors have been satisfied, the remaining assets are distributed on a pro rata basis among the shareholders. Certain classes of preferred stock (see Chapter 29) can be given priority to the extent of their contractual preference. If no preferences to distribution of assets upon liquidation are given to any class of stock, then the stockholders share the remaining assets equally.

Suppose a minority shareholder knows that the board of directors is mishandling corporate assets or is permitting a deadlock to threaten or irreparably injure the corporation's finances. The minority shareholder is not powerless to intervene. He or she can petition a court to appoint a receiver and to liquidate the business assets of the corporation.

The Model Business Corporation Act, in Section 97, and the Revised Model Business Corporation Act, in Section 14.30, permit any shareholder to institute such an action when it appears that:

1. The directors are deadlocked in the management of corporate affairs, shareholders are unable to break that deadlock, and irreparable injury to the corporation is being suffered or threatened.
2. The acts of the directors or those in control of the corporation are illegal, oppressive, or fraudulent.
3. Corporation assets are being misapplied or wasted.

❖ Liabilities of Shareholders

One of the hallmarks of the corporate organization is that shareholders are not personally liable for the debts of the corporation. If the corporation fails, shareholders can lose their investment, but that is generally the limit of their liability. In certain instances of fraud, undercapitalization, or careless observance of corporate formalities, a court will pierce the corporate veil (disregard the corporate entity) and hold the shareholders individually liable. But these situations are the exception, not the rule.

Although rare, there are certain other instances where a shareholder can be personally liable. One relates to illegal dividends, which were discussed previously, and two others relate to stock subscriptions and watered stock, which will be discussed here.

Stock Subscriptions

Sometimes stock-subscription agreements—written contracts by which one agrees to buy capital stock of a corporation—exist prior to incorporation. Normally, these agreements are treated as continuing offers and are usually irrevocable (for up to six months under the MBCA, Section 17). Once the corporation has been formed, it can sell shares to shareholder investors. In either case, once the subscription agreement or stock offer is accepted, a binding contract is formed. Any refusal to pay constitutes a breach resulting in the personal liability of the shareholder.

Watered Stock

Shares of stock can be paid for by property or by services rendered instead of cash. They cannot be purchased with promissory notes, however. The general rule is that for par-value shares sold (i.e., shares that have a specific face value, or formal cash-in value, written on them, such as one penny or one dollar), the corporation must receive a value at least equal to the par-value amount. For any no-par shares sold (i.e., shares that have no face value—no specific amount printed on their face), the corporation must receive the value of the shares as determined by the board or shareholders. When shares are issued by the corporation for less than these stated values, the shares are referred to as **watered stock.** In most cases, the shareholder who receives watered stock must pay the difference to the corporation (the shareholder is personally liable). In some states, the shareholder who receives watered stock may be liable to creditors of the corporation for unpaid corporate debts.

WATERED STOCK
Stock issued by a corporation as if fully paid for, when in fact less than par value has been paid.

To illustrate the concept of watered stock, suppose that during the formation of a corporation, Gomez, as one of the incorporators, transfers his property, Sunset Beach, to the corporation for 10,000 shares of stock at a par value of $100 per share for a total price of $1 million. After the property is transferred and the shares are issued, Sunset Beach is carried on the corporate books at a value of $1 million. Upon appraisal, it is discovered that the market value of the property at the time of transfer was only $500,000. The shares issued to Gomez are therefore watered stock, and he is liable to the corporation for the difference.

❖ Duties of Major Shareholders

In some cases, a majority shareholder is regarded as having a fiduciary duty to the corporation and to the minority shareholders. This occurs when a single shareholder (or a few shareholders acting in concert) owns a sufficient number of shares to exercise *de facto* control over the corporation. In these situations, majority shareholders owe a fiduciary duty to the minority shareholders and creditors when they sell their shares, because such a sale would be, in fact, a transfer of control of the corporation.

Application

Law and the Shareholder— Selling Shares in a Close Corporation

Remember that a close corporation is typically a family corporation or a privately held corporation in which very few people own all the shares in the corporation. Usually all shareholders know each other personally. There is no trading market for the shares in such a corporation, and it is often operated like a partnership. When such a corporation is formed, an important issue to address is each shareholder's future sale or gift of his or her stock or the disposition of that stock upon a shareholder's death. The reason that a close corporation is formed is to keep out "outsiders." That is to say, the shareholders want to keep management control within a small group. Therefore, the articles of incorporation normally should provide that the shares must be first offered for sale to the remaining shareholders who have the *right of first refusal*. For this right to be exerted, there must be a procedure for determining the price of the stock that must be sold. One way is to hire an appraiser or several appraisers who will value the business and therefore assign a "fair" price to the shares of stock to be sold.

As an alternative, the price can be specified as a multiple of the net after-tax earnings of the business. But what happens if there is a dispute among the shareholders, and one or more want to take control of the corporation or at least eliminate another shareholder? One possible solution is to allow one party to set the price and the other to decide whether to buy or to sell.

Checklist for the Close Corporation

☐ 1. Include in the articles of incorporation appropriate restrictions on the resale or disposition of the shares, including the right of first refusal.

☐ 2. In the initial formation of the corporation, establish a procedure for determining the price for the sale of a share of stock by any shareholder who wants to, or must, sell his or her shares. Do not wait until there is a heated dispute among shareholders to decide how shares are to be disposed.

❖ Chapter Summary: Rights and Duties of Directors, Managers, and Shareholders

DUTIES OF DIRECTORS	
Duty of Care	Directors are obligated to be honest and to use prudent business judgment in the conduct of corporate affairs. If a director fails to exercise this duty of care, he or she can be answerable to the corporation and to the shareholders for breaching the duty of care. In general, the duty of care requires that directors: 1. Carry out their responsibilities in an informed, businesslike manner and reasonably supervise those to whom they delegate any of their responsibilities. 2. Attend board of directors' meetings and, where appropriate, register dissent. 3. Be informed on corporate matters and understand legal and other professional advice rendered to the board.
Duty of Loyalty	Directors have a fiduciary duty to subordinate their own interests to those of the corporation in matters relating to the corporation. Loyalty to the corporation and its interests is required of all directors. 1. In situations where a director has a conflict of interests (e.g., being a director of two corporations negotiating a business transaction), the director must disclose this conflict to the board. 2. A director cannot operate in direct competition with the corporation or usurp a corporate opportunity.
RIGHTS OF DIRECTORS	
Participation	Directors have a right to be notified of all board of directors' meetings in order to participate in them.
Inspection	Directors have an absolute right to have access to corporate books and records in order to make decisions and to exercise necessary supervision.
Indemnification	Directors who acted in good faith may be indemnified by the corporation for legal costs, fees, and judgments involved in defending corporation-related suits. Corporations are permitted to purchase director liability insurance either by statute or under a corporation's implied powers.
Compensation	Many states permit the corporate articles or bylaws to authorize compensation for directors, or, in some cases, the board can set its own compensation.
RIGHTS OF SHAREHOLDERS	
Stock Certificate	Shareholders have the right to demand that the corporation issue a stock certificate to evidence their ownership of shares and to record their names and addresses in the corporate stock record books.
Preemptive Rights	A preemptive right is a common-law concept in which a preference is given to a shareholder over all other purchasers to subscribe to or purchase a new issue of stock. This allows the shareholder to maintain his or her portion of control, voting power, or financial interest in the corporation. The existence of preemptive rights is generally provided for, or denied, in the corporate charter.
Stock Warrants	When preemptive rights exist and a corporation is issuing additional shares, each shareholder is usually given stock warrants. A stock warrant is a transferable option to acquire a given number of shares from the corporation at a stated price (usually below the current market price).
Dividends	A dividend is a distribution of corporate profits or income ordered by the directors and paid to the shareholders of record in proportion to their respective shares in the corporation. When directors fail to pay a dividend, shareholders can ask a court of equity for an injunction to compel the directors to meet and to declare a dividend. Such will be granted only if it is shown that the directors have acted so unreasonably in withholding the dividend that their conduct is an abuse of discretion.

❖ Chapter Summary: Rights and Duties of Directors, Managers, and Shareholders—Continued

Voting Rights	Shareholders have the right to vote their shares, one vote per share. The articles of incorporation can exclude or limit voting rights for certain classes of shares, such as preferred shares. Treasury shares (held by the corporation) cannot be voted until reissued.
Inspection Rights	Shareholders have a right to inspect corporate records and books *for a proper purpose,* provided they make the request in advance. A corporation's improper refusal to allow access to its records to shareholders can result in severe and costly liability to the corporation.
Transfer of Shares	Corporate stock certificates are negotiable and freely transferable by indorsement and delivery, except in closely held corporations where transfer is generally restricted by contract or bylaws. 1. Right of first refusal—Sometimes transferability is restricted by a corporation by granting present shareholders the right of first refusal when any shares are offered for resale by a shareholder. 2. When shares are transferred, a new entry is made in the corporate stock book to indicate the new owner.
Dissolution	Upon the dissolution of a corporation, and after creditors have been satisfied, assets are distributed among the shareholders on a pro rata basis.
LIABILITIES AND DUTIES OF SHAREHOLDERS	
When the Corporate Entity is Disregarded	As discussed in Chapter 25, on rare occasions a court may "pierce the corporate veil" and hold shareholders personally liable for corporate debts.
Stock Subscriptions	As soon as preincorporation stock-subscription agreements are accepted by the corporation, a binding contract is formed. A refusal to pay constitutes a breach, resulting in the personal liability of the shareholder.
Watered Stock	If a shareholder purchases a corporation's shares for less than par value or for less than the value determined by the board or shareholders for no-par shares, these shares are referred to as *watered stock.* In most cases, the shareholder who receives watered stock must pay the difference to the corporation (the shareholder is personally liable). In some states, a shareholder who has received watered stock may be liable to creditors of the corporation for unpaid corporate debts.
Illegal Dividends	Whenever a dividend is paid while the corporation is insolvent, it is automatically an illegal dividend, and shareholders can be liable for returning the payment to the corporation or its creditors. Whenever a dividend is paid from unauthorized funds or when the dividend would render the corporation insolvent, (generally) shareholders are liable for return payment for the illegal dividend only if the shareholder knew the dividend was illegal when received.
Duties and Liabilities of Major Shareholders	In some cases, a majority shareholder who is selling his or her shares is regarded as having a fiduciary duty to the corporation and to the minority shareholders. This occurs when a single shareholder (or a few acting in concert) owns a sufficient number of shares to exercise *de facto* control over the corporation.

❖ Questions and Case Problems

27-1. Lisa owns 10,000 shares (10 percent) of Sundowner, Inc. Sundowner authorized 100,000 shares and issued all of them during its first six months in operation. Later, the company reacquired 10,000 of these shares. With shareholder approval, Sundowner amended its articles so as to authorize and issue another 100,000 shares and also, by a resolution of the board of directors, to reissue the 10,000 shares of treasury stock. There is no provision in the corporate articles for shareholder preemptive rights. Because of her previous ownership of 10 percent of Sundowner, Lisa claims that she has the preemptive right to purchase 10,000 shares of the new issue and 1,000 shares of the stock being reissued. Discuss her claims.

27-2. Abby has acquired one share of common stock of a multimillion-dollar corporation with over 500,000 shareholders. Abby's ownership is so small that she is questioning what her rights are as a shareholder. For example, she wants to know whether this one share entitles her to:

    a. Attend and vote at shareholder meetings.

    b. Inspect the corporate books.

    c. Receive yearly dividends.

Discuss Abby's rights in these three matters.

27-3. Mallard has made a preincorporation subscription agreement to purchase 500 shares of a newly formed corporation. The shares have a par value of $100 per share. The corporation is formed, and Mallard's subscription is accepted by the corporation. Mallard transfers a piece of land he owns to the corporation, and the corporation issues 250 shares for it. Mallard purchases no other shares. One year later, with the corporation in serious financial difficulty, the board declares and pays a $5-per-share dividend. It is now learned that the land transferred by Mallard had a market value of $18,000. Discuss any liability that shareholder Mallard has to the corporation or to the creditors of the corporation.

27-4. Arthur owned 1 percent of Exeter Corporation's outstanding shares. The board of directors of Exeter voted to sell to Arthur some equipment owned by the corporation. Although the equipment was worth $15,000, Exeter sold it to Arthur for only $11,500. Jennings, another shareholder, demanded that Arthur either return the equipment to the corporation or pay an additional $3,500 for it. Could Jennings enforce his demand? Explain.

27-5. Marsh Drugs, Inc., a thriving business, was considering plans for expansion. Upon hearing of Marsh's plans, Alderman approached one of the directors of the corporation, Owens, and offered to sell Marsh Drugs some property he owned adjacent to the current site of Marsh Drugs. Owens thought the price of Alderman's property was below market value and that it would be a good investment. Owens purchased the property for himself and never mentioned the offer to the other directors. A year later, Owens sold the property for a $10,000 profit. When one of the shareholders of Marsh Drugs discovered what Owens had done, the shareholder told Owens

that he would sue on behalf of the corporation if Owens did not turn over the $10,000 profit to the corporation. Could Owens be compelled by a court to turn over the $10,000 to the corporation? Explain.

27-6. Air Engineered Systems and Services, Inc., had three shareholders, Naquin, Dubois, and Hoffpauir. Each of the shareholders owned one-third of the corporation's outstanding shares. Naquin was fired after he had worked six years as an employee of the firm. He then formed a competing business, hired away one of the Air Engineered's employees, tried to hire another, and obtained a job for his own business which he had originally solicited for Air Engineered. Under Louisiana law, any shareholder who is also a business competitor is entitled to inspect the corporate records if he owns 25 percent of the outstanding shares for six months prior to the demand. When Naquin requested Air Engineered to allow him to inspect the corporate records, however, Air Engineered denied his request because Naquin refused to sign an indemnity agreement protecting Air Engineered from any damages it might suffer as a result of Naquin's use of the information contained in the corporate records. Shortly thereafter, Dubois and Hoffpauir voted to increase the capital stock of the corporation, and then they each purchased additional shares. This had the effect of reducing Naquin's percentage to less than 25 percent—which meant that Naquin was not entitled under Louisiana law to inspect Air Engineered's records. Naquin filed suit to require the corporation to permit him to inspect the books, since, at the time his request had been made, he owned more than 25 percent of the outstanding shares of Air Engineered. What was the result? [Naquin v. Air Engineered Systems and Services, Inc., 463 So.2d 992 (La.App. 1985)]

27-7. Midwest Management Corporation was looking for investment opportunities. Morris Stephens, one of Midwest's directors and chairman of the investment committee, proposed that Midwest provide financing for Stephens's son and his business colleagues who were in need of financing to open a broker-dealer business. Midwest agreed to propose to the shareholders for their approval an investment of $250,000 in the new business, on the condition that Stephens would manage the business and would purchase 100,000 shares of stock in the new firm. At each of two shareholder meetings, the directors informed the shareholders that Stephens agreed to the condition. Stephens was present at both meetings, and did not deny that he had agreed to purchase the 100,000 shares of stock and manage the new corporation. Upon the shareholders' approval, the $250,000 investment was made, and later another $150,000 when the new business suffered losses. About a year after it had opened, the business closed, and Midwest ended up losing over $325,000. Midwest then learned that Stephens had not kept his agreement to purchase stock in, or manage, the corporation. Midwest sued Stephens for breaching his fiduciary duties and asked for compensatory and punitive damages. Did

Midwest succeed? Explain. [Midwest Management Corp. v. Stephens, 353 N.W.2d 76 (Iowa 1984)]

27-8. Klinicki and Lundgren formed Berlinair, a closely held Oregon corporation, to provide air transportation out of West Germany. Klinicki, who owned 33 percent of the company stock, was the vice-president and a director. Lundgren, who also owned 33 percent of the stock, was the president and a director. Lelco, Inc., a corporation owned by Lundgren and his family, owned 33 percent of Berlinair, and Berlinair's attorney owned the last 1 percent of stock. One of the goals of Berlinair was to obtain a contract with BFR, a West German consortium of travel agents, to provide BFR with air charter service. Later, Lundgren learned that the BFR contract might become available. Lundgren then incorporated Air Berlin Charter Company, of which he was the sole owner, and bid for the BFR contract. Lundgren won the BFR contract for Air Berlin while using Berlinair working time, staff, money, and facilities without the knowledge of Klinicki. When Klinicki learned of the BFR contract, he filed a derivative suit, as a minority stockholder, against Air Berlin for usurping a corporate opportunity. Did Klinicki recover against Air Berlin? If so, what was Klinicki awarded as damages? [Klinicki v. Lundgren, 67 Or.App. 160, 678 P.2d 1250 (1984)]

27-9. Atlantic Properties, Inc., had only four shareholders, each of whom owned 25 percent of the capital stock. The bylaws required an 80 percent affirmative vote of the shareholders on all actions taken by the corporation. This provision had the effect of giving any of the four original shareholders a veto in corporate decisions. One shareholder refused for seven years to vote for any dividends, although he was warned that his actions might expose the corporation to Internal Revenue Service penalties for unreasonable accumulation of corporate earnings and profits. The Internal Revenue Service did impose such penalties on the corporation. Was the dissenting shareholder held personally liable for these penalties? Explain. [Smith v. Atlantic Properties, Inc., 12 Mass.App.Ct. 201, 422 N.E.2d 798 (1981)]

27-10. Dighton Grain, Inc., was a newly formed corporation operating a grain elevator business. Walter Gormley, the manager of the corporation, wrote $87,000 in corporate checks to himself during the first year of the firm's operation, kept inadequate records concerning grain shipments, and kept too short an inventory of grain. An auditor's report recommended that the directors have more frequent meetings, that Gormley discontinue his unauthorized use of the corporation's funds, and that new procedures be instituted by the corporation, such as requiring two signatures on corporate checks. None of these recommendations was followed, and Gormley continued to use corporate funds for his personal use. After it had been in business for two years, the firm went out of business, owing $400,000 to unsecured creditors. Gormley was convicted for misappropriating the firm's funds. One of the firm's creditors, Speer, brought a suit against the directors and officers of the corporation, alleging that they had been negligent in their duties and were thus personally liable for the debt to Speer. Did Speer succeed? [Speer v. Dighton Grain, Inc., 229 Kan. 272, 624 P.2d 952 (1981)]

Chapter 28

Corporations—Merger, Consolidation, and Termination

Corporations increase their holdings for a number of reasons. They may wish to enlarge their physical plants, increase their property or investment holdings, or acquire the assets, know-how, or goodwill of another corporation. Sometimes acquisition of another company is motivated by a desire to eliminate a competitor, to accomplish diversification, or to ensure adequate resources and markets for the acquiring corporation's product. Whatever the reason, in the business world of the 1980s, corporations acquiring other corporations has become a daily phenomenon and, to the uninformed observer, seems indeed to be represent a "scramble for the most daring" among the leading contenders, as Georges Bernanos predicted in the opening quote.

Typically, the corporation extends its operations by combining with another corporation in one of the following ways: merger, consolidation, purchase of assets, or purchase of a controlling interest in the other corporation. This chapter will examine the various ways that merger or consolidation alters the fundamental structure of the corporation. Dissolution and liquidation are the combined processes by which a corporation terminates its existence. The last part of this chapter will discuss the typical reasons for, and methods used in, terminating a corporation.

> *"The world belongs to risk. The world will soon be a matching of risks, a scramble for the most daring."*
>
> **Georges Bernanos (1888–1948) (French novelist and political commentator)**

❖ Merger and Consolidation

The terms *merger* and *consolidation* are often used interchangeably, but they refer to two legally distinct proceedings. The rights and liabilities of shareholders, the corporation, and its creditors are the same for both, however.

Merger

A **merger** involves the legal combination of two or more corporations in such a way that only one of the corporations continues to exist. For example, Corporation A and Corporation B decide to merge. It is agreed that A will absorb B, so upon merger, B ceases to exist as a separate entity and A continues as the *surviving corporation*.

After the merger, A is recognized as a single corporation, possessing all the rights, privileges, and powers of itself and B. It automatically acquires all of B's property and assets without the necessity of formal transfer or deed. Also, Corporation A

MERGER
A contractual process by which one corporation (the surviving corporation) acquires all the assets and liabilities of another corporation (the merged corporation). The shareholders of the merged corporation receive either payment for their shares or shares in the surviving corporation.

625

becomes liable for all of B's debts and obligations. Finally, A's articles of incorporation are deemed *amended* to include any changes that are stated in the *articles of merger*.

In the following case, the issue arose as to whether a business transaction constituted a sale or a merger.

Case 28.1
HAMAKER v. KENWEL-JACKSON MACHINE CO., INC.
Supreme Court of South Dakota, 1986.
387 N.W.2d 515.

FACTS On March 6, 1981, Carolyn Hamaker lost three fingers on her left hand while operating a notcher machine (a lathe) at her place of employment in South Dakota, Pallets and Wood Products. The notching machine had been manufactured by Kenwel Machine Company. On December 31, 1975, Kenwel sold its assets to John and Rosemary Jackson, who created a new company called Kenwel-Jackson Machine Company. Kenwel Machine Company terminated its existence in August of 1977. Kenwel-Jackson Machine Company continued to manufacture notchers, but they made several design changes and were in fact producing a different machine than the one that injured Carolyn Hamaker. The machine causing Hamaker's injury had been produced by Kenwel Machine Company.

As a result of her injuries, Hamaker brought a suit for damages against Kenwel-Jackson since Kenwel Machine Company no longer existed. The trial court granted Kenwel-Jackson's motion for summary judgment, and Hamaker appealed.

ISSUE The issue, in pertinent part, concerns whether the Jacksons' purchase of Kenwel Machine Company constituted a merger, in which they assumed both the assets and the liabilities of the Kenwel Machine Company. If so, under merger theory, Kenwel-Jackson could be held liable for Hamaker's injuries.

DECISION The appellate court affirmed the trial court's judgment in granting summary judgment to Kenwel-Jackson.

REASON Generally, a corporation that purchases the assets of another corporation does not succeed to the liabilities of the selling corporation. Exceptions to this rule exist, however, when (1) the purchasing corporation impliedly or expressly assumes the seller's liabilities; (2) the sale is really a merger, where one corporation absorbs another, assuming both the assets and the liabilities of the other, and where the other loses its existence as a separate entity; (3) when the purchaser continues the seller's corporation and retains the same personnel; and (4) when the sale is fraudulently executed to escape liability. Here the Jacksons accepted none of the liabilities of Kenwel Machine Company but only purchased its assets. Also, the Jacksons did not make any express or implied agreement to accept Kenwel Machine Company's liabilities. Finally, the personnel of the former corporation were not retained. Accordingly, the court concluded that Kenwel-Jackson was immune from any liability claims against Kenwel Machine Company.

CONSOLIDATION
A contractual and statutory process whereby two or more corporations join to become a completely new corporation. The original corporations cease to exist, and the new corporation acquires all their assets and liabilities.

Consolidation

In the case of a **consolidation,** two or more corporations combine in such a way that each corporation ceases to exist and a new one emerges. Corporation A and Corporation B consolidate to form an entirely new organization, Corporation C. In the process, A and B both terminate, and C comes into existence as an entirely new entity.

The results of a consolidation are essentially the same as the results of a merger. C is recognized as a new corporation and a single entity; A and B cease to exist. C accedes to all the rights, privileges, and powers previously held by A and B. Title to any property and assets owned by A and B passes to C without formal transfer. C assumes liability for all debts and obligations owed by A and B. The articles of consolidation *take the place of* A's and B's original corporate articles and are thereafter regarded as C's corporate articles.

Results of Merger or Consolidation

When a merger or a consolidation takes place, the surviving corporation or newly formed corporation issues shares to pay some fair consideration to the shareholders of the corporation that ceases to exist.

In a merger, the surviving corporation is vested with the disappearing corporation's preexisting legal rights and obligations. For example, if the disappearing corporation had a right of action against a third party, the surviving corporation can bring suit after the merger to recover the disappearing corporation's damages.

The corporation statutes of many states provide that a successor (surviving) corporation inherits a **chose in action** (a right to sue for a debt or sum of money) from a merging corporation as a matter of law. So, too, the common-law rule recognizes that a chose in action to enforce a property right upon merger will vest with the successor (surviving) corporation, and no right of action will remain with the disappearing corporation.

CHOSE IN ACTION
A right that can be enforced in court to recover a debt or to obtain damages.

Procedure for Merger or Consolidation

All states have statutes authorizing mergers and consolidations for domestic corporations, and most states allow the combination of domestic (in-state) and foreign (out-of-state) corporations. Although the procedures vary somewhat among jurisdictions, in each case the basic requirements are as follows:

1.   The board of directors of each corporation involved must approve a merger or consolidation plan.
2.   The shareholders of each corporation must vote approval of the plan at a shareholders' meeting. Most state statutes require the approval of two-thirds of the outstanding shares of voting stock, although some states require only a simple majority and others require a four-fifths vote. Frequently, statutes require that each class of stock approve the merger; thus, the holders of non-voting stock must also approve. A corporation's bylaws can dictate a stricter requirement.
3.   Once approved by all the directors and the shareholders, the plan (articles of merger or consolidation) is filed, usually with the secretary of state.
4.   When state formalities are satisfied, the state issues a certificate of merger to the surviving corporation or a certificate of consolidation to the newly consolidated corporation.

SHORT-FORM MERGER
A merger between a parent corporation and a subsidiary corporation where the parent corporation owns at least 90 percent of the outstanding shares of each class of stock issued by the subsidiary corporation. These mergers can be accomplished without shareholder approval of either corporation.

Short-Form Merger Statutes (Parent-Subsidiary Mergers)

The MBCA, Section 75, in most states provides a simplified procedure for the merger of a substantially owned subsidiary corporation into its parent corporation. Under these provisions, a **short-form merger** can be accomplished *without the approval of the shareholders* of either corporation.

The short-form merger can be utilized only when the parent corporation owns at least 90 percent of the outstanding shares of each class of stock of the subsidiary corporation. The simplified procedure requires that a plan for the merger be approved by the board of directors of the parent corporation before it is filed with the state. A copy of the merger plan must be sent to each shareholder of record of the subsidiary corporation. In the following case, a minority group of shareholders objected to a short-form merger undertaken to "cash out" public shareholders (including the plaintiffs in this case).

Case 28.2
ROLAND INTERNATIONAL CORP. v. NAJJAR
Supreme Court of Delaware, 1979.
407 A.2d 1032.

FACTS Roland International Corporation was 97.6 percent owned by Hyatt Corporation and others. This controlling group of shareholders created Landro Corporation for the purpose of merging it with Roland. All statutory requirements for a short-form merger were met, and the minority (public) shareholders were offered $5.25 per share for each share of Roland stock that they owned. If this price was not acceptable, the minority group could have their shares evaluated under the Delaware appraisal statute. Najjar brought a class action suit on behalf of the minority shareholders, seeking damages. Najjar claimed that the merger was simply an effort to eliminate the public shareholders and that it had been grossly inadequate and unfair to those shareholders. The defendants (the majority group) contended that a proper purpose is conclusively presumed when the conditions of the short-form merger

statutes are met, and the plaintiff had no cause of action. The defendants moved for dismissal on these grounds. The court of chancery denied the motion, and the defendants appealed.

ISSUE May a court examine a short-form merger to see if it was undertaken for a proper purpose?

DECISION Yes. The Supreme Court of Delaware affirmed the chancery court's denial of the defendants' motion to dismiss.

REASON The court held that the short-form merger statute does not create a presumption that the merger serves a valid purpose. The court may examine such mergers in order to determine whether the majority shareholders have met their fiduciary duty to the minority. When a merger is undertaken with the sole purpose of eliminating the minority shareholders, it constitutes a breach of that duty. The plaintiff thus had a cause of action, and the defendants' motion to dismiss was properly denied.

Appraisal Rights

APPRAISAL RIGHT
A dissenting shareholder's right to object to an extraordinary transaction of the corporation, such as a merger or consolidation, to have his or her shares appraised, and to be paid the fair-market value by the corporation.

What if a shareholder disapproves of the merger or consolidation but is outvoted by the other shareholders? The law recognizes that a dissenting shareholder should not be forced to become an unwilling shareholder in a corporation that is new or different from the one in which the shareholder originally invested. The shareholder has the right to dissent and may be entitled to be paid *fair value* for the number of shares held on the date of the merger or consolidation. (See MBCA, Section 80, and RMBCA, Section 13.02.)

This right is referred to as the shareholder's **appraisal right.** It is available only when a state statute specifically provides for it, and it may be lost if the elaborate

Profile

Robert Edward (Ted) Turner, III (1939–)

What do you do when your supplier raises the price of your goods, thus reducing your profits? One simple—if expensive—solution is to buy the supplier's business. This, at least, was Ted Turner's solution when MGM and other film studios raised the licensing fees for Hollywood films that Turner wanted to rerun on his WTBS cable TV channel.

Ted Turner is known for his "simple" solutions to major business problems and for avoiding the so-called fine print of contracts. Sometimes, this penchant has been costly—as in the attempted, but unsuccessful, takeover of CBS in 1985, in which he lost $23 million in fees to lawyers and investment bankers. More commonly, though, he has gambled and won. In the MGM deal, the results are not yet clear. Although he acquired the greatest film library in existence (3,650 films, approximately 35

percent of which are enduring classics), whether he can afford the debt incurred by the purchase of MGM—which amounted essentially to the film library of MGM, since he sold off the production facilities included in the purchase—remains to be seen.

To all who know him, Ted Turner is an enigmatic, energetic, and totally unpredictable individual. He is a risk-taker of dangerous proportions, adept at business "brinksmanship," and yet he never seems to lose sight of the appropriate "edge" in any bargaining situation.

Turner was raised by a wealthy Savannah, Georgia, family. Educated in his early years at a military academy, he later attended Brown University and embarked upon an education in the classics. In 1963, however, upon his father's death, Turner inherited a billboard business

worth approximately $1 million. Immediately, Ted Turner was faced with difficulties. His father, before his death, had made arrangements to sell the billboard firm. The younger Turner, however, determined to keep the business, convinced the prospective buyers that he would sabotage the firm before the deal was closed by transferring leases with landowners to another company which he had inherited. Turner ended up keeping the business; his career was launched.

Although he was only twenty-four years old when his father died, Turner caught on quickly to the necessities of the business world. He bought more billboard companies, then radio stations, and learned to live with debt. In 1969 he took his company public in a merger by which he acquired a small radio station, now known as WTBS. By

(continued on next page)

In 1980, Turner started Cable News Network (CNN), a 24-hour cable TV news channel.

Profile—Continued

1976 Turner transformed the small station into a nationwide satellite cable TV network that eventually reached 36 million U.S. homes. In 1980, Cable News Network (CNN) emerged—the 24-hour cable TV news channel. A further spin-off was "Headline News," a cable TV offering of condensed CNN programming.

All of Turner's major "deals" in the commercial world have been undertaken with the welfare of WTBS in mind. Certainly the CBS venture and the MGM venture were undertaken for that reason. Since about half of WTBS's programming consists of old movie classics, the increased fees charged by MGM and other Hollywood studios meant a significant decline in profits for WTBS. According to Turner's chief financial officer, Bill Bevins, the higher rates charged by MGM and other Hollywood studios would have reduced WTBS's profits from 40 percent of sales in 1985 to a meager 10 percent of sales in 1990.[1]

Although to all acquainted with the terms of the MGM/Turner transaction, Turner paid far too high a price for the film library, few who know Turner are willing to predict disaster for this particular gambler. In view of his past record, most observers simply bate their breath, and wait and see.

1. *Fortune* Magazine, July 7, 1986, p. 28.

statutory procedures are not precisely followed. Whenever the right is lost, the dissenting shareholder must go along with the objectionable transaction.

The appraisal right is normally extended to regular mergers, consolidations, short-form mergers, sales of substantially all the corporate assets not in the ordinary course of business, and, in certain states, adverse amendments to the articles of incorporation.

One of the usual procedures requires that a written notice of dissent be filed by dissenting shareholders prior to the vote of the shareholders on the proposed transaction. This notice of dissent is also basically a notice to all shareholders of costs that may be imposed by dissenting shareholders should the merger or consolidation be approved. In addition, after approval, the dissenting shareholders must make a written demand for payment and for fair value.

Valuation of shares is often a point of contention between the dissenting shareholder and the corporation. The MBCA, Section 81, provides that the "fair value of shares" is the value on the day prior to the date on which the vote was taken.[1] The corporation must make a *written* offer to purchase a dissenting shareholder's stock, accompanying the offer with a current balance sheet and income statement for the applicable (appropriate) corporation. If the shareholder and the corporation do not agree on the fair value, a court will determine it.

Once a dissenting shareholder elects appraisal rights under statute, most courts[2] hold that the shareholder may not withdraw from the appraisal process without securing the approval of the board of directors.

The following case illustrates the frequently encountered problem of determining the fair value of shares under appraisal rights.

---

1. Section 81(a)(3) of the MBCA says the fair value excludes any appreciation or depreciation of the stock in anticipation of the approval.

2. Exceptions include, for example, Rhode Island's provision that a stockholder may withdraw his or her demand at any time prior to the appraiser's report.

Case 28.3
WELSH v. INDEPENDENT BANK AND TRUST CO.
Appellate Court of Connecticut, 1983.
1 Conn.App. 14, 467 A.2d 941.

FACTS Two Connecticut banks, the Willimantic Trust Company and the Norwich State Bank and Trust Company, proposed a merger to their stockholders. Willimantic was to be the surviving bank. After the merger, the stockholders voted to change Willimantic's name to the Independent Bank and Trust Company, the named defendant in this case. The bank determined that the fair value of the stock was $76 on the day prior to the announcement of the merger by mail. The dissenting shareholders rejected the $76 valuation and sought judicial determination of the fair value of their shares. The trial judge set the value of the stock at $105 per share, on the ground that transfers of Willimantic stock had occurred at prices between $100 and $105.50 per share between the first newspaper announcement about the proposed merger and the end of the merger year. The bank appealed, arguing that the trial judge, in setting the value of the stock at $105 per share, erroneously relied on the "market value" approach in determining the "fair value" of the shares of stock instead of on book value, dividend yield, earnings value, and other methods of value determination.

ISSUE Was the trial court correct in appraising the shares on the basis of their market value?

DECISION Yes. The appellate court affirmed the trial judge's decision and held that using the "market value" approach in determining the fair value of the shares of stock was correct.

REASON The court disagreed with the bank's arguments, stating that the true value the stockholder is entitled to be paid is his or her proportionate interest in the "going concern" involved in the merger. It is up to the trier of fact to "determine the fair value of the share of the shareholders entitled to payment therefore," and in determining a fair value, "it is within the discretion of the trier of fact to select the most appropriate method of valuation under the facts."

Shareholder Approval

Shareholders invest in a corporate enterprise with the expectation that the board of directors will manage the enterprise and will approve ordinary business matters. Actions taken on extraordinary matters must be authorized by the board of directors and the shareholders. Often, modern statutes require that certain types of extraordinary matters—such as the sale, lease, or exchange of all or substantially all corporate assets outside of the corporation's regular course of business—be approved by a prescribed voter consent of the shareholders. Other examples of matters requiring shareholder approval include amendments to the articles of incorporation, transactions concerning merger or consolidation, and dissolution.

Hence, when any extraordinary matter arises, the corporation must proceed as authorized by law to obtain shareholder and board of director approval. Sometimes a transaction can be characterized in such a way as not to require shareholder approval, but, in that event, a court will use its equity powers to require such approval. In order to determine the nature of the transaction, the courts will look not only to the details of the transaction but also to its consequences.

Purchase of Assets

When a corporation acquires all or substantially all of the assets of another corporation by direct purchase, the purchasing, or *acquiring*, corporation simply extends its

Business Law in Action

Cashing Out—Too Soon

"Look before you leap"/"An ounce of caution is worth a pound of foolishness"/"You can't put spilt milk back into the glass." So the old maxims continue to instruct. And hindsight always proves them right, of course. But hindsight, unfortunately, is not available before the deed is done, as some of the minority shareholders of Kirby Lumber Corporation realized.

The problem arose as a result of a short-form merger between Kirby and another corporation, Forest Industries, Inc. In a short-form merger, as discussed in the text, approval of shareholders is not required because the short-form merger is allowed only in instances where a parent company is at least a 90-percent owner of a subsidiary corporation. Kirby was 95 percent

owned by Santa Fe Industries, Inc. Forest Industries was a wholly owned subsidiary of Santa Fe Natural Resources, Inc., which in turn was a wholly owned subsidiary of Santa Fe Industries. The lineage becomes complicated. Suffice it to say that Kirby's minority shareholders, as a result of the merger, were given notice of their right to *cash out* at $150 per share or to elect a judicial appraisal hearing. (Under Delaware law, which was applicable to the corporations in this case, the exclusive remedy for minority shareholders who disputed the fair value of their shares was to seek a judicial appraisal.)

Some of the minority shareholders opted to accept the $150-per-share offer, while others elected an appraisal. The appraisal proceeding resulted in a determination that the fair-market value of a Kirby share was $254.40.[1] The minority shareholders who had

accepted the $150 payment were, understandably, upset about their decision. They brought suit against Santa Fe, alleging that the merger was a "self-motivated" takeover, which fraudulently enriched the majority at the expense of the minority.

The court, however, disagreed. The minority shareholders had the option of the judicial appraisal. The fact that they did not elect to choose that option was nobody's fault but their own. The only other alternative for the minority shareholders was to fight the merger, but, since the minority shareholders controlled only 5 percent of Kirby stock, that would have been a patently useless endeavor.[2]

1. Bell v. Kirby Lumber Corp., 413 A.2d 137, 139 (Del. 1980).
2. See Loengard v. Santa Fe Industries, Inc., 639 F.Supp. 673 (S.D.N.Y. 1986).

ownership and control over more physical assets. Since no change in the legal entity occurs, the acquiring corporation is not required to obtain shareholder approval for the purchase.[3]

Although the acquiring corporation may not be required to obtain shareholder approval for such an acquisition, the Department of Justice has issued guidelines that significantly constrain and often prohibit mergers that could result from a purchase of assets, including takeover bids. These guidelines are part of the federal antitrust laws to enforce Section 7 of the Clayton Act (discussed in Chapter 30).

Note that the corporation that is selling all its assets is substantially changing its business position and perhaps its ability to carry out its corporate purposes. For that reason, the corporation whose assets are acquired must obtain both board of director and shareholder approval. In some states, a dissenting shareholder of the selling corporation can demand appraisal rights.

---

3. If the acquiring corporation plans to pay for the assets with its own corporate stock and not enough authorized unissued shares are available, the shareholders must vote to approve issuance of additional shares by amendment of the corporate articles. Also, acquiring corporations whose stock is traded in a national stock exchange can be required to obtain their own shareholders' approval if they plan to issue a significant number of shares, such as 20 percent or more of the outstanding shares.

To illustrate: The Southwestern Cotton Oil Company created a wholly owned subsidiary called Machine Works and transferred substantially all its assets to the subsidiary. A minority shareholder of Southwestern objected to the transaction and demanded appraisal rights, as provided in the Oklahoma statutes. The Oklahoma statute provided for appraisal rights for a dissenting shareholder when a corporation undertook the "sale, lease, exchange or other disposition of all or substantially all" of a corporation's assets. Southwestern refused the minority shareholder's demand. In a subsequent action the court denied Southwestern's claim that the transfer of its assets to a wholly owned subsidiary did not come within the statute. Therefore, shareholder approval was required, and the transfer created appraisal rights for dissenting shareholders.[4]

Purchase of Stock

An alternative to the purchase of another corporation's assets is the purchase of a substantial number of the voting shares of its stock. This enables the acquiring corporation to control the acquired, or *target*, corporation. The acquiring corporation deals directly with the shareholders in seeking to purchase the shares they hold.

A so-called takeover bid is subject to state and federal securities regulations. When the acquiring corporation makes a public offer to all shareholders of the target cor-

---

4. Campbell v. Vose, 515 F.2d 256 (10th Cir. 1975).

Drawing by Ed Fischer; © 1972, The New Yorker Magazine.

"When I agreed to the merger, Fairchild, I never contemplated this!"

poration, it is called a *tender offer* (an offer that is publicly advertised and addressed to all shareholders of the target company). The price of the stock in the tender offer is generally higher than the market price of the target stock prior to the announcement of the tender offer. The higher price induces shareholders to tender their shares to the acquiring firm.

The tender offer can be conditional upon the receipt of a specified number of outstanding shares by a specified date. The offering corporation can make an *exchange tender offer* in which it offers target stockholders its own securities in exchange for their target stock. In a *cash tender offer*, the offering corporation offers the target stockholders cash in exchange for their target stock.

Federal securities laws strictly control the terms, duration, and circumstances under which most tender offers are made. In addition, over thirty states have passed takeover statutes that impose additional regulations on tender offers. The use of the tender offer as a method of gaining corporate control began in the mid-1960s. Highly contested legal battles and enormous expenses involved in complying with federal and state regulations have worked in some cases to discourage the use of tender offers as a vehicle for obtaining control of a corporation through stock purchase. Recently, many tender offers have received national attention. In some cases, tenders have resulted in millions of dollars being made by the purchaser under a buyout agreement.

❖ Termination

DISSOLUTION
The formal disbanding of a partnership or a corporation. It can take place by (1) agreement of the parties or the shareholders and board or directors, (2) by the death of a partner, (3) by the expiration of a time period stated in a partnership agreement or a certificate of incorporation, (4) or by court order.

LIQUIDATION
The sale of assets of a business or an individual for cash and the distribution of the cash received to creditors with the balance going to the owner(s).

Termination of a corporate life has two phases. **Dissolution** is the legal death of the artificial "person" of the corporation. **Liquidation** is the process by which corporate assets are converted into cash and distributed among creditors and shareholders according to specific rules of preference.[5]

Dissolution can be brought about in any of the following ways:

1. An act of a legislature in the state of incorporation.
2. Expiration of the time provided in the certificate of incorporation.
3. Voluntary approval of the shareholders and the board of directors.
4. Unanimous action by all shareholders.
5. Court decree brought about by the attorney general of the state of incorporation for any of the following reasons: (a) the failure to comply with administrative requirements (for example, failure to pay annual franchise taxes or to submit an annual report or to have a designated registered agent); (b) the procurement of a corporation charter through fraud or misrepresentation upon the state; (c) the abuse of corporate powers (*ultra vires* acts); (d) the violation of the state criminal code after the demand to discontinue has been made by the secretary of the state; (e) the failure to commence business operations; or (f) the abandonment of operations before starting up.

Process of Liquidation

When dissolution takes place by voluntary action, the members of the board of directors act as trustees of the corporate assets. As trustees, they are responsible for

---

5.   Upon dissolution, the liquidated assets are first used to pay creditors. Any remaining assets are distributed to shareholders according to their respective stock rights; preferred stock has priority over common stock, generally by charter. See Chapter 29.

winding up the affairs of the corporation for the benefit of corporate creditors and shareholders. This makes the board members personally liable for any breach of their fiduciary trustee duties.

Liquidation can be accomplished without court supervision unless the members of the board do not wish to act in this capacity, or unless shareholders or creditors can show cause to the court why the board should not be permitted to assume the trustee function. In either case, the court will appoint a receiver to wind up the corporate affairs and liquidate corporate assets. A receiver is always appointed by the court if the dissolution is involuntary.

Involuntary Dissolution

Sometimes an involuntary dissolution of a corporation is necessary. For example, the board of directors may be deadlocked. Courts hesitate to order involuntary dissolution in such circumstances unless there is specific statutory authorization to do so, but if the deadlock cannot be resolved by the shareholders, and if it will irreparably injure the corporation, the court will proceed with an involuntary dissolution. Courts can also dissolve a corporation for mismanagement. In the following case, two of the shareholders in a close corporation petitioned for the dissolution of a corporation after they were fired as employees of the corporation.

Case 28.4
GUNZBERG v. ART-LLOYD METAL PRODUCTS CORP.

New York Supreme Court, Appellate Division, Second Department, 1985.
112 A.D.2d 423, 492 N.Y.S.2d 83.

FACTS In 1946 Fred Gunzberg helped his father form Art-Lloyd Metal Products Corporation, and together they built it into a successful company. In 1955 Fred's brother Lloyd joined the business, and the two brothers were responsible for the day-to-day running of the firm—although the father had the final say in business matters until a stroke incapacitated him. In 1961 another brother, Arthur, joined the firm. This lawsuit arose as a result of a falling out among the brothers in 1979, when Arthur was elected president of the corporation, and another brother and sister were elected as officers on the board of directors. After the election, Fred and Lloyd were fired as employees of the corporation, after which they sought judicial dissolution of the corporation based upon the majority faction's oppression. The trial court ordered the dissolution, and the corporation appealed.

ISSUE Should dissolution of the corporation be permitted?

DECISION Yes. The trial court's decision was affirmed by the appellate court.

REASON The New York court noted that, under New York corporate law, a judicial dissolution may be presented by "the holders of twenty percent or more of all outstanding shares of a corporation . . . who are entitled to vote in an election of directors." In this case, Fred and Lloyd jointly owned 41 percent of the corporate shares that had been issued. The court quoted the New York Court of Appeals that held where a petitioner has "set forth a prima facie case of oppressive conduct, it should be incumbent upon the parties seeking to forestall dissolution to demonstrate to the court the existence of an adequate, alternative remedy." In this case, the corporation had failed to suggest any alternative remedy—adequate or otherwise. Further quoting the New York Court of Appeals, the court stated that a "court has broad latitude in fashioning alternative relief, but when fulfillment of the oppressed petitioner's expectations by these means is doubtful, such as when there has been a complete deterioration of relations between the parties, a court should not hesitate to order dissolution."

❖ Chapter Summary: Corporations—Merger, Consolidation, and Termination

Merger and Consolidation	1. *Merger*—Involves the legal combination of two or more corporations whereby the surviving corporation acquires all the assets and obligations of the other corporation, which then ceases to exist.
	2. *Consolidation*—Involves two or more corporations combining so that each corporation ceases to exist and a new one emerges. The new corporation assumes all assets and obligations of the former corporations.
	3. *Procedure*—Determined by state statutes. Basic requirements are: a. The board of directors of each corporation involved must approve the merger or consolidation plan. b. The shareholders of each corporation must approve the merger or shareholder plan at a shareholders' meeting. c. Articles of merger or consolidation (the plan) must be filed, usually with the secretary of state. d. The state issues a certificate of merger (or consolidation) to the surviving (or newly consolidated) corporation.
	4. *Short-form mergers (parent-subsidy mergers)*—Possible when the parent corporation owns at least 90 percent of the outstanding shares of each class of stock of the subsidiary corporation. a. Shareholder approval not required. b. Must be approved only by the board of directors of the parent corporation. c. A copy of the merger plan must be sent to each shareholder of record. d. The merger plan must be filed with the state.
	5. *Appraisal rights*—Rights of shareholders (given by state statute) to receive the *fair value* for their shares when a merger or consolidation takes place. If the shareholder and the corporation do not agree on the fair value, a court will determine it.
	6. *Purchase of assets*—The acquisition by an acquiring corporation of all or substantially all of the assets of another corporation. a. The acquiring corporation is not required to obtain shareholder approval; the corporation is merely increasing its assets, and no fundamental business change occurs. b. The acquired corporation is required to obtain the approval of both its directors and its shareholders for the sale of its assets, since this creates a substantial change in its business position.
	7. *Purchase of stock*—Another way for an acquiring corporation to obtain control over the acquired (target) corporation is to purchase a substantial number of the voting shares of its stock. a. Tender offer—A public offer to all shareholders of the target corporation to purchase its stock (takeover bid) at a price generally higher than the market price of the target stock prior to the announcement of the tender offer. b. Federal and state securities laws strictly control the terms, duration, and circumstances under which most tender offers are made.
Termination	The termination of a corporation involves the following two phases:
	1. *Dissolution*—The legal death of the artificial "person" of the corporation. Dissolution can be brought about in any of the following ways: a. An act of a legislature in the state of incorporation. b. Expiration of the time provided in the corporate charter. c. Voluntary approval of the shareholders and the board of directors. d. Unanimous action by all shareholders. e. Court decree.
	2. *Liquidation*—The process by which corporate assets are converted into cash and distributed to creditors and shareholders according to specified rules of preference. May be supervised by members of the board of directors (when dissolution is voluntary) or by a receiver appointed by the court to wind up corporate affairs.

❖ Questions and Case Problems

28-1. Jolson is chairman of the board of directors of Artel, Inc., and Douglas is chairman of the board of directors of Fox Express, Inc. Artel is a manufacturing corporation, and Fox Express is a transportation corporation. Jolson and Douglas meet to consider the possibility of combining their corporations and activities into a single corporate entity. They consider two alternative courses of action: Artel acquiring all of the stock and assets of Fox Express, or both corporations combining to form a new corporation, called A&F Enterprises, Inc. Both chairmen are concerned about the necessity of a formal transfer of property, liability for existing debts, and the problem of amending the articles of incorporation. Discuss what the two proposed combinations are called and the legal effect each has on the transfer of property, the liabilities of the combined corporations, and the need to amend the articles of incorporation.

28-2. Tally Ho Company, Inc., was merged into Perfecto Corporation, Perfecto being the surviving corporation in the merger. Dawson, a creditor of Tally Ho, brought suit against Perfecto Corporation for payment of the debt. The directors of Perfecto refused to pay, stating that Tally Ho no longer existed and that Perfecto had never agreed to assume any of Tally Ho's liabilities. Discuss fully whether Dawson will be able to recover from Perfecto.

28-3. Ten-Four Corporation is a small midwestern business that owns a valuable patent. Ten-Four has approximately 1,000 shareholders with 100,000 authorized and outstanding shares. Bartlett Corporation would like to have use of the patent, but Ten-Four refuses to give Bartlett a license. Bartlett has tried to acquire Ten-Four by purchasing Ten-Four's assets, but Ten-Four's board of directors has refused to approve the acquisition. Ten-Four's shares are presently selling for $5 per share. Discuss how Bartlett Corporation might proceed in order to gain the control and use of Ten-Four's patent.

28-4. Frank Enterprises, Inc., purchased all the assets of Grosmont Corporation. The directors of both corporations approved of the sale, and 80 percent of Grosmont's shareholders approved. The shareholders of Frank Enterprises, however, were never consulted. Some of these shareholders claimed that the purchase was thus invalid. Are they correct? Explain.

28-5. Determine which of the following situations describes a consolidation:

    (a) Arkon Corporation purchases all of the assets of Hill Company, Inc.

    (b) Arkon Corporation and Hill Company, Inc., effect a combination of their firms, with Arkon Corporation being the surviving corporation.

    (c) Arkon Corporation and Hill Company, Inc., agree to combine their assets, dissolve their old corporations, and form a new corporation under a new name.

    (d) Arkon Corporation agrees to sell all its accounts receivable to Hill Company, Inc.

28-6. Gabhart was one of five shareholders in a corporation in which all the shareholders were also directors. Gabhart resigned as a director but refused to sell his shares. The other four shareholders formed a new corporation and merged the old one into it. Gabhart was not a stockholder in the new corporation, which was the surviving company. The only reason for the merger was to obtain Gabhart's shares. Was this action by the corporation viewed as a dissolution? If so, how did it affect Gabhart's rights? [Gabhart v. Gabhart, 267 Ind. 370, 370 N.E.2d 345 (1977)]

28-7. International General Industries, Inc. (IGI), purchased 81 percent of the outstanding shares of Kliklok and then merged Kliklok with an IGI subsidiary, KLK. All were Delaware corporations. IGI claimed that the purpose of the merger was to facilitate long-term debt financing of the parent corporation. All boards of directors and all shareholders approved, and the merger was carried out in accordance with Delaware statutes. The minority shareholders of Kliklok were paid $11 cash per share, with the understanding that they had the option to statutory appraisal rights if they disagreed with the $11 price. The minority shareholders of Kliklok brought suit against the directors of IGI, claiming that the merger was undertaken for the sole benefit of the parent corporation. When a merger is done in accordance with state laws but is solely for the benefit of the parent corporation, is it lawful? Explain. [Tanzer v. International General Industries, Inc., 379 A.2d 1121 (Del. 1977)]

28-8. Two couples, the Kimmelmans and the Zauderers, held approximately two-thirds of the outstanding shares of 79 Realty Corporation, a Madison Avenue firm. Alpert and three other shareholders (the Alpert group) owned 26 percent of the outstanding shares. Madison 28 Associates, a limited partnership formed by investors who wanted to purchase the 79 Realty Corporation, successfully negotiated with the Zimmermans and the Zauderers to purchase their shares. Once Madison Associates was in control, four of the Madison partners were appointed to the board of 79 Realty Corporation. The new directors, who now controlled 79 Realty, approved a plan to merge the 79 Realty Corporation with Williams Street, Realty Corporation, being the surviving corporation. A shareholders' meeting was called to approve the plan, with proper notice being sent to all shareholders as to the purpose of the meeting, and the merger was approved by a two-thirds vote of the shareholders. The Alpert group sued Madison Associates, alleging that the merger was illegal because it was undertaken for the sole benefit of the Madison group, and since the Madison group controlled both firms involved in the merger, there was a clear conflict of interest. The Madison group defended on the basis that the merger was beneficial to the 79 Realty's corporate interests because it advanced proper business interests: More capital would be available for necessary renovations of the 79 Realty building, and more tax advantages could be gained. Did Madison succeed in this defense? [Alpert v. 28 Williams St.

Corp., 63 N.Y.2d 557, 483 N.Y.S.2d 667, 473 N.E.2d 19 (1984)]

28-9. In 1956 the assets of Indiana Foundry Machine & Supply Company, Inc., were purchased by a newly incorporated firm who did business under the same name. There was no agreement to assume the liabilities of the purchased corporation. The old firm ceased doing business. Many of the old firm's products continued to be manufactured by the new firm, and several employees of the old firm were retained. None of the shareholders, officers, or directors of the new firm, however, had owned or managed the old firm. In 1962 the new firm merged with Union Tool Corporation, which, by written agreement, assumed all of the obligations of the Indiana Foundry Machine & Supply. In 1981 Marsha Bullington brought a products liability suit against Union Tool Corporation for damages suffered as a result of using a table saw manufactured by Indiana Foundry Machine & Supply (the old firm) sometime prior to 1956. The new Indiana Foundry Machine & Supply never manufactured table saws of any kind. Discuss whether Bullington can recover damages from Union Tool Corporation. [Bullington v. Union Tool Corp., 254 Ga. 283, 328 S.E.2d 726 (1985)]

28-10. Galdi was a shareholder of BankEast Corporation. BankEast proposed a merger with another bank, and Galdi voted against the merger and perfected her right to statutory appraisal. BankEast and Galdi could not agree on the value of the stock, so they each appointed an appraiser, who appointed a third appraiser. All three appraisers agreed on the value of the stock. Galdi, still not pleased with the price, withdrew from the appraisal process. BankEast went to court to compel Galdi to accept the appraisal and transfer the stock. What was the result? [BankEast Corporation v. Galdi, 125 N.H. 280, 480 A.2d 136 (1984)]

Chapter 29

Corporations—Financing, Financial Regulation, and Investor Protection

As discussed in the "Landmark" in this chapter, after the stock market crash of 1929, various studies showed a need for regulating securities markets. Basically, legislation for such regulation was enacted to provide investors with more information in order to help them to make buying and selling decisions and, as indicated by the opening quotation, to prohibit deceptive, unfair, and manipulative practices. Today, the sale and transfer of securities are heavily regulated by federal and state statutes and by government agencies. This is a complex area of the law. This chapter will first look at corporate financing and the sale of corporate securities, and then at the nature of federal securities regulations and their effect on the business world.

"It shall be unlawful for any person in the offer or sale of any security . . . to engage in any transaction, practice, or course of business which operates or would operate as a fraud or deceit upon the purchaser."

Securities Act of 1933, Section 17

SECURITIES
Stock certificates, bonds, notes, debentures, warrants, or other documents given as evidence of an ownership interest in the corporation or as a promise of repayment by the corporation.

EQUITY SECURITIES
Securities or shares of capital stock representing an ownership interest in a corporation rather than debt.

DEBT SECURITIES
Securities evidencing an obligation of the corporation to repay the holder, rather than an investment by the holder in exchange for stock.

❖ Corporate Financing

In order to obtain financing, corporations issue **securities**—evidence of the obligation to pay money or of the right to participate in earnings and the distribution of corporate trusts and other property. The principal method of long-term and initial corporate financing is the issuance of stocks (equity) and bonds (debt), both of which are sold to investors. Stocks, or **equity securities,** represent the purchase of ownership in the business firm. Bonds (debentures), or **debt securities,** represent the borrowing of money by firms (and governments).[1] Of course, not all debt is in the form of debt securities. Some is in the form of accounts payable, some is in the form of notes payable, and some is in the form of leaseholds. Accounts and notes payable are typically short-term debts. Bonds are simply a way for the corporation to split up its long-term debt so that it can market it more easily.

---

1. The term *bonds* is often used to describe both secured and unsecured obligations. Technically, however, bonds are secured by a lien or other security interest; debentures are unsecured.

Bonds

BOND
A certificate that evidences a corporate debt. It is a security that involves no ownership interest in the issuing corporation.

Bonds are issued by business firms and by governments at all levels as evidence of the funds they are borrowing from investors. Bonds almost always have a designated *maturity date*—the date when the principal or face amount of the bond (or loan) is returned to the investor—and are sometimes referred to as *fixed-income securities* because their owners receive a fixed-dollar interest payment during the period of time prior to maturity.

The characteristics of corporate bonds vary widely, in part because corporations differ in their ability to generate the earnings and cash flow necessary to make interest payments and to repay the principal amount of the bonds at maturity. Furthermore, corporate bonds are only a part of the total debt and the overall financial structure of corporate business.

In the bond trade, the word *bond* refers specifically to a debenture with a face value of $1,000. Bonds can be sold below their face value at a *discount* or above their face value at a *premium*. Bonds sold at a premium have yields that are less than their *coupon*, or stated (face), rate; those sold at a discount have yields that are greater than their face rate.

BOND INDENTURE
An instrument of secured indebtedness issued by a corporation.

Because debt financing represents a legal obligation on the part of the corporation, various features and terms of a particular bond issue are specified in a lending agreement called a **bond indenture**. A corporate trustee, often a commercial bank trust department, represents the collective well-being of all bondholders in ensuring that the terms of the bond issue are met by the corporation. The bond indenture specifies the maturity date of the bond and the pattern of interest payments until maturity. Most corporation bonds pay semiannually a coupon rate of interest on the $1,000 face amount of the bond.

Different types of corporate bonds exist. *Debentures* are bonds for which no specific assets of the corporation are pledged as backing; rather, they are backed by the general credit rating of the corporation, plus any assets that can be seized if the corporation allows the debentures to go into default. *Mortgage bonds*, however, pledge specific property. If the corporation defaults on the bonds, the bondholders can take the property. *Convertible bonds* are those that can be exchanged for a specified number of shares of common stock when and if the bondholder so desires. *Callable bonds* may be called in and the principal repaid at specified times or under conditions specified in the bond when it is issued.

Stocks

STOCK
An equity or ownership interest in a corporation, measured in units of shares.

Issuing **stocks** is another way corporations obtain financing. The ways in which stocks differ from bonds are summarized in Exhibit 29-1. Basically, stocks represent ownership in a business firm, whereas bonds represent borrowing by the firm. The most important characteristics of stocks are:

1. They need not be paid back.
2. The stockholder receives dividends only when so voted by the directors.
3. Stockholders are the last investors to be paid off upon dissolution.
4. Stockholders vote for management and on major issues.

◆ **Exhibit 29-1**
How Do Stocks and Bonds Differ?

STOCKS	BONDS
1. Stocks represent ownership.	1. Bonds represent owed debt.
2. Stocks (common) do not have a fixed dividend rate.	2. Interest on bonds must always be paid, whether or not any profit is earned.
3. Stockholders can elect a board of directors, which controls the corporation.	3. Bondholders usually have no voice in or control over management of the corporation.
4. Stocks do not have a maturity date; the corporation does not usually repay the stockholder.	4. Bonds have a maturity date when the bondholder is to be repaid the face value of the bond.
5. All corporations issue or offer to sell stocks. This is the usual definition of a corporation.	5. Corporations do not necessarily issue bonds.
6. Stockholders have a claim against the property and income of a corporation after all creditors' claims have been met.	6. Bondholders have a claim against the property and income of a corporation that must be met before the claims of stockholders.

Exhibit 29-2 offers a summary of the types of stocks issued by corporations. The two major types are *common stock* and *preferred stock*.

Common Stock   Common stock represents the true ownership of a corporation. It provides a threefold proportionate interest in the corporation with regard to (1) control,

COMMON STOCK
Shares of ownership in a corporation that are lowest in priority with respect to payment of dividends and distribution of the corporation's assets upon dissolution.

The common stocks of many larger corporations are traded on the floor of the New York Stock Exchange.

♦ **Exhibit 29-2**
   Stocks

Stocks	
TYPES	**DEFINITIONS**
Common Stock	Voting shares that represent ownership interests in a corporation with lowest priorities with respect to payment of dividends and distribution of assets upon the corporation's dissolution.
Preferred Stock	Shares of stock that have priority over common stock shares as to payment of dividends and distribution of assets upon corporate dissolution. Dividend payments are usually a fixed percentage of the face value of the share.
Cumulative Preferred Stock	Required dividends not paid in a given year must be paid in a subsequent year before any common stock dividends are paid.
Participating Preferred Stock	The owner is entitled to receive dividends from funds available after preferred shareholders receive required agreed dividends, and common shareholders receive prescribed dividends.
Convertible Preferred Stock	Preferred shareholders with the option to convert their shares into a specified number of common shares either in the issuing corporation or, sometimes, in another corporation.
Redeemable or Callable Preferred Stock	Preferred shares issued with the express condition that the issuing corporation has the right to repurchase the shares as specified.
Authorized Shares	Shares allowed to be issued by the articles of incorporation.
Issued Shares	Shares that are actually transferred to shareholders.
Outstanding Shares	Authorized and issued shares still held by shareholders.
Treasury Shares	Shares that are authorized and issued, but are not outstanding (reacquired by the corporation).
No Par Value	Shares issued with no stated value. The price is usually fixed by the board of directors or shareholders.
Par Value	Shares issued and priced at a stated value per share.
Watered Shares	Shares issued (as fully paid) for transfer of property or services rendered, where in fact the value of such property or services is less than the par value or stated board or shareholder price for no par shares.

(2) earning capacity, and (3) net assets. A shareholder's interest is generally in proportion to the number of shares owned out of the total number of shares issued.

Voting rights in a corporation apply to the election of the firm's board of directors and to any proposed changes in the ownership structure of the firm.[2] For example, a holder of common stock generally has the right to vote in a decision on a proposed merger, since mergers can change the proportion of ownership.

Firms are not obligated to return a principal amount per share to each holder of common stock, since no firm can ensure that the market price per share of its common

---

2. State corporation law specifies the types of issues on which shareholder approval must be obtained.

stock will not go down over time. Neither need the issuing firm guarantee a dividend; indeed, some business firms never pay dividends.

Holders of common stock are a group of investors who assume a *residual* position in the overall financial structure of a business. In terms of receiving payment for their investment, they are last in line. The earnings to which they are entitled also depend on all the other groups—suppliers, employees, managers, bankers, governments, bondholders, and holders of preferred stock—being paid what is due them first. Once those groups are paid, however, the owners of common stock may be entitled to *all* the remaining earnings. (But the board of directors is not normally under any duty to declare the remaining earnings as dividends.)

This is the central feature of ownership in any corporation, be it a corner grocery, a retail store, an architectural firm, or a giant international oil corporation. In each instance, the owners of common stock occupy the riskiest position, but they can expect a correspondingly greater return on their investment. Again, it can be seen why the return-and-risk pattern holds. As one moves from savings accounts and U.S. government bonds to corporate bonds with different ratings to preferred stock and, finally, to common stock, expected returns increase to compensate for the higher risks that are undertaken.

Preferred Stock   **Preferred stock** is stock with *preferences*. Usually, this means that holders of preferred stock have priority over holders of common stock as to dividends and to payment upon dissolution of the corporation. Preferred-stock shareholders may or may not have the right to vote.

From an investment standpoint, preferred stock is more similar to bonds than to common stock. It is not included among the liabilities of a business because it is equity. Like other equity securities, preferred shares have no fixed maturity date for when they must be retired by the firm. Although occasionally firms retire preferred stock, they are not legally obligated to do so.

Preferred shareholders receive periodic dividend payments, usually established as a fixed percentage of the face amount of each preferred share. A 9-percent preferred stock with a face amount of $100 per share would pay its owner a $9 dividend each year. This is not a legal obligation on the part of the firm. A sample cumulative convertible preferred-stock certificate is shown in Exhibit 29-3.

Position of Preferred Stockholder   Holders of preferred stock are investors who have assumed a rather cautious position in their relationship to the corporation. They have a stronger position than common shareholders with respect to dividends and claims on assets, but as a result, they will not share in the full prosperity of the firm if it grows successfully over time.

A preferred stockholder receives fixed dividends periodically, and there may be changes in the market price of the shares. The return and the risk for a share of preferred stock lie somewhere between those of bonds and those of common stock. As a result, preferred stock is often categorized with corporate bonds as a fixed-income security, even though the legal status is not the same. As just mentioned, preferred stock is more similar to a bond than to common stock, even though preferred stock appears in the ownership section of the firm's balance sheet (financial statement).

PREFERRED STOCK
Classes of stock that have priority over common stock both as to payment of dividends and distribution of assets upon the corporation's dissolution.

◆ **Exhibit 29-3**
Cumulative Convertible Preferred-Stock Certificate

❖ Securities Act of 1933

The Securities Act of 1933 [3] was designed to prohibit various forms of fraud and to stabilize the securities industry by requiring that all essential information concerning the issuance of stocks be made available to the investing public. Essentially, the purpose of this act is to require disclosure.

Registration Statement

Section 5 of the Securities Act of 1933 broadly provides that if a security does not qualify for an exemption, that security must be *registered* before it is offered to the public either through the mails or through any facility of interstate commerce, including securities exchanges. Issuing corporations must file a *registration statement* with the Securities and Exchange Commission (SEC), an agency created in 1934 to administer federal securities regulations (see the "Landmark" on the following page). Investors must be provided with a *prospectus* that describes the security being sold, the issuing corporation, and the investment or risk attaching to the security. In principle, the registration statement and the prospectus supply sufficient information to enable unsophisticated investors to evaluate the financial risk involved.

Contents of the Registration Statement The registration statement must include the following:

1. A description of the significant provisions of the security offered for sale, including the relationship between that security and the other capital securities of the registrant. Also, the corporation must disclose how it intends to use the proceeds of the sale.
2. A description of the registrant's properties and business.
3. A description of the management of the registrant, its security holdings, remuneration, and other benefits, including pensions and stock options. Any interests of directors or officers in any material transactions with the corporation must be disclosed.
4. A financial statement certified by an independent public accounting firm.
5. A description of threatened or pending lawsuits.

Other Requirements Before filing the registration statement and the prospectus with the SEC, the corporation is allowed to obtain an underwriter who will monitor the distribution of the new issue. There is a twenty-day waiting period after registration before the sale can take place. During this period, oral offers between interested investors and the issuing corporation concerning the purchase and sale of the proposed securities may take place; very limited written advertising is allowed. At this time the so-called *red herring prospectus* may be distributed. It gets its name from the red legend printed across it stating that the registration has been filed but has not become effective.

After the waiting period, the registered securities can be legally bought and sold. Written advertising is allowed in the form of a so-called *tombstone ad*, so named because the format resembles a tombstone. Such ads simply tell the investor where and how to obtain a prospectus. Normally, any other type of advertising is prohibited.

---

3. 15 U.S.C. Sections 77a through 77aa.

Landmark in the Law

The Securities and Exchange Commission

The creation of the Securities and Exchange Commission (SEC) was a direct result of the stock market crash of October 29, 1929. The crash and ensuing economic depression caused the public to focus on the importance of securities markets for the economic well-being of the nation. The feverish trading in securities during the preceding decade became the subject of widespread attention, and numerous reports were circulated concerning the speculative, manipulative, and at times unscrupulous trading that occurred in the stock markets.

The public, outraged by such practices, pressured Congress into action. As a result, in 1931 the Senate passed a resolution calling for an extensive investigation of securities trading. The investigation led, ultimately, to the passage by Congress of the Securities Act of 1933, which is also known as the *truth-in-securities* bill. In the following year, the Securities Exchange Act was passed by Congress. This 1934 act created the Securities and Exchange Commission as an independent regulatory agency whose function was to administer the 1933 and 1934 acts. Its major responsibilities in this respect are:

1. Requiring disclosure of facts concerning offerings of securities listed on national securities exchanges and of certain securities traded over the counter.
2. Regulating the trade in securities on the thirteen national and regional securities exchanges and in the over-the-counter markets.
3. Investigating securities frauds.
4. Regulating the activities of securities brokers, dealers, and investment advisers and requiring their registration.
5. Supervising the activities of mutual funds.
6. Recommending administrative sanctions, injunctive remedies, and criminal prosecution against those who violate securities laws.

In the early years of its existence, during Franklin Roosevelt's administration, the SEC was headed successively by Joseph P. Kennedy, James M. Landis, and William O. Douglas—all of whom contributed their leadership abilities to strengthening the powers of the

On October 19, 1987, the stock market plunged dramatically and created an environment in which tighter regulation of the securities industry became a topic for discussion.

commission. Douglas, who was chairman from 1937 until he was appointed to the U.S. Supreme Court in 1939, was particularly effective in transforming the New York Stock Exchange from what was often characterized as a "men's club" into a public institution.

From the time of its creation until the present, the SEC's regulatory functions have gradually been increased by legislation granting it authority in different areas. In recent years the SEC has been active in promoting stiffer penalties for *insider trading* and regulatory changes addressing the problem of the proliferation of hostile takeovers and corporate-control contests, in which outsiders attempt to wrest control of the corporation from its current board of directors. Another current major concern of the SEC is to effect fundamental changes in the basic regulatory framework applying to the financial services industry.

Main Exemptions

A corporation can avoid the high cost and complicated procedures associated with registration by taking advantage of certain exemptions. The SEC reworked the exemptions for offerings by small businesses in 1982, and the main exemptions now consist of the following:

- *Rule 504:* Offers up to $500,000 in any one year are exempt if no general solicitation or advertising is used.[4]
- *Rule 505:* Offers up to $5,000,000 in any one year with less than thirty-five unaccredited investors are exempt if no general solicitation or advertising is used.[5]
- *Rule 506:* Offers in unlimited amounts that are not generally solicited or advertised are exempt if the issuer believes that each unaccredited investor "has such knowledge and experience in financial and business matters that he is capable of evaluating the merits and the risks of the prospective investment."[6]

Transactions are also exempt if they do not involve a public offering. Some exempt transactions are private offerings to a limited number of persons, offerings to an institution that has access to the required information,[7] and offerings restricted to residents of the state in which the issuing company is organized and doing business (but these are still subject to state law).[8] The SEC also has the power to exempt small issues under $1,500,000 from the registration requirement.[9]

Additional Exemptions

Other exempt securities are as follows:

1. All bank securities sold prior to July 27, 1933.
2. Commercial paper if the maturity date does not exceed nine months.
3. Securities of charitable organizations.
4. Exchange securities where there has been a corporate reorganization.
5. Stock dividends and **stock splits.**
6. Securities issued by a common carrier or a contract carrier.
7. Any insurance, endowment, or annuity contract issued by an insurance company.

Registration violations of the 1933 act are not treated lightly. In the following case, the BarChris Construction Corporation was sued by the purchasers of the corporation's debentures under Section 11 of the Securities Act of 1933. Section 11 imposes liability when a registration statement or a prospectus contains material false statements or material omissions.

STOCK SPLIT
An action in which one share of stock is split into a larger number of shares. Stock splits involve no changes except adjustments in par value, or stated value per share, when applicable. They normally require action by the board of directors and advance shareholder approval if the articles of incorporation need to be amended to change the par value or stated value of the shares or to authorize additional shares. The common purpose of a stock split is to reduce the per-share market price to facilitate wider trading in the public securities markets.

---

4. Securities Act, Regulation D, 17 C.F.R., Section 230.504.
5. Securities Act, Regulation D, 17 C.F.R., Section 230.505.
6. Securities Act, Regulation D, 17 C.F.R., Section 230.506.
7. Securities Act, Section 4(2), 15 U.S.C., Section 77d(2).
8. Securities Act, Section 3(a)(11), 15 U.S.C., Section 77c(a)(11).
9. Securities Act, Section 3(b), 15 U.S.C., Section 77(b). For issues of less than $1,500,000, the commission has adopted a simplified registration process under Regulation A.

Case 29.1
ESCOTT v. BARCHRIS CONSTR. CORP.
United States District Court, Southern District of New York, 1968.
283 F.Supp. 643.

FACTS   This lawsuit was brought by purchasers of BarChris bonds under Section 11 of the Securities Act of 1933. The plaintiffs alleged that the registration statement filed with the Securities and Exchange Commission, which became effective May 16, 1961, contained material false statements and material omissions. There were three categories of defendants: the persons who signed the registration statement, the underwriters, and BarChris's auditors.

BarChris was an expanding bowling-alley building company, in constant need of cash to finance its operations. By early 1962 the company's financial difficulties became insurmountable, and BarChris defaulted on the interest due on the debentures one month after petitioning for bankruptcy. The plaintiffs challenged the accuracy of the registration statement accompanying the bond issue, and they charged that the text of the prospectus was false and that material information had been omitted.

ISSUE   Had BarChris violated the 1933 Securities Act requirements concerning its registration statement and prospectus accompanying the bond issue?

DECISION   Yes. BarChris Corporation and all the signers of the registration statement for the debentures, the underwriters, and the corporation's auditors were held liable.

REASON   The court found that the registration statement contained false statements of fact and omitted other facts that should have been stated in order to prevent the statement from being misleading. The misstatements included overstatement of sales and gross profits, understatement of contingent liabilities, overstatement of orders on hand, and failure to disclose true facts with respect to officers' loans, customers' delinquencies, application of proceeds, and the prospective operation of several bowling alleys. The facts that were falsely stated or omitted were "material" within the meaning of the Securities Act of 1933. The court found that "the average prudent investor is not concerned with minor inaccuracies or with errors as to matters which are of no interest to him. The facts which tend to deter him from purchasing a security are facts which have an important bearing upon the nature or condition of the issuing corporation or its business. . . . Judged by this test, there is no doubt that many of the misstatements and omissions in this prospectus were material."

❖ The Securities Exchange Act of 1934

The Securities Exchange Act provides for the regulation and registration of security exchanges, brokers, dealers, and national securities associations (such as NASD). It regulates the markets in which securities are traded by maintaining a continuous disclosure system for all corporations with securities on the securities exchanges and for those companies that have assets in excess of $5 million and 500 or more shareholders. These corporations are referred to as Section 12 companies, since they are required to register their securities under Section 12 of the 1934 act. The act regulates proxy solicitation for voting, and it allows the SEC to engage in market surveillance to regulate undesirable market practices such as fraud, market manipulation, misrepresentation, and stabilization. (*Stabilization* is a market-manipulating technique whereby securities underwriters bid for securities to stabilize their price during their issuance.)

INSIDER TRADING
Purchasing or selling securities according to information that has not been made available to the public.

Insider Trading

One of the most important parts of the 1934 act relates to so-called **insider trading.** Because of their positions, corporate directors and officers often obtain advance inside

In 1987, Wall Street was rocked by the insider trading scandal that involved millionaire investor Ivan Boesky.

information that can affect the future market value of the corporate stock. Obviously, their positions can give them a trading advantage over the general public and shareholders. The 1934 Securities Exchange Act defines and extends liability to officers and directors in their personal transactions for taking advantage of such information when they know it is unavailable to the person with whom they are dealing. In addition, in order to deter the use of inside information, the 1934 act requires officers, directors, and certain large shareholders (those holding 10 percent or more of the issued stock) to turn over to the corporation all short-term profits (within six months) realized on the purchase and sale of corporate stock.

Section 10(b) of the 1934 act and SEC **Rule 10b-5** cover not only corporate officers, directors, and majority shareholders but also any persons having access to or receiving information of a nonpublic nature on which trading is based. Those persons to whom the material information is transmitted are known as *tippees*.

In the following case a shareholder alleged that a corporate officer and a corporate director breached their fiduciary duties by trading corporate shares on the basis of nonpublic information.

RULE 10b-5
An SEC rule that makes it unlawful, in connection with the purchase or sale of any security, to make any untrue statement of a material fact or to omit a material fact if such omission causes the statement to be misleading.

Case 29.2
DIAMOND v. OREAMUNO
Court of Appeals of New York, 1969.
24 N.Y.2d 494, 301 N.Y.S.2d 78, 248 N.E.2d 910.

FACTS The defendants in this case were the chairman of the board (Oreamuno) and president (Gonzalez) of MAI (Management Assistance, Inc.), a corporation that bought and leased computers, with maintenance services being provided by IBM. The defendants learned that IBM was going to increase its maintenance prices dramatically, to the point where it would cut MAI's profits by 75 percent per month. Just before the IBM maintenance price increase was announced, the defendants sold their MAI stock for $28 per share. After IBM publicly announced its price increase, MAI stock fell to $11 per share. The plain-

Case 29.2—Continued

tiff (Diamond) brought a derivative action on behalf of MAI to recover the difference in profits.

ISSUE Where corporate fiduciaries have breached their duty to the corporation by the use of nonpublic information, may a derivative action be brought by a shareholder for any profit resulting from the breach of duty?

DECISION Yes. Those whose relationship with the corporation is such that they are privy to "inside information" may not use such knowledge for their own personal gain.

REASON The court pointed out that the Securities Exchange Act in Section 10(b) provides a general anti-fraud provision. Rule 10b-5 specifically renders it unlawful to engage in a variety of acts considered to be fraudulent. When the defendants sold their shares, they were guilty of withholding material information from the purchasers. Therefore, the activities of the defendants constituted a violation of Rule 10b-5. Any individual purchaser who could prove an injury as a result of this Rule 10b-5 violation could bring his or her own action, but in cases where securities are bought and sold in large public markets through anonymous transactions handled by brokers, it is virtually impossible to match the ultimate buyer with the ultimate seller. Thus, it would be difficult if not impossible for an individual to successfully prosecute under Rule 10b-5. Therefore, the court reasoned that it was possible to use an effective common-law remedy against the dishonest directors. The court held that the state attorney general could enforce proper behavior on the part of corporate officials through the medium of the derivative action brought in the name of the corporation. Even if the corporation had suffered no harm from the defendants' activities, the defendants' profits resulting from their use of inside information might still be recovered on behalf of the corporation.

Disclosure under Rule 10b-5

Any material omission or misrepresentation of material facts in connection with the purchase or sale of a security may violate Section 10(b) and Rule 10b-5. The key to liability (which can be civil or criminal) under this rule is whether the insider's information is *material*. Following are some examples of material facts calling for a disclosure under the rule:

1. A new ore discovery.
2. Fraudulent trading in the company stock by a broker-dealer.
3. A dividend change (whether up or down).
4. A contract for the sale of corporate assets.
5. A new discovery (process or product).
6. A significant change in the firm's financial condition.

When Must Disclosure under Rule 10b-5 Be Made? Courts have struggled with the problem of when information becomes public knowledge. Clearly, when inside information becomes public knowledge, all insiders should be allowed to trade without disclosure. The courts have suggested that insiders should refrain from trading for a "reasonable waiting period" when the news is not readily translatable into investment action. Presumably, this gives the news time to filter down and to be evaluated by the investing public. What constitutes a reasonable waiting period is not stipulated.

The following is one of the landmark cases interpreting Rule 10b-5. The SEC sued Texas Gulf Sulphur for issuing a misleading press release. The release underestimated the magnitude and the value of a mineral discovery. The SEC also sued several of Texas Gulf Sulphur's directors, officers, and employees under Rule 10b-5 after these persons had purchased large amounts of the corporate stock prior to the announcement of the corporation's rich ore discovery.

Case 29.3
SECURITIES AND EXCHANGE COMM. v. TEXAS GULF SULPHUR CO.

United States Court of Appeals, Second Circuit, 1968.
401 F.2d 833.

FACTS   The Texas Gulf Sulphur Company (TGS) drilled a hole on November 12, 1963, that appeared to yield a core with an exceedingly high mineral content. TGS kept secret the results of the core sample. Officers and employees of the company made substantial purchases of TGS's stock or accepted stock options after learning of the ore discovery, even though further drilling was necessary to establish whether there was enough ore to be mined commercially. On April 11, 1964, an unauthorized report of the mineral find appeared in the newspapers. On the following day, TGS issued a press release that played down the discovery and stated that it was too early to tell whether the ore finding would be a significant one. Later on, TGS announced a strike of at least 25 million tons of ore, substantially driving up the price of TGS stock. The SEC brought suit against the officers and employees of TGS for violating the insider-trading prohibition of Rule 10b-5. The officers and employees, however, argued that the prohibition did not apply because the information on which they had traded was not material since the mine had not been commercially proved. The trial court held that most of the defendants had not violated Rule 10b-5.

ISSUE   Had Rule 10b-5 been violated by the officers and employees of TGS by purchasing the stock, even though the extent and profit potential of the mine was not fully known at the time the stock was purchased?

DECISION   Yes. The Court of Appeals reversed and remanded the case to the trial court, holding that the employees and officers violated Rule 10b-5's prohibition against insider trading.

REASON   For Rule 10b-5, the test of materiality is not whether a company would be permitted to disclose the information if it were selling securities. Rather, the test is whether the information would affect the judgment of reasonable investors. Reasonable investors include speculative as well as conservative investors. "[A] major factor in determining whether the . . . discovery [of the ore] was a material fact is the importance attached to the drilling results by those who knew about it. . . . [T]he timing by those who knew of it of their stock purchases and their purchases of short-term calls [rights to buy shares at a specified price within a specified time period]—purchases in some cases by individuals who had never before purchased calls or even TGS stock—virtually compels the inference that the insiders were influenced by the drilling results. . . . We hold, therefore, that all transactions in TGS stock or calls by individuals apprised of the drilling results . . . were made in violation of Rule 10b-5."

COMMENTS   Texas Gulf Sulphur Company was not only sued by the SEC, but numerous civil actions for damages were brought against it by plaintiff-investors who had sold their TGS stock as a result of the deceptive press release of April 12 regarding the corporation's mineral exploration. All these suits were settled in 1972. [Cannon v. Texas Gulf Sulphur Co., 55 F.R.D. 308 (S.D.N.Y. 1972)] In a federal lawsuit filed against TGS some two years after the initial case, a court of appeals held that investors who had sold stock due to their reliance upon the representations in the press release could recover damages from the corporation and the officers who drafted the release. The court went on to state that the proper measure of damages was the difference between the selling price and the price at which the investors could have reinvested within a reasonable period of time after they became aware of a curative press release made by TGS.

After TGS issued its curative press release, the court held that a diligent and reasonable investor would have become informed of it within four days, and investors who sold their stock more than four days after the second press release was issued could not recover under the Securities Exchange Act on the basis of reliance on the earlier, deceptive release.

When Does Rule 10b-5 Apply?   Rule 10b-5 applies in virtually all cases concerning the trading of securities, whether on organized exchanges, in over-the-counter markets, or in private transactions. The rule covers notes, bonds, certificates of interest and participation in any profit-sharing agreement, agreements to form a corporation, and joint-venture agreements; in short, it covers just about any form of security. It is immaterial whether a firm has securities registered under the 1933 act for the 1934 act to apply.

Rule 10b-5 is applicable only when the requisites of federal jurisdiction, such as the use of the mails, of stock exchange facilities, or of any instrumentality of interstate commerce, are present. Virtually no commercial transaction, however, can be completed without such contact. In addition, the states have corporate securities laws, many of which include provisions similar to Rule 10b-5.

In the following case, the Supreme Court examines the liability of a person who had received material nonpublic information from insiders of a corporation with which he had no connection.

Case 29.4
DIRKS v. SECURITIES AND EXCHANGE COMMISSION
United States Supreme Court, 1983.
463 U.S. 646, 103 S.Ct. 3255, 77 L.Ed.2d 911.

FACTS Dirks was an officer of a New York broker-dealer firm that specialized in providing investment analysis of insurance company securities to institutional investors. In March 1973 Dirks received information from Ronald Secrist, a former officer of Equity Funding of America, who alleged that the assets of Equity Funding were vastly overstated as a result of fraudulent corporate practices. Secrist urged Dirks to verify the fraud and to disclose it publicly. Dirks decided to investigate the allegations, and through his investigation he openly discussed the information he had obtained with a number of clients and investors. The Securities and Exchange Commission (SEC) subsequently filed a complaint against Equity Funding and also found that Dirks had aided and abetted violations of Section 17(a) of the Securities Act of 1933, Section 10(b) of the Securities Exchange Act of 1934, and SEC Rule 10b-5 by repeating the allegations of fraud to members of the investment community who later sold their Equity stock. Dirks sought review in the court of appeals, which entered a judgment against him. The Supreme Court granted certiorari.

ISSUE Did Dirks have a duty to refrain from the use of inside information that he had acquired during his investigation of Equity Funding?

DECISION No. The decision of the court of appeals was reversed. The Supreme Court held that Dirks, under the circumstances, had no duty to refrain from the use of inside information that he had acquired.

REASON The SEC claimed that a breach of the common-law affirmative duty to disclose, which is imposed on corporate insiders—particularly officers, directors, and controlling stockholders—also established a violation of Rule 10b-5. Therefore, under the SEC's position, individuals (as tippees) other than corporate insiders could be obligated under Rule 10b-5 either to disclose material nonpublic information before trading or to abstain from trading altogether. In response, the Court stated that "there can be no duty to disclose where the person who has traded on inside information was not [the corporation's] agent, . . . was not a fiduciary, [or] was not a person in whom the sellers [of the securities] had placed their trust and confidence." Concluding that recipients of inside information do not invariably acquire a duty to disclose or abstain, the Court nonetheless stated that such tippees are not always free to trade on the information. In determining whether a tippee has a duty to disclose or abstain, it is necessary "to determine whether the insider's 'tip' constituted a breach of the insider's fiduciary duty. . . . Thus the test is whether the insider personally will benefit, directly or indirectly, from his disclosure. Absent some personal gain, there has been no breach of duty to stockholders. And absent a breach by the insider, there is no derivative breach." Therefore, because Dirks had no preexisting fiduciary duty to Equity Funding's shareholders, and because the insiders did not breach their common-law duty in disclosing nonpublic information to Dirks, he did not violate Rule 10b-5 by passing on the inside information he had acquired.

Business Law in Action

"Outsider" Trading and Rule 10b-5

The rationale behind Rule 10b-5 is to prevent "insiders"—corporate officers, directors, and others in a position enabling them to acquire information concerning a corporation—from using inside information to the detriment of a corporation's shareholders. Using inside information for personal gain is a breach of a director's or officer's fiduciary duty to shareholders. If a *tippee* (an outsider) acquires inside information, Rule 10b-5 will apply only if that acquisition of such information followed from an officer's or director's breach of his or her fiduciary duties. But what happens when inside information is obtained without the knowledge of any director or officer of the corporation, where no breach of fiduciary duty is involved, and when there is no use of interstate commerce, the mails, or any of the facilities of any national securities exchange? Does Rule 10b-5 apply in these cases?

This question came before the U. S. Supreme Court in 1980 in the case of *Chiarella* v. *United States*.[1] Chiarella was a printer who worked at a New York composing room and handled announcements of corporate takeover bids. Even though the documents that were delivered to the printer concealed the identity of the target corporations by blank spaces and false names, Chiarella was able to deduce the names of the target companies. Without disclosing his knowledge, he purchased stock in the target companies and sold the shares immediately after the takeover attempts were made public. He realized a gain of slightly more than $30,000 in the course of fourteen months.

In 1978 Chiarella was indicted on seventeen counts of violating Section 10b of the Securities Exchange Act of 1934 and SEC Rule 10b-5. The trial court convicted him on all counts, and the court of appeals affirmed that conviction. The Supreme Court, however, reversed. The Court held that Chiarella could not be convicted for his failure to disclose his knowledge to stockholders or to target companies since he was under no duty to disclose his knowledge. Chiarella was under no duty to disclose because he had no prior dealings with the stockholders and was not their agent, nor was he a person in whom sellers had placed their trust and confidence. Thus, an "outsider" such as Chiarella who comes into possession of nonpublic market information does not violate Rule 10b-5 if he or she fails to disclose this information. A duty to disclose does not arise from mere possession of nonpublic market information.

1. 445 U.S. 222, 100 S.Ct. 1108, 63 L.Ed.2d 348 (1980).

Insider Reporting and Trading—Section 16(b)

Officers, directors, and certain large stockholders[10] of Section 12 corporations are required to file reports with the SEC concerning their ownership and trading of the corporation's securities.[11] In order to discourage such insiders from using nonpublic information about their company to their personal benefit in the stock market, Section 16(b) of the 1934 act provides for the recapture by the corporation of all profits realized by the insider on any purchase and sale or sale and purchase of the corporation's

---

10. Those stockholders owning 10 percent of the class of equity securities registered under Section 12 of the 1934 act.
11. 15 U.S.C. Section 78*l*.

◆ **Exhibit 29-4**
Comparison of Coverage, Application, and Liabilities under Rule 10b-5 and Section 16(b)

	RULE 10b-5	SECTION 16(b)
1. Subject matter of transaction.	Any security (does not have to be registered).	Any security (does not have to be registered).
2. Transactions covered.	Purchase or sale.	Short-swing purchase and sale or short-swing sale and purchase.
3. Who is subject to liability?	Virtually anyone with inside information—including officers, directors, controlling stockholders, and tippees.	Officers, directors, and certain 10-percent stockholders.
4. Is omission, scheme, or misrepresentation necessary for liability?	Yes.	No.
5. Any exempt transactions?	No.	Yes, there are a variety of exemptions.
6. Is direct dealing with the party necessary?	No.	No.
7. Who can bring an action?	A person transacting with an insider or the SEC or a purchaser or a seller damaged by a wrongful act.	Corporation and shareholder by derivative action.

stock within any six-month period.[12] It is irrelevant whether the insider actually uses inside information; all such *short-swing* profits must be returned to the corporation.

Section 16(b) applies not only to stock but to warrants, options, and securities convertible into stock. In addition, the courts have fashioned complex rules for determining profits. Corporate insiders are wise to seek competent counsel prior to trading in the corporation's stock. Exhibit 29-4 compares the effects of Rule 10b-5 and Section 16(b).

In the following well-known case, the U. S. Supreme Court had to determine if Section 16(b) applied and whether the defendant would thus be liable for making *short-swing* profits by the purchase and sale of stock within a six-month period.

---

12. In a declining stock market, one can realize profits by selling at a high price and repurchasing at a later time at a lower price.

Case 29.5
RELIANCE ELECTRIC CO. v. EMERSON ELECTRIC CO.
United States Supreme Court, 1972.
404 U.S. 418, 92 S.Ct. 596, 30 L.Ed.2d 575.

FACTS Emerson Electric purchased 13.2 percent of Dodge Manufacturing Company's stock in an unsuccessful takeover attempt in June of 1967. Later, when Dodge merged with Reliance Electric Company, Emerson decided to sell its shares. To avoid being subject to the restrictions of Section 16 of the Securities Exchange Act of 1934, which pertain to any purchase and sale by any owner of 10 percent or more of a corporation's stock, Emerson decided on a two-step selling plan. First, it sold off sufficient shares to reduce its holdings to 9.96 percent, and then it sold the remaining stock—all within a six-month period. Since under Section 16(b) of the act, the owner must be a 10-percent owner "both at the time of the purchase and sale . . . of the security involved," Emerson in this way succeeded in avoiding Section 16(b) requirements.

Reliance demanded that Emerson return the profits made on both sales. Emerson sought a declaration from that court that it was not liable, arguing that since at the time of the second sale it had not owned 10 percent of Dodge stock, Section 16 did not apply.

The district court held for Reliance on the basis that, although two separate sales were involved and Emerson was not a 10-percent stockholder at the time of the second sale, nonetheless the two sales represented part of a "single plan," and Emerson was liable for its trading profits. Emerson appealed.

ISSUE Does Section 16 of the Securities Exchange Act of 1934 apply to Emerson's transactions, and is Emerson liable to Reliance for its profits?

DECISION No. The Court held that since Emerson was not a 10-percent stockholder at the time of the second sale, it was not liable to Reliance.

REASON The Court stated that the 10-percent requirement is one of the "objective standards" contained in Section 16(b), as is the six-month requirement. "Read literally," the court maintained, "this language clearly contemplates that a statutory insider might sell enough shares to bring his holdings below 10 percent and later—but still within six months—sell additional shares free from liability under the statute." The Supreme Court concluded that the district court had erred in its decision, which was not based on a literal reading of the 10-percent requirement. According to the Supreme Court, "A 'plan' to sell that is conceived within six months of purchase clearly would not fall within [Section] 16(b) if the sale were made after the six months had expired, and we see no basis in the statute for a different result where the 10 [percent] requirement is involved rather than the six-month limitation."

COMMENTS Three of the justices dissented to this decision. "By the simple expedient of dividing what would ordinarily be a single transaction into two parts—both of which could be performed on the same day, . . . a more-than-10 [percent] owner may reap windfall profits on 10 [percent] of his corporation's outstanding stock. This result [is] 'plainly at variance with the policy of the legislation as a whole.' "

Proxy Statements

Section 14(a) of the Securities Exchange Act of 1934 regulates the solicitation of proxies from shareholders of Section 12 companies. The SEC regulates the content of proxy statements sent to shareholders by corporate managers who are requesting authority to vote on behalf of the shareholders in a particular election on specified issues. Whoever solicits a proxy must fully and accurately disclose all facts that are pertinent to the matter to be voted on. SEC Rule 14a-9 is similar to the anti-fraud provisions of Rule 10b-5. Remedies for violation are extensive, ranging from injunctions to prevent a vote from being taken, to monetary damages.

❖ Regulation of Investment Companies

INVESTMENT COMPANIES
Companies that act on behalf of many smaller shareholders/owners by buying a large portfolio of securities and managing that portfolio professionally.

MUTUAL FUND
A specific type of investment company that continually buys or sells to investors shares of ownership in a portfolio.

Investment companies, and mutual funds in particular, grew rapidly after World War II. **Investment companies** act on behalf of many smaller shareholders/owners by buying a large portfolio of securities and managing that portfolio professionally. A **mutual fund** is a specific type of investment company that continually buys or sells to investors shares of ownership in a portfolio. Such companies are regulated by the Investment Company Act of 1940,[13] which provides for SEC regulation of their activities. It was expanded by the Investment Company Act Amendments of 1970. Further minor changes were made in the Securities Act Amendments of 1975.

The 1940 act requires that every investment company register with the SEC and imposes restrictions on the activities of such companies and persons connected with them. For the purposes of the act, an investment company is defined as any entity that (1) "is . . . engaged primarily . . . in the business of investing, reinvesting, or trading in securities" or (2) is engaged in such business and more than 40 percent of the company's assets consist of investment securities. Excluded from coverage of the act are banks, insurance companies, savings and loan associations, finance companies, oil and gas drilling firms, charitable foundations, tax-exempt pension funds, and other special types of institutions, such as closely held corporations.

Regulation of Mutual Funds

All investment companies must register with the SEC by filing a notification of registration. Each year registered companies must file reports with the SEC. In order to safeguard company assets, all securities must be held in the custody of a bank or stock-exchange member, and that bank or stock-exchange member must follow strict procedures established by the SEC. No dividends may be paid from any source other than accumulated, undistributed net income. Furthermore, there are some restrictions on investment activities.

The Foreign Corrupt Practices Act

In 1977 the Foreign Corrupt Practices Act (FCPA) was passed as an amendment to the Securities Exchange Act of 1934. Congress had discovered that several hundred American corporations had been giving bribes or other questionable payments, in their transactions abroad, to foreign government officials and others in order to obtain favorable business conditions or contracts. Those companies that made the payments argued that such payments were customary and necessary in many foreign countries. Since 1977 it has been a crime under the FCPA for any American firm to offer, promise, or make payments or gifts of anything of value to foreign officials in exchange for favored treatment. The FCPA also prohibits offers of payments to foreign political parties and to foreign candidates for political office.

Facilitating payments, often known as "grease payments," are currently made throughout the world to numerous lower-level government officials. The FCPA does not prohibit these payments as long as the recipient has no discretion in carrying out a government function. For example, if a payment is made by a firm to a foreign

---

13.　15 U.S.C. Sections 80a-1 through 80a-64.

government official simply to speed up an import licensing process, the FCPA has not been violated.

The FCPA provides for companies to be fined up to $1 million for violations of the act. Additionally, directors, officers, employees, or agents who participate in violations can be fined up to $10,000 and be given prison terms of up to five years.[14]

❖ State Securities Laws

Today, all states have their own corporate securities laws that regulate the offer and sale of securities within individual state borders.[15] Often referred to as *blue sky* laws, they are designed to prevent "speculative schemes which have no more basis than so many feet of blue sky."

Since the adoption of the 1933 and 1934 federal securities acts, the state and federal governments have regulated securities concurrently. Indeed, both acts specifically preserve state securities laws. Certain features are common to all state blue sky laws. They have antifraud provisions, many of which are patterned after Rule 10b-5. Also most state corporate securities laws regulate securities brokers and dealers.

Typically, these laws also provide for the registration or qualification of securities offered or issued for sale within the state. Unless an applicable exemption from registration is found, issuers must register or qualify their stock with the appropriate state official, often called a *corporations commissioner*. There is a difference in philosophy among state statutes. Many are like the Securities Act of 1933 and mandate certain disclosures before registration is effective and a permit to sell the securities is issued. Others have fairness standards that a corporation must meet in order to offer or sell stock in the state. The Uniform Securities Act, which has been adopted in part by several states, was drafted to be acceptable to states with differing regulatory philosophies.

---

14. See the "Landmark" Chapter 37 for a discussion of the FCPA in the context of ethics.
15. These laws are catalogued and annotated in CCH, *Blue Sky Law Reporter*, a loose-leaf service.

Application

Law and the Entrepreneur— Going Public

Virtually every week, some business "goes public." That phrase means selling shares in a company to the public. Once a firm has "gone public," it becomes regulated by the Securities and Exchange Commission at the federal level, and usually by the state's equivalent to the SEC as well. It may also be regulated by the National Asso-ciation of Securities Dealers (NASD), depending on the circumstances.

If you or anyone you know ever contemplates taking a business public, the checklist below indicates clearly what you should do.

Checklist for Going Public

☐ 1. Immediately visit the offices of a qualified securities law attorney.

❖ Chapter Summary: Corporations—Financing and Investor Protection

CORPORATE FINANCING	
Corporate Bonds	Corporate bonds are securities representing *corporate debt*—money borrowed by a corporation. Types of corporate bonds include: 1. *Debentures*—Bonds backed by the general credit rating of the corporation; no corporate assets are pledged as security. 2. *Mortgage bonds*—Bonds pledging as security specific corporate property. 3. *Convertible bonds*—Bonds that can be exchanged for a specified number of shares of common stock at the option of the bondholder. 4. *Callable bonds*—Bonds (debentures or other types of bonds) that may be called in and the principal repaid at specified times or under specified conditions.
Stocks	Equity securities issued by a corporation that represent the purchase of ownership in the business firms. 1. *Important characteristics of stock:* a. They need not be paid back. b. The stockholder receives dividends only when so voted by the directors. c. Stockholders are the last investors to be paid upon dissolution. d. Stockholders vote on director management and on major issues. 2. *Types of stock* (See Exhibit 29-2 for details): a. Common stock—Represents the true ownership of the firm; holders of common stock share in the control, earning capacity, and net assets of the corporation. Common stockholders carry more risk than preferred stockholders, but, if the corporation is successful, are compensated for this risk by greater returns on their investment. b. Preferred stock—Stock whose holders have a preferred status. Preferred stockholders have a stronger position than common shareholders with respect to dividends and claims on assets, but, as a result, they will not share in the full prosperity of the firm if it grows successfully over time. The return and risk for a share of preferred stock lie somewhere between those for bonds and common stock.

❖ Chapter Summary: Corporations—Financing and Investor Protection—Continued

FINANCIAL REGULATION AND INVESTOR PROTECTION	
The Securities and Exchange Commission (SEC)	An independent regulatory agency established by the Securities Exchange Act of 1934. It administers all federal securities laws.
The Securities Act of 1933	Prohibits fraud and stabilizes the securities industry by requiring disclosure of all essential information relating to the issuance of stocks to the investing public. 1. Securities, unless exempt, must be *registered* with the SEC before being offered to the public through the mails or any facility of interstate commerce (including securities exchanges). The *registration statement* must include detailed financial information about the issuing corporation, the intended use of the proceeds of the securities being issued, and certain disclosures, such as interests of directors or officers and pending lawsuits. 2. A *prospectus* must be provided to investors, describing the security being sold, the issuing corporation, and the risk attaching to the security. 3. Exemptions—The SEC has exempted certain offerings from the requirements of the Securities Act of 1933. Exemptions are determined on the basis of the size of the issuing corporation, whether the offering is private or public, and whether advertising is involved. Other exemptions include certain bank securities, securities of charitable organizations, corporate exchange securities where there has been a corporate reorganization, stock dividends and stock splits, securities issued by a common carrier, and insurance, endowment, or annuity contracts issued by an insurance company.

The Securities Exchange Act of 1934	Provides for the regulation and registration of security exchanges, brokers, dealers, and national securities associations (such as NASD). Maintains a continuous disclosure system for all corporations with securities on the securities exchanges and for those companies that have assets in excess of $5 million and 500 or more shareholders (Section 12 companies).
	
	1. *Insider trading*—To prevent corporate officers and directors from taking advantage of inside information (benefiting from information not available to the investing public), the 1934 act requires officers, directors, and shareholders owning 10 percent or more of the issued stock of a corporation to turn over to the corporation all short-term profits (within six months) realized from insider trading on the purchase and sale of corporate stock—under Section 16(b) of the 1934 act.
	
	2. *Rule 10b-5 (under Section 10(b) of the 1934 act):*
	  a. Applies to insider trading by corporate officers, directors, majority shareholders, and any persons (tippees) receiving information not available to the public who base their trading on this information.
	  b. Liability for violating Rule 10b-5 can be civil or criminal.
	  c. May be violated by failing to disclose "material facts" that are required to be disclosed under this rule.
	  d. Applies in virtually all cases concerning the trading of securities—a firm does not have to have its securities registered under the 1933 act for the 1934 act to apply.
	  e. Applies only when the requisites of federal jurisdiction (such as use of the mails, stock-exchange facilities, or any facility of interstate commerce) is present.
	
	3. *Proxies (under Section 14(a) of the 1934 act)*—The SEC regulates the content of proxy statements sent to shareholders by corporate managers of Section 12 companies who are requesting authority to vote on behalf of the shareholders in a particular election on specified issues; essentially a disclosure law, with provisions similar to the antifraud provisions of Rule 10b-5.

❖ Chapter Summary: Corporations—Financing and Investor Protection—Continued

Regulation of Investment Companies	The Investment Company Act of 1940 provides for SEC regulation of investment company activities. Altered and expanded by the amendments of 1970 and 1975.
State Securities Laws	All states have corporate securities laws (*blue sky* laws) that regulate the offer and sale of securities within their respective state borders; designed to prevent "speculative schemes which have no more basis than so many feet of blue sky." States regulate securities concurrently with the federal government.

❖ Questions and Case Problems

29-1. Langley Brothers, Inc., a corporation incorporated and doing business in Kansas, decides to sell $1,000,000 worth of its no-par common stock to the public. The stock will be sold only within the state of Kansas. Joseph Langley, the chairman of the board, says the offering need not be registered with the SEC. His brother, Harry, disagrees. Who is right? Explain.

29-2. Huron Corporation had 300,000 common shares outstanding. The owners of these outstanding shares lived in several different states. Huron decided to split the 300,000 shares two-for-one. Will Huron Corporation have to file a registration statement and prospectus on the 300,000 new shares to be issued as a result of the split? Explain.

29-3. Maresh, an experienced geologist, owned certain oil and gas leases covering land in Nebraska. To raise money for the drilling of a test well, he undertook to sell fractional interests in the leases. He approached Garfield, a man with whom he had done business in the past. Garfield had mentioned that he would be interested in investing in some of Maresh's future oil ventures. Garfield had wide business experience in the stock market and in oil stocks. He felt that the investment in Maresh's gas leases could be lucrative. Based on Garfield's promise to wire the money promptly, Maresh began drilling. Soon after, when Maresh realized that the land was dry, Garfield refused to pay his share of the investment. Garfield claimed that he could rescind the agreement to invest since the investment offered by Maresh was a security within the meaning of the Securities Act of 1933, and it had not been registered. Did Maresh offer a security within the meaning of the 1933 act? Explain. [Garfield v. Strain, 320 F.2d 116 (10th Cir. 1963)]

29-4. Leston Nay owned 90 percent of the stock of First Securities Company. Between the years 1942 and 1966, Hochfelder sent large sums of money to Nay to be invested in *escrow accounts*—accounts belonging to one entity but held by another entity—of First Securities. The whole investment scheme was a fraud, and Nay converted the money sent by Hochfelder to his own use. When Hochfelder discovered the fraud, he sued Ernst & Ernst, First Securities' auditor, for failing to use

proper auditing procedures and thus negligently failing to discover the fraudulent scheme. Was the firm of Ernst & Ernst found guilty of violating Section 10(b) and Rule 10b-5 of the 1934 Securities Exchange Act? Explain. [Ernst & Ernst v. Hochfelder, 425 U.S. 185, 96 S.Ct. 1375, 47 L.Ed.2d 668 (1976)]

29-5. Zabriskie purchased certain notes from Lewis in connection with a real estate venture that Lewis was trying to establish. The notes bore a maturity date of eight months after the date of purchase. The Securities Act of 1933 excludes from its definition of securities any note that has a maturity date not exceeding nine months at the time of issue. Knowing that the Securities Act is an attempt to control the sales of *investment* securities, discuss whether the court was able to devise a better test than this strict nine-month rule. [Zabriskie v. Lewis, 507 F.2d 546 (10th Cir. 1974)]

29-6. American Breeding Herds (ABH) offered a cattle-breeding plan for which Ronnett contracted to buy thirty-six Charolais cows at $3,000 per head and a one-quarter interest in a Charolais bull at $5,000, totaling $113,000. The ABH agreement described itself as a "tax shelter program . . . unlike the purchase of securities such as stocks and bonds." Ronnett entered into the agreement after receiving investment advice from Shannon, an investment counselor. The cows were tagged and sent to an ABH approved breeding ranch. Ronnett signed a maintenance agreement and paid a monthly maintenance fee. Was the ABH plan a security, and should it have been registered under Illinois securities law? Explain. [Ronnett v. American Breeding Herds, Inc., 124 Ill.App.3d 842, 80 Ill.Dec. 218, 464 N.E.2d 1201 (1984)]

29-7. Campbell was a financial columnist for a Los Angeles newspaper owned by Hearst Corporation. He often bought shares in companies on which he was about to give a favorable report, and then he would sell the shares at a profit after the columns appeared. In June of 1969 Campbell interviewed the officers of American Systems, Inc. (ASI). The ASI officers did not disclose to Campbell adverse information concerning its financial condition, and Campbell relied on the officers' presentation of ASI's financial status and made no independent investigation. Planning to write a favorable report, Campbell purchased 5,000 shares of ASI stock for $2 per share. Following the publication of Campbell's favorable, and misleading, article, ASI's stock rose rapidly, and on June 5 Campbell sold 2,000 of his shares at $5 per share. ASI had made plans with another corporation, RGC, in February of 1969 whereby RGC would merge with ASI and ASI would pay RGC stockholders enough ASI stock to equal a market value of $1.8 million on the closing date of June 10, 1969. Zweig and Bruno, who each owned one-third of RGC shares, brought suit against Hearst Corporation, alleging that because of the artificial rise in ASI stock due to Campbell's column, they ended up with a smaller percentage of the total outstanding shares of ASI than they would have otherwise received. Explain whether Hearst is liable under Rule 10b-5. [*Zweig v. Hearst Corp.*, 594 F.2d 1261 (9th Cir. 1979)]

29-8. On September 1, 1971, the Ecological Science Corporation issued a press release stating, in part, that it had renegotiated the terms of approximately $14 million in loans from its prime lender, and that under the renegotiated agreement, $4 million was due upon demand and the remainder on a specified date. The press release, however, failed to mention that, on the same date as the renegotiated loan agreement, an insurance and annuity association had refused to provide the corporation with the $4 million loan that it had planned to use to repay the demand loan. Moreover, while discussing its European prospects in the press release, Ecological Science Corporation failed to mention the proposed transfer of voting control among its European subsidiaries. Had Ecological Science Corporation violated any of the provisions of the Securities Exchange Act of 1934? [*Securities and Exchange Comm. v. Koenig*, 469 F.2d 198 (2d Cir. 1972)]

29-9. Lakeside Plastics and Engraving Company was a close corporation incorporated in Minnesota. The company suffered losses from the time it was incorporated in 1946. Of its four shareholders, only one was involved in the management of the firm. Notwithstanding its earlier difficulties, by 1954 the firm was apparently about to become profitable. Without informing the other shareholders of this fact, the shareholder-manager bought out the remaining shareholders. He accomplished this by making numerous misrepresentations to them. Assuming the shareholder-manager used none of the instrumentalities of interstate commerce, including the mails or the telephone, in making these misrepresentations, could the remaining shareholders bring an action under Section 10(b) of the Securities Exchange Act of 1934? If not, did the remaining shareholders have any legal recourse? [*Myzel v. Fields*, 386 F.2d 718 (8th Cir. 1967)]

29-10. Children's Hospital offered and sold a number of 8-percent mortgage bonds in order to raise enough money to begin operation. Its promoters solicited purchasers mainly through the mails and through local newspaper advertisements. Children's Hospital was to be a nonprofit medical organization established mainly to serve the needs of children in the local community. The promoters, however, expected to earn large profits from organizing the hospital. Were the promoters of Children's Hospital required to register the sale of the mortgage bonds with the Securities and Exchange Commission? Explain. [*Securities and Exchange Comm. v. Children's Hospital*, 214 F.Supp. 883 (D.Ariz. 1963)]

Unit Five

Government Regulation

❖ Why We Study Government Regulation

If this text were being written a hundred years ago, there would be little to say about government regulation. In the 1890s the beginnings of federal antitrust law were manifested in the form of the Interstate Commerce Commission Act and the Sherman Antitrust Act, but there was little or no legislation affecting consumer protection or environmental issues. And the right of unions to organize had not yet been fully practiced.

Today, in contrast, government regulation permeates the entire business community. A knowledge of what is and is not anticompetitive behavior is critical to the decision making of many businesspersons. State and federal regulations with respect to packaging and labeling, advertising, and the dumping of toxic waste affect numerous businesses; and the issues of employment discrimination, sexual harassment, and religious discrimination affect virtually every employer in this nation. In this unit, we will examine antitrust issues in Chapter 30, consumer and environmental law in Chapter 31, and employee and labor law in Chapter 32.

Chapter 30

Antitrust

Today's antitrust laws are the direct descendants of common-law actions intended to limit restraints on trade. Such actions date to the fifteenth century in England, and the antimonopoly attitude of the courts is clearly expressed by Sir Edward Coke, an eminent British jurist, in the opening quotation. In America, concern over monopolistic practices began following the Civil War with the growth of large corporate enterprises and their attempts to reduce or eliminate competition. They did this by legally tying themselves together in a **trust,** which is a legal entity in which a trustee holds title to property for the benefit of another. The participants in the most famous trust, Standard Oil (see this chapter's "Landmark"), transferred their stock to a trustee and received trust certificates in exchange. The trustee then made decisions fixing prices, controlling production, and determining the control of exclusive geographical markets for all of the oil companies that were in the Standard Oil trust. It became apparent that the trust wielded such economic power that corporations outside the trust could not compete effectively. Many states attempted to control such monopolistic behavior by enacting statutes outlawing the use of trusts. That is why all of the laws that regulate economic competition today are referred to as *antitrust* laws, whose purpose is to prevent monopolists from controlling our economy.

At the national level, the government recognized the problem in 1887 and passed the Interstate Commerce Act, followed by the Sherman Antitrust Act in 1890. We will examine the latter act, as well as other major federal antitrust acts that are enforced by both the Department of Justice and the Federal Trade Commission. Remember in reading this chapter that at the basis of antitrust legislation is the desire to foster competition. Antitrust legislation was initially created, and continues to be enforced, because of our belief that competition leads to lower prices, more product information, and a better distribution of wealth between consumers and producers.

> "A rule of such a nature as to bring all trade or traffic into the hands of one company, or one person, and to exclude all others, is illegal."
>
> **Sir Edward Coke, 1552–1634 (British jurist and legal scholar)**

TRUST
A legal entity in which a trustee holds title to property for the benefit of another.

❖ Sherman Antitrust Act

The author of the Sherman Act of 1890, Senator John Sherman, brother of the famed Civil War general and a recognized financial authority, had been concerned for years with the diminishing competition within American industry. This concern led to his introduction into Congress in 1888, 1889, and again in 1890 of bills

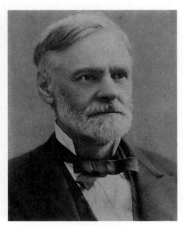

Senator John Sherman

designed to destroy the large combinations of capital that were, he felt, creating a lack of balance within the nation's economy. He told Congress that the Sherman Act "does not announce a new principle of law, but applies old and well-recognized principles of the common law." [1] The common law regarding trade regulation, however, was not always consistent. Certainly it was not very familiar to the legislators of the Fifty-first Congress of the United States. The public concern over large business integrations and trusts was familiar, however, and in 1890 Congress passed "An Act to Protect Trade and Commerce against Unlawful Restraints and Monopolies"—more commonly known as the Sherman Antitrust Act.

Sections 1 and 2 contain the main provisions of the Sherman Act:

1: Every contract, combination in the form of trust or otherwise, or conspiracy, in restraint of trade or commerce among the several States, or with foreign nations, is hereby declared to be illegal [and is a felony punishable by fine and/or imprisonment]. . . .

2: Every person who shall monopolize, or attempt to monopolize, or combine or conspire with any other person or persons, to monopolize any part of the trade or commerce among the several States, or with foreign nations, shall be deemed guilty of a felony [and is similarly punishable]. . . .

Sections 1 and 2 of the Sherman Antitrust Act Compared

The two main sections of the Sherman Act are quite different. Section 1 requires two or more persons, since a person cannot contract or combine or conspire alone. Thus, the essence of the illegal activity is *the act of joining together*. Section 2 applies both to an individual person and to several people, because it states, "[e]very person who. . . ." Thus, unilateral conduct can result in a violation of Section 2. The cases brought to the court under Section 1 of the Sherman Act differ from those brought under Section 2. Section 1 cases are often concerned with finding an agreement (written or oral) that leads to a restraint of trade. Section 2 cases deal with the structure of a monopoly that exists in the marketplace. Whereas Section 1 focuses on agreements that are restrictive—that is, agreements that have a wrongful purpose—Section 2 looks at the so-called misuse of monopoly power in the marketplace. Both sections seek to curtail market industrial practices that result in undesired monopoly pricing and output behavior. Any case brought under Section 2, however, must be one in which the "threshold" or "necessary" amount of monopoly power already exists.

Note that the Sherman Act does not tell businesses how they should act. It tells them how they should *not* act. In this sense, the act is *proscriptive* rather than *prescriptive*. It is the basis for *policing* rather than *regulating* business conduct.

Other Aspects of the Sherman Antitrust Act

Jurisdiction   The Sherman Act applies only to restraints that have a significant impact on commerce. Because Congress can regulate only interstate commerce, in principle only interstate commerce is affected by this act. [2] State regulation of anti-competitive practices addresses purely local restraints on competition. Courts, however, have construed the meaning of *interstate* commerce more and more broadly,

---

1.   21 Congressional Record 2456 (1890).
2.   See the discussion under "The Commerce Clause" in Chapter 1.

bringing even local activities within the purview of the Sherman Act if they have a significant anticompetitive effect on interstate commerce.

The Sherman Act extends to U. S. nationals abroad who are engaged in activities that will affect U. S. foreign commerce, a subject discussed in Chapter 36.

Standing   The Department of Justice is not the only entity that has standing to sue under the Sherman Act. Some private parties can also sue for damages or other remedies. The courts have determined that the test of ability to sue depends on the directness of the injury suffered by the would-be plaintiff. Thus, a person wishing to sue under the Sherman Act must prove (1) that the antitrust violation either directly caused or was at least a substantial factor in causing the injury that was suffered, and (2) the unlawful actions of the accused party affected business activities of the plaintiff that were protected by the antitrust laws.

One of the unique features of the Sherman Antitrust Act is that it allows any person injured as a result of violations of the act to bring a suit for treble damages against the defendants, in addition to reasonable attorneys' fees. In the 1960s General Electric Company, along with other major electrical equipment manufacturers, paid over $200 million in treble damage claims for price fixing. Certain of the corporate officers were fined, and some of them even went to jail.

Remedies and Sanctions   Any person found guilty of violating either Section 1 or Section 2 of the Sherman Act is subject to criminal prosecution for a felony. Currently, upon conviction, a person can be fined up to $100,000 or imprisoned for three years, or both. A corporation can be fined $1 million. The Department of Justice can simultaneously institute civil proceedings to restrain the conduct that is in violation of the act.

The various remedies that the Justice Department has asked the court to impose include **divestiture** (making a company give up one or more of its operating functions) and **dissolution.** A group of meat packers, for example, can be forced to divorce itself from controlling or owning butcher shops.

Early Court Responses to the Sherman Antitrust Act

Initially, the Sherman Act was stripped of any effectiveness because the courts interpreted it so narrowly. For example, five years after the passage of the act, the Supreme Court refused to apply the Sherman Act to a sugar trust.[3] The Court held that the law did not extend to restraints affecting only the manufacture of commodities. According to the Court, "commerce secedes to manufacturer, and is not a part of it." In other words, the manufacturer of a commodity does not control commerce and therefore cannot violate the Sherman Act.

Then the Court swung the other way and declared illegal certain price-fixing agreements and territorial divisions on the basis that, without exception, every restraint of trade was forbidden by Section 1 of the act.[4] This absolute position clearly could not hold for long. The Court retreated once again, first condemning only direct restraints,[5] then concluding that restraints held to be lawful at common law should not be prohibited by the Sherman Act.[6]

DIVESTITURE
The act of selling one or more of a company's parts, such as a subsidiary or a plant; often mandated by the courts in merger and monopolization cases.

DISSOLUTION
The ending or breaking up of a business; the ending of a corporation's existence.

---

3.   United States v. E. C. Knight Co., 156 U.S. 1, 15 S.Ct. 249, 39 L.Ed. 325 (1895).
4.   See U.S. v. TransMissouri Freight Ass'n, 166 U.S. 290, 17 S.Ct. 540, 41 L.Ed. 1007 (1897).
5.   Hopkins v. United States, 171 U.S. 578, 19 S.Ct. 40, 43 L.Ed. 290 (1898).
6.   United States v. Joint Traffic Ass'n, 171 U.S. 505, 19 S.Ct. 25, 43 L.Ed. 259 (1898).

Landmark in the Law

The Standard Oil Co. of New Jersey v. United States (1911)

By 1890 the Standard Oil trust had become the foremost petroleum manufacturing and marketing combination in the United States. Streamlined, integrated, centrally and efficiently controlled, its monopoly over the industry could not be disputed. By the time the Sherman Act was passed in 1890, Standard Oil controlled 90 percent of the U. S market for refined petroleum products, and small manufacturers were incapable of competing with such an industrial leviathan. The increasing consolidation occurring in American industry, and particularly the Standard Oil Trust, did not go unnoticed by the American public. In March of 1881 Henry Demarest Lloyd, a young journalist from Chicago, published an article in the *Atlantic Monthly* entitled "The Story of a Great Monopoly," which discussed the success of Standard Oil Company. The article brought to the public's attention for the first time the fact that the petroleum industry in America was dominated by one firm—Standard Oil. Lloyd's article, which was so popular that the issue was reprinted six times, marked the beginning of the growing awareness and concern of the American public over the growth of monopolies, a concern that eventually led to the passage of the Sherman Act of 1890.

Even after the passage of the Sherman Act, however, Standard Oil was able to evade for a decade and a half the arm of the new antitrust law. Technically, the trust confused the government by reorganizing itself from a trust structure into a holding company framework in 1892, thus avoiding the Sherman Act's prohibition of the trust device as a means of controlling an industry. For many years also, enforcement of the Sherman Act was not a high priority among government officials. By 1905, however, Congress mandated an investigation of the oil industry. James Garfield, the head of the bureau conducting the investigation, was determined to unveil as many facts as possible concerning Standard Oil, and the bureau's 1906 report led eventually to a suit filed by Theodore Roosevelt against Standard Oil Company of New Jersey and other corporations involved in the combination. In 1909 the federal court that heard the case rendered a unanimous decision that Standard Oil and the other corporations constituted an illegal monopoly and thus violated the Sherman Act.

The decision was appealed to the U. S. Supreme Court, and on May 15, 1911, the Supreme Court's decision[1] upheld the verdict of the lower federal court. Thirty-three of the firms involved in the Standard Oil trust were to sever their connections with the parent firm, and the Court forbade Standard Oil to engage in future combinations or conduct in violation of the Sherman Antitrust Act. Chief Justice White, in his decision, summarized how Standard Oil and the other firms in the alliance had gathered control over all phases of petroleum production and marketing, concluding that all of the evidence leads "the mind up to a conviction of a purpose and intent which we think is so certain as practically to cause the subject not to be within the domain of *reasonable* contention [emphasis added]." This *rule of reason* enunciated by the Court in this case has been interpreted and modified many times since in applying antitrust laws.

1.   221 U.S. 1, 31 S.Ct. 502, 55 L.Ed. 619 (1911).

In this now-famous cartoon entitled The Monster Monopoly, John D. Rockefeller's Standard Oil Company is depicted as an octopus-like monster preying on smaller corporations.

Rule of Reason

This change in the Court's view—from condemning every restraint of trade to making some exceptions—was expressed in its 1911 decision in the case against Standard Oil Company of New Jersey (see the "Landmark"). Beginning with this decision, a *rule of reason* was applied to determine the purpose of the arrangement, the powers of the parties, and the effect of their actions in restraining trade.

Development of Per Se Violations

According to the rule of reason, only unreasonable restraints were illegal at common law. With respect to certain restraints on competition, however, Section 1 is read literally. Certain kinds of restrictive contracts are deemed inherently anticompetitive—that is, in restraint of trade as a *matter of law*. In such *per se violations* of Section 1 there is no need to examine any other facts.

In *United States* v. *Socony-Vacuum Oil Co.*[7] the Supreme Court set forth a per se standard, condemning all price-fixing arrangements. Footnote 59 of that opinion has become the most famous footnote in antitrust law. In that footnote Justice Douglas wrote:

> [I]t is well established that a person "may be guilty of conspiring, although incapable of committing the objective offense". . . . And it is likewise well settled that conspiracies under the Sherman Act are not dependent on any overt action other than the act of conspiring. . . . It is the "contract, combination . . . or conspiracy, in restraint of trade or commerce" which Section 1 of the Act strikes down, whether the concerted activity be wholly nascent or abortive on the one hand, or successful on the other. . . . And the amount of interstate or foreign trade involved is not material, since Section 1 of the Act brands as illegal the character of the restraint not the amount of commerce affected. . . . In view of these considerations a conspiracy to fix prices violates Section 1 of the Act though no overt act is shown, though it is not established that the conspirators had the means available for accomplishment of their objective, and though the conspiracy embraced but a part of the interstate or foreign commerce in the commodity. Whatever may have been the status of price-fixing agreements at common law the Sherman Act has a *broader* [emphasis added] application to them than the common law prohibitions or sanctions. . . . Price-fixing agreements may or may not be aimed at complete elimination of price competition. The group making those agreements may or may not have the power to control the market. But the fact that the group cannot control the market prices does not necessarily mean that the agreement as to prices has no utility to the members of the combination. The effectiveness of price-fixing agreements is dependent on many factors, such as competitive tactics, position in the industry, the formula underlying price policies. Whatever economic justification particular price-fixing agreements may be thought to have, the law does not permit an inquiry into their reasonableness. They are all banned because of their actual or potential threat to the central nervous system of the economy. . . .

❖ Clayton Act

In 1914 Congress attempted to strengthen federal antitrust laws by enacting the Clayton Act, which was aimed at specific monopolistic practices. The important sections of the Clayton Act are Sections 2, 3, 7, and 8. Briefly, these sections state:

---

7. 310 U.S. 150, 60 S.Ct. 811, 84 L.Ed. 1129 (1940).

Business Law in Action

The Athletic Arm of the Sherman Act

An interesting problem in the application of antitrust laws arises in lawsuits involving nonprofit organizations. Although such entities operate in the commercial marketplace, they claim "noneconomic" motives for their actions. The problem has become an important one in recent years for nonprofit sports organizations, such as the National Collegiate Athletic Association (NCAA). Practices engaged in by the NCAA and other amateur sports organizations, if they were engaged in by other commercial competitors, would likely be deemed illegal per se by the courts. But should the fact that such organizations are not supposedly operated for economic motives exempt them from antitrust laws?

Until the late 1970s, most courts said yes. Then, gradually, the lower courts began to apply the rule of reason to allegedly anticompetitive conduct on the part of amateur sports organizations to determine if their conduct resulted in any unreasonable restraint of commerce. Based on a rule-of-reason analysis, however, the courts did not find, until 1984, that there was sufficient reason to consider the rules of sports organizations (which were termed "necessary to survival") violations of antitrust laws. The courts generally concluded that the challenged activities did not have an anticompetitive purpose, were related to legitimate noncommercial purposes, and did not have a

significant effect on free competition in the marketplace.[1]

The court took a distinctly different view in NCAA v. *Board of Regents of the University of Oklahoma*,[2] however. This case, which first came before a district court in Oklahoma in 1982, concerned NCAA contracts with television networks for the 1982–1985 football seasons. These contracts gave the ABC, CBS, and Turner broadcasting networks the exclusive rights to negotiate with NCAA colleges to televise games. The contracts limited the number of games that could be televised by the networks, the number of appearances that any one team could make on television, and the amount of money a school could have for televising its games. The NCAA plan also required that a certain number of games between small colleges be televised and prohibited any individual institution from contracting separately for television coverage of its games.

Not surprisingly, the NCAA plan drew criticism from major college teams, that felt they deserved more network appearances and more money than the smaller teams. Their efforts to gain a greater voice in the NCAA television policy, though supported by the College Football Association, proved unsuccessful. As a result, the Universities of

Oklahoma and Georgia brought an action against the NCAA, alleging that its contracts with the television networks violated Sections 1 and 2 of the Sherman Act. Specifically, the NCAA was charged with price fixing, horizontal limitations on production, group boycott, and monopolization.

The district court did not mince words in rejecting the NCAA's argument that its goals were "noneconomic" and that it should thus be subject to special treatment under antitrust laws:

> [I]t is cavil [trivial, petty objection] to suggest that college football, or indeed higher education itself, is not a business. The colleges of the nation are in competition for students, for faculty, for government grants, and for philanthropic support. It is a big business and millions of dollars are involved. The same is true of college football. . . . Like any business, the schools which play intercollegiate football seek to maximize revenue and minimize expense while at the same time maintaining the level of quality which makes their product attractive to the buying public.[3]

The court noted that NCAA rules do have legitimate noneconomic goals—preserving amateurism and a competitive balance among school programs, for example—but the court could not agree that the NCAA television plan was at all necessary to achieve such goals. "Noneconomic considerations, however worthy, cannot be used to justify restraints

1. See, for example, Hennessey v. NCAA, 564 F.2d 1136 (5th Cir. 1977), and Justice v. NCAA, 577 F.Supp. 356 (D.Ariz. 1983).
2. 468 U.S. 85, 104 S.Ct. 2948, 82 L.Ed.2d 70 (1984).

3. Board of Regents of the University of Oklahoma v. NCAA, 546 F.Supp. 1276 (W.D.Okla. 1982).

Business Law in Action—Continued

that adversely affect competition. . . ." When the case reached the Supreme Court, the justices concurred that a nonprofit organization engaged in anticompetitive behavior cannot, simply because of its nonprofit status, be exempted from antitrust legislation. The value of the NCAA in encouraging intercollegiate amateur athletics was stressed by the Court, and it recognized that "as the guardian of an important American tradition, the NCAA's motives must be accorded a respectful presumption of validity." At the same time, the Court noted that "it is . . . well-settled that good motives will not validate an otherwise anticompetitive practice."

Section 2: [It is illegal to] discriminate in price between different purchasers [except in cases where the differences are due to differences in selling or transportation costs].

Section 3: [Producers or lessors cannot sell or lease] on the condition, agreement or understanding that the . . . purchaser or lessee thereof shall not use or deal in the goods . . . of a competitor or competitors of the seller.

Section 7: [A person or business organization cannot hold stock and/or assets in another business] where the effect . . . may be to substantially lessen competition.

Section 8: . . . [N]o person at the same time shall be a director in any two or more competing corporations, any one of which has capital, surplus, and undivided profits aggregating more than $1 million, engaged in whole or in part in commerce, other than banks, banking associations, trust companies, and common carriers.

Thus, the Clayton Act outlaws price discrimination, exclusive dealing and tying contracts, the purchase of enough stock or assets in a competing business to reduce competition, and interlocking directorates. Most of these provisions are discussed later in this chapter in the context of antitrust enforcement.

> *"The commerce of the world is conducted by the strong, and usually it operates against the weak."*
>
> **Henry Ward Beecher, 1813–1887**
> *(American abolitionist leader)*

❖ Federal Trade Commission Act

In 1914 Congress passed the Federal Trade Commission Act, which created a bipartisan, independent administrative agency headed by five commissioners, no more than three of whom could be of the same political party.[8] Section 5 of the act gives the Federal Trade Commission (FTC) broad powers to prevent "unfair methods of competition in commerce and unfair or deceptive acts or practices in commerce." Amendments, particularly in 1975, have broadened the commission's powers.[9] The FTC also has the authority to conduct investigations relating to alleged violations of antitrust statutes and to make reports and recommendations to Congress regarding legislation. More importantly, the FTC can promulgate interpretive rules and general statements of policy with respect to unfair or deceptive acts or practices. It can also promulgate trade regulation rules, which *define* particular unfair or deceptive acts or practices, including requirements for the purpose of preventing such acts or practices. The commission has issued guidelines defining unfair practices, but these guidelines are very broad, and many seemingly unfair practices are allowed.[10]

---

8. 15 U.S.C.A. 41–51 (1914).
9. Magnuson-Moss FTC Improvement Act of 1975.
10. The commission, for example, has indicated that a practice is "unfair" if it offends public policy or is immoral, unethical, oppressive, unscrupulous, or causes substantial injury to consumers.

CEASE-AND-DESIST ORDER
An administrative or judicial order prohibiting a business firm from conducting activities that an agency or a court has deemed illegal.

The FTC initiates most of its investigations because of oral or written communications from the general public and private business firms. The primary enforcement mechanisms of the FTC are **cease-and-desist orders** (orders to stop certain activities or practices) against violators of the FTC Act. Furthermore, businesses that disregard these orders are subject to fines of up to $10,000 per day for each day of continued violation. Cease-and-desist orders can be appealed to the courts. Unlike the Sherman Act, the FTC Act does not allow for treble damage actions.

Section 5 of the FTC Act overlaps a number of other antitrust statutes, including the Sherman Act, the Clayton Act, and other laws designed to reduce unfair methods of competition. The FTC initiates investigations and issues cease-and-desist orders, particularly for violations of Sections 2, 3, 7, and 8 of the Clayton Act, as amended by the Celler-Kefauver Act, the Robinson-Patman Act, and other acts. The FTC has no jurisdiction per se over violations under the Sherman Act.

❖ Robinson-Patman Act

PRICE DISCRIMINATION
Exists when two competing buyers pay two different prices for an identical product sold by a seller.

One of the more important activities of the Federal Trade Commission has been the detection and prohibition of **price discrimination** (that is, charging different prices to different purchasers for identical goods) when such discrimination lessens competition or tends to create a monopoly.

Subsequent judicial interpretation and responses by businesses effectively circumvented the original intent of Section 2 of the Clayton Act, so in 1936 Congress responded by enacting the Robinson-Patman Act. This act tightened the prohibition against price discrimination. If goods of *similar grade and quality* were sold at different prices, and these differences could not be justified by differences in production and distribution costs, the practice would violate the Robinson-Patman Act even if the Clayton Act could be circumvented. In addition, the act prohibited sellers from cutting prices to levels substantially below those charged by their competitors.[11]

❖ Enforcement of Antitrust Laws

"Combinations are no less unlawful because they have not as yet resulted in restraint."

Hugo L. Black, 1886–1971
(Associate Justice of the U. S. Supreme Court, 1937–1971)

The probability of a costly prison sentence or the payment of damages deters most business people from *openly* entering into agreements or conspiracies to fix prices, boycott competitors, or perform other unlawful activities. Often, however, the courts must determine whether the parties acted in concert on the basis of an implicit agreement to perform such unlawful activities. Such implicit agreements are difficult to detect. The courts must also investigate business behavior suspected of violating the antitrust statutes or associated administrative rules.

Enforcement of prohibitions against certain activities has led to well-defined areas of antitrust action: concerted action, certain information exchanges, horizontal market divisions, group boycotts, monopolization, and other horizontal acts.

Horizontal Activities—Defining Concerted Action

Businesspersons are not likely to enter into open agreements to restrain trade. Consequently, the courts must infer the purpose of agreements, combinations, and contracts

11.   Robinson-Patman Act, Subsection B.

Profile

Louis D. Brandeis (1856–1941)

"A lawyer who has not studied economics and sociology is very apt to become a public enemy." Thus went the blunt caveat of Louis Brandeis—one that many later Supreme Court justices, particularly Earl Warren—readily endorsed. During his years in private legal practice and later, during his twenty-three-year tenure on the U. S. Supreme Court (1916–1939), Brandeis became renowned for his ability to garner armies of facts to support his arguments. Brandeis, along with Holmes, was a liberal voice on the bench ("radical," according to his opponents) in a time of dramatic change in the United States.

Brandeis, the son of a prosperous grain merchant, was born in Louisville, Kentucky, in 1856. Although he never attended college, Brandeis graduated first in his class from Harvard Law School in 1877. His brilliance was further manifested both in his private legal counsel and in his judicial decisions as a Supreme Court justice.

After graduation from Harvard, Brandeis began practicing law, first in St. Louis and then in Boston. His distrust of big business and large combinations was evident throughout his career, both in his early activities in Boston and in his Supreme Court decisions and other writings. In his long dissent in *Liggett* v. *Lee*,[1] for example, Brandeis favored a tax on Florida chain stores as being both constitutionally permissible and socially desirable—as a deterrent against the accumulation of too much power in the hands of a few. He favored the freedom of the individual and the interests of free competition within the economy. His views are clearly expressed in *The Curse of Bigness*, a collection of Brandeis's writings published in 1935, and in *Other People's Money*, published in 1914. He was an early forerunner in establishing the principle of the right to privacy, and his article on that subject, "The Right To Privacy,"[2] has become probably the most famous law review article of all time. Brandeis's progressive ideas about government decentralization, regulatory reform, and the necessity of restraint on arbitrary private power made an indelible mark on American jurisprudence.

Brandeis became well known, as mentioned earlier, for his emphasis on the value of sociological and economic data in the process of judicial decision making. By the early 1900s the courts were required to decide on questions of public policy that depended on a knowledge of such facts, and yet, according to one scholar, "Excursions into fields related to the law, as economics and sociology, were not [deemed] necessary" by the courts.[3] Brandeis, using a technique that he became famous for—the "Brandeis brief"—ensured that the judges or justices to whom he was presenting a case were sufficiently informed on the issue. His use of this technique in *Muller* v. *Oregon* in 1908[4] marked the beginning of a practice that today is commonplace in the courts.

The *Muller* case arose in 1907 when Curt Muller, who owned a laundry business in Portland, Oregon, was arrested for violating the state's ten-hour workday law for women. The U. S. Supreme Court had, two years before, struck down a New York statute limiting the working hours of bakers to ten hours a day,[5] and Muller contested his arrest on the grounds that the Oregon law was likewise unconstitutional because it was contrary to the constitutionally guaranteed freedom to contract.

When the case reached the U. S. Supreme Court, Brandeis was invited by the Oregon district attorney to

---

1. 288 U.S. 517, 548, 53 S.Ct. 481, 489, 77 L.Ed. 929, 944 (1933).
2. Louis D. Brandeis, "The Right to Privacy," 4 *Harvard Law Review* (December 1890), pp. 193–220.
3. Alpheus T. Mason, *Brandeis: Lawyer and Judge in the Modern State* (Princeton, N.J.: Princeton University Press, 1933), p. 103.
4. 208 U.S. 412, 28 S.Ct. 324, 52 L.Ed. 551 (1908).
5. *Lochner* v. *New York*, 198 U.S. 45, 25 S.Ct. 539, 49 L.Ed. 937 (1905).

(continued on next page)

Profile—Continued

defend the Oregon statute before the Court. Brandeis went to work. He gathered facts from all possible sources to justify the Oregon law. The result of his labors, the finished brief, contained two pages of "law" and over a hundred pages of extralegal sources. Included were extracts from over ninety reports of committees, commissioners of hygiene, factory inspectors, and committees. He had information based on European experiences as

well. "Production not only increased but improved in quality" as a result of a limitation on working hours. "Regulation of the working day acted as a stimulus to improvement in processes of manufacture. . . . Factory inspectors, physicians and working women were unanimous in advocating the ten-hour day. . . ." Even ten hours might be too long: "Long hours of labor are dangerous for women primarily because of their physical organization." And so on

and on. The Court was convinced. The constitutionality of the Oregon law was upheld, and the fact-finding activities of one Louis D. Brandeis were mentioned in the case opinion—an unusual departure from custom. The brief, which—along with its author—became famous, was later reprinted by the National Consumers' League under the title, *Women in Industry*.

to determine whether they violate the antitrust laws. In other words, what intent is evidenced by the conduct of the business?

Until recently, courts looked at the *effect* of the business practice to determine the intent of the participants. If the effect was to reduce competition in the market, a criminal conspiracy existed as a matter of law. In 1978, however, the Supreme Court reversed that trend in *United States* v. *United States Gypsum Co.*[12] The Supreme Court held that a defendant's *state of mind or intent* is an element that must be considered in determining guilt. The Court stated that "an effect on prices, without more, will not support a criminal conviction under the Sherman Act."[13]

Joint Refusals to Deal   Sellers of goods and services generally have the right to select customers, provided that such a selection is not based on a customer's religious beliefs, color, sex, or national origin. When two or more sellers act in concert to refuse to sell to a particular buyer or class of buyers, however, the courts have generally found such acts unlawful under either the Sherman Act or the Clayton Act, or both. In the following classic case, a group of automobile dealers encouraged General Motors to stop further sales to a discount automobile sales outlet.

Case 30.1
UNITED STATES v. GENERAL MOTORS CORP.
United States Supreme Court, 1966.
384 U.S. 127, 86 S.Ct. 1321, 16 L.Ed.2d 415.

FACTS   Beginning in the late 1950s, "discount houses" and "referral services" began offering to sell new cars to

the public at allegedly bargain prices. By 1960 about eighty-five Chevrolet dealers, without authorization from General Motors, furnished cars to the discount houses. As the volume of these sales grew, the nonparticipating Chevrolet dealers located near one or more of these discount outlets began to feel the financial pinch. These disgruntled dealers asked General Motors for help. General Motors obtained promises from each dealer not to

---

12.   438 U.S. 422, 98 S.Ct. 2864, 57 L.Ed.2d 845 (1978).
13.   438 U.S. 422, 435, 98 S.Ct. 2864, 2872, 57 L.Ed.2d 854, 868 (1978).

Case 30.1—Continued

do business with discounters, and dealer associations were subsequently asked to police these promises. Professional shoppers were used to buy cars from dealers suspected of cooperating with discounters. Dealers who were "caught" were required to repurchase the car sold at discount and promise to stop such sales activities in the future. The government charged that these practices constituted a conspiracy to restrain trade in violation of the Sherman Act.

ISSUE Did General Motors' activities constitute a violation of the Sherman Act?

DECISION Yes. The Supreme Court found that these activities were a violation of Section 1 of the Sherman Act.

REASON The Court found "joint, collaborative action by dealers, the appellee associations, and General Motors to eliminate a class of competitors by terminating business dealings between them and a minority of Chevrolet dealers and to deprive franchised dealers of their freedom to deal through discounters if they so choose." The Court found a "fabric interwoven by many strands of joint action to eliminate the discounters from participation in the market, [and] to inhibit the free choice of franchised dealers to select their own methods of trade. . . ." This conspiracy to restrain trade violated Section 1 of the Sherman Act.

Territorial and Customer Restrictions   It is a Section 1 violation of the Sherman Act for competitors to divide up territories or customers. For example, manufacturers A, B, and C compete against each other in the states of Kansas, Nebraska, and Iowa. By agreement, A sells products only in Kansas, B sells only in Nebraska, and C sells only in Iowa. This concerted action reduces costs and allows all three (assuming there is no other competition) to raise the price of the goods sold in their respective states.

The same violation would take place if A, B, and C had simply agreed that A would sell only to institutional purchasers (school districts, universities, state agencies and departments, cities, etc.) in the three states, B only to wholesalers, and C only to retailers.

Monopolization   Section 2 of the Sherman Act makes it unlawful to "monopolize or attempt to monopolize." In practice, "to monopolize" has often been interpreted to mean actions that aggressively exclude a competitor.

A number of factors are considered. In 1966 the Supreme Court defined two essential elements of monopolization:[14]

1.   The possession of monopoly power in the relevant market.
2.   The willful acquisition or maintenance of that power as distinguished from growth or development as a consequence of a superior product, business acumen, or historic accident.

Monopoly power is usually measured in terms of the size of the market share held by the defendant company. Significant monopoly is associated with a total market share of 75 percent or more, whereas a market share of 25 percent or less is generally considered to be insufficient market power to support most antitrust actions.

---

14.   United States v. Grinnell Corp., 384 U.S. 563, 86 S.Ct. 1698, 16 L.Ed.2d 778 (1966).

In 1985, AT&T was forced to announce its plans to divest and break up into smaller, regional companies that would be independently owned and managed.

Vertical Restraints—Distribution Restrictions

Vertical restraints involve the distribution of goods, the power of suppliers to engage in exclusionary practices, and price discrimination. They include those situations where manufacturers attempt to restrict the prices, locations, customers, or retailing methods of goods being sold. Restriction on the distribution of goods may involve resale price maintenance or territorial and customer restrictions.

Resale Price Maintenance   Resale-price-maintenance, or *fair-trade*, agreements arise when manufacturers specify what the retail price to consumers must be. Usually, this specification is in the form of either a minimum or a maximum price. In the well-known *Dr. Miles* decision the Supreme Court held that a manufacturer who sold medicine to wholesalers was not entitled to restrict resale of the medicine by specifying minimum prices for retailers.[15] Later, this rigid rule against vertical price-fixing was extended to prohibit the specifying of maximum as well as minimum prices.[16]

Territorial and Customer Restrictions   In arranging for the distribution of a firm's products, manufacturers often wish to insulate dealers from direct competition from other dealers selling the firm's product. In this endeavor, they may institute territorial restrictions, or they may attempt to prohibit wholesalers or retailers from reselling the products to certain classes of buyers, such as competing retailers. In *United States v. Arnold, Schwinn & Co.*,[17] such restrictions (of either the territorial or consumer type) in manufacturer contracts with wholesalers or retailers were held to be a Section 1 violation of the Sherman Act. As illustrated in the following case, territorial and customer restrictions are lawful unless their use unreasonably restricts trade.

---

15.   Dr. Miles Medical Co. v. John D. Park & Sons Co., 220 U.S. 373, 31 S.Ct. 376, 55 L.Ed.2d 502 (1911).
16.   Albrecht v. Herald Co., 390 U.S. 145, 88 S.Ct. 869, 19 L.Ed.2d 998 (1968).
17.   388 U.S. 365, 87 S.Ct. 1856, 18 L.Ed.2d 1249 (1967).

Case 30.2
CONTINENTAL T.V., INC. v. GTE SYLVANIA, INC.
United States Supreme Court, 1977.
433 U.S. 36, 97 S.Ct. 2549, 53 L.Ed.2d 568.

FACTS GTE Sylvania, Inc., a manufacturer of television sets, adopted a franchise plan limiting the number of franchises granted in any given geographic area and requiring each franchise to sell Sylvania products only from the location or locations at which they were franchised. A franchise did not constitute an exclusive territory, and Sylvania retained sole discretion to increase the number of retailers in an area, depending on the success or failure of existing retailers in developing their market. Continental T.V., Inc., was a retailer under Sylvania's franchise plan. Shortly after Sylvania proposed a new franchise that would compete with Continental, Continental brought an antitrust suit against Sylvania charging that its vertically restrictive franchise system violated Section 1 of the Sherman Act. The district court held for Continental.

ISSUE Did Sylvania's action violate Section 1 of the Sherman Act?

DECISION No. The Supreme Court reversed the district court's decision. Sylvania's vertical, non-price-restrictive system did not constitute a per se violation of Section 1 of the Sherman Act.

REASON The fact that Sylvania restricted franchise retailers in their locations, even though title in the televisions had passed to the retailers, was a violation of the Sherman Act only if the facts and circumstances indicated that the restrictions were unreasonable. Two facts militated against a per se rule here. The restrictions were between a manufacturer and a retailer instead of between two entities on the same level (for example, two retailers or two manufacturers), and no price restrictions were involved. Clearly, vertical restrictions can stimulate competition because they provide incentives to persons who wish to distribute competitive brands of a product in the market. Among these is the incentive for a new manufacturer to use restrictive systems "in order to induce competent and aggressive retailers to make the kind of investment of capital and labor that is often required in the distribution of products unknown to the consumer."

Vertical Restraints—Exclusionary Practices

Exclusionary practices involve *refusals to deal* and so-called *tying arrangements* in which firms refuse to sell or lease a good unless the buyer agrees to purchase other goods or articles produced or distributed by the seller. Exclusionary practices also include *exclusive-dealing* arrangements wherein the seller requires the purchaser, usually a retailer, not to sell products of competing firms.

Refusals to Deal Refusals to deal were discussed earlier as a prohibited horizontal activity. In vertical arrangements, the Supreme Court has generally given firms the freedom to refuse to sell to individual buyers. In *United States* v. *Colgate & Co.*,[18] for example, the Court held that a manufacturer's advance announcement that it would not sell to price cutters was not a violation of the Sherman Act.

Tying Arrangement In a tying arrangement, the seller of a product conditions the sale of that product upon the buyer's agreement to purchase another product produced or distributed by the seller. For example, the seller of a copier machine may tie the sale of a *tying product* (the copier) to the purchase of a *tied product* (the paper). The legality of such arrangements depends on many factors, particularly the business purpose or effect of the arrangement.

---

18. 250 U.S. 300, 39 S.Ct. 465, 63 L.Ed.2d 992 (1919).

In 1936 the Supreme Court held that International Business Machines' practice of requiring the purchase of cards (the tied product) as a condition of leasing its tabulation machines (the tying product) was unlawful.[19] The Court, however, has not applied a strict rule against tying arrangements. In *United States Steel Corp* v. *Fortner Enterprises, Inc.*,[20] the Court ruled in favor of U. S. Steel despite the existence of a tie-in between the purchase of prefabricated homes (the tying product) and credit (the tied product). Since there was no evidence that U. S. Steel had significant economic power in either the prefabricated-home market or the credit market, its arrangement was found to be lawful.

Is it a violation of antitrust laws for McDonald's, the fast-food chain, to require its franchisees to sell only Coca-Cola, when such a requirement reduces profits for the franchisees (because substitutes, such as Pepsi-Cola, could be purchased by the franchisees at much lower prices)? This was the issue in the following case.

Case 30.3
MARTINO v. McDONALD'S SYSTEM, INC.
United States District Court, Northern District of Illinois, 1985.
625 F.Supp. 356.

FACTS In each of its franchise contracts, McDonald's establishes the standards for food and drink to be provided by the franchisee. One such requirement is that Coca-Cola be the only sugar-sweetened cola beverage served. McDonald's sells approximately 18 percent of all Coca-Cola sold in the United States. Louis Martino and other franchisees wanted to sell Pepsi-Cola because it can be purchased at a lower price than Coca-Cola. The franchisees felt that the Coca-Cola requirement unfairly diminished their profit margins. Arguing that the Coca-Cola requirement was an illegal *tie-in* of a product and an illegal restraint of free trade, the franchisees brought suit against McDonald's.

ISSUE Is the requirement by McDonald's that its franchisees sell only Coca-Cola illegal under antitrust laws?

DECISION No. The district court found that the requirement was not illegal and granted the defendant's motion for summary judgment against the franchisees.

REASON The court looked at a number of factors in reaching its conclusion. First, it observed that McDonald's did not monopolize the fast-food industry: "McDonald's was a pioneer, but one need only step outside this courthouse to observe perhaps half a dozen fast food franchises within a block . . . [and] a continuous exposure to a cacophony of presumed gastronomical delights." Second, McDonald's did not so dominate the cola market through its purchases that competition was substantially lessened. And third, McDonald's did not directly receive any financial benefit from the Coca-Cola requirement. The Coca-Cola Company established its own prices, and McDonald's had no economic interest in the profits of the Coca-Cola firm. For these reasons, the Coca-Cola requirement was not illegal.

Exclusive Dealing Section 3 of the Clayton Act, as amended, prohibits *exclusive-dealing* contracts when the effect of these contracts would be "to substantially lessen competition or tend to create a monopoly." Exclusive-dealing contracts arise when a seller or manufacturer forbids the buyer to purchase the products of competitive sellers. Despite its similarity with a tying contract, an exclusive-dealing arrangement is subject to a different judicial standard. In general, the courts apply a modified *rule*

---

19. International Business Machines Corp. v. United States, 298 U.S. 131, 56 S.Ct. 701, 80 L.Ed. 1085 (1936).
20. 429 U.S. 610, 97 S.Ct. 861, 51 L.Ed.2d 80 (1977).

of reason in determining whether the arrangement will substantially lessen competition.

The leading exclusive-dealing decision is that of *Standard Oil Co. of California v. United States.*[21] In this case, the largest gasoline seller in the nation made exclusive-dealing contracts with independent stations in seven western states. The contracts involved 16 percent of all retail outlets, whose sales were approximately 7 percent of all retail sales in that market. The Supreme Court found that these contracts were a Section 3 violation of the Clayton Act.

Mergers

The statutory authority for enforcing anticompetitive mergers is Section 7 of the Clayton Act. This section was introduced because it was feared that concentration would potentially facilitate collusion among sellers in the market, and that such collusion would be difficult to detect.

Horizontal Mergers   Both the FTC and Antitrust Division of the Justice Department have established guidelines to determine the legality of **horizontal mergers** based on the degree of concentration or market shares of merging firms, although the Court has indicated that it will look at the likely effects of the merger as well. Thus, if a merger facilitates horizontal collusion without increasing production or marketing efficiencies, it will be declared unlawful.

HORIZONTAL MERGER
A merger between two businesses or persons competing in the marketplace.

Mergers are permitted when they enhance consumer welfare by increasing efficiency, as long as they do not increase the probability of horizontal collusion. In the case of *United States* v. *Philadelphia National Bank*,[22] the commission held that even in situations with low entry barriers, there may be a loss of actual competition. Thus, mergers can be declared illegal even where entry is relatively easy, as illustrated by the following case.

Case 30.4
UNITED STATES v. VON'S GROCERY CO.
United States Supreme Court, 1966.
384 U.S. 270, 86 S.Ct. 1478, 16 L.Ed.2d 555.

FACTS   In 1958 Von's, the third largest retail grocery business in the Los Angeles area, merged with its largest direct competitor, Shopping Bag Food Stores, the sixth largest retailer. This created the second largest grocery chain in Los Angeles. The number of small business owners operating single grocery stores in the area had been dropping prior to the merger, and after the merger the number dropped still further. The United States brought this action, charging that the merger violated Section 7 of the Clayton Act as amended by the Celler-Kefauver Anti-Merger Act of 1950, which provides that "no cor-

poration engaged in commerce . . . shall acquire the whole or any part of the assets of another corporation engaged also in commerce, where . . . the effect of such acquisition may be substantially to lessen competition. . . ." The district court found that the merger would not tend to substantially lessen competition. The government appealed.

ISSUE   Would the merger between Von's and the Shopping Bag Food Stores tend to substantially lessen competition in the retail grocery industry?

DECISION   Yes. The decision of the district court was reversed and the case remanded to the district court to order Von's to divest itself of Shopping Bag.

---

21.   337 U.S. 293, 69 S.Ct. 1051, 93 L.Ed. 1371 (1949).
22.   374 U.S. 321, 83 S.Ct. 1715, 10 L.Ed.2d 915 (1963).

Case 30.4—Continued

REASON The Court found that retail concentration in Los Angeles drove small businesspersons out of the market, a trend the Celler-Kefauver Amendment sought to prevent. The Court stated, "Congress sought to preserve competition among many small businesses by arresting a trend toward concentration in its incipiency before that trend developed to the point that a market was left in the grip of a few big companies." The Court found that the merger here could not be defended on the ground that one of the companies was about to fail or that the two had to compete with a larger and more powerful competitor. The Court stated, "What we have, on the contrary, is simply the case of two already powerful companies merging in a way which makes them even more powerful than they were before." This factor and the trend in the Los Angeles market toward fewer and fewer owner-competitors were held to constitute a violation of Section 7 of the Clayton Act.

COMMENTS This 1966 Supreme Court decision has since come under attack. In its opinion, the Court suggests that the rapid decline in the number of small grocery companies increases the very concentration that Congress wanted to halt. A declining number of firms in the market, however, does not necessarily increase concentration. Concentration pertains to the market shares held by the largest four to eight firms; it does not refer to the total number of firms in the market. Yet *United States* v. *Von's Grocery Co.* is illustrative of the emphasis the courts will place on the fact that Section 7 of the Clayton Act deals with probabilities, not certainties, since, by its terms, Section 7 looks to both the present and future effects of a proposed merger.

VERTICAL MERGER
A combining of two firms, one of which purchases goods for resale from the other. If a producer or wholesaler acquires a retailer, it is a *forward* vertical merger. If a retailer or distributor acquires its producer, it is a *backward* vertical merger.

Vertical Mergers **Vertical mergers** occur when a company at one stage of production acquires a company at a higher or lower stage of production. Thus, the acquisition of a tire plant by an automobile manufacturer would constitute a backward vertical integration, while acquisition of a car-renting agency would constitute a forward vertical integration. The FTC's approach to vertical mergers depends on a number of factors, including the definition of the relevant product in geographic markets as well as the characteristics identified as impeding competition. For example, the commission will attack any vertical merger that prevents competitors of either party from competing in a segment of the market that otherwise would be open to them.[23] Such a "foreclosure" of an otherwise open segment of a market is the subject of the following case concerning a backward merger.

Case 30.5
FORD MOTOR CO. v. UNITED STATES
United States Supreme Court, 1972.
405 U.S. 562, 92 S.Ct. 1142, 31 L.Ed.2d 492.

FACTS This case arose when Ford Motor Company purchased Autolite Company, a manufacturer of spark plugs. Ford, Chrysler, and General Motors together produced 90 percent of American automobiles. The spark-plug market was dominated by Champion (50 percent), General Motors (30 percent), and Autolite (15 percent). Ford had planned to begin manufacturing its own spark plugs but decided to buy Autolite instead. Following Ford's purchase of Autolite, Champion was the only independent spark-plug manufacturer and, six years after Ford's acquisition of Autolite, Champion's share of the spark-plug market was reduced from 50 percent to about 33 percent. The United States brought an action against Ford, claiming that this acquisition violated Section 7 of the Clayton Act because it substantially lessened competition in the spark-plug market. When the trial court ordered Ford to divest itself of the Autolite assets, Ford appealed to the U. S. Supreme Court.

---

23. Brown Shoe Co. v. United States, 370 U.S. 294, 82 S.Ct. 1502, 8 L.Ed.2d 510 (1962).

Case 30.5—Continued

ISSUE   Did Ford's acquisition of Autolite constitute a violation of Section 7 of the Clayton Act by foreclosing a sufficiently large segment of the spark-plug market to competition?

DECISION   Yes. The acquisition was declared to be unlawful and in violation of Section 7 of the Clayton Act. The ruling of the district court was affirmed.

REASON   The Court concluded that if the acquisition were allowed, the spark-plug industry would become as concentrated as the automobile industry, and entry into the spark-plug market by new firms would be impossible. According to the Court, "As a result of the acquisition of Autolite, the structure of the spark plug industry changed drastically. . . . Ford, which before the acquisition was the largest purchaser of spark plugs from the independent manufacturers, became a major manufacturer. The result was to foreclose to the remaining independent spark plug manufacturers the substantial segment of the market previously open to competitive selling."

Conglomerate Mergers   **Conglomerate mergers** often extend product lines at the retail level, particularly among products that are complementary, although mergers can also occur among firms using similar suppliers. A large number of conglomerate mergers, however, occur when the merging firms have no direct functional business link. In such mergers there are no changes in market structure, market shares, or concentration ratios. In many cases, conglomerate mergers serve to reduce overhead costs by spreading them over a larger range of output and reducing advertising and other promotional costs. The following case is illustrative of a *product-extension* conglomerate merger.

CONGLOMERATE MERGER
A merger between firms that do not compete with each other because they are in different industries, as opposed to horizontal and vertical mergers.

Case 30.6
FEDERAL TRADE COMM'N v. PROCTER & GAMBLE CO.
United States Supreme Court, 1967.
386 U.S. 568, 87 S.Ct. 1224, 18 L.Ed.2d 303.

FACTS   Procter & Gamble sought to acquire Clorox Chemical Company. At the time of the merger, Clorox was the leading manufacturer of household bleach (49 percent of the national market), and Procter & Gamble had over half of the national detergent market. The Federal Trade Commission (FTC) brought this action for divestiture of the merger on the grounds that it violated Section 7 of the Clayton Act. Arguing that the merger prevented other bleach products from entering the market, thereby eliminating potential competitors, the FTC ordered Procter & Gamble to divest itself of the Clorox Company.

ISSUE   Did the merger between Procter & Gamble and Clorox violate Section 7 of the Clayton Act?

DECISION   Yes. The Supreme Court held that the merger violated Section 7 of the Clayton Act.

REASON   Procter & Gamble had sought to expand its product line by adding household bleach to it. The Court noted that the markets for the products of each of the companies were highly concentrated markets; that is, they were already dominated by a few companies. Thus, barriers to entry by potential competitors were already high, and competition was at a minimum. Justice Douglas, who wrote the majority opinion, concluded, "In the marketing of soaps, detergents and cleansers, as in the marketing of household liquid bleach, advertising and sales promotion are vital. . . . [T]he substitution of Procter with its huge assets and advertising advantages for the already dominant Clorox would dissuade new entrants and discourage active competition from the firms already in the industry due to fear of retaliation by Procter."

❖ Organizations Exempt from Antitrust Laws

There are many legislative and constitutional limitations on antitrust enforcement. Most are statutory and judicially created exemptions applying to the following areas:

1. *Labor.* Section 6 of the Clayton Act generally permits labor unions to organize and bargain without violating antitrust laws. Section 20 of the Clayton Act specifies that strikes and other labor activities are not violations of any law of the United States. But a union can lose its exemption if it combines with a nonlabor group rather than acting simply in its own self-interest.

2. *Agricultural associations and fisheries.* Section 6 of the Clayton Act (along with the Capper-Volstead Act of 1922) exempts agricultural cooperatives from the antitrust laws. The Fisheries Cooperative Marketing Act of 1976 exempts from antitrust legislation individuals in the fishing industry who collectively catch, produce, and prepare for market their products. Both exemptions allow members of such co-ops to combine and set prices for a particular product, but they do not allow them to engage in exclusionary practices or restraints of trade directed at competitors.

3. *Insurance.* The McCarren-Ferguson Act of 1945 exempts the insurance business from the antitrust laws whenever state regulation exists. This exemption does not cover boycotts, coercion, or intimidation on the part of insurance companies.

4. *Foreign trade.* Under the provisions of the 1918 Webb-Pomerane Act, American exporters may engage in cooperative activity in order to compete with similar foreign associations. Such cooperative activity may not, however, restrain trade within the United States or injure other American exporters. In 1982 the Export Trading Company Act was passed, broadening the Webb-Pomerane Act by permitting the Department of Justice to certify properly qualified export trading companies. Any activity within the scope described by the certificate is exempt from public prosecution under the antitrust laws.

5. *Baseball.* In 1922 the Supreme Court held that professional baseball was not within the reach of federal antitrust laws because it was not "interstate commerce."[24] Under modern interpretations of the Constitution's *commerce clause,* this decision is clearly wrong. Nonetheless, professional baseball retains its antitrust exemption; but this exemption applies only to baseball and not to other sports.

6. *Oil Marketing.* The 1935 Interstate Oil Compact allows states to determine quotas on oil that will be marketed in interstate commerce.

---

24. Federal Baseball Club of Baltimore, Inc. v. National League of Professional Baseball Clubs, 259 U.S. 200, 42 S.Ct. 465, 66 L.Ed. 898 (1922).

Application

Law and the Businessperson—Avoiding Antitrust Problems

Antitrust law is subject to numerous interpretations by the courts. Also, businesspersons need to be aware of the various state antitrust laws in addition to federal laws. And states now have the power to bring civil suits to enforce federal antitrust laws; hence, the businessperson worried about potential antitrust violation must seek counsel from a competent attorney specializing in antitrust law. There is one checklist item that we can mention here, however.

Checklist for Avoiding Antitrust Problems

☐ 1. Be cautious about communicating with a direct competitor who offers products or services that are similar to your own. If you have heard of such communications causing problems in your line of business, you should probably arrange for the individual employees involved to attend a seminar given by professionals who will let your employees know what is legal and what is not in dealing with competitors.

❖ Chapter Summary: Antitrust Laws

MAJOR ANTITRUST LAWS	
Statutes Limiting Combinations	1. *Sherman Act* (1890)—Section 2* prohibits monopolies and attempts or conspiracies to monopolize.
	2. *Clayton Act* (1914)—Section 7 prohibits mergers where the effect may be to substantially lessen competition or to create a monopoly. Amended (1950)—Celler-Kefauver Act enlarged application of Section 7 to include acquisition of assets.
	3. *Clayton Act* (1914)—Section 8 prohibits interlocking directorates.
Statutes Limiting Contractual and Business Actions	1. *Sherman Act* (1890)—Section 1* prohibits contracts, combinations, and conspiracies in restraint of trade, including vertical and horizontal price fixing, group boycotts, division of markets, and other practices.
	2. *Clayton Act* (1914)—Section 2 prohibits price discrimination that substantially lessens sellers' competition (primary violation). Amended (1936)—Robinson-Patman Act prohibits a seller engaged in interstate commerce from selling to two or more buyers goods of similar grade and quality at different prices where the result is a substantial lessening of competition or the creation of a competitive injury.
	3. *Clayton Act* (1914)—Section 3 prohibits exclusive-dealing and tying arrangements where the effect may be to substantially lessen competition.
	4. *Federal Trade Commission Act* (1914)—Section 5** prohibits unfair methods of competition; this act established and defined the powers of the FTC.

*Amended in 1974 and 1976 to increase penalties and broaden enforcement.
**Amended in 1973 and 1975 to increase penalties and grant industry-wide, rule-making power.

❖ Chapter Summary: Antitrust Laws—Continued

Exemptions from Antitrust Laws	1. Labor unions (under Section 6 of the Clayton Act of 1914).
	2. Agricultural associations and fisheries (under Section 6 of the Clayton Act of 1914, the Capper-Volstead Act of 1922, and the Fisheries Cooperative Marketing Act of 1976).
	3. Insurance—when state regulation exists (under the McCarran-Ferguson Act of 1945, as amended).
	4. Export trading companies (under the Webb-Pomerane Act of 1918 and the Export Trading Company Act of 1982).
	5. Baseball (by 1922 judicial decision).
	6. Oil marketing (under the Interstate Oil Compact of 1935).
ACTIVITIES PROHIBITED BY ANTITRUST LAWS	
Horizontal Restraints	1. *Pricing and marketing practices*—When two or more competitive sellers act in concert, or enter into agreements, to fix prices or divide territories or other markets.
	2. *Joint refusals to deal or group boycotts*—When two or more sellers act in concert to refuse to sell to a particular buyer or class of buyers.
	3. *Monopolization*—The use of monopoly power in the relevant market or the willful acquisition or maintenance of that power.
Vertical Restraints	1. *Distribution restrictions*—Through resale-price-maintenance agreements or territorial and customer restrictions.
	2. *Exclusionary practices*—Through refusals to deal, tying arrangements, and exclusive-dealing contracts, provided such contracts substantially lessen competition or tend to create a monopoly.
Mergers	1. *Horizontal mergers*—The acquisition by merger or consolidation of a competing firm engaged in the same relevant market. Will be unlawful only if a merger results in a disproportionate share of the market held by the merging firms resulting in a substantial lessening of competition and if the merger does not enhance consumer welfare by increasing efficiency of production or marketing.
	2. *Vertical mergers*—The acquisition by a seller of a buyer or vice versa. Will be unlawful if the merger prevents competitors of either merging firm from competing in a segment of the market that otherwise would be open to them, resulting in a substantial lessening of competition.
	3. *Conglomerate mergers*—The acquisition of a noncompeting business. Will be unlawful if the merger prevents competitors of either merging firm from competing in a segment of the market that otherwise would be open to them, resulting in a substantial lessening of competition.

❖ Questions and Case Problems

30-1. Assume the following events take place. Discuss which antitrust law has been *primarily* violated.

    (a) Allitron, Inc., and Donovan, Ltd., are interstate competitors selling similar appliances principally in the states of Indiana, Kentucky, Illinois, and Ohio. Allitron and Donovan agree that Allitron will no longer sell in Ohio and Indiana, and Donovan will no longer sell in Kentucky and Illinois.

    (b) The partnership of Alvaredo and Parish is engaged in the oil-well-head service industry in the states of New Mexico and Colorado. They presently have about 40 percent of the market for this service.

Webb Corporation is engaged in competition with the Alvaredo-Parish partnership in the same state area. Webb has approximately 35 percent of the market. Alvaredo and Parish acquire the stock and assets of the Webb Corporation.

30-2. Super-Tech Industries presently controls 55 percent of the market in the manufacture and sale of computers. The balance of the market is controlled by five other manufacturers, with Alcan Corporation having 25 percent of the market. Alcan has an innovative research staff, but every time Alcan introduces a faster, more powerful and efficient computer in the market, Super-Tech immediately informs its customers of the upcoming development of a competing computer that they will sell at 30 percent below the Alcan price. Alcan claims that these activities on the part of Super-Tech are an antitrust violation. Discuss fully whether this unilateral action by Super-Tech violates antitrust law.

30-3. Jorge's Appliance Corporation is a new retail seller of appliances in Sunrise City. Jorge's innovative sales techniques and financing have caused a substantial loss of sales from the appliance department of No-Glow Department Store, a large chain store with substantial buying power. No-Glow told a number of appliance manufacturers that if they continued to sell to Jorge's, No-Glow would discontinue its large volume of purchases from these manufacturers. The manufacturers immediately stopped selling appliances to Jorge's. Jorge's filed suit against No-Glow and the manufacturers, claiming that their actions constituted an antitrust violation. No-Glow and the manufacturers were able to prove that Jorge's was a small retailer with a small portion of the market, and, since the relevant market was not substantially affected, they claimed that they were not guilty of restraint of trade. Discuss fully whether there was an antitrust violation.

30-4. Instant Foto Corporation is a manufacturer of photography film. At the present time Instant Foto has approximately 50 percent of the market. Instant Foto advertises that the purchase price for Instant Foto film includes photo processing by Instant Foto Corporation. Instant Foto claims that its film processing is specially designed to improve the quality of the finished photos when using Instant Foto's film. Is Instant Foto's combination of film purchase and film processing an antitrust violation? Explain.

30-5. The plaintiff, Spray-Rite, was an authorized distributor of Monsanto herbicides from 1957 to 1968, and the defendant, Monsanto Company, manufactures chemical products, including agricultural herbicides. Spray-Rite continually sold Monsanto products at a lower price than other distributors. In October 1968 Monsanto declined to renew Spray-Rite's distributorship. Spray-Rite subsequently brought an action under Section 1 of the Sherman Act. In its complaint, Spray-Rite alleged that Monsanto and some of its distributors conspired to fix the resale price of Monsanto herbicides. Monsanto contended, however, that Spray-Rite's distributorship had been terminated because of its failure to hire trained sales personnel

and to promote sales to dealers adequately. The court of appeals concluded that proof of Spray-Rite's termination subsequent to competitor complaints was sufficient to support an inference of concerted action. Could price fixing be inferred from the fact that a manufacturer terminated a price-cutting distributorship in response to complaints from other distributors? What was the standard of proof necessary to establish a vertical price-fixing conspiracy in violation of Section 1 of the Sherman Act? [Monsanto Co. v. Spray-Rite Service Corp., 465 U.S. 752, 104 S.Ct. 1464, 79 L.Ed.2d 775 (1984); rehearing denied 466 U.S. 994, 104 S.Ct. 2378, 80 L.Ed.2d 850 (1984)]

30-6. The plaintiff, Edwin G. Hyde, a certified anesthesiologist, applied for a position on the medical staff of the defendant, East Jefferson Parish Hospital. The hospital served approximately 30 percent of the patients in the area. Because the hospital had entered into a contract in which all anesthesiological services required by the hospital's patients were to be performed by a professional medical corporation, it denied the plaintiff's application. The plaintiff subsequently brought an action, alleging that the contract violated Section 1 of the Sherman Act. Tying arrangements are subject to the per se rule. Does this contract per se violate Section 1 of the Sherman Act, since every patient undergoing surgery at Jefferson Hospital must use the services of one firm of anesthesiologists? Explain. [Jefferson Parish Hospital District No. 2 v. Hyde, 466 U.S. 2, 104 S.Ct. 1551, 80 L.Ed.2d 2 (1984); remanded to Hyde v. Jefferson Parish Hosp. Dist. No. 2., 764 F.2d 1139 (5th Cir. 1985)]

30-7. Typically, a market will operate much more efficiently if sellers are well informed about how much buyers are willing to pay for a particular product, how much the industry is producing, what the capacity of various firms is, etc. The dissemination of information, however, is also likely to stabilize prices by reducing the *dispersion* of prices. The question then arises as to whether or not an exchange of price information for purposes of compliance with the Robinson-Patman Act is beyond the reach of the Sherman Act. (The Robinson-Patman Act forbids price discrimination—the discrimination in price between different purchasers of commodities of like grade and quality.) Consider, for example, a situation in which manufacturers of gypsum board were charged with a combination and conspiracy for allegedly contacting competitors about current and future prices before making price concessions to buyers. The defendants asserted that they had only contacted their competitors on prices and sales terms in order to meet the prices of competitors. Under the Robinson-Patman Act, a seller may justify its price discrimination by demonstrating that the lower price in one locality was charged "in good faith to meet an equally low price of a competitor." Thus, is there a conflict between the two antitrust statutes—the behavior proscribed by the Sherman Act and the meeting-competition defense of the Robinson-Patman Act? [United States v. United States Gypsum Co., 438 U.S. 422, 98 S.Ct. 2864, 57 L.Ed.2d 845 (1978)]

30-8. Blackwell leased and operated a gas station under a franchise agreement with a subsidiary of Power Test Petroleum Distributors. Under the terms of the franchise agreement, Blackwell was to sell only the gasoline products of Power Test Petroleum; if Blackwell purchased and sold gasoline produced by other petroleum firms, the agreement would be terminated. In May of 1980 Power Test increased the price of its gasoline. Blackwell, rather than pay the higher price for the gasoline and reduce his own profits, purchased his gasoline from other sources instead at lower price. When Power Test moved to terminate Blackwell's lease and franchise agreement, Blackwell sued for damages and injunctive relief, alleging that Power Test's tying arrangement violated the Sherman Act. The court determined that Power Test's share of the retail sales market for gasoline in the Greater New York Metropolitan Area was 6 percent. Did Power Test's tie-in of the lease and its own gasoline products violate the Sherman Act? Explain. [Blackwell v. Power Test Corp., 540 F.Supp. 802 (D.N.J. 1981)]

30-9. On August 5, 1969, at a hearing held before the Arizona Corporation Commission, the Arizona Water Company, a private corporation, sought and was granted the right to deliver water in a specified geographic area. Subsequently, the state of Arizona issued the company a "certificate of convenience and necessity," which confirmed the company's exclusive right to sell water in the specified area. In light of antitrust laws that prohibit the exercise of monopoly powers, could Arizona Water Company be granted this exclusive right? Under what conditions was the state of Arizona allowed to withdraw the "certificate of convenience and necessity" that it awarded Arizona Water Company? [Fernandez v. Arizona Water Co., 21 Ariz.App. 107, 516 P.2d 49 (1973)]

Chapter 31

Consumer and Environmental Law

Some have labeled the period from the mid-1960s as the age of the consumer because so much consumer-protection legislation has been passed. This legislation, in the words of Justice Douglas, "declared in terms well nigh conclusive" the public interest in protecting the consumer against the unfair practices and unsafe products of sellers. Both state and federal legislation has been enacted to regulate the manner in which businesses may advertise, engage in mail-order transactions, package and label their products, and so on. In addition, numerous local, state, and federal agencies have sprung up to aid the consumer in settling his or her grievances with sellers and producers. **Consumer-protection law** arises from common-law judicial rulings, as well as from federal, state, and local statutes. Additionally, administrative agencies, through their rule-making and enforcement activities, have influenced the way in which businesses can act.

In the first part of this chapter, we will examine some of the sources of consumer protection and some of the major issues. In the latter part of the chapter, we look at environmental protection as an even newer form of government regulation. The urban industrial society in our century has apparently strained the environment's capacity to handle the pollution that we are discharging into the air and water. In the last two decades, what has become known as **environmental law** has been of a statutory and administrative nature. We will examine some of the federal statutes that protect our environment.

"Subject to specific constitutional limitations, when the legislature has spoken, the public interest has been declared in terms well nigh conclusive."

William O. Douglas, 1898–1980
(Associate Justice of the U. S. Supreme Court, 1939–1975)

CONSUMER-PROTECTION LAW
State and federal laws specifying the duties of sellers and the rights of consumers in the sale and purchase of consumer goods.

ENVIRONMENTAL LAW
The body of legislation pertaining to environmental health and preservation; examples of such legislation include the Clean Air Act, the Clean Water Act, and numerous other statutes passed in recent decades to protect the environment.

❖ Sources of Consumer Protection

Sources of consumer protection exist at all levels of government. A number of federal laws—such as the Consumer Credit Protection Act and the Magnuson-Moss Warranty Act—have been passed to provide more explicit direction on the duties of sellers and the rights of consumers. Exhibit 31-1 lists a number of the major consumer-protection statutes. In addition to the Uniform Commercial Code's consumer-protection provisions, several of the states also have passed specific consumer-protection statutes. Administrative agencies, such as the Federal Trade Commission, also provide an important source of consumer protection. In nearly every agency and department of the government, there is an office of consumer affairs, and most states have one or more such offices to assist consumers. Numerous private organizations, such as the

◆ **Exhibit 31-1 Federal Consumer-Protection Statutes**

Popular Name	Purpose	Statute Reference
ADVERTISING		
Federal Trade Commission Act	Prohibits deceptive and unfair trade practices	15 U.S.C. 45, 341 *et seq.*
CERTIFICATION AND LABELING		
Child Protection and Toy Safety Act	Requires child-proof devices and special labeling	15 U.S.C. 1261 *et seq.*
Fair Packaging and Labeling Act	Requires accurate names, quantities, weights	15 U.S.C. 1451 *et seq.*
Fur Products Labeling Act	Prohibits misbranding of fur products	15 U.S.C. 69
Smoking Act	Requires labels warning of possible health hazards by surgeon general	15 U.S.C. 1331 *et seq.*
Smokeless Tobacco Act	Requires labels disclosing possible health hazards of smokeless tobacco; prohibits advertising via electronic media of smokeless tobacco products	15 U.S.C. 4401 *et seq.*
Wool Products Labeling Act	Requires accurate labeling of wool products	15 U.S.C. 68
HEALTH AND SAFETY		
Consumer Product Safety Act	Established the Consumer Product Safety Commission to regulate all potentially hazardous consumer products	15 U.S.C. 2051
Flammable Fabrics Act	Prohibits the sale of highly flammable clothing	15 U.S.C. 1191
Food and Drug Act/Food, Drug, and Cosmetic Act	Protects consumers from unsafe food products and from unsafe and/or ineffective drugs	21 U.S.C. 301
SALES AND WARRANTIES		
Magnuson-Moss Warranty Act	Provides rules that govern content of warranties	15 U.S.C. 2301 *et seq.*
Real Estate Settlement Procedures Act	Requires disclosure of home-buying costs	12 U.S.C. 2601 *et seq.*
Uniform Commercial Code (UCC)	Covers unconscionable sales contracts	UCC 2-302 (adopted by all states except Louisiana)
CREDIT		
Consumer Credit Protection Act	Offers comprehensive protection covering all phases of credit transactions	15 U.S.C. 1601 *et seq.*
Equal Credit Opportunity Act	Prohibits discrimination in the extending of credit	15 U.S.C. 1691 *et seq.*
Fair Credit Collection Practices Act	Prohibits debt collectors' abuses	15 U.S.C. 1692
Fair Credit Reporting Act	Protects consumers' credit reputations	15 U.S.C. 1681 *et seq.*
Truth-in-Lending Act	Requires full disclosure of credit terms	15 U.S.C. 1601 *et seq.*
Uniform Consumer Credit Code	Requires full disclosure of credit terms	Adopted by Colorado, Idaho, Indiana, Iowa, Kansas, Maine, Oklahoma, South Carolina, Utah, Wisconsin, and Wyoming

DECEPTIVE ADVERTISING
Advertising that misleads consumers, either by unjustified claims concerning a product's performance or by the omission of a material fact concerning the product's composition or performance.

Better Business Bureau system, also exist to aid consumers. Finally, consumers can use the courts to obtain remedies for their grievances. Various mechanisms have been developed—including free legal services, small claims courts, and the recovery of attorney's fees in class actions—to encourage consumer actions.

❖ Advertising

The increased protection received by consumers during the past two decades against **deceptive advertising** derives more from statutory and administrative sources than from common law. Common-law protection is based on fraud and requires proof of intent to misrepresent facts and other criteria. Statutory law and administrative regulations, on the other hand, focus on whether the advertising is likely to be misleading, regardless of intent. This approach arises from the reasoning that laws against false advertising should attempt to protect the consumer rather than to punish the seller or advertiser.

The Federal Trade Commission Act empowers the Federal Trade Commission (FTC) to determine what constitutes a deceptive practice within the meaning of Section 5 of the act. When the commission renders an opinion or issues an order, appeal can be taken through judicial channels, but a reviewing court generally accords great weight to the FTC's judgment. This is because the court recognizes that, as the administrative agency that deals continually with such cases, the FTC is often in a better position than the courts to determine when a practice is deceptive within the meaning of the act.

Defining Deceptive Advertising

As defined by the FTC, deceptive advertising generally means that the advertisement may be interpreted in more than one way and that one of those interpretations is false or misleading. Deception may arise from a false statement or claim about the product's quality, effects, price, origin, or availability; or it may arise from an omission of important information about the product. Some advertisements contain "half-truths," meaning that the presented information is true, but incomplete, leading consumers to a false conclusion. Others contain statements not supported by adequate scientific evidence. These may or may not be considered deceptive. When the claim is incapable of measurement, however, as in, "When you're out of Schlitz, you're out of beer," no problem of deception is perceived by the FTC. In the following case, the court addressed the question of allegedly deceptive advertising for an over-the-counter painkiller.

Case 31.1
THOMPSON MEDICAL COMPANY, INC. v. FEDERAL TRADE COMMISSION
United States Court of Appeals, District of Columbia Circuit, 1986.
253 U.S.App.D.C. 18, 791 F.2d 189.

FACTS This case concerned a complaint brought by the Federal Trade Commission against Thompson Medical Company, alleging that Thompson's advertising for "Aspercreme," a topical analgesic (painkiller) sold over-the-counter in drug stores, was false and misleading. According to Thompson's advertising, Aspercreme was supposed to help arthritis victims and others who seek relief from minor aches and pains. It was meant to be rubbed on the area where an analgesic effect is desired. Thompson's advertising strongly suggested that Aspercreme and aspirin were related. In one television advertisement, for example, Aspercreme was described as fol-

lows: "When you suffer from arthritis, imagine putting the strong relief of aspirin right where you hurt. Aspercreme is an odorless rub which concentrates the relief of aspirin. When you take regular aspirin, it goes throughout your body. . . . But, in seconds, Aspercreme starts concentrating all the temporary relief of two aspirin directly at the point of minor arthritis pain."

The Federal Trade Commission ordered Thompson to refrain from advertising Aspercreme as an effective painkiller until studies were conducted that proved its effectiveness. It also ordered Thompson to disclose in all advertising and labeling that Aspercreme does not contain aspirin. Thompson appealed the FTC decision, claiming that the FTC ruling was tantamount to an order to cease selling Aspercreme and would lead to the destruction of its business.

ISSUE Were the FTC's conclusions regarding Thompson's advertising of Aspercreme correct?

Case 31.1—Continued

DECISION   Yes. The appellate court affirmed the FTC order that Thompson refrain from deceptively advertising its product, Aspercreme.

REASON   The court found that the FTC adequately considered a large mass of technical evidence and concluded that Thompson had engaged in deceptive advertising with respect to Aspercreme. "We cannot find

fault," said the court, "in the Commission's conclusions or in the remedial measures it imposed. . . . If and when Thompson comes up with evidence that Aspercreme is effective, it will be free to again make efficacy claims in its advertising. Until that time, it should not say what it cannot prove. The FTC's requirement of aspirin-content disclaimers also is entirely appropriate."

Bait-and-Switch Advertising

BAIT-AND-SWITCH ADVERTISING

A selling technique that involves advertising a product (the "bait") at a very attractive price, then informing the consumer, once he or she is in the door, that the advertised product is either not available or is of poor quality, and promoting a more expensive item in its stead (the "switch").

In some cases, the FTC has promulgated specific rules to govern advertising. One of its more important rules is contained in the FTC "Guides on Bait Advertising." [1] The rule is designed to prohibit advertisements that specify a very low price for a particular item that will likely be unavailable to the consumer, who will then be encouraged to purchase a more expensive item. The low price is the "bait" to lure the consumer into the store. The salesperson is instructed to "switch" the consumer to a different item. According to the FTC guidelines, **bait-and-switch advertising** occurs if the seller refuses to show the advertised item, fails to have adequate quantities of it available, fails to promise to deliver the advertised item within a reasonable time, or discourages employees from selling the item.

In the following case, the plaintiff alleged that a car dealership had engaged in bait-and-switch advertising—as well as other forms of deceptive advertising. The court here distinguishes between price-bargaining activities, which are not illegal, and bait-and-switch techniques.

Case 31.2
GOLDBERG v. MANHATTAN FORD LINCOLN-MERCURY, INC.
Supreme Court, New York County, Part I, 1985.
129 Misc.2d 123, 492 N.Y.S.2d 318.

FACTS   Stuart Goldberg, in a phone conversation with an agent of Manhattan Ford Lincoln-Mercury, Inc. (Manhattan), had been told that he could buy a Lincoln he desired for 15 percent below the list price, less the trade-in allowance. Goldberg was told initially that he could get a $10,000 trade-in allowance for his 1981 Volvo, subject to appraisal, and that the sales manager would approve such a deal. When Goldberg went to the showroom, however, the sales agent said the used-car appraisal would

have to be reduced to $9,000, and when it was noticed that there had been some body damage to the Volvo, this amount was reduced even further, to $8,500. In addition, the price of the Lincoln Goldberg wanted to purchase, as it turned out, was not 15 percent below the list price, but $3,667 more than that amount. Because of these changes from the prices originally quoted to him, Goldberg contended the dealership had engaged in "deceptive" advertising. One of the allegations was that he had been the victim of a "bait-and-switch" operation; the quoted price and trade-in terms had lured him to the dealership, where he had been "switched" to another deal entirely. Goldberg sought damages of $1,500 for the reduction of the appraisal value of the Volvo and $3,667 for not getting the 15-percent discount below list price. He also sought

---
1.   16 C.F.R. 238 (1968).

Case 31.2—Continued

punitive damages for "wanton and willful fraud" on the part of Manhattan. Manhattan moved to dismiss the charges.

ISSUE   Can the charges of deceptive advertising be dismissed?

DECISION   Yes. The motion for dismissal was granted.

REASON   The court perceived the question in this case to be whether a cause of action for "deceptive practice" could be "predicated on the fact that one party in a contract negotiation continuously modified the proposed terms so that the deal fell through." The court showed little sympathy for the plaintiff, who alleged—as grounds for punitive damages—in a seventeen-page document the many details of the negotiations that had caused him frustration. The court found that the car dealership had done nothing more than engage in usual price-bargaining activities and held that the "practice of modifying proposed terms of a contract as the negotiations proceed is not at all analogous to 'bait and switch' selling." The bait-and-switch technique, the court noted, involved luring prospective

purchasers through the bait of a desirable item, and then talking the customer into a less desirable item—presumably with a greater profit margin for the seller. In this case, the court could find no evidence that Goldberg had been "lured" by the promise of a Lincoln, say, and "then switched over to an entirely different model, such as a 1928 DeSoto." Rather, the negotiations involved in this case were preliminary to any contract, and, absent a contract in which there has been a definite offer and acceptance, there can be no cause of action. In conclusion, the court noted that the plaintiff "suffered no damage, apart from loss of time and loss of pride. . . . No deceptive practice, no common-law fraud and no basis for punitive damages has been set forth." The court further noted, "Even when there has been an executed contract and a consummated sale, frustration and disappointed expectations do not of themselves give rise to a cognizable cause of action." The court stated, "It would be a revolutionary change in the law if we were to hold that a failure to agree on a contract created a new cause of action, or that a party to a negotiation could change the proposed terms or conditions only at the peril of being subjected to a lawsuit for 'deceptive practices.' "

Labeling and Packaging

A number of federal and state laws that govern labeling and packaging have been passed to provide the consumer with accurate information or warnings about the use or possible misuse of the product. The Fur Products Labeling Act, the Wool Products Labeling Act, the Flammable Fabrics Act, the Food, Drug and Cosmetic Act, the Cigarette Labeling and Advertising Act, the Smokeless Tobacco Health Education Act, and the Fair Packaging and Labeling Act are a few of the acts that have been enacted, in part, to reduce the amount of incorrect labeling and packaging in consumer products.

In general, labels must be accurate, which means that they must use words as they are ordinarily understood by consumers. For example, a regular size box of cereal cannot be labeled "giant" if that word would exaggerate the amount of cereal. Labels often must specify the raw materials used in the product, such as the percentage of cotton, nylon, or other fibers used in a shirt. The Fair Packaging and Labeling Act requires that consumer goods have labels that identify the product, the manufacturer, the packer or distributor and its place of business, the net quantity of the contents, and the quantity of each serving if the number of servings is stated.[2]

Additional authority is also included in this statute to add requirements governing words that are used to describe packages, terms that are associated with savings claims, information disclosure for ingredients in nonfood products, and standards for the

---

2.   15 U.S.C.A., Section 1451 *et seq.*

partial filling of packages. The provisions are enforced by the Federal Trade Commission and the Department of Health and Human Services.

❖ Sales

A number of statutes that protect the consumer in sales transactions concern the disclosure of certain terms in sales, rules governing home or door-to-door sales, mail-order transactions, referral sales, and unsolicited merchandise. The Federal Reserve Board of Governors, for example, has issued Regulation Z, which governs credit provisions associated with sales contracts, and numerous states have passed laws governing the remedies available to consumers in home sales. Furthermore, states have adopted a number of consumer-protection provisions by incorporating the UCC and the Uniform Consumer Credit Code into their statutory codes.

In 1968 Congress passed the first of a series of statutes regarding the content of credit information contained in written and oral messages. If, for instance, certain credit terms are used in an advertisement, other credit information is also required. Thus, if Prolific Pontiac Sales states in a newspaper advertisement that individuals have thirty-six months to pay, the firm must also include the cash price of the automobiles, the down payment, the finance charge, the amount of each periodic payment, and the annual percentage rate of interest.

The Postal Reorganization Act of 1970 provides that unsolicited merchandise sent by U. S. mail may be retained, used, discarded, or disposed of in any manner deemed appropriate, without the individual incurring any obligation to the sender.[3] In addition, the mailing of unordered merchandise (except for free samples) constitutes an unfair trade practice and is not permitted. (Exceptions are mailing by charitable agencies and those made by mistake.)

Door-to-Door Sales

Door-to-door sales are singled out for special treatment in the laws of most states. This special treatment stems in part from the nature of the sales transaction if the salesperson is able to gain entrance. A door-to-door seller usually has a captive audience because many individuals are actually immobilized at home. Since repeat purchases are not as likely as they are in stores, the seller has little incentive to cultivate the good will of the purchaser. Furthermore, the seller is unlikely to present alternative products and their prices. Thus, a number of states have passed statutes that permit the buyers of goods sold door-to-door to cancel their contracts within a specified period of time, usually two to three days after the sale.

A Federal Trade Commission regulation also makes it a Section 5 violation for door-to-door sellers to fail to give consumers three days to cancel any sale. This rule applies as well as state statutes so that consumers are given the most favorable benefits of the FTC rule and their own state statute. In addition, the FTC rule requires that the notification be given in Spanish if the oral negotiations for the sale were in that language.

---

3. 39 U.S.C.A. 3009.

Mail-Order Sales

Consumers buying from mail-order houses typically have been given less protection than when they purchase in stores. Many mail-order houses are outside the buyer's state, and it is more costly to seek **redress** for grievances in such situations. In addition to the federal statute that prevents the use of mails to defraud individuals, several states have passed statutes governing certain practices by sellers, including insurance companies, that solicit through the mails. The state statutes parallel the federal statutes governing mail fraud.

REDRESS
Satisfaction for damages incurred through the use of a product or a service or through the wrongdoing of another.

❖ Health Protection

As discussed in the "Landmark" in this chapter, in 1906 Congress passed its first act regulating food and drugs—the Food and Drug Act—which was the first step toward protecting consumers against adulteration and misbranding of food and drug products. In 1938 the Food, Drug and Cosmetic Act was passed to strengthen the protective features of the 1906 legislation. These acts, and subsequent amendments, established standards for foods, specification of safe levels of potentially dangerous food additives, and control of classifications of foods and food advertising. Drugs must be proved to be effective as well as safe before they can be marketed, and food additives that can be shown to be carcinogenic (cancer-causing) to humans or animals are forbidden. In general, food and drug laws make manufacturers responsible for ensuring that the food they offer for sale contains no substances that could cause injury to health. Most of the statutes involving food and drugs are monitored and enforced by the Food and Drug Administration.

Also in 1906, Congress passed the Meat Inspection Act, the beginning of legislation establishing inspection requirements for all meat and poultry sold for human consumption. The Food Safety and Quality Service of the Department of Agriculture enforces statutes relating to meat and poultry inspection.

Congress has enacted a number of statutes to protect individuals from harmful products as well. In response to public concern over the dangers of cigarette smoking, Congress has required warnings to be placed on cigarette and little cigar packages, as well as on containers of smokeless tobacco. For years, the statement: "Warning: The Surgeon General Has Determined That Cigarette Smoking Is Dangerous to Your Health" was required to appear on cigarette and little cigar packages. In 1985 major-brand cigarette producers were required to rotate four warning labels on a quarterly basis. Smaller companies may use all four warnings at the same time on a random basis. Each warning begins, "Surgeon General's Warning" and then states one of the following:

1.   Smoking Causes Lung Cancer, Heart Disease, Emphysema, and May Complicate Pregnancy.
2.   Quitting Smoking Now Greatly Reduces Serious Risks to Your Health.
3.   Smoking by Pregnant Women May Result in Fetal Injury, Premature Birth, and Low Birth Weight.
4.   Cigarette Smoke Contains Carbon Monoxide.

All cigarette advertising must carry one of the four warnings listed as well.

The Smokeless Tobacco Act of 1986 requires producers, packagers, and importers of smokeless tobacco to conspicuously label their products with one of three warnings:

1.   WARNING: This product may cause mouth cancer.
2.   WARNING: This product may cause gum disease and tooth loss.
3.   WARNING: This product is not a safe alternative to cigarettes.

All advertising, except outdoor billboards, must include these warnings.

❖ Consumer Product Safety Legislation

Consumer product safety legislation began in 1953 with the enactment of the Flammable Fabrics Act, which prohibits the sale of highly flammable clothing or materials. Between 1953 and 1972, Congress enacted legislation regulating specific classes of products or product design or composition, rather than the overall safety of consumer products. Finally, as a result of 1970 recommendations of the National Commission on Product Safety, the Consumer Product Safety Act was passed in 1972 to protect

---

Landmark in the Law
The Food and Drug Act of 1906

The Food and Drug Act of 1906, a legislative landmark in the area of consumer health protection, marked the beginning of federal regulation of food and drugs in the United States. Although the government had been considering the need for some form of regulation in this area and had been conducting investigations for over a quarter of a century, legislation had been stalled in Congress. The direct catalyst for the congressional action in 1906 was the public outrage generated by a novel published in 1905—Upton Sinclair's *The Jungle*. That novel, an exposé of the Chicago meatpacking industry, was a story so revolting that no one reading it could remain unaffected—including President Theodore Roosevelt, who received an advance copy of the book. It is said that the president demanded an immediate investigation of the Chicago meatpacking houses after reading the following paragraph:

> There was never the least attention paid to what was cut up for sausages; there would come all the way back from Europe old sausage that had been rejected, and that was mouldy and white—it would be dosed with borax and glycerine, and

dumped into the hoppers, and made over again for home consumption. There would be meat that had tumbled out on the floor, in the dirt and sawdust, where the workers had tramped and spit uncounted billions of consumption germs. . . . It was too dark in these storage places to see well, but a man could run his hand over these piles of meat and sweep off handfuls of the dried dung of rats. These rats were nuisances, and the packers would put poisoned bread out for them; they would die, and then rats, bread and meat would go into the hoppers together. This is no fairy story and no joke; . . . there were things that went into the sausage in comparison with which a poisoned rat was a tidbit.[1]

Whether it was this particular paragraph or others just as shocking that caused President Roosevelt's reaction, he did, in any event, write to Sinclair and promise to have the novelist's charges fully investigated. Sinclair wrote back, advising the president to make sure that the investigators did their work "under cover," as "official" visitors would not get the full truth. The investigation was ordered, and when the labor commissioner reported the results—confirming Sinclair's observations—the long-stalled Food and Drug Act of 1906 and the Meat Inspection Act of the same year were immediately passed.

1. Upton Sinclair, *The Jungle* (New York: Penguin Edition, 1985), p. 163.

---

consumers from unreasonable risk of injury from hazardous products. The act created the Consumer Product Safety Commission (CPSC). The purpose of the CPSC, as stated in the act, was:

1.   To protect the public against unreasonable risk of injury associated with consumer products.
2.   To assist consumers in evaluating the comparative safety of consumer products.
3.   To develop uniform safety standards for consumer products and to minimize conflicting state and local regulations.
4.   To promote research and investigation into the causes and prevention of product-related deaths, illnesses, and injuries.

"Unless I'm misinterpreting the signs, gentlemen, we are approaching the end of the golden age of shoddy merchandise."

Drawing by Weber; © 1972, The New Yorker Magazine.

Generally, the CPSC was authorized to set standards for consumer products and to ban the manufacture and sale of any product deemed potentially hazardous to consumers. The commission has the authority to remove products from the market if they are deemed imminently hazardous and to require manufacturers to report information about any products already sold or intended for sale that have proved to be hazardous.

The CPSC was also given the authority to administer other acts relating to product safety, such as the Child Protection and Toy Safety Act, the Federal Hazardous Substance Act, and the Flammable Fabrics Act. In the following case, a carpet manufacturer violated the requirements of the Flammable Fabrics Act and was required by the court to pay the damages ordered by the CPSC.

Case 31.3
UNITED STATES v. DANUBE CARPET MILLS, INC.

United States Court of Appeals, Eleventh Circuit, 1984.
737 F.2d 988.

FACTS Danube Carpet Mills prepares carpet yarn for the production of carpeting. Finished carpets are man-

ufactured by other firms who contract with Danube for its yarn. Because carpeting is flammable and a fabric, it must meet the minimum safety requirements set by the Flammable Fabrics Act (FFA). The authority to enforce this act passed from the Federal Trade Commission (FTC) to the Consumer Product Safety Commission (CPSC) in 1973. In 1972 Danube's carpet material was found by the FTC to exceed the FFA minimum flammability standards, but

Case 31.3—Continued

at that time, no fines were imposed. Rather, the FTC entered into a consent decree with Danube whereby Danube promised to comply with FFA requirements. During 1973 Danube made a change in its yarn-coloring process, which, though minor, affected the fabric's flammability. This was detected by the CPSC between November 1974 and March 1975 when it conducted tests on the carpet. Seven rolls of carpet failed to meet FFA requirements, and the CPSC ordered Danube to pay a penalty of $24,500 ($3,500 per roll of carpet). Danube argued that the penalty was inappropriate because no one had been harmed by the more flammable fabric. The district court granted the CPSC's motion for summary judgment, and Danube appealed.

ISSUE Was the imposition of fines by the CPSC appropriate in this case?

DECISION Yes. The appellate court affirmed the ruling of the trial court. Danube had to pay the $24,500.

REASON The court first noted that it is the CPSC's responsibility to assure that the public is safe from unnecessarily flammable fabric, and that, under the Flammable Fabrics Act, fines may be imposed when the act's requirements are not met. Had Danube made a good-faith effort to conduct testing according to the requirements of the FFA, damages might have been inappropriate. Danube, however, had never done more than random testing of its fabric, and had never once tested the fabric following the initiation of the new coloring process. Also, even though no harm had been caused to consumers by the more flammable carpet fabric, Danube had failed to comply with the flammability standards required by the FFA, and it was for this lack of compliance—and not harm done to users—that Danube was ordered to pay penalties. Finally, the court noted that given the net worth of Danube (almost $3.5 million) as of October 13, 1984, it was within the firm's ability to pay the $24,500 fine.

❖ Credit Protection

Because of the extensive use of credit by American consumers, credit protection has become one of the more important areas regulated by consumer-protection legislation. The Fair Debt Collection Practices Act of 1977 protects consumers from unfair debt-collection practices, such as the use of harassment or intimidation, contacting the debtor at unreasonable times or at work if the employer objects, or contacting third parties about the debt. More extensive in its application to the credit and credit-card industry is the Consumer Credit Protection Act (CCPA), commonly known as the Truth-in-Lending Act, passed by Congress in 1974.

Truth in Lending

The Truth-in-Lending Act (TILA) is basically a *disclosure law*, administered by the Federal Reserve Board, that requires sellers and lenders to disclose credit terms or loan terms so that individuals can shop around for the best financing arrangements. TILA requirements apply only to persons who, in the ordinary course of their business, lend money or sell on credit or arrange for the extension of credit. Thus, sales or loans made between two consumers do not come under the protection of the act. Also, only debtors who are *natural* persons (as opposed to the artificial "person" of the corporation) are protected by this law; other legal entities are not.

Transactions covered by the act typically include retail and installment sales and installment loans, car loans, home improvement loans, and certain real estate loans (if the amount being financed is under $25,000).

Under the terms of the TILA all terms of a credit instrument must be fully disclosed. In the following case, because a creditor failed to comply to the letter of the TILA, the defaulting debtor was not required to turn over to the creditor collateral that had been offered as security for a loan.

Case 31.4
KADLEC MOTORS, INC. v. KNUDSON
Court of Appeals of Minnesota, 1986.
383 N.W.2d 342.

FACTS In June of 1981 Bradley and Barbara Knudson purchased a 1978 Monte Carlo from Kadlec Motors pursuant to a motor vehicle retail installment contract and security agreement. The Knudsons traded in their 1975 Chevrolet Monza for a down payment, and, as security for its loan for the balance due on the Monte Carlo, Kadlec Motors took a security interest in both the Monte Carlo and a 1975 GMC High Sierra Jimmy that the Knudsons also owned. The security agreement for the GMC Jimmy, however, was separate from the security agreement for the Monte Carlo. Neither security agreement made reference to the other.

The Knudsons defaulted on the loan for the Monte Carlo, and both the Monte Carlo and the Jimmy were repossessed and sold by Kadlec Motors. Kadlec Motors then sought a deficiency judgment against the Knudsons for the balance of the loan. The Knudsons countersued, asserting wrongful repossession of the Jimmy and violation of the federal Truth-in-Lending Act (TILA). Under the TILA, a creditor is required to disclose in a consumer security agreement the property to which the security interest relates, and this disclosure must be on the same side as, and above or adjacent to, the place for the customer's signature. The Knudsons alleged that, since the motor vehicle contract for the Monte Carlo disclosed no security interest in the GMC Jimmy and referred in no way to the security agreement involving the Jimmy, Kadlec Motors violated the TILA and consequently was not entitled to repossess the Jimmy. The trial court entered judgment for the Knudsons, and Kadlec appealed to the Minnesota Court of Appeals.

ISSUE Did Kadlec violate the Truth-in-Lending Act, and, if so, did this violation make it legally impossible for Kadlec to take possession of the Jimmy?

DECISION Yes, to both issues. The appellate court affirmed the trial court's ruling.

REASON Kadlec failed to meet the requirements of the TILA by not clearly stating on the credit contract for the Monte Carlo, in the manner prescribed by the act, that the Jimmy was also being used as collateral for the loan. Kadlec argued that, notwithstanding this omission, the Knudsons knew of the joint relationship between the two security agreements and it therefore would be unfair in this case to apply the technical requirements of the TILA. The court, however, rejected Kadlec's argument, stating that the TILA was designed to protect consumers from inaccurate and unfair credit billing and that, consequently, creditors are required to comply with both the letter and the spirit of the law. By violating the TILA, Kadlec thus failed to have a security interest in the Jimmy. Therefore, the repossession and subsequent sale of the Jimmy was wrongful.

Equal Credit Opportunity The TILA also prohibits discrimination by lenders on the basis of race, religion, national origin, color, sex, marital status, age, or whether an individual is receiving certain types of income, such as public assistance benefits. Creditors are prohibited from requesting any information from a credit applicant that could be used for the type of discrimination covered in the act and its amendments.

Credit-Card Rules The TILA also contains provisions regarding credit cardholders. One provision limits the liability of a cardholder to $50 per card for unauthorized charges made prior to the time the creditor is notified. Another provision prohibits a credit-card company from billing a consumer for any unauthorized charges if the credit card is improperly issued by the company. Further provisions of the act concern billing disputes related to credit-card purchases. If a debtor thinks that an error has occurred in billing, or wishes to withhold payment for a faulty product purchased by credit card, the act outlines specific procedures for both the consumer and the credit-card company in settling the dispute.

Fair Credit Reporting Act

In order to ensure that consumers can determine and alter any inaccurate information about their credit records, Congress passed the Fair Credit Reporting Act (FCRA) in 1970. The FCRA covers all credit bureaus, investigative reporting companies, detective and collection agencies, and computerized information-reporting companies. Under the act, the consumer has the right to be notified of reporting activities, to have access to information contained in consumer reports, and to have corrected any erroneous information upon which a denial of credit, employment, or insurance might have been based. Upon request and proper identification, any consumer is entitled to know the nature and substance of information about him or her that is contained in the agency's file, as well as the sources of the information and the identity of those who have received a consumer credit report, such as businesses that may wish to extend credit to the consumer. The act requires that an investigative report cannot be prepared on an individual consumer unless that person is notified and given the right to request information on the nature and scope of the pending investigation.

A government poster informs consumers of their legal protection against discrimination in the granting of credit.

Uniform Consumer Credit Code

In 1968 the National Conference of Commissioners on Uniform State Laws promulgated the Uniform Consumer Credit Code (UCCC), which was revised in 1974. The UCCC has been controversial and only adopted by a few states, although bits and pieces of it have been extracted for inclusion in numerous state statutes. The UCCC is an attempt to promulgate a comprehensive body of rules governing the most important aspects of consumer credit. Sections of the UCCC, for example, focus on truth-in-lending disclosures, maximum credit ceilings, door-to-door sales, and referral sales. The UCCC is also concerned with materials contained in fine-print clauses and various provisions of creditor remedies, including deficiency judgments (personal judgments for the amount of a debt that remains unpaid after collateral is sold and the proceeds applied to the debt) and garnishments (proceedings where property, money, or wages controlled by a third person are transferred to the court to satisfy a judgment). The UCCC applies to most types of sales, including real estate. It also replaces existing state consumer credit laws, as well as installment-loan, usury, and retail-installment-sale acts.

❖ Environmental Protection

In one sense, concerns about the environment are not new. The English Parliament, for example, passed a number of acts that regulated the burning of soft coal in medieval England. Moreover, through common-law *nuisance statutes*, property owners were given relief from pollution in situations where the individual could identify a distinct harm separate from that affecting the general public. Thus, if a factory polluted the air and killed a farmer's crops, the farmer could seek an injunction and damages against the factory.

Needless to say, nuisance suits that granted specific relief for individuals were inadequate when the harm from pollution could not be attributed to groups separate from the public at large. Under the common law, citizens were denied *standing* (access to the courts) unless specific harm could be shown. Therefore, a group of citizens who wished to stop a new development that would cause significant water pollution would be denied access to the courts on the ground that the harm to them did not differ from the harm borne by the general public.[4] A public authority, however, could sue for public nuisance.

The common law further limited relief from pollution in situations where the harm was caused by two or more independent sources. For example, if a number of firms were polluting the air, a harmed individual could sue any individual firm; however, until early in the twentieth century, the plaintiff was not able to sue all of the factories simultaneously. Consequently, specific proof of damages in individual actions was often impossible. These difficulties in seeking relief in pollution cases, along with the forces creating additional pollution, have been largely responsible for the development of statutory regulation of environmental quality.

Regulation by Administrative Agencies

Beginning in 1970, Congress passed a number of federal statutes directing administrative agencies to study the effects of pollution on the environment. On January 1, 1970, the National Environmental Policy Act (NEPA) created the Council of Environmental Quality and mandated that an environmental statement be prepared for every recommendation or report on legislation or major federal action that significantly affects the quality of the environment.[5] Since that time, the government has passed a number of acts that govern air quality, such as the Clean Air Act. In addition, a number of regulations have been promulgated for water quality.[6] Additional regulations governing the use of pesticides,[7] radiation,[8] solid toxic substances,[9] and noise [10] have also been promulgated.

The Environmental Protection Agency (EPA) was created in 1970 to coordinate the various agencies responsible for environmental protection. It is primarily an administrative organization, employing approximately 10,000 individuals to carry out the directives of the numerous and complex regulations of federal statutes affecting the environment.

One of the important responsibilities of the EPA is to ensure that all proposed federal legislation affecting the environment is analyzed and an environmental impact statement is issued. This statement has become an instrument for private citizens,

---

4. Save the Bay Committee, Inc. v. Mayor of City of Savannah, 227 Ga. 436, 181 S.E.2d 351 (1971).

5. National Environmental Policy Act of 1969, 42 U.S.C.A. 4321 *et seq.*

6. Including the Federal Water Pollution Control Act of 1965, the Marine Protection and Research and Sanctuaries Act of 1972, and the Safe Drinking Water Act of 1974.

7. Federal Insecticide, Fungicide and Rodenticide Act of 1972, 7 U.S.C.A. 135 *et seq.* (1947), as amended May 12, 1964.

8. Resource Conservation Recovery Act of 1976, 42 U.S.C.A. 6901 *et seq.* (1976).

9. Toxic Substances Control Act of 1976, 15 U.S.C.A. 2602 (1976).

10. Noise Control Act of 1972, 42 U.S.C.A. 1604 (1972).

consumer interests, businesses, and federal agencies to help shape the final outcome of regulatory actions. Even if an agency's analysis concludes that the impact statement is unnecessary, a statement supporting that conclusion must be filed.[11]

Air Pollution from Automobiles

Federal involvement with air pollution goes back to the 1950s, when Congress authorized funds for air-pollution research. In 1963 the federal government passed the Clean Air Act, which focused on multistate air pollution and provided assistance to states. Various amendments, particularly in 1970 and 1977,[12] strengthened the government's authority to regulate the quality of air.

Regulations governing air pollution from automobiles and other mobile sources specify pollution standards and time schedules. For example, the 1970 Clean Air Act required a reduction of 90 percent in the amount of carbon monoxide and hydrocarbons emitted from automobiles by 1975.[13]

The 1977 amendments to the Clean Air Act establish multilevel standards. For example, they attempt to prevent the deterioration of air quality even in areas where the existing quality exceeds that required by federal law. Present regulations are meant to completely eliminate lead in gasoline sold within the next few years. In the following case the court reviewed an EPA order regulating the lead content of gasoline, the validity of which had been challenged by Ethyl Corporation.

---

11.   Arizona Public Serv. Co. v. Federal Power Comm'n, 483 F.2d 1275 (D.C.Cir. 1973).
12.   Clean Air Act Amendments of 1970, 42 U.S.C. 7521, and Clean Air Act Amendments of 1977, 42 U.S.C. 7521–25, 7541–51.
13.   Carbon monoxide, a colorless, odorless gas, can reduce mental performance and result in death if inhaled in sufficient quantities. Hydrocarbons are unburned fuel, one of the principal ingredients that generate smog.

California has the strictest automobile pollution standards in the United States.

Case 31.5
ETHYL CORP. v. ENVIRONMENTAL PROTECTION AGENCY

United States Court of Appeals, District of Columbia Circuit, 1976.
541 F.2d 1.

FACTS Ethyl Corporation, a leading producer of anti-knock compounds for increasing gasoline octane ratings, filed for review the Environmental Protection Agency (EPA) order that required annual reductions in the lead content of gasoline. The Clean Air Act authorized the agency to regulate gasoline additives that are a danger to public health or welfare.

ISSUE Had the EPA exceeded its authority by requiring a reduction in the lead content of gasoline?

DECISION No. The court found that the EPA did not abuse its discretion by requiring a reduction in the lead content of gasoline.

REASON The record in this case was massive—over 10,000 pages. The EPA relied on this evidence in its decision, and although the evidence was not wholly unassailable, it did provide a reasonable basis on which to make a decision. The court defined its scope of review as follows: "Our scope . . . requires us to strike 'agency action, findings, and conclusions' [only if] we find [them] to be 'arbitrary, capricious, an abuse of discretion, or otherwise not in accordance with law.' This standard of review is a highly deferential one. It presumes agency action to be valid. Moreover, it forbids the court's substituting its judgment for that of the agency. . . ."

Water Pollution

Federal regulations governing the pollution of water can be traced back nearly a century to the River and Harbor Act of 1886, as amended in 1899.[14] These regulations required a permit for discharging or depositing refuse in navigable waterways. The courts have determined that even hot water can be considered refuse.[15] In 1965 Congress passed the federal Water Pollution Control Act, which strengthened the EPA's enforcement powers.

Perhaps the most important regulations that govern the quality of water were instituted in 1972 by Congress. These regulations established goals to (1) make waters safe for swimming, (2) protect fish and wildlife, and (3) eliminate the discharge of pollutants into the water. They set forth specific time schedules, which were extended by amendment in 1977. The 1972 Clean Water Act also specifies a number of regulations with time schedules for controlling industrial water pollution. Regulations for the most part specify that the best available technology be installed.

The polluting party can be required to clean up the pollution or pay for the cost of doing so. In most cases, explicit penalties are also imposed on parties that pollute the water, as illustrated by the following case.

Case 31.6
UNITED STATES OF AMERICA v. ATLANTIC RICHFIELD CO.

United States District Court, Eastern District of Pennsylvania, 1977.
429 F.Supp. 830.

FACTS A number of oil companies, including Atlantic Richfield Company and Gulf Oil Company, were as-

sessed monetary civil penalties that included paying for the cost of cleaning up oil discharges. Atlantic Richfield argued that the imposition of penalties, over and above clean-up costs, for an accidental oil spill when the reporting and cleaning requirements had been satisfied constituted a criminal action. Therefore, the defendants believed that they had the right to a jury trial. The court had to determine whether these penalties denied due process.

14. 33 U.S.C.A. 407.
15. 33 U.S.C.A. 1254(t).

Case 31.6—Continued

ISSUE Did the levying of penalties on the oil companies constitute a denial of due process?

DECISION No. The penalties served the ends of civil regulation and were required by the Clean Water Act.

REASON Even though the defendant oil companies were not negligent in causing the oil spills, they were still subject to the statutory penalties. The statute does not make negligence or "fault" an element in imposing the penalty. The defendants claimed that "no regulatory purpose would be served by imposing a . . . penalty, an argument we reject because it proceeds from a faulty premise. . . . First, the principal goal of [the fines] is to *deter* spills. Second, the Congressional purpose here was to impose a standard of conduct higher than that related just to economic efficiency." Further, the court held no clean-up effort could guarantee against residual harm "too small or too well dispersed to be detectable." Therefore, the court concluded that "even where the defendants are not at fault, the penalty does not act only as a punishment but serves the ends of civil regulation."

Waste Disposal

Waste disposal can occur on land, in the water, or in the air; thus, regulations protecting these resources from pollution can also apply to waste disposal. In 1970 Congress passed the Materials Policy Act, an act designed to reduce solid-waste disposal by encouraging the recycling of waste and the reuse of materials by society. The act also provides for pilot waste-disposal projects utilizing modern technology. For example, the development and use of technology that converts garbage into useful products have been greatly encouraged by the solid-waste programs of the EPA.

Federal statutes also attempt to generate state and local community initiative for solving solid-waste disposal problems by providing monies and expert guidance for state and local studies. In response, a number of states have sought to reduce the problem of solid-waste disposal by requiring recycling or reuse of various products.

In 1976 Congress passed the Resource Conservation and Recovery Act (RCRA) in reaction to an ever-increasing concern with the effects of hazardous waste materials on the environment. The RCRA required the EPA to establish regulations to monitor and control hazardous waste disposal and to determine which forms of solid waste should be considered hazardous and thus subject to regulation. Under the authority granted by this act, the EPA has promulgated various technical requirements for limited types of facilities for storage and treatment of hazardous waste. It also requires all producers of hazardous waste materials to label and package properly any hazardous waste to be transported.

The RCRA was amended in 1984 to extend the program to 1988 and to add several new regulatory requirements to those already monitored and enforced by the EPA. The basic aims of the amendments are to decrease the use of land containment in disposing of hazardous waste and to reduce the *safe-harbor* provisions that had been created by the EPA in administering the 1976 act. Safe-harbor provisions had allowed some generators of hazardous waste—such as those generating less than 1,000 kilograms a month—to be excluded from regulation under the RCRA.

Toxic Substances

The Toxic Substances Control Act was passed in 1976 to regulate chemicals and chemical compounds that are known to be toxic and to institute investigation of any possible harmful effects from new chemical compounds. The regulations authorize the Environmental Protection Agency to require that manufacturers, processors, and other organizations planning to use chemicals first determine their effect on human health and the environment.

❖ Chapter Summary: Consumer and Environmental Law

MAJOR AREAS OF CONSUMER PROTECTION	
Advertising	1. *Deceptive advertising*—Advertising that may be false or misleading to consumers is prohibited by the Federal Trade Commission (FTC). 2. *Bait-and-switch advertising*—Advertising a lower-priced product when the intention is not to sell the advertised product but to lure the consumer into buying a higher-priced product is prohibited by the FTC.
Sales	1. *Credit terms*—If certain credit terms pertaining to the purchase of a product are advertised, other relevant credit and sale terms (such as cash price, down payment, payments, and annual percentage rate of interest) must be included. 2. *Unsolicited merchandise sent by U.S. mail*—May be retained, used, discarded, or disposed of in any manner by recipient without recipient incurring any contractual obligation (under Postal Reorganization Act of 1970). 3. *Door-to-door-sales*—The FTC requires all door-to-door sellers to give consumers three days to cancel any sale. 4. *Mail-order sales*—Federal and state statutes regulate certain practices of sellers who solicit through the mails and prohibit the use of the mails to defraud individuals.
Health Protection	Health-protection laws govern the processing and distribution of meat and poultry, poisonous substances, and drugs and cosmetics. For some products (such as cigarettes), explicit warnings about health hazards are required.
Product Safety	The Consumer Product Safety Act of 1972 protects consumers from risk of injury from hazardous products. The Consumer Product Safety Commission has the power to remove products from the market that are deemed imminently hazardous and to ban the manufacture and sale of hazardous products.
Credit Protection	1. *Fair Debt Collection Practices Act*—Prohibits debt collectors from using unfair debt-collection practices (such as contacting debtor at place of employment if employer objects or at unreasonable times, contacting third parties about the debt, harassment, intimidation, etc.). 2. *Consumer Credit Protection Act (Truth-in-Lending Act)*—A disclosure law regulated by the Federal Reserve Board; requires sellers and lenders to disclose credit terms or loan terms. Transactions covered by the act typically include retail and installment sales and loans, car loans, home-improvement loans, and certain real estate loans. Additionally, the Truth-in-Lending Act provides for: a. Equal credit opportunity (prohibits creditors from discriminating on the basis of race, religion, marital status, sex, etc.). b. Fair credit billing (allows credit-card users to withhold payment for a faulty product sold, or for an error in billing, until the dispute is resolved). c. Credit card protection (limits liability of cardholders prior to notice to $50 for unauthorized charges and protects consumers from liability for unauthorized charges made on unsolicited credit cards). 3. *Fair Credit Reporting Act*—Entitles consumers to be informed of a credit investigation, to request verification of accuracy of report, to have unverified information removed from their file, and to add "their side of the story" to the credit file.

❖ Chapter Summary: Consumer and Environmental Law—Continued

Credit Protection (Continued)	4. *Uniform Consumer Credit Code*—A comprehensive body of rules governing the most important aspects of consumer credit; adopted by only a minority of states.
ENVIRONMENTAL PROTECTION	
Environmental Protection Agency (EPA)	An administrative agency created in 1970 to coordinate the various agencies responsible for environmental protection. Ensures that all federal environmental legislation is analyzed and an environmental impact statement (EIS) is issued if necessary.
Major Protected Areas	1. *Air pollution by automobiles*—The amount of hydrocarbons and carbon monoxide emitted from automobiles is regulated by the Clean Air Act to prevent the deterioration of air quality.
	2. *Water pollution*—The River and Harbor Act of 1886, the Water Pollution Control Act of 1965, and the Clean Water Act of 1972 attempt to make waters safe for swimming, protect fish and wildlife, and eliminate the discharge of pollutants into the water.
	3. *Hazardous waste*—The Resource Conservation and Recovery Act of 1976 requires the Environmental Protection Agency (EPA) to regulate and monitor hazardous waste disposal, treatment, and storage.

❖ Questions and Case Problems

31-1. Alderman receives two new credit cards on May 1. One was solicited from Midtown Department Store and the other was unsolicited from High-Flying Airlines. During the month of May Alderman makes numerous credit-card purchases from Midtown Store, but she does not use the High-Flying Airlines card. On May 31 a burglar breaks into Alderman's home and, along with other items, steals both credit cards. Alderman notifies the Midtown Department Store of the theft on June 2, but she fails to notify High-Flying Airlines. Using the Midtown credit card, the burglar makes a $500 purchase on June 1 and a $200 purchase on June 3. The burglar then charges a vacation flight on the High-Flying Airlines card for $1,000 on June 5. Alderman receives the bills for these charges and refuses to pay them. Discuss Alderman's liability in these situations.

31-2. Fireside Rocking Chair Company advertised in the newspaper a special sale price of $159 on machine-caned rocking chairs. In the advertisement was a drawing of a natural-wood rocking chair with a caned back and seat. The average person would not be able to tell from the drawing whether the rocking chair was machine-caned or hand-caned. The hand-caned rocking chairs sold for $259. Lowell and Celia Carlisle went to Fireside because they had seen the ad for the machine-caned rocking chair and were very interested in purchasing one. The Carlisles arrived on the morning the sale opened. Fireside's agent said the only machine-caned rocking chairs he had were painted lime green and were priced at $159. He immediately turned the Carlisle's attention to the rocking chairs he had hand-caned, praising their workmanship and pointing

out that for the extra $100, the hand-caned chairs were surely a good value. The Carlisles, preferring the natural-wood, machine-caned rocking chair for $159 as pictured in the advertisement, said they would like to order the one in the ad. The Fireside agent said he could not order a natural-wood, machine-caned rocking chair. Discuss fully whether Fireside has violated any consumer-protection laws.

31-3. On June 28, a sales representative for Renowned Books called on the Petersons at their home. After a very persuasive sales pitch on the part of the sales agent, the Petersons agreed in writing to purchase a twenty-volume set of historical encyclopedias from Renowned Books for a total of $299. An initial down payment of $35 was required, with the remainder of the price to be paid in monthly payments over a one-year period. Two days later the Petersons, having second thoughts, contacted the book company and stated they had decided to rescind the contract. Renowned Books said this would be impossible. Has Renowned Books violated any consumer law by not allowing the Petersons to rescind their contract?

31-4. Fruitade, Inc., is a processor of a soft drink called "Freshen Up." Fruitade uses returnable bottles and uses a special acid to clean its bottles for further beverage processing. The acid is diluted by water and then allowed to pass into a navigable stream. Fruitade crushes its broken bottles and throws the crushed glass into the stream. Discuss *fully* any environmental laws that Fruitade has violated.

31-5. Dennis and Janice Geiger saw an advertisement in a newspaper for a Kimball Whitney Spinet piano on sale for $699 by McCormick Piano & Organ Company, Inc. Because the style of the piano drawn in the advertisement matched their furniture, the Geigers were particularly interested in the Kimball. When they went to McCormick Piano & Organ, however, they learned that the drawing closely resembled another, more expensive Crest piano, and that the Kimball spinet looked quite different than the piano sketched in the drawing. The salesperson told the Geigers that she was unable to order the spinet piano of the style requested by the Geigers. When the Geigers asked for the names of other customers who had purchased the advertised pianos, the salesperson became hysterical and said she would not, under any circumstances, sell the Geigers a piano. The Geigers then brought suit against the piano store, alleging that the store had engaged in deceptive advertising in violation of Indiana law. Was the McCormick Piano & Organ Company guilty of deceptive advertising? Explain. [McCormick Piano & Organ Co., Inc. v. Geiger, 412 N.E.2d 842 (Ind.App. 1980)]

31-6.   On July 16, 1982, the Semars signed a loan contract with Platte Valley Federal Savings & Loan Association, offering a second mortgage on their home as collateral. Under the Truth-in-Lending Act (TILA), borrowers are allowed three business days to rescind, without penalty, a consumer loan that uses their principal dwelling as security. The TILA requires lenders in such situations to state specifically the last date on which the borrower can rescind the loan agreement, and if they fail to include this date, the borrower may rescind the loan within three years after it was made. Platte Valley's form omitted the exact expiration date of the three-day period, although it stated that the rescission right expired three business days after July 16. In September of 1983, the Semars ceased making monthly payments on the loan and sent a Notice of Rescission to Platte Valley on February 15, 1984. The Semars claimed that Platte Valley had violated the TILA by failing to specify in the loan contract the exact date of the expiration of the three-day rescission period. Because of this violation, the Semars maintained they had three years in which to rescind the contract. Had Platte Valley violated the TILA? Explain. [Semar v. Platte Valley Federal Sav. & Loan Ass'n, 791 F.2d 699 (9th Cir. 1986)]

31-7.   Robert Martin loaned a business associate, E. L. McBride, his American Express credit card and told McBride he could charge up to $500 on the card. Approximately two months later, Martin received an American Express statement that showed a balance due of approximately $5,300. Martin refused to pay the amount, claiming that he had not signed any of the credit invoices and that his liability for the unauthorized charges was only $50 under the Truth-in-Lending Act. To what extent was Martin liable for payment to American Express on the $5,300? [Martin v. American Express, Inc., 361 So.2d 597 (Ala.Civ.App. 1978)]

31-8.   The Government Services Administration (GSA) entered into an agreement with a private individual under which the individual was to construct a building to GSA's specifications and lease it to the GSA. Under the contemplated lease provision, GSA would have use of the entire building for a five-year (renewable) period. As many as 2,300 government employees would be assigned to the building, and most would commute by automobile. The cost of the lease was approximately $11 million. GSA proceeded with its plans for the building without preparing any environmental impact statement. Was a statement necessary? Explain. [S. W. Neighborhood Assembly v. Eckard, 445 F.Supp. 1195 (D.D.C. 1978)]

31-9.   Josephine Rutyna was a 60-year-old widow who, in late 1976 and early 1977, had incurred a debt for medical treatment of her high blood pressure and epilepsy. She assumed that the cost of the services had been paid by either Medicare or her private insurance company. In July of 1978, however, she was contacted by an agent of Collection Accounts Terminal, Inc., who stated that Rutyna still owed a debt of $56 for those services. She denied that she owed the debt and the following month received a letter from the collection agency threatening to contact her neighbors and employer concerning the debt if the $56 was not paid immediately. Discuss fully whether the collection agency's letter violates any consumer-protection law. [Rutyna v. Collection Accounts Terminal, Inc., 478 F.Supp. 980 (N.D.Ill. 1979)]

Chapter 32

Employee and Labor Law

"Show me the country in which there are no strikes, and I'll show you the country in which there is no liberty."

Samuel Gompers, 1850–1924 (American labor leader)

Government regulation of employment and labor relations is very much present in our society. Businesses must operate within the confines established by statutes regulating employment and labor relations, and such legislation has increased over the years. This legislation affects the rights and liabilities of both employers and employees. Until the early 1930s, laws at the federal and state levels generally favored management. Collective activities such as unions were discouraged, sometimes forcibly, by employers. Early legislation protecting the rights of employees, such as the National War Labor Board that operated during World War I, was often temporary. Additionally, this type of legislation was frequently restricted to a particular industry, such as the Railway Labor Act of 1926, which required railroads and their employees to attempt to make employment agreements through representatives chosen by each side.

Beginning in 1932, however, a number of statutes were enacted that greatly increased employees' rights to join unions, to engage in collective bargaining, to receive retirement and income security benefits, to be protected against various discrimination practices, and to have a safe place to work. At the heart of labor rights is the right to unionize and bargain with management for improved working conditions, salaries, and benefits. The ultimate weapon of labor is, of course, the strike. As noted in the opening quotation, labor leader Samuel Gompers concluded that without the right to strike, there could be no liberty.

❖ Unions and Collective Bargaining

Most of the early legislation to protect employees focused on the rights of workers to join unions and to engage in collective bargaining.

Norris-LaGuardia Act

Congress protected peaceful strikes, picketing, and boycotts in 1932 in the Norris-LaGuardia Act.[1] The statute restricted federal courts in their power to issue injunctions

---

1. 29 U.S.C.A. 101–10, 113–15 (1973).

Congress protected the right of union members to peacefully strike, picket, and boycott in the 1932 Norris-LaGuardia Act.

against unions engaged in peaceful strikes. In effect, this act declared a national policy permitting employees to organize.

National Labor Relations Act

The National Labor Relations Act of 1935 (the Wagner Act)[2] established the rights of employees to engage in collective bargaining and to strike. The act also created the National Labor Relations Board to oversee union elections and to prevent employers from engaging in unfair and illegal union-labor activities and unfair labor practices. Details of the Wagner Act are given in the "Landmark" in this chapter.

Labor-Management Relations Act

CLOSED SHOP
A place of employment that requires union membership as a condition of employment. Unlawful under the Taft-Hartley Act.

UNION SHOP
A place of employment in which all workers, once employed, must become union members within a specified period of time as a condition of their continued employment.

The Labor-Management Relations Act (Taft-Hartley Act)[3] was signed into law by President Truman on June 23, 1947, after being passed over his veto. Intended to amend the Wagner Act, it contained provisions protecting employers as well as protecting employees. The act was bitterly opposed by organized labor groups. It provided a detailed list of unfair labor activities that unions as well as management were now forbidden to practice. Moreover, a *free-speech* amendment allowed employers to propagandize against unions prior to any National Labor Relations Board election.

Closed Shop Made Illegal   A **closed shop** is a firm that requires union membership by its workers as a condition of employment. It was made illegal under the Taft-Hartley Act. The act preserved the legality of the **union shop,** which does not require

2.   49 Stat. 449, 20 U.S.C.A. 151.
3.   61 Stat. 136, 29 U.S.C.A. 141.

membership as a prerequisite for employment but can, and usually does, require that workers join the union after a specified amount of time on the job. However, the Taft-Hartley Act allowed individual states to pass their own **right-to-work laws**—laws making it illegal for union membership to be required for *continued* employment in any establishment. Thus, union shops are technically illegal in states with right-to-work laws.

Eighty-Day Cooling-Off Period   One of the most controversial aspects of the Taft-Hartley Act was the eighty-day cooling-off period—a provision allowing federal courts to issue injunctions against strikes that would create a national emergency. The president of the United States can obtain a court injunction that will last for eighty days, and presidents have occasionally used this provision. For example, President Eisenhower applied the eighty-day injunction order to striking steelworkers in 1959, President Nixon applied it to striking longshoremen in 1971, and President Carter applied it to striking coal miners in 1978.

Labor-Management Reporting and Disclosure Act

The Labor-Management Reporting and Disclosure Act of 1959 (Landrum-Griffin Act)[4] established an employee bill of rights and reporting requirements for union activities. This act strictly regulated internal union business procedures.

Union elections, for example, are regulated by this act. The act requires that regularly scheduled elections of officers occur and that secret ballots be used. Ex-convicts and communists are prohibited from holding union office. Moreover, union officials are made accountable for union property and funds. Members have the right to attend and to participate in union meetings, to nominate officers, and to vote in most union proceedings.

The Landrum-Griffin Act also outlawed *hot-cargo contracts*—agreements wherein employers voluntarily agreed with unions not to handle, use, or deal in the nonunion-produced goods of other employers. In principle, the Taft-Hartley Act had made all such boycotts illegal. This particular type of secondary boycott was not made illegal by the Taft-Hartley Act, however, because that act only prevented unions from inducing *employees* to strike or otherwise act to force the employer not to handle such goods. Section 8(e) of the Landrum-Griffin Act addressed this problem:

> It shall be . . . [an] . . . unfair labor practice for any labor organization and any employer to enter into any contract or any agreement . . . whereby such employer . . . agrees to refrain from handling, using, selling, transporting or otherwise dealing in any of the products of any other employer, or to cease doing business with any other person. . . .

❖ Civil Rights Legislation and Employment

At common law, employment was terminable "at will." Any employer could establish all terms and conditions of employment. Labor unions were deemed private associations, so they could determine all membership requirements without oversight of

RIGHT-TO-WORK LAW
A state law generally providing that employees are not to be required to join a union as a condition of receiving or retaining employment.

---

4. 73 Stat. 519, 29 U.S.C.A. 401.

Landmark in the Law

The National Labor Relations Act (1935)

The National Labor Relations Act of 1935 is often referred to as the "Wagner Act" because it was sponsored by Senator Robert Wagner. Wagner emigrated from Germany to New York with his family when he was eight years old. He earned a law degree at New York Law School in 1990 and went on to serve in the state legislature and on the New York Supreme Court before he was elected to the U. S. Senate in 1926. He spent the next twenty-three years in the Senate and became one of its most prominent legislators during the New Deal era.

Wagner sponsored several pieces of New Deal legislation, particularly in the field of labor law. Until the early 1930s, an employer was free to establish the terms and conditions of employment. Collective activities by employees, such as participation in unions, were discouraged by employers. Thus, the employee was often left with little or no bargaining power in relation to the employer. In 1934, when Wagner introduced the bill subsequently enacted as the National Labor Relations Act (NLRA), he saw it as a vehicle through which the disparate balance of power between employers and employees could be corrected.

Section 1 of the NLRA justifies the act under the commerce clause of the Constitution. Section 1 states that unequal bargaining power between employees and employers leads to economic instability, whereas refusals of employers to bargain collectively lead to strikes. These disturbances impede the flow of interstate commerce. It is declared to be the policy of the United States, under the authority given to the federal government under the commerce clause, to ensure the free flow of commerce by encouraging collective bargaining and unionization.

The pervading purpose of the NLRA was to protect interstate commerce by securing for employees the rights established by Section 7 of the act: to organize, to bargain collectively through representatives of their own choosing, and to engage in concerted activities for that and other purposes. The act specifically defined a number of employer practices as unfair to labor:

1. Interference with the efforts of employees to form, join, or assist labor organizations or to engage in concerted activities for their mutual aid or protection. [Section 8(a)(1)]
2. An employer's domination of a labor organization or contribution of financial or other support to it. [Section 8(a)(2)]
3. Discrimination in the hiring or awarding of tenure to employees for reason of union affiliation. [Section 8(a)(3)]
4. Discrimination against employees for filing charges under the act or giving testimony under the act. [Section 8(a)(4)]
5. Refusal to bargain collectively with the duly designated representative of the employees. [Section 8(a)(5)]

Another purpose of the act was to promote fair and just settlements of disputes by peaceful processes and to avoid industrial warfare. The act created the National Labor Relations Board (NLRB) to oversee elections and to prevent employers from engaging in unfair and illegal union activities and unfair labor practices. The board was granted investigatory powers and was authorized to issue and serve complaints against employers in response to employee charges or unfair labor practices. The board was further empowered to issue cease-and-desist orders when violations were found, which could be enforced by a circuit court of appeals if necessary.

The Wagner Act was seen by employers as a drastic piece of legislation, and the bill elicited a great deal of opposition. Those who opposed the act claimed that it did not come under the commerce clause of the U. S. Constitution and therefore Congress had no power to act. In other words, it became an issue of states' rights for the opponents. Those who were willing to admit that it did fall under the commerce clause claimed that it created an undue burden, which therefore rendered it unconstitutional. The constitutionality of the act was tested in 1937 in *NLRB* v. *Jones & Laughlin Steel Corporation*.[1] In its decision, the U. S. Supreme Court held that the act and its application were constitutionally valid.

1.   301 U.S. 1, 57 S.Ct. 615, 81 L.Ed. 893 (1937).

the courts. In the past several decades, however, as a result of judicial decisions, administrative agency actions, and legislation, both employers and unions have been restricted in their ability to discriminate on the basis of race, religion, creed, age, or sex. The most important statute relating to fair employment practices is Title VII of the Civil Rights Act of 1964.[5]

General Provisions of the Civil Rights Act

Basically, the Civil Rights Act and its amendments eliminate job discrimination against employees, applicants, and union membership on the basis of race, color, national origin, religion, and sex at any stage of employment. Title VII of the act applies to employers with fifteen or more employees, to labor unions with fifteen or more members, to all labor unions that operate hiring halls (where members go regularly to be rationed jobs as they become available), and to all employment agencies. The 1972 amendments extend coverage to all state and local governments, government agencies, political subdivisions, and departments. A special section forbids discrimination in most federal government employment.

Race, Color, and National-Origin Discrimination   If a company's standards or policies for selecting or promoting employees have the effect of discriminating against minorities and do not have a substantial, demonstrable relationship to qualifications for the job in question, they are illegal. Discrimination in employment conditions and benefits is also illegal. An employer cannot maintain all-white or all-black crews for no demonstrable reason, nor can an employer grant higher average Christmas bonuses to whites than to blacks.

5.   78 Stat. 241, 42 U.S.C.A. 2000e *et seq.*

"All men think justice to be a sort of equality. But there still remains a question: equality or inequality of what?"

Aristotle, 384–322 B.C.
(Greek philosopher)

An employer subject to Title VII requirements can no longer maintain an all-white or all-male staff for no demonstrable reason.

Religious Discrimination   Employers in businesses are not allowed to discriminate in their employment practices on the basis of religion. Moreover, employers must make reasonable accommodation to the religious needs of their employees. The term "reasonable accommodation" has never been legislatively defined, but the U. S. Supreme Court has laid out certain guidelines. Employers do not have to bear more than a small cost to effect a reasonable accommodation, nor does an employer have to deny a shift or job preference to other employees or to take steps that are inconsistent with a valid collective-bargaining agreement.[6]

A few states have passed legislation that specifically allows employees to declare a certain day of the week as a "religious day." In those states employers cannot require an employee to work on such a day. A Connecticut statute, for example, provides, "No person who states that a particular day of the week is observed as his Sabbath may be required by his employer to work on such a day. An employee's refusal to work on his Sabbath shall not constitute grounds for his dismissal." This statute was challenged as going beyond the civil rights rule of reasonable accommodation to the religious needs of their employees and was declared unconstitutional by the Supreme Court in 1985.[7]

Sex Discrimination   Even though states have enacted laws to protect women, they also prohibit by statute the employment of women in certain occupations. Many state statutes have barred women from working during the night or from working more than a given number of hours per day or per week. Under the Equal Employment Opportunity Act of 1972, federal courts have struck down most of these laws: employers are forbidden from classifying jobs as male or female and from advertising in help-wanted columns that are designated male or female unless sex is a bona fide job qualification. Furthermore, employers cannot have separate male and female seniority lists.

The following case was brought by a woman who was fired from her job for behavior similar in character to that of male employees who were not fired because of their behavior. The court found sex discrimination to exist.

Case 32.1
WISE v. MEAD CORP.
United States District Court, Middle District of Georgia, 1985.
614 F.Supp. 1131.

FACTS   A female employee of Mead Corporation, Ms. Wise, became involved in a dispute in the lunchroom of her place of employment with another employee, Pruitt. A fight ensued, and Wise kicked and scratched Pruitt and used "abusive and uncivil" language. For her behavior, Wise's employment at Mead was terminated by her employer. Wise brought suit, alleging sex discrimination on the part of Mead Corporation in violation of Title VII of the Civil Rights Act of 1964, on the grounds that at least four

other fights at Mead had occurred under similar circumstances and none of the participants had been fired. None of the other fights had involved a female.

ISSUE   Was Wise's employment termination due to sex discrimination by Mead Corporation?

DECISION   Yes. Mead produced no convincing evidence that any other reason existed to terminate Wise's employment.

REASON   The court stated that a "plaintiff fired for misconduct makes out a prima facie case of discriminatory discharge if she shows (1) that she is a member of a

---

6.   Trans World Airline, Inc. v. Hardison, 432 U.S. 63, 97 S.Ct. 2264, 53 L.Ed.2d 113 (1977).
7.   Estate of Thornton et al. v. Caldor, Inc., 472 U.S. 703, 105 S.Ct. 2914, 86 L.Ed.2d 557 (1985).

Case 32.1—Continued

protected class, (2) that she was qualified for the job from which she was fired, and (3) that the misconduct for which she was discharged was nearly identical to that engaged in by an employee outside the protected class whom the employer retained." Wise had established a prima facie case because Mead did not dispute that she was qualified for her job and because three male employees had engaged in conduct nearly identical to that of Wise, but

the three men were retained in employment. Regardless of the fact that Mead produced grounds for firing Wise (the fighting), the court concluded that discrimination made a difference in the decision. "In this case, a review of the facts proves beyond a doubt that it is more likely that Mead was motivated by discrimination. Therefore, plaintiff has proved that Mead's proffered reasons for firing plaintiff are in fact pretext for discrimination. . . ."

Testing and Educational Requirements   Employers often find it necessary to use interviews and testing procedures in order to choose from among a large number of applicants for job openings. Consequently, personnel tests have been used as devices for screening applicants. Minimum educational requirements are also common. In the following case, the Supreme Court of the United States had to grapple with the thorny problem of whether minimum educational requirements and the use of standardized general intelligence tests as a condition for employment violated Title VII of the Civil Rights Act.

Case 32.2
GRIGGS v. DUKE POWER CO.
United States Supreme Court, 1971.
401 U.S. 424, 91 S.Ct. 849, 28 L.Ed.2d 158.

FACTS   The defendant, Duke Power Company, was sued by a number of its black employees for practicing racial discrimination in hiring and assigning employees at its Dan River plant. The plant was organized into five operating departments: (1) labor, (2) coal handling, (3) operation, (4) maintenance, and (5) laboratory testing. Blacks were employed only in the labor department, where the highest paying jobs paid less than the lowest paying jobs in the other four departments (which employed only whites). Promotions were normally made within each department on the basis of seniority. Transferees into a department usually began in the lowest position.

In 1955 the company began to require a high school education for an initial assignment into any department except the labor department. In addition, it required a high school education for any transfer from the coal handling department to any inside department (operations, maintenance, or laboratory). For ten years, this company-wide policy was enforced. In 1965, when the company abandoned its policy of restricting blacks to the labor department, a high school diploma or equivalency test

was nevertheless made a prerequisite to transfer from the labor department into any other department.

The equivalency test rendered a markedly disproportionate number of blacks ineligible for employment advancement in the company. The district court and the court of appeals found Duke Power Company not to be in violation of the Civil Rights Act.

ISSUE   Did the requirement of high school diplomas or equivalency tests in this case violate Title VII of the Civil Rights Act?

DECISION   Yes. The U.S. Supreme Court held that Duke Power's requirements respecting high school diplomas and equivalency tests violated the Civil Rights Act.

REASON   The Court noted that, ordinarily, requiring a high school education or the passing of a general intelligence test as a condition of employment does not violate a person's civil rights. When such requirements bear no relation to job performance, however, and when they operate to disqualify racial minorities at a substantially higher rate than white applicants, they amount to illegal barriers in violation of the Civil Rights Act. This is true even though Duke Power Company imposed the requirements without discriminatory *intent*. The Court explained its interpreta-

Case 32.2—Continued

tion of the law as follows: "Congress directed the thrust of the Act to the consequences of employment practices, not simply the motivation. . . . Nothing in the Act precludes the use of testing or measuring procedures; obviously they are useful. What the Congress has forbidden is giving these devices and mechanisms controlling force unless they are demonstrably a reasonable measure of job performance."

COMMENT   Recently, the Equal Employment Opportunity Commission (EEOC) adopted the so-called *four-fifths*

rule for determining when a standardized test has a discriminatory effect. If, for example, 50 percent of white male applicants pass the test and are hired, but only 30 percent of minority applicants pass the test and are hired, the four-fifths rule is violated and the EEOC would view the test as having a discriminatory impact (the rule requires that at least 40 percent of the minority applicants pass the test).

Lie-Detector Tests and Civil Rights

Polygraph experts are often used to test potential or actual employees. A polygraph expert presumably can determine whether a person is lying by examining a polygram—the graphic results of a polygraph—showing changes in pulse rate, blood pressure, and other physiological data that occur while answers are being given to the questions asked by the tester. Many consider such tests to represent an invasion of an employee's right to privacy and privilege against self-incrimination. Many union contracts have banned lie-detector tests, and some states prohibit employers from requiring prospective employees to undergo such tests. In the absence of legislation, however, the courts have not uniformly agreed on whether employees have the right to refuse a polygraph test.[8]

---

8.   See, for example, Cordle v. General Hugh Mercer Corp., 325 S.E.2d 111 (W.Va. 1984).

Some states have prohibited employers from requiring prospective employees to undergo lie detector tests.

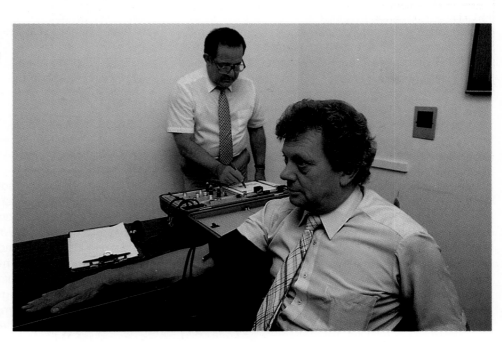

Profile

Sandra Day O'Connor (1930–)

"*A majority of litigants who come before us are people who are essentially unknown, not only to us but even within their own community. We resolve their problems and, in the process, resolve the problems of thousands or millions similarly situated.*"

On September 21, 1981, history was made when the Senate unanimously confirmed the nomination of Sandra Day O'Connor as the first woman justice of the United States Supreme Court. Born in El Paso, Texas, she was raised on her grandfather's 162,000-acre Lazy B Ranch near Duncan, Arizona. O'Connor graduated *magna cum laude* from Stanford University with a B.A. degree in economics in 1950. Two years later, she earned her LL.B. law degree from Stanford University Law School where she was an editor of the *Stanford Law Review* and a member of the Order of the Coif, an honorary society. In law school, she was a classmate of one of her future colleagues on the U.S. Supreme Court, William H. Rehnquist.

As was common for women professionals in the early 1950s, O'Connor had some difficulty in finding employment where she could use her legal training. After serving briefly as deputy county attorney for San Mateo County, California, from 1952 to 1953, she accompanied her husband to Germany during his

military service and worked as a civilian attorney for the army. Following a several-year interruption in her career to raise three sons—during which she worked part-time in the law—she became an assistant attorney general for the state of Arizona in 1965.

In 1969, she was appointed to fill a vacancy in the Arizona Senate and retained the seat in the next year's election. She was chosen Senate majority leader as a Republican in 1972—the first woman majority leader in history. Active in Republican politics, O'Connor also co-chaired the Arizona committee to Re-Elect the President (Nixon) in 1972. In 1974, she was elected to the Superior Court for Maricopa County, and five years later she was appointed to the Arizona Court of Appeals. On August 19, 1981, President Reagan nominated her as an associate justice to replace Potter Stewart, who had retired. Her first years on the Court have marked her as a conservative justice who believes in a relatively limited role for the Court in making national policy.

❖ Injury, Compensation, and Safety

Numerous state and federal statutes are designed to protect employees and their families from the risk of accidental injury, death, or disease resulting from their employment. This section discusses state workers' compensation acts and the Occupational Safety and Health Act of 1970, which are specifically designed to protect employees and their families.

State Workers' Compensation Acts

Workers' compensation laws are usually administered by some administrative agency or board that has quasi-judicial powers. All rulings of such boards are subject to review by the courts. In general, the right to recover under workers' compensation laws is determined without regard to the existence of negligence or of fault in the traditional sense. Rather, it is predicated wholly on the employment relationship and the fact that the injury *arose out of and/or was in the course of normal employment*. Some states require that just one of these conditions be satisfied, whereas other states require that both be satisfied. A simple, two-pronged test for determining whether an employee can receive workers' compensation is:

1. Was the injury accidental?
2. Did the injury arise out of and/or in the course of employment?

Intentionally inflicted self-injury, for example, would not be considered accidental and, hence, would not be covered under the workers' compensation laws. In the past, heart attacks or other medical problems arising out of preexisting disease or physical conditions were not covered, but recently some states have allowed recovery.

Basically, employers are under a system of strict liability. Few, if any, defenses (including the common-law defenses of contributory negligence, assumption of risk, or fellow-servant doctrines) exist for them. Therefore, the costs of treating workers' injuries are considered a cost of production and are passed on to consumers.

Health and Safety Protection

At the federal level the primary legislation for employee health and safety protection is the Occupational Safety and Health Act (OSHA) of 1970.[9] This act was passed to ensure safe and healthful working conditions for practically every employee in the country. The act requires that businesses be maintained free from recognized hazards.

Three federal agencies were created to develop and enforce the standards set by this act. The Occupational Safety and Health Administration is part of the Department of Labor and has the authority to promulgate standards, make inspections, and enforce the act. The National Institute for Occupational Safety and Health is part of the Department of Health and Human Services. Its main duty is to conduct research on safety and health problems and to recommend standards for OSHA administrators to adopt. Finally, the Occupational Safety and Health Review Commission is an independent agency set up to handle appeals from actions taken by OSHA administrators.

All employers affecting commerce who have one or more employees are covered by OSHA. Employees can file complaints of OSHA violations. Under the act, an employer cannot discharge an employee who files a complaint or who, in good faith, refuses to work in a high-risk area (where bodily harm or death might result). Employers with eleven or more employees are required to keep occupational injury and illness records for each employee. Each record must be kept and updated for a continuous five-year period and made available for inspection when requested by an OSHA inspector. Whenever a work-related injury or disease occurs, employers are required to make reports directly to OSHA. Whenever an employee is killed in a work-related accident, or if five or more employees are hospitalized in one accident, the Department of Labor must be notified within forty-eight hours. If it is not, the company is fined. Following the accident, a complete inspection of the premises is mandatory.

---

9.   84 Stat. 1590, 29 U.S.C.A. 553, 651–678.

OSHA-compliance officers may enter and inspect facilities of any establishment covered by OSHA. In the past, warrantless inspections were conducted. As illustrated in the following case, however, it is now recognized that such inspections violate the warrant clause of the Fourth Amendment.

Case 32.3
MARSHALL v. BARLOW'S, INC.
United States Supreme Court, 1978.
436 U.S. 307, 98 S.Ct. 1816, 56 L.Ed.2d 305.

FACTS In 1975 an OSHA inspector entered the customer service area of Barlow's, Inc., an electrical and plumbing installation business. After showing his credentials, the inspector informed the president and general manager, Barlow, that he wished to conduct a search of the working areas of the business. Upon inquiry, Barlow learned that no complaint had been received about his company. The inspection was simply the result of a random selection process, and the inspector did not have a search warrant. Thereupon, Barlow refused to permit the inspector to enter the working area of his business, claiming rights guaranteed by the Fourth Amendment of the United States Constitution. OSHA filed suit in the district court and received an order compelling Barlow to admit the inspector for purposes of conducting an occupational safety and health inspection. When the OSHA inspector presented himself, however, Barlow again refused admission. Barlow then sought an injunction against the warrantless search on the ground that it violated the Fourth Amendment. A panel of three judges issued a permanent injunction, and OSHA appealed.

ISSUE Was OSHA entitled to make a safety and health inspection of Barlow's work premises without a warrant?

DECISION No. The U.S. Supreme Court upheld the permanent injunction. OSHA inspections conducted without warrants were held to be unconstitutional, as the "warrant clause" of the Fourth Amendment was held to protect "commercial buildings as well as private homes."

REASON OSHA argued that the search-warrant requirement did not apply to "pervasively regulated businesses" covered under the Walsh-Healey Act and affecting interstate commerce. The Court disagreed that an exception should be granted on this basis, stating that nothing "but the most fictional sense of voluntary consent to later searches [can] be found in the single fact that one conducts a business affecting interstate commerce; under current practice and law, few businesses can be conducted without having some effect on interstate commerce."

COMMENTS The Fourth Amendment provides that, except upon *probable cause* supported by oath or affirmation, people have a right to be secure in their persons, houses, papers, and effects against unreasonable searches and seizures. Thus, OSHA inspectors are now required to obtain warrants before conducting an inspection. A warrant for an OSHA inspection, however, is much easier to obtain than one involving a criminal investigation. All that is required is proof that there was a reasonable and "uniformly applied" basis for selecting a particular workplace for inspection. In situations involving highly regulated businesses, such as the liquor business, warrantless searches are valid. [See Colonnade Catering Corp. v. United States, 397 U.S. 72, 90 S.Ct. 774, 25 L.Ed.2d 60 (1970), and United States v. Biswell, 406 U.S. 311, 92 S.Ct. 1593, 32 L.Ed.2d 87 (1972).]

❖ Retirement and Security Income

Federal and state governments participate in insurance programs designed to protect employees and their families by covering the financial impact of retirement, disability, death, hospitalization, and unemployment. The key federal law on this subject is the Social Security Act of 1935.[10]

---

10. 49 Stat. 620, 42 U.S.C.A. 301.

Old Age, Survivors, and Disability Insurance (OASDI)

Both employers and employees must "contribute" under the Federal Insurance Contributions Act (FICA)[11] to help pay for the loss of income benefits on retirement. The basis for the employee's contribution is the employee's annual wage base—the maximum amount of an employee's wages that are subject to the tax. Benefits are fixed by statute but increase automatically with increases in the cost of living if they exceed a certain minimum amount.

Medicare

A health insurance program, Medicare is administered by the Social Security Administration for people sixty-five years of age and older and for some under sixty-five who are disabled. It has two parts, one pertaining to hospital costs and the other to nonhospital medical costs, such as visits to doctors' offices. People who have Medicare hospital insurance can also obtain additional federal medical insurance if they pay small monthly premiums that increase as the cost of medical care increases.

Private Retirement Plans

There has been significant legislation to regulate retirement plans set up by employers to supplement social security benefits. The major piece of this type of legislation is the Employee Retirement Income Security Act (ERISA) of 1974.[12] This act empowers the Labor Management Services Administration of the Department of Labor to enforce its provisions to regulate individuals who operate private pension funds.

Unemployment Compensation

The United States has a system of unemployment insurance in which employers pay into a fund, the proceeds of which are paid out to qualified unemployed workers. The major piece of federal legislation involved is the Federal Unemployment Tax Act (FUTA).[13] This act created a state system that provides unemployment compensation to eligible individuals. Employers who fall under the provisions of the act are taxed quarterly. Taxes are typically collected by the employers and submitted to the states, which then deposit them with the federal government. The federal government maintains an Unemployment Insurance Fund, in which each state has an account.

❖ Other Employment Laws

Among the numerous other employment laws affecting U. S. workers and their employers are the Fair Labor Standards Act, the Davis-Bacon Act, and the Walsh-Healey Public Contracts Act.

---

11.   26 U.S.C.A. 3101.
12.   88 Stat. 829, 29 U.S.C.A. 1001.
13.   68A Stat. 439, 26 U.S.C.A., Chapter 23.

Fair Labor Standards Act

The Fair Labor Standards Act (also known as the Wage-Hour Law) was signed by the president on June 25, 1938.[14] It covers child labor, maximum hours, and minimum wages.

Child Labor   The act prohibits oppressive child labor. Children under sixteen years of age cannot be employed full time except by a parent under certain circumstances; nor can children between the ages of sixteen and eighteen be employed in hazardous jobs or in jobs detrimental to their health and well-being. Most states require children under sixteen years of age to obtain work permits.

Maximum Hours   Under the act, any employee who agrees to work more than forty hours per week must be paid no less than one and a half times his or her regular pay for all hours over forty. Exceptions are made for employees working under the terms of the collective-bargaining agreements and in some other circumstances. The following case illustrates a court's application of the Fair Labor Standards Act.

Case 32.4
CRENSHAW v. QUARLES DRILLING CORP.
United States Court of Appeals, Tenth Circuit, 1986.
798 F.2d. 1345.

FACTS   Fred Crenshaw was hired by Quarles Drilling Corporation (Quarles) as a drilling-equipment mechanic on September 16, 1980. Crenshaw was provided with a company truck, special tools, and a mobile telephone so that he could do routine maintenance and emergency repairs of Quarles's drilling equipment located in several states. Under the employment contract, Crenshaw was paid a biweekly salary based on a forty-hour regular work week and twenty hours of overtime per week. Crenshaw often worked more than sixty hours per week but was not given overtime pay for the additional hours. Nor were his hours of travel time between job sites included as "working" hours. In 1983, having left Quarles's employment, Crenshaw filed suit against the company for overtime compensation, claiming it had violated the Fair Labor Standards Act (FLSA).

Under the FLSA, employers are required to pay their employees time and a half for hours worked over forty hours during a given workweek. This applies to employees engaged in commerce or in the production of goods for commerce. An exception to the act exists, however, for employees (1) whose duties necessitate irregular

working hours, (2) who are employed pursuant to a bona fide individual contract or collective-bargaining agreement, (3) whose contracts specify a regular rate of pay for up to forty hours a week and one and a half times that rate for hours over forty, and (4) whose contracts provide a weekly pay guarantee for not more than sixty hours. If all four of these elements are present, the employee is exempted from the FLSA requirements. The trial court found that all four elements were not present and granted judgment for Crenshaw. Crenshaw was awarded $34,082.85 in overtime compensation and an equal amount in liquidated damages. Quarles appealed.

ISSUE   Had Quarles violated the FLSA by not paying Crenshaw overtime wages for the hours worked beyond the contractual sixty hours per week and for the travel time?

DECISION   Yes. The appellate court affirmed the trial court's decision that Quarles had violated the FLSA but remanded the case for further determination of the exact number of hours to be compensated.

REASON   The court noted that Quarles and Crenshaw had agreed to a sixty-hour week based on forty hours at a regular hourly rate and twenty hours at time and a half. As to the irregularity of Crenshaw's hours, for hours

---

14. 52 Stat. 1060, 29 U.S.C.A. 201.

Case 32.4—Continued

to be considered "irregular," they must, in a significant number of weeks, fluctuate both below forty hours per week as well as above. In this case, the court noted that only 6.7 percent of the weeks worked by Crenshaw involved less than 40 hours of work per week. Since this was not a significant percentage, the court found that Crenshaw did not work irregular hours. Therefore, Quarles could not claim exception to the FLSA on this basis and violated the FLSA by not paying Crenshaw overtime wages for the hours in excess of sixty hours per week. The appellate court also agreed with the trial court's conclusion that Crenshaw's travel time should be included in the computation of hours worked per week. The court reasoned that employees who transport equipment essential to well servicing are performing an activity that is so closely related to the work they are required to perform that it must be considered an integral and indispensable part of their principal activities. The appellate court affirmed the trial court's judgment that Crenshaw was entitled to compensation and damages, but, because of a discrepancy in the factual record concerning the hours worked during a certain period of weeks, the case was remanded to the trial court for further investigation in this respect.

Minimum Wage   The Fair Labor Standards Act provides that a minimum wage of a specified amount must be paid to employees in covered industries. Congress periodically revises such minimum wages. The term *wages* is meant to include the reasonable cost of the employer in furnishing employees with board, lodging, and other facilities if they are customarily furnished by that employer.

Other Government-Enforced Minimum-Wage Laws

In 1931, during the Great Depression, the president signed the Davis-Bacon Act,[15] which requires the payment of "prevailing wages" to employees of contractors or subcontractors working on government construction projects. In 1936 an act that extended the Davis-Bacon Act was put into effect—the Walsh-Healey Public Contract Act.[16] This act requires a minimum wage as well as overtime pay of time and a half to employees of manufacturers or suppliers entering into contracts with agencies of the federal government.

---

15.   46 Stat. 1494, 40 U.S.C.A. 276a.
16.   49 Stat. 2036, 41 U.S.C.A. 35.

Application

Law and the Employer— Avoiding Employment Discrimination

Discrimination against an employee can create numerous problems for the employer, so it is wise to review personnel practices with this in mind while analyzing your workforce. You must take an objective look at how many women and how many minorities have been hired and also at the positions they hold. Recruitment practices must also be scrutinized for inadvertent discrimination. For example, an employer who does no advertising but instead relies on word of mouth through employees and friends may have a problem. The result of such word-of-mouth recruitment can be a homogeneous workforce that well may be legally perceived as imbalanced with respect to women and minorities—even if the imbalance is unintentional.

Simply relying on supervisors to not discriminate may be inadequate. They must be aware of the employer's policies, and they must be made responsible for implementing them. The employer will be held liable whenever the supervisors discriminate in hiring and employment practices.

One way to avoid discrimination lawsuits is to have a formal grievance procedure for employees. They should easily be able to bring complaints of unfair treatment to the employer, who should have a formal procedure for the resolution of such complaints, giving employees due process. Courts are often impressed by a properly conducted, internal due process procedure.

Checklist for Avoiding Employment Discrimination

☐ 1. Establish a formal set of objectives and procedures to avoid discrimination.

☐ 2. Make sure supervisors are completely aware of such objectives and procedures.

☐ 3. Set up an internal mechanism for hearing and resolving complaints of employment discrimination.

☐ 4. Make sure that employment testing does not have an uneven impact on women and minority members. When in doubt, consult a qualified expert in industrial psychology.

❖ Chapter Summary: Employee and Labor Law

Unions and Collective Bargaining	1. *Norris-Laguardia Act* (1932)—Permitted employees to organize into unions and to engage in peaceful strikes.
	2. *National Labor Relations Act* (Wagner Act) (1935)—Established the right of employees to engage in collective bargaining and to strike. Created the National Labor Relations Board to oversee elections and to prevent employers from engaging in unfair and illegal union-labor activities and unfair labor practices.
	3. *Labor-Management Relations Act* (Taft-Hartley Act) (1947)—Amended the Wagner Act; allowed for protection of employers as well as of employees by providing a list of unfair labor activities which both unions and management were forbidden to practice. Prohibited *closed shops*, allowed states to pass right-to-work laws, and provided for eighty-day cooling-off period (whereby courts could enjoin employees from striking if strike would create a national emergency).

❖ Chapter Summary: Employee and Labor Law—Continued

Unions and Collective Bargaining (Continued)	4. *Labor-Management Reporting and Disclosure Act* (Landrum-Griffin Act) (1959)—Regulated internal union elections and procedures and established reporting requirements for union activities.
Civil Rights and Equal Opportunity	Title VII of the Civil Rights Act of 1964 (amended in 1972) prohibits discrimination by most employers, labor unions, employment agencies, and state and local governments against employees, job applicants, and union members on the basis of race, color, national origin, religion, or sex.
Injury, Compensation, and Safety	1. *State workers' compensation acts*—Allow compensation to workers whose injuries arose out of and during the course of their employment. Regulated by state agency or board. 2. *Health and safety protection*—The Occupational Safety and Health Act (OSHA) of 1970 ensures safe and healthful working conditions for employees.
Retirement and Security Income	1. *Social Security*—Old Age, Survivors, and Disability Insurance (OASDI) provides retired or disabled employees or their families with income created by mandatory employer and employee contributions. The Social Security Administration, created by the Social Security Act of 1935, also administers Medicare, a health insurance program for people sixty-five years of age and older and for some under age sixty-five who are disabled. 2. *Private retirement plans set up by employers*—These plans supplement social security income for retired individuals; most plans are regulated by the Employee Retirement Income Security Act (ERISA) of 1974. 3. *Unemployment compensation*—The Federal Unemployment Tax Act (FUTA) created a state system that provides unemployment compensation to eligible individuals; paid for by employer-paid taxes.
Other Employment Laws	1. *Fair Labor Standards Act* (1938)—Prohibits oppressive child labor, provides that a minimum hourly wage rate be paid to covered employees, and requires individuals working over forty hours a week to be paid overtime wages of no less than one and a half times the regular pay for hours worked beyond forty hours a week (with some exceptions). 2. *Other minimum-wage laws*—Employees must be paid at least a minimum wage rate (established and periodically revised by the federal government), and employees working on government construction projects must be paid "prevailing wages." Established by the Davis-Bacon Act of 1931 and extended by the Walsh-Healey Public Contract Act of 1936.

❖ Questions and Case Problems

32-1. Discuss fully which of the following constitutes a violation of the 1964 Civil Rights Act, Title VII, as amended:

(a) Tennington, Inc., is a consulting firm and has ten employees. These employees travel on consulting jobs in seven states. Tennington has an employment record of hiring only white males.

(b) Novo Films, Inc., is making a film about Africa and needs to employ approximately 100 extras for this picture. Novo advertises in all major newspapers in Southern California for the hiring of these extras. The ad states that only black persons need apply.

(c) Chinawa is a major processor of cheese sold throughout the United States, employing 100 employees at its principal processing plant. The plant is located in Heartland Corners, whose population is 50 percent white, 25 percent black, and the balance Hispanic, Asian, and other minorities. Chinawa requires a high school diploma as a condition of employment for its clean-up crew. Three-fourths of the white population complete high school, as compared to only one-fourth of the minority groups. Chinawa has an all-white cleaning crew.

32-2. Calzoni's is an interstate business engaged in manufacturing and selling boats. The company has 500 nonunion employees. Representatives of these employees are requesting a four-day, ten-hours-per-day workweek, and Calzoni is concerned that this would require paying time and a half after eight hours per day. Which federal act is Calzoni thinking of that might require this? Will it in fact require paying time and a half for all hours worked over eight hours per day if the employees' proposal is accepted? Explain.

32-3. Perlman is an employee of Jacobs, Inc., a cannery of peas that has a three-storied plant. On top of the third story is a flagpole. The company has a set lunch break, during which time the plant is shut down. The employees are not allowed to leave the plant property, and most eat their lunch outside on a grassy area. Some employees, however, eat their lunch on top of the third-story roof. Perlman, known as a cut-up, climbs the flagpole one afternoon, in order to show off, and while waving wildly at his fellow employees, loses his grip and falls, suffering numerous injuries. Is Perlman entitled to workers' compensation? Explain.

32-4. Denton and Carlo were employed at an appliance plant. Their job required them to do occasional maintenance work while standing on a wire mesh twenty feet above the plant floor. Other employees had fallen through the mesh, one of whom had been killed by the fall. When Denton and Carlo were asked by their supervisor to do work that would likely require them to walk on the mesh, they refused due to their fear of bodily harm or death. Because of their refusal to do the requested work, the two employees were fired from their jobs. Was their discharge wrongful? If so, under what federal employment law? To what federal agency or department should they turn for assistance?

32-5. Several black employees of the Connecticut Department of Income Maintenance who sought promotion to supervisory positions took the required written examination but failed to pass it. Of all who took the examination, 54 percent of the black employees passed it while nearly 80 percent of the white employees who took the test passed. Following the examination, the state of Connecticut promoted eleven black employees (representing 23 percent of all black employees) and thirty-five white employees (representing 14 percent of all white employees). Teal and three other black employees who failed the test sued the state of Connecticut and the Department of Income Maintenance. The employees asserted that the written test excluded a disproportionate number of black employees from promotion to supervisory positions and therefore violated Title VII of the Civil Rights Act. The state argued that since a greater percentage of black employees had been promoted, relative to white employees, the test was not discriminatory. Who was correct? [Connecticut v. Teal, 457 U.S. 440, 102 S.Ct. 2525, 73 L.Ed.2d 130 (1982)]

32-6. Gerwill, Inc., operated a taxicab business. Wages for the cab drivers were determined from the time the driver reported in as "ready to go" in the morning to the moment the

driver discharged his or her last passengers at the end of the day. Cab-cleaning time before the workday began, necessary for each driver, and the time it took each driver to return to the office, park the cab, and do daily paperwork were not included in computing the drivers' wages. The Secretary of Labor determined that because this work-related time was not included in the wage-determination calculations, the cab company had not met the minimum-wage standards required by federal law. Did the court rule that the time used by the cab drivers to prepare the cabs in the morning and to return to the office and complete the daily paperwork should be included as a part of the workday? Explain. [Marshall v. Gerwill, Inc., 495 F.Supp. 744 (D.Md. 1980)]

31-7. Robert Evjen, who worked full time for Boise Cascade, also attended a community college full time. When Evjen was laid off by Boise Cascade as part of a general cutback plan, Evjen applied for unemployment compensation. In order to qualify for unemployment compensation, a person must be available to work; and full-time enrollment in school, according to the Employment Appeals Board, created a "presumption" of nonavailability for work. Evidence was presented, however, that Evjen had never missed work in order to attend school, that he could not afford to attend college without working, and that his actions indicated that work always came first. Was Evjen allowed to receive unemployment compensation benefits? Explain. [Evjen v. Employment Division, 22 Or.App. 372, 539 P.2d 662 (1975)]

32-8. Beginning in June 1966, Corning Glass Works started to open up jobs on the night shift to women. The previously separate male and female seniority lists were consolidated, and the women became eligible to exercise their seniority on the same basis as men and to bid for higher-paid night inspection jobs as vacancies occurred. But on January 20, 1969, a new collective bargaining agreement went into effect; it established a new job evaluation system for setting wage rates. This agreement abolished (for the future) separate base wages for night and day shift inspectors and imposed a uniform base wage for inspectors that exceeded the wage rate previously in effect for the night shift. The agreement, however, did allow for a higher "red circle" rate for employees hired prior to January 20, 1969, when working as inspectors on the night shift. This "red circle" wage served essentially to perpetuate the differential in base wages between day and night inspectors. Was Corning in violation of the Civil Rights Act of 1964? [Corning Glass Works v. Brennan, 417 U.S. 188, 94 S.Ct. 2223, 41 L.Ed.2d 1 (1974)]

32-9. Local 1001 of the Retail Store Employees Union became the certified bargaining representative of some of the employees of Safeco Title Insurance Company in the state of Washington. Contract negotiations between Safeco and the union ended in a deadlock. At this point, the union began picketing the five local independent title companies, as well as the main Safeco office. The picketers carried signs indicating that Safeco was a nonunion employer. Safeco declared that

Local 1001 was engaging in a secondary boycott in violation of the National Labor Relations Act. It argued that the union was directing its appeal against Safeco insurance policies. The title companies that were being picketed were not owned by Safeco, and none of the daily operations of the title companies was controlled by Safeco. Rather, the title companies simply derived most of their income from the sale of Safeco title insurance policies. Was the Retail Store Employees Union indeed engaging in a secondary boycott? [NLRB v. Retail Store Employees Union, 447 U.S. 607, 100 S.Ct. 2372, 65 L.Ed.2d 377 (1980)]

Unit Six

Property, Its Protection, and the International Legal Environment

❖ Why We Study Laws Relating to Property, Its Protection, and International Trade

Property can be either movable,[1] in which case it is called *personal property* (or *chattel*), or not movable, in which case it is called *real property*. The law treats these two separate types of property in distinctly different ways. Consequently, we will discuss each in a separate chapter: personal property in Chapter 33 and real property in Chapter 34. Also included in Chapter 33 is an analysis of a situation in which personal property is temporarily delivered by its owner into the care of another person. This is called a *bailment*. What happens when you loan this law book to one of your friends and it gets destroyed in a fire? You need to know the law of bailments to give an answer. If your car is stolen in an attended parking lot, who is responsible? Again, you need to know the law of bailments to give an answer.

Both personal property and real property are usually insured. In Chapter 35 we examine insurance in general terms as it applies to personal and real property. We also look at wills, trusts, and estates, or how property is passed from one generation to another.

Finally, because we live in an increasingly international economic community, an entire chapter is devoted to international law. Many businesspersons find themselves engaged in selling goods and services to other countries. These are exports. Others find that they are buying goods and services from other countries. These are imports. Additionally, numerous other types of financial dealings with other countries are possible. Often money capital is raised abroad to finance a project at home. And some businesses are discovering that they can make higher profits by investing money capital in other countries or by actually producing goods in other countries for sale in those countries, as well as for sale elsewhere, including the United States.

---

1. This also includes intangible property.

Chapter 33

Personal Property and Bailments

Property consists of the legally protected rights and interests a person has in anything with an ascertainable value that is subject to ownership. Property would have little value (and the word would have little meaning) if the law did not define the right to use it, to sell or dispose of it, and to prevent trespassing upon it. In the United States, the ownership of property receives unique protection under the law. The Bill of Rights states that "no person shall . . . be deprived of life, liberty, or property, without due process of law; nor shall private property be taken for public use, without just compensation." The Fourteenth Amendment provides that "no State shall . . . deprive any person of life, liberty, or property, without due process of law." Indeed, John Locke, as indicated in the opening quotation, considered the preservation of property to be the primary reason for the establishment of government.

In the first part of this chapter, we will look at the nature of personal property, property rights and ownership title, the methods of acquiring ownership and personal property, and issues relating to mislaid, lost, and abandoned personal property. In the second part of the chapter, we will look at a bailment relationship, where personal property is temporarily delivered into the care of another without transferring title. This is the distinguishing characteristic of a bailment as compared to a sale or a gift—there is no passage of title, or no intent to transfer title.

❖ The Nature of Personal Property

As discussed in the introduction to this unit, property is divided into two categories. **Real property** consists of the land and everything permanently attached to the land. Where structures are permanently attached to the land, then everything attached permanently to the structures is also real property, or *realty*. All other property is **personal property,** or *personalty*. Attorneys sometimes refer to all personal property as **chattel,** a more comprehensive term than *goods* because it includes living as well as inanimate property.

Personal property can be tangible or intangible. Tangible personal property, like a TV set or a car, has physical substance. Intangible personal property represents some set of rights and duties, but has no real physical existence. Stocks and bonds, patents, and copyrights are examples of intangible personal property.

"The great and chief end . . . of men united into commonwealths, and putting themselves under government, is the preservation of their property."

John Locke, 1632–1704 *(English political philosopher)*

REAL PROPERTY
Property consisting of land and buildings thereupon, which are stationary, as opposed to personal property, which can be moved. In the absence of a contract, real property includes things growing on the land before they are severed (such as timber) as well as fixtures.

PERSONAL PROPERTY
Property that is movable; any property that is not real property.

CHATTEL
Tangible and intangible personal property.

727

In a dynamic society, the concept of personal property must expand to take account of new types of ownership rights. For example, gas, water, and telephone services are now considered personal property for the purpose of criminal prosecution when they are stolen or used without authorization. Federal and state statutes protect against the copying of musical compositions. It is a crime now to engage in the "bootleg-ging"—illegal copying for resale—of records and tapes. The theft of computer programs is usually considered a theft of personal property.

❖ Property Ownership

"Personal property has no locality."

Lord Loughborough, 1733–1805
(British jurist)

FEE SIMPLE
Exists when the owner or owners of property are entitled to use, possess, or dispose of that property as they choose during their lifetime, and, upon death, their interests in the property descend to their heirs.

TENANCY IN COMMON
Co-ownership of property whereby each party owns an undivided interest that passes to his or her heirs at death.

JOINT TENANCY WITH RIGHT OF SURVIVORSHIP
The ownership interest of two or more co-owners of property whereby each owns an undivided portion of the property. Upon the death of one of the joint tenants, his or her interest automatically passes to the others and cannot be transferred by the will of the deceased.

Property ownership can be viewed as a bundle of rights, including the right to possession of the property and disposition—by sale, gift, rental, lease, and so on—of the property. There are three principal ways for one or more persons to hold this bundle of rights at one time.

1. *Fee simple.* A person (or persons) who holds the entire bundle of rights is said to be the owner (or owners) in a **fee simple.** The owner or owners in a fee simple are entitled to use, possess, or dispose of the property as they choose during their lifetimes, and upon death their interests in the property descend to their heirs.
2. *Tenancy in common.* When two or more persons own an undivided fractional interest in the property, and one tenant dies, that interest passes to his or her heirs. This is called a **tenancy in common.** For example, Rosalind and Chad own a rare stamp collection as tenants in common. Should Rosalind die before Chad, one-half of the stamp collection would become the property of Rosalind's heirs. If Rosalind sold her interest to Fred before she died, Fred and Chad would be co-owners as tenants in common. If Fred died, his interest in the personal property would pass to his heirs, and they in turn would own the property with Chad as tenants in common.
3. *Joint tenancy with right of survivorship.* Two or more persons who own an undivided interest in the whole (personal property), with the deceased's interest passing to the survivor, constitute a **joint tenancy with right of survivorship.** This can be terminated at any time before a joint tenant's death by gift or by sale. If no termination occurs, then upon the death of a joint tenant, his or her interest transfers to the remaining joint tenants, not to the heirs of the deceased joint tenant. In the preceding example, if Rosalind and Chad held their stamp collection in a joint tenancy with right of survivorship, and if Rosalind dies before Chad, the entire collection becomes the property of Chad. Rosalind's heirs receive absolutely no interest in the collection. If, prior to Rosalind's death, she sells her interest to Fred, Fred and Chad become co-owners. Rosalind's sale, however, terminates the joint tenancy with the right of survivorship, and Fred and Chad become owners as tenants in common.

Concurrent ownership of property can also take the form of a *tenancy by the entirety*—a form of co-ownership with right of survivorship between a husband and wife in which a spouse cannot transfer separately his or her interest during his or her lifetime. Property can also be held as *community property*—in which each spouse technically owns an *undivided* one-half interest in property acquired during the marriage. The latter type of ownership occurs in only a few states. These forms of property ownership are discussed further in the following chapter. In this chapter we will discuss various ways in which the ownership of personal property can be acquired.

Possession

A particularly interesting example of acquiring ownership by possession is the capture of wild animals. Wild animals belong to no one in their natural state, and the first person to take possession of a wild animal normally owns it. The killing of a wild animal amounts to assuming ownership of it. Merely being in hot pursuit does not give title, however. There are two exceptions to this basic rule. First, any wild animals captured by a trespasser are the property of the landowner, not the trespasser. Second, if wild animals are captured or killed in violation of wild game statutes, the capturer does not obtain title to the animals; rather, the state does. Other illustrations of acquiring ownership by possession are presented later in this chapter.

Purchase or Production

Purchase is one of the most common means of acquiring and transferring ownership of personal property. The purchase or sale of personal property (called *goods*) falls under the Uniform Commercial Code and was discussed in detail in Chapters 11 to 13.

Production—the fruits of labor—is another means of acquiring ownership of personal property. Nearly everyone in the United States today is involved in some sort of production. For example, writers, inventors, and manufacturers all produce personal property and thereby acquire title to it. (In some situations—for example, where researchers are hired for that purpose—the producer does not own what is produced, however.)

Gifts

A **gift** is another fairly common means of both acquiring and transferring ownership of real and personal property. A gift is essentially a voluntary transfer of property ownership. It is not supported by legally sufficient consideration since the very essence of a gift is giving without consideration. Moreover, a gift must be transferred or delivered in the present rather than in the future. For example, if your aunt tells you that she is going to give you a new Mercedes-Benz for your next birthday, this is a promise, not a gift. It does not become a gift until the Mercedes-Benz is delivered to you, the donee (recipient of the gift).

Three conditions determine whether an effective gift exists:

1. *Donative intent.* There must be evidence of the donor's intent to give the donee the gift. Such donative intent is determined from the language of the donor and the surrounding circumstances. Thus, when a gift is challenged in court, the court may look at the relationship between the parties and the size of the gift in relation to the donor's other assets. A gift to an arch-enemy is viewed with suspicion. Likewise, when a gift represents a large portion of a person's assets, the courts scrutinize the transaction closely to determine the mental capacity of the donor and whether there is any element of fraud or duress present.

2. *Delivery.* An effective delivery requires giving up *complete control and dominion* (ownership rights) over the subject matter of the gift. Delivery is obvious in most cases. But suppose that you want to make a gift of various old rare coins that you have stored in a safety deposit box. You certainly cannot deliver the box itself to the donee, and you do not want to take the coins out of the bank. In such a case, when

GIFT
Any voluntary transfer of property made without consideration, past or present.

CONSTRUCTIVE DELIVERY
An act equivalent to the actual, physical delivery of property that cannot be physically delivered because of difficulty or impossibility; to illustrate, the transfer of a key to a safe constructively delivers the contents of the safe.

the physical object cannot be delivered, a symbolic, or *constructive*, delivery will be sufficient. **Constructive delivery** is a general term for all those acts that the law holds to be equivalent to acts of real delivery. In the preceding example, the delivery of the key to the safety deposit box constitutes a constructive delivery of the contents of the box. The delivery of intangible property—such as stocks, bonds, insurance policies, contracts, and so on—is always accomplished by symbolic, or constructive, delivery.

Delivery may be accomplished by means of a third party. If the third party is the agent of the donor, the delivery is effective when the agent delivers to the donee. If, on the other hand, the third party is the agent of the donee, then the gift is effectively delivered when the donor delivers the property to the donee's agent.[1] Naturally, no delivery is necessary if the gift is already in the hands of the donee.

3.   *Acceptance.* The final requirement of a valid gift is acceptance by the donee. This rarely presents any problems since most donees readily accept their gifts. The courts generally assume acceptance unless shown otherwise.

In the following case, the court considered the factors that must be present before an effective gift exists.

Case 33.1
IN RE ESTATE OF PIPER
Missouri Court of Appeals, 1984.
676 S.W.2d 897.

FACTS   Gladys Piper died intestate (without a will) in 1982. At her death, she owned miscellaneous personal property worth $5,000 and had in her purse $200 in cash and two diamond rings known as the "Andy Piper" rings. The contents of her purse were taken by her niece Wanda Brown, allegedly to preserve them for the estate. Clara Kaufmann, a friend of Gladys's, filed a claim against the estate for $4,800 because from October 1974 until Gladys's death, Clara took Gladys to the doctor, beauty shop, grocery store, wrote her checks to pay her bills, and helped her care for her home. Clara maintained that Gladys had promised to pay her for these services and that the diamond rings were a gift. The trial court denied her request for payment, finding her services had been voluntary. Clara then filed a petition for delivery of personal property, the rings (as a gift), which was granted by the trial court. Wanda, other heirs, and the administrator of Gladys's estate appealed.

ISSUE   Had Gladys Piper made an effective gift of the rings to Clara Kaufmann?

DECISION   No. The appellate court reversed the judgment of the trial court on the ground that Gladys had never delivered the rings to Clara.

REASON   Clara claimed the rings belonged to her by reason of a "consummated gift long prior to the death of Gladys Piper." Two witnesses testified for Clara at the trial that Gladys had told them the rings belonged to Clara, but that she was going to wear them until she died. The appellate court found "no evidence of any actual delivery." The court held that "[t]he essentials of a gift are (1) a present intention to make a gift on the part of the donor, (2) a delivery of the property by the donor to the donee, and (3) an acceptance by the donee. . . ." Since the evidence in the case showed only an intent to make a gift, and there was no delivery—either actual, constructive, or symbolic—a valid gift was not made. For Gladys to have made a gift, her intention had to have been executed by a complete and unconditional delivery of the property, or delivery of a proper written instrument evidencing the gift. Since this did not occur, the court found that there had been no gift.

---

1.   Bickford v. Mattocks, 95 Me. 547, 50 A. 894 (1901).

Gifts *Inter Vivos* and Gifts *Causa Mortis*

Gifts *inter vivos* are gifts made during one's lifetime, whereas **gifts *causa mortis*** (so-called *death-bed gifts*) are made in contemplation of imminent death. Gifts *causa mortis* do not become absolute until the donor dies from the contemplated illness. Moreover, the donee must survive to take the gift, and the donor must not have revoked the gift prior to death. A gift *causa mortis* is revocable at any time up to the death of the donor and is automatically revoked if the donor recovers.

GIFT *INTER VIVOS*
A gift made during one's lifetime and not in contemplation of imminent death, in contrast to a gift *causa mortis*.

GIFT *CAUSA MORTIS*
A gift made in contemplation of death. If the donor does not die of that ailment, the gift is revoked.

Will or Inheritance

Ownership of personal property may be transferred by will or by inheritance under state statutes. These transfers, called *bequests*, *devises*, or *inheritances*, are dealt with in Chapter 35.

Accession

Accession means "adding on" to something. It occurs when someone adds value to a piece of personal property by either labor or materials. Generally, there is no dispute about who owns the property after accession has occurred, especially when the accession is accomplished with the owner's consent.

If accession occurred without the permission of the owner, the courts will tend to favor the owner over the improver, provided the accession was caused wrongfully and in bad faith. In addition, many courts would deny the improver (wrongdoer) any compensation for the value added; for example, a car thief who put new tires on the stolen car would obviously not be compensated for the value of the new tires.

If the accession is performed in good faith, however, even without the owner's consent, ownership of the improved item most often depends on whether the accession increased the value of the property or changed its identity. The greater the increase in value, the more likely it is that ownership will pass to the improver. If ownership so passes, the improver obviously must compensate the original owner for the value of the property prior to the accession. If the increase in value is not sufficient to pass ownership to the improver, most courts will require the owner to compensate the improver for the value added.

To illustrate: Suppose Juarez is walking in a large country field and discovers a huge stone lying near a fence that is shaped approximately like a horse. For twenty-seven weeks Juarez works on the stone and eventually transforms it into an exact replica of the Lone Ranger's horse, Silver. Juarez's artist friends are very impressed and convince him to move the stone horse to a gallery, where it is valued at $50,000. The owner of the field where Juarez found the stone now wants to claim title to it. Normally, the courts would give Juarez title to the stone because the changes he made greatly increased its value, and the accession was performed in good faith. But Juarez would have to pay the owner of the field for the reasonable value of the stone before it was altered.

ACCESSION
The changing (for example, through manufacturing) of one good into a new good (for example, flour into bread); the right, upon payment for the original materials, to keep an article manufactured out of goods that were innocently converted.

Confusion

Confusion is defined as the commingling of goods such that one person's personal property cannot be distinguished from another's. It frequently occurs when the goods

CONFUSION
The mixing together of goods of two or more owners so that the independent goods cannot be identified.

are *fungible*, meaning that each particle is identical with every other particle, such as with grain and oil. For example, if two farmers were to put their Number 2–grade winter wheat into the same silo, confusion would occur.

If confusion of goods is caused by a person who wrongfully and willfully mixes them in order to render them indistinguishable, the innocent party acquires title to the total. If confusion occurs as a result of agreement, an honest mistake, or the act of some third party, the owners share ownership as *tenants in common* and will share any loss in proportion to their share of ownership of the property.

❖ Mislaid, Lost, and Abandoned Property

Mislaid Property

MISLAID PROPERTY
Property that the owner has voluntarily parted with and then cannot find or recover.

Property that has been placed somewhere by the owner voluntarily and then inadvertently forgotten is **mislaid property.** Suppose you go to the theater and leave your gloves on the concession stand. The gloves are mislaid property, and the theater owner is entrusted with the duty of reasonable care for the goods. Whenever mislaid property is found, the finder does not obtain title to the goods, but becomes an *involuntary bailee* (to be discussed later in this chapter). This is because it is highly likely that the true owner will return for the property.

Lost Property

LOST PROPERTY
Property that the owner has involuntarily parted with and then cannot find or recover.

Property that is involuntarily left and forgotten is **lost property.** A finder of the property can claim title to the property against the whole world, *except the true owner*. The leading case in the rights of a finder to lost property is *Armory* v. *Delamirie*, a case discussed in this chapter's "Landmark." If the true owner demands that the lost property be returned, the finder must return it. If a third party attempts to take possession of lost property from a finder, the third party cannot assert a better title than the finder. Whenever a finder knows who the true owners of property are and fails to return it to them, that finder is guilty of the tort of *conversion* (see Chapter 3). Finally, many states require the finder to make a reasonably diligent search to locate the true owner of lost property.

To illustrate the above rules, suppose Kormian works in a large library at night. In the courtyard on her way home, she finds a piece of gold jewelry that looks like it has several precious stones in it. She takes it to a jeweler to have it appraised. While pretending to weigh the jewelry, an employee of the jeweler removes several of the stones. If Kormian brings an action to recover the stones from the jeweler, she will win, because she found lost property and holds valid title against everyone *except the true owner*. Since the property was lost, rather than mislaid, the owner of the library is not the caretaker of the jewelry. Instead, Kormian acquires title good against the whole world (except the true owner).[2]

---

2.   If Kormian had found the jewelry during the course of her employment, however, her employer would be the involuntary bailee. Further, many courts now say that lost property recovered in a private place allows the owner of the place, rather than the finder, to become the bailee (even if the finder is not a trespasser).

Landmark in the Law

The *Armory* Rule (1722) and Trover Lawsuits

Armory v. *Delamirie*[1] is an interesting case, not only because it has become a well-known landmark in the law of finders' rights to property but also because it illustrates an *action in trover*—an early form of recovery of damages for the conversion of property. The plaintiff in this case, Armory, was a chimney sweep who found a jewel in its setting during the course of his work. He took the jewel to a goldsmith to have it appraised. The goldsmith, however, refused to return the jewel to Armory, claiming that Armory was not the rightful owner of the property. Armory brought an action in trover for damages to the extent of the value of the jewel and its setting, which the court awarded him. The court was careful to point out that its decision did not accord absolute ownership rights in the property to Armory: "[T]he finder of a jewel, though he does not by such finding acquire an absolute property or ownership, yet . . . has such a property as will enable him to keep it against all but the rightful owner, and consequently may maintain trover."

Trover actions emerged late in the fifteenth century in cases where a finder of lost property did not return the goods but either used them or sold or gave them to someone else. These actions largely replaced earlier *actions of detinue*—actions brought to regain possession of lost property from a finder. A plaintiff's chances of recovering lost property in detinue actions were often narrowed by the "wager of law," which allowed the defendant to win the case if he could find eleven friends or neighbors to swear the property belonged to him. The potential for perjury under the wager law goes without saying. Once trover actions became common, detinue fell into complete disuse.

The *Armory* rule established the precedent that even a finder of lost property can sue in trover for damages against all except the true owner of the chattel. As such, *Armory* was the first example of the doctrine of the *relativity of title to property*. This means that if two contestants are before the court, neither of whom can claim absolute title to the chattel, the one who can claim prior possession to the goods will likely have established sufficient rights to the property to win the case.

A curious situation arises when goods wrongfully obtained by one person are, in turn, wrongfully obtained by another, and the two parties contest their rights to possession. In such a case, does the *Armory* rule still apply—that is, does the first possessor have more rights in the property than the second? In a case that came before the Minnesota Supreme Court in 1892, *Anderson* v. *Gouldberg*,[2] the court said yes.

In the *Anderson* case, the plaintiffs had trespassed on another's land and wrongfully cut timber. The defendants later took the logs from the mill site, allegedly in the name of the owner of the property where the timber was cut. The evidence at trial indicated that both parties had illegally acquired the property. The court instructed the jury that even if the plaintiffs were trespassers when they had cut the logs, they were entitled to recover them from later possessors—except the true owner or an agent of the true owner. The jury found for the plaintiffs, a decision affirmed later by the Minnesota Supreme Court. The latter court held that the plaintiff's possession, "though wrongfully obtained," justified an action to repossess against another who took it from him.

1. 93 Eng.Rep. 664 (1 Strange 505), K.B. (1722).

2. 51 Minn. 294, 53 N.W. 636 (1892).

Many states have **estray statutes** to encourage and facilitate the return of property to its true owner and then to reward a finder for honesty if the property remains unclaimed. Such statutes provide an incentive for finders to report their discoveries by making it possible for them, after passage of a specified period of time, to acquire legal title to the property they have found. The statute usually requires the county clerk to advertise the property in an attempt to enhance the opportunity of the owner to recover what has been lost.

There are always some preliminary questions to be resolved before the estray statute can be employed. The item must be *lost property*, not merely mislaid or

ESTRAY STATUTE
A statute dealing with a person's rights in property whose ownership is unknown.

abandoned property. When the situation indicates that the property was probably lost and not mislaid or abandoned, as a matter of public policy, loss is presumed, and the estray statute applies.

Abandoned Property

ABANDONED PROPERTY
Property that the owner has voluntarily parted with, having no intention of recovering it.

Property that has been discarded by the true owner with no intention of claiming title to it is **abandoned property.** Someone who finds abandoned property acquires title to it, and such title is good against the whole world, *including the original owner*. The owner of lost property who eventually gives up any further attempt to find the lost property is frequently held to have abandoned the property. In cases where the finder is trespassing on the property of another and finds abandoned property, title does not vest in the finder but in the owner of the land. In the following case, the issue was whether some valuable property found by the plaintiff was "lost" or "abandoned" property.

Case 33.2
MICHAEL v. FIRST CHICAGO CORP.
Appellate Court of Illinois, Second District, 1985.
139 Ill.App.3d 374, 93 Ill.Dec. 736, 487 N.E.2d 403.

FACTS In June of 1983 the First National Bank of Chicago (First Chicago) sold some of its used office furniture to Walter Zibton, a new and secondhand office supply and furniture dealer. Included among the items of furniture were some file cabinets that were locked and presumed to be empty. Keys for the file cabinets were unavailable. Zibton sold one of the file cabinets to Charles Strayve, throwing three other file cabinets into the deal free of charge. Strayve later gave one of the cabinets to his friend Richard Michael, the plaintiff in this case. About six weeks after Michael had received the cabinet, it fell over in Michael's garage, burst open, and exposed the contents: $6,687,948.85 worth of certificates of deposit. Michael took the certificates to the FBI for safekeeping and brought action to determine ownership of the certificates, claiming that they were abandoned property and that he, as the finder, was thus the rightful owner. The trial court disagreed with Michael and gave the First Chicago possession, holding that the certificates had not been abandoned but were instead lost property. As such, First Chicago was the rightful owner.

ISSUE Were the certificates abandoned property or lost property?

DECISION The appellate court upheld the trial court's judgment. First Chicago was the rightful owner of the certificates.

REASON The court noted that if the property was lost property, Michael could claim possession against all others except the rightful owner. If it were abandoned property, however, Michael, as the finder, could claim possession against all others including the owner. According to the court, "As a general rule, abandonment is not presumed, and the party seeking to declare an abandonment must prove the abandoning party intended to do so. . . . Plaintiffs failed to show that First Chicago intended to abandon the certificates of deposit. It is readily apparent from the evidence that the certificates of deposit were to be transferred to other storage and some simply were overlooked and left in the file cabinets. The relinquishment of possession, under the circumstances here, without a showing of an intention to permanently give up all right to the certificates of deposit is not enough to show an abandonment."

❖ Bailments

Virtually every individual or business is affected by the law of bailments at one time or another (and sometimes even on a daily basis). When individuals deal with bailments, whether they realize it or not, they are subject to the obligations and duties that arise from the bailment relationship. A **bailment** is formed by the delivery of personal property, without transfer of title, by one person, called a **bailor,** to another, called a **bailee,** usually under an agreement for a particular purpose (for example, loan, storage, repair, or transportation). Upon completion of the purpose, the bailee is obligated to return the bailed property to the bailor or to a third person or to dispose of it as directed.

Most bailments are created by agreement, but not necessarily by contract, because in many bailments not all of the elements of a contract (such as mutual assent or consideration) are present. For example, if you loan your bicycle to a friend, a bailment is created, but not by contract because there is no consideration. On the other hand, many commercial bailments, such as the delivery of your suit or dress to the cleaners for dry cleaning, are based on contract.

The number, scope, and importance of bailments created daily in the business community and in everyday life make it desirable for any person to understand the elements necessary for the creation of a bailment and to know what rights, duties, and liabilities flow from bailments.

BAILMENT
An agreement in which goods or personal property of one person (bailor) are entrusted to another (bailee), who is obligated to return the bailed property to the bailor or dispose of it as directed.

BAILOR
One who entrusts goods to a bailee.

BAILEE
One to whom goods are entrusted by a bailor.

Elements of a Bailment

Not all transactions involving the delivery of property from one person to another create a bailment. In order for such a transfer to become a bailment, the following three conditions must be met:

1. *Personal property.* Bailment involves only personal property; a bailment of persons is not possible. Although a bailment of your luggage is created when it is transported by an airline, as a passenger you are not the subject of a bailment. Also, you cannot bail realty; thus, leasing your house to a tenant is not a bailment.

2. *Delivery of possession.* Possession of the property must be transferred to the bailee in such a way that the bailee is given both exclusive possession and control over the property. Also, the bailee must *knowingly* accept the personal property.[3] If either of these conditions for effective *delivery of possession* is lacking, there is no bailment relationship.

To illustrate: You take a friend out to dinner at an expensive restaurant. Upon arrival, you turn over your car to the parking attendant. Has a bailment of your car been created? Yes. As a general rule, valet parking constitutes a bailment, but self-parking does not. The difference is found in the control of the car keys. If you parked the car yourself, locked it, and kept the keys, this would be considered a lease of space from the restaurant or owner of the parking place. The owner would be a *lessor* and you would be a *lessee* of the space. To carry our example further: When you enter the restaurant, your friend checks her coat. In the pocket of the coat is a $20,000 diamond necklace. The bailee, by accepting the coat, does not *knowingly* accept also the necklace; thus, a bailment of the coat exists—because the restaurant has exclusive possession and control over the coat—but a bailment of the necklace does not exist.

Two types of delivery—*physical* and *constructive*—will result in the bailee's exclusive possession of and control over the property. As discussed earlier, in the context of effective delivery concerning gifts, constructive delivery is a substitute, or symbolic, delivery. What is delivered to the bailee is not the actual property bailed, but something so related to the property that the requirement of delivery is satisfied.

---

3. We are dealing here with *voluntary* bailments.

If you give up your keys to a parking attendant, a bailment is created because you are giving up temporary control of your personal property by handing over the keys to someone else.

In certain unique situations a bailment is found despite the apparent lack of requisite elements of control or knowledge. In particular, rental of safe-deposit boxes is usually held to constitute a bailor-bailee relationship between the bank and its customer, despite the bank's lack of knowledge of the contents and its inability to have exclusive control of the property.[4] Another example of such a situation is where the bailee acquires the property accidentally or by mistake—such as in finding someone else's lost or mislaid property. A bailment is created even though the bailor did not voluntarily deliver the property to the bailee. These are called *constructive* or *involuntary* bailments.

3. *Bailment agreement.* A bailment agreement can be *express* or *implied*. Although a written agreement is not required for bailments of less than one year (that is, the Statute of Frauds does not apply—see Chapter 8), it is a good idea to have one, especially when valuable property is involved.

The bailment agreement expressly or impliedly provides for the return of the bailed property to the bailor or to a third person, or it provides for disposal by the bailee. The agreement presupposes that the bailee will return the identical goods originally given by the bailor. In certain types of bailments, however, such as bailments of *fungible goods* (uniformly identical goods), only equivalent property must be returned.

For example, if Holman stores his grain (fungible goods) in Joe's Warehouse, a bailment is created. But at the end of the storage period, the warehouse is not obligated to return to Holman exactly the same grain that was stored. As long as the warehouse returns goods of the same *type, grade,* and *quantity,* the warehouse—the bailee—has performed its obligation.

In a bailment with an option to purchase, the prospective buyer becomes a bailee while deciding whether to purchase the property. At the end of an agreed-upon

---

4.   By statute or by express contract, however, a safe-deposit box may be a lease of space or license, depending on the jurisdiction or the facts, or both.

period, the bailee must either return the property to the bailor-seller or agree to purchase the property.

Ordinary Bailments

Bailments are either *ordinary* or *special (extraordinary)*. There are three types of ordinary bailments. The distinguishing feature among them is *which party receives a benefit from the bailment*. Ultimately, the courts will use this factor to determine the standard of care required by the bailee while in possession of the personal property, and this factor will dictate the rights and liabilities of the parties. Modern courts tend to use *reasonable standards of care* regardless of the type of bailment arrangement in effect, but, obviously, who derives the benefit of the bailment does affect the amount of care required.

The three types of bailments are:

1.   *Bailment for the sole benefit of the bailor.* This is a type of gratuitous bailment for the convenience and benefit of the bailor.
2.   *Bailment for the sole benefit of the bailee.* This is typically a loan of an article to a person (the bailee) solely for that person's convenience and benefit.
3.   *Bailment for the mutual benefit of the bailee and the bailor.* The most common kind, involving some form of compensation for storing items or holding property.

The standard of care required by the bailee often depends on the type of bailment. See Exhibit 33-1.

Rights of the Bailee   Certain rights are implicit in the bailment agreement. A hallmark of the bailment agreement is that the bailee acquires the *right to temporarily control and possess the property*. The bailee's right of possession permits the bailee to recover damages from any third persons for damage or loss to the property, and if the personal property is stolen, the bailee has a legal right to regain possession of the goods or obtain damages from any third person who has wrongfully interfered with the bailee's possessory rights. Depending on the type of bailment and the terms

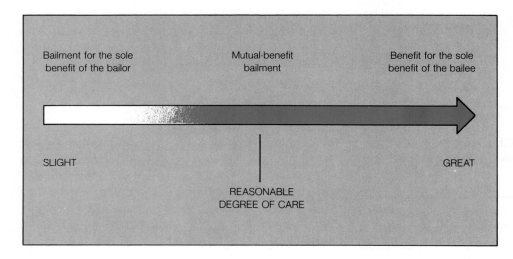

◆ **Exhibit 33-1**
Standard of Care
Required of a Bailee

of the bailment agreement, a bailee also may have a *right to use the bailed property*. When leasing drilling machinery, for example, the bailee is expected to use the equipment to drill. On the other hand, in long-term storage of a car, the bailee is not expected to use the car because the ordinary purpose of a storage bailment does not include use of the property.

Unless it is a gratuitous bailment, a bailee has a *right to be compensated* as provided for in the bailment agreement or reimbursed for costs and services rendered in the keeping of the bailed property, or both. Even in a gratuitous bailment, a bailee has a right to be reimbursed or compensated for costs incurred in the keeping of the bailed property. For example, Margo loses her pet dog, which is found by Judith. Judith takes Margo's dog to her home and feeds it. Even though she takes good care of the dog, it becomes ill, and a veterinarian is called. The bill for the veterinarian's services and the medicine is paid for by Judith. Judith is normally entitled to be reimbursed by Margo for all reasonable costs incurred in the keeping of her dog. To enforce a bailee's right of compensation, the bailee has a right to place a *possessory lien* (claim) on the specific bailed property until he or she has been fully compensated. This type of lien, sometimes referred to as an *artisan's* or *bailee's lien*, was discussed in Chapter 20.

Ordinary bailees have the *right to limit their liability* as long as the limitations are called to the attention of the bailor and the limitations are not against public policy. The bailee is not required to read orally or interpret the limitation, but it is essential that the bailor in some way know of the limitation. Even if the bailor has notice, certain types of disclaimers of liability have been considered to be against public policy and therefore illegal. Certain exculpatory clauses limiting a person's liability for his or her own wrongful acts are often scrutinized by the courts and, in the case of bailments, are routinely held to be illegal.

Duties of the Bailee   The bailee has two basic responsibilities: (1) to take proper care of the property and (2) to surrender or dispose of the property at the end of the bailment. The first duty (of "care") involves standards and principles of tort law discussed in Chapter 3. A bailee's failure to exercise appropriate care in handling the bailor's property results in tort liability. The second duty (to relinquish the property at the end of the bailment) is grounded in both contract and tort law principles. Failure to return the property constitutes a breach of contract or a tort of conversion, and, with one exception, the bailee is liable for damages. The exception is when the obligation is excused because the goods or chattel have been destroyed, lost, or stolen through no fault of the bailee (or claimed by a third party with a superior claim). In the following case, in which the bailee was unable to return bailed property to the bailor because it had been stolen, the question of fault is at issue.

Case 33.3
FREEMAN v. GARCIA
Court of Appeal of Louisiana, Second Circuit, 1986.
495 So.2d 351.

FACTS   Robert Freeman owned a broken Bulova watch that was encrusted with gold nuggets and two jade stones on the band. He took the watch to John Garcia's jewelry store for repairs. Garcia did not have the necessary equipment to make all the repairs so he sent the watch to Douglas Viers Base Watch Repair Lab. While it was at Mr. Viers's shop, the watch, along with several others, was stolen. Mr. Viers did not have insurance, nor did he have any burglar alarm or other safeguards on the premises. Freeman, claiming the watch had been worth $25,000, sued both Garcia and Viers for the value of the watch.

Case 33.3—Continued

The trial court found Garcia to be free of negligence but held that Mr. Viers was liable for the value of the watch, which the court adjudged to be $1,000. Since Mr. Viers had no insurance, Freeman appealed, claiming that Garcia was also liable.

ISSUE Which party (or parties) is liable for the loss of the watch?

DECISION Both Garcia and Viers were held liable by the appellate court. Garcia was ordered to pay Freeman $1,000 and to recover half of this amount from Viers.

REASON When an individual deposits property with a depositary, the depositary has the duty to use the same diligence in preserving the deposit that he or she uses in preserving his or her own property. This duty is strictly enforced when the depositary receives money for his or her services, as in the case of both Garcia and Viers. It is also the law that when one depositary accepts the property of another, then delivers that property to another for repair, and the property is lost while in the possession of the co-depositary, both parties are equally liable unless they can show they were not negligent. Since Viers did not have burglar alarms or other safeguards to protect his property, he was negligent. Because Garcia failed to inquire as to whether Viers had a burglar alarm system, guards, or other safeguarding equipment and did not check to find out whether Viers was insured against loss of property kept on his premises, Garcia was also negligent.

The law of bailments recognizes a rule whereby a bailor's proof that damage or loss to the property has occurred will, in and of itself, raise a *presumption* that the bailee is guilty of negligence or conversion. This situation arose in the following case. Because the bailee could not *rebut* (contradict) the presumption, the bailee was held liable.

Case 33.4
LEHMAN v. LEHMAN
United States District Court, Southern District of New York, 1984. 591 F.Supp. 1523.

FACTS While living in London in 1971, Mr. and Mrs. Lehman separated. Mr. Lehman left forty-three pieces of artwork in London with his wife for safekeeping with the understanding that he owned them and could repossess them upon demand. Mrs. Lehman later moved to Paris and took the artwork with her. During the course of pre- and post-divorce negotiations, Mr. Lehman, either personally or through his attorneys, demanded the return of the artwork. Mrs. Lehman refused the demand, claiming ownership of the art. During these negotiations it was discovered that certain pieces of the art had disappeared. Mr. Lehman finally sued in district court to recover possession or the value of the artwork. At trial, he alleged that Mrs. Lehman breached a bailment agreement because she refused to return the art to him and could not adequately explain the whereabouts of the missing pieces.

ISSUE Was Mrs. Lehman a bailee in this case and, if so, was she liable as a bailee for the missing pieces of art?

DECISION Yes, to both issues. The court held that Mrs. Lehman became a bailee when Mr. Lehman left the artwork in her possession. Further, under New York law, Mr. Lehman could recover on his *prima facie* case when Mrs. Lehman failed to explain what happened to the property.

REASON The bailor (Mr. Lehman) did not need to prove the negligence of the bailee (Mrs. Lehman) in this case. The court first found that Mr. Lehman owned the artwork, primarily because Mrs. Lehman had taken inconsistent positions before and during trial with respect to her ownership of the property. The court held that Mr. Lehman "established a *prima facie* case for conversion by showing that he owned the artwork, that he placed the property in his wife's possession [thereby creating a bailment], and that she refused to return it [to him] upon demand." Moreover, Mrs. Lehman's explanation of what happened to the missing artwork was "incredible" and was supported by no corroborating evidence. As a result, she was liable to Mr. Lehman as a converter.

Duties of the Bailor   It goes without saying that the rights of a bailor are essentially the same as the duties of a bailee. The major duty of the bailor is to provide the bailee with goods or chattel that are free from known defects that could cause injury to the bailee. In the case of a mutual-benefit bailment, the bailor must also notify the bailee of any hidden defects that the bailor could have discovered with reasonable diligence and proper inspection.

The bailor's duty to reveal defects is based on a negligence theory of tort law. A bailor who fails to give the appropriate notice is liable to the bailee and to any other person who might reasonably be expected to come into contact with the defective article. For example, if an equipment rental firm leases equipment with a *discoverable* defect, and the lessee (bailee) is not notified of such a defect and is harmed because of it, the rental firm is liable for negligence under tort law.

An exception to this rule exists, however, if the bailment was created for the sole benefit of the bailee. Thus, if you loan your car to a friend as a favor to your friend and not for any direct return benefit to yourself, you would be required to notify your friend of any *known* defect of the automobile that could cause injury, but not of a defect of which you were unaware (even if it is a *discoverable* defect). If your friend were injured in an accident as a result of a defect unknown to you, you would not be liable.

A bailor can also incur *warranty liability* based on contract law for injuries resulting from bailment of defective articles. Property leased by a bailor must be *fit for the intended purpose of the bailment*. Warranties of fitness arise by law in sales contracts and by judicial interpretation in the case of *bailments for hire*.

Termination of Bailments   Bailments that are for a specific term end when the stated period lapses. When no stated period is specified, the bailment can be terminated at any time by (1) the mutual agreement of both parties, (2) a demand by either party, (3) completion of the purpose of the bailment, (4) an act by the bailee that is inconsistent with the terms of the bailment, and (5) the operation of law.

Special Bailments

To this point, this section has been concerned with ordinary bailments. *Special*, or *extraordinary*, *bailments* include common carriers, warehouse companies, and inn-keepers or hotel owners.

Common Carriers   Common carriers are publicly licensed to provide transportation services to the general public. They are distinguished from private carriers that operate transportation facilities for a select clientele. Whereas a private carrier is not bound to provide service to every person or company making a request, a common carrier must arrange carriage for all who apply, within certain limitations.[5] The delivery of goods to a common carrier creates a bailment relationship between the shipper (bailor) and the common carrier (bailee). Unlike ordinary bailments, the common carrier is held to a standard of care based on *strict liability*, rather than reasonable care, in protecting the bailed personal property. This means that the common carrier is

---

5.   A common carrier is not required to take any and all property anywhere in all instances. Public regulatory agencies, such as the Interstate Commerce Commission, govern commercial carriers, and carriers can be restricted to geographical areas. They can also be limited to carrying certain kinds of goods or to providing only special types of transportation equipment.

absolutely liable, regardless of negligence, for all loss or damage to goods except damage caused by one of the following common law exceptions: (1) an act of God, (2) an act of a public enemy, (3) an order of a public authority, (4) an act of the shipper, and (5) the inherent nature of the goods. Common carriers cannot contract away this liability for damaged goods; but, subject to government regulations, they are permitted to limit their dollar liability to an amount stated on the shipment contract.[6] Even when their liability is limited on the shipment contract, unless the shipper is fully aware of this provision and its implications when signing the contract, the carrier may still be held liable for property damages by the court, as the following case illustrates.

Case 33.5
SOLOMON v. NATIONAL MOVERS CO., INC.
Supreme Court, New York County, 1986.
131 Misc. 2d 992, 502 N.Y.S.2d 644.

FACTS When Fran Solomon moved from Beverly Hills, California, to New Jersey, she hired Bekins Van Lines to move her personal belongings. When filling out the shipping contract, she valued her belongings at $25,000. She read the contract but was urged by the Bekins agent to write in that amount. Solomon stated that the agent "never advised me that the $25,000 represented a limit on the carrier's total liability. He assured me that the $25,000 on the form provided sufficient insurance coverage." The actual value of the goods was $397,075. Bekins delivered Solomon's belongings to a warehouse operated by National Movers. The warehouse, along with everything in it, was destroyed by a fire. Solomon then sought recovery of the full value of her belongings from National Movers and Bekins. Bekins responded that they were only liable up to the $25,000 valuation that Solomon had put on the Bill of Lading covering the shipment and sought a dismissal of any damages beyond that limit.

ISSUE Should the court grant Bekins's motion to dis-

miss Solomon's claim on the ground that its liability for Solomon's property was limited by contract?

DECISION No. The court denied the motion for dismissal and stated a trial would be necessary.

REASON The court noted that, as a general rule, statements releasing the carrier from expensive insurance are binding on the shipper. But, stated the court, this law is applied only to commercial shippers who use carriers on an everyday basis. It is not as applicable in cases dealing with the transport of household goods. Individuals move rarely and are therefore inexperienced in the dealings of common carriers. To protect consumers, release agreements that limit the liability of common carriers are strictly construed against the carrier. The law also mandates that agreements releasing the carrier from liability beyond a certain limit be entered into only after the individual has been completely informed of the agreement's purpose and implications. Solomon alleged that she was not informed as to the meaning of the agreement and was not informed that it established the carrier's total liability for harm to her household goods. Because of this, the court refused Bekins's motion for dismissal and held that a trial would be necessary to determine the true facts and circumstances surrounding the signing of the release agreement.

Warehouse Companies Warehousing is the business of providing storage of property for compensation.[7] A warehouse company is a professional bailee whose responsibility differs from an ordinary bailee in two important aspects. First, a warehouse company

---

6. State and federal laws and Interstate Commerce Commission regulations require common carriers to offer shippers the opportunity to obtain higher dollar limits for loss by paying a higher fee for the transport.
7. UCC 7-102(h) defines the person engaged in the storing of goods for hire as a "warehouseman."

is empowered to issue documents of title, in particular, warehouse receipts.[8] Second, warehouse companies are subject to an extraordinary network of state and federal statutes and Article 7 of the UCC (as are carriers).

Like ordinary bailees, a warehouse company is liable for loss or damage to property and possession resulting from *negligence* (and therefore does not have the same liability as a common carrier). The duty is one of reasonable care to protect and preserve the goods. A warehouse company can limit the dollar amount of liability, but the bailor must be given the option of paying an increased storage rate for an increase in the liability limit.

A warehouse company accepts goods for storage and issues a warehouse receipt describing the property and the terms of the bailment contract. The warehouse receipt can be negotiable or nonnegotiable, depending on how it is written. It is negotiable if its terms provide that the warehouse company will deliver the goods "to the bearer" of the receipt, or "to the order of" a person named on the receipt.[9]

The warehouse receipt serves multiple functions. It is a receipt for the goods stored; it is a contract of bailment; it also represents the goods (that is, it indicates title) and hence has value and utility in financing commercial transactions. For example, Ossip, a processor and canner of corn, delivers 6,000 cases of corn to Shaneyfelt, the owner of a warehouse. Shaneyfelt issues a negotiable warehouse receipt payable "to bearer" and gives it to Ossip. Ossip sells and delivers the warehouse receipt to a large supermarket chain, "Better Foods, Inc." Better Foods is now the owner of the corn and has the right to obtain the cases from Shaneyfelt. It will present the warehouse receipt to Shaneyfelt, who in return will release the cases of corn to the grocery chain.

"All saints can do miracles, but few of them can keep a hotel."

Mark Twain (Samuel Clemens), 1835–1910 *(American author and humorist)*

Innkeepers   At common law, innkeepers, hotel owners, or similar operators were held to the same strict liability as common carriers with respect to property brought into the rooms by guests. Today, only those who provide lodging to the public for compensation as a *regular* business are covered under this rule of strict liability. Moreover, the rule applies only to those who are guests, as opposed to lodgers. A lodger is a permanent resident of the hotel or inn, whereas a guest is a traveler.

In many states, innkeepers can avoid strict liability for loss of guests' valuables and money by providing a safe in which to keep them. Each guest must be clearly notified of the availability of such a safe. When articles are not kept in the safe, or when they are of such a nature that they are not normally kept in a safe, statutes will often limit the liability of innkeepers.

To illustrate: Jiminez stays for a night at the Harbor Hotel. When he returns from eating breakfast in the hotel restaurant, he discovers that the people in the room next door have forced the lock on the door between the two rooms and stolen his suitcase. Jiminez claims that the hotel is liable for his loss. The hotel maintains that since it was not negligent, it is not liable. Although at common law, innkeepers were

---

8.   A document of title is defined in UCC 1-201(15) as any "document which in the regular course of business or financing is treated as adequately evidencing that the person in possession of it is entitled to receive, hold, and dispose of the document and the goods it covers. To be a document of title, a document must purport to be issued by or addressed to a bailee and purport to cover goods in the bailee's possession. . . ."

9.   UCC 7-104.

actually insurers of the property of their guests, so the hotel would have been liable, today state statutes limit the strict liability of the common law. These statutes vary from state to state, but in many states they limit the amount of monetary damages for which the innkeeper is liable and may even provide that the innkeeper has no liability in the absence of negligence. Many statutes require these limitations to be posted or the guest to be notified, and the posting (notice) is frequently found on the door of each room in the motel or hotel.

Normally, the innkeeper (a motel keeper, for example) assumes no responsibility for the safety of a guest's automobile because the guest usually retains possession and control over it. If, on the other hand, the innkeeper provides parking facilities, and the guest's car is entrusted to the innkeeper or to an employee, the innkeeper will be liable under the rules that pertain to parking-lot bailees (ordinary bailments).

In the following case, a hotel patron brought an action against a Marriott Hotel when his cashmere coat, which he had placed on a rack outside a seminar room, was missing. As you read through the case, try to determine if the elements of a bailment are present.

Case 33.6
AUGUSTINE v. MARRIOTT HOTEL
Town Court, Amherst, New York, 1986.
132 Misc.2d 180, 503 N.Y.S.2d 498.

FACTS The plaintiff (Augustine) attended a dental seminar held at a Marriott Hotel. The sponsor of the seminar had rented the banquet room in which the seminar was held and had requested the hotel to place a movable coat rack outside the room, in the public lobby. Augustine placed his coat on the rack before entering the seminar. When he tried to find the coat at the noon recess, however, he noted that the rack had been moved a distance down the lobby and around a corner, near an exit. To his dismay, his cashmere coat was missing. Claiming the hotel was liable for the loss, Augustine brought this action.

ISSUE Was the hotel a bailee of the coat and thus liable to its owner for the loss?

DECISION No. The court held that the hotel was not liable to Augustine for the loss of the coat and dismissed the claim.

REASON The court stated that the relationship of bailor-bailee never came into existence here because Augustine had not entrusted his coat to the hotel. There had been no delivery to the hotel, nor was the hotel, in the eyes of the court, ever in actual or constructive custody of the coat. Furthermore, Augustine was not even a guest of the hotel directly. The court likened Augustine's status vis-à-vis the hotel to that of a "wedding guest of individuals who rent banquet facilities from a hotel." The court concluded that "a reasonable man would have wondered about the safety of his coat which he hung on a rack in a public lobby of a hotel, without ascertaining if there were a guard." The court could find no evidence that users of the rack were led to assume that the rack would be guarded, and hence users placed their coats there at their own risk.

Application

Law and the Warehouser— Problems with Being a Bailee

A warehouser is a bailee—specifically in business to store goods. But the warehouser must exercise a reasonable amount of care for the stored goods. And what is reasonable will be a function of the value of those stored goods.

Reasoning that they are not acting as insurers of stored goods, warehousers may believe that they can limit liability for lost, stolen, or destroyed bailed property by including a liability-limiting provision on a warehouse receipt. It is possible for the liability on stored goods to be limited by the terms of a warehouse receipt (or storage agreement), but the receipt must set forth the liability per article. It normally must also provide to the individual leaving the property (the bailor) the option of increasing the valuation for liability purposes at a correspondingly higher price.

Checklist for the Bailee:

☐ 1. Even though you may not be the insurer of stored goods, taking out insurance for them might still be appropriate.

☐ 2. You must exercise reasonable care in proportion to the value of the stored goods.

☐ 3. You may choose to limit your liability, but if so, make such limitation plainly readable and understandable on the warehouse receipt or storage agreement.

❖ Chapter Summary: Personal Property and Bailments

PERSONAL PROPERTY	
Definition of Personal Property	Personal property (personalty) is considered to include all property not classified as real property (realty). It can be tangible (such as a TV set or a car) or intangible (such as stocks or bonds). Referred to legally as *chattel*—a term that includes both living and inanimate property.
Property Rights	Possession and disposition (by sale, gift, will, and so on).
Common Types of Ownership of Personal Property	1. *Fee simple*—Exists when individuals have the right to possess, use, or dispose of the property as they choose during their lifetime and to pass on the property to their heirs at death. 2. *Tenancy in common*—Co-ownership in which two or more persons own an undivided fractional interest in the property; upon one tenant's death, the property interest passes to his or her heirs. 3. *Joint tenancy with right of survivorship*—Exists when two or more persons own an undivided interest in property; upon the death of a joint tenant, the property interest transfers to the remaining tenant(s), not to the heirs of the deceased.
How Ownership of Personal Property is Acquired	1. *Possession*—Ownership may be acquired by possession if no other person has ownership title (e.g., wild animals or abandoned property). 2. *Purchase*—The most common means of acquiring and transferring ownership of personal property.

❖ Chapter Summary: Personal Property and Bailments—Continued

How Ownership of Personal Property is Acquired (Continued)	3. *Production*—Any product or item produced by an individual (with minor exceptions) becomes the property of that individual.
	4. *Gift*—An effective gift exists when: a. The gift is delivered (physically or constructively) to the donee or the donee's agent. b. There is evidence of *intent* to make a gift of the property in question. c. The gift is accepted by the donee or the donee's agent.
	5. *Will or inheritance*—Upon death, the property of the deceased passes by bequest or devise to named beneficiaries if there is a valid will, or, if no valid will exists, to heirs by intestacy laws.
	6. *Accession*—When someone adds value to a piece of property by labor or materials. Generally, the added value becomes the property of the owner of the original property (including bad-faith or wrongful accessions). Substantial (in value) accessions, or accessions that change the identity of the property, may pass title to the improver.
	7. *Confusion*—In the case of fungible goods, if a person wrongfully and willfully commingles goods with those of another in order to render them indistinguishable, the innocent party acquires title to the total. Otherwise, the owners become tenants in common of the intermingled goods.
Mislaid, Lost, and Abandoned Property	1. *Mislaid property*—Property that is placed somewhere *voluntarily* by the owner and then inadvertently forgotten. A finder of mislaid property will not acquire title to the goods, and the owner of the place where the property was mislaid becomes a caretaker of the mislaid property.
	2. *Lost property*—Property that is *involuntarily* left and forgotten. A finder of lost property can claim title to the property against the whole world *except the true owner*.
	3. *Abandoned property*—Property that has been discarded by the true owner with no intention of claiming title to the property in the future. A finder of abandoned property can claim title to it against the whole world, *including the original owner*.
BAILMENTS	
Elements of a Bailment	1. *Personal property*—Bailments involve only personal property.
	2. *Delivery of possession*—The bailee (one receiving the property) must be given exclusive possession and control over the property, and in a voluntary bailment the bailee must knowingly accept the personal property for an effective bailment to exist.
	3. *The bailment agreement*—Expressly or impliedly provides for the return of the bailed property to the bailor or to a third party, or provides for disposal by the bailee.
Ordinary Bailments	1. *Bailment for the sole benefit of the bailor*—A gratuitous bailment undertaken for the sole benefit of the bailor (e.g., as a favor to the bailor). Only slight care to preserve the bailed property is required of the bailee.
	2. *Bailment for the sole benefit of the bailee*—A gratuitous loan of an article to a person (the bailee) solely for the bailee's benefit. Great care to preserve the bailed property is required of the bailee.
	3. *Mutual-benefit (contractual) bailment*—The most common kind of bailment; involves compensation between the bailee and bailor for the service provided. Reasonable care to preserve the bailed property is required of the bailee.
Special Bailments	1. *Common carriers*—Carriers that are publicly licensed to provide transportation services to the general public. A common-carrier contract of transportation creates a mutual-benefit bailment, and the common carrier is held to a standard of care based on *strict liability* (with limited exceptions) in protecting the bailed property.

❖ Chapter Summary: Personal Property and Bailments—Continued

Special Bailments (Continued)	2. *Warehouse companies*—Professional bailees that differ from ordinary bailees because they (1) can issue documents of title (warehouse receipts) and (2) are subject to state and federal statutes and Article 7 of the UCC (as are common carriers). They must exercise a high degree of reasonable care over the bailed property and are liable for loss or damage of property due to negligence.
	3. *Innkeepers* (hotel operators)—The common-law strict-liability standard to which innkeepers (those who provide lodging to the public for compensation as a *regular* business) were held is today limited by state statutes, which vary from state to state.
Rights of a Bailee (Duties of a Bailor)	1. *The right to be compensated and reimbursed for expenses*—In the event of nonpayment, the bailee has the right to place a bailee's lien on the bailed property and the right to foreclose.
	2. *The right to limit liability*—An ordinary bailee can limit liability for risk or monetary amount, or both, provided proper notice is given and the limitation is not against public policy. In special bailments, limitations on types of risk are usually not allowed, but limitations on the monetary amount of liability are permitted.
	3. *The right of possession*—Allows actions against third persons who damage or convert the bailed property, and allows actions against the bailor for wrongful breach of the bailment.
Duties of a Bailee (Rights of a Bailor)	1. A bailee must exercise reasonable care over property entrusted to him or her. A common carrier (special bailee) is held to a standard of care based on *strict liability* unless the bailed property is lost or destroyed due to (a) an act of God, (b) an act of a public enemy, (c) an act of a governmental authority, (d) an act of a shipper, or (e) the inherent nature of the goods.
	2. Bailed goods in a bailee's possession must be either returned to the bailor or disposed of according to the bailor's directions.
	3. A bailee cannot use or profit from bailed goods except by agreement or where the use is implied to further the bailment purpose (e.g., road-testing a car after major engine repairs).

❖ Questions and Case Problems

33-1. Reineken, very old and ill, wanted to make a gift to his nephew, Gerald. He had a friend obtain $2,500 in cash for him from his bank account, placed this cash in an envelope, and wrote on the envelope, "This is for my nephew, Gerald." Reineken then placed the envelope in his dresser drawer. When Reineken died a month later, his family found the envelope and Gerald got word of the intended gift. Gerald then demanded that Reineken's daughter, the executrix of Reineken's estate, turn over the gift to him. The daughter refused to do so. Discuss fully whether Gerald can successfully claim ownership rights to the $2,500.

33-2. In 1968 Lloyd was about to be shipped to Vietnam for active duty with the U. S. Marines. Shortly before he left, he gave an expensive stereo set and other personal belongings to his girlfriend, Sara, saying "I'll probably not return from this war, so I'm giving these to you." Lloyd returned eighteen months later and requested that Sara return the property. Sara said that

since Lloyd had given her these items to keep, she was not required to return them. What kind of gift was made in this instance, and can Lloyd recover his property?

33-3. Candice went to Seastone Department Store to do some Christmas shopping. She became engrossed in looking at some silk blouses and did not notice the time. Suddenly, she realized she had to leave quickly in order to meet her date for dinner. She hastily departed from the store, inadvertently leaving her purse on a sales counter. Pam, a sales clerk, noticed the purse on the counter but left it there, expecting Candice to return for it. Later, when Candice returned to retrieve the purse, it was gone. Candice filed an action against Seastone Department Store for the loss of her purse. Will she be able to recover damages for her loss?

33-4. Louis Bardozo has a son named Richard. Louis wants to give his son a new car that he has recently purchased. Louis and his son have not gotten along during the past few years, and Louis feels part of this is his fault. He goes to his son's house, wanting to make amends by giving the car to Richard. When Louis arrives at Richard's house, his daughter-in-law (Richard's wife) tells Louis that Richard is out of town and will return the next day. Louis gives the keys to the new car to his daughter-in-law, tells her to hold the keys for his son, and says that he will return the next day. Two hours later, Louis has second thoughts about giving Richard a car. He retrieves the keys from his daughter-in-law before she can turn them over to Richard. Richard returns from his trip, learns of the events, and demands possession of the car, claiming a gift was made. Is Richard entitled to the car?

33-5. Discuss the standard of care required from the bailee for the bailed property in the following situations, and determine whether the bailee breached that duty.

   (a) Dick borrows Steve's lawn mower because his own lawn mower needs repair. Dick mows his front yard. In order to mow the back yard, he needs to move some hoses and lawn furniture. He leaves the mower in front of his house while doing so. When he returns to the front yard, he discovers the mower has been stolen.

   (b) Tricia owns a valuable speedboat. She is going on vacation and asks her neighbor, Maureen, to store the boat in one stall of Maureen's double garage. Maureen consents, and the boat is moved into the garage. In need of some grocery items for dinner, Maureen drives to the store. She leaves the garage door open while she is gone, as is her custom, and the speedboat is stolen during that time.

33-6. Rena, in her will, bequeathed her jewelry to her daughter Linda. Upon Rena's death, her husband, Edward (Linda's stepfather), gave Linda one ring, a gift to Rena from a prior husband, but he put the other jewelry in his home in a dresser drawer. While Edward was in the hospital with a heart ailment, the jewelry was stolen from the dresser drawer. Edward never told Linda about the theft and never filed an insurance claim or a police report. When Linda found out, she sued her stepfather for negligence for failure to exercise reasonable care over her bailed property. What was the result? [Estate of Murrell v. Quin, 454 So. 2d 437 (Miss. 1984)]

33-7. Welton, an experienced businessperson, transferred to Gallagher *bearer bonds*, stating that the bonds were hers with "no strings attached" and that she should place the bonds in her safe-deposit box for safekeeping. Later, Welton wanted Gallagher to return the bonds to him, claiming that he was still the owner. Gallagher refused, claiming that Welton's transfer was a gift. Was it? Discuss fully. [Welton v. Gallagher, 2 Hawaii App. 242, 630 P.2d 1077 (1981)]

33-8. Several individuals placed personal property in a stor-age facility offered by the Winnebago County Fair Association. All who stored property in the building were required by the County Fair Association to sign a storage agreement that included the following provision: "No liability exists for damage or loss to the stored equipment from the perils of fire." The storage building burned down and all the property within was destroyed. A number of the people who had stored their property in the building brought suit against the fair association, claiming that the fire resulted from the fair association's negligence. Allstate Insurance Company, which had paid a number of claims for losses incurred due to the fire, joined the plaintiffs in the lawsuit. The County Fair Association claimed that the exculpatory clause in its contract relieved it from any and all liability. The issue before the court was whether the bailee (the fair association) could validly contract away *all* liability for fire damage. What was the result? [Allstate Ins. Co. v. Winnebago County Fair Association, Inc., 131 Ill. App. 3d 225, 86 Ill. Dec. 233, 475 N.E. 2d 230 (1985)]

33-9. David Ross was a corporate officer and director of Equitable Life and Casualty Insurance, a family-owned corporation. David wanted to make a gift of some of his stock to his son, Rod, to reward Rod for his work with Equitable Life, so he exchanged some of his own stock in Equitable for shares issued in Rod's name. The stock certificates and corporate records listed Rod as the owner of this stock. Rod attended shareholders' meetings, voted his stock, and received dividends from it. The stock certificates themselves, along with other family certificates, were kept by David in a safe to which only he and his brother had access. At the time of his death, David had transferred 25 percent of his stock in the family business to Rod. In addition to the stock given to him by his father, Rod acquired, as did his brother and sister, an equal share in his father's estate. This meant that Rod effectively received, through gift and by will, a total of 50 percent of his father's stock, while the other two children received 25 percent each. The brother and sister alleged that the stock transfers made to Rod during David's lifetime were not valid gifts because David had failed to deliver the stock certificates to Rod. Were they correct? Explain. [Estate of Ross v. Ross, 626 P.2d 489 (Utah 1981)]

33-10. Hook owned an airplane and rented tie-down space annually from Stubbs' Aviation Service. Stubbs provided the tie-down equipment and possessed a set of keys for the airplane in order to be able to move it when necessary. On one occasion, when Hook came to the airport, he noticed that his plane had been damaged, apparently from a ground vehicle. Hook brought an action against Stubbs, claiming that Stubbs was a bailee and was liable for damages due to negligence. Discuss whether a bailment relationship existed between Hook and Stubbs. [Stubbs v. Hook, 467 N.E. 2d 29 (Ind. App. 1984)]

Chapter 34

Real Property

From earliest times, property has provided a means for survival. Primitive peoples lived off the fruits of the land, eating the vegetation and wildlife. Later, as the wildlife was domesticated and the vegetation cultivated, property provided pasturage and farmland. In the twelfth and thirteenth centuries the power of feudal lords was exemplified by the amount of land that they held; the more land they held, the more powerful they were. After the age of feudalism passed, property continued to be an indicator of family wealth and social position. In the western world, the protection of an individual's right to his or her property has become, in the words of Jean Jacques Rousseau, one of the "most sacred rights of citizenship."

❖ The Nature of Real Property

Real property consists of land and the buildings, plants, and trees that it contains. Whereas personal property is movable, real property—also called *real estate* or *realty*—is immovable. Real property usually means land, but it also includes subsurface and air rights, plant life and vegetation, and *fixtures*—things attached to realty.

Land

Land includes the soil on the surface of the earth and the natural or artificial structures that are attached to it. It further includes all the waters contained on or under the surface and much, but not necessarily all, of the air space above it. The exterior boundaries of land extend straight down to the center of the earth and straight up to the furthest reaches of the atmosphere (subject to certain qualifications).

Subsurface and Air Rights

The owner of real property has relatively exclusive rights to the air space above the land as well as the soil and minerals underneath it. Until fifty years ago, the right to use air space was not too significant, but in today's world of commercial airlines and high-rise office buildings and apartments, it is.

Early cases involving air rights dealt with matters such as the right to run a telephone wire across a person's property when the wire did not touch any of the property [1] and whether a bullet shot over a person's land constituted trespass.[2] Today such cases involve the right of commercial and private planes to fly over property, and the right of individuals and governments to seed clouds and produce artificial rain. Flights over private land do not normally violate the property owners' rights unless the flights are low and frequent, causing a direct interference with the enjoyment and the use of the land.[3]

Significant limitations on either air rights or subsurface rights normally have to be indicated on the deed transferring title at the time of purchase. Where no such encumbrances are noted, a purchaser can expect unfettered right to possession of the property. If any preexisting **covenant** unknown to the purchaser interferes with these rights, the purchaser can sue the seller for breach of warranty of title. Most state statutes, however, limit the time period in which the purchaser can sue. An alternative lawsuit is for breach of the **covenant of quiet enjoyment.** There is also a limit on the time for bringing such a suit, but it does not begin to run until after the discovery of the breach.

COVENANT
Any agreement between two or more parties by deed, in writing, signed, and delivered, promising that something is either done, shall be done, or shall not be done. The term is currently used with respect to promises contained in instruments relating to real estate.

COVENANT OF QUIET ENJOYMENT
A promise by a grantor (or landlord) that the grantee (or tenant) will not be evicted or disturbed by the grantor or a person having a lien or superior title.

Separation of Surface and Subsurface Rights

In many states, the owner of the surface of a piece of land is not the owner of the subsurface, and hence the land ownership may be separated. Subsurface rights can be extremely valuable, as these rights include the ownership of minerals and, in most states, oil and natural gas. Water rights are also extremely valuable, especially in the west.

When the ownership is separated into surface and subsurface rights, each owner can pass title to what he or she owns without the consent of the other. Each owner has the right to use the land owned, and in some cases a conflict will arise between a surface owner's use and the subsurface owner's need to extract minerals, oil, and natural gas.

Plant Life and Vegetation

Plant life, both natural and cultivated, is also considered to be real property. In many instances, the natural vegetation, such as trees, adds greatly to the value of the realty. When a parcel of land is sold and the land has growing crops on it, the sale includes the crops, unless otherwise specified in the sales contract. When crops are sold by themselves, however, they are considered to be personal property or goods. Consequently, the sale of crops is a sale of goods, and it is governed by the Uniform Commercial Code rather than by real property law. [UCC 2-107(2)]

1. Butler v. Frontier Telephone Co., 186 N.Y. 486, 79 N.E. 716 (1906). Stringing a wire across someone's property violates the air rights of that person. Leaning walls, buildings, projecting eave spouts, and roofs also violate the air rights of the property owner.
2. Herrin v. Sutherland, 74 Mont. 587, 241 P. 328 (1925). Shooting over a person's land constitutes trespass.
3. United States v. Causby, 328 U.S. 256, 66 S.Ct. 1062, 90 L.Ed. 1206 (1946).

Fixtures

FIXTURE

A thing that was once personal property but has become attached to real property in such a way that it takes on the characteristics of real property and becomes part of that real property.

Certain personal property can become so closely associated with the real property to which it is attached that the law views it as real property. Such property is known as a **fixture**—a thing *affixed* to realty, meaning it is attached to it by roots, embedded in it, or permanently attached by means of cement, plaster, bolts, nails, or screws. The fixture can be physically attached to real property, be attached to another fixture, or even be without any actual physical attachment to the land. As long as the owner *intends* the property to be a fixture, it will be a fixture.

Fixtures are included in the sale of land if the sales contract does not provide otherwise. The sale of a house includes the land and the house and the garage on it, as well as the cabinets, plumbing, and windows. Since these are permanently affixed to the property, they are considered to be a part of it. Unless otherwise agreed, however, the curtains and throw rugs are not included. Items such as drapes and window-unit air conditioners are difficult to classify. Thus, a contract for the sale of a house or commercial realty should indicate which items of this sort are included in the sale.

The following case illustrates the court's interpretation of whether a grain-storage silo became a fixture to the realty or remained personal property.

Case 34.1
METROPOLITAN LIFE INS. CO. v. REEVES

Supreme Court of Nebraska, 1986.
223 Neb. 299, 389 N.W.2d 295.

FACTS Lawrence Reeves was a landowning farmer whose land was being foreclosed upon by his mortgage holder, Metropolitan Life Insurance Company. Prior to the foreclosure, Mr. Reeves had contracted with Production Sale Company to erect a grain-storage facility on the farm. Its total cost was $171,185.30. Prior to the foreclosure Mr. Reeves had paid only $16,137.77. When Metropolitan brought the foreclosure proceedings, the question arose as to whether the grain-storage facility was a fixture to the realty or personal property. If it was considered to be a fixture, Metropolitan would receive the proceeds from the sale; if it was considered to be personal property, the proceeds would go to Production Sale Company. The trial court held that the facility was a fixture, and Production Sale Company appealed to the Supreme Court of Nebraska.

ISSUE Was the facility a fixture to the real property or was it personal property?

DECISION The Supreme Court of Nebraska reversed the district court's ruling and deemed the storage facility to be personal property.

REASON The court cited three factors that determine whether an article, or combination of articles, is a fixture: (1) Is the article actually annexed to the realty? (2) Has the article been appropriated to the use or purpose of that part of the realty with which it is connected? and (3) Was it the intention of the parties making the contract to make the article permanent to the land? The last factor was the most important in determining this case, and the court gave much weight to the circumstances of the purchase agreement between Reeves and Production Sales. The court concluded that, under the provisions of that agreement, the parties had not intended the grain-storage facility to become a part of the real property until full payment had been made. Since full payment had not been made, the facility had not become a fixture.

❖ Estates in Land

Ownership of property is an abstract concept that cannot exist independently of the legal system. No one can actually possess or *hold* a piece of land, the air above, the earth below, and all the water contained on it. The legal system therefore recognizes certain rights and duties that constitute the ownership interest in real property.

Rights of ownership in real property, called **estates**, are classified according to their nature, interest, and extent. Two major categories of estates are *freehold estates*, which are held indefinitely, and *less-than-freehold estates*, which are held for a predetermined time.

Freehold Estates

There are two kinds of freehold estates—*estates in fee* and *life estates*.

Estates in Fee   The most common type of property ownership today is the **fee simple absolute**, referred to as the *fee simple*, in which the owner has the greatest aggregation of rights, privileges, and power possible. The fee simple is limited absolutely to a person and his or her heirs and is assigned forever without limitation or condition. The rights that accompany a fee simple include the right to use the land for whatever purpose the owner sees fit, subject to laws that prevent the owner from unreasonably interfering with another person's land, and subject to applicable zoning laws.

A fee simple is potentially infinite in duration and can be disposed of by deed or by will (by selling or giving it away). When there is no will, the fee simple passes to the owner's legal heirs. The owner of a fee simple absolute also has the rights of *exclusive possession* and *use*. *Exclusive possession* and *use* means that the owner can use the land without replenishing what is used. Thus, if Johnny Carter has fee simple absolute ownership of fifteen acres in the mountains, he can mine any ore on that land without replacing it.

The **fee simple defeasible** [4] is essentially a fee simple that can end if a specified condition or event occurs. A conveyance, for example, "to A and his heirs as long as the land is used for charitable purposes" creates a fee simple defeasible. The original owner retains a *partial* ownership interest in that as long as the specified condition occurs, A has full ownership rights, but if the specified condition does not occur, and the land ceases to be used for charitable purposes, then the land reverts, or returns, to the original owner. [5] The interest that the original owner retains is called a *future interest* since, if it arises, it will arise in the future. [6] (But a so-called future interest is still a form of present property ownership that has a current market value.)

Life Estates   A **life estate** is an estate that lasts for the life of some specified individual. A conveyance "to A for his life" creates a life estate. [7] Estates for life can be created by an act of law or by an act of the parties.

ESTATE
Broadly, all that a person owns, including both real and personal property; in real-estate law, the extent of ownership or interest that one has in realty.

"All inferior estates and interests in land are derived out of the fee simple."

William Cruise, ?—1824 (English historian)

FEE SIMPLE ABSOLUTE
An estate or interest in land with no time, disposition, or descendibility limitations.

FEE SIMPLE DEFEASIBLE
An estate that can be taken away (by the prior grantor) upon the occurrence or nonoccurrence of a specified event.

LIFE ESTATE
An interest in land that exists only for the duration of the life of some person, usually the holder of the estate.

---

4.   The word *defeasible* refers to an owner's ability to lose ownership of property, whether the loss is voluntary or involuntary.

5.   If the original owner is not living at the time, the land passes to his or her heirs. In other words, once the condition does or does not occur (depending on what was specified), A is divested of rights regardless of whether the original owner to (or through) whom the land reverts is alive.

6.   In the specific example given in the text, the future interest that the owner holds is known as a *possibility of reverter*. In the conveyance, "to A, but if the premises are ever used for the sale of alcoholic beverages then to B," the original owner has conveyed the entire interest. The owner has conveyed a fee simple defeasible to A and a future interest to B.

7.   A less common type of life estate is created by the conveyance "to A for the life of B." This is known as an estate *pur autre vie*, or an estate for the life of another.

In a life estate, the life tenant has fewer rights of ownership than the holder of a fee simple defeasible. The life tenant has the right to use the land provided no waste (injury to the land) is committed. In other words, the life tenant cannot injure the land in a manner that would adversely affect the owner of the future interest in it. The life tenant can use the land to harvest crops or, if mines and oil wells are already on the land, can extract minerals and oil from it, but the life tenant cannot exploit the land by creating new wells or mines.

The life tenant has the right to mortgage the life estate and create liens, easements, and leases; but none can extend beyond the life of the tenant. In addition, the owner of a life estate has an exclusive right to possession during his or her life. Exclusive possession, however, is subject to the rights of the future-interest holder to come onto the land and protect the future interest.

Along with these rights, the life tenant also has some duties—to keep the property in repair and to pay property taxes. In short, the owner of the life estate has the same rights as a fee simple owner except that the value of the property must be kept intact for the future-interest holder, less the decrease in value resulting from normal use of the property allowed by the life tenancy.

Nonfreehold Estates

LESS-THAN-FREEHOLD ESTATE
A possessory real-estate interest in which the tenant has a qualified right to exclusive possession for a specified period of time, such as occurs in a leasehold estate.

LEASEHOLD ESTATE
An estate in realty held by a tenant under a lease. In every leasehold estate, the tenant has a qualified right to possess and/or use the land.

TENANCY FOR YEARS
A nonfreehold estate/lease for a specified period of time, after which the interest reverts to the grantor.

TENANCY FROM PERIOD TO PERIOD
A nonfreehold estate/lease for an unspecified period where specified rent payments are made at certain intervals (for example, every month); automatically renewed for a like period until terminated.

Less-than-freehold (nonfreehold) **estates** are possessory real estate interests treated for some purposes as personal rather than real property. They are covered in this chapter for the sake of convenience because they relate to ownership of an interest in land. These estates include (1) a tenancy for years, (2) a tenancy from period to period, (3) a tenancy at will, and (4) a tenancy by sufferance. All, except a tenancy by sufferance, involve the transfer of the right to possession for a specified period of time; that is, the owner or lessor (landlord) conveys the property to the lessee (tenant) for a certain period of time, and the tenant has a *qualified* right to exclusive possession (qualified by the right of the landlord to enter upon the premises to assure that no waste is being committed). An example is the **leasehold estate**, in which the tenant can use the land—for example, by harvesting crops—but cannot injure the land (by such activities as cutting down timber for sale or extracting oil).

Tenancy for Years   A **tenancy for years** is created by express contract (which can sometimes be oral) by leasing the property for any specified period of time (even for less than a year). For example, signing a one-year lease to rent an apartment creates a tenancy for years. At the end of the period specified in the lease, the lease ends (without notice), and possession of the apartment returns to the lessor. If the tenant dies during the period of the lease, the lease passes to the tenant's heirs as personal property. Often, leases include renewal or extension provisions.

Tenancy from Period to Period   A **tenancy from period to period** is created by a lease that does not specify how long it is to last but does specify that rent is to be paid at certain intervals. This type of tenancy is automatically renewed for another rental period unless properly terminated. For example, a tenancy from period to period is created by a lease that states, "Rent is due on the tenth day of every month." This provision creates a tenancy from month to month, but the tenancy can also be from week to week or from year to year. Also, a tenancy from period to period sometimes arises when a tenancy for years ends but the landlord allows the tenant to continue paying monthly or weekly rent.

At common law, in order to terminate a tenancy from period to period, the landlord or tenant must give one period's notice to the other party. If the tenancy is month to month, one month's notice must be given. If the tenancy is week to week, one week's notice must be given. State statutes often define the required notice of termination in a tenancy from period to period. Therefore, the particular state statute in question should be referred to in order to determine the proper time for notice of termination.

Tenancy at Will   Suppose a landlord rents an apartment to a tenant "for as long as both agree." In such a case, the tenant receives a leasehold estate known as a **tenancy at will**. At common law, either party can terminate the tenancy without notice. This type of estate usually arises when a tenant who has been under a tenancy for years retains possession after the termination date of that tenancy with the landlord's consent. Before the tenancy has been converted into a tenancy from period to period (by the periodic payment of rent), it is a tenancy at will, terminable by either party without notice. Once the tenancy is treated as a tenancy from period to period, a termination notice must conform to the one already discussed. The death of either party or the voluntary commission of waste by the tenant will terminate a tenancy at will.

TENANCY AT WILL
The right of a tenant to remain in possession of land with permission of the landlord until either the tenant or the landlord chooses to terminate the tenancy.

Tenancy by Sufferance   A **tenancy by sufferance** is not a true tenancy. It is the mere possession of land without right. It is also not an estate, since it is created by a tenant *wrongfully* retaining possession of property. Whenever a life estate, tenancy for years, tenancy from period to period, or tenancy at will ends, and the tenant continues to retain possession of the premises without the owner's permission, a tenancy by sufferance is created. Many states do not recognize the concept of tenancy by sufferance and have abolished it by statute.

TENANCY BY SUFFERANCE
Tenancy by one who, after rightfully being in possession of leased premises, continues (wrongfully) to occupy the property after the lease has been terminated. The tenant has no estate in the land and occupies it only because the person entitled to evict has not done so.

Wrongful Termination of Tenancy   As long as a tenancy exists, a landlord can collect rent in full, regardless of whether the premises are actually occupied by the tenant. Thus, when a tenant wrongfully abandons the premises and refuses to pay rent, the landlord can permit the premises to remain vacant, refuse to recognize the attempted surrender by the tenant, and bring a lawsuit to collect the rent as it comes due. A tenant who wrongfully abandons the premises and refuses to pay rent cannot require that the landlord find another tenant to pay the rent. In many circumstances, however, the landlord has a duty created by statute or judicial decisions to mitigate his or her damages. As a result, if other tenants are available, the landlord may be unable to collect damages for the tenant's breach of the lease.

❖ Relationship of Landlord and Tenant

Much real property is used by those who do not own it. A **lease** is a contract by which the owner—the landlord—grants the tenant an exclusive right to use and possess the land, usually for an ascertainable period of time. The basic characteristic of this particular estate is that it continues for the ascertainable term and carries with it the obligation by the tenant to pay rent to the landlord. Thus an individual who leases property must pay rent unless some other form of payment is agreed upon. Usually, the creation of the leasehold estate by contract for terms longer than a year (or three years in some jurisdictions) must be in writing.

LEASE
A transfer by the landlord/lessor of real or personal property to the tenant/lessee for a period of time, for a consideration (usually the payment of rent). Upon termination of the lease, the property reverts to the lessor.

Warranties of Landlord

WARRANTY OF POSSESSION
In a lease contract, a warranty by the landlord that the premises have been leased to only one tenant and that the premises will be available at the agreed time.

When a landlord leases premises to a tenant, a *warranty of possession* and a *covenant of quiet enjoyment* are implied by law. Under the **warranty of possession,** the landlord warrants that the premises have been leased to only one tenant, and that the premises will be available for occupancy at the agreed time. This is particularly important in leasing apartments, offices, and the like in buildings under construction.

Under the **covenant of quiet enjoyment,** the landlord promises that the tenant or grantee shall enjoy the possession of the premises in peace and without disturbance. Generally, questions regarding a breach of the covenant of quiet enjoyment arise when the landlord's action (or inaction) affects the tenant's use and enjoyment of the premises in such a way that the tenant is *constructively evicted,* meaning that the landlord's failure to perform one or more of the undertakings required by the lease has caused a substantial and lasting injury to the tenant's beneficial enjoyment of the premises. This failure is regarded as an eviction of the tenant.

To illustrate: Emerson, a quiet minister, rents half of a duplex from Hawthorne. Hawthorne rents the other half of the duplex to three members of a rock band. The band rehearses in the duplex every night from about 11:00 in the evening to 5:00 in the morning. Emerson complains to Hawthorne that strange people are constantly entering and leaving the premises and that the noise is unbearable. If Hawthorne fails to take any action, he has breached his covenant of quiet enjoyment to Emerson and has *constructively evicted* him from the premises. Emerson can probably rescind the rental agreement.

At common law, the landlord was under no duty to repair the premises rented by a tenant or to warrant that the premises were habitable or suitable for the particular purpose for which they were rented. Under most state statutes today, however, and under judicial decisions, a landlord of residential premises impliedly warrants that

Drawing by Chon Day; © 1970, The New Yorker Magazine.

"Yes, the walls are paper-thin. But you'll find your neighbor possesses a rapierlike wit, full of amusing double-entendres and profusely studded with literary allusions."

the premises are *habitable* (properly maintained and repaired) and cannot disclaim this **warranty of habitability** unless the landlord and the tenant have equal bargaining power. Additionally, unless otherwise stated in the lease, a landlord is under an affirmative duty to repair and maintain the structure and all its *common areas* and fixtures. The landlord can be held liable for injuries resulting from negligent failure to maintain the rented premises.

WARRANTY OF HABITABILITY
An implied warranty by a landlord that rental premises are properly maintained and repaired and fit for human habitation.

Duties of Tenant

The basic duty of the tenant to the landlord is the implied obligation to pay reasonable rent to the landlord. Most lease contracts contain an express promise, known as a *covenant*, that indicates that the tenant is to pay a specific amount at specified times. Generally, if the express promise is not in the lease agreement, then the tenant is obliged to pay only rent that is reasonable and only at the end of the term.

The following case illustrates some of the consequences that ensue when a tenant fails to pay the rent due under the terms of the lease contract. In this instance, the tenant vacated the premises prior to the end of the lease, and the question was raised as to whether the lease had been terminated or whether the tenant should be forced to pay rent until the lease expired.

Case 34.2
PROVIDENT MUTUAL LIFE INSURANCE CO. v. TACHTRONIC INSTRUMENTS, INC.
Court of Appeals of Minnesota, 1986.
394 N.W.2d 161.

FACTS Tachtronic Instruments, a small Minnesota corporation, leased office and warehouse space in a building owned by Provident Mutual Life Insurance Company. The three-year lease ran until October 31, 1985, and specified monthly payments to Provident in the amount of $2,463. Within the first year of the lease term, Tachtronic defaulted on its payments. When Provident brought an action to evict Tachtronic, the small firm paid a portion of the rent due and the action was dismissed. By February of 1984 Tachtronic had largely vacated the premises. On March 1, 1984, Tachtronic met with representatives of Provident at the "leased" premises. The premises were inspected by Provident, and Tachtronic removed its remaining possessions, broom-swept the floor, and turned over the keys to Provident. Immediately thereafter, Provident sought a new tenant for the premises. A new tenant was found, and a lease beginning November 1, 1984, was created between Provident and the new tenant. The new lease was even more lucrative for Provident than the one with Tachtronic had been. In June of 1984 Provident commenced an action to recover the rent due from Tachtronic

prior to its vacation of the leased premises and also for the rent due and payable for the remainder of the lease. The trial court jury found the lease between Provident and Tachtronic had been terminated on March 1, 1984, and $15,235.12 plus interest was awarded as damages to Provident. The trial court did not hold Tachtronic liable for lease payments after March of 1984. Provident appealed.

ISSUE Was the jury's finding that the lease had been terminated on March 1, 1984, a reasonable one, or should Tachtronic be required to pay the payments due for the remainder of the lease period?

DECISION The appellate court affirmed the trial court's ruling. By accepting the keys from Tachtronic on March 1, 1984, Provident had effectively accepted the termination of the lease.

REASON A lease may be terminated by express agreement or by implied agreement. The latter is sometimes called *termination,* or *surrender, by operation of law.* A surrender by operation of law arises from a condition of fact that is voluntarily assumed and that is incompatible with the existence of a landlord-tenant relationship. In this case, although the lease was not specifically terminated when Tachtronic vacated the premises. Provident's

Case 34.2—Continued

actions—accepting the keys from Tachtronic and seeking another tenant—evidenced its intention to treat the lease as terminated. Therefore, the appellate court found that the trial court jury had been reasonable in deciding the lease was terminated on March 1, 1984, freeing Tachtronic from future liabilities under the lease.

Assignment   An assignment of a tenant's lease to another is an agreement to transfer all rights, title, and interest in the lease to the assignee. It is a complete transfer. Many leases require that the assignment have the landlord's written consent, and an assignment that lacks consent can be avoided by the landlord. A landlord who knowingly accepts rent from the assignee, however, will be held to have waived the requirement. Once waived, it cannot later be revised unless new grounds appear.

A tenant does not end his or her liabilities on a lease upon assignment, because the tenant may assign rights but not duties. Thus, even though the assignee of the lease is required to pay rent, the original tenant is not released from the contractual obligation to pay rent. Whenever the assignee fails to pay, the landlord can look to the original tenant for compensation.

Subleasing   Subleasing involves a partial transfer of the original tenant's rights to the lease. Frequently, the tenant is prohibited from subleasing the premises without the landlord's consent. By subleasing, the original tenant is not relieved of any obligations to the landlord under the lease.

To illustrate: A student named Tami leases an apartment for a two-year period. Although Tami had planned on attending summer school, she is offered a vacation job in Europe for the summer months and accepts. Since she does not wish to pay three months' rent for an unoccupied apartment, she subleases the apartment to another student (sublessee). (She may have to obtain her landlord's permission for this if her lease requires it.) The sublessee is bound by the same terms of the lease as the tenant, and should the sublessee violate the lease, Tami can be held liable by the landlord.

Rent Payment When Premises Are Destroyed   At common law, destruction by fire or flood of a building leased by a tenant did not relieve the tenant of the obligation to pay rent or permit the termination of the lease. Today, however, state statutes have altered the common-law rule. If the building burns down, apartment dwellers in most states are not continuously liable to the landlord for the payment of rent.

❖ Concurrent Ownership

CONCURRENT ESTATES
Ownership of property by two or more persons at the same time; e.g., joint tenancy.

Property owned by one person is said to be held *severally*, that is, apart from others. When two or more persons own property, it is said to be held *concurrently*. There are several types of **concurrent estates,** including tenancy in common, joint tenancy, tenancy by the entirety, and community property.

TENANCY IN COMMON
Co-ownership of property whereby each party owns an undivided interest that passes to his or her heirs at death.

Tenancy in Common

Suppose Shaw conveys land "to Browning, Keats, and Byron." This conveyance creates a **tenancy in common** among Browning, Keats, and Byron, whereby each takes a one-third interest. In a tenancy in common, each tenant has the right to convey his or her interest in the property. When one of the tenants dies, that tenant's interest passes to his or her heirs (or, by will, to someone else). Essentially, tenants in a tenancy in common each own an undivided fractional share of the property, an interest that can be conveyed to another.

Joint Tenancy

In a **joint tenancy**, each tenant owns an undivided interest in the property. Unlike a tenancy in common, however, each joint tenant has a *right of survivorship*. For example, if there are two joint tenants and one dies, the other becomes the sole owner of this interest. No property passes to the heirs of the deceased—not even by will. At common law, unless a clear intention to create a tenancy in common was shown, there was a presumption that any co-tenancy was a joint tenancy. Modern statutes, however, reverse this presumption. Most statutes now presume that a co-tenancy is a tenancy in common unless there is a clear intention to establish a joint tenancy. A joint tenancy is transformed into a tenancy in common when one of the joint tenants transfers his or her interest to another party.

JOINT TENANCY
The ownership interest of two or more co-owners of property whereby each owns an undivided portion of the property. The key feature of joint tenancy is the right of survivorship, whereby, upon the death of one of the joint tenants, his or her interest automatically passes to the others and cannot be transferred by the will of the deceased.

Tenancy by the Entirety

Another type of concurrent estate is the **tenancy by the entirety**—a joint tenancy between a husband and wife. At common law, a tenancy by the entirety could be created between a husband and wife only by specific language such as "to David and Helga Carson, husband and wife, and their heirs and assigns." A tenancy by the entirety differs from a joint tenancy and tenancy in common in that neither spouse can convey his or her interest without the express consent of the other. Since neither can voluntarily convey his or her interest, the creditors of one spouse cannot levy on the property. Divorce terminates a tenancy by the entirety and, in most states, creates a tenancy in common. The tenancy by the entirety is not recognized in many states.[8]

TENANCY BY THE ENTIRETY
The joint ownership of property by husband and wife. Neither party can alienate or encumber the property without the consent of the other. The property is inherited by the survivor of the two, and dissolution of marriage transforms the tenancy by the entirety to a tenancy in common.

Community Property

Nine states provide for concurrent ownership of property by what is called community property.[9] Generally, any property acquired by a husband and wife during the period of their marriage becomes community property, with each owning an undivided half-interest. Property acquired after marriage by gift or inheritance, however, is not included in this category.

The community-property systems are based upon the theory that both spouses contribute to acquisitions during marriage. It is thus recognized that the activity of each spouse is directed toward making the marriage a "going concern," and it is consequently immaterial who actually earns or acquires the property. There is an irrefutable presumption of equal contribution.

---

8.   See *Dorf v. Tuscarora Pipe Line Co.*, 48 N.J.Super. 26, 136 A.2d 778 (1957) and *Lindenfelser v. Lindenfelser*, 396 Pa. 530, 153 A.2d 901 (1959). Some of the states that recognize tenancy by the entirety require express language to create it.
9.   Arizona, California, Idaho, Louisiana, Nevada, New Mexico, Texas, Washington, and Wisconsin.

❖ Transfer of Ownership

Ownership of real property can pass from one person to another by a number of ways, including transfer by inheritance or will, eminent domain, adverse possession, and deed. Conveyance by deed includes transfer by sale and by gift.

Transfer by Inheritance or Will

Property that is transferred on an owner's death is passed either by inheritance or will. If the owner of land dies with a will, the land that the owner had prior to death passes according to the terms of the will. If the owner dies without a will, state statutes prescribe how and to whom the property will pass (see Chapter 35).

Eminent Domain

"The right of eminent domain . . . gives the Legislature the control of private property for public use."

Thomas Wharton, 1648–1715 (British politician)

Even where ownership in real property is fee simple absolute, there is still a superior ownership that limits the fee simple absolute. It is called **eminent domain,** and it is sometimes referred to as the *condemnation power* of the government to take land for public use. It gives a right to the government to acquire possession of real property in the manner directed by the Constitution and the laws of the state whenever the public interest so requires.

For example, when a new public highway is to be built, the government must decide where to build it and how much land to condemn. The power of eminent domain is generally invoked through condemnation proceedings. After the government determines that a particular parcel of land is necessary for public use, if a voluntary sale cannot be consummated, it brings a judicial proceeding to obtain title to the land. Then, in another proceeding, the court further determines the *fair value* of the land, which is usually approximately equal to the market value. Under the Fifth Amendment, private property may not be taken for public use without "just compensation."

EMINENT DOMAIN
The power of a government to take land for public use from private citizens for fair compensation.

Adverse Possession

ADVERSE POSSESSION
The acquisition of title to real property by occupying it openly, with the knowledge but without the consent of the owner, for a period of time specified by state statutes.

Adverse possession is a means of obtaining title to land without a deed being delivered. Essentially, when one person possesses the property of another for a certain statutory period of time (three to thirty years, with ten years being most common), that person, called the *adverse possessor,* acquires title to the land and cannot be removed from the land by the original owner. The adverse possessor is vested with a perfect title just as if there had been a conveyance by deed.

In order to hold property adversely, four elements must be satisfied:

1.   Possession must be actual and exclusive; that is, the possessor must take sole physical occupancy of the property.
2.   Possession must be open, visible, and notorious, not secret or clandestine. In other words, the possessor must occupy the land for all the world to see.
3.   Possession must be continuous and peaceable for the required period of time. This requirement means that the possessor must not be interrupted in the occupancy by the true owner or by the courts.

4. Possession must be hostile and adverse. In other words, the possessor must claim the property as against the whole world. If he or she lives on the property with the permission of the owner, possession is not adverse. "Hostile" does not here mean displaying evil intent or emotion against the title owner. Rather, it means that the possession is asserted against the claim of ownership of all others.

In the following case, the court ruled that a couple had obtained title to a certain portion of land by adverse possession.

Case 34.3
KLOS v. MOLENDA
Superior Court of Pennsylvania, 1986.
355 Pa. Super. 399, 513 A.2d 490.

FACTS In September of 1950 Michael and Albina Klos purchased part of some property owned by John and Anne Molenda. The Kloses' lot was 50 feet wide and 135 feet deep. Rather than surveying the property, the seller and buyer paced off the lot and placed stakes in the ground as boundary markers. The Kloses built a house on the lot in 1952 and put in a sidewalk along the full front. They also put in a driveway 30 inches from the stake line. They planted grass and a hedge in that 30 inches and maintained it until 1984. In 1983 Mr. Molenda died, and his widow hired a surveyor to inventory the land holdings. The survey located the rightful property line between Molenda's and the Kloses' land as being 30 inches closer to the Kloses' house than it currently was. This placed the property line right along the Kloses' driveway, instead of 30 inches to the side of the driveway. Upon learning this, Mrs. Molenda dug up the grass strip and the hedgerow and erected a fence right along the Kloses' driveway, marking the property line. The Kloses brought this action challenging Mrs. Molenda's conduct, claiming they

held title to the land by adverse possession. The trial court held that the Kloses had title to the land. Mrs. Molenda appealed.

ISSUE Who has title to the 30-inch strip of land?

DECISION The appellate court affirmed the trial court's decision. The Kloses held rightful title to the land.

REASON The rule of adverse possession holds that if a person has actual, continuous, exclusive, visible, notorious, distinct, and hostile possession of land for a long period of time (in Pennsylvania, twenty-one years), that person gains title to the land. This means that the adverse possessor must use the land in a regular, normal, and obvious manner so that the original title owner would know, upon inspection, of the possessor's use. If the original title owner does not evict the possessor or otherwise exercise his or her ownership, then the possessor will obtain title once the statutory time period has lapsed. Here the Kloses were certainly open, hostile, and notorious in their possession of the land in question, and they possessed the land for over thirty years, thereby passing the time limit. They therefore obtained title to the land by adverse possession.

Conveyance by Deed

Possession and title to land are also passed from person to person by means of a **deed**—the instrument of conveyance of real property. A deed is a writing signed by the owner who is transferring title to his or her property to another.

Requirements of a Valid Deed Unlike a contract, a deed does not have to be supported by legally sufficient consideration. Gifts of real property are common, and they require deeds even though there is no consideration for the gift. A valid deed must contain the following elements:

DEED
A document by which title to property (usually real property) is passed.

1. The names of the buyer (grantee) and seller (grantor).

2. Words evidencing an intent to convey (for example, "I hereby bargain, sell, grant, or give").
3. A legally sufficient description of the land.
4. The grantor's (and usually the spouse's) signature.

Finally, to be valid, a deed must be delivered.

Types of Deeds   Different types of deeds provide different degrees of protection against defects of title. A **general warranty deed** warrants the greatest number of things and thus provides the greatest protection. In most states, special language is required to make a general warranty deed; but, in essence, it must include a written promise to protect the buyer against all claims of ownership of the property.

A **quit-claim deed** offers the least amount of protection against defects in the title. Basically, it conveys to the grantee whatever interest the grantor had; so if the grantor had no interest, then the grantee receives no interest.

Recording Statutes   **Recording statutes** are in force in every jurisdiction in order to provide prospective buyers with a way to check whether there has been an earlier transaction concerning particular real property. Once a deed is properly recorded, any subsequent purchaser takes the property subject to the interest of the recorded owner. Most deeds are recorded in the presence of a notary public in the county where the property is recorded.

❖ Future Interests

The common law recognizes a number of estates that are nonpossessory, such as **future estates,** which are in direct contrast to possessory estates such as the estates in fee discussed earlier. The holder of a future estate does not actually possess the estate but *may* or *will* possess it in the future. The holder of an estate for life has a *present possessory interest* in the real property, which is accompanied by a *residuary,* or *future interest,* on the part of the grantor. This future interest can take several forms. If it remains with the grantor, it is called a *reversion,* a *possibility of reverter,* or a *power of termination.* If not retained by the grantor, it is called either a *remainder* or an *executory interest.*

Reversionary Interests

When an owner of a fee simple estate in land conveys the estate to another for a specified period of time, the owner retains a future interest in the undisposed residue of the estate. That undisposed residue is called a **reversion.**

Suppose that Oliver owns a fee simple estate and conveys a life estate in Blackwood Hills to Alice. Oliver has not disposed of the interest in the land remaining after Alice's life, so he has automatically retained a reversion that will become possessory, upon Alice's death, in Oliver or his heirs. Alice's life estate is an estate in possession, whereas Oliver has a *vested* future interest—that is, an absolute right to possession of Blackwood Hills at some point in the future. Furthermore, even though Oliver holds such a future interest, this interest exists in the present in the sense that Oliver can convey his future interest.

GENERAL WARRANTY DEED
A deed that warrants that the title to land being conveyed is free of all encumbrances, except as noted in the document; warrants the most extensive protection against defects of title.

QUIT-CLAIM DEED
A deed intended to pass any title, interest, or claim that the grantor may have in the premises but not professing that such title is valid nor containing any warranty or covenants for title.

RECORDING STATUTES
Statutes enacted to provide notice to future purchasers, creditors, and encumbrancers of an existing claim on real property.

FUTURE ESTATE
An estate that is not at present possessory but will or may be possessory in the future. Remainders and reversions are future estates.

REVERSION
A future interest under which a grantor retains a present right to a future interest in property that the grantor conveys to another; usually the residue of a life estate. The reversion is always a vested property right.

Suppose, however, that Oliver conveys Blackwood Hills "to Alice and her heirs." It is clear that there is no future interest in Blackwood Hills since Oliver has conveyed his entire estate to Alice as a fee simple absolute. If, on the other hand, Oliver conveys a *fee simple defeasible* (which is one of the estates that is less than a fee simple, such as "to Alice and her heirs as long as the property is used for educational purposes"), Oliver has retained a **possibility of reverter,** which is a future interest in favor of the grantor that is contingent on the happening of the event named in the conveyance. The conveyance of a fee simple determinable that gives rise to a possibility of reverter usually includes the words "as long as," "until," "while," or "during."

Remainders and Executory Interests

When an owner of real property conveys an estate that is less than a fee simple absolute and does not retain the residuary interest, then that interest will take the form of either a **remainder** or an **executory interest.** A remainder differs from an executory interest in that a remainder occurs upon the *natural termination* of a preceding estate—such as a life estate. Executory interests, however, take effect either before or after the natural termination of a preceding estate. To illustrate: Oliver conveys Blackwood Hills "to Alice for twenty years, but if Alice should divorce, then Blackwood Hills is to pass immediately to Carrie." Carrie has a future interest in Blackwood Hills that will become a present possessory interest if Alice becomes divorced. Carrie's future interest is known as a *shifting executory interest,* since the possessory interest would shift from Alice to Carrie if Alice should divorce.

❖ Nonpossessory Interests

Some interests in land do not include any rights of possession. These nonpossessory interests include easements, profits, and licenses. Because easements and profits are similar, and the same rules apply to both, they will be discussed together.

Easements and Profits

An **easement** is the right of a person to make limited use of another person's property without taking anything from the property. An easement, for example, can be the right to walk across another's property. In contrast, a **profit** is the right to go onto land in possession of another and take away some part of the land itself or some product of the land. For example, Oliver gives Alice the right to go into Blackwood Hills and remove all the sand and gravel that Alice needs for her cement business. Alice has a profit. The difference between an easement and a profit is that an easement merely allows a person to use land without taking anything from it, whereas a profit allows a person to take something from the land.

Classification of Easements and Profits   Easements and profits can be classified as either *appurtenant* or *in gross.* The first arises when the owner of one parcel of land has the right to go onto (or remove things from) an adjacent parcel of land owned by another. Thus, if Oliver, the owner of Blackwood Hills, has a right to drive his car across Mulligan's land, White Sands, this right of way over White Sands is an easement appurtenant to Blackwood Hills. Oliver can convey the easement when he

POSSIBILITY OF REVERTER
A future interest in land that a grantor retains after conveying property subject to a condition subsequent (e.g., if a certain future event occurs, the interest in the estate will terminate automatically).

REMAINDER
A future interest in property, held by a person other than the grantor, that occurs at the natural termination of the preceding estate.

EXECUTORY INTEREST
A future interest, held by a person other than the grantor, that either cuts short or begins some time after the natural termination of the preceding estate.

EASEMENT
A nonpossessory right to use another's property in a manner established by either express or implied agreement.

PROFIT
In real property law, the right to enter upon and remove things from the property of another (for example, the right to enter onto a person's land and remove sand and gravel therefrom).

conveys Blackwood Hills. The outstanding feature of an easement appurtenant is that it involves two neighboring parcels of land owned by two different persons.

An easement or profit in gross exists when the right to use or take things from another's land is not dependent upon *the owner of the easement or profit also owning an adjacent tract of land*. Suppose Oliver owns a parcel of land with a marble quarry. He conveys to the XYZ Corporation, which owns no land, the right to come onto his land and remove up to 500 pounds of marble per day. XYZ Corporation owns a profit in gross. An easement or profit in gross requires the existence of only one parcel of land that must be owned by someone other than the owner of the easement or profit in gross. Another illustration is that of a utility company that is granted an easement to run its power lines across another's property.

Effect of Sale of Property   Whenever a parcel of land that is *benefited* by an easement or profit appurtenant is sold, the property carries the easement or profit along with it. Thus, if Oliver sells Blackwood Hills to Trueblood and includes the appurtenant right of way across White Sands in the deed to Trueblood, Trueblood will own both the property and the easement that benefits it.

When a piece of land that has the *burden* of an easement or profit appurtenant is sold, the new owner is required to recognize its existence only if he or she knew or should have known of it or if it is recorded in the appropriate office of the county. Thus, if Oliver records his easement across White Sands in the appropriate county office before Mulligan conveys the land, the new owner of White Sands will have to allow Oliver, or any subsequent owner of Blackwood Hills, such as Trueblood, to continue to use the path across White Sands.

Creation of Easements (and Profits)   Easements and profits can be created by deed, will, implication, necessity, or prescription. Creation by deed or will simply involves the delivery of a deed or a disposition in a will by the owner of an easement stating that the grantee (the person receiving the profit or easement) is granted the rights in the easement or profit that the grantor had. An easement or profit, however, may be created by *implication* when the circumstances surrounding the division of a piece of property imply its creation. If Bailey divides a parcel of land that has only one well for drinking water and conveys the half without a well to David, a profit by implication arises, since David needs drinking water.

An easement may also be created by *necessity*, which does not require division of property for its existence. A person who rents an apartment, for example, has an easement by necessity in the private road leading up to it.

Easements and profits by *prescription* arise when one person uses another person's land for a period of time equal to the applicable statute of limitations (usually the same as for acquiring title by adverse possession). If the owner of the land does not object to the use of the land for the required period of time, the person using the land has an easement or profit by prescription.

Termination of Easements (and Profits)   Easements and profits can be terminated, or extinguished, in several ways. The simplest way is to deed them back to the owner of the land burdened by them. A second way is for the owners to abandon them and create evidence of their intent to relinquish the right to use them. Mere nonuse will not extinguish an easement or profit *unless it is accompanied by an intent to abandon*. A third way is for the owner of the easement or profit to become the owner of the property burdened by it; then it is merged into the property.

Licenses

A license is the revocable right of a person to come onto another person's land. It is a personal privilege that arises from the consent of the owner of the land and that can be revoked by the owner. A ticket to attend a movie at a theater is an example of a license. If a theater owner issues a ticket entitling the holder to enter the property of the owner, and another person subsequently acquires the ticket and is refused entry into the theater, that other person has no right to force his or her way into the theater. The ticket is only a revocable license, not a conveyance of an interest in property.

Application

Law and the Seller of Real Estate

At some time in your life you may wish to sell real property (or buy it, for that matter, which requires many of the same steps to be outlined here). The first step in selling your real property is to locate a buyer. This can be done by putting your property on *open listing*, which allows you, the seller, to find a buyer yourself or to hire brokers with nonexclusive rights to sell the property. The first broker who produces a bona fide buyer is entitled to a brokerage commission. If you have an exclusive-agency agreement with the broker, that broker has the exclusive right to sell the property but can employ other brokers with whom the commission is shared. With both an open listing and an exclusive agency, if you sell the property without the assistance of a broker, you need not pay a commission. On the other hand, if you sign a contract giving a broker an *exclusive right to sell* the real estate, then, no matter who sells the real estate, that particular broker is entitled to a commission.

Once you find a buyer for your real estate, a contract for the sale of the property must be negotiated. Its essential elements are (1) an identification of the parties, (2) a description of the property to be conveyed, (3) the purchase price, and (4) the signatures of the buyer and seller. Today a buyer will often purchase title insurance to protect the buyer in the event that someone is shown to have a better title.

After the sales contract has been negotiated, the buyer or the buyer's attorney (or even a broker, an escrow agent, or a title insurance company) needs to begin the title search, in which an examination of all past transfers and sales of the piece of property in question is undertaken.

The buyer of your property typically will seek a mortgage—that is, borrow in order to pay for much of the purchase price of the property. Usually, the property is put up as collateral for the mortgage, because the mortgage is essentially a lien against the property that enables the lender to foreclose and sell the real estate if the bor-

rower fails to make timely payments. As the seller, you may decide to offer the mortgage yourself.

The final stage of the sale of real estate is called the *closing*. At the closing, normally the buyer pays the purchase price and the seller delivers the deed to the buyer. Prior to the closing, a number of activities must take place, including the title search and having the documents drafted and signed. During this period of time, the property is put *in escrow*, meaning that the seller has placed the property in the hands of a broker or escrow agent who will deliver the property to the purchaser when all the conditions of the sale have been performed. Legal title to the property will remain in your hands, however, until the escrow conditions are fully performed. Even if there has been a deposit of the deed in escrow, that does not pass title to your buyer until all escrow agreement terms have been performed. At the time the terms and conditions of the contract of sale have been completed, the escrow is closed by the designated escrow agent. A closing statement is then prepared in which the details of the transactions are listed, including the purchase price of the property, the proration of taxes, obligations chargeable to each party, real estate broker's commission, and title company charges.

Checklist for the Sale of Real Estate

☐ 1. For almost all real-estate sales, it is advisable to utilize the services of a qualified attorney who specializes in real-estate law.

☐ 2. Make sure that the prospective buyer of your property fully understands all the terms and conditions that you require.

☐ 3. If you have doubts about the potential buyer's ability to obtain financing for the purchase of your real estate, make sure that you are not tying up the property for very long while that buyer seeks a mortgage.

❖ Chapter Summary: Real Property

Nature of Real Property	Real property—also called real estate or realty—is immovable. It includes land, subsurface and air rights, plant life and vegetation, and fixtures.

Ownership of Real Property (Estates in Land)	1. *Freehold estates* (estates held indefinitely):
	  a. Estates in fee:
	    (1) Fee simple absolute—Most complete form of ownership.
	    (2) Fee simple defeasible—Fee simple that can end if the specified event or condition occurs.
	  b. Life estates—Estates that last for the life of a specified individual; these rights are subject to the rights of the future-interest holder.
	
	2. *Nonfreehold (less-than-freehold) estates* (possessory interests held for a specified period of time):
	  a. Tenancy for years—Tenancy for period of time stated by express contract.
	  b. Tenancy from period to period—Tenancy for period determined by frequency of rent payments; automatically renewed unless proper notice is given.
	  c. Tenancy at will—Tenancy for as long as both parties agree; no notice of termination required.
	  d. Tenancy by sufferance—Possession of land without legal right.
	
	3. *Concurrent ownership* (jointly held ownership):
	  a. Tenancy in common—Each tenant owns an undivided fractional share of the property. Such interests can be conveyed without the consent of the other owner(s), and, upon death, pass to the tenant's heirs.
	  b. Joint tenancy (with right of survivorship)—Each tenant owns an undivided share of the property. Such interest can be conveyed without the consent of the other owner(s), converting the interest to a tenancy in common. Upon death, the decedent's interest passes to the surviving joint tenant, not to the decedent's heirs.
	  c. Tenancy by the entirety—Joint tenancy with right of survivorship between husband and wife.
	  d. Community property—Most property acquired during marriage by either spouse or both spouses is owned equally by each spouse.

Landlord-Tenant Relationship	1. *Warranties of the landlord:*
	  a. Warranty of possession—The tenant has an exclusive right to the use and possession of leased property, and the premises must be available to the tenant at the agreed-upon time.
	  b. Covenant of quiet enjoyment—The tenant shall enjoy the possession of the premises in peace and without disturbance.
	  c. Warranty of habitability—Under most state statutes, a landlord of residential property warrants that the premises are *habitable* (properly maintained and repaired) and may be liable for injuries resulting from negligent failure to maintain the leased premises.
	
	2. *Duties of the tenant:*
	  a. The tenant's major duty is to pay rent to the landlord. If the amount is not expressly stated in a lease contract, then the tenant is obliged to pay only rent that is reasonable and only at the end of the term.
	  b. Unless prohibited (landlord's express or implied consent required), tenants may assign their rights, but not their duties, under a lease contract to a third person.
	  c. Unless prohibited (landlord's express or implied consent required), tenants may *sublease* leased property to a third person, but the original tenant is not relieved of any obligations to the landlord under the lease.

Transfer of Property	1. *By inheritance or will*—If the owner dies *intestate* (without a will), the heirs inherit according to state intestacy laws. If the owner dies *testate* (with a valid will), the land passes to the devisees named in the will. 2. *By eminent domain*—The taking of private land by the government (by condemnation) for public use, for just compensation, when the public interest requires it.

❖ Chapter Summary: Real Property—Continued

Transfer of Property (Continued)	3. *By adverse possession*—When a person possesses the property of another for a statutory period of time (three to thirty years, with ten years being most common), that person acquires title to the property provided the possession is (1) actual and exclusive, (2) open and visible, (3) continuous and peaceable, and (4) hostile and adverse (without the permission of the owner).
	4. *By deed*—The instrument of conveyance of real property. A deed must meet specific legal requirements; can be a *general warranty deed* (warrants the most extensive protection against defects of title) or a *quit-claim deed* (conveys to the grantee whatever interest the grantor had; warrants less than any other deed). Deeds may be recorded in the manner prescribed by *recording statutes* in the appropriate jurisdiction to give third parties notice of the owner's interest.
Future Interests	1. A *future estate* is an estate that may or will become possessory in the future (in contrast to a *possessory estate*). Consists of the residuary interest not granted by the grantor when conveying an estate to another for life, for a specified period of time, or conditioned by the occurrence (or nonoccurrence) of a specified event.
	2. When the residuary interest remains with the grantor, it is called a *reversion* (where title will revert to the grantor after a specified period of time) or a *possibility of reverter* (where title will revert to the grantor upon the happening of a specified event).
	3. When the future interest is not retained by the grantor but given to a third person, then it is called a *remainder* or an *executory interest*.
Nonpossessory Interests	1. *Easement*—The right of a person to make limited use of another person's property without taking anything from the property.
	2. *Profit*—The right of a person to go onto land in another's possession and remove some part of the land or products of the land.
	3. *License*—The revocable right of a person to come onto another person's land (e.g., a ticket to attend a movie).

❖ Questions and Case Problems

34-1. Boris Nolan owned a number of homes in Bloomsville. Because his widowed Aunt Willet was rather pressed for funds, he conveyed one of these homes to her as a life estate. This meant that his aunt could possess the property until her death, at which time the property would revert to Boris. When his Aunt Willet died, her son Jeremy inherited all of Willet's property. Jeremy maintained that he had title to the property by adverse possession, because his mother had lived there for twenty years before her death. Discuss the merits of Jeremy's claim.

34-2. Calvin and Dora Knudson lived in a community-property state. Dora had a savings account in her name only into which she had deposited a considerable sum of money that she had acquired prior to her marriage to Calvin. Dora died, leaving all of her property to her niece, Sonja. Calvin claimed that one-half of the money in the savings account was rightfully his, since they lived in a community property state. Was Calvin right? Explain.

34-3. Elkins owned a tract of land, but he was not sure that he had full title to the property. When Maves expressed an interest in buying the property, Elkins sold Maves the land and executed a quit-claim deed. Maves properly recorded the deed immediately. Several months later, Elkins learned that he had had full title to the tract of land. He then sold the land to Jones by general warranty deed. Jones knew of the earlier purchase by Maves but took the deed anyway and later sued to have Maves evicted from the land. Jones claimed that since he had a general warranty deed, his title to the land was better than that of Maves's quit-claim deed. Will Jones succeed in claiming title to the land? Discuss.

34-4. Lorenz was a wanderer twenty-two years ago. It was at that time that he decided to settle down on a vacant three-acre piece of land, which he did not own. People in the area indicated to him that they had no idea who owned it. Lorenz built a house on the land, got married, and raised three children while living there. He fenced in the land, placed a gate with a sign, "Lorenz's Homestead," above it, and had trespassers removed. Lorenz is now confronted by Joe Reese, who has a deed in his name as owner of the property. Reese orders Lorenz and his family off the property, claiming his title ownership. Discuss who has the better "title" to the property.

34-5. Tony is the owner of a lakeside house and lot. He deeds the house and lot to "my wife, Angela, for life, with remainder to my son, Charles, providing he graduates from college with a B or better average during Angela's lifetime." Given these facts, answer the following questions:

    (a) Does Tony have any interest in the deeded lakeside house? Explain.

    (b) What is Angela's interest called? Explain.

    (c) What is Charles's interest called? Explain.

34-6. Bernadine and Robert Meyers married in 1947 and lived in Robert's house until 1948, when Robert enlisted in the army and moved to California. Robert never thereafter lived in the house. It was maintained and cared for solely by Bernadine, and Bernadine made all the tax payments on the property. Bernadine had never asserted her ownership of the property to her children, to Robert, or to any others; by all appearances, Bernadine lived in the house by Robert's permission. The couple divorced in 1954, and nothing was mentioned in the divorce papers concerning the residence. In 1979 Robert requested the local authorities to send property tax statements to his California address, and Bernadine brought an action for adverse possession. Under Minnesota law, adverse possession for a period of fifteen years was necessary to claim title to property. Discuss the probability of Bernadine's success in her claim of title to the property by adverse possession. [Meyers v. Meyers, 368 N.W.2d 391 (Minn.App. 1985)]

34-7. Ralph Swafford purchased three prefabricated, metal buildings and had them assembled and installed on his ranch. The buildings, which were bolted to concrete slabs when they were installed, included a horse barn, an open-air hay shed with no siding, and a building for use as an office, trophy room, and tack room. Swafford later obtained a loan from Kerman, using his ranch as collateral for the mortgage loan. When Swafford defaulted on the debt, Kerman foreclosed on the property and, at the foreclosure sale, bought the property himself. Kerman maintained that the three prefabricated buildings were part of the real property. Swafford alleged that the portable buildings were his personal property and not a part of the real estate now owned by Kerman. Discuss who will prevail in court. [Kerman v. Swafford, 101 N.M.App. 241, 680 P.2d 622 (1984)]

34-8. A landlord of residential premises leased a building he owned nearby for use as a cocktail lounge. The residential tenants complained to the landlord about the late-evening and early-morning music and disturbances coming from the lounge. Although the lease for the lounge provided that entertainment had to be conducted so that it could not be heard outside the building and would not disturb residents of the apartments, the landlord was unsuccessful in remedying the problem. The tenants vacated their apartments. Was the landlord successful in his suit to collect rent from the tenants who vacated? [Blackett v. Olanoff, 371 Mass. 714, 358 N.E.2d 817 (1977)]

34-9. As the result of a survey in 1976, the Nolans discovered that their neighbor's garage extended more than a foot onto their property. As a result, Nolan requested that his neighbor, Naab, tear down the garage. The Naabs refused to do this, stating that the garage had been built in 1952 and was on the property when the Naabs purchased it in 1973. In West Virginia, there is a ten-year statute of limitations covering adverse possession of property. Were the Naabs able to claim title to the land on which the garage was situated by adverse possession? [Naab v. Nolan, 327 S.E.2d 151 (W.Va.1985)]

Chapter 35

Insurance, Wills, and Trusts

Most individuals insure both real and personal property (as well as their lives). As Calvin Coolidge asserted, insurance is "all common sense"—by insuring our property, we protect ourselves against damage and loss. After discussing insurance, a foremost concern of all property owners, we will examine how property is passed upon the death of its owner. Certainly, the laws of succession of property are a necessary corollary to the concept of private ownership of property. Our laws require that upon death, title to the property of a decedent (one who has recently died) must be delivered in full somewhere. In this chapter we will see that this can be done by will, through trusts, or through state law prescribing distribution of property among heirs or next of kin.

❖ The Nature of Insurance

Insurance is a contract by which the insurance company (insurer) promises to pay a sum of money or give something of value to another (to either the insured or the beneficiary) in the event that the insured is injured or sustains damage as a result of particular, stated contingencies. Basically, insurance is an arrangement for *transferring and allocating risk*. In many cases, *risk* can be described as a prediction concerning potential loss based on known and unknown factors. Insurance, however, involves much more than a game of chance, and insurers have an interest in seeing that risk is minimized. Many familiar safety devices are now commonplace because of insurer concerns or insurance laws—automobile seat belts, fire escapes, train whistles, railroad-crossing lights, reflecting road signs, and break-away highway light-posts, among others.

Terminology

An insurance contract is called a **policy;** the consideration paid to the insurer is called a **premium;** and the insurance company is sometimes called an **underwriter.**

POLICY
In insurance, the contract of indemnity against a contingent loss between the insurer and insured.

PREMIUM
In insurance, the price for insurance protection for a specified period of exposure.

UNDERWRITER
In insurance law, the one assuming a risk in return for the payment of a premium; the insurer.

Parties   The *parties* to an insurance policy are the *insurer* (the insurance company) and the *insured* (the person covered by its provisions). Insurance contracts are usually obtained through an *agent*, who ordinarily works for the insurance company, or through a *broker*, who is ordinarily an independent contractor. When a broker deals with an applicant for insurance, the broker is, in effect, the applicant's agent. By contrast, an insurance agent is an agent of the insurance company, not the applicant. Thus, an insurance agent's relationship with the applicant for insurance is controlled by ordinary rules of agency law (see Chapter 22).

As a general rule, the insurance company is bound by the acts of its agents when they act within the agency relationship. On the other hand, a broker has no relationship with the insurance company and is an agent of the applicant for insurance. In most situations, state law determines the status of all parties writing or obtaining insurance. The status of agent or broker can be extremely important in determining liability, as is evident in the following case.

Case 35.1
GRAY v. GREAT AMERICA RESERVE INS. CO.
Supreme Court of Alabama, 1986.
495 S.2d 602.

FACTS   On April 12, 1984, James and Hazel Gray signed a joint application for health insurance coverage with Great American. The application was taken by John L. Sides, who at that time was not an agent for Great American but an independent insurance broker. Upon signing the application, the Grays gave Sides $188.50, the first month's premium, and later alleged that Sides had told them the policy would become effective when the first payment was made. Sides then sent the application to Great American, including his own application to become a salesperson for Great American. Sides subsequently was allowed to sell Great American insurance policies. After several initial problems, Great American received the Grays' policy application on June 29, 1984, and only then began to process the application.

Two days before Great American had received the policy application, Mr. Gray was thrown from a horse and was injured. Mrs. Gray notified Sides of the injury, but Sides learned from Great American that the Grays were not covered as of the date of the injury. James Gray then brought suit against Great American and Sides for breach of an insurance contract. The trial court granted Great American's motion for summary judgment, and Gray appealed.

ISSUE   Did the Grays have a valid insurance policy with Great American on the date of Mr. Gray's injury?

DECISION   No. The Supreme Court of Alabama affirmed the trial court's ruling.

REASON   Because an application for insurance is a mere offer, it does not become a contract until the insurer accepts it. No matter what Sides may have said to the Grays, he had no authority to accept the Grays' offer and thus bind Great American in a contractual relationship as he was not at that time an agent for Great American, but an independent broker. Therefore, Great American was not liable under contract to Gray.

Insurable Interest   A person can insure anything in which he or she has an **insurable interest**. Without this insurable interest, there is no enforceable contract, and a transaction to insure would have to be treated as a wager. In the case of real and personal property, an insurable interest exists when the insured derives a pecuniary benefit from the preservation and continued existence of the property. Put another way, one has an insurable interest in property when one would sustain a pecuniary loss from its destruction. In the case of life insurance, a person must have a reasonable

INSURABLE INTEREST
An interest either in a person's life or well-being or in property which is sufficiently substantial that insuring against injury to the person or damage to the property does not amount to a mere wagering (betting) contract.

expectation of benefit from the continued life of another in order to have an insurable interest in that person's life. The benefit may be pecuniary (such as so-called *key-person insurance*, insuring the lives of important officers, usually in small companies), or it may be founded upon the relationship between the parties (by blood or affinity). Also, the insurable interest in life insurance must exist at the time the policy is obtained. This is exactly the opposite of property insurance, where the insurable interest must exist at the time the loss occurs and not necessarily when the policy is purchased. The existence of an insurable interest is a primary concern when determining liability under an insurance policy.

Indemnity   In fire insurance policies, insurance coverage is usually an *indemnity*; that is, the insurance pays only for what is actually lost. This is usually the replacement value of the property minus any depreciation. In addition, once payment is made, the insurance company is entitled to "stand in the shoes" of the insured in pursuing any lawsuits arising from the incident. This is called the *right of subrogation*.

❖ Insurance Contract

An insurance contract is governed by the general principles of contract law, although the insurance industry is heavily regulated by each state. The filled-in application form for insurance is usually attached to the policy and made a part of the insurance contract. Thus, an insurance applicant is bound by any false statements that appear in the application (subject to certain exceptions). Because the insurance company evaluates the risk factors based on the information included in the insurance application, misstatements or misrepresentations can void a policy, especially if the insurance company can show that it would not have extended insurance if it had known the facts.

Timing

The effective date of an insurance contract is important. In some instances, the insurance applicant is not protected until a formal written policy is issued. In other situations, the applicant is protected between the time an application is received and the time the insurance company either accepts or rejects it. Four facts should be kept in mind:

1.   A broker is merely the agent of an applicant. Therefore, if the broker fails to procure a policy, the applicant is not insured. According to general principles of agency law, if the broker fails to obtain policy coverage and the applicant is damaged as a result, then the broker is liable to the damaged applicant/principal for the loss.
2.   A person who seeks insurance from an insurance company's agent will usually be protected from the moment the application is made, provided—in the case of life insurance—that some form of premium has been paid. Between the time the application is received and either rejected or accepted, the applicant is covered (possibly subject to medical examination). Usually, the agent will write a memorandum, or **binder,** indicating that a policy is pending and stating its essential terms.
3.   If the parties agree that the policy will be issued and delivered at a later time, the contract is not effective until the policy is issued and delivered or sent to the

BINDER
A written, temporary insurance policy.

applicant, depending upon the agreement. Thus, any loss sustained between the time of application and the delivery of the policy is not covered.

4. Parties may agree that a life insurance policy will be binding at the time the insured pays the first premium, or the policy may be expressly contingent upon the applicant's passing a physical examination. (If the applicant pays the premium and passes the examination, then the policy coverage is continuously in effect.) If the applicant pays the premium but dies before having the physical examination, then, in order to collect, the applicant's estate must show that the applicant would have passed the examination had he or she not died.

Coverage on an insurance policy can begin when a binder is written, when the policy is issued, or, depending on the terms of the contract, after a certain period of time has elapsed.

Defenses against Payment

An insurance company can raise any of the defenses that would be valid in any ordinary action on a contract and some defenses that do not apply in ordinary contract actions. If the insurance company can show that the policy was procured by fraud, misrepresentation, or violation of warranties, it may have a valid defense for not paying on a claim, as happened in a case discussed in the "Business Law in Action" in this chapter. (The insurance company may also have the right to disaffirm or rescind an insurance contract.) Improper actions, such as those that are against public policy or that are otherwise illegal, can also give the insurance company a defense against the payment of a claim or allow it to rescind the contract. In the following case, an inaccurate answer to a pertinent question on an application for a mortgage life insurance policy was successfully used by the insurance company to deny a claim following the policyowner's death.

Case 35.2
BERTHIAUME v. MINNESOTA MUTUAL LIFE INS. CO.
Court of Appeals of Minnesota, 1986.
388 N.W.2d 15.

FACTS On April 16, 1982, Frances and Michael Berthiaume made a written application for mortgage life insurance with the Minnesota Mutual Life Insurance Company. The policy sought was to provide $44,308.37 in insurance coverage to cover the amount of the Berthiaumes' loan balance on the mortgage for their house, for a monthly premium of $12.42. Mr. Berthiaume did not take a physical examination for the policy, but in filling out the application he answered "no" to a question asking whether he had ever been treated for or had ever been advised that he had high blood pressure. The answer Mr. Berthiaume gave was incorrect; in fact, he had been di-

agnosed as having hypertension four months before the application was made.

In October of 1982 Mr. Berthiaume became ill and died two months later. When his widow submitted a claim for the mortgage insurance, the insurance company denied payment, citing Mr. Berthiaume's inaccurate answer on the application. Minnesota Mutual sought summary judgment, which was granted by the trial court. Mrs. Berthiaume appealed.

ISSUE Did Mr. Berthiaume's inaccurate answer on the insurance policy application void Minnesota Mutual's obligation to pay on the policy?

DECISION Yes. The Minnesota Court of Appeals affirmed the trial court's decision to grant summary judgment to the insurance company.

Case 35.2—Continued

REASON   The state law of Minnesota allows an insurer to void an insurance policy issued without a prior medical examination if the insured willfully misstates necessary information or intentionally misleads the insurance company. The materiality of a misrepresentation is measured by the extent to which the disclosure influenced the insurer's decision to accept the risk of coverage, not by the degree of causal connection between the false statement and the loss protected by the policy. Here it is clear that Mr. Berthiaume failed to disclose he had been advised by his doctor that he had high blood pressure and had been treated by the doctor for that condition. Thus, the court concluded that the insurance company deserved summary judgment in this case.

❖ Wills and Trusts

"When it comes time to divide an estate, the politest men quarrel."

**Ralph Waldo Emerson,
1803–1882
(American essayist and poet)**

INTESTATE
A person who dies without making a valid will.

Private ownership of property leads logically to both the protection of that property by insurance coverage while the owner is alive and the transfer of that property upon the death of the owner to those designated by the owner. At common law, people had no way to control the distribution of their property after death. The power of transfer or distribution is derived solely from statutes originating in feudal England, where the transfer of property at death was strictly controlled. The heir (the one who inherited) was required to pay the feudal lord a sum of money [1] for the privilege of succeeding to his or her ancestor's lands. When a tenant died without heirs, the land *escheated* (titled passed) to the feudal lord of the manor. [2]

Sweeping land reforms in England during the 1920s replaced inheritance payments and escheat to the feudal lord with the right of the crown to receive inheritance taxes and to take property of an **intestate** without heirs. Modern legislation has

"To my one true-blue ever-faithful companion . . ."

© 1985 by D. Robert White. Illustrations © 1985, Mike Goodman.

---

1.   The sum, called a *relief*, was usually equivalent to one year's rent.
2.   C. J. Moynihan, *Introduction to the Law of Real Property* (St. Paul, Minn.: West Publishing Co., 1962), p. 22.

Business Law in Action

Mr. Knight's Sunken Treasure

Economists have a term for irrecoverable costs. They are called "sunk costs"—costs that have, for all practical purposes, sunk to the bottom of the ocean, figuratively speaking. Frederick Knight faced sunk costs, both literally and figuratively, when the *Aliakmon Runner*, a ship transporting his collection of Buddha statues and fable gods from Singapore to the Greek port of Piraeus, sank deep into the Indian Ocean on February 7, 1983. Knight's collection of antique bronze and stone Buddhas and fable gods had been obtained in Bangkok, Thailand, during the late 1970s. Over a course of several years, Knight had purchased the statuary, which, according to a Bangkok appraiser, was worth $30,307,500 in 1981. (The year before, however, the same appraiser had valued the collection at $20,205,000.)

In late 1982 Knight began careful arrangements for the shipment of his collection to a Greek buyer, George Papalios. On the basis of the Bangkok appraiser's evaluation and a letter of intent to purchase from the buyer, a group of New York insurance companies insured the shipment for $30,307,500. Thus assured of protection, Knight arranged for the collection to be shipped in January of 1983 on the ill-fated *Aliakmon Runner*.

Mr. Knight did not realize that he had not only lost his collection but also his insurance coverage until February 10, 1986, when a New York district court agreed with the underwriters of Knight's insurance policy (of $30 million) that they could rightfully cancel the policy *ab initio* (from its beginning). The reason? Mr. Knight had failed to disclose material information on his insurance application.

The material information that Knight had failed to disclose was that a previous policy covering the statuary had been cancelled. That policy had been obtained from Hogg Robinson, a London brokerage firm, in 1981 to cover a planned shipment of the statues from Singapore to a buyer in Marseilles. The policy had been for $20 million—based on the Bangkok appraiser's first valuation of the collection. After Knight had obtained the policy, however, the London underwriters received two anonymous phone calls from individuals who had a "score to settle" with Knight. These individuals told the London group that Knight was attempting to perpetrate a fraud and alleged that Knight's collection was nowhere near $20 million in value. Hogg Robinson, upon hearing this, arranged for an independent appraisal of the statues—which were in Singapore awaiting shipment. Shortly after receiving the results of their investigation, they sent a telex to Knight stating that they had voided his policy because the statues were "grossly over-valued . . . and in some, if not all cases, replicas" and that the real value of the consignment was "possibly approximately one percent of the value declared."

Knight had not disclosed this cancellation of the earlier policy in his application to the New York underwriters, who learned of the earlier policy only upon investigation of the claim after the sinking of the *Aliakmon Runner*. Knight argued that he did not consider it materially relevant to his application. The insurance companies thought it highly relevant. Unfortunately for Mr. Knight, the court agreed with the insurers.[1]

1. Knight v. United States Fire Ins. Co., 651 F.Supp. 477 (S.D.N.Y. 1986).

changed the terminology but not the result. In all states, title to land of persons who die intestate and without heirs vests in the state; the right to make a will and the ways to make one are determined by state law. To be valid, wills normally must follow statutory requirements.

Wills

A **will** is the final declaration of how a person desires to have his or her property disposed of after death, as opposed to an *inter vivos* trust (discussed later), which is created and becomes effective during one's lifetime. A will is referred to as a *testamentary disposition* of property. It is a formal instrument that must follow exactly

WILL
An instrument directing what is to be done with a person's property upon his or her death, made by that person and revocable during his or her lifetime; no interests pass until the testator dies.

the requirements of the Statute of Wills in order to be effective. The reasoning behind such a strict requirement is obvious. A will becomes effective only after death. No attempts to modify it after the death of the maker are allowed because the court cannot ask the maker to confirm the attempted modifications. (But sometimes the wording of the will must be "interpreted" by the courts.)

A will can serve other purposes besides the distribution of property. It can appoint a guardian for minor children or incapacitated adults. It can also appoint a personal representative to settle the affairs of the deceased.

Vocabulary of Wills   Every area of law has its own special vocabulary, and the area of wills is no exception. A man who makes out a will is known as a **testator,** and a woman who makes out a will is called a **testatrix.** The court responsible for administering any legal problems surrounding a will is called a **probate court.** When a person dies, a *personal representative* settles the affairs of the deceased. An **executor** or **executrix** is the personal representative named in the will; an **administrator** or **administratrix** is the personal representative appointed by the court for a decedent who dies without a will, who fails to name an executor in the will, who names an executor lacking the capacity to serve, or who writes a will that the court refuses to admit to probate. A gift of real estate by will is generally called a **devise,** and a gift of personal property by will is called a **bequest** or **legacy.**

Types of Gifts   Gifts by will can be specific, general, or residuary. A *specific* devise or bequest (legacy) describes particular property (for example, an inscribed gold watch, a specific collection of rare books, or a particular piece of real estate) that can be distinguished from all the rest of the testator's property. A *general* devise or bequest (legacy) does not single out any particular item of property to be transferred by will but usually specifies a sum of money. If the assets of an estate are insufficient to pay in full all general bequests provided for in the will, an *abatement*, by which the **legatees** receive reduced benefits, takes place. If the legatee dies prior to the death of the testator or testatrix or before the legacy is payable, a *lapsed legacy* results. At common law, the legacy failed. Today, the legacy may not lapse if the legatee is in a certain blood relationship to the testator or testatrix (such as a child, grandchild, brother, or sister) and has also left a child or other surviving descendant.

Sometimes a will provides that any assets remaining after specific gifts are made and debts are paid are to be distributed through a *residuary* clause. This is necessary when the exact amount to be distributed cannot be determined until all other gifts and payouts are made. A residuary estate can pose problems, however, when the will does not specifically name the beneficiaries to receive the residue. In such a case, if the court cannot determine the testator's intent, the remainder of the residuary passes according to state laws of intestacy. In the following case, the court had to decide how to distribute the residual assets of an estate.

TESTATOR (-TRIX)
One who makes and executes a will.

PROBATE COURT
A special court, in some jurisdictions, having jurisdiction over proceedings concerning the settlement of a person's estate.

EXECUTOR (-TRIX)
A person either expressly or by implication named by a testator to see that his or her will is administered appropriately.

ADMINISTRATOR (-TRIX)
One who is appointed by a court to handle the probate (disposition) of a person's estate if that person dies intestate (without leaving a will).

DEVISE
A gift by will of real property.

BEQUEST OR LEGACY
A gift by will of personal property

LEGATEE
A person who inherits personal property under a will.

Case 35.3
ESTATE OF CANCIK
Appellate Court of Illinois,
First District, Fifth Division, 1984.
122 Ill. App. 3d 113, 76 Ill. Dec. 659, 459 N.E. 2d 296.

FACTS   Edward Cancik, the testator, died with a net estate valued at more than $200,000. Edward had intentionally omitted the names of all his relatives from the will except his cousin Charles Cancik, to whom he specifically willed all his personal and household goods. He placed the residue of the estate in a testamentary trust for the maintenance of the Cancik family mausoleum. After Edward's death, Charles filed a complaint alleging that the value of the trust corpus vastly exceeded the amount necessary to accomplish its purpose (to maintain the

Case 35.3—Continued

mausoleum), and asked that the *residuum* be distributed to him as the testator's only heir at law. Thomas, another relative of Edward's, acting as guardian for any unknown heirs, filed a petition to have the residuum distributed to all the testator's heirs by intestacy, twelve of whom were later found to be living in Czechoslovakia. The trial court held that the residue passed to all the heirs by the laws of intestacy. The court reasoned that "the residuary bequest was against public policy and invalid because of the inexhaustible residuum that would result from the investment of the trust funds," and therefore was actually a lapsed legacy. The court further noted that the will did not effectively disinherit Cancik's other heirs or make an alternate gift to Charles. Charles appealed.

ISSUE   Should the residuum of Edward's estate go to Charles or to Edward's other heirs?

DECISION   The court held that the residuum of Edward's estate must go to his heirs rather than to Charles, who was merely the beneficiary of Edward's personal property.

REASON   The court reasoned that "the object of testamentary construction is to ascertain the intention of the testator" through the language of the will. "Although there is a presumption against intestacy, it . . . may not be used to overcome language of the will or to supply language which has been omitted." Moreover, the court will not rewrite the will for the testator. Since a testator cannot disinherit heirs by a simple declaration that they are excluded from the will, the testator must give the property specifically to someone else. Thus, the testator is presumed to know that when a testamentary gift fails for any reason, and no alternate gift is made, the property passes by intestacy to his heirs. A gift by implication will be recognized only if there is no reasonable doubt that it is necessary to effectuate the intent of the testator. Therefore, in this case, Edward's statement that he had intentionally omitted the name of the heirs from his will did "not give rise to an implication so strong as to leave no reasonable doubt that [he] intended Charles to inherit the entire excess residuum. . . ." The court found Edward's major concern to be in the care of the family mausoleum. Even though the division of property between Charles and the trust was "vastly disproportionate," the court declined to write into the will an alternate residuary bequest to Charles.

Probate versus Nonprobate   To **probate** a will means to establish its validity and to carry the administration of the estate through a court process. The process of probate is time-consuming and costly, and the court is involved in every step of the proceedings. Attorneys and personal representatives of decedents' estates often become involved in probate.

Many states have statutes that allow for the distribution of assets without probate proceedings. Faster and less expensive methods are then used. For example, property can be transferred by affidavit, and problems or questions can be handled during an administrative hearing. In addition, some state statutes provide that title to cars, savings and checking accounts, and certain other property can be passed merely by filling out forms. This is particularly true when most of the property is held in joint tenancy with right of survivorship or when there is only one heir.

Family settlement agreements.   A majority of states provide for *family settlement agreements*, which are private agreements among the beneficiaries. Once a will is admitted to probate, the family members can agree to settle among themselves the distribution of the decedent's assets. Although a family settlement agreement speeds the settlement process, a court order is still needed to protect the estate from future creditors and to clear title to the assets involved.

PROBATE
The process of proving and validating a will, and the settling of all matters pertaining to administration, guardianship, and like matters concerning the decedent's estate.

Summary procedures.   The use of summary procedures in estate administration can save time and money. The expenses of a personal representative's commission, attorneys' fees, appraisers' fees, and so forth, can be eliminated or at least minimized if the parties utilize summary administration procedures. But in some situations— for example, where a guardian for minor children or for an incompetent person must be appointed and a trust has been created to protect the minor or the incompetent person—probate procedures cannot be avoided. In the ordinary situation, a person can employ various will substitutes to avoid the cost of probate—for example, *inter vivos* trusts (discussed later), life insurance policies with named beneficiaries, or joint-tenancy arrangements. Not all methods are suitable for every estate, but there are alternatives to a complete probate administration.

Uniform Probate Code   Probate laws vary from state to state. In 1969 the American Bar Association and the National Conference of Commissioners on Uniform State Laws approved the Uniform Probate Code (UPC). The UPC codifies general principles and procedures for the resolution of conflicts in settling estates and relaxes some of the requirements for a valid will contained in earlier state laws. Fourteen states have adopted some form of the UPC. References to its provisions will be included in the remainder of this chapter where general practice in most states is consistent. Since succession and inheritance laws vary widely among different states, however, one should always check the particular laws of the state involved.[3]

Testamentary Capacity   Not everyone who owns property necessarily qualifies to make a valid disposition of that property by will. *Testamentary capacity* requires the testator to be of legal age and sound mind *at the time the will is made.* The legal age for executing a will varies, but in most states and under the UPC the minimum age is eighteen years. [UPC 2-501] Thus, a will of a twenty-one-year-old decedent written when the person was sixteen is invalid.

The concept of "being of sound mind" refers to the testator's ability to formulate and to comprehend a personal plan for the disposition of property. Further, a testator must intend the document to be his or her will.

Formal Requirements of Wills   A will must comply with statutory formalities designed to ensure that the testator or testatrix understood his or her actions at the time the will was made. These formalities are intended to help prevent fraud. Unless they are followed, the will is declared void and the decedent's property is distributed according to the laws of intestacy of that state. The requirements are not uniform among the jurisdictions. Most states, however, uphold the following basic requirements for executing a will.

1.   *A will must be in writing.* A written document is generally required, although in some cases oral wills, called *nuncupative* wills (to be discussed later), are found valid. [UPC 2-502] The writing itself can be informal as long as it substantially complies with the statutory requirements. In some states a will can be handwritten in crayon or ink. It can be written on a sheet or scrap of paper, on a paper bag, or on a piece of cloth. A will that is completely in the handwriting of the testator is called a **holographic** (or olographic) **will.**

HOLOGRAPHIC WILL
A will written entirely in the signer's handwriting and usually not witnessed.

---

3.   For example, California law differs substantially from the UPC.

first. To all my blood relatives I leave One-twelfth of my estate. —

second. To Hughes Medical Institute of Miami, Fla. I leave one-sixth of all my assets. —

Third: One-sixth of my estate to be divided among the University of Nevada and the University of California. —

fourth: one-sixth of my estate to be divided among the Universities of Texas and the University of Mexico City, Mex. —

fifth: One-twelfth of my estate to be divided among the blind and homeless children of America and to the ones with medical needs. —

sixth: One-sixth of all my assets to be divided among ten living American individuals, bearers of this social security account numbers. —

The settlement of the estate of Howard R. Hughes, Jr., a wealthy industrialist who died in April 1976, has been contested on several grounds. Pictured here is an excerpt from one of the more than forty wills that appeared after Hughes's death. In 1982, however, a Texas probate judge ruled that Hughes left no will, thereby formalizing earlier decisions by juries that the wills were forgeries.

A will also can refer to a written memorandum that itself is not a will but that contains information necessary to carry out the will. For example, Fran's will provides that a certain sum of money be divided among a group of charities named in a written memorandum that Fran gave to the trustee *the same day the will was signed.* The written list of charities will be "incorporated by reference" into the will only if it was in existence when the will was executed (signed) and if it is sufficiently described so that it can be identified.

2. *A formal (nonholographic) will must be signed by the testator.* It is a fundamental requirement in almost all jurisdictions that the testator's or testatrix's signature appear, generally at the end of the will. Each jurisdiction dictates by statute and court decision what constitutes a signature. Initials, an "X" or other mark, and words like "Mom" have all been upheld as valid when it was shown that the testator intended them to be a signature.

3. *A formal (nonholographic) will must be witnessed.* A will must be attested by two and sometimes three witnesses. The number of witnesses, their qualifications, and the manner in which the witnessing must be done are generally set out in a statute.

A witness can be required to be disinterested—that is, not a beneficiary under the will. By contrast, the UPC provides that a will is valid even if it is attested by an interested witness. [UPC 2-505] There are no age requirements for witnesses, but they must be mentally competent.

The purpose of witnesses is to verify that the testator actually executed (signed) the will and had the requisite intent and capacity at the time. A witness does not have to read the contents of the will. Usually, the testator and witnesses must all sign in the sight or the presence of one another, but the UPC deems it sufficient if the testator acknowledges his or her signature to the witnesses. [UPC 2-502] The UPC does not require all parties to sign in the presence of one another.

4. *Sometimes a will must be published.* A will is *published* by an oral declaration by the maker to the witnesses that the document they are about to sign is his or her "last will and testament." Publication is becoming an unnecessary formality in most states, and it is not required under the UPC.

In general, strict compliance with the preceding formalities (except for the one relating to witnesses and the one relating to publication) is required before a formal document is accepted as the decedent's will. Holographic wills constitute another exception in some jurisdictions. Nevertheless, holographic wills must be signed by the decedent, and their material provisions must be in the testator's handwriting in order for them to be probated. [UPC 2-503]

NUNCUPATIVE WILL
An oral (usually deathbed) will made before witnesses; limited to transfers of personal property.

Nuncupative Wills   A **nuncupative will** is an oral will made before witnesses. It is not permitted in most states. Where authorized by statute, such wills are generally valid only if made during the last illness of the testator or testatrix and are sometimes referred to as *death-bed wills*. Only personal property (not real property) can be transferred by a nuncupative will. Statutes frequently permit soldiers and sailors to make nuncupative wills when on active duty.

"A son can bear with equanimity the loss of his father, but the loss of his inheritance may drive him to despair."

Niccolo Machiavelli, 1469–1527
(Italian political theorist)

Undue Influence   A valid will is one that represents the maker's intention to transfer and distribute his or her property. When it can be shown that the decedent's plan of distribution was the result of improper pressure brought by another person, the will is declared invalid.

Undue influence may be inferred by the court if the testator or testatrix ignores blood relatives and names as beneficiary a nonrelative who is in constant close contact and in a position to influence the making of the will. For example, if a nurse or friend caring for the deceased at the time of death is named as beneficiary to the exclusion of all family members, the validity of the will might well be challenged on the basis of undue influence. One of the charges in the following case is that a sister exerted undue influence over her brother in the drafting of his will.

Case 35.4
THE MATTER OF ESTATE OF PRIGGE
Court of Appeals of Minnesota, 1984.
352 N.W.2d 443.

FACTS   John Prigge had never married and had spent his life in farming. It was undisputed that he had often needed direction, and that his mother had often balanced his checkbook and taken care of his book-work. His memory was somewhat faulty, and he required constant re-

minding as to household chores and other duties. In 1980 he sold his farm and moved in with one of his sisters, Marian. In 1981 Prigge executed a will in which he left his entire estate to Marian and her six children. He specifically excluded another sister, Jean, and a brother, Louis. When Prigge first drafted the will, he had asked Marian to help him by writing down his intentions for him. Prigge then took Marian's handwritten instructions to a lawyer, who created a will based on the contents of the document prepared by Marian.

Case 35.4—Continued

When Prigge died in 1982, Louis and Jean contested the will, charging that John Prigge lacked testamentary capacity and that Marian had exerted undue influence over her brother. The trial court ruled that the will was valid, and Jean and Louis appealed.

ISSUE   The issue was twofold: (1) Did John Prigge have testamentary capacity? (2) Did Marian exert undue influence over her brother when the will was prepared?

DECISION   Yes to the first issue, no to the second. The appellate court upheld the trial court's finding that the will was valid.

REASON   The court stated that a "testator will be found to have testamentary capacity if, when making the will, he understands the nature, situation, and extent of his property and the claims of others on his bounty or his remembrance, and he is able to hold these things in his mind long enough to form a rational judgment concerning them. Less mental capacity is required to make a will than to conduct regular business affairs." Evidence given by the lawyer who prepared the will and by others who had dealt with John Prigge attested to Prigge's testamentary capacity. As to undue influence, the court concluded that the "relationship between John and his brothers and sisters negated undue influence. Whereas Marian and her husband had helped John on many occasions for at least eight years before he sold the family farm, John had an estranged relationship with Louis and Jean and had not associated with them except on a very limited basis." Based on the relationship between John and his brother and sisters and on the fact that the attorney testified that John had been quite clear about what his holdings were and exactly how he wanted to dispose of them, the court found that no undue influence was present.

Revocation of Wills   An executed will is revocable by the maker at any time during the maker's lifetime. Wills can also be revoked by operation of law. Revocation can be partial or complete, and it must follow certain strict formalities.

Revocation of an executed will by the *act of the maker* can be effected by a physical act such as burning the will or by a writing revoking the will. The physical acts by which a testator or testatrix may revoke a will may include, in addition to intentionally burning it, intentionally tearing, canceling, obliterating, or destroying it, or having someone else do so in the presence of the maker and at the maker's direction.[4] In some states, partial revocation by physical act of the maker is recognized. Thus, those portions of a will lined out or torn away are dropped, and the remaining parts of the will are valid. In no case, however, can a provision be crossed out and an additional or substitute provision written in. Such altered portions require reexecution (resigning) and reattestation (rewitnessing). To revoke a will by physical act, it is necessary to follow the mandates of a state statute exactly. Where a state statute prescribes the exact methods for revoking a will by physical act, those are the only methods that will revoke the will.

A will may also be revoked by another writing, a **codicil,** a written instrument separate from the will that amends or revokes provisions in the will. A codicil eliminates the necessity of redrafting an entire will merely to add to it or amend it. It can also be used to revoke an entire will. The codicil must be executed with the same formalities required for a will, and it must refer expressly to the will. In effect, it updates a will because the will is "incorporated by reference" into the codicil.

A *second,* or *new will,* can be executed that may or may not revoke the first or a prior will, depending on the language used. The second will must use specific

CODICIL
A written supplement to, or modification of, a will. Codicils must be executed with the same formalities as a will.

---

4.   The destruction cannot be inadvertent. The maker's intent to revoke must be shown. Consequently, where a will has been burned or torn accidentally, it is normally recommended that the maker have a new document created so that it will not falsely appear that the maker intended to revoke the will.

language like, "This will hereby revokes all prior wills." If the second will is otherwise valid and properly executed, it will revoke all prior wills. If the express *declaration of revocation* is missing, then both wills are read together. If any of the dispositions made in the second will are inconsistent with the prior will, the second will controls. Where a state statute details the requirements for revoking a will with another writing, those requirements must be strictly complied with, as illustrated in the following case.

Case 35.5
ESTATE OF THOMPSON
Supreme Court of Nebraska, 1983.
214 Neb. 899, 336 N.W.2d 590.

FACTS Frances Thompson, the decedent, executed a will in 1964 in Nebraska. Upon her death, Victor Thompson, her husband, filed a petition for the probate of her will. John Finley, son of the decedent through a prior marriage, filed a petition seeking a formal adjudication of his deceased mother's estate by intestacy. Finley's petition claimed that his mother executed a subsequent will that revoked the 1964 document offered for probate by the husband. Finley, however, could not find the subsequent will. The probate court denied Finley's petition and admitted the 1964 will for probate. Finley appealed.

ISSUE Could the 1964 will be revoked on the basis of Finley's allegations that a second will existed?

DECISION No. The Supreme Court of Nebraska held that the testatrix did not revoke her validly executed will by writing a second will because, as far as the alleged second will was concerned, she did not adhere strictly to the state formalities of a properly executed will.

REASON In Nebraska, a person can revoke a will by writing a new one, which revokes the prior will entirely or to the extent it is inconsistent with the new will. Evidence of revocation, however, must be "clear, unequivocal, and convincing." Finley testified that he had seen a new will containing a clause revoking all prior wills. But the court looked to Nebraska law and stated: "If revocation is by a subsequent will, it must be properly executed." At trial no evidence was presented as to where the second will was executed, if the testatrix signed it, whether the required witnesses observed the formalities in affixing their signatures to the document, or what role, if any, a notary public played in the process. It was not shown clearly, convincingly, and unequivocally that the second will was properly executed. Therefore, the husband's petition for the probate of the 1964 will governed the disposition of the decedent's estate.

Revocation by *operation of law* occurs when marriage, divorce or annulment, or the birth of children takes place after a will has been executed. In the vast majority of states, when a testator marries after executing a will that does not include the new spouse, the spouse can still receive the amount the spouse would have taken had the testator died intestate. In effect, this revokes the will to the point of providing the spouse with an intestate share. The rest of the estate is passed under the will. [UPC 2-301, 2-508] If, however, the omission of a future spouse is intentional in the existing will, or the spouse is otherwise provided for in the will (or by transfer of property outside of the will), the omitted spouse will not be given an intestate amount.

At common law and under the UPC, divorce does not necessarily revoke the entire will. A divorce or an annulment occurring after a will has been executed will revoke those dispositions of property made under the will to the former spouse. [UPC 2-508]

If a child is born after a will has been executed and if it appears that the testator would have made a provision for the child, then the child is entitled to receive whatever portion of the estate he or she is allowed under state intestacy laws. Most state laws allow a child to receive some portion of the estate if no provision is made in a will, unless it appears from the terms of the will that the testator intended to disinherit the child. Under the UPC, the rule is the same. The effect is to partially revoke the parent's will. [UPC 2-302]

Property Distribution Absent a Will—Intestacy Laws   The rules of descent are governed by statutes of descent and distribution. That means each state can regulate how property shall be distributed when a person dies without a will. State laws attempt to carry out the likely intent and wishes of the decedent. These statutes are called **intestacy laws.**

The rules of descent vary widely from state to state. There is, however, usually a special statutory provision for the rights of the surviving spouse and children. In addition, the law provides that first the debts of the decedent must be satisfied out of his or her estate, and then the remaining assets can pass to the surviving spouse and to the children.

A surviving spouse usually receives a share of the estate—one-half if there is also a surviving child and one-third if there are two or more children. Only where no children or grandchildren survive the decedent will a surviving spouse succeed to the entire estate. The UPC is more generous to the surviving spouse than most state statutes. [UPC 2-102]

Assume that Allen dies intestate and is survived by his wife, Della, and his children, Duane and Tara. Allen's property passes according to intestacy laws. After Allen's outstanding debts are paid, Della will receive the homestead (either in fee simple or as a life estate) and ordinarily a one-third to one-half interest in all other property. The remaining real and personal property will pass to Duane and Tara in equal portions.

State statutes of descent and distribution specify the order in which heirs of an intestate share in the estate. When there is no surviving spouse or child, then grandchildren, brothers and sisters, and, in some states, parents of the decedent are the next in line to share. These relatives are usually called *lineal descendants*. If there are no lineal descendants, then *collateral heirs*—nieces, nephews, aunts, and uncles of the decedent—are the next group to share.

If there are no survivors in any of those groups of people related to the decedent, most statutes provide that the property shall be distributed among the next of kin of any of the collateral heirs. Stepchildren are not considered kin. Legally adopted children, however, are recognized as lawfuls heirs of their adoptive parents. The degree to which illegitimate children are permitted to inherit is the topic of this chapter's "Landmark."

Because state statutes differ so widely, few generalizations can be made about the laws of descent and distribution. It is extremely important to refer to the exact terms of the applicable state statutes when addressing any problem of intestacy distribution.

The UPC provides that a surviving spouse, in addition to taking an elective share of one-third of the decedent's estate, is entitled to the following:

1. A homestead allowance of $5,000.
2. A household and personal effects exemption to a value not to exceed $3,500.
3. A family allowance for a period of up to one year after the death occurs to provide for daily expenses before the estate is settled, up to the amount of $6,000. [UPC 2-401, 402, 403, and 404]

INTESTACY LAWS
State laws determining the division and descent of the estate of an intestate (one who dies without a valid will).

Landmark in the Law

Trimble v. *Gordon* (1977)

In the ancient world, illegitimacy was often dealt with expeditiously by simply destroying the mother of the future illegitimate child. In biblical days, an adulteress was stoned to death—unless, as in the case of David and Bathsheba, a marriage could be arranged. In Bathsheba's case, David saved her life at the expense of her husband, Uriah, whom David arranged to have killed in battle so he could then marry Bathsheba. Under Islamic law, stoning was also the proper punishment for adultery. In the Christian world, illegitimate children and their mothers were always allowed to live, even though they were usually regarded as outcasts and pariahs until fairly recently.[1]

At common law, the illegitimate child was regarded as a *filius nullius* (Latin for "child of no one") and had no right to inherit. Today, statutes vary from state to state in regard to the inheritance laws regarding illegitimate offspring. Generally, an illegitimate child is treated as the child of the mother and can inherit from her and her relatives. The child is usually not regarded as the legal child of the father unless paternity is established through some legal proceeding. Many state statutes permit the illegitimate child to inherit from the father, however, if paternity has been established prior to the father's death.

A landmark case in establishing the rights of illegitimate children was decided by the U. S. Supreme Court in 1977. In *Trimble* v. *Gordon*[2] an illegitimate child sought to inherit property from her deceased natural father on the grounds that an Illinois statute prohibiting inheritance by illegitimate children in the absence of a will was unconstitutional. The child was Deta Mona Trimble, daughter of Jessie Trimble and Sherman Gordon. The paternity of the father had been established before a Cook County,

1. Jenny Teichman, *Illegitimacy: A Philosophical Examination* (Oxford: Blackwell, 1982), pp. 53–55.
2. 430 U.S. 762, 97 S.Ct. 1459, 52 L.Ed.2d 31 (1977).

Illinois, circuit court in 1973. Gordon died intestate in 1974. The mother filed a petition on behalf of the child in the probate division of the county circuit court, which was denied by the court on the basis of an Illinois law disallowing the child's inheritance because she was illegitimate. Had she been legitimate, she would have been her father's sole heir. The Illinois Supreme Court in 1975 affirmed the petition's dismissal.

When the case came before the Supreme Court of the United States in 1977, the Court acknowledged that the "judicial task here is the difficult one of vindicating constitutional rights without interfering unduly with the State's primary responsibility in this area. . . . and the need for the States to draw 'arbitrary lines . . . to facilitate potentially difficult problems of proof.'" The Court found it hard to perceive any justification for the Illinois statute, nor for the lower court's insistence that the father could have avoided the problem had he just made a will. In reversing the Illinois Supreme Court decision, the high court stated that the section of the Illinois Probate Act that forbade Deta Mona to inherit her father's property "cannot be squared with the command of the Equal Protection Clause of the Fourteenth Amendment." Even though the Illinois statute rested to some extent on public policy supporting the family unit, the Court "expressly considered and rejected the argument that a State may attempt to influence the actions of men and women by imposing sanctions on the children born of their illegitimate relationships."

By declaring the Illinois statute unconstitutional, the Court thereby invalidated similar laws of several other states. That does not mean that all illegitimate children will have inheritance rights identical to those of all legitimate children. Those state statutes that discriminate between the two classes of individuals for a legitimate state purpose have been thus far allowed to stand, in the interests of the need of each state to create an appropriate legal framework for the legal disposition of property at death.

PER STIRPES
A method of distribution of property whereby the heirs to an intestate's estate take the share to which their deceased ancestor would have been entitled.

When an intestate is survived by descendants of deceased children, a question arises as to what share the descendants (that is, grandchildren of the intestate) will receive. **Per stirpes** is a method of dividing an intestate share where a class or group of distributees (for example, grandchildren) take the share that their deceased parent *would have been* entitled to inherit had that child lived.

Assume that Michael, a widower, has three children, Scott, Jonathan, and David. Scott has two children (Becky and Holly), Jonathan has one child (Paul), and David has one child (Beth). At the time of Michael's death, Scott and Jonathan have predeceased their father. If Michael's estate is distributed per stirpes, the following distribution would take place:

1. Becky and Holly: one-sixth each, taking Scott's share.
2. Paul: one-third, taking Jonathan's share.
3. David: one-third, as the surviving child (Beth does not inherit).

Another type of distribution of an estate is on a **per capita** basis. This means that each person takes an equal share of the estate. Assume that Michael, a widower, has two children, Scott and Jonathan. Scott has two children (Becky and Holly), and Jonathan has one child (Paul). At the time of Michael's death, Scott and Jonathan have predeceased their father. If Michael's estate is distributed per capita, Becky, Holly, and Paul will each receive a one-third share.

In most states and under the Uniform Probate Code, in-laws do not share in an estate. If a child dies before his or her parents, the child's spouse will not receive an inheritance. Assume that Michael, a widower, has two married children, Scott and Jonathan, and no grandchildren. If Scott predeceases his father, Michael's entire estate will go to Jonathan. Scott's surviving wife will not inherit.

PER CAPITA
A method of distribution of property whereby the heirs to an intestate's estate inherit equal portions of the estate.

Trusts

A **trust** involves any arrangement whereby property is transferred from one person to a trustee to be administered for the first person's or another party's benefit. It can also be defined as a right or property, real or personal, held by one party for the benefit of another. A trust can be created for any purpose that is not illegal or against public policy. Its essential elements are:

1. A designated beneficiary.
2. A designated trustee.
3. A fund sufficiently identified to enable title to pass to the trustee.
4. Actual delivery by the settlor or grantor to the trustee with the intention of passing title.

If James conveys his farm to the First Bank of Minnesota to be held for the benefit of his daughters, he has created a trust. James is the settlor, First Bank of Minnesota is the trustee, and James's daughters are the beneficiaries.

TRUST
A legal entity in which a trustee holds title to property for the benefit of another.

Express Trusts An *express trust* is one created or declared in expressed terms, usually in writing. It differs from one that is inferred by the law from the conduct or dealings of the parties (an *implied trust*, to be discussed later). The two types of express trusts that will be discussed here are *inter vivos* trusts and testamentary trusts.

An **inter vivos** trust is a trust executed by a grantor during his or her lifetime. The grantor executes a *trust deed*, and legal title to the trust property passes to the named trustee. The trustee has a duty to administer the property as directed by the grantor for the benefit and in the interest of the beneficiaries. The trustee must

INTER VIVOS TRUST
A trust created and effected by the grantor (settlor) during the grantor's lifetime (that is, a trust not established by a will).

preserve the trust property, make it productive, and, if required by the terms of the trust agreement, pay income to the beneficiaries, all in accordance with the terms of the trust. Once the *inter vivos* trust is created, the grantor has, in effect, given over the property for the benefit of beneficiaries. Often, tax-related benefits exist in setting up this type of trust.

A **testamentary trust** is a trust created by a will to come into existence upon the settlor's death. Although a testamentary trust has a trustee who maintains legal title to the trust property, actions of the trustee are subject to judicial approval. This trustee can be named in the will or be appointed by the court. Unlike an *inter vivos* trust, a testamentary trust does not fail because a trustee has not been named in the will. The legal responsibilities of the trustees are the same in both kinds of trusts, however. If the will setting up a testamentary trust is invalid, then the trust will also be invalid. The property that was supposed to be in the trust will then pass according to intestacy laws, not according to the terms of the trust.

Implied Trusts   Sometimes a trust will be imposed by law, even in the absence of an express trust. Customarily, these *implied trusts* are divided into constructive and resulting trusts.

A **constructive trust** differs from an express trust in that it arises by operation of law. Whenever a transaction takes place in which the person who takes the legal estate in property cannot also enjoy the beneficial interest without violating some established principle of equity, the court will create a constructive trust. In effect, the legal owner becomes a trustee for the parties who, in equity, are actually entitled to the beneficial enjoyment that flows from the trust. One element of a constructive trust is a wrongful action, whether it be active or constructive.

To illustrate: Kraft and Lattimore are partners in buying, developing, and selling real estate. Kraft learns through the staff of the partnership that a piece of land will soon come on the market that the staff will recommend that the partnership purchase. Kraft purchases the property secretly in his own name, violating his fiduciary relationship. When these facts are discovered, a court will determine that Kraft must hold the property in trust for the partnership.

A **resulting trust** arises from the conduct of the parties. Here the trust results from, or is created by, the *apparent intention* of the parties. Since the trust is created by law, the conduct of the parties evidencing the intent to create a trust relationship is carefully scrutinized.

To illustrate: Garrison purchases one acre of land from Villard. Because Garrison is going out of the country for a period of two years and will be unable to attend the closing, she asks Villard, at the closing, to deed the property to her (Garrison's) good friend, Oswald. Villard does indeed convey the property to Oswald. Since the intent of the transaction is not to make a gift of the land to Oswald, the property will be held in trust (a resulting trust) with Oswald as the trustee for the benefit of Garrison.

Other Kinds of Trusts   Certain trusts are created for special purposes. Three such trusts that warrant discussion are charitable, spendthrift, and totten trusts. A trust designed for the benefit of a segment of the public or of the public in general is a **charitable trust.** It differs from a private trust in that the identities of the beneficiaries are uncertain. Usually, to be deemed a charitable trust, a trust must be created for charitable, educational, religious, or scientific purposes.

A trust created to provide for the maintenance of a beneficiary by preventing his or her improvidence with the bestowed funds is a **spendthrift trust.** Essentially, the

TESTAMENTARY TRUST
A trust that is created by will and therefore does not take effect until the death of the testator or testatrix.

CONSTRUCTIVE TRUST
A trust created by operation of law against one who wrongfully has obtained or holds legal right to property that he or she should not, in equity and good conscience, hold and enjoy.

RESULTING TRUST
A trust implied in law from the intentions of the parties to a given transaction. In this trust, a party holds legal title for the benefit of another, although without expressed intent to do so, because the presumption of such intent arises by operation of law.

CHARITABLE TRUST
A trust in which property held by a trustee must be used for charitable purposes (such as advancement of health or religion).

SPENDTHRIFT TRUST
A trust created to protect the beneficiary from spending all the money to which he or she is entitled. Only a certain portion of the total amount is given to the beneficiary at any one time, and most states prohibit creditors from attaching assets of the trust.

beneficiary is permitted to draw only a certain portion of the total amount to which he or she is entitled at any one time. The majority of states allow spendthrift trust provisions that prohibit creditors from attaching such trusts.

A special type of trust created when one person deposits money in his or her own name as a trustee for another is a **totten trust.** This trust is tentative in that it is revocable at will until the depositor dies or completes the gift in his or her lifetime by some unequivocal act or declaration (for example, delivery of the funds to the intended beneficiary). If the depositor should die before the beneficiary dies and if the depositor has not revoked the trust expressly or impliedly, a presumption arises that an absolute trust has been created for the benefit of the beneficiary. At the death of the depositor, the beneficiary obtains property rights to the balance on hand.

TOTTEN TRUST
A trust created by the deposit of a person's own money in his or her own name as a trustee for another. This is a tentative trust, revocable at will until the depositor dies or completes the gift in his or her lifetime by some unequivocal act or declaration.

Application

Law and the Partner—The Insurance of Partners and Close Corporation Shareholders

Life insurance on the lives of partners or shareholders may be a valuable tool for you as a participant in a partnership or a closely held corporation should one partner or co-shareholder die. Typically, the others will want to buy that partner's interest, particularly if they wish to continue in the business, and the partnership or corporation may wish to purchase life insurance on each partner or co-shareholder to help fund the buy-out. Problems arise, however, when the partners or co-shareholders are not all the same age or do not all have the same financial interest in the partnership or corporation. How does one arrange an insurance and buy-out agreement so as to be fair to everyone?

First, you must determine the current value of the business and then provide a method for determining the value of the business when one of the owners dies. There are numerous ways to accomplish such a valuation. The important point is that all partners agree on the method to be used. Each must be satisfied that if he or she were the first to die, the valuation method would provide a fair and equitable way to buy that interest from the estate.

Next, you must determine how much life insurance to purchase. Insurance can be used to fund the entire amount of the purchase price of the deceased's share or it can be used to purchase just a part of that purchase price. Because the premiums for some of the owners may cost more (due to more advanced age or poorer health), an agreement may be reached to buy less insurance for them in order to reduce the current cost of the life in-

surance policy. The remaining part of the buy-out purchase price will presumably be made in installments that draw current interest rates.

Owners can negotiate a variety of payment plans to fit each partner's or co-shareholder's individual needs in the event a buy-out becomes necessary. For example, for an older partner, the payments may be spread over only a few years, and for younger partners, over a longer period of time. All these points are negotiable. It should be possible to draft an agreement that provides for insurance and/or a buy-out purchase plan that protects the interest of each person.

Checklist for Partners and Close Shareholders

- ☐ 1. If anyone in your partnership or closely held corporation can be considered a "key" person, then you should buy *key-person life insurance* on that individual.

- ☐ 2. Estimate the amount of loss that the partnership or closely held corporation would suffer if a key person should die or become incapacitated. Insure for only that amount (the partnership or close corporation should not benefit from a partner or shareholder's death, but rather "be left in an equal financial position compared to prior to the death").

- ☐ 3. Establish a buy-out purchase plan for the partnership or close corporation members in the case of one key person's death.

❖ Chapter Summary: Insurance, Wills, and Trusts

INSURANCE	
Terminology	1. *Policy*—The insurance contract. 2. *Premium*—The consideration paid to the insurer for a policy. 3. *Underwriter*—The insurance company. 4. *Parties*—Include the insurer (the insurance company), the insured (the person covered by insurance), an agent (representative of the insurance company), or a broker (ordinarily an independent contractor). 5. *Insurable interest*—Exists whenever an individual or entity benefits from the preservation of the health or life of the insured, or the property to be insured.
The Insurance Contract	1. *Laws governing*—The general principles of contract law are applied. 2. *When coverage begins*—Coverage on an insurance policy can begin when a *binder* (a written memorandum indicating a policy is pending and stating its essential terms) is written, when the policy is issued, or, depending on the terms of the contract, when a certain period of time has elapsed. 3. *Defenses against payment to the insured*—Misrepresentation, fraud, or violation of warranties by applicant.

WILLS	
Laws Governing Wills	1. *State statutes* (probate laws)—Vary from state to state. 2. *Uniform Probate Code (UPC)*—Codifies general principles and procedures concerning wills and probate; adopted in some form by fourteen states.
Types of Wills	1. *Holographic*—A will completely in the handwriting of the testator; valid where permitted by state statute. 2. *Attested*—A written will, signed by the testator, properly witnessed, and, where required, published; one that meets formal statutory requirements for a valid will. 3. *Nuncupative*—An oral will made before witnesses during the death-bed illness of the testator; it is valid only to transfer personal property, not real property.
Formal Requirements of a Will	1. A will must be in writing (except for nuncupative wills). 2. A nonholographic will must be signed by the testator; what constitutes a signature varies from jurisdiction to jurisdiction. 3. A nonholographic will must be witnessed in the manner prescribed by state statute. 4. A will may be required to be *published*—i.e., the testator may be required to announce to witnesses that this is his or her "last will and testament." Not required under the UPC.

Methods of Revoking or Modifying a Will	1. *By acts of the maker:*
	  a. Physical act—Tearing up, canceling, obliterating, or deliberately destroying part or all of a will.
	  b. Codicil—A formal separate document to amend or revoke an existing will.
	  c. Second, or new will—A new, properly executed will, expressly revoking the existing will.
	
	2. *By operation of law:*
	  a. Marriage—Generally revokes a will written before the marriage.
	  b. Divorce or annulment—Revokes dispositions made under a will to a former spouse.
	  c. Subsequently born child—It is *implied* that the child is entitled to receive the portion of the estate granted under intestacy distribution laws.

❖ Chapter Summary: Insurance, Wills, and Trusts—Continued

Gifts by Will	1. *Specific*—A devise or bequest of a particular piece of property in the testator's estate.
	2. *General*—A devise or bequest that does not single out a particular item in the testator's estate, usually a sum of money.
	3. *Residuary*—A devise or bequest of any properties left in the estate after all specific and general gifts have been made.
Intestacy Laws (Statutes of Descent and Distribution)	1. Vary widely from state to state. Usually, the law provides that the surviving spouse and children inherit the property of the decedent (after the decedent's debts are paid). The spouse usually will inherit the entire estate if there are no children, one-half of the estate if there is one child, and one-third of the estate if there are two or more children.
	2. If there is no surviving spouse or child, then lineal descendants (grandchildren, brothers and sisters, and—in some states—parents of the decedent) inherit. If there are no lineal descendants, then collateral heirs (nieces, nephews, aunts, and uncles of the decedent) inherit.
TRUSTS	
Definition	Any arrangement whereby property is transferred from one person to be administered by a trustee for a third party's benefit. The essential elements of a trust are (1) a designated beneficiary, (2) a designated trustee, (3) a fund sufficiently identified to enable title to pass to the trustee, and (4) actual delivery to the trustee with the intention of passing title.
Types of Trusts	1. *Express trusts*—Created by expressed terms, usually in writing. a. *Inter vivos* trust—A trust executed by a grantor during his or her lifetime. b. Testamentary trust—A trust created by will and coming into existence upon the death of the grantor.
	2. *Implied trusts*—Trusts imposed by law. a. Constructive trust—Arises by operation of law whenever a transaction takes place whereby the person who takes title to or possession of the property is in equity not entitled to enjoy the beneficial interest therein. b. Resulting trust—Arises from the conduct of the parties where an *apparent intention* to create a trust is present.
	3. *Other kinds of trusts:* a. Charitable trust—A trust designed for the benefit of a public group or the public in general. b. Spendthrift trust—A trust created to provide for the maintenance of a beneficiary by allowing only a certain portion of the total amount to be received by the beneficiary at any one time. c. Totten trust—A special type of trust created when one person deposits money in his or her own name as a trustee for another.

❖ Questions and Case Problems

35-1. On October 10, Bonnie Lang applied for a $50,000 life insurance policy with Magnum Life Insurance Company, naming her husband, William, as the beneficiary. Bonnie paid the insurance company the first year's policy premium upon making the application. Two days later, before she had a chance to take the physical examination required by the insurance company and before the policy was issued, Bonnie was killed in an automobile accident. William submitted a claim to the insurance company for the $50,000. Can William collect? Explain.

35-2. Merlin Winters had three sons. Winters and his youngest son, Abraham, had a falling out in 1984 and had not spoken to each other since. Winters made a formal will in 1986, leaving all his property to the two older children and deliberately excluding Abraham. Winters's health began to deteriorate, and by 1987 he was under the full-time care of a nurse, Julia. In 1988 he made a new will expressly revoking the 1986 will and leaving all his property to Julia. Upon Winters's death, the two older children contested the 1988 will, claiming that Julia had exercised undue influence over their father. Abraham claimed that both wills were invalid, because the first one had been revoked by the second will, and the second will was invalid on the grounds of undue influence. Is Abraham's contention correct? Explain.

35-3. Gary Mendel drew up a will in which he left his favorite car, a 1966 red Ferrari, to his daughter, Roberta. A year prior to his death, Mendel sold the 1966 Ferrari and purchased a 1969 Ferrari. Discuss whether Roberta will inherit the 1969 Ferrari under the terms of her father's will.

35-4. Benjamin is a widower who has two married children, Edward and Patricia. Patricia has two children, Perry and Paul. Edward has no children. Benjamin dies, leaving a typewritten will that leaves all his property equally to his children, Edward and Patricia, and provides that should a child predecease him, the grandchildren are to take per stirpes. The will was witnessed by Patricia and Benjamin's lawyer and was signed by Benjamin in their presence. Patricia has predeceased Benjamin. Edward claims the will is invalid.

    (a) Discuss whether the will is valid.

    (b) Discuss the distribution of Benjamin's estate if the will is invalid.

    (c) Discuss the distribution of Benjamin's estate if the will is valid.

35-5. Bill was a bachelor. While single, he made out a will naming his mother, Carrie as the sole beneficiary. Later Bill married Emily. Discuss the results of each of the following possible events:

    (a) If Bill died while married to Emily without changing his will, would the estate go to his mother, Carrie? Explain.

    (b) Assume Bill made out a new will upon his marriage to Emily, leaving his entire estate to Emily. Later, he divorces Emily and marries Helen, but he does not change his will. Discuss the rights of Emily and Helen to his estate when he dies.

    (c) Assume Bill divorces Emily, marries Helen, and changes his will leaving his estate to Helen. Later a daughter, Margaret, is born. Bill dies without having included Margaret in his will. Discuss fully whether Margaret has any rights in the estate.

35-6. Claude and Mildred owned their home in Lexington and had a fire insurance policy on the home. Claude and Mildred contracted with Benjamin to build a new home for them in exchange for cash and transfer of their present home. After conveying the home to Benjamin, Claude and Mildred continued living there and paid both rent and the insurance premium. The fire insurance policy was never assigned to Benjamin. While Claude and Mildred were still living in their old home, a fire occurred. The insurance company would not pay because they claimed Claude and Mildred had no insurable interest in the property at the time of the loss. Discuss fully how the court ruled. [O'Donnell v. MFA Insurance Company, 671 S.W.2d 302 (Mo.App. 1984)]

35-7. Robert M. Daly prepared his own will, without re-ceiving advice from his attorney, on December 29, 1976. Although Daly was married and had three children, by will he left his entire estate, valued at approximately $176,000, to friends of his. Daly had two of his employees sign the will as witnesses. One of the witnesses later testified that he was not told what he was signing, that Daly did not sign the will in his presence, and that Daly did not acknowledge that the signature on the will was his own or that he had even signed the document. Because of the way the paper was folded when the witness signed it, the witness could not see whether Daly had signed it. The second witness was not sure if Daly's signature was on the document, but the witness was sure that Daly had not acknowledged any signature to the witness. Under these circumstances, was Daly's will valid? Explain. [Matter of Estate of Daly, 93 Misc.2d 241, 402 N.Y.S.2d 747 (N.Y. Surrogate Court 1978)]

35-8. Tennie Joyner was eighty years old and about to be hospitalized for an illness. In order to provide for her son, Calvin, Joyner wrote a will and took it to her neighbors for them to type and witness. In the document, she stated that she was giving all her possessions to Calvin because he had taken care of her for years. The will was contested on the basis that Joyner had not met the formal requirement of publication, since she did not tell her neighbors explicitly that the document was her "last will and testament." Joyner had merely told her neighbors that she wanted "a piece of paper fixed up so I can sign it and Calvin will have a place to live." Joyner intended the document to dispose of her property, and the neighbors were fully aware of her intention. Does Joyner's failure to state "this is my last will and testament" invalidate the will? Explain. [Faith v. Singleton, 286 Ark. 403, 692 S.W.2d 239 (1985)]

35-9. In 1925 Campbell died, leaving a will in which the ninth clause read as follows: "My good friends Clark and Smith I appoint as my trustees. Each of my trustees is competent by reason of familiarity with the property, my wishes and friend-ships, to wisely distribute some portion at least of said property. I therefore give and bequeath to my trustees all my property in trust to make disposal by the way of a memento from myself, of such articles to such of my friends as they, my trustees, shall select. All of said property, not so disposed of by them, my trustees are directed to sell and the proceeds of such sale or sales to become and be disposed of as a part of the residue of my estate." Was this a valid trust? Explain. [Clark v. Campbell, 82 N.H. 281, 133 A. 166 (1926)]

35-10. An elderly, childless widow had nine nieces and neph-ews. She devised her entire estate to be divided equally among two nieces and the husband of one of the nieces, who was also the attorney-draftsman of the will and the executor named in the will. The testatrix was definitely of sound mind when the will was executed. If you were one of the seven nieces or nephews omitted from the will, could you think of any way to have the will invalidated? [Estate of Eckert, 93 Misc.2d 677, 403 N.Y.S.2d 633 (1978)]

Chapter 36

International Law
in a Global Economy

INTERNATIONAL LAW
The law that governs relations between nations. International customs and treaties are generally considered to be two of the most important sources of international law.

Since World War II, business has become increasingly multinational in character. It is not uncommon, for example, for a U.S. corporation to have investments or manufacturing plants in a foreign country, or for a foreign corporation to have operations within the United States. Because the exchange of goods, services, and ideas on a global level is now a common phenomenon, it is important for the student of business law to be familiar with the laws pertaining to international business transactions.

International law is a body of laws observed by otherwise independent nations. It governs the acts of individuals as well as states. Although no sovereign nation can be compelled to obey a law external to itself, nations can and do voluntarily agree to be governed in certain respects by international law for the purpose of facilitating international trade and commerce and civilized discourse. In general, nations attempt to balance their need to have sovereign control over their own affairs and those of their citizens against their interest in maintaining harmonious relationships with other countries. This is not always easy. As the opening quotation by William Coplin illustrates, the fact that international law has traditionally recognized the absolute sovereignty of each nation over affairs within its territorial boundaries can pose difficulties for those wishing to engage in international business transactions.

In this chapter we first examine some of the sources of international law and then some legal principles and doctrines guiding judicial settlement of disputes where a foreign element is involved. We next look at some selected areas relating to business activities in a global context and at the application of U.S. antitrust laws in a transnational setting.

❖ Sources of International Law

One important source of international law consists of international customs that have evolved among nations in their relations with one another. Under Article 38(1) of the Statute of the International Court of Justice, international custom is referred to as "evidence of a general practice accepted as law." Even though customary law serves as an independent form of law, it is subject to challenges upon various applications. When, for example, does a particular custom evolve into a general practice

Many international disputes are settled at the International Court of Justice at The Hague.

constituting a law? Conversely, when does a custom traditionally accepted as law become so outdated or impractical in a modern context that it should no longer be considered law? Just as customs within a nation change, often necessitating changes in that nation's laws, so do customs among nations change, thus affecting international law.

Treaties between or among foreign nations provide another source of international law. A *treaty* is an agreement or contract between two or more nations that must be authorized and ratified by the supreme power of each nation. Under Article II, Section 2, of the U.S. Constitution, the president has the power "by and with the consent of the Senate, to make treaties, provided two-thirds of the Senators present concur."

International organizations and conferences further contribute to what is known as international law. These organizations adopt resolutions, declarations, and other types of standards that often require a particular behavior of nations. The General Assembly of the United Nations, for example, has adopted numerous resolutions and declarations that embody principles of international law. Disputes with respect to these resolutions and declarations may be brought before the United Nations International Court of Justice. In general, however, the Court has jurisdiction to settle legal disputes only when nations voluntarily submit to its jurisdiction. In the past decade, a significant step has been made toward establishing more uniformity in international law relating to trade and commerce by the United Nations Commission on International Trade Law (UNCITRAL); this organization is the topic of this chapter's "Landmark."

❖ Conflicts between National and International Law

National law, or **municipal law,** is law that pertains to a particular nation. Because the legal system of each country reflects its own unique cultural, historical, economic,

MUNICIPAL LAW
Laws that pertain to a particular nation (national law), as opposed to international law.

and political background, the laws of each nation differ. Consequently, it is not uncommon for a country's municipal law to come into conflict with international law. Two important principles that have guided the settlement of such conflicts are the *act of state doctrine* and the *principle of comity*.

Act of State Doctrine

ACT OF STATE DOCTRINE
A judicially created doctrine that provides that the judicial branch of one country will not examine the validity of public acts committed by a recognized foreign government within its own territory.

The **act of state doctrine** is a judicially created doctrine that provides that the judicial branch of one country will not examine the validity of public acts committed by a recognized foreign government within its own territory. As indicated by the court in *Libra Bank Ltd.* v. *Banco Nacional de Costa Rica, S.A.*, this doctrine is premised on the theory that the judicial branch should not "pass upon the validity of foreign acts when to do so would vex the harmony of our international relations with that foreign nation." [1]

EXPROPRIATION
The seizure by a government of privately owned business or personal property for a proper public purpose and with just compensation.

The act of state doctrine is usually employed in cases of **expropriation,** wherein a government seizes a privately owned business or privately owned goods for a proper public purpose and awards just compensation. A **confiscation,** in contrast, occurs when there is a taking without a proper public purpose or an award of just compensation.

CONFISCATION
Taking privately owned business or personal property without proper public purpose or an award of just compensation.

Principle of Comity

COMITY
A deference by which one nation gives effect to the laws and judicial decrees of another nation. This recognition is based primarily upon respect.

When municipal and international law conflict, the principle of **comity** may also arise—a deference by which one nation gives effect to the laws and judicial decrees of another nation. This recognition is based primarily upon respect.

In the recent case of *Allied Bank International* v. *Banco Credito Agricola de Cartago*, the Second Circuit concluded that the act of state doctrine was inapplicable to a dispute between a syndicate of thirty-nine creditor banks and three Costa Rican banks. [2] The court found that the acts of the Costa Rican government had an *extraterritorial effect*—meaning one that exists beyond the country's borders—and hence fell outside the scope and protection of this doctrine. Comity principles were then applied.

In applying the principle of comity, the Second Circuit concluded that the acts of foreign governments having an extraterritorial effect should be recognized by courts only when they are consistent with the laws and policy of the United States. Since the Costa Rican government attempted to repudiate private, commercial obligations, the court held that such repudiation was inconsistent with the law and policy of the United States. Even though the Costa Rican government was experiencing international debt problems, the court recognized the fact that the U.S. government has procedures for resolving these types of difficulties.

❖ Doctrine of Sovereign Immunity

SOVEREIGN IMMUNITY
A doctrine that, when certain conditions are satisfied, immunizes foreign nations from the jurisdiction of U.S. courts; codified in the Foreign Sovereign Immunities Act of 1976.

When certain conditions are satisfied, the doctrine of **sovereign immunity** immunizes foreign nations from the jurisdiction of the United States. In 1976 Congress codified

---

1.   570 F.Supp. 870, 883 (S.D.N.Y. 1983).
2.   757 F.2d 516 (2d Cir. 1985).

Landmark in the Law

UNCITRAL

In 1966 the United Nations Commission on International Trade Law (UNCITRAL) had its initial meeting for the purpose of promoting "the progressive harmonization and unification of the law of international trade." [1] The function of UNCITRAL on the international level is similar to that of the National Conference of Commissioners on Uniform State Laws on the national level in the United States. UNCITRAL's purpose is also to draft and promulgate "model" laws establishing uniformity in the legal relations of trading partners. The scope of the UNCITRAL's task, however, cannot be compared to that of the National Conference, because of the innumerable difficulties that are necessarily involved when trying to obtain consensus among nations. The achievement of UNCITRAL to date, within the span of little more than two decades, is indeed impressive when you recall the length of time it took to draft the Uniform Commercial Code and secure its adoption by the states. And the differences among the states in the United States, while significant, cannot compare to the differences among the member countries of UNCITRAL.

UNCITRAL is composed of government and university representatives from thirty-six countries. Its size is limited to thirty-six members in order to allow effective decision making. Despite its small size, all regions of the world are represented by the commission. Africa has nine representatives; Asia, seven; Eastern Europe, five; Latin America, six; and Western Europe, Australia, and North America have nine representatives. This allocation of seats on the commission has led to a rough equivalence between developing countries and industrialized states. Because seats are allocated on the basis of region instead of country, and because countries within a region compete to obtain and retain membership on the commission, the result has been that the most influential countries of each region

1. General Assembly Resolution 2205 (XXI) of December 17, 1966, 1 *Yearbook* 65.

are represented on the commission. This, in turn, has made commission decisions very influential.

The representatives to the commission meet two to six weeks a year. All issues and proposals are extensively debated, and compromise is always the goal. In spite of the differing legal and economic histories of its members, the commission has been successful in promulgating model laws in the areas of international sales, shipping, arbitration, and negotiable instruments. In 1978 the commission unanimously approved the text of the Draft Convention on Contracts for the International Sale of Goods. The United Nations as a whole adopted the draft in 1980. The draft is similar in scope to Article 2 of the Uniform Commercial Code, as it governs contract formation and the obligations of the parties to a contract. The commission also drafted and submitted to the United Nations a Convention on the Carriage of Goods by Sea, which concerns the transportation of goods between countries over the oceans and seas. The commission's proposal provides rules governing such issues as liability for lost or damaged goods, delays in shipment, and the conveyance of bills of lading. In 1977 UNCITRAL began work on a Uniform Law on International Bills of Exchange and International Promissory Notes to help in the prevention and settlement of controversies arising among nations in this complex aspect of international trade.

Finally, UNCITRAL has provided rules governing arbitration of contract disputes among international trading parties. Those involved in international business transactions, if they include in their contract an agreement to apply UNCITRAL's arbitration rules, need not worry about uncertainty as to which laws govern a potential contractual dispute.

The model laws created by UNCITRAL are not binding unless they are specifically adopted by the nations. But because most of the commission-promulgated laws were drafted and adopted by the most influential countries in the world, the commission's conventions have assumed as much importance in international trade as the Uniform Commercial Code has in commercial transactions in the United States.

the law of sovereign immunity in the Foreign Sovereign Immunities Act (FSIA). The FSIA also modified the law of sovereign immunity in certain respects by expanding the rights that plaintiff creditors have against foreign nations.

Foreign Sovereign Immunities Act (FSIA)

The FSIA exclusively governs the circumstances in which an action may be brought in the United States against a foreign nation. Attachment of a foreign nation's property is also covered by this act. One of the primary purposes of the FSIA was to have federal courts, rather than the Department of State, determine claims of foreign sovereign immunity. It was thought that a determination of such an immunity by the courts would increase the degree of certainty in the law of sovereign immunity.

Section 1605 of the FSIA

Section 1605 of the FSIA sets forth the major exceptions to the jurisdictional immunity of a foreign state (country). A foreign state is not immune from the jurisdiction of the courts of the United States when the state has "waived its immunity either explicitly or by implication" or when the action is "based upon a commercial activity carried on in the United States by the foreign state." [3]

Issues frequently arise as to the entities that fall within the category of *foreign state*. The question of what is a *commercial activity* has also been the subject of dispute. Under Section 1603 of the FSIA, a *foreign state* is defined to include both a political subdivision of a foreign state and an instrumentality of a foreign state. A *commercial activity* is defined under Section 1603 to mean a commercial activity that is carried on by the foreign state having substantial contact with the United States. In the following case, the court had to determine whether the defense of sovereign immunity was available under the FSIA.

Case 36.1
CHISHOLM & CO. v. BANK OF JAMAICA

United States District Court, Southern District of Florida, 1986.
643 F.Supp. 1393.

FACTS   The Bank of Jamaica, which is wholly owned by the government of Jamaica, contracted with Chisholm & Company in January of 1981 for Chisholm to arrange for lines of credit from various U.S. banks and obtain $50 million in credit insurance from the Export-Import Bank of the United States. This Chisholm successfully did, but subsequently the deals arranged for by Chisholm were refused by the Bank of Jamaica. The bank had decided to do its own negotiating while still having Chisholm work as well. When the bank refused to pay Chisholm for its services, Chisholm brought this action to obtain relief for the bank's breach of the implied contract. The Bank of Jamaica brought a motion to dismiss, claiming sovereign immunity and state action (act of state doctrine) as defenses.

ISSUES   Is the Bank of Jamaica immune from Chisholm's action for breach of contract in a U.S. federal court?

DECISION   No. The court ruled that, although the bank is an arm of a foreign government, its actions here met the requirements for an exception to the Foreign Sovereign Immunities Act; therefore, the bank was not immune from Chisholm's action.

REASON   The Foreign Sovereign Immunities Act (FSIA) grants foreign states immunity from suits in U.S. federal and state courts subject to certain exceptions, one being when the foreign state deals in a commercial activity that causes a direct effect in the United States. *Commercial activity* is defined as a regular course of commercial conduct or a particular commercial transaction or act and includes contracting for lines of credit or credit insurance. Another test for commercial activity is whether the activity is solely within the realm of governing or if any private enterprise could do the same thing. Here private banks can and do seek lines of credit and credit insurance; so the Bank of Jamaica is not the only party that can perform this activity. Further, a court does not look at the purpose for an activity, only at the activity itself. Thus, although the bank argued that the money was needed for a governmental purpose, the court ignored this and looked only at the contract itself. It found that the Bank of Jamaica's

---

3.   U.S.C.A., Section 1605(a)(1), (2).

Case 36.1—Continued

action was commercial activity and thus met the requirements of an exception to the FSIA.

The bank also argued that the contract was an act of state, meaning that the court, if it judged the case solely on its merit, would be judging the validity of the public acts of a sovereign state performed within its own territory. The court responded that the act of state doctrine was not applicable because the court need not adjudicate the legality or propriety of any act of the government of Jamaica performed solely within its own borders. A judicial decision does not threaten to embarrass the executive branch in its foreign affairs and hence does not seriously implicate the relevant policy considerations of the act of state doctrine.

❖ Transacting Business Abroad

Transacting business abroad involves peculiar risks since buyers and sellers are often separated by thousands of miles. Sellers want to avoid delivering goods for which they might not be paid. Buyers desire the assurance that sellers will not be paid until there is evidence that the goods have been shipped. Thus, **letters of credit** have been increasingly used to facilitate international business transactions.

Letters of Credit

In a simple letter-of-credit transaction, the *issuer* (a bank) agrees to issue a letter of credit and to ascertain the occurrence of certain acts by the *beneficiary* (seller). In return, the *account party* (buyer) promises to reimburse the issuer for the amount paid to the beneficiary. There may also be an *advising bank* that transmits information, and a *paying bank* may be involved to expedite payment under the letter of credit. See Exhibit 36-1 for the letter-of-credit "life cycle."

"Commerce is the great equalizer. We exchange ideas when we exchange fabrics."

R. G. Ingersoll, 1833–1899
(American lawyer and orator)

LETTER OF CREDIT
A written instrument, usually issued by a bank on behalf of a customer or other person, in which the issuer promises to honor drafts or other demands for payment by third persons in accordance with the terms of the instrument.

Transacting business abroad involves peculiar risks since buyers and sellers are often separated by thousands of miles.

◆ **Exhibit 36.1 The "Life Cycle" of a Letter of Credit**

Although the letter of credit appears quite complex at first, it is not difficult to understand. This cycle merely involves the exchange of documents (and money) through intermediaries. The following steps depict the letter-of-credit procurement cycle.

Step 1:   The buyer and seller agree upon the terms of sale. The sales contract dictates that a letter of credit is to be used to finance the transaction.

Step 2:   The buyer completes an application for a letter of credit and forwards it to his or her bank which will issue the letter of credit.

Step 3:   The issuing buyer's bank then forwards the letter of credit to a correspondent bank in the seller's country.

Step 4:   The correspondent bank relays the letter of credit to the seller.

Step 5:   Having received assurance of payment, the seller makes the necessary shipping arrangements.

Step 6:   The seller prepares the documents required under the letter of credit and delivers them to the correspondent bank.

Step 7:   The correspondent bank negotiates the documents. If it finds them in order, it sends them to the issuing bank, and pays the seller in accordance with the terms of the letter of credit.

Step 8:   The issuing bank, having received the documents, examines them. If they are in order, the issuing bank will charge the buyer's account and send the documents on to the buyer or his or her customs broker. The issuing bank also will reimburse the correspondent bank.

Step 9:   The buyer or broker receives the documents and picks up the merchandise from the shipper (carrier).

Source: National Association of Purchasing Management.

Under a letter of credit, the issuer is bound to pay the beneficiary (seller) when the beneficiary has complied with the terms and conditions of the letter of credit. The beneficiary looks to the issuer, not to the account party (buyer), when it presents the documents required by the letter of credit. Typically, the letter of credit will require that the beneficiary deliver a *bill of lading* to prove that shipment has been made. Letters of credit assure beneficiaries (sellers) of payment while at the same time they assure account parties (buyers) that payment will not be made until the beneficiaries have complied with the terms and conditions of the credit.

The Value of Letter of a Credit   The basic principle behind letters of credit is that payment is made against the documents presented by the beneficiary and not against the facts that the documents purport to reflect. Thus, in a letter-of-credit transaction, the issuer does not police the underlying contract: A letter of credit is independent of the underlying contract between the buyer and the seller. Eliminating the need for banks (issuers) to inquire into whether or not actual conditions have been satisfied greatly reduces the costs of letters of credit. Moreover, the use of a letter of credit protects both buyers and sellers.

Compliance with a Letter of Credit   In a letter-of-credit transaction, there are generally at least three separate and distinct contracts involved: the contract between the account party (buyer) and the beneficiary (seller), the one between the issuer (bank) and the account party (buyer), and finally the letter of credit itself, which involves the issuer and the beneficiary. Given the fact that these contracts are separate and distinct, the issuer's obligations under the letter of credit do not concern the underlying contract between the buyer and the seller. Rather, it is the issuer's duty to ascertain whether the documents presented by the beneficiary (seller) comply with the terms of the letter of credit.

If the documents presented by the beneficiary comply with the terms of the letter of credit, the issuer (bank) must honor the letter of credit. Sometimes, however, it is difficult to determine exactly what a letter of credit requires. Moreover, the courts are divided as to whether *strict* or *substantial* compliance with the terms of the letter of credit is required. Traditionally, courts required strict compliance with the terms of a letter of credit, but in recent years some courts have moved to a standard of *reasonable* compliance.

Is it possible for a creditor to attach open letters of credit on which the debtor is the beneficiary, when those are the only "assets" of a foreign firm within the creditor's country? This was the issue addressed in the following case.

Case 36.2
FERROSTAAL METALS CORPORATION v. S. S. LASH PACIFICO

United States District Court, Southern District of New York, 1987. 652 F.Supp. 420.

FACTS In this case, the plaintiff, Ferrostaal Metals Corporation, sued Prudential Lines, Inc. (PLI), one of the defendants in this case, for damage to a shipment of seamless pipes. PLI brought in Metal Importexport (MIE), the supplier of the pipes, claiming that the damage was the result of MIE's negligence. PLI, as a judgment creditor, served restraining notices upon various New York and New Jersey banks, enjoining their payment under any open letter of credit that named MIE as the beneficiary. MIE countered this action by stating that it was an agency of the state of Romania, and since the restraining notices were not preceded by a court order consistent with the requirements of the Foreign Sovereign Immunities Act of 1976, they were invalid. MIE further argued that, even if the restraining notices were otherwise valid, they were ineffective against the type of asset represented by an open letter of credit.

ISSUE The central issue presented to the court was whether the interest of a foreign beneficiary in an open letter of credit could be effectively attached by a creditor.

DECISION The court held for the beneficiary, MIE, and vacated the restraining order that had been placed on the letters of credit by PLI.

REASON The court held that MIE was an agency of the state of Romania and thus normally would be subject to the provisions of the Foreign Sovereign Immunities Act. Romania, however, had explicitly waived its immunity under the act from post-judgment attachment of property in a bilateral trade agreement with the United States. As to whether open letters of credit could be construed as "property" subject to attachment, the Foreign Sovereign Immunities Act and federal law offered the court little guidance. The court thus looked to a New York precedent [Diakan Love, S.A. v. Al-Haddad Bros. Enterprises, Inc., 584 F.Supp. 782 (S.D.N.Y. 1984)] that had vacated a similar attachment of an open letter of credit, claiming a letter of credit was not "attachable as a debt or property since prior to the presentation of conforming documents, a confirming bank is neither indebted to the beneficiary nor holds any of its property."

In *Diakan,* the New York court had emphasized the importance of letters of credit to international trade and the uncertainties that would result if attachments of open letters of credit were permitted: "In all such cases, the expectations supported by letters of credit will be unfulfilled. It is likely that the entire chain of interlinked contracts necessary to accomplish a completed purchase and sale in international trade will be frustrated. Innocent parties will be injured. Law suits will proliferate. But most importantly, if uncertainties of this order surround letters of credit, financiers will cease to extend credit in reliance on them." The court hearing the instant case agreed with this reasoning and thus ruled for MIE.

Sales Contracts

As with all commercial contracts, the transnational business contract should be in writing. In addition, it should contain a clause that designates the official language to be used in interpreting the terms of the contract, since such a clause promotes a clear and precise understanding of the contract terms by each of the parties. The basic contract of sale should include a legal definition of terms, the price and manner of payment, and a provision specifying the acceptable currency for payment. A *force majeure* clause, which protects the parties from forces beyond their control, is also advisable.

It is also important that the parties to a transnational business contract agree in advance as to what law will be applied in the event of a dispute or breach of contract. Such an agreement can be written into the contract in the form of a *choice-of-law* clause, which designates the forum in which adjudication will take place and what substantive law will be applied in the event of any disputes. An *arbitration* clause may also be included in the contract. When providing for arbitration, it is important that the forum, choice of law, and expertise of the arbitrator be specified in the contract. Many countries recognize the validity of choice-of-law and arbitration clauses and will enforce them in their courts. It is of critical importance, however, that before entering into a transnational business contract, both parties be familiar with the laws of the foreign country involved.

International Dispute Resolution

As discussed in Chapter 2, arbitration of civil disputes is becoming an increasingly attractive alternative to costly litigation through the court system. This is true on the international level as well. As mentioned in the preceding section, arbitration clauses are frequently found in contracts governing the international sale of goods. By means of such clauses, the parties agree in advance to be bound by the decision of a specified third party in the event a dispute should arise. The third party may be a neutral entity such as the International Chamber of Commerce, a panel of individuals representing both parties' interests, or some other group or organization. The United Nations Convention on the Recognition and Enforcement of Foreign Arbitral Awards, which has been implemented in more than fifty countries, including the United States— assists in the enforcement of arbitration clauses, as do provisions in specific treaties between nations.

If no arbitration clause is contained in the sales contract, litigation may occur. In this case, if forum and choice-of-law clauses are included in the contract, the lawsuit will be heard by a court in the forum country specified and decided according to that country's law. Also, each country has choice-of-law rules governing particular types of international transactions with certain nations. If no forum and choice of law have been specified, then legal proceedings may take place in two or more countries, with each country applying its own choice-of-law rules to determine which substantive law will be applied to the particular transaction.

Investment Protection

To counter the deterrent effect that the possibility of expropriation may have on potential investors, many countries guarantee compensation to foreign investors in the event any foreign assets are expropriated. Such guarantees can be in the form of national constitutional or statutory laws or provisions in international treaties. As further protection for foreign investments, some western countries, including the United States, provide insurance for their citizens covering their investment risks abroad. In the United States, for example, the Overseas Private Investment Corporation (OPIC), a government agency, insures U.S. citizens and businesses against losses incurred as a result of expropriation or confiscation of their assets by foreign governments, war, or other causes. The premium charged by OPIC for such coverage depends on the nature and extent of the business risk covered. In addition to OPIC, several private firms offer international investment insurance.

❖ U.S. Antitrust Laws in a Transnational Setting

U.S. antitrust laws (see Chapter 30) have a wide application. They may *subject* persons in foreign nations to their provisions as well as *protect* foreign consumers and competitors from antitrust-violation acts committed by U.S. citizens. Consequently, *foreign persons*, a term that by definition includes foreign governments, may sue under U.S. antitrust laws in U.S. courts.

Section 1 of the Sherman Act provides for the extraterritorial effect of the U.S. antitrust laws.[4] The United States is a major proponent of free competition in the global economy, and thus any conspiracy that has a substantial effect on U.S. commerce is within the reach of the Sherman Act. The act of violation may even occur outside the United States, and foreign governments as well as persons can be sued in violation of U.S. antitrust laws. Yet before U.S. courts will exercise jurisdiction and apply antitrust laws, it must be shown that the alleged violation had a *substantial effect* on U.S. commerce. U.S. jurisdiction is automatically invoked, however, when a per se violation occurs.[5]

A per se violation may consist of resale price-fixing and tying, or tie-in, contracts. If a domestic firm, for example, joins a foreign cartel to control the production, price, or distribution of goods, and this cartel has a *substantial restraining effect* on U.S. commerce, a per se violation may exist. Hence, both the domestic firm and the foreign cartel have the potential to be sued in violation of the U.S. antitrust laws. Likewise, if foreign firms doing business in the United States enter into a price-fixing or other anticompetitive agreement to control a portion of U.S. markets, a per se violation may exist. An alleged conspiracy on the part of Japanese television manufacturers to gain control of the electronic products market in the United States—in violation of the Sherman Act and other antitrust and tariff legislation—is explored in "Business Law in Action" in this chapter.

With the enactment of Title IV, the United States has amended the Sherman Act and the Federal Trade Commission Act. Sections 402 and 403 of Title IV limit the application of the Sherman Act and the Federal Trade Commission Act in their application to unfair methods of competition, when such methods or conduct involve U.S. export trade or commerce with foreign nations. The acts are not limited, however, where there is a "direct, substantial, and reasonably foreseeable effect" upon U.S. domestic commerce that results in a claim for damages.

---

4.   Extraterritorial effect refers to the effect of U.S. antitrust laws outside the United States.
5.   Certain types of restrictive contracts are deemed inherently anticompetitive and thus in restraint of trade as a matter of law. When such a restrictive contract is entered into, there is said to be a per se violation of the antitrust laws. See Chapter 30.

Business Law in Action

The Price of Competition

Antitrust laws were created to foster competition. Is it possible that they also can be used to the opposite effect—that is, to squelch competition? Price-cutting—selling goods at prices lower than those of competing firms—for example, is often viewed as a sign of healthy competition within an economy. If, however, a firm or group of firms engages in "predatory pricing" (selling below cost with the aim of gaining future monopoly control over a certain market), that will constitute a violation of antitrust laws. It is not always easy for the courts to distinguish between competitive and anticompetitive price-cutting techniques. And, when a firm alleges a competitor is engaging in price-fixing or other acts in violation of antitrust legislation, the court must determine whether its agreement with such an allegation would, in fact, remove a bona fide competitor from the market (and thus reduce competition) or further the purpose for which antitrust laws were created (to enhance competition).

A case that came before the U.S. Supreme Court in 1986 is illustrative. In *Matsushita Electric Industrial Co., Ltd.*, v. *Zenith Radio Corporation*,[1] several U.S. manufacturers of television sets alleged that Matsushita and other Japanese firms "illegally conspired to drive American firms from the consumer electronic products market" by means of a "scheme to raise, fix and maintain

1. 475 U.S. 574, 106 S.Ct. 1348, 89 L.Ed.2d 538 (1986).

artificially *high* prices for television receivers sold by [Matsushita and others] in Japan and, at the same time, to fix and maintain *low* prices for television receivers exported to and sold in the United States." The alleged conspiracy began, according to Zenith, in 1953. The American firms claimed that the Japanese were engaged in a "predatory pricing" arrangement whereby the losses sustained by selling at such low prices in the United States were offset by monopoly profits obtained in Japan. Once the Japanese gained control over an overwhelming portion of the American market for electronic products, their monopoly power would enable them to recover their losses by charging artificially high prices in America as well.

In his opinion, Justice Powell found the allegation to be "implausible" and one "that simply makes no economic sense." Citing numerous authorities on predatory pricing, he argued that the risk of suffering real, immediate losses in the present in the mere hope of not only establishing monopoly power, but maintaining it for a sufficiently long period to recoup the losses at some point in the distant future, was one rarely, if ever, taken by any firm. For a cartel, or alliance of firms, to undertake such a risk was even more unlikely. The difficulties involved in allocating losses and future profits among a group of firms and in ensuring that none of them cheated on the others—which would be especially tempting given the uncertainty of the future monopoly profits—were unlikely to be overcome.

Justice Powell further contended that the "alleged predatory scheme

makes sense only if petitioners can recoup their losses. In light of the large number of firms involved here, petitioners can achieve this only by engaging in some form of price-fixing *after* they have succeeded in driving competitors from the market. Such price-fixing would, of course, be an independent violation of Section 1 of the Sherman Act." Thus, even if the cartel could overcome the difficulties mentioned above by consistently pricing below cost, the existence of antitrust legislation in the United States would still make it extremely difficult, if not impossible, to realize their goal of monopoly profits.

Finally, and perhaps most persuasively, Justice Powell noted a relevant fact: In 1953 the two leading television producers in the United States, RCA and Zenith, controlled approximately 40 percent of that market. During the twenty years during which the Japanese were implementing their alleged plan, that percentage remained approximately constant and had not changed significantly. "The alleged conspiracy's failure to achieve its ends in the two decades of its asserted operation," stated the Court, "is strong evidence that the conspiracy does not in fact exist." To claim such a conspiracy exists simply "makes no practical sense."

Justice Powell clearly indicated to both potential future litigants and to the courts that "cutting price in order to increase business often is the very essence of competition." To infer otherwise in cases such as this one can be "especially costly, because they chill the very conduct the antitrust laws are designed to protect."

❖ Chapter Summary: International Law

Sources of International Law	International customs, international treaties, and international organizations (such as the United Nations) and conferences.
Act of State Doctrine	A judicially created doctrine that provides that the judicial branch of one country will not examine the validity of public acts committed by a recognized foreign government within its own territory.
Principle of Comity	A principle whereby nations, for reasons of courtesy and international harmony, give effect to the laws and judicial decrees of other nations.
Doctrine of Sovereign Immunity	When certain conditions are satisfied, under the Foreign Sovereign Immunities Act (FSIA) of 1976 foreign nations are immune from U.S. jurisdiction. Exceptions are (1) when the foreign state has "waived its immunity either explicitly or by implication," and (2) when the action is "based upon a commercial activity carried on in the United States by the foreign state."
Transacting Business Abroad	1. *Letters of credit*—These facilitate international transactions by ensuring payment to sellers and ensuring to buyers that payment will not be made until the sellers have complied with the terms of the letter of credit (e.g., delivery of the goods to the buyer or a bill of lading to the issuer bank). See Exhibit 36-1 for the chronology of a letter-of-credit transaction. 2. *Sales contracts*—These should (1) be in writing, (2) include a clause that designates the official language to be used in interpreting the terms of the contract, and (3) include choice-of-law and forum clauses. It is also advisable to include a *force majeure* clause (protecting parties from forces beyond their control). It is important for both parties to be familiar with the laws of the foreign country involved. 3. *Dispute settlement*—Arbitration is a speedier, less costly, and increasingly attractive method of settling disputes. Many transnational sales contracts include arbitration clauses. When such clauses are included in the contract, it is important that the arbitrator's identity and expertise be specified. 4. *Protection for foreign investments*—Insurance covering foreign assets can be obtained from the Overseas Private Investment Corporation (a U.S. agency) or other private insurance groups to protect investors against expropriation or confiscation or loss of assets in foreign nations.
Antitrust Laws	May subject persons in foreign nations to their provisions as well as protect foreign consumers and competitors from antitrust violations committed by U.S. citizens. Under Section 1 of the Sherman Act, any conspiracy that has a *substantial effect* on U.S. commerce is within the reach of the Sherman Act. The violation may occur outside the United States, and foreign governments as well as persons can be sued in violation of U.S. antitrust laws.

❖ Questions and Case Problems

36-1. James Reynolds entered into an agreement to purchase dental supplies from Tooth-Tech, Inc. Reynolds further secured an irrevocable letter of credit from Central Bank. When Tooth-Tech placed the sixty crates of dental supplies on board a steamship, it received in return the invoices required under the letter of credit. The purchaser, Reynolds, subsequently learned that Tooth-Tech, Inc. filled the sixty crates with rubbish, not dental supplies. Given the fact that an issuer's obligation under a letter of credit is independent of the underlying contract between the buyer and seller, would the issuer be required to pay the draft? Explain. See UCC 5-114(1)(2).

36-2. Verlinden B.V., the plaintiff, entered into a contract for the purchase of 240,000 metric tons of cement by the Federal Republic of Nigeria, the defendant. Verlinden B.V., a Dutch corporation, subsequently sued the Central Bank of Nigeria and alleged that Central Bank's actions constituted an anticipatory breach. May a federal court exercise subject-matter jurisdiction over an action brought by a foreign corporation against a foreign sovereign? Did Congress exceed the scope of Article III by granting federal district courts this jurisdiction? Explain. [Verlinden B.V. v. Central Bank of Nigeria, 461 U.S. 480, 103 S.Ct. 1962, 76 L.Ed.2d 81 (1983)]

36-3. Issues frequently arise as to whether or not a particular instrument is a letter of credit or an ordinary guaranty contract. A letter of credit creates a primary liability, whereas a guaranty contract imposes a secondary liability on the preexisting obligation of another. State statutes prohibit banks from guarantying the debt of another. Consider an instrument that is labeled as a letter of credit but requires that the bank (issuer) do more than simply deal in documents. Discuss whether such an instrument is a letter of credit or an ordinary guaranty contract. [Wichita Eagle & Beacon Pub. Co., Inc. v. Pacific Nat. Bk., San Fran., 493 F.2d 1285 (9th Cir. 1974)]

36-4. A letter of credit was issued by North Carolina National Bank for its customer, Adastra Knitting Mills, Inc. The credit was to cover Adastra's purchases of acrylic yarn from Courtaulds, the beneficiary. Under the letter of credit, Courtaulds was to present a draft accompanied by a commercial invoice stating that it covered 100 percent acrylic yarn. When Courtaulds presented the draft, the accompanying invoices stated that the goods were "Imported Acrylic Yarn." The packing lists, however, disclosed that the packages contained 100 percent acrylic yarn. The bank refused to honor the draft. Under the traditional view, should the bank be liable to Courtaulds for the amount of the draft? Explain. [Courtaulds North America, Inc. v. North Carolina Nat. Bank, 528 F.2d 802 (4th Cir. 1975)]

36-5. Section 1610(d)(1) of the Foreign Sovereign Immunities Act (FSIA) provides that the property of a foreign state that is used for a commercial activity in the United States shall not be immune from attachment prior to the entry of a judgment if the foreign state has "explicitly waived its immunity from attachment prior to judgment." Banco Nacional, an in-strumentality of the government of Costa Rica, entered into a written agreement with Libra Bank Ltd., the plaintiffs. In the agreement, Banco Nacional stated that it did not have "any right of immunity from suit with respect to the Borrower's obligations" under the particular agreement. Did Banco Nacional, the defendant, "explicitly" waive its immunity from prejudgment attachment as required by Section 1610(d)(1) of the FSIA? [Libra Bank Ltd. v. Banco Nacional De Costa Rica, 676 F.2d 47 (2d Cir. 1982)]

36-6. Harris Corporation, the plaintiff, entered into a contract with the defendant, National Iranian Radio and Television (NIRT), to manufacture and deliver 144 FM broadcast transmitters to Teheran, Iran. Due to the revolution in Iran, the plaintiff was unable to complete delivery of the transmitters. NIRT attempted to collect on a letter of credit that had been set up to guarantee performance. The plaintiff subsequently brought an action against the defendant seeking to enjoin receipt of payment on the letter of credit. Bank Melli Iran, the issuer, was also made a defendant. Both defendants alleged that the district court lacked jurisdiction over them. From 1969 to 1982, Melli maintained an office in New York City where it carried out significant business transactions. Moreover, NIRT entered into this contract that required performance by Harris in the United States and also the training of NIRT personnel in the United States. Was this action consistent with due process? Was the "minimum contacts" standard established by International Shoe Co. v. Washington [326 U.S. 10, 66 S.Ct. 154, 98 L.Ed. 95 (1945)], discussed in Chapter 25, satisfied? [Harris Corp. v. National Iranian Radio, Etc., 691 F.2d 1344 (11th Cir. 1982)]

Ethics and Social Responsibility

❖ Why We Study Ethics

For business people, ethical issues arise because of competing interests in the business world among buyers, sellers, managers, nonmanagers, employers, employees, and others. Obviously, individuals enter into business to make a profit. But to what extent should the profit motive control policy decisions? What weight should be given to the desire of others in society for a clean environment or for safe, effective products when such aims conflict with the company's profit motive?

Conflict sometimes arises between the goals of different departments of the same company. In these cases it is frequently difficult to determine who has the responsibility to voice concern over, for example, the quality or safety of a product being manufactured by the firm. What if, as an employee, you have knowledge that a product being manufactured by your company may be potentially harmful to consumers, but those in authority choose to ignore that danger and continue manufacturing the product? Is it your ethical responsibility to disclose the problem to someone higher up in the company—or even to the public or a governmental authority?

It is often middle-management personnel who have the knowledge upon which an ethical dilemma turns. All too often the manager in such a case is in a no-win situation. He or she must be concerned with the reaction of upper-management personnel as well as with the reactions of fellow employees; and the course of action that pleases one may displease the other. A middle manager most likely has also developed a loyalty to the reputation of the company and its long-run interests. Thus, disclosing or not disclosing problems in product safety or quality involves an ethical decision for these middle managers.

It is important for anyone embarking on a career in business today to be able to both recognize and deal effectively with ethical problems. For that reason, we present in this final unit an examination of the nature of ethical issues and numerous examples of the ways in which ethical concerns affect individuals within the business context.

Chapter 37

Ethics and Social Responsibility

As Justice Cardozo stated, standards of prudent conduct—that is to say, ethical standards—are not created by the courts but arise from the "facts of life." The customs, religious beliefs, and other moral values of a community or a nation determine what is considered ethical. The circumstances in which a particular action takes place also determine whether an action is ethical or not.

Business ethics, of course, relate to the ethical principles employed in business decisions. "Good faith," "honesty," "reasonability," and other similar terms used in business law ultimately rest on ethical premises—that is, on collectively held opinions as to right and wrong behavior. Since many decisions faced by business people are complicated, they often involve an ethical dimension. A course of action that may mean relatively high short-run profits, for example, may also involve conduct that, though legal, may produce harmful long-run effects on society. Thus, every manager should be prepared to face ethical issues in reaching certain business decisions.

"Standards of prudent conduct are declared at times by the courts, but they are taken over from the facts of life."

Benjamin Cardozo, 1870–1938
(Associate Justice of the U.S. Supreme Court, 1932–1938)

❖ The Nature of Ethical Issues

Essentially, an **ethical issue** is one that transcends its subject matter to pose a fundamental, structural question such as: What is fair? What is just? Or what makes this outcome more socially desirable than another? One of the best definitions of **ethics** from a business point of view appeared in *Ethics in the Corporate Policy Process: An Introduction:*

> Ethics is a process by which individuals, sòcial groups, and societies evaluate their actions from the perspective of moral principles and values. This evaluation may be on the basis of traditional convictions, of ideals sought, of goals desired, of moral laws to be obeyed, of an improved quality of relations among humans and with the environment. When we speak of 'ethics' and ethical reflection, we mean the activity of applying these various yardsticks to the actions of persons and groups.[1]

ETHICAL ISSUE
One having to do with normative rules of conduct governing social behavior. Ethical issues concern the inherent fairness, justness, and appropriateness of actions of individuals (or businesses or governments) within a specific social context.

ETHICS
Moral principles and values applied to social behavior.

---

1. C. McCoy, et al., *Ethics in the Corporate Policy Process: An Introduction* (Berkeley Calif.: Center for Ethics and Social Policy, Graduate Theological Union, 1976), p. 2.

Thus, a society's ethical values, whether related to business or otherwise, rest on a collection of shared beliefs. Indeed, it is the sharing of beliefs and the desire to spread these beliefs that cause people to organize as groups. The collection of basic values accepted by most members of society constitutes the prevailing morality of that society. We must bear in mind, however, that what constitutes an ethical concern of a society may change as the values of that society change. What was ethical conduct in the United States ten years ago may be considered unethical today, although ten years from now it may once again be considered ethical.

❖ Changing Societal Values and the Law

"Legal principles represent the prevailing mores of our time, and with the mores, they must necessarily be born, survive for the appointed season, and perish."

Sir William Reynell Anson, 1843–1914
(English jurist and Member of Parliament)

Since law reflects societal values, when values change, the law also changes. Law is a response, however, so there is a time lag between any changes in society's values and corresponding changes in the law. It is during this interval that someone questions the fairness of an existing law, asking whether it truly represents society's values; and this is what leads to a change in the law. It would be a mistake to focus on understanding the content of current laws without exploring why they exist or why they have changed.

For example, it was only recently that the commercial bribery of foreign government officials was raised as an ethical issue. (See this chapter's "Landmark.") It took several scandals involving large payoffs to bring this issue to the forefront. Because enough groups concluded that this type of behavior was unethical, Congress was induced to pass a law prohibiting it.

Every advance in technology seems to be accompanied by new situations in which unethical behavior becomes possible. In the past, for example, manufacturers of computer software marketed their programs in an unreadable form stored in a silicon chip. But then technology advanced to the point where programs stored in these silicon chips could be "pirated." For many years, the uncertainty of the law on this subject encouraged program piracy, though it was deemed by many to be unethical behavior. Recently, however, courts have begun to impose liability on this unethical behavior and extend copyright protection to computer programs and codes (see the "Landmark" in Chapter 3). Congress has also addressed this issue to a certain extent with the passage in 1984 of the Semiconductor Chip Protection Act.[2]

Another interesting problem has been posed by the computer age: Should the unauthorized use of another's computer constitute "theft" of another's property and thus come under larceny statutes? The following case illustrates such a situation.

Case 37.1
INDIANA v. McGRAW
Court of Appeals of Indiana, 1984.
459 N.E.2d 61.

FACTS McGraw was a computer operator for the Indianapolis Department of Planning and Zoning. The computer system had been leased by the city on a flat-fee basis, and employees were not authorized to use the computer for private matters. McGraw, however, used the computer fairly extensively for his own private business and, upon discovering this, the city charged McGraw with, among other things, two counts of theft. The trial court granted a motion to dismiss, filed by McGraw on

---

2.   17 U.S.C.A. Section 901 *et seq.*

Case 37.1—Continued

the grounds that his activities and the facts as stated by the city did not constitute an offense. The city appealed.

ISSUE Can the unauthorized use of another person's computer for private business be considered theft under Indiana law?

DECISION Yes. The trial court's judgment was reversed, and the trial court was ordered to sentence McGraw for theft of property.

REASON According to Indiana statutory law, "A person who knowingly and intentionally exerts unauthorized control over property of another person with intent to deprive the other person of any part of its value or use, commits theft." The court stated, "Computer services, leased or owned, are a part of our market economy in huge dollar amounts. . . . Computer time is 'services' for which money is paid. Such services may reasonably be regarded as valuable assets to the beneficiary. Thus, computer services are property within the meaning of the definition of property subject to theft. . . ."

❖ Ethics and Positive Law

Virtually all of what you have read in this text involves **positive law,** sometimes called *black-letter law.* In a sense, positive law represents the basic social ethic on a matter; it gives individuals knowledge of which actions are prohibited and assurance that society (via its government) will punish the violators. As a consequence, individuals know that when they do not follow positive law, they will be punished, and they are typically prepared for it. Some may choose to reject society's rules, or positive law, for ethical reasons that they deem more important. Robin Hood robbing the rich to give to the poor is an example, albeit a fictional one. A major problem arises from individuals "taking the law into their own hands" supposedly for higher ethical reasons: What is to stop governments from doing the same thing and thereby, for example, trampling on the Bill of Rights for some "higher reason"? When an individual can exempt himself or herself from a positive law, the social contract that keeps us together as a civilized entity starts to break down. Then government officials can exempt themselves also.

While it may not be appropriate to justify conduct disallowed by positive law simply for ethical reasons, there is certainly nothing to prevent individuals in their capacity as citizens or businesspersons from raising the level or standard of their conduct above positive law—for ethical or other reasons. Positive law does not require individuals to be charitable or to come to the aid of others, yet ethical considerations may well cause individuals to do so.

POSITIVE LAW
The objective laws legally created by a society, as opposed to natural law or social customs; also called *black-letter law.*

❖ Ethics in the Workplace

Laws relating to the rights of employers and employees have given rise to numerous ethical concerns. This is nowhere more evident than in the area of employment discrimination (or antidiscrimination) practices.

Employment Discrimination

Society has definitely changed its thinking with respect to employment. In the past, traditional concerns in the area of **employment discrimination** centered on the failure

EMPLOYMENT DISCRIMINATION
Treating employees or job applicants unequally on the basis of race, sex, nationality, religion, or age; prohibited by Title VII of the Civil Rights Act of 1964 as amended.

Landmark in the Law

The Foreign Corrupt Practices Act of 1977

In the 1970s the U.S. press, and government officials as well, uncovered a number of business scandals involving large side payments by American corporations—such as Lockheed Aircraft—to foreign representatives for the purpose of securing advantageous international trade contracts. In response to this unethical behavior, Congress passed the Foreign Corrupt Practices Act (FCPA) in 1977.[1]

The act is divided into two major parts. The first part, which applies to all U.S. companies and their directors, officers, shareholders, employers, or agents, prohibits bribes (giving anything of value) to foreign government officials where the purpose is to obtain or retain business for the U.S. company. The second part is directed toward accountants, because previously bribes were often concealed in corporate financial records. The act requires all companies to keep detailed records that "accurately and fairly" reflect the company's financial activities, and to have an accounting system that provides "reasonable assurance" that all transactions entered into by the company are accounted for and legal. Although these requirements are broad in scope, they should assist in detecting illegal foreign bribes.

The act further prohibits any person in a U.S. company from making any false entry in any record or account. Any violation of the act results in fines of up to $1 million and the incarceration of officers or directors of convicted companies for up to a maximum of five years. Those officers and directors can also be fined up to $10,000, and the fine cannot be paid by the company.

Notice that the act does not prohibit paying substantial sums to minor officials, as long as their duties are ministerial, or clerical. Such payments are often referred to as "grease," or facilitating, payments. They are to ensure that customary services that might be performed at a rather slow pace are speeded up.

1. 15 U.S.C.A. Section 78 *et seq.*

Ethics versus Economic Reality

American corporations wishing to do business abroad, particularly in less developed countries and in the Middle East, have probably always engaged in some sort of *side-payment* system in order to win contracts. Whereas in America the majority of contracts are decided upon in the private sector, in many foreign countries, the majority of major construction contracts and manufacturing contracts are decided upon by government officials because of extensive government regulation and control over trade and industry. (For example, in Mexico all production and exportation of oil is under the control of a government agency—PEMEX.) Therefore, U.S. corporations wishing to do business in less-developed countries have to contend with numerous government officials, many of whom depend on what Americans would call "bribes" for their regular income. And such side payments are not considered unethical behavior in such countries, but rather a kind of direct use tax for official services. Given this attitude, it is not surprising that foreign government personnel in charge of making decisions about multimillion-dollar contracts have sometimes been influenced by payments on the side.

This has created an ethical dilemma for American business firms seeking to do business abroad: An employee of an American corporation has a fiduciary responsibility to do what is in the best interest of the corporation's shareholders. In many cases, that necessitates some sort of side payment to a foreign official or officials in order to obtain a profitable contract abroad. But such offers of side payments are in violation of the FCPA. Since the passage of the FCPA in 1977, managers in American corporations have been at a competitive disadvantage vis-à-vis foreign corporations from other countries that are not subject to any type of legislation governing side payments. In short, the FCPA did not change international trade practices in other countries, while it effectively tied the hands of American firms trying to secure foreign contracts.

This ethical dilemma has not escaped the attention of the U.S. legislature, and beginning in 1982, some modifications to the FCPA have been made. The rigorous accounting standards of the act have been relaxed somewhat, and corporations are now required only to ensure that "reasonable assurances" exist about the authorization and use of business enterprise funds.

In the well-known case of Regents of the University of California v. Bakke, *Alan Bakke sued the University of California regents alleging reverse discrimination.*

to hire, retain, and promote with equality. Equal opportunity regulations were therefore designed to reduce or eliminate discriminatory practices. Today, however, subsequent attempts at "making up" for past patterns of discrimination have resulted in **affirmative action** programs, some of which have resulted in what has been termed **reverse discrimination** against majority groups. Such reverse discrimination raises the ethical issue of how far society should go in trying to remedy the effects of past discrimination against minorities.

In the well-known case of *Regents of the University of California* v. *Bakke,*[3] for example, Alan Bakke, a Vietnam veteran and engineer who had been turned down for medical school at the Davis campus of the University of California, discovered that his academic record was better than those of some of the minority applicants who had been admitted to the program. He sued the University of California regents, alleging reverse discrimination. The U.S. Supreme Court held that a public university may give favorable weight to minority applicants as part of a plan to increase minority enrollment. The Court, however, stated that a quota system, in which a certain number of seats is explicitly reserved for minority applicants, is unconstitutional. In other words, public universities may consider race or ethnic background as a factor in attempting to obtain the benefits that flow from an ethnically diverse student body, but they may not utilize a quota system for the benefit of minorities.

Reverse discrimination was also addressed in the recent case of *Firefighters Local Union No. 1784* v. *Stotts.*[4] In this case, Stotts, a black member of the Memphis, Tennessee, Fire Department filed a class action alleging that the department and certain city officials were violating Title VII of the Civil Rights Act of 1964 by engaging in a pattern or practice of making hiring and promotion decisions on the basis of race. A **consent decree** was subsequently entered into for the purpose of remedying the department's hiring and promotion practices with respect to blacks.

AFFIRMATIVE ACTION
Job-hiring policies that give special consideration or compensatory treatment to minority groups in an effort to overcome present effects of past discrimination.

REVERSE DISCRIMINATION
A type of discrimination in which majority groups are purportedly discriminated against in favor of minority groups, usually via affirmative action programs.

CONSENT DECREE
A settlement in which a person, company, or government agency agrees to take certain actions without admitting fault or guilt for the situation that caused the original lawsuit.

3.   438 U.S. 265, 98 S.Ct. 2733, 57 L.Ed.2d 750 (1978).
4.   467 U.S. 561, 104 S.Ct. 2576, 81 L.Ed.2d 482 (1984).

After the consent decree was entered into, the city of Memphis announced that projected budget deficits necessitated a reduction of city employees. The district court proceeded to enjoin the department from adhering to its seniority system in determining who would be laid off. The court concluded that the proposed layoffs would have a racially discriminatory effect and that the seniority system was not a bona fide one. The court of appeals affirmed, and the Supreme Court granted the petition for certiorari.

The Supreme Court held that the consent decree did not include the displacement of white employees with seniority over blacks, and hence the district court's injunction did not merely enforce the agreement of the parties as embodied in the consent decree. The Court concluded that, while Title VII protects bona fide seniority systems, it is inappropriate to deny an innocent employee the benefits of his or her seniority in order to provide a remedy in a **pattern-or-practice** suit. Thus, the Supreme Court's decision prevented the use of reverse discrimination in the area of seniority in hiring in order to remedy past discrimination.

PATTERN OR PRACTICE
Repeated, regular, and intentional conduct.

How much should the current generation of white employees and other members of majority groups have to pay for past discriminatory practices of employers? To what extent, and in what ways, should the government regulate employment conditions to ensure equal opportunity? These are the questions facing society—and the courts—today. In *Johnson* v. *Transportation Agency*, the court focused on alleged "reverse" gender discrimination, where a male employee contested the promotion of a less-qualified female.

Case 37.2
JOHNSON v. TRANSPORTATION AGENCY, SANTA CLARA COUNTY, CALIFORNIA
Supreme Court of the United States, 1987.
——— U.S. ———, 107 S.Ct. 1442, 94 L.Ed.2d 615.

FACTS Paul Johnson, a male public transit authority employee in Santa Clara, California, challenged the promotion of a female employee, Diane Joyce, who had lower test scores than some of the employees not promoted. Johnson and Joyce were both among the final seven candidates for the promotional position of road dispatcher for the County of Santa Clara, and a strong factor in awarding the job to Joyce was the fact that she was a female. Joyce was promoted to the position pursuant to an affirmative action plan designed to increase the number of females in higher levels of a governmental agency. At the time of Joyce's promotion, not one of the 238 positions in the pertinent job classification was held by a woman. Johnson contended that this promotion violated Title VII of the 1964 Civil Rights Act, which prohibits discrimination in employment on the basis of race, color, religion, sex, or national origin. The district court held for Johnson, but the Ninth Circuit Court of Appeals reversed, maintaining that this promotion was a lawful effort to rem-

edy long-standing imbalances in the workforce. Johnson appealed to the U. S. Supreme Court.

ISSUE Did the Transportation Agency's affirmative action plan and promotion of Joyce over Johnson violate Title VII of the Civil Rights Act?

DECISION No. The U. S. Supreme Court affirmed the appellate court's judgment.

REASON In an employment discrimination case, the plaintiff bears the burden of proving that race or sex was taken into account in the employer's employment decision. If the plaintiff succeeds in establishing a prima facie case of discrimination, then the burden shifts to the employer to justify its decision on nondiscriminatory grounds. The existence of an affirmative action plan is an acceptable justification for considering race or sex in employment decisions, and since the Transportation Agency made its decision pursuant to such a plan, the burden again shifted to the plaintiff to demonstrate that the plan was in any way invalid.

This Johnson was unable to do. A conspicuous imbalance in traditionally segregated job categories is sufficient reason for an employer to adopt an affirmative

Case 37.2—Continued

action plan, and the goal and method of implementation of the Transportation Agency's plan were deemed reasonable by the Court. Since the purpose of an affirmative action plan is to further Title VII's purpose of eliminating the effects of discrimination in the workplace, Title VII should not be used to thwart the implementation of an affirmative action plan—as Johnson had attempted to do.

The Court noted that it was addressing only the issue of the prohibitory scope of Title VII and not the broader issue of the constitutional right to equal protection under the Fourteenth Amendment, which had been neither raised nor addressed in the litigation. Insofar as Title VII was concerned, the Court could find no indication that this legislation had been violated by the Transportation Agency. "The Agency plan did not unnecessarily trammel male employees' rights or create an absolute bar to their advancement. . . . Denial of the promotion to petitioner [Johnson] unsettled no legitimate firmly rooted expectation on his part, since the Agency director was authorized to select any of the seven applicants deemed qualified for the job."

Whistleblowing

A major ethical dilemma is posed to employees when they are forced to choose between ignoring unethical, unsafe, or illegal activities in their workplace or "blowing the whistle" on their employer. Choosing the first alternative compromises their own ethical standards and perhaps requires their participation in the unethical or illegal actions. Choosing the second alternative, however, may lead to undesirable results: employees who blow the whistle often find themselves disciplined or even fired by their employers as a result.

At common law, an employee can be hired and discharged *at will* by an employer. Except to the extent that employers are limited by contract or statute, they are free to determine the conditions and terms of employment and to conduct their affairs without judicial or administrative interference. Some states[5] have passed special laws with respect to workers and whistleblowing, and federal legislation covers employees in certain areas. Yet many states still uphold the common law at-will doctrine, and in such states whistleblowers have had as yet relatively little protection.

The case of *Geary* v. *United States Steel Corporation*[6] illustrates some possible consequences of an ethical dilemma. George Geary was employed by the United States Steel Corporation to sell tubular products to the oil and gas industry. His employment was at will. Geary alleged that he believed that one of the company's new products, a tubular casing, had not been adequately tested and constituted a serious danger to anyone who used it. Even though Geary at all times performed his duties to the best of his ability, he continued to express his reservations with respect to the company's new product. Geary alleged that because of the above events, he was summarily discharged without notice.

The Supreme Court of Pennsylvania held that Geary had no right of action against his employer for wrongful discharge. The court stated that Geary vigorously expressed his own point of view by bypassing his immediate superiors and by taking his case to a vice-president of the company. It concluded that the most natural inference from the chain of events was that Geary had made a nuisance of himself and, hence, the company had discharged him to preserve administrative order. In addition, the court acknowledged the fact that Geary did not possess any expert

---

5. Including California, Connecticut, Maine, Michigan, and New York.
6. 456 Pa. 171, 319 A.2d 174 (1974).

qualifications. He was involved only in the sale of company products. The mere fact that Geary may have had "good intentions" was not found to be sufficient to establish a right to litigate a case such as this one.

The court in *Geary* recognized the potential for abuse if it upheld a nonstatutory exception to the at-will discharge in this case. Vexatious suits brought by disgruntled employees against a company could severely disrupt its normal operational procedures. Furthermore, there would also be substantial problems of establishing proof in creating a legal forum for this type of plaintiff. How does one actually prove that an employee is discharged for one reason as opposed to another?

Clearly, there are conflicting interests in this area to which our laws must address themselves. On the one hand, our laws must be structured in such a way as to discourage frivolous suits that unnecessarily disrupt business. On the other hand, our legal system serves to encourage individuals to acknowledge their ethical responsibilities because it is in the public interest to do so. Consequently, a small, but increasing, number of courts are allowing exceptions to the at-will doctrine on the basis of public policy, as discussed in the "Business Law in Action."

The movement for greater protection of whistleblowers, however, has not been totally successful. And how many working men or women are willing to risk their jobs, or, at best, face subtle types of punishment, in order to expose business behavior that they know is unethical or unsafe—or even illegal? Whistleblowing is usually in the public interest, and it should be encouraged; but the pressure upon individuals to tolerate or ignore unethical behavior is often too great to overcome.

❖ Ethics and the Corporation

Relating ethics and ethical concepts to corporate activities is difficult because no one person controls a corporation. Consider a corporation with literally millions of shareholders. Does any one shareholder affect the way in which the modern corporation governs itself? The answer has to be no. Indeed, the question of the separation of ownership and management is basic. Management of a corporation apparently can do whatever it wants within the scope of the charter of the corporation. The directors and officers have a duty to perform, but perform for whom? If a director's action cannot be controlled by the owners of the corporation, then by what means is such an action controlled?

There is an ethical question at the heart of all actions of directors and officers: What is the nature of their duty to the entity called the corporation? Furthermore, what is the nature of their duty to society? What is the nature of their duty to the corporation's employees and shareholders and to consumers who purchase their products? All of these ethical responsibilities can be considered elements of the question of corporate social responsibility.

Corporate Social Responsibility

For a number of years now, numerous speakers have debated the social responsibility of the corporation as an institution. What should be the primary corporate goal? Should the growth of the firm or long-term profit maximization be the primary corporate goal, or should social responsibility be given considerable weight in assessing corporate goals? The way in which corporate goals and social responsibility are perceived inevitably involves ethical considerations.

Business Law in Action

Whistleblowing and Public Policy

Whistleblowers who bring suits against their employers for wrongful discharge often pose a special problem for the courts. In situations where neither an employment contract nor whistleblowing statutes protect the worker, the case must be decided on the basis of common law and the employment-at-will doctrine. The modern trend by the courts, however, has been to modify the at-will employment doctrine by finding exceptions to its operation.

One such exception is created when a court construes that an "implied" contract exists between an employer and an employee. An increasing number of courts, for example, have held that an employer who discharges an employee who entered a good-faith agreement with the employer is in breach of an implied employment contract—unless the employer can prove that the discharge was a reasonable action.

A second exception is based on public policy. Under this exception, an employee should not be discharged because he or she performed an act encouraged by public policy—or because he or she refused to perform an act counter to public policy. But what public policies are significant enough to warrant protection by the courts? This

is a difficult question, and one the courts can answer only on a case-by-case basis. In the *Geary* case already discussed, the court found that Geary's discharge by his employer, U.S. Steel Corporation, did not constitute a violation of public policy and that the employer had reasonable cause to discharge Geary for his actions. In *Harless* v. *First National Bank in Fairmont* (1978),[1] however, a court ruled that it did violate public policy when a bank employee was discharged because he pressured his employer to comply with state and federal consumer credit laws.

In a recent case, *Wagner* v. *City of Globe* (1986),[2] the issue of what constitutes public policy was further addressed when a probationary officer and an at-will employee (Wagner) of the police department of the city of Globe, Arizona, discovered that a man had been arrested for vagrancy under an obsolete statute and had been sentenced to ten days in prison. Wagner further learned that the arrested man had been in jail for twenty-one, not ten, days. Wagner pointed out to a magistrate that such arrest and detention were illegal, and the magistrate informed Wagner that he would talk to the police chief about it. The police chief later told Wagner that "he [the police chief] did not appreciate 'big city cops'

1. 162 W.Va. 116, 246 S.E.2d 270 (1978).
2. 150 Ariz. 82, 722 P.2d 250 (1986).

telling him how to run his department." Subsequently, Wagner was fired and brought an action against the city of Globe for wrongful discharge.

In evaluating Wagner's claim, the court decided that discharge in Wagner's case represented a violation of public policy. The court maintained, "Whistleblowing activity that serves a public purpose should be protected. So long as employees' actions are not merely private or proprietary, but instead seek to further the public good, the decision to expose illegal or unsafe practices should be encouraged . . . . There is no public policy more important or fundamental than the one favoring the effective protection of the lives, liberty, and property of the people. The officer's successful attempt to free the arrestee from illegal confinement was a refreshing and laudable exercise that should be protected, not punished."

These are encouraging words to potential whistleblowers. Although public-policy exceptions to at-will discharge are relatively recent and represent a fairly narrow trend in the courts, it is apparent that whistleblowers are gaining a measure of judicial protection in those areas not governed by statutory or contract law.

At one end of the spectrum is the notion that the corporation's sole responsibility is to maximize profits within the limits set by the law. Commentators at this end of the spectrum assert that the social duty of a business enterprise is actually long-term profit maximization. From this perspective, professional managers are regarded as trustees, and the corporation is simply viewed as an extension of its shareholders. Thus, nonprofit-making activities will diminish the shareholders' wealth and therefore are not considered appropriate corporate conduct. Residual profits belong to the stockholders and are not to be devoted to the public interest.

At the other end of the spectrum is the notion that the directors and officers of a corporation have a duty higher than that of mere profit maximization or growth of the firm. According to this view, corporate management should engage only in those activities that benefit society as a whole. Therefore, if the corporation produces a type of baby food that babies like and that mothers buy but that is not nutritionally satisfactory for babies because of a high MSG or sugar content, the corporation should not market the baby food.

Defining Corporate Responsibility   One of the major problems in discussing corporate social responsibility is our inability to define it objectively. We might have some notion of the nature of socially responsible actions when publicly appointed or elected officials are under study, but we have much less clear-cut notions when the directors or officers of a private corporation are concerned. In addition, critics of the entire concept of corporate social responsibility argue that they do not want private citizens, in their roles as directors and officers of private corporations, deciding what is socially responsible. Besides, are business executives equipped to fashion appropriate corporate responses to social demands? What exactly is in society's best interest? This last query has been a subject of dispute for decades, and hence many critics contend that the political process is the appropriate forum for decisions concerning social responsibility, and not the corporate boardroom.

Safety Standards and Ethics   The 1984 Union Carbide tragedy in Bhopal, India, has raised numerous ethical considerations. Was this company exhibiting corporate responsibility in its Bhopal operations? When the U.S.–owned Union Carbide company leaked twenty-five tons of the agricultural pesticide methyl isocyanate from its Bhopal plant, 2,000 deaths and 100,000 injuries resulted in the city of Bhopal. Union Carbide insisted that the Bhopal factory was built according to the same safety standards as its U.S. factories. There was, however, no computerized safety system installed in the Bhopal plant, even though one was installed in a sister plant in West Virginia.

Many experts contend that U.S. companies frequently locate factories in developing countries in order to escape the many U.S. environmental and safety regulations. Such companies are not violating any laws, but is it ethical for them to take advantage of lax regulations in Third World countries?

It is further alleged that companies such as Union Carbide are lacking in social responsibility when they locate factories with lethal materials in areas of high population density. Many of the survivors of the Bhopal tragedy alleged that they were completely unaware of the fact that lethal materials were manufactured so near to them. Do companies have a responsibility to inform residents near their factories as to the nature of their products? If so, how far should this responsibility extend?

Corporate Social Responsiveness

At early common law, a corporation was absolutely prohibited from giving to charity. The law has changed, however, and now allows private corporations to give to charity. Corporate nonprofit activity is justified by public-policy reasons. The argument is that the wealth of the nation is no longer primarily in the hands of private individuals. Much of the nation's wealth is in corporate hands. Additionally, since the size of

There was no computerized safety system installed in the Bhopal plant even though one was installed in a similar plant in West Virginia.

government has increased dramatically since the 1930s, taxation has increased accordingly, and the philanthropic abilities of private individuals have been correspondingly diminished.

Despite charges against them of a general lack of corporate social responsiveness, most major corporations do engage in philanthropic activities. Corporations routinely donate to hospitals, the arts, universities, and the like. Most major corporations employ one or more individuals to screen charitable requests and to determine which organizations should be the recipients of charitable contributions. B. Dalton Bookseller, for example, put up $3 million to launch a massive drive against functional illiteracy. Over the next four years, this contribution will help support 50,000 volunteer literacy tutors. The Bank of America has created a $10 million revolving-loan program in which funds are loaned to community development groups at a 3 percent interest rate.

A considerable number of corporations have also acknowledged moral and political considerations in their social responsiveness. In 1983 the Bank of America announced that future loans would be barred to the South African government or to its government entities until concrete steps have been taken to dismantle the apartheid laws. Coca-Cola has established the National Hispanic Business Agenda—a major program to expand ties with the Hispanic community. This corporation has agreed to patronize more Hispanic firms, employ more Hispanic employees, and support Hispanic educational and job-training programs.

Social Investing

Social investing, the buying and selling of securities on the basis of moral or social criteria, has become a popular subject of debate. The question frequently arises: how do you determine whether a company is socially responsible? Socially conscious investors have begun using social-responsibility criteria—such as pollution control,

SOCIAL INVESTING
Investments made on the basis of moral or ethical judgments; buying stock in a corporation based on the ethical behavior of the corporation or on its benefits to society.

McDonald's Corporation has been donating funds to Ronald McDonald houses for a number of years. These houses provide a cost-free and supportive environment for the parents of children who suffer from cancer while the latter are being treated.

charitable donations, safety conditions, and equal employment opportunities—in identifying socially responsible companies. Some investment advisors rely upon the nature of the products or services that a company provides in order to determine whether a company is socially responsible. Others, however, look to the internal operations of a company in evaluating social responsibility.

Yet, irrespective of the widespread attention recently given to the subject of social investing, the goal of most people is still simply to make a profit. Even though people claim to be, and probably are, concerned with social responsibility, they still are reluctant to commit their funds on any basis other than expected profits. The idea of moral and social scrutiny is appealing, but in practice it does have its problems. How exactly do you determine which company is socially responsible and which is not? How deeply must you examine a company to determine whether it is socially responsible? Furthermore, does social investing make good financial sense? Trustees of investment funds, for example, may be held liable under the prudent investor rule if they fail to invest the funds at their disposal prudently. Many individuals allege, however, that when social investing is done properly, the corporation and the public both benefit.

The Corporation's Duty to Its Employees and Shareholders

What are the corporation's duties to its employees? The answer to this ethical question is complicated by the trade-offs required. To the extent that the corporation provides higher than competitive wages, better than "reasonable" working conditions, and the like, its costs per unit of production will be higher. That means that the price of the product will be higher. Who has a greater "right," the employee or the consumer? Also, as previously mentioned, there is a conflict between the shareholder and the employee. The more employees obtain, presumably the less shareholders will obtain. No easy solution to such a conflict is available.

Particular ethical problems arise with respect to the relationship between the shareholders and the corporate management. The *shareholders' derivative suit* is the principal means available to minority shareholders to correct abuses committed by corporate management. Through the application of the *business judgment rule,*

Does Honda Motor Company have a duty to warn parents about the potential misuse of the company's high speed motor bike by teenage consumers? This bike can easily attain speeds of one hundred and fifty miles per hour; many teenagers in California race the bikes on dangerous mountain roads.

however, courts have begun to limit the availability of this action. The business judgment rule allows the board of directors to dismiss the shareholders' demand if it believes that such a demand is not in the corporation's best interests. The directors, however, must be disinterested in the sense that they must not have participated in the challenged transactions or have a personal interest in the outcome of the suit. Therefore, ethically, interested directors cannot vote on a suit brought against them. Yet how exactly do you go about determining a personal interest? How strong or how weak can this personal interest be? How do you know whether the directors have exercised good faith in their business decisions?

The Corporation's Duty to Consumers

What is the nature of the corporation's duty to the consumer? This issue often dominates discussions of product quality, pricing, and advertising. The layperson's notion is that he or she has absolutely no effect on the pricing, quality, and nature of the products and services offered by the modern-day giant corporation. Therefore, some consumers believe that corporations should be severely regulated by the government and the courts in order to maintain the consumer's rights.

But what, really, is at issue here? Can the corporation willfully ignore the well-being of the consumer? As previously discussed, the critics of modern-day corporations assert that profit maximization is basically the only goal of those corporations. The supporters of modern-day corporations, however, claim that it is impossible for the well-being of the consumer to be ignored by the corporation, and that, indeed, the ultimate control of the corporation actually lies in the hands of the consumer. After all, they argue, the consumer freely chooses to buy or not to buy a corporation's product. Even in the absence of effective competition, the consumer can purchase a smaller quantity of the product being offered. Thus, it is in the corporation's best interest to attempt to satisfy the consumer.

Assuming that this alleged power of the consumer to control the corporation exists, an ethical question still remains. The process of competition takes time. Information is costly to obtain and never perfect. If corporate leaders know or suspect that certain of their products may have deleterious long-run effects on the consumer, do not such corporate leaders have an ethical responsibility to inform the consumer? Eli Lilly, for example, failed to recognize an ethical responsibility that resulted in the death of an eighty-one-year-old woman who had taken Lilly's arthritis drug, Oraflex, and a $6 million punitive verdict was rendered against Lilly. Lilly had had Oraflex approved for sale in the United States without informing the Food and Drug Administration of thirty-two overseas deaths associated with the use of this drug.

Furthermore, what about an ethical responsibility to citizens in other countries? If the Food and Drug Administration has prohibited the sale of a particular substance in the United States because it might have long-run carcinogenic effects, should the producer attempt to sell it in those countries where its sale is legal?

The question is often raised, however, as to the extent of the corporation's duty to the consumer. To what extent should the manufacturer be liable for the use or abuse of its products, and to what extent should such responsibility rest with the consumer? Consider, for example, a recent case where a boy was injured while riding a minibike on a public road.[7] The father had repeatedly told the boy not to ride the minibike in the street, and the owner's manual stated in bold print that the bike was intended for off-the-road use only. This warning was also given on a sticker prominently displayed on the bike. Is the consumer responsible for the injury because of misuse of the product? Or should the manufacturer be held responsible? The court in this case held that Honda Motor Company, the manufacturer, had performed its duty to warn consumers by instructing that the bikes were intended for off-the-road use only.

The following case involves another situation in which a child's unforeseeable use of a product caused harm—in this case, the death of an infant. It again raises the question of whether the consumer or the producer should bear the responsibility for the misuse of a product.

> *"Neither equity nor the law relieves those who seek aid in Court merely to avoid the effects of their own negligence. . . . Negligence always has misfortune for a companion."*
>
> **Henry Lamm, 1846–1926**
> *(Missouri jurist)*

Case 37.3
LANDRINE v. MEGO CORPORATION
Supreme Court of New York, Appellate Division, 1983.
95 A.D.2d 759, 464 N.Y.S.2d 516.

FACTS Beverly Landrine sued on behalf of her infant daughter, who died after she swallowed a balloon while playing with a doll known as "Bubble Yum Baby." When a balloon was inserted into the doll's mouth, and the doll's arm was pumped, thereby inflating the balloon, the doll simulated the blowing of a bubble gum bubble. The balloon was made by defendant Perfect Product Company and distributed by Mego. Landrine alleged that the balloon was defectively made or inherently unsafe when used by children and that Perfect failed to warn of the danger associated with the balloon's usage. The trial court denied Perfect's motion for summary judgment, and Perfect appealed.

ISSUE Should the producer of the balloon be liable for damages on the basis of product liability laws?

DECISION No. The appellate court reversed the trial court's ruling and granted summary judgment to Perfect, thereby freeing it of any liability for the infant's death.

REASON The court stated that "a cause of action in strict liability arises when a manufacturer places on the

---

7. Baughn v. Honda Motor Co., Ltd., 107 Wash.2d 127, 727 P.2d 655 (1986).

Case 37.3—Continued

market a product which has a defect that causes injury." A design defect exists when the product is sold in "a condition not reasonably contemplated by the ultimate consumer and is unreasonably dangerous for its intended use. . . ." The court found that Landrine had not demonstrated that the balloon was unreasonably dangerous or defectively made. Thus, Perfect had a duty to warn of possible danger only if all balloons are inherently dangerous, a position that the court rejected. Moreover, no duty to warn existed when the consumer is already aware, through common knowledge or learning, of a specific hazard. Here, eating the balloon was not an intended use, and to the extent it was foreseeable, it was a misuse of the product for which the guardian of the child "must be wary." Otherwise, "anything capable of being swallowed would have to be kept from children."

Environmental Concerns

To what extent is a business firm required to concern itself with the conservation of natural resources? Does a company have to wait until it is besieged by protesters before it acts, such as in the case of Weyerhauser in the Northwest? This forest products company found itself under attack by protesters who accused it of raping the forest. It ultimately set up an extensive program of replanting trees and became more selective in its cutting, thereafter cutting in a manner to conserve natural resources.

For business enterprises generally, the emphasis has been on maximizing short-term profits and thus taking the minimal environmental precautions required by law. Yet the effect that large corporations' activities have on the environment has now become a subject of public concern. Throughout this nation's history, Americans have tended to view large corporations with a somewhat critical eye. Whereas in the past corporations have been criticized for failing to create enough jobs or for failing to produce a sufficient quantity or quality of goods and services, these same corporations are now being criticized for failing to consider as their ethical responsibility the protection of the environment. Yet companies usually cannot protect the environment without incurring higher production costs, costs that are ultimately passed on to the consumer, and this result is not happily received by stockholders—even those having environmentalist leanings. Pollution control clearly involves costs that must be absorbed somewhere—by paying out smaller dividends, raising prices, or lowering employee wages.

In a competitive economic system, one company cannot be socially responsible by itself. If an individual firm tries to accept this responsibility, and other firms do not, the socially responsible firm is likely to lose profits and eventually cease operation. Consequently, we can argue that it is because of our competitive system that we require government regulation and that this need is particularly great in the environmental protection area.

But does this mean that it is only through government regulation of all competitors that we will achieve a reduction in the amount of environmental destruction due to production processes? Is it possible to combine profit-making activities with environmental protection programs? Dow Chemical thought so. That firm devised and implemented a massive program of pollution control directed toward waste reduction and the conservation of raw materials. Manufacturing processes were closely scrutinized to increase operating efficiency, to recycle raw materials formerly vented into the air or lost to the sewer, and to use waste products. Dow emphasized its good citizenship, but it nonetheless profited by these programs. Pollution control meant savings that could be transferred directly into higher company profits.

❖ Other Ethical Concerns of Business

It is obvious that ethical concerns arise in the business world, just as they do in the private lives of individuals. To discuss all of the ways in which ethics affects business would be impossible in this chapter. In this concluding section we touch upon three further areas relating to business that frequently elicit ethical questions and debate.

Consumer Credit

Consider an example of a court decision and the ethical versus the economic issues involved. To purchase furniture and consumer durable goods, residents in low-income areas must sign an agreement with a clause stating that if they fail to make timely payment, not only the goods purchased under the instant contract will be repossessed, but also any prior goods purchased under similar contracts from the same vendor. This provision is often referred to as an **add-on clause.**

ADD-ON CLAUSE
A clause in an installment contract that makes an individual's earlier purchase from a firm security for a new purchase.

Suppose that Mrs. Brown, a poor, single mother of three children, makes three separate purchases at a furniture store. First she buys a television set, then a stereo, and then a couch. Each one of these items is purchased on credit. Each time she purchases an item, she makes a down payment and signs a contract containing the add-on clause. She duly makes payments on the first two items but fails to make payments on time for the last item. The vendor, invoking its rights under the add-on clause, repossesses not only the couch but also the stereo and television. Mrs. Brown sues.

What should the court decide? The add-on clause offends many people's sense of justice. After all, why should Mrs. Brown relinquish those items for which she has properly paid according to the sales agreement? Indeed, when such cases have reached the courts, judgments have tended to favor the plaintiffs on the grounds of public policy.

But now consider the long-run implications of such court decision. Add-on clauses allowing for the repossession *(replevin)* of previously purchased items, in addition to the one under contract, give vendors in low-income areas additional security to reduce the costs of nonperformance. The reason, presumably, that one does not find such add-on clauses in similar sales agreements in middle-income areas is because vendors do not find it necessary to seek the additional security. Without this additional security in a low-income area, vendors will reduce the amount of credit offered. How? They will screen applicants more carefully, eliminating those who previously might have been able to obtain credit. The long-term result of Mrs. Brown's successful litigation will be a reduction in the amount of credit given in low-income areas. Those buyers with the lowest credit ratings are the ones who will be hurt. How appealing is this result?

Now try to determine whether the vendor's business conduct in repossessing the stereo and the television, in addition to the couch, was ethically appropriate.

Insurance and Negligence

MORAL HAZARD
A term used in the insurance industry to describe a situation in which insurance coverage provides individuals or business entities with little disincentive to be negligent.

In the area of insurance, one of the major ethical questions involves what has been named **moral hazard,** which occurs when individuals or companies have little disincentive to act negligently or to engage in activities that will result in payment by an insurance company. For example, the businessperson who takes out a large insurance policy on a building has less incentive to take care that the building is protected from potential fire than an individual without an insurance policy. What is the ethical responsibility of the owner of the building when insurance is in effect? Is he or she exempt from taking precautions against a fire?

The same issue arises for insurance policies that cover losses due to theft. The smaller the deductible in such policies, the less incentive the property owner has to prevent loss due to theft. For example, with insurance in effect, the property owner may have less incentive to install alarm systems, to pay for private patrol service, and so on. Of course, the more claims made on such insurance policies, the higher the average insurance rate per dollar amount insured. Thus, those individuals who are careless about protecting their own property impose costs on all individuals who buy property insurance.

Moral hazard exists with medical insurance also. The smaller the deductible, the less the incentive is for the individual to practice preventive medicine. What is the ethical responsibility of the individual citizen in terms of providing for his or her own well-being? Because health insurance is available for most individuals in the United States, does that mean that individuals should not be concerned about smoking, being overweight, too much sugar in their diets, and so on? Indeed, it is argued that in the United States, too many resources are devoted to the care of those who are already sick and too few resources to preventive medicine.

Concerning the insurer of property, consider what his or her ethical viewpoint must be. Should the insurer settle when there is a doubt, or should he or she require litigation before making payment?

Bankruptcy

As discussed in Chapter 20, the first goal of bankruptcy law is to provide relief and protection, and a fresh start, to debtors who have "gotten in over their heads." But consider the concept of bankruptcy from the point of view of the creditor. The creditor has extended a transfer of purchasing power from himself or herself to the debtor. That transfer of purchasing power represents a transfer of an asset for an asset. The debtor obtains the asset of money, goods, or services; and the creditor obtains the asset called a *secured* or *unsecured* legal obligation on the part of the debtor to pay. Once the debtor is in bankruptcy, voluntarily or involuntarily, the asset that the creditor owns most often has a diminished value. Indeed, in many circumstances that asset will have a zero value.

Society has generally concluded that everyone should be given the chance to start over again. Thus, bankruptcy law is a balancing act between providing such a chance and ensuring that creditors are given "a fair shake." But the question of *moral hazard* arises with bankruptcy law just as it does with insurance law: The easier it becomes for debtors to hide behind bankruptcy laws, the greater will be the incentive for debtors to use such laws to avoid payment of legally owed sums of money. That also means that the more easily a debtor can hide behind bankruptcy laws, the more a creditor will charge for a higher degree of risk-taking.

The total number of bankruptcies has more than doubled since the enactment of the Bankruptcy Reform Act of 1978. Creditors therefore know that they incur higher risks in making loans today. In order to compensate for these higher risks, creditors will do one or more of the following: increase the interest rates charged to everyone, require more security (collateral), or be more selective in the granting of credit. Thus, a trade-off situation exists: The more lenient bankruptcy laws are, the better off will be those debtors who find themselves in bankruptcy; but those debtors who will never be in bankruptcy will be worse off. Ethical concerns here must be matched with the economic concerns of other groups of individuals affected by the law.

Chapter 11 Filing   Particularly controversial is the question concerning at what point and in which circumstances companies should be entitled to file a Chapter 11 petition for reorganization under the Bankruptcy Reform Act of 1978. Filing a Chapter 11 petition automatically stays the commencement, continuation, or enforcement of proceedings against the debtor by a creditor or creditors. As previously stated, the bankruptcy law attempts to provide a refuge to the honest debtor who is unable to pay his or her debts. The "rehabilitation" of the debtor, rather than the liquidation of the debtor's estate (as occurs under Chapter 7), is the primary purpose of Chapter 11.

Manville Corporation's Chapter 11 filing (see Chapter 20) raises many ethical issues. When the Manville Corporation filed for Chapter 11 reorganization on August 26, 1982, the corporation's reported assets were valued at $2.2 billion. The fact that Manville Corporation was solvent when it filed for Chapter 11 reorganization led many people to question the fairness of Chapter 11. Manville officials countered that the petition for reorganization was the only way to save the corporation from the pending 16,500 lawsuits for asbestos-related diseases. A research firm commissioned by Manville in 1982 estimated liability as high as $4.8 billion by the year 2009. Furthermore, the Bankruptcy Code is drafted so as to allow the filing for Chapter 11 reorganization by a solvent debtor, the theory being that creditors will be better protected if debtors file for reorganization while their assets are still available to pay creditors' claims. So long as a debtor is "honest," bankruptcy courts have been willing to discharge the debtor from pre-petition debts and some post-petition debts.

But is it right for a bankruptcy court to be used by a solvent company facing potential tort liability? Do companies such as Manville deserve the "fresh start" available under Chapter 11—which allows debtors to escape the pressures that drove them into bankruptcy? Even though the filing by Manville may stick to the letter of the Bankruptcy Code, these questions still arise. Evidence suggests that Manville knew that exposure to asbestos resulted in asbestos-related diseases such as asbestosis, lung cancer, and cancer of the stomach, colon, and rectum. Also, court cases revealed that Manville had withheld this knowledge from its employees. Given this evidence of social irresponsibility, does Manville deserve a fresh start?

In another bankruptcy case, *N.L.R.B.* v. *Bildisco and Bildisco*,[8] an employer was able to avoid its obligations under a collective-bargaining agreement by filing for Chapter 11 reorganization. Bildisco, the debtor firm, filed a voluntary petition for Chapter 11 reorganization and was thereafter authorized by the bankruptcy court to operate the business as a debtor-in-possession. The debtor's employees were represented by the union with whom the debtor had negotiated a collective-bargaining agreement. When the debtor became unable to meet some of its obligations under the agreement, it requested and received permission from the bankruptcy court to reject the agreement. The U.S. Supreme Court, upon granting the petition for certiorari, held that collective-bargaining agreements subject to the National Labor Relations Act are executory contracts, and hence they are subject to rejection by debtors-in-possession. Is such a result ethical? Should the "fresh start" policy of the Bankruptcy Code extend to the rejection of collective-bargaining agreements? Does

8.   465 U.S. 513, 104 S.Ct. 1188, 79 L.Ed.2d 482 (1984).

this opinion give businesses an unfair bargaining advantage in dealing with unions? If the unions refuse to take pay cuts or other concessions, will not businesses just turn to Chapter 11?

The 1984 Bankruptcy Amendments attempted to answer some of these questions. In general, a collective-bargaining contract can be rejected in a Chapter 11 bankruptcy if the debtor has first proposed "necessary" contractual modifications to the union, and if the union has rejected the modification without good cause. Good-faith negotiations to reach an agreement are required from both sides.

Competition and Chapter 11 Competition often induces manufacturers to take risks that may subsequently harm society, thus precipitating the manufacturer's own economic downfall. Some critics argue, however, that the remedy to this—the imposition of punitive damages in product liability cases—may in effect be "overkill," since it will probably spur the company to file a petition for Chapter 11 reorganization. Thus, the economic consequences of our devices for punishment and deterrence are complex. How can we punish and deter unethical conduct by a company that has done much good in the past and has the potential to do much good in the future without inviting it to file for Chapter 11 reorganization? Remember, the filing of a petition in bankruptcy automatically stays the commencement of proceedings against the debtor. What happens to potential and existing plaintiffs then?

Application

Law and the Money Manager

Assume you are a money manager for a large corporation. You have complete discretion at your disposal to invest certain assets of the company in stocks, bonds, and related investment outlets. If you decide that you want to be a "moral" investor for your company's dollars, you will seek out investment vehicles that stay away from companies whose behavior you think is reprehensible.

You now have two problems facing you: The first is to analyze the company to determine whether its financial future is rosy enough to warrant purchasing its stock; the second is to analyze the company for its social, or ethical, value. Although there are many tried-and-true methods of determining the financial wisdom of investing in a particular company, there are certainly fewer tried methods, and probably no true ones, for deciding which company or companies engage in ethical, or socially responsible, behavior. The answer is completely subjective and open to endless debate. But there exist so-called *ethical funds* whose money managers scan the universe of over 8,500 publicly held companies in order to determine which ones meet their ethical standards. In recent years companies that have direct or indirect dealings with South Africa head the list of firms to be avoided by ethical-investment seekers. But then less obvious ethical issues arise. Should defense contractors be fair game? What about firms that sell alcohol or tobacco? What about those that have something to do with nuclear power plants? And what about those that might be adding to environmental pollution, such as steel companies? Conflicts also arise, as in the case of Johnson & Johnson, which has a great record as a corporate citizen, yet has operations in South Africa.

In a sentence, your job is not easy. A number of mutual funds have claimed to invest only in socially responsible companies and still make profits for their clients. Several studies at the beginning of 1987, however, showed that those mutual funds applying ethical criteria had, on average, below-average rates of return relative to other investment funds that were using traditional criteria for making their investing decisions. Look at Exhibit 37-1, which presents a scorecard for ethical funds. You see that in 1986 of the eight mutual funds that use social and ethical criteria in stock selection, none outperformed the Dow Jones Industrial Average, which rose 22.6 percent. And only two did better than the typical mutual fund, which rose 15.1 percent. Of the four ethical funds that had been in business for five years, only one outdid either the Dow or the average mutual fund. Will your choice to invest in socially responsible companies make a difference? Probably not, in a capital market that is so large. Of course, that is no reason to abandon the idea of investing only in socially responsible businesses. It may simply make people feel more comfortable. Essentially, socially conscious investing appeals to that segment of individuals who want to put their money where their mouths and minds are.

◆ **Exhibit 37-1**
Scorecard on Ethical Funds

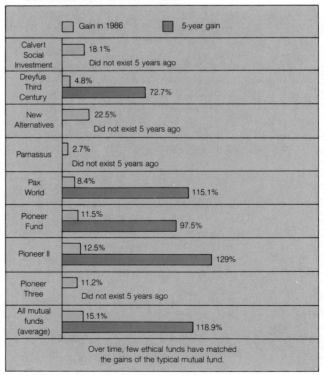

Over time, few ethical funds have matched the gains of the typical mutual fund.

❖ Chapter Summary: Ethics and Social Responsibility

Definitions	1. *Business ethics*—Moral principles and values applied to business decisions.
	2. *Ethical issue*—One that raises questions relating to fairness and justice or what is socially desirable. What is deemed to be ethical changes over time as the social context of decisions changes and societal customs and values change.
	3. *Positive law*—Law created by governmental authority and representing a basic social ethic; also called *black-letter law*.
Ethics in the Workplace	1. Ethical issues are raised in the areas of employment, particularly regarding affirmative action programs that result in reverse discrimination.
	2. Whistleblowing ("blowing the whistle" on the illegal or improper acts of one's employer) presents an ethical issue as it brings into conflict two public policies—the right of employers to manage their affairs (including the hiring and firing of employees) without government or judicial interference, and the right of the public to be protected from unsafe products, criminal activities, and so forth.
Ethics and the Corporation	1. The directors and officers of a corporation owe a fiduciary duty to its shareholders and have a responsibility for the welfare of its employees. Today most corporations believe that they also have a social responsibility to consumers and to the public. Quite often these duties and responsibilities come into conflict, and ethical issues arise over which group should be favored.
	2. One of the most significant ethical questions facing modern corporations is the extent to which they should be responsible to society for the effects of their products and methods of manufacturing, including liability for the misuse of its products by consumers.
	3. Despite criticisms of a lack of corporate social responsiveness, most major corporations engage in philanthropic activities and make generous donations to worthy causes.
	4. Social investing (purchasing stock only in corporations that are socially responsible) is a recent trend receiving widespread debate.
	5. Corporations face an ethical issue when they devote financial resources to and take actions in the conservation of natural resources when such conservation reduces profits (and thus the income of shareholders and employees).
Other Ethical Concerns of Business	Other ethical concerns of business arise in the following areas:
	1. *Consumer credit*—Add-on clause (a statement in a purchase agreement for consumer goods that failure to make timely payment can result in repossession not only of the goods purchased under the instant contract but also of any prior goods purchased under similar contracts from the same vendor).
	2. *Insurance*—Moral hazard (occurs when individuals or companies have little disincentive to act negligently or to engage in activities that will result in payment by an insurance company).
	3. *Bankruptcy*—Is it ethical to allow solvent businesses to declare bankruptcy in order to stay law suits, break union contracts, and so forth?

❖ Questions and Case Problems

37-1. What is a company's ethical responsibility toward its competitors? Toward its suppliers?

37-2. What is a company's ethical responsibility to its workers? How can a company balance its ethical responsibilities to its workers and its legal responsibilities to its shareholders?

37-3. Should ethics be a concern of top management alone, or should it be a shared concern of all employees, distributors, suppliers, and so on?

37-4. If shareholders as individuals own too small a percentage of a corporation to have an effect on its actions, how do shareholders exert control over the corporation? Some argue that their control is via the sale of shares in companies with whose actions they are dissatisfied. How would such a sale of shares have any effect on the company's future activities?

37-5. Should conservation of natural resources and other environmental considerations be ethical concerns of businesses?

37-6. Michael Hauck was a deckhand for Sabine Pilot Service, Inc. His employment was at-will. One of his duties each day was to pump the bilges of one of his employer's boats into the waterways. Hauck had noticed a sign on the boat that stated it was illegal to pump the bilges (inner hulls) into the water. He had also called the U.S. Coast Guard concerning this, and a Coast Guard officer confirmed that it was indeed illegal to empty the bilges into the water. Hauck thereafter refused to perform the illegal act for his employer and was fired from his job because of this refusal. Hauck brought an action against Sabine for wrongful discharge. Texas was an employment-at-will state, and the Texas courts had steadfastly refused to grant any exception to this doctrine. On what basis might the Texas court to which this case was appealed create an exception to the at-will doctrine? Discuss. [Sabine Pilot Service, Inc. v. Hauck, 687 S.W.2d 733 (Tex. 1985)]

37-7. A husband whose wife's death had been caused by lung cancer caused by her forty-year history of cigarette smoking sued the Liggett Group of tobacco producers for damages. The husband contended that the Liggett Group should be liable for damages under product liability laws because it not only manufactured and marketed a harmful product but failed to stress adequately to consumers the harmful consequences of cigarette smoking. This and similar cases raise the question as to whether cigarette producers should be liable for the ultimate harm caused to consumers using their products, even though the consumers who use their products voluntarily assume the health risk associated with cigarette smoking. What public policies must be weighed in answering this question? [Cipollone v. Liggett Group, Inc., 644 F.Supp. 283 (D.N.J. 1986)]

Appendix A

The Constitution of the United States

PREAMBLE

We the People of the United States, in Order to form a more perfect Union, establish Justice, insure domestic Tranquility, provide for the common defence, promote the general Welfare, and secure the Blessings of Liberty to ourselves and our Posterity, do ordain and establish this Constitution for the United States of America.

ARTICLE I

Section 1. All legislative Powers herein granted shall be vested in a Congress of the United States, which shall consist of a Senate and House of Representatives.

Section 2. The House of Representatives shall be composed of Members chosen every second Year by the People of the several States, and the Electors in each State shall have the Qualifications requisite for Electors of the most numerous Branch of the State Legislature.

No Person shall be a Representative who shall not have attained to the Age of twenty five Years, and been seven Years a Citizen of the United States, and who shall not, when elected, be an Inhabitant of that State in which he shall be chosen.

Representatives and direct Taxes shall be apportioned among the several States which may be included within this Union, according to their respective Numbers, which shall be determined by adding to the whole Number of free Persons, including those bound to Service for a Term of Years, and excluding Indians not taxed, three fifths of all other Persons. The actual Enumeration shall be made within three Years after the first Meeting of the Congress of the United States, and within every subsequent Term of ten Years, in such Manner as they shall by Law direct. The Number of Representatives shall not exceed one for every thirty Thousand, but each State shall have at Least one Representative; and until such enumeration shall be made, the State of New Hampshire shall be entitled to chuse three, Massachusetts eight, Rhode Island and Providence Plantations one, Connecticut five, New York six, New Jersey four, Pennsylvania eight, Delaware one, Maryland six, Virginia ten, North Carolina five, South Carolina five, and Georgia three.

When vacancies happen in the Representation from any State, the Executive Authority thereof shall issue Writs of Election to fill such Vacancies.

The House of Representatives shall chuse their Speaker and other Officers; and shall have the sole Power of Impeachment.

Section 3. The Senate of the United States shall be composed of two Senators from each State, chosen by the Legislature thereof, for six Years; and each Senator shall have one Vote.

Immediately after they shall be assembled in Consequence of the first Election, they shall be divided as equally as may be into three Classes. The Seats of the Senators of the first Class shall be vacated at the Expiration of the second Year, of the second Class at the Expiration of the fourth Year, and of the third Class at the Expiration of the sixth Year, so that one third may be chosen every second Year; and if Vacancies happen by Resignation, or otherwise, during the Recess of the Legislature of any State, the Executive thereof may make temporary Appointments until the next Meeting of the Legislature, which shall then fill such Vacancies.

No Person shall be a Senator who shall not have attained to the Age of thirty Years, and been nine Years a Citizen of the United States, and who shall not, when elected, be an Inhabitant of that State for which he shall be chosen.

The Vice President of the United States shall be President of the Senate, but shall have no Vote, unless they be equally divided.

The Senate shall chuse their other Officers, and also a President pro tempore, in the Absence of the Vice President, or when he shall exercise the Office of President of the United States.

The Senate shall have the sole Power to try all Impeachments. When sitting for that Purpose, they shall be on Oath or Affirmation. When the President of the United States is tried, the Chief Justice shall preside: And no Person shall be convicted without the Concurrence of two thirds of the Members present.

Judgment in Cases of Impeachment shall not extend further than to removal from Office, and disqualification to hold and enjoy any Office of honor, Trust, or Profit under the United States: but the Party convicted shall nevertheless be liable and subject to Indictment, Trial, Judgment, and Punishment, according to Law.

Section 4. The Times, Places and Manner of holding Elections for Senators and Representatives, shall be prescribed in each State by the Legislature thereof; but the Congress may at any time by Law make or alter such Regulations, except as to the Places of chusing Senators.

The Congress shall assemble at least once in every Year, and such Meeting shall be on the first Monday in December, unless they shall by Law appoint a different Day.

Section 5. Each House shall be the Judge of the Elections, Returns, and Qualifications of its own Members, and a Majority of each shall constitute a Quorum to do Business; but a smaller Number may adjourn from day to day, and may be authorized to compel the Attendance of absent Members, in such Manner, and under such Penalties as each House may provide.

Each House may determine the Rules of its Proceedings, punish its Members for disorderly Behavior, and, with the Concurrence of two thirds, expel a Member.

Each House shall keep a Journal of its Proceedings, and from time to time publish the same, excepting such Parts as may in their Judgment require Secrecy; and the Yeas and Nays of the Members of either House on any question shall, at the Desire of one fifth of those Present, be entered on the Journal.

Neither House, during the Session of Congress, shall, without the Consent of the other, adjourn for more than three days, nor to any other Place than that in which the two Houses shall be sitting.

Section 6.   The Senators and Representatives shall receive a Compensation for their Services, to be ascertained by Law, and paid out of the Treasury of the United States. They shall in all Cases, except Treason, Felony and Breach of the Peace, be privileged from Arrest during their Attendance at the Session of their respective Houses, and in going to and returning from the same; and for any Speech or Debate in either House, they shall not be questioned in any other Place.

No Senator or Representative shall, during the Time for which he was elected, be appointed to any civil Office under the Authority of the United States, which shall have been created, or the Emoluments whereof shall have been increased during such time; and no Person holding any Office under the United States, shall be a Member of either House during his Continuance in Office.

Section 7.   All Bills for raising Revenue shall originate in the House of Representatives; but the Senate may propose or concur with Amendments as on other Bills.

Every Bill which shall have passed the House of Representatives and the Senate, shall, before it become a Law, be presented to the President of the United States; If he approve he shall sign it, but if not he shall return it, with his Objections to the House in which it shall have originated, who shall enter the Objections at large on their Journal, and proceed to reconsider it. If after such Reconsideration two thirds of that House shall agree to pass the Bill, it shall be sent together with the Objections, to the other House, by which it shall likewise be reconsidered, and if approved by two thirds of that House, it shall become a Law. But in all such Cases the Votes of both Houses shall be determined by Yeas and Nays, and the Names of the Persons voting for and against the Bill shall be entered on the Journal of each House respectively. If any Bill shall not be returned by the President within ten Days (Sundays excepted) after it shall have been presented to him, the Same shall be a Law, in like Manner as if he had signed it, unless the Congress by their Adjournment prevent its Return in which Case it shall not be a Law.

Every Order, Resolution, or Vote, to which the Concurrence of the Senate and House of Representatives may be necessary (except on a question of Adjournment) shall be presented to the President of the United States; and before the Same shall take Effect, shall be approved by him, or being disapproved by him, shall be repassed by two thirds of the Senate and House of Representatives, according to the Rules and Limitations prescribed in the Case of a Bill.

Section 8.   The Congress shall have Power To lay and collect Taxes, Duties, Imposts and Excises, to pay the Debts and provide for the common Defence and general Welfare of the United States; but all Duties, Imposts and Excises shall be uniform throughout the United States;

To borrow Money on the credit of the United States;

To regulate Commerce with foreign Nations, and among the several States, and with the Indian Tribes;

To establish an uniform Rule of Naturalization, and uniform Laws on the subject of Bankruptcies throughout the United States;

To coin Money, regulate the Value thereof, and of foreign Coin, and fix the Standard of Weights and Measures;

To provide for the Punishment of counterfeiting the Securities and current Coin of the United States;

To establish Post Offices and post Roads;

To promote the Progress of Science and useful Arts, by securing for limited Times to Authors and Inventors the exclusive Right to their respective Writings and Discoveries;

To constitute Tribunals inferior to the supreme Court;

To define and punish Piracies and Felonies committed on the high Seas, and Offenses against the Law of Nations;

To declare War, grant Letters of Marque and Reprisal, and make Rules concerning Captures on Land and Water;

To raise and support Armies, but no Appropriation of Money to that Use shall be for a longer Term than two Years;

To provide and maintain a Navy;

To make Rules for the Government and Regulation of the land and naval Forces;

To provide for calling forth the Militia to execute the Laws of the Union, suppress Insurrections and repel Invasions;

To provide for organizing, arming, and disciplining, the Militia, and for governing such Part of them as may be employed in the Service of the United States, reserving to the States respectively, the Appointment of the Officers, and the Authority of training the Militia according to the discipline prescribed by Congress;

To exercise exclusive Legislation in all Cases whatsoever, over such District (not exceeding ten Miles square) as may, by Cession of particular States, and the Acceptance of Congress, become the Seat of the Government of the United States, and to exercise like Authority over all Places purchased by the Consent of the Legislature of the State in which the Same shall be, for the Erection of Forts, Magazines, Arsenals, dock-Yards, and other needful Buildings;—And

To make all Laws which shall be necessary and proper for carrying into Execution the foregoing Powers, and all other Powers vested by this Constitution in the Government of the United States, or in any Department or Officer thereof.

Section 9.   The Migration or Importation of such Persons as any of the States now existing shall think proper to admit, shall not be prohibited by the Congress prior to the Year one thousand eight hundred and eight, but a Tax or duty may be imposed on such Importation, not exceeding ten dollars for each Person.

The privilege of the Writ of Habeas Corpus shall not be suspended, unless when in Cases of Rebellion or Invasion the public Safety may require it.

No Bill of Attainder or ex post facto Law shall be passed.

No Capitation, or other direct, Tax shall be laid, unless in Proportion to the Census or Enumeration herein before directed to be taken.

No Tax or Duty shall be laid on Articles exported from any State.

No Preference shall be given by any Regulation of Commerce or Revenue to the Ports of one State over those of another: nor shall Vessels bound to, or from, one State be obliged to enter, clear, or pay Duties in another.

No Money shall be drawn from the Treasury, but in Consequence of Appropriations made by Law; and a regular Statement and Account of the Receipts and Expenditures of all public Money shall be published from time to time.

No Title of Nobility shall be granted by the United States: And no Person holding any Office of Profit or Trust under them, shall, without the Consent of the Congress, accept of any present, Emolument, Office, or Title, of any kind whatever, from any King, Prince, or foreign State.

Section 10.   No State shall enter into any Treaty, Alliance, or Confederation; grant Letters of Marque and Reprisal; coin Money; emit Bills of Credit; make any Thing but gold and silver Coin a Tender in Payment of Debts; pass any Bill of Attainder, ex post facto Law, or Law impairing the Obligation of Contracts, or grant any Title of Nobility.

No State shall, without the Consent of the Congress, lay any Imposts or Duties on Imports or Exports, except what may be absolutely necessary for executing it's inspection Laws: and the net Produce of all Duties and Imposts, laid by any State on Imports or Exports, shall be for the Use of the Treasury of the United States; and all such Laws shall be subject to the Revision and Controul of the Congress.

No State shall, without the Consent of Congress, lay any Duty of Tonnage, keep Troops, or Ships of War in time of Peace, enter into any Agreement or Compact with another State, or with a foreign Power, or engage in War, unless actually invaded, or in such imminent Danger as will not admit of delay.

ARTICLE II

Section 1.   The executive Power shall be vested in a President of the United States of America. He shall hold his Office during the Term of four Years, and, together with the Vice President, chosen for the same Term, be elected, as follows:

Each State shall appoint, in such Manner as the Legislature thereof may direct, a Number of Electors, equal to the whole Number of Senators and Representatives to which the State may be entitled in the Congress; but no Senator or Representative, or Person holding an Office of Trust or Profit under the United States, shall be appointed an Elector.

The Electors shall meet in their respective States, and vote by Ballot for two Persons, of whom one at least shall not be an Inhabitant of the same State with themselves. And they shall make a List of all the Persons voted for, and of the Number of Votes for each; which List they shall sign and certify, and transmit sealed to the Seat of the Government of the United States, directed to the President of the Senate. The President of the Senate shall, in the Presence of the Senate and House of Representatives, open all the Certificates, and the Votes shall then be counted. The Person having the greatest Number of Votes shall be the President, if such Number be a Majority of the whole Number of Electors appointed; and if there be more than one who have such Majority, and have an equal Number of Votes, then the House of Representatives shall immediately chuse by Ballot one of them for President; and if no Person have a Majority, then from the five highest on the List the said House shall in like Manner chuse the President. But in chusing the President, the Votes shall be taken by States, the Representation from each State having one Vote; A quorum for this Purpose shall consist of a Member or Members from two thirds of the States, and a Majority of all the States shall be necessary to a Choice. In every Case, after the Choice of the President, the Person having the greater Number of Votes of the Electors shall be the Vice President. But if there should remain two or more who have equal Votes, the Senate shall chuse from them by Ballot the Vice President.

The Congress may determine the Time of chusing the Electors, and the Day on which they shall give their Votes; which Day shall be the same throughout the United States.

No person except a natural born Citizen, or a Citizen of the United States, at the time of the Adoption of this Constitution, shall be eligible to the Office of President; neither shall any Person be eligible to that Office who shall not have attained to the Age of thirty five Years, and been fourteen Years a Resident within the United States.

In Case of the Removal of the President from Office, or of his Death, Resignation or Inability to discharge the Powers and Duties of the said Office, the same shall devolve on the Vice President, and the Congress may by Law provide for the Case of Removal, Death, Resignation or Inability, both of the President and Vice President, declaring what Officer shall then act as President, and such Officer shall act accordingly, until the Disability be removed, or a President shall be elected.

The President shall, at stated Times, receive for his Services, a Compensation, which shall neither be increased nor diminished during the Period for which he shall have been elected, and he shall not receive within that Period any other Emolument from the United States, or any of them.

Before he enter on the Execution of his Office, he shall take the following Oath or Affirmation: "I do solemnly swear (or affirm) that I will faithfully execute the Office of President of the United States, and will to the best of my Ability, preserve, protect and defend the Constitution of the United States."

Section 2.   The President shall be Commander in Chief of the Army and Navy of the United States, and of the Militia of the several States, when called into the actual Service of the United

States; he may require the Opinion, in writing, of the principal Officer in each of the executive Departments, upon any Subject relating to the Duties of their respective Offices, and he shall have Power to grant Reprieves and Pardons for Offenses against the United States, except in Cases of Impeachment.

He shall have Power, by and with the Advice and Consent of the Senate to make Treaties, provided two thirds of the Senators present concur; and he shall nominate, and by and with the Advice and Consent of the Senate, shall appoint Ambassadors, other public Ministers and Consuls, Judges of the supreme Court, and all other Officers of the United States, whose Appointments are not herein otherwise provided for, and which shall be established by Law; but the Congress may by Law vest the Appointment of such inferior Officers, as they think proper, in the President alone, in the Courts of Law, or in the Heads of Departments.

The President shall have Power to fill up all Vacancies that may happen during the Recess of the Senate, by granting Commissions which shall expire at the End of their next Session.

Section 3. He shall from time to time give to the Congress Information of the State of the Union, and recommend to their Consideration such Measures as he shall judge necessary and expedient; he may, on extraordinary Occasions, convene both Houses, or either of them, and in Case of Disagreement between them, with Respect to the Time of Adjournment, he may adjourn them to such Time as he shall think proper; he shall receive Ambassadors and other public Ministers; he shall take Care that the Laws be faithfully executed, and shall Commission all the Officers of the United States.

Section 4. The President, Vice President and all civil Officers of the United States, shall be removed from Office on Impeachment for, and Conviction of, Treason, Bribery, or other high Crimes and Misdemeanors.

ARTICLE III

Section 1. The judicial Power of the United States, shall be vested in one supreme Court, and in such inferior Courts as the Congress may from time to time ordain and establish. The Judges, both of the supreme and inferior Courts, shall hold their Offices during good Behaviour, and shall, at stated Times, receive for their Services a Compensation, which shall not be diminished during their Continuance in Office.

Section 2. The judicial Power shall extend to all Cases, in Law and Equity, arising under this Constitution, the Laws of the United States, and Treaties made, or which shall be made, under their Authority;—to all Cases affecting Ambassadors, other public Ministers and Consuls;—to all Cases of admiralty and maritime Jurisdiction;—to Controversies to which the United States shall be a Party;—to Controversies between two or more States;—between a State and Citizens of another State;—between Citizens of different States;—between Citizens of the same State claiming Lands under Grants of different States, and between a State, or the Citizens thereof, and foreign States, Citizens or Subjects.

In all Cases affecting Ambassadors, other public Ministers and Consuls, and those in which a State shall be a Party, the supreme Court shall have original Jurisdiction. In all the other Cases before mentioned, the supreme Court shall have appellate Jurisdiction, both as to Law and Fact, with such Exceptions, and under such Regulations as the Congress shall make.

The Trial of all Crimes, except in Cases of Impeachment, shall be by Jury; and such Trial shall be held in the State where the said Crimes shall have been committed; but when not committed within any State, the Trial shall be at such Place or Places as the Congress may by Law have directed.

Section 3. Treason against the United States, shall consist only in levying War against them, or, in adhering to their Enemies, giving them Aid and Comfort. No Person shall be convicted of Treason unless on the Testimony of two Witnesses to the same overt Act, or on Confession in open Court.

The Congress shall have Power to declare the Punishment of Treason, but no Attainder of Treason shall work Corruption of Blood, or Forfeiture except during the Life of the Person attainted.

ARTICLE IV

Section 1. Full Faith and Credit shall be given in each State to the public Acts, Records, and judicial Proceedings of every other State. And the Congress may by general Laws prescribe the Manner in which such Acts, Records and Proceedings shall be proved, and the Effect thereof.

Section 2. The Citizens of each State shall be entitled to all Privileges and Immunities of Citizens in the several States.

A Person charged in any State with Treason, Felony, or other Crime, who shall flee from Justice, and be found in another State, shall on Demand of the executive Authority of the State from which he fled, be delivered up, to be removed to the State having Jurisdiction of the Crime.

No Person held to Service or Labour in one State, under the Laws thereof, escaping into another, shall, in Consequence of any Law or Regulation therein, be discharged from such Service or Labour, but shall be delivered up on Claim of the Party to whom such Service or Labour may be due.

Section 3. New States may be admitted by the Congress into this Union; but no new State shall be formed or erected within the Jurisdiction of any other State; nor any State be formed by the Junction of two or more States, or Parts of States, without the Consent of the Legislatures of the States concerned as well as of the Congress.

The Congress shall have Power to dispose of and make all needful Rules and Regulations respecting the Territory or other Property belonging to the United States; and nothing in this Constitution shall be so construed as to Prejudice any Claims of the United States, or of any particular State.

Section 4. The United States shall guarantee to every State in this Union a Republican Form of Government, and shall protect each of them against Invasion; and on Application of the Legislature, or of the Executive (when the Legislature cannot be convened) against domestic Violence.

ARTICLE V

The Congress, whenever two thirds of both Houses shall deem it necessary, shall propose Amendments to this Constitution, or, on the Application of the Legislatures of two thirds of the several States, shall call a Convention for proposing Amendments, which, in either Case, shall be valid to all Intents and Purposes, as part of this Constitution, when ratified by the Legislatures of three fourths of the several States, or by Conventions in three fourths thereof, as the one or the other Mode of Ratification may be proposed by the Congress; Provided that no Amendment which may be made prior to the Year One thousand eight hundred and eight shall in any Manner affect the first and fourth Clauses in the Ninth Section of the first Article; and that no State, without its Consent, shall be deprived of its equal Suffrage in the Senate.

ARTICLE VI

All Debts contracted and Engagements entered into, before the Adoption of this Constitution shall be as valid against the United States under this Constitution, as under the Confederation.

This Constitution, and the Laws of the United States which shall be made in Pursuance thereof; and all Treaties made, or which shall be made, under the Authority of the United States, shall be the supreme Law of the Land; and the Judges in every State shall be bound thereby, any Thing in the Constitution or Laws of any State to the Contrary notwithstanding.

The Senators and Representatives before mentioned, and the Members of the several State Legislatures, and all executive and judicial Officers, both of the United States and of the several States, shall be bound by Oath or Affirmation, to support this Constitution; but no religious Test shall ever be required as a Qualification to any Office or public Trust under the United States.

ARTICLE VII

The Ratification of the Conventions of nine States shall be sufficient for the Establishment of this Constitution between the States so ratifying the Same.

AMENDMENT I [1791]

Congress shall make no law respecting an establishment of religion, or prohibiting the free exercise thereof; or abridging the freedom of speech, or of the press; or the right of the people peaceably to assembly, and to petition the Government for a redress of grievances.

AMENDMENT II [1791]

A well regulated Militia, being necessary to the security of a free State, the right of the people to keep and bear Arms, shall not be infringed.

AMENDMENT III [1791]

No Soldier shall, in time of peace be quartered in any house, without the consent of the Owner, nor in time of war, but in a manner to be prescribed by law.

Amendment IV [1791]

The right of the people to be secure in their persons, houses, papers, and effects, against unreasonable searches and seizures, shall not be violated, and no Warrants shall issue, but upon probable cause, supported by Oath or affirmation, and particularly describing the place to be searched, and the persons or things to be seized.

AMENDMENT V [1791]

No person shall be held to answer for a capital, or otherwise infamous crime, unless on a presentment or indictment of a Grand Jury, except in cases arising in the land or naval forces, or in the Militia, when in actual service in time of War or public danger; nor shall any person be subject for the same offence to be twice put in jeopardy of life or limb; nor shall be compelled in any criminal case to be a witness against himself, nor be deprived of life, liberty, or property, without due process of law; nor shall private property be taken for public use, without just compensation.

AMENDMENT VI [1791]

In all criminal prosecutions, the accused shall enjoy the right to a speedy and public trial, by an impartial jury of the State and district wherein the crime shall have been committed, which district shall have been previously ascertained by law, and to be informed of the nature and cause of the accusation; to be confronted with the witnesses against him; to have compulsory process for obtaining witnesses in his favor, and to have the Assistance of Counsel for his defence.

AMENDMENT VII [1791]

In Suits at common law, where the value in controversy shall exceed twenty dollars, the right of trial by jury shall be preserved, and no fact tried by jury, shall be otherwise re-examined in any Court of the United States, than according to the rules of the common law.

AMENDMENT VIII [1791]

Excessive bail shall not be required, nor excessive fines imposed, nor cruel and unusual punishments inflicted.

AMENDMENT IX [1791]

The enumeration in the Constitution, of certain rights, shall not be construed to deny or disparage others retained by the people.

AMENDMENT X [1791]

The powers not delegated to the United States by the Constitution, nor prohibited by it to the States, are reserved to the States respectively, or to the people.

AMENDMENT XI [1798]

The Judicial power of the United States shall not be construed to extend to any suit in law or equity, commenced or prosecuted against one of the United States by Citizens of another State, or by Citizens or Subjects of any Foreign State.

AMENDMENT XII [1804]

The Electors shall meet in their respective states, and vote by ballot for President and Vice-President, one of whom, at least, shall not be an inhabitant of the same state with themselves; they shall name in their ballots the person voted for as President, and in distinct ballots the person voted for as Vice-President, and they shall make distinct lists of all persons voted for as President, and of all persons voted for as Vice-President, and of the number of votes for each, which lists they shall sign and certify, and transmit sealed to the seat of the government of the United States, directed to the President of the Senate;—The President of the Senate shall, in the presence of the Senate and House of Representatives, open all the certificates and the votes shall then be counted;—The person having the greatest number of votes for President, shall be the President, if such number be a majority of the whole number of Electors appointed; and if no person have such majority, then from the persons having the highest numbers not exceeding three on the list of those voted for as President, the House of Representatives shall choose immediately, by ballot, the President. But in choosing the President, the votes shall be taken by states, the representation from each state having one vote; a quorum for this purpose shall consist of a member or members from two-thirds of the states, and a majority of all states shall be necessary to a choice. And if the House of Representatives shall not choose a President whenever the right of choice shall devolve upon them, before the fourth day of March next following, then the Vice-President shall act as President, as in the case of the death or other constitutional disability of the President.—The person having the greatest number of votes as Vice-President, shall be the Vice-President, if such number be a majority of the whole number of Electors appointed, and if no person have a majority, then from the two highest numbers on the list, the Senate shall choose the Vice-President; a quorum for the purpose shall consist of two-thirds of the whole number of Senators, and a majority of the whole number shall be necessary to a choice. But no person constitutionally ineligible to the office of President shall be eligible to that of Vice-President of the United States.

AMENDMENT XIII [1865]

Section 1.   Neither slavery nor involuntary servitude, except as a punishment for crime whereof the party shall have been duly convicted, shall exist within the United States, or any place subject to their jurisdiction.

Section 2.   Congress shall have power to enforce this article by appropriate legislation.

AMENDMENT XIV [1868]

Section 1.   All persons born or naturalized in the United States, and subject to the jurisdiction thereof, are citizens of the United States and of the State wherein they reside. No State shall make or enforce any law which shall abridge the privileges or immunities of citizens of the United States; nor shall any State deprive any person of life, liberty, or property, without due process of law; nor deny to any person within its jurisdiction the equal protection of the laws.

Section 2.   Representatives shall be apportioned among the several States according to their respective numbers, counting the whole number of persons in each State, excluding Indians not taxed. But when the right to vote at any election for the choice of electors for President and Vice President of the United States, Representatives in Congress, the Executive and Judicial officers of a State, or the members of the Legislature thereof, is denied to any of the male inhabitants of such State, being twenty-one years of age, and citizens of the United States, or in any way abridged, except for participation in rebellion, or other crime, the basis of representation therein shall be reduced in the proportion which the number of such male citizens shall bear to the whole number of male citizens twenty-one years of age in such State.

Section 3.   No person shall be a Senator or Representative in Congress, or elector of President and Vice President, or hold any office, civil or military, under the United States, or under any State, who having previously taken an oath, as a member of Congress, or as an officer of the United States, or as a member of any State legislature, or as an executive or judicial officer of any State, to support the Constitution of the United States, shall have engaged in insurrection or rebellion against the same, or given aid or comfort to the enemies thereof. But Congress may by a vote of two-thirds of each House, remove such disability.

Section 4.   The validity of the public debt of the United States, authorized by law, including debts incurred for payment of pensions and bounties for services in suppressing insurrection or rebellion, shall not be questioned. But neither the United States nor any State shall assume or pay any debt or obligation incurred in aid of insurrection or rebellion against the United States, or any claim for the loss or emancipation of any slave; but all such debts, obligations and claims shall be held illegal and void.

Section 5.   The Congress shall have power to enforce, by appropriate legislation, the provisions of this article.

AMENDMENT XV [1870]

Section 1.   The right of citizens of the United States to vote shall not be denied or abridged by the United States or by any State on account of race, color, or previous condition of servitude.

Section 2.   The Congress shall have power to enforce this article by appropriate legislation.

AMENDMENT XVI [1913]

The Congress shall have power to lay and collect taxes on incomes, from whatever source derived, without apportionment among the several States, and without regard to any census or enumeration.

AMENDMENT XVII [1913]

[1] The Senate of the United States shall be composed of two Senators from each State, elected by the people thereof, for six years; and each Senator shall have one vote. The electors in each State shall have the qualifications requisite for electors of the most numerous branch of the State legislatures.

[2] When vacancies happen in the representation of any State in the Senate, the executive authority of such State shall issue writs of election to fill such vacancies: *Provided*, That the legislature of any State may empower the executive thereof to make temporary appointments until the people fill the vacancies by election as the legislature may direct.

[3] This amendment shall not be so construed as to affect the election or term of any Senator chosen before it becomes valid as part of the Constitution.

AMENDMENT XVIII [1919]

Section 1.   After one year from the ratification of this article the manufacture, sale, or transportation of intoxicating liquors within, the importation thereof into, or the exportation thereof from the United States and all territory subject to the jurisdiction thereof for beverage purposes is hereby prohibited.

Section 2.   The Congress and the several States shall have concurrent power to enforce this article by appropriate legislation.

Section 3.   This article shall be inoperative unless it shall have been ratified as an amendment to the Constitution by the legislatures of the several States, as provided in the Constitution, within seven years from the date of the submission hereof to the States by the Congress.

AMENDMENT XIX [1920]

[1] The right of citizens of the United States to vote shall not be denied or abridged by the United States or by any State on account of sex.

[2] Congress shall have power to enforce this article by appropriate legislation.

AMENDMENT XX [1933]

Section 1.   The terms of the President and Vice President shall end at noon on the 20th day of January, and the terms of Senators and Representatives at noon on the 3d day of January, of the years in which such terms would have ended if this article had not been ratified; and the terms of their successors shall then begin.

Section 2.   The Congress shall assemble at least once in every year, and such meeting shall begin at noon on the 3d day of January, unless they shall by law appoint a different day.

Section 3.   If, at the time fixed for the beginning of the term of the President, the President elect shall have died, the Vice President elect shall become President. If the President shall not

have been chosen before the time fixed for the beginning of his term, or if the President elect shall have failed to qualify, then the Vice President elect shall act as President until a President shall have qualified; and the Congress may by law provide for the case wherein neither a President elect nor a Vice President elect shall have qualified, declaring who shall then act as President, or the manner in which one who is to act shall be selected, and such person shall act accordingly until a President or Vice President shall have qualified.

Section 4.   The Congress may by law provide for the case of the death of any of the persons from whom the House of Representatives may choose a President whenever the right of choice shall have devolved upon them, and for the case of the death of any of the persons from whom the Senate may choose a Vice President whenever the right of choice shall have devolved upon them.

Section 5.   Sections 1 and 2 shall take effect on the 15th day of October following the ratification of this article.

Section 6.   This article shall be inoperative unless it shall have been ratified as an amendment to the Constitution by the legislatures of three-fourths of the several States within seven years from the date of its submission.

AMENDMENT XXI [1933]

Section 1.   The eighteenth article of amendment to the Constitution of the United States is hereby repealed.

Section 2.   The transportation or importation into any State, Territory, or possession of the United States for delivery or use therein of intoxicating liquors, in violation of the laws thereof, is hereby prohibited.

Section 3.   This article shall be inoperative unless it shall have been ratified as an amendment to the Constitution by conventions in the several States, as provided in the Constitution, within seven years from the date of the submission hereof to the States by the Congress.

AMENDMENT XXII [1951]

Section 1.   No person shall be elected to the office of the President more than twice, and no person who has held the office of President, or acted as President, for more than two years of a term to which some other person was elected President shall be elected to the office of President more than once. But this Article shall not apply to any person holding the office of President when this Article was proposed by the Congress, and shall not prevent any person who may be holding the office of President, or acting as President, during the term within which this Article becomes operative from holding the office of President or acting as President during the remainder of such term.

Section 2.   This article shall be inoperative unless it shall have been ratified as an amendment to the Constitution by the legislatures of three-fourths of the several States within seven years from the date of its submission to the States by the Congress.

AMENDMENT XXIII [1961]

Section 1. The District constituting the seat of Government of the United States shall appoint in such manner as the Congress may direct:

A number of electors of President and Vice President equal to the whole number of Senators and Representatives in Congress to which the District would be entitled if it were a State, but in no event more than the least populous state; they shall be in addition to those appointed by the states, but they shall be considered, for the purposes of the election of President and Vice President, to be electors appointed by a state; and they shall meet in the District and perform such duties as provided by the twelfth article of amendment.

Section 2. The Congress shall have power to enforce this article by appropriate legislation.

AMENDMENT XXIV [1964]

Section 1. The right of citizens of the United States to vote in any primary or other election for President or Vice President, for electors for President or Vice President, or for Senator or Representative in Congress, shall not be denied or abridged by the United States, or any State by reason of failure to pay any poll tax or other tax.

Section 2. The Congress shall have power to enforce this article by appropriate legislation.

AMENDMENT XXV [1967]

Section 1. In case of the removal of the President from office or of his death or resignation, the Vice President shall become President.

Section 2. Whenever there is a vacancy in the office of the Vice President, the President shall nominate a Vice President who shall take office upon confirmation by a majority vote of both Houses of Congress.

Section 3. Whenever the President transmits to the President pro tempore of the Senate and the Speaker of the House of Representatives his written declaration that he is unable to discharge the powers and duties of his office, and until he transmits to them a written declaration to the contrary, such powers and duties shall be discharged by the Vice President as Acting President.

Section 4. Whenever the Vice President and a majority of either the principal officers of the executive departments or of such other body as Congress may by law provide, transmit to the President pro tempore of the Senate and the Speaker of the House of Representatives their written declaration that the President is unable to discharge the powers and duties of his office, the Vice President shall immediately assume the powers and duties of the office as Acting President.

Thereafter, when the President transmits to the President pro tempore of the Senate and the Speaker of the House of Representatives his written declaration that no inability exists, he shall resume the powers and duties of his office unless the Vice President and a majority of either the principal officers of the executive department or of such other body as Congress may by law provide, transmit within four days to the President pro tempore of the Senate and the Speaker of the House of Representatives their written declaration and the President is unable to discharge the powers and duties of his office. Thereupon Congress shall decide the issue, assembling within forty-eight hours for that purpose if not in session. If the Congress, within twenty-one days after receipt of the latter written declaration, or, if Congress is not in session, within twenty-one days after Congress is required to assemble, determines by two-thirds vote of both Houses that the President is unable to discharge the powers and duties of his office, the Vice President shall continue to discharge the same as Acting President; otherwise, the President shall resume the powers and duties of his office.

AMENDMENT XXVI [1971]

Section 1. The right of citizens of the United States, who are eighteen years of age or older, to vote shall not be denied or abridged by the United States or by any State on account of age.

Section 2. The Congress shall have power to enforce this article by appropriate legislation.

Appendix B

The Uniform Commercial Code

(Adopted in 52 jurisdictions; all 50 States, although Louisiana has adopted only Articles 1, 3, 4, and 5; the District of Columbia, and the Virgin Islands.)

The Code consists of 10 Articles as follows:

Art.

1. GENERAL PROVISIONS

2. Sales
   2A. Leases

3. Commercial Paper

4. Bank Deposits and Collections

5. Letters of Credit

6. Bulk Transfers

7. Warehouse Receipts, Bills of Lading and Other Documents of Title

8. Investment Securities

9. Secured Transactions: Sales of Accounts and Chattel Paper

10. Effective Date and Repealer

Article 1
GENERAL PROVISIONS

Part 1 Short Title, Construction, Application and Subject Matter of the Act

§ 1—101. Short Title.

This Act shall be known and may be cited as Uniform Commercial Code.

§ 1—102. Purposes; Rules of Construction; Variation by Agreement.

(1) This Act shall be liberally construed and applied to promote its underlying purposes and policies.

(2) Underlying purposes and policies of this Act are

(a) to simplify, clarify and modernize the law governing commercial transactions;

(b) to permit the continued expansion of commercial practices through custom, usage and agreement of the parties;

(c) to make uniform the law among the various jurisdictions.

(3) The effect of provisions of this Act may be varied by agreement, except as otherwise provided in this Act and except that the obligations of good faith, diligence, reasonableness and care prescribed by this Act may not be disclaimed by agreement but the parties may by agreement determine the standards by which the performance of such obligations is to be measured if such standards are not manifestly unreasonable.

(4) The presence in certain provisions of this Act of the words "unless otherwise agreed" or words of similar import does not imply that the effect of other provisions may not be varied by agreement under subsection (3).

(5) In this Act unless the context otherwise requires

(a) words in the singular number include the plural, and in the plural include the singular;

(b) words of the masculine gender include the feminine and the neuter, and when the sense so indicates words of the neuter gender may refer to any gender.

§ 1—103. Supplementary General Principles of Law Applicable.

Unless displaced by the particular provisions of this Act, the principles of law and equity, including the law merchant and the law relative to capacity to contract, principal and agent, estoppel, fraud, misrepresentation, duress, coercion, mistake, bankruptcy, or other validating or invalidating cause shall supplement its provisions.

§ 1—104. Construction Against Implicit Repeal.

This Act being a general act intended as a unified coverage of its subject matter, no part of it shall be deemed to be impliedly repealed by subsequent legislation if such construction can reasonably be avoided.

§ 1—105. Territorial Application of the Act; Parties' Power to Choose Applicable Law.

(1) Except as provided hereafter in this section, when a transaction bears a reasonable relation to this state and also to another state or nation the parties may agree that the law either of this state or of such other state or nation shall govern their rights and duties. Failing such agreement this Act applies to transactions bearing an appropriate relation to this state.

(2) Where one of the following provisions of this Act specifies the applicable law, that provision governs and a contrary agreement is effective only to the extent permitted by the law (including the conflict of laws rules) so specified:

Rights of creditors against sold goods. Section 2—402.

Applicability of the Article on Leases. Sections 2A—105 and 2A—106.

Applicability of the Article on Bank Deposits and Collections. Section 4—102.

Bulk transfers subject to the Article on Bulk Transfers. Section 6—102.

Applicability of the Article on Investment Securities. Section 8—106.

Perfection provisions of the Article on Secured Transactions. Section 9—103.

§ 1—106. Remedies to Be Liberally Administered.

(1) The remedies provided by this Act shall be liberally administered to the end that the aggrieved party may be put in as good

a position as if the other party had fully performed but neither consequential or special nor penal damages may be had except as specifically provided in this Act or by other rule of law.

(2) Any right or obligation declared by this Act is enforceable by action unless the provision declaring it specifies a different and limited effect.

§ 1—107. Waiver or Renunciation of Claim or Right After Breach.

Any claim or right arising out of an alleged breach can be discharged in whole or in part without consideration by a written waiver or renunciation signed and delivered by the aggrieved party.

§ 1—108. Severability.

If any provision or clause of this Act or application thereof to any person or circumstances is held invalid, such invalidity shall not affect other provisions or applications of the Act which can be given effect without the invalid provision or application, and to this end the provisions of this Act are declared to be severable.

§ 1—109. Section Captions.

Section captions are parts of this Act.

Part 2 General Definitions and Principles of Interpretation

§ 1—201. General Definitions.

Subject to additional definitions contained in the subsequent Articles of this Act which are applicable to specific Articles or Parts thereof, and unless the context otherwise requires, in this Act:

(1) "Action" in the sense of a judicial proceeding includes recoupment, counterclaim, set-off, suit in equity and any other proceedings in which rights are determined.

(2) "Aggrieved party" means a party entitled to resort to a remedy.

(3) "Agreement" means the bargain of the parties in fact as found in their language or by implication from other circumstances including course of dealing or usage of trade or course of performance as provided in this Act (Sections 1—205 and 2—208). Whether an agreement has legal consequences is determined by the provisions of this Act, if applicable; otherwise by the law of contracts (Section 1—103). (Compare "Contract".)

(4) "Bank" means any person engaged in the business of banking.

(5) "Bearer" means the person in possession of an instrument, document of title, or certificated security payable to bearer or indorsed in blank.

(6) "Bill of lading" means a document evidencing the receipt of goods for shipment issued by a person engaged in the business of transporting or forwarding goods, and includes an airbill. "Airbill" means a document serving for air transportation as a bill of lading does for marine or rail transportation, and includes an air consignment note or air waybill.

(7) "Branch" includes a separately incorporated foreign branch of a bank.

(8) "Burden of establishing" a fact means the burden of persuading the triers of fact that the existence of the fact is more probable than its non-existence.

(9) "Buyer in ordinary course of business" means a person who in good faith and without knowledge that the sale to him is in violation of the ownership rights or security interest of a third party in the goods buys in ordinary course from a person in the business of selling goods of that kind but does not include a pawnbroker. All persons who sell minerals or the like (including oil and gas) at wellhead or minehead shall be deemed to be persons in the business of selling goods of that kind. "Buying" may be for cash or by exchange of other property or on secured or unsecured credit and includes receiving goods or documents of title under a preexisting contract for sale but does not include a transfer in bulk or as security for or in total or partial satisfaction of a money debt.

(10) "Conspicuous": A term or clause is conspicuous when it is so written that a reasonable person against whom it is to operate ought to have noticed it. A printed heading in capitals (as: NON-NEGOTIABLE BILL OF LADING) is conspicuous. Language in the body of a form is "conspicuous" if it is in larger or other contrasting type or color. But in a telegram any stated term is "conspicuous". Whether a term or clause is "conspicuous" or not is for decision by the court.

(11) "Contract" means the total legal obligation which results from the parties' agreement as affected by this Act and any other applicable rules of law. (Compare "Agreement".)

(12) "Creditor" includes a general creditor, a secured creditor, a lien creditor and any representative of creditors, including an assignee for the benefit of creditors, a trustee in bankruptcy, a receiver in equity and an executor or administrator of an insolvent debtor's or assignor's estate.

(13) "Defendant" includes a person in the position of defendant in a cross-action or counterclaim.

(14) "Delivery" with respect to instruments, documents of title, chattel paper, or certificated securities means voluntary transfer of possession.

(15) "Document of title" includes bill of lading, dock warrant, dock receipt, warehouse receipt or order for the delivery of goods, and also any other document which in the regular course of business or financing is treated as adequately evidencing that the person in possession of it is entitled to receive, hold and dispose of the document and the goods it covers. To be a document of title a document must purport to be issued by or addressed to a bailee and purport to cover goods in the bailee's possession which are either identified or are fungible portions of an identified mass.

(16) "Fault" means wrongful act, omission or breach.

(17) "Fungible" with respect to goods or securities means goods or securities of which any unit is, by nature or usage of trade, the equivalent of any other like unit. Goods which are not fungible

shall be deemed fungible for the purposes of this Act to the extent that under a particular agreement or document unlike units are treated as equivalents.

(18) "Genuine" means free of forgery or counterfeiting.

(19) "Good faith" means honesty in fact in the conduct or transaction concerned.

(20) "Holder" means a person who is in possession of a document of title or an instrument or a certificated investment security drawn, issued, or indorsed to him or his order or to bearer or in blank.

(21) To "honor" is to pay or to accept and pay, or where a credit so engages to purchase or discount a draft complying with the terms of the credit.

(22) "Insolvency proceedings" includes any assignment for the benefit of creditors or other proceedings intended to liquidate or rehabilitate the estate of the person involved.

(23) A person is "insolvent" who either has ceased to pay his debts in the ordinary course of business or cannot pay his debts as they become due or is insolvent within the meaning of the federal bankruptcy law.

(24) "Money" means a medium of exchange authorized or adopted by a domestic or foreign government as a part of its currency.

(25) A person has "notice" of a fact when

    (a) he has actual knowledge of it; or

    (b) he has received a notice or notification of it; or

    (c) from all the facts and circumstances known to him at the time in question he has reason to know that it exists.

A person "knows" or has "knowledge" of a fact when he has actual knowledge of it. "Discover" or "learn" or a word or phrase of similar import refers to knowledge rather than to reason to know. The time and circumstances under which a notice or notification may cease to be effective are not determined by this Act.

(26) A person "notifies" or "gives" a notice or notification to another by taking such steps as may be reasonably required to inform the other in ordinary course whether or not such other actually comes to know of it. A person "receives" a notice or notification when

    (a) it comes to his attention; or

    (b) it is duly delivered at the place of business through which the contract was made or at any other place held out by him as the place for receipt of such communications.

(27) Notice, knowledge or a notice or notification received by an organization is effective for a particular transaction from the time when it is brought to the attention of the individual conducting that transaction, and in any event from the time when it would have been brought to his attention if the organization had exercised due diligence. An organization exercises due diligence if it maintains reasonable routines for communicating significant information to the person conducting the transaction and there is reasonable compliance with the routines. Due diligence does not require an individual acting for the organization to communicate information unless such communication is part of his regular duties or unless he has reason to know of the transaction and that the transaction would be materially affected by the information.

(28) "Organization" includes a corporation, government or governmental subdivision or agency, business trust, estate, trust, partnership or association, two or more persons having a joint or common interest, or any other legal or commercial entity.

(29) "Party", as distinct from "third party", means a person who has engaged in a transaction or made an agreement within this Act.

(30) "Person" includes an individual or an organization (See Section 1—102).

(31) "Presumption" or "presumed" means that the trier of fact must find the existence of the fact presumed unless and until evidence is introduced which would support a finding of its nonexistence.

(32) "Purchase" includes taking by sale, discount, negotiation, mortgage, pledge, lien, issue or re-issue, gift or any other voluntary transaction creating an interest in property.

(33) "Purchaser" means a person who takes by purchase.

(34) "Remedy" means any remedial right to which an aggrieved party is entitled with or without resort to a tribunal.

(35) "Representative" includes an agent, an officer of a corporation or association, and a trustee, executor or administrator of an estate, or any other person empowered to act for another.

(36) "Rights" includes remedies.

37) "Security interest" means an interest in personal property or fixtures which secures payment or performance of an obligation. The retention or reservation of title by a seller of goods notwithstanding shipment or delivery to the buyer (Section 2—401) is limited in effect to a reservation of a "security interest". The term also includes any interest of a buyer of accounts or chattel paper which is subject to Article 9. The special property interest of a buyer of goods on identification of those goods to a contract for sale under Section 2—401 is not a "security interest", but a buyer may also acquire a "security interest" by complying with Article 9. Unless a consignment is intended as security, reservation of title thereunder is not a "security interest," but a consignment is in any event subject to the provisions on consignment sales (Section 2—326).

Whether a transaction creates a lease or security interest is determined by the facts of each case; however, a transaction creates a security interest if the consideration the lessee is to pay the lessor for the right to possession and use of the goods is an obligation for the term of the lease not subject to termination by the lessee, and

    (a) the original term of the lease is equal to or greater than the remaining economic life of the goods,

(b) the lessee is bound to renew the lease for the remaining economic life of the goods or is bound to become the owner of the goods,

(c) the lessee has an option to renew the lease for the remaining economic life of the goods for no additional consideration or nominal additional consideration upon compliance with the lease agreement, or

(d) the lessee has an option to become the owner of the goods for no additional consideration or nominal additional consideration upon compliance with the lease agreement.

A transaction does not create a security interest merely because it provides that

(a) the present value of the consideration the lessee is obligated to pay the lessor for the right to possession and use of the goods is substantially equal to or is greater than the fair market value of the goods at the time the lease is entered into,

(b) the lessee assumes risk of loss of the goods, or agrees to pay taxes, insurance, filing, recording, or registration fees, or service or maintenance costs with respect to the goods,

(c) the lessee has an option to renew the lease or to become the owner of the goods,

(d) the lessee has an option to renew the lease for a fixed rent that is equal to or greater than the reasonably predictable fair market rent for the use of the goods for the term of the renewal at the time the option is to be performed, or

(e) the lessee has an option to become the owner of the goods for a fixed price that is equal to or greater than the reasonably predictable fair market value of the goods at the time the option is to be performed.

For purposes of this subsection (37):

(x) Additional consideration is not nominal if (i) when the option to renew the lease is granted to the lessee the rent is stated to be the fair market rent for the use of the goods for the term of the renewal determined at the time the option is to be performed, or (ii) when the option to become the owner of the goods is granted to the lessee the price is stated to be the fair market value of the goods determined at the time the option is to be performed. Additional consideration is nominal if it is less than the lessee's reasonably predictable cost of performing under the lease agreement if the option is not exercised;

(y) "Reasonably predictable" and "remaining economic life of the goods" are to be determined with reference to the facts and circumstances at the time the transaction is entered into; and

(z) "Present value" means the amount as of a date certain of one or more sums payable in the future, discounted to the date certain. The discount is determined by the interest rate specified by the parties if the rate is not manifestly unreasonable at the time the transaction is entered into; otherwise, the discount is determined by a commercially reasonable rate that takes into account the facts and circumstances of each case at the time the transaction was entered into.

(38) "Send" in connection with any writing or notice means to deposit in the mail or deliver for transmission by any other usual means of communication with postage or cost of transmission provided for and properly addressed and in the case of an instrument to an address specified thereon or otherwise agreed, or if there be none to any address reasonable under the circumstances. The receipt of any writing or notice within the time at which it would have arrived if properly sent has the effect of a proper sending.

(39) "Signed" includes any symbol executed or adopted by a party with present intention to authenticate a writing.

(40) "Surety" includes guarantor.

(41) "Telegram" includes a message transmitted by radio, teletype, cable, any mechanical method of transmission, or the like.

(42) "Term" means that portion of an agreement which relates to a particular matter.

(43) "Unauthorized" signature or indorsement means one made without actual, implied or apparent authority and includes a forgery.

(44) "Value". Except as otherwise provided with respect to negotiable instruments and bank collections (Sections 3—303, 4—208 and 4—209) a person gives "value" for rights if he acquires them

(a) in return for a binding commitment to extend credit or for the extension of immediately available credit whether or not drawn upon and whether or not a chargeback is provided for in the event of difficulties in collection; or

(b) as security for or in total or partial satisfaction of a preexisting claim; or

(c) by accepting delivery pursuant to a preexisting contract for purchase; or

(d) generally, in return for any consideration sufficient to support a simple contract.

(45) "Warehouse receipt" means a receipt issued by a person engaged in the business of storing goods for hire.

(46) "Written" or "writing" includes printing, typewriting or any other intentional reduction to tangible form.

Amended in 1962, 1972, 1977, and 1987.

§ 1—202. Prima Facie Evidence by Third Party Documents.

A document in due form purporting to be a bill of lading, policy or certificate of insurance, official weigher's or inspector's certificate, consular invoice, or any other document authorized or required by the contract to be issued by a third party shall be prima facie evidence of its own authenticity and genuineness and of the facts stated in the document by the third party.

§ 1—203. Obligation of Good Faith.

Every contract or duty within this Act imposes an obligation of good faith in its performance or enforcement.

§ 1—204. Time; Reasonable Time; "Seasonably".

(1) Whenever this Act requires any action to be taken within a reasonable time, any time which is not manifestly unreasonable may be fixed by agreement.

(2) What is a reasonable time for taking any action depends on the nature, purpose and circumstances of such action.

(3) An action is taken "seasonably" when it is taken at or within the time agreed or if no time is agreed at or within a reasonable time.

§ 1—205. Course of Dealing and Usage of Trade.

(1) A course of dealing is a sequence of previous conduct between the parties to a particular transaction which is fairly to be regarded as establishing a common basis of understanding for interpreting their expressions and other conduct.

(2) A usage of trade is any practice or method of dealing having such regularity of observance in a place, vocation or trade as to justify an expectation that it will be observed with respect to the transaction in question. The existence and scope of such a usage are to be proved as facts. If it is established that such a usage is embodied in a written trade code or similar writing the interpretation of the writing is for the court.

(3) A course of dealing between parties and any usage of trade in the vocation or trade in which they are engaged or of which they are or should be aware give particular meaning to and supplement or qualify terms of an agreement.

(4) The express terms of an agreement and an applicable course of dealing or usage of trade shall be construed wherever reasonable as consistent with each other; but when such construction is unreasonable express terms control both course of dealing and usage of trade and course of dealing controls usage trade.

(5) An applicable usage of trade in the place where any part of performance is to occur shall be used in interpreting the agreement as to that part of the performance.

(6) Evidence of a relevant usage of trade offered by one party is not admissible unless and until he has given the other party such notice as the court finds sufficient to prevent unfair surprise to the latter.

§ 1—206. Statute of Frauds for Kinds of Personal Property Not Otherwise Covered.

(1) Except in the cases described in subsection (2) of this section a contract for the sale of personal property is not enforceable by way of action or defense beyond five thousand dollars in amount or value of remedy unless there is some writing which indicates that a contract for sale has been made between the parties at a defined or stated price, reasonably identifies the subject matter, and is signed by the party against whom enforcement is sought or by his authorized agent.

(2) Subsection (1) of this section does not apply to contracts for the sale of goods (Section 2—201) nor of securities (Section 8—319) nor to security agreements (Section 9—203).

§ 1—207. Performance or Acceptance Under Reservation of Rights.

A party who with explicit reservation of rights performs or promises performance or assents to performance in a manner demanded or offered by the other party does not thereby prejudice the rights reserved. Such words as "without prejudice", "under protest" or the like are sufficient.

§ 1—208. Option to Accelerate at Will.

A term providing that one party or his successor in interest may accelerate payment or performance or require collateral or additional collateral "at will" or "when he deems himself insecure" or in words of similar import shall be construed to mean that he shall have power to do so only if he in good faith believes that the prospect of payment or performance is impaired. The burden of establishing lack of good faith is on the party against whom the power has been exercised.

§ 1—209. Subordinated Obligations

An obligation may be issued as subordinated to payment of another obligation of the person obligated, or a creditor may subordinate his right to payment of an obligation by agreement with either the person obligated or another creditor of the person obligated. Such a subordination does not create a security interest as against either the common debtor or a subordinated creditor. This section shall be construed as declaring the law as it existed prior to the enactment of this section and not as modifying it. Added 1966.

Note: *This new section is proposed as an optional provision to make it clear that a subordination agreement does not create a security interest unless so intended.*

Article 2
SALES

Part 1
Short Title, General Construction and Subject Matter

§ 2—101. Short Title.

This Article shall be known and may be cited as Uniform Commercial Code—Sales.

§ 2—102. Scope; Certain Security and Other Transactions Excluded From This Article.

Unless the context otherwise requires, this Article applies to transactions in goods; it does not apply to any transaction which al-

A-17

though in the form of an unconditional contract to sell or present sale is intended to operate only as a security transaction nor does this Article impair or repeal any statute regulating sales to consumers, farmers or other specified classes of buyers.

§ 2—103. Definitions and Index of Definitions.

(1) In this Article unless the context otherwise requires

(a) "Buyer" means a person who buys or contracts to buy goods.

(b) "Good faith" in the case of a merchant means honesty in fact and the observance of reasonable commercial standards of fair dealing in the trade.

(c) "Receipt" of goods means taking physical possession of them.

(d) "Seller" means a person who sells or contracts to sell goods.

(2) Other definitions applying to this Article or to specified Parts thereof, and the sections in which they appear are:
"Acceptance". Section 2—606.
"Banker's credit". Section 2—325.
"Between merchants". Section 2—104.
"Cancellation". Section 2—106(4).
"Commercial unit". Section 2—105.
"Confirmed credit". Section 2—325.
"Conforming to contract". Section 2—106.
"Contract for sale". Section 2—106.
"Cover". Section 2—712.
"Entrusting". Section 2—403.
"Financing agency". Section 2—104.
"Future goods". Section 2—105.
"Goods". Section 2—105.
"Identification". Section 2—501.
"Installment contract". Section 2—612.
"Letter of Credit". Section 2—325.
"Lot". Section 2—105.
"Merchant". Section 2—104.
"Overseas". Section 2—323.
"Person in position of seller". Section 2—707.
"Present sale". Section 2—106.
"Sale". Section 2—106.
"Sale on approval". Section 2—326.
"Sale or return". Section 2—326.
"Termination". Section 2—106.

(3) The following definitions in other Articles apply to this Article:
"Check". Section 3—104.
"Consignee". Section 7—102.
"Consignor". Section 7—102.
"Consumer goods". Section 9—109.
"Dishonor". Section 3—507.
"Draft". Section 3—104.

(4) In addition Article 1 contains general definitions and principles of construction and interpretation applicable throughout this Article.

§ 2—104. Definitions: "Merchant"; "Between Merchants"; "Financing Agency".

(1) "Merchant" means a person who deals in goods of the kind or otherwise by his occupation holds himself out as having knowledge or skill peculiar to the practices or goods involved in the transaction or to whom such knowledge or skill may be attributed by his employment of an agent or broker or other intermediary who by his occupation holds himself out as having such knowledge or skill.

(2) "Financing agency" means a bank, finance company or other person who in the ordinary course of business makes advances against goods or documents of title or who by arrangement with either the seller or the buyer intervenes in ordinary course to make or collect payment due or claimed under the contract for sale, as by purchasing or paying the seller's draft or making advances against it or by merely taking it for collection whether or not documents of title accompany the draft. "Financing agency" includes also a bank or other person who similarly intervenes between persons who are in the position of seller and buyer in respect to the goods (Section 2—707).

(3) "Between merchants" means in any transaction with respect to which both parties are chargeable with the knowledge or skill of merchants.

§ 2—105. Definitions: Transferability; "Goods"; "Future" Goods; "Lot"; "Commercial Unit".

(1) "Goods" means all things (including specially manufactured goods) which are movable at the time of identification to the contract for sale other than the money in which the price is to be paid, investment securities (Article 8) and things in action. "Goods" also includes the unborn young of animals and growing crops and other identified things attached to realty as described in the section on goods to be severed from realty (Section 2—107).

(2) Goods must be both existing and identified before any interest in them can pass. Goods which are not both existing and identified are "future" goods. A purported present sale of future goods or of any interest therein operates as a contract to sell.

(3) There may be a sale of a part interest in existing identified goods.

(4) An undivided share in an identified bulk of fungible goods is sufficiently identified to be sold although the quantity of the bulk is not determined. Any agreed proportion of such a bulk or any quantity thereof agreed upon by number, weight or other measure may to the extent of the seller's interest in the bulk be sold to the buyer who then becomes an owner in common.

(5) "Lot" means a parcel or a single article which is the subject matter of a separate sale or delivery, whether or not it is sufficient to perform the contract.

(6) "Commercial unit" means such a unit of goods as by commercial usage is a single whole for purposes of sale and division

of which materially impairs its character or value on the market or in use. A commercial unit may be a single article (as a machine) or a set of articles (as a suite of furniture or an assortment of sizes) or a quantity (as a bale, gross, or carload) or any other unit treated in use or in the relevant market as a single whole.

§ 2—106. **Definitions: "Contract"; "Agreement"; "Contract for Sale"; "Sale"; "Present Sale"; "Conforming" to Contract; "Termination"; "Cancellation".**

(1) In this Article unless the context otherwise requires "contract" and "agreement" are limited to those relating to the present or future sale of goods. "Contract for sale" includes both a present sale of goods and a contract to sell goods at a future time. A "sale" consists in the passing of title from the seller to the buyer for a price (Section 2—401). A "present sale" means a sale which is accomplished by the making of the contract.

(2) Goods or conduct including any part of a performance are "conforming" or conform to the contract when they are in accordance with the obligations under the contract.

(3) "Termination" occurs when either party pursuant to a power created by agreement or law puts an end to the contract otherwise than for its breach. On "termination" all obligations which are still executory on both sides are discharged but any right based on prior breach or performance survives.

(4) "Cancellation" occurs when either party puts an end to the contract for breach by the other and its effect is the same as that of "termination" except that the cancelling party also retains any remedy for breach of the whole contract or any unperformed balance.

§ 2—107. **Goods to Be Severed From Realty: Recording.**

(1) A contract for the sale of minerals or the like (including oil and gas) or a structure or its materials to be removed from realty is a contract for the sale of goods within this Article if they are to be severed by the seller but until severance a purported present sale thereof which is not effective as a transfer of an interest in land is effective only as a contract to sell.

(2) A contract for the sale apart from the land of growing crops or other things attached to realty and capable of severance without material harm thereto but not described in subsection (1) or of timber to be cut is a contract for the sale of goods within this Article whether the subject matter is to be severed by the buyer or by the seller even though it forms part of the realty at the time of contracting, and the parties can by identification effect a present sale before severance.

(3) The provisions of this section are subject to any third party rights provided by the law relating to realty records, and the contract for sale may be executed and recorded as a document transferring an interest in land and shall then constitute notice to third parties of the buyer's rights under the contract for sale.

Part 2 Form, Formation and Readjustment of Contract

§ 2—201. **Formal Requirements; Statute of Frauds.**

(1) Except as otherwise provided in this section a contract for the sale of goods for the price of $500 or more is not enforceable by way of action or defense unless there is some writing sufficient to indicate that a contract for sale has been made between the parties and signed by the party against whom enforcement is sought or by his authorized agent or broker. A writing is not insufficient because it omits or incorrectly states a term agreed upon but the contract is not enforceable under this paragraph beyond the quantity of goods shown in such writing.

(2) Between merchants if within a reasonable time a writing in confirmation of the contract and sufficient against the sender is received and the party receiving it has reason to know its contents, its satisfies the requirements of subsection (1) against such party unless written notice of objection to its contents is given within ten days after it is received.

(3) A contract which does not satisfy the requirements of subsection (1) but which is valid in other respects is enforceable

(a) if the goods are to be specially manufactured for the buyer and are not suitable for sale to others in the ordinary course of the seller's business and the seller, before notice of repudiation is received and under circumstances which reasonably indicate that the goods are for the buyer, has made either a substantial beginning of their manufacture or commitments for their procurement; or

(b) if the party against whom enforcement is sought admits in his pleading, testimony or otherwise in court that a contract for sale was made, but the contract is not enforceable under this provision beyond the quantity of goods admitted; or

(c) with respect to goods for which payment has been made and accepted or which have been received and accepted (Sec. 2—606).

§ 2—202. **Final Written Expression: Parol or Extrinsic Evidence.**

Terms with respect to which the confirmatory memoranda of the parties agree or which are otherwise set forth in a writing intended by the parties as a final expression of their agreement with respect to such terms as are included therein may not be contradicted by evidence of any prior agreement or of a contemporaneous oral agreement but may be explained or supplemented

(a) by course of dealing or usage of trade (Section 1—205) or by course of performance (Section 2—208); and

(b) by evidence of consistent additional terms unless the court finds the writing to have been intended also as a complete and exclusive statement of the terms of the agreement.

§ 2—203. **Seals Inoperative.**

The affixing of a seal to a writing evidencing a contract for sale or an offer to buy or sell goods does not constitute the writing a sealed instrument and the law with respect to sealed instruments does not apply to such a contract or offer.

§ 2—204. Formation in General.

(1) A contract for sale of goods may be made in any manner sufficent to show agreement, including conduct by both parties which recognizes the existence of such a contract.

(2) An agreement sufficient to constitute a contract for sale may be found even though the moment of its making is undetermined.

(3) Even though one or more terms are left open a contract for sale does not fail for indefiniteness if the parties have intended to make a contract and there is a reasonably certain basis for giving an appropriate remedy.

§ 2—205. Firm Offers.

An offer by a merchant to buy or sell goods in a signed writing which by its terms gives assurance that it will be held open is not revocable, for lack of consideration, during the time stated or if no time is stated for a reasonable time, but in no event may such period of irrevocability exceed three months; but any such term of assurance on a form supplied by the offeree must be separately signed by the offeror.

§ 2—206. Offer and Acceptance in Formation of Contract.

(1) Unless other unambiguously indicated by the language or circumstances

(a) an offer to make a contract shall be construed as inviting acceptance in any manner and by any medium reasonable in the circumstances;

(b) an order or other offer to buy goods for prompt or current shipment shall be construed as inviting acceptance either by a prompt promise to ship or by the prompt or current shipment of conforming or nonconforming goods, but such a shipment of non-conforming goods does not constitute an acceptance if the seller seasonably notifies the buyer that the shipment is offered only as an accommodation to the buyer.

(2) Where the beginning of a requested performance is a reasonable mode of acceptance an offeror who is not notified of acceptance within a reasonable time may treat the offer as having lapsed before acceptance.

§ 2—207. Additional Terms in Acceptance or Confirmation.

(1) A definite and seasonable expression of acceptance or a written confirmation which is sent within a reasonable time operates as an acceptance even though it states terms additional to or different from those offered or agreed upon, unless acceptance is expressly made conditional on assent to the additional or different terms.

(2) The additional terms are to be construed as proposals for addition to the contract. Between merchants such terms become part of the contract unless:

(a) the offer expressly limits acceptance to the terms of the offer;

(b) they materially alter it; or

(c) notification of objection to them has already been given or is given within a reasonable time after notice of them is received.

(3) Conduct by both parties which recognizes the existence of a contract is sufficient to establish a contract for sale although the writings of the parties do not otherwise establish a contract. In such case the terms of the particular contract consist of those terms on which the writings of the parties agree, together with any supplementary terms incorporated under any other provisions of this Act.

§ 2—208. Course of Performance or Practical Construction.

(1) Where the contract for sale involves repeated occasions for performance by either party with knowledge of the nature of the performance and opportunity for objection to it by the other, any course of performance accepted or acquiesced in without objection shall be relevant to determine the meaning of the agreement.

(2) The express terms of the agreement and any such course of performance, as well as any course of dealing and usage of trade, shall be construed whenever reasonable as consistent with each other; but when such construction is unreasonable, express terms shall control course of performance and course of performance shall control both course of dealing and usage of trade (Section 1—205).

(3) Subject to the provisions of the next section on modification and waiver, such course of performance shall be relevant to show a waiver or modification of any term inconsistent with such course of performance.

§ 2—209. Modification, Rescission and Waiver.

(1) An agreement modifying a contract within this Article needs no consideration to be binding.

(2) A signed agreement which excludes modification or rescission except by a signed writing cannot be otherwise modified or rescinded, but except as between merchants such a requirement on a form supplied by the merchant must be separately signed by the other party.

(3) The requirements of the statute of frauds section of this Article (Section 2—201) must be satisfied if the contract as modified is within its provisions.

(4) Although an attempt at modification or rescission does not satisfy the requirements of subsection (2) or (3) it can operate as a waiver.

(5) A party who has made a waiver affecting an executory portion of the contract may retract the waiver by reasonable notification received by the other party that strict performance will be required of any term waived, unless the retraction would be unjust in view of a material change of position in reliance on the waiver.

§ 2—210. Delegation of Performance; Assignment of Rights.

(1) A party may perform his duty through a delegate unless otherwise agreed or unless the other party has a substantial interest in

having his original promisor perform or control the acts required by the contract. No delegation of performance relieves the party delegating of any duty to perform or any liability for breach.

(2) Unless otherwise agreed all rights of either seller or buyer can be assigned except where the assignment would materially change the duty of the other party, or increase materially the burden or risk imposed on him by his contract, or impair materially his chance of obtaining return performance. A right to damages for breach of the whole contract or a right arising out of the assignor's due performance of his entire obligation can be assigned despite agreement otherwise.

(3) Unless the circumstances indicate the contrary a prohibition of assignment of "the contract" is to be construed as barring only the delegation to the assignee of the assignor's performance.

(4) An assignment of "the contract" or of "all my rights under the contract" or an assignment in similar general terms is an assignment of rights and unless the language or the circumstances (as in an assignment for security) indicate the contrary, it is a delegation of performance of the duties of the assignor and its acceptance by the assignee constitutes a promise by him to perform those duties. This promise is enforceable by either the assignor or the other party to the original contract.

(5) The other party may treat any assignment which delegates performance as creating reasonable grounds for insecurity and may without prejudice to his rights against the assignor demand assurances from the assignee (Section 2—609).

Part 3 General Obligation and Construction of Contract

§ 2—301. General Obligations of Parties.

The obligation of the seller is to transfer and deliver and that of the buyer is to accept and pay in accordance with the contract.

§ 2—302. Unconscionable Contract or Clause.

(1) If the court as a matter of law finds the contract or any clause of the contract to have been unconscionable at the time it was made the court may refuse to enforce the contract, or it may enforce the remainder of the contract without the unconscionable clause, or it may so limit the application of any unconscionable clause as to avoid any unconscionable result.

(2) When it is claimed or appears to the court that the contract or any clause thereof may be unconscionable the parties shall be afforded a reasonable opportunity to present evidence as to its commercial setting, purpose and effect to aid the court in making the determination.

§ 2—303. Allocations or Division of Risks.

Where this Article allocates a risk or a burden as between the parties "unless otherwise agreed", the agreement may not only shift the allocation but may also divide the risk or burden.

§ 2—304. Price Payable in Money, Goods, Realty, or Otherwise.

(1) The price can be made payable in money or otherwise. If it is payable in whole or in part in goods each party is a seller of the goods which he is to transfer.

(2) Even though all or part of the price is payable in an interest in realty the transfer of the goods and the seller's obligations with reference to them are subject to this Article, but not the transfer of the interest in realty or the transferor's obligations in connection therewith.

§ 2—305. Open Price Term.

(1) The parties if they so intend can conclude a contract for sale even though the price is not settled. In such a case the price is a reasonable price at the time for delivery if

(a) nothing is said as to price; or

(b) the price is left to be agreed by the parties and they fail to agree; or

(c) the price is to be fixed in terms of some agreed market or other standard as set or recorded by a third person or agency and it is not so set or recorded.

(2) A price to be fixed by the seller or by the buyer means a price for him to fix in good faith.

(3) When a price left to be fixed otherwise than by agreement of the parties fails to be fixed through fault of one party the other may at his option treat the contract as cancelled or himself fix a reasonable price.

(4) Where, however, the parties intend not to be bound unless the price be fixed or agreed and it is not fixed or agreed there is no contract. In such a case the buyer must return any goods already received or if unable so to do must pay their reasonable value at the time of delivery and the seller must return any portion of the price paid on account.

§ 2—306. Output, Requirements and Exclusive Dealings.

(1) A term which measures the quantity by the output of the seller or the requirements of the buyer means such actual output or requirements as may occur in good faith, except that no quantity unreasonably disproportionate to any stated estimate or in the absence of a stated estimate to any normal or otherwise comparable prior output or requirements may be tendered or demanded.

(2) A lawful agreement by either the seller or the buyer for exclusive dealing in the kind of goods concerned imposes unless otherwise agreed an obligation by the seller to use best efforts to supply the goods and by the buyer to use best efforts to promote their sale.

§ 2—307. Delivery in Single Lot or Several Lots.

Unless otherwise agreed all goods called for by a contract for sale must be tendered in a single delivery and payment is due only on such tender but where the circumstances give either party the right to make or demand delivery in lots the price if it can be apportioned may be demanded for each lot.

§ 2—308. Absence of Specified Place for Delivery.

Unless otherwise agreed

(a) the place for delivery of goods is the seller's place of business or if he has none his residence; but

(b) in a contract for sale of identified goods which to the knowledge of the parties at the time of contracting are in some other place, that place is the place for their delivery; and

(c) documents of title may be delivered through customary banking channels.

§ 2—309. Absence of Specific Time Provisions; Notice of Termination.

(1) The time for shipment or delivery or any other action under a contract if not provided in this Article or agreed upon shall be a reasonable time.

(2) Where the contract provides for successive performances but is indefinite in duration it is valid for a reasonable time but unless otherwise agreed may be terminated at any time by either party.

(3) Termination of a contract by one party except on the happening of an agreed event requires that reasonable notification be received by the other party and an agreement dispensing with notification is invalid if its operation would be unconscionable.

§ 2—310. Open Time for Payment or Running of Credit; Authority to Ship Under Reservation.

Unless otherwise agreed

(a) payment is due at the time and place at which the buyer is to receive the goods even though the place of shipment is the place of delivery; and

(b) if the seller is authorized to send the goods he may ship them under reservation, and may tender the documents of title, but the buyer may inspect the goods after their arrival before payment is due unless such inspection is inconsistent with the terms of the contract (Section 2—513); and

(c) if delivery is authorized and made by way of documents of title otherwise than by subsection (b) then payment is due at the time and place at which the buyer is to receive the documents regardless of where the goods are to be received; and

(d) where the seller is required or authorized to ship the goods on credit the credit period runs from the time of shipment but post-dating the invoice or delaying its dispatch will correspondingly delay the starting of the credit period.

§ 2—311. Options and Cooperation Respecting Performance.

(1) An agreement for sale which is otherwise sufficiently definite (subsection (3) of Section 2—204) to be a contract is not made invalid by the fact that it leaves particulars of performance to be specified by one of the parties. Any such specification must be made in good faith and within limits set by commercial reasonableness.

(2) Unless otherwise agreed specifications relating to assortment of the goods are at the buyer's option and except as otherwise provided in subsections (1)(c) and (3) of Section 2—319 specifications or arrangements relating to shipment are at the seller's option.

(3) Where such specification would materially affect the other party's performance but is not seasonably made or where one party's cooperation is necessary to the agreed performance of the other but is not seasonably forthcoming, the other party in addition to all other remedies

(a) is excused for any resulting delay in his own performance; and

(b) may also either proceed to perform in any reasonable manner or after the time for a material part of his own performance treat the failure to specify or to cooperate as a breach by failure to deliver or accept the goods.

§ 2—312. Warranty of Title and Against Infringement; Buyer's Obligation Against Infringement.

(1) Subject to subsection (2) there is in a contract for sale a warranty by the seller that

(a) the title conveyed shall be good, and its transfer rightful; and

(b) the goods shall be delivered free from any security interest or other lien or encumbrance of which the buyer at the time of contracting has no knowledge.

(2) A warranty under subsection (1) will be excluded or modified only by specific language or by circumstances which give the buyer reason to know that the person selling does not claim title in himself or that he is purporting to sell only such right or title as he or a third person may have.

(3) Unless otherwise agreed a seller who is a merchant regularly dealing in goods of the kind warrants that the goods shall be delivered free of the rightful claim of any third person by way of infringement or the like but a buyer who furnishes specifications to the seller must hold the seller harmless against any such claim which arises out of compliance with the specifications.

§ 2—313. Express Warranties by Affirmation, Promise, Description, Sample.

(1) Express warranties by the seller are created as follows:

(a) Any affirmation of fact or promise made by the seller to the buyer which relates to the goods and becomes part of the basis of the bargain creates an express warranty that the goods shall conform to the affirmation or promise.

(b) Any description of the goods which is made part of the basis of the bargain creates an express warranty that the goods shall conform to the description.

(c) Any sample or model which is made part of the basis of the bargain creates an express warranty that the whole of the goods shall conform to the sample or model.

(2) It is not necessary to the creation of an express warranty that the seller use formal words such as "warrant" or "guarantee" or that he have a specific intention to make a warranty, but an affirmation merely of the value of the goods or a statement purporting to be merely the seller's opinion or commendation of the goods does not create a warranty.

§ 2—314. Implied Warranty: Merchantability; Usage of Trade.

(1) Unless excluded or modified (Section 2—316), a warranty that the goods shall be merchantable is implied in a contract for their sale if the seller is a merchant with respect to goods of that kind. Under this section the serving for value of food or drink to be consumed either on the premises or elsewhere is a sale.

(2) Goods to be merchantable must be at least such as

(a) pass without objection in the trade under the contract description; and

(b) in the case of fungible goods, are of fair average quality within the description; and

(c) are fit for the ordinary purposes for which such goods are used; and

(d) run, within the variations permitted by the agreement, of even kind, quality and quantity within each unit and among all units involved; and

(e) are adequately contained, packaged, and labeled as the agreement may require; and

(f) conform to the promises or affirmations of fact made on the container or label if any.

(3) Unless excluded or modified (Section 2—316) other implied warranties may arise from course of dealing or usage of trade.

§ 2—315. Implied Warranty: Fitness for Particular Purpose.

Where the seller at the time of contracting has reason to know any particular purpose for which the goods are required and that the buyer is relying on the seller's skill or judgment to select or furnish suitable goods, there is unless excluded or modified under the next section an implied warranty that the goods shall be fit for such purpose.

§ 2—316. Exclusion or Modification of Warranties.

(1) Words or conduct relevant to the creation of an express warranty and words or conduct tending to negate or limit warranty shall be construed wherever reasonable as consistent with each other; but subject to the provisions of this Article on parol or extrinsic evidence (Section 2—202) negation or limitation is inoperative to the extent that such construction is unreasonable.

(2) Subject to subsection (3), to exclude or modify the implied warranty of merchantability or any part of it the language must mention merchantability and in case of a writing must be conspicuous, and to exclude or modify any implied warranty of fitness the exclusion must be by a writing and conspicuous. Language to exclude all implied warranties of fitness is sufficient if it states, for example, that "There are no warranties which extend beyond the description on the face hereof."

(3) Notwithstanding subsection (2)

(a) unless the circumstances indicate otherwise, all implied warranties are excluded by expressions like "as is", "with all faults" or other language which in common understanding calls the buyer's attention to the exclusion of warranties and makes plain that there is no implied warranty; and

(b) when the buyer before entering into the contract has examined the goods or the sample or model as fully as he desired or has refused to examine the goods there is no implied warranty with regard to defects which an examination ought in the circumstances to have revealed to him; and

(c) an implied warranty can also be excluded or modified by course of dealing or course of performance or usage of trade.

(4) Remedies for breach of warranty can be limited in accordance with the provisions of this Article on liquidation or limitation of damages and on contractual modification of remedy (Sections 2—718 and 2—719).

§ 2—317. Cumulation and Conflict of Warranties Express or Implied.

Warranties whether express or implied shall be construed as consistent with each other and as cumulative, but if such construction is unreasonable the intention of the parties shall determine which warranty is dominant. In ascertaining that intention the following rules apply:

(a) Exact or technical specifications displace an inconsistent sample or model or general language of description.

(b) A sample from an existing bulk displaces inconsistent general language of description.

(c) Express warranties displace inconsistent implied warranties other than an implied warranty of fitness for a particular purpose.

§ 2—318. Third Party Beneficiaries of Warranties Express or Implied.

Note: If this Act is introduced in the Congress of the United States this section should be omitted. (States to select one alternative.)

Alternative A

A seller's warranty whether express or implied extends to any natural person who is in the family or household of his buyer or who is a guest in his home if it is reasonable to expect that such person may use, consume or be affected by the goods and who is injured in person by breach of the warranty. A seller may not exclude or limit the operation of this section.

Alternative B

A seller's warranty whether express or implied extends to any natural person who may reasonably be expected to use, consume or be affected by the goods and who is injured in person by breach of the warranty. A seller may not exclude or limit the operation of this section.

Alternative C

A seller's warranty whether express or implied extends to any person who may reasonably be expected to use, consume or be affected by the goods and who is injured by breach of the warranty. A seller may not exclude or limit the operation of this section with respect to injury to the person of an individual to whom the warranty extends. As amended 1966.

§ 2—319. F.O.B. and F.A.S. Terms.

(1) Unless otherwise agreed the term F.O.B. (which means "free on board") at a named place, even though used only in connection with the stated price, is a delivery term under which

(a) when the term is F.O.B. the place of shipment, the seller must at that place ship the goods in the manner provided in this Article (Section 2—504) and bear the expense and risk of putting them into the possession of the carrier; or

(b) when the term is F.O.B. the place of destination, the seller must at his own expense and risk transport the goods to that place and there tender delivery of them in the manner provided in this Article (Section 2—503);

(c) when under either (a) or (b) the term is also F.O.B. vessel, car or other vehicle, the seller must in addition at his own expense and risk load the goods on board. If the term is F.O.B. vessel the buyer must name the vessel and in an appropriate case the seller must comply with the provisions of this Article on the form of bill of lading (Section 2—323).

(2) Unless otherwise agreed the term F.A.S. vessel (which means "free alongside") at a named port, even though used only in connection with the stated price, is a delivery term under which the seller must

(a) at his own expense and risk deliver the goods alongside the vessel in the manner usual in that port or on a dock designated and provided by the buyer; and

(b) obtain and tender a receipt for the goods in exchange for which the carrier is under a duty to issue a bill of lading.

(3) Unless otherwise agreed in any case falling within subsection (1)(a) or (c) or subsection (2) the buyer must seasonably give any needed instructions for making delivery, including when the term is F.A.S. or F.O.B. the loading berth of the vessel and in an appropriate case its name and sailing date. The seller may treat the failure of needed instructions as a failure of cooperation under this Article (Section 2—311). He may also at his option move the goods in any reasonable manner preparatory to delivery or shipment.

(4) Under the term F.O.B. vessel or F.A.S. unless otherwise agreed the buyer must make payment against tender of the required documents and the seller may not tender nor the buyer demand delivery of the goods in substitution for the documents.

§ 2—320. C.I.F. and C. & F. Terms.

(1) The term C.I.F. means that the price includes in a lump sum the cost of the goods and the insurance and freight to the named destination. The term C. & F. or C.F. means that the price so includes cost and freight to the named destination.

(2) Unless otherwise agreed and even though used only in connection with the stated price and destination, the term C.I.F.

destination or its equivalent requires the seller at his own expense and risk to

(a) put the goods into the possession of a carrier at the port for shipment and obtain a negotiable bill or bills of lading covering the entire transportation to the named destination; and

(b) load the goods and obtain a receipt from the carrier (which may be contained in the bill of lading) showing that the freight has been paid or provided for; and

(c) obtain a policy or certificate of insurance, including any war risk insurance, of a kind and on terms then current at the port of shipment in the usual amount, in the currency of the contract, shown to cover the same goods covered by the bill of lading and providing for payment of loss to the order of the buyer or for the account of whom it may concern; but the seller may add to the price the amount of the premium for any such war risk insurance; and

(d) prepare an invoice of the goods and procure any other documents required to effect shipment or to comply with the contract; and

(e) forward and tender with commercial promptness all the documents in due form and with any indorsement necessary to perfect the buyer's rights.

(3) Unless otherwise agreed the term C. & F. or its equivalent has the same effect and imposes upon the seller the same obligations and risks as a C.I.F. term except the obligation as to insurance.

(4) Under the term C.I.F. or C. & F. unless otherwise agreed the buyer must make payment against tender of the required documents and the seller may not tender nor the buyer demand delivery of the goods in substitution for the documents.

§ 2—321. C.I.F. or C. & F.: "Net Landed Weights"; "Payment on Arrival"; Warranty of Condition on Arrival.

Under a contract containing a term C.I.F. or C. & F.

(1) Where the price is based on or is to be adjusted according to "net landed weights", "delivered weights", "out turn" quantity or quality or the like, unless otherwise agreed the seller must reasonably estimate the price. The payment due on tender of the documents called for by the contract is the amount so estimated, but after final adjustment of the price a settlement must be made with commercial promptness.

(2) An agreement described in subsection (1) or any warranty of quality or condition of the goods on arrival places upon the seller the risk of ordinary deterioration, shrinkage and the like in transportation but has no effect on the place or time of identification to the contract for sale or delivery or on the passing of the risk of loss.

(3) Unless otherwise agreed where the contract provides for payment on or after arrival of the goods the seller must before payment allow such preliminary inspection as is feasible; but if the goods

are lost delivery of the documents and payment are due when the goods should have arrived.

§ 2—322. Delivery "Ex-Ship".

(1) Unless otherwise agreed a term for delivery of goods "ex-ship" (which means from the carrying vessel) or in equivalent language is not restricted to a particular ship and requires delivery from a ship which has reached a place at the named port of destination where goods of the kind are usually discharged.

(2) Under such a term unless otherwise agreed

(a) the seller must discharge all liens arising out of the carriage and furnish the buyer with a direction which puts the carrier under a duty to deliver the goods; and

(b) the risk of loss does not pass to the buyer until the goods leave the ship's tackle or are otherwise properly unloaded.

§ 2—323. Form of Bill of Lading Required in Overseas Shipment; "Overseas".

(1) Where the contract contemplates overseas shipment and contains a term C.I.F. or C. & F. or F.O.B. vessel, the seller unless otherwise agreed must obtain a negotiable bill of lading stating that the goods have been loaded on board or, in the case of a term C.I.F. or C. & F., received for shipment.

(2) Where in a case within subsection (1) a bill of lading has been issued in a set of parts, unless otherwise agreed if the documents are not to be sent from abroad the buyer may demand tender of the full set; otherwise only one part of the bill of lading need be tendered. Even if the agreement expressly requires a full set

(a) due tender of a single part is acceptable within the provisions of this Article on cure of improper delivery (subsection (1) of Section 2—508); and

(b) even though the full set is demanded, if the documents are sent from abroad the person tendering an incomplete set may nevertheless require payment upon furnishing an indemnity which the buyer in good faith deems adequate.

(3) A shipment by water or by air or a contract contemplating such shipment is "overseas" insofar as by usage of trade or agreement it is subject to the commercial, financing or shipping practices characteristic of international deep water commerce.

§ 2—324. "No Arrival, No Sale" Term.

Under a term "no arrival, no sale" or terms of like meaning, unless otherwise agreed,

(a) the seller must properly ship conforming goods and if they arrive by any means he must tender them on arrival but he assumes no obligation that the goods will arrive unless he has caused the non-arrival; and

(b) where without fault of the seller the goods are in part lost or have so deteriorated as no longer to conform to the contract or arrive after the contract time, the buyer may proceed as if there had been casualty to identified goods (Section 2—613).

§ 2—325. "Letter of Credit" Term; "Confirmed Credit".

(1) Failure of the buyer seasonably to furnish an agreed letter of credit is a breach of the contract for sale.

(2) The delivery to seller of a proper letter of credit suspends the buyer's obligation to pay. If the letter of credit is dishonored, the seller may on seasonable notification to the buyer require payment directly from him.

(3) Unless otherwise agreed the term "letter of credit" or "banker's credit" in a contract for sale means an irrevocable credit issued by a financing agency of good repute and, where the shipment is overseas, of good international repute. The term "confirmed credit" means that the credit must also carry the direct obligation of such an agency which does business in the seller's financial market.

§ 2—326. Sale on Approval and Sale or Return; Consignment Sales and Rights of Creditors.

(1) Unless otherwise agreed, if delivered goods may be returned by the buyer even though they conform to the contract, the transaction is

(a) a "sale on approval" if the goods are delivered primarily for use, and

(b) a "sale or return" if the goods are delivered primarily for resale.

(2) Except as provided in subsection (3), goods held on approval are not subject to the claims of the buyer's creditors until acceptance; goods held on sale or return are subject to such claims while in the buyer's possession.

(3) Where goods are delivered to a person for sale and such person maintains a place of business at which he deals in goods of the kind involved, under a name other than the name of the person making delivery, then with respect to claims of creditors of the person conducting the business the goods are deemed to be on sale or return. The provisions of this subsection are applicable even though an agreement purports to reserve title to the person making delivery until payment or resale or uses such words as "on consignment" or "on memorandum". However, this subsection is not applicable if the person making delivery

(a) complies with an applicable law providing for a consignor's interest or the like to be evidenced by a sign, or

(b) establishes that the person conducting the business is generally known by his creditors to be substantially engaged in selling the goods of others, or

(c) complies with the filing provisions of the Article on Secured Transactions (Article 9).

(4) Any "or return" term of a contract for sale is to be treated as a separate contract for sale within the statute of frauds section of this Article (Section 2—201) and as contradicting the sale aspect of the contract within the provisions of this Article on parol or extrinsic evidence (Section 2—202).

§ 2—327. Special Incidents of Sale on Approval and Sale or Return.

(1) Under a sale on approval unless otherwise agreed

(a) although the goods are identified to the contract the risk of loss and the title do not pass to the buyer until acceptance; and

(b) use of the goods consistent with the purpose of trial is not acceptance but failure seasonably to notify the seller of election to return the goods is acceptance, and if the goods conform to the contract acceptance of any part is acceptance of the whole; and

(c) after due notification of election to return, the return is at the seller's risk and expense but a merchant buyer must follow any reasonable instructions.

(2) Under a sale or return unless otherwise agreed

(a) the option to return extends to the whole or any commercial unit of the goods while in substantially their original condition, but must be exercised seasonably; and

(b) the return is at the buyer's risk and expense.

§ 2—328. Sale by Auction.

(1) In a sale by auction if goods are put up in lots each lot is the subject of a separate sale.

(2) A sale by auction is complete when the auctioneer so announces by the fall of the hammer or in other customary manner. Where a bid is made while the hammer is falling in acceptance of a prior bid the auctioneer may in his discretion reopen the bidding or declare the goods sold under the bid on which the hammer was falling.

(3) Such a sale is with reserve unless the goods are in explicit terms put up without reserve. In an auction with reserve the auctioneer may withdraw the goods at any time until he announces completion of the sale. In an auction without reserve, after the auctioneer calls for bids on an article or lot, that article or lot cannot be withdrawn unless no bid is made within a reasonable time. In either case a bidder may retract his bid until the auctioneer's announcement of completion of the sale, but a bidder's retraction does not revive any previous bid.

(4) If the auctioneer knowingly receives a bid on the seller's behalf or the seller makes or procures such as bid, and notice has not been given that liberty for such bidding is reserved, the buyer may at his option avoid the sale or take the goods at the price of the last good faith bid prior to the completion of the sale. This subsection shall not apply to any bid at a forced sale.

Part 4 Title, Creditors and Good Faith Purchasers

§ 2—401. Passing of Title; Reservation for Security; Limited Application of This Section.

Each provision of this Article with regard to the rights, obligations and remedies of the seller, the buyer, purchasers or other third parties applies irrespective of title to the goods except where the provision refers to such title. Insofar as situations are not covered by the other provisions of this Article and matters concerning title became material the following rules apply:

(1) Title to goods cannot pass under a contract for sale prior to their identification to the contract (Section 2—501), and unless otherwise explicitly agreed the buyer acquires by their identification a special property as limited by this Act. Any retention or reservation by the seller of the title (property) in goods shipped or delivered to the buyer is limited in effect to a reservation of a security interest. Subject to these provisions and to the provisions of the Article on Secured Transactions (Article 9), title to goods passes from the seller to the buyer in any manner and on any conditions explicitly agreed on by the parties.

(2) Unless otherwise explicitly agreed title passes to the buyer at the time and place at which the seller completes his performance with reference to the physical delivery of the goods, despite any reservation of a security interest and even though a document of title is to be delivered at a different time or place; and in particular and despite any reservation of a security interest by the bill of lading

(a) if the contract requires or authorizes the seller to send the goods to the buyer but does not require him to deliver them at destination, title passes to the buyer at the time and place of shipment; but

(b) if the contract requires delivery at destination, title passes on tender there.

(3) Unless otherwise explicitly agreed where delivery is to be made without moving the goods,

(a) if the seller is to deliver a document of title, title passes at the time when and the place where he delivers such documents; or

(b) if the goods are at the time of contracting already identified and no documents are to be delivered, title passes at the time and place of contracting.

(4) A rejection or other refusal by the buyer to receive or retain the goods, whether or not justified, or a justified revocation of acceptance revests title to the goods in the seller. Such revesting occurs by operation of law and is not a "sale".

§ 2—402. Rights of Seller's Creditors Against Sold Goods.

(1) Except as provided in subsections (2) and (3), rights of unsecured creditors of the seller with respect to goods which have been identified to a contract for sale are subject to the buyer's rights to recover the goods under this Article (Sections 2—502 and 2—716).

(2) A creditor of the seller may treat a sale or an identification of goods to a contract for sale as void if as against him a retention of possession by the seller is fraudulent under any rule of law of the state where the goods are situated, except that retention of possession in good faith and current course of trade by a merchant-

seller for a commercially reasonable time after a sale or identification is not fraudulent.

(3) Nothing in this Article shall be deemed to impair the rights of creditors of the seller

(a) under the provisions of the Article on Secured Transactions (Article 9); or

(b) where identification to the contract or delivery is made not in current course of trade but in satisfaction of or as security for a pre-existing claim for money, security or the like and is made under circumstances which under any rule of law of the state where the goods are situated would apart from this Article constitute the transaction a fraudulent transfer or voidable preference.

§ 2—403. Power to Transfer; Good Faith Purchase of Goods; "Entrusting".

(1) A purchaser of goods acquires all title which his transferor had or had power to transfer except that a purchaser of a limited interest acquires rights only to the extent of the interest purchased. A person with voidable title has power to transfer a good title to a good faith purchaser for value. When goods have been delivered under a transaction of purchase the purchaser has such power even though

(a) the transferor was deceived as to the identity of the purchaser, or

(b) the delivery was in exchange for a check which is later dishonored, or

(c) it was agreed that the transaction was to be a "cash sale", or

(d) the delivery was procured through fraud punishable as larcenous under the criminal law.

(2) Any entrusting of possession of goods to a merchant who deals in goods of that kind gives him power to transfer all rights of the entruster to a buyer in ordinary course of business.

(3) "Entrusting" includes any delivery and any acquiescence in retention of possession regardless of any condition expressed between the parties to the delivery or acquiescence and regardless of whether the procurement of the entrusting or the possessor's disposition of the goods have been such as to be larcenous under the criminal law.

(4) The rights of other purchasers of goods and of lien creditors are governed by the Articles on Secured Transactions (Article 9), Bulk Transfers (Article 6) and Documents of Title (Article 7).

Part 5 Performance

§ 2—501. Insurable Interest in Goods; Manner of Identification of Goods.

(1) The buyer obtains a special property and an insurable interest in goods by identification of existing goods as goods to which the contract refers even though the goods so identified are non-con-forming and he has an option to return or reject them. Such identification can be made at any time and in any manner explicitly agreed to by the parties. In the absence of explicit agreement identification occurs

(a) when the contract is made if it is for the sale of goods already existing and identified;

(b) if the contract is for the sale of future goods other than those described in paragraph (c), when goods are shipped, marked or otherwise designated by the seller as goods to which the contract refers;

(c) when the crops are planted or otherwise become growing crops or the young are conceived if the contract is for the sale of unborn young to be born within twelve months after contracting or for the sale of crops to be harvested within twelve months or the next normal harvest season after contracting whichever is longer.

(2) The seller retains an insurable interest in goods so long as title to or any security interest in the goods remains in him and where the identification is by the seller alone he may until default or insolvency or notification to the buyer that the identification is final substitute other goods for those identified.

(3) Nothing in this section impairs any insurable interest recognized under any other statute or rule of law.

§ 2—502. Buyer's Right to Goods on Seller's Insolvency.

(1) Subject to subsection (2) and even though the goods have not been shipped a buyer who has paid a part or all of the price of goods in which he has a special property under the provisions of the immediately preceding section may on making and keeping good a tender of any unpaid portion of their price recover them from the seller if the seller becomes insolvent within ten days after receipt of the first installment on their price.

(2) If the identification creating his special property has been made by the buyer he acquires the right to recover the goods only if they conform to the contract for sale.

§ 2—503. Manner of Seller's Tender of Delivery.

(1) Tender of delivery requires that the seller put and hold conforming goods at the buyer's disposition and give the buyer any notification reasonably necessary to enable him to take delivery. The manner, time and place for tender are determined by the agreement and this Article, and in particular

(a) tender must be at a reasonable hour, and if it is of goods they must be kept available for the period reasonably necessary to enable the buyer to take possession; but

(b) unless otherwise agreed the buyer must furnish facilities reasonably suited to the receipt of the goods.

(2) Where the case is within the next section respecting shipment tender requires that the seller comply with its provisions.

(3) Where the seller is required to deliver at a particular destination tender requires that he comply with subsection (1) and also

in any appropriate case tender documents as described in subsections (4) and (5) of this section.

(4) Where goods are in the possession of a bailee and are to be delivered without being moved

(a) tender requires that the seller either tender a negotiable document of title covering such goods or procure acknowledgment by the bailee of the buyer's right to possession of the goods; but

(b) tender to the buyer of a non-negotiable document of title or of a written direction to the bailee to deliver is sufficient tender unless the buyer seasonably objects, and receipt by the bailee of notification of the buyer's rights fixes those rights as against the bailee and all third persons; but risk of loss of the goods and of any failure by the bailee to honor the non-negotiable document of title or to obey the direction remains on the seller until the buyer has had a reasonable time to present the document or direction, and a refusal by the bailee to honor the document or to obey the direction defeats the tender.

(5) Where the contract requires the seller to deliver documents

(a) he must tender all such documents in correct form, except as provided in this Article with respect to bills of lading in a set (subsection (2) of Section 2—323); and

(b) tender through customary banking channels is sufficient and dishonor of a draft accompanying the documents constitutes non-acceptance or rejection.

§ 2—504. Shipment by Seller.

Where the seller is required or authorized to send the goods to the buyer and the contract does not require him to deliver them at a particular destination, then unless otherwise agreed he must

(a) put the goods in the possession of such a carrier and make such a contract for their transportation as may be reasonable having regard to the nature of the goods and other circumstances of the case; and

(b) obtain and promptly deliver or tender in due form any document necessary to enable the buyer to obtain possession of the goods or otherwise required by the agreement or by usage of trade; and

(c) promptly notify the buyer of the shipment.

Failure to notify the buyer under paragraph (c) or to make a proper contract under paragraph (a) is a ground for rejection only if material delay or loss ensues.

§ 2—505. Seller's Shipment Under Reservation.

(1) Where the seller has identified goods to the contract by or before shipment:

(a) his procurement of a negotiable bill of lading to his own order or otherwise reserves in him a security interest in the goods. His procurement of the bill to the order of a financing agency or of the buyer indicates in addition only the seller's expectation of transferring that interest to the person named.

(b) a non-negotiable bill of lading to himself or his nominee reserves possession of the goods as security but except in a case of conditional delivery (subsection (2) of Section 2—507) a non-negotiable bill of lading naming the buyer as consignee reserves no security interest even though the seller retains possession of the bill of lading.

(2) When shipment by the seller with reservation of a security interest is in violation of the contract for sale it constitutes an improper contract for transportation within the preceding section but impairs neither the rights given to the buyer by shipment and identification of the goods to the contract nor the seller's powers as a holder of a negotiable document.

§ 2—506. Rights of Financing Agency.

(1) A financing agency by paying or purchasing for value a draft which relates to a shipment of goods acquires to the extent of the payment or purchase and in addition to its own rights under the draft and any document of title securing it any rights of the shipper in the goods including the right to stop delivery and the shipper's right to have the draft honored by the buyer.

(2) The right to reimbursement of a financing agency which has in good faith honored or purchased the draft under commitment to or authority from the buyer is not impaired by subsequent discovery of defects with reference to any relevant document which was apparently regular on its face.

§ 2—507. Effect of Seller's Tender; Delivery on Condition.

(1) Tender of delivery is a condition to the buyer's duty to accept the goods and, unless otherwise agreed, to his duty to pay for them. Tender entitles the seller to acceptance of the goods and to payment according to the contract.

(2) Where payment is due and demanded on the delivery to the buyer of goods or documents of title, his right as against the seller to retain or dispose of them is conditional upon his making the payment due.

§ 2—508. Cure by Seller of Improper Tender or Delivery; Replacement.

(1) Where any tender or delivery by the seller is rejected because non-conforming and the time for performance has not yet expired, the seller may seasonably notify the buyer of his intention to cure and may then within the contract time make a conforming delivery.

(2) Where the buyer rejects a non-conforming tender which the seller had reasonable grounds to believe would be acceptable with or without money allowance the seller may if he seasonably notifies the buyer have a further reasonable time to substitute a conforming tender.

§ 2—509. Risk of Loss in the Absence of Breach.

(1) Where the contract requires or authorizes the seller to ship the goods by carrier

(a) if it does not require him to deliver them at a particular destination, the risk of loss passes to the buyer when the goods are duly delivered to the carrier even though the shipment is under reservation (Section 2—505); but

(b) if it does require him to deliver them at a particular destination and the goods are there duly tendered while in the possession of the carrier, the risk of loss passes to the buyer when the goods are there duly so tendered as to enable the buyer to take delivery.

(2) Where the goods are held by a bailee to be delivered without being moved, the risk of loss passes to the buyer

(a) on his receipt of a negotiable document of title covering the goods; or

(b) on acknowledgment by the bailee of the buyer's right to possession of the goods; or

(c) after his receipt of a non-negotiable document of title or other written direction to deliver, as provided in subsection (4)(b) of Section 2—503.

(3) In any case not within subsection (1) or (2), the risk of loss passes to the buyer on his receipt of the goods if the seller is a merchant; otherwise the risk passes to the buyer on tender of delivery.

(4) The provisions of this section are subject to contrary agreement of the parties and to the provisions of this Article on sale on approval (Section 2—327) and on effect of breach on risk of loss (Section 2—510).

§ 2—510. Effect of Breach on Risk of Loss.

(1) Where a tender or delivery of goods so fails to conform to the contract as to give a right of rejection the risk of their loss remains on the seller until cure or acceptance.

(2) Where the buyer rightfully revokes acceptance he may to the extent of any deficiency in his effective insurance coverage treat the risk of loss as having rested on the seller from the beginning.

(3) Where the buyer as to conforming goods already identified to the contract for sale repudiates or is otherwise in breach before risk of their loss has passed to him, the seller may to the extent of any deficiency in his effective insurance coverage treat the risk of loss as resting on the buyer for a commercially reasonable time.

§ 2—511. Tender of Payment by Buyer; Payment by Check.

(1) Unless otherwise agreed tender of payment is a condition to the seller's duty to tender and complete any delivery.

(2) Tender of payment is sufficient when made by any means or in any manner current in the ordinary course of business unless the seller demands payment in legal tender and gives any extension of time reasonably necessary to procure it.

(3) Subject to the provisions of this Act on the effect of an instrument on an obligation (Section 3—802), payment by check is conditional and is defeated as between the parties by dishonor of the check on due presentment.

§ 2—512. Payment by Buyer Before Inspection.

(1) Where the contract requires payment before inspection non-conformity of the goods does not excuse the buyer from so making payment unless

(a) the non-conformity appears without inspection; or

(b) despite tender of the required documents the circumstances would justify injunction against honor under the provisions of this Act (Section 5—114).

(2) Payment pursuant to subsection (1) does not constitute an acceptance of goods or impair the buyer's right to inspect or any of his remedies.

§ 2—513. Buyer's Right to Inspection of Goods.

(1) Unless otherwise agreed and subject to subsection (3), where goods are tendered or delivered or identified to the contract for sale, the buyer has a right before payment or acceptance to inspect them at any reasonable place and time and in any reasonable manner. When the seller is required or authorized to send the goods to the buyer, the inspection may be after their arrival.

(2) Expenses of inspection must be borne by the buyer but may be recovered from the seller if the goods do not conform and are rejected.

(3) Unless otherwise agreed and subject to the provisions of this Article on C.I.F. contracts (subsection (3) of Section 2—321), the buyer is not entitled to inspect the goods before payment of the price when the contract provides

(a) for delivery "C.O.D." or on other like terms; or

(b) for payment against documents of title, except where such payment is due only after the goods are to become available for inspection.

(4) A place or method of inspection fixed by the parties is presumed to be exclusive but unless otherwise expressly agreed it does not postpone identification or shift the place for delivery or for passing the risk of loss. If compliance becomes impossible, inspection shall be as provided in this section unless the place or method fixed was clearly intended as an indispensable condition failure of which avoids the contract.

§ 2—514. When Documents Deliverable on Acceptance; When on Payment.

Unless otherwise agreed documents against which a draft is drawn are to be delivered to the drawee on acceptance of the draft if it is payable more than three days after presentment; otherwise, only on payment.

§ 2—515. Preserving Evidence of Goods in Dispute.

In furtherance of the adjustment of any claim or dispute

(a) either party on reasonable notification to the other and for the purpose of ascertaining the facts and preserving evidence has the right to inspect, test and sample the goods including such of them as may be in the possession or control of the other; and

(b) the parties may agree to a third party inspection or survey to determine the conformity or condition of the goods and may agree that the findings shall be binding upon them in any subsequent litigation or adjustment.

Part 6 Breach, Repudiation and Excuse

§ 2—601. Buyer's Rights on Improper Delivery.

Subject to the provisions of this Article on breach in installment contracts (Section 2—612) and unless otherwise agreed under the sections on contractual limitations of remedy (Sections 2—718 and 2—719), if the goods or the tender of delivery fail in any respect to conform to the contract, the buyer may

(a) reject the whole; or

(b) accept the whole; or

(c) accept any commercial unit or units and reject the rest.

§ 2—602. Manner and Effect of Rightful Rejection.

(1) Rejection of goods must be within a reasonable time after their delivery or tender. It is ineffective unless the buyer seasonably notifies the seller.

(2) Subject to the provisions of the two following sections on rejected goods (Sections 2—603 and 2—604),

(a) after rejection any exercise of ownership by the buyer with respect to any commercial unit is wrongful as against the seller; and

(b) if the buyer has before rejection taken physical possession of goods in which he does not have a security interest under the provisions of this Article (subsection (3) of Section 2—711), he is under a duty after rejection to hold them with reasonable care at the seller's disposition for a time sufficient to permit the seller to remove them; but

(c) the buyer has no further obligations with regard to goods rightfully rejected.

(3) The seller's rights with respect to goods wrongfully rejected are governed by the provisions of this Article on Seller's remedies in general (Section 2—703).

§ 2—603. Merchant Buyer's Duties as to Rightfully Rejected Goods.

(1) Subject to any security interest in the buyer (subsection (3) of Section 2—711), when the seller has no agent or place of business at the market of rejection a merchant buyer is under a duty after rejection of goods in his possession or control to follow any reasonable instructions received from the seller with respect to the goods and in the absence of such instructions to make reasonable efforts to sell them for the seller's account if they are perishable or threaten to decline in value speedily. Instructions are not reasonable if on demand indemnity for expenses is not forthcoming.

(2) When the buyer sells goods under subsection (1), he is entitled to reimbursement from the seller or out of the proceeds for reasonable expenses of caring for and selling them, and if the expenses include no selling commission then to such commission as is usual in the trade or if there is none to a reasonable sum not exceeding ten per cent on the gross proceeds.

(3) In complying with this section the buyer is held only to good faith and good faith conduct hereunder is neither acceptance nor conversion nor the basis of an action for damages.

§ 2—604. Buyer's Options as to Salvage of Rightfully Rejected Goods.

Subject to the provisions of the immediately preceding section on perishables if the seller gives no instructions within a reasonable time after notification of rejection the buyer may store the rejected goods for the seller's account or reship them to him or resell them for the seller's account with reimbursement as provided in the preceding section. Such action is not acceptance or conversion.

§ 2—605. Waiver of Buyer's Objections by Failure to Particularize.

(1) The buyer's failure to state in connection with rejection a particular defect which is ascertainable by reasonable inspection precludes him from relying on the unstated defect to justify rejection or to establish breach

(a) where the seller could have cured it if stated seasonably; or

(b) between merchants when the seller has after rejection made a request in writing for a full and final written statement of all defects on which the buyer proposes to rely.

(2) Payment against documents made without reservation of rights precludes recovery of the payment for defects apparent on the face of the documents.

§ 2—606. What Constitutes Acceptance of Goods.

(1) Acceptance of goods occurs when the buyer

(a) after a reasonable opportunity to inspect the goods signifies to the seller that the goods are conforming or that he will take or retain them in spite of their nonconformity; or

(b) fails to make an effective rejection (subsection (1) of Section 2—602), but such acceptance does not occur until the buyer has had a reasonable opportunity to inspect them; or

(c) does any act inconsistent with the seller's ownership; but if such act is wrongful as against the seller it is an acceptance only if ratified by him.

(2) Acceptance of a part of any commercial unit is acceptance of that entire unit.

§ 2—607. Effect of Acceptance; Notice of Breach; Burden of Establishing Breach After Acceptance; Notice of Claim or Litigation to Person Answerable Over.

(1) The buyer must pay at the contract rate for any goods accepted.

(2) Acceptance of goods by the buyer precludes rejection of the goods accepted and if made with knowledge of a non-conformity

cannot be revoked because of it unless the acceptance was on the reasonable assumption that the non-conformity would be seasonably cured but acceptance does not of itself impair any other remedy provided by this Article for non-conformity.

(3) Where a tender has been accepted

(a) the buyer must within a reasonable time after he discovers or should have discovered any breach notify the seller of breach or be barred from any remedy; and

(b) if the claim is one for infringement or the like (subsection (3) of Section 2—312) and the buyer is sued as a result of such a breach he must so notify the seller within a reasonable time after he receives notice of the litigation or be barred from any remedy over for liability established by the litigation.

(4) The burden is on the buyer to establish any breach with respect to the goods accepted.

(5) Where the buyer is sued for breach of a warranty or other obligation for which his seller is answerable over

(a) he may give his seller written notice of the litigation. If the notice states that the seller may come in and defend and that if the seller does not do so he will be bound in any action against him by his buyer by any determination of fact common to the two litigations, then unless the seller after seasonable receipt of the notice does come in and defend he is so bound.

(b) if the claim is one for infringement or the like (subsection (3) of Section 2—312) the original seller may demand in writing that his buyer turn over to him control of the litigation including settlement or else be barred from any remedy over and if he also agrees to bear all expense and to satisfy any adverse judgment, then unless the buyer after seasonable receipt of the demand does turn over control the buyer is so barred.

(6) The provisions of subsections (3), (4) and (5) apply to any obligation of a buyer to hold the seller harmless against infringement or the like (subsection (3) of Section 2—312).

§ 2—608. Revocation of Acceptance in Whole or in Part.

(1) The buyer may revoke his acceptance of a lot or commercial unit whose non-conformity substantially impairs its value to him if he has accepted it

(a) on the reasonable assumption that its nonconformity would be cured and it has not been seasonably cured; or

(b) without discovery of such non-conformity if his acceptance was reasonably induced either by the difficulty of discovery before acceptance or by the seller's assurances.

(2) Revocation of acceptance must occur within a reasonable time after the buyer discovers or should have discovered the ground for it and before any substantial change in condition of the goods which is not caused by their own defects. It is not effective until the buyer notifies the seller of it.

(3) A buyer who so revokes has the same rights and duties with regard to the goods involved as if he had rejected them.

§ 2—609. Right to Adequate Assurance of Performance.

(1) A contract for sale imposes an obligation on each party that the other's expectation of receiving due performance will not be impaired. When reasonable grounds for insecurity arise with respect to the performance of either party the other may in writing demand adequate assurance of due performance and until he receives such assurance may if commercially reasonable suspend any performance for which he has not already received the agreed return.

(2) Between merchants the reasonableness of grounds for insecurity and the adequacy of any assurance offered shall be determined according to commercial standards.

(3) Acceptance of any improper delivery or payment does not prejudice the aggrieved party's right to demand adequate assurance of future performance.

(4) After receipt of a justified demand failure to provide within a reasonable time not exceeding thirty days such assurance of due performance as is adequate under the circumstances of the particular case is a repudiation of the contract.

§ 2—610. Anticipatory Repudiation.

When either party repudiates the contract with respect to a performance not yet due the loss of which will substantially impair the value of the contract to the other, the aggrieved party may

(a) for a commercially reasonable time await performance by the repudiating party; or

(b) resort to any remedy for breach (Section 2—703 or Section 2—711), even though he has notified the repudiating party that he would await the latter's performance and has urged retraction; and

(c) in either case suspend his own performance or proceed in accordance with the provisions of this Article on the seller's right to identify goods to the contract notwithstanding breach or to salvage unfinished goods (Section 2—704).

§ 2—611. Retraction of Anticipatory Repudiation.

(1) Until the repudiating party's next performance is due he can retract his repudiation unless the aggrieved party has since the repudiation cancelled or materially changed his position or otherwise indicated that he considers the repudiation final.

(2) Retraction may be by any method which clearly indicates to the aggrieved party that the repudiating party intends to perform, but must include any assurance justifiably demanded under the provisions of this Article (Section 2—609).

(3) Retraction reinstates the repudiating party's rights under the contract with due excuse and allowance to the aggrieved party for any delay occasioned by the repudiation.

§ 2—612. "Installment Contract"; Breach.

(1) An "installment contract" is one which requires or authorizes the delivery of goods in separate lots to be separately accepted,

even though the contract contains a clause "each delivery is a separate contract" or its equivalent.

(2) The buyer may reject any installment which is non-conforming if the non-conformity substantially impairs the value of that installment and cannot be cured or if the non-conformity is a defect in the required documents; but if the non-conformity does not fall within subsection (3) and the seller gives adequate assurance of its cure the buyer must accept that installment.

(3) Whenever non-conformity or default with respect to one or more installments substantially impairs the value of the whole contract there is a breach of the whole. But the aggrieved party reinstates the contract if he accepts a non-conforming installment without seasonably notifying of cancellation or if he brings an action with respect only to past installments or demands performance as to future installments.

§ 2—613. Casualty to Identified Goods.

Where the contract requires for its performance goods identified when the contract is made, and the goods suffer casualty without fault of either party before the risk of loss passes to the buyer, or in a proper case under a "no arrival, no sale" term (Section 2—324) then

(a) if the loss is total the contract is avoided; and

(b) if the loss is partial or the goods have so deteriorated as no longer to conform to the contract the buyer may nevertheless demand inspection and at his option either treat the contract as voided or accept the goods with due allowance from the contract price for the deterioration or the deficiency in quantity but without further right against the seller.

§ 2—614. Substituted Performance.

(1) Where without fault of either party the agreed berthing, loading, or unloading facilities fail or an agreed type of carrier becomes unavailable or the agreed manner of delivery otherwise becomes commercially impracticable but a commercially reasonable substitute is available, such substitute performance must be tendered and accepted.

(2) If the agreed means or manner of payment fails because of domestic or foreign governmental regulation, the seller may withhold or stop delivery unless the buyer provides a means or manner of payment which is commercially a substantial equivalent. If delivery has already been taken, payment by the means or in the manner provided by the regulation discharges 'the buyer's obligation unless the regulation is discriminatory, oppressive or predatory.

§ 2—615. Excuse by Failure of Presupposed Conditions.

Except so far as a seller may have assumed a greater obligation and subject to the preceding section on substituted performance:

(a) Delay in delivery or non-delivery in whole or in part by a seller who complies with paragraphs (b) and (c) is not a breach of his duty under a contract for sale if performance as agreed has been made impracticable by the occurrence of a contingency the nonoccurrence of which was a basic assumption on which the contract was made or by compliance in good faith with any applicable foreign or domestic governmental regulation or order whether or not it later proves to be invalid.

(b) Where the causes mentioned in paragraph (a) affect only a part of the seller's capacity to perform, he must allocate production and deliveries among his customers but may at his option include regular customers not then under contract as well as his own requirements for further manufacture. He may so allocate in any manner which is fair and reasonable.

(c) The seller must notify the buyer seasonably that there will be delay or non-delivery and, when allocation is required under paragraph (b), of the estimated quota thus made available for the buyer.

§ 2—616. Procedure on Notice Claiming Excuse.

(1) Where the buyer receives notification of a material or indefinite delay or an allocation justified under the preceding section he may by written notification to the seller as to any delivery concerned, and where the prospective deficiency substantially impairs the value of the whole contract under the provisions of this Article relating to breach of installment contracts (Section 2—612), then also as to the whole,

(a) terminate and thereby discharge any unexecuted portion of the contract; or

(b) modify the contract by agreeing to take his available quota in substitution.

(2) If after receipt of such notification from the seller the buyer fails so to modify the contract within a reasonable time not exceeding thirty days the contract lapses with respect to any deliveries affected.

(3) The provisions of this section may not be negated by agreement except in so far as the seller has assumed a greater obligation under the preceding section.

Part 7 Remedies

§ 2—701. Remedies for Breach of Collateral Contracts Not Impaired.

Remedies for breach of any obligation or promise collateral or ancillary to a contract for sale are not impaired by the provisions of this Article.

§ 2—702. Seller's Remedies on Discovery of Buyer's Insolvency.

(1) Where the seller discovers the buyer to be insolvent he may refuse delivery except for cash including payment for all goods theretofore delivered under the contract, and stop delivery under this Article (Section 2—705).

(2) Where the seller discovers that the buyer has received goods on credit while insolvent he may reclaim the goods upon demand

made within ten days after the receipt, but if misrepresentation of solvency has been made to the particular seller in writing within three months before delivery the ten day limitation does not apply. Except as provided in this subsection the seller may not base a right to reclaim goods on the buyer's fraudulent or innocent misrepresentation of solvency or of intent to pay.

(3) The seller's right to reclaim under subsection (2) is subject to the rights of a buyer in ordinary course or other good faith purchaser under this Article (Section 2—403). Successful reclamation of goods excludes all other remedies with respect to them.

§ 2—703. Seller's Remedies in General.

Where the buyer wrongfully rejects or revokes acceptance of goods or fails to make a payment due on or before delivery or repudiates with respect to a part or the whole, then with respect to any goods directly affected and, if the breach is of the whole contract (Section 2—612), then also with respect to the whole undelivered balance, the aggrieved seller may

(a) withhold delivery of such goods;

(b) stop delivery by any bailee as hereafter provided (Section 2—705);

(c) proceed under the next section respecting goods still unidentified to the contract;

(d) resell and recover damages as hereafter provided (Section 2—706);

(e) recover damages for non-acceptance (Section 2—708) or in a proper case the price (Section 2—709);

(f) cancel.

§ 2—704. Seller's Right to Identify Goods to the Contract Notwithstanding Breach or to Salvage Unfinished Goods.

(1) An aggrieved seller under the preceding section may

(a) identify to the contract conforming goods not already identified if at the time he learned of the breach they are in his possession or control;

(b) treat as the subject of resale goods which have demonstrably been intended for the particular contract even though those goods are unfinished.

(2) Where the goods are unfinished an aggrieved seller may in the exercise of reasonable commercial judgment for the purposes of avoiding loss and of effective realization either complete the manufacture and wholly identify the goods to the contract or cease manufacture and resell for scrap or salvage value or proceed in any other reasonable manner.

§ 2—705. Seller's Stoppage of Delivery in Transit or Otherwise.

(1) The seller may stop delivery of goods in the possession of a carrier or other bailee when he discovers the buyer to be insolvent (Section 2—702) and may stop delivery of carload, truckload, planeload or larger shipments of express or freight when the buyer repudiates or fails to make a payment due before delivery or if for any other reason the seller has a right to withhold or reclaim the goods.

(2) As against such buyer the seller may stop delivery until

(a) receipt of the goods by the buyer; or

(b) acknowledgment to the buyer by any bailee of the goods except a carrier that the bailee holds the goods for the buyer; or

(c) such acknowledgment to the buyer by a carrier by reshipment or as warehouseman; or

(d) negotiation to the buyer of any negotiable document of title covering the goods.

(3) (a) To stop delivery the seller must so notify as to enable the bailee by reasonable diligence to prevent delivery of the goods.

(b) After such notification the bailee must hold and deliver the goods according to the directions of the seller but the seller is liable to the bailee for any ensuing charges or damages.

(c) If a negotiable document of title has been issued for goods the bailee is not obliged to obey a notification to stop until surrender of the document.

(d) A carrier who has issued a non-negotiable bill of lading is not obliged to obey a notification to stop received from a person other than the consignor.

§ 2—706. Seller's Resale Including Contract for Resale.

(1) Under the conditions stated in Section 2—703 on seller's remedies, the seller may resell the goods concerned or the undelivered balance thereof. Where the resale is made in good faith and in a commercially reasonable manner the seller may recover the difference between the resale price and the contract price together with any incidental damages allowed under the provisions of this Article (Section 2—710), but less expenses saved in consequence of the buyer's breach.

(2) Except as otherwise provided in subsection (3) or unless otherwise agreed resale may be at public or private sale including sale by way of one or more contracts to sell or of identification to an existing contract of the seller. Sale may be as a unit or in parcels and at any time and place and on any terms but every aspect of the sale including the method, manner, time, place and terms must be commercially reasonable. The resale must be reasonably identified as referring to the broken contract, but it is not necessary that the goods be in existence or that any or all of them have been identified to the contract before the breach.

(3) Where the resale is at private sale the seller must give the buyer reasonable notification of his intention to resell.

(4) Where the resale is at public sale

(a) only identified goods can be sold except where there is a recognized market for a public sale of futures in goods of the kind; and

(b) it must be made at a usual place or market for public sale if one is reasonably available and except in the case of goods which are perishable or threaten to decline in value speedily the seller must give the buyer reasonable notice of the time and place of the resale; and

(c) if the goods are not to be within the view of those attending the sale the notification of sale must state the place where the goods are located and provide for their reasonable inspection by prospective bidders; and

(d) the seller may buy.

(5) A purchaser who buys in good faith at a resale takes the goods free of any rights of the original buyer even though the seller fails to comply with one or more of the requirements of this section.

(6) The seller is not accountable to the buyer for any profit made on any resale. A person in the position of a seller (Section 2—707) or a buyer who has rightfully rejected or justifiably revoked acceptance must account for any excess over the amount of his security interest, as hereinafter defined (subsection (3) of Section 2—711).

§ 2—707. "Person in the Position of a Seller".

(1) A "person in the position of a seller" includes as against a principal an agent who has paid or become responsible for the price of goods on behalf of his principal or anyone who otherwise holds a security interest or other right in goods similar to that of a seller.

(2) A person in the position of a seller may as provided in this Article withhold or stop delivery (Section 2—705) and resell (Section 2—706) and recover incidental damages (Section 2—710).

§ 2—708. Seller's Damages for Non-Acceptance or Repudiation.

(1) Subject to subsection (2) and to the provisions of this Article with respect to proof of market price (Section 2—723), the measure of damages for non-acceptance or repudiation by the buyer is the difference between the market price at the time and place for tender and the unpaid contract price together with any incidental damages provided in this Article (Section 2—710), but less expenses saved in consequence of the buyer's breach.

(2) If the measure of damages provided in subsection (1) is inadequate to put the seller in as good a position as performance would have done then the measure of damages is the profit (including reasonable overhead) which the seller would have made from full performance by the buyer, together with any incidental damages provided in this Article (Section 2—710), due allowance for costs reasonably incurred and due credit for payments or proceeds of resale.

§ 2—709. Action for the Price.

(1) When the buyer fails to pay the price as it becomes due the seller may recover, together with any incidental damages under the next section, the price

(a) of goods accepted or of conforming goods lost or damaged within a commercially reasonable time after risk of their loss has passed to the buyer; and

(b) of goods identified to the contract if the seller is unable after reasonable effort to resell them at a reasonable price or the circumstances reasonably indicate that such effort will be unavailing.

(2) Where the seller sues for the price he must hold for the buyer any goods which have been identified to the contract and are still in his control except that if resale becomes possible he may resell them at any time prior to the collection of the judgment. The net proceeds of any such resale must be credited to the buyer and payment of the judgment entitles him to any goods not resold.

(3) After the buyer has wrongfully rejected or revoked acceptance of the goods or has failed to make a payment due or has repudiated (Section 2—610), a seller who is held not entitled to the price under this section shall nevertheless be awarded damages for non-acceptance under the preceding section.

§ 2—710. Seller's Incidental Damages.

Incidental damages to an aggrieved seller include any commercially reasonable charges, expenses or commissions incurred in stopping delivery, in the transportation, care and custody of goods after the buyer's breach, in connection with return or resale of the goods or otherwise resulting from the breach.

§ 2—711. Buyer's Remedies in General; Buyer's Security Interest in Rejected Goods.

(1) Where the seller fails to make delivery or repudiates or the buyer rightfully rejects or justifiably revokes acceptance then with respect to any goods involved, and with respect to the whole if the breach goes to the whole contract (Section 2—612), the buyer may cancel and whether or not he has done so may in addition to recovering so much of the price as has been paid

(a) "cover" and have damages under the next section as to all the goods affected whether or not they have been identified to the contract; or

(b) recover damages for non-delivery as provided in this Article (Section 2—713).

(2) Where the seller fails to deliver or repudiates the buyer may also

(a) if the goods have been identified recover them as provided in this Article (Section 2—502); or

(b) in a proper case obtain specific performance or replevy the goods as provided in this Article (Section 2—716).

(3) On rightful rejection or justifiable revocation of acceptance a buyer has a security interest in goods in his possession or control for any payments made on their price and any expenses reasonably incurred in their inspection, receipt, transportation, care and custody and may hold such goods and resell them in like manner as an aggrieved seller (Section 2—706).

§ 2—712. "Cover"; Buyer's Procurement of Substitute Goods.

(1) After a breach within the preceding section the buyer may "cover" by making in good faith and without unreasonable delay any reasonable purchase of or contract to purchase goods in substitution for those due from the seller.

(2) The buyer may recover from the seller as damages the difference between the cost of cover and the contract price together with any incidental or consequential damages as hereinafter defined (Section 2—715), but less expenses saved in consequence of the seller's breach.

(3) Failure of the buyer to effect cover within this section does not bar him from any other remedy.

§ 2—713. Buyer's Damages for Non-Delivery or Repudiation.

(1) Subject to the provisions of this Article with respect to proof of market price (Section 2—723), the measure of damages for non-delivery or repudiation by the seller is the difference between the market price at the time when the buyer learned of the breach and the contract price together with any incidental and consequential damages provided in this Article (Section 2—715), but less expenses saved in consequence of the seller's breach.

(2) Market price is to be determined as of the place for tender or, in cases of rejection after arrival or revocation of acceptance, as of the place of arrival.

§ 2—714. Buyer's Damages for Breach in Regard to Accepted Goods.

(1) Where the buyer has accepted goods and given notification (subsection (3) of Section 2—607) he may recover as damages for any non-conformity of tender the loss resulting in the ordinary course of events from the seller's breach as determined in any manner which is reasonable.

(2) The measure of damages for breach of warranty is the difference at the time and place of acceptance between the value of the goods accepted and the value they would have had if they had been as warranted, unless special circumstances show proximate damages of a different amount.

(3) In a proper case any incidental and consequential damages under the next section may also be recovered.

§ 2—715. Buyer's Incidental and Consequential Damages.

(1) Incidental damages resulting from the seller's breach include expenses reasonably incurred in inspection, receipt, transportation and care and custody of goods rightfully rejected, any commercially reasonable charges, expenses or commissions in connection with effecting cover and any other reasonable expense incident to the delay or other breach.

(2) Consequential damages resulting from the seller's breach include

(a) any loss resulting from general or particular requirements and needs of which the seller at the time of contracting had

reason to know and which could not reasonably be prevented by cover or otherwise; and

(b) injury to person or property proximately resulting from any breach of warranty.

§ 2—716. Buyer's Right to Specific Performance or Replevin.

(1) Specific performance may be decreed where the goods are unique or in other proper circumstances.

(2) The decree for specific performance may include such terms and conditions as to payment of the price, damages, or other relief as the court may deem just.

(3) The buyer has a right of replevin for goods identified to the contract if after reasonable effort he is unable to effect cover for such goods or the circumstances reasonably indicate that such effort will be unavailing or if the goods have been shipped under reservation and satisfaction of the security interest in them has been made or tendered.

§ 2—717. Deduction of Damages From the Price.

The buyer on notifying the seller of his intention to do so may deduct all or any part of the damages resulting from any breach of the contract from any part of the price still due under the same contract.

§ 2—718. Liquidation or Limitation of Damages; Deposits.

(1) Damages for breach by either party may be liquidated in the agreement but only at an amount which is reasonable in the light of the anticipated or actual harm caused by the breach, the difficulties of proof of loss, and the inconvenience or nonfeasibility of otherwise obtaining an adequate remedy. A term fixing unreasonably large liquidated damages is void as a penalty.

(2) Where the seller justifiably withholds delivery of goods because of the buyer's breach, the buyer is entitled to restitution of any amount by which the sum of his payments exceeds

(a) the amount to which the seller is entitled by virtue of terms liquidating the seller's damages in accordance with subsection (1), or

(b) in the absence of such terms, twenty per cent of the value of the total performance for which the buyer is obligated under the contract or $500, whichever is smaller.

(3) The buyer's right to restitution under subsection (2) is subject to offset to the extent that the seller establishes

(a) a right to recover damages under the provisions of this Article other than subsection (1), and

(b) the amount or value of any benefits received by the buyer directly or indirectly by reason of the contract.

(4) Where a seller has received payment in goods their reasonable value or the proceeds of their resale shall be treated as payments for the purposes of subsection (2); but if the seller has notice of the buyer's breach before reselling goods received in part performance, his resale is subject to the conditions laid down in this Article on resale by an aggrieved seller (Section 2—706).

§ 2—719. **Contractual Modification or Limitation of Remedy.**

(1) Subject to the provisions of subsections (2) and (3) of this section and of the preceding section on liquidation and limitation of damages,

(a) the agreement may provide for remedies in addition to or in substitution for those provided in this Article and may limit or alter the measure of damages recoverable under this Article, as by limiting the buyer's remedies to return of the goods and repayment of the price or to repair and replacement of nonconforming goods or parts; and

(b) resort to a remedy as provided is optional unless the remedy is expressly agreed to be exclusive, in which case it is the sole remedy.

(2) Where circumstances cause an exclusive or limited remedy to fail of its essential purpose, remedy may be had as provided in this Act.

(3) Consequential damages may be limited or excluded unless the limitation or exclusion is unconscionable. Limitation of consequential damages for injury to the person in the case of consumer goods is prima facie unconscionable but limitation of damages where the loss is commercial is not.

§ 2—720. **Effect of "Cancellation" or "Rescission" on Claims for Antecedent Breach.**

Unless the contrary intention clearly appears, expressions of "cancellation" or "rescission" of the contract or the like shall not be construed as a renunciation or discharge of any claim in damages for an antecedent breach.

§ 2—721. **Remedies for Fraud.**

Remedies for material misrepresentation or fraud include all remedies available under this Article for non-fraudulent breach. Neither rescission or a claim for rescission of the contract for sale nor rejection or return of the goods shall bar or be deemed inconsistent with a claim for damages or other remedy.

§ 2—722. **Who Can Sue Third Parties for Injury to Goods.**

Where a third party so deals with goods which have been identified to a contract for sale as to cause actionable injury to a party to that contract

(a) a right of action against the third party is in either party to the contract for sale who has title to or a security interest or a special property or an insurable interest in the goods; and if the goods have been destroyed or converted a right of action is also in the party who either bore the risk of loss under the contract for sale or has since the injury assumed that risk as against the other;

(b) if at the time of the injury the party plaintiff did not bear the risk of loss as against the other party to the contract for sale and there is no arrangement between them for disposition of the recovery, his suit or settlement is, subject to his own interest, as a fiduciary for the other party to the contract;

(c) either party may with the consent of the other sue for the benefit of whom it may concern.

§ 2—723. **Proof of Market Price: Time and Place.**

(1) If an action based on anticipatory repudiation comes to trial before the time for performance with respect to some or all of the goods, any damages based on market price (Section 2—708 or Section 2—713) shall be determined according to the price of such goods prevailing at the time when the aggrieved party learned of the repudiation.

(2) If evidence of a price prevailing at the times or places described in this Article is not readily available the price prevailing within any reasonable time before or after the time described or at any other place which in commercial judgment or under usage of trade would serve as a reasonable substitute for the one described may be used, making any proper allowance for the cost of transporting the goods to or from such other place.

(3) Evidence of a relevant price prevailing at a time or place other than the one described in this Article offered by one party is not admissible unless and until he has given the other party such notice as the court finds sufficient to prevent unfair surprise.

§ 2—724. **Admissibility of Market Quotations.**

Whenever the prevailing price or value of any goods regularly bought and sold in any established commodity market is in issue, reports in official publications or trade journals or in newspapers or periodicals of general circulation published as the reports of such market shall be admissible in evidence. The circumstances of the preparation of such a report may be shown to affect its weight but not its admissibility.

§ 2—725. **Statute of Limitations in Contracts for Sale.**

(1) An action for breach of any contract for sale must be commenced within four years after the cause of action has accrued. By the original agreement the parties may reduce the period of limitation to not less than one year but may not extend it.

(2) A cause of action accrues when the breach occurs, regardless of the aggrieved party's lack of knowledge of the breach. A breach of warranty occurs when tender of delivery is made, except that where a warranty explicitly extends to future performance of the goods and discovery of the breach must await the time of such performance the cause of action accrues when the breach is or should have been discovered.

(3) Where an action commenced within the time limited by subsection (1) is so terminated as to leave available a remedy by another action for the same breach such other action may be commenced after the expiration of the time limited and within six months after the termination of the first action unless the termination resulted from voluntary discontinuance or from dismissal for failure or neglect to prosecute.

(4) This section does not alter the law on tolling of the statute of limitations nor does it apply to causes of action which have accrued before this Act becomes effective.

Article 2A
LEASES

Part 1 General Provisions

§ 2A—101. Short Title.

This Article shall be known and may be cited as the Uniform Commercial Code—Leases.

§ 2A—102. Scope.

This Article applies to any transaction, regardless of form, that creates a lease.

§ 2A—103. Definitions and Index of Definitions.

(1) In this Article unless the context otherwise requires:

(a) "Buyer in ordinary course of business" means a person who in good faith and without knowledge that the sale to him [or her] is in violation of the ownership rights or security interest or leasehold interest of a third party in the goods buys in ordinary course from a person in the business of selling goods of that kind but does not include a pawnbroker. "Buying" may be for cash or by exchange of other property or on secured or unsecured credit and includes receiving goods or documents of title under a pre-existing contract for sale but does not include a transfer in bulk or as security for or in total or partial satisfaction of a money debt.

(b) "Cancellation" occurs when either party puts an end to the lease contract for default by the other party.

(c) "Commercial unit" means such a unit of goods as by commercial usage is a single whole for purposes of lease and division of which materially impairs its character or value on the market or in use. A commercial unit may be a single article, as a machine, or a set of articles, as a suite of furniture or a line of machinery, or a quantity, as a gross or carload, or any other unit treated in use or in the relevant market as a single whole.

(d) "Conforming" goods or performance under a lease contract means goods or performance that are in accordance with the obligations under the lease contract.

(e) "Consumer lease" means a lease that a lessor regularly engaged in the business of leasing or selling makes to a lessee, except an organization, who takes under the lease primarily for a personal, family, or household purpose, if the total payments to be made under the lease contract, excluding payments for options to renew or buy, do not exceed $25,000.

(f) "Fault" means wrongful act, omission, breach, or default.

(g) "Finance lease" means a lease in which (i) the lessor does not select, manufacture or supply the goods, (ii) the lessor acquires the goods or the right to possession and use of the goods in connection with the lease, and (iii) either the lessee receives a copy of the contract evidencing the lessor's purchase of the goods on or before signing the lease contract, or the lessee's approval of the contract evidencing the lessor's purchase of the goods is a condition to effectiveness of the lease contract.

(h) "Goods" means all things that are movable at the time of identification to the lease contract, or are fixtures (Section 2A—309), but the term does not include money, documents, instruments, accounts, chattel paper, general intangibles, or minerals or the like, including oil and gas, before extraction. The term also includes the unborn young of animals.

(i) "Installment lease contract" means a lease contract that authorizes or requires the delivery of goods in separate lots to be separately accepted, even though the lease contract contains a clause "each delivery is a separate lease" or its equivalent.

(j) "Lease" means a transfer of the right to possession and use of goods for a term in return for consideration, but a sale, including a sale on approval or a sale or return, or retention or creation of a security interest is not a lease. Unless the context clearly indicates otherwise, the term includes a sublease.

(k) "Lease agreement" means the bargain, with respect to the lease, of the lessor and the lessee in fact as found in their language or by implication from other circumstances including course of dealing or usage of trade or course of performance as provided in this Article. Unless the context clearly indicates otherwise, the term includes a sublease agreement.

(l) "Lease contract" means the total legal obligation that results from the lease agreement as affected by this Article and any other applicable rules of law. Unless the context clearly indicates otherwise, the term includes a sublease contract.

(m) "Leasehold interest" means the interest of the lessor or the lessee under a lease contract.

(n) "Lessee" means a person who acquires the right to possession and use of goods under a lease. Unless the context clearly indicates otherwise, the term includes a sublessee.

(o) "Lessee in ordinary course of business" means a person who in good faith and without knowledge that the lease to him [or her] is in violation of the ownership rights or security interest or leasehold interest of a third party in the goods, leases in ordinary course from a person in the business of selling or leasing goods of that kind but does not include a pawnbroker. "Leasing" may be for cash or by exchange of other property or on secured or unsecured credit and includes receiving goods or documents of title under a pre-existing lease contract but does not include a transfer in bulk or as security for or in total or partial satisfaction of a money debt.

(p) "Lessor" means a person who transfers the right to possession and use of goods under a lease. Unless the context clearly indicates otherwise, the term includes a sublessor.

(q) "Lessor's residual interest" means the lessor's interest in the goods after expiration, termination, or cancellation of the lease contract.

(r) "Lien" means a charge against or interest in goods to secure payment of a debt or performance of an obligation, but the term does not include a security interest.

(s) "Lot" means a parcel or a single article that is the subject matter of a separate lease or delivery, whether or not it is sufficient to perform the lease contract.

(t) "Merchant lessee" means a lessee that is a merchant with respect to goods of the kind subject to the lease.

(u) "Present value" means the amount as of a date certain of one or more sums payable in the future, discounted to the date certain. The discount is determined by the interest rate specified by the parties if the rate was not manifestly unreasonable at the time the transaction was entered into; otherwise, the discount is determined by a commercially reasonable rate that takes into account the facts and circumstances of each case at the time the transaction was entered into.

(v) "Purchase" includes taking by sale, lease, mortgage, security interest, pledge, gift, or any other voluntary transaction creating an interest in goods.

(w) "Sublease" means a lease of goods the right to possession and use of which was acquired by the lessor as a lessee under an existing lease.

(x) "Supplier" means a person from whom a lessor buys or leases goods to be leased under a finance lease.

(y) "Supply contract" means a contract under which a lessor buys or leases goods to be leased.

(z) "Termination" occurs when either party pursuant to a power created by agreement or law puts an end to the lease contract otherwise than for default.

(2) Other definitions applying to this Article and the sections in which they appear are:

"Accessions". Section 2A—310(1).
"Construction mortgage". Section 2A—309(1)(d).
"Encumbrance". Section 2A—309(1)(e).
"Fixtures". Section 2A—309(1)(a).
"Fixture filing". Section 2A—309(1)(b).
"Purchase money lease". Section 2A—309(1)(c).

(3) The following definitions in other Articles apply to this Article:

"Accounts". Section 9—106.
"Between merchants". Section 2—104(3).
"Buyer". Section 2—103(1)(a).
"Chattel paper". Section 9—105(1)(b).
"Consumer goods". Section 9—109(1).
"Documents". Section 9—105(1)(f).
"Entrusting". Section 2—403(3).
"General intangibles". Section 9—106.
"Good faith". Section 2—103(1)(b).
"Instruments". Section 9—105(1)(i).
"Merchant". Section 2—104(1).
"Mortgage". Section 9—105(1)(j).

"Pursuant to commitment". Section 9—105(1)(k).
"Receipt". Section 2—103(1)(c).
"Sale". Section 2—106(1).
"Sale on Approval". Section 2—326.
"Sale or Return". Section 2—326.
"Seller". Section 2—103(1)(d).

(4) In addition Article 1 contains general definitions and principles of construction and interpretation applicable throughout this Article.

§ 2A—104. Leases Subject to Other Statutes.

(1) A lease, although subject to this Article, is also subject to any applicable:

(a) statute of the United States;

(b) certificate of title statute of this State: (list any certificate of title statutes covering automobiles, trailers, mobile homes, boats, farm tractors, and the like);

(c) certificate of title statute of another jurisdiction (Section 2A—105); or

(d) consumer protection statute of this State.

(2) In case of conflict between the provisions of this Article, other than Sections 2A—105, 2A—304(3) and 2A—305(3), and any statute referred to in subsection (1), the provisions of that statute control.

(3) Failure to comply with any applicable statute has only the effect specified therein.

§ 2A—105. Territorial Application of Article to Goods Covered by Certificate of Title.

Subject to the provisions of Sections 2A—304(3) and 2A—305(3), with respect to goods covered by a certificate of title issued under a statute of this State or of another jurisdiction, compliance and the effect of compliance or noncompliance with a certificate of title statute are governed by the law (including the conflict of laws rules) of the jurisdiction issuing the certificate until the earlier of (a) surrender of the certificate, or (b) four months after the goods are removed from that jurisdiction and thereafter until a new certificate of title is issued by another jurisdiction.

§ 2A—106. Limitation on Power of Parties to Consumer Lease to Choose Applicable Law and Judicial Forum.

(1) If the law chosen by the parties to a consumer lease is that of a jurisdiction other than a jurisdiction in which the lessee resides at the time the lease agreement becomes enforceable or within 30 days thereafter or in which the goods are to be used, the choice is not enforceable.

(2) If the judicial forum chosen by the parties to a consumer lease is a forum that would not otherwise have jurisdiction over the lessee, the choice is not enforceable.

§ 2A—107. **Waiver or Renunciation of Claim or Right After Default.**

Any claim or right arising out of an alleged default or breach of warranty may be discharged in whole or in part without consideration by a written waiver or renunciation signed and delivered by the aggrieved party.

§ 2A—108. **Unconscionability.**

(1) If the court as a matter of law finds a lease contract or any clause of a lease contract to have been unconscionable at the time it was made the court may refuse to enforce the lease contract, or it may enforce the remainder of the lease contract without the unconscionable clause, or it may so limit the application of any unconscionable clause as to avoid any unconscionable result.

(2) With respect to a consumer lease, if the court as a matter of law finds that a lease contract or any clause of a lease contract has been induced by unconscionable conduct or that unconscionable conduct has occurred in the collection of a claim arising from a lease contract, the court may grant appropriate relief.

(3) Before making a finding of unconscionability under subsection (1) or (2), the court, on its own motion or that of a party, shall afford the parties a reasonable opportunity to present evidence as to the setting, purpose, and effect of the lease contract or clause thereof, or of the conduct.

(4) In an action in which the lessee claims unconscionability with respect to a consumer lease:

(a) If the court finds unconscionability under subsection (1) or (2), the court shall award reasonable attorney's fees to the lessee.

(b) If the court does not find unconscionability and the lessee claiming unconscionability has brought or maintained an action he [or she] knew to be groundless, the court shall award reasonable attorney's fees to the party against whom the claim is made.

(c) In determining attorney's fees, the amount of the recovery on behalf of the claimant under subsections (1) and (2) is not controlling.

§ 2A—109. **Option to Accelerate at Will.**

(1) A term providing that one party or his [or her] successor in interest may accelerate payment or performance or require collateral or additional collateral "at will" or "when he [or she] deems himself [or herself] insecure" or in words of similar import must be construed to mean that he [or she] has power to do so only if he [or she] in good faith believes that the prospect of payment or performance is impaired.

(2) With respect to a consumer lease, the burden of establishing good faith under subsection (1) is on the party who exercised the power; otherwise the burden of establishing lack of good faith is on the party against whom the power has been exercised.

Part 2 Formation and Construction of Lease Contract

§ 2A—201. **Statute of Frauds.**

(1) A lease contract is not enforceable by way of action or defense unless:

(a) the total payments to be made under the lease contract, excluding payments for options to renew or buy, are less than $1,000; or

(b) there is a writing, signed by the party against whom enforcement is sought or by that party's authorized agent, sufficient to indicate that a lease contract has been made between the parties and to describe the goods leased and the lease term.

(2) Any description of leased goods or of the lease term is sufficient and satisfies subsection (1)(b), whether or not it is specific, if it reasonably identifies what is described.

(3) A writing is not insufficient because it omits or incorrectly states a term agreed upon, but the lease contract is not enforceable under subsection (1)(b) beyond the lease term and the quantity of goods shown in this writing.

(4) A lease contract that does not satisfy the requirements of subsection (1), but which is valid in other respects, is enforceable:

(a) if the goods are to be specially manufactured or obtained for the lessee and are not suitable for lease or sale to others in the ordinary course of the lessor's business, and the lessor, before notice of repudiation is received and under circumstances that reasonably indicate that the goods are for the lessee, has made either a substantial beginning of their manufacture or commitments for their procurement;

(b) if the party against whom enforcement is sought admits in that party's pleading, testimony or otherwise in court that a lease contract was made, but the lease contract is not enforceable under this provision beyond the quantity of goods admitted; or

(c) with respect to goods that have been received and accepted by the lessee.

(5) The lease term under a lease contract referred to in subsection (4) is:

(a) if there is a writing signed by the party against whom enforcement is sought or by that party's authorized agent specifying the lease term, the term so specified;

(b) if the party against whom enforcement is sought admits in that party's pleading, testimony, or otherwise in court a lease term, the term so admitted; or

(c) a reasonable lease term.

§ 2A—202. **Final Written Expression: Parol or Extrinsic Evidence.**

Terms with respect to which the confirmatory memoranda of the parties agree or which are otherwise set forth in a writing intended by the parties as a final expression of their agreement with respect to such terms as are included therein may not be contradicted by evidence of any prior agreement or of a contemporaneous oral agreement but may be explained or supplemented:

(a) by course of dealing or usage of trade or by course of performance; and

(b) by evidence of consistent additional terms unless the court finds the writing to have been intended also as a complete and exclusive statement of the terms of the agreement.

§ 2A—203. Seals Inoperative.

The affixing of a seal to a writing evidencing a lease contract or an offer to enter into a lease contract does not render the writing a sealed instrument and the law with respect to sealed instruments does not apply to the lease contract or offer.

§ 2A—204. Formation in General.

(1) A lease contract may be made in any manner sufficient to show agreement, including conduct by both parties which recognizes the existence of a lease contract.

(2) An agreement sufficient to constitute a lease contract may be found although the moment of its making is undetermined.

(3) Although one or more terms are left open, a lease contract does not fail for indefiniteness if the parties have intended to make a lease contract and there is a reasonably certain basis for giving an appropriate remedy.

§ 2A—205. Firm Offers.

An offer by a merchant to lease goods to or from another person in a signed writing that by its terms gives assurance it will be held open is not revocable, for lack of consideration, during the time stated or, if no time is stated, for a reasonable time, but in no event may the period of irrevocability exceed 3 months. Any such term of assurance on a form supplied by the offeree must be separately signed by the offeror.

§ 2A—206. Offer and Acceptance in Formation of Lease Contract.

(1) Unless otherwise unambiguously indicated by the language or circumstances, an offer to make a lease contract must be construed as inviting acceptance in any manner and by any medium reasonable in the circumstances.

(2) If the beginning of a requested performance is a reasonable mode of acceptance, an offeror who is not notified of acceptance within a reasonable time may treat the offer as having lapsed before acceptance.

§ 2A—207. Course of Performance or Practical Construction.

(1) If a lease contract involves repeated occasions for performance by either party with knowledge of the nature of the performance and opportunity for objection to it by the other, any course of performance accepted or acquiesced in without objection is relevant to determine the meaning of the lease agreement.

(2) The express terms of a lease agreement and any course of performance, as well as any course of dealing and usage of trade, must be construed whenever reasonable as consistent with each other; but if that construction is unreasonable, express terms control course of performance, course of performance controls both course of dealing and usage of trade, and course of dealing controls usage of trade.

(3) Subject to the provisions of Section 2A—208 on modification and waiver, course of performance is relevant to show a waiver or modification of any term inconsistent with the course of performance.

§ 2A—208. Modification, Rescission and Waiver.

(1) An agreement modifying a lease contract needs no consideration to be binding.

(2) A signed lease agreement that excludes modification or rescission except by a signed writing may not be otherwise modified or rescinded, but, except as between merchants, such a requirement on a form supplied by a merchant must be separately signed by the other party.

(3) Although an attempt at modification or rescission does not satisfy the requirements of subsection (2), it may operate as a waiver.

(4) A party who has made a waiver affecting an executory portion of a lease contract may retract the waiver by reasonable notification received by the other party that strict performance will be required of any term waived, unless the retraction would be unjust in view of a material change of position in reliance on the waiver.

§ 2A—209. Lessee under Finance Lease as Beneficiary of Supply Contract.

(1) The benefit of the supplier's promises to the lessor under the supply contract and of all warranties, whether express or implied, under the supply contract, extends to the lessee to the extent of the lessee's leasehold interest under a finance lease related to the supply contract, but subject to the terms of the supply contract and all of the supplier's defenses or claims arising therefrom.

(2) The extension of the benefit of the supplier's promises to the lessee does not: (a) modify the rights and obligations of the parties to the supply contract, whether arising therefrom or otherwise, or (b) impose any duty or liability under the supply contract on the lessee.

(3) Any modification or rescission of the supply contract by the supplier and the lessor is effective against the lessee unless, prior to the modification or rescission, the supplier has received notice that the lessee has entered into a finance lease related to the supply contract. If the supply contract is modified or rescinded after the lessee enters the finance lease, the lessee has a cause of action against the lessor, and against the supplier if the supplier has notice of the lessee's entering the finance lease when the supply contract is modified or rescinded. The lessee's recovery from such action shall put the lessee in as good a position as if the modification or rescission had not occurred.

§ 2A—210. **Express Warranties.**

(1) Express warranties by the lessor are created as follows:

(a) Any affirmation of fact or promise made by the lessor to the lessee which relates to the goods and becomes part of the basis of the bargain creates an express warranty that the goods will conform to the affirmation or promise.

(b) Any description of the goods which is made part of the basis of the bargain creates an express warranty that the goods will conform to the description.

(c) Any sample or model that is made part of the basis of the bargain creates an express warranty that the whole of the goods will conform to the sample or model.

(2) It is not necessary to the creation of an express warranty that the lessor use formal words, such as "warrant" or "guarantee," or that the lessor have a specific intention to make a warranty, but an affirmation merely of the value of the goods or a statement purporting to be merely the lessor's opinion or commendation of the goods does not create a warranty.

§ 2A—211. **Warranties Against Interference and Against Infringement; Lessee's Obligation Against Infringement.**

(1) There is in a lease contract a warranty that for the lease term no person holds a claim to or interest in the goods that arose from an act or omission of the lessor, other than a claim by way of infringement or the like, which will interfere with the lessee's enjoyment of its leasehold interest.

(2) Except in a finance lease there is in a lease contract by a lessor who is a merchant regularly dealing in goods of the kind a warranty that the goods are delivered free of the rightful claim of any person by way of infringement or the like.

(3) A lessee who furnishes specifications to a lessor or a supplier shall hold the lessor and the supplier harmless against any claim by way of infringement or the like that arises out of compliance with the specifications.

§ 2A—212. **Implied Warranty of Merchantability.**

(1) Except in a finance lease, a warranty that the goods will be merchantable is implied in a lease contract if the lessor is a merchant with respect to goods of that kind.

(2) Goods to be merchantable must be at least such as

(a) pass without objection in the trade under the description in the lease agreement;

(b) in the case of fungible goods, are of fair average quality within the description;

(c) are fit for the ordinary purposes for which goods of that type are used;

(d) run, within the variation permitted by the lease agreement, of even kind, quality, and quantity within each unit and among all units involved;

(e) are adequately contained, packaged, and labeled as the lease agreement may require; and

(f) conform to any promises or affirmations of fact made on the container or label.

(3) Other implied warranties may arise from course of dealing or usage of trade.

§ 2A—213. **Implied Warranty of Fitness for Particular Purpose.**

Except in a finance of lease, if the lessor at the time the lease contract is made has reason to know of any particular purpose for which the goods are required and that the lessee is relying on the lessor's skill or judgment to select or furnish suitable goods, there is in the lease contract an implied warranty that the goods will be fit for that purpose.

§ 2A—214. **Exclusion or Modification of Warranties.**

(1) Words or conduct relevant to the creation of an express warranty and words or conduct tending to negate or limit a warranty must be construed wherever reasonable as consistent with each other; but, subject to the provisions of Section 2A—202 on parol or extrinsic evidence, negation or limitation is inoperative to the extent that the construction is unreasonable.

(2) Subject to subsection (3), to exclude or modify the implied warranty of merchantability or any part of it the language must mention "merchantability", be by a writing, and be conspicuous. Subject to subsection (3), to exclude or modify any implied warranty of fitness the exclusion must be by a writing and be conspicuous. Language to exclude all implied warranties of fitness is sufficient if it is conspicuous and states, for example, "There is no warranty that the goods will be fit for a particular purpose".

(3) Notwithstanding subsection (2), but subject to subsection (4),

(a) unless the circumstances indicate otherwise, all implied warranties are excluded by expressions like "as is" or "with all faults" or by other language that in common understanding calls the lessee's attention to the exclusion of warranties and makes plain that there is no implied warranty, and is conspicuous;

(b) if the lessee before entering into the lease contract has examined the goods or the sample or model as fully as desired or has refused to examine the goods, there is no implied warranty with regard to defects that an examination ought in the circumstances to have revealed; and

(c) an implied warranty may also be excluded or modified by course of dealing, course of performance, or usage of trade.

(4) To exclude or modify a warranty against interference or against infringement (Section 2A—211) or any part of it, the language must be specific, be by a writing, and be conspicuous, unless the circumstances, including course of performance, course of dealing, or usage of trade, give the lessee reason to know that the goods are being leased subject to a claim or interest of any person.

§ 2A—215. **Cumulation and Conflict of Warranties Express or Implied.**

Warranties, whether express or implied, must be construed as consistent with each other and as cumulative, but if that construction is unreasonable, the intention of the parties determines which warranty is dominant. In ascertaining that intention the following rules apply:

(a) Exact or technical specifications displace an inconsistent sample or model or general language of description.

(b) A sample from an existing bulk displaces inconsistent general language of description.

(c) Express warranties displace inconsistent implied warranties other than an implied warranty of fitness for a particular purpose.

§ 2A—216. Third-Party Beneficiaries of Express and Implied Warranties.

Alternative A

A warranty to or for the benefit of a lessee under this Article, whether express or implied, extends to any natural person who is in the family or household of the lessee or who is a guest in the lessee's home if it is reasonable to expect that such person may use, consume, or be affected by the goods and who is injured in person by breach of the warranty. This section does not displace principles of law and equity that extend a warranty to or for the benefit of a lessee to other persons. The operation of this section may not be excluded, modified, or limited, but an exclusion, modification, or limitation of the warranty, including any with respect to rights and remedies, effective against the lessee is also effective against any beneficiary designated under this section.

Alternative B

A warranty to or for the benefit of a lessee under this Article, whether express or implied, extends to any natural person who may reasonably be expected to use, consume, or be affected by the goods and who is injured in person by breach of the warranty. This section does not displace principles of law and equity that extend a warranty to or for the benefit of a lessee to other persons. The operation of this section may not be excluded, modified, or limited, but an exclusion, modification, or limitation of the warranty, including any with respect to rights and remedies, effective against the lessee is also effective against the beneficiary designated under this section.

Alternative C

A warranty to or for the benefit of a lessee under this Article, whether express or implied, extends to any person who may reasonably be expected to use, consume, or be affected by the goods and who is injured by breach of the warranty. The operation of this section may not be excluded, modified, or limited with respect to injury to the person of an individual to whom the warranty extends, but an exclusion, modification, or limitation of the warranty, including any with respect to rights and remedies, effective against the lessee is also effective against the beneficiary designated under this section.

§ 2A—217. Identification.

Identification of goods as goods to which a lease contract refers may be made at any time and in any manner explicitly agreed to by the parties. In the absence of explicit agreement, identification occurs:

(a) when the lease contract is made if the lease contract is for a lease of goods that are existing and identified;

(b) when the goods are shipped, marked, or otherwise designated by the lessor as goods to which the lease contract refers, if the lease contract is for a lease of goods that are not existing and identified; or

(c) when the young are conceived, if the lease contract is for a lease of unborn young of animals.

§ 2A—218. Insurance and Proceeds.

(1) A lessee obtains an insurable interest when existing goods are identified to the lease contract even though the goods identified are nonconforming and the lessee has an option to reject them.

(2) If a lessee has an insurable interest only by reason of the lessor's identification of the goods, the lessor, until default or insolvency or notification to the lessee that identification is final, may substitute other goods for those identified.

(3) Notwithstanding a lessee's insurable interest under subsections (1) and (2), the lessor retains an insurable interest until an option to buy has been exercised by the lessee and risk of loss has passed to the lessee.

(4) Nothing in this section impairs any insurable interest recognized under any other statute or rule of law.

(5) The parties by agreement may determine that one or more parties have an obligation to obtain and pay for insurance covering the goods and by agreement may determine the beneficiary of the proceeds of the insurance.

§ 2A—219. Risk of Loss.

(1) Except in the case of a finance lease, risk of loss is retained by the lessor and does not pass to the lessee. In the case of a finance lease, risk of loss passes to the lessee.

(2) Subject to the provisions of this Article on the effect of default on risk of loss (Section 2A—220), if risk of loss is to pass to the lessee and the time of passage is not stated, the following rules apply:

(a) If the lease contract requires or authorizes the goods to be shipped by carrier.

(i) and it does not require delivery at a particular destination, the risk of loss passes to the lessee when the goods are duly delivered to the carrier; but

(ii) if it does require delivery at a particular destination and the goods are there duly tendered while in the possession of the carrier, the risk of loss passes to the lessee when the goods are there duly so tendered as to enable the lessee to take delivery.

(b) If the goods are held by a bailee to be delivered without being moved, the risk of loss passes to the lessee on acknowledgment by the bailee of the lessee's right to possession of the goods.

(c) In any case not within subsection (a) or (b), the risk of loss passes to the lessee on the lessee's receipt of the goods if the lessor, or, in the case of a finance lease, the supplier, is a merchant; otherwise the risk passes to the lessee on tender of delivery.

§ 2A—220. Effect of Default on Risk of Loss.

(1) Where risk of loss is to pass to the lessee and the time of passage is not stated:

(a) If a tender or delivery of goods so fails to conform to the lease contract as to give a right of rejection, the risk of their loss remains with the lessor, or, in the case of a finance lease, the supplier, until cure or acceptance.

(b) If the lessee rightfully revokes acceptance, he [or she], to the extent of any deficiency in his [or her] effective insurance coverage, may treat the risk of loss as having remained with the lessor from the beginning.

(2) Whether or not risk of loss is to pass to the lessee, if the lessee as to conforming goods already identified to a lease contract repudiates or is otherwise in default under the lease contract, the lessor, or, in the case of a finance lease, the supplier, to the extent of any deficiency in his [or her] effective insurance coverage may treat the risk of loss as resting on the lessee for a commercially reasonable time.

§ 2A—221. Casualty to Identified Goods.

If a lease contract requires goods identified when the lease contract is made, and the goods suffer casualty without fault of the lessee, the lessor or the supplier before delivery, or the goods suffer casualty before risk of loss passes to the lessee pursuant to the lease agreement or Section 2A—219, then:

(a) if the loss is total, the lease contract is avoided; and

(b) if the loss is partial or the goods have so deteriorated as to no longer conform to the lease contract, the lessee may nevertheless demand inspection and at his [or her] option either treat the lease contract as avoided or, except in a finance lease that is not a consumer lease, accept the goods with due allowance from the rent payable for the balance of the lease term for the deterioration or the deficiency in quantity but without further right against the lessor.

Part 3 Effect Of Lease Contract

§ 2A—301. Enforceability of Lease Contract.

Except as otherwise provided in this Article, a lease contract is effective and enforceable according to its terms between the parties, against purchasers of the goods and against creditors of the parties.

§ 2A—302. Title to and Possession of Goods.

Except as otherwise provided in this Article, each provision of this Article applies whether the lessor or a third party has title to the goods, and whether the lessor, the lessee, or a third party has possession of the goods, notwithstanding any statute or rule of law that possession or the absence of possession is fraudulent.

§ 2A—303. Alienability of Party's Interest Under Lease Contract or of Lessor's Residual Interest in Goods; Delegation of Performance; Assignment of Rights.

(1) Any interest of a party under a lease contract and the lessor's residual interest in the goods may be transferred unless

(a) the transfer is voluntary and the lease contract prohibits the transfer; or

(b) the transfer materially changes the duty of or materially increases the burden or risk imposed on the other party to the lease contract, and within a reasonable time after notice of the transfer the other party demands that the transferee comply with subsection (2) and the transferee fails to comply.

(2) Within a reasonable time after demand pursuant to subsection (1)(b), the transferee shall:

(a) cure or provide adequate assurance that he [or she] will promptly cure any default other than one arising from the transfer;

(b) compensate or provide adequate assurance that he [or she] will promptly compensate the other party to the lease contract and any other person holding an interest in the lease contract, except the party whose interest is being transferred, for any loss to that party resulting from the transfer;

(c) provide adequate assurance of future due performance under the lease contract; and

(d) assume the lease contract.

(3) Demand pursuant to subsection (1)(b) is without prejudice to the other party's rights against the transferee and the party whose interest is transferred.

(4) An assignment of "the lease" or of "all my rights under the lease" or an assignment in similar general terms is a transfer of rights, and unless the language or the circumstances, as in an assignment for security, indicate the contrary, the assignment is a delegation of duties by the assignor to the assignee and acceptance by the assignee constitutes a promise by him [or her] to perform those duties. This promise is enforceable by either the assignor or the other party to the lease contract.

(5) Unless otherwise agreed by the lessor and the lessee, no delegation of performance relieves the assignor as against the other party of any duty to perform or any liability for default.

(6) A right to damages for default with respect to the whole lease contract or a right arising out of the assignor's due performance of his [or her] entire obligation can be assigned despite agreement otherwise.

(7) To prohibit the transfer of an interest of a party under a lease contract, the language of prohibition must be specific, by a writing, and conspicuous.

§ 2A—304. **Subsequent Lease of Goods by Lessor.**

(1) Subject to the provisions of Section 2A—303, a subsequent lessee from a lessor of goods under an existing lease contract obtains, to the extent of the leasehold interest transferred, the leasehold interest in the goods that the lessor had or had power to transfer, and except as provided in subsection (2) and Section 2A—527(4), takes subject to the existing lease contract. A lessor with voidable title has power to transfer a good leasehold interest to a good faith subsequent lessee for value, but only to the extent set forth in the preceding sentence. When goods have been delivered under a transaction of purchase the lessor has that power even though:

(a) the lessor's transferor was deceived as to the identity of the lessor;

(b) the delivery was in exchange for a check which is later dishonored;

(c) it was agreed that the transaction was to be a "cash sale"; or

(d) the delivery was procured through fraud punishable as larcenous under the criminal law.

(2) A subsequent lessee in the ordinary course of business from a lessor who is a merchant dealing in goods of that kind to whom the goods were entrusted by the existing lessee before the interest of the subsequent lessee became enforceable against the lessor obtains, to the extent of the leasehold interest transferred, all of the lessor's and the existing lessee's rights to the goods, and takes free of the existing lease contract.

(3) A subsequent lessee from the lessor of goods that are subject to an existing lease contract and are covered by a certificate of title issued under a statute of this State or of another jurisdiction takes no greater rights than those provided both by this section and by the certificate of title statute.

§ 2A—305. **Sale or Sublease of Goods by Lessee.**

(1) Subject to the provisions of Section 2A—303, a buyer or sublessee from the lessee of goods under an existing lease contract obtains, to the extent of the interest transferred, the leasehold interest in the goods that the lessee had or had power to transfer, and except as provided in subsection (2) and Section 2A—511(4), takes subject to the existing lease contract. A lessee with a voidable leasehold interest has power to transfer a good leasehold interest to a good faith buyer for value or a good faith sublessee for value, but only to the extent set forth in the preceding sentence. When goods have been delivered under a transaction of lease the lessee has that power even though:

(a) the lessor was deceived as to the identity of the lessee;

(b) the delivery was in exchange for a check which is later dishonored; or

(c) the delivery was procured through fraud punishable as larcenous under the criminal law.

(2) A buyer in the ordinary course of business or a sublessee in the ordinary course of business from a lessee who is a merchant dealing in goods of that kind to whom the goods were entrusted by the lessor obtains, to the extent of the interest transferred, all of the lessor's and lessee's rights to the goods, and takes free of the existing lease contract.

(3) A buyer or sublessee from the lessee of goods that are subject to an existing lease contract and are covered by a certificate of title issued under a statute of this State or of another jurisdiction takes no greater rights than those provided both by this section and by the certificate of title statute.

§ 2A—306. **Priority of Certain Liens Arising by Operation of Law.**

If a person in the ordinary course of his [or her] business furnishes services or materials with respect to goods subject to a lease contract, a lien upon those goods in the possession of that person given by statute or rule of law for those materials or services takes priority over any interest of the lessor or lessee under the lease contract or this Article unless the lien is created by statute and the statute provides otherwise or unless the lien is created by rule of law and the rule of law provides otherwise.

§ 2A—307. **Priority of Liens Arising by Attachment or Levy on, Security Interests in, and Other Claims to Goods.**

(1) Except as otherwise provided in Section 2A—306, a creditor of a lessee takes subject to the lease contract.

(2) Except as otherwise provided in subsections (3) and (4) of this section and in Sections 2A—306 and 2A—308, a creditor of a lessor takes subject to the lease contract:

(a) unless the creditor holds a lien that attached to the goods before the lease contract became enforceable, or

(b) unless the creditor holds a security interest in the goods that under the Article on Secured Transactions (Article 9) would have priority over any other security interest in the goods perfected by a filing covering the goods and made at the time the lease contract became enforceable, whether or not any other security interest existed.

(3) A lessee in the ordinary course of business takes the leasehold interest free of a security interest in the goods created by the lessor even though the security interest is perfected and the lessee knows of its existence.

(4) A lessee other than a lessee in the ordinary course of business takes the leasehold interest free of a security interest to the extent that it secures future advances made after the secured party acquires knowledge of the lease or more than 45 days after the lease contract becomes enforceable, whichever first occurs, unless the future advances are made pursuant to a commitment entered into without knowledge of the lease and before the expiration of the 45-day period.

§ 2A—308. **Special Rights of Creditors.**

(1) A creditor of a lessor in possession of goods subject to a lease contract may treat the lease contract as void if as against the creditor retention of possession by the lessor is fraudulent under any statute or rule of law, but retention of possession in good faith and current course of trade by the lessor for a commercially reasonable time after the lease contract becomes enforceable is not fraudulent.

(2) Nothing in this Article impairs the rights of creditors of a lessor if the lease contract (a) becomes enforceable, not in current course of trade but in satisfaction of or as security for a pre-existing claim for money, security, or the like, and (b) is made under circumstances which under any statute or rule of law apart from this Article would constitute the transaction a fraudulent transfer or voidable preference.

(3) A creditor of a seller may treat a sale or an identification of goods to a contract for sale as void if as against the creditor retention of possession by the seller is fraudulent under any statute or rule of law, but retention of possession of the goods pursuant to a lease contract entered into by the seller as lessee and the buyer as lessor in connection with the sale or identification of the goods is not fraudulent if the buyer bought for value and in good faith.

§ 2A—309. **Lessor's and Lessee's Rights When Goods Become Fixtures.**

(1) In this section:

(a) goods are "fixtures" when they become so related to particular real estate that an interest in them arises under real estate law;

(b) a "fixture filing" is the filing, in the office where a mortgage on the real estate would be recorded or registered, of a financing statement concerning goods that are or are to become fixtures and conforming to the requirements of subsection (5) of Section 9—402;

(c) a lease is a "purchase money lease" unless the lessee has possession or use of the goods or the right to possession or use of the goods before the lease agreement is enforceable;

(d) a mortgage is a "construction mortgage" to the extent it secures an obligation incurred for the construction of an improvement on land including the acquisition cost of the land, if the recorded writing so indicates; and

(e) "encumbrance" includes real estate mortgages and other liens on real estate and all other rights in real estate that are not ownership interests.

(2) Under this Article a lease may be of goods that are fixtures or may continue in goods that become fixtures, but no lease exists under this Article of ordinary building materials incorporated into an improvement on land.

(3) This Article does not prevent creation of a lease of fixtures pursuant to real estate law.

(4) The perfected interest of a lessor of fixtures has priority over a conflicting interest of an encumbrancer or owner of the real estate if:

(a) the lease is a purchase money lease, the conflicting interest of the encumbrancer or owner arises before the goods become fixtures, the interest of the lessor is perfected by a fixture filing before the goods become fixtures or within ten days thereafter, and the lessee has an interest of record in the real estate or is in possession of the real estate; or

(b) the interest of the lessor is perfected by a fixture filing before the interest of the encumbrancer or owner is of record, the lessor's interest has priority over any conflicting interest of a predecessor in title of the encumbrancer or owner, and the lessee has an interest of record in the real estate or is in possession of the real estate.

(5) The interest of a lessor of fixtures, whether or not perfected, has priority over the conflicting interest of an encumbrancer or owner of the real estate if:

(a) the fixtures are readily removable factory or office machines, readily removable equipment that is not primarily used or leased for use in the operation of the real estate, or readily removable replacements of domestic appliances that are goods subject to a consumer lease, and before the goods become fixtures the lease contract is enforceable; or

(b) the conflicting interest is a lien on the real estate obtained by legal or equitable proceedings after the lease contract is enforceable; or

(c) the encumbrancer or owner has consented in writing to the lease or has disclaimed an interest in the goods as fixtures; or

(d) the lessee has a right to remove the goods as against the encumbrancer or owner. If the lessee's right to remove terminates, the priority of the interest of the lessor continues for a reasonable time.

(6) Notwithstanding paragraph (a) of subsection (4) but otherwise subject to subsections (4) and (5), the interest of a lessor of fixtures is subordinate to the conflicting interest of an encumbrancer of the real estate under a construction mortgage recorded before the goods become fixtures if the goods become fixtures before the completion of the construction. To the extent given to refinance a construction mortgage, the conflicting interest of an encumbrancer of the real estate under a mortgage has this priority to the same extent as the encumbrancer of the real estate under the construction mortgage.

(7) In cases not within the preceding subsections, priority between the interest of a lessor of fixtures and the conflicting interest of an encumbrancer or owner of the real estate who is not the lessee is determined by the priority rules governing conflicting interests in real estate.

(8) If the interest of a lessor has priority over all conflicting interests of all owners and encumbrancers of the real estate, the lessor or the lessee may (a) on default, expiration, termination, or cancellation of the lease agreement by the other party but subject to the provisions of the lease agreement and this Article, or (b) if nec-

essary to enforce his [or her] other rights and remedies under this Article, remove the goods from the real estate, free and clear of all conflicting interests of all owners and encumbrancers of the real estate, but he [or she] must reimburse any encumbrancer or owner of the real estate who is not the lessee and who has not otherwise agreed for the cost of repair of any physical injury, but not for any diminution in value of the real estate caused by the absence of the goods removed or by any necessity of replacing them. A person entitled to reimbursement may refuse permission to remove until the party seeking removal gives adequate security for the performance of this obligation.

(9) Even though the lease agreement does not create a security interest, the interest of a lessor of fixtures is perfected by filing a financing statement as a fixture filing for leased goods that are or are to become fixtures in accordance with the relevant provisions of the Article on Secured Transactions (Article 9).

§ 2A—310. Lessor's and Lessee's Rights When Goods Become Accessions.

(1) Goods are "accessions" when they are installed in or affixed to other goods.

(2) The interest of a lessor or a lessee under a lease contract entered into before the goods became accessions is superior to all interests in the whole except as stated in subsection (4).

(3) The interest of a lessor or a lessee under a lease contract entered into at the time or after the goods became accessions is superior to all subsequently acquired interests in the whole except as stated in subsection (4) but is subordinate to interests in the whole existing at the time the lease contract was made unless the holders of such interests in the whole have in writing consented to the lease or disclaimed an interest in the goods as part of the whole.

(4) The interest of a lessor or a lessee under a lease contract described in subsection (2) or (3) is subordinate to the interest of

(a) a buyer in the ordinary course of business or a lessee in the ordinary course of business of any interest in the whole acquired after the goods became accessions; or

(b) a creditor with a security interest in the whole perfected before the lease contract was made to the extent that the creditor makes subsequent advances without knowledge of the lease contract.

(5) When under subsections (2) or (3) and (4) a lessor or a lessee of accessions holds an interest that is superior to all interests in the whole, the lessor or the lessee may (a) on default, expiration, termination, or cancellation of the lease contract by the other party but subject to the provisions of the lease contract and this Article, or (b) if necessary to enforce his [or her] other rights and remedies under this Article, remove the goods from the whole, free and clear of all interests in the whole, but he [or she] must reimburse any holder of an interest in the whole who is not the lessee and who has not otherwise agreed for the cost of repair of any physical injury but not for any diminution in value of the whole caused by the absence of the goods removed or by any

necessity for replacing them. A person entitled to reimbursement may refuse permission to remove until the party seeking removal gives adequate security for the performance of this obligation.

Part 4 Performance Of Lease Contract: Repudiated, Substituted And Excused

§ 2A—401. Insecurity: Adequate Assurance of Performance.

(1) A lease contract imposes an obligation on each party that the other's expectation of receiving due performance will not be impaired.

(2) If reasonable grounds for insecurity arise with respect to the performance of either party, the insecure party may demand in writing adequate assurance of due performance. Until the insecure party receives that assurance, if commercially reasonable the insecure party may suspend any performance for which he [or she] has not already received the agreed return.

(3) A repudiation of the lease contract occurs if assurance of due performance adequate under the circumstances of the particular case is not provided to the insecure party within a reasonable time, not to exceed 30 days after receipt of a demand by the other party.

(4) Between merchants, the reasonableness of grounds for insecurity and the adequacy of any assurance offered must be determined according to commercial standards.

(5) Acceptance of any nonconforming delivery or payment does not prejudice the aggrieved party's right to demand adequate assurance of future performance.

§ 2A—402. Anticipatory Repudiation.

If either party repudiates a lease contract with respect to a performance not yet due under the lease contract, the loss of which performance will substantially impair the value of the lease contract to the other, the aggrieved party may:

(a) for a commercially reasonable time, await retraction of repudiation and performance by the repudiating party;

(b) make demand pursuant to Section 2A—401 and await assurance of future performance adequate under the circumstances of the particular case; or

(c) resort to any right or remedy upon default under the lease contract or this Article, even though the aggrieved party has notified the repudiating party that the aggrieved party would await the repudiating party's performance and assurance and has urged retraction. In addition, whether or not the aggrieved party is pursuing one of the foregoing remedies, the aggrieved party may suspend performance or, if the aggrieved party is the lessor, proceed in accordance with the provisions of this Article on the lessor's right to identify goods to the lease contract notwithstanding default or to salvage unfinished goods (Section 2A—524).

§ 2A—403. Retraction of Anticipatory Repudiation.

(1) Until the repudiating party's next performance is due, the repudiating party can retract the repudiation unless, since the

repudiation, the aggrieved party has cancelled the lease contract or materially changed the aggrieved party's position or otherwise indicated that the aggrieved party considers the repudiation final.

(2) Retraction may be by any method that clearly indicates to the aggrieved party that the repudiating party intends to perform under the lease contract and includes any assurance demanded under Section 2A—401.

(3) Retraction reinstates a repudiating party's rights under a lease contract with due excuse and allowance to the aggrieved party for any delay occasioned by the repudiation.

§ 2A—404. **Substituted Performance.**

(1) If without fault of the lessee, the lessor and the supplier, the agreed berthing, loading, or unloading facilities fail or the agreed type of carrier becomes unavailable or the agreed manner of delivery otherwise becomes commercially impracticable, but a commercially reasonable substitute is available, the substitute performance must be tendered and accepted.

(2) If the agreed means or manner of payment fails because of domestic or foreign governmental regulation:

(a) the lessor may withhold or stop delivery or cause the supplier to withhold or stop delivery unless the lessee provides a means or manner of payment that is commercially a substantial equivalent; and

(b) if delivery has already been taken, payment by the means or in the manner provided by the regulation discharges the lessee's obligation unless the regulation is discriminatory, oppressive, or predatory.

§ 2A—405. **Excused Performance.**

Subject to Section 2A—404 on substituted performance, the following rules apply:

(a) Delay in delivery or nondelivery in whole or in part by a lessor or a supplier who complies with paragraphs (b) and (c) is not a default under the lease contract if performance as agreed has been made impracticable by the occurrence of a contingency the nonoccurrence of which was a basic assumption on which the lease contract was made or by compliance in good faith with any applicable foreign or domestic governmental regulation or order, whether or not the regulation or order later proves to be invalid.

(b) If the causes mentioned in paragraph (a) affect only part of the lessor's or the supplier's capacity to perform, he [or she] shall allocate production and deliveries among his [or her] customers but at his [or her] option may include regular customers not then under contract for sale or lease as well as his [or her] own requirements for further manufacture. He [or she] may so allocate in any manner that is fair and reasonable.

(c) The lessor seasonally shall notify the lessee and in the case of a finance lease the supplier seasonally shall notify the lessor and the lessee, if known, that there will be delay or nondelivery and, if allocation is required under paragraph (b), of the estimated quota thus made available for the lessee.

§ 2A—406. **Procedure on Excused Performance.**

(1) If the lessee receives notification of a material or indefinite delay or an allocation justified under Section 2A—405, the lessee may by written notification to the lessor as to any goods involved, and with respect to all of the goods if under an installment lease contract the value of the whole lease contract is substantially impaired (Section 2A—510):

(a) terminate the lease contract (Section 2A—505(2)); or

(b) except in a finance lease that is not a consumer lease, modify the lease contract by accepting the available quota in substitution, with due allowance from the rent payable for the balance of the lease term for the deficiency but without further right against the lessor.

(2) If, after receipt of a notification from the lessor under Section 2A—405, the lessee fails so to modify the lease agreement within a reasonable time not exceeding 30 days, the lease contract lapses with respect to any deliveries affected.

§ 2A—407. **Irrevocable Promises: Finance Leases.**

(1) In the case of a finance lease that is not a consumer lease the lessee's promises under the lease contract become irrevocable and independent upon the lessee's acceptance of the goods.

(2) A promise that has become irrevocable and independent under subsection (1):

(a) is effective and enforceable between the parties or against third parties including assignees of the parties, and

(b) is not subject to cancellation, termination, modification, repudiation, excuse, or substitution without the consent of the party to whom the promise runs.

Part 5 Default
A. In General

§ 2A—501. **Default: Procedure.**

(1) Whether the lessor or the lessee is in default under a lease contract is determined by the lease agreement and this Article.

(2) If the lessor or the lessee is in default under the lease contract, the party seeking enforcement has rights and remedies as provided in this Article and, except as limited by this Article, as provided in the lease agreement.

(3) If the lessor or the lessee is in default under the lease contract, the party seeking enforcement may reduce the party's claim to judgment, or otherwise enforce the lease contract by self-help or any available judicial procedure or nonjudicial procedure, including administrative proceeding, arbitration, or the like, in accordance with this Article.

(4) Except as otherwise provided in this Article or the lease agreement, the rights and remedies referred to in subsections (2) and (3) are cumulative.

(5) If the lease agreement covers both real property and goods, the party seeking enforcement may proceed under this Part as to the goods, or under other applicable law as to both the real property and the goods in accordance with his [or her] rights and remedies in respect of the real property, in which case this Part does not apply.

§ 2A—502. Notice After Default.

Except as otherwise provided in this Article or the lease agreement, the lessor or lessee in default under the lease contract is not entitled to notice of default or notice of enforcement from the other party to the lease agreement.

§ 2A—503. Modification or Impairment of Rights and Remedies.

(1) Except as otherwise provided in this Article, the lease agreement may include rights and remedies for default in addition to or in substitution for those provided in this Article and may limit or alter the measure of damages recoverable under this Article.

(2) Resort to a remedy provided under this Article or in the lease agreement is optional unless the remedy is expressly agreed to be exclusive. If circumstances cause an exclusive or limited remedy to fail of its essential purpose, or provision for an exclusive remedy is unconscionable, remedy may be had as provided in this Article.

(3) Consequential damages may be liquidated under Section 2A—504, or may otherwise be limited, altered, or excluded unless the limitation, alteration, or exclusion is unconscionable. Limitation of consequential damages for injury to the person in the case of consumer goods is prima facie unconscionable but limitation of damages where the loss is commercial is not.

(4) Rights and remedies on default by the lessor or the lessee with respect to any obligation or promise collateral or ancillary to the lease contract are not impaired by this Article.

§ 2A—504. Liquidation of Damages.

(1) Damages payable by either party for default, or any other act or omission, including indemnity for loss or diminution of anticipated tax benefits or loss or damage to lessor's residual interest, may be liquidated in the lease agreement but only at an amount or by a formula that is reasonable in light of the then anticipated harm caused by the default or other act or omission.

(2) If the lease agreement provides for liquidation of damages, and such provision does not comply with subsection (1), or such provision is an exclusive or limited remedy that circumstances cause to fail of its essential purpose, remedy may be had as provided in this Article.

(3) If the lessor justifiably withholds or stops delivery of goods because of the lessee's default or insolvency (Section 2A—525 or 2A—526), the lessee is entitled to restitution of any amount by which the sum of his [or her] payments exceeds:

(a) the amount to which the lessor is entitled by virtue of terms liquidating the lessor's damages in accordance with subsection (1); or

(b) in the absence of those terms, 20 percent of the then present value of the total rent the lessee was obligated to pay for the balance of the lease term, or, in the case of a consumer lease, the lesser of such amount or $500.

(4) A lessee's right to restitution under subsection (3) is subject to offset to the extent the lessor establishes:

(a) a right to recover damages under the provisions of this Article other than subsection (1); and

(b) the amount or value of any benefits received by the lessee directly or indirectly by reason of the lease contract.

§ 2A—505. Cancellation and Termination and Effect of Cancellation, Termination, Rescission, or Fraud on Rights and Remedies.

(1) On cancellation of the lease contract, all obligations that are still executory on both sides are discharged, but any right based on prior default or performance survives, and the cancelling party also retains any remedy for default of the whole lease contract or any unperformed balance.

(2) On termination of the lease contract, all obligations that are still executory on both sides are discharged but any right based on prior default or performance survives.

(3) Unless the contrary intention clearly appears, expressions of "cancellation," "rescission," or the like of the lease contract may not be construed as a renunciation or discharge of any claim in damages for an antecedent default.

(4) Rights and remedies for material misrepresentation or fraud include all rights and remedies available under this Article for default.

(5) Neither rescission nor a claim for rescission of the lease contract nor rejection or return of the goods may bar or be deemed inconsistent with a claim for damages or other right or remedy.

§ 2A—506. Statute of Limitations.

(1) An action for default under a lease contract, including breach of warranty or indemnity, must be commenced within 4 years after the cause of action accrued. By the original lease contract the parties may reduce the period of limitation to not less than one year.

(2) A cause of action for default accrues when the act or omission on which the default or breach of warranty is based is or should have been discovered by the aggrieved party, or when the default occurs, whichever is later. A cause of action for indemnity accrues when the act or omission on which the claim for indemnity is based is or should have been discovered by the indemnified party, whichever is later.

(3) If an action commenced within the time limited by subsection (1) is so terminated as to leave available a remedy by another action for the same default or breach of warranty or indemnity, the other action may be commenced after the expiration of the time limited and within 6 months after the termination of the first

action unless the termination resulted from voluntary discontinuance or from dismissal for failure or neglect to prosecute.

(4) This section does not alter the law on tolling of the statute of limitations nor does it apply to causes of action that have accrued before this Article becomes effective.

§ 2A—507. Proof of Market Rent: Time and Place.

(1) Damages based on market rent (Section 2A—519 or 2A—528) are determined according to the rent for the use of the goods concerned for a lease term identical to the remaining lease term of the original lease agreement and prevailing at the time of the default.

(2) If evidence of rent for the use of the goods concerned for a lease term identical to the remaining lease term of the original lease agreement and prevailing at the times or places described in this Article is not readily available, the rent prevailing within any reasonable time before or after the time described or at any other place or for a different lease term which in commercial judgment or under usage of trade would serve as a reasonable substitute for the one described may be used, making any proper allowance for the difference, including the cost of transporting the goods to or from the other place.

(3) Evidence of a relevant rent prevailing at a time or place or for a lease term other than the one described in this Article offered by one party is not admissible unless and until he [or she] has given the other party notice the court finds sufficient to prevent unfair surprise.

(4) If the prevailing rent or value of any goods regularly leased in any established market is in issue, reports in official publications or trade journals or in newspapers or periodicals of general circulation published as the reports of that market are admissible in evidence. The circumstances of the preparation of the report may be shown to affect its weight but not its admissibility.

B. Default by Lessor

§ 2A—508. Lessee's Remedies.

(1) If a lessor fails to deliver the goods in conformity to the lease contract (Section 2A—509) or repudiates the lease contract (Section 2A—402), or a lessee rightfully rejects the goods (Section 2A—509) or justifiably revokes acceptance of the goods (Section 2A—517), then with respect to any goods involved, and with respect to all of the goods if under an installment lease contract the value of the whole lease contract is substantially impaired (Section 2A—510), the lessor is in default under the lease contract and the lessee may:

(a) cancel the lease contract (Section 2A—505(1));

(b) recover so much of the rent and security as has been paid, but in the case of an installment lease contract the recovery is that which is just under the circumstances;

(c) cover and recover damages as to all goods affected whether or not they have been identified to the lease contract (Sections 2A—518 and 2A—520), or recover damages for nondelivery (Sections 2A—519 and 2A—520).

(2) If a lessor fails to deliver the goods in conformity to the lease contract or repudiates the lease contract, the lessee may also:

(a) if the goods have been identified, recover them (Section 2A—522); or

(b) in a proper case, obtain specific performance or replevy the goods (Section 2A—521).

(3) If a lessor is otherwise in default under a lease contract, the lessee may exercise the rights and remedies provided in the lease contract and this Article.

(4) If a lessor has breached a warranty, whether express or implied, the lessee may recover damages (Section 2A—519(4)).

(5) On rightful rejection or justifiable revocation of acceptance, a lessee has a security interest in goods in the lessee's possession or control for any rent and security that has been paid and any expenses reasonably incurred in their inspection, receipt, transportation, and care and custody and may hold those goods and dispose of them in good faith and in a commercially reasonable manner, subject to the provisions of Section 2A—527(5).

(6) Subject to the provisions of Section 2A—407, a lessee, on notifying the lessor of the lessee's intention to do so, may deduct all or any part of the damages resulting from any default under the lease contract from any part of the rent still due under the same lease contract.

§ 2A—509. Lessee's Rights on Improper Delivery; Rightful Rejection.

(1) Subject to the provisions of Section 2A—510 on default in installment lease contracts, if the goods or the tender or delivery fail in any respect to conform to the lease contract, the lessee may reject or accept the goods or accept any commercial unit or units and reject the rest of the goods.

(2) Rejection of goods is ineffective unless it is within a reasonable time after tender or delivery of the goods and the lessee seasonably notifies the lessor.

§ 2A—510. Installment Lease Contracts: Rejection and Default.

(1) Under an installment lease contract a lessee may reject any delivery that is nonconforming if the nonconformity substantially impairs the value of that delivery and cannot be cured or the nonconformity is a defect in the required documents; but if the nonconformity does not fall within subsection (2) and the lessor or the supplier gives adequate assurance of its cure, the lessee must accept that delivery.

(2) Whenever nonconformity or default with respect to one or more deliveries substantially impairs the value of the installment lease contract as a whole there is a default with respect to the whole. But, the aggrieved party reinstates the installment lease contract as a whole if the aggrieved party accepts a nonconforming

delivery without seasonably notifying of cancellation or brings an action with respect only to past deliveries or demands performance as to future deliveries.

§ 2A—511. Merchant Lessee's Duties as to Rightfully Rejected Goods.

(1) Subject to any security interest of a lessee (Section 2A—508(5)), if a lessor or a supplier has no agent or place of business at the market of rejection, a merchant lessee, after rejection of goods in his [or her] possession or control, shall follow any reasonable instructions received from the lessor or the supplier with respect to the goods. In the absence of those instructions, a merchant lessee shall make reasonable efforts to sell, lease, or otherwise dispose of the goods for the lessor's account if they threaten to decline in value speedily. Instructions are not reasonable if on demand indemnity for expenses is not forthcoming.

(2) If a merchant lessee (subsection (1)) or any other lessee (Section 2A—512) disposes of goods, he [or she] is entitled to reimbursement either from the lessor or the supplier or out of the proceeds for reasonable expenses of caring for and disposing of the goods and, if the expenses include no disposition commission, to such commission as is usual in the trade, or if there is none, to a reasonable sum not exceeding 10 percent of the gross proceeds.

(3) In complying with this section or Section 2A—512, the lessee is held only to good faith. Good faith conduct hereunder is neither acceptance or conversion nor the basis of an action for damages.

(4) A purchaser who purchases in good faith from a lessee pursuant to this section or Section 2A—512 takes the goods free of any rights of the lessor and the supplier even though the lessee fails to comply with one or more of the requirements of this Article.

§ 2A—512. Lessee's Duties as to Rightfully Rejected Goods.

(1) Except as otherwise provided with respect to goods that threaten to decline in value speedily (Section 2A—511) and subject to any security interest of a lessee (Section 2A—508(5)):

(a) the lessee, after rejection of goods in the lessee's possession, shall hold them with reasonable care at the lessor's or the supplier's disposition for a reasonable time after the lessee's seasonable notification of rejection;

(b) if the lessor or the supplier gives no instructions within a reasonable time after notification of rejection, the lessee may store the rejected goods for the lessor's or the supplier's account or ship them to the lessor or the supplier or dispose of them for the lessor's or the supplier's account with reimbursement in the manner provided in Section 2A—511; but

(c) the lessee has no further obligations with regard to goods rightfully rejected.

(2) Action by the lessee pursuant to subsection (1) is not acceptance or conversion.

§ 2A—513. Cure by Lessor of Improper Tender or Delivery; Replacement.

(1) If any tender or delivery by the lessor or the supplier is rejected because nonconforming and the time for performance has not yet expired, the lessor or the supplier may seasonably notify the lessee of the lessor's or the supplier's intention to cure and may then make a conforming delivery within the time provided in the lease contract.

(2) If the lessee rejects a nonconforming tender that the lessor or the supplier had reasonable grounds to believe would be acceptable with or without money allowance, the lessor or the supplier may have a further reasonable time to substitute a conforming tender if he [or she] seasonably notifies the lessee.

§ 2A—514. Waiver of Lessee's Objections.

(1) In rejecting goods, a lessee's failure to state a particular defect that is ascertainable by reasonable inspection precludes the lessee from relying on the defect to justify rejection or to establish default:

(a) if, stated seasonably, the lessor or the supplier could have cured it (Section 2A—513); or

(b) between merchants if the lessor or the supplier after rejection has made a request in writing for a full and final written statement of all defects on which the lessee proposes to rely.

(2) A lessee's failure to reserve rights when paying rent or other consideration against documents precludes recovery of the payment for defects apparent on the face of the documents.

§ 2A—515. Acceptance of Goods.

(1) Acceptance of goods occurs after the lessee has had a reasonable opportunity to inspect the goods and

(a) the lessee signifies or acts with respect to the goods in a manner that signifies to the lessor or the supplier that the goods are conforming or that the lessee will take or retain them in spite of their nonconformity; or

(b) the lessee fails to make an effective rejection of the goods (Section 2A—509(2)).

(2) Acceptance of a part of any commercial unit is acceptance of that entire unit.

§ 2A—516. Effect of Acceptance of Goods; Notice of Default; Burden of Establishing Default after Acceptance; Notice of Claim or Litigation to Person Answerable Over.

(1) A lessee must pay rent for any goods accepted in accordance with the lease contract, with due allowance for goods rightfully rejected or not delivered.

(2) A lessee's acceptance of goods precludes rejection of the goods accepted. In the case of a finance lease, if made with knowledge of a nonconformity, acceptance cannot be revoked because of it. In any other case, if made with knowledge of a nonconformity, acceptance cannot be revoked because of it unless the acceptance was on the reasonable assumption that the nonconformity would

be seasonably cured. Acceptance does not of itself impair any other remedy provided by this Article or the lease agreement for nonconformity.

(3) If a tender has been accepted:

(a) within a reasonable time after the lessee discovers or should have discovered any default, the lessee shall notify the lessor and the supplier, or be barred from any remedy.

(b) except in the case of a consumer lease, within a reasonable time after the lessee receives notice of litigation for infringement or the like (Section 2A—211) the lessee shall notify the lessor or be barred from any remedy over for liability established by the litigation; and

(c) the burden is on the lessee to establish any default.

(4) If a lessee is sued for breach of a warranty or other obligation for which a lessor or a supplier is answerable over:

(a) The lessee may give the lessor or the supplier written notice of the litigation. If the notice states that the lessor or the supplier may come in and defend and that if the lessor or the supplier does not do so he [or she] will be bound in any action against him [or her] by the lessee by any determination of fact common to the two litigations, then unless the lessor or the supplier after seasonable receipt of the notice does come in and defend he [or she] is so bound.

(b) The lessor or the supplier may demand in writing that the lessee turn over control of the litigation including settlement if the claim is one for infringement or the like (Section 2A—211) or else be barred from any remedy over. If the demand states that the lessor or the supplier agrees to bear all expense and to satisfy any adverse judgment, then unless the lessee after seasonable receipt of the demand does turn over control the lessee is so barred.

(5) The provisions of subsections (3) and (4) apply to any obligation of a lessee to hold the lessor or the supplier harmless against infringement or the like (Section 2A—211).

§ 2A—517. Revocation of Acceptance of Goods.

(1) A lessee may revoke acceptance of a lot or commercial unit whose nonconformity substantially impairs its value to the lessee if he [or she] has accepted it:

(a) except in the case of a finance lease, on the reasonable assumption that its nonconformity would be cured and it has not been seasonably cured; or

(b) without discovery of the nonconformity if the lessee's acceptance was reasonably induced either by the lessor's assurances or, except in the case of a finance lease, by the difficulty or discovery before acceptance.

(2) Revocation of acceptance must occur within a reasonable time after the lessee discovers or should have discovered the ground for it and before any substantial change in condition of the goods which is not caused by the nonconformity. Revocation is not effective until the lessee notifies the lessor.

(3) A lessee who so revokes has the same rights and duties with regard to the goods involved as if the lessee had rejected them.

§ 2A—518. Cover; Substitute Goods.

(1) After default by a lessor under the lease contract (Section 2A—508(1)), the lessee may cover by making in good faith and without unreasonable delay any purchase or lease of or contract to purchase or lease goods in substitution for those due from the lessor.

(2) Except as otherwise provided with respect to damages liquidated in the lease agreement (Section 2A—504) or determined by agreement of the parties (Section 1—102(3)), if a lessee's cover is by lease agreement substantially similar to the original lease agreement and the lease agreement is made in good faith and in a commercially reasonable manner, the lessee may recover from the lessor as damages (a) the present value, as of the date of default, of the difference between the total rent for the lease term of the new lease agreement and the total rent for the remaining lease term of the original lease agreement and (b) any incidental or consequential damages less expenses saved in consequence of the lessor's default.

(3) If a lessee's cover does not qualify for treatment under subsection (2), the lessee may recover from the lessor as if the lessee had elected not to cover and Section 2A—519 governs.

§ 2A—519. Lessee's Damages for Non-Delivery, Repudiation, Default and Breach of Warranty in Regard to Accepted Goods.

(1) If a lessee elects not to cover or a lessee elects to cover and the cover does not qualify for treatment under Section 2A—518(2), the measure of damages for non-delivery or repudiation by the lessor or for rejection or revocation of acceptance by the lessee is the present value as of the date of the default of the difference between the then market rent and the original rent, computed for the remaining lease term of the original lease agreement together with incidental and consequential damages, less expenses saved in consequence of the lessor's default.

(2) Market rent is to be determined as of the place for tender or, in cases of rejection after arrival or revocation of acceptance, as of the place of arrival.

(3) If the lessee has accepted goods and given notification (Section 2A—516(3)), the measure of damages for non-conforming tender or delivery by a lessor is the loss resulting in the ordinary course of events from the lessor's default as determined in any manner that is reasonable together with incidental and consequential damages, less expenses saved in consequence of the lessor's default.

(4) The measure of damages for breach of warranty is the present value at the time and place of acceptance of the difference between the value of the use of the goods accepted and the value if they had been as warranted for the lease term, unless special circumstances show proximate damages of a different amount, together with incidental and consequential damages, less expenses saved in consequence of the lessor's default or breach of warranty.

§ 2A—520. Lessee's Incidental and Consequential Damages.

(1) Incidental damages resulting from a lessor's default include expenses reasonably incurred in inspection, receipt, transportation, and care and custody of goods rightfully rejected or goods the acceptance of which is justifiably revoked, any commercially reasonable charges, expenses or commissions in connection with effecting cover, and any other reasonable expense incident to the default.

(2) Consequential damages resulting from a lessor's default include:

(a) any loss resulting from general or particular requirements and needs of which the lessor at the time of contracting had reason to know and which could not reasonably be prevented by cover or otherwise; and

(b) injury to person or property proximately resulting from any breach of warranty.

§ 2A—521. Lessee's Right to Specific Performance or Replevin.

(1) Specific performance may be decreed if the goods are unique or in other proper circumstances.

(2) A decree for specific performance may include any terms and conditions as to payment of the rent, damages, or other relief that the court deems just.

(3) A lessee has a right of replevin, detinue, sequestration, claim and delivery, or the like for goods identified to the lease contract if after reasonable effort the lessee is unable to effect cover for those goods or the circumstances reasonably indicate that the effort will be unavailing.

§ 2A—522. Lessee's Right to Goods on Lessor's Insolvency.

(1) Subject to subsection (2) and even though the goods have not been shipped, a lessee who has paid a part or all of the rent and security for goods identified to a lease contract (Section 2A—217) on making and keeping good a tender of any unpaid portion of the rent and security due under the lease contract may recover the goods identified from the lessor if the lessor becomes insolvent within 10 days after receipt of the first installment of rent and security.

(2) A lessee acquires the right to recover goods identified to a lease contract only if they conform to the lease contract.

C. Default by Lessee

§ 2A—523. Lessor's Remedies.

(1) If a lessee wrongfully rejects or revokes acceptance of goods or fails to make a payment when due or repudiates with respect to a part or the whole, then, with respect to any goods involved, and with respect to all of the goods if under an installment lease contract the value of the whole lease contract is substantially impaired (Section 2A—510), the lessee is in default under the lease contract and the lessor may:

(a) cancel the lease contract (Section 2A—505(1));

(b) proceed respecting goods not identified to the lease contract (Section 2A—524);

(c) withhold delivery of the goods and take possession of goods previously delivered (Section 2A—525);

(d) stop delivery of the goods by any bailee (Section 2A—526);

(e) dispose of the goods and recover damages (Section 2A—527), or retain the goods and recover damages (Section 2A—528), or in a proper case recover rent (Section 2A—529).

(2) If a lessee is otherwise in default under a lease contract, the lessor may exercise the rights and remedies provided in the lease contract and this Article.

§ 2A—524. Lessor's Right to Identify Goods to Lease Contract.

(1) A lessor aggrieved under Section 2A—523(1) may:

(a) identify to the lease contract conforming goods not already identified if at the time the lessor learned of the default they were in the lessor's or the supplier's possession or control; and

(b) dispose of goods (Section 2A—527(1)) that demonstrably have been intended for the particular lease contract even though those goods are unfinished.

(2) If the goods are unfinished, in the exercise of reasonable commercial judgment for the purposes of avoiding loss and of effective realization, an aggrieved lessor or the supplier may either complete manufacture and wholly identify the goods to the lease contract or cease manufacture and lease, sell, or otherwise dispose of the goods for scrap or salvage value or proceed in any other reasonable manner.

§ 2A—525. Lessor's Right to Possession of Goods.

(1) If a lessor discovers the lessee to be insolvent, the lessor may refuse to deliver the goods.

(2) The lessor has on default by the lessee under the lease contract the right to take possession of the goods. If the lease contract so provides, the lessor may require the lessee to assemble the goods and make them available to the lessor at a place to be designated by the lessor which is reasonably convenient to both parties. Without removal, the lessor may render unusable any goods employed in trade or business, and may dispose of goods on the lessee's premises (Section 2A—527).

(3) The lessor may proceed under subsection (2) without judicial process if that can be done without breach of the peace or the lessor may proceed by action.

§ 2A—526. Lessor's Stoppage of Delivery in Transit or Otherwise.

(1) A lessor may stop delivery of goods in the possession of a carrier or other bailee if the lessor discovers the lessee to be insolvent and may stop delivery of carload, truckload, planeload, or larger shipments of express or freight if the lessee repudiates or

fails to make a payment due before delivery, whether for rent, security or otherwise under the lease contract, or for any other reason the lessor has a right to withhold or take possession of the goods.

(2) In pursuing its remedies under subsection (1) the lessor may stop delivery until

(a) receipt of the goods by the lessee;

(b) acknowledgment to the lessee by any bailee of the goods, except a carrier, that the bailee holds the goods for the lessee; or

(c) such an acknowledgment to the lessee by a carrier via reshipment or as warehouseman.

(3) (a) To stop delivery, a lessor shall so notify as to enable the bailee by reasonable diligence to prevent delivery of the goods.

(b) After notification, the bailee shall hold and deliver the goods according to the directions of the lessor, but the lessor is liable to the bailee for any ensuing charges or damages.

(c) A carrier who has issued a nonnegotiable bill of lading is not obliged to obey a notification to stop received from a person other than the consignor.

§ 2A—527. **Lessor's Rights to Dispose of Goods.**

(1) After a default by a lessee under the lease contract (Section 2A—523(1)) or after the lessor refuses to deliver or take possession of goods (Section 2A—525 or 2A—526), the lessor may dispose of the goods concerned or the undelivered balance thereof in good faith and without unreasonable delay by lease, sale or otherwise.

(2) If the disposition is by lease contract substantially similar to the original lease contract and the lease contract is made in good faith and in a commercially reasonable manner, the lessor may recover from the lessee as damages (a) accrued and unpaid rent as of the date of default, (b) the present value as of the date of default of the difference between the total rent for the remaining lease term of the original lease contract and the total rent for the lease term of the new lease contract, and (c) any incidental damages allowed under Section 2A—530, less expenses saved in consequence of the lessee's default.

(3) If the lessor's disposition is by lease contract that for any reason does not qualify for treatment under subsection (2), or is by sale or otherwise, the lessor may recover from the lessee as if the lessor had elected not to dispose of the goods and Section 2A—528 governs.

(4) A subsequent buyer or lessee who buys or leases from the lessor in good faith for value as a result of a disposition under this section takes the goods free of the original lease contract and any rights of the original lessee even though the lessor fails to comply with one or more of the requirements of this Article.

(5) The lessor is not accountable to the lessee for any profit made on any disposition. A lessee who has rightfully rejected or justifiably revoked acceptance shall account to the lessor for any excess over the amount of the lessee's security interest (Section 2A—508(5)).

§ 2A—528. **Lessor's Damages for Non-Acceptance or Repudiation.**

(1) Except as otherwise provided with respect to damages liquidated in the lease agreement (Section 2A—504) or determined by agreement of the parties (Section 1—102(3)), if a lessor elects to retain the goods or a lessor elects to dispose of the goods and disposition is by lease agreement that for any reason does not qualify for treatment under Section 2A—527(2), or is by sale or otherwise, the lessor may recover from the lessee as damages for non-acceptance or repudiation by the lessee (a) accrued and unpaid rent as of the date of default, (b) the present value as of the date of default of the difference between the total rent for the remaining lease term of the original lease agreement and the market rent at the time and place for tender computed for the same lease term, and (c) any incidental damages allowed under Section 2A—530, less expenses saved in consequence of the lessee's default.

(2) If the measure of damages provided in subsection (1) is inadequate to put a lessor in as good a position as performance would have, the measure of damages is the profit, including reasonable overhead, the lessor would have made from full performance by the lessee, together with any incidental damages allowed under Section 2A—530, due allowance for costs reasonably incurred and due credit for payments or proceeds of disposition.

§ 2A—529. **Lessor's Action for the Rent.**

(1) After default by the lessee under the lease contract (Section 2A—523(1)), if the lessor complies with subsection (2), the lessor may recover from the lessee as damages:

(a) for goods accepted by the lessee and for conforming goods lost or damaged within a commercially reasonable time after risk of loss passes to the lessee (Section 2A—219), (i) accrued and unpaid rent as of the date of default, (ii) the present value as of the date of default of the rent for the remaining lease term of the lease agreement, and (iii) any incidental damages allowed under Section 2A—530, less expenses saved in consequence of the lessee's default; and

(b) for goods identified to the lease contract if the lessor is unable after reasonable effort to dispose of them at a reasonable price or the circumstances reasonably indicate that effort will be unavailing, (i) accrued and unpaid rent as of the date of default, (ii) the present value as of the date of default of the rent for the remaining lease term of the lease agreement, and (iii) any incidental damages allowed under Section 2A—530, less expenses saved in consequence of the lessee's default.

(2) Except as provided in subsection (3), the lessor shall hold for the lessee for the remaining lease term of the lease agreement any goods that have been identified to the lease contract and are in the lessor's control.

(3) The lessor may dispose of the goods at any time before collection of the judgment for damages obtained pursuant to subsection (1) and the lessor may proceed against the lessee for damages pursuant to Section 2A—527 or Section 2A—528.

(4) Payment of the judgment for damages obtained pursuant to subsection (1) entitles the lessee to use and possession of the goods not then disposed of for the remaining lease term of the lease agreement.

(5) After a lessee has wrongfully rejected or revoked acceptance of goods, has failed to pay rent then due, or has repudiated (Section 2A—402), a lessor who is held not entitled to rent under this section must nevertheless be awarded damages for non-acceptance under Sections 2A—527 and 2A—528.

§ 2A—530. Lessor's Incidental Damages.

Incidental damages to an aggrieved lessor include any commercially reasonable charges, expenses, or commissions incurred in stopping delivery, in the transportation, care and custody of goods after the lessee's default, in connection with return or disposition of the goods, or otherwise resulting from the default.

§ 2A—531. Standing to Sue Third Parties for Injury to Goods.

(1) If a third party so deals with goods that have been identified to a lease contract as to cause actionable injury to a party to the lease contract (a) the lessor has a right of action against the third party, and (b) the lessee also has a right of action against the third party if the lessee:

    (i)   has a security interest in the goods;

    (ii) has an insurable interest in the goods; or

    (iii) bears the risk of loss under the lease contract or has since the injury assumed that risk as against the lessor and the goods have been converted or destroyed.

(2) If at the time of the injury the party plaintiff did not bear the risk of loss as against the other party to the lease contract and there is no arrangement between them for disposition of the recovery, his [or her] suit or settlement, subject to his [or her] own interest, is as a fiduciary for the other party to the lease contract.

(3) Either party with the consent of the other may sue for the benefit of whom it may concern.

Article 3
COMMERCIAL PAPER

Part 1 Short Title, Form and Interpretation

§ 3—101. Short Title.

This Article shall be known and may be cited as Uniform Commercial Code—Commercial Paper.

§ 3—102. Definitions and Index of Definitions.

(1) In this Article unless the context otherwise requires

    (a) "Issue" means the first delivery of an instrument to a holder or a remitter.

    (b) An "order" is a direction to pay and must be more than an authorization or request. It must identify the person to pay with reasonable certainty. It may be addressed to one or more such persons jointly or in the alternative but not in succession.

    (c) A "promise" is an undertaking to pay and must be more than an acknowledgment of an obligation.

    (d) "Secondary party" means a drawer or indorser.

    (e) "Instrument" means a negotiable instrument.

(2) Other definitions applying to this Article and the sections in which they appear are:
"Acceptance". Section 3—410.
"Accommodation party". Section 3—415.
"Alteration". Section 3—407.
"Certificate of deposit". Section 3—104.
"Certification". Section 3—411.
"Check". Section 3—104.
"Definite time". Section 3—109.
"Dishonor". Section 3—507.
"Draft". Section 3—104.
"Holder in due course". Section 3—302.
"Negotiation". Section 3—202.
"Note". Section 3—104.
"Notice of dishonor". Section 3—508.
"On demand". Section 3—108.
"Presentment". Section 3—504.
"Protest". Section 3—509.
"Restrictive Indorsement". Section 3—205.
"Signature". Section 3—401.

(3) The following definitions in other Articles apply to this Article:
"Account". Section 4—104.
"Banking Day". Section 4—104.
"Clearing House". Section 4—104.
"Collecting Bank". Section 4—105.
"Customer". Section 4—104.
"Depositary Bank". Section 4—105.
"Documentary Draft". Section 4—104.
"Intermediary Bank". Section 4—105.
"Item". Section 4—104.
"Midnight deadline". Section 4—104.
"Payor Bank". Section 4—105.

(4) In addition Article 1 contains general definitions and principles of construction and interpretation applicable throughout this Article.

§ 3—103. Limitations on Scope of Article.

(1) This Article does not apply to money, documents of title or investment securities.

(2) The provisions of this Article are subject to the provisions of the Article on Bank Deposits and Collections (Article 4) and Secured Transactions (Article 9).

§ 3—104. **Form of Negotiable Instruments; "Draft";** **"Check"; "Certificate of Deposit"; "Note".**

(1) Any writing to be a negotiable instrument within this Article must

    (a) be signed by the maker or drawer; and

    (b) contain an unconditional promise or order to pay a sum certain in money and no other promise, order, obligation or power given by the maker or drawer except as authorized by this Article; and

    (c) be payable on demand or at a definite time; and

    (d) be payable to order or to bearer.

(2) A writing which complies with the requirements of this section is

    (a) a "draft" ("bill of exchange") if it is an order;

    (b) a "check" if it is a draft drawn on a bank and payable on demand;

    (c) a "certificate of deposit" if it is an acknowledgment by a bank receipt of money with an engagement to repay it;

    (d) a "note" if it is a promise other than a certificate of deposit.

(3) As used in other Articles of this Act, and as the context may require, the terms "draft", "check", "certificate of deposit" and "note" may refer to instruments which are not negotiable within this Article as well as to instruments which are so negotiable.

§ 3—105. **When Promise or Order Unconditional.**

(1) A promise or order otherwise unconditional is not made conditional by the fact that the instrument

    (a) is subject to implied or constructive conditions; or

    (b) states its consideration, whether performed or promised, or the transaction which gave rise to the instrument, or that the promise or order is made or the instrument matures in accordance with or "as per" such transaction; or

    (c) refers to or states that it arises out of a separate agreement or refers to a separate agreement for rights as to prepayment or acceleration; or

    (d) states that it is drawn under a letter of credit; or

    (e) states that it is secured, whether by mortgage, reservation of title or otherwise; or

    (f) indicates a particular account to be debited or any other fund or source from which reimbursement is expected; or

    (g) is limited to payment out of a particular fund or the proceeds of a particular source, if the instrument is issued by a government or governmental agency or unit; or

    (h) is limited to payment out of the entire assets of a partnership, unincorporated association, trust or estate by or on behalf of which the instrument is issued.

 (2) A promise or order is not unconditional if the instrument

    (a) states that it is subject to or governed by any other agreement; or

    (b) states that it is to be paid only out of a particular fund or source except as provided in this section.

§ 3—106. **Sum Certain.**

(1) The sum payable is a sum certain even though it is to be paid

    (a) with stated interest or by stated installments; or

    (b) with stated different rates of interest before and after default or a specified date; or

    (c) with a stated discount or addition if paid before or after the date fixed for payment; or

    (d) with exchange or less exchange, whether at a fixed rate or at the current rate; or

    (e) with costs of collection or an attorney's fee or both upon default.

(2) Nothing in this section shall validate any term which is otherwise illegal.

§ 3—107. **Money.**

(1) An instrument is payable in money if the medium of exchange in which it is payable is money at the time the instrument is made. An instrument payable in "currency" or "current funds" is payable in money.

(2) A promise or order to pay a sum stated in a foreign currency is for a sum certain in money and, unless a different medium of payment is specified in the instrument, may be satisfied by payment of that number of dollars which the stated foreign currency will purchase at the buying sight rate for that currency on the day on which the instrument is payable or, if payable on demand, on the day of demand. If such an instrument specifies a foreign currency as the medium of payment the instrument is payable in that currency.

§ 3—108. **Payable on Demand.**

Instruments payable on demand include those payable at sight or on presentation and those in which no time for payment is stated.

§ 3—109. **Definite Time.**

(1) An instrument is payable at a definite time if by its terms it is payable

    (a) on or before a stated date or at a fixed period after a stated date; or

    (b) at a fixed period after sight; or

    (c) at a definite time subject to any acceleration; or

    (d) at a definite time subject to extension at the option of the holder, or to extension to a further definite time at the option of the maker or acceptor or automatically upon or after a specified act or event.

(2) An instrument which by its terms is otherwise payable only upon an act or event uncertain as to time of occurrence is not

payable at a definite time even though the act or event has occurred.

§ 3—110. Payable to Order.

(1) An instrument is payable to order when by its terms it is payable to the order or assigns of any person therein specified with reasonable certainty, or to him or his order, or when it is conspicuously designated on its face as "exchange" or the like and names a payee. It may be payable to the order of

(a) the maker or drawer; or

(b) the drawee; or

(c) a payee who is not maker, drawer or drawee; or

(d) two or more payees together or in the alternative; or

(e) an estate, trust or fund, in which case it is payable to the order of the representative of such estate, trust or fund or his successors; or

(f) an office, or an officer by his title as such in which case it is payable to the principal but the incumbent of the office or his successors may act as if he or they were the holder; or

(g) a partnership or unincorporated association, in which case it is payable to the partnership or association and may be indorsed or transferred by any person thereto authorized.

(2) An instrument not payable to order is not made so payable by such words as "payable upon return of this instrument properly indorsed."

(3) An instrument made payable both to order and to bearer is payable to order unless the bearer words are handwritten or typewritten.

§ 3—111. Payable to Bearer.

An instrument is payable to bearer when by its terms it is payable to

(a) bearer or the order of bearer; or

(b) a specified person or bearer; or

(c) "cash" or the order of "cash", or any other indication which does not purport to designate a specific payee.

§ 3—112. Terms and Omissions Not Affecting Negotiability.

(1) The negotiability of an instrument is not affected by

(a) the omission of a statement of any consideration or of the place where the instrument is drawn or payable; or

(b) a statement that collateral has been given to secure obligations either on the instrument or otherwise of an obligor on the instrument or that in case of default on those obligations the holder may realize on or dispose of the collateral; or

(c) a promise or power to maintain or protect collateral or to give additional collateral; or

(d) a term authorizing a confession of judgment on the instrument if it is not paid when due; or

(e) a term purporting to waive the benefit of any law intended for the advantage or protection of any obligor; or

(f) a term in a draft providing that the payee by indorsing or cashing it acknowledges full satisfaction of an obligation of the drawer; or

(g) a statement in a draft drawn in a set of parts (Section 3—801) to the effect that the order is effective only if no other part has been honored.

(2) Nothing in this section shall validate any term which is otherwise illegal.

§ 3—113. Seal.

An instrument otherwise negotiable is within this Article even though it is under a seal.

§ 3—114. Date, Antedating, Postdating.

(1) The negotiability of an instrument is not affected by the fact that it is undated, antedated or postdated.

(2) Where an instrument is antedated or postdated the time when it is payable is determined by the stated date if the instrument is payable on demand or at a fixed period after date.

(3) Where the instrument or any signature thereon is dated, the date is presumed to be correct.

§ 3—115. Incomplete Instruments.

(1) When a paper whose contents at the time of signing show that it is intended to become an instrument is signed while still incomplete in any necessary respect it cannot be enforced until completed, but when it is completed in accordance with authority given it is effective as completed.

(2) If the completion is unauthorized the rules as to material alteration apply (Section 3—407), even though the paper was not delivered by the maker or drawer; but the burden of establishing that any completion is unauthorized is on the party so asserting.

§ 3—116. Instruments Payable to Two or More Persons.

An instrument payable to the order of two or more persons

(a) if in the alternative is payable to any one of them and may be negotiated, discharged or enforced by any of them who has possession of it;

(b) if not in the alternative is payable to all of them and may be negotiated, discharged or enforced only by all of them.

§ 3—117. Instruments Payable With Words of Description.

An instrument made payable to a named person with the addition of words describing him

(a) as agent or officer of a specified person is payable to his principal but the agent or officer may act as if he were the holder;

(b) as any other fiduciary for a specified person or purpose is payable to the payee and may be negotiated, discharged or enforced by him;

(c) in any other manner is payable to the payee unconditionally and the additional words are without effect on subsequent parties.

§ 3—118. Ambiguous Terms and Rules of Construction.

The following rules apply to every instrument:

(a) Where there is doubt whether the instrument is a draft or a note the holder may treat it as either. A draft drawn on the drawer is effective as a note.

(b) Handwritten terms control typewritten and printed terms, and typewritten control printed.

(c) Words control figures except that if the words are ambiguous figures control.

(d) Unless otherwise specified a provision for interest means interest at the judgment rate at the place of payment from the date of the instrument, or if it is undated from the date of issue.

(e) Unless the instrument otherwise specifies two or more persons who sign as maker, acceptor or drawer or indorser and as a part of the same transaction are jointly and severally liable even though the instrument contains such words as "I promise to pay."

(f) Unless otherwise specified consent to extension authorizes a single extension for not longer than the original period. A consent to extension, expressed in the instrument, is binding on secondary parties and accommodation makers. A holder may not exercise his option to extend an instrument over the objection of a maker or acceptor or other party who in accordance with Section 3—604 tenders full payment when the instrument is due.

§ 3—119. Other Writings Affecting Instrument.

(1) As between the obligor and his immediate obligee or any transferee the terms of an instrument may be modified or affected by any other written agreement executed as a part of the same transaction, except that a holder in due course is not affected by any limitation of his rights arising out of the separate written agreement if he had no notice of the limitation when he took the instrument.

(2) A separate agreement does not affect the negotiability of an instrument.

§ 3—120. Instruments "Payable Through" Bank.

An instrument which states that it is "payable through" a bank or the like designates that bank as a collecting bank to make presentment but does not of itself authorize the bank to pay the instrument.

§ 3—121. Instruments Payable at Bank.

Note: If this Act is introduced in the Congress of the United States this section should be omitted.
(States to select either alternative)

Alternative A—

A note or acceptance which states that it is payable at a bank is the equivalent of a draft drawn on the bank payable when it falls due out of any funds of the maker or acceptor in current account or otherwise available for such payment.

Alternative B—

A note or acceptance which states that it is payable at a bank is not of itself an order or authorization to the bank to pay it.

§ 3—122. Accrual of Cause of Action.

(1) A cause of action against a maker or an acceptor accrues

(a) in the case of a time instrument on the day after maturity;

(b) in the case of a demand instrument upon its date or, if no date is stated, on the date of issue.

(2) A cause of action against the obligor of a demand or time certificate of deposit accrues upon demand, but demand on a time certificate may not be made until on or after the date of maturity.

(3) A cause of action against a drawer of a draft or an indorser of any instrument accrues upon demand following dishonor of the instrument. Notice of dishonor is a demand.

(4) Unless an instrument provides otherwise, interest runs at the rate provided by law for a judgment

(a) in the case of a maker, acceptor or other primary obligor of a demand instrument, from the date of demand;

(b) in all other cases from the date of accrual of the cause of action.

Part 2 Transfer and Negotiation

§ 3—201. Transfer: Right to Indorsement.

(1) Transfer of an instrument vests in the transferee such rights as the transferor has therein, except that a transferee who has himself been a party to any fraud or illegality affecting the instrument or who as a prior holder had notice of a defense or claim against it cannot improve his position by taking from a later holder in due course.

(2) A transfer of a security interest in an instrument vests the foregoing rights in the transferee to the extent of the interest transferred.

(3) Unless otherwise agreed any transfer for value of an instrument not then payable to bearer gives the transferee the specifically enforceable right to have the unqualified indorsement of the transferor. Negotiation takes effect only when the indorsement is made and until that time there is no presumption that the transferee is the owner.

§ 3—202. Negotiation.

(1) Negotiation is the transfer of an instrument in such form that the transferee becomes a holder. If the instrument is payable to order it is negotiated by delivery with any necessary indorsement; if payable to bearer it is negotiated by delivery.

(2) An indorsement must be written by or on behalf of the holder and on the instrument or on a paper so firmly affixed thereto as to become a part thereof.

(3) An indorsement is effective for negotiation only when it conveys the entire instrument or any unpaid residue. If it purports to be of less it operates only as a partial assignment.

(4) Words of assignment, condition, waiver, guaranty, limitation or disclaimer of liability and the like accompanying an indorsement do not affect its character as an indorsement.

§ 3—203. **Wrong or Misspelled Name.**

Where an instrument is made payable to a person under a misspelled name or one other than his own he may indorse in that name or his own or both; but signature in both names may be required by a person paying or giving value for the instrument.

§ 3—204. **Special Indorsement; Blank Indorsement.**

(1) A special indorsement specifies the person to whom or to whose order it makes the instrument payable. Any instrument specially indorsed becomes payable to the order of the special indorsee and may be further negotiated only by his indorsement.

(2) An indorsement in blank specifies no particular indorsee and may consist of a mere signature. An instrument payable to order and indorsed in blank becomes payable to bearer and may be negotiated by delivery alone until specially indorsed.

(3) The holder may convert a blank indorsement into a special indorsement by writing over the signature of the indorser in blank any contract consistent with the character of the indorsement.

§ 3—205. **Restrictive Indorsements.**

An indorsement is restrictive which either

(a) is conditional; or

(b) purports to prohibit further transfer of the instrument; or

(c) includes the words "for collection", "for deposit", "pay any bank", or like terms signifying a purpose of deposit or collection; or

(d) otherwise states that it is for the benefit or use of the indorser or of another person.

§ 3—206. **Effect of Restrictive Indorsement.**

(1) No restrictive indorsement prevents further transfer or negotiation of the instrument.

(2) An intermediary bank, or a payor bank which is not the depositary bank, is neither given notice nor otherwise affected by a restrictive indorsement of any person except the bank's immediate transferor or the person presenting for payment.

(3) Except for an intermediary bank, any transferee under an indorsement which is conditional or includes the words "for collection", "for deposit", "pay any bank", or like terms (subparagraphs (a) and (c) of Section 3—205) must pay or apply any value given by him for or on the security of the instrument consistently with the indorsement and to the extent that he does so he becomes a holder for value. In addition such transferee is a holder in due course if he otherwise complies with the requirements of Section 3—302 on what constitutes a holder in due course.

(4) The first taker under an indorsement for the benefit of the indorser or another person (subparagraph (d) of Section 3—205) must pay or apply any value given by him for or on the security of the instrument consistently with the indorsement and to the extent that he does so he becomes a holder for value. In addition such taker is a holder in due course if he otherwise complies with the requirements of Section 3—302 on what constitutes a holder in due course. A later holder for value is neither given notice nor otherwise affected by such restrictive indorsement unless he has knowledge that a fiduciary or other person has negotiated the instrument in any transaction for his own benefit or otherwise in breach of duty (subsection (2) of Section 3—304).

§ 3—207. **Negotiation Effective Although It May Be Rescinded.**

(1) Negotiation is effective to transfer the instrument although the negotiation is

(a) made by an infant, a corporation exceeding its powers, or any other person without capacity; or

(b) obtained by fraud, duress or mistake of any kind; or

(c) part of an illegal transaction; or

(d) made in breach of duty.

(2) Except as against a subsequent holder in due course such negotiation is in an appropriate case subject to rescission, the declaration of a constructive trust or any other remedy permitted by law.

§ 3—208. **Reacquisition.**

Where an instrument is returned to or reacquired by a prior party he may cancel any indorsement which is not necessary to his title and reissue or further negotiate the instrument, but any intervening party is discharged as against the reacquiring party and subsequent holders not in due course and if his indorsement has been cancelled is discharged as against subsequent holders in due course as well.

Part 3 Rights of a Holder

§ 3—301. **Rights of a Holder.**

The holder of an instrument whether or not he is the owner may transfer or negotiate it and, except as otherwise provided in Section 3—603 on payment or satisfaction, discharge it or enforce payment in his own name.

§ 3—302. **Holder in Due Course**

(1) A holder in due course is a holder who takes the instrument

(a) for value; and

(b) in good faith; and

(c) without notice that it is overdue or has been dishonored or of any defense against or claim to it on the part of any person.

(2) A payee may be a holder in due course.

(3) A holder does not become a holder in due course of an instrument:

(a) by purchase of it at judicial sale or by taking it under legal process; or

(b) by acquiring it in taking over an estate; or

(c) by purchasing it as part of a bulk transaction not in regular course of business of the transferor.

(4) A purchaser of a limited interest can be a holder in due course only to the extent of the interest purchased.

§ 3—303. **Taking for Value.**

A holder takes the instrument for value

(a) to the extent that the agreed consideration has been performed or that he acquires a security interest in or a lien on the instrument otherwise than by legal process; or

(b) when he takes the instrument in payment of or as security for an antecedent claim against any person whether or not the claim is due; or

(c) when he gives a negotiable instrument for it or makes an irrevocable commitment to a third person.

§ 3—304. **Notice to Purchaser.**

(1) The purchaser has notice of a claim or defense if

(a) the instrument is so incomplete, bears such visible evidence of forgery or alteration, or is otherwise so irregular as to call into question its validity, terms or ownership or to create an ambiguity as to the party to pay; or

(b) the purchaser has notice that the obligation of any party is voidable in whole or in part, or that all parties have been discharged.

(2) The purchaser has notice of a claim against the instrument when he has knowledge that a fiduciary has negotiated the instrument in payment of or as security for his own debt or in any transaction for his own benefit or otherwise in breach of duty.

(3) The purchaser has notice that an instrument is overdue if he has reason to know

(a) that any part of the principal amount is overdue or that there is an uncured default in payment of another instrument of the same series; or

(b) that acceleration of the instrument has been made; or

(c) that he is taking a demand instrument after demand has been made or more than a reasonable length of time after its issue. A reasonable time for a check drawn and payable within the states and territories of the United States and the District of Columbia is presumed to be thirty days.

(4) Knowledge of the following facts does not of itself give the purchaser notice of a defense or claim

(a) that the instrument is antedated or postdated;

(b) that it was issued or negotiated in return for an executory promise or accompanied by a separate agreement, unless the purchaser has notice that a defense or claim has arisen from the terms thereof;

(c) that any party has signed for accommodation;

(d) that an incomplete instrument has been completed, unless the purchaser has notice of any improper completion;

(e) that any person negotiating the instrument is or was a fiduciary;

(f) that there has been default in payment of interest on the instrument or in payment of any other instrument, except one of the same series.

(5) The filing or recording of a document does not of itself constitute notice within the provisions of this Article to a person who would otherwise be a holder in due course.

(6) To be effective notice must be received at such time and in such manner as to give a reasonable opportunity to act on it.

§ 3—305. **Rights of a Holder in Due Course.**

To the extent that a holder is a holder in due course he takes the instrument free from

(1) all claims to it on the part of any person; and

(2) all defenses of any party to the instrument with whom the holder has not dealt except

(a) infancy, to the extent that it is a defense to a simple contract; and

(b) such other incapacity, or duress, or illegality of the transaction, as renders the obligation of the party a nullity; and

(c) such misrepresentation as has induced the party to sign the instrument with neither knowledge nor reasonable opportunity to obtain knowledge of its character or its essential terms; and

(d) discharge in insolvency proceedings; and

(e) any other discharge of which the holder has notice when he takes the instrument.

§ 3—306. **Rights of One Not Holder in Due Course.**

Unless he has the rights of a holder in due course any person takes the instrument subject to

(a) all valid claims to it on the part of any person; and

(b) all defenses of any party which would be available in an action on a simple contract; and

(c) the defenses of want or failure of consideration, nonperformance of any condition precedent, non-delivery, or delivery for a special purpose (Section 3—408); and

(d) the defense that he or a person through whom he holds the instrument acquired it by theft, or that payment or satisfaction to such holder would be inconsistent with the terms of a restrictive indorsement. The claim of any third person to the instrument is not otherwise available as a defense to any party liable thereon unless the third person himself defends the action for such party.

§ 3—307. Burden of Establishing Signatures, Defenses and Due Course.

(1) Unless specifically denied in the pleadings each signature on an instrument is admitted. When the effectiveness of a signature is put in issue

(a) the burden of establishing it is on the party claiming under the signature; but

(b) the signature is presumed to be genuine or authorized except where the action is to enforce the obligation of a purported signer who has died or become incompetent before proof is required.

(2) When signatures are admitted or established, production of the instrument entitles a holder to recover on it unless the defendant establishes a defense.

(3) After it is shown that a defense exists a person claiming the rights of a holder in due course has the burden of establishing that he or some person under whom he claims is in all respects a holder in due course.

Part 4 Liability of Parties

§ 3—401. Signature.

(1) No person is liable on an instrument unless his signature appears thereon.

(2) A signature is made by use of any name, including any trade or assumed name, upon an instrument, or by any word or mark used in lieu of a written signature.

§ 3—402. Signature in Ambiguous Capacity.

Unless the instrument clearly indicates that a signature is made in some other capacity it is an indorsement.

§ 3—403. Signature by Authorized Representative.

(1) A signature may be made by an agent or other representative, and his authority to make it may be established as in other cases of representation. No particular form of appointment is necessary to establish such authority.

(2) An authorized representative who signs his own name to an instrument

(a) is personally obligated if the instrument neither names the person represented nor shows that the representative signed in a representative capacity;

(b) except as otherwise established between the immediate parties, is personally obligated if the instrument names the person represented but does not show that the representative signed in a representative capacity, or if the instrument does not name

the person represented but does show that the representative signed in a representative capacity.

(3) Except as otherwise established the name of an organization preceded or followed by the name and office of an authorized individual is a signature made in a representative capacity.

§ 3—404. Unauthorized Signatures.

(1) Any unauthorized signature is wholly inoperative as that of the person whose name is signed unless he ratifies it or is precluded from denying it; but it operates as the signature of the unauthorized signer in favor of any person who in good faith pays the instrument or takes it for value.

(2) Any unauthorized signature may be ratified for all purposes of this Article. Such ratification does not of itself affect any rights of the person ratifying against the actual signer.

§ 3—405. Impostors; Signature in Name of Payee.

(1) An indorsement by any person in the name of a named payee is effective if

(a) an impostor by use of the mails or otherwise has induced the maker or drawer to issue the instrument to him or his confederate in the name of the payee; or

(b) a person signing as or on behalf of a maker or drawer intends the payee to have no interest in the instrument; or

(c) an agent or employee of the maker or drawer has supplied him with the name of the payee intending the latter to have no such interest.

(2) Nothing in this section shall affect the criminal or civil liability of the person so indorsing.

§ 3—406. Negligence Contributing to Alteration or Unauthorized Signature.

Any person who by his negligence substantially contributes to a material alteration of the instrument or to the making of an unauthorized signature is precluded from asserting the alteration or lack of authority against a holder in due course or against a drawee or other payor who pays the instrument in good faith and in accordance with the reasonable commercial standards of the drawee's or payor's business.

§ 3—407. Alteration.

(1) Any alteration of an instrument is material which changes the contract of any party thereto in any respect, including any such change in

(a) the number or relations of the parties; or

(b) an incomplete instrument, by completing it otherwise than as authorized; or

(c) the writing as signed, by adding to it or by removing any part of it.

(2) As against any person other than a subsequent holder in due course

(a) alteration by the holder which is both fraudulent and material discharges any party whose contract is thereby changed unless that party assents or is precluded from asserting the defense;

(b) no other alteration discharges any party and the instrument may be enforced according to its original tenor, or as to incomplete instruments according to the authority given.

(3) A subsequent holder in due course may in all cases enforce the instrument according to its original tenor, and when an incomplete instrument has been completed, he may enforce it as completed.

§ 3—408. **Consideration.**

Want or failure of consideration is a defense as against any person not having the rights of a holder in due course (Section 3—305), except that no consideration is necessary for an instrument or obligation thereon given in payment of or as security for an antecedent obligation of any kind. Nothing in this section shall be taken to displace any statute outside this Act under which a promise is enforceable notwithstanding lack or failure of consideration. Partial failure of consideration is a defense pro tanto whether or not the failure is in an ascertained or liquidated amount.

§ 3—409. **Draft Not an Assignment.**

(1) A check or other draft does not of itself operate as an assignment of any funds in the hands of the drawee available for its payment, and the drawee is not liable on the instrument until he accepts it.

(2) Nothing in this section shall affect any liability in contract, tort or otherwise arising from any letter of credit or other obligation or representation which is not an acceptance.

§ 3—410. **Definition and Operation of Acceptance.**

(1) Acceptance is the drawee's signed engagement to honor the draft as presented. It must be written on the draft, and may consist of his signature alone. It becomes operative when completed by delivery or notification.

(2) A draft may be accepted although it has not been signed by the drawer or is otherwise incomplete or is overdue or has been dishonored.

(3) Where the draft is payable at a fixed period after sight and the acceptor fails to date his acceptance the holder may complete it by supplying a date in good faith.

§ 3—411. **Certification of a Check.**

(1) Certification of a check is acceptance. Where a holder procures certification the drawer and all prior indorsers are discharged.

(2) Unless otherwise agreed a bank has no obligation to certify a check.

(3) A bank may certify a check before returning it for lack of proper indorsement. If it does so the drawer is discharged.

§ 3—412. **Acceptance Varying Draft.**

(1) Where the drawee's proffered acceptance in any manner varies the draft as presented the holder may refuse the acceptance and treat the draft as dishonored in which case the drawee is entitled to have his acceptance cancelled.

(2) The terms of the draft are not varied by an acceptance to pay at any particular bank or place in the United States, unless the acceptance states that the draft is to be paid only at such bank or place.

(3) Where the holder assents to an acceptance varying the terms of the draft each drawer and indorser who does not affirmatively assent is discharged.

§ 3—413. **Contract of Maker, Drawer and Acceptor.**

(1) The maker or acceptor engages that he will pay the instrument according to its tenor at the time of his engagement or as completed pursuant to Section 3—115 on incomplete instruments.

(2) The drawer engages that upon dishonor of the draft and any necessary notice of dishonor or protest he will pay the amount of the draft to the holder or to any indorser who takes it up. The drawer may disclaim this liability by drawing without recourse.

(3) By making, drawing or accepting the party admits as against all subsequent parties including the drawee the existence of the payee and his then capacity to indorse.

§ 3—414. **Contract of Indorser; Order of Liability.**

(1) Unless the indorsement otherwise specifies (as by such words as "without recourse") every indorser engages that upon dishonor and any necessary notice of dishonor and protest he will pay the instrument according to its tenor at the time of his indorsement to the holder or to any subsequent indorser who takes it up, even though the indorser who takes it up was not obligated to do so.

(2) Unless they otherwise agree indorsers are liable to one another in the order in which they indorse, which is presumed to be the order in which their signatures appear on the instrument.

§ 3—415. **Contract of Accommodation Party.**

(1) An accommodation party is one who signs the instrument in any capacity for the purpose of lending his name to another party to it.

(2) When the instrument has been taken for value before it is due the accommodation party is liable in the capacity in which he has signed even though the taker knows of the accommodation.

(3) As against a holder in due course and without notice of the accommodation oral proof of the accommodation is not admissible to give the accommodation party the benefit of discharges dependent on his character as such. In other cases the accommodation character may be shown by oral proof.

(4) An indorsement which shows that it is not in the chain of title is notice of its accommodation character.

(5) An accommodation party is not liable to the party accommodated, and if he pays the instrument has a right of recourse on the instrument against such party.

§ 3—416. **Contract of Guarantor.**

(1) "Payment guaranteed" or equivalent words added to a signature mean that the signer engages that if the instrument is not paid when due he will pay it according to its tenor without resort by the holder to any other party.

(2) "Collection guaranteed" or equivalent words added to a signature mean that the signer engages that if the instrument is not paid when due he will pay it according to its tenor, but only after the holder has reduced his claim against the maker or acceptor to judgment and execution has been returned unsatisfied, or after the maker or acceptor has become insolvent or it is otherwise apparent that it is useless to proceed against him.

(3) Words of guaranty which do not otherwise specify guarantee payment.

(4) No words of guaranty added to the signature of a sole maker or acceptor affect his liability on the instrument. Such words added to the signature of one of two or more makers or acceptors create a presumption that the signature is for the accommodation of the others.

(5) When words of guaranty are used presentment, notice of dishonor and protest are not necessary to charge the user.

(6) Any guaranty written on the instrument is enforcible notwithstanding any statute of frauds.

§ 3—417. **Warranties on Presentment and Transfer.**

(1) Any person who obtains payment or acceptance and any prior transferor warrants to a person who in good faith pays or accepts that

(a) he has a good title to the instrument or is authorized to obtain payment or acceptance on behalf of one who has a good title; and

(b) he has no knowledge that the signature of the maker or drawer is unauthorized, except that this warranty is not given by a holder in due course acting in good faith

(i) to a maker with respect to the maker's own signature; or

(ii) to a drawer with respect to the drawer's own signature, whether or not the drawer is also the drawee; or

(iii) to an acceptor of a draft if the holder in due course took the draft after the acceptance or obtained the acceptance without knowledge that the drawer's signature was unauthorized; and

(c) the instrument has not been materially altered, except that this warranty is not given by a holder in due course acting in good faith

(i) to the maker of a note; or

(ii) to the drawer of a draft whether or not the drawer is also the drawee; or

(iii) to the acceptor of a draft with respect to an alteration made prior to the acceptance if the holder in due course took the draft after the acceptance, even though the acceptance provided "payable as originally drawn" or equivalent terms; or

(iv) to the acceptor of a draft with respect to an alteration made after the acceptance.

(2) Any person who transfers an instrument and receives consideration warrants to his transferee and if the transfer is by indorsement to any subsequent holder who takes the instrument in good faith that

(a) he has a good title to the instrument or is authorized to obtain payment or acceptance on behalf of one who has a good title and the transfer is otherwise rightful; and

(b) all signatures are genuine or authorized; and

(c) the instrument has not been materially altered; and

(d) no defense of any party is good against him; and

(e) he has no knowledge of any insolvency proceeding instituted with respect to the maker or acceptor or the drawer of an unaccepted instrument.

(3) By transferring "without recourse" the transferor limits the obligation stated in subsection (2) (d) to a warranty that he has no knowledge of such a defense.

(4) A selling agent or broker who does not disclose the fact that he is acting only as such gives the warranties provided in this section, but if he makes such disclosure warrants only his good faith and authority.

§ 3—418. **Finality of Payment or Acceptance.**

Except for recovery of bank payments as provided in the Article on Bank Deposits and Collections (Article 4) and except for liability for breach of warranty on presentment under the preceding section, payment or acceptance of any instrument is final in favor of a holder in due course, or a person who has in good faith changed his position in reliance on the payment.

§ 3—419. **Conversion of Instrument; Innocent Representative.**

(1) An instrument is converted when

(a) a drawee to whom it is delivered for acceptance refuses to return it on demand; or

(b) any person to whom it is delivered for payment refuses on demand either to pay or to return it; or

(c) it is paid on a forged indorsement.

(2) In an action against a drawee under subsection (1) the measure of the drawee's liability is the face amount of the instrument. In any other action under subsection (1) the measure of liability is presumed to be the face amount of the instrument.

(3) Subject to the provisions of this Act concerning restrictive indorsements a representative, including a depository or collecting bank, who has in good faith and in accordance with the reasonable commercial standards applicable to the business of such representative dealt with an instrument or its proceeds on behalf of one who was not the true owner is not liable in conversion or otherwise to the true owner beyond the amount of any proceeds remaining in his hands.

(4) An intermediary bank or payor bank which is not a depositary bank is not liable in conversion solely by reason of the fact that proceeds of an item indorsed restrictively (Sections 3—205 and 3—206) are not paid or applied consistently with the restrictive indorsement of an indorser other than its immediate transferor.

Part 5 Presentment, Notice of Dishonor and Protest

§ 3—501. When Presentment, Notice of Dishonor, and Protest Necessary or Permissible.

(1) Unless excused (Section 3—511) presentment is necessary to charge secondary parties as follows:

(a) presentment for acceptance is necessary to charge the drawer and indorsers of a draft where the draft so provides, or is payable elsewhere than at the residence or place of business of the drawee, or its date of payment depends upon such presentment. The holder may at his option present for acceptance any other draft payable at a stated date;

(b) presentment for payment is necessary to charge any indorser;

(c) in the case of any drawer, the acceptor of a draft payable at a bank or the maker of a note payable at a bank, presentment for payment is necessary, but failure to make presentment discharges such drawer, acceptor or maker only as stated in Section 3—502(1)(b).

(2) Unless excused (Section 3—511)

(a) notice of any dishonor is necessary to charge any indorser;

(b) in the case of any drawer, the acceptor of a draft payable at a bank or the maker of a note payable at a bank, notice of any dishonor is necessary, but failure to give such notice discharges such drawer, acceptor or maker only as stated in Section 3—502(1)(b).

(3) Unless excused (Section 3—511) protest of any dishonor is necessary to charge the drawer and indorsers of any draft which on its face appears to be drawn or payable outside of the states, territories, dependencies, and possessions of the United States, the District of Columbia and the Commonwealth of Puerto Rico. The holder may at his option make protest of any dishonor of any other instrument and in the case of a foreign draft may on insolvency of the acceptor before maturity make protest for better security.

(4) Notwithstanding any provision of this section, neither presentment nor notice of dishonor nor protest is necessary to charge an indorser who has indorsed an instrument after maturity.

§ 3—502. Unexcused Delay; Discharge.

(1) Where without excuse any necessary presentment or notice of dishonor is delayed beyond the time when it is due

(a) any indorser is discharged; and

(b) any drawer or the acceptor of a draft payable at a bank or the maker of a note payable at a bank who because the drawee or payor bank becomes insolvent during the delay is deprived of funds maintained with the drawee or payor bank to cover the instrument may discharge his liability by written assignment to the holder of his rights against the drawee or payor bank in respect of such funds, but such drawer, acceptor or maker is not otherwise discharged.

(2) Where without excuse a necessary protest is delayed beyond the time when it is due any drawer or indorser is discharged.

§ 3—503. Time of Presentment.

(1) Unless a different time is expressed in the instrument the time for any presentment is determined as follows:

(a) where an instrument is payable at or a fixed period after a stated date any presentment for acceptance must be made on or before the date it is payable;

(b) where an instrument is payable after sight it must either be presented for acceptance or negotiated within a reasonable time after date or issue whichever is later;

(c) where an instrument shows the date on which it is payable presentment for payment is due on that date;

(d) where an instrument is accelerated presentment for payment is due within a reasonable time after the acceleration;

(e) with respect to the liability of any secondary party presentment for acceptance or payment of any other instrument is due within a reasonable time after such party becomes liable thereon.

(2) A reasonable time for presentment is determined by the nature of the instrument, any usage of banking or trade and the facts of the particular case. In the case of an uncertified check which is drawn and payable within the United States and which is not a draft drawn by a bank the following are presumed to be reasonable periods within which to present for payment or to initiate bank collection:

(a) with respect to the liability of the drawer, thirty days after date or issue whichever is later; and

(b) with respect to the liability of an indorser, seven days after his indorsement.

(3) Where any presentment is due on a day which is not a full business day for either the person making presentment or the party to pay or accept, presentment is due on the next following day which is a full business day for both parties.

(4) Presentment to be sufficient must be made at a reasonable hour, and if at a bank during its banking day.

§ 3—504. How Presentment Made.

(1) Presentment is a demand for acceptance or payment made upon the maker, acceptor, drawee or other payor by or on behalf of the holder.

(2) Presentment may be made

(a) by mail, in which event the time of presentment is determined by the time of receipt of the mail; or

(b) through a clearing house; or

(c) at the place of acceptance or payment specified in the instrument or if there be none at the place of business or residence of the party to accept or pay. If neither the party to accept or pay nor anyone authorized to act for him is present or accessible at such place presentment is excused.

(3) It may be made

(a) to any one of two or more makers, acceptors, drawees or other payors; or

(b) to any person who has authority to make or refuse the acceptance or payment.

(4) A draft accepted or a note made payable at a bank in the United States must be presented at such bank.

(5) In the cases described in Section 4—210 presentment may be made in the manner and with the result stated in that section.

§ 3—505. Rights of Party to Whom Presentment Is Made.

(1) The party to whom presentment is made may without dishonor require

(a) exhibition of the instrument; and

(b) reasonable identification of the person making presentment and evidence of his authority to make it if made for another; and

(c) that the instrument be produced for acceptance or payment at a place specified in it, or if there be none at any place reasonable in the circumstances; and

(d) a signed receipt on the instrument for any partial or full payment and its surrender upon full payment.

(2) Failure to comply with any such requirement invalidates the presentment but the person presenting has a reasonable time in which to comply and the time for acceptance or payment runs from the time of compliance.

§ 3—506. Time Allowed for Acceptance or Payment.

(1) Acceptance may be deferred without dishonor until the close of the next business day following presentment. The holder may also in a good faith effort to obtain acceptance and without either dishonor of the instrument or discharge of secondary parties allow postponement of acceptance for an additional business day.

(2) Except as a longer time is allowed in the case of documentary drafts drawn under a letter of credit, and unless an earlier time is agreed to by the party to pay, payment of an instrument may be deferred without dishonor pending reasonable examination to determine whether it is properly payable, but payment must be made in any event before the close of business on the day of presentment.

§ 3—507. Dishonor; Holder's Right of Recourse; Term Allowing Re-Presentment.

(1) An instrument is dishonored when

(a) a necessary or optional presentment is duly made and due acceptance or payment is refused or cannot be obtained within the prescribed time or in case of bank collections the instrument is seasonably returned by the midnight deadline (Section 4—301); or

(b) presentment is excused and the instrument is not duly accepted or paid.

(2) Subject to any necessary notice of dishonor and protest, the holder has upon dishonor an immediate right of recourse against the drawers and indorsers.

(3) Return of an instrument for lack of proper indorsement is not dishonor.

(4) A term in a draft or an indorsement thereof allowing a stated time for re-presentment in the event of any dishonor of the draft by nonacceptance if a time draft or by nonpayment if a sight draft gives the holder as against any secondary party bound by the term an option to waive the dishonor without affecting the liability of the secondary party and he may present again up to the end of the stated time.

§ 3—508. Notice of Dishonor.

(1) Notice of dishonor may be given to any person who may be liable on the instrument by or on behalf of the holder or any party who has himself received notice, or any other party who can be compelled to pay the instrument. In addition an agent or bank in whose hands the instrument is dishonored may give notice to his principal or customer or to another agent or bank from which the instrument was received.

(2) Any necessary notice must be given by a bank before its midnight deadline and by any other person before midnight of the third business day after dishonor or receipt of notice of dishonor.

(3) Notice may be given in any reasonable manner. It may be oral or written and in any terms which identify the instrument and state that it has been dishonored. A misdescription which does not mislead the party notified does not vitiate the notice. Sending the instrument bearing a stamp, ticket or writing stating that acceptance or payment has been refused or sending a notice of debit with respect to the instrument is sufficient.

(4) Written notice is given when sent although it is not received.

(5) Notice to one partner is notice to each although the firm has been dissolved.

(6) When any party is in insolvency proceedings instituted after the issue of the instrument notice may be given either to the party or to the representative of his estate.

(7) When any party is dead or incompetent notice may be sent to his last known address or given to his personal representative.

(8) Notice operates for the benefit of all parties who have rights on the instrument against the party notified.

§ 3—509. **Protest; Noting for Protest.**

(1) A protest is a certificate of dishonor made under the hand and seal of a United States consul or vice consul or a notary public or other person authorized to certify dishonor by the law of the place where dishonor occurs. It may be made upon information satisfactory to such person.

(2) The protest must identify the instrument and certify either that due presentment has been made or the reason why it is excused and that the instrument has been dishonored by nonacceptance or nonpayment.

(3) The protest may also certify that notice of dishonor has been given to all parties or to specified parties.

(4) Subject to subsection (5) any necessary protest is due by the time that notice of dishonor is due.

(5) If, before protest is due, an instrument has been noted for protest by the officer to make protest, the protest may be made at any time thereafter as of the date of the noting.

§ 3—510. **Evidence of Dishonor and Notice of Dishonor.**

The following are admissible as evidence and create a presumption of dishonor and of any notice of dishonor therein shown:

(a) a document regular in form as provided in the preceding section which purports to be a protest;

(b) the purported stamp or writing of the drawee, payor bank or presenting bank on the instrument or accompanying it stating that acceptance or payment has been refused for reasons consistent with dishonor;

(c) any book or record of the drawee, payor bank, or any collecting bank kept in the usual course of business which shows dishonor, even though there is no evidence of who made the entry.

§ 3—511. **Waived or Excused Presentment, Protest or Notice of Dishonor or Delay Therein.**

(1) Delay in presentment, protest or notice of dishonor is excused when the party is without notice that it is due or when the delay is caused by circumstances beyond his control and he exercises reasonable diligence after the cause of the delay ceases to operate.

(2) Presentment or notice or protest as the case may be is entirely excused when

(a) the party to be charged has waived it expressly or by implication either before or after it is due; or

(b) such party has himself dishonored the instrument or has countermanded payment or otherwise has no reason to expect or right to require that the instrument be accepted or paid; or

(c) by reasonable diligence the presentment or protest cannot be made or the notice given.

(3) Presentment is also entirely excused when

(a) the maker, acceptor or drawee of any instrument except a documentary draft is dead or in insolvency proceedings instituted after the issue of the instrument; or

(b) acceptance or payment is refused but not for want of proper presentment.

(4) Where a draft has been dishonored by nonacceptance a later presentment for payment and any notice of dishonor and protest for nonpayment are excused unless in the meantime the instrument has been accepted.

(5) A waiver of protest is also a waiver of presentment and of notice of dishonor even though protest is not required.

(6) Where a waiver of presentment or notice or protest is embodied in the instrument itself it is binding upon all parties; but where it is written above the signature of an indorser it binds him only.

Part 6 Discharge

§ 3—601. **Discharge of Parties.**

(1) The extent of the discharge of any party from liability on an instrument is governed by the sections on

(a) payment or satisfaction (Section 3—603); or

(b) tender of payment (Section 3—604); or

(c) cancellation or renunciation (Section 3—605); or

(d) impairment of right of recourse or of collateral (Section 3—606); or

(e) reacquisition of the instrument by a prior party (Section 3—208); or

(f) fraudulent and material alteration (Section 3—407); or

(g) certification of a check (Section 3—411); or

(h) acceptance varying a draft (Section 3—412); or

(i) unexcused delay in presentment or notice of dishonor or protest (Section 3—502).

(2) Any party is also discharged from his liability on an instrument to another party by any other act or agreement with such party which would discharge his simple contract for the payment of money.

(3) The liability of all parties is discharged when any party who has himself no right of action or recourse on the instrument

(a) reacquires the instrument in his own right; or

(b) is discharged under any provision of this Article, except as otherwise provided with respect to discharge for impairment of recourse or of collateral (Section 3—606).

§ 3—602. **Effect of Discharge Against Holder in Due Course.**

No discharge of any party provided by this Article is effective against a subsequent holder in due course unless he has notice thereof when he takes the instrument.

§ 3—603. **Payment or Satisfaction.**

(1) The liability of any party is discharged to the extent of his payment or satisfaction to the holder even though it is made with

knowledge of a claim of another person to the instrument unless prior to such payment or satisfaction the person making the claim either supplies indemnity deemed adequate by the party seeking the discharge or enjoins payment or satisfaction by order of a court of competent jurisdiction in an action in which the adverse claimant and the holder are parties. This subsection does not, however, result in the discharge of the liability

(a) of a party who in bad faith pays or satisfies a holder who acquired the instrument by theft or who (unless having the rights of a holder in due course) holds through one who so acquired it; or

(b) of a party (other than an intermediary bank or a payor bank which is not a depositary bank) who pays or satisfies the holder of an instrument which has been restrictively indorsed in a manner not consistent with the terms of such restrictive indorsement.

(2) Payment or satisfaction may be made with the consent of the holder by any person including a stranger to the instrument. Surrender of the instrument to such a person gives him the rights of a transferee (Section 3—201).

§ 3—604. Tender of Payment.

(1) Any party making tender of full payment to a holder when or after it is due is discharged to the extent of all subsequent liability for interest, costs and attorney's fees.

(2) The holder's refusal of such tender wholly discharges any party who has a right of recourse against the party making the tender.

(3) Where the maker or acceptor of an instrument payable otherwise than on demand is able and ready to pay at every place of payment specified in the instrument when it is due, it is equivalent to tender.

§ 3—605. Cancellation and Renunciation.

(1) The holder of an instrument may even without consideration discharge any party

(a) in any manner apparent on the face of the instrument or the indorsement, as by intentionally cancelling the instrument or the party's signature by destruction or mutilation, or by striking out the party's signature; or

(b) by renouncing his rights by a writing signed and delivered or by surrender of the instrument to the party to be discharged.

(2) Neither cancellation nor renunciation without surrender of the instrument affects the title thereto.

§ 3—606. Impairment of Recourse or of Collateral.

(1) The holder discharges any party to the instrument to the extent that without such party's consent the holder

(a) without express reservation of rights releases or agrees not to sue any person against whom the party has to the knowledge of the holder a right of recourse or agrees to suspend the right to enforce against such person the instrument or collateral or

otherwise discharges such person, except that failure or delay in effecting any required presentment, protest or notice of dishonor with respect to any such person does not discharge any party as to whom presentment, protest or notice of dishonor is effective or unnecessary; or

(b) unjustifiably impairs any collateral for the instrument given by or on behalf of the party or any person against whom he has a right of recourse.

(2) By express reservation of rights against a party with a right of recourse the holder preserves

(a) all his rights against such party as of the time when the instrument was originally due; and

(b) the right of the party to pay the instrument as of that time; and

(c) all rights of such party to recourse against others.

Part 7 Advice of International Sight Draft

§ 3—701. Letter of Advice of International Sight Draft.

(1) A "letter of advice" is a drawer's communication to the drawee that a described draft has been drawn.

(2) Unless otherwise agreed when a bank receives from another bank a letter of advice of an international sight draft the drawee bank may immediately debit the drawer's account and stop the running of interest pro tanto. Such a debit and any resulting credit to any account covering outstanding drafts leaves in the drawer full power to stop payment or otherwise dispose of the amount and creates no trust or interest in favor of the holder.

(3) Unless otherwise agreed and except where a draft is drawn under a credit issued by the drawee, the drawee of an international sight draft owes the drawer no duty to pay an unadvised draft but if it does so and the draft is genuine, may appropriately debit the drawer's account.

Part 8 Miscellaneous

§ 3—801. Drafts in a Set.

(1) Where a draft is drawn in a set of parts, each of which is numbered and expressed to be an order only if no other part has been honored, the whole of the parts constitutes one draft but a taker of any part may become a holder in due course of the draft.

(2) Any person who negotiates, indorses or accepts a single part of a draft drawn in a set thereby becomes liable to any holder in due course of that part as if it were the whole set, but as between different holders in due course to whom different parts have been negotiated the holder whose title first accrues has all rights to the draft and its proceeds.

(3) As against the drawee the first presented part of a draft drawn in a set is the part entitled to payment, or if a time draft to acceptance and payment. Acceptance of any subsequently presented part renders the drawee liable thereon under subsection

(2). With respect both to a holder and to the drawer payment of a subsequently presented part of a draft payable at sight has the same effect as payment of a check notwithstanding an effective stop order (Section 4—407).

(4) Except as otherwise provided in this section, where any part of a draft in a set is discharged by payment or otherwise the whole draft is discharged.

§ 3—802. Effect of Instrument on Obligation for Which It Is Given.

(1) Unless otherwise agreed where an instrument is taken for an underlying obligation

(a) the obligation is pro tanto discharged if a bank is drawer, maker or acceptor of the instrument and there is no recourse on the instrument against the underlying obligor; and

(b) in any other case the obligation is suspended pro tanto until the instrument is due or if it is payable on demand until its presentment. If the instrument is dishonored action may be maintained on either the instrument or the obligation; discharge of the underlying obligor on the instrument also discharges him on the obligation.

(2) The taking in good faith of a check which is not postdated does not of itself so extend the time on the original obligation as to discharge a surety.

§ 3—803. Notice to Third Party.

Where a defendant is sued for breach of an obligation for which a third person is answerable over under this Article he may give the third person written notice of the litigation, and the person notified may then give similar notice to any other person who is answerable over to him under this Article. If the notice states that the person notified may come in and defend and that if the person notified does not do so he will in any action against him by the person giving the notice be bound by any determination of fact common to the two litigations, then unless after seasonable receipt of the notice the person notified does come in and defend he is so bound.

§ 3—804. Lost, Destroyed or Stolen Instruments.

The owner of an instrument which is lost, whether by destruction, theft or otherwise, may maintain an action in his own name and recover from any party liable thereon upon due proof of his ownership, the facts which prevent his production of the instrument and its terms. The court may require security indemnifying the defendant against loss by reason of further claims on the instrument.

§ 3—805. Instruments Not Payable to Order or to Bearer.

This Article applies to any instrument whose terms do not preclude transfer and which is otherwise negotiable within this Article but which is not payable to order or to bearer, except that there can be no holder in due course of such an instrument.

Article 4
BANK DEPOSITS AND COLLECTIONS

Part 1 General Provisions and Definitions

§ 4—101. Short Title.

This Article shall be known and may be cited as Uniform Commercial Code—Bank Deposits and Collections.

§ 4—102. Applicability.

(1) To the extent that items within this Article are also within the scope of Articles 3 and 8, they are subject to the provisions of those Articles. In the event of conflict the provisions of this Article govern those of Article 3 but the provisions of Article 8 govern those of this Article.

(2) The liability of a bank for action or non-action with respect to any item handled by it for purposes of presentment, payment or collection is governed by the law of the place where the bank is located. In the case of action or non-action by or at a branch or separate office of a bank, its liability is governed by the law of the place where the branch or separate office is located.

§ 4—103. Variation by Agreement; Measure of Damages; Certain Action Constituting Ordinary Care.

(1) The effect of the provisions of this Article may be varied by agreement except that no agreement can disclaim a bank's responsibility for its own lack of good faith or failure to exercise ordinary care or can limit the measure of damages for such lack or failure; but the parties may by agreement determine the standards by which such responsibility is to be measured if such standards are not manifestly unreasonable.

(2) Federal Reserve regulations and operating letters, clearing house rules, and the like, have the effect of agreements under subsection (1), whether or not specifically assented to by all parties interested in items handled.

(3) Action or nonaction approved by this Article or pursuant to Federal Reserve regulations or operating letters constitutes the exercise of ordinary care and, in the absence of special instructions, action or nonaction consistent with clearing house rules and the like or with a general banking usage not disapproved by this Article, prima facie constitutes the exercise of ordinary care.

(4) The specification or approval of certain procedures by this Article does not constitute disapproval of other procedures which may be reasonable under the circumstances.

(5) The measure of damages for failure to exercise ordinary care in handling an item is the amount of the item reduced by an amount which could not have been realized by the use of ordinary care, and where there is bad faith it includes other damages, if any, suffered by the party as a proximate consequence.

§ 4—104. **Definitions and Index of Definitions.**

(1) In this Article unless the context otherwise requires

(a) "Account" means any account with a bank and includes a checking, time, interest or savings account;

(b) "Afternoon" means the period of a day between noon and midnight;

(c) "Banking day" means that part of any day on which a bank is open to the public for carrying on substantially all of its banking functions;

(d) "Clearing house" means any association of banks or other payors regularly clearing items;

(e) "Customer" means any person having an account with a bank or for whom a bank has agreed to collect items and includes a bank carrying an account with another bank;

(f) "Documentary draft" means any negotiable or nonnegotiable draft with accompanying documents, securities or other papers to be delivered against honor of the draft;

(g) "Item" means any instrument for the payment of money even though it is not negotiable but does not include money;

(h) "Midnight deadline" with respect to a bank is midnight on its next banking day following the banking day on which it receives the relevant item or notice or from which the time for taking action commences to run, whichever is later;

(i) "Properly payable" includes the availability of funds for payment at the time of decision to pay or dishonor;

(j) "Settle" means to pay in cash, by clearing house settlement, in a charge or credit or by remittance, or otherwise as instructed. A settlement may be either provisional or final;

(k) "Suspends payments" with respect to a bank means that it has been closed by order of the supervisory authorities, that a public officer has been appointed to take it over or that it ceases or refuses to make payments in the ordinary course of business.

(2) Other definitions applying to this Article and the sections in which they appear are:

"Collecting bank" Section 4—105.
"Depositary bank" Section 4—105.
"Intermediary bank" Section 4—105.
"Payor bank" Section 4—105.
"Presenting bank" Section 4—105.
"Remitting bank" Section 4—105.

(3) The following definitions in other Articles apply to this Article:

"Acceptance" Section 3—410.
"Certificate of deposit" Section 3—104.
"Certification" Section 3—411.
"Check" Section 3—104.
"Draft" Section 3—104.
"Holder in due course" Section 3—302.
"Notice of dishonor" Section 3—508.

"Presentment" Section 3—504.
"Protest" Section 3—509.
"Secondary party" Section 3—102.

(4) In addition Article 1 contains general definitions and principles of construction and interpretation applicable throughout this Article.

§ 4—105. **"Depositary Bank"; "Intermediary Bank"; "Collecting Bank"; "Payor Bank"; "Presenting Bank"; "Remitting Bank".**

In this Article unless the context otherwise requires:

(a) "Depositary bank" means the first bank to which an item is transferred for collection even though it is also the payor bank;

(b) "Payor bank" means a bank by which an item is payable as drawn or accepted;

(c) "Intermediary bank" means any bank to which an item is transferred in course of collection except the depositary or payor bank;

(d) "Collecting bank" means any bank handling the item for collection except the payor bank;

(e) "Presenting bank" means any bank presenting an item except a payor bank;

(f) "Remitting bank" means any payor or intermediary bank remitting for an item.

§ 4—106. **Separate Office of a Bank.**

A branch or separate office of a bank [maintaining its own deposit ledgers] is a separate bank for the purpose of computing the time within which and determining the place at or to which action may be taken or notices or orders shall be given under this Article and under Article 3.

Note: *The brackets are to make it optional with the several states whether to require a branch to maintain its own deposit ledgers in order to be considered to be a separate bank for certain purposes under Article 4. In some states "maintaining its own deposit ledgers" is a satisfactory test. In others branch banking practices are such that this test would not be suitable.*

§ 4—107. **Time of Receipt of Items.**

(1) For the purpose of allowing time to process items, prove balances and make the necessary entries on its books to determine its position for the day, a bank may fix an afternoon hour of 2 P.M. or later as a cut-off hour for the handling of money and items and the making of entries on its books.

(2) Any item or deposit of money received on any day after a cut-off hour so fixed or after the close of the banking day may be treated as being received at the opening of the next banking day.

§ 4—108. **Delays.**

(1) Unless otherwise instructed, a collecting bank in a good faith effort to secure payment may, in the case of specific items and with or without the approval of any person involved, waive, modify or extend time limits imposed or permitted by this Act for a period

not in excess of an additional banking day without discharge of secondary parties and without liability to its transferor or any prior party.

(2) Delay by a collecting bank or payor bank beyond time limits prescribed or permitted by this Act or by instructions is excused if caused by interruption of communication facilities, suspension of payments by another bank, war, emergency conditions or other circumstances beyond the control of the bank provided it exercises such diligence as the circumstances require.

§ 4—109. Process of Posting.

The "process of posting" means the usual procedure followed by a payor bank in determining to pay an item and in recording the payment including one or more of the following or other steps as determined by the bank:

(a) verification of any signature;

(b) ascertaining that sufficient funds are available;

(c) affixing a "paid" or other stamp;

(d) entering a charge or entry to a customer's account;

(e) correcting or reversing an entry or erroneous action with respect to the item.

Part 2 Collection of Items: Depositary and Collecting Banks

§ 4—201. Presumption and Duration of Agency Status of Collecting Banks and Provisional Status of Credits; Applicability of Article; Item Indorsed "Pay Any Bank".

(1) Unless a contrary intent clearly appears and prior to the time that a settlement given by a collecting bank for an item is or becomes final (subsection (3) of Section 4—211 and Sections 4—212 and 4—213) the bank is an agent or sub-agent of the owner of the item and any settlement given for the item is provisional. This provision applies regardless of the form of indorsement or lack of indorsement and even though credit given for the item is subject to immediate withdrawal as of right or is in fact withdrawn; but the continuance of ownership of an item by its owner and any rights of the owner to proceeds of the item are subject to rights of a collecting bank such as those resulting from outstanding advances on the item and valid rights of setoff. When an item is handled by banks for purposes of presentment, payment and collection, the relevant provisions of this Article apply even though action of parties clearly establishes that a particular bank has purchased the item and is the owner of it.

(2) After an item has been indorsed with the words "pay any bank" or the like, only a bank may acquire the rights of a holder

(a) until the item has been returned to the customer initiating collection; or

(b) until the item has been specially indorsed by a bank to a person who is not a bank.

§ 4—202. Responsibility for Collection; When Action Seasonable.

(1) A collecting bank must use ordinary care in

(a) presenting an item or sending it for presentment; and

(b) sending notice of dishonor or non-payment or returning an item other than a documentary draft to the bank's transferor [or directly to the depositary bank under subsection (2) of Section 4—212] *(see note to Section 4—212)* after learning that the item has not been paid or accepted as the case may be; and

(c) settling for an item when the bank receives final settlement; and

(d) making or providing for any necessary protest; and

(e) notifying its transferor of any loss or delay in transit within a reasonable time after discovery thereof.

(2) A collecting bank taking proper action before its midnight deadline following receipt of an item, notice or payment acts seasonably; taking proper action within a reasonably longer time may be seasonable but the bank has the burden of so establishing.

(3) Subject to subsection (1)(a), a bank is not liable for the insolvency, neglect, misconduct, mistake or default of another bank or person or for loss or destruction of an item in transit or in the possession of others.

§ 4—203. Effect of Instructions.

Subject to the provisions of Article 3 concerning conversion of instruments (Section 3—419) and the provisions of both Article 3 and this Article concerning restrictive indorsements only a collecting bank's transferor can give instructions which affect the bank or constitute notice to it and a collecting bank is not liable to prior parties for any action taken pursuant to such instructions or in accordance with any agreement with its transferor.

§ 4—204. Methods of Sending and Presenting; Sending Direct to Payor Bank.

(1) A collecting bank must send items by reasonably prompt method taking into consideration any relevant instructions, the nature of the item, the number of such items on hand, and the cost of collection involved and the method generally used by it or others to present such items.

(2) A collecting bank may send

(a) any item direct to the payor bank;

(b) any item to any non-bank payor if authorized by its transferor; and

(c) any item other than documentary drafts to any non-bank payor, if authorized by Federal Reserve regulation or operating letter, clearing house rule or the like.

(3) Presentment may be made by a presenting bank at a place where the payor bank has requested that presentment be made.

§ 4—205. Supplying Missing Indorsement; No Notice from Prior Indorsement.

(1) A depositary bank which has taken an item for collection may supply any indorsement of the customer which is necessary to title unless the item contains the words "payee's indorsement required" or the like. In the absence of such a requirement a statement placed on the item by the depositary bank to the effect that the item was deposited by a customer or credited to his account is effective as the customer's indorsement.

(2) An intermediary bank, or payor bank which is not a depositary bank, is neither given notice nor otherwise affected by a restrictive indorsement of any person except the bank's immediate transferor.

§ 4—206. Transfer Between Banks.

Any agreed method which identifies the transferor bank is sufficient for the item's further transfer to another bank.

§ 4—207. Warranties of Customer and Collecting Bank on Transfer or Presentment of Items; Time for Claims.

(1) Each customer or collecting bank who obtains payment or acceptance of an item and each prior customer and collecting bank warrants to the payor bank or other payor who in good faith pays or accepts the item that

(a) he has a good title to the item or is authorized to obtain payment or acceptance on behalf of one who has a good title; and

(b) he has no knowledge that the signature of the maker or drawer is unauthorized, except that this warranty is not given by any customer or collecting bank that is a holder in due course and acts in good faith

(i) to a maker with respect to the maker's own signature; or

(ii) to a drawer with respect to the drawer's own signature, whether or not the drawer is also the drawee; or

(iii) to an acceptor of an item if the holder in due course took the item after the acceptance or obtained the acceptance without knowledge that the drawer's signature was unauthorized; and

(c) the item has not been materially altered, except that this warranty is not given by any customer or collecting bank that is a holder in due course and acts in good faith

(i) to the maker of a note; or

(ii) to the drawer of a draft whether or not the drawer is also the drawee; or

(iii) to the acceptor of an item with respect to an alteration made prior to the acceptance if the holder in due course took the item after the acceptance, even though the acceptance provided "payable as originally drawn" or equivalent terms; or

(iv) to the acceptor of an item with respect to an alteration made after the acceptance.

(2) Each customer and collecting bank who transfers an item and receives a settlement or other consideration for it warrants to his transferee and to any subsequent collecting bank who takes the item in good faith that

(a) he has a good title to the item or is authorized to obtain payment or acceptance on behalf of one who has a good title and the transfer is otherwise rightful; and

(b) all signatures are genuine or authorized; and

(c) the item has not been materially altered; and

(d) no defense of any party is good against him; and

(e) he has no knowledge of any insolvency proceeding instituted with respect to the maker or acceptor or the drawer of an unaccepted item.

In addition each customer and collecting bank so transferring an item and receiving a settlement or other consideration engages that upon dishonor and any necessary notice of dishonor and protest he will take up the item.

(3) The warranties and the engagement to honor set forth in the two preceding subsections arise notwithstanding the absence of indorsement or words of guaranty or warranty in the transfer or presentment and a collecting bank remains liable for their breach despite remittance to its transferor. Damages for breach of such warranties or engagement to honor shall not exceed the consideration received by the customer or collecting bank responsible plus finance charges and expenses related to the item, if any.

(4) Unless a claim for breach of warranty under this section is made within a reasonable time after the person claiming learns of the breach, the person liable is discharged to the extent of any loss caused by the delay in making claim.

§ 4—208. Security Interest of Collecting Bank in Items, Accompanying Documents and Proceeds.

(1) A bank has a security interest in an item and any accompanying documents or the proceeds of either

(a) in case of an item deposited in an account to the extent to which credit given for the item has been withdrawn or applied;

(b) in case of an item for which it has given credit available for withdrawal as of right, to the extent of the credit given whether or not the credit is drawn upon and whether or not there is a right of charge-back; or

(c) if it makes an advance on or against the item.

(2) When credit which has been given for several items received at one time or pursuant to a single agreement is withdrawn or applied in part the security interest remains upon all the items, any accompanying documents or the proceeds of either. For the purpose of this section, credits first given are first withdrawn.

(3) Receipt by a collecting bank of a final settlement for an item is a realization on its security interest in the item, accompanying documents and proceeds. To the extent and so long as the bank

does not receive final settlement for the item or give up possession of the item or accompanying documents for purposes other than collection, the security interest continues and is subject to the provisions of Article 9 except that

(a) no security agreement is necessary to make the security interest enforceable (subsection (1)(a) of Section 9—203); and

(b) no filing is required to perfect the security interest; and

(c) the security interest has priority over conflicting perfected security interests in the item, accompanying documents or proceeds.

§ 4—209. When Bank Gives Value for Purposes of Holder in Due Course.

For purposes of determining its status as a holder in due course, the bank has given value to the extent that it has a security interest in an item provided that the bank otherwise complies with the requirements of Section 3—302 on what constitutes a holder in due course.

§ 4—210. Presentment by Notice of Item Not Payable by, Through or at a Bank; Liability of Secondary Parties.

(1) Unless otherwise instructed, a collecting bank may present an item not payable by, through or at a bank by sending to the party to accept or pay a written notice that the bank holds the item for acceptance or payment. The notice must be sent in time to be received on or before the day when presentment is due and the bank must meet any requirement of the party to accept or pay under Section 3—505 by the close of the bank's next banking day after it knows of the requirement.

(2) Where presentment is made by notice and neither honor nor request for compliance with a requirement under Section 3—505 is received by the close of business on the day after maturity or in the case of demand items by the close of business on the third banking day after notice was sent, the presenting bank may treat the item as dishonored and charge any secondary party by sending him notice of the facts.

§ 4—211. Media of Remittance; Provisional and Final Settlement in Remittance Cases.

(1) A collecting bank may take in settlement of an item

(a) a check of the remitting bank or of another bank on any bank except the remitting bank; or

(b) a cashier's check or similar primary obligation of a remitting bank which is a member of or clears through a member of the same clearing house or group as the collecting bank; or

(c) appropriate authority to charge an account of the remitting bank or of another bank with the collecting bank; or

(d) if the item is drawn upon or payable by a person other than a bank, a cashier's check, certified check or other bank check or obligation.

(2) If before its midnight deadline the collecting bank properly dishonors a remittance check or authorization to charge on itself or presents or forwards for collection a remittance instrument of or on another bank which is of a kind approved by subsection (1) or has not been authorized by it, the collecting bank is not liable to prior parties in the event of the dishonor of such check, instrument or authorization.

(3) A settlement for an item by means of a remittance instrument or authorization to charge is or becomes a final settlement as to both the person making and the person receiving the settlement

(a) if the remittance instrument or authorization to charge is of a kind approved by subsection (1) or has not been authorized by the person receiving the settlement and in either case the person receiving the settlement acts seasonably before its midnight deadline in presenting, forwarding for collection or paying the instrument or authorization,—at the time the remittance instrument or authorization is finally paid by the payor by which it is payable;

(b) if the person receiving the settlement has authorized remittance by a non-bank check or obligation or by a cashier's check or similar primary obligation of or a check upon the payor or other remitting bank which is not of a kind approved by subsection (1)(b),—at the time of the receipt of such remittance check or obligation; or

(c) if in a case not covered by sub-paragraphs (a) or (b) the person receiving the settlement fails to seasonably present, forward for collection, pay or return a remittance instrument or authorization to it to charge before its midnight deadline,—at such midnight deadline.

§ 4—212. Right of Charge-Back or Refund.

(1) If a collecting bank has made provisional settlement with its customer for an item and itself fails by reason of dishonor, suspension of payments by a bank or otherwise to receive a settlement for the item which is or becomes final, the bank may revoke the settlement given by it, charge back the amount of any credit given for the item to its customer's account or obtain refund from its customer whether or not it is able to return the items if by its midnight deadline or within a longer reasonable time after it learns the facts it returns the item or sends notification of the facts. These rights to revoke, charge-back and obtain refund terminate if and when a settlement for the item received by the bank is or becomes final (subsection (3) of Section 4—211 and subsections (2) and (3) of Section 4—213).

[(2) Within the time and manner prescribed by this section and Section 4—301, an intermediary or payor bank, as the case may be, may return an unpaid item directly to the depositary bank and may send for collection a draft on the depositary bank and obtain reimbursement. In such case, if the depositary bank has received provisional settlement for the item, it must reimburse the bank drawing the draft and any provisional credits for the item between banks shall become and remain final.]

Note: *Direct returns is recognized as an innovation that is not yet established bank practice, and therefore, Paragraph 2 has been bracketed. Some lawyers have doubts whether it should be included in legislation or left to development by agreement.*

(3) A depositary bank which is also the payor may chargeback the amount of an item to its customer's account or obtain refund in accordance with the section governing return of an item received by a payor bank for credit on its books (Section 4—301).

(4) The right to charge-back is not affected by

(a) prior use of the credit given for the item; or

(b) failure by any bank to exercise ordinary care with respect to the item but any bank so failing remains liable.

(5) A failure to charge-back or claim refund does not affect other rights of the bank against the customer or any other party.

(6) If credit is given in dollars as the equivalent of the value of an item payable in a foreign currency the dollar amount of any charge-back or refund shall be calculated on the basis of the buying sight rate for the foreign currency prevailing on the day when the person entitled to the charge-back or refund learns that it will not receive payment in ordinary course.

§ 4—213. Final Payment of Item by Payor Bank; When Provisional Debits and Credits Become Final; When Certain Credits Become Available for Withdrawal.

(1) An item is finally paid by a payor bank when the bank has done any of the following, whichever happens first:

(a) paid the item in cash; or

(b) settled for the item without reserving a right to revoke the settlement and without having such right under statute, clearing house rule or agreement; or

(c) completed the process of posting the item to the indicated account of the drawer, maker or other person to be charged therewith; or

(d) made a provisional settlement for the item and failed to revoke the settlement in the time and manner permitted by statute, clearing house rule or agreement.

Upon a final payment under subparagraphs (b), (c) or (d) the payor bank shall be accountable for the amount of the item.

(2) If provisional settlement for an item between the presenting and payor banks is made through a clearing house or by debits or credits in an account between them, then to the extent that provisional debits or credits for the item are entered in accounts between the presenting and payor banks or between the presenting and successive prior collecting banks seriatim, they become final upon final payment of the item by the payor bank.

(3) If a collecting bank receives a settlement for an item which is or becomes final (subsection (3) of Section 4—211, subsection (2) of Section 4—213) the bank is accountable to its customer for the amount of the item and any provisional credit given for the item in an account with its customer becomes final.

(4) Subject to any right of the bank to apply the credit to an obligation of the customer, credit given by a bank for an item in an account with its customer becomes available for withdrawal as of right

(a) in any case where the bank has received a provisional settlement for the item,—when such settlement becomes final and the bank has had a reasonable time to learn that the settlement is final;

(b) in any case where the bank is both a depositary bank and a payor bank and the item is finally paid,—at the opening of the bank's second banking day following receipt of the item.

(5) A deposit of money in a bank is final when made but, subject to any right of the bank to apply the deposit to an obligation of the customer, the deposit becomes available for withdrawal as of right at the opening of the bank's next banking day following receipt of the deposit.

§ 4—214. Insolvency and Preference.

(1) Any item in or coming into the possession of a payor or collecting bank which suspends payment and which item is not finally paid shall be returned by the receiver, trustee or agent in charge of the closed bank to the presenting bank or the closed bank's customer.

(2) If a payor bank finally pays an item and suspends payments without making a settlement for the item with its customer or the presenting bank which settlement is or becomes final, the owner of the item has a preferred claim against the payor bank.

(3) If a payor bank gives or a collecting bank gives or receives a provisional settlement for an item and thereafter suspends payments, the suspension does not prevent or interfere with the settlement becoming final if such finality occurs automatically upon the lapse of certain time or the happening of certain events (subsection (3) of Section 4—211, subsections (1)(d), (2) and (3) of Section 4—213).

(4) If a collecting bank receives from subsequent parties settlement for an item which settlement is or becomes final and suspends payments without making a settlement for the item with its customer which is or becomes final, the owner of the item has a preferred claim against such collecting bank.

Part 3 Collection of Items: Payor Banks

§ 4—301. Deferred Posting; Recovery of Payment by Return of Items; Time of Dishonor.

(1) Where an authorized settlement for a demand item (other than a documentary draft) received by a payor bank otherwise than for immediate payment over the counter has been made before midnight of the banking day of receipt the payor bank may revoke the settlement and recover any payment if before it has made final payment (subsection (1) of Section 4—213) and before its midnight deadline it

(a) returns the item; or

(b) sends written notice of dishonor or nonpayment if the item is held for protest or is otherwise unavailable for return.

(2) If a demand item is received by a payor bank for credit on its books it may return such item or send notice of dishonor and may

revoke any credit given or recover the amount thereof withdrawn by its customer, if it acts within the time limit and in the manner specified in the preceding subsection.

(3) Unless previous notice of dishonor has been sent an item is dishonored at the time when for purposes of dishonor it is returned or notice sent in accordance with this section.

(4) An item is returned:

(a) as to an item received through a clearing house, when it is delivered to the presenting or last collecting bank or to the clearing house or is sent or delivered in accordance with its rules; or

(b) in all other cases, when it is sent or delivered to the bank's customer or transferor or pursuant to his instructions.

§ 4—302. **Payor Bank's Responsibility for Late Return of Item.**

In the absence of a valid defense such as breach of a presentment warranty (subsection (1) of Section 4—207), settlement effected or the like, if an item is presented on and received by a payor bank the bank is accountable for the amount of

(a) a demand item other than a documentary draft whether properly payable or not if the bank, in any case where it is not also the depositary bank, retains the item beyond midnight of the banking day of receipt without settling for it or, regardless of whether it is also the depositary bank, does not pay or return the item or send notice of dishonor until after its midnight deadline; or

(b) any other properly payable item unless within the time allowed for acceptance or payment of that item the bank either accepts or pays the item or returns it and accompanying documents.

§ 4—303. **When Items Subject to Notice, Stop-Order, Legal Process or Setoff; Order in Which Items May Be Charged or Certified.**

(1) Any knowledge, notice or stop-order received by, legal process served upon or setoff exercised by a payor bank, whether or not effective under other rules of law to terminate, suspend or modify the bank's right or duty to pay an item or to charge its customer's account for the item, comes too late to so terminate, suspend or modify such right or duty if the knowledge, notice, stop-order or legal process is received or served and a reasonable time for the bank to act thereon expires or the setoff is exercised after the bank has done any of the following:

(a) accepted or certified the item;

(b) paid the item in cash;

(c) settled for the item without reserving a right to revoke the settlement and without having such right under statute, clearing house rule or agreement;

(d) completed the process of posting the item to the indicated account of the drawer, maker or other person to be charged

therewith or otherwise has evidenced by examination of such indicated account and by action its decision to pay the item; or

(e) become accountable for the amount of the item under subsection (1)(d) of Section 4—213 and Section 4—302 dealing with the payor bank's responsibility for late return of items.

(2) Subject to the provisions of subsection (1) items may be accepted, paid, certified or charged to the indicated account of its customer in any order convenient to the bank.

Part 4 Relationship Between Payor Bank and Its Customer

§ 4—401. **When Bank May Charge Customer's Account.**

(1) As against its customer, a bank may charge against his account any item which is otherwise properly payable from that account even though the charge creates an overdraft.

(2) A bank which in good faith makes payment to a holder may charge the indicated account of its customer according to

(a) the original tenor of his altered item; or

(b) the tenor of his completed item, even though the bank knows the item has been completed unless the bank has notice that the completion was improper.

§ 4—402. **Bank's Liability to Customer for Wrongful Dishonor.**

A payor bank is liable to its customer for damages proximately caused by the wrongful dishonor of an item. When the dishonor occurs through mistake liability is limited to actual damages proved. If so proximately caused and proved damages may include damages for an arrest or prosecution of the customer or other consequential damages. Whether any consequential damages are proximately caused by the wrongful dishonor is a question of fact to be determined in each case.

§ 4—403. **Customer's Right to Stop Payment; Burden of Proof of Loss.**

(1) A customer may by order to his bank stop payment of any item payable for his account but the order must be received at such time and in such manner as to afford the bank a reasonable opportunity to act on it prior to any action by the bank with respect to the item described in Section 4—303.

(2) An oral order is binding upon the bank only for fourteen calendar days unless confirmed in writing within that period. A written order is effective for only six months unless renewed in writing.

(3) The burden of establishing the fact and amount of loss resulting from the payment of an item contrary to a binding stop payment order is on the customer.

§ 4—404. **Bank Not Obligated to Pay Check More Than Six Months Old.**

A bank is under no obligation to a customer having a checking account to pay a check, other than a certified check, which is presented more than six months after its date, but it may charge its customer's account for a payment made thereafter in good faith.

§ 4—405. Death or Incompetence of Customer.

(1) A payor or collecting bank's authority to accept, pay or collect an item or to account for proceeds of its collection if otherwise effective is not rendered ineffective by incompetence of a customer of either bank existing at the time the item is issued or its collection is undertaken if the bank does not know of an adjudication of incompetence. Neither death nor incompetence of a customer revokes such authority to accept, pay, collect or account until the bank knows of the fact of death or of an adjudication of incompetence and has reasonable opportunity to act on it.

(2) Even with knowledge a bank may for 10 days after the date of death pay or certify checks drawn on or prior to that date unless ordered to stop payment by a person claiming an interest in the account.

§ 4—406. Customer's Duty to Discover and Report Unauthorized Signature or Alteration.

(1) When a bank sends to its customer a statement of account accompanied by items paid in good faith in support of the debit entries or holds the statement and items pursuant to a request or instructions of its customer or otherwise in a reasonable manner makes the statement and items available to the customer, the customer must exercise reasonable care and promptness to examine the statement and items to discover his unauthorized signature or any alteration on an item and must notify the bank promptly after discovery thereof.

(2) If the bank establishes that the customer failed with respect to an item to comply with the duties imposed on the customer by subsection (1) the customer is precluded from asserting against the bank

(a) his unauthorized signature or any alteration on the item if the bank also establishes that it suffered a loss by reason of such failure; and

(b) an unauthorized signature or alteration by the same wrongdoer on any other item paid in good faith by the bank after the first item and statement was available to the customer for a reasonable period not exceeding fourteen calendar days and before the bank receives notification from the customer of any such unauthorized signature or alteration.

(3) The preclusion under subsection (2) does not apply if the customer establishes lack of ordinary care on the part of the bank in paying the item(s).

(4) Without regard to care or lack of care of either the customer or the bank a customer who does not within one year from the time the statement and items are made available to the customer (subsection (1)) discover and report his unauthorized signature or any alteration on the face or back of the item or does not within three years from that time discover and report any unauthorized indorsement is precluded from asserting against the bank such unauthorized signature or indorsement or such alteration.

(5) If under this section a payor bank has a valid defense against a claim of a customer upon or resulting from payment of an item and waives or fails upon request to assert the defense the bank may not assert against any collecting bank or other prior party presenting or transferring the item a claim based upon the unauthorized signature or alteration giving rise to the customer's claim.

§ 4—407. Payor Bank's Right to Subrogation on Improper Payment.

If a payor bank has paid an item over the stop payment order of the drawer or maker or otherwise under circumstances giving a basis for objection by the drawer or maker, to prevent unjust enrichment and only to the extent necessary to prevent loss to the bank by reason of its payment of the item, the payor bank shall be subrogated to the rights

(a) of any holder in due course on the item against the drawer or maker; and

(b) of the payee or any other holder of the item against the drawer or maker either on the item or under the transaction out of which the item arose; and

(c) of the drawer or maker against the payee or any other holder of the item with respect to the transaction out of which the item arose.

Part 5 Collection of Documentary Drafts

§ 4—501. Handling of Documentary Drafts; Duty to Send for Presentment and to Notify Customer of Dishonor.

A bank which takes a documentary draft for collection must present or send the draft and accompanying documents for presentment and upon learning that the draft has not been paid or accepted in due course must seasonably notify its customer of such fact even though it may have discounted or bought the draft or extended credit available for withdrawal as of right.

§ 4—502. Presentment of "On Arrival" Drafts.

When a draft or the relevant instructions require presentment "on arrival", "when goods arrive" or the like, the collecting bank need not present until in its judgment a reasonable time for arrival of the goods has expired. Refusal to pay or accept because the goods have not arrived is not dishonor; the bank must notify its transferor of such refusal but need not present the draft again until it is instructed to do so or learns of the arrival of the goods.

§ 4—503. Responsibility of Presenting Bank for Documents and Goods; Report of Reasons for Dishonor; Referee in Case of Need.

Unless otherwise instructed and except as provided in Article 5 a bank presenting a documentary draft

(a) must deliver the documents to the drawee on acceptance of the draft if it is payable more than three days after presentment; otherwise, only on payment; and

(b) upon dishonor, either in the case of presentment for acceptance or presentment for payment, may seek and follow instructions from any referee in case of need designated in the draft or if the presenting bank does not choose to utilize his services it must use diligence and good faith to ascertain the reason for dishonor, must notify its transferor of the dishonor and of the results of its effort to ascertain the reasons therefor and must request instructions.

But the presenting bank is under no obligation with respect to goods represented by the documents except to follow any reasonable instructions seasonably received; it has a right to reimbursement for any expense incurred in following instructions and to prepayment of or indemnity for such expenses.

§ 4—504. Privilege of Presenting Bank to Deal With Goods; Security Interest for Expenses.

(1) A presenting bank which, following the dishonor of a documentary draft, has seasonably requested instructions but does not receive them within a reasonable time may store, sell, or otherwise deal with the goods in any reasonable manner.

(2) For its reasonable expenses incurred by action under subsection (1) the presenting bank has a lien upon the goods or their proceeds, which may be foreclosed in the same manner as an unpaid seller's lien.

Article 5
LETTERS OF CREDIT

§ 5—101. Short Title.

This Article shall be known and may be cited as Uniform Commercial Code—Letters of Credit.

§ 5—102. Scope.

(1) This Article applies

(a) to a credit issued by a bank if the credit requires a documentary draft or a documentary demand for payment; and

(b) to a credit issued by a person other than a bank if the credit requires that the draft or demand for payment be accompanied by a document of title; and

(c) to a credit issued by a bank or other person if the credit is not within subparagraphs (a) or (b) but conspicuously states that it is a letter of credit or is conspicuously so entitled.

(2) Unless the engagement meets the requirements of subsection (1), this Article does not apply to engagements to make advances or to honor drafts or demands for payment, to authorities to pay or purchase, to guarantees or to general agreements.

(3) This Article deals with some but not all of the rules and concepts of letters of credit as such rules or concepts have developed prior to this act or may hereafter develop. The fact that this Article states a rule does not by itself require, imply or negate application of the same or a converse rule to a situation not provided for or to a person not specified by this Article.

§ 5—103. Definitions.

(1) In this Article unless the context otherwise requires

(a) "Credit" or "letter of credit" means an engagement by a bank or other person made at the request of a customer and of a kind within the scope of this Article (Section 5—102) that the issuer will honor drafts or other demands for payment upon compliance with the conditions specified in the credit. A credit may be either revocable or irrevocable. The engagement may be either an agreement to honor or a statement that the bank or other person is authorized to honor.

(b) A "documentary draft" or a "documentary demand for payment" is one honor of which is conditioned upon the presentation of a document or documents. "Document" means any paper including document of title, security, invoice, certificate, notice of default and the like.

(c) An "issuer" is a bank or other person issuing a credit.

(d) A "beneficiary" of a credit is a person who is entitled under its terms to draw or demand payment.

(e) An "advising bank" is a bank which gives notification of the issuance of a credit by another bank.

(f) A "confirming bank" is a bank which engages either that it will itself honor a credit already issued by another bank or that such a credit will be honored by the issuer or a third bank.

(g) A "customer" is a buyer or other person who causes an issuer to issue a credit. The term also includes a bank which procures issuance or confirmation on behalf of that bank's customer.

(2) Other definitions applying to this Article and the sections in which they appear are:
"Notation of Credit". Section 5—108.
"Presenter". Section 5—112(3).

(3) Definitions in other Articles applying to this Article and the sections in which they appear are:
"Accept" or "Acceptance". Section 3—410.
"Contract for sale". Section 2—106.
"Draft". Section 3—104.
"Holder in due course". Section 3—302.
"Midnight deadline". Section 4—104.
"Security". Section 8—102.

(4) In addition, Article 1 contains general definitions and principles of construction and interpretation applicable throughout this Article.

§ 5—104. Formal Requirements; Signing.

(1) Except as otherwise required in subsection (1)(c) of Section 5—102 on scope, no particular form of phrasing is required for a credit. A credit must be in writing and signed by the issuer and

a confirmation must be in writing and signed by the confirming bank. A modification of the terms of a credit or confirmation must be signed by the issuer or confirming bank.

(2) A telegram may be a sufficient signed writing if it identifies its sender by an authorized authentication. The authentication may be in code and the authorized naming of the issuer in an advice of credit is a sufficient signing.

§ 5—105. Consideration.

No consideration is necessary to establish a credit or to enlarge or otherwise modify its terms.

§ 5—106. Time and Effect of Establishment of Credit.

(1) Unless otherwise agreed a credit is established

(a) as regards the customer as soon as a letter of credit is sent to him or the letter of credit or an authorized written advice of its issuance is sent to the beneficiary; and

(b) as regards the beneficiary when he receives a letter of credit or an authorized written advice of its issuance.

(2) Unless otherwise agreed once an irrevocable credit is established as regards the customer it can be modified or revoked only with the consent of the customer and once it is established as regards the beneficiary it can be modified or revoked only with his consent.

(3) Unless otherwise agreed after a revocable credit is established it may be modified or revoked by the issuer without notice to or consent from the customer or beneficiary.

(4) Notwithstanding any modification or revocation of a revocable credit any person authorized to honor or negotiate under the terms of the original credit is entitled to reimbursement for or honor of any draft or demand for payment duly honored or negotiated before receipt of notice of the modification or revocation and the issuer in turn is entitled to reimbursement from its customer.

§ 5—107. Advice of Credit; Confirmation; Error in Statement of Terms.

(1) Unless otherwise specified an advising bank by advising a credit issued by another bank does not assume any obligation to honor drafts drawn or demands for payment made under the credit but it does assume obligation for the accuracy of its own statement.

(2) A confirming bank by confirming a credit becomes directly obligated on the credit to the extent of its confirmation as though it were its issuer and acquires the rights of an issuer.

(3) Even though an advising bank incorrectly advises the terms of a credit it has been authorized to advise the credit is established as against the issuer to the extent of its original terms.

(4) Unless otherwise specified the customer bears as against the issuer all risks of transmission and reasonable translation or interpretation of any message relating to a credit.

§ 5—108. "Notation Credit"; Exhaustion of Credit.

(1) A credit which specifies that any person purchasing or paying drafts drawn or demands for payment made under it must note the amount of the draft or demand on the letter or advice of credit is a "notation credit".

(2) Under a notation credit

(a) a person paying the beneficiary or purchasing a draft or demand for payment from him acquires a right to honor only if the appropriate notation is made and by transferring or forwarding for honor the documents under the credit such a person warrants to the issuer that the notation has been made; and

(b) unless the credit or a signed statement that an appropriate notation has been made accompanies the draft or demand for payment the issuer may delay honor until evidence of notation has been procured which is satisfactory to it but its obligation and that of its customer continue for a reasonable time not exceeding thirty days to obtain such evidence.

(3) If the credit is not a notation credit

(a) the issuer may honor complying drafts or demands for payment presented to it in the order in which they are presented and is discharged pro tanto by honor of any such draft or demand;

(b) as between competing good faith purchasers of complying drafts or demands the person first purchasing his priority over a subsequent purchaser even though the later purchased draft or demand has been first honored.

§ 5—109. Issuer's Obligation to Its Customer.

(1) An issuer's obligation to its customer includes good faith and observance of any general banking usage but unless otherwise agreed does not include liability or responsibility

(a) for performance of the underlying contract for sale or other transaction between the customer and the beneficiary; or

(b) for any act or omission of any person other than itself or its own branch or for loss or destruction of a draft, demand or document in transit or in the possession of others; or

(c) based on knowledge or lack of knowledge of any usage of any particular trade.

(2) An issuer must examine documents with care so as to ascertain that on their face they appear to comply with the terms of the credit but unless otherwise agreed assumes no liability or responsibility for the genuineness, falsification or effect of any document which appears on such examination to be regular on its face.

(3) A non-bank issuer is not bound by any banking usage of which it has no knowledge.

§ 5—110. Availability of Credit in Portions; Presenter's Reservation of Lien or Claim.

(1) Unless otherwise specified a credit may be used in portions in the discretion of the beneficiary.

(2) Unless otherwise specified a person by presenting a documentary draft or demand for payment under a credit relinquishes

upon its honor all claims to the documents and a person by transferring such draft or demand or causing such presentment authorizes such relinquishment. An explicit reservation of claim makes the draft or demand noncomplying.

§ 5—111. Warranties on Transfer and Presentment.

(1) Unless otherwise agreed the beneficiary by transferring or presenting a documentary draft or demand for payment warrants to all interested parties that the necessary conditions of the credit have been complied with. This is in addition to any warranties arising under Articles 3, 4, 7 and 8.

(2) Unless otherwise agreed a negotiating, advising, confirming, collecting or issuing bank presenting or transferring a draft or demand for payment under a credit warrants only the matters warranted by a collecting bank under Article 4 and any such bank transferring a document warrants only the matters warranted by an intermediary under Articles 7 and 8.

§ 5—112. Time Allowed for Honor or Rejection; Withholding Honor or Rejection by Consent; "Presenter".

(1) A bank to which a documentary draft or demand for payment is presented under a credit may without dishonor of the draft, demand or credit

(a) defer honor until the close of the third banking day following receipt of the documents; and

(b) further defer honor if the presenter has expressly or impliedly consented thereto.

Failure to honor within the time here specified constitutes dishonor of the draft or demand and of the credit [except as otherwise provided in subsection (4) of Section 5—114 on conditional payment].

Note: *The bracketed language in the last sentence of subsection (1) should be included only if the optional provisions of Section 5—114(4) and (5) are included.*

(2) Upon dishonor the bank may unless otherwise instructed fulfill its duty to return the draft or demand and the documents by holding them at the disposal of the presenter and sending him an advice to that effect.

(3) "Presenter" means any person presenting a draft or demand for payment for honor under a credit even though that person is a confirming bank or other correspondent which is acting under an issuer's authorization.

§ 5—113. Indemnities.

(1) A bank seeking to obtain (whether for itself or another) honor, negotiation or reimbursement under a credit may give an indemnity to induce such honor, negotiation or reimbursement.

(2) An indemnity agreement inducing honor, negotiation or reimbursement

(a) unless otherwise explicitly agreed applies to defects in the documents but not in the goods; and

(b) unless a longer time is explicitly agreed expires at the end of ten business days following receipt of the documents by the ultimate customer unless notice of objection is sent before such expiration date. The ultimate customer may send notice of objection to the person from whom he received the documents and any bank receiving such notice is under a duty to send notice to its transferor before its midnight deadline.

§ 5—114. Issuer's Duty and Privilege to Honor; Right to Reimbursement.

(1) An issuer must honor a draft or demand for payment which complies with the terms of the relevant credit regardless of whether the goods or documents conform to the underlying contract for sale or other contract between the customer and the beneficiary. The issuer is not excused from honor of such a draft or demand by reason of an additional general term that all documents must be satisfactory to the issuer, but an issuer may require that specified documents must be satisfactory to it.

(2) Unless otherwise agreed when documents appear on their face to comply with the terms of a credit but a required document does not in fact conform to the warranties made on negotiation or transfer of a document of title (Section 7—507) or of a certificated security (Section 8—306) or is forged or fraudulent or there is fraud in the transaction:

(a) the issuer must honor the draft or demand for payment if honor is demanded by a negotiating bank or other holder of the draft or demand which has taken the draft or demand under the credit and under circumstances which would make it a holder in due course (Section 3—302) and in an appropriate case would make it a person to whom a document of title has been duly negotiated (Section 7—502) or a bona fide purchaser of a certificated security (Section 8—302); and

(b) in all other cases as against its customer, an issuer acting in good faith may honor the draft or demand for payment despite notification from the customer of fraud, forgery or other defect not apparent on the face of the documents but a court of appropriate jurisdiction may enjoin such honor.

(3) Unless otherwise agreed an issuer which has duly honored a draft or demand for payment is entitled to immediate reimbursement of any payment made under the credit and to be put in effectively available funds not later than the day before maturity of any acceptance made under the credit.

[(4) When a credit provides for payment by the issuer on receipt of notice that the required documents are in the possession of a correspondent or other agent of the issuer

(a) any payment made on receipt of such notice is conditional; and

(b) the issuer may reject documents which do not comply with the credit if it does so within three banking days following its receipt of the documents; and

(c) in the event of such rejection, the issuer is entitled by charge back or otherwise to return of the payment made.]

[(5) In the case covered by subsection (4) failure to reject documents within the time specified in sub-paragraph (b) constitutes acceptance of the documents and makes the payment final in favor of the beneficiary.]

Note: *Subsections (4) and (5) are bracketed as optional. If they are included the bracketed language in the last sentence of Section 5—112(1) should also be included.*

§ 5—115. Remedy for Improper Dishonor or Anticipatory Repudiation.

(1) When an issuer wrongfully dishonors a draft or demand for payment presented under a credit the person entitled to honor has with respect to any documents the rights of a person in the position of a seller (Section 2—707) and may recover from the issuer the face amount of the draft or demand together with incidental damages under Section 2—710 on seller's incidental damages and interest but less any amount realized by resale or other use or disposition of the subject matter of the transaction. In the event no resale or other utilization is made the documents, goods or other subject matter involved in the transaction must be turned over to the issuer on payment of judgment.

(2) When an issuer wrongfully cancels or otherwise repudiates a credit before presentment of a draft or demand for payment drawn under it the beneficiary has the rights of a seller after anticipatory repudiation by the buyer under Section 2—610 if he learns of the repudiation in time reasonably to avoid procurement of the required documents. Otherwise the beneficiary has an immediate right of action for wrongful dishonor.

§ 5—116. Transfer and Assignment.

(1) The right to draw under a credit can be transferred or assigned only when the credit is expressly designated as transferable or assignable.

(2) Even through the credit specifically states that it is nontransferable or nonassignable the beneficiary may before performance of the conditions of the credit assign his right to proceeds. Such an assignment is an assignment of an account under Article 9 on Secured Transactions and is governed by that Article except that

(a) the assignment is ineffective until the letter of credit or advice of credit is delivered to the assignee which delivery constitutes perfection of the security interest under Article 9; and

(b) the issuer may honor drafts or demands for payment drawn under the credit until it receives a notification of the assignment signed by the beneficiary which reasonably identifies the credit involved in the assignment and contains a request to pay the assignee; and

(c) after what reasonably appears to be such a notification has been received the issuer may without dishonor refuse to accept or pay even to a person otherwise entitled to honor until the letter of credit or advice of credit is exhibited to the issuer.

(3) Except where the beneficiary has effectively assigned his right to draw or his right to proceeds, nothing in this section limits his right to transfer or negotiate drafts or demands drawn under the credit.

§ 5—117. Insolvency of Bank Holding Funds for Documentary Credit.

(1) Where an issuer or an advising or confirming bank or a bank which has for a customer procured issuance of a credit by another bank becomes insolvent before final payment under the credit and the credit is one to which this Article is made applicable by paragraphs (a) or (b) of Section 5—102(1) on scope, the receipt or allocation of funds or collateral to secure or meet obligations under the credit shall have the following results:

(a) to the extent of any funds or collateral turned over after or before the insolvency as indemnity against or specifically for the purpose of payment of drafts or demands for payment drawn under the designated credit, the drafts or demands are entitled to payment in preference over depositors or other general creditors of the issuer or bank; and

(b) on expiration of the credit or surrender of the beneficiary's rights under it unused any person who has given such funds or collateral is similarly entitled to return thereof; and

(c) a charge to a general or current account with a bank if specifically consented to for the purpose of indemnity against or payment of drafts or demands for payment drawn under the designated credit falls under the same rules as if the funds had been drawn out in cash and then turned over with specific instructions.

(2) After honor or reimbursement under this section the customer or other person for whose account the insolvent bank has acted is entitled to receive the documents involved.

Article 6
BULK TRANSFERS

§ 6—101. Short Title.

This Article shall be known and may be cited as Uniform Commercial Code—Bulk Transfers.

§ 6—102. "Bulk Transfers"; Transfers of Equipment; Enterprises Subject to This Article; Bulk Transfers Subject to This Article.

(1) A "bulk transfer" is any transfer in bulk and not in the ordinary course of the transferor's business of a major part of the materials, supplies, merchandise or other inventory (Section 9—109) of an enterprise subject to this Article.

(2) A transfer of a substantial part of the equipment (Section 9—109) of such an enterprise is a bulk transfer if it is made in connection with a bulk transfer of inventory, but not otherwise.

(3) The enterprises subject to this Article are all those whose principal business is the sale of merchandise from stock, including those who manufacture what they sell.

(4) Except as limited by the following section all bulk transfers of goods located within this state are subject to this Article.

§ 6—103. **Transfers Excepted From This Article.**

The following transfers are not subject to this Article:

(1) Those made to give security for the performance of an obligation;

(2) General assignments for the benefit of all the creditors of the transferor, and subsequent transfers by the assignee thereunder;

(3) Transfers in settlement or realization of a lien or other security interests;

(4) Sales by executors, administrators, receivers, trustees in bankruptcy, or any public officer under judicial process;

(5) Sales made in the course of judicial or administrative proceedings for the dissolution or reorganization of a corporation and of which notice is sent to the creditors of the corporation pursuant to order of the court or administrative agency;

(6) Transfers to a person maintaining a known place of business in this State who becomes bound to pay the debts of the transferor in full and gives public notice of that fact, and who is solvent after becoming so bound;

(7) A transfer to a new business enterprise organized to take over and continue the business, if public notice of the transaction is given and the new enterprise assumes the debts of the transferor and he receives nothing from the transaction except an interest in the new enterprise junior to the claims of creditors;

(8) Transfers of property which is exempt from execution.

Public notice under subsection (6) or subsection (7) may be given by publishing once a week for two consecutive weeks in a newspaper of general circulation where the transferor had its principal place of business in this state an advertisement including the names and addresses of the transferor and transferee and the effective date of the transfer.

§ 6—104. **Schedule of Property, List of Creditors.**

(1) Except as provided with respect to auction sales (Section 6—108), a bulk transfer subject to this Article is ineffective against any creditor of the transferor unless:

(a) The transferee requires the transferor to furnish a list of his existing creditors prepared as stated in this section; and

(b) The parties prepare a schedule of the property transferred sufficient to identify it; and

(c) The transferee preserves the list and schedule for six months next following the transfer and permits inspection of either or both and copying therefrom at all reasonable hours by any creditor of the transferor, or files the list and schedule in (a public office to be here identified).

(2) The list of creditors must be signed and sworn to or affirmed by the transferor or his agent. It must contain the names and business addresses of all creditors of the transferor, with the amounts when known, and also the names of all persons who are known to the transferor to assert claims against him even though such claims are disputed. If the transferor is the obligor of an outstanding issue of bonds, debentures or the like as to which there is an indenture trustee, the list of creditors need include only the name and address of the indenture trustee and the aggregate outstanding principal amount of the issue.

(3) Responsibility for the completeness and accuracy of the list of creditors rests on the transferor, and the transfer is not rendered ineffective by errors or omissions therein unless the transferee is shown to have had knowledge.

§ 6—105. **Notice to Creditors.**

In addition to the requirements of the preceding section, any bulk transfer subject to this Article except one made by auction sale (Section 6—108) is ineffective against any creditor of the transferor unless at least ten days before he takes possession of the goods or pays for them, whichever happens first, the transferee gives notice of the transfer in the manner and to the persons hereafter provided (Section 6—107).

[§ 6—106. **Application of the Proceeds.**

In addition to the requirements of the two preceding sections:
(1) Upon every bulk transfer subject to this Article for which new consideration becomes payable except those made by sale at auction it is the duty of the transferee to assure that such consideration is applied so far as necessary to pay those debts of the transferor which are either shown on the list furnished by the transferor (Section 6—104) or filed in writing in the place stated in the notice (Section 6—107) within thirty days after the mailing of such notice. This duty of the transferee runs to all the holders of such debts, and may be enforced by any of them for the benefit of all.

(2) If any of said debts are in dispute the necessary sum may be withheld from distribution until the dispute is settled or adjudicated.

(3) If the consideration payable is not enough to pay all of the said debts in full distribution shall be made pro rata.]

Note: *This section is bracketed to indicate division of opinion as to whether or not it is a wise provision, and to suggest that this is a point on which State enactments may differ without serious damage to the principle of uniformity. In any State where this section is omitted, the following parts of sections, also bracketed in the text, should also be omitted, namely:*
        Section 6—107(2)(e).
                6—108(3)(c).
                6—109(2).
    In any State where this section is enacted, these other provisions should be also.

Optional Subsection (4)

[(4) The transferee may within ten days after he takes possession of the goods pay the consideration into the (specify court) in the county where the transferor had its principal place of business in this state and thereafter may discharge his duty under this section by giving notice by registered or certified mail to all the persons to whom the duty runs that the consideration has been paid into that court and that they should file their claims there. On motion of any interested party, the court may order the distribution of the consideration to the persons entitled to it.]

Note: *Optional subsection (4) is recommended for those states which do not have a general statute providing for payment of money into court.*

§ 6—107. The Notice.

(1) The notice to creditors (Section 6—105) shall state:

(a) that a bulk transfer is about to be made; and

(b) the names and business addresses of the transferor and transferee, and all other business names and addresses used by the transferor within three years last past so far as known to the transferee; and

(c) whether or not all the debts of the transferor are to be paid in full as they fall due as a result of the transaction, and if so, the address to which creditors should send their bills.

(2) If the debts of the transferor are not to be paid in full as they fall due or if the transferee is in doubt on that point then the notice shall state further:

(a) the location and general description of the property to be transferred and the estimated total of the transferor's debts;

(b) the address where the schedule of property and list of creditors (Section 6—104) may be inspected;

(c) whether the transfer is to pay existing debts and if so the amount of such debts and to whom owing;

(d) whether the transfer is for new consideration and if so the amount of such consideration and the time and place of payment; [and]

[(e) if for new consideration the time and place where creditors of the transferor are to file their claims.]

(3) The notice in any case shall be delivered personally or sent by registered or certified mail to all the persons shown on the list of creditors furnished by the transferor (Section 6—104) and to all other persons who are known to the transferee to hold or assert claims against the transferor.

§ 6—108. Auction Sales; "Auctioneer".

(1) A bulk transfer is subject to this Article even though it is by sale at auction, but only in the manner and with the results stated in this section.

(2) The transferor shall furnish a list of his creditors and assist in the preparation of a schedule of the property to be sold, both prepared as before stated (Section 6—104).

(3) The person or persons other than the transferor who direct, control or are responsible for the auction are collectively called the "auctioneer". The auctioneer shall:

(a) receive and retain the list of creditors and prepare and retain the schedule of property for the period stated in this Article (Section 6—104);

(b) give notice of the auction personally or by registered or certified mail at least ten days before it occurs to all persons shown on the list of creditors and to all other persons who are known to him to hold or assert claims against the transferor; [and]

[(c) assure that the net proceeds of the auction are applied as provided in this Article (Section 6—106).]

(4) Failure of the auctioneer to perform any of these duties does not affect the validity of the sale or the title of the purchasers, but if the auctioneer knows that the auction constitutes a bulk transfer such failure renders the auctioneer liable to the creditors of the transferor as a class for the sums owing to them from the transferor up to but not exceeding the net proceeds of the auction. If the auctioneer consists of several persons their liability is joint and several.

§ 6—109. What Creditors Protected; [Credit for Payment to Particular Creditors].

(1) The creditors of the transferor mentioned in this Article are those holding claims based on transactions or events occurring before the bulk transfer, but creditors who become such after notice to creditors is given (Sections 6—105 and 6—107) are not entitled to notice.

[(2) Against the aggregate obligation imposed by the provisions of this Article concerning the application of the proceeds (Section 6—106 and subsection (3)(c) of 6—108) the transferee or auctioneer is entitled to credit for sums paid to particular creditors of the transferor, not exceeding the sums believed in good faith at the time of the payment to be properly payable to such creditors.]

§ 6—110. Subsequent Transfers.

When the title of a transferee to property is subject to a defect by reason of his noncompliance with the requirements of this Article, then:

(1) a purchaser of any of such property from such transferee who pays no value or who takes with notice of such noncompliance takes subject to such defect, but

(2) a purchaser for value in good faith and without such notice takes free of such defect.

§ 6—111. Limitation of Actions and Levies.

No action under this Article shall be brought nor levy made more than six months after the date on which the transferee took possession of the goods unless the transfer has been concealed. If the transfer has been concealed, actions may be brought or levies made within six months after its discovery.

Note to Article 6: *Section 6—106 is bracketed to indicate division of opinion as to whether or not it is a wise provision, and to suggest that this is a point on which State enactments may differ without serious damage to the principle of uniformity.*

In any State where Section 6—106 is not enacted, the following parts of sections, also bracketed in the text, should also be omitted, namely:
Sec. 6—107(2)(e).
    6—108(3)(c).
    6—109(2).
In any State where Section 6—106 is enacted, these other provisions should be also.

Article 7
Warehouse Receipts, Bills of Lading and Other Documents of Title

Part 1 General

§ 7—101. **Short Title.**

This Article shall be known and may be cited as Uniform Commercial Code—Documents of Title.

§ 7—102. **Definitions and Index of Definitions.**

(1) In this Article, unless the context otherwise requires:

(a) "Bailee" means the person who by a warehouse receipt, bill of lading or other document of title acknowledges possession of goods and contracts to deliver them.

(b) "Consignee" means the person named in a bill to whom or to whose order the bill promises delivery.

(c) "Consignor" means the person named in a bill as the person from whom the goods have been received for shipment.

(d) "Delivery order" means a written order to deliver goods directed to a warehouseman, carrier or other person who in the ordinary course of business issues warehouse receipts or bills of lading.

(e) "Document" means document of title as defined in the general definitions in Article 1 (Section 1—201).

(f) "Goods" means all things which are treated as movable for the purposes of a contract of storage or transportation.

(g) "Issuer" means a bailee who issues a document except that in relation to an unaccepted delivery order it means the person who orders the possessor of goods to deliver. Issuer includes any person for whom an agent or employee purports to act in issuing a document if the agent or employee has real or apparent authority to issue documents, notwithstanding that the issuer received no goods or that the goods were misdescribed or that in any other respect the agent or employee violated his instructions.

(h) "Warehouseman" is a person engaged in the business of storing goods for hire.

(2) Other definitions applying to this Article or to specified Parts thereof, and the sections in which they appear are:
"Duly negotiate". Section 7—501.

"Person entitled under the document". Section 7—403(4).

(3) Definitions in other Articles applying to this Article and the sections in which they appear are:
"Contract for sale". Section 2—106.
"Overseas". Section 2—323.
"Receipt" of goods. Section 2—103.

(4) In addition Article 1 contains general definitions and principles of construction and interpretation applicable throughout this Article.

§ 7—103. **Relation of Article to Treaty, Statute, Tariff, Classification or Regulation.**

To the extent that any treaty or statute of the United States, regulatory statute of this State or tariff, classification or regulation filed or issued pursuant thereto is applicable, the provisions of this Article are subject thereto.

§ 7—104. **Negotiable and Nonnegotiable Warehouse Receipt, Bill of Lading or Other Document of Title.**

(1) A warehouse receipt, bill of lading or other document of title is negotiable

(a) if by its terms the goods are to be delivered to bearer or to the order of a named person; or

(b) where recognized in overseas trade, if it runs to a named person or assigns.

(2) Any other document is nonnegotiable. A bill of lading in which it is stated that the goods are consigned to a named person is not made negotiable by a provision that the goods are to be delivered only against a written order signed by the same or another named person.

§ 7—105. **Construction Against Negative Implication.**

The omission from either Part 2 or Part 3 of this Article of a provision corresponding to a provision made in the other Part does not imply that a corresponding rule of law is not applicable.

Part 2 Warehouse Receipts: Special Provisions

§ 7—201. **Who May Issue a Warehouse Receipt; Storage Under Government Bond.**

(1) A warehouse receipt may be issued by any warehouseman.

(2) Where goods including distilled spirits and agricultural commodities are stored under a statute requiring a bond against withdrawal or a license for the issuance of receipts in the nature of warehouse receipts, a receipt issued for the goods has like effect as a warehouse receipt even though issued by a person who is the owner of the goods and is not a warehouseman.

§ 7—202. **Form of Warehouse Receipt; Essential Terms; Optional Terms.**

(1) A warehouse receipt need not be in any particular form.

(2) Unless a warehouse receipt embodies within its written or printed terms each of the following, the warehouseman is liable for damages caused by the omission to a person injured thereby:

(a) the location of the warehouse where the goods are stored;

(b) the date of issue of the receipt;

(c) the consecutive number of the receipt;

(d) a statement whether the goods received will be delivered to the bearer, to a specified person, or to a specified person or his order;

(e) the rate of storage and handling charges, except that where goods are stored under a field warehousing arrangement a statement of that fact is sufficient on a nonnegotiable receipt;

(f) a description of the goods or of the packages containing them;

(g) the signature of the warehouseman, which may be made by his authorized agent;

(h) if the receipt is issued for goods of which the warehouseman is owner, either solely or jointly or in common with others, the fact of such ownership; and

(i) a statement of the amount of advances made and of liabilities incurred for which the warehouseman claims a lien or security interest (Section 7—209). If the precise amount of such advances made or of such liabilities incurred is, at the time of the issue of the receipt, unknown to the warehouseman or to his agent who issues it, a statement of the fact that advances have been made or liabilities incurred and the purpose thereof is sufficient.

(3) A warehouseman may insert in his receipt any other terms which are not contrary to the provisions of this Act and do not impair his obligation of delivery (Section 7—403) or his duty of care (Section 7—204). Any contrary provisions shall be ineffective.

§ 7—203. Liability for Nonreceipt or Misdescription.

A party to or purchaser for value in good faith of a document of title other than a bill of lading relying in either case upon the description therein of the goods may recover from the issuer damages caused by the nonreceipt or misdescription of the goods, except to the extent that the document conspicuously indicates that the issuer does not know whether any part or all of the goods in fact were received or conform to the description, as where the description is in terms of marks or labels or kind, quantity or condition, or the receipt or description is qualified by "contents, condition and quality unknown", "said to contain" or the like, if such indication be true, or the party or purchaser otherwise has notice.

§ 7—204. Duty of Care; Contractual Limitation of Warehouseman's Liability.

(1) A warehouseman is liable for damages for loss of or injury to the goods caused by his failure to exercise such care in regard to them as a reasonably careful man would exercise under like circumstances but unless otherwise agreed he is not liable for damages which could not have been avoided by the exercise of such care.

(2) Damages may be limited by a term in the warehouse receipt or storage agreement limiting the amount of liability in case of loss or damage, and setting forth a specific liability per article or item, or value per unit of weight, beyond which the warehouseman shall not be liable; provided, however, that such liability may on written request of the bailor at the time of signing such storage agreement or within a reasonable time after receipt of the warehouse receipt be increased on part or all of the goods thereunder, in which event increased rates may be charged based on such increased valuation, but that no such increase shall be permitted contrary to a lawful limitation of liability contained in the warehouseman's tariff, if any. No such limitation is effective with respect to the warehouseman's liability for conversion to his own use.

(3) Reasonable provisions as to the time and manner of presenting claims and instituting actions based on the bailment may be included in the warehouse receipt or tariff.

(4) This section does not impair or repeal . . .

Note: *Insert in subsection (4)* a reference to any statute which imposes a higher responsibility upon the warehouseman or invalidates contractual limitations which would be permissible under this Article.

§ 7—205. Title Under Warehouse Receipt Defeated in Certain Cases.

A buyer in the ordinary course of business of fungible goods sold and delivered by a warehouseman who is also in the business of buying and selling such goods takes free of any claim under a warehouse receipt even though it has been duly negotiated.

§ 7—206. Termination of Storage at Warehouseman's Option.

(1) A warehouseman may on notifying the person on whose account the goods are held and any other person known to claim an interest in the goods require payment of any charges and removal of the goods from the warehouse at the termination of the period of storage fixed by the document, or, if no period is fixed, within a stated period not less than thirty days after the notification. If the goods are not removed before the date specified in the notification, the warehouseman may sell them in accordance with the provisions of the section on enforcement of a warehouseman's lien (Section 7—210).

(2) If a warehouseman in good faith believes that the goods are about to deteriorate or decline in value to less than the amount of his lien within the time prescribed in subsection (1) for notification, advertisement and sale, the warehouseman may specify in the notification any reasonable shorter time for removal of the goods and in case the goods are not removed, may sell them at public sale held not less than one week after a single advertisement or posting.

(3) If as a result of a quality or condition of the goods of which the warehouseman had no notice at the time of deposit the goods are a hazard to other property or to the warehouse or to persons, the warehouseman may sell the goods at public or private sale without advertisement on reasonable notification to all persons

known to claim an interest in the goods. If the warehouseman after a reasonable effort is unable to sell the goods he may dispose of them in any lawful manner and shall incur no liability by reason of such disposition.

(4) The warehouseman must deliver the goods to any person entitled to them under this Article upon due demand made at any time prior to sale or other disposition under this section.

(5) The warehouseman may satisfy his lien from the proceeds of any sale or disposition under this section but must hold the balance for delivery on the demand of any person to whom he would have been bound to deliver the goods.

§ 7—207. **Goods Must Be Kept Separate; Fungible Goods.**

(1) Unless the warehouse receipt otherwise provides, a warehouseman must keep separate the goods covered by each receipt so as to permit at all times identification and delivery of those goods except that different lots of fungible goods may be commingled.

(2) Fungible goods so commingled are owned in common by the persons entitled thereto and the warehouseman is severally liable to each owner for that owner's share. Where because of overissue a mass of fungible goods is insufficient to meet all the receipts which the warehouseman has issued against it, the persons entitled include all holders to whom overissued receipts have been duly negotiated.

§ 7—208. **Altered Warehouse Receipts.**

Where a blank in a negotiable warehouse receipt has been filled in without authority, a purchaser for value and without notice of the want of authority may treat the insertion as authorized. Any other unauthorized alteration leaves any receipt enforceable against the issuer according to its original tenor.

§ 7—209. **Lien of Warehouseman.**

(1) A warehouseman has a lien against the bailor on the goods covered by a warehouse receipt or on the proceeds thereof in his possession for charges for storage or transportation (including demurrage and terminal charges), insurance, labor, or charges present or future in relation to the goods, and for expenses necessary for preservation of the goods or reasonably incurred in their sale pursuant to law. If the person on whose account the goods are held is liable for like charges or expenses in relation to other goods whenever deposited and it is stated in the receipt that a lien is claimed for charges and expenses in relation to other goods, the warehouseman also has a lien against him for such charges and expenses whether or not the other goods have been delivered by the warehouseman. But against a person to whom a negotiable warehouse receipt is duly negotiated a warehouseman's lien is limited to charges in an amount or at a rate specified on the receipt or if no charges are so specified then to a reasonable charge for storage of the goods covered by the receipt subsequent to the date of the receipt.

(2) The warehouseman may also reserve a security interest against the bailor for a maximum amount specified on the receipt for charges other than those specified in subsection (1), such as for money advanced and interest. Such a security interest is governed by the Article on Secured Transactions (Article 9).

(3) (a) A warehouseman's lien for charges and expenses under subsection (1) or a security interest under subsection (2) is also effective against any person who so entrusted the bailor with possession of the goods that a pledge of them by him to a good faith purchaser for value would have been valid but is not effective against a person as to whom the document confers no right in the goods covered by it under Section 7—503.

(b) A warehouseman's lien on household goods for charges and expenses in relation to the goods under subsection (1) is also effective against all persons if the depositor was the legal possessor of the goods at the time of deposit. "Household goods" means furniture, furnishings and personal effects used by the depositor in a dwelling.

(4) A warehouseman loses his lien on any goods which he voluntarily delivers or which he unjustifiably refuses to deliver.

§ 7—210. **Enforcement of Warehouseman's Lien.**

(1) Except as provided in subsection (2), a warehouseman's lien may be enforced by public or private sale of the goods in bloc or in parcels, at any time or place and on any terms which are commercially reasonable, after notifying all persons known to claim an interest in the goods. Such notification must include a statement of the amount due, the nature of the proposed sale and the time and place of any public sale. The fact that a better price could have been obtained by a sale at a different time or in a different method from that selected by the warehouseman is not of itself sufficient to establish that the sale was not made in a commercially reasonable manner. If the warehouseman either sells the goods in the usual manner in any recognized market therefor, or if he sells at the price current in such market at the time of his sale, or if he has otherwise sold in conformity with commercially reasonable practices among dealers in the type of goods sold, he has sold in a commercially reasonable manner. A sale of more goods than apparently necessary to be offered to ensure satisfaction of the obligation is not commercially reasonable except in cases covered by the preceding sentence.

(2) A warehouseman's lien on goods other than goods stored by a merchant in the course of his business may be enforced only as follows:

(a) All persons known to claim an interest in the goods must be notified.

(b) The notification must be delivered in person or sent by registered or certified letter to the last known address of any person to be notified.

(c) The notification must include an itemized statement of the claim, a description of the goods subject to the lien, a demand for payment within a specified time not less than ten days after receipt of the notification, and a conspicuous statement that unless the claim is paid within the time the goods will be advertised for sale and sold by auction at a specified time and place.

(d) The sale must conform to the terms of the notification.

(e) The sale must be held at the nearest suitable place to that where the goods are held or stored.

(f) After the expiration of the time given in the notification, an advertisement of the sale must be published once a week for two weeks consecutively in a newspaper of general circulation where the sale is to be held. The advertisement must include a description of the goods, the name of the person on whose account they are being held, and the time and place of the sale. The sale must take place at least fifteen days after the first publication. If there is no newspaper of general circulation where the sale is to be held, the advertisement must be posted at least ten days before the sale in not less than six conspicuous places in the neighborhood of the proposed sale.

(3) Before any sale pursuant to this section any person claiming a right in the goods may pay the amount necessary to satisfy the lien and the reasonable expenses incurred under this section. In that event the goods must not be sold, but must be retained by the warehouseman subject to the terms of the receipt and this Article.

(4) The warehouseman may buy at any public sale pursuant to this section.

(5) A purchaser in good faith of goods sold to enforce a warehouseman's lien takes the goods free of any rights of persons against whom the lien was valid, despite noncompliance by the warehouseman with the requirements of this section.

(6) The warehouseman may satisfy his lien from the proceeds of any sale pursuant to this section but must hold the balance, if any, for delivery on demand to any person to whom he would have been bound to deliver the goods.

(7) The rights provided by this section shall be in addition to all other rights allowed by law to a creditor against his debtor.

(8) Where a lien is on goods stored by a merchant in the course of his business the lien may be enforced in accordance with either subsection (1) or (2).

(9) The warehouseman is liable for damages caused by failure to comply with the requirements for sale under this section and in case of willful violation is liable for conversion.

Part 3 Bills of Lading: Special Provisions

§ 7—301. Liability for Nonreceipt or Misdescription; "Said to Contain"; "Shipper's Load and Count"; Improper Handling.

(1) A consignee of a nonnegotiable bill who has given value in good faith or a holder to whom a negotiable bill has been duly negotiated relying in either case upon the description therein of the goods, or upon the date therein shown, may recover from the issuer damages caused by the misdating of the bill or the nonreceipt or misdescription of the goods, except to the extent that the document indicates that the issuer does not know whether any part of all of the goods in fact were received or conform to the description, as where the description is in terms of marks or labels or kind, quantity, or condition or the receipt or description is qualified by "contents or condition of contents of packages unknown", "said to contain", "shipper's weight, load and count" or the like, if such indication be true.

(2) When goods are loaded by an issuer who is a common carrier, the issuer must count the packages of goods if package freight and ascertain the kind and quantity if bulk freight. In such cases "shipper's weight, load and count" or other words indicating that the description was made by the shipper are ineffective except as to freight concealed by packages.

(3) When bulk freight is loaded by a shipper who makes available to the issuer adequate facilities for weighing such freight, an issuer who is a common carrier must ascertain the kind and quantity within a reasonable time after receiving the written request of the shipper to do so. In such cases "shipper's weight" or other words of like purport are ineffective.

(4) The issuer may by inserting in the bill the words "shipper's weight, load and count" or other words of like purport indicate that the goods were loaded by the shipper; and if such statement be true the issuer shall not be liable for damages caused by the improper loading. But their omission does not imply liability for such damages.

(5) The shipper shall be deemed to have guaranteed to the issuer the accuracy at the time of shipment of the description, marks, labels, number, kind, quantity, condition and weight, as furnished by him; and the shipper shall indemnify the issuer against damage caused by inaccuracies in such particulars. The right of the issuer to such indemnity shall in no way limit his responsibility and liability under the contract of carriage to any person other than the shipper.

§ 7—302. Through Bills of Lading and Similar Documents.

(1) The issuer of a through bill of lading or other document embodying an undertaking to be performed in part by persons acting as its agents or by connecting carriers is liable to anyone entitled to recover on the document for any breach by such other persons or by a connecting carrier of its obligation under the document but to the extent that the bill covers an undertaking to be performed overseas or in territory not contiguous to the continental United States or an undertaking including matters other than transportation this liability may be varied by agreement of the parties.

(2) Where goods covered by a through bill of lading or other document embodying an undertaking to be performed in part by persons other than the issuer are received by any such person, he is subject with respect to his own performance while the goods are in his possession to the obligation of the issuer. His obligation is discharged by delivery of the goods to another such person

pursuant to the document, and does not include liability for breach by any other such persons or by the issuer.

(3) The issuer of such through bill of lading or other document shall be entitled to recover from the connecting carrier or such other person in possession of the goods when the breach of the obligation under the document occurred, the amount it may be required to pay to anyone entitled to recover on the document therefor, as may be evidenced by any receipt, judgment, or transcript thereof, and the amount of any expense reasonably incurred by it in defending any action brought by anyone entitled to recover on the document therefor.

§ 7—303. Diversion; Reconsignment; Change of Instructions.

(1) Unless the bill of lading otherwise provides, the carrier may deliver the goods to a person or destination other than that stated in the bill or may otherwise dispose of the goods on instructions from

(a) the holder of a negotiable bill; or

(b) the consignor on a nonnegotiable bill notwithstanding contrary instructions from the consignee; or

(c) the consignee on a nonnegotiable bill in the absence of contrary instructions from the consignor, if the goods have arrived at the billed destination or if the consignee is in possession of the bill; or

(d) the consignee on a nonnegotiable bill if he is entitled as against the consignor to dispose of them.

(2) Unless such instructions are noted on a negotiable bill of lading, a person to whom the bill is duly negotiated can hold the bailee according to the original terms.

§ 7—304. Bills of Lading in a Set.

(1) Except where customary in overseas transportation, a bill of lading must not be issued in a set of parts. The issuer is liable for damages caused by violation of this subsection.

(2) Where a bill of lading is lawfully drawn in a set of parts, each of which is numbered and expressed to be valid only if the goods have not been delivered against any other part, the whole of the parts constitute one bill.

(3) Where a bill of lading is lawfully issued in a set of parts and different parts are negotiated to different persons, the title of the holder to whom the first due negotiation is made prevails as to both the document and the goods even though any later holder may have received the goods from the carrier in good faith and discharged the carrier's obligation by surrender of his part.

(4) Any person who negotiates or transfers a single part of a bill of lading drawn in a set is liable to holders of that part as if it were the whole set.

(5) The bailee is obliged to deliver in accordance with Part 4 of this Article against the first presented part of a bill of lading lawfully drawn in a set. Such delivery discharges the bailee's obligation on the whole bill.

§ 7—305. Destination Bills.

(1) Instead of issuing a bill of lading to the consignor at the place of shipment a carrier may at the request of the consignor procure the bill to be issued at destination or at any other place designated in the request.

(2) Upon request of anyone entitled as against the carrier to control the goods while in transit and on surrender of any outstanding bill of lading or other receipt covering such goods, the issuer may procure a substitute bill to be issued at any place designated in the request.

§ 7—306. Altered Bills of Lading.

An unauthorized alteration or filling in of a blank in a bill of lading leaves the bill enforceable according to its original tenor.

§ 7—307. Lien of Carrier.

(1) A carrier has a lien on the goods covered by a bill of lading for charges subsequent to the date of its receipt of the goods for storage or transportation (including demurrage and terminal charges) and for expenses necessary for preservation of the goods incident to their transportation or reasonably incurred in their sale pursuant to law. But against a purchaser for value of a negotiable bill of lading a carrier's lien is limited to charges stated in the bill or the applicable tariffs, or if no charges are stated then to a reasonable charge.

(2) A lien for charges and expenses under subsection (1) on goods which the carrier was required by law to receive for transportation is effective against the consignor or any person entitled to the goods unless the carrier had notice that the consignor lacked authority to subject the goods to such charges and expenses. Any other lien under subsection (1) is effective against the consignor and any person who permitted the bailor to have control or possession of the goods unless the carrier had notice that the bailor lacked such authority.

(3) A carrier loses his lien on any goods which he voluntarily delivers or which he unjustifiably refuses to deliver.

§ 7—308. Enforcement of Carrier's Lien.

(1) A carrier's lien may be enforced by public or private sale of the goods, in bloc or in parcels, at any time or place and on any terms which are commercially reasonable, after notifying all persons known to claim an interest in the goods. Such notification must include a statement of the amount due, the nature of the proposed sale and the time and place of any public sale. The fact that a better price could have been obtained by a sale at a different time or in a different method from that selected by the carrier is not of itself sufficient to establish that the sale was not made in a commercially reasonable manner. If the carrier either sells the goods in the usual manner in any recognized market therefor or if he sells at the price current in such market at the time of his sale or if he has otherwise sold in conformity with commercially reasonable practices among dealers in the type of goods sold he has sold in a commercially reasonable manner. A sale of more

goods than apparently necessary to be offered to ensure satisfaction of the obligation is not commercially reasonable except in cases covered by the preceding sentence.

(2) Before any sale pursuant to this section any person claiming a right in the goods may pay the amount necessary to satisfy the lien and the reasonable expenses incurred under this section. In that event the goods must not be sold, but must be retained by the carrier subject to the terms of the bill and this Article.

(3) The carrier may buy at any public sale pursuant to this section.

(4) A purchaser in good faith of goods sold to enforce a carrier's lien takes the goods free of any rights of persons against whom the lien was valid, despite noncompliance by the carrier with the requirements of this section.

(5) The carrier may satisfy his lien from the proceeds of any sale pursuant to this section but must hold the balance, if any, for delivery on demand to any person to whom he would have been bound to deliver the goods.

(6) The rights provided by this section shall be in addition to all other rights allowed by law to a creditor against his debtor.

(7) A carrier's lien may be enforced in accordance with either subsection (1) or the procedure set forth in subsection (2) of Section 7—210.

(8) The carrier is liable for damages caused by failure to comply with the requirements for sale under this section and in case of willful violation is liable for conversion.

§ 7—309. Duty of Care; Contractual Limitation of Carrier's Liability.

(1) A carrier who issues a bill of lading whether negotiable or nonnegotiable must exercise the degree of care in relation to the goods which a reasonably careful man would exercise under like circumstances. This subsection does not repeal or change any law or rule of law which imposes liability upon a common carrier for damages not caused by its negligence.

(2) Damages may be limited by a provision that the carrier's liability shall not exceed a value stated in the document if the carrier's rates are dependent upon value and the consignor by the carrier's tariff is afforded an opportunity to declare a higher value or a value as lawfully provided in the tariff, or where no tariff is filed he is otherwise advised of such opportunity; but no such limitation is effective with respect to the carrier's liability for conversion to its own use.

(3) Reasonable provisions as to the time and manner of presenting claims and instituting actions based on the shipment may be included in a bill of lading or tariff.

Part 4 Warehouse Receipts and Bills of Lading: General Obligations

§ 7—401. Irregularities in Issue of Receipt or Bill or Conduct of Issuer.

The obligations imposed by this Article on an issuer apply to a document of title regardless of the fact that

(a) the document may not comply with the requirements of this Article or of any other law or regulation regarding its issue, form or content; or

(b) the issuer may have violated laws regulating the conduct of his business; or

(c) the goods covered by the document were owned by the bailee at the time the document was issued; or

(d) the person issuing the document does not come within the definition of warehouseman if it purports to be a warehouse receipt.

§ 7—402. Duplicate Receipt or Bill; Overissue.

Neither a duplicate nor any other document of title purporting to cover goods already represented by an outstanding document of the same issuer confers any right in the goods, except as provided in the case of bills in a set, overissue of documents for fungible goods and substitutes for lost, stolen or destroyed documents. But the issuer is liable for damages caused by his overissue or failure to identify a duplicate document as such by conspicuous notation on its face.

§ 7—403. Obligation of Warehouseman or Carrier to Deliver; Excuse.

(1) The bailee must deliver the goods to a person entitled under the document who complies with subsections (2) and (3), unless and to the extent that the bailee establishes any of the following:

(a) delivery of the goods to a person whose receipt was rightful as against the claimant;

(b) damage to or delay, loss or destruction of the goods for which the bailee is not liable [, but the burden of establishing negligence in such cases is on the person entitled under the document];

Note: *The brackets in (1)(b) indicate that State enactments may differ on this point without serious damage to the principle of uniformity.*

(c) previous sale or other disposition of the goods in lawful enforcement of a lien or on warehouseman's lawful termination of storage;

(d) the exercise by a seller of his right to stop delivery pursuant to the provisions of the Article on Sales (Section 2—705);

(e) a diversion, reconsignment or other disposition pursuant to the provisions of this Article (Section 7—303) or tariff regulating such right;

(f) release, satisfaction or any other fact affording a personal defense against the claimant;

(g) any other lawful excuse.

(2) A person claiming goods covered by a document of title must satisfy the bailee's lien where the bailee so requests or where the bailee is prohibited by law from delivering the goods until the charges are paid.

(3) Unless the person claiming is one against whom the document confers no right under Sec. 7—503(1), he must surrender for

cancellation or notation of partial deliveries any outstanding negotiable document covering the goods, and the bailee must cancel the document or conspicuously note the partial delivery thereon or be liable to any person to whom the document is duly negotiated.

(4) "Person entitled under the document" means holder in the case of a negotiable document, or the person to whom delivery is to be made by the terms of or pursuant to written instructions under a nonnegotiable document.

§ 7—404. No Liability for Good Faith Delivery Pursuant to Receipt or Bill.

A bailee who in good faith including observance of reasonable commercial standards has received goods and delivered or otherwise disposed of them according to the terms of the document of title or pursuant to this Article is not liable therefor. This rule applies even though the person from whom he received the goods had no authority to procure the document or to dispose of the goods and even though the person to whom he delivered the goods had no authority to receive them.

Part 5 Warehouse Receipts and Bills of Lading: Negotiation and Transfer

§ 7—501. Form of Negotiation and Requirements of "Due Negotiation".

(1) A negotiable document of title running to the order of a named person is negotiated by his indorsement and delivery. After his indorsement in blank or to bearer any person can negotiate it by delivery alone.

(2) (a) A negotiable document of title is also negotiated by delivery alone when by its original terms it runs to bearer.

(b) When a document running to the order of a named person is delivered to him the effect is the same as if the document had been negotiated.

(3) Negotiation of a negotiable document of title after it has been indorsed to a specified person requires indorsement by the special indorsee as well as delivery.

(4) A negotiable document of title is "duly negotiated" when it is negotiated in the manner stated in this section to a holder who purchases it in good faith without notice of any defense against or claim to it on the part of any person and for value, unless it is established that the negotiation is not in the regular course of business or financing or involves receiving the document in settlement or payment of a money obligation.

(5) Indorsement of a nonnegotiable document neither makes it negotiable nor adds to the transferee's rights.

(6) The naming in a negotiable bill of a person to be notified of the arrival of the goods does not limit the negotiability of the bill nor constitute notice to a purchaser thereof of any interest of such person in the goods.

§ 7—502. Rights Acquired by Due Negotiation.

(1) Subject to the following section and to the provisions of Section 7—205 on fungible goods, a holder to whom a negotiable document of title has been duly negotiated acquires thereby:

(a) title to the document;

(b) title to the goods;

(c) all rights accruing under the law of agency or estoppel, including rights to goods delivered to the bailee after the document was issued; and

(d) the direct obligation of the issuer to hold or deliver the goods according to the terms of the document free of any defense or claim by him except those arising under the terms of the document or under this Article. In the case of a delivery order the bailee's obligation accrues only upon acceptance and the obligation acquired by the holder is that the issuer and any indorser will procure the acceptance of the bailee.

(2) Subject to the following section, title and rights so acquired are not defeated by any stoppage of the goods represented by the document or by surrender of such goods by the bailee, and are not impaired even though the negotiation or any prior negotiation constituted a breach of duty or even though any person has been deprived of possession of the document by misrepresentation, fraud, accident, mistake, duress, loss, theft or conversion, or even though a previous sale or other transfer of the goods or document has been made to a third person.

§ 7—503. Document of Title to Goods Defeated in Certain Cases.

(1) A document of title confers no right in goods against a person who before issuance of the document had a legal interest or a perfected security interest in them and who neither

(a) delivered or entrusted them or any document of title covering them to the bailor or his nominee with actual or apparent authority to ship, store or sell or with power to obtain delivery under this Article (Section 7—403) or with power of disposition under this Act (Sections 2—403 and 9—307) or other statute or rule of law; nor

(b) acquiesced in the procurement by the bailor or his nominee of any document of title.

(2) Title to goods based upon an unaccepted delivery order is subject to the rights of anyone to whom a negotiable warehouse receipt or bill of lading covering the goods has been duly negotiated. Such a title may be defeated under the next section to the same extent as the rights of the issuer or a transferee from the issuer.

(3) Title to goods based upon a bill of lading issued to a freight forwarder is subject to the rights of anyone to whom a bill issued by the freight forwarder is duly negotiated; but delivery by the carrier in accordance with Part 4 of this Article pursuant to its own bill of lading discharges the carrier's obligation to deliver.

§ 7—504. Rights Acquired in the Absence of Due Negotiation; Effect of Diversion; Seller's Stoppage of Delivery.

(1) A transferee of a document, whether negotiable or nonnegotiable, to whom the document has been delivered but not duly negotiated, acquires the title and rights which his transferor had or had actual authority to convey.

(2) In the case of a nonnegotiable document, until but not after the bailee receives notification of the transfer, the rights of the transferee may be defeated

(a) by those creditors of the transferor who could treat the sale as void under Section 2—402; or

(b) by a buyer from the transferor in ordinary course of business if the bailee has delivered the goods to the buyer or received notification of his rights; or

(c) as against the bailee by good faith dealings of the bailee with the transferor.

(3) A diversion or other change of shipping instructions by the consignor in a nonnegotiable bill of lading which causes the bailee not to deliver to the consignee defeats the consignee's title to the goods if they have been delivered to a buyer in ordinary course of business and in any event defeats the consignee's rights against the bailee.

(4) Delivery pursuant to a nonnegotiable document may be stopped by a seller under Section 2—705, and subject to the requirement of due notification there provided. A bailee honoring the seller's instructions is entitled to be indemnified by the seller against any resulting loss or expense.

§ 7—505. Indorser Not a Guarantor for Other Parties.

The indorsement of a document of title issued by a bailee does not make the indorser liable for any default by the bailee or by previous indorsers.

§ 7—506. Delivery Without Indorsement: Right to Compel Indorsement.

The transferee of a negotiable document of title has a specifically enforceable right to have his transferor supply any necessary indorsement but the transfer becomes a negotiation only as of the time the indorsement is supplied.

§ 7—507. Warranties on Negotiation or Transfer of Receipt or Bill.

Where a person negotiates or transfers a document of title for value otherwise than as a mere intermediary under the next following section, then unless otherwise agreed he warrants to his immediate purchaser only in addition to any warranty made in selling the goods

(a) that the document is genuine; and

(b) that he has no knowledge of any fact which would impair its validity or worth; and

(c) that his negotiation or transfer is rightful and fully effective with respect to the title to the document and the goods it represents.

§ 7—508. Warranties of Collecting Bank as to Documents.

A collecting bank or other intermediary known to be entrusted with documents on behalf of another or with collection of a draft or other claim against delivery of documents warrants by such delivery of the documents only its own good faith and authority. This rule applies even though the intermediary has purchased or made advances against the claim or draft to be collected.

§ 7—509. Receipt or Bill: When Adequate Compliance With Commercial Contract.

The question whether a document is adequate to fulfill the obligations of a contract for sale or the conditions of a credit is governed by the Articles on Sales (Article 2) and on Letters of Credit (Article 5).

Part 6 Warehouse Receipts and Bills of Lading: Miscellaneous Provisions

§ 7—601. Lost and Missing Documents.

(1) If a document has been lost, stolen or destroyed, a court may order delivery of the goods or issuance of a substitute document and the bailee may without liability to any person comply with such order. If the document was negotiable the claimant must post security approved by the court to indemnify any person who may suffer loss as a result of non-surrender of the document. If the document was not negotiable, such security may be required at the discretion of the court. The court may also in its discretion order payment of the bailee's reasonable costs and counsel fees.

(2) A bailee who without court order delivers goods to a person claiming under a missing negotiable document is liable to any person injured thereby, and if the delivery is not in good faith becomes liable for conversion. Delivery in good faith is not conversion if made in accordance with a filed classification or tariff or, where no classification or tariff is filed, if the claimant posts security with the bailee in an amount at least double the value of the goods at the time of posting to indemnify any person injured by the delivery who files a notice of claim within one year after the delivery.

§ 7—602. Attachment of Goods Covered by a Negotiable Document.

Except where the document was originally issued upon delivery of the goods by a person who had no power to dispose of them, no lien attaches by virtue of any judicial process to goods in the possession of a bailee for which a negotiable document of title is outstanding unless the document be first surrendered to the bailee or its negotiation enjoined, and the bailee shall not be compelled to deliver the goods pursuant to process until the document is surrendered to him or impounded by the court. One who purchases the document for value without notice of the process or injunction takes free of the lien imposed by judicial process.

§ 7—603. **Conflicting Claims; Interpleader.**

If more than one person claims title or possession of the goods, the bailee is excused from delivery until he has had a reasonable time to ascertain the validity of the adverse claims or to bring an action to compel all claimants to interplead and may compel such interpleader, either in defending an action for nondelivery of the goods, or by original action, whichever is appropriate.

Article 8
INVESTMENT SECURITIES

Part 1 Short Title and General Matters

§ 8—101. **Short Title.**

This Article shall be known and may be cited as Uniform Commercial Code—Investment Securities.

§ 8—102. **Definitions and Index of Definitions.**

(1) In this Article, unless the context otherwise requires:

(a) A "certificated security" is a share, participation, or other interest in property of or an enterprise of the issuer or an obligation of the issuer which is

(i) represented by an instrument issued in bearer or registered form;

(ii) of a type commonly dealt in on securities exchanges or markets or commonly recognized in any area in which it is issued or dealt in as a medium for investment; and

(iii) either one of a class or series or by its terms divisible into a class or series of shares, participations, interests, or obligations.

(b) An "uncertificated security" is a share, participation, or other interest in property or an enterprise of the issuer or an obligation of the issuer which is

(i) not represented by an instrument and the transfer of which is registered upon books maintained for that purpose by or on behalf of the issuer;

(ii) of a type commonly dealt in on securities exchanges or markets; and

(iii) either one of a class or series or by its terms divisible into a class or series of shares, participations, interests, or obligations.

(c) A "security" is either a certificated or an uncertificated security. If a security is certificated, the terms "security" and "certificated security" may mean either the intangible interest, the instrument representing that interest, or both, as the context requires. A writing that is a certificated security is governed by this Article and not by Article 3, even though it also meets the requirements of that Article. This Article does not apply to money. If a certificated security has been retained by or

surrendered to the issuer or its transfer agent for reasons other than registration of transfer, other temporary purpose, payment, exchange, or acquisition by the issuer, that security shall be treated as an uncertificated security for purposes of this Article.

(d) A certificated security is in "registered form" if

(i) it specifies a person entitled to the security or the rights it represents; and

(ii) its transfer may be registered upon books maintained for that purpose by or on behalf of the issuer, or the security so states.

(e) A certificated security is in "bearer form" if it runs to bearer according to its terms and not by reason of any indorsement.

(2) A "subsequent purchaser" is a person who takes other than by original issue.

(3) A "clearing corporation" is a corporation registered as a "clearing agency" under the federal securities laws or a corporation:

(a) at least 90 percent of whose capital stock is held by or for one or more organizations, none of which, other than a national securities exchange or association, holds in excess of 20 percent of the capital stock of the corporation, and each of which is

(i) subject to supervision or regulation pursuant to the provisions of federal or state banking laws or state insurance laws,

(ii) a broker or dealer or investment company registered under the federal securities laws, or

(iii) a national securities exchange or association registered under the federal securities laws; and

(b) any remaining capital stock of which is held by individuals who have purchased it at or prior to the time of their taking office as directors of the corporation and who have purchased only so much of the capital stock as is necessary to permit them to qualify as directors.

(4) A "custodian bank" is a bank or trust company that is supervised and examined by state or federal authority having supervision over banks and is acting as custodian for a clearing corporation.

(5) Other definitions applying to this Article or to specified Parts thereof and the sections in which they appear are:
"Adverse claim". Section 8—302.
"Bona fide purchaser". Section 8—302.
"Broker". Section 8—303.
"Debtor". Section 9—105.
"Financial intermediary". Section 8—313.
"Guarantee of the signature". Section 8—402.
"Initial transaction statement". Section 8—408.
"Instruction". Section 8—308.
"Intermediary bank". Section 4—105.
"Issuer". Section 8—201.
"Overissue". Section 8—104.

"Secured Party". Section 9—105.

"Security Agreement". Section 9—105.

(6) In addition, Article 1 contains general definitions and principles of construction and interpretation applicable throughout this Article.

Amended in 1962, 1973 and 1977.

§ 8—103. Issuer's Lien.

A lien upon a security in favor of an issuer thereof is valid against a purchaser only if:

(a) the security is certificated and the right of the issuer to the lien is noted conspicuously thereon; or

(b) the security is uncertificated and a notation of the right of the issuer to the lien is contained in the initial transaction statement sent to the purchaser or, if his interest is transferred to him other than by registration of transfer, pledge, or release, the initial transaction statement sent to the registered owner or the registered pledgee.

Amended in 1977.

§ 8—104. Effect of Overissue; "Overissue".

(1) The provisions of this Article which validate a security or compel its issue or reissue do not apply to the extent that validation, issue, or reissue would result in overissue; but if:

(a) an identical security which does not constitute an overissue is reasonably available for purchase, the person entitled to issue or validation may compel the issuer to purchase the security for him and either to deliver a certificated security or to register the transfer of an uncertificated security to him, against surrender of any certificated security he holds; or

(b) a security is not so available for purchase, the person entitled to issue or validation may recover from the issuer the price he or the last purchaser for value paid for it with interest from the date of his demand.

(2) "Overissue" means the issue of securities in excess of the amount the issuer has corporate power to issue.

Amended in 1977.

§ 8—105. Certificated Securities Negotiable; Statements and Instructions Not Negotiable; Presumptions.

(1) Certificated securities governed by this Article are negotiable instruments.

(2) Statements (Section 8—408), notices, or the like, sent by the issuer of uncertificated securities and instructions (Section 8—308) are neither negotiable instruments nor certificated securities.

(3) In any action on a security:

(a) unless specifically denied in the pleadings, each signature on a certificated security, in a necessary indorsement, on an initial transaction statement, or on an instruction, is admitted;

(b) if the effectiveness of a signature is put in issue, the burden of establishing it is on the party claiming under the signature, but the signature is presumed to be genuine or authorized;

(c) if signatures on a certificated security are admitted or established, production of the security entitles a holder to recover on it unless the defendant establishes a defense or a defect going to the validity of the security;

(d) if signatures on an initial transaction statement are admitted or established, the facts stated in the statement are presumed to be true as of the time of its issuance; and

(e) after it is shown that a defense or defect exists, the plaintiff has the burden of establishing that he or some person under whom he claims is a person against whom the defense or defect is ineffective (Section 8—202).

Amended in 1977.

§ 8—106. Applicability.

The law (including the conflict of laws rules) of the jurisdiction of organization of the issuer governs the validity of a security, the effectiveness of registration by the issuer, and the rights and duties of the issuer with respect to:

(a) registration of transfer of a certificated security;

(b) registration of transfer, pledge, or release of an uncertificated security; and

(c) sending of statements of uncertificated securities.

Amended in 1977.

§ 8—107. Securities Transferable; Action for Price.

(1) Unless otherwise agreed and subject to any applicable law or regulation respecting short sales, a person obligated to transfer securities may transfer any certificated security of the specified issue in bearer form or registered in the name of the transferee, or indorsed to him or in blank, or he may transfer an equivalent uncertificated security to the transferee or a person designated by the transferee.

(2) If the buyer fails to pay the price as it comes due under a contract of sale, the seller may recover the price of:

(a) certificated securities accepted by the buyer;

(b) uncertificated securities that have been transferred to the buyer or a person designated by the buyer; and

(c) other securities if efforts at their resale would be unduly burdensome or if there is no readily available market for their resale.

Amended in 1977.

§ 8—108. Registration of Pledge and Release of Uncertificated Securities.

A security interest in an uncertificated security may be evidenced by the registration of pledge to the secured party or a person designated by him. There can be no more than one registered pledge of an uncertificated security at any time. The registered owner of an uncertificated security is the person in whose name the security is registered, even if the security is subject to a registered pledge. The rights of a registered pledgee of an uncertificated security under this Article are terminated by the registration of release.

Added in 1977.

Part 2 Issue—Issuer

§ 8—201. "Issuer"

(1) With respect to obligations on or defenses to a security, "issuer" includes a person who:

(a) places or authorizes the placing of his name on a certificated security (otherwise than as authenticating trustee, registrar, transfer agent, or the like) to evidence that it represents a share, participation, or other interest in his property or in an enterprise, or to evidence his duty to perform an obligation represented by the certificated security;

(b) creates shares, participations, or other interests in his property or in an enterprise or undertakes obligations, which shares, participations, interests, or obligations are uncertificated securities;

(c) directly or indirectly creates fractional interests in his rights or property, which fractional interests are represented by certificated securities; or

(d) becomes responsible for or in place of any other person described as an issuer in this section.

(2) With respect to obligations on or defenses to a security, a guarantor is an issuer to the extent of his guaranty, whether or not his obligation is noted on a certificated security or on statements of uncertificated securities sent pursuant to Section 8—408.

(3) With respect to registration of transfer, pledge, or release (Part 4 of this Article), "issuer" means a person on whose behalf transfer books are maintained.

Amended in 1977.

§ 8—202. Issuer's Responsibility and Defenses; Notice of Defect or Defense.

(1) Even against a purchaser for value and without notice, the terms of a security include:

(a) if the security is certificated, those stated on the security;

(b) if the security is uncertificated, those contained in the initial transaction statement sent to such purchaser or, if his interest is transferred to him other than by registration of transfer, pledge, or release, the initial transaction statement sent to the registered owner or registered pledgee; and

(c) those made part of the security by reference, on the certificated security or in the initial transaction statement, to

another instrument, indenture, or document or to a constitution, statute, ordinance, rule, regulation, order or the like, to the extent that the terms referred to do not conflict with the terms stated on the certificated security or contained in the statement. A reference under this paragraph does not of itself charge a purchaser for value with notice of a defect going to the validity of the security, even though the certificated security or statement expressly states that a person accepting it admits notice.

(2) A certificated security in the hands of a purchaser for value or an uncertificated security as to which an initial transaction statement has been sent to a purchaser for value, other than a security issued by a government or governmental agency or unit, even though issued with a defect going to its validity, is valid with respect to the purchaser if he is without notice of the particular defect unless the defect involves a violation of constitutional provisions, in which case the security is valid with respect to a subsequent purchaser for value and without notice of the defect. This subsection applies to an issuer that is a government or governmental agency or unit only if either there has been substantial compliance with the legal requirements governing the issue or the issuer has received a substantial consideration for the issue as a whole or for the particular security and a stated purpose of the issue is one for which the issuer has power to borrow money or issue the security.

(3) Except as provided in the case of certain unauthorized signatures (Section 8—205), lack of genuineness of a certificated security or an initial transaction statement is a complete defense, even against a purchaser for value and without notice.

(4) All other defenses of the issuer of a certificated or uncertificated security, including nondelivery and conditional delivery of a certificated security, are ineffective against a purchaser for value who has taken without notice of the particular defense.

(5) Nothing in this section shall be construed to affect the right of a party to a "when, as and if issued" or a "when distributed" contract to cancel the contract in the event of a material change in the character of the security that is the subject of the contract or in the plan or arrangement pursuant to which the security is to be issued or distributed.

Amended in 1977.

§ 8—203. Staleness as Notice of Defects or Defenses.

(1) After an act or event creating a right to immediate performance of the principal obligation represented by a certificated security or that sets a date on or after which the security is to be presented or surrendered for redemption or exchange, a purchaser is charged with notice of any defect in its issue or defense of the issuer if:

(a) the act or event is one requiring the payment of money, the delivery of certificated securities, the registration of transfer of uncertificated securities, or any of these on presentation or surrender of the certificated security, the funds or securities are available on the date set for payment or exchange, and he takes the security more than one year after that date; and

(b) the act or event is not covered by paragraph (a) and he takes the security more than 2 years after the date set for surrender or presentation or the date on which performance became due.

(2) A call that has been revoked is not within subsection (1).

Amended in 1977.

§ 8—204. Effect of Issuer's Restrictions on Transfer.

A restriction on transfer of a security imposed by the issuer, even if otherwise lawful, is ineffective against any person without actual knowledge of it unless:

(a) the security is certificated and the restriction is noted conspicuously thereon; or

(b) the security is uncertificated and a notation of the restriction is contained in the initial transaction statement sent to the person or, if his interest is transferred to him other than by registration of transfer, pledge, or release, the initial transaction statement sent to the registered owner or the registered pledgee.

Amended in 1977.

§ 8—205. Effect of Unauthorized Signature on Certificated Security or Initial Transaction Statement.

An unauthorized signature placed on a certificated security prior to or in the course of issue or placed on an initial transaction statement is ineffective, but the signature is effective in favor of a purchaser for value of the certificated security or a purchaser for value of an uncertificated security to whom the initial transaction statement has been sent, if the purchaser is without notice of the lack of authority and the signing has been done by:

(a) an authenticating trustee, registrar, transfer agent, or other person entrusted by the issuer with the signing of the security, of similar securities, or of initial transaction statements or the immediate preparation for signing of any of them; or

(b) an employee of the issuer, or of any of the foregoing, entrusted with responsible handling of the security or initial transaction statement.

Amended in 1977.

§ 8—206. Completion or Alteration of Certificated Security or Initial Transaction Statement.

(1) If a certificated security contains the signatures necessary to its issue or transfer but is incomplete in any other respect:

(a) any person may complete it by filling in the blanks as authorized; and

(b) even though the blanks are incorrectly filled in, the security as completed is enforceable by a purchaser who took it for value and without notice of the incorrectness.

(2) A complete certificated security that has been improperly altered, even though fraudulently, remains enforceable, but only according to its original terms.

(3) If an initial transaction statement contains the signatures necessary to its validity, but is incomplete in any other respect:

(a) any person may complete it by filling in the blanks as authorized; and

(b) even though the blanks are incorrectly filled in, the statement as completed is effective in favor of the person to whom it is sent if he purchased the security referred to therein for value and without notice of the incorrectness.

(4) A complete initial transaction statement that has been improperly altered, even though fraudulently, is effective in favor of a purchaser to whom it has been sent, but only according to its original terms.

Amended in 1977.

§ 8—207. Rights and Duties of Issuer With Respect to Registered Owners and Registered Pledgees.

(1) Prior to due presentment for registration of transfer of a certificated security in registered form, the issuer or indenture trustee may treat the registered owner as the person exclusively entitled to vote, to receive notifications, and otherwise to exercise all the rights and powers of an owner.

(2) Subject to the provisions of subsections (3), (4), and (6), the issuer or indenture trustee may treat the registered owner of an uncertificated security as the person exclusively entitled to vote, to receive notifications, and otherwise to exercise all the rights and powers of an owner.

(3) The registered owner of an uncertificated security that is subject to a registered pledge is not entitled to registration of transfer prior to the due presentment to the issuer of a release instruction. The exercise of conversion rights with respect to a convertible uncertificated security is a transfer within the meaning of this section.

(4) Upon due presentment of a transfer instruction from the registered pledgee of an uncertificated security, the issuer shall:

(a) register the transfer of the security to the new owner free of pledge, if the instruction specifies a new owner (who may be the registered pledgee) and does not specify a pledgee;

(b) register the transfer of the security to the new owner subject to the interest of the existing pledgee, if the instruction specifies a new owner and the existing pledgee; or

(c) register the release of the security from the existing pledge and register the pledge of the security to the other pledgee, if the instruction specifies the existing owner and another pledgee.

(5) Continuity of perfection of a security interest is not broken by registration of transfer under subsection (4)(b) or by registration of release and pledge under subsection (4)(c), if the security interest is assigned.

(6) If an uncertificated security is subject to a registered pledge:

(a) any uncertificated securities issued in exchange for or distributed with respect to the pledged security shall be registered subject to the pledge;

(b) any certificated securities issued in exchange for or distributed with respect to the pledged security shall be delivered to the registered pledgee; and

(c) any money paid in exchange for or in redemption of part or all of the security shall be paid to the registered pledgee.

(7) Nothing in this Article shall be construed to affect the liability of the registered owner of a security for calls, assessments, or the like.

Amended in 1977.

§ 8—208. Effect of Signature of Authenticating Trustee, Registrar, or Transfer Agent.

(1) A person placing his signature upon a certificated security or an initial transaction statement as authenticating trustee, registrar, transfer agent, or the like, warrants to a purchaser for value of the certificated security or a purchaser for value of an uncertificated security to whom the initial transaction statement has been sent, if the purchaser is without notice of the particular defect, that:

(a) the certificated security or initial transaction statement is genuine;

(b) his own participation in the issue or registration of the transfer, pledge, or release of the security is within his capacity and within the scope of the authority received by him from the issuer; and

(c) he has reasonable grounds to believe the security is in the form and within the amount the issuer is authorized to issue.

(2) Unless otherwise agreed, a person by so placing his signature does not assume responsibility for the validity of the security in other respects.

Amended in 1962 and 1977.

Part 3 Transfer

§ 8—301. Rights Acquired by Purchaser.

(1) Upon transfer of a security to a purchaser (Section 8—313), the purchaser acquires the rights in the security which his transferor had or had actual authority to convey unless the purchaser's rights are limited by Section 8—302(4).

(2) A transferee of a limited interest acquires rights only to the extent of the interest transferred. The creation or release of a security interest in a security is the transfer of a limited interest in that security.

Amended in 1977.

§ 8—302. "Bona Fide Purchaser"; "Adverse Claim"; Title Acquired by Bona Fide Purchaser.

(1) A "bona fide purchaser" is a purchaser for value in good faith and without notice of any adverse claim:

(a) who takes delivery of a certificated security in bearer form or in registered form, issued or indorsed to him or in blank;

(b) to whom the transfer, pledge, or release of an uncertificated security is registered on the books of the issuer; or

(c) to whom a security is transferred under the provisions of paragraph (c), (d)(i), or (g) of Section 8—313(1).

(2) "Adverse claim" includes a claim that a transfer was or would be wrongful or that a particular adverse person is the owner of or has an interest in the security.

(3) A bona fide purchaser in addition to acquiring the rights of a purchaser (Section 8—301) also acquires his interest in the security free of any adverse claim.

(4) Notwithstanding Section 8—301(1), the transferee of a particular certificated security who has been a party to any fraud or illegality affecting the security, or who as a prior holder of that certificated security had notice of an adverse claim, cannot improve his position by taking from a bona fide purchaser.

Amended in 1977.

§ 8—303. "Broker".

"Broker" means a person engaged for all or part of his time in the business of buying and selling securities, who in the transaction concerned acts for, buys a security from, or sells a security to, a customer. Nothing in this Article determines the capacity in which a person acts for purposes of any other statute or rule to which the person is subject.

§ 8—304. Notice to Purchaser of Adverse Claims.

(1) A purchaser (including a broker for the seller or buyer, but excluding an intermediary bank) of a certificated security is charged with notice of adverse claims if:

(a) the security, whether in bearer or registered form, has been indorsed "for collection" or "for surrender" or for some other purpose not involving transfer; or

(b) the security is in bearer form and has on it an unambiguous statement that it is the property of a person other than the transferor. The mere writing of a name on a security is not such a statement.

(2) A purchaser (including a broker for the seller or buyer, but excluding an intermediary bank) to whom the transfer, pledge, or release of an uncertificated security is registered is charged with notice of adverse claims as to which the issuer has a duty under Section 8—403(4) at the time of registration and which are noted in the initial transaction statement sent to the purchaser or, if his interest is transferred to him other than by registration of transfer, pledge, or release, the initial transaction statement sent to the registered owner or the registered pledgee.

(3) The fact that the purchaser (including a broker for the seller or buyer) of a certificated or uncertificated security has notice that the security is held for a third person or is registered in the name of or indorsed by a fiduciary does not create a duty of inquiry into

the rightfulness of the transfer or constitute constructive notice of adverse claims. However, if the purchaser (excluding an intermediary bank) has knowledge that the proceeds are being used or that the transaction is for the individual benefit of the fiduciary or otherwise in breach of duty, the purchaser is charged with notice of adverse claims.

Amended in 1977.

§ 8—305. Staleness as Notice of Adverse Claims.

An act or event that creates a right to immediate performance of the principal obligation represented by a certificated security or sets a date on or after which a certificated security is to be presented or surrendered for redemption or exchange does not itself constitute any notice of adverse claims except in the case of a transfer:

(a) after one year from any date set for presentment or surrender for redemption or exchange; or

(b) after 6 months from any date set for payment of money against presentation or surrender of the security if funds are available for payment on that date.

Amended in 1977.

§ 8—306. Warranties on Presentment and Transfer of Certificated Securities; Warranties of Originators of Instructions.

(1) A person who presents a certificated security for registration of transfer or for payment or exchange warrants to the issuer that he is entitled to the registration, payment, or exchange. But, a purchaser for value and without notice of adverse claims who receives a new, reissued, or re-registered certificated security on registration of transfer or receives an initial transaction statement confirming the registration of transfer of an equivalent uncertificated security to him warrants only that he has no knowledge of any unauthorized signature (Section 8—311) in a necessary indorsement.

(2) A person by transferring a certificated security to a purchaser for value warrants only that:

(a) his transfer is effective and rightful;

(b) the security is genuine and has not been materially altered; and

(c) he knows of no fact which might impair the validity of the security.

(3) If a certificated security is delivered by an intermediary known to be entrusted with delivery of the security on behalf of another or with collection of a draft or other claim against delivery, the intermediary by delivery warrants only his own good faith and authority, even though he has purchased or made advances against the claim to be collected against the delivery.

(4) A pledgee or other holder for security who redelivers a certificated security received, or after payment and on order of the debtor delivers that security to a third person, makes only the warranties of an intermediary under subsection (3).

(5) A person who originates an instruction warrants to the issuer that:

(a) he is an appropriate person to originate the instruction; and

(b) at the time the instruction is presented to the issuer he will be entitled to the registration of transfer, pledge, or release.

(6) A person who originates an instruction warrants to any person specially guaranteeing his signature (subsection 8—312(3)) that:

(a) he is an appropriate person to originate the instruction; and

(b) at the time the instruction is presented to the issuer

(i) he will be entitled to the registration of transfer, pledge, or release; and

(ii) the transfer, pledge, or release requested in the instruction will be registered by the issuer free from all liens, security interests, restrictions, and claims other than those specified in the instruction.

(7) A person who originates an instruction warrants to a purchaser for value and to any person guaranteeing the instruction (Section 8—312(6)) that:

(a) he is an appropriate person to originate the instruction;

(b) the uncertificated security referred to therein is valid; and

(c) at the time the instruction is presented to the issuer

(i) the transferor will be entitled to the registration of transfer, pledge, or release;

(ii) the transfer, pledge, or release requested in the instruction will be registered by the issuer free from all liens, security interests, restrictions, and claims other than those specified in the instruction; and

(iii) the requested transfer, pledge, or release will be rightful.

(8) If a secured party is the registered pledgee or the registered owner of an uncertificated security, a person who originates an instruction of release or transfer to the debtor or, after payment and on order of the debtor, a transfer instruction to a third person, warrants to the debtor or the third person only that he is an appropriate person to originate the instruction and, at the time the instruction is presented to the issuer, the transferor will be entitled to the registration of release or transfer. If a transfer instruction to a third person who is a purchaser for value is originated on order of the debtor, the debtor makes to the purchaser the warranties of paragraphs (b), (c)(ii) and (c)(iii) of subsection (7).

(9) A person who transfers an uncertificated security to a purchaser for value and does not originate an instruction in connection with the transfer warrants only that:

(a) his transfer is effective and rightful; and

(b) the uncertificated security is valid.

(10) A broker gives to his customer and to the issuer and a purchaser the applicable warranties provided in this section and has

the rights and privileges of a purchaser under this section. The warranties of and in favor of the broker, acting as an agent are in addition to applicable warranties given by and in favor of his customer.

Amended in 1962 and 1977.

§ 8—307. Effect of Delivery Without Indorsement; Right to Compel Indorsement.

If a certificated security in registered form has been delivered to a purchaser without a necessary indorsement he may become a bona fide purchaser only as of the time the indorsement is supplied; but against the transferor, the transfer is complete upon delivery and the purchaser has a specifically enforceable right to have any necessary indorsement supplied.

Amended in 1977.

§ 8—308. Indorsements; Instructions.

(1) An indorsement of a certificated security in registered form is made when an appropriate person signs on it or on a separate document an assignment or transfer of the security or a power to assign or transfer it or his signature is written without more upon the back of the security.

(2) An indorsement may be in blank or special. An indorsement in blank includes an indorsement to bearer. A special indorsement specifies to whom the security is to be transferred, or who has power to transfer it. A holder may convert a blank indorsement into a special indorsement.

(3) An indorsement purporting to be only of part of a certificated security representing units intended by the issuer to be separately transferable is effective to the extent of the indorsement.

(4) An "instruction" is an order to the issuer of an uncertificated security requesting that the transfer, pledge, or release from pledge of the uncertificated security specified therein be registered.

(5) An instruction originated by an appropriate person is:

(a) a writing signed by an appropriate person; or

(b) a communication to the issuer in any form agreed upon in a writing signed by the issuer and an appropriate person.

If an instruction has been originated by an appropriate person but is incomplete in any other respect, any person may complete it as authorized and the issuer may rely on it as completed even though it has been completed incorrectly.

(6) "An appropriate person" in subsection (1) means the person specified by the certificated security or by special indorsement to be entitled to the security.

(7) "An appropriate person" in subsection (5) means:

(a) for an instruction to transfer or pledge an uncertificated security which is then not subject to a registered pledge, the registered owner; or

(b) for an instruction to transfer or release an uncertificated security which is then subject to a registered pledge, the registered pledgee.

(8) In addition to the persons designated in subsections (6) and (7), "an appropriate person" in subsections (1) and (5) includes:

(a) if the person designated is described as a fiduciary but is no longer serving in the described capacity, either that person or his successor;

(b) if the persons designated are described as more than one person as fiduciaries and one or more are no longer serving in the described capacity, the remaining fiduciary or fiduciaries, whether or not a successor has been appointed or qualified;

(c) if the person designated is an individual and is without capacity to act by virtue of death, incompetence, infancy, or otherwise, his executor, administrator, guardian, or like fiduciary;

(d) if the persons designated are described as more than one person as tenants by the entirety or with right of survivorship and by reason of death all cannot sign, the survivor or survivors;

(e) a person having power to sign under applicable law or controlling instrument; and

(f) to the extent that the person designated or any of the foregoing persons may act through an agent, his authorized agent.

(9) Unless otherwise agreed, the indorser of a certificated security by his indorsement or the originator of an instruction by his origination assumes no obligation that the security will be honored by the issuer but only the obligations provided in Section 8—306.

(10) Whether the person signing is appropriate is determined as of the date of signing and an indorsement made by or an instruction originated by him does not become unauthorized for the purposes of this Article by virtue of any subsequent change of circumstances.

(11) Failure of a fiduciary to comply with a controlling instrument or with the law of the state having jurisdiction of the fiduciary relationship, including any law requiring the fiduciary to obtain court approval of the transfer, pledge, or release, does not render his indorsement or an instruction originated by him unauthorized for the purposes of this Article.

Amended in 1962 and 1977.

§ 8—309. Effect of Indorsement Without Delivery.

An indorsement of a certificated security, whether special or in blank, does not constitute a transfer until delivery of the certificated security on which it appears or, if the indorsement is on a separate document, until delivery of both the document and the certificated security.

Amended in 1977.

§ 8—310. Indorsement of Certificated Security in Bearer Form.

An indorsement of a certificated security in bearer form may give notice of adverse claims (Section 8—304) but does not otherwise affect any right to registration the holder possesses.

Amended in 1977.

§ 8—311. Effect of Unauthorized Indorsement or Instruction.

Unless the owner or pledgee has ratified an unauthorized indorsement or instruction or is otherwise precluded from asserting its ineffectiveness:

(a) he may assert its ineffectiveness against the issuer or any purchaser, other than a purchaser for value and without notice of adverse claims, who has in good faith received a new, reissued, or re-registered certificated security on registration of transfer or received an initial transaction statement confirming the registration of transfer, pledge, or release of an equivalent uncertificated security to him; and

(b) an issuer who registers the transfer of a certificated security upon the unauthorized indorsement or who registers the transfer, pledge, or release of an uncertificated security upon the unauthorized instruction is subject to liability for improper registration (Section 8—404).

Amended in 1977.

§ 8—312. Effect of Guaranteeing Signature, Indorsement or Instruction.

(1) Any person guaranteeing a signature of an indorser of a certificated security warrants that at the time of signing:

(a) the signature was genuine;

(b) the signer was an appropriate person to indorse (Section 8—308); and

(c) the signer had legal capacity to sign.

(2) Any person guaranteeing a signature of the originator of an instruction warrants that at the time of signing:

(a) the signature was genuine;

(b) the signer was an appropriate person to originate the instruction (Section 8—308) if the person specified in the instruction as the registered owner or registered pledgee of the uncertificated security was, in fact, the registered owner or registered pledgee of the security, as to which fact the signature guarantor makes no warranty;

(c) the signer had legal capacity to sign; and

(d) the taxpayer identification number, if any, appearing on the instruction as that of the registered owner or registered pledgee was the taxpayer identification number of the signer or of the owner or pledgee for whom the signer was acting.

(3) Any person specially guaranteeing the signature of the originator of an instruction makes not only the warranties of a signature guarantor (subsection (2)) but also warrants that at the time the instruction is presented to the issuer:

(a) the person specified in the instruction as the registered owner or registered pledgee of the uncertificated security will be the registered owner or registered pledgee; and

(b) the transfer, pledge, or release of the uncertificated security requested in the instruction will be registered by the issuer free from all liens, security interests, restrictions, and claims other than those specified in the instruction.

(4) The guarantor under subsections (1) and (2) or the special guarantor under subsection (3) does not otherwise warrant the rightfulness of the particular transfer, pledge, or release.

(5) Any person guaranteeing an indorsement of a certificated security makes not only the warranties of a signature guarantor under subsection (1) but also warrants the rightfulness of the particular transfer in all respects.

(6) Any person guaranteeing an instruction requesting the transfer, pledge, or release of an uncertificated security makes not only the warranties of a special signature guarantor under subsection (3) but also warrants the rightfulness of the particular transfer, pledge, or release in all respects.

(7) No issuer may require a special guarantee of signature (subsection (3)), a guarantee of indorsement (subsection (5)), or a guarantee of instruction (subsection (6)) as a condition to registration of transfer, pledge, or release.

(8) The foregoing warranties are made to any person taking or dealing with the security in reliance on the guarantee, and the guarantor is liable to the person for any loss resulting from breach of the warranties.

Amended in 1977.

§ 8—313. When Transfer to Purchaser Occurs; Financial Intermediary as Bona Fide Purchaser; "Financial Intermediary".

(1) Transfer of a security or a limited interest (including a security interest) therein to a purchaser occurs only:

(a) at the time he or a person designated by him acquires possession of a certificated security;

(b) at the time the transfer, pledge, or release of an uncertificated security is registered to him or a person designated by him;

(c) at the time his financial intermediary acquires possession of a certificated security specially indorsed to or issued in the name of the purchaser;

(d) at the time a financial intermediary, not a clearing corporation, sends him confirmation of the purchase and also by book entry or otherwise identifies as belonging to the purchaser

(i) a specific certificated security in the financial intermediary's possession;

(ii) a quantity of securities that constitute or are part of a fungible bulk of certificated securities in the financial intermediary's possession or of uncertificated securities registered in the name of the financial intermediary; or

(iii) a quantity of securities that constitute or are part of a fungible bulk of securities shown on the account of the financial intermediary on the books of another financial intermediary;

(e) with respect to an identified certificated security to be delivered while still in the possession of a third person, not a financial intermediary, at the time that person acknowledges that he holds for the purchaser;

(f) with respect to a specific uncertificated security the pledge or transfer of which has been registered to a third person, not a financial intermediary, at the time that person acknowledges that he holds for the purchaser;

(g) at the time appropriate entries to the account of the purchaser or a person designated by him on the books of a clearing corporation are made under Section 8—320;

(h) with respect to the transfer of a security interest where the debtor has signed a security agreement containing a description of the security, at the time a written notification, which, in the case of the creation of the security interest, is signed by the debtor (which may be a copy of the security agreement) or which, in the case of the release or assignment of the security interest created pursuant to this paragraph, is signed by the secured party, is received by

(i) a financial intermediary on whose books the interest of the transferor in the security appears;

(ii) a third person, not a financial intermediary, in possession of the security, if it is certificated;

(iii) a third person, not a financial intermediary, who is the registered owner of the security, if it is uncertificated and not subject to a registered pledge; or

(iv) a third person, not a financial intermediary, who is the registered pledgee of the security, if it is uncertificated and subject to a registered pledge;

(i) with respect to the transfer of a security interest where the transferor has signed a security agreement containing a description of the security, at the time new value is given by the secured party; or

(j) with respect to the transfer of a security interest where the secured party is a financial intermediary and the security has already been transferred to the financial intermediary under paragraphs (a), (b), (c), (d), or (g), at the time the transferor has signed a security agreement containing a description of the security and value is given by the secured party.

(2) The purchaser is the owner of a security held for him by a financial intermediary, but cannot be a bona fide purchaser of a security so held except in the circumstances specified in paragraphs (c), (d)(i), and (g) of subsection (1). If a security so held is part of a fungible bulk, as in the circumstances specified in paragraphs (d)(ii) and (d)(iii) of subsection (1), the purchaser is the owner of a proportionate property interest in the fungible bulk.

(3) Notice of an adverse claim received by the financial intermediary or by the purchaser after the financial intermediary takes delivery of a certificated security as a holder for value or after the transfer, pledge, or release of an uncertificated security has been registered free of the claim to a financial intermediary who has given value is not effective either as to the financial intermediary or as to the purchaser. However, as between the financial intermediary and the purchaser the purchaser may demand transfer of an equivalent security as to which no notice of adverse claim has been received.

(4) A "financial intermediary" is a bank, broker, clearing corporation, or other person (or the nominee of any of them) which in the ordinary course of its business maintains security accounts for its customers and is acting in that capacity. A financial intermediary may have a security interest in securities held in account for its customer.

Amended in 1962 and 1977.

§ 8—314. Duty to Transfer, When Completed

(1) Unless otherwise agreed, if a sale of a security is made on an exchange or otherwise through brokers:

(a) the selling customer fulfills his duty to transfer at the time he:

(i) places a certificated security in the possession of the selling broker or a person designated by the broker;

(ii) causes an uncertificated security to be registered in the name of the selling broker or a person designated by the broker;

(iii) if requested, causes an acknowledgment to be made to the selling broker that a certificated or uncertificated security is held for the broker; or

(iv) places in the possession of the selling broker or of a person designated by the broker a transfer instruction for an uncertificated security, providing the issuer does not refuse to register the requested transfer if the instruction is presented to the issuer for registration within 30 days thereafter; and

(b) the selling broker, including a correspondent broker acting for a selling customer, fulfills his duty to transfer at the time he:

(i) places a certificated security in the possession of the buying broker or a person designated by the buying broker;

(ii) causes an uncertificated security to be registered in the name of the buying broker or a person designated by the buying broker;

(iii) places in the possession of the buying broker or of a person designated by the buying broker a transfer instruction for an uncertificated security, providing the issuer does not refuse to register the requested transfer if the instruction is presented to the issuer for registration within 30 days thereafter; or

(iv) effects clearance of the sale in accordance with the rules of the exchange on which the transaction took place.

(2) Except as provided in this section or unless otherwise agreed, a transferor's duty to transfer a security under a contract of purchase is not fulfilled until he:

(a) places a certificated security in form to be negotiated by the purchaser in the possession of the purchaser or of a person designated by the purchaser;

(b) causes an uncertificated security to be registered in the name of the purchaser or a person designated by the purchaser; or

(c) if the purchaser requests, causes an acknowledgment to be made to the purchaser that a certificated or uncertificated security is held for the purchaser.

(3) Unless made on an exchange, a sale to a broker purchasing for his own account is within subsection (2) and not within subsection (1).

Amended in 1977.

§ 8—315. Action Against Transferee Based Upon Wrongful Transfer

(1) Any person against whom the transfer of a security is wrongful for any reason, including his incapacity, as against anyone except a bona fide purchaser, may:

(a) reclaim possession of the certificated security wrongfully transferred;

(b) obtain possession of any new certificated security representing all or part of the same rights;

(c) compel the origination of an instruction to transfer to him or a person designated by him an uncertificated security constituting all or part of the same rights; or

(d) have damages.

(2) If the transfer is wrongful because of an unauthorized indorsement of a certificated security, the owner may also reclaim or obtain possession of the security or a new certificated security, even from a bona fide purchaser, if the ineffectiveness of the purported indorsement can be asserted against him under the provisions of this Article on unauthorized indorsements (Section 8—311).

(3) The right to obtain or reclaim possession of a certificated security or to compel the origination of a transfer instruction may be specifically enforced and the transfer of a certificated or uncertificated security enjoined and a certificated security impounded pending the litigation.

Amended in 1977.

§ 8—316. Purchaser's Right to Requisites for Registration of Transfer, Pledge, or Release on Books

Unless otherwise agreed, the transferor of a certificated security or the transferor, pledgor, or pledgee of an uncertificated security on due demand must supply his purchaser with any proof of his authority to transfer, pledge, or release or with any other requisite necessary to obtain registration of the transfer, pledge, or release of the security; but if the transfer, pledge, or release is not for value, a transferor, pledgor, or pledgee need not do so unless the purchaser furnishes the necessary expenses. Failure within a reasonable time to comply with a demand made gives the purchaser the right to reject or rescind the transfer, pledge, or release.

Amended in 1977.

§ 8—317. Creditors' Rights

(1) Subject to the exceptions in subsections (3) and (4), no attachment or levy upon a certificated security or any share or other interest represented thereby which is outstanding is valid until the security is actually seized by the officer making the attachment or levy, but a certificated security which has been surrendered to the issuer may be reached by a creditor by legal process at the issuer's chief executive office in the United States.

(2) An uncertificated security registered in the name of the debtor may not be reached by a creditor except by legal process at the issuer's chief executive office in the United States.

(3) The interest of a debtor in a certificated security that is in the possession of a secured party not a financial intermediary or in an uncertificated security registered in the name of a secured party not a financial intermediary (or in the name of a nominee of the secured party) may be reached by a creditor by legal process upon the secured party.

(4) The interest of a debtor in a certificated security that is in the possession of or registered in the name of a financial intermediary or in an uncertificated security registered in the name of a financial intermediary may be reached by a creditor by legal process upon the financial intermediary on whose books the interest of the debtor appears.

(5) Unless otherwise provided by law, a creditor's lien upon the interest of a debtor in a security obtained pursuant to subsection (3) or (4) is not a restraint on the transfer of the security, free of the lien, to a third party for new value; but in the event of a transfer, the lien applies to the proceeds of the transfer in the hands of the secured party or financial intermediary, subject to any claims having priority.

(6) A creditor whose debtor is the owner of a security is entitled to aid from courts of appropriate jurisdiction, by injunction or otherwise, in reaching the security or in satisfying the claim by means allowed at law or in equity in regard to property that cannot readily be reached by ordinary legal process.

Amended in 1977.

§ 8—318. No Conversion by Good Faith Conduct

An agent or bailee who in good faith (including observance of reasonable commercial standards if he is in the business of buying, selling, or otherwise dealing with securities) has received certificated securities and sold, pledged, or delivered them or has sold or caused the transfer or pledge of uncertificated securities over which he had control according to the instructions of his principal, is not liable for conversion or for participation in breach of fiduciary duty although the principal had no right so to deal with the securities.

Amended in 1977.

§ 8—319. Statute of Frauds

A contract for the sale of securities is not enforceable by way of action or defense unless:

(a) there is some writing signed by the party against whom enforcement is sought or by his authorized agent or broker, sufficient to indicate that a contract has been made for sale of a stated quantity of described securities at a defined or stated price;

(b) delivery of a certificated security or transfer instruction has been accepted, or transfer of an uncertificated security has been registered and the transferee has failed to send written objection to the issuer within 10 days after receipt of the initial transaction statement confirming the registration, or payment has been made, but the contract is enforceable under this provision only to the extent of the delivery, registration, or payment;

(c) within a reasonable time a writing in confirmation of the sale or purchase and sufficient against the sender under paragraph (a) has been received by the party against whom enforcement is sought and he has failed to send written objection to its contents within 10 days after its receipt; or

(d) the party against whom enforcement is sought admits in his pleading, testimony, or otherwise in court that a contract was made for the sale of a stated quantity of described securities at a defined or stated price.

Amended in 1977.

§ 8—320. Transfer or Pledge Within Central Depository System

(1) In addition to other methods, a transfer, pledge, or release of a security or any interest therein may be effected by the making of appropriate entries on the books of a clearing corporation reducing the account of the transferor, pledgor, or pledgee and increasing the account of the transferee, pledgee, or pledgor by the amount of the obligation or the number of shares or rights transferred, pledged, or released, if the security is shown on the account of a transferor, pledgor, or pledgee on the books of the clearing corporation; is subject to the control of the clearing corporation; and

(a) if certificated,

(i) is in the custody of the clearing corporation, another clearing corporation, a custodian bank, or a nominee of any of them; and

(ii) is in bearer form or indorsed in blank by an appropriate person or registered in the name of the clearing corporation, a custodian bank, or a nominee of any of them; or

(b) if uncertificated, is registered in the name of the clearing corporation, another clearing corporation, a custodian bank, or a nominee of any of them.

(2) Under this section entries may be made with respect to like securities or interests therein as a part of a fungible bulk and may refer merely to a quantity of a particular security without reference to the name of the registered owner, certificate or bond number, or the like, and, in appropriate cases, may be on a net basis taking into account other transfers, pledges, or releases of the same security.

(3) A transfer under this section is effective (Section 8—313) and the purchaser acquires the rights of the transferor (Section 8—301). A pledge or release under this section is the transfer of a limited interest. If a pledge or the creation of a security interest is intended, the security interest is perfected at the time when both value is given by the pledgee and the appropriate entries are made (Section 8—321). A transferee or pledgee under this section may be a bona fide purchaser (Section 8—302).

(4) A transfer or pledge under this section is not a registration of transfer under Part 4.

(5) That entries made on the books of the clearing corporation as provided in subsection (1) are not appropriate does not affect the validity or effect of the entries or the liabilities or obligations of the clearing corporation to any person adversely affected thereby.

Added in 1962; amended in 1977.

§ 8—321. Enforceability, Attachment, Perfection and Termination of Security Interests

(1) A security interest in a security is enforceable and can attach only if it is transferred to the secured party or a person designated by him pursuant to a provision of Section 8—313(1).

(2) A security interest so transferred pursuant to agreement by a transferor who has rights in the security to a transferee who has given value is a perfected security interest, but a security interest that has been transferred solely under paragraph (i) of Section 8—313(1) becomes unperfected after 21 days unless, within that time, the requirements for transfer under any other provision of Section 8—313(1) are satisfied.

(3) A security interest in a security is subject to the provisions of Article 9, but:

(a) no filing is required to perfect the security interest; and

(b) no written security agreement signed by the debtor is necessary to make the security interest enforceable, except as provided in paragraph (h), (i), or (j) of Section 8—313(1). The secured party has the rights and duties provided under Section

9—207, to the extent they are applicable, whether or not the security is certificated, and, if certificated, whether or not it is in his possession.

(4) Unless otherwise agreed, a security interest in a security is terminated by transfer to the debtor or a person designated by him pursuant to a provision of Section 8—313(1). If a security is thus transferred, the security interest, if not terminated, becomes unperfected unless the security is certificated and is delivered to the debtor for the purpose of ultimate sale or exchange or presentation, collection, renewal, or registration of transfer. In that case, the security interest becomes unperfected after 21 days unless, within that time, the security (or securities for which it has been exchanged) is transferred to the secured party or a person designated by him pursuant to a provision of Section 8—313(1).

Added in 1977.

Part 4 Registration

§ 8—401. Duty of Issuer to Register Transfer, Pledge, or Release

(1) If a certificated security in registered form is presented to the issuer with a request to register transfer or an instruction is presented to the issuer with a request to register transfer, pledge, or release, the issuer shall register the transfer, pledge, or release as requested if:

(a) the security is indorsed or the instruction was originated by the appropriate person or persons (Section 8—308);

(b) reasonable assurance is given that those indorsements or instructions are genuine and effective (Section 8—402);

(c) the issuer has no duty as to adverse claims or has discharged the duty (Section 8—403);

(d) any applicable law relating to the collection of taxes has been complied with; and

(e) the transfer, pledge, or release is in fact rightful or is to a bona fide purchaser.

(2) If an issuer is under a duty to register a transfer, pledge, or release of a security, the issuer is also liable to the person presenting a certificated security or an instruction for registration or his principal for loss resulting from any unreasonable delay in registration or from failure or refusal to register the transfer, pledge, or release.

Amended in 1977.

§ 8—402. Assurance that Indorsements and Instructions Are Effective

(1) The issuer may require the following assurance that each necessary indorsement of a certificated security or each instruction (Section 8—308) is genuine and effective:

(a) in all cases, a guarantee of the signature (Section 8—312(1) or (2)) of the person indorsing a certificated security or originating an instruction including, in the case of an instruction, a warranty of the taxpayer identification number or, in the absence thereof, other reasonable assurance of identity;

(b) if the indorsement is made or the instruction is originated by an agent, appropriate assurance of authority to sign;

(c) if the indorsement is made or the instruction is originated by a fiduciary, appropriate evidence of appointment or incumbency;

(d) if there is more than one fiduciary, reasonable assurance that all who are required to sign have done so; and

(e) if the indorsement is made or the instruction is originated by a person not covered by any of the foregoing, assurance appropriate to the case corresponding as nearly as may be to the foregoing.

(2) A "guarantee of the signature" in subsection (1) means a guarantee signed by or on behalf of a person reasonably believed by the issuer to be responsible. The issuer may adopt standards with respect to responsibility if they are not manifestly unreasonable.

(3) "Appropriate evidence of appointment or incumbency" in subsection (1) means:

(a) in the case of a fiduciary appointed or qualified by a court, a certificate issued by or under the direction or supervision of that court or an officer thereof and dated within 60 days before the date of presentation for transfer, pledge, or release; or

(b) in any other case, a copy of a document showing the appointment or a certificate issued by or on behalf of a person reasonably believed by the issuer to be responsible or, in the absence of that document or certificate, other evidence reasonably deemed by the issuer to be appropriate. The issuer may adopt standards with respect to the evidence if they are not manifestly unreasonable. The issuer is not charged with notice of the contents of any document obtained pursuant to this paragraph (b) except to the extent that the contents relate directly to the appointment or incumbency.

(4) The issuer may elect to require reasonable assurance beyond that specified in this section, but if it does so and, for a purpose other than that specified in subsection (3)(b), both requires and obtains a copy of a will, trust, indenture, articles of co-partnership, by-laws, or other controlling instrument, it is charged with notice of all matters contained therein affecting the transfer, pledge, or release.

Amended in 1977.

§ 8—403. Issuer's Duty as to Adverse Claims

(1) An issuer to whom a certificated security is presented for registration shall inquire into adverse claims if:

(a) a written notification of an adverse claim is received at a time and in a manner affording the issuer a reasonable opportunity to act on it prior to the issuance of a new, reissued, or re-registered certificated security, and the notification identifies the claimant, the registered owner, and the issue of which the security is a part, and provides an address for communications directed to the claimant; or

(b) the issuer is charged with notice of an adverse claim from a controlling instrument it has elected to require under Section 8—402(4).

(2) The issuer may discharge any duty of inquiry by any reasonable means, including notifying an adverse claimant by registered or certified mail at the address furnished by him or, if there be no such address, at his residence or regular place of business that the certificated security has been presented for registration of transfer by a named person, and that the transfer will be registered unless within 30 days from the date of mailing the notification, either:

(a) an appropriate restraining order, injunction, or other process issues from a court of competent jurisdiction; or

(b) there is filed with the issuer an indemnity bond, sufficient in the issuer's judgment to protect the issuer and any transfer agent, registrar, or other agent of the issuer involved from any loss it or they may suffer by complying with the adverse claim.

(3) Unless an issuer is charged with notice of an adverse claim from a controlling instrument which it has elected to require under Section 8—402(4) or receives notification of an adverse claim under subsection (1), if a certificated security presented for registration is indorsed by the appropriate person or persons the issuer is under no duty to inquire into adverse claims. In particular:

(a) an issuer registering a certificated security in the name of a person who is a fiduciary or who is described as a fiduciary is not bound to inquire into the existence, extent, or correct description of the fiduciary relationship; and thereafter the issuer may assume without inquiry that the newly registered owner continues to be the fiduciary until the issuer receives written notice that the fiduciary is no longer acting as such with respect to the particular security;

(b) an issuer registering transfer on an indorsement by a fiduciary is not bound to inquire whether the transfer is made in compliance with a controlling instrument or with the law of the state having jurisdiction of the fiduciary relationship, including any law requiring the fiduciary to obtain court approval of the transfer; and

(c) the issuer is not charged with notice of the contents of any court record or file or other recorded or unrecorded document even though the document is in its possession and even though the transfer is made on the indorsement of a fiduciary to the fiduciary himself or to his nominee.

(4) An issuer is under no duty as to adverse claims with respect to an uncertificated security except:

(a) claims embodied in a restraining order, injunction, or other legal process served upon the issuer if the process was served at a time and in a manner affording the issuer a reasonable opportunity to act on it in accordance with the requirements of subsection (5);

(b) claims of which the issuer has received a written notification from the registered owner or the registered pledgee if the notification was received at a time and in a manner af-

fording the issuer a reasonable opportunity to act on it in accordance with the requirements of subsection (5);

(c) claims (including restrictions on transfer not imposed by the issuer) to which the registration of transfer to the present registered owner was subject and were so noted in the initial transaction statement sent to him; and

(d) claims as to which an issuer is charged with notice from a controlling instrument it has elected to require under Section 8—402(4).

(5) If the issuer of an uncertificated security is under a duty as to an adverse claim, he discharges that duty by:

(a) including a notation of the claim in any statements sent with respect to the security under Sections 8—408(3), (6), and (7); and

(b) refusing to register the transfer or pledge of the security unless the nature of the claim does not preclude transfer or pledge subject thereto.

(6) If the transfer or pledge of the security is registered subject to an adverse claim, a notation of the claim must be included in the initial transaction statement and all subsequent statements sent to the transferee and pledgee under Section 8—408.

(7) Notwithstanding subsections (4) and (5), if an uncertificated security was subject to a registered pledge at the time the issuer first came under a duty as to a particular adverse claim, the issuer has no duty as to that claim if transfer of the security is requested by the registered pledgee or an appropriate person acting for the registered pledgee unless:

(a) the claim was embodied in legal process which expressly provides otherwise;

(b) the claim was asserted in a written notification from the registered pledgee;

(c) the claim was one as to which the issuer was charged with notice from a controlling instrument it required under Section 8—402(4) in connection with the pledgee's request for transfer; or

(d) the transfer requested is to the registered owner.

Amended in 1977.

§ 8—404. Liability and Non-Liability for Registration

(1) Except as provided in any law relating to the collection of taxes, the issuer is not liable to the owner, pledgee, or any other person suffering loss as a result of the registration of a transfer, pledge, or release of a security if:

(a) there were on or with a certificated security the necessary indorsements or the issuer had received an instruction originated by an appropriate person (Section 8—308); and

(b) the issuer had no duty as to adverse claims or has discharged the duty (Section 8—403).

(2) If an issuer has registered a transfer of a certificated security to a person not entitled to it, the issuer on demand shall deliver a like security to the true owner unless:

(a) the registration was pursuant to subsection (1);

(b) the owner is precluded from asserting any claim for registering the transfer under Section 8—405(1); or

(c) the delivery would result in overissue, in which case the issuer's liability is governed by Section 8—104.

(3) If an issuer has improperly registered a transfer, pledge, or release of an uncertificated security, the issuer on demand from the injured party shall restore the records as to the injured party to the condition that would have obtained if the improper registration had not been made unless:

(a) the registration was pursuant to subsection (1); or

(b) the registration would result in overissue, in which case the issuer's liability is governed by Section 8—104.

Amended in 1977.

§ 8—405. Lost, Destroyed, and Stolen Certificated Securities

(1) If a certificated security has been lost, apparently destroyed, or wrongfully taken, and the owner fails to notify the issuer of that fact within a reasonable time after he has notice of it and the issuer registers a transfer of the security before receiving notification, the owner is precluded from asserting against the issuer any claim for registering the transfer under Section 8—404 or any claim to a new security under this section.

(2) If the owner of a certificated security claims that the security has been lost, destroyed, or wrongfully taken, the issuer shall issue a new certificated security or, at the option of the issuer, an equivalent uncertificated security in place of the original security if the owner:

(a) so requests before the issuer has notice that the security has been acquired by a bona fide purchaser;

(b) files with the issuer a sufficient indemnity bond; and

(c) satisfies any other reasonable requirements imposed by the issuer.

(3) If, after the issue of a new certificated or uncertificated security, a bona fide purchaser of the original certificated security presents it for registration of transfer, the issuer shall register the transfer unless registration would result in overissue, in which event the issuer's liability is governed by Section 8—104. In addition to any rights on the indemnity bond, the issuer may recover the new certificated security from the person to whom it was issued or any person taking under him except a bona fide purchaser or may cancel the uncertificated security unless a bona fide purchaser or any person taking under a bona fide purchaser is then the registered owner or registered pledgee thereof.

Amended in 1977.

§ 8—406. Duty of Authenticating Trustee, Transfer Agent, or Registrar

(1) If a person acts as authenticating trustee, transfer agent, registrar, or other agent for an issuer in the registration of transfers of its certificated securities or in the registration of transfers, pledges, and releases of its uncertificated securities, in the issue of new securities, or in the cancellation of surrendered securities:

(a) he is under a duty to the issuer to exercise good faith and due diligence in performing his functions; and

(b) with regard to the particular functions he performs, he has the same obligation to the holder or owner of a certificated security or to the owner or pledgee of an uncertificated security and has the same rights and privileges as the issuer has in regard to those functions.

(2) Notice to an authenticating trustee, transfer agent, registrar or other agent is notice to the issuer with respect to the functions performed by the agent.

Amended in 1977.

§ 8—407. Exchangeability of Securities

(1) No issuer is subject to the requirements of this section unless it regularly maintains a system for issuing the class of securities involved under which both certificated and uncertificated securities are regularly issued to the category of owners, which includes the person in whose name the new security is to be registered.

(2) Upon surrender of a certificated security with all necessary indorsements and presentation of a written request by the person surrendering the security, the issuer, if he has no duty as to adverse claims or has discharged the duty (Section 8—403), shall issue to the person or a person designated by him an equivalent uncertificated security subject to all liens, restrictions, and claims that were noted on the certificated security.

(3) Upon receipt of a transfer instruction originated by an appropriate person who so requests, the issuer of an uncertificated security shall cancel the uncertificated security and issue an equivalent certificated security on which must be noted conspicuously any liens and restrictions of the issuer and any adverse claims (as to which the issuer has a duty under Section 8—403(4)) to which the uncertificated security was subject. The certificated security shall be registered in the name of and delivered to:

(a) the registered owner, if the uncertificated security was not subject to a registered pledge; or

(b) the registered pledgee, if the uncertificated security was subject to a registered pledge.

Added in 1977.

§ 8—408. Statements of Uncertificated Securities

(1) Within 2 business days after the transfer of an uncertificated security has been registered, the issuer shall send to the new registered owner and, if the security has been transferred subject to a registered pledge, to the registered pledgee a written statement containing:

(a) a description of the issue of which the uncertificated security is a part;

(b) the number of shares or units transferred;

(c) the name and address and any taxpayer identification number of the new registered owner and, if the security has been transferred subject to a registered pledge, the name and address and any taxpayer identification number of the registered pledgee;

(d) a notation of any liens and restrictions of the issuer and any adverse claims (as to which the issuer has a duty under Section 8—403(4)) to which the uncertificated security is or may be subject at the time of registration or a statement that there are none of those liens, restrictions, or adverse claims; and

(e) the date the transfer was registered.

(2) Within 2 business days after the pledge of an uncertificated security has been registered, the issuer shall send to the registered owner and the registered pledgee a written statement containing:

(a) a description of the issue of which the uncertificated security is a part;

(b) the number of shares or units pledged;

(c) the name and address and any taxpayer identification number of the registered owner and the registered pledgee;

(d) a notation of any liens and restrictions of the issuer and any adverse claims (as to which the issuer has a duty under Section 8—403(4)) to which the uncertificated security is or may be subject at the time of registration or a statement that there are none of those liens, restrictions, or adverse claims; and

(e) the date the pledge was registered.

(3) Within 2 business days after the release from pledge of an uncertificated security has been registered, the issuer shall send to the registered owner and the pledgee whose interest was released a written statement containing:

(a) a description of the issue of which the uncertificated security is a part;

(b) the number of shares or units released from pledge;

(c) the name and address and any taxpayer identification number of the registered owner and the pledgee whose interest was released;

(d) a notation of any liens and restrictions of the issuer and any adverse claims (as to which the issuer has a duty under Section 8—403(4)) to which the uncertificated security is or may be subject at the time of registration or a statement that there are none of those liens, restrictions, or adverse claims; and

(e) the date the release was registered.

(4) An "initial transaction statement" is the statement sent to:

(a) the new registered owner and, if applicable, to the registered pledgee pursuant to subsection (1);

(b) the registered pledgee pursuant to subsection (2); or

(c) the registered owner pursuant to subsection (3).

Each initial transaction statement shall be signed by or on behalf of the issuer and must be identified as "Initial Transaction Statement".

(5) Within 2 business days after the transfer of an uncertificated security has been registered, the issuer shall send to the former registered owner and the former registered pledgee, if any, a written statement containing:

(a) a description of the issue of which the uncertificated security is a part;

(b) the number of shares or units transferred;

(c) the name and address and any taxpayer identification number of the former registered owner and of any former registered pledgee; and

(d) the date the transfer was registered.

(6) At periodic intervals no less frequent than annually and at any time upon the reasonable written request of the registered owner, the issuer shall send to the registered owner of each uncertificated security a dated written statement containing:

(a) a description of the issue of which the uncertificated security is a part;

(b) the name and address and any taxpayer identification number of the registered owner;

(c) the number of shares or units of the uncertificated security registered in the name of the registered owner on the date of the statement;

(d) the name and address and any taxpayer identification number of any registered pledgee and the number of shares or units subject to the pledge; and

(e) a notation of any liens and restrictions of the issuer and any adverse claims (as to which the issuer has a duty under Section 8—403(4)) to which the uncertificated security is or may be subject or a statement that there are none of those liens, restrictions, or adverse claims.

(7) At periodic intervals no less frequent than annually and at any time upon the reasonable written request of the registered pledgee, the issuer shall send to the registered pledgee of each uncertificated security a dated written statement containing:

(a) a description of the issue of which the uncertificated security is a part;

(b) the name and address and any taxpayer identification number of the registered owner;

(c) the name and address and any taxpayer identification number of the registered pledgee;

(d) the number of shares or units subject to the pledge; and

(e) a notation of any liens and restrictions of the issuer and any adverse claims (as to which the issuer has a duty under Section 8—403(4)) to which the uncertificated security is or may be subject or a statement that there are none of those liens, restrictions, or adverse claims.

(8) If the issuer sends the statements described in subsections (6) and (7) at periodic intervals no less frequent than quarterly, the issuer is not obliged to send additional statements upon request unless the owner or pledgee requesting them pays to the issuer the reasonable cost of furnishing them.

(9) Each statement sent pursuant to this section must bear a conspicuous legend reading substantially as follows: "This statement is merely a record of the rights of the addressee as of the time of its issuance. Delivery of this statement, of itself, confers no rights on the recipient. This statement is neither a negotiable instrument nor a security."

Added in 1977.

Article 9
SECURED TRANSACTIONS; SALES OF ACCOUNTS AND CHATTEL PAPER

Note: *The adoption of this Article should be accompanied by the repeal of existing statutes dealing with conditional sales, trust receipts, factor's liens where the factor is given a nonpossessory lien, chattel mortgages, crop mortgages, mortgages on railroad equipment, assignment of accounts and generally statutes regulating security interests in personal property.*

Where the state has a retail installment selling act or small loan act, that legislation should be carefully examined to determine what changes in those acts are needed to conform them to this Article. This Article primarily sets out rules defining rights of a secured party against persons dealing with the debtor; it does not prescribe regulations and controls which may be necessary to curb abuses arising in the small loan business or in the financing of consumer purchases on credit. Accordingly there is no intention to repeal existing regulatory acts in those fields by enactment or re-enactment of Article 9. See Section 9—203(4) and the Note thereto.

Part 1 Short Title, Applicability and Definitions

§ 9—101. **Short Title.**

This Article shall be known and may be cited as Uniform Commercial Code—Secured Transactions.

§ 9—102. **Policy and Subject Matter of Article.**

(1) Except as otherwise provided in Section 9—104 on excluded transactions, this Article applies

(a) to any transaction (regardless of its form) which is intended to create a security interest in personal property or fixtures including goods, documents, instruments, general intangibles, chattel paper or accounts; and also

(b) to any sale of accounts or chattel paper.

(2) This Article applies to security interests created by contract including pledge, assignment, chattel mortgage, chattel trust, trust deed, factor's lien, equipment trust, conditional sale, trust receipt, other lien or title retention contract and lease or consignment

intended as security. This Article does not apply to statutory liens except as provided in Section 9—310.

(3) The application of this Article to a security interest in a secured obligation is not affected by the fact that the obligation is itself secured by a transaction or interest to which this Article does not apply.

§ 9—103. **Perfection of Security Interest in Multiple State Transactions**

(1) Documents, instruments and ordinary goods.

(a) This subsection applies to documents and instruments and to goods other than those covered by a certificate of title described in subsection (2), mobile goods described in subsection (3), and minerals described in subsection (5).

(b) Except as otherwise provided in this subsection, perfection and the effect of perfection or non-perfection of a security interest in collateral are governed by the law of the jurisdiction where the collateral is when the last event occurs on which is based the assertion that the security interest is perfected or unperfected.

(c) If the parties to a transaction creating a purchase money security interest in goods in one jurisdiction understand at the time that the security interest attaches that the goods will be kept in another jurisdiction, then the law of the other jurisdiction governs the perfection and the effect of perfection or non-perfection of the security interest from the time it attaches until thirty days after the debtor receives possession of the goods and thereafter if the goods are taken to the other jurisdiction before the end of the thirty-day period.

(d) When collateral is brought into and kept in this state while subject to a security interest perfected under the law of the jurisdiction from which the collateral was removed, the security interest remains perfected, but if action is required by Part 3 of this Article to perfect the security interest,

(i) if the action is not taken before the expiration of the period of perfection in the other jurisdiction or the end of four months after the collateral is brought into this state, whichever period first expires, the security interest becomes unperfected at the end of that period and is thereafter deemed to have been unperfected as against a person who became a purchaser after removal;

(ii) if the action is taken before the expiration of the period specified in subparagraph (i), the security interest continues perfected thereafter;

(iii) for the purpose of priority over a buyer of consumer goods (subsection (2) of Section 9—307), the period of the effectiveness of a filing in the jurisdiction from which the collateral is removed is governed by the rules with respect to perfection in subparagraphs (i) and (ii).

(2) Certificate of title.

(a) This subsection applies to goods covered by a certificate of title issued under a statute of this state or of another jurisdiction under the law of which indication of a security interest on the certificate is required as a condition of perfection.

(b) Except as otherwise provided in this subsection, perfection and the effect of perfection or non-perfection of the security interest are governed by the law (including the conflict of laws rules) of the jurisdiction issuing the certificate until four months after the goods are removed from that jurisdiction and thereafter until the goods are registered in another jurisdiction, but in any event not beyond surrender of the certificate. After the expiration of that period, the goods are not covered by the certificate of title within the meaning of this section.

(c) Except with respect to the rights of a buyer described in the next paragraph, a security interest, perfected in another jurisdiction otherwise than by notation on a certificate of title, in goods brought into this state and thereafter covered by a certificate of title issued by this state is subject to the rules stated in paragraph (d) of subsection (1).

(d) If goods are brought into this state while a security interest therein is perfected in any manner under the law of the jurisdiction from which the goods are removed and a certificate of title is issued by this state and the certificate does not show that the goods are subject to the security interest or that they may be subject to security interests not shown on the certificate, the security interest is subordinate to the rights of a buyer of the goods who is not in the business of selling goods of that kind to the extent that he gives value and receives delivery of the goods after issuance of the certificate and without knowledge of the security interest.

(3) Accounts, general intangibles and mobile goods.

(a) This subsection applies to accounts (other than an account described in subsection (5) on minerals) and general intangibles (other than uncertificated securities) and to goods which are mobile and which are of a type normally used in more than one jurisdiction, such as motor vehicles, trailers, rolling stock, airplanes, shipping containers, road building and construction machinery and commercial harvesting machinery and the like, if the goods are equipment or are inventory leased or held for lease by the debtor to others, and are not covered by a certificate of title described in subsection (2).

(b) The law (including the conflict of laws rules) of the jurisdiction in which the debtor is located governs the perfection and the effect of perfection or non-perfection of the security interest.

(c) If, however, the debtor is located in a jurisdiction which is not a part of the United States, and which does not provide for perfection of the security interest by filing or recording in that jurisdiction, the law of the jurisdiction in the United States in which the debtor has its major executive office in the United States governs the perfection and the effect of perfection or non-perfection of the security interest through filing. In the alternative, if the debtor is located in a jurisdiction which is not a part of the United States or Canada and the collateral

is accounts or general intangibles for money due or to become due, the security interest may be perfected by notification to the account debtor. As used in this paragraph, "United States" includes its territories and possessions and the Commonwealth of Puerto Rico.

(d) A debtor shall be deemed located at his place of business if he has one, at his chief executive office if he has more than one place of business, otherwise at his residence. If, however, the debtor is a foreign air carrier under the Federal Aviation Act of 1958, as amended, it shall be deemed located at the designated office of the agent upon whom service of process may be made on behalf of the foreign air carrier.

(e) A security interest perfected under the law of the jurisdiction of the location of the debtor is perfected until the expiration of four months after a change of the debtor's location to another jurisdiction, or until perfection would have ceased by the law of the first jurisdiction, whichever period first expires. Unless perfected in the new jurisdiction before the end of that period, it becomes unperfected thereafter and is deemed to have been unperfected as against a person who became a purchaser after the change.

(4) Chattel paper.

The rules stated for goods in subsection (1) apply to a possessory security interest in chattel paper. The rules stated for accounts in subsection (3) apply to a nonpossessory security interest in chattel paper, but the security interest may not be perfected by notification to the account debtor.

(5) Minerals.

Perfection and the effect of perfection or non-perfection of a security interest which is created by a debtor who has an interest in minerals or the like (including oil and gas) before extraction and which attaches thereto as extracted, or which attaches to an account resulting from the sale thereof at the wellhead or minehead are governed by the law (including the conflict of laws rules) of the jurisdiction wherein the wellhead or minehead is located.

(6) Uncertificated securities.

The law (including the conflict of laws rules) of the jurisdiction of organization of the issuer governs the perfection and the effect of perfection or non-perfection of a security interest in uncertificated securities.

Amended in 1972 and 1977.

§ 9—104. **Transactions Excluded From Article.**

This Article does not apply

(a) to a security interest subject to any statute of the United States, to the extent that such statute governs the rights of parties to and third parties affected by transactions in particular types of property; or

(b) to a landlord's lien; or

(c) to a lien given by statute or other rule of law for services or materials except as provided in Section 9—310 on priority of such liens; or

(d) to a transfer of a claim for wages, salary or other compensation of an employee; or

(e) to a transfer by a government or governmental subdivision or agency; or

(f) to a sale of accounts or chattel paper as part of a sale of the business out of which they arose, or an assignment of accounts or chattel paper which is for the purpose of collection only, or a transfer of a right to payment under a contract to an assignee who is also to do the performance under the contract or a transfer of a single account to an assignee in whole or partial satisfaction of a preexisting indebtedness; or

(g) to a transfer of an interest in or claim in or under any policy of insurance, except as provided with respect to proceeds (Section 9—306) and priorities in proceeds (Section 9—312); or

(h) to a right represented by a judgment (other than a judgment taken on a right to payment which was collateral); or

(i) to any right of set-off; or

(j) except to the extent that provision is made for fixtures in Section 9—313, to the creation or transfer of an interest in or lien on real estate, including a lease or rents thereunder; or

(k) to a transfer in whole or in part of any claim arising out of tort; or

(l) to a transfer of an interest in any deposit account (subsection (1) of Section 9—105), except as provided with respect to proceeds (Section 9—306) and priorities in proceeds (Section 9—312).

Amended in 1972.

§ 9—105. Definitions and Index of Definitions

(1) In this Article unless the context otherwise requires:

(a) "Account debtor" means the person who is obligated on an account, chattel paper or general intangible;

(b) "Chattel paper" means a writing or writings which evidence both a monetary obligation and a security interest in or a lease of specific goods, but a charter or other contract involving the use or hire of a vessel is not chattel paper. When a transaction is evidenced both by such a security agreement or a lease and by an instrument or a series of instruments, the group of writings taken together constitutes chattel paper;

(c) "Collateral" means the property subject to a security interest, and includes accounts and chattel paper which have been sold;

(d) "Debtor" means the person who owes payment or other performance of the obligation secured, whether or not he owns or has rights in the collateral, and includes the seller of accounts or chattel paper. Where the debtor and the owner of the collateral are not the same person, the term "debtor" means the owner of the collateral in any provision of the Article

dealing with the collateral, the obligor in any provision dealing with the obligation, and may include both where the context so requires;

(e) "Deposit account" means a demand, time, savings, passbook or like account maintained with a bank, savings and loan association, credit union or like organization, other than an account evidenced by a certificate of deposit;

(f) "Document" means document of title as defined in the general definitions of Article 1 (Section 1—201), and a receipt of the kind described in subsection (2) of Section 7—201;

(g) "Encumbrance" includes real estate mortgages and other liens on real estate and all other rights in real estate that are not ownership interests;

(h) "Goods" includes all things which are movable at the time the security interest attaches or which are fixtures (Section 9—313), but does not include money, documents, instruments, accounts, chattel paper, general intangibles, or minerals or the like (including oil and gas) before extraction. "Goods" also includes standing timber which is to be cut and removed under a conveyance or contract for sale, the unborn young of animals, and growing crops;

(i) "Instrument" means a negotiable instrument (defined in Section 3—104), or a certificated security (defined in Section 8—102) or any other writing which evidences a right to the payment of money and is not itself a security agreement or lease and is of a type which is in ordinary course of business transferred by delivery with any necessary indorsement or assignment;

(j) "Mortgage" means a consensual interest created by a real estate mortgage, a trust deed on real estate, or the like;

(k) An advance is made "pursuant to commitment" if the secured party has bound himself to make it, whether or not a subsequent event of default or other event not within his control has relieved or may relieve him from his obligation;

(l) "Security agreement" means an agreement which creates or provides for a security interest;

(m) "Secured party" means a lender, seller or other person in whose favor there is a security interest, including a person to whom accounts or chattel paper have been sold. When the holders of obligations issued under an indenture of trust, equipment trust agreement or the like are represented by a trustee or other person, the representative is the secured party;

(n) "Transmitting utility" means any person primarily engaged in the railroad, street railway or trolley bus business, the electric or electronics communications transmission business, the transmission of goods by pipeline, or the transmission or the production and transmission of electricity, steam, gas or water, or the provision of sewer service.

(2) Other definitions applying to this Article and the sections in which they appear are:

"Account". Section 9—106.
"Attach". Section 9—203.
"Construction mortgage". Section 9—313(1).
"Consumer goods". Section 9—109(1).
"Equipment". Section 9—109(2).
"Farm products". Section 9—109(3).
"Fixture". Section 9—313(1).
"Fixture filing". Section 9—313(1).
"General intangibles". Section 9—106.
"Inventory". Section 9—109(4).
"Lien creditor". Section 9—301(3).
"Proceeds". Section 9—306(1).
"Purchase money security interest". Section 9—107.
"United States". Section 9—103.

(3) The following definitions in other Articles apply to this Article:
"Check". Section 3—104.
"Contract for sale". Section 2—106.
"Holder in due course". Section 3—302.
"Note". Section 3—104.
"Sale". Section 2—106.

(4) In addition Article 1 contains general definitions and principles of construction and interpretation applicable throughout this Article.

Amended in 1966, 1972 and 1977.

§ 9—106. Definitions: "Account"; "General Intangibles".

"Account" means any right to payment for goods sold or leased or for services rendered which is not evidenced by an instrument or chattel paper, whether or not it has been earned by performance. "General intangibles" means any personal property (including things in action) other than goods, accounts, chattel paper, documents, instruments, and money. All rights to payment earned or unearned under a charter or other contract involving the use or hire of a vessel and all rights incident to the charter or contract are accounts.

§ 9—107. Definitions: "Purchase Money Security Interest".

A security interest is a "purchase money security interest" to the extent that it is

(a) taken or retained by the seller of the collateral to secure all or part of its price; or

(b) taken by a person who by making advances or incurring an obligation gives value to enable the debtor to acquire rights in or the use of collateral if such value is in fact so used.

§ 9—108. When After-Acquired Collateral Not Security for Antecedent Debt.

Where a secured party makes an advance, incurs an obligation, releases a perfected security interest, or otherwise gives new value which is to be secured in whole or in part by after-acquired property his security interest in the after-acquired collateral shall be deemed to be taken for new value and not as security for an antecedent debt if the debtor acquires his rights in such collateral either in the ordinary course of his business or under a contract of purchase made pursuant to the security agreement within a reasonable time after new value is given.

§ 9—109. Classification of Goods; "Consumer Goods"; "Equipment"; "Farm Products"; "Inventory".

Goods are

(1) "consumer goods" if they are used or bought for use primarily for personal, family or household purposes;

(2) "equipment" if they are used or bought for use primarily in business (including farming or a profession) or by a debtor who is a non-profit organization or a governmental subdivision or agency or if the goods are not included in the definitions of inventory, farm products or consumer goods;

(3) "farm products" if they are crops or livestock or supplies used or produced in farming operations or if they are products of crops or livestock in their unmanufactured states (such as ginned cotton, wool-clip, maple syrup, milk and eggs), and if they are in the possession of a debtor engaged in raising, fattening, grazing or other farming operations. If goods are farm products they are neither equipment nor inventory;

(4) "inventory" if they are held by a person who holds them for sale or lease or to be furnished under contracts of service or if he has so furnished them, or if they are raw materials, work in process or materials used or consumed in a business. Inventory of a person is not to be classified as his equipment.

§ 9—110. Sufficiency of Description.

For purposes of this Article any description of personal property or real estate is sufficient whether or not it is specific if it reasonably identifies what is described.

§ 9—111. Applicability of Bulk Transfer Laws.

The creation of a security interest is not a bulk transfer under Article 6 (see Section 6—103).

§ 9—112. Where Collateral Is Not Owned by Debtor.

Unless otherwise agreed, when a secured party knows that collateral is owned by a person who is not the debtor, the owner of the collateral is entitled to receive from the secured party any surplus under Section 9—502(2) or under Section 9—504(1), and is not liable for the debt or for any deficiency after resale, and he has the same right as the debtor

(a) to receive statements under Section 9—208;

(b) to receive notice of and to object to a secured party's proposal to retain the collateral in satisfaction of the indebtedness under Section 9—505;

(c) to redeem the collateral under Section 9—506;

(d) to obtain injunctive or other relief under Section 9—507(1); and

(e) to recover losses caused to him under Section 9—208(2).

§ 9—113. Security Interests Arising Under Article on Sales or Under Article on Leases.

A security interest arising solely under the Article on Sales (Article 2) or the Article on Leases is subject to the provisions of this Article except that to the extent that and so long as the debtor does not have or does not lawfully obtain possession of the goods

(a) no security agreement is necessary to make the security interest enforceable; and

(b) no filing is required to perfect the security interest; and

(c) the rights of the secured party on default by the debtor are governed (i) by the Article on Sales (Article 2) in the case of a security interest arising solely under such Article or (ii) by the Article on Leases (Article 2A) in the case of a security interest arising solely under such Article.

§ 9—114. Consignment.

(1) A person who delivers goods under a consignment which is not a security interest and who would be required to file under this Article by paragraph (3)(c) of Section 2—326 has priority over a secured party who is or becomes a creditor of the consignee and who would have a perfected security interest in the goods if they were the property of the consignee, and also has priority with respect to identifiable cash proceeds received on or before delivery of the goods to a buyer, if

(a) the consignor complies with the filing provision of the Article on Sales with respect to consignments (paragraph (3)(c) of Section 2—326) before the consignee receives possession of the goods; and

(b) the consignor gives notification in writing to the holder of the security interest if the holder has filed a financing statement covering the same types of goods before the date of the filing made by the consignor; and

(c) the holder of the security interest receives the notification within five years before the consignee receives possession of the goods; and

(d) the notification states that the consignor expects to deliver goods on consignment to the consignee, describing the goods by item or type.

(2) In the case of a consignment which is not a security interest and in which the requirements of the preceding subsection have not been met, a person who delivers goods to another is subordinate to a person who would have a perfected security interest in the goods if they were the property of the debtor.

Part 2 Validity of Security Agreement and Rights of Parties Thereto

§ 9—201. General Validity of Security Agreement.

Except as otherwise provided by this Act a security agreement is effective according to its terms between the parties, against pur-

chasers of the collateral and against creditors. Nothing in this Article validates any charge or practice illegal under any statute or regulation thereunder governing usury, small loans, retail installment sales, or the like, or extends the application of any such statute or regulation to any transaction not otherwise subject thereto.

§ 9—202. Title to Collateral Immaterial.

Each provision of this Article with regard to rights, obligations and remedies applies whether title to collateral is in the secured party or in the debtor.

§ 9—203. Attachment and Enforceability of Security Interest; Proceeds; Formal Requisites

(1) Subject to the provisions of Section 4—208 on the security interest of a collecting bank, Section 8—321 on security interests in securities and Section 9—113 on a security interest arising under the Article on Sales, a security interest is not enforceable against the debtor or third parties with respect to the collateral and does not attach unless:

(a) the collateral is in the possession of the secured party pursuant to agreement, or the debtor has signed a security agreement which contains a description of the collateral and in addition, when the security interest covers crops growing or to be grown or timber to be cut, a description of the land concerned;

(b) value has been given; and

(c) the debtor has rights in the collateral.

(2) A security interest attaches when it becomes enforceable against the debtor with respect to the collateral. Attachment occurs as soon as all of the events specified in subsection (1) have taken place unless explicit agreement postpones the time of attaching.

(3) Unless otherwise agreed a security agreement gives the secured party the rights to proceeds provided by Section 9—306.

(4) A transaction, although subject to this Article, is also subject to . . . .*, and in the case of conflict between the provisions of this Article and any such statute, the provisions of such statute control. Failure to comply with any applicable statute has only the effect which is specified therein.

Amended in 1972 and 1977.

Note: *At * in subsection (4) insert reference to any local statute regulating small loans, retail installment sales and the like.*

The foregoing subsection (4) is designed to make it clear that certain transactions, although subject to this Article, must also comply with other applicable legislation.

This Article is designed to regulate all the "security" aspects of transactions within its scope. There is, however, much regulatory legislation, particularly in the consumer field, which supplements this Article and should not be repealed by its enactment. Examples are small loan acts, retail installment selling acts and the like. Such acts may provide for licensing and rate regulation and may prescribe particular forms of contract. Such provisions should remain in force despite the enactment of this Article. On the other hand if a retail installment selling act contains provisions on filing, rights on default, etc., such provisions should be repealed as incon-

sistent with this Article except that inconsistent provisions as to deficiencies, penalties, etc., in the Uniform Consumer Credit Code and other recent related legislation should remain because those statutes were drafted after the substantial enactment of the Article and with the intention of modifying certain provisions of this Article as to consumer credit.

§ 9—204. After-Acquired Property; Future Advances.

(1) Except as provided in subsection (2), a security agreement may provide that any or all obligations covered by the security agreement are to be secured by after-acquired collateral.

(2) No security interest attaches under an after-acquired property clause to consumer goods other than accessions (Section 9—314) when given as additional security unless the debtor acquires rights in them within ten days after the secured party gives value.

(3) Obligations covered by a security agreement may include future advances or other value whether or not the advances or value are given pursuant to commitment (subsection (1) of Section 9—105).

§ 9—205. Use or Disposition of Collateral Without Accounting Permissible.

A security interest is not invalid or fraudulent against creditors by reason of liberty in the debtor to use, commingle or dispose of all or part of the collateral (including returned or repossessed goods) or to collect or compromise accounts or chattel paper, or to accept the return of goods or make repossessions, or to use, commingle or dispose of proceeds, or by reason of the failure of the secured party to require the debtor to account for proceeds or replace collateral. This section does not relax the requirements of possession where perfection of a security interest depends upon possession of the collateral by the secured party or by a bailee.

§ 9—206. Agreement Not to Assert Defenses Against Assignee; Modification of Sales Warranties Where Security Agreement Exists.

(1) Subject to any statute or decision which establishes a different rule for buyers or lessees of consumer goods, an agreement by a buyer or lessee that he will not assert against an assignee any claim or defense which he may have against the seller or lessor is enforceable by an assignee who takes his assignment for value, in good faith and without notice of a claim or defense, except as to defenses of a type which may be asserted against a holder in due course of a negotiable instrument under the Article on Commercial Paper (Article 3). A buyer who as part of one transaction signs both a negotiable instrument and a security agreement makes such an agreement.

(2) When a seller retains a purchase money security interest in goods the Article on Sales (Article 2) governs the sale and any disclaimer, limitation or modification of the seller's warranties.

§ 9—207. Rights and Duties When Collateral is in Secured Party's Possession.

(1) A secured party must use reasonable care in the custody and preservation of collateral in his possession. In the case of an in-strument or chattel paper reasonable care includes taking necessary steps to preserve rights against prior parties unless otherwise agreed.

(2) Unless otherwise agreed, when collateral is in the secured party's possession

   (a) reasonable expenses (including the cost of any insurance and payment of taxes or other charges) incurred in the custody, preservation, use or operation of the collateral are chargeable to the debtor and are secured by the collateral;

   (b) the risk of accidental loss or damage is on the debtor to the extent of any deficiency in any effective insurance coverage;

   (c) the secured party may hold as additional security any increase or profits (except money) received from the collateral, but money so received, unless remitted to the debtor, shall be applied in reduction of the secured obligation;

   (d) the secured party must keep the collateral identifiable but fungible collateral may be commingled;

   (e) the secured party may repledge the collateral upon terms which do not impair the debtor's right to redeem it.

(3) A secured party is liable for any loss caused by his failure to meet any obligation imposed by the preceding subsections but does not lose his security interest.

(4) A secured party may use or operate the collateral for the purpose of preserving the collateral or its value or pursuant to the order of a court of appropriate jurisdiction or, except in the case of consumer goods, in the manner and to the extent provided in the security agreement.

§ 9—208. Request for Statement of Account or List of Collateral.

(1) A debtor may sign a statement indicating what he believes to be the aggregate amount of unpaid indebtedness as of a specified date and may send it to the secured party with a request that the statement be approved or corrected and returned to the debtor. When the security agreement or any other record kept by the secured party identifies the collateral a debtor may similarly request the secured party to approve or correct a list of the collateral.

(2) The secured party must comply with such a request within two weeks after receipt by sending a written correction or approval. If the secured party claims a security interest in all of a particular type of collateral owned by the debtor he may indicate that fact in his reply and need not approve or correct an itemized list of such collateral. If the secured party without reasonable excuse fails to comply he is liable for any loss caused to the debtor thereby; and if the debtor has properly included in his request a good faith statement of the obligation or a list of the collateral or both the secured party may claim a security interest only as shown in the statement against persons misled by his failure to comply. If he no longer has an interest in the obligation or collateral at the time the request is received he must disclose the name and address of any successor in interest known to him and he is liable for any loss caused to the debtor as a result of failure to disclose. A suc-

cessor in interest is not subject to this section until a request is received by him.

(3) A debtor is entitled to such a statement once every six months without charge. The secured party may require payment of a charge not exceeding $10 for each additional statement furnished.

Part 3 Rights of Third Parties; Perfected and Unperfected Security Interests; Rules of Priority

§ 9—301. Persons Who Take Priority Over Unperfected Security Interests; Rights of "Lien Creditor".

(1) Except as otherwise provided in subsection (2), an unperfected security interest is subordinate to the rights of

(a) persons entitled to priority under Section 9—312;

(b) a person who becomes a lien creditor before the security interest is perfected;

(c) in the case of goods, instruments, documents, and chattel paper, a person who is not a secured party and who is a transferee in bulk or other buyer not in ordinary course of business or is a buyer of farm products in ordinary course of business, to the extent that he gives value and receives delivery of the collateral without knowledge of the security interest and before it is perfected;

(d) in the case of accounts and general intangibles, a person who is not a secured party and who is a transferee to the extent that he gives value without knowledge of the security interest and before it is perfected.

(2) If the secured party files with respect to a purchase money security interest before or within ten days after the debtor receives possession of the collateral, he takes priority over the rights of a transferee in bulk or of a lien creditor which arise between the time the security interest attaches and the time of filing.

(3) A "lien creditor" means a creditor who has acquired a lien on the property involved by attachment, levy or the like and includes an assignee for benefit of creditors from the time of assignment, and a trustee in bankruptcy from the date of the filing of the petition or a receiver in equity from the time of appointment.

(4) A person who becomes a lien creditor while a security interest is perfected takes subject to the security interest only to the extent that it secures advances made before he becomes a lien creditor or within 45 days thereafter or made without knowledge of the lien or pursuant to a commitment entered into without knowledge of the lien.

§ 9—302. When Filing Is Required to Perfect Security Interest; Security Interests to Which Filing Provisions of This Article Do Not Apply

(1) A financing statement must be filed to perfect all security interests except the following:

(a) a security interest in collateral in possession of the secured party under Section 9—305;

(b) a security interest temporarily perfected in instruments or documents without delivery under Section 9—304 or in proceeds for a 10 day period under Section 9—306;

(c) a security interest created by an assignment of a beneficial interest in a trust or a decedent's estate;

(d) a purchase money security interest in consumer goods; but filing is required for a motor vehicle required to be registered; and fixture filing is required for priority over conflicting interests in fixtures to the extent provided in Section 9—313;

(e) an assignment of accounts which does not alone or in conjunction with other assignments to the same assignee transfer a significant part of the outstanding accounts of the assignor;

(f) a security interest of a collecting bank (Section 4—208) or in securities (Section 8—321) or arising under the Article on Sales (see Section 9—113) or covered in subsection (3) of this section;

(g) an assignment for the benefit of all the creditors of the transferor, and subsequent transfers by the assignee thereunder.

(2) If a secured party assigns a perfected security interest, no filing under this Article is required in order to continue the perfected status of the security interest against creditors of and transferees from the original debtor.

(3) The filing of a financing statement otherwise required by this Article is not necessary or effective to perfect a security interest in property subject to

(a) a statute or treaty of the United States which provides for a national or international registration or a national or international certificate of title or which specifies a place of filing different from that specified in this Article for filing of the security interest; or

(b) the following statutes of this state; [list any certificate of title statute covering automobiles, trailers, mobile homes, boats, farm tractors, or the like, and any central filing statute.]; but during any period in which collateral is inventory held for sale by a person who is in the business of selling goods of that kind, the filing provisions of this Article (Part 4) apply to a security interest in that collateral created by him as debtor; or

(c) a certificate of title statute of another jurisdiction under the law of which indication of a security interest on the certificate is required as a condition of perfection (subsection (2) of Section 9—103).

(4) Compliance with a statute or treaty described in subsection (3) is equivalent to the filing of a financing statement under this Article, and a security interest in property subject to the statute or treaty can be perfected only by compliance therewith except as provided in Section 9—103 on multiple state transactions. Duration and renewal of perfection of a security interest perfected by compliance with the statute or treaty are governed by the provisions of the statute or treaty; in other respects the security interest is subject to this Article.

Amended in 1972 and 1977.

§ 9—303. When Security Interest Is Perfected; Continuity of Perfection.

(1) A security interest is perfected when it has attached and when all of the applicable steps required for perfection have been taken. Such steps are specified in Sections 9—302, 9—304, 9—305 and 9—306. If such steps are taken before the security interest attaches, it is perfected at the time when it attaches.

(2) If a security interest is originally perfected in any way permitted under this Article and is subsequently perfected in some other way under this Article, without an intermediate period when it was unperfected, the security interest shall be deemed to be perfected continuously for the purposes of this Article.

§ 9—304. Perfection of Security Interest in Instruments, Documents, and Goods Covered by Documents; Perfection by Permissive Filing; Temporary Perfection Without Filing or Transfer of Possession

(1) A security interest in chattel paper or negotiable documents may be perfected by filing. A security interest in money or instruments (other than certificated securities or instruments which constitute part of chattel paper) can be perfected only by the secured party's taking possession, except as provided in subsections (4) and (5) of this section and subsections (2) and (3) of Section 9—306 on proceeds.

(2) During the period that goods are in the possession of the issuer of a negotiable document therefor, a security interest in the goods is perfected by perfecting a security interest in the document, and any security interest in the goods otherwise perfected during such period is subject thereto.

(3) A security interest in goods in the possession of a bailee other than one who has issued a negotiable document therefor is perfected by issuance of a document in the name of the secured party or by the bailee's receipt of notification of the secured party's interest or by filing as to the goods.

(4) A security interest in instruments (other than certificated securities) or negotiable documents is perfected without filing or the taking of possession for a period of 21 days from the time it attaches to the extent that it arises for new value given under a written security agreement.

(5) A security interest remains perfected for a period of 21 days without filing where a secured party having a perfected security interest in an instrument (other than a certificated security), a negotiable document or goods in possession of a bailee other than one who has issued a negotiable document therefor

(a) makes available to the debtor the goods or documents representing the goods for the purpose of ultimate sale or exchange or for the purpose of loading, unloading, storing, shipping, transshipping, manufacturing, processing or otherwise dealing with them in a manner preliminary to their sale or exchange, but priority between conflicting security interests in the goods is subject to subsection (3) of Section 9—312; or

(b) delivers the instrument to the debtor for the purpose of ultimate sale or exchange or of presentation, collection, renewal or registration of transfer.

(6) After the 21 day period in subsections (4) and (5) perfection depends upon compliance with applicable provisions of this Article.

Amended in 1972 and 1977.

§ 9—305. When Possession by Secured Party Perfects Security Interest Without Filing

A security interest in letters of credit and advices of credit (subsection (2)(a) of Section 5—116), goods, instruments (other than certificated securities), money, negotiable documents, or chattel paper may be perfected by the secured party's taking possession of the collateral. If such collateral other than goods covered by a negotiable document is held by a bailee, the secured party is deemed to have possession from the time the bailee receives notification of the secured party's interest. A security interest is perfected by possession from the time possession is taken without a relation back and continues only so long as possession is retained, unless otherwise specified in this Article. The security interest may be otherwise perfected as provided in this Article before or after the period of possession by the secured party.

Amended in 1972 and 1977.

§ 9—306. "Proceeds"; Secured Party's Rights on Disposition of Collateral.

(1) "Proceeds" includes whatever is received upon the sale, exchange, collection or other disposition of collateral or proceeds. Insurance payable by reason of loss or damage to the collateral is proceeds, except to the extent that it is payable to a person other than a party to the security agreement. Money, checks, deposit accounts, and the like are "cash proceeds". All other proceeds are "noncash proceeds".

(2) Except where this Article otherwise provides, a security interest continues in collateral notwithstanding sale, exchange or other disposition thereof unless the disposition was authorized by the secured party in the security agreement or otherwise, and also continues in any identifiable proceeds including collections received by the debtor.

(3) The security interest in proceeds is a continuously perfected security interest if the interest in the original collateral was perfected but it ceases to be a perfected security interest and becomes unperfected ten days after receipt of the proceeds by the debtor unless

(a) a filed financing statement covers the original collateral and the proceeds are collateral in which a security interest may be perfected by filing in the office or offices where the financing statement has been filed and, if the proceeds are acquired with cash proceeds, the description of collateral in the financing statement indicates the types of property constituting the proceeds; or

(b) a filed financing statement covers the original collateral and the proceeds are identifiable cash proceeds; or

(c) the security interest in the proceeds is perfected before the expiration of the ten day period.

Except as provided in this section, a security interest in proceeds can be perfected only by the methods or under the circumstances permitted in this Article for original collateral of the same type.

(4) In the event of insolvency proceedings instituted by or against a debtor, a secured party with a perfected security interest in proceeds has a perfected security interest only in the following proceeds:

(a) in identifiable noncash proceeds and in separate deposit accounts containing only proceeds;

(b) in identifiable cash proceeds in the form of money which is neither commingled with other money nor deposited in a deposit account prior to the insolvency proceedings;

(c) in identifiable cash proceeds in the form of checks and the like which are not deposited in a deposit account prior to the insolvency proceedings; and

(d) in all cash and deposit accounts of the debtor in which proceeds have been commingled with other funds, but the perfected security interest under this paragraph (d) is

(i) subject to any right to set-off; and

(ii) limited to an amount not greater than the amount of any cash proceeds received by the debtor within ten days before the institution of the insolvency proceedings less the sum of (I) the payments to the secured party on account of cash proceeds received by the debtor during such period and (II) the cash proceeds received by the debtor during such period to which the secured party is entitled under paragraphs (a) through (c) of this subsection (4).

(5) If a sale of goods results in an account or chattel paper which is transferred by the seller to a secured party, and if the goods are returned to or are repossessed by the seller or the secured party, the following rules determine priorities:

(a) If the goods were collateral at the time of sale, for an indebtedness of the seller which is still unpaid, the original security interest attaches again to the goods and continues as a perfected security interest if it was perfected at the time when the goods were sold. If the security interest was originally perfected by a filing which is still effective, nothing further is required to continue the perfected status; in any other case, the secured party must take possession of the returned or repossessed goods or must file.

(b) An unpaid transferee of the chattel paper has a security interest in the goods against the transferor. Such security interest is prior to a security interest asserted under paragraph (a) to the extent that the transferee of the chattel paper was entitled to priority under Section 9—308.

(c) An unpaid transferee of the account has a security interest in the goods against the transferor. Such security interest is subordinate to a security interest asserted under paragraph (a).

(d) A security interest of an unpaid transferee asserted under paragraph (b) or (c) must be perfected for protection against creditors of the transferor and purchasers of the returned or repossessed goods.

§ 9—307. **Protection of Buyers of Goods.**

(1) A buyer in ordinary course of business (subsection (9) of Section 1—201) other than a person buying farm products from a person engaged in farming operations takes free of a security interest created by his seller even though the security interest is perfected and even though the buyer knows of its existence.

(2) In the case of consumer goods, a buyer takes free of a security interest even though perfected if he buys without knowledge of the security interest, for value and for his own personal, family or household purposes unless prior to the purchase the secured party has filed a financing statement covering such goods.

(3) A buyer other than a buyer in ordinary course of business (subsection (1) of this section) takes free of a security interest to the extent that it secures future advances made after the secured party acquires knowledge of the purchase, or more than 45 days after the purchase, whichever first occurs, unless made pursuant to a commitment entered into without knowledge of the purchase and before the expiration of the 45 day period.

§ 9—308. **Purchase of Chattel Paper and Instruments.**

A purchaser of chattel paper or an instrument who gives new value and takes possession of it in the ordinary course of his business has priority over a security interest in the chattel paper or instrument

(a) which is perfected under Section 9—304 (permissive filing and temporary perfection) or under Section 9—306 (perfection as to proceeds) if he acts without knowledge that the specific paper or instrument is subject to a security interest; or

(b) which is claimed merely as proceeds of inventory subject to a security interest (Section 9—306) even though he knows that the specific paper or instrument is subject to the security interest.

§ 9—309. **Protection of Purchasers of Instruments, Documents and Securities**

Nothing in this Article limits the rights of a holder in due course of a negotiable instrument (Section 3—302) or a holder to whom a negotiable document of title has been duly negotiated (Section 7—501) or a bona fide purchaser of a security (Section 8—302) and the holders or purchasers take priority over an earlier security interest even though perfected. Filing under this Article does not constitute notice of the security interest to such holders or purchasers.

Amended in 1977.

§ 9—310. Priority of Certain Liens Arising by Operation of Law.

When a person in the ordinary course of his business furnishes services or materials with respect to goods subject to a security interest, a lien upon goods in the possession of such person given by statute or rule of law for such materials or services takes priority over a perfected security interest unless the lien is statutory and the statute expressly provides otherwise.

§ 9—311. Alienability of Debtor's Rights: Judicial Process.

The debtor's rights in collateral may be voluntarily or involuntarily transferred (by way of sale, creation of a security interest, attachment, levy, garnishment or other judicial process) notwithstanding a provision in the security agreement prohibiting any transfer or making the transfer constitute a default.

§ 9—312. Priorities Among Conflicting Security Interests in the Same Collateral

(1) The rules of priority stated in other sections of this Part and in the following sections shall govern when applicable: Section 4—208 with respect to the security interests of collecting banks in items being collected, accompanying documents and proceeds; Section 9—103 on security interests related to other jurisdictions; Section 9—114 on consignments.

(2) A perfected security interest in crops for new value given to enable the debtor to produce the crops during the production season and given not more than three months before the crops become growing crops by planting or otherwise takes priority over an earlier perfected security interest to the extent that such earlier interest secures obligations due more than six months before the crops become growing crops by planting or otherwise, even though the person giving new value had knowledge of the earlier security interest.

(3) A perfected purchase money security interest in inventory has priority over a conflicting security interest in the same inventory and also has priority in identifiable cash proceeds received on or before the delivery of the inventory to a buyer if

(a) the purchase money security interest is perfected at the time the debtor receives possession of the inventory; and

(b) the purchase money secured party gives notification in writing to the holder of the conflicting security interest if the holder had filed a financing statement covering the same types of inventory (i) before the date of the filing made by the purchase money secured party, or (ii) before the beginning of the 21 day period where the purchase money security interest is temporarily perfected without filing or possession (subsection (5) of Section 9—304); and

(c) the holder of the conflicting security interest receives the notification within five years before the debtor receives possession of the inventory; and

(d) the notification states that the person giving the notice has or expects to acquire a purchase money security interest in

inventory of the debtor, describing such inventory by item or type.

(4) A purchase money security interest in collateral other than inventory has priority over a conflicting security interest in the same collateral or its proceeds if the purchase money security interest is perfected at the time the debtor receives possession of the collateral or within ten days thereafter.

(5) In all cases not governed by other rules stated in this section (including cases of purchase money security interests which do not qualify for the special priorities set forth in subsections (3) and (4) of this section), priority between conflicting security interests in the same collateral shall be determined according to the following rules:

(a) Conflicting security interests rank according to priority in time of filing or perfection. Priority dates from the time a filing is first made covering the collateral or the time the security interest is first perfected, whichever is earlier, provided that there is no period thereafter when there is neither filing nor perfection.

(b) So long as conflicting security interests are unperfected, the first to attach has priority.

(6) For the purposes of subsection (5) a date of filing or perfection as to collateral is also a date of filing or perfection as to proceeds.

(7) If future advances are made while a security interest is perfected by filing, the taking of possession, or under Section 8—321 on securities, the security interest has the same priority for the purposes of subsection (5) with respect to the future advances as it does with respect to the first advance. If a commitment is made before or while the security interest is so perfected, the security interest has the same priority with respect to advances made pursuant thereto. In other cases a perfected security interest has priority from the date the advance is made.

Amended in 1972 and 1977.

§ 9—313. Priority of Security Interests in Fixtures.

(1) In this section and in the provisions of Part 4 of this Article referring to fixture filing, unless the context otherwise requires

(a) goods are "fixtures" when they become so related to particular real estate that an interest in them arises under real estate law

(b) a "fixture filing" is the filing in the office where a mortgage on the real estate would be filed or recorded of a financing statement covering goods which are or are to become fixtures and conforming to the requirements of subsection (5) of Section 9—402

(c) a mortgage is a "construction mortgage" to the extent that it secures an obligation incurred for the construction of an improvement on land including the acquisition cost of the land, if the recorded writing so indicates.

(2) A security interest under this Article may be created in goods which are fixtures or may continue in goods which become fix-

tures, but no security interest exists under this Article in ordinary building materials incorporated into an improvement on land.

(3) This Article does not prevent creation of an encumbrance upon fixtures pursuant to real estate law.

(4) A perfected security interest in fixtures has priority over the conflicting interest of an encumbrancer or owner of the real estate where

(a) the security interest is a purchase money security interest, the interest of the encumbrancer or owner arises before the goods become fixtures, the security interest is perfected by a fixture filing before the goods become fixtures or within ten days thereafter, and the debtor has an interest of record in the real estate or is in possession of the real estate; or

(b) the security interest is perfected by a fixture filing before the interest of the encumbrancer or owner is of record, the security interest has priority over any conflicting interest of a predecessor in title of the encumbrancer or owner, and the debtor has an interest of record in the real estate or is in possession of the real estate; or

(c) the fixtures are readily removable factory or office machines or readily removable replacements of domestic appliances which are consumer goods, and before the goods become fixtures the security interest is perfected by any method permitted by this Article; or

(d) the conflicting interest is a lien on the real estate obtained by legal or equitable proceedings after the security interest was perfected by any method permitted by this Article.

(5) A security interest in fixtures, whether or not perfected, has priority over the conflicting interest of an encumbrancer or owner of the real estate where

(a) the encumbrancer or owner has consented in writing to the security interest or has disclaimed an interest in the goods as fixtures; or

(b) the debtor has a right to remove the goods as against the encumbrancer or owner. If the debtor's right terminates, the priority of the security interest continues for a reasonable time.

(6) Notwithstanding paragraph (a) of subsection (4) but otherwise subject to subsections (4) and (5), a security interest in fixtures is subordinate to a construction mortgage recorded before the goods become fixtures if the goods become fixtures before the completion of the construction. To the extent that it is given to refinance a construction mortgage, a mortgage has this priority to the same extent as the construction mortgage.

(7) In cases not within the preceding subsections, a security interest in fixtures is subordinate to the conflicting interest of an encumbrancer or owner of the related real estate who is not the debtor.

(8) When the secured party has priority over all owners and encumbrancers of the real estate, he may, on default, subject to the provisions of Part 5, remove his collateral from the real estate but

he must reimburse any encumbrancer or owner of the real estate who is not the debtor and who has not otherwise agreed for the cost of repair of any physical injury, but not for any diminution in value of the real estate caused by the absence of the goods removed or by any necessity of replacing them. A person entitled to reimbursement may refuse permission to remove until the secured party gives adequate security for the performance of this obligation.

§ 9—314. **Accessions.**

(1) A security interest in goods which attaches before they are installed in or affixed to other goods takes priority as to the goods installed or affixed (called in this section "accessions") over the claims of all persons to the whole except as stated in subsection (3) and subject to Section 9—315(1).

(2) A security interest which attaches to goods after they become part of a whole is valid against all persons subsequently acquiring interests in the whole except as stated in subsection (3) but is invalid against any person with an interest in the whole at the time the security interest attaches to the goods who has not in writing consented to the security interest or disclaimed an interest in the goods as part of the whole.

(3) The security interests described in subsections (1) and (2) do not take priority over

(a) a subsequent purchaser for value of any interest in the whole; or

(b) a creditor with a lien on the whole subsequently obtained by judicial proceedings; or

(c) a creditor with a prior perfected security interest in the whole to the extent that he makes subsequent advances

if the subsequent purchase is made, the lien by judicial proceedings obtained or the subsequent advance under the prior perfected security interest is made or contracted for without knowledge of the security interest and before it is perfected. A purchaser of the whole at a foreclosure sale other than the holder of a perfected security interest purchasing at his own foreclosure sale is a subsequent purchaser within this section.

(4) When under subsections (1) or (2) and (3) a secured party has an interest in accessions which has priority over the claims of all persons who have interests in the whole, he may on default subject to the provisions of Part 5 remove his collateral from the whole but he must reimburse any encumbrancer or owner of the whole who is not the debtor and who has not otherwise agreed for the cost of repair of any physical injury but not for any diminution in value of the whole caused by the absence of the goods removed or by any necessity for replacing them. A person entitled to reimbursement may refuse permission to remove until the secured party gives adequate security for the performance of this obligation.

§ 9—315. **Priority When Goods Are Commingled or Processed.**

(1) If a security interest in goods was perfected and subsequently the goods or a part thereof have become part of a product or mass, the security interest continues in the product or mass if

(a) the goods are so manufactured, processed, assembled or commingled that their identity is lost in the product or mass; or

(b) a financing statement covering the original goods also covers the product into which the goods have been manufactured, processed or assembled.

In a case to which paragraph (b) applies, no separate security interest in that part of the original goods which has been manufactured, processed or assembled into the product may be claimed under Section 9—314.

(2) When under subsection (1) more than one security interest attaches to the product or mass, they rank equally according to the ratio that the cost of the goods to which each interest originally attached bears to the cost of the total product or mass.

§ 9—316. Priority Subject to Subordination.

Nothing in this Article prevents subordination by agreement by any person entitled to priority.

§ 9—317. Secured Party Not Obligated on Contract of Debtor.

The mere existence of a security interest or authority given to the debtor to dispose of or use collateral does not impose contract or tort liability upon the secured party for the debtor's acts or omissions.

§ 9—318. Defenses Against Assignee; Modification of Contract After Notification of Assignment; Term Prohibiting Assignment Ineffective; Identification and Proof of Assignment.

(1) Unless an account debtor has made an enforceable agreement not to assert defenses or claims arising out of a sale as provided in Section 9—206 the rights of an assignee are subject to

(a) all the terms of the contract between the account debtor and assignor and any defense or claim arising therefrom; and

(b) any other defense or claim of the account debtor against the assignor which accrues before the account debtor receives notification of the assignment.

(2) So far as the right to payment or a part thereof under an assigned contract has not been fully earned by performance, and notwithstanding notification of the assignment, any modification of or substitution for the contract made in good faith and in accordance with reasonable commercial standards is effective against an assignee unless the account debtor has otherwise agreed but the assignee acquires corresponding rights under the modified or substituted contract. The assignment may provide that such modification or substitution is a breach by the assignor.

(3) The account debtor is authorized to pay the assignor until the account debtor receives notification that the amount due or to become due has been assigned and that payment is to be made to the assignee. A notification which does not reasonably identify the rights assigned is ineffective. If requested by the account debtor, the assignee must seasonably furnish reasonable proof that the assignment has been made and unless he does so the account debtor may pay the assignor.

(4) A term in any contract between an account debtor and an assignor is ineffective if it prohibits assignment of an account or prohibits creation of a security interest in a general intangible for money due or to become due or requires the account debtor's consent to such assignment or security interest.

Part 4 Filing

§ 9—401. Place of Filing; Erroneous Filing; Removal of Collateral.

First Alternative Subsection (1)

(1) The proper place to file in order to perfect a security interest is as follows:

(a) when the collateral is timber to be cut or is minerals or the like (including oil and gas) or accounts subject to subsection (5) of Section 9—103, or when the financing statement is filed as a fixture filing (Section 9—313) and the collateral is goods which are or are to become fixtures, then in the office where a mortgage on the real estate would be filed or recorded;

(b) in all other cases, in the office of the [Secretary of State].

Second Alternative Subsection (1)

(1) The proper place to file in order to perfect a security interest is as follows:

(a) when the collateral is equipment used in farming operations, or farm products, or accounts or general intangibles arising from or relating to the sale of farm products by a farmer, or consumer goods, then in the office of the . . . . in the county of the debtor's residence or if the debtor is not a resident of this state then in the office of the . . . . in the county where the goods are kept, and in addition when the collateral is crops growing or to be grown in the office of the . . . . in the county where the land is located;

(b) when the collateral is timber to be cut or is minerals or the like (including oil and gas) or accounts subject to subsection (5) of Section 9—103, or when the financing statement is filed as a fixture filing (Section 9—313) and the collateral is goods which are or are to become fixtures, then in the office where a mortgage on the real estate would be filed or recorded;

(c) in all other cases, in the office of the [Secretary of State].

Third Alternative Subsection (1)

(1) The proper place to file in order to perfect a security interest is as follows:

(a) when the collateral is equipment used in farming operations, or farm products, or accounts or general intangibles arising from or relating to the sale of farm products by a farmer, or consumer goods, then in the office of the . . . . in the county of the debtor's residence or if the debtor is not a resident of this state then in the office of the . . . . in the county where the goods are kept, and in addition when the collateral is crops growing or to be grown in the office of the . . . . in the county where the land is located;

(b) when the collateral is timber to be cut or is minerals or the like (including oil and gas) or accounts subject to subsection (5) of Section 9—103, or when the financing statement is filed as a fixture filing (Section 9—313) and the collateral is goods which are or are to become fixtures, then in the office where a mortgage on the real estate would be filed or recorded;

(c) in all other cases, in the office of the [Secretary of State] and in addition, if the debtor has a place of business in only one county of this state, also in the office of . . . . of such county, or, if the debtor has no place of business in this state, but resides in the state, also in the office of . . . . of the county which he resides.

Note: *One of the three alternatives should be selected as subsection (1).*

(2) A filing which is made in good faith in an improper place or not in all of the places required by this section is nevertheless effective with regard to any collateral as to which the filing complied with the requirements of this Article and is also effective with regard to collateral covered by the financing statement against any person who has knowledge of the contents of such financing statement.

(3) A filing which is made in the proper place in this state continues effective even though the debtor's residence or place of business or the location of the collateral or its use, whichever controlled the original filing, is thereafter changed.

Alternative Subsection (3)

[(3) A filing which is made in the proper county continues effective for four months after a change to another county of the debtor's residence or place of business or the location of the collateral, whichever controlled the original filing. It becomes ineffective thereafter unless a copy of the financing statement signed by the secured party is filed in the new county within said period. The security interest may also be perfected in the new county after the expiration of the four-month period; in such case perfection dates from the time of perfection in the new county. A change in the use of the collateral does not impair the effectiveness of the original filing.]

(4) The rules stated in Section 9—103 determine whether filing is necessary in this state.

(5) Notwithstanding the preceding subsections, and subject to subsection (3) of Section 9—302, the proper place to file in order to perfect a security interest in collateral, including fixtures, of a transmitting utility is the office of the [Secretary of State]. This filing constitutes a fixture filing (Section 9—313) as to the collateral described therein which is or is to become fixtures.

(6) For the purposes of this section, the residence of an organization is its place of business if it has one or its chief executive office if it has more than one place of business.

Note: *Subsection (6) should be used only if the state chooses the Second or Third Alternative Subsection (1).*

§ 9—402. Formal Requisites of Financing Statement; Amendments; Mortgage as Financing Statement.

(1) A financing statement is sufficient if it gives the names of the debtor and the secured party, is signed by the debtor, gives an address of the secured party from which information concerning the security interest may be obtained, gives a mailing address of the debtor and contains a statement indicating the types, or describing the items, of collateral. A financing statement may be filed before a security agreement is made or a security interest otherwise attaches. When the financing statement covers crops growing or to be grown, the statement must also contain a description of the real estate concerned. When the financing statement covers timber to be cut or covers minerals or the like (including oil and gas) or accounts subject to subsection (5) of Section 9—103, or when the financing statement is filed as a fixture filing (Section 9—313) and the collateral is goods which are or are to become fixtures, the statement must also comply with subsection (5). A copy of the security agreement is sufficient as a financing statement if it contains the above information and is signed by the debtor. A carbon, photographic or other reproduction of a security agreement or a financing statement is sufficient as a financing statement if the security agreement so provides or if the original has been filed in this state.

(2) A financing statement which otherwise complies with subsection (1) is sufficient when it is signed by the secured party instead of the debtor if it is filed to perfect a security interest in

(a) collateral already subject to a security interest in another jurisdiction when it is brought into this state, or when the debtor's location is changed to this state. Such a financing statement must state that the collateral was brought into this state or that the debtor's location was changed to this state under such circumstances; or

(b) proceeds under Section 9—306 if the security interest in the original collateral was perfected. Such a financing statement must describe the original collateral; or

(c) collateral as to which the filing has lapsed; or

(d) collateral acquired after a change of name, identity or corporate structure of the debtor (subsection (7)).

(3) A form substantially as follows is sufficient to comply with subsection (1):

Name of debtor (or assignor) . . . .
Address . . . .
Name of secured party (or assignee) . . . .
Address . . . .
1. This financing statement covers the following types (or items) of property:
    (Describe) . . . .
2. (If collateral is crops) The above described crops are growing or are to be grown on:
    (Describe Real Estate) . . . .

3. (If applicable) The above goods are to become fixtures on *

*Where appropriate substitute either "The above timber is standing on . . . ." or "The above minerals or the like (including oil and gas) or accounts will be financed at the wellhead or minehead of the well or mine located on . . . ."
            (Describe Real Estate) . . . .
and this financing statement is to be filed [for record] in the real estate records. (If the debtor does not have an interest of record) The name of a record owner is . . . .
4. (If products of collateral are claimed) Products of the collateral are also covered.

(use
whichever   . . . .
                        Signature of Debtor (or Assignor)

is
applicable)   . . . .
                        Signature of Secured Party
                              (or Assignee)

(4) A financing statement may be amended by filing a writing signed by both the debtor and the secured party. An amendment does not extend the period of effectiveness of a financing statement. If any amendment adds collateral, it is effective as to the added collateral only from the filing date of the amendment. In this Article, unless the context otherwise requires, the term "financing statement" means the original financing statement and any amendments.

(5) A financing statement covering timber to be cut or covering minerals or the like (including oil and gas) or accounts subject to subsection (5) of Section 9—103, or a financing statement filed as a fixture filing (Section 9—313) where the debtor is not a transmitting utility, must show that it covers this type of collateral, must recite that it is to be filed [for record] in the real estate records, and the financing statement must contain a description of the real estate [sufficient if it were contained in a mortgage of the real estate to give constructive notice of the mortgage under the law of this state]. If the debtor does not have an interest of record in the real estate, the financing statement must show the name of a record owner.

(6) A mortgage is effective as a financing statement filed as a fixture filing from the date of its recording if

(a) the goods are described in the mortgage by item or type; and

(b) the goods are or are to become fixtures related to the real estate described in the mortgage; and

(c) the mortgage complies with the requirements for a financing statement in this section other than a recital that it is to be filed in the real estate records; and

(d) the mortgage is duly recorded.

No fee with reference to the financing statement is required other than the regular recording and satisfaction fees with respect to the mortgage.

(7) A financing statement sufficiently shows the name of the debtor if it gives the individual, partnership or corporate name of the debtor, whether or not it adds other trade names or names of partners. Where the debtor so changes his name or in the case of an organization its name, identity or corporate structure that a filed financing statement becomes seriously misleading, the filing is not effective to perfect a security interest in collateral acquired by the debtor more than four months after the change, unless a new appropriate financing statement is filed before the expiration of that time. A filed financing statement remains effective with respect to collateral transferred by the debtor even though the secured party knows of or consents to the transfer.

(8) A financing statement substantially complying with the requirements of this section is effective even though it contains minor errors which are not seriously misleading.

Note: *Language in brackets is optional.*

Note: *Where the state has any special recording system for real estate other than the usual grantor-grantee index (as, for instance, a tract system or a title registration or Torrens system) local adaptations of subsection (5) and Section 9—403(7) may be necessary. See Mass.Gen.Laws Chapter 106, Section 9—409.*

§ 9—403. **What Constitutes Filing; Duration of Filing; Effect of Lapsed Filing; Duties of Filing Officer.**

(1) Presentation for filing of a financing statement and tender of the filing fee or acceptance of the statement by the filing officer constitutes filing under this Article.

2) Except as provided in subsection (6) a filed financing statement is effective for a period of five years from the date of filing. The effectiveness of a filed financing statement lapses on the expiration of the five year period unless a continuation statement is filed prior to the lapse. If a security interest perfected by filing exists at the time insolvency proceedings are commenced by or against the debtor, the security interest remains perfected until termination of the insolvency proceedings and thereafter for a period of sixty days or until expiration of the five year period, whichever occurs later. Upon lapse the security interest becomes unperfected, unless it is perfected without filing. If the security interest becomes unperfected upon lapse, it is deemed to have been unperfected as against a person who became a purchaser or lien creditor before lapse.

(3) A continuation statement may be filed by the secured party within six months prior to the expiration of the five year period specified in subsection (2). Any such continuation statement must be signed by the secured party, identify the original statement by file number and state that the original statement is still effective. A continuation statement signed by a person other than the secured party of record must be accompanied by a separate written statement of assignment signed by the secured party of record and complying with subsection (2) of Section 9—405, including payment of the required fee. Upon timely filing of the continuation statement, the effectiveness of the original statement is continued for five years after the last date to which the filing was effective

whereupon it lapses in the same manner as provided in subsection (2) unless another continuation statement is filed prior to such lapse. Succeeding continuation statements may be filed in the same manner to continue the effectiveness of the original statement. Unless a statute on disposition of public records provides otherwise, the filing officer may remove a lapsed statement from the files and destroy it immediately if he has retained a microfilm or other photographic record, or in other cases after one year after the lapse. The filing officer shall so arrange matters by physical annexation of financing statements to continuation statements or other related filings, or by other means, that if he physically destroys the financing statements of a period more than five years past, those which have been continued by a continuation statement or which are still effective under subsection (6) shall be retained.

(4) Except as provided in subsection (7) a filing officer shall mark each statement with a file number and with the date and hour of filing and shall hold the statement or a microfilm or other photographic copy thereof for public inspection. In addition the filing officer shall index the statement according to the name of the debtor and shall note in the index the file number and the address of the debtor given in the statement.

(5) The uniform fee for filing and indexing and for stamping a copy furnished by the secured party to show the date and place of filing for an original financing statement or for a continuation statement shall be $. . . . . . . if the statement is in the standard form prescribed by the [Secretary of State] and otherwise shall be $. . . . . . ., plus in each case, if the financing statement is subject to subsection (5) of Section 9—402, $. . . . . . . The uniform fee for each name more than one required to be indexed shall be $. . . . . . . The secured party may at his option show a trade name for any person and an extra uniform indexing fee of $. . . . . . . shall be paid with respect thereto.

(6) If the debtor is a transmitting utility (subsection (5) of Section 9—401) and a filed financing statement so states, it is effective until a termination statement is filed. A real estate mortgage which is effective as a fixture filing under subsection (6) of Section 9—402 remains effective as a fixture filing until the mortgage is released or satisfied of record or its effectiveness otherwise terminates as to the real estate.

(7) When a financing statement covers timber to be cut or covers minerals or the like (including oil and gas) or accounts subject to subsection (5) of Section 9—103, or is filed as a fixture filing, [it shall be filed for record and] the filing officer shall index it under the names of the debtor and any owner of record shown on the financing statement in the same fashion as if they were the mortgagors in a mortgage of the real estate described, and, to the extent that the law of this state provides for indexing of mortgages under the name of the mortgagee, under the name of the secured party as if he were the mortgagee thereunder, or where indexing is by description in the same fashion as if the financing statement were a mortgage of the real estate described.

Note: *In states in which writings will not appear in the real estate records and indices unless actually recorded the bracketed language in subsection (7) should be used.*

§ 9—404. **Termination Statement.**

(1) If a financing statement covering consumer goods is filed on or after . . . ., then within one month or within ten days following written demand by the debtor after there is no outstanding secured obligation and no commitment to make advances, incur obligations or otherwise give value, the secured party must file with each filing officer with whom the financing statement was filed, a termination statement to the effect that he no longer claims a security interest under the financing statement, which shall be identified by file number. In other cases whenever there is no outstanding secured obligation and no commitment to make advances, incur obligations or otherwise give value, the secured party must on written demand by the debtor send the debtor, for each filing officer with whom the financing statement was filed, a termination statement to the effect that he no longer claims a security interest under the financing statement, which shall be identified by file number. A termination statement signed by a person other than the secured party of record must be accompanied by a separate written statement of assignment signed by the secured party of record complying with subsection (2) of Section 9—405, including payment of the required fee. If the affected secured party fails to file such a termination statement as required by this subsection, or to send such a termination statement within ten days after proper demand therefor, he shall be liable to the debtor for one hundred dollars, and in addition for any loss caused to the debtor by such failure.

(2) On presentation to the filing officer of such a termination statement he must note it in the index. If he has received the termination statement in duplicate, he shall return one copy of the termination statement to the secured party stamped to show the time of receipt thereof. If the filing officer has a microfilm or other photographic record of the financing statement, and of any related continuation statement, statement of assignment and statement of release, he may remove the originals from the files at any time after receipt of the termination statement, or if he has no such record, he may remove them from the files at any time after one year after receipt of the termination statement.

(3) If the termination statement is in the standard form prescribed by the [Secretary of State], the uniform fee for filing and indexing the termination statement shall be $. . . . . . ., and otherwise shall be $. . . . . . ., plus in each case an additional fee of $. . . . . . . for each name more than one against which the termination statement is required to be indexed.

Note: *The date to be inserted should be the effective date of the revised Article 9.*

§ 9—405. **Assignment of Security Interest; Duties of Filing Officer; Fees.**

(1) A financing statement may disclose an assignment of a security interest in the collateral described in the financing statement by

indication in the financing statement of the name and address of the assignee or by an assignment itself or a copy thereof on the face or back of the statement. On presentation to the filing officer of such a financing statement the filing officer shall mark the same as provided in Section 9—403(4). The uniform fee for filing, indexing and furnishing filing data for a financing statement so indicating an assignment shall be $. . . . . if the statement is in the standard form prescribed by the [Secretary of State] and otherwise shall be $. . . . ., plus in each case an additional fee of $. . . . . . . for each name more than one against which the financing statement is required to be indexed.

(2) A secured party may assign of record all or part of his rights under a financing statement by the filing in the place where the original financing statement was filed of a separate written statement of assignment signed by the secured party of record and setting forth the name of the secured party of record and the debtor, the file number and the date of filing of the financing statement and the name and address of the assignee and containing a description of the collateral assigned. A copy of the assignment is sufficient as a separate statement if it complies with the preceding sentence. On presentation to the filing officer of such a separate statement, the filing officer shall mark such separate statement with the date and hour of the filing. He shall note the assignment on the index of the financing statement, or in the case of a fixture filing, or a filing covering timber to be cut, or covering minerals or the like (including oil and gas) or accounts subject to subsection (5) of Section 9—103, he shall index the assignment under the name of the assignor as grantor and, to the extent that the law of this state provides for indexing the assignment of a mortgage under the name of the assignee, he shall index the assignment of the financing statement under the name of the assignee. The uniform fee for filing, indexing and furnishing filing data about such a separate statement of assignment shall be $. . . . . . if the statement is in the standard form prescribed by the [Secretary of State] and otherwise shall be $. . . . . ., plus in each case an additional fee of $. . . . . . for each name more than one against which the statement of assignment is required to be indexed. Notwithstanding the provisions of this subsection, an assignment of record of a security interest in a fixture contained in a mortgage effective as a fixture filing (subsection (6) of Section 9—402) may be made only by an assignment of the mortgage in the manner provided by the law of this state other than this Act.

(3) After the disclosure or filing of an assignment under this section, the assignee is the secured party of record.

§ 9—406. Release of Collateral; Duties of Filing Officer; Fees.

A secured party of record may by his signed statement release all or a part of any collateral described in a filed financing statement. The statement of release is sufficient if it contains a description of the collateral being released, the name and address of the debtor, the name and address of the secured party, and the file number of the financing statement. A statement of release signed by a person other than the secured party of record must be accompanied by a separate written statement of assignment signed by the secured

party of record and complying with subsection (2) of Section 9—405, including payment of the required fee. Upon presentation of such a statement of release to the filing officer he shall mark the statement with the hour and date of filing and shall note the same upon the margin of the index of the filing of the financing statement. The uniform fee for filing and noting such a statement of release shall be $. . . . . if the statement is in the standard form prescribed by the [Secretary of State] and otherwise shall be $. . . . . ., plus in each case an additional fee of $. . . . . . for each name more than one against which the statement of release is required to be indexed. Amended in 1972.

§ 9—407. Information From Filing Officer.

[(1) If the person filing any financing statement, termination statement, statement of assignment, or statement of release, furnishes the filing officer a copy thereof, the filing officer shall upon request note upon the copy the file number and date and hour of the filing of the original and deliver or send the copy to such person.]

[(2) Upon request of any person, the filing officer shall issue his certificate showing whether there is on file on the date and hour stated therein, any presently effective financing statement naming a particular debtor and any statement of assignment thereof and if there is, giving the date and hour of filing of each such statement and the names and addresses of each secured party therein. The uniform fee for such a certificate shall be $. . . . . . if the request for the certificate is in the standard form prescribed by the [Secretary of State] and otherwise shall be $. . . . . . . Upon request the filing officer shall furnish a copy of any filed financing statement or statement of assignment for a uniform fee of $. . . . . . per page.]

Note: *This section is proposed as an optional provision to require filing officers to furnish certificates. Local law and practices should be consulted with regard to the advisability of adoption.*

§ 9—408. Financing Statements Covering Consigned or Leased Goods.

A consignor or lessor of goods may file a financing statement using the terms "consignor," "consignee," "lessor," "lessee" or the like instead of the terms specified in Section 9—402. The provisions of this Part shall apply as appropriate to such a financing statement but its filing shall not of itself be a factor in determining whether or not the consignment or lease is intended as security (Section 1—201(37)). However, if it is determined for other reasons that the consignment or lease is so intended, a security interest of the consignor or lessor which attaches to the consigned or leased goods is perfected by such filing.

Part 5 Default

§ 9—501. Default; Procedure When Security Agreement Covers Both Real and Personal Property.

(1) When a debtor is in default under a security agreement, a secured party has the rights and remedies provided in this Part and except as limited by subsection (3) those provided in the security agreement. He may reduce his claim to judgment, fo-

reclose or otherwise enforce the security interest by any available judicial procedure. If the collateral is documents the secured party may proceed either as to the documents or as to the goods covered thereby. A secured party in possession has the rights, remedies and duties provided in Section 9—207. The rights and remedies referred to in this subsection are cumulative.

(2) After default, the debtor has the rights and remedies provided in this Part, those provided in the security agreement and those provided in Section 9—207.

(3) To the extent that they give rights to the debtor and impose duties on the secured party, the rules stated in the subsections referred to below may not be waived or varied except as provided with respect to compulsory disposition of collateral (subsection (3) of Section 9—504 and Section 9—505) and with respect to redemption of collateral (Section 9—506) but the parties may by agreement determine the standards by which the fulfillment of these rights and duties is to be measured if such standards are not manifestly unreasonable:

(a) subsection (2) of Section 9—502 and subsection (2) of Section 9—504 insofar as they require accounting for surplus proceeds of collateral;

(b) subsection (3) of Section 9—504 and subsection (1) of Section 9—505 which deal with disposition of collateral;

(c) subsection (2) of Section 9—505 which deals with acceptance of collateral as discharge of obligation;

(d) Section 9—506 which deals with redemption of collateral; and

(e) subsection (1) of Section 9—507 which deals with the secured party's liability for failure to comply with this Part.

(4) If the security agreement covers both real and personal property, the secured party may proceed under this Part as to the personal property or he may proceed as to both the real and the personal property in accordance with his rights and remedies in respect of the real property in which case the provisions of this Part do not apply.

(5) When a secured party has reduced his claim to judgment the lien of any levy which may be made upon his collateral by virture of any execution based upon the judgment shall relate back to the date of the perfection of the security interest in such collateral. A judicial sale, pursuant to such execution, is a foreclosure of the security interest by judicial procedure within the meaning of this section, and the secured party may purchase at the sale and thereafter hold the collateral free of any other requirements of this Article.

§ 9—502. Collection Rights of Secured Party.

(1) When so agreed and in any event on default the secured party is entitled to notify an account debtor or the obligor on an instrument to make payment to him whether or not the assignor was theretofore making collections on the collateral, and also to take control of any proceeds to which he is entitled under Section 9—306.

(2) A secured party who by agreement is entitled to charge back uncollected collateral or otherwise to full or limited recourse against the debtor and who undertakes to collect from the account debtors or obligors must proceed in a commercially reasonable manner and may deduct his reasonable expenses of realization from the collections. If the security agreement secures an indebtedness, the secured party must account to the debtor for any surplus, and unless otherwise agreed, the debtor is liable for any deficiency. But, if the underlying transaction was a sale of accounts or chattel paper, the debtor is entitled to any surplus or is liable for any deficiency only if the security agreement so provides.

§ 9—503. Secured Party's Right to Take Possession After Default.

Unless otherwise agreed a secured party has on default the right to take possession of the collateral. In taking possession a secured party may proceed without judicial process if this can be done without breach of the peace or may proceed by action. If the security agreement so provides the secured party may require the debtor to assemble the collateral and make it available to the secured party at a place to be designated by the secured party which is reasonably convenient to both parties. Without removal a secured party may render equipment unusable, and may dispose of collateral on the debtor's premises under Section 9—504.

§ 9—504. Secured Party's Right to Dispose of Collateral After Default; Effect of Disposition.

(1) A secured party after default may sell, lease or otherwise dispose of any or all of the collateral in its then condition or following any commercially reasonable preparation or processing. Any sale of goods is subject to the Article on Sales (Article 2). The proceeds of disposition shall be applied in the order following to

(a) the reasonable expenses of retaking, holding, preparing for sale or lease, selling, leasing and the like and, to the extent provided for in the agreement and not prohibited by law, the reasonable attorneys' fees and legal expenses incurred by the secured party;

(b) the satisfaction of indebtedness secured by the security interest under which the disposition is made;

(c) the satisfaction of indebtedness secured by any subordinate security interest in the collateral if written notification of demand therefor is received before distribution of the proceeds is completed. If requested by the secured party, the holder of a subordinate security interest must seasonably furnish reasonable proof of his interest, and unless he does so, the secured party need not comply with his demand.

(2) If the security interest secures an indebtedness, the secured party must account to the debtor for any surplus, and, unless otherwise agreed, the debtor is liable for any deficiency. But if the underlying transaction was a sale of accounts or chattel paper, the debtor is entitled to any surplus or is liable for any deficiency only if the security agreement so provides.

(3) Disposition of the collateral may be by public or private proceedings and may be made by way of one or more contracts. Sale or other disposition may be as a unit or in parcels and at any time and place and on any terms but every aspect of the disposition including the method, manner, time, place and terms must be commercially reasonable. Unless collateral is perishable or threatens to decline speedily in value or is of a type customarily sold on a recognized market, reasonable notification of the time and place of any public sale or reasonable notification of the time after which any private sale or other intended disposition is to be made shall be sent by the secured party to the debtor, if he has not signed after default a statement renouncing or modifying his right to notification of sale. In the case of consumer goods no other notification need be sent. In other cases notification shall be sent to any other secured party from whom the secured party has received (before sending his notification to the debtor or before the debtor's renunciation of his rights) written notice of a claim of an interest in the collateral. The secured party may buy at any public sale and if the collateral is of a type customarily sold in a recognized market or is of a type which is the subject of widely distributed standard price quotations he may buy at private sale.

(4) When collateral is disposed of by a secured party after default, the disposition transfers to a purchaser for value all of the debtor's rights therein, discharges the security interest under which it is made and any security interest or lien subordinate thereto. The purchaser takes free of all such rights and interests even though the secured party fails to comply with the requirements of this Part or of any judicial proceedings

 (a) in the case of a public sale, if the purchaser has no knowledge of any defects in the sale and if he does not buy in collusion with the secured party, other bidders or the person conducting the sale; or

 (b) in any other case, if the purchaser acts in good faith.

(5) A person who is liable to a secured party under a guaranty, indorsement, repurchase agreement or the like and who receives a transfer of collateral from the secured party or is subrogated to his rights has thereafter the rights and duties of the secured party. Such a transfer of collateral is not a sale or disposition of the collateral under this Article.

§ 9—505. Compulsory Disposition of Collateral; Acceptance of the Collateral as Discharge of Obligation.

(1) If the debtor has paid sixty per cent of the cash price in the case of a purchase money security interest in consumer goods or sixty per cent of the loan in the case of another security interest in consumer goods, and has not signed after default a statement renouncing or modifying his rights under this Part a secured party who has taken possession of collateral must dispose of it under Section 9—504 and if he fails to do so within ninety days after he takes possession the debtor at his option may recover in conversion or under Section 9—507(1) on secured party's liability.

(2) In any other case involving consumer goods or any other collateral a secured party in possession may, after default, propose to retain the collateral in satisfaction of the obligation. Written notice of such proposal shall be sent to the debtor if he has not signed after default a statement renouncing or modifying his rights under this subsection. In the case of consumer goods no other notice need be given. In other cases notice shall be sent to any other secured party from whom the secured party has received (before sending his notice to the debtor or before the debtor's renunciation of his rights) written notice of a claim of an interest in the collateral. If the secured party receives objection in writing from a person entitled to receive notification within twenty-one days after the notice was sent, the secured party must dispose of the collateral under Section 9—504. In the absence of such written objection the secured party may retain the collateral in satisfaction of the debtor's obligation. Amended in 1972.

§ 9—506. Debtor's Right to Redeem Collateral.

At any time before the secured party has disposed of collateral or entered into a contract for its disposition under Section 9—504 or before the obligation has been discharged under Section 9—505(2) the debtor or any other secured party may unless otherwise agreed in writing after default redeem the collateral by tendering fulfillment of all obligations secured by the collateral as well as the expenses reasonably incurred by the secured party in retaking, holding and preparing the collateral for disposition, in arranging for the sale, and to the extent provided in the agreement and not prohibited by law, his reasonable attorneys' fees and legal expenses.

§ 9—507. Secured Party's Liability for Failure to Comply With This Part.

(1) If it is established that the secured party is not proceeding in accordance with the provisions of this Part disposition may be ordered or restrained on appropriate terms and conditions. If the disposition has occurred the debtor or any person entitled to notification or whose security interest has been made known to the secured party prior to the disposition has a right to recover from the secured party any loss caused by a failure to comply with the provisions of this Part. If the collateral is consumer goods, the debtor has a right to recover in any event an amount not less than the credit service charge plus ten per cent of the principal amount of the debt or the time price differential plus 10 per cent of the cash price.

(2) The fact that a better price could have been obtained by a sale at a different time or in a different method from that selected by the secured party is not of itself sufficient to establish that the sale was not made in a commercially reasonable manner. If the secured party either sells the collateral in the usual manner in any recognized market therefor or if he sells at the price current in such market at the time of his sale or if he has otherwise sold in conformity with reasonable commercial practices among dealers in the type of property sold he has sold in a commercially reasonable manner. The principles stated in the two preceding sentences with respect to sales also apply as may be appropriate t

other types of disposition. A disposition which has been approved in any judicial proceeding or by any bona fide creditors' committee or representative of creditors shall conclusively be deemed to be commercially reasonable, but this sentence does not indicate that any such approval must be obtained in any case nor does it indicate that any disposition not so approved is not commercially reasonable.

Article 10
EFFECTIVE DATE AND REPEALER

§ 10—101. Effective Date.

This Act shall become effective at midnight on December 31st following its enactment. It applies to transactions entered into and events occurring after that date.

§ 10—102. Specific Repealer; Provision for Transition.

(1) The following acts and all other acts and parts of acts inconsistent herewith are hereby repealed:
(Here should follow the acts to be specifically repealed including the following:
    Uniform Negotiable Instruments Act
    Uniform Warehouse Receipts Act
    Uniform Sales Act
    Uniform Bills of Lading Act
    Uniform Stock Transfer Act
    Uniform Conditional Sales Act
    Uniform Trust Receipts Act
      Also any acts regulating:
    Bank collections
    Bulk sales
    Chattel mortgages
    Conditional sales
    Factor's lien acts
    Farm storage of grain and similar acts
    Assignment of accounts receivable)

(2) Transactions validly entered into before the effective date specified in Section 10—101 and the rights, duties and interests flowing from them remain valid thereafter and may be terminated, completed, consummated or enforced as required or permitted by any statute or other law amended or repealed by this Act as though such repeal or amendment had not occurred.

Note: *Subsection (1) should be separately prepared for each state. The foregoing is a list of statutes to be checked.*

§ 10—103. General Repealer.

Except as provided in the following section, all acts and parts of acts inconsistent with this Act are hereby repealed.

§ 10—104. Laws Not Repealed.

(1) The Article on Documents of Title (Article 7) does not repeal or modify any laws prescribing the form or contents of documents of title or the services or facilities to be afforded by bailees, or otherwise regulating bailees' businesses in respects not specifically dealt with herein; but the fact that such laws are violated does not affect the status of a document of title which otherwise complies with the definition of a document of title (Section 1—201).

[(2) This Act does not repeal . . . .*, cited as the Uniform Act for the Simplification of Fiduciary Security Transfers, and if in any respect there is any inconsistency between that Act and the Article of this Act on investment securities (Article 8) the provisions of the former Act shall control.]

Note: *At * in subsection (2) insert the statutory reference to the Uniform Act for the Simplification of Fiduciary Security Transfers if such Act has previously been enacted. If it has not been enacted, omit subsection (2).*

Article 11
(REPORTERS' DRAFT)
EFFECTIVE DATE AND TRANSITION PROVISIONS

This material has been numbered Article 11 to distinguish it from Article 10, the transition provision of the 1962 Code, which may still remain in effect in some states to cover transition problems from pre-Code law to the original Uniform Commercial Code. Adaptation may be necessary in particular states. The terms "[old Code]" and "[new Code]" and "[old U.C.C.]" and "[new U.C.C.]" are used herein, and should be suitably changed in each state.

Note: *This draft was prepared by the Reporters and has not been passed upon by the Review Committee, the Permanent Editorial Board, the American Law Institute, or the National Conference of Commissioners on Uniform State Laws. It is submitted as a working draft which may be adapted as appropriate in each state.*

§ 11—101. Effective Date.

This Act shall become effective at 12:01 A.M. on _____, 19___

§ 11—102. Preservation of Old Transition Provision.

The provisions of [here insert reference to the original transition provision in the particular state] shall continue to apply to [the new U.C.C.] and for this purpose the [old U.C.C. and new U.C.C.] shall be considered one continuous statute.

§ 11—103. Transition to [New Code]—General Rule.

Transactions validly entered into after [effective date of old U.C.C.] and before [effective date of new U.C.C.], and which were subject to the provisions of [old U.C.C.] and which would be subject to this Act as amended if they had been entered into after the effective date of [new U.C.C.] and the rights, duties and interests flowing from such transactions remain valid after the latter date and may be terminated, completed, consummated or enforced as required or permitted by the [new U.C.C.]. Security interests arising out of such transactions which are perfected when [new U.C.C.] becomes effective shall remain perfected until they lapse as provided in [new U.C.C.], and may be continued as permitted by [new U.C.C.], except as stated in Section 11—105.

§ 11—104. Transition Provision on Change of Requirement of Filing.

A security interest for the perfection of which filing or the taking of possession was required under [old U.C.C.] and which attached prior to the effective date of [new U.C.C.] but was not perfected shall be deemed perfected on the effective date of [new U.C.C.] if [new U.C.C.] permits perfection without filing or authorizes filing in the office or offices where a prior ineffective filing was made.

§ 11—105. Transition Provision on Change of Place of Filing.

(1) A financing statement or continuation statement filed prior to [effective date of new U.C.C.] which shall not have lapsed prior to [the effective date of new U.C.C.] shall remain effective for the period provided in the [old Code], but not less than five years after the filing.

(2) With respect to any collateral acquired by the debtor subsequent to the effective date of [new U.C.C.], any effective financing statement or continuation statement described in this section shall apply only if the filing or filings are in the office or offices that would be appropriate to perfect the security interests in the new collateral under [new U.C.C.].

(3) The effectiveness of any financing statement or continuation statement filed prior to [effective date of new U.C.C.] may be continued by a continuation statement as permitted by [new U.C.C.], except that if [new U.C.C.] requires a filing in an office where there was no previous financing statement, a new financing statement conforming to Section 11—106 shall be filed in that office.

(4) If the record of a mortgage of real estate would have been effective as a fixture filing of goods described therein if [new U.C.C.] had been in effect on the date of recording the mortgage, the mortgage shall be deemed effective as a fixture filing as to such goods under subsection (6) of Section 9—402 of the [new U.C.C.] on the effective date of [new U.C.C.].

§ 11—106. Required Refilings.

(1) If a security interest is perfected or has priority when this Act takes effect as to all persons or as to certain persons without any filing or recording, and if the filing of a financing statement would be required for the perfection or priority of the security interest against those persons under [new U.C.C.], the perfection and priority rights of the security interest continue until 3 years after the effective date of [new U.C.C.]. The perfection will then lapse unless a financing statement is filed as provided in subsection (4) or unless the security interest is perfected otherwise than by filing.

(2) If a security interest is perfected when [new U.C.C.] takes effect under a law other than [U.C.C.] which requires no further filing, refiling or recording to continue its perfection, perfection

continues until and will lapse 3 years after [new U.C.C.] takes effect, unless a financing statement is filed as provided in subsection (4) or unless the security interest is perfected otherwise than by filing, or unless under subsection (3) of Section 9—302 the other law continues to govern filing.

(3) If a security interest is perfected by a filing, refiling or recording under a law repealed by this Act which required further filing, refiling or recording to continue its perfection, perfection continues and will lapse on the date provided by the law so repealed for such further filing, refiling or recording unless a financing statement is filed as provided in subsection (4) or unless the security interest is perfected otherwise than by filing.

(4) A financing statement may be filed within six months before the perfection of a security interest would otherwise lapse. Any such financing statement may be signed by either the debtor or the secured party. It must identify the security agreement, statement or notice (however denominated in any statute or other law repealed or modified by this Act), state the office where and the date when the last filing, refiling or recording, if any, was made with respect thereto, and the filing number, if any, or book and page, if any, of recording and further state that the security agreement, statement or notice, however denominated, in another filing office under the [U.C.C.] or under any statute or other law repealed or modified by this Act is still effective. Section 9—401 and Section 9—103 determine the proper place to file such a financing statement. Except as specified in this subsection, the provisions of Section 9—403(3) for continuation statements apply to such a financing statement.

§ 11—107. Transition Provisions as to Priorities.

Except as otherwise provided in [Article 11], [old U.C.C.] shall apply to any questions of priority if the positions of the parties were fixed prior to the effective date of [new U.C.C.]. In other cases questions of priority shall be determined by [new U.C.C.].

§ 11—108. Presumption that Rule of Law Continues Unchanged.

Unless a change in law has clearly been made, the provisions of [new U.C.C.] shall be deemed declaratory of the meaning of the [old U.C.C.].

1978 OFFICIAL TEXT—UCC

The preceding articles and sections constitute the 1978 official text of the Uniform Commercial Code. As of January 1, 1987, the following states had adopted most of the proposed amendments of 1972, which was the year of the most recent major changes. The other states basically follow the original text plus amendments proposed in the 1960s.

States	Effective Date	States	Effective Date
Alabama	2/01/82	Nebraska	7/19/80
Alaska	7/01/83	Nevada	7/01/75
Arizona	1/01/76	New Hampshire	8/21/79
Arkansas	1/01/74	New Jersey	12/01/81
California	1/01/76	New Mexico	6/14/85
Colorado	1/01/78	New York	7/02/78
Connecticut	10/01/76	North Carolina	7/01/76
Delaware	1/01/84	North Dakota	1/01/74
Florida	1/01/80	Ohio	1/01/79
Georgia	7/01/78	Oklahoma	10/19/81
Hawaii	7/01/79	Oregon	1/01/74
Idaho	7/01/79	Pennsylvania	5/25/83
Illinois	7/01/73	Rhode Island	1/01/80
Indiana	1/01/86	South Dakota	7/01/83
Iowa	1/01/75	Tennessee	1/01/86
Kansas	1/01/76	Texas	1/01/74
Kentucky	7/01/87	Utah	7/01/77
Maine	1/01/78	Virginia	7/01/74
Maryland	1/01/81	Washington	7/01/82
Massachusetts	1/01/80	West Virginia	7/01/75
Michigan	1/01/79	Wisconsin	7/01/74
Minnesota	1/01/77	Wyoming	9/01/83
Mississippi	4/01/78		
Montana	10/01/83	District of Columbia	3/16/82

Appendix C

The Uniform Partnership Act

(Adopted in 48 States [except Georgia and Louisiana], the District of Columbia, the Virgin Islands, and Guam. The adoptions by Alabama and Nebraska do not follow the official text in every respect, but are substantially similar, with local variations.)

The Act consists of 7 Parts as follows:

I. Preliminary Provisions

II. Nature of Partnership

III. Relations of Partners to Persons Dealing with the Partnership

IV. Relations of Partners to One Another

V. Property Rights of a Partner

VI. Dissolution and Winding Up

VII. Miscellaneous Provisions

An Act to make uniform the Law of Partnerships

Be it enacted, etc.:

Part I Preliminary Provisions

Sec. 1. Name of Act

This act may be cited as Uniform Partnership Act.

Sec. 2. Definition of Terms

In this act, "Court" includes every court and judge having jurisdiction in the case.

"Business" includes every trade, occupation, or profession.

"Person" includes individuals, partnerships, corporations, and other associations.

"Bankrupt" includes bankrupt under the Federal Bankruptcy Act or insolvent under any state insolvent act.

"Conveyance" includes every assignment, lease, mortgage, or encumbrance.

"Real property" includes land and any interest or estate in land.

Sec. 3. Interpretation of Knowledge and Notice

(1) A person has "knowledge" of a fact within the meaning of this act not only when he has actual knowledge thereof, but also when he has knowledge of such other facts as in the circumstances shows bad faith.

(2) A person has "notice" of a fact within the meaning of this act when the person who claims the benefit of the notice:

(a) States the fact to such person, or

(b) Delivers through the mail, or by other means of communication, a written statement of the fact to such person or to a proper person at his place of business or residence.

Sec. 4. Rules of Construction

(1) The rule that statutes in derogation of the common law are to be strictly construed shall have no application to this act.

(2) The law of estoppel shall apply under this act.

(3) The law of agency shall apply under this act.

(4) This act shall be so interpreted and construed as to effect its general purpose to make uniform the law of those states which enact it.

(5) This act shall not be construed so as to impair the obligations of any contract existing when the act goes into effect, nor to affect any action or proceedings begun or right accrued before this act takes effect.

Sec. 5. Rules for Cases Not Provided for in this Act.

In any case not provided for in this act the rules of law and equity, including the law merchant, shall govern.

Part II Nature of Partnership

Sec. 6. Partnership Defined

(1) A partnership is an association of two or more persons to carry on as co-owners a business for profit.

(2) But any association formed under any other statute of this state, or any statute adopted by authority, other than the authority of this state, is not a partnership under this act, unless such association would have been a partnership in this state prior to the adoption of this act; but this act shall apply to limited partnerships except in so far as the statutes relating to such partnerships are inconsistent herewith.

Sec. 7. Rules for Determining the Existence of a Partnership

In determining whether a partnership exists, these rules shall apply:

(1) Except as provided by Section 16 persons who are not partners as to each other are not partners as to third persons.

(2) Joint tenancy, tenancy in common, tenancy by the entireties, joint property, common property, or part ownership does not of itself establish a partnership, whether such co-owners do or do not share any profits made by the use of the property.

(3) The sharing of gross returns does not of itself establish a partnership, whether or not the persons sharing them have a joint or common right or interest in any property from which the returns are derived.

(4) The receipt by a person of a share of the profits of a business is prima facie evidence that he is a partner in the business, but no such inference shall be drawn if such profits were received in payment:

(a) As a debt by installments or otherwise,

(b) As wages of an employee or rent to a landlord,

(c) As an annuity to a widow or representative of a deceased partner,

(d) As interest on a loan, though the amount of payment vary with the profits of the business.

(e) As the consideration for the sale of a good-will of a business or other property by installments or otherwise.

Sec. 8. Partnership Property

(1) All property originally brought into the partnership stock or subsequently acquired by purchase or otherwise, on account of the partnership, is partnership property.

(2) Unless the contrary intention appears, property acquired with partnership funds is partnership property.

(3) Any estate in real property may be acquired in the partnership name. Title so acquired can be conveyed only in the partnership name.

(4) A conveyance to a partnership in the partnership name, though without words of inheritance, passes the entire estate of the grantor unless a contrary intent appears.

Part III Relations of Partners to Persons Dealing with the Partnership

Sec. 9. Partner Agent of Partnership as to Partnership Business

(1) Every partner is an agent of the partnership for the purpose of its business, and the act of every partner, including the execution in the partnership name of any instrument, for apparently carrying on in the usual way the business of the partnership of which he is a member binds the partnership, unless the partner so acting has in fact no authority to act for the partnership in the particular matter, and the person with whom he is dealing has knowledge of the fact that he has no such authority.

(2) An act of a partner which is not apparently for the carrying on of the business of the partnership in the usual way does not bind the partnership unless authorized by the other partners.

(3) Unless authorized by the other partners or unless they have abandoned the business, one or more but less than all the partners have no authority to:

(a) Assign the partnership property in trust for creditors or on the assignee's promise to pay the debts of the partnership,

(b) Dispose of the good-will of the business,

(c) Do any other act which would make it impossible to carry on the ordinary business of a partnership,

(d) Confess a judgment,

(e) Submit a partnership claim or liability to arbitration or reference.

(4) No act of a partner in contravention of a restriction on authority shall bind the partnership to persons having knowledge of the restriction.

Sec. 10. Conveyance of Real Property of the Partnership

(1) Where title to real property is in the partnership name, any partner may convey title to such property by a conveyance executed in the partnership name; but the partnership may recover such property unless the partner's act binds the partnership under the provisions of paragraph (1) of section 9, or unless such property has been conveyed by the grantee or a person claiming through such grantee to a holder for value without knowledge that the partner, in making the conveyance, has exceeded his authority.

(2) Where title to real property is in the name of the partnership, a conveyance executed by a partner, in his own name, passes the equitable interest of the partnership, provided the act is one within the authority of the partner under the provisions of paragraph (1) of section 9.

(3) Where title to real property is in the name of one or more but not all the partners, and the record does not disclose the right of the partnership, the partners in whose name the title stands may convey title to such property, but the partnership may recover such property if the partners' act does not bind the partnership under the provisions of paragraph (1) of section 9, unless the purchaser or his assignee, is a holder for value, without knowledge.

(4) Where the title to real property is in the name of one or more or all the partners, or in a third person in trust for the partnership, a conveyance executed by a partner in the partnership name, or in his own name, passes the equitable interest of the partnership, provided the act is one within the authority of the partner under the provisions of paragraph (1) of section 9.

(5) Where the title to real property is in the names of all the partners a conveyance executed by all the partners passes all their rights in such property.

Sec. 11. Partnership Bound by Admission of Partner

An admission or representation made by any partner concerning partnership affairs within the scope of his authority as conferred by this act is evidence against the partnership.

Sec. 12. Partnership Charged with Knowledge of or Notice to Partner

Notice to any partner of any matter relating to partnership affairs, and the knowledge of the partner acting in the particular matter, acquired while a partner or then present to his mind, and the knowledge of any other partner who reasonably could and should have communicated it to the acting partner, operate as notice to or knowledge of the partnership, except in the case of a fraud on the partnership committed by or with the consent of that partner.

Sec. 13. Partnership Bound by Partner's Wrongful Act

Where, by any wrongful act or omission of any partner acting in the ordinary course of the business of the partnership or with the authority of his co-partners, loss or injury is caused to any person, not being a partner in the partnership, or any penalty is incurred, the partnership is liable therefor to the same extent as the partner so acting or omitting to act.

Sec. 14. Partnership Bound by Partner's Breach of Trust

The partnership is bound to make good the loss:

(a) Where one partner acting within the scope of his apparent authority receives money or property of a third person and misapplies it; and

(b) Where the partnership in the course of its business receives money or property of a third person and the money or property so received is misapplied by any partner while it is in the custody of the partnership.

Sec. 15. **Nature of Partner's Liability**

All partners are liable

(a) Jointly and severally for everything chargeable to the partnership under sections 13 and 14.

(b) Jointly for all other debts and obligations of the partnership; but any partner may enter into a separate obligation to perform a partnership contract.

Sec. 16. **Partner by Estoppel**

(1) When a person, by words spoken or written or by conduct, represents himself, or consents to another representing him to any one, as a partner in an existing partnership or with one or more persons not actual partners, he is liable to any such person to whom such representation has been made, who has, on the faith of such representation, given credit to the actual or apparent partnership, and if he has made such representation or consented to its being made in a public manner he is liable to such person, whether the representation has or has not been made or communicated to such person so giving credit by or with the knowledge of the apparent partner making the representation or consenting to its being made.

> (a) When a partnership liability results, he is liable as though he were an actual member of the partnership.

> (b) When no partnership liability results, he is liable jointly with the other persons, if any, so consenting to the contract or representation as to incur liability, otherwise separately.

(2) When a person has been thus represented to be a partner in an existing partnership, or with one or more persons not actual partners, he is an agent of the persons consenting to such representation to bind them to the same extent and in the same manner as though he were a partner in fact, with respect to persons who rely upon the representation. Where all the members of the existing partnership consent to the representation, a partnership act or obligation results; but in all other cases it is the joint act or obligation of the person acting and the persons consenting to the representation.

Sec. 17. **Liability of Incoming Partner**

A person admitted as a partner into an existing partnership is liable for all the obligations of the partnership arising before his admission as though he had been a partner when such obligations were incurred, except that this liability shall be satisfied only out of partnership property.

Part IV Relations of Partners to One Another

Sec. 18. **Rules Determining Rights and Duties of Partners**

The rights and duties of the partners in relation to the partnership shall be determined, subject to any agreement between them, by the following rules:

(a) Each partner shall be repaid his contributions, whether by way of capital or advances to the partnership property and share equally in the profits and surplus remaining after all liabilities, including those to partners, are satisfied; and must contribute towards the losses, whether of capital or otherwise, sustained by the partnership according to his share in the profits.

(b) The partnership must indemnify every partner in respect of payments made and personal liabilities reasonably incurred by him in the ordinary and proper conduct of its business, or for the preservation of its business or property.

(c) A partner, who in aid of the partnership makes any payment or advance beyond the amount of capital which he agreed to contribute, shall be paid interest from the date of the payment or advance.

(d) A partner shall receive interest on the capital contributed by him only from the date when repayment should be made.

(e) All partners have equal rights in the management and conduct of the partnership business.

(f) No partner is entitled to remuneration for acting in the partnership business, except that a surviving partner is entitled to reasonable compensation for his services in winding up the partnership affairs.

(g) No person can become a member of a partnership without the consent of all the partners.

(h) Any difference arising as to ordinary matters connected with the partnership business may be decided by a majority of the partners; but no act in contravention of any agreement between the partners may be done rightfully without the consent of all the partners.

Sec. 19. **Partnership Books**

The partnership books shall be kept, subject to any agreement between the partners, at the principal place of business of the partnership, and every partner shall at all times have access to and may inspect and copy any of them.

Sec. 20. **Duty of Partners to Render Information**

Partners shall render on demand true and full information of all things affecting the partnership to any partner or the legal representative of any deceased partner or partner under legal disability.

Sec. 21. **Partner Accountable as a Fiduciary**

(1) Every partner must account to the partnership for any benefit, and hold as trustee for it any profits derived by him without the consent of the other partners from any transaction connected with the formation, conduct, or liquidation of the partnership or from any use by him of its property.

(2) This section applies also to the representatives of a deceased partner engaged in the liquidation of the affairs of the partnership as the personal representatives of the last surviving partner.

Sec. 22. Right to an Account

Any partner shall have the right to a formal account as to partnership affairs:

(a) If he is wrongfully excluded from the partnership business or possession of its property by his co-partners,

(b) If the right exists under the terms of any agreement,

(c) As provided by section 21,

(d) Whenever other circumstances render it just and reasonable.

Sec. 23. Continuation of Partnership Beyond Fixed Term

(1) When a partnership for a fixed term or particular undertaking is continued after the termination of such term or particular undertaking without any express agreement, the rights and duties of the partners remain the same as they were at such termination, so far as is consistent with a partnership at will.

(2) A continuation of the business by the partners or such of them as habitually acted therein during the term, without any settlement or liquidation of the partnership affairs, is prima facie evidence of a continuation of the partnership.

Part V Property Rights of a Partner

Sec. 24. Extent of Property Rights of a Partner

The property rights of a partner are (1) his rights in specific partnership property, (2) his interest in the partnership, and (3) his right to participate in the management.

Sec. 25. Nature of a Partner's Right in Specific Partnership Property

(1) A partner is co-owner with his partners of specific partnership property holding as a tenant in partnership.

(2) The incidents of this tenancy are such that:

(a) A partner, subject to the provisions of this act and to any agreement between the partners, has an equal right with his partners to possess specific partnership property for partnership purposes; but he has no right to possess such property for any other purpose without the consent of his partners.

(b) A partner's right in specific partnership property is not assignable except in connection with the assignment of rights of all the partners in the same property.

(c) A partner's right in specific partnership property is not subject to attachment or execution, except on a claim against the partnership. When partnership property is attached for a partnership debt the partners, or any of them, or the representatives of a deceased partner, cannot claim any right under the homestead or exemption laws.

(d) On the death of a partner his right in specific partnership property vests in the surviving partner or partners, except where the deceased was the last surviving partner, when his right in such property vests in his legal representative. Such surviving partner or partners, or the legal representative of the last surviving partner, has no right to possess the partnership property for any but a partnership purpose.

(e) A partner's right in specific partnership property is not subject to dower, curtesy, or allowances to widows, heirs, or next of kin.

Sec. 26. Nature of Partner's Interest in the Partnership

A partner's interest in the partnership is his share of the profits and surplus, and the same is personal property.

Sec. 27. Assignment of Partner's Interest

(1) A conveyance by a partner of his interest in the partnership does not of itself dissolve the partnership, nor, as against the other partners in the absence of agreement, entitle the assignee, during the continuance of the partnership, to interfere in the management or administration of the partnership business or affairs, or to require any information or account of partnership transactions, or to inspect the partnership books; but it merely entitles the assignee to receive in accordance with his contract the profits to which the assigning partner would otherwise be entitled.

(2) In case of a dissolution of the partnership, the assignee is entitled to receive his assignor's interest and may require an account from the date only of the last account agreed to by all the partners.

Sec. 28. Partner's Interest Subject to Charging Order

(1) On due application to a competent court by any judgment creditor of a partner, the court which entered the judgment, order, or decree, or any other court, may charge the interest of the debtor partner with payment of the unsatisfied amount of such judgment debt with interest thereon; and may then or later appoint a receiver of his share of the profits, and of any other money due or to fall due to him in respect of the partnership, and make all other orders, directions, accounts and inquiries which the debtor partner might have made, or which the circumstances of the case may require.

(2) The interest charged may be redeemed at any time before foreclosure, or in case of a sale being directed by the court may be purchased without thereby causing a dissolution:

(a) With separate property, by any one or more of the partners, or

(b) With partnership property, by any one or more of the partners with the consent of all the partners whose interests are not so charged or sold.

(3) Nothing in this act shall be held to deprive a partner of his right, if any, under the exemption laws, as regards his interest in the partnership.

Part VI Dissolution and Winding up

Sec. 29. Dissolution Defined

The dissolution of a partnership is the change in the relation of the partners caused by any partner ceasing to be associated in the carrying on as distinguished from the winding up of the business.

Sec. 30. Partnership not Terminated by Dissolution

On dissolution the partnership is not terminated, but continues until the winding up of partnership affairs is completed.

Sec. 31. Causes of Dissolution

Dissolution is caused:

(1) Without violation of the agreement between the partners,

(a) By the termination of the definite term or particular undertaking specified in the agreement,

(b) By the express will of any partner when no definite term or particular undertaking is specified,

(c) By the express will of all the partners who have not assigned their interests or suffered them to be charged for their separate debts, either before or after the termination of any specified term or particular undertaking,

(d) By the expulsion of any partner from the business bona fide in accordance with such a power conferred by the agreement between the partners;

(2) In contravention of the agreement between the partners, where the circumstances do not permit a dissolution under any other provision of this section, by the express will of any partner at any time;

(3) By any event which makes it unlawful for the business of the partnership to be carried on or for the members to carry it on in partnership;

(4) By the death of any partner;

(5) By the bankruptcy of any partner or the partnership;

(6) By decree of court under section 32.

Sec. 32. Dissolution by Decree of Court

(1) On application by or for a partner the court shall decree a dissolution whenever:

(a) A partner has been declared a lunatic in any judicial proceeding or is shown to be of unsound mind,

(b) A partner becomes in any other way incapable of performing his part of the partnership contract,

(c) A partner has been guilty of such conduct as tends to affect prejudicially the carrying on of the business,

(d) A partner wilfully or persistently commits a breach of the partnership agreement, or otherwise so conducts himself in matters relating to the partnership business that it is not reasonably practicable to carry on the business in partnership with him,

(e) The business of the partnership can only be carried on at a loss,

(f) Other circumstances render a dissolution equitable.

(2) On the application of the purchaser of a partner's interest under sections 28 or 29 [should read 27 or 28];

(a) After the termination of the specified term or particular undertaking,

(b) At any time if the partnership was a partnership at will when the interest was assigned or when the charging order was issued.

Sec. 33. General Effect of Dissolution on Authority of Partner

Except so far as may be necessary to wind up partnership affairs or to complete transactions begun but not then finished, dissolution terminates all authority of any partner to act for the partnership,

(1) With respect to the partners,

(a) When the dissolution is not by the act, bankruptcy or death of a partner; or

(b) When the dissolution is by such act, bankruptcy or death of a partner, in cases where section 34 so requires.

(2) With respect to persons not partners, as declared in section 35.

Sec. 34. Rights of Partner to Contribution from Co-partners After Dissolution

Where the dissolution is caused by the act, death or bankruptcy of a partner, each partner is liable to his copartners for his share of any liability created by any partner acting for the partnership as if the partnership had not been dissolved unless

(a) The dissolution being by act of any partner, the partner acting for the partnership had knowledge of the dissolution, or

(b) The dissolution being by the death or bankruptcy of a partner, the partner acting for the partnership had knowledge or notice of the death or bankruptcy.

Sec. 35. Power of Partner to Bind Partnership to Third Persons After Dissolution

(1) After dissolution a partner can bind the partnership except as provided in Paragraph (3).

(a) By any act appropriate for winding up partnership affairs or completing transactions unfinished at dissolution;

(b) By any transaction which would bind the partnership if dissolution had not taken place, provided the other party to the transaction

(I) Had extended credit to the partnership prior to dissolution and had no knowledge or notice of the dissolution; or

(II) Though he had not so extended credit, had nevertheless known of the partnership prior to dissolution, and, having no knowledge or notice of dissolution, the fact of dissolution had not been advertised in a newspaper of general circulation in the place (or in each place if more than one) at which the partnership business was regularly carried on.

(2) The liability of a partner under paragraph (1b) shall be satisfied out of partnership assets alone when such partner had been prior to dissolution

(a) Unknown as a partner to the person with whom the contract is made; and

(b) So far unknown and inactive in partnership affairs that the business reputation of the partnership could not be said to have been in any degree due to his connection with it.

(3) The partnership is in no case bound by any act of a partner after dissolution

(a) Where the partnership is dissolved because it is unlawful to carry on the business, unless the act is appropriate for winding up partnership affairs; or

(b) Where the partner has become bankrupt; or

(c) Where the partner has no authority to wind up partnership affairs; except by a transaction with one who

(I) Had extended credit to the partnership prior to dissolution and had no knowledge or notice of his want of authority; or

(II) Had not extended credit to the partnership prior to dissolution, and, having no knowledge or notice of his want of authority, the fact of his want of authority has not been advertised in the manner provided for advertising the fact of dissolution in paragraph (1bII).

(4) Nothing in this section shall affect the liability under Section 16 of any person who after dissolution represents himself or consents to another representing him as a partner in a partnership engaged in carrying on business.

Sec. 36. Effect of Dissolution on Partner's Existing Liability

(1) The dissolution of the partnership does not of itself discharge the existing liability of any partner.

(2) A partner is discharged from any existing liability upon dissolution of the partnership by an agreement to that effect between himself, the partnership creditor and the person or partnership continuing the business; and such agreement may be inferred from the course of dealing between the creditor having knowledge of the dissolution and the person or partnership continuing the business.

(3) Where a person agrees to assume the existing obligations of a dissolved partnership, the partners whose obligations have been assumed shall be discharged from any liability to any creditor of the partnership who, knowing of the agreement, consents to a material alteration in the nature or time of payment of such obligations.

(4) The individual property of a deceased partner shall be liable for all obligations of the partnership incurred while he was a partner but subject to the prior payment of his separate debts.

Sec. 37. Right to Wind Up

Unless otherwise agreed the partners who have not wrongfully dissolved the partnership or the legal representative of the last surviving partner, not bankrupt, has the right to wind up the partnership affairs; provided, however, that any partner, his legal representative or his assignee, upon cause shown, may obtain winding up by the court.

Sec. 38. Rights of Partners to Application of Partnership Property

(1) When dissolution is caused in any way, except in contravention of the partnership agreement, each partner, as against his co-partners and all persons claiming through them in respect of their interests in the partnership, unless otherwise agreed, may have the partnership property applied to discharge its liabilities, and the surplus applied to pay in cash the net amount owing to the respective partners. But if dissolution is caused by expulsion of a partner, bona fide under the partnership agreement and if the expelled partner is discharged from all partnership liabilities, either by payment or agreement under section 36(2), he shall receive in cash only the net amount due him from the partnership.

(2) When dissolution is caused in contravention of the partnership agreement the rights of the partners shall be as follows:

(a) Each partner who has not caused dissolution wrongfully shall have,

(I) All the rights specified in paragraph (1) of this section, and

(II) The right, as against each partner who has caused the dissolution wrongfully, to damages for breach of the agreement.

(b) The partners who have not caused the dissolution wrongfully, if they all desire to continue the business in the same name, either by themselves or jointly with others, may do so, during the agreed term for the partnership and for that purpose may possess the partnership property, provided they secure the payment by bond approved by the court, or pay to any partner who has caused the dissolution wrongfully, the value of his interest in the partnership at the dissolution, less any damages recoverable under clause (2a II) of the section, and in like manner indemnify him against all present or future partnership liabilities.

(c) A partner who has caused the dissolution wrongfully shall have:

(I) If the business is not continued under the provisions of paragraph (2b) all the rights of a partner under paragraph (1), subject to clause (2a II), of this section,

(II) If the business is continued under paragraph (2b) of this section the right as against his co-partners and all claiming through them in respect of their interests in the partnership, to have the value of his interest in the partnership, less any damages caused to his co-partners by the dissolution, ascertained and paid to him in cash, or the payment secured by bond approved by the court, and to be released from all existing liabilities of the partnership; but in ascertaining the value of the partner's interest the value of the good-will of the business shall not be considered.

Sec. 39. Rights Where Partnership is Dissolved for Fraud or Misrepresentation

Where a partnership contract is rescinded on the ground of the fraud or misrepresentation of one of the parties thereto, the party entitled to rescind is, without prejudice to any other right, entitled,

(a) To a lien on, or right of retention of, the surplus of the partnership property after satisfying the partnership liabilities to third persons for any sum of money paid by him for the purchase of an interest in the partnership and for any capital or advances contributed by him; and

(b) To stand, after all liabilities to third persons have been satisfied, in the place of the creditors of the partnership for any payments made by him in respect of the partnership liabilities; and

(c) To be indemnified by the person guilty of the fraud or making the representation against all debts and liabilities of the partnership.

Sec. 40. Rules for Distribution

In settling accounts between the partners after dissolution, the following rules shall be observed, subject to any agreement to the contrary:

(a) The assets of the partnership are:

(I) The partnership property,

(II) The contributions of the partners necessary for the payment of all the liabilities specified in clause (b) of this paragraph.

(b) The liabilities of the partnership shall rank in order of payment, as follows:

(I) Those owing to creditors other than partners,

(II) Those owing to partners other than for capital and profits,

(III) Those owing to partners in respect of capital,

(IV) Those owing to partners in respect of profits.

(c) The assets shall be applied in the order of their declaration in clause (a) of this paragraph to the satisfaction of the liabilities.

(d) The partners shall contribute, as provided by section 18(a) the amount necessary to satisfy the liabilities; but if any, but not all, of the partners are insolvent, or, not being subject to process, refuse to contribute, the other partners shall contribute their share of the liabilities, and, in the relative proportions in which they share the profits, the additional amount necessary to pay the liabilities.

(e) An assignee for the benefit of creditors or any person appointed by the court shall have the right to enforce the contributions specified in clause (d) of this paragraph.

(f) Any partner or his legal representative shall have the right to enforce the contributions specified in clause (d) of this paragraph, to the extent of the amount which he has paid in excess of his share of the liability.

(g) The individual property of a deceased partner shall be liable for the contributions specified in clause (d) of this paragraph.

(h) When partnership property and the individual properties of the partners are in possession of a court for distribution, partnership creditors shall have priority on partnership property and separate creditors on individual property, saving the rights of lien or secured creditors as heretofore.

(i) Where a partner has become bankrupt or his estate is insolvent the claims against his separate property shall rank in the following order:

(I) Those owing to separate creditors,

(II) Those owing to partnership creditors,

(III) Those owing to partners by way of contribution.

Sec. 41. Liability of Persons Continuing the Business in Certain Cases

(1) When any new partner is admitted into an existing partnership, or when any partner retires and assigns (or the representative of the deceased partner assigns) his rights in partnership property to two or more of the partners, or to one or more of the partners and one or more third persons, if the business is continued without liquidation of the partnership affairs, creditors of the first or dissolved partnership are also creditors of the partnership so continuing the business.

(2) When all but one partner retire and assign (or the representative of a deceased partner assigns) their rights in partnership property to the remaining partner, who continues the business without liquidation of partnership affairs, either alone or with others, creditors of the dissolved partnership are also creditors of the person or partnership so continuing the business.

(3) When any partner retires or dies and the business of the dissolved partnership is continued as set forth in paragraphs (1) and (2) of this section, with the consent of the retired partners or the representative of the deceased partner, but without any assignment of his right in partnership property, rights of creditors of the dissolved partnership and of the creditors of the person or partnership continuing the business shall be as if such assignment had been made.

(4) When all the partners or their representatives assign their rights in partnership property to one or more third persons who promise to pay the debts and who continue the business of the dissolved partnership, creditors of the dissolved partnership are also creditors of the person or partnership continuing the business.

(5) When any partner wrongfully causes a dissolution and the remaining partners continue the business under the provisions of section 38(2b), either alone or with others, and without liquidation of the partnership affairs, creditors of the dissolved partnership are also creditors of the person or partnership continuing the business.

(6) When a partner is expelled and the remaining partners continue the business either alone or with others, without liquidation of the partnership affairs, creditors of the dissolved partnership are also creditors of the person or partnership continuing the business.

(7) The liability of a third person becoming a partner in the partnership continuing the business, under this section, to the creditors of the dissolved partnership shall be satisfied out of partnership property only.

(8) When the business of a partnership after dissolution is continued under any conditions set forth in this section the creditors of the dissolved partnership, as against the separate creditors of the retiring or deceased partner or the representative of the deceased partner, have a prior right to any claim of the retired partner or the representative of the deceased partner against the person or partnership continuing the business, on account of the retired or deceased partner's interest in the dissolved partnership or on account of any consideration promised for such interest or for his right in partnership property.

(9) Nothing in this section shall be held to modify any right of creditors to set aside any assignment on the ground of fraud.

(10) The use by the person or partnership continuing the business of the partnership name, or the name of a deceased partner as part thereof, shall not of itself make the individual property of the deceased partner liable for any debts contracted by such person or partnership.

Sec. 42. Rights of Retiring or Estate of Deceased Partner When the Business is Continued

When any partner retires or dies, and the business is continued under any of the conditions set forth in section 41 (1, 2, 3, 5, 6), or section 38(2b) without any settlement of accounts as between him or his estate and the person or partnership continuing the business, unless otherwise agreed, he or his legal representative as against such persons or partnership may have the value of his interest at the date of dissolution ascertained, and shall receive as an ordinary creditor an amount equal to the value of his interest in the dissolved partnership with interest, or, at his option or at the option of his legal representative, in lieu of interest, the profits attributable to the use of his right in the property of the dissolved partnership; provided that the creditors of the dissolved partnership as against the separate creditors, or the representative of the retired or deceased partner, shall have priority on any claim arising under this section, as provided by section 41(8) of this act.

Sec. 43. Accrual of Actions

The right to an account of his interest shall accrue to any partner, or his legal representative, as against the winding up partners or the surviving partners or the person or partnership continuing the business, at the date of dissolution, in the absence of any agreement to the contrary.

Part VII Miscellaneous Provisions

Sec. 44. When Act Takes Effect

This act shall take effect on the ___ day of ___ one thousand nine hundred and ___.

Sec. 45. Legislation Repealed

All acts or parts of acts inconsistent with this act are hereby repealed.

Appendix D

Spanish Equivalents for Important Legal Terms in English

Abandoned property: bienes abandonados

Acceptance: aceptación; consentimiento; acuerdo

Acceptor: aceptante

Accession: toma de posesión; aumento; accesión

Accommodation indorser: avalista de favor

Accommodation party: firmante de favor

Accord: acuerdo; convenio; arregio

Accord and satisfaction; transacción ejecutada

Act of state doctrine: doctrina de acto de gobierno

Administrative law: derecho administrativo

Administrative process: procedimiento o metódo administrativo

Administrator (-trix): administrador (-a)

Adverse possession: posesión de hecho susceptible de proscripción adquisitiva

Affirmative action: acción afirmativa

Affirmative defense: defensa afirmativa

After-acquired property: bienes adquiridos con posterioridad a un hecho dado

Agency: mandato; agencia

Agent: mandatorio; agente; representante

Agreement: convenio; acuerdo; contrato

Alien corporation: empresa extranjera

Allonge: hojas adicionales de endosos

Answer: contestación de la demande; alegato

Anticipatory breach, or anticipatory repudiation: anuncio previo de las partes de su imposibilidad de cumplir con el contrato

Appeal: apelación; recurso de apelación

Appellate jurisdiction: jurisdicción de apelaciones

Appraisal right: derecho de valuación

Abritration: arbitraje

Arson: incendio intencional

Articles of partnership: contrato social

Artisian's lien: derecho de retención que ejerce al artesano

Assault: asalto; ataque; agresión

Assignment of rights: transmisión; transferencia; cesión

Assumption of risk: no resarcimiento por exposición voluntaria al peligro

Attachment: auto judicial que autoriza el embargo; embargo

Bailee: depositario

Bailment: depósito; constitución en depósito

Bailor: depositante

Bankruptcy trustee: síndico de la quiebra

Battery: agresión; física

Bearer: portador; tenedor

Bearer instrument: documento al portador

Bequest or legacy: legado (de bienes muebles)

Bilateral contract: contrato bilateral

Bill of lading: conocimiento de embarque; carta de porte

Bill of Rights: declaración de derechos

Binder: póliza de seguro provisoria; recibo de pago a cuenta del precio

Blank indorsement: endoso en blanco

Blue Sky laws: leyes reguladoras del comercio bursátil

Bond: título de crédito; garantía; caución

Bond indenture: contrato de emisión de bonos; contrato del empréstito

Breach of contract: incumplimiento de contrato

Brief: escrito; resumen; informe

Burglary; violación de domicilio

Business judgment rule: regla de juicio comercial

Business tort: agravio comercial

Case law: ley de casos; derecho casuístico

Cashier's check: cheque de caja

Causation in fact: causalidad en realidad

Cease-and-desist order: orden para cesar y desistir

Certificate of deposit: certificado de depósito

Certified check: cheque certificado

Charitable trust: fideicomiso para fines benéficos

Chattel: bien mueble

Check: cheque

Chose in action: derecho inmaterial; derecho de acción

Civil law: derecho civil

Close corporation: sociedad de un solo accionista o de un grupo restringido de accionistas

Closed shop: taller agremiado (emplea solamente a miembros de un gremio)

Closing argument: argumento al final

Codicil: codicilo

Collateral: guarantía; bien objeto de la guarantía real

Comity: cortesía; cortesía entre naciones

Commercial paper: instrumentos negociables; documentos a valores commerciales

Common law: derecho consuetudinario; derecho común; ley común

Common stock: acción ordinaria

Comparative negligence: negligencia comparada

Compensatory damages: daños y perjuicios reales o compensatorios

Concurrent conditions: condiciones concurrentes

Concurrent estates: condominio

Concurrent jurisdiction: competencia concurrente de varios tribunales para entender en una misma causa

Concurring opinion: opinión concurrente

Condition: condición

Condition precedent: condición suspensiva

Condition subsequent: condición resolutoria

Confiscation: confiscación

Confusion: confusión; fusión

Conglomerate merger: fusión de firmas que operan en distintos mercados

Consent decree: acuerdo entre las partes aprobado por un tribunal

Consequential damages: daños y perjuicios indirectos

Consideration: consideración; motivo; contraprestación

Consolidation: consolidación

Constructive delivery: entrega simbólica

Constructive trust: fideicomiso creado por aplicación de la ley

Consumer-protection law: ley para proteger el consumidor

Contract: contrato

Contracts under seal: contrato formal o sellado

Contributory negligence: negligencia de la parte actora

Conversion: usurpación; conversión de valores

Copyright: derecho de autor

Corporation: sociedad anónima; corporación; persona juridica

Co-sureties: cogarantes

Counterclaim, or cross-complaint: reconvención; contrademanda
Counteroffer: contraoferta
Course of dealing: curso de transacciones
Course of performance: curso de cumplimiento
Covenant: pacto; garantía; contrato
Covenant not to sue: pacto or contrato a no demandar
Covenant of quiet enjoyment: garantía del uso y goce pacífico del inmueble
Creditors' composition agreement: concordato preventivo
Crime: crimen; delito; contravención
Criminal law: derecho penal
Cross-examination: contrainterrogatorio
Cure: cura; cuidado; derecho de remediar un vicio contractual
Customs receipts: recibos de derechos aduaneros

Damages: daños; indemnización por daños y perjuicios
Debit card: tarjeta de débito
Debtor: deudor
Debt securities: seguridades de deuda
Deceptive advertising: publicidad engañosa
Deed: escritura; título; acta translativa de domino
Defamation: difamación
Delegation of duties: delegación de obligaciones
Demand deposit: depósito a la vista
Depositions: declaración de un testigo fuera del tribunal
Derivative suit: acción judicial entablada por un accionista en nombre de la sociedad
Devise: legado; deposición testamentaria (bienes inmuebles)
Directed verdict: veredicto según orden del juez y sin participación activa del jurado
Direct examination: interrogatorio directo; primer interrogatorio
Disaffirmance: repudiación; renuncia; anulación
Discharge: descargo; liberación; cumplimiento
Disclosed principal: mandante revelado
Discovery: descubrimiento; producción de la prueba
Dissenting opinion: opinión disidente

Dissolution: disolución; terminación
Diversity of citizenship: competencia de los tribunales federales para entender en causas cuyas partes intervinientes son cuidadanos de distintos estados
Divestiture: extinción premature de derechos reales
Dividend: dividendo
Docket: orden del día; lista de causas pendientes
Domestic corporation: sociedad local
Draft: orden de pago; letrade cambio
Drawee: girado; beneficiario
Drawer: librador
Duress: coacción; violencia

Easement: servidumbre
Embezzlement: desfalco; malversación
Eminent domain: poder de expropiación
Employment discrimination: discriminación en el empleo
Entrepreneur: empresario
Environmental law: ley ambiental
Equal dignity rule: regla de dignidad egual
Equity security: tipo de participación en una sociedad
Estate: propiedad; patrimonio; derecho
Estop: impedir; prevenir
Ethical issue: cuestión ética
Exclusive jurisdiction: competencia exclusiva
Exculpatory clause: cláusula eximente
Executed contract: contrato ejecutado
Execution: ejecución; cumplimiento
Executor (-trix): albacea
Executory contract: contrato aún no completamente consumado
Executory interest: derecho futuro
Express contract: contrato expreso
Expropriation: expropriación

Federal question: caso federal
Fee simple: pleno dominio; dominio absoluto
Fee simple absolute: dominio absoluto
Fee simple defeasible: dominio sujeta a una condición resolutoria
Felony: crimen; delito grave
Fictitious payee: beneficiario ficticio
Fiduciary: fiduciaro
Firm offer: oferta en firme

Fixture: inmueble por destino, incorporación a anexación
Floating lien: gravamen continuado
Foreign corporation: sociedad extranjera; U.S. sociedad constituída en otro estado
Forgery: falso; falsificación
Formal contract: contrato formal
Franchise: privilegio; franquicia; concesión
Franchisee: persona que recibe una concesión
Franchisor: persona que vende una concesión
Fraud: fraude; dolo; engaño
Future estate; bien futuro

Garnishment: embargo de derechos
General partner: socio comanditario
General warranty deed: escritura translativa de domino con garantía de título
Gift: donación
Gift *causa mortis:* donación por causa de muerte
Gift *inter vivos:* donación entre vivos
Good faith: buena fe
Good-faith purchaser: comprador de buena fe

Holder: tenedor por contraprestación
Holder in due course: tenedor legítimo
Holographic will: testamento ológrafico
Homestead exemption laws: leyes que exceptúan las casas de familia de ejecución por duedas generales
Horizontal merger: fusión horizontal

Identification: identificación
Implied-in-fact contract: contrato implícito en realidad
Implied warranty: guarantía implícita
Implied warranty of merchantability: garantía implícita de vendibilidad
Impossibility of performance: imposibilidad de cumplir un contrato
Imposter: imposter
Incidental beneficiary: beneficiario incidental; beneficiario secundario
Incidental damages: daños incidentales
Indictment: auto de acusación; acusación
Indorsee: endorsatario
Indorsement: endoso

Indorser: endosante

Informal contract: contrato no formal; contrato verbal

Information: acusación hecha por el ministerio público

Injunction: mandamiento; orden de no innovar

Innkeeper's lien: derecho de retención que ejerce el posadero

Installment contract: contrato de pago en cuotas

Insurable interest: interés asegurable

Intended beneficiary: beneficiario destinado

Intentional tort: agravio; cuasi-delito intenciónal

International law: derecho internaciónal

Interrogatories: preguntas escritas sometidas por una parte a la otra o a un testigo

Inter vivos **trust:** fideicomiso entre vivos

Intestacy laws: leyes de la condición de morir intestado

Intestate: intestado

Investment company: compañia de inversiones

Issue: emisión

Joint tenancy: derechos conjuntos en un bien inmueble

Joint tenancy with right of survivorship: derechos conjuntos en un bien inmueble en favor del beneficiario sobreviviente

Judgment n.o.v.: juicio no obstante veredicto

Judgment rate of interest: interés de juicio

Judicial process: acto de procedimiento; proceso jurídico

Judicial review: revisión judicial

Jurisdiction: jurisdicción

Larceny: robo; hurto

Law: derecho; ley; jurisprudencia

Lease: contrato de locación; contrato de alquiler

Leasehold estate: bienes forales

Legal rate of interest: interés legal

Legatee: legatario

Less-than-freehold estate: menos de derecho de dominio absoluto

Letter of credit: carta de crédito

Levy: embargo; comiso

Libel: libelo; difamación escrita

Life estate: usufructo

Limited partner: comanditario

Limited partnership: sociedad en comandita

Liquidation: liquidación; realización

Lost property: objetos perdidos

Majority opinion: opinión de la mayoría

Maker: persona que realiza u ordena; librador

Mechanic's lien: gravamen de constructor

Mediation: mediación; intervención

Merger: fusión

Mirror-image rule: fallo de reflejo

Misdemeanor: infracción; contravención

Mislaid property: bienes extraviados

Mitigation of damages: reducción de daños

Moral hazard: riesgo moral

Mortgage: hypoteca

Motion to dismiss, or demurrer: excepción parentoria

Municipal law: derecho municipal

Mutual fund: fondo mutual

Negotiable instrument: instrumento negociable

Negotiation: negociación

Nominal damages: daños y perjuicios nominales

Novation: novación

Nuncupative will: testamento nuncupativo

Objective theory of contracts: teoria objetiva de contratos

Offer: oferta

Offeree: persona que recibe una oferta

Offeror: oferente

Order paper: instrumento o documento a la orden

Original jurisdiction: jurisdicción de primera instancia

Output contract: contrato de producción

Parol evidence rule: regla relativa a la prueba oral

Partially disclosed principal: mandante revelado en parte

Partnership: sociedad colectiva; asociación; asociación de participación

Past consideration: causa o contraprestación anterior

Patent: patente; privilegio

Pattern or practice: muestra o práctica

Payee: beneficiario de un pago

Penalty: pena; penalidad

Per capita: por cabeza

Perfection: perfeción

Performance: cumplimiento; ejecución

Personal defenses: excepciones personales

Personal property: bienes muebles

Per stirpes: por estirpe

Plea bargaining: regateo por un alegato

Pleadings: alegatos

Pledge: prenda

Police powers: poderes de policia y de prevención del crimen

Policy: póliza

Positive law: derecho positivo; ley positiva

Possibility of reverter: posibilidad de reversión

Precedent: precedente

Preemptive right: derecho de prelación

Preferred stock: acciones preferidas

Premium: recompensa; prima

Presentment warranty: garantía de presentación

Price discrimination: discriminación en los precios

Principal: mandante; principal

Privity: nexo jurídico

Privity of contract: relación contractual

Probable cause: causa probable

Probate: verificación; verificación del testamento

Probate court: tribunal de sucesiones y tutelas

Proceeds: resultados; ingresos

Profit: beneficio; utilidad; lucro

Promise: promesa

Promisee: beneficiario de una promesa

Promisor: promtente

Promissory estoppel: impedimento promisorio

Promissory note: pagaré; nota de pago

Promoter: promotor; fundador

Proximate cause: causa inmediata o próxima

Proxy: apoderado; poder

Punitive, or exemplary, damages: daños y perjuicios punitivos o ejemplares

Qualified indorsement: endoso con reservas
Quasi-contract: contrato tácito o implícito
Quit-claim deed: acto de transferencia de una propiedad por finiquito, pero sin ninguna garantía sobre la validez del título transferido

Ratification: ratificación
Real defenses: defensas legitimas o legales
Real property: bienes inmuebles
Reasonable doubt: duda razonable
Rebuttal: refutación
Recognizance: promesa; compromiso; reconocimiento
Recording statutes: leyes estatales sobre registros oficiales
Redress: reparación
Reformation: rectificación; reforma; corrección
Rejoinder: dúplica; contrarréplica
Release: liberación; renuncia a un derecho
Remainder: substitución; reversión
Remedy: recurso; remedio; reparación
Replevin: acción reivindicatoria; reivindicación
Reply: réplica
Requirements contract: contrato de suministro
Rescission: rescisión
Res judicata: cosa juzgada; res judicata
Respondeat superior: responsabilidad del mandante o del maestro
Restitution: restitución
Restrictive indorsement: endoso restrictivo
Resulting trust: fideicomiso implícito
Reversion: reversión; sustitución
Revocation: revocación; derogación
Right of contribution: derecho de contribución
Right of reimbursement: derecho de reembolso
Right of subrogation: derecho de subrogación
Right-to-work law: ley de libertad de trabajo

Robbery: robo
Rule 10b-5: Regla 10b-5

Sale: venta; contrato de compreventa
Sale on approval: venta a ensayo; venta sujeta a la aprobación del comprador
Sale or return: venta con derecho de devolución
Sales contract: contrato de compraventa; boleto de compraventa
Satisfaction: satisfacción; pago
Scienter: a sabiendas
S corporation: S corporación
Secured party: acreedor garantizado
Secured transaction: transacción garantizada
Securities: volares; titulos; seguridades
Security agreement: convenio de seguridad
Security interest: interés en un bien dado en garantía que permite a quien lo detenta venderlo en caso de incumplimiento
Service mark: marca de identificación de servicios
Signature: firma; rúbrica
Slander: difamación oral; calumnia
Sovereign immunity: immunidad soberana
Special indorsement: endoso especial; endoso a la orden de una person en particular
Specific performance: ejecución precisa, según los términos del contrato
Spendthrift trust: fideicomiso para pródigos
Stale check: cheque vencido
Stare decisis: acatar las decisiones, observar los precedentes
State exemption laws: leyes que exceptúan los estados
Statutory law: derecho estatutario; derecho legislado; derecho escrito
Stock: acciones
Stock split: fraccionamiento de acciones
Stock warrant: certificado para la compra de acciones
Stop-payment order: orden de suspensión del pago de un cheque dada por el librador del mismo
Strict liability: responsabilidad unconditional
Summary judgment: fallo sumario

Tangible property: bienes corpóreos
Tenancy at will: inguilino por tiempo indeterminado (según la voluntad del propietario)
Tenancy by sufferance: posesión por tolerancia
Tenancy by the entirety: locación conyugal conjunta
Tenancy for years: inguilino por un término fijo
Tenancy in common: specie de copropiedad indivisa
Tender: oferta de pago; oferta de ejecución
Testamentary trust: fideicomiso testamentario
Testator (-trix): testador (-a)
Third-party-beneficiary contract: contrato para el beneficio del tercero-beneficiario
Tort: agravio; cuasi-delito
Totten trust: fideicomiso creado por un depósito bancario
Trade acceptance: letra de cambio aceptada
Trademark: marca registrada
Trade name: nombre comercial; razón social
Traveler's check: cheque del viajero
Trespass to land: ingreso no authorizado a las tierras de otro
Trespass to personalty: violación de los derechos posesorios de un tercero con respecto a bienes muebles
Trust: fideicomiso; trust

Ultra vires: ultra vires; fuera de la facultad (de una sociedad anónima)
Unanimous opinion: opinión unánime
Unconscionable contract or clause: contrato leonino; cláusula leonino
Underwriter: subscriptor; asegurador
Unenforceable contract: contrato que no se puede hacer cumplir
Unilateral contract: contrato unilateral
Union shop: taller agremiado; empresa en la que todos los empleados son miembros del gremio o sindicato
Usge of trade: uso comercial
Usury: usura

Valid contract: contrato válido
Venue: lugar; sede del proceso

Vertical merger: fusión vertical de empresas

Voidable contract: contrato anulable

Void contract: contrato nulo; contrato inválido, sin fuerza legal

Voir dire: examen preliminar de un testigo a jurado por el tribunal para determinar su competencia

Voting trust: fideicomiso para ejercer el derecho de voto

Waiver: renuncia; abandono

Warranty of habitability: garantía de habitabilidad

Warranty of possession: garantía de posesión

Watered stock: acciones diluídos; capital inflado

White-collar crime: crimen administrativo

Writ of attachment: mandamiento de ejecución; mandamiento de embargo

Writ of certiorari: auto de avocación; auto de certiorari

Writ of execution: auto ejecutivo; mandamiento de ejecución

Writ of mandamus: auto de mandamus; mandamiento; orden judicial

Glossary

ABANDONED PROPERTY Property that the owner has voluntarily parted with, having no intention of recovering it.

ACCELERATION CLAUSE A clause in a contract for installment payments that provides for all future payments to become due immediately upon the failure to tender timely payments or upon the occurrence of a specified event.

ACCEPTANCE In contract law, the offeree's notification to the offeror that the offeree agrees to the terms of the offer and will be bound by them.

ACCEPTOR A drawee who accepts a draft and who engages to be primarily responsible for its payment.

ACCESSION The changing (for example, through manufacturing) of one good into a new good (for example, flour into bread); the right, upon payment for the original materials, to keep an article manufactured out of goods that were innocently converted.

ACCOMMODATION INDORSER An indorser who signs an instrument for the purpose of lending his or her credit to another indorser.

ACCOMMODATION PARTY A person who signs an instrument for the purpose of lending that person's credit to another party on that instrument.

ACCORD An agreement between two persons, one of whom has a right of action against the other, to settle a contractual obligation.

ACCORD AND SATISFACTION A method of discharging a claim in which the parties agree to give and accept something different from the performance originally promised in settlement of the claim. The accord is the agreement, and the satisfaction is its execution, or performance. Normally, an accord and satisfaction results in a full release, that is, the discharge of the original contractual obligation.

ACT OF STATE DOCTRINE A judicially created doctrine that provides that the judicial branch of one country will not examine the validity of public acts committed by a recognized foreign government within its own territory.

ADD-ON CLAUSE A clause in an installment contract that makes an individual's earlier purchase from a firm security for a new purchase.

ADMINISTRATIVE LAW A body of law created by administrative agencies—such as the Securities and Exchange Commission (SEC) and the Federal Trade Commission (FTC)—in the form of rules, regulations, orders, and decisions in order to carry out their duties and responsibilities. This law can initially be enforced by these agencies outside the judicial process.

ADMINISTRATIVE PROCESS The procedure used by administrative agencies in the administration of law.

ADMINISTRATOR (-TRIX) One who is appointed by a court to handle the probate (disposition) of a person's estate if that person dies intestate (without leaving a will).

ADVERSE POSSESSION The acquisition of title to real property by occupying it openly, with the knowledge but without the consent of the owner, for a period of time specified by state statutes.

AFFIRMATIVE ACTION Job-hiring policies that give special consideration or compensatory treatment to minority groups in an effort to overcome present effects of past discrimination.

AFFIRMATIVE DEFENSE Any response to the plaintiff's claim that does not deny the plaintiff's facts, but asserts a new basis for nonliability. Examples are fraud, duress, and the expiration of the statute of limitations.

AFTER-ACQUIRED PROPERTY Property of the debtor that is acquired after a security interest in the debtor's property is created.

AGENCY A relationship between two persons where, by agreement or otherwise, one (the principal) is bound by the words and acts of the other (the agent).

AGENT A person authorized by another to act for or in place of him or her.

AGREEMENT A meeting of two or more minds. Often used as a synonym for contract.

ALIEN CORPORATION A corporation formed in another country but doing business in the United States.

ALLONGE A piece of paper firmly attached to a negotiable instrument, upon which transferees can make indorsements if there is no room left on the instrument itself.

AMERICAN ARBITRATION ASSOCIATION (AAA) The major organization offering arbitration services in the United States.

ANSWER Procedurally, a defendant's response to the complaint.

ANTICIPATORY BREACH OR ANTICIPATORY REPUDIATION An assertion or action by a party indicating that he or she will not perform an obligation that the party is contractually obligated to perform at a future time.

APPEAL Resort to a superior (i.e., appellate) court to review the decision of an inferior (i.e., trial) court.

APPELLATE JURISDICTION The power of a court to hear and decide an appeal; that is to say, the power and authority of a court to review cases that have already been in the lower court for trial, and the power to make decisions about them without actually holding a trial—this process is called appellate review.

APPRAISAL RIGHT A dissenting shareholder's right to object to an extraordinary transaction of the corporation, such as a merger or consolidation, to have his or her shares appraised, and to be paid the fair-market value by the corporation.

ARBITRATION The settling of a dispute by submitting it to a disinterested third party (other than a court), who renders a legally binding decision.

ARSON The malicious burning of another's dwelling. Some statutes have expanded this to include any real property regardless of ownership and the destruction of property by other means—for example, by explosion.

ARTICLES OF PARTNERSHIP A written agreement that sets forth each partner's rights in, and obligations to, the partnership.

ARTISAN'S LIEN A possessory lien given to a person who has made improvements and added value to another person's personal property as security for payment for services performed.

ASSAULT Any word or action intended to make another person fearful of immediate physical harm; a reasonably believable threat.

ASSIGNMENT OF RIGHTS The act of transferring to another all or part of one's rights arising under a contract.

ASSUMPTION OF RISK A doctrine whereby a plaintiff may not recover for injuries or damages suffered from risks he or she knows of and assents to. A defense against negligence that can be used when the plaintiff has knowledge of and appreciates a danger and voluntarily exposes himself or herself to the danger.

ATTACHMENT In a secured transaction, the process by which a security interest in the property of another becomes enforceable; the legal process of seizing another's property in accordance with a writ or judicial order for the purpose of securing satisfaction of a judgment yet to be rendered.

BAILEE One to whom goods or property owned by another (a bailor) are entrusted. The bailee is obligated to return the bailed goods or property to the bailor or dispose of them as directed by the bailor.

BAILMENT An agreement in which goods or personal property of one person (bailor) are entrusted to another (bailee), who is obligated to return the bailed property to the bailor or dispose of it as directed.

BAILOR One who entrusts goods to a bailee.

BAIT-AND-SWITCH ADVERTISING A selling technique that involves advertising a product (the "bait") at a very attractive price, then informing the consumer, once he or she is in the door, that the advertised product is either not available or is of poor quality, and promoting a more expensive item in its stead (the "switch").

BANKRUPTCY TRUSTEE A person appointed by the bankruptcy court (or a permanent trustee appointed by the U.S. Attorney General) to take charge of a bankrupt estate or business, to collect assets, to bring suit on the bankrupt's claims, and to defend actions against it.

BATTERY The unprivileged, intentional touching of another.

BEARER A person in the possession of an instrument payable to bearer or indorsed in blank.

BEARER INSTRUMENT In the law of commercial paper, any instrument that runs to the bearer, including instruments payable to the bearer or to "cash."

BEQUEST OR LEGACY A gift by will of personal property

BILATERAL CONTRACT A contract that includes the exchange of a promise for a promise.

BILL OF LADING A document of title given by a carrier, such as a shipping company, that lists the goods accepted for transport. Additionally, the bill of lading lists the terms of the shipping agreement.

BILL OF RIGHTS The first ten amendments to the Constitution.

BINDER A written, temporary insurance policy.

BLANK INDORSEMENT One made by the mere writing of the indorser's name on the back of an instrument. Such indorsement causes an instrument, otherwise payable to order, to become payable to bearer and negotiated only by delivery.

BLUE SKY LAWS Laws that regulate the offer and sale of securities.

BOND A certificate that evidences a corporate debt. It is a security that involves no ownership interest in the issuing corporation.

BOND INDENTURE An instrument of secured indebtedness issued by a corporation.

BREACH OF CONTRACT Failure, without legal excuse, of a promisor to perform the obligations of a contract.

BRIEF A written summary or statement prepared by one side in a lawsuit to explain its case to the judge; a typical brief has a facts summary, a law summary, and an argument about how the law applies to the facts.

BURGLARY The unlawful entry into a building with the intent to commit theft. (Some state statutes expand this to include the intent to commit any crime.)

BUSINESS JUDGMENT RULE A rule that immunizes corporate management from liability for actions that are undertaken in good faith, when the action was within both the power of the corporation and the authority of management.

BUSINESS TORT A tort occurring within the business context; typical business torts are wrongful interference with the business or contractual relationships of others and unfair competition.

CASE LAW Rules of law announced in court decisions. Case law includes the aggregate of reported cases that interpret judicial precedents, statutes, regulations, and constitutional provisions.

CASHIER'S CHECK A draft drawn by a bank on itself.

CAUSATION IN FACT An act or omission without which an event would not have occurred.

CEASE-AND-DESIST ORDER An administrative or judicial order prohibiting a business firm from conducting activities that an agency or a court has deemed illegal.

CERTIFICATE OF DEPOSIT An instrument evidencing a promissory acknowledgment by a bank of a receipt of money with an engagement to repay it.

CERTIFIED CHECK A check drawn by an individual on his or her own account but bearing a guarantee (acceptance) by a bank that the bank will pay the check regardless of whether the drawer's account contains adequate funds at the time the check is presented.

CHARITABLE TRUST A trust in which property held by a trustee must be used for charitable purposes (such as advancement of health or religion).

CHATTEL Tangible and intangible personal property.

CHATTEL PAPER Any writing or writings that show both a debt and the fact that the debt is secured by personal property. In many instances, chattel paper consists of a negotiable instrument coupled with a security agreement.

CHECK A draft drawn by a drawer ordering the drawee bank to pay a certain amount of money to the holder on demand.

CHECKS AND BALANCES SYSTEM The national government is composed of three separate branches: the executive, the legislative, and the judicial. Each branch of the government exercises a check upon the actions of the others.

CHOSE IN ACTION A right that can be enforced in court to recover a debt or to obtain damages.

CIVIL LAW (1) The branch of law dealing with the definition and enforcement of all private or public rights, as opposed to criminal matters. (2) Codified law, such as that compiled by the early Roman jurists.

CLOSE CORPORATION A corporation whose shareholders are limited to a small group of persons, often including only family members. The rights of shareholders of a close corporation usually are restricted regarding the transfer of shares to others.

CLOSED SHOP A place of employment that requires union membership as a condition of employment. Unlawful under the Taft-Hartley Act.

CLOSING ARGUMENT Made after the plaintiff and defendant have rested their cases. Closing arguments are made prior to the jury charges.

CODICIL A written supplement to, or modification of, a will. Codicils must be executed with the same formalities as a will.

COLLATERAL In a broad sense, any property used as security for a loan. Under the UCC, property in which a debtor has an interest or a right.

COLLECTING BANK Any bank handling an item for collection, except the payor bank.

COMITY A deference by which one nation gives effect to the laws and judicial decrees of another nation. This recognition is based primarily upon respect.

COMMERCIAL PAPER Under UCC Article 3, negotiable instruments, which are signed writings that contain an unconditional promise or order to pay an exact sum of money, either when demanded or at an exact future time. Includes bills of exchange (i.e., drafts), promissory notes, certificates of deposits, and checks.

COMMON LAW That body of law developed from custom or judicial decisions in English and American courts, not attributable to a legislature.

COMMON STOCK Shares of ownership in a corporation that are lowest in priority with respect to payment of dividends and distribution of the corporation's assets upon dissolution.

COMPARATIVE NEGLIGENCE A concept in tort law whereby liability for injuries resulting from negligent acts is shared by all persons who were guilty of negligence (including the injured party), on the basis of each person's proportionate carelessness.

COMPENSATORY DAMAGES A money award equivalent to the actual value of injuries or damages sustained by the aggrieved party.

CONCURRENT CONDITIONS Conditions that must occur or be performed at the same time; they are mutually dependent. No obligations arise until these conditions are simultaneously performed.

CONCURRENT ESTATES Ownership of property by two or more persons at the same time; e.g., joint tenancy.

CONCURRENT JURISDICTION Concurrent jurisdiction exists when two different courts have the power to hear a case. For example, some cases can be heard in a federal or a state court.

CONCURRING OPINION An opinion, separate from that which embodies the view and decision of the majority of the court, prepared by a judge or justice who agrees in general but wants to make or clarify a particular point or to voice disapproval of the grounds on which the decision was made, but not the decision itself.

CONDITION A qualification, provision, or clause in a contractual agreement, the occurrence of which creates, suspends, or terminates the obligations of the contracting parties.

CONDITION PRECEDENT In a contractual agreement, a condition that must be met before the other party's obligations arise.

CONDITION SUBSEQUENT A condition in a contract which, if not met, discharges an existing obligation of the other party.

CONFISCATION Taking privately owned business or personal property without proper public purpose or an award of just compensation.

CONFUSION The mixing together of goods of two or more owners so that the independent goods cannot be identified.

CONGLOMERATE MERGER A merger between firms that do not compete with each other because they are in different industries, as opposed to horizontal and vertical mergers.

CONSENT DECREE A settlement in which a person, company, or government agency agrees to take certain actions without admitting fault or guilt for the situation that caused the original lawsuit.

CONSEQUENTIAL DAMAGES Special damages, which compensate for a loss that is not direct or immediate (i.e., lost profits). The special damages must have been reasonably foreseeable at the time the breach or injury occurred in order for the plaintiff to collect them.

CONSIDERATION That which motivates the exchange of promises or performance in a contractual agreement. The consideration, which must be present to make the contract legally binding, must result in a detriment to the promisee (something of legal value, legally sufficient, and bargained for) or a benefit to the promisor.

CONSOLIDATION A contractual and statutory process whereby two or more corporations join to become a completely new corporation. The original corporations cease to exist, and the new corporation acquires all their assets and liabilities.

CONSTRUCTIVE DELIVERY An act equivalent to the actual, physical delivery of property that cannot be physically delivered because of difficulty or impossibility; to illustrate, the transfer of a key to a safe constructively delivers the contents of the safe.

CONSTRUCTIVE TRUST A trust created by operation of law against one who wrongfully has obtained or holds legal right to property that he or she should not, in equity and good conscience, hold and enjoy.

CONSUMER-PROTECTION LAW State and federal laws specifying the duties of sellers and the rights of consumers in the sale and purchase of consumer goods.

CONTRACT An agreement affecting the legal relationships between two or more parties.

CONTRACTS UNDER SEAL Formal agreements in which the seal is a substitute for consideration. A court will not invalidate a contract under seal for lack of consideration.

CONTRIBUTORY NEGLIGENCE A concept in tort law whereby a complaining party's own negligence contributed to or caused his or her injuries. Contributory negligence is an absolute bar to recovery in some jurisdictions.

CONVERSION Wrongfully taking or retaining possession of personal property that belongs to another.

COPYRIGHT The exclusive right of "authors" to publish, print, or sell an intellectual production for a statutory period of time (currently, for an identified author, his or her lifetime plus fifty years; for anonymous or pseudonymous authors, seventy-five years from publication or one hundred years from creation). A copyright has the same monopolistic nature as a patent or trademark, but it differs in that it applies exclusively to works of art and literature.

CORPORATION A legal entity created under the authority of the laws of a state or the federal government. The entity exists distinctly from its several members.

CO-SURETIES Joint sureties; two or more sureties to the same obligation.

COUNTERCLAIM, OR CROSS-COMPLAINT A claim made by a defendant in a civil lawsuit that in effect sues the plaintiff; it can be based on entirely different grounds than those given in the plaintiff's complaint.

COUNTEROFFER An offeree's response to an offer in which the offeree rejects the original offer and at the same time makes a new offer.

COURSE OF DEALING A sequence of previous conduct between the parties to a particular transaction that establishes a common basis for their understanding.

COURSE OF PERFORMANCE The conduct that occurs under the terms of a particular agreement; such conduct indicates what the parties to an agreement intended it to mean.

COVENANT Any agreement between two or more parties by deed, in writing, signed, and delivered, promising that something is either done, shall be done, or shall not be done. The term is currently used with respect to promises contained in instruments relating to real estate.

COVENANT NOT TO SUE An agreement to substitute a contractual obligation for some other type of action.

COVENANT OF QUIET ENJOYMENT A promise by the grantor (or landlord) that the grantee (or tenant) will not be evicted or disturbed by the grantor or a person having a lien or superior title.

CREDITORS' COMPOSITION AGREEMENT An agreement formed between a debtor and his or her creditors whereby the creditors agree to accept a lesser sum than that owed by the debtor in full satisfaction of the debt.

CRIME A broad term for violations of law that are punishable by the state and are codified by legislatures. The objective of criminal law is to protect the public.

CRIMINAL LAW Governs and defines those actions which are crimes and which subject the convicted offender to punishment imposed by the government.

CROSS-EXAMINATION The questioning of an opposing witness during the trial.

CURE The right of a party who tenders nonconforming performance to correct, without liability, his or her performance within the contract period.

CUSTOMS RECEIPTS Receipts evidencing payment of taxes due on goods imported from other countries.

DAMAGES Money sought as a remedy for a breach-of-contract action or for tortious acts.

DEBIT CARD A plastic card, similar in appearance to a credit card, that allows bank customers access to automated teller machines.

DEBTOR A person who owes a sum of money or other obligations to another; in secured transactions law, the party who owes payment or performance of the secured obligation, whether or not that party actually owns or has rights in the collateral, is a debtor.

DEBT SECURITIES Securities that are of such duration that they evidence an obligation of the corporation to repay the holder, rather than evidencing an investment by the holder in exchange for stock.

DECEPTIVE ADVERTISING Advertising that misleads consumers, either by unjustified claims concerning a product's performance or by the omission of a material fact concerning the product's composition or performance.

DEED A document by which title to property (usually real property) is passed.

DEFAMATION Anything published or publicly spoken that causes injury to another's good name, reputation, or character.

DELEGATION OF DUTIES The act of transferring to another all or part of one's duties arising under a contract.

DEMAND DEPOSIT Funds (accepted by a bank) subject to immediate withdrawal, in contrast to a time deposit which requires that a depositor wait a specific time before withdrawing or pay a penalty for early withdrawal.

DEPOSITARY BANK The first bank to which an item is transferred for collection, even though it may also be the payor bank.

DEPOSITIONS A generic term that refers to any evidence verified by oath. As a legal term, it is often limited to the testimony of a witness taken under oath before a trial, with the opportunity of cross-examination.

DERIVATIVE SUIT A suit by a shareholder to enforce a corporate cause of action against a third person.

DEVISE A gift by will of real property.

DIRECTED VERDICT The verdict in which the judge takes the decision out of the hands of the jury by telling the jury what they must decide, or by actually making the decision.

DIRECT EXAMINATION In a trial, the first questioning of a witness, by the side that called the particular witness.

DISAFFIRMANCE The repudiation of an obligation.

DISCHARGE The termination of one's obligation. In contract law, discharge occurs when the parties have fully performed their contractual obligations or when events, conduct of the parties, or operation of the law release the parties from further performance.

DISCLOSED PRINCIPAL A principal whose identity and existence as a principal is known by a third person at the time a transaction is conducted by an agent.

DISCOVERY A method by which opposing parties may obtain information from each other to prepare for trial. Generally governed by rules of procedure, but may be controlled by the court.

DISSENTING OPINION A separate opinion in which a judge or justice does not agree with the conclusion reached by the majority of the court and expounds his or her views on the case.

DISSOLUTION The formal disbanding of a partnership or a corporation. It can take place by (1) agreement of the parties or the shareholders and board or directors, (2) by the death of a partner, (3) by the expiration of a time period stated in a partnership agreement or a certificate of incorporation, (4) or by court order.

DIVERSITY OF CITIZENSHIP A situation occurring when persons on one side of a case in federal court come from a different state than persons on the other side. This may also involve a foreign country or citizens or subjects of a foreign country and citizens of a state.

DIVESTITURE The act of selling one or more of a company's parts, such as a subsidiary or a plant; often mandated by the courts in merger and monopolization cases.

DIVIDEND A distribution to corporate shareholders, disbursed in proportion to the number of shares held.

DOCKET The list of cases entered on a court's calendar and thus scheduled to be heard by the court.

DOMESTIC CORPORATION In a given state, a corporation that does business in, and is organized under the laws of, that state.

DRAFT Any instrument drawn on a drawee (including a bank) which orders the drawee to pay a certain sum of money.

DRAWEE The person who is ordered to pay a draft or check. With a check, the bank is always the drawee.

DRAWER A person who initiates a draft (including a check) ordering the drawee to pay.

DURESS Unlawful pressure brought to bear on a person, overcoming that person's free will and causing him or her to do what he or she would not otherwise have done.

EASEMENT A nonpossessory right to use another's property in a manner established by either express or implied agreement.

EMBEZZLEMENT The fraudulent appropriation of money or other property by a person to whom the money or property has been entrusted.

EMINENT DOMAIN The power of a government to take land for public use from private citizens for fair compensation.

EMPLOYMENT DISCRIMINATION Treating employees or job applicants unequally on the basis of race, sex, nationality, religion, or age; prohibited by Title VII of the Civil Rights Act of 1964 as amended.

ENTREPRENEUR One who initiates and assumes the financial risks of a new enterprise and one who undertakes to provide or control its management.

ENVIRONMENTAL LAW The body of legislation pertaining to environmental health and preservation; examples of such legislation include the Clean Air Act, the Clean Water Act, and numerous other statutes passed in recent decades to protect the environment.

EQUAL DIGNITY RULE In most states, express authority given to an agent must be in writing if the contract to be made on behalf of the principal is required to be in writing.

EQUITABLE PRINCIPLES AND MAXIMS Propositions or general statements of rules of laws; frequently involved in equity jurisdiction.

EQUITY SECURITIES Securities or shares of capital stock representing an ownership interest in a corporation rather than debt.

ESTATE Broadly, all that a person owns, including both real and personal property; in real-estate law, the extent of ownership or interest that one has in realty.

ESTOPPED Barred, impeded, or precluded.

ESTRAY STATUTE A statute dealing with a person's rights in property whose ownership is unknown.

ETHICAL ISSUE One having to do with normative rules of conduct governing social behavior. Ethical issues concern the inherent fairness, justness, and appropriateness of actions of individuals (or businesses or governments) within a specific social context.

ETHICS Moral principles and values applied to social behavior.

EXCLUSIVE JURISDICTION Jurisdiction is exclusive when a case can only be heard in one particular court.

EXCULPATORY CLAUSES Clauses that release a party (to a contract) from liability for his or her wrongful acts.

EXECUTED CONTRACT A contract that has been completely performed by both parties.

EXECUTION An action to carry into effect the directions in a decree or judgment; otherwise stated, an official carrying out of a court's order or judgment.

EXECUTOR (-TRIX) A person either expressly or by implication named by a testator to see that his or her will is administered appropriately.

EXECUTORY CONTRACT A contract that has not as yet been fully performed.

EXECUTORY INTEREST A future interest, held by a person other than the grantor, that either cuts short or begins some time after the natural termination of the preceding estate.

EXPRESS CONTRACT A contract that is oral and/or written (as opposed to an implied contract).

EXPRESS WARRANTY A promise, ancillary to an underlying sales agreement, that is included in the written or oral terms of the sales agreement under which the promisor assures the quality, description, or performance of the goods.

EXPROPRIATION The seizure by a government of privately owned business or personal property for a proper public purpose and with just compensation.

FEDERAL QUESTION A federal question provides jurisdiction for federal courts. This jurisdiction arises from Article III, Section 2, of the Constitution. Federal questions may pertain to the U.S. Constitution, acts of Congress, or treaties.

FEE SIMPLE Exists when the owner or owners of property are entitled to use, possess, or dispose of that property as they choose during their lifetime, and, upon death, their interests in the property descend to their heirs.

FEE SIMPLE ABSOLUTE An estate or interest in land with no time, disposition, or descendibility limitations.

FEE SIMPLE DEFEASIBLE An estate that can be taken away (by the prior grantor) upon the occurrence or nonoccurrence of a specified event.

FELONIES Crimes—such as arson, murder, rape, and robbery—that carry the most severe sanctions, usually ranging from one year in a state or federal prison to the forfeiture of one's life.

FICTITIOUS PAYEE A payee on a negotiable instrument whom the maker or drawer does not intend to have an interest in the instrument and whose name is supplied by an agent or employee of the drawer or maker. Indorsements by fictitious payees are not forgeries under negotiable instruments law.

FIDUCIARY As a noun, a person having a duty created by his or her undertaking to act primarily for another's benefit in matters connected with the undertaking. As an adjective, a relationship founded upon trust and confidence.

FIRM OFFER An offer (by a merchant) that is irrevocable without consideration for a period of time. A firm offer by a merchant must be in writing, must be signed by the offeror, and must state that the offer is to remain open for a stated or a reasonable period of time (not more than three months).

FIXTURE A thing that was once personal property but has become attached to real property in such a way that it takes on the characteristics of real property and becomes part of that real property.

FLOATING LIEN A security interest retained in collateral even when the collateral changes in character, classification, or location.

FOREIGN CORPORATION In a given state, a corporation that does business in the state without being incorporated therein.

FORGERY The false or unauthorized signature of a document, or the false making of a document, with the intent to defraud.

FORMAL CONTRACTS Agreements or contracts that by law require for their validity a specific form, such as executed under seal.

FRANCHISE A written agreement whereby an owner of a trademark, trade name, or copyright licenses another to use that trademark, trade name, or copyright in selling goods and services.

FRANCHISEE One receiving a license to use another's (the franchisor's) trademark, trade name, or copyright in the sale of goods and services.

FRANCHISOR One licensing another (the franchisee) to use his or her trademark, trade name, or copyright in the sale of goods or services.

FRAUD Any misrepresentation, either by misstatement or omission of a material fact, knowingly made with the intention of misrepresentation to another and on which a reasonable person would and does rely, to his or her detriment.

FUTURE ESTATE An estate that is not at present possessory but will or may be possessory in the future. Remainders and reversions are future estates.

GARNISHMENT A legal process whereby a creditor appropriates the debtor's property or wages that are in the hands of a third party.

GENERAL PARTNER In a limited partnership, a partner who assumes responsibility for the management of the partnership and liability for all partnership debts.

GENERAL WARRANTY DEED A deed that warrants that the title to land being conveyed is free of all encumbrances, except as noted in the document; warrants the most extensive protection against defects of title.

GIFT Any voluntary transfer of property made without consideration, past or present.

GIFT *CAUSA MORTIS* A gift made in contemplation of death. If the donor does not die of that ailment, the gift is revoked.

GIFT *INTER VIVOS* A gift made during one's lifetime and not in contemplation of imminent death, in contrast to a gift *causa mortis*.

GOOD FAITH Honesty in fact; for a merchant, the observance of reasonable commercial standards of fair dealing.

GOOD-FAITH PURCHASER A purchaser who buys without notice of circumstance, which would put a person of ordinary prudence on inquiry as to the title, or as to an impediment on the title, of a seller. Sometimes used interchangeably with a "buyer in the ordinary course of business."

HOLDER A person "who is in possession of a document of title or negotiable instrument or a certificated investment security drawn, issued, or indorsed to him or his order or to bearer or blank." [UCC 1-201(20)]

HOLDER IN DUE COURSE Any holder who acquires a negotiable instrument for value, in good faith, and without notice that the instrument is defective or overdue.

HOLOGRAPHIC WILL A will written entirely in the signer's handwriting and usually not witnessed.

HOMESTEAD EXEMPTION A law allowing an owner to designate his or her house and adjoining land as a homestead and thus exempt it from liability for his or her general debt.

HORIZONTAL MERGER A merger between two businesses or persons competing in the marketplace.

IDENTIFICATION Proof that a thing is what it is purported or represented to be. In the sale of goods, the express designation of the goods as provided in the contract.

IMPLIED-IN-FACT CONTRACT A contract formed in whole or in part from the conduct of the parties (as opposed to an express contract).

IMPLIED WARRANTY A warranty that the law implies either through the situation of the parties or the nature of the transaction.

IMPLIED WARRANTY OF MERCHANTABILITY A promise by a merchant seller of goods that the goods are reasonably fit for the general purpose for which they are sold, are properly packaged and labeled, and are of proper quality.

IMPOSSIBILITY OF PERFORMANCE A doctrine under which a party to a contract is relieved of his or her duty to perform when performance becomes impossible or totally impracticable (through no fault of either party).

IMPOSTER One who, with the intent to deceive, pretends to be somebody else.

INCIDENTAL BENEFICIARY A third party who incidentally benefits from a contract but whose benefit was not the reason the contract was formed; incidental beneficiaries have no rights in a contract and cannot sue the promisor if the contract is breached.

INCIDENTAL DAMAGES Damages resulting from a breach of contract, including all reasonable expenses incurred because of the breach.

INDICTMENT A charge or written accusation, issued by a grand jury, that a named person has committed a crime.

INDORSEE The one to whom a negotiable instrument is transferred by indorsement.

INDORSEMENT A signature placed on an instrument or a document of title for the purpose of transferring one's ownership in the instrument or document of title.

INDORSER One who, being the payee or holder of a negotiable instrument, signs by indorsement on the back of it.

INFORMAL CONTRACTS Contracts that do not require a specified form or formality for their validity.

INFORMATION A formal accusation or complaint (without an indictment) issued in certain types of actions by a prosecuting attorney or other law officer, such as a magistrate. The types of actions are set forth in the rules of states or in the Federal Rules of Criminal Procedure.

INJUNCTION A court decree ordering a person to refrain from a certain act or activity.

INNKEEPER'S LIEN A possessory or statutory lien allowing the innkeeper to take the personal property of a guest, brought into the hotel, as security for nonpayment of the guest's bill (debt).

INSIDER TRADING Purchasing or selling securities according to information that has not been made available to the public.

INSTALLMENT CONTRACT A contract whereby payments due are made periodically. Also may allow for delivery of goods in separate lots with payment made for each.

INSURABLE INTEREST An interest either in a person's life or well-being or in property which is sufficiently substantial that insuring against injury to the person or damage to the property does not amount to a mere wagering (betting) contract.

INTENDED BENEFICIARY A third party for whose benefit a contract is formed; intended beneficiaries can sue the promisor if such a contract is breached.

INTENTIONAL TORT A tort in which the actor is expressly or impliedly judged to have injured another intentionally or purposefully.

INTERMEDIARY BANK Any bank to which an item is transferred in the course of collection, except the depositary or payor bank.

INTERNATIONAL LAW The law that governs relations between nations. International customs and treaties are generally considered to be two of the most important sources of international law.

INTERROGATORIES A series of written questions for which written answers are prepared and then signed under oath by a party (plaintiff or defendant) to the lawsuit.

INTER VIVOS TRUST A trust created and effected by the grantor (settlor) during the grantor's lifetime (that is, a trust not established by a will).

INTESTACY LAWS State laws determining the division and descent of the estate of an intestate (one who dies with no will).

INTESTATE A person who dies without making a valid will.

INVESTMENT COMPANIES Companies that act on behalf of many smaller shareholders/owners by buying a large portfolio of securities and managing that portfolio professionally.

ISSUE The first transfer, or delivery, of an instrument to a holder.

JOINT TENANCY The ownership interest of two or more co-owners of property whereby each owns an undivided portion of the property. The key feature of joint tenancy is the right of survivorship, see Joint Tenancy with Right of Survivorship.

JOINT TENANCY WITH RIGHT OF SURVIVORSHIP The ownership interest of two or more co-owners of property whereby each owns an undivided portion of the property. Upon the death of one of the joint tenants, his or her interest automatically passes to the others and cannot be transferred by the will of the deceased.

JUDGMENT N.O.V. A judgment notwithstanding the verdict; may be entered by the court for the plaintiff (or the defendant) after there has been a jury verdict for the defendant (or the plaintiff).

JUDGMENT RATE OF INTEREST A rate of interest fixed by statute which is applied to a monetary judgment from the moment the judgment is awarded by a court until the judgment is paid or terminated.

JUDICIAL PROCESS The procedures relating to or connected with the administration of justice through the judicial system.

JUDICIAL REVIEW The authority of a court to reexamine a previously considered dispute; the process by which a court decides on the constitutionality of legislative acts.

JURISDICTION The authority of a court to hear and decide a specific action.

LARCENY The act of taking another person's personal property unlawfully. Some states classify larceny as either grand or petit, depending on the property's value.

LAW A body of rules of conduct with legal force and effect, prescribed by the controlling authority.

LEASE A transfer by the landlord/lessor of real or personal property to the tenant/lessee for a period of time, for a consideration (usually the payment of rent). Upon termination of the lease, the property reverts to the lessor.

LEASEHOLD ESTATE An estate in realty held by a tenant under a lease. In every leasehold estate, the tenant has a qualified right to possess and/or use the land.

LEGAL RATE OF INTEREST A rate of interest fixed by statute as either the maximum rate of interest allowed by law, or a rate of interest applied when the parties to a contract intend, but do not fix, an interest rate in the contract. In the latter case, the rate is frequently the same as the statutory maximum rate permitted.

LEGATEE A person who inherits personal property under a will.

LESS-THAN-FREEHOLD ESTATE A possessory real-estate interest in which the tenant has a qualified right to exclusive possession for a specified period of time, such as occurs in a leasehold estate.

LETTER OF CREDIT A written instrument, usually issued by a bank on behalf of a customer or other person, in which the issuer promises to honor drafts or other demands for payment by third persons in accordance with the terms of the instrument.

LEVY The obtaining of money by legal process through seizure and sale of property, usually done after an execution has been issued.

LIBEL A written defamation of one's character, reputation, business, or property rights. The First Amendment, to a limited degree, protects the press from libel actions.

LIFE ESTATE An interest in land that exists only for the duration of the life of some person, usually the holder of the estate.

LIMITED PARTNER In a limited partnership, a partner who contributes capital to the partnership but has no right to participate in the management and operation of the business. The limited partner assumes no liability for partnership debts beyond the capital contributed.

LIMITED PARTNERSHIP A partnership consisting of one or more general partners, who carry on the business and who are liable to the full extent of their personal assets for debts of the partnership, and of one or more limited partners, who contribute only assets and who are liable only up to the amount contributed by them.

LIQUIDATED DAMAGES An amount, stipulated in the contract, which the parties believe to be a reasonable estimation of the damages that will occur in the event of a breach.

LIQUIDATION The sale of assets of a business or an individual for cash and the distribution of the cash received to creditors with the balance going to the owner(s).

LONG-ARM STATUTE Through long-arm statutes, states permit personal jurisdiction to be obtained over nonresident individuals and corporations. Individuals or corporations, however, must have certain "minimum contacts" with that state.

LOST PROPERTY Property that the owner has involuntarily parted with and then cannot find or recover.

MAILBOX RULE A rule providing that an acceptance of an offer becomes effective upon dispatch (upon being placed in a mailbox), if mail is, expressly or impliedly, an authorized means of communication of acceptance to the offeror.

MAJORITY OPINION A court opinion supported by a majority of the judges or justices involved in deciding the case.

MAKER One who issues a promissory note or certificate of deposit (*i.e.*, one who promises to pay a certain sum to the holder of the note or CD).

MECHANIC'S LIEN A statutory lien upon the real property of another, created to ensure priority of payment for work performed and materials furnished in erecting or repairing a building or other structure.

MEDIATION A method of settling disputes outside of court by using the services of a neutral third party, who acts as a communicating agent between the parties; a method of dispute settlement less formal than arbitration.

MERGER A contractual process by which one corporation (the surviving corporation) acquires all the assets and liabilities of another corporation (the merged corporation). The shareholders of the merged corporation receive either payment for their shares or shares in the surviving corporation.

MIRROR-IMAGE RULE A common-law rule that requires, for a valid contractual agreement, that the terms of the offeree's acceptance adhere exactly to the terms of the offeror's offer.

MISDEMEANORS Lesser crimes than felonies, punishable by a fine or imprisonment in other than a state or federal penitentiary.

MISLAID PROPERTY Property that the owner has voluntarily parted with and then cannot find or recover.

MITIGATION OF DAMAGES The rule requiring the party suing to have done whatever was reasonable to minimize damages caused by the defendant.

MORAL HAZARD A term used in the insurance industry to describe a situation in which insurance coverage provides individuals or business entities with little disincentive to be negligent.

MORTGAGE A written instrument giving a creditor (the mortgagee) an interest (lien) in the debtor's (mortgagor's) property as security for a debt.

MOTION TO DISMISS OR DEMURRER A pleading in which a defendant admits to the facts as alleged by the plaintiff but asserts that the plaintiff's claim fails to state a cause of action (i.e., has no basis in law).

MUNICIPAL LAW Laws that pertain to a particular nation (national law), as opposed to international law.

MUTUAL FUND A specific type of investment company that continually buys or sells to investors shares of ownership in a portfolio.

NEGOTIABLE INSTRUMENT A written and signed unconditional promise or order to pay a specified sum of money on demand or at a definite time payable to order (a specific entity) or bearer.

NEGOTIATION The transferring of a negotiable instrument to another in such form that the transferee becomes a holder.

NOMINAL DAMAGES A small monetary award (often one dollar) granted to a plaintiff when no actual damage was suffered.

NOVATION The substitution, by agreement, of a new contract for an old one, with the rights under the old one being terminated. Typically, there is a substitution of a new person who is responsible for the contract and the removal of the original party's rights and duties under the contract.

NUNCUPATIVE WILL An oral (usually deathbed) will made before witnesses; limited to transfers of personal property.

OBJECTIVE THEORY OF CONTRACTS The view taken by American law that contracting parties shall only be bound by terms that can actually be inferred from promises made. Contract law does not examine a contracting party's subjective intent or underlying motive.

OFFER An offeror's proposal to do something, which creates in the offeree accepting the offer a legal power to bind the offeror to the terms of the proposal.

OFFEREE A person to whom an offer is made.

OFFEROR A person who makes an offer.

ORDER PAPER A negotiable instrument that is payable to a specific payee or to any person the payee by indorsement designates.

ORIGINAL JURISDICTION The power of a court to take a case, try it, and decide it.

OUTPUT CONTRACT A binding agreement whereby a seller agrees to deliver/sell the seller's entire output of a good (an unspecified amount at the time of agreement) to a buyer, and the buyer agrees to buy all the goods supplied.

PAROL EVIDENCE RULE A substantive rule of contracts under which a court will not receive into evidence oral or written statements made prior to or contemporaneous with a written agreement.

PARTIALLY DISCLOSED PRINCIPAL A principal whose identity is unknown by a third person, but the third person knows that the agent is or may be acting for a principal at the time the contract is made.

PARTNERSHIP An association of two or more persons to carry on, as co-owners, a business for profit. [UPA Section 6(1)]

PAST CONSIDERATION An act done before the contract is made, which ordinarily, by itself, cannot be consideration for a later promise to pay for the act.

PATENT A government grant that gives an inventor the exclusive right or privilege to make, use, or sell his or her invention for a limited time period (currently, seventeen years). The word *patent* usually refers to some invention and designates either the instrument by which patent rights are evidenced or the patent itself.

PATTERN OR PRACTICE Repeated, regular, and intentional conduct.

PAYEE A person to whom an instrument is made payable.

PAYOR BANK A bank on which an item is payable as drawn (or is payable as accepted).

PENALTY A sum inserted into a contract, not as a measure of compensation for its breach, but rather as punishment for a default. The agreement as to the amount will not be enforced, and recovery will be limited to actual damages.

PER CAPITA A method of distribution of property whereby the heirs to an intestate's estate inherit equal portions of the estate.

PERFECTION A process in which certain steps are legally required to give a secured party a priority interest over the debtor's collateral against other parties with claims to the same collateral.

PERFORMANCE In contract law, the fulfillment of one's duties arising under a contract with another; the normal way of discharging one's obligations in a contract.

PERSONAL DEFENSES Defenses that can be used to avoid payment to an ordinary holder of a negotiable instrument. Personal defenses cannot be used to avoid payment to an HDC or a holder through an HDC (the shelter principle).

PERSONAL PROPERTY Property that is movable; any property that is not real property.

PER STIRPES A method of distribution of property whereby the heirs to an intestate's estate take the share to which their deceased ancestor would have been entitled.

PLEA BARGAINING Discussions between a prosecutor and a criminal defendant's lawyer. Typically, the defendant agrees to plead guilty in exchange for the prosecutor's agreement to accept a plea to a less serious charge or to drop some charges or to request a light sentence from the judge for the defendant.

PLEADINGS Statements by the plaintiff and the defendant which detail the facts, charges, and defenses. Modern rules simplify common law pleading, often requiring only the complaint, answer, and sometimes a reply to the answer.

PLEDGE The bailment of personal property to a creditor as security for the payment of a debt.

POLICE POWERS Powers possessed by states as part of their inherent sovereignty. These powers may be exercised to protect or promote public health, safety, morals, or the general welfare.

POLICY In insurance, the contract of indemnity against a contingent loss between the insurer and insured.

POSITIVE LAW The objective laws legally created by a society, as opposed to natural law or social customs; also called *black-letter law*.

POSSIBILITY OF REVERTER A future interest in land that a grantor retains after conveying property subject to a condition subsequent (e.g., if a certain future event occurs, the interest in the estate will terminate automatically).

PRECEDENT A court decision that furnishes an example or authority for deciding subsequent cases in which identical or similar facts are presented.

PREEMPTIVE RIGHT A shareholder's right to purchase newly issued stock of a corporation before it is offered to any outside buyers, equal in percentage to shares presently held, enabling the shareholder to maintain proportionate ownership and voice in the corporation.

PREFERRED STOCK Classes of stock that have priority over common stock both as to payment of dividends and distribution of assets upon the corporation's dissolution.

PREMIUM In insurance, the price for insurance protection for a specified period of exposure.

PRESENTMENT WARRANTY A warranty impliedly made by any person who seeks payment or acceptance of a negotiable instrument to any other person who in good faith pays or accepts the instrument that (1) the party presenting has good title to the instrument, or is authorized to obtain payment or acceptance on behalf of a person who has good title, and (2) the party presenting has no knowledge that the signature of a maker or the drawer is unauthorized, and (3) the instrument has not been materially altered.

PRICE DISCRIMINATION Exists when two competing buyers pay two different prices for an identical product sold by a seller.

PRINCIPAL In agency law, a person who, by agreement or otherwise, authorizes an agent to act on his or her behalf in such a way that the acts of the agent become binding on the principal.

PRIVITY The relationship that exists between the promisor and the promisee of a contract.

PRIVITY OF CONTRACT The relationship that exists between the promisor and the promisee of a contract.

PROBABLE CAUSE Reasonable grounds to believe the existence of facts warranting certain actions, such as the search or arrest of a person.

PROBATE The process of proving and validating a will, and the settling of all matters pertaining to administration, guardianship, and like matters concerning the decedent's estate.

PROBATE COURT A special court, in some jurisdictions, having jurisdiction over proceedings concerning the settlement of a person's estate.

PROCEEDS In secured transactions law, whatever is received when the collateral is sold, exchanged, collected, or otherwise disposed of, such as insurance payments for destroyed or lost collateral. Money, checks, and the like are *cash proceeds*, while all other proceeds received are *noncash proceeds*.

PROFIT In real property law, the right to enter upon and remove things from the property of another (for example, the right to enter onto a person's land and remove sand and gravel therefrom).

PROMISE A declaration that binds the person who makes it (promisor) to do or not to do a certain act. The person to whom the promise is made (promisee) has a right to expect or demand the performance of some particular thing.

PROMISEE A person to whom a promise is made.

PROMISOR A person who makes a promise.

PROMISSORY ESTOPPEL A doctrine that applies when a promisor reasonably expects a promise to induce definite and substantial action or forbearance by the promisee, and which does induce such action or forbearance in reliance thereon; such a promise is binding if injustice can be avoided only by enforcing the promise.

PROMISSORY NOTE A written instrument signed by a maker unconditionally promising to pay a certain sum in money to a payee or a holder on demand or on a specified date.

PROMOTER An entrepreneur who participates in the organization of a corporation in its formative stage, usually by issuing a prospectus, procuring subscriptions to the stock, making contract purchases, securing a charter, and the like.

PROXIMATE CAUSE The "next" or "substantial" cause; in tort law, a concept used to determine whether a plaintiff's injury was the natural and continuous result of a defendant's negligent act. If the negligent act of a defendant was the sole cause or a substantial cause of injuries to a plaintiff, the defendant is liable.

PROXY In corporation law, a written agreement between a stockholder and another under which the stockholder authorizes the other to vote the stockholder's shares in a certain manner.

PUNITIVE, OR EXEMPLARY, DAMAGES Compensation in excess of actual or consequential damages. Awarded in order to punish the wrongdoer; awarded only in cases involving willful or malicious misconduct.

PURCHASE MONEY SECURITY INTEREST A security interest to the extent that it is (1) taken or retained by a seller of the collateral to secure all or part of its price; or (2) taken by a creditor who, by making advances or incurring an obligation, gives value to enable the debtor to acquire rights in or use of collateral, if such value is in fact so used.

QUALIFIED INDORSEMENT An indorsement on a negotiable instrument under which the indorser disclaims to subsequent holders secondary liability on the instrument; the most common qualified indorsement is "without recourse."

QUASI-CONTRACT An obligation or contract imposed by law, in the absence of agreement, to prevent unjust enrichment. Sometimes referred to as an implied-in-law contract (a legal fiction) to distinguish it from an implied-in-fact contract.

QUIT-CLAIM DEED A deed intended to pass any title, interest, or claim that the grantor may have in the premises but not professing that such title is valid nor containing any warranty or covenants for title.

RATIFICATION The approval or validation of a previous action; in contract law, giving legal force to an obligation that was previously unenforceable.

REAL DEFENSES Defenses that can be used to avoid payment to all holders of a negotiable instrument, including an HDC or a holder through an HDC (the shelter principle).

REAL PROPERTY Property consisting of land and buildings thereupon, which are stationary, as opposed to personal property, which can be moved. In the absence of a contract, real property includes things growing on the land before they are severed (such as timber) as well as fixtures.

REASONABLE DOUBT The standard used to determine the guilt or innocence of a person charged with a criminal offense. To be guilty of a crime, one must be proved guilty "beyond and to the exclusion of every reasonable doubt." A reasonable doubt is one that would cause prudent or "reasonable" persons to hesitate before acting in matters important to them.

REBUTTAL Refers to evidence given by the plaintiff's attorney to refute (rebut) evidence introduced by the defendant's attorney.

RECOGNIZANCE A formal obligation to perform a certain act as recorded and required by a court, such as reappearing in court.

RECORDING STATUTES Statutes enacted to provide notice to future purchasers, creditors, and encumbrancers of an existing claim on real property.

REDRESS Satisfaction for damages incurred through the use of a product or a service or through the wrongdoing of another.

REFORMATION A court-ordered correction of a written contract so that it reflects the true intentions of the parties.

REJOINDER The defendant's attorney's answer to the plaintiff's rebuttal.

RELEASE The relinquishment, concession, or giving up of a right, claim, or privilege, by the person in whom it exists or to whom it accrues, to the person against whom it might have been enforced or demanded.

REMAINDER A future interest in property, held by a person other than the grantor, that occurs at the natural termination of the preceding estate.

REMEDY Refers to the relief given to innocent parties, by law or by contract, when a contract is breached.

REMEDY AT LAW A remedy available under the particular circumstances of a case in a court of law.

REMEDY IN EQUITY A remedy allowed by courts in situations where remedies at law are not appropriate. Based on settled rules of fairness, justice, and honesty.

REPLEVIN An action in equity brought in order to recover possession of personal property unlawfully held by another.

REPLY Procedurally, a plaintiff's response to a defendant's answer.

REQUIREMENTS CONTRACT An agreement under which a promisor promises to supply the promisee with all the goods and/or services the promisee might require from period to period.

RESCISSION A remedy whereby a contract is canceled and the parties are returned to the positions they occupied before the contract was made; may be effected through the mutual consent of the parties, by their conduct, or by the decree of a court of equity.

RES JUDICATA A rule that prohibits the same factual dispute between two parties to be retried by a court after final judgment has been entered by a trial court and all appeals have been exhausted (or the time for appeal has passed).

RESPONDEAT SUPERIOR In Latin, "Let the master respond." The employer is responsible for acts of an employee that are committed during the course of employment.

RESTITUTION An equitable remedy under which a person is restored to his or her original position prior to loss or injury, or placed in the position he or she would have been, had the breach not occurred.

RESTRICTIVE INDORSEMENT Any indorsement of a negotiable instrument that purports to condition or prohibit further transfer of the instrument. As against payor and intermediary banks, such indorsements are usually ineffective.

RESULTING TRUST A trust implied in law from the intentions of the parties to a given transaction. In this trust, a party holds legal title for the benefit of another, although without expressed intent to do so, because the presumption of such intent arises by operation of law.

REVERSE DISCRIMINATION A type of discrimination in which majority groups are purportedly discriminated against in favor of minority groups, usually via affirmative action programs.

REVERSION A future interest under which a grantor retains a present right to a future interest in property that the grantor conveys to another; usually the residue of a life estate. The reversion is always a vested property right.

REVOCATION In contract law, the withdrawal of an offer by an offeror; unless the offer is irrevocable, it can be revoked at any time prior to acceptance without liablity.

RIGHT OF CONTRIBUTION The act of any one or several of a number of co-sureties in reimbursing one of their number who has paid the whole debt, each to the extent of his or her proportionate share.

RIGHT OF REIMBURSEMENT The legal right of a person to be restored, repaid, or indemnified for costs, expenses, or losses incurred or expended on behalf of another.

RIGHT OF SUBROGATION The right of a person to substitute one person in the place of another, giving the substituted party the same legal rights that the original party had.

RIGHT-TO-WORK LAW A state law generally providing that employees are not to be required to join a union as a condition of receiving or retaining employment.

ROBBERY Theft from a person, accompanied by force or fear of force.

RULE 10b-5 An SEC rule that makes it unlawful, in connection with the purchase or sale of any security, to make any untrue statement of a material fact or to omit a material fact if such omission causes the statement to be misleading.

SALE The passing of title from the seller to the buyer for a price, where title refers to the formal right of ownership of property.

SALE ON APPROVAL A type of conditional sale that becomes absolute only when the buyer approves or is satisfied with the good(s) sold. Besides express approval of goods, approval may be inferred if the buyer keeps the goods beyond a reasonable time, or uses the goods in any way that is inconsistent with the seller's ownership.

SALE OR RETURN A type of conditional sale wherein title and possession pass from the seller to the buyer; however, the buyer retains the option to rescind or return the goods during a specified period even though the goods conform to the contract.

SALES CONTRACT A contract by means of which the ownership of goods is transferred from a seller to a buyer for a fixed price in money, paid or agreed to be paid by the buyer.

SATISFACTION The tender of substitute performance in return for the relinquishing of the right of action on a prior obligation.

SCIENTER Knowledge by the misrepresenting party that material facts have been falsely represented or omitted with an intent to deceive.

S CORPORATION A close business corporation, which has met certain requirements as set out by the Internal Revenue Code, that qualifies for special income-tax treatment. Essentially, an S corporation is taxed the same as a partnership but its owners enjoy the privilege of limited liability.

SECURED PARTY A lender, seller, or any other person in whose favor there is a security interest, including a person to whom accounts or chattel paper have been sold.

SECURED TRANSACTION Any transaction, regardless of its form, that is intended to create a security interest in personal property or fixtures, including goods, documents, and other intangibles.

SECURITIES Stock certificates, bonds, notes, debentures, warrants, or other documents given as evidence of an ownership interest in the corporation or as a promise of repayment by the corporation.

SECURITY AGREEMENT The agreement that creates or provides for a security interest between the debtor and a secured party.

SECURITY INTEREST Every interest "in *personal property or fixtures* [emphasis added] which secures payment or performance of an obligation." [UCC 1-201(37)]

SERVICE MARK A mark used in the sale or the advertising of services, such as to distinguish the services of one person from the services of others. Titles, character names, and other distinctive features of radio and television programs may be registered as service marks.

SHELTER PRINCIPLE The principle that the holder of a negotiable instrument who cannot qualify as a holder in due course, but who derives his or her title through a holder in due course, acquires the rights of a holder in due course.

SHORT-FORM MERGER A merger between a parent corporation and a subsidiary corporation where the parent corporation owns at least 90 percent of the outstanding shares of each class of stock issued by the subsidiary corporation. These mergers can be accomplished without shareholder approval of either corporation.

SIGNATURE The name or mark of a person, written by that person or at his or her direction. In commercial law, any name, word, or mark used with the intention to authenticate a writing constitutes a signature.

SLANDER An oral defamation of one's character, reputation, business, or property rights.

SOCIAL INVESTING Investments made on the basis of moral or ethical judgments; buying stock in a corporation based on the ethical behavior of the corporation or on its benefits to society.

SOVEREIGN IMMUNITY A doctrine that, when certain conditions are satisfied, immunizes foreign nations from the jurisdiction of U.S. courts; codified in the Foreign Sovereign Immunities Act of 1976.

SPECIAL INDORSEMENT An indorsement of an instrument specifying to whom or to whose order the instrument is payable.

SPECIFIC PERFORMANCE A remedy requiring *exactly* the performance that was specified in a contract.

SPENDTHRIFT TRUST A trust created to protect the beneficiary from spending all the money to which he or she is entitled. Only a certain portion of the total amount is given to the beneficiary at any one time, and most states prohibit creditors from attaching assets of the trust.

STALE CHECK A check, other than a certified check, that is presented for payment more than six months after its date.

STARE DECISIS A flexible doctrine of the courts, recognizing the value of following prior decisions (precedents) in cases similar to the one before the court; the courts' practice of being consistent with prior decisions based on similar facts. See precedent.

STATE EXEMPTION LAWS Laws passed by individual states describing the property of the debtor that cannot be attached by a judgment creditor or trustee in bankruptcy to satisfy a debt.

STATUTORY LAW Laws enacted by a legislative body (as opposed to constitutional law, administrative law, or case law).

STOCK An equity or ownership interest in a corporation, measured in units of shares.

STOCK SPLIT An action in which one share of stock is split into a larger number of shares. Stock splits involve no changes except adjustments in par value, or stated value per share, when applicable. They normally require action by the board of directors and advance shareholder approval if the articles of incorporation need to be amended to change the par value or stated value of the shares or to authorize additional shares. The common purpose of a stock split is to reduce the per-share market price to facilitate wider trading in the public securities markets.

STOCK WARRANT A certificate granting a transferable option to buy a given number of shares of stock, usually within a set time period.

STOP-PAYMENT ORDER An order by the drawer of a draft or check directing the drawer's bank not to pay the check.

STRICT LIABILITY Liability regardless of fault. Under tort law, strict liability is imposed on a merchant who introduces into commerce a good that is unreasonably dangerous when in a defective condition.

SUMMARY JUDGMENT A judgment entered by a trial court prior to trial which is based on the valid assertion by one of the parties that there are no disputed issues of fact which would necessitate a trial.

TANGIBLE PROPERTY Property that has physical existence and can be distinguished by the senses of touch, sight, and so on. A car is tangible property; a patent right is intangible property.

TENANCY AT WILL The right of a tenant to remain in possession of land with permission of the landlord until either the tenant or the landlord chooses to terminate the tenancy.

TENANCY BY SUFFERANCE Tenancy by one who, after rightfully being in possession of leased premises, continues (wrongfully) to occupy the property after the lease has been terminated. The tenant has no estate in the land and occupies it only because the person entitled to evict has not done so.

TENANCY BY THE ENTIRETY The joint ownership of property by husband and wife. Neither party can alienate or encumber the property without the consent of the other. The property is inherited by the survivor of the two, and dissolution of marriage transforms the tenancy by the entirety to a tenancy in common.

TENANCY FOR YEARS A nonfreehold estate/lease for a specified period of time, after which the interest reverts to the grantor.

TENANCY FROM PERIOD TO PERIOD A nonfreehold estate/lease for an unspecified period where specified rent payments are made at certain intervals (for example, every month); automatically renewed for a like period until terminated.

TENANCY IN COMMON Co-ownership of property whereby each party owns an undivided interest that passes to his or her heirs at death.

TENDER A timely offer, or expression of willingness, to pay a debt or perform an obligation.

TESTAMENTARY TRUST A trust that is created by will and therefore does not take effect until the death of the testator or testatrix.

TESTATOR (-TRIX) One who makes and executes a will.

THIRD-PARTY-BENEFICIARY CONTRACT A contract between two or more parties, the performance of which is intended to directly benefit a third party, thus giving the third party a right to file suit for breach of contract by either of the original contract parties.

TOTTEN TRUST A trust created by the deposit of a person's own money in his or her own name as a trustee for another. This is a tentative trust, revocable at will until the depositor dies or completes the gift in his or her lifetime by some unequivocal act or declaration.

TRADE ACCEPTANCE A bill of exchange/draft drawn by the seller of goods on the purchaser and accepted by the purchaser's written promise to pay the draft. Once accepted, the purchaser becomes primarily liable to pay the draft.

TRADEMARK A word or symbol that has become sufficiently associated with a good (in common law) or has been registered with a government agency. Once a trademark is established, the owner has exclusive use of it and has the right to bring a legal action against those who infringe upon the protection given the trademark.

TRADE NAME A name used in commercial activity to designate a particular business, a place where a business is located, or a class of goods. Trade names are not usually affixed to goods sent into the market.

TRAVELER'S CHECK An instrument purchased from a bank, express company, or the like, in various denominations, that can be used as cash upon a second signature by the purchaser. It has the characteristics of a cashier's check.

TRESPASS TO LAND In common law, the intentional or unintentional passing over another person's land uninvited, regardless of whether any physical damage is done to the land. Today a majority of courts find trespass only in cases of intentional intrusion, negligence, or some "abnormally dangerous activity" on the part of the defendant.

TRESPASS TO PERSONALTY Any wrongful transgression or offense against the personal property of another.

TRUST A legal entity in which a trustee holds title to property for the benefit of another.

ULTRA VIRES Activities of a corporation's managers that are outside the scope of the power granted them by its charter or the laws of the state of incorporation.

UNANIMOUS OPINION A court opinion supported by all the judges or justices involved in deciding the case.

UNCONSCIONABLE CONTRACT OR CLAUSE A contract or clause that is void as against public policy because one party, as a result of his or her disproportionate bargaining power, is forced to accept terms that are unfairly burdensome and that unfairly benefit the dominating party.

UNDERWRITER In insurance law, the one assuming a risk in return for the payment of a premium; the insurer.

UNDISCLOSED PRINCIPAL A principal whose identity is unknown by a third person, and the third person has no knowledge that the agent is acting in an agency capacity at the time the contract is made.

UNENFORCEABLE CONTRACT A valid contract having no legal effect or force in a court action.

UNILATERAL CONTRACT A contract that includes the exchange of a promise for an act.

UNION SHOP A place of employment in which all workers, once employed, must become union members within a specified period of time as a condition of their continued employment.

USAGE OF TRADE Any practice or method of dealing having such regularity of observance in a place, vocation, or trade as to justify an expectation that it will be observed with respect to the transaction in question.

USURY Charging an illegal rate of interest.

VALID CONTRACT A properly constituted contract having legal strength or force.

VENUE The geographical district in which the action is tried and from which the jury is selected.

VERTICAL MERGER A combining of two firms, one of which purchases goods for resale from the other. If a producer or wholesaler acquires a retailer, it is a *forward* vertical merger. If a retailer or distributor acquires its producer, it is a *backward* vertical merger.

VOIDABLE CONTRACT A contract that may be legally annulled at the option of one of the parties.

VOID CONTRACT A contract having no legal force or binding effect.

VOIR DIRE From the French, meaning "to speak the truth." A phrase denoting the preliminary examination used for potential jurors (or witnesses) where competency, interests, etc., may be objected to.

VOTING TRUST The transfer of title by stockholders of shares of a corporation to a trustee who is authorized to vote the shares on their behalf.

WAIVER An intentional, knowing relinquishment of a legal right.

WARRANTY OF HABITABILITY An implied warranty by a landlord that rental premises are properly maintained and repaired and fit for human habitation.

WARRANTY OF POSSESSION In a lease contract, a warranty by the landlord that the premises have been leased to only one tenant and that the premises will be available at the agreed time.

WATERED STOCK Stock issued by a corporation as if fully paid for, when in fact less than par value has been paid.

WHITE-COLLAR CRIME Nonviolent crimes committed by corporations and individuals. Embezzlement and commercial bribery are two examples of white-collar crime.

WILL An instrument directing what is to be done with a person's property upon his or her death, made by that person and revocable during his or her lifetime; no interests pass until the testator dies.

WORKOUT A common law or bankruptcy out-of-court negotiation with creditors whereby a debtor enters into an agreement with a creditor or creditors for a payment or plan to discharge the debtor's debt(s).

WRIT OF ATTACHMENT A writ employed to enforce obedience to an order or judgment of the court. The writ may take the form of taking or seizing property to bring it under the control of the court.

WRIT OF CERTIORARI A writ from a higher court asking the lower court for the record of a case. A request for certiorari (or "cert" for short) is similar to an appeal, but one which the higher court is not required to take for decision.

WRIT OF EXECUTION A writ that puts in force a court's decree or judgment.

WRIT OF MANDAMUS A court order telling a public official or governmental department to do something.

Table of Cases

The principal cases are in bold type. Principal cases that can also be retrieved on CLERK (Computer Legal Research Key System) are indicated with a color dot. Cases cited or discussed are in roman type.

Index

A

Abatement, 774
AAA. *See* American Arbitration Association
Ability, legal. *See* Capacity
Acceleration clause, 347
Acceptance:
  of a gift, 730
  of an offer. *See* Contracts, acceptance of
    offer in
  of plan, in Chapter 11 reorganization,
    466–467
  revocation of, 287-288
  of a sales contract, 244–246
  trade, 333
Acceptor:
  defined, 331
  liability of, 374–375
Accession, personal property and, 731
Accommodation:
  indorsers, 375
  party, 331–332, 377
    and negotiable instruments, 375–376
  shipment, notice of, 245
Accord:
  defined, 209
  and satisfaction, 139–140, 209, 211
    case illustrating, 140–141
Account party, to a letter of credit, 795
Accounting:
  agent's duty of, 506–507
  of partnership assets, partners' right to,
    551
Accounts, security interest in, 423 n.3, 427
Act:
  criminal *(actus reus)*, 84

case illustrating, 84–85
  of state doctrine, in international law,
    792
Act for the Prevention of Frauds and
  Perjuries, An, 179
Act to Regulate Commerce (1887), 17
  as *Landmark*, 665
Activity, commercial, *defined*, 794
Actus reus (criminal act), 84 n.1
Add-on clause, 820
Adequacy of consideration, 135
Adequate protection, concept of, 45
Administrative agencies, 8
  and environmental protection, 700–701
Administrative law, 8, 25
Administrative process, 8
Administrator (administratrix), 774
Advances, future, security interest in, 428
Adverse possession, transfer of real estate by,
  758
Advertisements, and contractual offers, 122,
  125
Advertising:
  bait-and-switch, 690
    case illustrating, 690–691
  and consumer protection, 688–692
  deceptive, *defined*, 688–689
    case illustrating, 689–690
  and the First Amendment, 23–24
  labeling and packaging regulations and,
    691–692
  sale of securities and, 645
Affiliation doctrine, 16–17
Affirmative action, and reverse
  discrimination, 809–810
Age:
  of majority, 147
  misrepresentation of, by a minor, 149

Agency, 499–526
  administrative, 8
    and environmental protection, 700–
      701
  coupled with an interest, termination of,
    520
  defined, 499
  exclusive, 764
  minors and, 503
  nature of, 499
  relationships, types of, 500–502
    case illustrating, 501–502
    formation of, 502–504
    rights and remedies in, 508
  termination of, 518–521
    by act of the parties, 518–520
    notice required in, 521
    by operation of law, 520–521
Agent:
  authority of, 508–514
  corporate, 605
  defined, 499
  and delivery of gifts, 730
  duty of, to principal, 504–507
  escrow, 764
  indorsement by, 356
  insurance, 769
    compared to insurance broker, *case
      illustrating*, 769
  legal capacity of, 502–503
  liability of,
    for contracts, 514–515
    personal, 341
    for torts, 515–518
  principal and, relationship between, 500
  registered, of a corporation, 579
  remedies of, against principal, 508
  signature of, 341